Hippocrene
Practical Dictionaries

English – Español
Spanish – Inglés

Arthur Swift Butterfield

HIPPOCRENE BOOKS, New York

Front cover photo © Robert Phillips/The Image Bank

Second printing, 1988

First Hippocrene Edition, 1983

© Laurence Urdang Associates, 1982

Glossary of Menu Terms and special American usage entries © Hippocrene Books, 1983

ISBN 0-88254-814-X

Abbreviations/Abreviaciones

adj adjective, adjetivo
adv adverb, adverbio
aero aeronautics, aeronáutica
agr agriculture, agricultura
anat anatomy, anatomía
arch architecture
arq arquitectura
art article, artículo
astrol astrology, astrología
astron astronomy, astronomía
auto automobile, automóvil
bot botany, botánica
chem chemistry
coll colloquial
com comercio
comm commerce
conj conjunction, conjunción
culin culinario
derog derogatory
econ economics, economía
elec electricity, electricidad
f feminine, femenino
fam familiar, colloquial
ferr ferrocarril
fig figurative, figurativo
foto fotografía
geog geography, geografía
geol geology, geología
gram gramática
gramm grammar
impol impolite

interj interjection, interjección
interrog interrogative,
    interrogativo
invar invariable
jur jurisprudencia
m masculine, masculino
mar marítimo
mat matemáticas
math mathematics
mec mecánica
mech mechanics
med medicine, medicina
mil military, militar
mot motoring
n noun
naut nautical
phone telephone
phot photography
pl plural
pol politics, política
prep preposition, preposición
pron pronoun, pronombre
psych psychology
quím química
rail railways
rel religion, religión
s sustantivo
sing singular
tech technology, technical
tecn tecnología
v verb, verbo
V vide (see, vea)
zool zoology, zoología

Spanish pronunciation

a cada ['kaða]
e entre ['entre]
i libro ['liβro]
o loco ['loko]
u lunes ['lunes]
j nieve ['njeβe]
b bueno ['bweno]
d desde ['desðe]
f fácil ['faθil]
g grande ['grande]
k poco ['poko]
l salud [sa'luð]

m hombre ['ombre]
n noche ['notʃe]
p lápiz ['lapiθ]
r cerca ['θerka]
rr perro ['perro]
s servir [ser'βir]
t todo ['toðo]
w luego ['lwego]
θ cerveza [θer'βeθa]
β hábil ['aβil]
tʃ muchacho [mu'tʃatʃo]
ð ciudad [θju'ðað]
ʎ calle ['kaʎe]
ɲ señor [se'ɲor]
x ojo, ágil ['oxo], ['axil]

The symbol ' indicates that the following syllable should be stressed.

Pronunciación del inglés

a hat [hat]
e bell [bel]
i big [big]
ɒ dot [dot]
ʌ bun [bʌn]
u book [buk]
ə alone [ə'loun]
a: card [ᵏa:d]
ə: word [wə:d]
i: team [ti:m]
o: torn [to:n]
u: spoon [spu:n]
ai die [dai]
ei ray [rei]
oi toy [toi]
au how [hau]
ou road [roud]
eə lair [leə]
iə fear [fiə]
uə poor [puə]
b back [bak]
d dull [dʌl]
f find [faind]

g gaze [geiz]
h hop [hop]
j yell [jel]
k cat [kat]
l life [laif]
m mouse [maus]
n night [nait]
p pick [pik]
r rose [rouz]
s sit [sit]
t toe [tou]
v vest [vest]
w week [wi:k]
z zoo [zu:]
ө think [өiŋk]
ð those [ðouz]
ʃ shoe [ʃu:]
ʒ treasure ['treʒə]
tʃ chalk [tʃo:k]
dʒ jump [dʒʌmp]
ŋ sing [siŋ]

El signo de acentuación ' se coloca directamente delante de la sílaba aguda.

El signo ˌ se coloca delante de la sílaba aguda secundaria.

Guide to the dictionary

The infinitives of all irregular verbs appearing in the headword list are marked with an asterisk. These and examples of Spanish stem-changing verbs, and the tenses in which such changes occur, can be found in the following verb tables. Composite verbs, such as *deshacer* from *hacer*, are also included under the parent verb.

The Spanish alphabet includes three symbols or combinations of letters that are not found in the English alphabet. These are **ch, ll,** and **ñ,** which are treated as individual letters and follow **c, l,** and **n** respectively in the alphabetical order.

The plurals of almost all Spanish nouns are formed regularly by the addition of *s* or *es* to the singular form. Occasional irregular plural forms are shown immediately after the part of speech referring to the headword. Some nouns do not change in the plural and these are marked *invar* (invariable).

Adverbs are regularly formed by adding -*mente* to the feminine (or occasionally masculine) form of the adjective, and are not normally shown unless a different translation is called for.

Guía al diccionario

Los plurales irregulares de los sustantivos se hallen junto al encabezamiento. Las categorías siguientes de los plurales se consideran regulares en inglés:

cat	cats
glass	glasses
fly	flies
half	halves
wife	wives

Los verbos irregulares en la lista de encabezamientos se señalan por medio de un asterisco y se hallen en las tablas de los verbos.

Los adverbios regulares no se indican. Los adverbios ingleses que se forman añadiendo -(al)ly al adjetivo, se consideran regulares. Los adverbios españoles que se forman añadiendo -mente al adjetivo femenino (de vez en cuando masculino), se consideran regulares y no se indican sino exigiendo una traducción diferente.

Spanish verb tables

1. The final consonants preceding the infinitive endings (**-ar, -er,** and **-(u)ir**) change, for reasons of euphony, when they occur before certain vowels.

Infinitives	Change	Before
-car	the **c** to **qu**	e
-cer	the **c** to **z**	a or o
-cir	the **c** to **z**	a or o
-gir	the **g** to **j**	a or o
-guir	the **gu** to **g**	a or o
-quir	the **qu** to **c**	a or o
-gar	the **ga** to **gu**	e
-zar	the **z** to **c**	e

2. Verbs adding **z**. There are numerous verbs ending in **-ecer** (*e.g.* **parecer**) and other verbs ending in a vowel + **-cer** (*e.g.* **conocer**). When the ending of these verbs is **a** or **o** (specifically, present indicative 1 *sing*, and present subjunctive, all persons), a **z** is added before the **c** (*e.g.* **parezco, conozco**).

3. Verbs in the following tables change the vowels in their stems in certain persons and tenses. The sections below are arranged according to the vowel change involved and are followed by a selection of verbs exemplifying the change. Note that composite verbs (*e.g.* **desplegar**) are conjugated in the same way as their base forms (*e.g.* **plegar**).

    (i) Stem changes **e** to **ie** in present indicative and present subjunctive 1, 2, 3 *sing* and 3 *pl*, and in imperative *sing*.

acertar	aterrar	comenzar	dentar	entender
acrecentar	aventar	concertar	desalentar	entesar
aferrar	calentar	confesar	descender	fregar
apretar	cegar	contender	desempedrar	gobernar
arrendar	cerner	decentar	despernar	hacendar
ascender	cerrar	defender	despertar	heder

helar	merendar	recentar	sembrar	tentar
hender	negar	recomendar	sentar	trascender
herrar	nevar	regar	serrar	trasegar
incensar	pensar	remendar	sosegar	trasverter
invernar	perder	restregar	soterrar	tropezar
manifestar	plegar	reventar	temblar	verter
mentar	quebrar	segar	tender	

(ii) Stem changes **o** to **ue** in present indicative and present subjunctive 1, 2, 3 *sing* and 3 *pl*, and in imperative *sing*.

acordar	colar	jugar	resollar	soñar
acostar	colgar	moler	rodar	torcer
aforar	contar	mostrar	rogar	tostar
almorzar	costar	mover	solar	trocar
apostar	doler	poblar	soldar	tronar
aprobar	encontrar	probar	soler	voler
avergonzar	forzar	recordar	soltar	volcar
azolar	holgar	renovar	sonar	volver

(iii) Stem changes from **e** to **i** in present indicative 1, 2, 3 *sing* and 3 *pl*; preterite 3 *sing* and *pl*; present, imperfect, and future subjunctives, all persons; imperative *sing* and present participle.

colegir	derretir	henchir	regir	seguir
concebir	elegir	medir	rendir	servir
corregir	gemir	pedir	repetir	vestir

(iv) Stem changes **e** to **ie** in present indicative and present subjunctive 1, 2, 3 *sing* and 3 *pl*; imperative *sing*.
Stem changes **e** to **i** in preterite 3 *sing* and *pl*; present subjunctive 1, 2 *pl*; imperfect and future subjunctives, all persons; present participle.

advertir	digerir	hervir	preferir
cernir	divertir	inferir	requerir
convertir	hendir	ingerir	sentir
diferir	herir	mentir	sugerir

4. The verbs shown below change in various ways. In the table, 1 and 3 *sing* are shown under the present indicative and 1 *sing* under the preterite and future.

Infinitive	Present Indicative	Preterite	Future	Past Participle
andar	ando, anda	anduve	andaré	andado
caber	quepo, cabe	cupe	cabré	cabido
caer	caigo, cae	caí	caeré	caido
dar	doy, da	di	daré	dado
decir	digo, dice	dije	diré	dicho
dormir	duermo, duerme	dormí	dormiré	dormido
erguir	yergo, yergue	erguí	erguiré	erguido
errar	yerro, yerra	erré	erraré	errado
estar	estoy, está	estuve	estaré	estado
haber	he, ha	hube	habré	habido
hacer	hago, hace	hice	haré	hecho
huir	huyo, huye	huí	huiré	huido
ir	voy, va	fui	iré	ido
oír	oigo, oye	oí	oiré	oido
oler	huelo, huele	olí	oleré	olido
poder	puedo, puede	pude	podré	podido
poner	pongo, pone	puse	pondré	puesto
querer	quiero, quiere	quise	querré	querido
reducir	reduzco, reduce	reduje	reduciré	reducido
reír	río, ríe	reí	reiré	reido
saber	sé, sabe	supe	sabré	sabido
ser	soy, es	fui	seré	sido
tener	tengo, tiene	tuve	tendré	tenido
traer	traigo, trae	traje	traeré	traído
valer	valgo, vale	valí	valdré	valido
venir	vengo, viene	vine	vendré	venido
ver	veo, ve	vi	veré	visto

Verbos irregulares ingleses

Infinitivo	Pretérito	Participo Pasado	Infinitive	Pretérito	Participo Pasado
abide	abode	abode	**deal**	dealt	dealt
arise	arose	arisen	**dig**	dug	dug
awake	awoke	awoken	**do**	did	done
be	was	been	**draw**	drew	drawn
bear	bore	borne	**dream**	dreamed	dreamed
		or born		*or* dreamt	*or* dreamt
beat	beat	beaten	**drink**	drank	drunk
become	became	become	**drive**	drove	driven
begin	began	begun	**dwell**	dwelt	dwelt
behold	beheld	beheld	**eat**	ate	eaten
bend	bent	bent	**fall**	fell	fallen
bet	bet	bet	**feed**	fed	fed
beware			**feel**	felt	felt
bid	bid	bidden	**fight**	fought	fought
		or bid	**find**	found	found
bind	bound	bound	**flee**	fled	fled
bite	bit	bitten	**fling**	flung	flung
bleed	bled	bled	**fly**	flew	flown
blow	blew	blown	**forbid**	forbade	forbidden
break	broke	broken	**forget**	forgot	forgotten
breed	bred	bred	**forgive**	forgave	forgiven
bring	brought	brought	**forsake**	forsook	forsaken
build	built	built	**freeze**	froze	frozen
burn	burnt	burnt	**get**	got	got
	or burned	*or* burned	**give**	gave	given
burst	burst	burst	**go**	went	gone
buy	bought	bought	**grind**	ground	ground
can	could		**grow**	grew	grown
cast	cast	cast	**hang**	hung	hung
catch	caught	caught		*or* hanged	*or* hanged
choose	chose	chosen	**have**	had	had
cling	clung	clung	**hear**	heard	heard
come	came	come	**hide**	hid	hidden
cost	cost	cost	**hit**	hit	hit
creep	crept	crept	**hold**	held	held
cut	cut	cut	**hurt**	hurt	hurt

Infinitivo	Pretérito	Participo Pasado	Infinitivo	Pretérito	Participo Pasado
keep	kept	kept	**say**	said	said
kneel	knelt	knelt	**see**	saw	seen
knit	knitted	knitted	**seek**	sought	sought
	or knit	or knit	**sell**	sold	sold
know	knew	known	**send**	sent	sent
lay	laid	laid	**set**	set	set
lead	led	led	**sew**	sewed	sewn
lean	leant	leant			or sewed
	or leaned	or leaned	**shake**	shook	shaken
leap	leapt	leapt	**shear**	sheared	sheared
	or leaped	or leaped			or shorn
learn	learnt	learnt	**shed**	shed	shed
	or learned	or learned	**shine**	shone	shone
leave	left	left	**shoe**	shod	shod
lend	lent	lent	**shoot**	shot	shot
let	let	let	**show**	showed	shown
lie	lay	lain	**shrink**	shrank	shrunk
light	lit	lit	**shut**	shut	shut
	or lighted	or lighted	**sing**	sang	sung
lose	lost	lost	**sink**	sank	sunk
make	made	made	**sit**	sat	sat
may	might		**sleep**	slept	slept
mean	meant	meant	**slide**	slid	slid
meet	met	met	**sling**	slung	slung
mow	mowed	mown	**slink**	slunk	slunk
must			**slit**	slit	slit
ought			**smell**	smelt	smelt
pay	paid	paid		or smelled	or smelled
put	put	put	**sow**	sowed	sown
quit	quitted	quitted			or sowed
	or quit	or quit	**speak**	spoke	spoken
read	read	read	**speed**	sped	sped
rid	rid	rid		or speeded	or speeded
ride	rode	ridden	**spell**	spelt	spelt
ring	rang	rung		or spelled	or spelled
rise	rose	risen	**spend**	spent	spent
run	ran	run	**spill**	spilt	spilt
saw	sawed	sawn		or spilled	or spilled
		or sawed	**spin**	spun	spun

Infinitivo	Pretérito	Participo Pasado	Infinitivo	Pretérito	Participo Pasado
spit	spat	spat	**swim**	swam	swum
split	split	split	**swing**	swung	swung
spread	spread	spread	**take**	took	taken
spring	sprang	sprung	**teach**	taught	taught
stand	stood	stood	**tear**	tore	torn
steal	stole	stolen	**tell**	told	told
stick	stuck	stuck	**think**	thought	thought
sting	stung	stung	**throw**	threw	thrown
stink	stank	stunk	**thrust**	thrust	thrust
	or stunk		**tread**	trod	trodden
stride	strode	stridden	**wake**	woke	woken
strike	struck	struck	**wear**	wore	worn
string	strung	strung	**weave**	wove	woven
strive	strove	striven	**weep**	wept	wept
swear	swore	sworn	**win**	won	won
sweep	swept	swept	**wind**	wound	wound
swell	swelled	swollen	**wring**	wrung	wrung
	or swelled		**write**	wrote	written

Glossary of menu terms

Americans dining in Spain, Mexico, and the Spanish Caribbean are in for a pleasant surprise, for Spanish cooking is far more diverse than the few dishes that have become part of the American diet would indicate. Neither is it as hot and spicy (**picante**) as the food often served in the Southwest. Food in Spain is tasty but relatively bland; even in Mexico, the "hot" comes mainly from the red and green sauces found on the table.

The Spanish menu lacks the gourmet tradition of France. Dishes tend to be less delicate, heartier and more filling. Menu items not imported are those that are grown locally, hence many ingredients are those that have always been readily available: rice and olive oil, for instance, are used over and over. Caribbean cooking makes frequent use of such fruits as pineapples, bananas and the smaller plaintain, and other, less familiar, tropical fruits. Mexican cooking combines corn, beans, tomatoes (both red and green), and countless varieties of peppers and **chiles** in intriguing combinations.

A first-time visitor to Spanish-speaking countries may find the times for eating more exotic than the food itself. Full breakfasts are seldom found in Spain outside of large hotels catering to tourists. In the Americas, however, a large breakfast is easy to get — often to be eaten about the middle of the morning rather than first thing (coffee or hot chocolate help tide you over). The midday meal, the **comida,** is taken between 1:00 and 3:00 p.m. in Mexico, 2:00 and 4:00 in Spain. Most "business dinners" take place at **comida.** Traditionally, most offices closed for the delightful custom, the **siesta,** although long commuting times have made the break for a nap less common in large cities. The last meal of the day, the **cena,** is much lighter than **comida** and is eaten late in the evening, sometimes very late (any time between 8:00 and midnight with the emphasis on the later hours).

You would have to work hard, however, to go hungry. It often seems that Spanish-speaking societies never stop eating. Snacking is not only common, but the occasion for sampling some of the most representative local foods. Spain has even institutionalized the between-meal snack, the **merienda,** which consists of a variety of hors d'oeuvre eaten with a few **copas** of wine around 6:00 p.m. No visitor should leave Spain without visiting a few taverns for **merienda** and sampling the local specialties, **tapas.** Indeed, it is considered customary to have a light snack whenever one stops for morning coffee or after-work cocktails.

In general, restaurants of comparable quality are less expensive than their U.S. counterparts, especially in Mexico and the Caribbean. Service appears more formal, although it is often acceptable to attract a waiter's attention by hissing, making a kissing sound, or slapping hands, depending on local custom. Better not try it until you see someone else do it first! The economy-minded visitor should be warned that such ordinary extras as soft drinks, coffee, even bread, are sometimes priced out of proportion to the rest of the menu; second cups of coffee are seldom free. On the other hand, one is never rushed to pay the bill and leave; you may linger forever over one drink or coffee. Indeed, getting a waiter to bring the check (**cuenta**) can be a major challenge. You have to ask for it and probably remind the waiter a few times before he produces it. Finally, as a general rule, the more American-looking a restaurant, the higher its prices.

A typical Spanish menu is completely à la carte. The standard headings include **entremeses** and/or **tapas** (appetizers); **sopas** (soups); sometimes **sopas secas** (literally dry soups, usually a pasta or rice course); **carnes** (red meats); **aves** (poultry); **pescados** (fish); **mariscos** (shellfish); **ensaladas** (salads); **legumbres** (vegetables); **postres** (desserts); and **bebidas** (beverages). The people who live in the country you are visiting will probably eat an astonishing number of courses, but you can order from as many or as few categories as you like to make up a meal that suits your tastes and appetite.

An exception to the à la carte menu is the multicourse combination usually available at the midday meal, the **comida**. Called the **menu turístico, comida corrida,** or simply **comida,** it offers few choices and (sometimes) smaller portions, but it is a good bargain. Be sure to inform the waiter that you are having the set meal and restrict yourself to the choices offered.

Finally, it is important to remind yourself that although the menu may be in English, the waiter does not always speak English. Spanish and English entrées are usually listed in the same order for this reason.

Basic Terms

a la mexicana Mexican-style: mixed with peppers, tomatoes, onions, and **chiles**

caldo thick stew-like soup with solid ingredients

cilantro fresh coriander; if you don't like the taste, ask for your food **sin** (without) **cilantro**

mole a spicy sauce with many variations, some quite **picante,** others bland; the famous dish is **mole poblano de guajolote,** turkey in dark chocolate-flavored sauce in the style of Puebla

rellenos stuffed, often vegetables with stuffing

salsa sauce; some common ones are **salsa mexicana** (see above), **salsa verde** (made with green tomatoes called **tomatillos**), and **salsa ranchera** (quite hot, used for **huevos rancheros**)

sofrito common base of tomatoes, vegetables, onions, garlic lightly fried in olive oil

tortillas The Mexican tortilla is, with beans and peppers, the basic ingredient in Mexican cooking. A tortilla is a flat pancake made from **masa harina,** a flour made of corn from which the husks and germ have been removed, and water. Tortillas are baked on an ungreased griddle and are used as bread with many meals and combined with other ingredients to make a number of common Mexican menu items:

chalupas small tortillas filled with meat or other toppings, served as hors d'oeuvre

chilaquiles strips of stale tortillas fried, then combined with meat or chicken, sauces, and meats and baked; green chilaquiles feature chicken and green **tomatillo** sauce while red chilaquiles usually have beef and red tomato (**jitomate**) sauce; both topped with cheese

enchiladas tortillas dipped in **chile** sauce, then fried to receive various fillings, e.g. chicken, cheese, and sour cream to make **enchiladas suizas** (Swiss enchiladas)

nachos similar to chalupas

quesadillas small raw tortillas, filled with cheese or other savory fillings, sealed, and baked or fried on a grill

taco ubiquitous Mexican counterpart of the American sandwich; a tortilla is rolled around filling and either eaten as is or fried on a grill; **taco al carbón:** a taco made with meat only

tamales not tortillas, but soft dumplings made by wrapping tortilla dough around various fillings, securing the whole in corn husks, and steaming

tostado taco for which the tortilla is first fried until crisp in deep fat

Entremeses or Tapas (Appetizers)

ceviche a seafood cocktail made of raw fish or shellfish "cooked" by marinat-

ing in lime juice and mixed with spices;
many different versions exist

chalupas see **tortillas**

cóctel de camarones shrimp cocktail

cóctel de ostiones oyster-like cocktail;
shellfish is served out of the shell in
cocktail sauce

nachos see **tortillas**

pescado Santo Domingo cold sea bass
served as hors d'oeuvre

quesadillas see **tortillas**

Sopas (Soups)

albóndigas very thick soup made with
ground beef and rice

caldo de pescado fish soup

caldo Tlalpeño rich clear chicken soup
with vegetables and dried **chiles**; very
good

gazpacho classic cold soup made of raw
tomatoes and other vegetables and oil
and vinegar

menudo tripe soup; very hearty and
filling

pozole soup made of pork, hominy, and
chiles; often very hot, always very filling

sopa de ajo popular garlic soup prepared by browning garlic cloves and
bread in oil

sopa de cebolla onion soup, often with
cheese

sopa de frijol negro black bean soup

sopa de judías coloradas black bean
soup with ham and hard-cooked egg

sopa de tortilla delicious soup made
with chicken broth, tortilla strips, and
many flavorings

Entrées or Platillo Fuerte or Platos Principales (Main Dishes)

Carnes (Red Meats)

albóndigas meat balls, often very **picante**, sometimes served as an appetizer
as well

carne asada literally grilled meat, this
is almost always filet of beef sliced fair-

ly thin **with** the grain, broiled medium-
well, and served with any combination
of a number of side dishes; a safe dish to
order almost anywhere

cocido popular stew with many variations but usually including meat, chicken,
bacon, chick peas, and vegetables

cocido de riñones kidney stew in a sofrito base

cochinillo asado roast suckling pig; no
one should go through life without it

cochinillo pibil Yucatecan-style barbe-
cued pork

chiles rellenos stuffed **chile poblanos**
(stuffing is usually ground pork but can
be cheese)

chorizo popular red-colored sausage

empanada Galacian hot turnover usually filled with a meat mixture

fabada stew of pork, beans, and spices

guisado stew, usually of meat and other
vegetables

higado liver

jamón en dulce ham preserved in
sugar, i.e. sugar-cured ham, served cold

lechón asada another name for roast
suckling pig

lengua de res ox tongue

lomo de cerdo loin of pork

olla podrida same as **cocido**

piononos deep-fried plaintain rings with
tasty ground-beef filling

pote same as **cocido**

puchero same as **cocido**

puerco en mole verde pork in green
mole sauce; also called **pipián verde**
sauce (**pipián** means a sauce made with
ground nuts or seeds, in this case with
green pumpkin seeds, **pepitas**)

riñones kidneys

Aves (Poultry)

arroz con pollo common rice with
chicken dish including saffron, peas,
and other vegetables and seasonings in
endless variations; always a good and
safe bet

guisado de pollo chicken stew with potatoes, peas, and wine sauce

mole poblano one of the national dishes of Mexico, traditionally made with turkey, though chicken is often used

pato duck

pechuga de pollo breast of chicken

pollo a la chilindrón chicken sautéed with peppers, tomatoes, and olives

pollo en pipián rojo chicken in a red sauce flavored with sesame seeds; may be referred to as **en pipián colorado** (red **pipián**)

Huevos (Eggs)

huevos a la flamenca fried eggs on a sofrito base

huevos motuleños as they are made in the town of Motul in Yucatán, incorporating chopped ham and peas

huevos rancheros soft fried eggs on tortillas covered with hot sauce (**salsa ranchera**) served with refried beans; guaranteed to wake you up

huevos revueltos a la mexicana eggs scrambled with chopped tomatoes, onions, and **chiles**

pisto manchego mixed vegetables, bits of ham, and eggs, a sort of omelette, easy on the eggs; there are many variations from region to region

tortilla in Spain only, a sturdy omelette containing many combinations of ingredients other than eggs

Pescados y Mariscos (Fish and Shellfish)

adobo de pescado fish casserole with tomatoes

aguacates rellenos literally stuffed avocados; often the stuffing is a seafood salad or a vegetable mixture; sometimes served as an appetizer or first course

asopao Puerto Rican rice stew with seafood

bacalao a la Vizcaina salt cod and tomatoes, of Basque origin

blanco de Pátzcuaro white fish from Lake Pátzcauro in Mexico

calamares en su tinta squid in a sauce made with their ink; much tastier than it sounds

camarones shrimp

huachinango a la Veracruzana red snapper in the style of Veracruz: baked with tomatoes, onions, and chiles

paella famous rice-based casserole usually containing shellfish, chicken, peas, and sometimes sausages; spices include saffron; every chef has his own version, but be prepared to wait because it is always cooked to order

pescado guisado fish stew

zarzuela mixed seafood stew in a sauce of wine and brandy; many variations, almost all delicious

Snacks, Side Dishes, etc.

bocadillo literally sandwich, it is also the standard hard roll, very soft inside; a real staple

bolillo the Mexican standard roll

bombas de camarones deep-fried potato cakes with shrimp in the dough

burritos wheat-flour tortillas rolled around a variety of fillings similar to those used for the corn tortillas; if then fried, usually called **chimachangas**

churros long deep-fried pastry made from a doughnut-like dough and dipped in granulated sugar; served for breakfast in Spain and also for late-night **merienda** with coffee or chocolate in Mexico

frijoles refritos "refried" beans; actually the beans are cooked tender, then fried only once, being mashed in the process; served with practically everything in Mexico

guacamole avocado purée with onions, peppers, often fresh coriander (**cilantro**), and possibly chopped tomatoes; usually bland, it is sometimes made with hot **chiles**, so taste cautiously

migas bread bits fried in olive oil and flavored with garlic; a distinctively Spanish crouton

pan dulce literally sweet bread, this term covers a huge variety of pastries and sweet breads made in bakeries that seem to be on every corner; don't miss these delicious sweets, but buy only what you will eat in one day since they lose their bloom if kept longer

torta Mexico City only: a carved out bolillo filled with meat, avocado, tomato, etc.; a great takeout

Postres (Desserts)

Spanish desserts are relatively simple and not difficult to understand. Fruits are popular, sometimes in cream (**con crema**) or with whipped cream (**nata,** thicker than the American version). One can order a variety of pastries (**pastales** or, in Spain, **tortas**) or ice cream (**helado**).

arroz con leche rice pudding

chongos a kind of cross between custard and cheese made by letting gently heated milk separate into curds and whey, these are served with a sweet syrup; don't miss them

natillas universally available soft custard served cold

flan sometimes called **crème caramel,** this custard baked with caramel syrup on the bottom is probably the best known distinctly Spanish dessert; usually on every menu

Bebidas (Beverages)

atole a hot drink made with **masa harina,** rather like a thin cornmeal mush sweetened and flavored in various ways; not everybody's cup, but interesting to try — perhaps the chocolate version, called **champurrado**

café coffee; be careful how you order:

café americano American-style coffee

café con crema American-style coffee with cream (in small or very rural places, the cream may be evaporated milk, so be advised)

café con leche coffee with warm milk (**café au lait**)

café de olla coffee made in a clay pot served black flavored with stick cinnamon and sweetened with raw brown sugar

café solo espresso-style black coffee

chocolate spelled the same way but pronounced choco-LAHT-tay, this popular beverage in Mexico comes in many styles among which are mexicana (made with water) and francesca (made with milk and, possibly, an egg)

cerveza beer; light is **clara,** dark is **negra;** dark Mexican beer is labeled **oscura** and the very dark, once-a-year treat around Christmas is **nochebuena**

coñac brandy (no particular brand)

jerez sherry, our corruption of the name of the city that gave rise to the wine, Jerez, Spain, pronounced (both city and drink) *hereth*

jugo de naranja orange juice

Kalaúa the coffee-flavored, chocolatey liqueur of Mexico

refresco any soft drink, usually ordered by brand

tequila Mexican liquor distilled from the agave plant; other forms of agave products, including **mescal** and **pulque;** ask local advice

vino wine; red (**tinto**), rose (**rosado**), or white (**blanco**); local table wine is **vino corriente, vino de mesa,** or **vino del país**

English—Español

A

a, an [ə, ən] *art* un, -a.
aback [ə'bak] *adv* be taken aback quedar desconcertado.
abandon [ə'bandən] *v* abandonar. *n* abandono *m*.
abashed [ə'baʃt] *adj* avergonzado, confundido.
abate [ə'beit] *v* disminuir. **abatement** *n* disminución *f*.
abattoir ['abətwaɪ] *n* matadero *m*.
abbey ['abi] *n* abadía *f*. **abbess** *n* abadesa *f*. **abbot** *n* abad *m*.
abbreviate [ə'briːvieit] *v* abreviar. **abbreviation** *n* abreviación *f*.
abdicate ['abdikeit] *v* abdicar. **abdication** *n* abdicación *f*.
abdomen ['abdəmən] *n* abdomen *m*. **abdominal** *adj* abdominal.
abduct [əb'dʌkt] *v* raptar. **abduction** *n* rapto *m*.
aberration [abə'reiʃən] *n* extravío *m*, engaño *m*. **aberrant** *adj* extraviado.
abet [ə'bet] *v* instigar, inducir.
abeyance [ə'beiəns] *n* in abeyance en suspenso.
abhor [əb'hoɪ] *v* aborrecer, odiar. **abhorrence** *n* aborrecimiento *m*, odio *m*. **abhorrent** *adj* aborrecible.
*abide [ə'baid] *v* residir, habitar; (*tolerate*) aguantar, sufrir. **abide by** atenerse a, cumplir con.
ability [ə'biləti] *n* habilidad *f*, capacidad *f*. **to the best of one's ability** lo mejor que pueda.
abject [,abdʒekt] *adj* abyecto.
ablaze [ə'bleiz] *adj* en llamas.
able ['eibl] *adj* capaz; (*talented*) hábil.

able-bodied *adj* entero. **able-bodied seaman** marinero de primera *m*. **be able** poder. **ably** *adv* hábilmente.
abnormal [ab'noɪml] *adj* anormal. **abnormality** *n* anormalidad *f*.
aboard [ə'boɪd] *adv, prep* a bordo (de). **all aboard!** ¡viajeros a bordo! **go aboard** embarcarse.
abode [ə'boud] *n* domicilio *m*.
abolish [ə'boliʃ] *v* abolir. **abolition** *n* abolición *f*.
abominable [ə'bominəbl] *adj* abominable. **abominate** *v* abominar (de). **abomination** *n* abominación *f*.
Aborigine [abə'ridʒini] *n* aborigen *m*.
abortion [ə'boɪʃən] *n* aborto *m*. **abort** *v* abortar.
abound [ə'baund] *v* abundar.
about [ə'baut] *adv* (*approximately*) casi, alrededor de, más o menos. **all about** por todas partes. *prep* (*place*) alrededor de; (*near*) cerca de; (*concerning*) de, acerca de.
above [ə'bʌv] *adv* encima, arriba. *prep* (*place*) encima de, sobre; (*number*) más de; (*rank*) superior a. **above-mentioned** *adj* susodicho, citado.
abrasion [ə'breiʒən] *n* raspadura *f*. **abrasive** *adj* raspante.
abreast [ə'brest] *adv* de frente. **keep abreast of** *or* **with** ir al paso de.
abridge [ə'bridʒ] *v* abreviar, resumir. **abridgement** *n* abreviación *f*, resumen *m*.
abroad [ə'broɪd] *adv* en el extranjero.
abrupt [ə'brʌpt] *adj* abrupto, brusco.
abscess ['abses] *n* absceso *m*.
abscond [əb'skond] *v* fugarse.
absent ['absənt] *adj* ausente. **absent-minded** *adj* distraído. **absent oneself** ausentarse. **absence** *n* ausencia *f*. **absentee** *n* ausente *m, f*. **absenteeism** *n* absentismo *m*.

absolute [ˈæbsəluːt] *adj* absoluto. **absolutely** *adv* absolutamente; (*interj*) categóricamente. **absolutism** *n* absolutismo *m*.

absolve [əbˈzolv] *v* absolver. **absolution** *n* absolución *f*.

absorb [əbˈzoːb] *v* absorber. **be absorbed in** enfrascarse en. **absorbent** *adj* absorbente. **absorbing** *adj* (*coll*) sumamente interesante.

abstain [əbˈsteɪn] *v* abstenerse (de). **abstention** *n* abstención *f*. **abstinence** *n* abstinencia *f*.

abstemious [əbˈstiːmɪəs] *adj* abstemio.

abstract [ˈæbstrækt; *v* æbˈstrækt] *adj* abstracto. *n* resumen *m*. *v* extractar. **abstractedly** *adv* distraidamente. **abstraction** *n* abstracción *f*.

absurd [əbˈsoːd] *adj* absurdo. **absurdity** *n* absurdidad *f*.

abundance [əˈbʌndəns] *n* abundancia *f*. **abundant** *adj* abundante.

abuse [əˈbjuːz; *n* əˈbjuːs] *v* abusar (de). *n* abuso *m*; injuria *f*. **abusive** *adj* abusivo; injurioso.

abyss [əˈbɪs] *n* abismo *m*. **abysmal** *adj* abismal; profundo.

academy [əˈkædəmɪ] *n* academia *f*. **academic** *adj* académico.

accede [ækˈsiːd] *v* acceder.

accelerate [əkˈseləreɪt] *v* acelerar. **acceleration** *n* aceleración *f*. **accelerator** *n* acelerador *m*.

accent [ˈæksənt] *n* acento *m*. *v* acentuar.

accept [əkˈsept] *v* aceptar. **acceptable** *adj* aceptable. **acceptance** *n* aceptación *f*.

access [ˈækses] *n* acceso *m*. **accessible** *adj* asequible.

accessory [əkˈsesərɪ] *nm, adj* accessorio. *n* (*law*) cómplice *m, f*. **accessories** *pl n* (*mot, etc.*) complementos *m pl*.

accident [ˈæksɪdənt] *n* accidente *m*. **by accident** sin querer, por casualidad. **accidental** *adj* accidental.

acclaim [əˈkleɪm] *v* aclamar, aplaudir. *n also* **acclamation** aclamación *f*, aplauso *m*.

acclimatize [əˈklaɪmətaɪz] *v* aclimatar.

accolade [ˈækəleɪd] *n* acolada *f*.

accommodate [əˈkomədeɪt] *v* acomodar; (*lodge*) alojar, hospedar; adaptar; (*provide*) proveer (de). **accommodating** *adj* complaciente. **accommodation** *n* alojamiento *m*.

accompany [əˈkʌmpənɪ] *v* acompañar. **accompaniment** *n* acompañamiento *m*. **accompanist** *n* acompañante, -a *m, f*.

accomplice [əˈkʌmplɪs] *n* cómplice *m, f*.

accomplish [əˈkʌmplɪʃ] *v* cumplir. **accomplished** *adj* (*talented*) talentoso. **accomplishment** *n* efectuación *f*; talentos *m pl*.

accord [əˈkoːd] *v* conceder; concordar. *n* acuerdo *m*. **of one's own accord** espontáneamente. **in accordance with** conforme a. **accordingly** *adv* en consecuencia. **according to** según.

accordion [əˈkoːdɪən] *n* acordeón *m*.

accost [əˈkost] *v* abordar.

account [əˈkaunt] *n* (*bank, etc.*) cuenta *f*; (*narrative*) relato *m*; (*status*) importancia *f*. **on account of** a causa de. **on no account** de ninguna manera. **take into account** tener en cuenta. **account for** dar una explicación de. **accountant** *n* contador *m*; (*chartered*) contador colegiado.

accrue [əˈkruː] *v* crecer.

accumulate [əˈkjuːmjuleɪt] *v* acumular. **accumulation** *n* acumulación *f*.

accurate [ˈækjurət] *adj* exacto. **accuracy** *n* precisión *f*.

accuse [əˈkjuːz] *v* acusar. **accusation** *n* acusación *f*. **the accused** acusado, -a *m, f*.

accustom [əˈkʌstəm] *v* acostumbrar.

ace [eis] *n* as *m*. **within an ace of** de dos dedos de.

ache [eik] *n* dolor *m*. *v* doler.

achieve [əˈtʃiːv] *v* ejecutar. **achievement** *n* ejecución *f*; (*feat*) hazaña *f*.

acid [ˈæsɪd] *nm, adj* ácido. **acidity** *n* acidez *f*.

acknowledge [əkˈnolɪdʒ] *v* reconocer, aceptar. **acknowledge receipt of** acusar recibo de. **acknowledgement** *n* reconocimiento *m*; acuse de recibo *m*.

acne [ˈækni] *n* acné *m*.

acorn [ˈeikoːn] *n* bellota *f*.

acoustic [əˈkuːstɪk] *adj* acústico. **acoustics** *pl n* acústica *f sing*.

acquaint [əˈkweint] *v* informar, avisar. **acquaintance** *n* (*knowledge*) conocimiento *m*; (*person*) conocido, -a *m, f*. **be acquainted with** conocer(a).

acquiesce [ækwiˈes] *v* consentir, conformarse. **acquiescence** *n* conformidad *f*. **acquiescent** *adj* sumiso.

acquire [əˈkwaiə] *v* adquirir. **acquisition** *n* adquisición *f*. **acquisitive** *adj* adquisitivo; (*derog*) ahorrativo.

acquit [ə'kwit] v absolver. **acquit oneself** portarse. **acquittal** (law) absolución f.

acrid ['akrid] adj acre.

acrimony ['akriməni] n acrimonia f. **acrimonious** adj áspero.

acrobat ['akrəbat] n acróbata m, f. **acrobatic** adj acrobático. **acrobatics** pl n acrobacia f sing.

across [ə'kros] adv a través, al través. prep a través de, al través de, de través de; al otro lado de, del otro lado de.

acrylic [ə'krilik] adj acrílico.

act [akt] v (theatre) representar; (function) funcionar, marchar; (behave) comportarse; (take action) obrar, tomar medidas; (affect) afectar. n acto m, acción f; obra f; (law) decreto; (theatre) acto m. **actor** n actor m. **actress** n actriz f.

action ['akʃən] n acción f, hecho m; (mil) acción f, batalla f; (mech) mecanismo m. **bring an action against** entablar demanda contra. **put out of action** inutilizar.

active ['aktiv] adj activo. **activate** v activar. **activist** n activista m, f. **activity** n actividad f; movimiento m.

actual ['aktʃuəl] adj verdadero, efectivo. **actually** adv en realidad.

actuate ['aktjueit] v mover; accionar.

acupuncture ['akjupʌŋktʃə] n acupuntura f.

acute [ə'kjuːt] adj agudo.

adamant ['adəmənt] adj firme, seguro.

Adam's apple [adəm'zapl] n nuez de la garganta f.

adapt [ə'dapt] v adaptar; ajustar; (play, book) refundir; (music) arreglar. **adaptable** adj adaptable. **adaptation** n adaptación f; refundición f; arreglo m. **adapter** n (theatre) refundidor m; (elec) enchufe de reducción m.

add [ad] v añadir; (increase) aumentar. **add up** sumar. **add up to** subir a. **addition** n el añadir m; (math) suma f, adición f. **additional** adj adicional.

addendum [ə'dendəm] n invar adenda f.

adder ['adə] n víbora f.

addict ['adikt] n partidario, -a m, f; (drugs) toxicómano, -a m, f. **addiction** n adicción f; propensión f. **be addicted to** ser adicto a.

additive ['aditiv] n aditivo m.

address [ə'dres] v (letter) dirigir; (meeting, etc.) pronunciar un discurso ante. **address oneself to** dirigirse. n (postal) dirección f; (speech) discurso m; (envelope) sobrescrito m. **addressee** n destinatario, -a m, f.

adenoids ['adənoidz] pl n amígdalas vegetaciones f pl.

adept [ə'dept] nm, adj experto.

adequate ['adikwət] adj adecuado, suficiente.

adhere [əd'hiə] v pegarse; (to a policy) adherirse a. **adhesion** n adhesión f. **adhesive** adj adhesivo. **adhesive tape** esparadrapo m.

adherent [əd'hiərənt] n partidario, -a m, f.

adjacent [ə'dʒeisənt] adj próximo, contiguo.

adjective ['adʒiktiv] n adjetivo m.

adjoin [ə'dʒoin] v lindar (con). **adjoining** adj contiguo.

adjourn [ə'dʒəːn] v aplazar; (session) levantar la sesión. **adjournment** n aplazamiento m; (of a session) suspensión f.

adjudicate [ə'dʒuːdikeit] v adjudicar; (law) juzgar. **adjudication** n adjudicación f; (law) fallo m. **adjudicator** n árbitro m.

adjust [ə'dʒʌst] v arreglar; (tech) ajustar. **adjustment** n arreglo m; ajuste m.

ad-lib ['ad'lib] adv a voluntad, a discreción. v improvisar.

administer [əd'ministə] v administrar; (law) aplicar; (med) suministrar. **administration** n administración f; (ministry) gobierno m. **administrative** adj administrativo. **administrator** n administrador m.

admiral ['admərəl] n almirante m.

admire [əd'maiə] v admirar. **admirable** adj admirable. **admiration** n admiración f.

admit [əd'mit] v dar entrada a; (concede) conceder; (acknowledge) reconocer. **admission** n entrada f; (acknowledgement) confesión f.

adolescence [adə'lesns] n adolescencia f. **adolescent** n(m+f), adj adolescente.

adopt [ə'dopt] v adoptar; (report) aprobar. **adopted** adj (child) adoptivo. **adoption** n adopción f.

adore [ə'doː] v adorar. **adoration** n adoración f.

adorn [ə'doːn] v adornar, embellecer. **adornment** n adorno m.

adrenaline [ə'drenəlin] n adrenalina f.

adrift [ə'drift] *adv* a la deriva.
adroit [ə'droit] *adj* diestro, hábil.
adulation [adju'leiʃən] *n* adulación *f*.
adult ['adʌlt] *n, adj* adulto, -a.
adulterate [ə'dʌltəreit] *v* adulterar.
adultery [ə'dʌltəri] *n* adulterio *m*. **adulter-**
er *n* adúltero, -a *m, f*.
advance [əd'vains] *v* adelantar; avanzar. *n*
progreso *m*, avance *m*, adelanto *m*;
(*cash*) anticipo *m*.
advantage [əd'vaintidʒ] *n* ventaja *f*. **take**
advantage of aprovecharse de. **advanta-**
geous *adj* ventajoso.
advent ['advənt] *n* advenimiento *m*.
Advent *n* Adviento *m*.
adventure [əd'ventʃə] *n* aventura *f*;
(*comm*) especulación *f*. **adventurer** *n*
aventurero *m*. **adventurous** *adj* aventurero.
adverb ['advəib] *n* adverbio *m*.
adversary ['advəsəri] *n* adversario, -a *m,*
f.
adverse ['advəis] *adj* adverso. **adversity** *n*
adversidad *f*.
advertise ['advətaiz] *v* anunciar; publicar.
advertisement *n* anuncio *m*. **advertising** *n*
publicidad *f*.
advise [əd'vaiz] *v* aconsejar; avisar. **advis-**
able *adj* conveniente. **advisedly** *adv* con
intención. **adviser** *n* consejero *m*. **advice**
n consejo *m*.
advocate ['advəkeit] *v* recomendar.
aerial ['eəriəl] *adj* aéreo. *n* antena *f*.
aerodynamics [eərədai'namiks] *n* aerodinámica *f sing*.
aeronautics [eərə'noitiks] *n* aeronáutica *f*
sing.
aeroplane ['eərəplein] *n* avión *m*.
aerosol ['eərəsol] *n* aerosol *m*.
aesthetic [iis'θetik] *adj* estético. **aesthetics**
n estética *f sing*.
affair [ə'feə] *n* asunto *m*; episodio *m*;
(*love*) aventura amorosa *f*. **affairs** (*busi-*
ness) negocios *m pl*.
affect[1] [ə'fekt] *v* (*influence*) influir en;
(*move*) conmover.
affect[2] [ə'fekt] *v* (*pretend*) afectar.
affection [ə'fekʃən] *n* cariño *m*.
affiliate [ə'filieit] *v* afiliarse (a). **affiliation**
n afiliación *f*.
affinity [ə'finəti] *n* afinidad *f*.
affirm [ə'fəim] *v* afirmar. **affirmation** *n*
afirmación *f*. **affirmative** *adj* afirmativo.
affix [ə'fiks] *v* fijar; añadir; pegar; poner.

afflict [ə'flikt] *v* afligir, aquejar. **affliction** *n*
aflicción *f*, dolor *m*.
affluent ['afluənt] *adj* afluente, opulento.
affluence *n* afluencia *f*, opulencia *f*.
afford [ə'foid] *v* tener medios; (*produce*)
dar; ofrecer.
affront [ə'frʌnt]‚ *v* afrentar. *n* afrenta *f*,
ofensa *f*.
afloat [ə'flout] *adv* a flote.
afoot [ə'fut] *adv* a pie; (*fig*) en proyecto.
aforesaid [ə'foised] *adj* susodicho, men-
cionado.
afraid [ə'freid] *adj* temeroso, espantado.
be afraid tener miedo (a *or* de).
afresh [ə'freʃ] *adv* de nuevo.
Africa ['afrikə] *n* África *f*. **African** *n, adj*
africano, -a.
aft [aift] *adv* a popa.
after ['aiftə] *prep* (*time*) después de;
(*place*) detrás de; tras. *adv* (*time*)
después; (*place*) detrás. *conj* después (de)
que. **after all** con todo. **afterwards** *adv*
después. **after-effect** *n* consecuencia *f*.
aftershave *n* loción de afeitar *f*.
afternoon [,aiftə'nuin] *n* tarde *f*. **good**
afternoon! ¡buenas tardes!
again [ə'gen] *adv* de nuevo, otra vez;
además. **again and again** aún una y otra
vez. **now and again** de vez en cuando.
against [ə'genst] *prep* contra; (*touching*)
tocante.
age [eidʒ] *n* edad *f*; (*era*) época *f*. **of age**
mayor de edad. **under age** menor de
edad. *v* envejecer. **aged** *adj* de la edad
de; (*old*) viejo.
agency ['eidʒənsi] *n* agencia *f*; mediación
f.
agenda [ə'dʒendə] *n* agenda *f*.
agent ['eidʒənt] *n* agente *m, f*; (*comm*)
representante *m, f*.
aggravate ['agrəveit] *v* agravar; (*coll*)
exasperar. **aggravation** *n* agravamiento
m; (*coll*) irritación *f*.
aggregate ['agrigət] *m, adj* agregado. *v*
agregar, juntar.
aggression [ə'greʃən] *n* agresión *f*. **aggres-**
sive *adj* agresivo. **aggressiveness** *n*
belicosidad *f*. **aggressor** *n* agresor, -a *m, f*.
aghast [ə'gaist] *adj* horrorizado.
agile ['adʒail] *adj* ágil, ligero. **agility** *n*
agilidad *f*.
agitate ['adʒiteit] *v* agitar, excitar. **agitate**
for luchar por. **agitation** *n* agitación *f*;
perturbación *f*.

agnostic [ag'nostik] *n, adj* agnóstico, -a.
agnosticism *n* agnosticismo *m*.
ago [ə'gou] *adv* hace. ha. **long ago** hace mucho tiempo. **a short time ago** hace poco.
agog [ə'gog] *adj* ansioso.
agony ['agəni] *n* agonía *f*. angustia *f*. **agonize** *v* atormentar.
agree [ə'griː] *v* estar de acuerdo. convenir (en): (*consent*) consentir (en): (*gram*) concordar: (*correspond*) estar conforme (con). **agreeable** *adj* agradable. **agreement** *n* (*pact*) pacto *m*; (*comm*) contrato *m*.
agriculture ['agrikʌltʃə] *n* agricultura *f*. **agricultural** *adj* agrícola.
aground [ə'graund] *adv* encallado. **run aground** encallar, varar.
ahead [ə'hed] *adv* delante, al frente. **be ahead** estar adelante. **go ahead!** ¡adelante!
aid [eid] *v* ayudar. socorrer. *n* ayuda *f*. **in aid of** en beneficio de. **first aid** primera cura. **go to the aid of** acudir en defensa de.
aim [eim] *v* (*weapon*) apuntar (a): (*remark*) dirigir (a). *n* (*weapon*) puntería *f*: (*fig*) propósito *m*, meta *f*, blanco *m*. **aimless** *adj* sin objeto. **aimlessly** *adv* a la ventura.
air [eə] *n* aire *m*; (*music*) aire *m*, tonada *f*; (*aspect*) aspecto *m*. *v* airear, ventilar.
airbed ['eəbed] *n* colchón de viento *m*.
airborne ['eəbɔin] *adj* en el aire.
aircraft ['eəkraːft] *n* avión *m*. **aircraft-carrier** *n* portaaviones *m invar*.
airfield ['eəfiːld] *n* campo de aviación *m*.
air force *n* fuerza *or* flota aérea *f*.
air-hostess *n* azafata *f*.
air lift *n* puente aéreo *m*.
airline ['eəlain] *n* línea aérea *f*.
airmail ['eəmeil] *n* correo aéreo *m*.
airport ['eəpɔit] *n* aeropuerto *m*.
air-raid *n* bombardeo aéreo *m*.
airtight ['eətait] *adj* hermético, herméticamente cerrado.
airy ['eəri] *adj* aéreo; (*flippant*) frívolo.
aisle [ail] *n* nave lateral *f*.
ajar [ə'dʒaɪ] *adv* entreabierto, entornado.
alabaster ['aləbaistə] *n* alabastro *m*. *adj* alabastrino.
alarm [ə'laim] *n* alarma *f*. *v* alarmar. **alarm clock** *n* despertador *m*.
alas [ə'las] *interj* ¡ay!

Albania [al'beinjə] *n* Albania *f*. **Albanian** *n, adj* albanés, -esa.
albatross ['albətros] *n* albatros *m*.
albino [al'biinou] *n, adj* albino, -a.
album ['albəm] *n* álbum *m*.
alchemy ['alkəmi] *n* alquimia *f*. **alchemist** *n* alquimista *m*.
alcohol ['alkəhol] *n* alcohol *m*. **alcoholic** *n, adj* alcohólico, -a. **alcoholism** *n* alcoholismo *m*.
alcove ['alkouv] *n* nicho *m*, hueco *m*.
alderman ['oildəmən] *n* teniente de alcalde *m*, concejal *m*.
ale [eil] *n* cerveza *f*.
alert [ə'ləit] *adj* alerto, vivo, despierto. *v* poner sobre aviso, alertar.
algebra ['aldʒibrə] *n* álgebra *f*.
Algeria [al'dʒiəriə] *n* Argelia *f*. **Algerian** *n, adj* argelino, -a.
alias ['eiliəs] *nm, adv* alias.
alibi ['alibai] *n* coartada *f*.
alien ['eiliən] *n, adj* extranjero, -a. **alienate** *v* enajenar, alejar. **alienation** *n* alienación *f*.
alight[1] [ə'lait] *v* desmontar, bajar, apearse.
alight[2] [ə'lait] *adj* encendido, iluminado, en llamas.
align [ə'lain] *v* alinear. **alignment** *n* alineación *f*.
alike [ə'laik] *adj* igual, parecido, semejante. *adv* igualmente, del mismo modo.
alimentary canal [ali'mentəri] *n* tubo digestivo *m*.
alimony ['aliməni] *n* alimentos *m pl*.
alive [ə'laiv] *adj* vivo, activo. **alive to** sensible de. **alive with** rebosante de.
alkali ['alkəlai] *n* álcali *m*.
all [oil] *adj* todo. *pron* todo el mundo. *n* todo *m*, totalidad *f*. *adv* todo, enteramente. **all but** casi. **all right** está bien. **all the more** cuanto más. **all the same** sin embargo.
allay [ə'lei] *v* aliviar, calmar.
allege [ə'ledʒ] *v* alegar, afirmar.
allegiance [ə'liidʒəns] *n* fidelidad *f*, lealtad *f*.
allegory ['aligəri] *n* alegoría *f*.
allergy ['alədʒi] *n* alergia *f*. **allergic** *adj* alérgico.
alleviate [ə'liivieit] *v* aliviar. **alleviation** *n* alivio *m*.
alley ['ali] *n* callejuela *f*, paseo *m*. **blind alley** callejón sin salida *m*.
alliance [ə'laiəns] *n* alianza *f*.

allied ['alaid] *adj* aliado.

alligator ['aligeitə] *n* caimán *m*.

alliteration [əlitə'reiʃən] *n* aliteración *f*.

allocate ['aləkeit] *v* asignar, distribuir.

allocation *n* asignación *f*, repartimiento *m*.

allot [ə'lot] *v* asignar. **allotment** *n* lote *m*.

allow [ə'lau] *v* permitir, admitir. **allow for** tener en cuenta. **allowable** *adj* permisible, legítimo. **allowance** *n* ración *f*; pensión *f*. monthly allowance mesada *f*.

alloy ['aloi; *v* ə'loi] *n* aleación *f*; (*fig*) mezcla *f*. *v* alear, ligar.

allude [ə'luːd] *v* aludir. **allusion** *n* alusión *f*. **allusive** *adj* alusivo.

allure [ə'ljuə] *v* seducir, fascinar. **allurement** *n* incentivo *m*, anzuelo *m*. **alluring** *adj* halagüeño, tentador.

ally ['alai; *v* ə'lai] *n* aliado, -a *m*, *f*, asociado, -a *m*, *f*. *v* unir.

almanac ['oɪlmənak] *n* almanaque *m*.

almighty [oɪl'maiti] *adj* omnipotente, todopoderoso.

almond ['aɪmənd] *n* (*nut*) almendra *f*; (*tree*) almendro *m*.

almost ['oɪlmoust] *adv* casi.

alms [aɪmz] *n* limosna *f*. **almsgiving** *n* caridad *f*. **almshouse** *n* hospicio *m*.

aloft [ə'loft] *adv* en alto, arriba.

alone [ə'loun] *adj* solo, único. *adv* solamente, a solas. **leave alone** dejar en paz.

along [ə'loŋ] *prep* a lo largo de. **along with** en compañía de, junto con. **come along!** ¡ven! **alongside** *adv* al lado; (*naut*) al costado de.

aloof [ə'luːf] *adv* a distancia. *adj* altanero, reservado. **keep aloof** mantenerse alejado. **aloofness** *n* alejamiento *m*.

aloud [ə'laud] *adv* en voz alta, recio, alto.

alphabet ['alfəbit] *n* alfabeto *m*.

Alps [alps] *n* Alpes *m pl*.

already [oɪl'redi] *adv* ya.

also ['oɪlsou] *adv* también, además.

altar [oɪltə] *n* altar *m*. **high altar** altar mayor. **altar boy** monaguillo *m*. **altarpiece** retablo *m*.

alter ['oɪltə] *v* cambiar, modificar, corregir, transformar; (*clothes*) arreglar. **alteration** *n* cambio *m*, modificación *f*; (*building*) reforma *f*.

alternate [oɪl'təɪnət; *v* 'oɪltəneit] *adj* alterno. *v* alternar. **alternating current** corriente alterna.

alternative [oɪl'təɪnətiv] *n* alternativa *f*.

adj alternativo. **have no alternative but** ... no poder menos de ... .

although [oɪl'ðou] *conj* aunque.

altitude ['altitjuɪd] *n* altura *f*, altitud *f*.

altogether [oɪltə'geðə] *adv* en total, en conjunto, del todo.

altruistic [altruː'istik] *adj* altruista. **altruism** *n* altruismo. **altruist** *n* altruista *m*, *f*.

aluminium [alju'miniəm] *n* aluminio *m*.

always ['oɪlweiz] *adv* siempre.

am [am] *V* **be**.

amalgamate [ə'malgəmeit] *v* amalgamar, combinar, unir; combinarse, unirse. **amalgamation** *n* amalgamación *f*; mezcla *f*.

amass [ə'mas] *v* acumular, amontonar.

amateur ['amətə] *n*, *adj* aficionado, -a. **amateurish** *adj* de aficionado, superficial.

amaze [ə'meiz] *v* asombrar, sorprender, confundir. **amazement** *n* asombro *m*. **amazing** *adj* asombroso.

ambassador [am'basədə] *n* embajador *m*.

amber ['ambə] *n* ámbar *m*. *adj* ambarino.

ambidextrous [ambi'dekstrəs] *adj* ambidextro.

ambiguous [am'bigjuəs] *adj* ambiguo. **ambiguity** *n* ambigüedad *f*.

ambition [am'biʃən] *n* ambición *f*. **ambitious** *adj* ambicioso.

ambivalent [am'bivələnt] *adj* ambivalente.

amble ['ambl] *v* amblar, andar lentamente. *n* paso de andadura *m*.

ambulance ['ambjuləns] *n* ambulancia *f*.

ambush ['ambuʃ] *n* emboscada *f*, asechanza *f*. *v* emboscar, asechar.

ameliorate [ə'miːliəreit] *v* mejorar. **amelioration** *n* mejora *f*.

amenable [ə'miːnəbl] *adj* tratable, dócil, sujeto.

amend [ə'mend] *v* enmendar, modificar, rectificar. **amendment** *n* enmienda *f*. **make amends** dar satisfacción, indemnizar.

amenity [ə'miːnəti] *n* amenidad *f*, comodidad *f*.

America [ə'merikə] *n* América *f*. **American** *n*, *adj* americano, -a *m*, *f*.

amethyst ['aməθist] *n* amatista *f*.

amiable ['eimiəbl] *adj* amistoso, afable.

amicable ['amikəbl] *adj* amigable.

amid [ə'mid] *prep* entre, rodeado por, en medio de.

amiss [ə'mis] *adv* mal, de más, impropiamente. **take amiss** llevar a mal.

ammonia [ə'mouniə] *n* amoníaco *m*.

ammunition [amju'niʃən] *n* municiones *f pl*.

amnesia [am'niːziə] *n* amnesia *f*.

amnesty ['amnəsti] *n* amnistía *f*.

amoeba [ə'miːbə] *n* ameba *f*.

among [ə'mʌŋ] *prep* entre, en medio de.

amoral [ei'morəl] *adj* amoral.

amorous ['amərəs] *adj* amoroso.

amorphous [ə'mɔːfəs] *adj* amorfo.

amount [ə'maunt] *n* cantidad *f*, importe *m*, suma *f*. *v* llegar a, subir a, valer. **gross amount** importe bruto *m*. **net amount** importe neto *m*. **it amounts to this** se reduce a esto.

ampere ['ampeə] *n* amperio *m*.

amphetamine [am'fetəmiːn] *n* anfetamina *f*.

amphibian [am'fibiən] *nm*, *adj* anfibio.

amphitheatre ['amfiθiətə] *n* anfiteatro *m*.

ample ['ampl] *adj* amplio, abundante; (*enough*) bastante, suficiente.

amplify ['amplifai] *v* ampliar, amplificar, aumentar. **amplifier** *n* amplificador *m*.

amputate ['ampjuteit] *v* amputar. **amputation** *n* amputación *f*.

amuse [ə'mjuːz] *v* divertir, distraer, entretener. **amuse oneself** divertirse. **amusement** *n* diversión *f*, entretenimiento *m*, recreo *m*; (*hobby*) pasatiempo *m*. **amusement park** parque de atracciones *m*. **amusing** *adj* divertido, gracioso.

anachronism [ə'nakrənizəm] *n* anacronismo *m*. **anachronistic** *adj* anacrónico.

anaemia [ə'niːmiə] *n* anemia *f*. **anaemic** *adj* anémico.

anaesthetic [anəs'θetik] *nm*, *adj* anestésico.

anagram ['anəgram] *n* anagrama *m*.

analogy [ə'nalədʒi] *n* analogía *f*. **analogous** *adj* análogo.

analysis [ən'aləsis] *n*, *pl* **-ses** análisis *m*. **analyst** *n* analista *m*, *f*. **analytic(al)** *adj* analítico.

anarchy ['anəki] *n* anarquía *f*. **anarchic** *adj* anárquico. **anarchist** *n* anarquista *m*, *f*.

anathema [ə'naθəmə] *n* anatema *m*, *f*.

anatomy [ə'natəmi] *n* anatomía *f*. **anatomical** *adj* anatómico.

ancestor ['ansestə] *n* antepasado *m*. **ancestral** *adj* ancestral, hereditario. **ancestry** *n* linaje *m*.

anchor ['aŋkə] *n* ancla *f*; (*fig*) áncora *f*. *v* anclar, fijar, fondear.

anchovy ['antʃəvi] *n* anchoa *f*.

ancient ['einʃənt] *adj* anciano, antiguo. **ancients** *pl n* los antiguos *m pl*. **from ancient times** de antiguo.

ancillary [an'siləri] *adj* auxiliar.

and [and] *conj* y, e.

anecdote ['anikdout] *n* anécdota *f*.

anemone [ə'neməni] *n* anémona *f*.

anew [ə'njuː] *adv* de nuevo, otra vez.

angel ['eindʒəl] *n* ángel *m*. **angelic** *adj* angélico.

anger ['aŋgə] *n* cólera *f*, ira *f*, enojo *m*. *v* enojar, enfadar, encolerizar. **angry** *adj* enojado, enfadado.

angina [an'dʒainə] *n* angina *f*. **angina pectoris** angina de pecho.

angle ['aŋgl] *n* ángulo *m*, rincón *m*; (*viewpoint*) punto de vista *m*.

angling ['aŋgliŋ] *n* pesca con caña *f*. **angler** *n* pescador, -a *m*, *f*.

anguish ['aŋgwiʃ] *n* angustia *f*, agonía *f*, dolor *m*.

animal ['animəl] *n* animal *m*, bestia *f*. *adj* animal. **animal kingdom** reino animal *m*. **animal spirits** brío *m*, energía *f*, exuberancia vital *f*.

animate ['animeit; *adj* 'animət] *v* animar, alentar, vivificar. *adj* viviente, animado. **animated** *adj* animado, vivo. **animated cartoon** dibujo animado.

animosity [ani'mosəti] *n* animosidad *f*, hostilidad *f*.

aniseed ['anisiːd] *n* grano de anís *m*.

ankle ['aŋkl] *n* tobillo *m*.

annals ['anlz] *pl n* anales *m pl*.

annex ['aneks; *v* ə'neks] *n* anexo *m*. *v* anexar, anexionar; unir, juntar. **annexation** *n* anexión *f*.

annihilate [ə'naiəleit] *v* aniquilar. **annihilation** *n* aniquilación *f*.

anniversary [,ani'vɔːsəri] *n* aniversario *m*.

annotate ['anəteit] *v* anotar, acotar, glosar. **annotation** *n* anotación *f*, nota *f*.

announce [ə'nauns] *v* anunciar, publicar, proclamar. **announcement** *n* anuncio *m*, aviso *m*, publicación *f*; (*of engagement*) participación *f*. **announcer** *n* annuncidor, -a *m*, *f*; (*radio*) locutor, -a *m*, *f*.

annoy [ə'noi] *v* molestar, irritar, fastidiar. **annoyance** *n* molestia *f*, disgusto *m*. **annoyed** *adj* enojado. **annoying** *adj* fastidioso, enojoso, molesto.

annual ['anjuəl] *adj* anual. *n* (*book*) anuario *m*; (*plant*) planta anual *f*.
annul [ə'nʌl] *v* anular; (*law*) abrogar. **annulment** *n* anulación *f*.
Annunciation [əˌnʌnsi'eiʃən] *n* (*rel*) Anunciación *f*.
anode ['anoud] *n* ánodo *m*.
anomaly [ə'noməli] *n* anomalía *f*. **anomalous** *adj* anómalo.
anonymous [ə'noniməs] *adj* anónimo.
anorak ['anərak] *n* anorak *m*.
another [ə'nʌðə] *adj* otro. *pron* otro, -a *m, f.* **one after another** uno después de otro.
answer ['ainsə] *n* contestación *f*, respuesta *f*; (*solution*) solución *f*; (*math*) resultado *m. v* contestar, responder; (*a bell*) acudir; (*door*) abrir. **answer back** replicar. **answer by return** contestar a vuelta de correo. **answerable** *adj* responsable.
ant [ant] *n* hormiga *f.*
antagonize [an'tagənaiz] *v* antagonizar, contender. **antagonism** *n* antagonismo *m*, oposición *f.* **antagonist** *n* antagonista *m, f.* **antagonistic** *adj* antagónico.
antecedent [anti'siidənt] *nm, adj* antecedente.
antelope ['antəloup] *n* antilope *m.*
antenatal [anti'neitl] *adj* antenatal.
antenna [an'tenə] *n* antena *f.*
anthem ['anθəm] *n* motete *m.* **national anthem** himno nacional *m.*
anthology [an'θolədʒi] *n* antología *f.*
anthropology [anθrə'polədʒi] *n* antropología *f.*
anti-aircraft [anti'eəkraift] *adj* anti-aéreo.
antibiotic [antibai'otik] *nm, adj* antibiótico.
antibody ['antiˌbodi] *n* anticuerpo *m.*
anticipate [an'tisipeit] *v* prever, esperar; anticiparse a. **anticipation** *n* anticipación *f*, esperanza *f*, adelantamiento *m.* **in anticipation of** en espera de.
anticlimax [anti'klaimaks] *n* anticlimax *m.*
anticlockwise [anti'klokwaiz] *adj* en dirección contraria a las agujas del reloj.
antics ['antiks] *pl n* cabriola *f sing*, travesura *f sing*, payasadas *f pl.*
anticyclone [anti'saikloun] *n* anticiclón *m.*
antidote ['antidout] *n* antídoto *m*, contraveneno *m.*
antifreeze ['antifriiz] *n* anticongelante *m.*
antipathy [an'tipəθi] *n* antipatía *f*, aversión *f.*

antique [an'tiik] *n* antigualla *f*, antigüedad *f. adj* antiguo. **antique dealer** anticuario *m.* **antique shop** tienda de antigüedades. **antiquity** *n* antigüedad *f.*
anti-Semitic [antisə'mitik] *adj* antisemítico. **anti-Semitism** *n* antisemitismo *m.*
antiseptic [anti'septik] *nm, adj* antiséptico.
antisocial [anti'souʃəl] *adj* antisocial.
anti-tank [anti'taŋk] *adj* antitanque.
antithesis [an'tiθəsis] *n, pl* -ses antítesis *f.*
antler ['antlə] *n* asta *f*, cuerno *m.*
antonym ['antənim] *n* antónimo *m.*
anus ['einəs] *n* ano *m.* **anal** *adj* anal.
anvil ['anvil] *n* yunque *m.*
anxious ['aŋkʃəs] *adj* ancioso, preocupado, inquieto. **anxiety** *n* inquietud *f*, ansiedad *f*, intranquilidad *f.*
any ['eni] *adv* cualquier; (*some*) algún, ningún; (*every*) todo. *pron* alguno, -a *m, f*; cualquiera *m, f*; ninguno, -a *m, f. adv* algo. **anybody** *or* **anyone** *pron* cualquiera, alguien, nadie. **anyhow** *adv* de cualquier modo. **anything** *n* algo *m*; (*negative*) nada *f.* **anywhere** *adv* dondequiera.
apart [ə'pait] *adv* aparte.
apartment [ə'paitmənt] *n* apartamento *m*, cuarto *m*, habitación *f*; (*flat*) piso *m.*
apathy ['apəθi] *n* apatía *f*, indiferencia *f.* **apathetic** *adj* apático.
ape [eip] *n* simio *m*, mono, -a *m, f. v* imitar.
aperitive [ə'peritiv] *nm, adj* aperitivo.
aperture ['apətjuə] *n* abertura *f*, orificio *m*, agujero *m.*
apex ['eipeks] *n* ápice *m.*
aphrodisiac [afrə'diziak] *n* afrodisíaco *m.*
apiece [ə'piis] *adv* por persona, por cabeza, cada uno.
apology [ə'polədʒi] *n* disculpa *f*, apología *f*, excusa *f.* **apologize** *v* disculparse, pedir perdón; (*regret*) sentir.
apoplexy ['apəpleksi] *n* apoplejía *f.* **apoplectic** *adj* apoplético.
apostle [ə'posl] *n* apóstol *m.*
apostrophe [ə'postrəfi] *n* (*punctuation*) apóstrofo *m*; (*speech*) apóstrofe *m, f.*
appal [ə'poil] *v* espantar, aterrar. **appalling** *adj* espantoso, horrible.
apparatus [apə'reitəs] *n* aparato *m*, máquina *f.*
apparent [ə'parənt] *adj* aparente; notable, obvio, evidente, claro. **apparently** *adv* al parecer.

apparition [apə'riʃən] *n* aparición *f*, fantasma *m*.

appeal [ə'piːl] *v* (*law*) apelar; (*attract*) atraer. *n* (*law*) apelación *f*; atractivo *m*. **appeal against** suplicar de.

appear [ə'piə] *v* aparecer; (*seem*) parecer; (*in court*) comparecer. **appearance** *n* aparición *f*; (*aspect*) apariencia *f*, aspecto *m*; (*arrival*) llegada *f*.

appease [ə'piːz] *v* aplacar, apaciguar. **appeasement** *n* aplacamiento *m*, apaciguamiento *m*.

appendix [ə'pendiks] *n* apéndice *m*. **appendicitis** *n* apendicitis *f*.

appetite ['apitait] *n* apetito *m*. **have an appetite** tener ganas. **appetizing** *adj* apetitoso.

applaud [ə'plɔːd] *v* aplaudir. **applause** *n* aplauso *m*.

apple ['apl] *n* (*fruit*) manzana *f*; (*tree*) manzano *m*. **apple sauce** compota de manzanes *f*.

apply [ə'plai] *v* dirigirse a, recurrir; aplicar; (*use*) emplear; (*for a job*) proponerse a. **apply oneself** to dedicarse a. **appliance** *n* aparato *m*. **applicable** *adj* aplicable. **applicant** *n* aspirante *m*, *f*. **application** *n* aplicación *f*.

appoint [ə'point] *v* nombrar, designar. **be appointed to** colocarse a. **be appointed as** ser nombrado. **appointment** *n* puesto *m*, empleo *m*; (*assignation*) cita *f*. **make an appointment with** citar.

apportion [ə'pɔːʃən] *v* distribuir, repartir.

appraisal [ə'preizl] *n* valoración *f*, estimación *f*. **appraise** *v* valorizar, tasar.

appreciate [ə'priːʃieit] *v* apreciar, darse cuenta de; (*affection*) encarecer; (*in value*) tener en alza. **appreciation** *n* apreciación *f*, aprecio *m*; (*understanding*) percepción *f*; (*of shares, etc.*) aumento de valor *m*.

apprehend [apri'hend] *v* (*arrest*) prender, capturar; (*understand*) aprehender, percibir; (*fear*) temer. **apprehension** *n* (*arrest*) aprehensión *f*; (*understanding*) comprensión *f*; (*fear*) aprensión *f*. **apprehensive** *adj* aprensivo.

apprentice [ə'prentis] *n* aprendiz *m*. **apprenticeship** *n* aprendizaje *m*.

approach [ə'prəutʃ] *v* acercarse a, aproximar; (*speak to*) hablar con. *n* acercamiento *m*, aproximación *f*; (*arrival*) llegada *f*; (*entrance*) entrada *f*.

appropriate [ə'prouprieit; *adj* ə'proupriət] *v* tomar posesión de, apropiar; (*assign*) asignar, destinar. *adj* propio, pertinente, correspondiente. **appropriateness** *n* conveniencia *f*.

approve [ə'pruːv] *v* aprobar. **approval** *n* aprobación *f*. **on approval** a prueba. **approved** *adj* bien visto.

approximate [ə'proksimeit; *adj* ə'proksimət] *v* aproximar, aproximarse. *adj* aproximado. **approximately** *adv* poco más o menos.

apricot ['eiprikot] *n* (*fruit*) albaricoque *m*; (*tree*) albaricoquero *m*.

April ['eiprəl] *n* abril *m*.

apron ['eiprən] *n* delantal *m*; (*stage*) proscenio *m*.

apt [apt] *adj* apto; propenso; (*suitable*) apropiado.

aptitude ['aptitjuːd] *n* aptitud *f*.

aqualung ['akwəlʌŋ] *n* aparato de aire comprimido *m*.

aquarium [ə'kweəriəm] *n* acuario *m*.

Aquarius [ə'kweəriəs] *n* Acuario *m*.

aquatic [ə'kwatik] *adj* acuático.

aqueduct ['akwidʌkt] *n* acueducto *m*.

Arab ['arəb] *n*(*m*+*f*), *adj* árabe. **Arabia** *n* Arabia *f*. **Arabic** *adj* arábigo.

arable ['arəbl] *adj* arable.

arbitrary ['aːbitrəri] *adj* arbitrario.

arbitrate ['aːbitreit] *v* arbitrar. **arbitration** *n* arbitraje *m*. **arbiter** *or* **arbitrator** *n* árbitro *m*.

arc [aːk] *n* arco *m*. **arc lamp** lámpara de arco *f*.

arcade [aː'keid] *n* arcada *f*, galería *f*.

arch[1] [aːtʃ] *n* arco *m*. *v* arquear.

arch[2] [aːtʃ] *adj* (*chief*) principal; archi-.

archaeology [aːki'olədʒi] *n* arqueología *f*. **archaeologist** *n* arqueólogo *m*.

archaic [aː'keiik] *adj* arcaico, arcaizante.

archbishop [aːtʃ'biʃəp] *n* arzobispo *m*.

archduke [aːtʃ'djuːk] *n* archiduque *m*.

archery ['aːtʃəri] *n* tiro con arco *m*. **archer** *n* arquero, -a *m*, *f*.

archetype ['aːkitaip] *n* arquetipo *m*.

archipelago [aːki'peləgou] *n* archipiélago *m*.

architect ['aːkitekt] *n* arquitecto *m*. **architecture** *n* arquitectura *f*.

archives ['aːkaivz] *n pl* archivo *m sing*.

arctic ['aːktik] *adj* ártico. **the Arctic** el Ártico.

ardent ['aːdənt] *adj* ardiente, apasionado.

ardour ['aɪdə] n ardor m.
arduous ['aɪdjuəs] adj arduo.
are [aɪ] V be.
area ['eərɪə] n área f, superficie f; extensión f.
arena [ə'riːnə] n arena f, liza f.
Argentina [aɪdʒən'tiːnə] n Argentina f.
Argentinian n, adj argentino, -a.
argue ['aɪgjuɪ] v debatir, disputar, discutir. **argue against** oponer. **arguable** adj discutible. **argument** n argumento m.
argumentative adj contencioso.
arid ['arid] adj árido, seco.
Aries ['eəriːz] n (astrol) Aries m.
***arise** [ə'raɪz] v elevarse, subir; (revolt) sublevarse; (from bed) levantarse.
aristocracy [ari'stokrəsi] n aristocracia f. **aristocrat** n aristócrata m, f. **aristocratic** adj aristocrático.
arithmetic [ə'riθmətik] n aritmética f.
ark [aɪk] n arca f. **Noah's Ark** arca de Noé f.
arm¹ [aɪm] n (limb) brazo m. **armchair** n sillón m. **arm in arm** de bracete, de bracero. **armpit** n sobaco m. **within arm's reach** al alcance del brazo.
arm² [aɪm] n arma f. v armar. **to arms!** ¡a las armas! **take up arms** alzarse en armas. **under arms** sobre las armas.
armistice ['aɪmistis] n armisticio m.
armour ['aɪmə] n armadura f, arnés m; (ships, vehicles) blindaje m. v blindar, acorazar. **armour-plate** n coraza f. **armoury** n armería f.
army ['aɪmi] n ejército m.
aroma [ə'roumə] n aroma m, fragancia f. **aromatic** adj aromático.
around [ə'raund] prep alrededor de, cerca de; a la vuelta de. adv alrededor, en torno, por todas partes.
arouse [ə'rauz] v despertar, excitar.
arrange [ə'reindʒ] v arreglar, disponer; organizar; (music) adaptar; concertarse. **arrangement** n arreglo m; (agreement) acuerdo m; (music) adaptación f. **arrangements** pl n preparativos m pl.
array [ə'rei] v ataviar, poner en orden de batalla. n (dress) atavío m; (troops) formación f.
arrears [ə'riəz] pl n atrasos m pl. **in arrears** atrasado en pagos.
arrest [ə'rest] v arrestar, detener. n (stop) parada f; (detention) detención f. **under arrest** bajo arresto.

arrive [ə'raiv] v llegar. **arrival** n llegada f, venida f. **on arrival** al llegar.
arrogant ['arəgənt] adj arrogante, altanero. **arrogance** n arrogancia f.
arrow ['arou] n flecha f, saeta f.
arse [aɪs] n (vulgar) culo m, ojete m.
arsenal ['aɪsənl] n arsenal m.
arsenic ['aɪsnik] n arsénico m.
arson ['aɪsn] n incendiarismo m, incendio premeditado m.
art [aɪt] n arte m; (cunning) artificio m. **art gallery** museo de pinturas m. **artful** adj artero, mañoso.
artery ['aɪtəri] n arteria f.
arthritis [aɪ'θraitis] n artritis f.
artichoke ['aɪtitʃouk] n alcachofa f.
article ['aɪtikl] n artículo m; (object) objeto m.
articulate [aɪ'tikjuleit; adj aɪ'tikjulət] v articular. adj claro, distinto.
artifice ['aɪtifis] n artificio m.
artificial [aɪti'fiʃəl] adj artificial, falso. **artificiality** n lo artificial. **artificial respiration** respiración artificial f.
artillery [aɪ'tiləri] n artillería f.
artisan [aɪti'zan] n artesano, -a m, f.
artist ['aɪtist] n artista m, f. **artistic** adj artístico.
as [az] adv tan. prep, conj como, ya que, según, a medida que; (when) cuando; (since) puesto que; (because) porque; (although) aunque. **as a rule** por regla general. **as far as** en cuanto a. **as from** desde. **as good as** tan bueno como. **as if** como si. **as it were** en cierto modo. **as soon as** en cuanto. **as soon as possible** cuanto antes. **as usual** como de costumbre. **as well** también. **as well as** además de.
asbestos [az'bestos] n asbesto m.
ascend [ə'send] v subir. **ascendancy** n ascendiente m. **be in the ascendant** ir en aumento. **ascension** n subida f. **ascent** n subida f; (slope) cuesta f.
ascetic [ə'setik] adj ascético. n asceta m, f.
ash¹ [aʃ] n (cinder) ceniza f, cenizas f pl. **ashtray** n cenicero m.
ash² [aʃ] n (tree) fresno m.
ashamed [ə'ʃeimd] adj avergonzado.
ashore [ə'ʃoɪ] adv a tierra. **go ashore** desembarcar.
Ash Wednesday n miércoles de ceniza m.

Asia ['eiʃə] *n* Asia *f.* **Asian** *n, adj* asiático, -a.

aside [ə'said] *adv* aparte, a un lado. *n* (*theatre*) aparte *m.*

ask [aisk] *v* preguntar, pedir, invitar. **ask for trouble** buscársela. **for the asking** sin más que pedirlo.

askew [ə'skjuɪ] *adj* oblicuamente, a un lado.

asleep [ə'sliːp] *adj, adv* dormido. **fall asleep** dormirse.

asparagus [ə'spærəgəs] *n* espárrago *m.*

aspect ['aspekt] *n* aspecto *m,* vista *f.*

asphalt ['asfalt] *n* asfalto *m.*

asphyxiate [əs'fiksieit] *v* asfixiar.

aspire [ə'spaiə] *v* aspirar. **aspiration** *n* aspiración *f.*

aspirin ['aspərin] *n* aspirina *f.*

ass [as] *n* asno *m.* **asinine** *adj* asnal.

assail [ə'seil] *v* atacar. **assailant** *n* asaltador, -a *m, f.*

assassinate [ə'sasineit] *v* asesinar. **assassin** *n* asesino *m, f.* **assassination** *n* asesinato *m.*

assault [ə'soɪlt] *n* asalto *m. v* asaltar.

assemble [ə'sembl] *v* (*people*) convocar; (*things*) juntar; (*machines*) armar. **assemblage** *n* reunión *f.* **assembly** *n* asamblea *f.* **assembly line** línea de montaje *f.*

assent [ə'sent] *v* asentir. *n* asentimiento *m.*

assert [ə'sɔɪt] *v* afirmar, declarar. **assertion** *n* afirmación *f,* aserción *f.*

assess [ə'ses] *v* evaluar, asesorar. **assessment** *n* valoración *f.*

asset ['aset] *n* ventaja *f.* **assets** *pl n* activo *m sing,* haber *m sing,* bienes *m pl.*

assiduous [ə'sidjuəs] *adj* asiduo, aplicado.

assign [ə'sain] *v* asignar, señalar; (*law*) consignar; (*goods*) traspasar. **assignment** *n* asignación *f.*

assimilate [ə'simileit] *v* asimilar, incorporarse. **assimilation** *n* asimilación *f.*

assist [ə'sist] *v* asistir, ayudar. **assistance** *n* ayuda *f.* **assistant** *n* ayudante *m,* colaborador *m.*

associate [ə'sousiət; *v* ə'sousieit] *n* socio, -a *m, f,* compañero, -a *m, f,* cómplice *m, f. v* asociar, juntar. **associate with** ir con. **association** *n* asociación *f,* sociedad *f.*

assorted [ə'sɔɪtid] *adj* surtido, mezclado. **assortment** *n* clasificación *f,* mezcla *f.*

assume [ə'sjuɪm] *v* asumir, tomar; (*suppose*) suponer. **assumed** *adj* fingido.

assuming that dado que. **assumption** *n* asunción *f.*

assure [ə'ʃuə] *v* asegurar, garantizar. **assurance** *n* seguridad *f,* certeza *f;* (*comm*) seguro *m.* **assuredly** *adv* seguramente.

asterisk ['astərisk] *n* asterisco *m.*

asthma ['asmə] *n* asma *f.*

astonish [ə'stoniʃ] *v* asombrar. **astonishment** *n* asombro *m.*

astound [ə'staund] *v* aturdir. **be astounded** quedarse muerto.

astray [ə'strei] *adv* desviado. **go astray** perderse.

astride [ə'straid] *adv* a horcajadas. *prep* a horcajadas sobre.

astringent [ə'strindʒənt] *adj* astringente.

astrology [ə'strolədʒi] *n* astrología *f.* **astrologer** *n* astrólogo, -a *m, f.*

astronaut ['astrənoɪt] *n* astronauta *m, f.*

astronomy [ə'stronəmi] *n* astronomía *f.* **astronomer** *n* astrónomo *m.* **astronomical** *adj* astronómico.

astute [ə'stjuɪt] *adj* astuto, agudo. **astuteness** *n* astucia *f,* sagacidad *f.*

asunder [ə'sʌndə] *adv* separadamente, en dos.

asylum [ə'sailəm] *n* (*refuge*) asilo *m;* (*for the insane*) manicomio *m.*

at [at] *prep* a, en.

ate [et] *V* eat.

atheism ['eiθiizəm] *n* ateísmo *m.* **atheist** *n* ateo, -a *m, f.*

Athens ['aθinz] *n* Atenas *f.* **Athenian** *n*(*m+f*), *adj* ateniense.

athlete ['aθliɪt] *n* atleta *m, f.* **athletic** *adj* atlético. **athletics** *n* atletismo *m.*

Atlantic [ət'lantik] *n* Atlántico *m. adj* atlántico.

atlas ['atləs] *n* atlas *m.*

atmosphere ['atməsfiə] *n* atmósfera *f,* aire *m;* (*feeling*) ambiente *m.* **atmospheric** *adj* atmosférico. **atmospherics** *pl n* perturbaciones atmosféricas *f pl.*

atom ['atəm] *n* átomo *m.* **atomic** *adj* atómico.

atone [ə'toun] *v* expiar. **atonement** *n* expiación *f.*

atrocious [ə'trouʃəs] *adj* atroz. **atrocity** *n* atrocidad *f.*

attach [ə'tatʃ] *v* atar, adherir, pegar. **attach oneself to** asociarse con. **attachment** *n* unión *f;* (*hook*) enganche *m;* (*friendship*) amistad *f.*

attaché [ə'taʃei] n agregado m. **attaché case** maletín m.

attack [ə'tak] v atacar. n ataque m; (*mil*) ofensiva f. **attacker** n atacador, -a m, f.

attain [ə'tein] v lograr, alcanzar. **attainable** adj asequible, realizable. **attainment** n logro m. **attainments** pl n prendas f pl.

attempt [ə'tempt] n tentativa f. v procurar, tratar de.

attend [ə'tend] v atender, servir; concurrir; (*the sick*) asistir; (*listen*) escuchar. **attendance** n servicio m, asistencia f; (*audience*) auditorio m. **attendant** n criado, -a m, f, servidor, -a m, f.

attention [ə'tenʃən] n atención f. **call attention to** destacar, hacer presente. **pay attention** prestar atención. **attentive** adj atento, cortés. **attentiveness** n cuidado m.

attic ['atik] n desván m, sotabanco m.

attire [ə'taiə] n atavió m, ropaje m, traje m, adorno m. v ataviar, vestir.

attitude ['atitjuːd] n actitud f, postura f, ademán m.

attorney [ə'təːni] n (*agent*) apoderado, -a m, f; (*solicitor*) abogado, -a m, f. **power of attorney** poderes m pl.

attract [ə'trakt] v atraer, llamar. **attraction** n atracción f, imán m. **attractive** adj atractivo, atrayente.

attribute ['atribjuːt; v ə'tribjuːt] n atributo m. v atribuir. **attributable** adj atribuible. **attribution** n atributo m.

attrition [ə'triʃən] n atrición f.

atypical [ei'tipikl] adj atípico.

aubergine ['oubəʒiːn] n berenjena f.

auburn ['oːbən] adj castaño rojizo.

auction ['oːkʃən] n remate m, almoneda f, subasta f. v rematar, subastar. **auctioneer** n subastador m.

audacious [oː'deiʃəs] adj audaz, arrojado. **audacity** n audacia f, arrojo m, atrevimiento m.

audible ['oːdəbl] adj audible. **audibility** n audibilidad f.

audience ['oːdjəns] n audiencia f; oyentes m pl.

audiovisual [oːdiou'viʒuəl] adj audiovisual.

audit ['oːdit] v intervenir. n intervención f, ajuste (de cuentas) m. **auditor** n inteventor m, contador m.

audition [oː'diʃən] n audición f. v dar audición.

auditorium [oːdi'toːriəm] n auditorio m, sala de espectáculos f.

augment [oːg'ment] v aumentar, engrosar; acrecentarse.

august [oː'gʌst] adj augusto.

August ['oːgəst] n agosto m.

aunt [aːnt] n tía f. **great-aunt** n tía abuela f.

aura ['oːrə] n aura f; exhalación f.

auspicious [oː'spiʃəs] adj propicio.

austere [oː'stiə] adj austero, severo. **austerity** n austeridad f, severidad f.

Australia [o'streiljə] n Australia f. **Australian** n, adj australiano, -a.

Austria ['oːstriə] n Austria f. **Austrian** n, adj austríaco, -a.

authentic [oː'θentik] adj auténtico.

author ['oːθə] n autor, -a m, f.

authority [oː'θorəti] n autoridad f. **on good authority** de buena fuente. **authoritarian** adj autoritario.

authorize ['oːθəraiz] v autorizar. **authorization** n autorización f.

autobiography [oːtoubai'ogrəfi] n autobiografía f. **autobiographical** adj autobiográfico.

autocratic [oːtou'kratik] adj autocrático. **autocrat** n autócrata m, f.

autograph ['oːtəgraːf] n autógrafo m. v firmar, dedicar.

automatic [oːtə'matik] adj automático. **automation** n automatización f.

automobile ['oːtəməbiːl] n automóvil m.

autonomous [oː'tonəməs] adj autónomo.

autopsy ['oːtopsi] n autopsia f.

autumn ['oːtəm] n otoño m. **autumnal** adj otoñal.

auxiliary [oːg'ziljəri] adj auxiliar. n auxiliador m.

avail [ə'veil] v servir, valer, importar; aprovechar. **avail oneself of** aprovecharse de. **to no avail** en balde.

available [ə'veiləbl] adj útil, disponible. **availability** n utilidad f, disponibilidad f.

avalanche ['avəlaːnʃ] n avalancha f, alud m.

avarice ['avəris] n avaricia f, codicia f. **avaricious** adj avariento.

avenge [ə'vendʒ] v vengar, vindicar. **avenge oneself** vengarse de. **avenger** n vengador, -a m, f.

avenue ['avinjuː] n avenida f.

average ['avəridʒ] n promedio m, término medio m. adj de promedio, corriente. v hallar el término medio. **on average** por regla general.

aversion [ə'vɜːʃən] n aversión f. **averse** adj opuesto. **be averse to** ser enemigo de.
avert [ə'vɜːt] v apartar; (avoid) evitar.
aviary ['eiviəri] n avería f.
aviation [eivi'eiʃən] n aviación f. **aviator** n aviador, -a m, f.
avid ['avid] adj ávido, codicioso, voraz. **avidity** n avidez f, codicia f.
avocado [avə'kaːdou] n aguacate m.
avoid [ə'void] v evitar, eludir, evadir. **avoidance** n evitación f.
await [ə'weit] v esperar, aguardar.
***awake** [ə'weik] v despertar; despertarse. adj despierto, atento (a). **awakening** n despertamiento m.
award [ə'wɔːd] n fallo m, premio m, recompensa f. v otorgar, conceder, conferir.
aware [ə'weə] adj enterado, vigilante, consciente. **become aware of** darse cuenta de. **make aware of** hacer saber. **awareness** n conocimiento m.
away [ə'wei] adv a lo lejos, ausente, fuera, en otro lugar.
awe [ɔː] n temor m, pasmo m; reverencia f. v intimidar, atemorizar. **awesome** adj pavoroso, imponente.
awful ['ɔːful] adj tremendo, atroz, terrible, espantoso. **how awful!** ¡qué barbaridad! **awfully** adv (coll) muy.
awkward ['ɔːkwəd] adj difícil; (clumsy) desmañado; (ungraceful) sin gracia.
awl [ɔːl] n punzón m, lezna f.
awning ['ɔːniŋ] n toldo m.
axe [aks] n hacha f.
axiom ['aksiəm] n axioma m.
axis ['aksis] n eje m.
axle ['aksl] n eje m, peón m, árbol m.

B

babble ['babl] v balbucear; garlar. n murmullo m, cháchara f.
baboon [bə'buːn] n babuino m.
baby ['beibi] n bebé m, criatura f, nene m; (animals) crío m. **babyhood** n niñez f. **babyish** adj infantil.
bachelor ['batʃələ] n soltero m; (of Arts or Science) licenciado m, bachiller m.
back [bak] n (anat) espalda f; dorso m;

(sport) defensa f. adj trasero, posterior, de atrás; (of pay, etc.) atrasado. adv atrás; detrás; otra vez, de nuevo. v retroceder; (support) apoyar; (bet on) apostar a. **back down** abandonar. **back out** echarse atrás; (retract) desdecirse.
backache ['bakeik] n dolor de espaldas m.
backbone ['bakboun] n espinazo m.
backdate [bak'deit] v poner fecha atrasada.
backfire [bak'faiə] n petardeo m. v petardear.
backgammon ['bakgamən] n chaquete m.
backhand ['bakhand] n (sport) revés m. **back-handed** adj de revés; (fig) ambiguo.
backing ['bakiŋ] n forro m; (support) apoyo m; (lining) refuerzo m; (betting) el apostar (a) m.
backlash ['baklaʃ] n reacción f.
backlog ['baklog] n atrasos m pl.
backside ['baksaid] n trasero m, parte trasera f.
backward ['bakwəd] adj atrasado, vuelto hacia atrás. **backwardness** n atraso m, torpeza f. **backward and forward** de acá para allá.
backwards ['bakwədz] adv hacia atrás, al revés.
backwater ['bakwɔːtə] n (pool) remanso m.
bacon ['beikən] n tocino m.
bacteria [bak'tiəriə] n pl bacteria f pl.
bad [bad] adj malo; (ill) enfermo; (rotten) podrido; (debt) incobrable; (dangerous) peligroso; (coin) falso; (pain) fuerte; (unlucky) desgraciado. **bad-tempered** adj de mal genio. **from bad to worse** de mal en peor. **badly** adv mal; (seriously) gravemente.
badge [badʒ] n insignia f, marca f, divisa f.
badger ['badʒə] n tejón m. v molestar.
badminton ['badmintən] n volante m, badminton m.
baffle ['bafl] v frustrar, desconcertar, confundir. **baffling** adj desconcertante, difícil; (person) enigmático.
bag [bag] n bolsa f, saco m, valija f; (sewing) costurera f; (suitcase) maleta f. v ensacar; (coll, esp. game) matar, tomar. **pack one's bags** liar el petate. **baggage** m equipaje m.
baggy ['bagi] adj holgado.

bagpipes ['bagpaips] *n pl* gaita *f.*
bail¹ [beil] *n* (*law*) fianza *f.* caución *f.* v
poner bajo fianza.
bail² *or* **bale** [beil] *v* **bail out** (*flooded boat*)
achicar, baldear; (*from aircraft*) lanzarse
en paracaídas.
bailiff ['beilif] *n* (*law*) alguacil *m*; (*of
estate*) capataz *m.*
bait [beit] *n* (*fishing*) cebo *m*, anzuelo *m*;
(*lure*) añagaza *f.* v cebar, azuzar; (*annoy*)
molestar.
bake [beik] *v* cocer al horno. **baker's doz-
en** la docena del fraile *f.* **baker** *m*
panadero *m.* **bakery** *n* panadería *f.* **baking powder** levadura en polvo *f.*
balance ['baləns] *n* equilibrio *m*; (*scales*)
balanza *f*; (*comm*) balance *m.* v
equilibrar; (*comm*) saldar.
balcony ['balkəni] *n* balcón *m*, galería *f*;
(*theatre*) anfiteatro *m.*
bald [boild] *adj* calvo, pelado; (*tyre*)
desgastado. **baldness** *n* calvicie *f.*
bale¹ [beil] *n* fardo *m*, bala *f.* v embalar.
bale² *V* **bail²**.
ball¹ [boil] *n* pelota *f*; globo *m*, bola *f*;
(*shot*) bala *f*; (*of wool*) ovillo *m*; (*of the
foot*) planta del pie *f.* **ball-and-socket
joint** articulación esférica *f.* **ball bearings**
cojinete de bolas *m sing.* **ball-point pen**
bolígrafo *m.*
ball² [boil] *n* (*dance*) baile *m.* **fancy-dress
ball** baile de disfraces. **ballroom** *n* salón
de baile *m.*
ballad ['baləd] *n* balada *f*, romance *m*,
trova *f*; (*music*) canción *f.*
ballast ['baləst] *n* lastre. v lastrar.
ballet ['balei] *n* ballet *m*, danza *f.* **ballet
dancer** bailarín, bailarina *m, f.*
ballistic [bə'listik] *adj* balístico. **ballistic
missile** proyectil balístico *m.*
balloon [bə'luɪn] *n* globo *m.* **balloonist** *n*
aeronauta *m, f.*
ballot ['balət] *n* votación *f*, sufragio *m.* v
votar, balotar. **ballot-box** *n* urna electoral *f.*
bamboo [bam'buɪ] *n* bambú *m.*
ban [ban] *n* prohibición *f*, interdicción *f.*
v prohibir, proscribir.
banal [bə'naɪl] *adj* trivial, trillado.
banana [bə'naɪnə] *n* (*fruit and tree*) plátano *m*; (*S. Am.*) (*fruit*) banana, (*tree*)
banano *m.*
band¹ [band] *n* (*troop*) grupo *m*, banda *f*;
(*music*) orquesta *f*, banda *f.* v congregar,
unir, asociar.

band² [band] *n* (*strip*) lista *f*, tira *f*, banda
f.
bandage ['bandidʒ] *n* venda *f.* v vendar.
bandit ['bandit] *n* bandido *m.*
bandy ['bandi] *adj also* **bandy-legged**
estevado. v trocar.
bang [baŋ] *n* golpazo *m*, detonación *f*,
golpe *m.* v golpear, estallar.
bangle ['baŋgl] *n* ajorca *f*, pulseta *f*,
brazalete *m.*
banish ['baniʃ] *v* desterrar, despedir, exilar, deportar. **banishment** *n* destierro *m.*
banister ['banistə] *n* baranda *f*, pasamano
m.
banjo ['bandʒou] *n* banjo *m.*
bank¹ [baŋk] *n* (*of river, etc.*) ribera *f*,
orilla *f*, margen *m.*
bank² [baŋk] *n* banco *m.* **bank account**
cuenta bancaria *f.* **bank holiday** día festivo *m.* v depositar en el banco. **banker** *n*
banquero *m.*
bankrupt ['baŋkrʌpt] *n* quebrado, -a *m, f.*
adj insolvente, quebrado. **go bankrupt**
hacer bancarrota, declararse en quiebra.
bankruptcy *n* bancarrota *f*, quiebra *f.*
banner ['banə] *n* bandera *f*, estandarte *m.*
banns [banz] *n pl* amonestaciones *f pl.*
publish the banns decir las amonestaciones.
banquet ['baŋkwit] *m* banquete *m.* v ban-
quetear.
bantam ['bantəm] *n* gallina enana *f.* **ban-
tamweight** *n* peso gallo *m.*
banter ['bantə] *n* burla *f*, chanza *f.* v
burlarse, tomar el pelo a.
baptize [bap'taiz] *v* bautizar. **baptism** *n*
bautismo *m.* **baptist** *n* bautista *m.* **baptis-
try** *n* baptisterio *m*, bautisterio *m.*
bar [baɪ] *n* barra *f*; (*soap, chocolate, etc.*)
pastilla *f*; (*music*) barra *f*, compás *m*;
(*barrier*) barrera *f*; (*refreshments*) bar *m*;
(*law*) foro *m*, curia *f*; v atrancar,
obstruir, impedir. **barman** *m* mozo de bar
m. **barmaid** *n* camarera *f.*
barb [baɪb] *n* púa *f*; (*fish-hook*) lengüeta *f.*
barbarian [baɪ'beəriən] *n, adj* bárbaro, -a
m, f. **barbaric** *adj* barbárico. **barbarity** *n*
barbaridad *f.*
barbecue ['baɪbikjuɪ] *n* barbacoa *f.*
barber ['baɪbə] *n* barbero *m*, peluquero
m. **barber's shop** barbería *f*, peluquería *f.*
barbiturate [baɪ'bitjurət] *n* barbitúrico *m.*
bare [beə] *adj* desnudo, descubierto. v
desnudar, descubrir. **barefaced** *adj*

descarado. **barefoot** adj descalzo. **bare-
headed** adj sin sombrero. **barely** adv
apenas.

bargain ['bɑːgin] n (cheap) ganga f;
(agreement) pacto m, ajuste m, convenio
m. v negociar, regatear. **bargain sale**
saldo m. **into the bargain** por más señas.

barge [bɑːdʒ] n barca f, bote m, barcaza
f. **barge in** irrumpir. **barge into** entrometerse.

baritone ['bæritoun] n barítono m.

bark[1] [bɑːk] n (dog) ladrido m. v ladrar.

bark[2] [bɑːk] n (tree) corteza f.

barley ['bɑːli] n cebada f. **barley water** n
hordiate m.

barn [bɑːn] n granero m, pajar m.

barometer [bə'rɒmitə] n barómetro m.

baron ['bærən] n barón m. **baroness** n
baronesa f. **baronet** n baronet m.

baroque [bə'rɒk] adj barroco.

barracks ['bærəks] pl n cuartel m, barraca
f.

barrage ['bærɑːʒ] n presa f; (mil)
bombardeo m, cortina de fuego f.

barrel ['bærəl] n (cask) barril m; (gun,
etc.) cañón m. **barrel organ** organillo m.

barren ['bærən] adj (land) yermo, árido;
estéril. **barrenness** n aridez f; esterilidad
f.

barricade [bæri'keid] n barrera f, barricada f, empalizada f. v barrear, obstruir.

barrier ['bæriə] n barrera f; impedimento
m; valla f.

barrister ['bæristə] n abogado, -a m, f.

barrow ['bærou] n carretilla f.

barter ['bɑːtə] v cambiar, trocar. n
trueque m, cambio m, tráfico m.

base[1] [beis] n base f, fundamento m, pie
m. v fundar, apoyarse, basar. **baseless**
adj sin base.

base[2] [beis] adj bajo, vil, impuro. **base-
ness** n bajeza f, vileza f.

baseball ['beisbɔːl] n béisbol m.

basement ['beismənt] n sótano m.

bash [bæʃ] n golpe m. v golpear.

bashful ['bæʃful] adj vergonzoso, tímido,
encogido. **bashfulness** n vergüenza f,
encogimiento m.

basic ['beisik] adj fundamental; (chem)
básico.

basil ['bæzl] n albahaca f.

basilica [bə'zilikə] n basílica f.

basin ['beisin] n bacía f, jofaina f; (wash-
basin) palangana f; (dock) dársena f;
(river) cuenca f.

basis ['beisis] n base f, fundamento m.

bask [bɑːsk] v calentarse.

basket ['bɑːskit] n cesta f, canasta f. **basketball** n baloncesto m.

Basque [bɑːsk] n, adj vasco, -a m, f; (language) vascuence m.

bas-relief ['bæsri,liːf] n bajorrelieve m.

bass[1] [beis] n (voice) bajo m. **bass clef** n
clave de fa f.

bass[2] [bæs] n (freshwater) róbalo m; (sea)
lobina f.

bassoon [bə'suːn] n bajón m.

bastard ['bɑːstəd] n bastardo, -a m, f.

baste [beist] v (cookery) enlardar, pringar; (sewing) bastear, hilvanar.

bastion ['bæstjən] n bastión m, baluarte
m.

bat[1] [bæt] n maza f, palo m; (cricket)
paleta f; (table tennis) pala f. v golpear
con le paleta.

bat[2] [bæt] n (zool) murciélago m.

batch [bætʃ] n grupo m; (loaves) hornada
f.

bath [bɑːθ] n baño m. v bañar, lavar,
tomar un baño. **bath-chair** n cochecillo
de inválido m. **bathrobe** n albornoz m.
bathroom n cuarto de baño m. **bathtowel**
n toalla de baño f. **swimming baths** n pl
piscina f sing.

bathe [beið] v bañar, bañarse. **bathing cap**
gorra de baño f. **bathing costume** traje de
baño m. **bathing pool** piscina f. **bathing
trunks** pantalones de baño m pl.

baton ['bætn] n (mil) bastón de mando m;
(police) porra f; (music) batuta f.

battalion [bə'taljən] n batallón m.

batter[1] ['bætə] v apalear, golpear, derribar.

batter[2] ['bætə] n (cookery) batido m, pasta
f.

battery ['bætəri] n (elec) pila f, batería f;
(mil) batería; (law) agresión f. **storage
battery** acumulador m. **battery cell** pila
de batería eléctrica f.

battle ['bætl] n batalla f, combate m. v
batallar, luchar. **battlefield** n campo de
batalla m. **battlement** n almenaje m. **bat-
tleship** n buque de guerra m.

bawdy ['bɔːdi] adj obsceno, escabroso.

bawl [bɔːl] v vocear.

bay[1] [bei] n (geog) bahía f.

bay[2] [bei] v (cry) aullar. **at bay** acor-
ralado.

bay[3] [bei] n (tree) laurel m.

bayonet ['beiənit] *n* bayoneta *f*. *v* dar un bayonetazo.

bay window *n* mirador *m*.

bazaar [bə'zɑː] *n* bazar *m*.

*****be** [biː] *v* ser, existir; estar; (*place*) encontrarse, quedar.

beach [biːtʃ] *n* playa *f*; costa *f*. *v* varar, encallar en la costa.

beacon ['biːkən] *n* fanal *m*, faro *m*; (*naut*) boya *f*.

bead [biːd] *n* cuenta *f*, perla *f*, gota *f*. **beads** *n pl* rosario *m sing*.

beagle ['biːgl] *n* sabueso *m*.

beak [biːk] *n* pico *m*; punta *f*. **beaked** *adj* picudo.

beaker ['biːkə] *n* vaso *m*, copa *f*.

beam [biːm] *n* (*light*) rayo *m*, destello *m*; (*arch*) madero *m*; (*width of a ship*) manga *f*; (*smile*) sonrisa brillante *f*. *v* irradiar; (*smile*) sonreír radiantemente.

bean [biːn] *n* (*broad*) haba *f*; (*black*) fréjol *m*; (*kidney*) habichuela *f*, alubia *f*, judía *f*.

*****bear¹** [beə] *v* soportar, aguantar, sufrir; (*carry*) llevar; (*have*) tener, (*fruit*) dar; (*give birth to*) parir; (*a strain*) resistir. **bear in mind** tener presente. **bearing** *n* porte *m*, aspecto *m*; relación *f*.

bear² [beə] *n* oso *m*.

beard [biəd] *n* barba *f*. *v* enfrentarse con, mesar la barba a. **bearded** *adj* barbudo. **beardless** *adj* imberbe.

bearings ['beəriŋz] *n pl* situación *f sing*, relación *f sing*, camino *m sing*. **lose one's bearings** desorientarse, desatinar. **take one's bearings** orientarse.

beast [biːst] *n* bestia *f*; res *f*; (*wild*) fiera *f*. **beastly** *adj* bestial; desagradable.

*****beat** [biːt] *v* batir; (*games*) derrotar, vencer; (*with weapon*) golpear; (*carpet*) sacudir. **beat down** atropellar. *n* (*med*) latido *m*, pulsación *f*; golpe *m*; (*music*) compás *m*.

beauty ['bjuːti] *n* hermosura *f*, belleza *f*; (*coll*) lo mejor. **beauty spot** lunar *m*. **beautiful** *adj* bello, hermoso; guapo. **beautify** *v* embellecer.

beaver ['biːvə] *n* castor *m*.

because [bi'koz] *conj* porque. **because of** a causa de.

beckon ['bekən] *v* llamar con señas, atraer, invitar.

*****become** [bi'kʌm] *v* convenir; llegar a ser, ponerse; hacerse. **becoming** *adj* que sienta bien, propio, decoroso. **becomingly** *adv* con gracia.

bed [bed] *n* cama *f*, lecho *m*; (*coal, etc.*) yacimiento *m*; (*flowers*) macizo *m*. **bedding** *n* ropa de cama *f*. **bedroom** *n* dormitorio *m*. **bedsitter** *n* salón con cama *m*. **bedspread** *n* colcha *f*.

bedbug ['bedbʌg] *n* chinche *f*.

bedraggled [bi'dragld] *adj* mojado y sucio, enlodado.

bee [biː] *n* abeja *f*. **bee line** línea recta *f*. **beehive** *n* colmena *f*. **bumble-bee** *n* abejorro *m*.

beech [biːtʃ] *n* (*tree*) haya *f*; (*nut*) hayuco *m*.

beef [biːf] *n* carne de vaca *f*. **roast beef** rosbif *m*.

been [biːn] *V* be.

beer [biə] *n* cerveza *f*.

beetle ['biːtl] *n* (*zool*) escarabajo *m*; (*tech*) pisón *m*. **death-watch beetle** carcoma *f*. **beetle-browed** *adj* cejijunto.

beetroot ['biːtruːt] *n* remolacha *f*.

before [bi'foː] *adv* delante; al frente; (*time*) antes; (*already*) ya. *prep* delante de; frente de; (*time*) ante; (*rather than*) antes de. *conj* antes (que). **beforehand** *adv* de antemano.

befriend [bi'frend] *v* favorecer, amistar, proteger, ayudar.

beg [beg] *v* pedir, suplicar; mendigar. **I beg your pardon?** ¿cómo dice? **I beg your pardon!** ¡Vd dispense! **beg the question** dejar a un lado. **beggar** *n* mendigo *m*.

*****begin** [bi'gin] *v* comenzar, empezar, iniciar. **to begin with** en primer lugar. **beginner** *n* principiante, -a *m, f*. **beginning** *n* principio *m*.

begrudge [bi'grʌdʒ] *v* envidiar; conceder de mala gana.

beguile [bi'gail] *v* engañar; (*charm*) encantar.

behalf [bi'haːf] *n* provecho *m*. **on behalf of** en nombre de, a favor de.

behave [bi'heiv] *v* comportarse, manejarse, portarse; funcionar, obrar. **behaviour** *n* comportamiento *m*, conducta *f*; funcionamiento *m*.

behead [bi'hed] *v* decapitar.

behind [bi'haind] *adv* atrás, detrás, hacia atrás; (*time*) después; (*late*) con retraso. *prep* detrás de, por detrás de. *n* (*coll*) trasero *m*. **fall behind** retrasarse. **behind the times** pasado de moda.

*behold [bi'hould] v mirar, contemplar.
interj ¡aqui está!, ¡he aqui!
beige [beiʒ] *adj* beige.
being ['biiŋ] n ser m, existencia f, estado
m. **human being** ser humano m. **well-
being** n bienestar m.
belated [bi'leitid] *adj* tardio.
belch [beltʃ] n eructo m, v eructar,
arrojar.
belfry ['belfri] n campanario m.
Belgium ['beldʒəm] m Bélgica f. **Belgian**
n(m+f), *adj* belga.
believe [bi'liiv] v creer, pensar; opinar.
believer n creyente m, f, fiel m. **belief** n,
pl -s creencia f; opinión f.
bell [bel] n campana f, campanilla f;
(*electric*) timbre m; (*hand*) esquila f.
belligerent [bi'lidʒərənt] n, *adj* beligerante, -a m, f.
bellow ['belou] v bramar, rugir. n
bramido m.
bellows ['belouz] n pl fuelle m sing.
belly ['beli] n barriga f, panza f, vientre
m. **bellyful** n hartón m.
belong [bi'loŋ] v pertenecer, tocar a.
belong to ser de. **belongings** n pl bienes
m pl.
beloved [bi'lʌvid] n amado, -a m, f, querido, -a m, f. **favorito, -a** m, f.
below [bi'lou] *adv* abajo, debajo. *prep*
(por) debajo de.
belt [belt] n cinturón m, cinto m, faja f;
(*tech*) correa f; (*geog*) zona f. v ceñir,
rodear, fajar.
bench [bentʃ] n banco m, banca f, escaño
m, (*law*) tribunal m.
*bend [bend] v torcer, doblar; inclinar,
encorvar. n recodo m, curva f.
beneath [bi'niiθ] *adv* abajo, debajo. (*prep*)
bajo, debajo de. **beneath regard** indigno
de consideración.
benefactor ['benəfaktə] n bienhechor m,
patrono m.
benefit ['benəfit] n beneficio m, provecho
m. v beneficiar. **beneficial** *adj* ventajoso.
beneficiary n beneficiaro m.
benevolent [bi'nevələnt] *adj* benévolo;
caritativo. **benevolence** n benevolencia f,
caridad f.
benign [bi'nain] *adj* benigno.
bent [bent] *adj* torcido, encorvado; (*on a
course of action*) resuelto a (a); (*fam*) inver-
tido. n talento m, inclinación f.
bequeath [bi'kwiθ] v legar; transmitir.
bequest n legado m.

bereaved [bi'riivd] *adj* afligido. **bereave** v
quitar; afligir. **bereavement** n pérdida f,
aflicción f.
beret ['berei] n boina f.
berry ['beri] n baya f, grano m.
berserk [bə'sɔik] *adj* demente.
berth [bɔiθ] n camarote m; (*dock*)
fondeadero m. v fondear. **give a wide
berth to** apartarse de.
beside [bi'said] *prep* junto a, cerca de.
beside oneself fuera de si. **beside the
point** no venir al caso. **besides** *adv* (*as
well*) también; (*moreover*) ademas.
besiege [bi'siidʒ] v asediar, sitiar.
bespoke [bi'spouk] *adj* hecho a medida.
bespeak v reservar.
best [best] *adj, adv* mejor. **at best** a lo
mejor. **do one's best** hacer todo lo
posible. **make the best of** sacar el mayor
provecho de. **best man** padrino de boda
m. **best-seller** n éxito de librería m.
bestow [bi'stou] v conferir, otorgar.
*bet [bet] v apostar; jugar. n apuesta f,
postura f. **better, bettor** n apostador, -a
m, f. **betting shop** establecimiento de
apuesta m.
betray [bi'trei] v traicionar; engañar;
revelar. **betrayal** n traición f.
better ['betə] *adj, adv* mejor. **get better**
mejorarse. **better half** (*coll*) media
naranja f. **better off** mejor situado. **so
much the better** tanto mejor. v
mejorarse.
between [bi'twiin] *prep* entre. *adv* entre
los dos. **far between** a grandes intervalos.
between ourselves entre nosotros.
beverage ['bevəridʒ] n bebida f, brebaje
m.
*beware [bi'weə] v tener cuidado de.
interj ¡atención!
bewilder [bi'wildə] v desconcertar, aturrullar, aturdir. **bewilderment** n
aturdimiento m, anonadamiento m.
beyond [bi'jond] *adv* más alla, más lejos.
prep superior a, fuera de. **beyond doubt**
fuera de duda. **beyond measure**
sobremanera. **beyond question** indiscutible.
bias ['baiəs] n sesgo m, través m; propensión f, prejuicio m. v sesgar; influir,
predisponer. **biased** *adj* predispuesto. **cut
on the bias** contar al sesgo.
bib [bib] n babero m, pechera f.

Bible ['baibl] n Biblia f. **biblical** adj bíblico.

bibliography [bibli'ɔgrəfi] n bibliografía f. **bibliographer** n bibliógrafo m. **bibliographical** adj bibliográfico.

biceps ['baiseps] n biceps m.

bicker ['bikə] v disputar, reñir, altercar. **bickering** n altercado m.

bicycle ['baisikl] n bicicleta f.

*****bid** [bid] v ofrecer, pujar; (*command*) mandar; rogar. n oferta f; (*attempt*) tentativa f. **make a bid for** procurar. **no bid** (*cards*) paso. **bidder** n postor m.

bidet ['biːdei] n bidé m.

biennial [bai'eniəl] adj bienal, bianual.

bifocals [bai'foukəlz] pl n lentes bifocales m pl.

big [big] adj grande; grueso; abultado; importante.

bigamy ['bigəmi] n bigamia f. **bigamist** n bígamo, -a m, f. **bigamous** adj bígamo.

bigot ['bigət] n beatón, -ona m, f, fanático, -a m, f. **bigoted** adj fanático, intolerante. **bigotry** n fanatismo m, intolerancia f.

bikini [bi'kiːni] n bikini m.

bilingual [bai'lingwəl] adj bilingüe.

bilious ['biljəs] adj bilioso. **bile** n bilis f.

bill¹ [bil] n (*comm*) cuenta f, factura f; (*poster*) cartel m; (*pol*) proyecto de ley m; anuncio m. **billboard** n cartelera f. **bill of lading** conocimiento de embarque m. **bill of sale** escritura de venta f. v enviar una cuenta; anunciar. **bill and coo** arrullar; (*coll*) besuquearse.

bill² [bil] n (*beak*) pico m.

billiards ['biljədz] n billar m.

billion ['biljən] n (*10¹²*) billón m; (*10⁹*) mil millones m pl.

bin [bin] n arcón m, hucha f; papelera f; (*wine*) estante m.

binary ['bainəri] adj binario.

*****bind** [baind] v atar; ligar, unir; (*bandage*) vendar; (*sheaves*) agavillar, (*books*) encuadernar; (*captive*) aprisionar; (*sewing*) ribetear; (*oblige*) comprometer. **binding** ['baindiŋ] n (*books*) encuadernación f; atadura f. adj válido; obligatorio.

binge [bindʒ] n (*coll*) parranda f. **go on the binge** ir de parranda.

binoculars [bi'nokjuləz] n pl binóculos m pl, prismáticos m pl, gemelos m pl.

biography [bai'ɔgrəfi] n biografía f. **biographer** n biógrafo, -a m, f. **biographical** adj biográfico.

biology [bai'ɔlədʒi] n biología f. **biological** adj biológico. **biologist** n biólogo m.

birch [bəitʃ] n abedul m. v varear.

bird [bəid] n pájaro m, ave f; (*slang*) chica f. **bird's eye view** vista de pájaro f. **birdcage** n jaula f. **birdseed** n alpiste m.

birth [bəiθ] n nacimiento m, parto m; linaje m; comienzo m. **give birth to** dar a luz; parir. **birth certificate** partida de nacimiento f. **birth control** anticoncepcionismo m. **birthday** n cumpleaños m. **birthplace** n lugar de nacimiento m. **birthrate** n natalidad f. **birthright** n herencia f.

biscuit ['biskit] n bizcocho m, galleta f.

bishop ['biʃəp] n obispo m; (*chess*) alfil m.

bison ['baisən] n bisonte m.

bit¹ [bit] n (*drill*) barrena f, taladro m; (*horse*) bocado m. **take the bit between one's teeth** desbocarse.

bit² [bit] n pedazo m, poco m, trocito m; (*time*) ratito m; (*jot*) jota f. **bit by bit** poco a poco. **not a bit** nada de eso.

bitch [bitʃ] n (*dog*) perra f; (*slang*) zorra f.

*****bite** [bait] v morder; (*insect, etc.*) picar. n mordedura f; picadura f. **biting** adj (*remark, etc.*) mordaz.

bitter ['bitə] adj amargo, áspero. **to the bitter end** hasta la muerte. **bitterness** n amargura f.

bizarre [bi'zaɪ] adj extravagante, grotesco.

black [blak] n, adj negro, -a m, f. **blacken** v ennegrecer; (*character*) denigrar.

blackberry ['blakbəri] n (*bush*) zarza f; (*fruit*) zarzamora f.

blackbird ['blakbəid] n mirlo m.

blackboard ['blakbɔid] n pizarra f.

blackcurrant [,blak'kʌrənt] n grosella negra f.

black eye n ojo a la funerala m.

blackhead ['blakhed] n espinilla f.

blackleg ['blakleg] n esquirol m.

blackmail ['blakmeil] n chantaje m. v hacer chantaje. **blackmailer** n chantajista m, f.

black market n mercado negro m.

blackout ['blakaut] n apagón m, apagamiento m; (*fainting*) desmayo m.

black pudding n morcilla f.

blacksmith ['blaksmiθ] n herrero m.

bladder ['bladə] n vejiga f.

blade [bleid] n (*grass*) brizna f; (*razor*) hoja f; (*propeller*) paleta f; (*oar*) pala f.

blame [bleim] *n* culpa *f*. *v* culpar. **blameless** *adj* inculpable. **blameworthy** *adj* culpable.

bland [bland] *adj* afable; dulce.

blank [blaŋk] *adj* en blanco; (*empty*) vacío; confuso. *n* blanco *m*, hueco *m*; vacío *m*. **blank cartridge** cartucho para salvas *m*. **blank verse** verso libre *m*, verso suelto *m*.

blanket ['blaŋkit] *n* manta *f*, frazada *f*; (*of dust*) capa *f*. *v* cubrir con manta. *adj* comprensivo.

blare [bleə] *v* vociferar, rugir. *n* trompetazo *m*, fragor *m*; estrépito *m*.

blaspheme [blas'fiːm] *v* blasfema. **blasphemer** *n* blasfemador, -a *m*, *f*. **blasphemous** *adj* blasfemo. **blasphemy** *n* blasfemia *f*.

blast [blaɪst] *n* explosión *f*; (*trumpet*) trompetazo *m*; (*wind*) ráfaga *f*. *v* (*rocks*) barrenar; (*wither*) marchitar; (*curse*) maldecir. **full blast** en plena marcha. **blast furnace** alto horno *m*.

blatant ['bleitənt] *adj* discarado, vinciglero, llamativo.

blaze [bleiz] *n* incendio *m*, llamarada *f*, conflagración *f*. *v* llamear, flamear; arder. **blaze a trail** abrir un camino. **blaze of colour** masa de color *f*. **blazer** *n* chaqueta deportiva *f*.

bleach [bliːtʃ] *v* blanquear, descolorar. *n* lejía *f*.

bleak [bliːk] *adj* desabrido, desierto, crudo; (*prospect*) sombrío.

bleat [bliːt] *v* balar. *n* balido *m*.

*****bleed** [bliːd] *v* sangrar. **bleed to death** morir desangrado. **bleeding** *n* hemorragia *f*.

blemish ['blemiʃ] *n* mácula *f*, defecto *m*, mancha *f*. *v* empañar, manchar.

blend [blend] *v* mezclar, combinar, fundir; (*colour*) matizar. *n* mezcla *f*, combinación *f*.

bless [bles] *v* bendecir; consagrar; favorecer. **blessedness** *n* felicidad *f*. **blessing** *n* bendición *f*; merced *f*; favor *m*.

blew [bluː] *V* **blow²**.

blight [blait] *n* (*plants*) tizne *m*; (*fig*) influencia maligna *f*. *v* atizonar; (*fig*) malograr.

blind [blaind] *adj* ciego. *n* pretexto *m*; (*window*) persiana *f*. *v* cegar. **blindness** *n* ceguera *f*. **turn a blind eye** hacer la vista gorda.

blindfold ['blaindfould] *n* venda *f*. *v* vendar los ojos de.

blink [bliŋk] *v* parpadear, pestañear, guiñar. *n* parpadeo *m*, guiño *m*; (*of light*) destello *m*. **blinkers** *pl n* anteojeras *f pl*.

bliss [blis] *n* bienaventuranza *f*, felicidad *f*. **blissful** *adj* bienaventurado, feliz.

blister ['blistə] *n* vesícula *f*, ampolla *f*. *v* ampollar.

blizzard ['blizəd] *n* ventisca *f*.

bloated ['bloutid] *adj* abotagado.

blob [blob] *n* gota *f*, goterón *m*; borrón *m*.

bloc [blok] *n* (*pol*) bloque *m*.

block [blok] *n* bloque *m*; (*butcher's*) tajo *m*; (*houses*) manzana *f*; (*obstruction*) atasco *m*. *v* bloquear, obstruir, cerrar el paso. **block and tackle** polea con aparejo *f*.

blockade [blo'keid] *n* bloqueo *m*. *v* bloquear.

bloke [blouk] *n* (*coll*) tío *m*, fulano *m*.

blond [blond] *adj* rubio. **blonde** *n* rubia *f*.

blood [blʌd] *n* sangre *f*; (*lineage*) parentesco *m*. **bloodless** *adj* exangüe. **blood donor** donante de sangre *m*, *f*. **blood group** grupo sanguíneo *m*. **blood poisoning** envenenamiento de la sangre *m*. **blood pressure** *n* presión arterial *f*. **bloodshed** *n* matanza *f*. **bloodshot** *adj* inyectado de sangre. **bloodstream** *n* corriente sanguínea *f*. **bloodthirsty** *adj* sanguinario. **bloody** *adj* sangriento; (*slang*) maldito.

bloom [bluːm] *n* flor *f*; florecimiento *m*; (*prime*) lozanía *f*. *v* florecer. **in bloom** en flor. **blooming** *adj* floreciente.

blossom ['blosəm] *n* flor *f*. *v* florecer.

blot [blot] *n* borrón *m*; mancha *f*. *v* manchar, tachar; (*dry*) secar. **blot out** borrar. **blotter** *n* libro borrador *m*. **blotting paper** papel secante *m*.

blotch [blotʃ] *n* mancha *f*; (*med*) erupción *f*. *v* manchar, ennegrecer.

blouse [blauz] *n* blusa *f*.

blow¹ [blou] *n* (*hit*) golpe *m*, bofetada *f*; (*shock*) choque *m*; (*misfortune*) revés *m*. **come to blows** venir a las manos.

*****blow²** [blou] *n* soplido *m*. *v* soplar, hacer viento; (*pant*) jadear; (*fuse*) fundirse; (*music*) tocar. **blow away** disipar. **blow one's nose** sonarse las narices. **blow out** (*a light*) apagar soplando. **blow up** (*explode*) volar; (*inflate*) inflar.

blubber ['blʌbə] n grasa de ballena f. v gimotear.

blue [bluː] adj azul; (mournful) deprimido; (obscene) verde. **bluebell** n campanilla f. **bluebottle** n moscón m. **blueprint** n fotocopia f, plan m.

bluff [blʌf] v fanfarronear. n fanfarronada f; (cliff) morro m, tisco m, peñasco. adj campechano, brusco.

blunder [blʌndə] n desatino m, yerro m. v desatinar; tropezar (con); (coll) meter la pata. **blunderer** n desatinado m.

blunt [blʌnt] adj desafilado, embotado; (abrupt) franco, descortés; (plain) claro. v despuntar, desafilar, embotar; (pain) mitigar. **bluntness** n embotamiento m.

blur [bləː] v empañar; emborronar. n borrón m. **blurred** adj borroso.

blush [blʌʃ] v ruborizarse, enrojecerse. n rubor m, sonrojo m; (of shame) bochorno m.

boar [boː] n jabalí m.

board [boːd] n tabla f; (chess, draughts) tablero m; (for notices) tablón m; (table) mesa f; (food) comida f; (committee) junta f, tribunal m; (naut) bordo m. v (carpentry) enmaderar, entablar; (embark) embarcarse en.

boast [boust] n jactancia f, alarde m, baladronada f. v jactarse, presumir. **boastful** adj jactancioso.

boat [bout] n bote m, lancha f, barca f; buque m, barco m. v navegar, ir en bote. **boatman** n barquero m. **boatswain** n contramaestre m. **lifeboat** n lancha de socorro f.

boater ['boutə] n (hat) canotié m, canotier m.

bob [bob] v bambolean, menear. n balanceo m; borla f.

bobbin ['bobin] n (sewing-machine, loom) bobina f.

bobsleigh ['bobslei] n trineo doble m. v ir en trineo.

bodice ['bodis] n corpiño m.

body ['bodi] n cuerpo m, masa f, entidad f; (corpse) cadáver m; (mot) carrocería f. **bodyguard** n guardia de corps f.

bog [bog] n pantano m.

bogus ['bougəs] adj espurio, fingido, falso.

bohemian [bə'hiːmiən] adj bohemio.

boil¹ [boil] v hervir. n hervor m. **boil over** irse. **boiler** n caldera f. **boiling point** punto de ebullición m.

boil² [boil] n divieso m, grano m, furúnculo m.

boisterous ['boistərəs] adj borrascoso, bullicioso. **boisterousness** n bullicio m.

bold [bould] adj osado, arrojado, atrevido; resuelto; (showy) llamativo. **bold-faced** adj descarado. **bold-faced type** letra negra f. **boldness** n temeridad f, intrepidez f.

Bolivia [bə'liviə] n Bolivia f. **Bolivian** adj, n boliviano, -a m, f.

bolster ['boulstə] n travesaño m; almohada f. v estribar, levantar, apoyar.

bolt [boult] n (door) cerraja f, cerrojo m; (for nut) perno m; rayo m. v (run) huir; (secure) empernar; (food) zampar. **bolt upright** enhiesto. **thunderbolt** n rayo m.

bomb [bom] n bomba f. v bombardear.

bombard [bəm'baɪd] v bombardear. **bombardment** n bombardeo m.

bonafide [bounə'faidi] adj fidedigno.

bond [bond] n lazo m, unión f, vínculo m; (comm) obligación f; (security) fianza f; (customs) depósito m. v unir, ligar; dar fianza. **bonds** n pl cadenas f pl. **bondage** n esclavitud f.

bone [boun] n hueso m; (fish) espina f. v desosar. **bony** adj huesudo. **all skin and bones** estar en los huesos. **pick a bone with** arreglar las cuentas con.

bonfire ['bonfaiə] n hoguera f.

bonnet ['bonit] n capota f, gorra f; (mot) capó m.

bonus ['bounəs] n extra m, prima f.

booby trap ['buːbi] n trampa f; (mil) mina f.

book [buk] n libro m; tomo m. v (a seat) tomar; (reserve) reservar; (engage) contratar.

bookcase ['bukkeis] n librería f.

book-ends ['bukendz] n pl sujetalibros m pl.

booking ['bukin] n taquilla f.

book-keeper ['buk,kiːpə] n tenedor de libros m.

booklet ['buklit] n folleto m.

bookmark ['bukmaːk] n marcador m.

bookseller ['bukselə] n librero m.

bookshop ['bukʃop] n librería f.

boom [buːm] n (noise) ruido m; (econ) auge repentino m. v (comm) prosperar, estar en bonanza; sonar, bramar.

boost [buːst] v (advertise) dar bombo (a); (coll) empujar. n (coll) empujón m.

boot [buːt] *n* (*shoe*) bota *f*; (*mot*) maleta *f*.
get the boot ser despedido.
booth [buːð] *n* cabina *f*, quiosco *m*.
booze [buːz] *n* (*coll*) bebida alcohólica *f*. *v*
(*coll*) emborracharse, coger una turca.
border ['bɔɪdə] *n* confín *m*; frontera *f*;
margen *m*; (*sewing*) ribete *m*; (*garden*)
arriate *m*. *v* lindar con. **borderline** *n*
límite *m*.
bore¹ [bɔɪ] *v* (*hole, etc.*) perforar, horadar,
taladrar. *n* taladro *m*, barreno *m*; (*gun*)
calibre *m*.
bore² [bɔɪ] *v* aburrir, fastidiar. *n* aburrimiento *m*; (*person*) pelmazo *m*. **boredom** *n* tedio *m*, hastío *m*. **boring** *adj*
aburrido, tedioso.
bore³ [bɔɪ] *V* **bear¹**.
born [bɔɪn] *adj* nacido, nato. **be born**
nacer.
borne [bɔɪn] *V* **bear¹**.
borough ['bʌrə] *n* municipio *m*.
borrow ['bɔrou] *v* tomar prestado, pedir
prestado. **borrower** *n* prestatario *m*.
bosom ['buzəm] *n* seno *m*; pecho *m*.
boss [bos] *n* amo *m*, jefe *m*, patrón *m*;
(*political*) cacique *m*. *v* dominar, dirigir.
botany ['botəni] *n* botánica *f*. **botanical**
adj botánico. **botanist** *n* botánico, -a *m*,
f.
both [bouθ] *adj*, *pron* ambos, los dos.
bother ['boðə] *v* molestar; (*worry*) preocuparse. *n* molestia *f*; preocupación *f*.
bottle ['botl] *n* botella *f*, frasco *m*; (*water*)
cantimplora *f*; (*wine*) porrón *m*. *v*
embotellar.
bottom ['botəm] *n* fondo *m*; casco *m*;
(*anat*) trasero *m*, (*vulgar*) culo *m*; (*river*)
lecho *m*; (*page*) pie *m*; (*chair*) asiento *m*.
adj más bajo. **bottomless** *adj* sin fondo.
boudoir ['buːdwaɪ] *n* tocador *m*, gabinete
m.
bough [bau] *n* rama *f*.
bought [bɔɪt] *V* **buy**.
boulder ['bouldə] *n* peñasco *m*, pedrusco
m.
bounce [bauns] *v* rebotar, botar, saltar;
(*cheque*) ser rechazado. *n* rebote *m*, resp-
ingo *m*.
bound¹ [baund] *v* (*leap*) saltar, brincar. *n*
salto *m*, brinco *m*.
bound² [baund] *n* límite *m*. **within bounds**
dentro del límite.
bound³ [baund] *V* **bind**.
bound⁴ [baund] *adj* **bound for** destinado
a, con rumbo a.

boundary ['baundəri] *n* lindero *m*, término *m*.
bouquet [buːkei] *n* ramo *m*, ramillete *m*;
perfume *m*; (*wine*) nariz *f*.
bourgeois ['buəʒwaɪ] *adj* burgués.
bout [baut] *n* turno *m*; (*illness*) ataque *m*.
bow¹ [bau] *v* (*bend*) inclinarse, saludar;
(*submit*) someterse (a). *n* inclinación *f*;
reverencia *f*.
bow² [bou] *n* (*music, weapon*) arco *m*;
(*ribbon*) lazo *m*. **bow-legged** *adj* paties-
tevado. **bow window** ventana arqueada *f*.
bow³ [bau] *n* (*naut*) proa *f*.
bowels ['bauəlz] *n pl* intestinos *m pl*,
entrañas *f pl*.
bowl¹ [boul] *n* receptáculo *m*; (*soup*)
escudilla *f*; (*washing*) jofaina *f*.
bowl² [boul] *v* tirar; (*cricket*) sacar. **bowl
over** (*fig*) desconcertar. **bowls** *pl n* juego
de bolos *m sing*.
bowler hat *n* hongo *m*.
box¹ [boks] *n* caja *f*, cajón *m*; (*luggage*)
baúl *m*; (*theatre*) palco *m*; (*sentry*) garita
f, casilla *f*. *v* encajonar. **box office** taquilla *f*. **post-office box** apartado de correos
m.
box² [boks] *v* (*sport*) boxear. **boxer** *n* boxeador *m*, puglista *m*. **boxing** *n* boxeo *m*,
pugilato *m*.
Boxing Day *n* Día de San Esteban *m*.
boy [boi] *n* muchacho *m*, niño *m*, chico
m. **boyfriend** *n* novio *m*. **boy scout**
muchacho explorador *m*. **boyhood** niñez
f.
boycott ['boikot] *n* boicot *m*. *v* boicotear.
bra [braɪ] *n* (*coll*) sostén *m*.
brace [breis] *n* refuerzo *m*; (*tech*)
abrazadera *f*; (*pair*) par *m*. *v* reforzar;
refrescar. **braces** *n pl* tirantes *m pl*. **brac-
ing** *adj* tónico.
bracelet ['breislit] *n* pulsera *f*; brazalete
m.
bracken ['brakən] *n* helecho *m*.
bracket ['brakit] *n* soporte *m*; (*writing*)
paréntesis *m*, corchete *m*.
brag [brag] *v* jactarse. *n* jactancia *f*.
Braille [breil] *n* Braille *m*, alfabeto para
los ciegos *m*.
brain [brein] *n* cerebro *m*, sesos *m pl*. *v*
romper la crisma. **brains** *n pl* talento *m
sing*. **brainwash** *v* lavar el cerebro.
brainwave *n* idea luminosa *f*. **brainy** *adj*
sesudo. **rack one's brains** devanarse los
sesos.

braise [breiz] v estofar.
brake [breik] n freno m. v frenar.
bramble ['brambl] n zarza f, maleza f.
bramble patch breña f, matorral m.
bran [bran] n salvado m.
branch [braintʃ] n rama f; (of learning) ramo m; (river) tributario m; (road, rail) ramal m; (company) dependencia f. v echar ramas, dividirse.
brand [brand] n (manufacture) marca f; (animals) hierro m; (fire) tizón m; (stigma) estigma m. v marcar; tildar. **brand-new** adj enteramente nuevo.
brandish ['brandiʃ] v blandir.
brandy ['brandi] n coñac m.
brass [brais] n latón m; (music) cobre m, metal m; (coll) pasta f. **brassy** adj de latón; (coll) presuntuoso.
brassière ['brasiə] V **bra**.
brave [breiv] adj valiente, intrépido. v desafiar. **bravery** n valentía f.
brawl [broil] n alboroto m, riña f. v alborotar.
brawn [broin] n carnosidad f, músculo m; (food) carne de cerdo adobada f. **brawny** adj musculoso.
brazen ['breizn] adj (metal) de latón; (fig) desahogado.
Brazil [brəˈzil] n (el) Brasil m. **Brazilian** n, adj brasileño, -a m, f. **Brazil nut** nuez del Brasil f.
breach [briitʃ] n brecha f. v abrir brecha; romper. **breach of promise** infracción f. **breach of the peace** alteración de orden público f.
bread [bred] n pan m. **breadcrumb** n migaja f. **breadcrumbs** n pl pan rallado m sing. **slice of bread** rebanada f.
breadth [bredθ] n anchura f.
*break [breik] v romper; quebrar; quebrantar; (burst) reventar; (violate) infringir. **break away** desprenderse. **break down** (mech) averiarse; (cry) deshacerse en lágrimas. **break in** forzar la entrada. **break out** estallar. **break up** desmenuzar. n ruptura f, rotura f; (opening) abertura f; (interruption) interrupción f. **breakdown** n colapso m. **breakthrough** n avance m.
breakfast ['brekfəst] n desayuno m. v desayunar.
breast [brest] n pecho m; (female) mama f, teta f. **breastbone** n esternón m. **breast pocket** bolsillo de pecho m. **breaststroke** n brazada de pecho f.

breath [breθ] n respiración f, aliento m; (breeze) soplo m. **breathless** adj sin aliento. **under one's breath** en voz baja.
breathalyser ['breθəlaizə] n alcohómetro m.
breathe [briið] v respirar, exhalar, inspirar. **breathing** n respiración f.
*breed [briid] v criar, engendrar. n raza f, casta f. **breeding** n cría f, reproducción f; (upbringing) crianza f, educación f.
breeze [briiz] n brisa f. **breezy** adj fresco; (of manner) animado.
brew [bruі] v (infuse) infusionar; (beer) fabricar. n poción f. **brewery** n fábrica de cerveza f.
bribe [braib] n soborno m. v sobornar. **bribery** n soborno m.
brick [brik] n ladrillo m. v enladrillar. **bricklayer** n albañil m. **brickyard** n ladrillar m.
bride [braid] n novia f, desposada f. **bridal** adj nupcial. **bridegroom** m novio m, desposado m. **bridesmaid** n dama de honor f, madrina de boda f.
bridge¹ [bridʒ] n puente m. **drawbridge** n puente levadizo m. **suspension bridge** puente colgante m. v pontear.
bridge² [bridʒ] n (cards) bridge m.
bridle ['braidl] n brida f, freno m. v enfrenar; picarse.
brief [briif] adj breve. n resumen m; (law) escrito m, relación f. v (law) instruir. **briefcase** n cartera f. **briefly** adv brevemente.
brigade [briˈgeid] n brigada f.
bright [brait] adj brillante; (intelligent) inteligente. **brighten** v hacer brillar; (make happy) alegrar; (polish) pulir; (weather) aclarar. **brightness** n brillantez f; (intelligence) talento m.
brilliant ['briljənt] adj brillante. **brilliance** n brillo m, fulgor m.
brim [brim] n (of a container) borde m; (hat) ala f.
brine [brain] n salmuera f.
*bring [briŋ] v traer, llevar, conducir. **bring about** causar, ocasionar. **bring down** rebajar. **bring in** introducir. **bring off** lograr, conseguir. **bring out** sacar; publicar. **bring together** reunir. **bring to light** descubrir. **bring up** criar, educar.
brink [briŋk] n borde m. **on the brink of a** dos dedos de.

brisk [brisk] *adj* animado, vivo.
bristle ['brisl] *n* cerda *f*. *v* erizarse. **bristly**
adj erizado.
Britain ['britn] *n* Gran Bretaña *f*. **British**
adj británico. **Briton** *n* britano, -a *m*, *f*,
británico, -a *m*, *f*.
brittle ['britl] *adj* quebradizo.
broad [broid] *adj* ancho; (*fig*) lato,
amplio; (*accent*) fuerte. **broad-minded** *adj*
tolerante. **broaden** *v* ensanchar. **broadly**
adv en general. **broadness** *n* anchura *f*.
broadcast ['broidkaist] *n* emisión *f*, radiodifusión *f*; *v* emitir, radiar. **broadcasting
station** *n* emisora *f*.
broccoli ['brokəli] *n* bróculi *m*, brécol *m*.
brochure ['brouʃuə] *n* folleto *m*.
broke [brouk] *V* **break**. *adj* (*coll*) pelado,
sin blanca.
broken ['broukn] *V* **break**.
broker ['broukə] *n* corredor de bolsa *m*.
bronchitis [bronʲkaitis] *m* bronquitis *f*.
bronze [bronz] *n* bronce *m*.
brooch [broutʃ] *n* broche *m*.
brood [bruid] *n* (*chickens*) pollada *f*;
(*birds*) nidada *f*; (*other animals*) cría *f*. *v*
empollar. **brood over** rumiar.
brook [bruk] *n* arroyo *m*.
broom [bruim] *n* escoba *f*; (*bot*) retama *f*.
broth [broθ] *n* caldo *m*.
brothel ['broθl] *n* burdel *m*, lupanar *m*.
brother ['brʌðə] *n* hermano *m*. **brother-in-
law** *n* cuñado *m*. **brotherhood** *n*
fraternidad *f*. **brotherly** *adv* fraternal.
brow [brau] *n* frente *f*; (*hill*) cumbre *f*.
browbeat *v* intimidar verbalmente.
brown [braun] *adj* castaño, moreno. *v*
(*cookery*) dorar; (*tan*) tostar. **brown
paper** papel de estraza *m*. **brownish** *adj*
pardusco.
browse [brauz] *v* pacer.
bruise [bruiz] *n* contusión *f*, magulladura
f. *v* magullar.
brunette [bruiʲnet] *n* morena *f*.
brush [brʌʃ] *n* cepillo *m*; (*broom*) escoba
f; (*for painting*) pincel *m*; (*undergrowth*)
matorral *m*. *v* cepillar; (*sweep*) barrer;
(*touch*) rozar. **brush aside** echar a un
lado. **brush off** sacudir(se).
brusque [brusk] *adj* brusco, rudo.
Brussels ['brʌsəlz] *n* Bruselas. **Brussels
sprouts** coles de Bruselas *f pl*.
brute [bruit] *n* bruto *m*, bestia *m*, *f*. **brutal**
adj brutal, bestial. **brutality** *n* brutalidad
f.

bubble ['bʌbl] *n* burbuja *f*; borbollón *m*.
v burbujear, borbollar.
buck [bʌk] *n* gamo *m*. *v* encorvarse. **buck
up** animarse.
bucket ['bʌkit] *n* cubo *m*, balde *m*.
buckle ['bʌkl] *n* hebilla *f*. *v* enhebillar;
doblarse.
buck-tooth *n* diente saliente *m*.
bud [bʌd] *n* brote *m*. *v* brotar, germinar.
budge [bʌdʒ] *v* mover, moverse,
menearse.
budgerigar ['bʌdʒərigaı] *n* periquito *m*.
budget ['bʌdʒit] *n* presupuesto *m*. *v*
presupuestar.
buffalo ['bʌfəlou] *n* búfalo *m*.
buffer ['bʌfə] *n* parochoque *m*.
buffet[1] ['bʌfit] *n* (*blow*) bofetón *m*,
bofetada *f*. *v* abofetear, golpear.
buffet[2] ['bufei] *n* fonda *f*, bar *m*.
bug [bʌg] *n* chinche *m*. *v* (*coll*) ocultar un
micrófono en.
bugger ['bʌgə] *n* sodomita *m*. *v* cometer
sodomía. *interj* ¡joder! **bugger off!** ¡vete a
la mierda! **buggery** *m* sodomía *f*.
bugle ['bjuːgl] *n* corneta *f*. **bugler** *n*
trompetero *m*.
***build** [bild] *v* construir; edificar; fundar.
building *n* edificio *m*. **building site** *n* solar
m. **built-up area** *n* zona urbana *f*.
bulb [bʌlb] *n* (*elec*) bombilla *f*; (*bot*)
bulbo *m*.
Bulgaria [bʌlʲgeəriə] *n* Bulgaria *f*. **Bulgarian** *n*, *adj* búlgaro, -a *m*, *f*.
bulge [bʌldʒ] *n* hinchazón *f*, bulto *m*. *v*
hincharse. **bulging** *adj* hinchado (de).
bulk [bʌlk] *n* bulto *m*; masa *f*; (*larger
part*) grueso *m*. **in bulk** (*comm*) en bruto.
bulky *adj* voluminoso.
bull [bul] *n* toro *m*. **bullfight** *n* corrida de
toros *f*. **bullfighter** *n* torero *m*. **bull in a
china shop** un caballo loco en una
cacharrería *m*. **bullring** *n* plaza de toros *f*.
bull's-eye *n* centro del blanco *m*.
bulldozer ['buldouzə] *n* bulldozer *m*,
excavadora *f*.
bullet ['bulit] *n* bala *f*. **bullet-proof** *adj* a
prueba de balas.
bulletin ['bulətin] *n* boletín *m*.
bullion ['buliən] *n* (*gold*) oro en barras *m*;
(*silver*) plata en barras *f*.
bully ['buli] *n* valentón *m*, rufián *m*. *v*
intimidar.
bum [bʌm] *n* (*coll*) posaderas *f pl*. *v* holgazanear.

bump [bʌmp] *n* (*swelling*) hinchazón *f*; (*blow*) golpe *m*. *v* chocar, golpear.

bumper ['bʌmpə] *n* (*mot*) parachoques *m* *invar*. *adj* abundante.

bun [bʌn] *n* buñuelo *m*; (*hair*) moño *m*.

bunch [bʌntʃ] *n* (*flowers*) ramo *m*; (*fruit*) racimo *m*; (*coll*: *gang*) pandilla *f*. *v* agruparse.

bundle ['bʌndl] *n* fardo *m*, bulto *m*. *v* enfardar, liar.

bungalow ['bʌŋgəlou] *n* chalet *m*, casa de un solo piso *f*.

bungle ['bʌŋgl] *v* estropear, chapucear. *n* chapucería *f*. **bungler** *n* chapucero, -a *m*, *f*. **bungling** *adj* chapucero.

bunion ['bʌnjən] *n* juanete *m*.

bunk [bʌŋk] *n* litera *f*; (*coll*: *nonsense*) palabrería *f*. **do a bunk** pirarse.

bunker ['bʌŋkə] *n* (*refuge*) refugio *m*; (*coal*) carbonera *f*; (*golf*) bunker *m*, hoya de arena *f*. ,

buoy [boi] *n* boya *f*. **buoyancy** *n* fluctuación *f*. **buoyant** *adj* boyante.

burden ['bəːdn] *n* carga *f*. *v* cargar.

bureau ['bjuərou] *n* (*desk*) escritorio *m*; (*office*) oficina *f*; departamento *m*.

bureaucracy [bju'rokrəsi] *n* burocracia *f*. **bureaucrat** *n* burócrata *m*, *f*. **bureaucratic** *adj* burocrático.

burglar ['bəːglə] *n* ladrón *m*. **burglar alarm** alarma contra ladrones *f*. **burglary** *n* robo *m*. **burgle** *v* robar.

***burn** [bəːn] *v* quemar, incendiar. *n* quemadura *f*. **burner** *n* quemador *m*. **burning** *adj* ardiente.

burrow ['bʌrou] *n* madriguera *f*. *v* amadrigar, minar.

***burst** [bəːst] *n* estallido *m*, explosión *f*. *v* reventar, estallar. **burst into tears** romper a llorar. **burst open** forzar.

bury ['beri] *v* enterrar, sepultar. **burial** *n* entierro *m*.

bus [bʌs] *n* autobús *m*, ómnibus *m*. **double-decker bus** ómnibus de dos pisos *m*. **bus station** término *m*. **bus-stop** *n* parada de autobús *or* ómnibus.

bush [buʃ] *n* arbusto *m*; (*undergrowth*) maleza *f*. **bushy** *adj* denso, espeso, matoso.

business ['biznis] *n* negocio *m*, comercio *m*; ocupación *f*. **business hours** horas de trabajo *f pl*. **businesslike** *adj* práctico,

sistemático. **businessman** *n* hombre de negocios *m*. **mean business** estar resuelto. **mind one's own business** no meterse donde no le llaman.

bust[1] [bʌst] *n* (*anat*) pecho *m*; (*art*) busto *m*.

bust[2] [bʌst] *adj* (*fam*) quebrado, reventado. **go bust** quebrar.

bustle ['bʌsl] *n* animación *f*. *v* menearse, dar prisa (a).

busy ['bizi] *adj* ocupado; activo, diligente. **busybody** *n* entrometido *m*.

but [bʌt] *conj* pero, sino. *prep* excepto. *adv* solamente. **but for** a no ser por. **nothing but** nada más que.

butane ['bjuːtein] *n* butano *m*.

butcher [butʃə] *n* carnicero *m*. **butcher's shop** carnicería *f*. *v* matar, destrozar.

butler ['bʌtlə] *n* mayordomo *m*.

butt[1] [bʌt] *n* (*gun*) culata *f*; (*cigarette*, *etc*.) colilla *f*.

butt[2] [bʌt] *n* (*of jokes*, *etc*.) objeto *m*.

butt[3] [bʌt] *v* topar, acornear. **butt in** entrometerse.

butter ['bʌtə] *n* mantequilla *f*; *v* untar con mantequilla.

buttercup ['bʌtəkʌp] *n* ranúnculo *m*.

butterfly ['bʌtəflai] *n* mariposa *f*.

butterscotch ['bʌtəskotʃ] *n* dulce de azúcar y mantequilla *m*.

buttocks ['bʌtəks] *n pl* nalgas *f pl*.

button ['bʌtn] *n* botón *m*. *v* abotonear. **buttonhole** *n* ojal *m*. *v* (*coll*) importunar.

buttress ['bʌtris] *n* estribo *m*, contrafuerte *m*; (*fig*) apoyo *m*. *v* estribar.

***buy** [bai] *v* comprar. *n* compra *f*. **buy up** acaparar. **buyer** *n* comprador, -a *m*, *f*.

buzz [bʌz] *v* zumbar. *n* zumbido *m*. **buzzer** *n* zumbador *m*; (*bell*) timbre *m*.

by [bai] *prep* por, de, a; (*near*) cerca de. *adv* al lado, cerca; aparte. **by all means** naturalmente. **by and large** en general. **by the way** de paso.

bye-law ['bailoː] *n* reglamento *m*.

by-election ['baii,lekʃən] *n* elección parcial *f*.

bypass ['bai,pais] *n* desviación *f*. *v* desviar.

by-product ['baiprodəkt] *n* subproducto *m*.

bystander ['bai,standə] *n* espectador, -a *m*, *f*.

C

cab [kab] *n* taxi *m*; (*lorry*) cabina *f*.
cabaret ['kabərei] *n* cabaret *m*; (*show*) atracciones *f pl*.
cabbage ['kabidʒ] *n* col *f*. repollo *m*.
cabin ['kabin] *n* cabaña *f*; (*naut*) camarote *m*; (*aircraft, etc*.) cabina *f*. **cabin cruiser** *n* motonave *f*.
cabinet ['kabinit] *n* (*cupboard*) armario *m*; (*display*) vitrina *f*; (*pol*) gabinete *m*, consejo de ministros *m*. **medicine cabinet** botiquín *m*. **cabinet-maker** *n* ebanista *m*.
cable ['keibl] *n* (*rope, wire*) cable *m*; (*message*) cablegrama *m*. **cable address** dirección telegráfica *f*. **cable car** funicular *m*. *v* cablegrafiar.
cackle ['kakl] *v* carcarear. *n* carcareo *m*.
cactus ['kaktəs] *n pl* -i *or* -uses cacto *m*.
caddie ['kadi] *n* caddy *m*; (*trolley*) carrito *m*.
cadence ['keidəns] *n* cadencia *f*.
cadet [kə'det] *n* cadete *m*.
café ['kafei] *n* café *m*. restaurante *m*.
cafeteria [kafə'tiəriə] *n* cafetería *f*. restaurante de autoservicio *m*.
caffeine ['kafiɪn] *n* cafeína *f*.
cage [keidʒ] *n* jaula *f*. *v* enjaular.
cake [keik] *n* pastel *m*; (*soap*) pastilla *f*. Christmas cake tarta de Navidad *f*. a piece of cake (*coll*) ser pan comido. **sell like hot cakes** (*coll*) venderse como rosquillas. **take the cake** (*coll*) llevarse la palma. *v* endurecerse.
calamine ['kaləmain] *n* calamina *f*.
calamity [kə'laməti] *n* calamidad *f*.
calcium ['kalsiəm] *n* calcio *m*.
calculate ['kalkjuleit] *v* calcular; (*guess, suppose*) confiar en. **calculated** *adj* intencional, deliberado. **calculating** *adj* calculador. **calculation** *n* cálculo *m*. **calculator** *n* calculador *m*.
calendar ['kaləndə] *n* calendario *m*. **calendar month** mes civil *m*.
calf¹ [kaɪf] *n* (*zool*) becerro *m*, ternero *m*.
calf² [kaɪf] *n* (*anat*) pantorrilla *f*.
calibre ['kalibə] *n* (*measurement*) calibre *m*; (*talent*) capacidad *f*, talento *m*.
call [koɪl] *n* llamada *f*, llamamiento *m*; (*cry*) grito *m*; (*visit*) visita *f*. on call de guardia. **trunk call** conferencia *f*. *v* llamar. **call for** pedir. **call off** cancelar. **call on** visitar. **call up** evocar; convocar.

callous ['kaləs] *adj* insensible, duro.
calm [kaɪm] *adj* calmoso, sosegado, tranquilo. *n* calma *f*, tranquilidad *f*. *v* calmar, sosegar.
calorie ['kaləri] *n* caloría *f*.
came [keim] *V* **come**.
camel ['kaməl] *n* camello *m*.
camera ['kamərə] *n* máquina fotográfica *f*. **in camera** a puerta cerrada. **cameraman** *n* cameraman *m*.
camouflage ['kaməflɑːʒ] *n* camuflaje *m*. *v* camuflar.
camp¹ [kamp] *n* (*site*) campamento *m*. **camp-bed** *n* cama plegable *f*. **holiday camp** campamento de vacaciones *m*. *v* acampar.
camp² [kamp] *adj* (*coll*) afeminado; afectado; homosexual.
campaign [kam'pein] *n* campaña *f*. **advertising campaign** campaña publicitaria *f*. **election campaign** campaña electoral *f*. *v* hacer (una) campaña.
campus ['kampəs] *n* recinto universitario *m*, campus *m*, ciudad universitaria *f*.
***can¹** [kan] *v* (*be able*) poder; (*know how to*) saber.
can² [kan] *n* (*container*) lata *f*. **can-opener** *n* abrelatas *m invar*. *v* enlatar, conservar en lata. **canned** *adj* enlatado.
Canada ['kanədə] *n* Canadá *m*. **Canadian** *n(m+f)*, *adj* canadiense.
canal [kə'nal] *n* canal *m*.
canary [kə'neəri] *n* canario *m*.
Canary Islands *n pl* (islas) Canarias *f pl*.
cancel ['kansəl] *v* (*contract, decree, etc*.) cancelar; (*cheque, order, invitation*) anular; (*delete*) tachar; (*maths*) eliminar. **cancel out** anularse. **cancellation** *n* cancelación *f*; anulación *f*.
cancer ['kansə] *n* cáncer *m*. **cancerous** *adj* canceroso.
Cancer ['kansə] *n* Cáncer *m*.
candid ['kandid] *adj* franco, sincero.
candidate ['kandidət] *n* candidato *m*. **candidacy** *n* candidatura *f*.
candle ['kandl] *n* vela *f*; (*in a church*) cirio *m*. **burn the candle at both ends** hacer de la noche día. **candlestick** *n* candelero *m*.
candour ['kandə] *n* franqueza *f*, sinceridad *f*.
candy ['kandi] *n* caramelo *m*. *v* escarchar, cristalizar.

cane [kein] *n* caña *f*; (*walking stick*) bastón *m*; (*school*) palmeta *f*, vara *f*. **sugar cane** caña de azúcar *f*. **cane furniture** muebles de mimbre *m pl*. *v* castigar con la palmeta *or* vara.

canine ['keinain] *adj* canino. **canine tooth** diente canino *m*.

cannabis ['kanəbis] *n* marijuana *f*.

cannibal ['kanibəl] *n*(*m*+*f*), *adj* canibal. **cannibalism** *n* canibalismó *m*.

cannon ['kanən] *n* cañón *m*. **cannonball** *n* bala de cañón *f*.

canoe [kə'nuː] *n* canoa *f*. *v* ir en canoa.

canon ['kanən] *n* canónigo *m*. **canonical** *adj* canónico. **canonize** *v* canonizar. **canonization** *n* canonización *f*.

canopy ['kanəpi] *n* (*awning*) toldo *m*; (*over a bed*) dosel *m*, baldaquin *m*.

canteen [kan'tiːn] *n* (*restaurant*) cantina *f*; (*flask*) cantimplora *f*; (*cutlery*) juego de cubiertos *m*.

canter ['kantə] *n* medio galope *m*. *v* ir a medio galope.

canton ['kantən] *n* cantón *m*.

canvas ['kanvəs] *n* (*fabric*) lona *f*; (*art*) lienzo.

canvass ['kanvəs] *v* solicitar votos de; (*comm*) buscar clientes; (*public opinion*) sondear.

canyon ['kanjən] *n* cañón *m*.

cap [kap] *n* gorra *f*; (*military or bathing*) gorro *m*; (*cover*) tapa *f*; (*bottle*) chapa *f*; (*pen*) capuchón *m*. *v* (*fig: crown*) coronar; (*do better than*) superar.

capable ['keipəbl] *adj* capaz, hábil. **capability** *n* capacidad *f*, habilidad *f*.

capacity [kə'pasəti] *n* capacidad *f*; (*mot*) cilindrada *f*.

cape[1] [keip] *n* (*cloak*) capa *f*; (*cycling*) impermeable de hule *m*.

cape[2] [keip] *n* (*geog*) cabo *m*.

caper ['keipə] *n* (*jump*) cabriola *f*; (*prank*) travesura *f*; (*cookery*) alcaparra *f*.

capillary [kə'piləri] *n* capilar *m*.

capital ['kapitl] *adj* capital. **capital punishment** pena capital *f*. *n* (*letter*) mayúscula *f*; (*city*) capital *f*; (*money*) fondo de operaciones *m*. **capitalism** *n* capitalismo *m*. **capitalist** *n* capitalista *m*, *f*. **capitalistic** *adj* capitalista. **capitalize** *v* capitalizar. **capitalization** *n* capitalización *f*.

capitulate [kə'pitjuleit] *v* capitular. **capitulation** *n* capitulación *f*.

capricious [kə'priʃəs] *adj* caprichoso. **caprice**, **capriciousness** *n* capricho *m*.

Capricorn ['kaprikoɪn] *n* Capricornio *m*.

capsicum ['kapsikəm] *n* pimiento *m*, chile *m*.

capsize [kap'saiz] *v* volcar, zozobrar.

capsule ['kapsjuːl] *n* cápsula *f*.

captain ['kaptin] *n* capitán *m*. *v* capitanear. **captaincy** *n* capitanía *f*.

caption ['kapʃən] *n* encabezamiento *m*, pie *m*. *v* poner pie a.

captive ['kaptiv] *n*, *adj* cautivo, -a. **captivate** *v* cautivar. **captivity** *n* cautividad *f*.

capture ['kaptʃə] *v* capturar; (*place*) tomar; (*market*) acaparar; (*fig*) atraer. *n* captura *f*, apresamiento *m*; (*place*) toma *f*.

car [kaɪ] *n* coche *m*, automóvil *m*; (*rail*) vagón *m*; (*cable*) cabina *f*. **car park** aparcamiento *m*. **car wash** lavado de coches *m*. **dining car** coche comedor *m*. **racing car** coche de carreras *m*. **sleeping car** coche cama *m*.

caramel ['karəmel] *n* caramelo *m*, azúcar quemado *m*.

carat ['karət] *n* quilate *m*.

caravan ['karəvan] *n* (*mot*) remolque *m*; (*travellers*) caravana *f*; (*gipsy*) carromato *m*.

caraway ['karəwei] *n* (*seed*) carvi *m*; (*plant*) alcaravea *f*.

carbohydrate [kaɪbə'haidreit] *n* carbohidrato *m*.

carbon ['kaɪbən] *n* (*chem*) carbono *m*; carbón *m*. **carbon dioxide** bióxido de carbono *m*. **carbon paper** papel carbón *m*.

carbuncle ['kaɪbʌŋkl] *n* (*med*) carbunco *m*, carbunclo *m*.

carburettor ['kaɪbjuretə] *n* carburador *m*.

carcass ['kaɪkəs] *n* (*animal*) res muerta *f*.

card [kaɪd] *n* tarjeta *f*; (*visiting*) tarjeta de visita *f*; (*postcard*) tarjeta postal *f*; (*playing card*) carta *f*, naipe *m*; (*membership*) carnet *m*; (*thin cardboard*) cartulina *f*; (*coll*) gracioso, -a *m*, *f*. **cardboard** *n* cartón *m*. **card index** fichero *m*.

cardiac ['kaɪdiak] *adj* cardiaco.

cardigan ['kaɪdigən] *n* rebeca *f*.

cardinal ['kaɪdənl] *n* (*church*, *bird*) cardenal *m*. *adj* cardinal, esencial. **cardinal number** número cardinal *m*.

care [keə] *n* cuidado *m*, atención *f*; (*worry*) inquietud *f*; (*responsibility*) cargo *m*. **medical care** asistencia médica *f*. **care of** para entregar a. **handle with care** frágil. **take care!** ¡ojo! *v* importar, preocuparse por. **take care of** guardar, tener cuidado de. **careful** *adj* cuidadoso. **carefulness** *n* cuidado *m*, esmero *m*. **careless** *adj* descuidado, desatento.

career [kə'riə] *n* carrera *f*, curso *m*. *v* correr a toda velocidad.

caress [kə'res] *n* caricia *f*. *v* acariciar.

cargo ['kɑːgou] *n* carga *f*, cargamento *m*.

caricature ['karikətjuə] *n* caricatura *f*. *v* caricaturizar.

carnage ['kɑːnidʒ] *n* carnicería *f*.

carnal ['kɑːnl] *adj* carnal. **carnality** *n* carnalidad *f*.

carnation [kɑː'neiʃən] *n* clavel *m*.

carnival ['kɑːnivəl] *n* carnaval *m*.

carnivorous [kɑː'nivərəs] *adj* carnívoro. **carnivore** *n* carnívoro, -a *m*, *f*.

carol ['karəl] *n* villancico *m*.

carpenter ['kɑːpəntə] *n* carpintero *m*. **carpentry** *n* carpintería *f*.

carpet ['kɑːpit] *n* alfombra *f*; (*fitted*) moqueta *f*. **carpet-sweeper** escoba mecánica *f*. *v* alfombrar.

carriage ['karidʒ] *n* carruaje *m*, carro *m*; vagón *m*; (*posture*) manera de andar *f*; (*comm*) porte *m*. **carriageway** *n* calzada *f*. **dual carriageway** carretera de doble calzada *f*.

carrier ['kariə] *n* portador *m*; (*comm*) empresa de transportes *f*; (*med*) portador, -a *m*, *f*.

carrot ['karət] *n* zanahoria *f*.

carry ['kari] *v* llevar; (*bring*) traer; (*a load*) transportar; (*by pipes*) conducir; (*sustain*) sostener. **carry forward** (*comm*) pasar. **carry out** realizar. **carrycot** *n* cuna portátil *f*.

cart [kɑːt] *n* carro *m*; (*handcart*) carro de mano *m*; (*trolley*) carrito *m*. *v* carretear. **cart horse** caballo de tiro *m*.

cartilage ['kɑːtəlidʒ] *n* cartílago *m*.

cartography [kɑː'togrəfi] *n* cartografía *f*.

carton ['kɑːtən] *n* cartón *m*, caja de cartón *f*.

cartoon [kɑː'tuːn] *n* caricatura *f*, chiote *m*; (*art*) cartón *m*; (*film*) dibujos animados *m pl*. **cartoonist** *n* caricaturista *m*, *f*, humorista *m*, *f*.

cartridge ['kɑːtridʒ] *n* cartucho *m*; (*blank*) cartucho sin bala *m*.

carve [kɑːv] *v* (*meat*) trinchar; (*cut*) cortar; (*sculpture*) tallar. **carve up** (*divide*) dividir; (*stab*) acuchillar. **carving knife** cuchillo de trinchar *m*.

cascade [kas'keid] *n* cascada *f*, salto de agua *m*. *v* caer en cascada.

case[1] [keis] *n* caso *m*; (*affair*) asunto *m*. **in any case** en todo caso. **in case** en caso. **in no case** de ningún modo. **in the case of** en cuanto a. **it's not a case of . . .** no se trata de . . . . **just in case** por si acaso. **state the case** exponer los hechos.

case[2] [keis] *n* (*box*) caja *f*; (*rigid*) estuche *m*; (*soft*) funda. **suitcase** *n* maleta *f*. *v* encajonar, embalar.

cash [kaʃ] *n* dinero al constante *m*; (*comm*) pago al contado *m*. **cash account** cuenta de caja *f*. **cash book** libro de caja *m*. **cash discount** descuento por pago al contado *m*. **cash on delivery** envío contra reembolso *m*. **cash register** caja registradora *f*. **petty cash** dinero para gastos menores *m*.

cashier[1] [ka'ʃiə] *n* (*bank*) cajero, -a *m*, *f*.

cashier[2] [ka'ʃiə] *v* (*mil*) dar de baja.

cashmere [kaʃ'miə] *n* cachemira *f*.

casing ['keisiŋ] *n* cubierta *f*; (*wrapping*) envoltura *f*; (*cylinder*) camisa *f*.

casino [kə'siːnou] *n* casino *m*.

cask [kɑːsk] *n* barril *m*.

casket ['kɑːskit] *n* joyero *m*, cofre *m*.

casserole ['kasəroul] *n* (*dish*) cacerola *f*; (*food*) cazuela *f*.

cassette [kə'set] *n* (*tape*) cassette *m*; (*phot*) cartucho *m*.

cassock ['kasək] *n* sotana *f*.

*****cast** ['kɑːst] *n* (*acting*) reparto *m*; (*throw*) lanzamiento *m*; (*appearance*) aspecto *m*; (*tech*) molde *m*; (*squint*) estrabismo *m*; (*plaster*) escayola *f*. *v* echar, arrojar; (*tech*) moldear, fundir. **castaway** *n* náufrago *m*. **cast aside** desechar. **cast down** bajar. **cast iron** hierro colado *m*. **cast off** abandonar; (*naut*) desamarrar.

castanets [kastə'nets] *pl n* castañuelas *f pl*.

caste [kɑːst] *n* casta *f*.

castle ['kɑːsl] *n* castillo *m*.

castor ['kɑːstə] *n* (*wheel*) ruedecilla *f*.

castor oil *n* aceite de ricino *m*.

castrate [kə'streit] *v* castrar. **castration** *n* castración *f*.

casual ['kaʒuəl] *adj* casual, informal; (*carefree*) despreocupado. **casual clothes** ropa de sport *f sing*. **casually** *adv* de paso.

casualty ['kaʒuəlti] *n* accidente *m*; víctima *f*; (*mil*) baja *f*.

cat [kat] *n* gato, -a *m, f*. **let the cat out of the bag** descubrir el pastel.

catalogue ['katəlog] *n* catálogo *m*. *v* catalogar.

catalyst ['katəlist] *n* catalizador *m*.

catapult ['katəpʌlt] *n* catapulta *f*, honda *f*. *v* catapultar.

cataract ['katərakt] *n* catarata *f*.

catarrh [kə'taɪ] *n* catarro *m*.

catastrophe [kə'tastrəfi] *n* catástrofe *f*. **catastrophic** *adj* catastrófico.

***catch** [katʃ] *v* (*seize*) agarrar, coger; (*capture*) prender, atrapar; (*disease*) contraer; (*hook*) engancharse. **catch on** (*coll*) comprender. **catch out** sorprender. **catch up** alcanzar. *n* (*act of catching*) cogida *f*; (*prey*) presa *f*; (*bolt*) pestillo *m*; (*buckle*) hebijón *m*; (*drawback*) trampa *f*; (*trick*) truco *m*. **safety catch** fiador *m*. **catching** *adj* contagioso. **catchy** *adj* pegadizo.

category ['katəgəri] *n* categoría *f*. **categorical** *adj* categórico, rotundo. **categorize** *v* clasificar.

cater ['keitə] *v* proveer de comida. **cater for** atender a. **caterer** *n* proveedor, -a *m, f*. **catering** *n* abastecimiento *m*.

caterpillar ['katəpilə] *n* oruga *f*.

cathedral [kə'θiːdrəl] *n* catedral *f*.

cathode ['kaθoud] *n* cátodo *m*. **cathode-ray tube** tubo de rayos catódicos *m*.

catholic ['kaθəlik] *n, adj* católico, -a. *adj* universal; ortodoxo. **catholicism** *n* catolicismo *m*. **catholicity** *n* catolicidad *f*.

catkin ['katkin] *n* candelilla *f*.

cattle ['katl] *n* ganado *m*.

catty ['kati] *adj* malicioso.

caught [koɪt] *V* **catch**.

cauliflower ['koliflauə] *n* coliflor *m*.

cause [koɪz] *n* causa *f*, motivo *m*. *v* causar, provocar. **in the cause of** por.

causeway ['koɪzwei] *n* terraplén *m*.

caustic ['koɪstik] *adj* cáustico, mordaz.

caution ['koɪʃən] *n* cautela *f*, cuidado *m*; (*warning*) advertencia *f*. *v* (*reprimand*) amonestar; (*warn*) advertir. **cautionary** *adj* amonestador. **cautious** *adj* cauteloso, precavido.

cavalry ['kavəlri] *n* caballería *f*.

cave [keiv] *n* cueva *f*, caverna *f*. **cave in** derrumbarse. **cavernous** *adj* cavernoso.

caviar ['kaviaɪ] *n* caviar *m*.

cavity ['kavəti] *n* cavidad *f*; (*dental*) cavies *f invar*.

cayenne [kei'en] *n* pimentón *m*.

cease [siɪs] *v* cesar. **cease-fire** *n* alto el fuego. **ceaseless** *adj* incesante.

cedar ['siɪdə] *n* cedro *m*.

cedilla [si'dilə] *n* cedilla *f*.

ceiling ['siɪliŋ] *n* techo *m*; (*aero*) altura *f*; (*fig*) tope *m*, limite *m*. **hit the ceiling** subirse por las paredes.

celebrate ['seləbreit] *v* celebrar, festejar. **celebrated** *adj* célebre. **celebration** *n* celebración *f*. **celebrant** *n* celebrante *m*.

celery ['seləri] *n* apio *m*.

celestial [sə'lestiəl] *adj* celestial; (*astron*) celeste.

celibate ['selibət] *n*(*m+f*), *adj* célibe. **celibacy** *n* celibato *m*.

cell [sel] *n* celda *f*; (*biol*) célula *f*; (*elec*) pila *f*.

cellar ['selə] *n* sótano *m*; (*wine*) bodega *f*.

cello ['tʃelou] *n* violoncelo *m*. **cellist** *n* violoncelista *m, f*.

cellular ['seljulə] *adj* celular.

cement [sə'ment] *n* cemento *m*. *v* (*tech*) cementar; (*fig*) cimentar.

cemetery ['semətri] *n* cementerio *m*.

cenotaph ['senətaːf] *n* cenotafio *m*.

censor ['sensə] *n* censor *m*. *v* censurar; (*delete*) tachar. **censorious** *adj* censorador. **censorship** *n* censura *f*.

censure ['senʃə] *n* censura *f*. *v* censurar. **censurable** *adv* censurable.

census ['sensəs] *n* censo *m*. **take a census of** empadronar.

cent [sent] *n* centavo *m*.

centenary [sen'tiɪnəri] *nm, adj* centenario. **centenarian** *n, adj* centenario, -a. **centennial** *adj* centenario.

centigrade ['sentigreid] *adj* centígrado.

centimetre ['sentimiɪtə] *n* centímetro *m*.

centipede ['sentipiɪd] *n* ciempiés *m invar*.

centre ['sentə] *n* centro *m*. **community centre** centro social *m*. *v* centrar. **central** *adj* central, céntrico. **central heating** calefacción central *f*. **centralize** *v* centralizar. **centralization** *n* centralización *f*.

centrifugal [sen'trifjugəl] *adj* centrífugo.

century ['sentʃuri] *n* siglo *m*.

ceramic [sə'ramik] *adj* cerámico. **ceramics** *n* cerámica *f sing*.

cereal ['siəriəl] *nm, adj* cereal.

ceremony ['serəməni] *n* ceremonia *f*. **stand on ceremony** andarse con ceremonias. **ceremonial** *nm, adj* ceremonial. **ceremonious** *adj* ceremonioso.

certain ['səɪtn] *adj* cierto, seguro. **make certain** asegurarse. **certainly** *adv* desde luego, naturalmente. **certainly not** de ninguna manera. **certainty** *n* certeza *f*, certidumbre *f*; seguridad *f*.

certificate [sə'tifikət] *n* certificado *m*; (*academic*) título *m*, diploma *f*. **birth certificate** partida de nascimiento *f*. **death certificate** partida de defunción *f*. **marriage certificate** partida de matrimonio *f*. **certify** *v* certificar; garantizar.

cesspool ['sespuːl] *n* pozo negro *m*.

chafe [tʃeif] *v* (*rub*) rozar; (*irritate*) irritar; (*for warmth*) frotar; (*fig*) enfadar. *n* rozadura *f*; irritación *f*.

chaffinch ['tʃafintʃ] *n* pinzón *m*.

chain [tʃein] *n* cadena *f*. **chain store** sucursal *m*. *v* encadenar.

chair [tʃeə] *n* silla *f*; (*university*) cátedra *f*; (*meeting*) presidencia *f*. **folding chair** silla plegable *f*. **take the chair** tomar la presidencia. **chairman** *n* presidente *m*. *v* presidir.

chalet ['ʃalei] *n* chalet *m*.

chalk [tʃɔːk] *n* (*geol*) creta *f*; (*for writing*) tiza *f*. **not by a long chalk** ni mucho menos. *v* marcar con tiza. **chalk up** apuntarse. **chalky** *adj* cretáceo, yesoso.

challenge ['tʃalindʒ] *n* reto *m*, desafío *m*; (*sentry*) alto *m*; (*incentive*) estímulo *m*; (*law*) recusación *f*. *v* desafiar, retar. **challenger** *n* desafiador *m*, retador *m*.

chamber ['tʃeimbə] *n* (*room, legislative body*) cámara *f*; (*tech*) recámara *f*. **chambermaid** *n* doncella *f*, camarera *f*. **chamber music** música de cámara *f*. **chamber pot** orinal *m*.

chameleon [kəmiːliən] *n* camaleón *m*.

chamois ['ʃamwaː] *n* gamuza *f*.

champagne [ʃam'pein] *n* champaña *f*.

champion ['tʃampiən] *n, adj* campeón, -ona. *v* defender, hacerse el campeón de. **championship** *n* campeonato *m*.

chance [tʃaːns] *n* casualidad *f*, suerte *f*, azar *m*; oportunidad *f*, ocasión *f*; posibilidad *f*; riesgo *m*. *adj* casual, fortuito. *v* arriesgar; probar; (*happen*) acaecer. **chance upon** tropezarse con.

chancellor ['tʃaːnsələ] *n* canciller *m*. **chancellery** *n* cancillería *f*.

chandelier [ʃandə'liə] *n* araña *f*.

change [tʃeindʒ] *n* cambio *m*; (*money*) suelto *m*; (*clothes*) muda *f*. **for a change** para variar. *v* cambiar; mudar. **changeable** *adj* (*character, weather*) variable; (*inconsistent*) cambiadizo; (*able to be*

changed) cambiable. **changing room** vestuario *m*.

channel ['tʃanl] *n* canal *m*; (*of a river*) cauce *m*; (*fig*) vía *f*; (*groove*) ranura *f*. **English Channel** Canal de la Mancha *m*.

chant [tʃaːnt] *n* canción *f*, canto *m*. *v* cantar; entonar.

chaos ['keiɔs] *n* caos *m*. **chaotic** *adj* caótico.

chap[1] [tʃap] *v* (*skin*) agrietar. *n* grieta *f*.

chap[2] [tʃap] *n* (*coll*) tipo *m*, sujeto *m*.

chapel ['tʃapəl] *n* capilla *f*.

chaperon ['ʃapəroun] *n* carabina *f*. *v* acompañar.

chaplain ['tʃaplin] *n* capellán *m*.

chapter ['tʃaptə] *n* capítulo *m*; (*rel*) cabildo *m*. **quote chapter and verse** citar literalmente.

char[1] [tʃaː] *v* (*burn*) carbonizar.

char[2] [tʃaː] *n* (*charwoman*) asistenta *f*.

character ['karəktə] *n* carácter *m*; (*person*) personaje *m*; (*role*) papel *m*; (*coll*) tipo *m*. **character reference** informe *m*. **characterize** *v* caracterizar. **characterization** *n* caracterización *f*.

characteristic [ˌkarəktə'ristik] *adj* característico. *n* característica *f*.

charcoal ['tʃaːkoul] *n* carbón de leña *m*.

charge [tʃaːdʒ] *n* (*responsibility*) cargo *m*; (*task*) tarea *f*; (*battery, explosive, attack*) carga *f*. **charge account** cuenta a cargo *f*. **in charge of** encargado de. **take charge of** hacerse cargo de. *v* (*accuse*) acusar; (*bill*) cobrar; (*mil*) atacar.

chariot ['tʃariət] *n* carro *m*.

charity ['tʃarəti] *n* caridad *f*; (*alms*) limosna *f*; (*society*) sociedad benéfica *f*. **charitable** *adj* caritativo.

charm [tʃaːm] *n* encanto *m*; (*spell*) hechizo *m*. *v* encantar; hechizar. **charming** *adj* encantador, simpático.

chart [tʃaːt] *n* (*naut*) carta marina *f*; (*map*) mapa *m*; (*table*) tabla *f*; (*graph*) gráfico *m*. *v* tabular; trazar.

charter ['tʃaːtə] *n* (*law*) carta; (*comm*) flete *m*, fletamento *m*, fletamiento *m*; (*transport*) alquiler *m*. *v* fletar; alquilar; (*grant a charter*) conceder carta a. **charter flight** vuelo charter' m. **charter member** socio fundador *m*.

chase [tʃeis] *v* perseguir; (*hunt*) cazar. **chase after** ir detrás de. **chase away/off** ahuyentar. *n* persecución *f*; caza *f*.

chasm ['kazəm] *n* sima *f*, abismo *m*.

chassis ['ʃasi] *n* (*mech*) chasis *m*.
chaste [tʃeist] *adj* casto; (*style*) sobrio.
chastity *n* castidad *f*.
chastise [tʃas'taiz] *v* castigar.
chat [tʃat] *n* charla *f*. *v* charlar. **chatty** *adj*
charlador.
chatter ['tʃatə] *v* chacharear, parlotear;
(*teeth*) castañetear. *n* cháchara *f*,
parloteo *m*; castañeteo *m*. **chatterbox** *n*
charlatán, -ana *m*, *f*.
chauffeur ['ʃoufə] *n* chófer *m*, conductor,
-a *m*, *f*.
chauvinism ['ʃouvinizəm] *n* chauvinismo
m. **chauvinist** *n*(*m+f*), *adj* chauvinista.
cheap [tʃiːp] *adj* barato. **dirt cheap**
baratísimo *adj*, *adv*. **cheapen** *v* abaratar.
cheat [tʃiːt] *v* (*swindle*) timar, estafar;
(*deceive*) engañar; (*at games*) hacer
trampas; (*in exams*) copiar. *n* timador,
-a *m*, *f*, estafador, -a *m*, *f*; tramposo, -a
m, *f*; (*trick*) trampa *f*.
check [tʃek] *v* parar, detener; (*restrain*)
reprimir, refrenar; (*inspect*) inspeccionar;
(*facts*) comprobar; (*mark*) poner contraseña a; (*chess*) dar jaque a. **check in**
registrarse. **check on** averiguar. **check
with** cotejar con. *n* parada *f*, detención *f*;
(*restraint*) restricción *f*; (*control*) inspección *f*; (*pattern*) cuadro *m*; (*chess*) jaque
m. **checkmate** *v* dar el mate; *n* jaque
mate *m*. **checkpoint** *n* control *m*. **check-
up** *n* (*med*) reconocimiento general *m*.
cheek [tʃiːk] *n* carrillo *m*, mejilla *f*; (*coll*)
cara dura *f*. **turn the other cheek** poner la
otra mejilla. **cheekbone** *n* pómulo *m*.
cheeky *adj* descarado.
cheer [tʃiə] *v* (*shout*) vitorear, aclamar;
(*gladden*) alegrar. **cheer on** animar. **cheer
up** alentar. *n* (*shout*) viva *m*; (*comfort*)
consuelo *m*; (*joy*) ánimo *m*. **cheers!** *interj*
¡a su salud! **cheerful** *adj* alegre, animado.
cheerfulness *n* alegría *f*. **cheerio!** *interj*
¡hasta luego! **cheerless** *adj* triste.
cheese [tʃiːz] *n* queso *m*. **cheesecake** *n*
pastel de queso *m*. **cheesecloth** *n* estopi-
lla *f*.
cheetah ['tʃiːtə] *n* leopardo cazador *m*.
chef [ʃef] *n* jefe de cocina *m*.
chemistry ['kemistri] *n* química *f*. **chemi-
cal** *adj* químico. **chemist** *n* químico *m*;
farmacéutico *m*. **chemist's shop** farmacia
f.
check [tʃek] *n* cheque *m*. **checkbook** *n*
talonario de cheques *m*. **check card**

tarjeta de crédito *f*. **traveler's check**
cheque de viaje *m*.
cherish ['tʃeriʃ] *v* (*love*) querer; (*nourish*)
abrigar; (*take care of*) cuidar.
cherry ['tʃeri] *n* (*fruit*) cereza *f*; (*tree*) cerezo *m*.
chess [tʃes] *n* ajedrez *m*. **chessboard** *n*
tablero de ajedrez *m*. **chessman** *n* pieza
de ajedrez *f*.
chest [tʃest] *n* (*anat*) pecho *m*; (*box*) caja
f. **chest of drawers** *n* cómoda *f*. **chesty** *adj*
(*cough*) delicado de los broncios.
chestnut ['tʃesnʌt] *n* (*fruit*) castaña *f*;
(*tree*) castaño *m*. *adj* (*hair*) castaño.
chew [tʃuː] *v* masticar. **chewing gum** chicle *m*. **chew the cud** rumiar. **chew up**
estropear.
chick pea ['tʃik,piː] *n* garbanzo *m*.
chicken ['tʃikin] *n* (*coffee*) achicoria *f*;
varicela *f*. **chicken out** (*slang*) ser una
gallina.
chicory ['tʃikəri] *n* (*coffee*) achicoria *f*;
(*salad*) escarola *f*.
chief [tʃiːf] *n* *pl* -s jefe *m*, *f*. *adj* principal.
chiefly *adv* principalmente; sobre todo.
chilblain ['tʃilblein] *n* sabañón *m*.
child [tʃaild] *n* *pl* -ren niño, -a *m*, *f*. **childbirth** *n* parto *m*. **childhood** *n* niñez *f*.
childish *adj* infantil, pueril. **childless** *adj*
sin hijos.
Chile ['tʃili] *n* Chile *m*. **Chilean** *n*, *adj*
chileno, -a.
chill [tʃil] *n* frío *m*; (*med*) tiritona *f*; (*shiver*) escalofrío *m*; (*fig*) frialdad *f*. *v*
enfriar. **chilled to the bone** enfriado hasta los huesos. **chilly** *adj* fresco.
chilli ['tʃili] *n* chile *m*.
chime [tʃaim] *v* sonar, repicar. **chime in**
intervenir. *n* carillón *m*.
chimney ['tʃimni] *n* chimenea *f*. **chimney
pot** cañón de chimenea *m*. **chimney
sweep** deshollinador *m*.
chimpanzee [tʃimpən'ziː] *n* chimpancé *m*.
chin [tʃin] *n* barbilla *f*, mentón *m*.
china ['tʃainə] *n* porcelana *f*.
China ['tʃainə] *n* China *f*. **Chinese** *n*, *adj*
chino, -a. **the Chinese** los chinos.
chink[1] [tʃiŋk] *n* (*fissure*) raja *f*, grieta *m*.
chink[2] [tʃiŋk] *n* (*sound*) sonido metálico
m. *v* hacer tintinear.
chip [tʃip] *n* (*fragment*) pedacito *m*; (*in
cup, etc.*) desportilladura *f*; (*gambling*)
ficha *f*. **chipboard** *n* madera aglomerada
f. **chips** *pl* *n* (*cookery*) patata frita *f*. *v*

astillar. **chip in** (*interrupt*) interrumpir; (*contribute money*) poner.

chiropodist [ki'ropədist] *n* pedicuro, -a *m*, *f*. **chiropody** *n* quiropodia *f*.

chirp [tʃɜɪp] *v* (*birds*) gorjear; (*crickets*) chirriar. *n* gorjeo *m*; chirrido *m*. **chirpy** *adj* animado.

chisel ['tʃɪzl] *n* cincel *m*. *v* cincelar.

chivalry ['ʃivəlri] *n* caballerosidad *f*. **chivalrous** *adj* caballeroso.

chive [tʃaiv] *n* cebolleta *f*.

chlorine ['klɔtriːn] *n* cloro *m*. **chlorinate** *v* tratar con cloro.

chloroform ['klɔrəfɔtm] *n* cloroformo *m*. *v* cloroformizar.

chlorophyll ['klɔrəfil] *n* clorofila *f*.

chocolate ['tʃokələt] *n* chocolate *m*. **drinking chocolate** chocolate a la taza *m*.

choice [tʃois] *n* elección *f*, selección *f*; preferencia *f*. *adj* (*best*) flor y nata.

choir ['kwaiə] *n* coro *m*, coral *f*. **choirboy** *n* niño de coro *m*. **choirmaster** *n* director de coro *m*.

choke [tʃouk] *v* (*strangle*) estrangular; (*block*) obstruir. *n* (*mot*) estrangulador *m*.

cholera ['kolərə] *n* cólera *m*.

*****choose** [tʃuːz] *v* escoger, elegir.

chop[1] [tʃop] *n* (*meat*) chuleta *f*; (*blow*) golpe *m*. *v* (*cut*) cortar; (*mince*) picar; (*lop*) tronchar. **chop down** talar. **chopper** *n* hacha *f*; (*slang*) helicóptero *m*.

chop[2] [tʃop] *v* **chop and change** cambiar de opinión. **choppy** *adj* (*sea*) picado.

chops [tʃops] *pl n* (*jaws*) morros *m pl*. **lick one's chops** relamerse.

chopstick ['tʃopstik] *n* palillo *m*.

chord [kɔtd] *n* (*music*) acorde *m*; (*anat*) cuerda *f*.

chore [tʃɔt] *n* (*unpleasant*) tarea penosa *f*. **chores** *pl n* (*household*) faenas de la casa *f pl*.

choreography [kori'ogrəfi] *n* coreografía *f*. **choreographer** *n* coreógrafo *m*.

chorus ['kɔtrəs] *n* (*refrain*) estribillo *m*; (*singers*) coro *m*. **chorus girl** corista *f*. **choral** *adj* coral. **choral society** orfeón *m*.

chose [tʃouz] *V* **choose**.

christen ['krisn] *v* bautizar; (*nickname*) llamar. **christening** *n* bautismo *m*.

Christian ['kristʃən] *n, adj* cristiano, -a *m, f*. **Christian name** nombre de pila *m*. **Christianity** *n* cristianismo *m*.

Christmas ['krisməs] *n* Navidad *f*. **Christmas Day** día de Navidad *m*. **Christmas Eve** Nochebuena *f*.

chromatic [krə'matik] *adj* cromático.

chrome [kroum] *n* cromo *m*.

chromium ['kroumiəm] *n* cromo *m*. **chromium-plated** *adj* cromado.

chronic ['kronik] *adj* crónico; (*coll: dreadful*) terrible.

chronicle ['kronikl] *n* crónica *f*.

chronological [kronə'lodʒikəl] *adj* cronológico.

chrysalis ['krisəlis] *n* crisálida *f*.

chrysanthemum [kri'sanθəməm] *n* crisantemo *m*.

chubby ['tʃʌbi] *adj* gordinflón.

chuck [tʃʌk] *v* (*coll: throw*) tirar; (*give up*) abandonar.

chuckle ['tʃʌkl] *v* reir entre de dientes. *n* risa *f*.

chunk [tʃʌŋk] *n* pedazo *m*; (*large amount*) cantidad grande *f*.

church [tʃɜtʃ] *n* iglesia *f*. **church service** oficio religioso *m*. **churchyard** *n* cementerio *m*.

churn [tʃɜin] *n* mantequera *f*. *v* batir. **churn out** producir en profusión.

chute [ʃuːt] *n* tolva *f*.

cider ['saidə] *n* sidra *f*.

cigar [si'gat] *n* cigarro puro *m*.

cigarette [sigə'ret] *n* cigarillo *m*. **cigarette case** pitillera *f*. **cigarette holder** boquilla *f*. **cigarette lighter** encendedor *m*, mechero *m*. **cigarette paper** papel de fumar *m*.

cinder ['sində] *n* carbonilla *f*, ceniza *f*.

cinema ['sinəmə] *n* cine *m*. **cinematography** *n* cinematografía *f*.

cinnamon ['sinəmən] *n* canela *f*.

circle ['sɜtkl] *n* círculo *m*; (*theatre*) piso principal *m*. **go round in circles** dar vueltas. *v* rodear; (*surround*) circundar. **circular** *adj*, *n* circular *f*.

circuit ['sɜtkit] *n* (*route*) circuito *m*; (*perimeter*) perímetro *m*; (*law*) distrito *m*; (*cinemas, theatres*) cadena *f*. **short circuit** cortocircuito *m*. **circuitous** *adj* indirecto.

circulate ['sɜtkjuleit] *v* circular. **circulation** *n* circulación *f*.

circumcise ['sɜtkəmsaiz] *v* circuncidar. **circumcision** *n* circuncisión *f*.

circumference [sər'kʌmfərəns] *n* circunferencia *f*.

circumflex ['sɜtkəmfleks] *n* circunflejo *m*.

circumscribe ['sɔɪkəmskraib] v circunscribir. **circumscription** n circunscripción f.

circumstance ['sɔɪkəmstans] n circunstancia f. **extenuating circumstances** circunstancias atenuantes f pl. **under no circumstances** de ninguna manera. **under the circumstances** en estas circunstancias. **circumstantial** adj (incidental) circunstancial; (detailed) circunstanciado. **circumstantial evidence** testimonio indirecto m.

circus ['sɔɪkəs] n circo m.

cistern ['sistən] n cisterna f, aljibe m.

cite [sait] v citar. **citation** n citación f; (mil) mención f.

citizen ['sitizn] n ciudadano, -a m, f. **citizenship** n ciudadanía f.

citrus ['sitrəs] n cidro m. **citrus fruit** n agrios m pl. **citric acid** ácido cítrico m.

city ['siti] n ciudad f.

civic ['sivik] adj cívico.

civil ['sivl] adj civil; (polite) cortés. **civil engineering** ingeniería civil f. **civil rights** derechos civiles m pl. **civil servant** funcionario, -a m, f. **civil service** administración pública f. **civil war** guerra civil f.

civilian [sə'viljən] adj civil, de paisano. n paisano, -a m, f.

civilization [,sivilai'zeifən] n civilización f. **civilize** v civilizar.

clad [klad] adj vestido (de).

claim [kleim] v (damages) exigir; (a right) reclamar; (assert) declarar; (need) requerir. n (right) derecho m; (demand) demanda f, reclamación f; (statement) declaración f; (land) propiedad f. **claimant** (law) n demandante m, f; (pretender) pretendiente m, f.

clairvoyant [kleə'voiənt] n(m+f), adj clarividente. **clairvoyance** n clarividencia f.

clam [klam] n almeja f.

clamber ['klambə] v trepar.

clammy ['klami] adj pegajoso.

clamour ['klamə] n clamor m. v clamar, vociferar.

clamp [klamp] n abrazadera f. v sujetar con abrazadera. **clamp down on** suprimir.

clan [klan] n clan m. **clannish** adj exclusivista.

clandestine [klan'destin] adj clandestino.

clang [klaŋ] v sonar estripitosamente. n sonido metálico m.

clap [klap] v aplaudir, dar palmadas. n (with hands) palmada f; (noise) ruido seco m. **clap of thunder** trueno m.

claret ['klarət] n clarete m.

clarify ['klarəfai] v aclarar; (liquid) clarificar. **clarification** n aclaración f; clarificación f.

clarinet [klarə'net] n clarinete m.

clarity ['klarəti] n claridad f.

clash [klaʃ] v (collide) chocar; (cymbals) golpear; (interests) estar en desacuerdo; (dates) coincidir; (colours) matarse. n ruido metálico m; (encounter) choque m; (interests) conflicto m; coincidencia f; disparidad f.

clasp [klaɪsp] v (grasp) agarrar; (fasten) abrochar. n (hands) apretón m; (fastening) cierre m; (belt) broche m.

class [klaɪs] n clase f.

classic ['klasik] adj clásico. **classical** adj clásico. **classics** n pl clásicas f pl.

classify ['klasifai] v clasificar. **classification** n clasificación f. **classified advertisement** anuncio por palabras m.

clatter ['klatə] n estruendo m; (hooves) chacoloteo m. v sonar con estrépito; chacolotear.

clause [klɔɪz] n (law) cláusula f; (gramm) oración f.

claustrophobia [klɔɪstrə'foubiə] n claustrofobia f.

claw [klɔɪ] n (talon) garra f; (cat) uña f; (crab) pinza f; (tech) garfio m. v agarrar; arañar; (tear) desgarrar.

clay [klei] n arcilla f, barro m.

clean [kliɪn] adj limpio; (irreproachable) sin tocha. v limpiar. **clean out** (empty) vaciar. **clean up** (tidy) ordenar; (win) ganarse. **clean-cut** adj bien hecho, perfilado. **cleaner** (person) n asistenta f. **cleanliness** n limpieza f. **clean-shaven** adj bien afeitado.

cleanse [klenz] v limpiar, purificar.

clear [kliə] adj claro, transparente; (conscience) tranquilo; evidente; (free) libre; (unobstructed) despejado; (profit) neto. adv claramente. v aclarar; despejar; (law) absolver. **clearance** n espacio m, altura libre f, margen m; despeje m; acreditación f. **clearance sale** liquidación f.

clef [klef] n clave f.

clench [klentʃ] v apretar, sujetar.

clergy ['klɔɪdʒi] n clero m. **clergyman** n clérigo m.

clerical ['klerikəl] adj (clerk) de oficina; (rel) clerical. **clerical error** error de copia m.

clerk [klɑːk] n oficinista m, f; (law) escribano m.

clever ['klevə] adj listo; inteligente; (skilful) hábil; (cunning) astuto. **cleverness** n habilidad f; ingenio m.

cliché ['kliːʃei] n cliché m, clisé m.

click [klik] n chasquido m; taconeo m. v chascar, chasquear; taconear.

client ['klaiənt] n cliente m, f.

cliff [klif] n (coast) acantilado m; (crag) risco m.

climate ['klaimət] n clima m; (atmosphere) ambiente m. **climatic** adj climático.

climax ['klaimaks] n punto culminante m; clímax m. v llevar al punto culminante.

climb [klaim] v subir, escalar; (plants) trepar. n subida f, escalada f. **climber** n escalador, -a m, f; (mountaineer) alpinista m, f; (plant) planta trepadora f.

*cling [kliŋ] v agarrarse; (stick to) adherirse a, pegarse a. **clinging** adj ceñido; pegajoso.

clinic ['klinik] n dispensario m; clínica f. **clinical** adj clínico.

clip¹ [klip] v (trim) recortar; (animals) esquilar; (ticket) picar; (coll: cuff) abofetear. n (film) fragmento; (cuff) bofetada f.

clip² [klip] v (fasten) sujetar. n grapa f; sujetapapeles m invar; (hair) horquilla f; (pen, pencil) prendedor m.

cloak [klouk] n capa f; (fig) manto m; (mil) capote m. **cloak-and-dagger** adj de capa y espada. **cloakroom** n guardarropa m; (toilet) servicios m pl. v encubrir, cubrir, encapotar.

clock [klok] n reloj m. **against the clock** contra reloj. **alarm clock** despertador m. **around the clock** durante 24 horas. **clockwise** adj en el sentido de las agujas del reloj. **clockwork** n aparato de relojería m. v registrar.

clog [klog] n zueco m. v atascar, obstruir.

cloister ['kloistə] n claustro m. v enclaustrar.

close [klouz; adj, adv klous] v cerrar; (block) tapar; (end) acabar; (account) saldar; (distance) acortar. **close in** acercarse. n conclusión f; final m. adj cercano; íntimo; (air) cargado; (game) reñido. adv cerca. **close-up** n primer plano m.

closet ['klozit] n (WC) retrete m. water m; armario m.

clot [klot] n (blood) coágulo m; (liquid) grumo m. v coagular, cuajar.

cloth [kloθ] n (rag) trapo m; (fabric) paño m; (tablecloth) mantel m.

clothe [klouð] v vestir; (cover) cubrir.

clothes [klouðz] pl n also **clothing** ropa f sing; vestidos m pl. **clothes basket** cesta de la ropa sucia f. **clothes brush** cepillo de la ropa m. **clothes line** tendedero m. **clothes peg** pinza f.

cloud [klaud] n nube f; (gas) capa f. v nublar; (darken) ensombrecer, oscurecer. **cloudburst** n chaparrón m. **cloudiness** n nubosidad f. **cloudless** adj despejado. **cloudy** adj nuboso; nublado.

clove¹ [klouv] n (spice) clavo m.

clove² [klouv] n (of garlic, etc.) diente m.

clover ['klouvə] n trébol m.

clown [klaun] n payaso m. v hacer el payaso.

club [klʌb] n (association) club m; (stick) porra f, garrote m; (golf) palo m. v (beat) aporrear. **clubfoot** n pie zopo m.

clue [kluː] n (police lead) pista f; (piece of evidence) indicio m.

clump [klʌmp] n (trees) grupo m; (flowers) matar f; (earth) terrón m; (noise) pisada fuerte f. v agrupar; andar con pisadas fuertes.

clumsy ['klʌmzi] adj (awkward) torpe; (unskilful) desmañado; (tactless) sin tacto. **clumsiness** n torpeza f; desmaña f.

cluster ['klʌstə] n grupo m; (fruits) racimo m. v agruparse, arracimarse.

clutch [klʌtʃ] v agarrar, apretar. n (grip) agarrón m; (mot) embrague m. **engage the clutch** embragar.

clutter ['klʌtə] n desorden m, confusión f. v desordenar, atentar.

coach [koutʃ] n (carriage) coche m; (ceremonial carriage) carroza f; (mot) autocar m; (tutor) profesor particular m; (trainer) entrenador m. v dar clases particulares; entrenar.

coagulate [kou'agjuleit] v coagular. **coagulation** n coagulación f.

coal [koul] n carbón m, hulla f. **coal cellar** carbonera f. **coalman** n carbonero m. **coalmine** n mina de carbón f. **coalminer** n minero de carbón m. **coal scuttle** cubo para el carbón m.

coalesce [kouə'les] v (unite) unirse; (merge) fundirse.

coalition [kouə'liʃən] n coalición f.

coarse [kɔɪs] adj (gross) grosero; (ill-made) basto. coarse-grained adj de grano grueso. coarseness n grosería f; basteza f.

coast [koust] n costa f. the coast is clear no hay moros en la costa. v (freewheel) deslizarse cuesta abajo. coastguard n guardacostas m invar. coastline n litoral m.

coat [kout] n chaqueta f; (overcoat) abrigo m; (animal) pelo m. coat-hanger percha f. coat of arms escudo de armas m. coat of paint mano de pintura f. v cubrir; dar una mano de pintura; (cookery) rebozar. coating n capa f; mano f; rebozo m.

coax [kouks] v engatusar.

cobbler ['koblə] n zapatero m.

cobra ['koubrə] n cobra f.

cobweb ['kobweb] n telaraña f.

cocaine [kə'kein] n cocaína f.

cock¹ [kok] n (male fowl) gallo m; (male bird) macho m; (impol: penis) polla f. cocky adj engreído.

cock² [kok] v (gun) amartillar; (ears) aguzar el oído.

cockle ['kokl] n berberecho m.

cockpit ['kokpit] n (aero) cabina del piloto f; (cockfighting) reñidero m.

cockroach ['kokroutʃ] n cucaracha f.

cocktail ['kokteil] n cóctel m. cocktail shaker coctelera f.

cocoa ['koukou] n cacao m.

coconut ['koukənʌt] n coco m. coconut palm cocotero m.

cocoon [kə'kuɪn] n capullo m.

cod [kod] n bacalao m.

code [koud] n código m; (signals) cifra f, clave f; (area code) prefijo m. highway code codigo de la circulación m. Morse code alfabeto Morse m. v cifrar.

codeine ['koudiɪn] n codeína f.

coeducation [kouedju'keiʃən] n coeducación f.

coerce [kou'əɪs] v forzar, obligar.

coexist [kouig'zist] v coexistir. coexistence n coexistencia f.

coffee ['kofi] n café m. black/white coffee café solo/con leche m. coffee bean grano de café m. coffee pot cafetera f. coffee table mesita de café f.

coffin ['kofin] n ataúd m.

cog [kog] n diente m; (wheel) rueda dentada f.

cognac ['konjak] n coñac m.

cohabit [kou'habit] v cohabitar, vivir juntos. cohabitation n cohabitación f.

cohere [kə'hiə] v adherirse, pegarse. coherence n coherencia f. coherent adj coherente.

coil [koil] n (rope) rollo m; (smoke) espiral m; (elec) carrete m. coil spring muelle en espiral m. v enrollar, arrollar.

coin [koin] n moneda f. toss a coin echar a cara o cruz. v acuñar; inventar. coinage n moneda f.

coincide [kouin'said] v coincidir. coincidence n coincidencia f. coincidental adj coincidente.

colander ['koləndə] n escurridor m.

cold [kould] adj frío. be cold (person) tener frío; (weather) hacer frío. cold front frente frío m. cold storage conservación f. cold war guerra fría f. catch a cold resfriarse. cold-blooded adj (biol) de sangre fría; (fig) insensible.

colic ['kolik] n cólico m.

collaborate [kə'labəreit] v colaborar. collaboration n colaboración f. collaborator n (colleague) colaborador, -a m, f; (pol) colaboracionista m, f.

collapse [kə'laps] v derrumbar; (med) sufrir un colapso. n derrumbamiento m; colapso; (failure) fracaso m. collapsible adj plegable.

collar ['kolə] n cuello m; (dog, etc.) collar m. collarbone n clavícula f. v (seize) agarrar por el cuello; (put a collar on) acollarar.

collate [ko'leit] v cotejar. collation n (food) colación f; (texts) cotejo m.

colleague ['koliːg] n colega m, f.

collect [kə'lekt] v (bring together) juntar, reunir; (hobby) coleccionar; (funds) allegar; (taxes) recaudar; (bills) cobrar; (gather) recoger. collected works obras completas f pl. collection (hobby) colección f; (charity) colecta f; (people) grupo m; (things) reunión f; (rent, bills) cobro m; (taxes) recaudación f; (postal) recogida f. collective adj colectivo. collector n (tax) recaudador, -a m, f; (bills, rent) cobrador m; (hobbies) coleccionista m, f.

college ['kolidʒ] n colegio m. collegiate adj colegiado.

collide [kə'laid] v chocar. **collision** n choque m.

colloquial [kə'loukwiəl] adj familiar, popular. **colloquialism** n expresión familiar f.

Colombia [kə'lombiə] n Colombia f. **Colombian** n, adj colombiano, -a.

colon ['koulon] n dos puntos m pl; (anat) colon m.

colonel ['kɜːnl] n coronel m.

colony ['koləni] n colonia f. **colonial** adj colonial. **colonialist** n(m+f), adj colonialista. **colonist** n colono m. **colonization** n colonización f. **colonize** v colonizar.

colossal [kə'losəl] adj colosal.

colour ['kʌlə] n color m. **colour bar** barrera racial f. **colour-blind** adj daltoniano. **colourful** adj animado. **fast colour** color sólido m. **in colour** en colores. v colorear; (dye) teñir.

colt [koult] n potro m.

column ['koləm] n columna f. **columnist** n columnista m, f.

coma ['koumə] n coma m.

comb [koum] n peine m; (honey) panal m. v peinar.

combat ['kombat] n combate m. v combatir, luchar contra. **combatant** n(m+f), adj combatiente.

combine [kəm'bain; n 'kombain] v combinar, reunir. n (comm) cártel m. **combination** n combinación f, asociación f.

combustion [kəm'bʌstʃən] n combustión f. **combustible** adj combustible.

*__come__ [kʌm] v venir, llegar; proceder; salir. **come about** ocurrir. **come across** dar con. **come along!** ¡vamos! **come back** volver. **comeback** n restablecimiento m. **come off** desprender; (succeed) tener éxito. **come out** salir. **come to** (from faint) volver ensí; (total) ascender a.

comedy ['komədi] n comedia f. **comedian** n cómico m.

comet ['komit] n cometa m.

comfort ['kʌmfət] n (relief) alivio m; (consolation) consuelo m; (well-being) bienestar m; (convenience) comodidad f. v aliviar; consolar; animar. **comfortable** adj cómodo; agradable. **comfortably** adv cómodamente; confortablemente.

comic ['komik] adj cómico, divertido. n (magazine) tebeo m. **comical** adj cómico.

comma ['komə] n coma f. **inverted commas** comillas f pl.

command [kə'maind] n (order) orden f; (authority) mando m; (mastery) dominio m. v mandar, ordenar; dominar. **commandant** n comandante m. **commander** n comandante m; (leader) jefe m. **commander-in-chief** n comandante-en-jefe m. **commandment** n mandamiento m.

commandeer [komən'diə] v expropiar.

commando [kə'maindou] n comando m.

commemorate [kə'meməreit] v conmemorar. **commemoration** n conmemoración f. **commemorative** adj conmemorativo.

commence [kə'mens] v empezar, comenzar. **commencement** n comienzo m.

commend [kə'mend] v (recommend) recomendar; (entrust) encomendar; (praise) alabar. **commendable** adj recomendable. **commendation** n alabanza f, elogio m, encomio m.

comment ['koment] n observación f; (explanation) comentario. **no comment** sin comentarios. v comentar, hacer observaciones. **commentary** n comentario m, observación f. **running commentary** reportaje en directo m.

commerce ['komɜːs] n comercio m. **commercial** adj comercial. **commercial traveller** agente comercial m. **commercialism** n mercantilismo m. **commercialize** v comercializar.

commiserate [kə'mizəreit] v compadecerse. **commiseration** n conmiseración f.

commission [kə'miʃən] n (profit) comisión f; (to a post, etc.) nombramiento m; (assignment) cometido m; (charge) encargo; (crime) ejecución f; (mil) grado de oficial m. v comisionar; encargar; (mil) nombrar. **commissionaire** n portero m. **commissioner** n comisionado m. **High Commissioner** alto comisario m.

commit [kə'mit] v (crime) cometer; (entrust) confiar; (imprison) encarcelar. **commit oneself** comprometerse. **commitment** n (assignment) cometido m; (pledge) compromiso m.

committee [kə'miti] n comité m, comisión f.

commodity [kə'modəti] n mercancia f, producto m, artículo m.

common ['komən] adj común; público; ordinario; frecuente. **commoner** n plebeyo, -a m, f. **Common Market** Mercado Común m. **commonness** n frecuencia f; vulgaridad f. **commonplace**

adj común, trivial. **commonsense** *adj* lógico. **commonwealth** *n* república *f*.

commotion [kə'mouʃən] *n* disturbio *m*; tumulto *m*.

commune¹ [kə'mjuɪn] *v* (*communicate*) comunicarse; (*meditate*) meditar. **communion** *n* comunión *f*.

commune² ['komjuɪn] *n* comuna *f*. **communal** *adj* comunal.

communicate [kə'mjuɪnikeit] *v* comunicar. **communication** *n* comunicación *f*. **communicative** *adj* comunicativo.

communism ['komjunizəm] *n* comunismo *m*. **communist** *n*(*m*+*f*), *adj* comunista.

community [kə'mjuɪnəti] *n* comunidad *f*. **community centre** centro social *m*.

commute [kə'mjuɪt] *v* (*travel*) viajar; (*law*) conmutar. **commuter** *n*, *adj* viajero, -a.

compact¹ [kəm'pakt] *adj* compacto; recogido; conciso; denso. *v* condensar; comprimir.

compact² ['kompakt] *n* pacto *m*; (*powder*) polvera *f*.

companion [kəm'panjən] *n* compañero, -a *m*, *f*; (*professional*) acompañante *m*, *f*. **companionship** *n* compañerismo *m*.

company ['kʌmpəni] *n* (*comm*) compañiá *f*, empresa *f*; (*companionship*) compañerismo *m*, sociedad *f*.

compare [kəm'peə] *v* comparar. **comparable** *adj* comparable. **comparative** *adj* relativo; (*gram*) comparativo. **comparison** *n* comparación *f*.

compartment [kəm'paɪtmənt] *n* compartimiento *m*, departamento *m*.

compass ['kʌmpəs] *n* (*naut*) brújula *f*; (*extent*) extensión *f*. **compasses** *n pl* (*maths*) compás *m*.

compassion [kəm'paʃən] *n* compasión *f*. **compassionate** *adj* compasivo.

compatible [kəm'patəbl] *adj* compatible. **compatibility** *n* compatibilidad *f*.

compel [kəm'pel] *v* compeler, obligar. **compelling** *adj* convincente.

compensate ['kompənseit] *v* (*make up for*) compensar; (*repay*) indemnizar. **compensation** *n* compensación *f*; indemnización *f*; (*reward*) recompensa *f*.

compete [kəm'piɪt] *v* competir. **competition** *n* competición *f*; (*contest*) concurso *m*; (*comm*) competencia *f*. **competitive** *adj* competitivo; (*spirit*) de competencia. **competitor** *n* competidor, -a *m*, *f*. (*contestant*) concursante *m*, *f*.

competent ['kompətənt] *adj* competente; (*suitable*) adecuado. **competence** *n* competencia *f*, aptitud *f*.

compile [kəm'pail] *v* compilar. **compilation** *n* compilación *f*. **compiler** *n* compilador, -a *m*, *f*.

complacent [kəm'pleisnt] *adj* complaciente. **complacence, complacency** *n* satisfacción de si mismo *f*.

complain [kəm'plein] *v* quejarse. **complaint** *n* queja *f*; (*med*) enfermedad *f*; (*law*) demanda *f*.

complement ['kompləmənt] *n* complemento *m*. *v* complementar. **complementary** *adj* complementario.

complete [kəm'pliɪt] *adj* completo; (*finished*) acabado, concluido, terminado; (*entire*) entero. *v* completar; terminar; (*fill in*) llenar. **completion** *n* cumplimiento *m*; terminación *f*.

complex ['kompleks] *adj* complejo, complicado. *n* complejo *m*. **complexity** *n* complejidad *f*.

complexion [kəm'plekʃən] *n* tez *f*, cutis *m*; aspecto *m*.

complicate ['komplikeit] *v* complicar. **complicated** *adj* complicado. **complication** *n* complicación *f*.

complicity [kəm'plisəti] *n* complicidad *f*.

compliment ['kompləmənt] *n* cumplido *m*. **compliments** *n pl* saludos *m pl*. **complimentary** *adj* elogioso; (*gratis*) de favor.

comply [kəm'plai] *v* conformarse; (*obey*) obeceder.

component [kəm'pounənt] *nm*, *adj* componente.

compose [kəm'pouz] *v* componer; calmar. **composed** *adj* sereno. **be composed of** constar de. **composer** *n* compositor, -a *m*, *f*. **composite** *adj* compuesto. **composition** *n* composición *f*.

compost ['kompost] *n* abono *m*.

composure [kəm'pouʒə] *n* calma *f*, serenidad *f*.

compound¹ [kəm'paund; *n*, *adj* 'kompaund] *v* componer; mezclar. *nm*, *adj* compuesto. **compound fracture** fractura complicada *f*.

compound² ['kompaund] *n* (*enclosure*) recinto cercado *m*.

comprehend [kompri'hend] *v* comprender. **comprehensible** *adj* comprensible. **comprehension** *n* comprensión *f*.

comprehensive *adj* extenso, amplio. **comprehensive insurance** seguro a todo riesgo *m*. **comprehensive school** colegio integrado *m*.

compress ['kompres; *v* kəm'pres] *n* (*med*) compresa *f*. *v* comprimir; (*condense*) condensar. **compression** *n* compresión *f*.

comprise [kəm'praiz] *v* comprender.

compromise ['komprəmaiz] *n* compromiso *m*, arreglo *m*. *v* (*agree*) llegar a un arreglo; (*yield*) transigir; (*endanger*) comprometer. **compromising** *adj* comprometedor.

compulsion [kəm'pʌlʃən] *n* obligación *f*; (*coercion*) coacción *f*; (*impulse*) impulso *m*. **compulsive** *adj* compulsivo. **compulsory** *adj*

computer [kəm'pjuːtə] *n* computador *m*, computadora *f*, ordenador *m*. **compute** *v* computar, calcular. **computerize** *v* tratar.

comrade ['komrid] *n* camarada *m*, *f* compañero, -a *m*, *f*. **comradeship** *n* camaradería *f*.

concave [kon'keiv] *adj* cóncavo. **concavity** *n* concavidad *f*.

conceal [kən'siːl] *v* ocultar. **concealed** *adj* oculto. **concealment** *n* encubrimiento *m*.

concede [kən'siːd] *v* conceder; (*admit*) reconocer. **concede victory** darse por vencido.

conceit [kən'siːt] *n* presunción *f*, vanidad *f*. **conceited** *adj* engreido, vanidoso.

conceive [kən'siːv] *v* concebir. **conceive of** imaginarse. **conceivable** *adj* concebible.

concentrate ['konsəntreit] *v* concentrar. *n* concentrado. **concentration** *n* concentración *f*. **concentration camp** campo de concentración *m*.

concentric [kən'sentrik] *adj* concéntrico.

concept ['konsept] *n* concepto *m*. **conception** *n* concepción *f*; idea *f*.

concern [kən'səːn] *n* asunto *m*; (*interest*) interés *m*; (*business*) empresa *f* (*worry*) preocupación *f*. *v* (*have as a subject*) tratar de; (*affect*) afectar; (*be related to*) referirse a. **concerned** *adj* preocupado. **concerning** *prep* con respecto a.

concert ['konsət; *v* kən'səːt] *n* concierto *m*. *v* concertar.

concertina [konsə'tiːnə] *n* concertina *f*.

concerto [kən'tʃəːtou] *n* concierto *m*.

concession [kən'seʃən] *n* concesión *f*.

conciliate [kən'silieit] *v* conciliar. **conciliation** *n* conciliación *f*. **conciliator** *n* conciliador, -a *m*, *f*. **conciliatory** *adj* conciliatorio.

concise [kən'sais] *adj* conciso.

conclude [kən'kluːd] *v* acabar, terminar; (*treaty*) concertar; (*deduce*) concluir. **conclusion** *n* conclusión *f*. **conclusive** *adj* conclusivo; concluyente.

concoct [kən'kokt] *v* (*mix*) confeccionar; (*plot*) urdir; inventar. **concoction** *n* (*mixture*) mezcla *f*; (*lies*) fabricación *f*.

concrete ['koŋkriːt] *n* hormigón *m*. **concrete mixer** hormigonera *f*. **reinforced concrete** hormigón armado *m*. *adj* concreto; (*tech*) de hormigón.

concussion [kən'kʌʃən] *n* conmoción cerebral *f*. **concuss** *v* conmocionar.

condemn [kən'dem] *v* condenar; (*building*) declarar en ruina. **condemnation** *n* condenación *f*. **condemnatory** *adj* condenatorio. **condemned** *adj* condenado.

condense [kən'dens] *v* (*cut*) abreviar, resumir; (*physics*) condensar. **condensation** *n* condensación *f*; (*vapour*) vaho *m*; (*abbreviation*) resumen *m*. **condenser** *n* condensador *m*.

condescend [kondi'send] *v* condescender, dignarse. **condescending** *adj* condescendiente, superior. **condescension** *n* condescendencia *f*.

condition [kən'diʃən] *n* condición *f*, estado *m*. *v* condicionar, determinar. **conditional** *adj* condicional. **conditionally** *adv* con reservas. **conditioning** *n* condicionamiento *m*.

condolence [kən'douləns] *n* condolencia *f*, pésame *m*. **condole** *v* condolerse, dar el pésame.

condom ['kondom] *n* condón *m*.

condone [kən'doun] *v* condonar, perdonar.

conducive [kən'djuːsiv] *adj* conducivo; (*helpful*) propicio.

conduct ['kondʌkt; *v* kən'dʌkt] *n* conducta *f*, comportamiento *m*. *v* (*lead*) conducir; (*music, business*) dirigir; (*behave*) comportarse. **conductance** *n* conductancia *f*. **conduction** *n* conducción *f*. **conductivity** *n* conductividad *f*.

conductor [kən'dʌktə] *n* (*music*) director, -a *m*, *f*; (*guide*) guia *m*; (*bus*) cobrador *m*; (*physics*) conductor *m*. **lightning conductor** pararrayos *m sing*.

cone [koun] *n* cono *m*; (*bot*) piña *f*; (*ice*

cream) cucurucho de helado *m*. **cone-shaped** *adj* cónico.

confectioner [kən'fekʃənə] *n* confitero, -a *m, f*. **confection** *n* dulce *m*. **confectionery** *n* (*sweets*) dulces *m pl*; (*shop*) confitería *f*; (*cake shop*) repostería *f*.

confederate [kən'fedərət] *nm, adj* confederado. *v* confederar. **confederation** *n* confederación *f*.

confer [kən'fəː] *v* consultar, conferir; (*hold a conference*) conferenciar. **conference** *n* consulta *f*; (*meeting*) conferencia *f*; (*talks*) entrevista *f*.

confess [kən'fes] *v* confesar. **confession** *n* confesión *f*. **confessional** *n* (*rel*) confesionario *m*. **confessor** *n* confesor *m*; (*priest*) director espiritual *m*.

confetti [kən'feti] *n* confeti *m*.

confide [kən'faid] *v* confiar. **confidence** *n* (*trust*) confianza *f*; (*secret*) confidencia *f*; (*self-reliance*) seguridad en si mismo *f*. **confidence trick** estafa *f*. **confident** *adj* lleno de confianza. **confidential** *adj* confidencial. **confidentially** *adv* en confianza.

confine [kən'fain] *n* confín *m*; límite *m*. *v* confinar; limitar; (*med*) estar de parto. **confined** *adj* reducido. **confinement** *n* encierro *m*; (*med*) parto *m*.

confirm [kən'fəːm] *v* confirmar; (*treaty*) ratificar. **confirmation** *n* confirmación *f*; ratificación *f*. **confirmed** *adj* confirmado; (*inveterate*) empedernido.

confiscate ['konfiskeit] *v* confiscar. **confiscation** *n* confiscación *f*.

conflict ['konflikt; *v* kən'flikt] *n* conflicto *m*. *v* luchar; (*clash*) chocar. **conflicting** *adj* contrapuesto.

conform [kən'foːm] *v* conformarse. **conformist** *n*(*m* + *f*), *adj* conformista. **conformity** *n* conformidad *f*.

confound [kən'faund] *v* confundir; (*foil*) frustrar; (*disconcert*) desconcertar.

confront [kən'frʌnt] *v* hacer frente a; (*present with*) presentarse; (*bring face to face*) enfrentar, confrontar. **confrontation** *n* confrontación *f*.

confuse [kən'fjuːz] *v* confundir; desconcertar; complicar. **confused** *adj* confuso; perplejo. **confusing** *adj* confuso; desconcertante. **confusion** *n* confusión *f*, desorden *m*.

congeal [kən'dʒiːl] *v* congelar; coagular.

congenial [kən'dʒiːniəl] *adj* (*pleasant*) agradable; (*suitable*) conveniente; (*similar*) compatible.

congenital [kən'dʒenitl] *adj* congénito.

congested [kən'dʒestid] *adj* congestionado; (*crowded*) superpoblado. **congestion** *n* congestión *f*; superpoblación *f*.

conglomeration [kən,glomə'reiʃən] *n* conglomeración *f*. **conglomerate** *v* conglomerar.

congratulate [kən'gratjuleit] *v* felicitar, dar la enhorabuena. **congratulations** *pl n* felicitaciones *f pl*; *interj* ¡felicidades!

congregate ['kongrigeit] *v* congregarse. **congregation** *n* congregación *f*, asamblea *f*; (*rel*) feligreses *m pl*.

congress ['kongres] *n* congreso *m*.

conical ['konikəl] *adj* cónico.

conifer ['konifə] *n* conífera *f*. **coniferous** *adj* conífero.

conjecture [kən'dʒektʃə] *n* conjetura *f*. *v* conjeturar. **conjectural** *adj* conjetural.

conjugal ['kondʒugəl] *adj* conyugal.

conjugate ['kondʒugeit] *v* conjugar. **conjugation** *n* conjugación *f*.

conjunction [kən'dʒʌŋkʃən] *n* (*gramm*) conjunción *f*. **conjunctive** *adj* conjuntivo. **conjunctivitis** [kən,dʒʌŋkti'vaitis] *n* conjuntivitis *f*.

conjure ['kʌndʒə; (*appeal to*) kən'dʒuə] *v* (*magic*) hacer juegos de manos; (*appeal to*) conjurar. **conjurer** *n* ilusionista *m*, prestidigitador *m*. **conjuring trick** juego de manos *m*.

connect [kə'nekt] *v* (*join*) unir, juntar; (*relate*) relacionar; (*elec*) conectar. **connected** *adj* (*joined*) conectado, unido; (*related*) emparentado; (*associated*) relacionado; coherente. **connection** *n* relación *f*; (*transport*) empalme *m*; (*elec*) conexión *f*; (*joint*) unión *f*; (*relative*) pariente *m*. **in connection with** con respecto a.

connoisseur [konə'səː] *n* experto, -a *m, f*, conocedor, -a *m, f*.

connotation [konə'teiʃən] *n* connotación *f*.

conquer ['koŋkə] *v* vencer, triunfar. **conquering** *adj* victorioso. **conqueror** *n* conquistador *m*, vencedor, -a *m, f*. **conquest** *n* conquista *f*.

conscience ['konʃəns] *n* conciencia *f*.

conscientious [konʃi'enʃəs] *adj* concienzudo. **conscientious objector** objetor de conciencia *m*. **conscientiousness** *n* escrupulosidad *f*.

conscious ['kɒnʃəs] *adj* (*aware*) consciente; (*deliberate*) intencional. **be conscious** tener conocimiento. **be conscious of** tener conciencia de. **become conscious** volver en sí. **become conscious of** darse cuenta de. **consciousness** *n* conocimiento *m*.

conscript ['kɒnskript] *n* recluta *m*.

consecrate ['kɒnsikreit] *v* consagrar. **consecration** *n* consagración *f*.

consecutive [kən'sekjutiv] *adj* consecutivo.

consensus [kən'sensəs] *n* consenso *m*.

consent [kən'sent] *n* consentimiento *m*. **by common consent** de acuerdo mutuo. *v* consentir (en).

consequence ['kɒnsikwəns] *n* consecuencia *f*, resultado *m*. **consequent** *adj* consiguiente. **consequently** *adv* consecuentemente, por lo tanto.

conserve [kən'səːv] *v* conservar. *n* conserva *f*. **conservation** *n* conservación *f*. **conservative** *adj* conservador, moderado. **conservatory** *n* (*plants*) invernadero *m*; (*music*) conservatorio *m*.

consider [kən'sidə] *v* considerar; (*think*) pensar (en); (*study*) examinar; (*realize*) darse cuenta de; (*take into account*) tener en cuenta. **considerable** *adj* considerable. **considerably** *adv* considerablemente. **consideration** *n* consideración *f*; (*payment*) retribución *f*. **considerate** *adj* considerado.

consign [kən'sain] *v* consignar; (*send*) enviar; (*entrust*) confiar. **consignee** *n* consignatorio *m*. **consignment** *n* consignación *f*; envío *m*.

consist [kən'sist] *v* consistir; (*made up of*) constar, componerse. **consistency** *n* (*density*) consistencia *f*; (*agreement*) conformidad *f*. **consistent** *adj* de acuerdo; firme. **consistently** *adv* constantemente; consecuentemente.

console¹ ['kɒnsoul] *n* (*table, organ*) consola *f*; (*support*) ménsula *f*; mesa de control *f*; pupitre *m*.

console² [kən'soul] *v* consolar. **consolation** *n* consuelo *m*. **consolation prize** premio de consolación *m*.

consolidate [kən'sɒlideit] *v* consolidar. **consolidation** *n* consolidación *f*.

consommé [kən'sɒmei] *n* consomé *m*, caldo *m*.

consonant ['kɒnsənənt] *n* consonante *f*. *adj* conforme.

consortium [kən'sɔːtiəm] *n* consorcio *m*.

conspicuous [kən'spikjuəs] *adj* visible; (*remarkable*) notable; (*attracting attention*) llamativo.

conspire [kən'spaiə] *v* conspirar. **conspiracy** *n* conspiración *f*. **conspirator** *n* conspirador, -a *m*, *f*.

constable ['kʌnstəbl] *n* policía *m*, guardia *m*. **constabulary** *n* policía *f*.

constant ['kɒnstənt] *adj* (*continuous*) constante; (*faithful*) fiel, leal. **constancy** *n* constancia *f*; fidelidad *f*, lealdad *f*.

constellation [kɒnstə'leiʃən] *n* constelación *f*.

constipation [kɒnsti'peiʃən] *n* estreñimiento *m*. **constipated** *adj* estreñido.

constitute ['kɒnstitjuːt] *v* constituir. **constituency** *n* distrito electoral *m*. **constituent** *n* (*component*) componente *m*; (*pol*) votante *m*. *adj* (*component*) constitutivo, constituyente; electoral. **constitution** *n* constitución *f*. **constitutional** *adj* constitucional. *n* (*coll*) paseo *m*.

constraint [kən'streint] *n* (*restriction*) encierro *m*; (*compulsion*) coacción *f*; (*inhibition*) turbación *f*. **constrain** *v* encerrar; (*compel*) constreñir; (*inhibit*) incomodar.

constrict [kən'strikt] *v* (*narrow*) estrechar; (*compress*) oprimir. **constricted** *adj* estrecho. **constriction** *n* constricción *f*.

construct [kən'strʌkt] *v* construir. **construction** *n* construcción *f*; (*structure*) estructura *f*; (*meaning*) interpretación *f*. **constructive** *adj* constructivo. **constructor** *n* constructor *m*.

consul ['kɒnsəl] *n* cónsul *m*. **consular** *adj* consular. **consulate** *n* consulado *m*.

consult [kən'sʌlt] *v* consultar. **consultant** *n* (*adviser*) asesor *m*; (*med*) especialista *m*; (*tech*) consejero técnico *m*. **consultation** *n* consulta *f*. **consulting room** consultorio *m*.

consume [kən'sjuːm] *v* consumir; (*time*) tomar; (*food*) comerse; (*drink*) beberse. **consumer** *n* consumidor, -a *m*, *f*. **consumer goods** bienes de consumo *m pl*. **consumption** *n* consumo *m*; (*med: tuberculosis*) tisis *f*. **consumptive** *n*, *adj* (*med*) tísico, -a.

contact ['kɒntakt] *n* contacto *m*. **contact lens** lente de contacto *f*. *v* ponerse en contacto con.

contagious [kən'teidʒəs] *adj* contagioso.
contagion *n* contagio *m*.
contain [kən'tein] *v* contener. **container** *n* (*package*) envase *m*; (*receptacle*) recipiente *m*. (*transport*) contenedor *m*.
containment *n* contención *f*.
contaminate [kən'taməneit] *v* contaminar.
contamination *n* contaminación *f*.
contemplate ['kontəmpleit] *v* contemplar; (*expect*) contar con; (*consider*) considerar. **contemplation** *n* contemplación *f*, meditación *f*; consideración *f*. **contemplative** *adj* contemplativo.
contemporary [kən'tempərəri] *nm, adj* contemporáneo.
contempt [kən'tempt] *n* desprecio *m*, desdén *m*. **contempt of court** desacato a los tribunales *m*. **hold in contempt** despreciar. **contemptible** *adj* despreciable, desdeñable. **contemptuous** *adj* despreciativo, desdeñoso.
contend [kən'tend] *v* (*struggle*) contender; (*compete*) competir; (*dispute*) disputir; (*affirm*) afirmar. **contender** *n* competidor, -a *m, f*. **contention** *n* contienda *f*; (*argument*) discusión *f*; (*opinion*) opinión *f*. **contentious** *adj* (*person*) pendenciero; (*issue*) discutible. **contentiousness** *n* carácter pendenciero *m*.
content¹ ['kontent] *n* contenido *m*.
content² [kən'tent] *adj* **also contented** contento, satisfecho. **be contented with** contentarse con. **contentment** *n* contento *m*.
contest [kən'test; *n* 'kontest] *v* (*dispute*) disputar; (*question*) impugnar. *n* (*struggle*) contienda *f*; (*competition*) competición *f*; (*controversy*) controversia *f*. **contestant** *n* contrincante *m*; (*election*) candidato, -a *m, f*.
context ['kontekst] *n* contexto *m*.
continent ['kontinənt] *n* continente *m*. **the Continent** el continente europeo *m*. **continental** *adj* continental.
contingency [kən'tindʒənsi] *n* (*possibility*) contingencia *f*, eventualidad *f*; (*event*) acontecimiento fortuito *m*. **contingent** *adj* (*accidental*) fortuito; (*probable*) contingente; (*incidental*) derivado; (*dependent*) subordinado; (*dependent on chance*) aleatorio.
continue [kən'tinjut] *v* continuar, seguir; (*extend*) prolongar. **continual** *adj* continuo. **continually** *adv* constantemente.

continuation *n* continuación *f*. **continuity** *n* continuidad *f*; (*cinema, radio*) guión *m*.
continuous *adj* continuo.
contort [kən'tott] *v* retorcer, torcer. **contortion** *n* contorsión *f*; deformación *f*. **contortionist** *n* contorsionista *m, f*.
contour ['kontuə] *n* (*map*) curva de nivel *f*; (*outline*) contorno *m*.
contraband ['kontrəband] *n* contrabando *m*. *adj* de contrabando.
contraception [kontrə'sepʃən] *n* contracepción *f*. **contraceptive** *nm, adj* contraceptivo. **contraceptive pill** pildora contraceptiva *f*.
contract ['kontrakt; *v* kən'trakt] *n* contrato *m*. *v* (*shrink*) contraer; (*make a contract*) contratar; (*ailment*) coger. **contraction** *n* contracción *f*. **contractor** *n* contratista *m*. **contractual** *adj* contractual.
contradict [kontrə'dikt] *v* contradecir. **contradiction** *n* contradicción *f*. **contradictory** *adj* contradictorio.
contralto [kən'traltou] *n* contralto *m, f*.
contraption [kən'trapʃən] *n* (*coll*) chisme *m*.
contrary ['kontrəri] *adj* contrario. **on the contrary** al contrario.
contrast [kən'traist; *n* 'kontraist] *v* contrastar. *n* contraste *m*. **in contrast** por contrasté. **in contrast to** a diferencia de. **contrasting** *adj* contrastante.
contravene [kontrə'viin] *v* contravenir. **contravention** *n* contravención *f*.
contribute [kən'tribjut] *v* contribuir (con); (*write*) escribir; (*give information*) aportar. **contribution** *n* contribución *f*; artículo *m*; aportación *f*; (*to conversation*) intervención *f*. **contributive** *adj* contributivo. **contributor** *n* contribuyente *m, f*; (*writer*) colaborador, -a *m, f*. **contributory** *adj* contribuyente.
contrive [kən'traiv] *v* idear, inventar; (*manage*) conseguir. **contrived** *adj* artificial. **contrivable** *adj* realizable; imaginable. **contrivance** *n* aparato *m*; invención *f*; (*resourcefulness*) ingenio *m*.
control [kən'troul] *n* control *m*; autoridad *f*; dominación *f*; (*standard of comparison*) testigo *m*. **remote control** mando a distancia *m*. **controls** *pl n* mandos *m pl*. *v* controlar; tener autoridad sobre; (*direct*) dirigir; (*regulate*) regular; (*vehicle*)

manejar. **controller** *n* director *m*. **air traffic controller** controlador del tráfico aéreo *m*. **controlling** *adj* predominante: (*decisive*) determinante.
controversy [kən'trɒvəsi] *n* controversia *f*. **controversial** *adj* discutible.
convalesce [kɒnvə'les] *v* convalecer. **convalescence** *n* convalecencia *f*.
convector [kən'vektə] *n* estufa de convección *f*. **convection** *n* convección *f*.
convenience [kən'viːnjəns] *n* conveniencia *f*: (*comfort*) comodidad *f*: (*advantage*) ventaja *f*: (*useful object*) dispositivo útil *m*. **at your convenience** cuando le sea posible. **public convenience** servicios *m pl*. **convenient** *adj* (*handy*) cómodo: (*suitable*) conveniente: (*place*) bien situado: (*time*) oportuno.
convent ['kɒnvənt] *n* convento *m*.
convention [kən'venʃən] *n* (*usage*) convención *f*: (*assembly*) asamblea *f*: (*international agreement*) convenio *m*. **conventions** *n pl* conveniencias *f pl*. **conventional** *adj* (*not original*) convencional: (*traditional*) clásico.
converge [kən'vɜːdʒ] *v* convergir, converger. **convergence** *n* convergencia *f*. **converging** *adj* convergente.
converse[1] [kən'vɜːs] *v* conversar, hablar. **conversant** *adj* versado, familiarizado. **conversation** *n* conversación *f*.
converse[2] ['kɒnvɜːs] *n* lo opuesto *m*. *adj* opuesto, contrario.
convert ['kɒnvɜːt; *v* kən'vɜːt] *n* converso, -a *m*. *f*. *v* convertir. **conversion** *n* conversión *f*: transformación *f*.
convertible [kən'vɜːtəbl] *adj* convertible: transformable. *n* (*mot*) descapotable *m*.
convex ['kɒnveks] *adj* convexo.
convey [kən'vei] *v* (*carry*) llevar, transportar: (*suggest*) sugerir, dar a entender: (*transmit*) transmitir: (*meaning*) expresar. **conveyance** *n* transporte *m*: transmisión *f*: (*deed*) escritura de traspaso *f*. **conveyancer** *n* notario que hace escritura de traspaso *m*. **conveyancing** *n* redacción de una escritura de traspaso *f*.
convict ['kɒnvikt; *v* kən'vikt] *n* presidiario, -a *m*. *f*. *v* (*prove guilty*) condenar: (*betray*) traicionar.
conviction [kən'vikʃən] *n* condena *f*: (*belief*) convicción *f*.
convince [kən'vins] *v* convencer. **convincing** *adj* convincente.

convivial [kən'viviəl] *adj* alegre, sociable, festivo.
convoy ['kɒnvoi] *n* convoy *m*. *v* convoyar.
convulsion [kən'vʌlʃən] *n* (*med*) convulsión *f*: (*laughter*) carcajadas *f pl*. **convulse** *v* convulsionar.
cook [kuk] *v* cocinar: (*coll: the books*) falsificar. *n* cocinero, -a *m*. *f*. **cooker** *n* cocina *f*: olla *f*. **pressure cooker** olla de presión *f*. **cookery** *n* arte de cocina *m*: cocción *f*: cocina *f*. **cookery book** libro de cocina *m*. **do the cooking** guisar.
cool [kuːl] *adj* fresco: (*calm*) tranquilo: (*unenthusiastic*) frío. *v* enfriar: calmar. **cooler** *n* enfriador *m*. **cooling** *adj* refrescante. **cooling system** *n* sistema de refrigeración *m*. **coolish** *adj* fresquito. **coolly** *adv* friamente: tranquilamente. **coolness** *n* frescor *m*: frialdad *f*: serenidad *f*: sangre fria *f*.
coop [kuːp] *n* (*poultry*) gallinero *m*. **coop up** encerrar.
cooperate [kou'ɒpəreit] *v* cooperar. **cooperation** *n* cooperación *f*. **cooperative** *adj* cooperativo.
coordinate [kou'ɔːdineit] *n* coordenada *f*. *adj* igual. *v* coordinar. **coordination** *n* coordinación *f*.
cope[1] [koup] *v* arreglárselas: dar abasto: poder con.
cope[2] [koup] *n* (*rel*) capa pluvial *f*.
Copenhagen [koupən'heigən] *n* Copenhague.
copious ['koupiəs] *adj* copioso, abundante.
copper[1] ['kɒpə] *n* (*metal*) cobre *m*. *adj* de cobre: (*colour*) cobrizo. **copper plate** plancha de cobre *f*.
copper[2] ['kɒpə] *n* *also* cop (*slang*) poli *m*.
copulate ['kɒpjuleit] *v* copular. **copulation** *n* cópula *f*.
copy ['kɒpi] *n* copia *f*: (*book*) ejemplar *m*: (*pattern*) modelo *m*: (*reportage*) asunto *m*. **carbon copy** papel carbón *m*. **fair copy** copia en limpio *f*. **rough copy** borrador *m*. *v* copiar: imitar. **copyright** *n* propiedad literaria.
coral ['kɒrəl] *n* coral *m*. *adj* coralino.
cord [kɔːd] *n* (*string, rope*) cuerda *f*: (*insulated wire*) cordón *m*. **spinal cord** médula espinal *f*. **umbilical cord** cordón umbilical *m*. **vocal cords** cuerdas vocales *f pl*.
cordial ['kɔːdiəl] *adj, nm* cordial. **cordiality** *n* cordialidad *f*.

cordon ['kɔɪdn] *n* cordón *m*. **cordon off** acordonar.

corduroy ['kɔɪdərɔɪ] *n* pana *f*.

core [kɔɪ] *n* (*fruit*) corazón *m*; (*geol*) núcleo; (*fig*) centro *m*, esencia *f*. *v* quitar el corazón de.

cork [kɔɪk] *n* (*bot*) corcho *m*; (*stopper*) tapón *m*. **cork tree** alcornoque *m*. **cork-tipped** *adj* con boquilla de corcho. *v* taponar. **uncork** *v* (*bottle*) descorchar. **corked** *adj* (*bottle*) taponado; (*wine*) que sabe a corcho. **corkscrew** *n* sacacorchos *m invar*.

corn¹ [kɔɪn] *n* (*wheat*) trigo *m*; (*maize*) maíz *m*; (*cereals*) granos cereales *m pl*. **corn on the cob** maíz en la mazorca *m*.

corn² [kɔɪn] *n* (*med*) callo *m*.

corner ['kɔɪnə] *n* (*inside angle*) rincón *m*; (*outside angle*) esquina *f*; (*of an object*) pico *m*. **cut corners** tomar atajos. *v* poner en un aprieto; (*accost*) abordar; (*mot*) tomar una curva; (*comm*) monopolizar.

cornet ['kɔɪnit] *n* corneta *f*; (*ice cream*) cucurucho *m*.

coronary ['kɔrənəri] *adj* coronario. **coronary thrombosis** trombosis coronaria *f*.

coronation [kɔrə'neiʃən] *n* coronación *f*.

corporal¹ ['kɔɪpərəl] *adj* corporal. **corporal punishment** castigo corporal *m*.

corporal² ['kɔɪpərəl] *n* (*mil*) cabo *m*.

corporation [kɔɪpə'reiʃən] *n* corporación *f*; sociedad anónima *f*. **municipal corporation** ayuntamiento *m*. **corporate** *adj* colectivo, corporativo.

corps [kɔɪ] *n* cuerpo *m*. **corps de ballet** cuerpo de ballet. **diplomatic corps** cuerpo diplomático.

corpse [kɔɪps] *n* cadáver *m*.

correct [kə'rekt] *adj* (*accurate*) exacto; (*behaviour*) correcto; (*right*) justo. *v* corregir. **correction** *n* corrección *f*. **corrective** *adj* correctivo. **correctness** *n* corrección *f*; exactitud *f*; (*judgment*) rectitud *f*.

correlate ['kɔrəleit] *v* correlacionar. **correlation** *n* correlación *f*.

correspond [kɔrə'spond] *v* corresponder; (*write*) escribirse. **correspondence** *n* correspondencia *f*. **correspondent** *n* correspondiente *m*, *f*; (*newspaper*) corresponsal *m*, *f*.

corridor ['kɔridɔɪ] *n* pasillo *m*, corredor *m*.

corroborate [kə'robəreit] *v* corroborar. **corroboration** *n* corroboración *f*.

corrode [kə'roud] *v* corroer. **corrosion** *n* corrosión *f*. **corrosive** *adj* corrosivo.

corrugated ['kɔrəgeitid] *adj* ondulado.

corrupt [kə'rʌpt] *adj* corrupto; corrompido; (*rotten*) estragado; (*perverted*) pervertido; (*bribable*) venal. *v* corromper; (*bribe*) sobornar. **corruptible** *adj* corruptible. **corruption** *n* corrupción *f*.

corset ['kɔɪset] *n* faja *f*.

Corsica ['kɔɪsikə] *n* Córcega *f*. **Corsican** *n*, *adj* corso, -a *m*, *f*.

cosmetic [koz'metik] *nm*, *adj* cosmético.

cosmic ['kozmik] *adj* cósmico.

cosmopolitan [kozmə'politən] *n*(*m*+*f*), *adj* cosmopolita.

***cost** [kost] *n* costo *m*, coste *m*; (*price*) precio *m*; (*expenses*) gastos *m pl*. **costs** *pl n* (*law*) costas *f pl*. **at all costs** cueste lo que cueste. **cost of living** coste de vida *m*. **to one's cost** a expensas de uno. *v* costar; valer. **costly** *adj* caro.

Costa Rica [kostə'riːkə] *n* Costa Rica. **Costa Rican** *n*(*m*+*f*), *adj* costarriquense; *n*, *adj* costarriqueño, -a *m*, *f*.

costume ['kostjuːm] *n* traje *m*. **bathing costume** traje de baño. **costume jewellery** bisutería *f*.

cosy ['kouzi] *adj* confortable; (*place*) acogedor.

cot [kot] *n* cuna *f*.

cottage ['kotidʒ] *n* casa de campo *f*; chalet *m*. **cottage cheese** requesón *m*.

cotton ['kotn] *n* algodón *m*. *adj* de algodón. **cotton-wool** *n* algodón hidrófilo *m*.

couch [kautʃ] *n* sofá *m*; (*bed*) lecho *m*. *v* (*express*) expresar.

cough [kof] *n* tos *f*. *v* toser. **cough up** (*coll*) cascar.

could [kud] *V* **can¹**.

council ['kaunsəl] *n* consejo *m*; (*assembly*) ayuntamiento *m*. **council house** vivienda protegida *f*. **town council** concejo municipal *m*. **councillor** *n* concejal *m*.

counsel ['kaunsəl] *n* consejo *m*; (*lawyer*) abogado *m*; (*legal adviser*) asesor jurídico *m*. *v* aconsejar; pedir consejo.

count¹ [kaunt] *v* contar, calcular; (*consider*) considerar. **count against** ir en contra de. **count for** valer por. **countable** *adj* contable. **countdown** *n* cuenta atrás *f*. **countless** *adj* incontable. *n* cuenta *f*, cálculo *m*; (*sum*) total *m*; (*votes*) escrutinio *m*.

count² [kaunt] *n* (*noble*) conde *m*. **countess** *n* condesa *f*.
countenance ['kauntinəns] *n* semblante *m*, cara *f*. *v* (*approve*) aprobar; (*support*) apoyar.
counter¹ ['kauntə] *n* (*disc*) ficha *f*; (*table top*) mostrador *m*, contador *m*. **Geiger counter** contador Geiger *m*. **under the counter** bajo mano.
counter² ['kauntə] *adj* (*opposed*) contrario, opuesto. *v* contraatacar; oponerse. **go counter to** ir en contra de.
counterattack ['kauntərə,tak] *n* contraataque *m*. *v* contraatacar.
counterfeit ['kauntəfit] *adj* falso, falsificado. *v* falsificar. *n* falsificación *f*.
counterfoil ['kauntə,foil] *n* talón *m*.
counterpart ['kauntə,pait] *n* contraparte *f*.
country ['kʌntri] *n* (*state*) país *m*; (*out of town*) campo. **country estate** finca *f*. **country house** casa de campo *f*. **countryman** *n* campesino *m*; compatriota *m*. **countryside** *n* campo *m*; (*landscape*) paisaje *m*.
county ['kaunti] *n* condado *m*. **county council** diputación provincial *f*.
coup [kuː] *n* golpe *m*. **coup d'état** golpe de estado *m*.
couple ['kʌpl] *n* par *m*; (*married, engaged, etc.*) pareja *f*. *v* emparejar; (*associate*) asociar; (*vehicles*) enganchar; (*elec*) conectar; (*copulate*) copular.
coupon ['kuːpon] *n* cupón *m*; (*pools*) boleto *m*.
courage ['kʌridʒ] *n* valor *m*, valentía *f*. **pluck up courage** armarse de valor. **take courage** cobrar ánimo. **courageous** *adj* valiente.
courgette [kuə'ʒet] *n* calabacín *m*.
courier ['kuriə] *n* guía *m*, *f*; agente de turismo *m*, *f*; mensajero, -a *m*, *f*.
course [kɔːs] *n* (*direction*) dirección *f*, rumbo *m*; (*progress*) curso *m*; (*way, means*) camino *m*; (*action, conduct*) línea *f*; (*meal*) plato *m*; (*track*) pista *f*; (*golf*) campo *m*. **in due course** a su debido tiempo. **main course** plato fuerte *m*. **of course** claro, por supuesto. **set course for** hacer rumbo a. *v* (*hunt*) cazar; (*run: liquid*) correr.
court [kɔːt] *n* (*royalty*) corte *f*; (*alley*) callejón sin salida *m*; (*law*) audiencia *f*, tribunal *m*; (*sport*) cancha *f*. **court order** orden judicial *f*. **go to court** acudir a los tribunales. **courtyard** *n* patio *m*. *v* (*woo*)

cortejar, hacer la corte a; buscar; pedir, solicitar. **courtier** *n* cortesano *m*. **courtly** *adj* cortés. **court-martial** *n* consejo de guerra *m*. **courtship** *n* noviazgo *m*.
courteous ['kɔːtiəs] *adj* cortés. **courtesy** *n* cortesía *f*.
cousin ['kʌzn] *n* primo, -a *m*, *f*. **first cousin** primo, -a carnal *m*, *f*.
cove [kouv] *n* cala *f*; (*slang*) tío *m*.
cover ['kʌvə] *n* cubierta *f*; (*lid*) tapa *f*; (*bed*) colcha *f*; (*table*) tapete *m*; (*refuge*) refugio *m*; (*parcel*) envoltura *f*; (*envelope*) sobre *m*; (*pretence*) excusa *f*; (*protection*) amparo *m*. **cover charge** precio del cubierto *m*. **take cover** ponerse a cubierto. *v* cubrir, tapar. **coverage** *n* alcance *m*.
cow [kau] *n* vaca *f*; (*female animal*) hembra *f*. *v* intimidar. **cowboy** *n* vaquero *m*, (*Amer*) gaucho *m*. **cowshed** *n* establo *m*.
cowslip *n* prímula *f*.
coward ['kauəd] *n* cobarde *m*, *f*. **cowardice** *n* cobardía *f*. **cowardly** *adj* cobarde.
cower ['kauə] *v* encogerse; agacharse.
coy [koi] *adj* (*shy*) tímido; (*demure*) remilgado.
crab [krab] *n* cangrejo *m*. **crab apple** manzana silvestre *f*. **crabbed** *adj* (*bad-tempered*) malhumorado; (*writing*) indecifrable.
crack [krak] *n* (*noise*) restallido *m*, chasquido *m*; (*opening*) abertura *f*; (*split*) raja *f*; (*in walls, etc.*) hendidura *f*; (*slit*) rendija *f*; (*blow*) golpe *m*; (*coll: joke*) chiste *m*. **crack of dawn** al amanecer. **have a crack at** intentar. *v* restallar, chasquear; golpear; (*break*) romper; (*a nut*) cascar; hender; rajar; (*burst*) reventar; (*give in*) ceder; (*break down*) hundirse; (*coll: joke*) bromear; (*coll: safe*) forzar. **get cracking** darse prisa. **crackpot** *n*, *adj* (*coll*) chiflado, -a *m*, *f*.
cracker ['krakə] *n* (*Christmas*) sorpresa *f*; (*firework*) buscapiés *m invar*; (*biscuit*) galleta *f*.
crackle ['krakl] *n* crepitación *f*, crujido *m*. *v* crepitar, crujir. **crackling** *n* (*cookery*) chicharrón *m*.
cradle ['kreidl] *n* cuna *f*; soporte *m*. *v* acunar; (*in one's arms*) mecer; soportar.
craft [kraːft] *n* (*trade*) trabajo manual *m*; (*skill*) arte *m*; (*guild*) gremio *m*; (*cunning*) astucia *f*, maña *f*; (*ship*) embarcación *f*; (*aircraft*) avión *m*. **craftily** *adv* astutamente. **craftsman** *n* artesano *m*.

craftsmanship n artesanía f. **crafty** adj astuto, socarrón.

cram [kram] v (fill up) aborratar; (force in) meter a la fuerza; (for exam) empollar.

cramp [kramp] n (med) calambre m. v dar calambre a. **cramped** adj (crowded) apiñado; (writing) apretado.

cranberry ['kranbəri] n arándano m.

crane [krein] n (hoist) grúa f; (bird) grulla f. v (neck) estirar.

crank [krank] n (tech) manivela f; (fool) chiflado, -a m, f. v arrancar con la manivela. **crankcase** n cárter m. **crankiness** n irritabilidad f; excentricidad f; chifladura f. **crankshaft** n cigueñal m.

crap [krap] n (slang: nonsense) disparate; (impol) mierda f. v (impol) cagar.

crash [kraʃ] n accidente m, choque m; (noise) estrépito m; (aircraft) caída f; (business) quiebra f. **crash course** curso intensivo m. **crash helmet** casco protector m. v chocar; caer; quebrar; (make a loud noise) retumbar. **crash-land** hacer un aterrizaje de emergencia.

crate [kreit] n cajón de embalaje m. v embalar.

crater ['kreitə] n cráter m.

crave [kreiv] v (desire) ansiar; (beg) suplicar; (attention) reclamar. **craving** n ansia f.

crawl [kroːl] v arrastrarse, andar a gatas; (move slowly) andar lentamente. n arrastramiento m; marcha lenta f.

crayfish ['kreifiʃ] n ástaco m, cangrejo de río m.

crayon ['kreiən] n lápiz de tiza m. v dibujar al pastel.

craze [kreiz] n (wild enthusiasm) locura f; (fad) manía f; (fashion) moda f. v enloquecer. **craziness** n locura f. **crazy** adj loco.

creak [kriːk] n crujido m. v crujir. **creaky** adj que cruje.

cream [kriːm] n nata f, crema f. **whipped cream** nata batida. adj color crema. v (beat) batir; (skim) desnatar. **cream cheese** queso de nata m.

crease [kriːs] n (fold) pliegue m; (wrinkle) arruga f; (trousers) raya f. **crease-resistant** adj inarrugable. v plegar; arrugar; hacer la raya de.

create [kri'eit] v crear. **creation** n creación f. **creator** n creador, -a m, f.

credentials [kri'denʃəlz] pl n credenciales f pl.

credible ['kredəbl] adj creíble. **credibility** n credibilidad f.

credit[1] ['kredit] n crédito m; (comm) haber m; (prestige) honor m. **credits** pl n (film) ficha técnica f sing. **credit balance** saldo acreedor m. **credit card** tarjeta de crédito f. **credit rating** solvabilidad f. **on credit** a plazos. **we do not give credit** no se fía.

credit[2] ['kredit] v (believe) creer; (fig) atribuir; (an account) abonar en cuenta. **creditable** adj (believable) digno de crédito; (praiseworthy) encomiable; (well spoken of) de buena reputación. **creditably** adv honrosamente. **creditor** n acreedor, -a m, f.

credulous ['kredjuləs] adj crédulo.

creed [kriːd] n credo m.

*****creep** [kriːp] v deslizarse, arrastrarse; (flesh) ponerse a uno la carne de gallina. n (coll) pelotillero, -a m, f. **creepy** adj horripilante.

cremate [kri'meit] v incinerar. **cremation** n incineración f. **crematorium** n horno crematorio m.

crescent ['kresnt] n medialuna f, luna creciente f. adj creciente.

cress [kres] n berro m.

crest [krest] n (on animal's head, wave) cresta f; (hill) cima f, cumbre f; (heraldry) timbre m. **crested** adj crestado. **crestfallen** adj alicaído.

crevice ['krevis] n grieta f; hendedura f.

crew [kruː] n (body of workers) equipo m; (ship, aircraft) tripulación f; (mob) banda f. **ground crew** personal de tierra m.

crib [krib] n (rack) pesebre m; (small cot) cuna f; (coll: exam) chuleta f. v plagiar.

cricket[1] ['krikit] n (insect) grillo m.

cricket[2] ['krikit] n (sport) criquet m.

crime [kraim] n crimen m; criminalidad f. **criminal** nm, adj criminal.

crimson ['krimzn] nm, adj carmesí.

cringe [krindʒ] v agacharse, encogerse. **cringing** adj servil.

crinkle ['krinkl] n arruga f. v arrugarse.

cripple ['kripl] n, adj tullido, -a m, f. v (person) tullir; (object) estropear; (fig) paralizar.

crisis ['kraisis] n pl -ses crisis f invar.

crisp [krisp] adj fresco; (bread) curruscante; (style) crespo; (snow) crujiente; (talk) animado. v encrespar, rizar. **potato**

crisp patata frita a la inglesa *f*. **crispness** *n* encrespado *m*.
criterion [krai'tiərɪən] *n pl* **-a** criterio *m*.
criticize ['kriti,saiz] *v* criticar. **critic** (*fault-finder*) criticón, **-ona** *m*, *f*; (*reviewer*) crítico *m*. **critical** *adj* crítico. **criticism** *n* crítica *f*.
crochet ['krouʃei] *n* croché *m*. ganchillo *m*. *v* hacer a ganchillo.
crockery ['krokəri] *n* loza *f*. vajilla *f*.
crocodile ['krokə,dail] *n* cocodrilo *m*.
crocus ['kroukəs] *n* azafrán *m*.
crook [kruk] *n* (*shepherd's*) cayado *m*; (*bishop's*) báculo *m*; (*coll*) ladrón *m*, timador *m*.
crooked ['krukid] *adj* (*bent*) curvado; (*twisted*) torcido; (*path*) sinuoso; (*nose*) ganchudo; (*coll*) poco limpio. **crookedness** *n* sinuosidad *f*. (*coll*) falta de honradez *f*.
crop [krop] *n* (*harvest*) cosecha *f*; (*cultivated produce*) cultiva *f*; (*whip*) fusta *f*; (*bird*) buche *m*; (*haircut*) corte de pelo *m*. **crop rotation** rotación de cultivos *f*. *v* (*graze*) pacer; (*ears*) desorejar; (*tail*) cortar la cola de; (*hair*) cortar muy corto. **come a cropper** darse un batacazo.
croquet ['kroukei] *n* croquet *m*.
cross [kros] *n* cruz *f*; (*breeding*) cruce *f*. **make the sign of the cross** santiguarse. *adj* cruzado; (*angry*) enfadado. *v* (*move*) atravesar; (*limbs*) cruzar; (*oppose*) contrariar; (*mark*) marcar con una cruz. **cross out** tachar. **cross one's mind** ocurrírsele el.
cross-country *adj* a campo traviesa.
cross-current *n* contracorriente *f*.
cross-examination *n* repregunta *f*.
cross-eyed *adj* bizco.
crossfire ['kros,faiə] *n* fuego cruzado *m*.
crossing ['krosiŋ] *n* (*intersection*) cruce *f*; (*voyage*) travesía *f*; (*pedestrian*) paso de peatones *m*.
cross-purposes *pl n* fines opuestos *m pl*.
cross-reference *n* remisión *f*.
crossroads ['kros,roudz] *pl n* cruce *f sing*; (*fig*) encrucijada *f sing*.
cross section *n* sección transversal *f*.
crossword ['kros,wəɪd] *n* crucigrama *m*.
crotchet ['krotʃit] *n* (*music*) negra *f*. **crotchety** *adj* de mal genio.
crouch [krautʃ] *v* agacharse, encogerse.
crow[1] [krou] *n* (*bird*) cuervo *m*. **as the crow flies** en línea recta. **crowbar** *n* palanca *f*.

crow[2] [krou] *v* cantar; cacarear. *n* cacareo *m*.
crowd [kraud] *n* muchedumbre *f*, multitud *f*. *v* amontonar; congregarse. **crowded** *adj* lleno.
crown [kraun] *n* corona *f*; (*hat*) copa *f*; (*hill*) cumbre *f*; (*head*) coronilla *f*. **crown jewels** joyas reales *f pl*. **crown prince** príncipe heredero *m*. *v* coronar. **to crown it all** para rematarlo todo. **crowning** *adj* supremo.
crucial ['kruɪʃəl] *adj* crucial, decisivo.
crucify ['kruɪsi,fai] *v* crucificar. **crucifix** *n* crucifijo *m*. **crucifixion** *n* crucifixión *f*.
crude [kruɪd] *adj* (*raw*) crudo; (*steel*) bruto; (*oil*) sin refinar; (*vulgar*) basto; (*ill-made*) tosco. **crudeness**, **crudity** *n* crudeza *f*; tosquedad *f*.
cruel ['kruɪəl] *adj* cruel. **cruelty** *n* crueldad *f*.
cruise [kruɪz] *n* crucero *m*. *v* hacer un crucero; (*patrol*) patrullar; (*at cruising speed*) ir a una velocidad de crucero. **cruiser** *n* (*naut*) crucero *m*.
crumb [krʌm] *n* migaja *f*, miga *f*.
crumble ['krʌmbl] *v* desmenuzar; desmigar. **crumbly** *adj* desmenuzable.
crumple ['krʌmpl] *v* arrugar, ajar. **crumple up** desplomarse.
crunch [krʌntʃ] *n* crujido *m*; (*coll*) punto decisivo *m*. *v* crujir; mascar. **crunchy** *adj* crujiente.
crusade [kruɪ'seid] *n* cruzada *f*; (*fig*) campaña *f*. *v* hacer una cruzada. **crusader** *n* cruzado *m*.
crush [krʌʃ] *n* aplastamiento *m*; (*crowd*) aglomeración *f*; (*squeeze*) apretón *m*. **have a crush on** (*coll*) estar loco perdido por. *v* aplastar; apretar; (*pulverize*) machacar; (*overwhelm*) abrumar. **crushing** *adj* aplastante.
crust [krʌst] *n* (*of a loaf*) corteza *f*. **upper crust** la flor y nata *f*. **crusty** *adj* de corteza dura; (*coll*) brusco.
crutch [krʌtʃ] *n* (*support*) muleta *f*; (*fig*) apoyo *m*.
crux [krʌks] *n* quid *m*.
cry [krai] *n* grito *m*. *v* (*call*) gritar; (*weep*) llorar. **cry out** clamar.
crypt [kript] *n* cripta *f*. **cryptic** *adj* secreto; enigmático.
crystal ['kristl] *n* cristal *m*. *adj* de cristal. **crystal clear** cristalino. **crystallize** *v* cristalizar.

cub [kʌb] *n* (*bear, lion, tiger, wolf*) cachorro *m*; (*other animals*) cría *f*. **cub scout** niño explorador *m*.

Cuba ['kjuːbə] *n* Cuba *f*. **Cuban** *n, adj* cubano, -a.

cube [kjuːb] *n* (*math*) cubo *m*; (*sugar, etc.*) terrón *m*. *v* (*math*) cubicar. **cube root** raíz cúbica *f*. **cubic** *adj* cúbico.

cubicle ['kjuːbikl] *n* cubículo *m*; (*for sleeping*) cubilla *f*; (*for changing*) caseta *f*.

cuckoo ['kukuː] *n* cuco *m*, cuclillo *m*.

cucumber [kjuˈkʌmbə] *n* pepino *m*.

cuddle ['kʌdl] *n* abrazo *m*. *v* abrazar. **cuddly** *adj* mimoso.

cue[1] [kjuː] *n* (*theatre*) señal *f*; entrada *f*. *v* indicar.

cue[2] [kjuː] *n* (*billiards*) taco *m*.

cuff[1] [kʌf] *n* (*shirt*) puño *m*. **cufflinks** *pl n* gemelos *m pl*. **off the cuff** de improviso.

cuff[2] [kʌf] *n* (*hit*) bofetada *f*. *v* abofetear.

culinary ['kʌlinəri] *adj* culinario.

culminate ['kʌlmiˌneit] *v* culminar. **culmination** *n* culminación *f*.

culprit ['kʌlprit] *n* culpado, -a *m, f*; culpable *m, f*.

cult [kʌlt] *n* culto *m*.

cultivate ['kʌltiˌveit] *v* cultivar. **cultivated** *adj* (*land*) cultivado; (*person*) culto. **cultivation** *n* cultivo *m*.

culture ['kʌltʃə] *n* cultura *f*; cultivo *m*. **cultured** *adj* culto.

cumbersome ['kʌmbəsəm] *adj* molesto; (*annoying*) incómodo.

cunning ['kʌnin] *adj* (*sly*) taimado; (*clever*) astuto; (*skilful*) mañoso. *n* astucia *f*; maña *f*.

cup [kʌp] *n* taza *f*; (*prize*) copa *f*.

cupboard ['kʌbəd] *n* armario *m*.

curate ['kjuərət] *n* cura *m*.

curator [kjuəˈreitə] *n* conservador, -a *m, f*.

curb [kəːb] *v* contener, refrenar. *n* (*obstacle*) estorbo *m*; (*fig*) freno *m*.

curdle ['kəːdl] *v* cuajar, cuajarse. **curd** cuajada *f*.

cure [kjuə] *n* (*course of treatment; smoking food*) cura *f*; (*remedy*) remedio *m*; (*of leather*) curtido *m*; (*salting*) salazón *m*. *v* curar; remediar; salar; curtir. **cure-all** *n* curalotodo *m*.

curfew ['kəːfjuː] *n* toque de queda *m*.

curious ['kjuəriəs] *adj* curioso. **curiosity** *n* curiosidad *f*.

curl [kəːl] *n* (*hair*) bucle *m*; (*smoke*) voluta *f*; (*twist*) torcedura *f*; serpenteo *m*.

v (*hair*) rizar. **curl oneself up** hacerse un ovillo. **curler** *n* rulo *m*. **curly** *adj* rizado; sinuoso; en espiral.

currant ['kʌrənt] *n* (*dried grape*) pasa *f*; (*berry*) grosella *f*; (*bush*) grosellero *m*.

currency ['kʌrənsi] *n* moneda *f*; (*general use*) uso corriente *m*.

current ['kʌrənt] *n* corriente *f*; curso *m*. **alternating/direct current** corriente alterna/continua *f*. *adj* (*general*) corriente, prevalente; (*now*) actual; (*accepted*) admitido. **current account** cuenta corriente *f*. **current affairs** actualidades *f pl*. **current rate of exchange** cambio del día *m*. **current year** año en curso. **currently** *adv* corrientemente; actualmente.

curry ['kʌri] *n* cari *m*, curry *m*. *v* preparar con cari. **curry powder** especias en polvo *f pl*.

curse [kəːs] *n* maldición *f*. *v* maldecir; (*swear*) decir palabrotas; (*blaspheme*) blasfemar.

curt [kəːt] *adj* brusco. **curtness** *n* brusquedad *f*.

curtail [kəːˈteil] *v* (*cut short*) abreviar; (*expenses*) reducir. **curtailment** *n* abreviación *f*; reducción *f*.

curtain ['kəːtn] *n* cortina *f*; (*theatre*) telón *m*. **curtain call** llamada a escena *f*. **draw the curtain** correr la cortina. *v* poner cortinas en; encubrir.

curtsy ['kəːtsi] *n* reverencia *f*. *v* hacer una reverencia.

curve [kəːv] *n* curva *f*; vuelta *f*. *v* doblar; encorvar. **curvature** *n* curvatura *f*; (*earth*) esfericidad *f*; (*spine*) encorvamiento *m*. **curved** *adj* curvo; doblado.

cushion ['kuʃən] *n* cojín *m*, almohadón *m*. *v* amortiguar, acolchar.

custard ['kʌstəd] *n* natillas *f pl*.

custody ['kʌstədi] *n* custodia *f*, guardia *f*; prisión *f*. **in custody** bajo custodia. **take into custody** detener. **custodian** *n* custodio *m*; guardián, -ana *m, f*.

custom ['kʌstəm] *n* (*habit*) costumbre *f*; (*customers*) clientela *f sing*. **customs** *n* derechos de aduana *m pl*. **customary** *adj* de costumbre. **custom-built** *adj* hecho de encargo. **customer** *n* cliente *m, f*.

*cut [kʌt] *n* corte *m*; (*wound*) herida *f*; (*notch*) muesca *f*; (*reduction*) reducción *f*; (*med*) incisión *f*. **short cut** atajo *m*. **cut-and-dried** previsto. **cut and thrust** la lucha *f*. *v* cortar; reducir; (*reap*) segar; (*shorten*) acortar. **cut short** cortar en

seco. *adj* cortado; reducido. **cut-price** *adj*
a precio reducido.
cute [kjuɪt] *adj* (*attractive*) mono, lindo;
(*clever*) astuto. **cuteness** *n* monería *f*;
astucia *f*.
cuticle ['kjuːtikl] *n* cutícula *f*.
cutlery ['kʌtləri] *n* cubiertos *m pl*.
cutlet ['kʌtlit] *n* chuleta *f*.
cycle ['saikl] *n* ciclo *m*; bicicleta *f*. *v* pasar
por un ciclo; ir en bicicleta. **cyclical** *adj*
cíclico. **cycling** *n* ciclismo *m*. **cyclist** *n*
ciclista *m, f*.
cyclone ['saikloun] *n* ciclón *m*.
cylinder ['silində] *n* cilindro *m*. **cylinder
block** bloque de cilindros *m*. **cylindrical**
adj cilíndrico.
cymbal ['simbəl] *n* címbalo *m*, platillo *m*.
cynic ['sinik] *n*, *adj* cínico, -a *m, f*. **cynical**
adj cínico. **cynicism** *n* cinicismo *m*.
cypress ['saiprəs] *n* ciprés *m*.
Cyprus ['saiprəs] *n* Chipre. **Cypriot**
n(*m*+*f*), *adj* chipriota.
cyst [sist] *n* quiste *m*. **cystitis** *n* cistitis *f*.
Czechoslovakia [‚tʃekəslə'vakiə] *n*
Checoslovaquia *f*. **Czechoslovakian,
Czechoslovak, Czech** *n, adj* checoslovaco, -a.

D

dab [dab] *n* (*light blow*) golpe ligero *m*;
(*touch*) toque *m*; (*bit*) pizca *f*. *v* golpear
ligeramente; dar unos toques de. *adj* **be
a dab hand at** ser un hacha en.
dabble ['dabl] *v* (*splash*) salpicar; (*wet*)
mojar. **dabble in** (*water*) chapotear; (*participation*) meterse en.
dad [dad] *n* (*coll*) papá *m*.
daffodil ['dafədil] *n* narciso *m*.
daft [daːft] *adj* (*coll*) tonto.
dagger ['dagə] *n* daga *f*; puñal *m*.
daily ['deili] *adj* diario, cotidiano. *adv*
diariamente, cada día. *n* (*coll: newspaper*)
diario *m*.
dainty ['deinti] *adj* (*taste*) delicado, fino;
(*fussy*) difícil. **daintiness** *n* delicadeza *f*;
elegancia *f*.
dairy ['deəri] *n* lechería *f*. **dairy cattle**
vacas lecheras *f pl*. **dairy farm** granja de
vacas *f*. **dairy products** productos lácteos
m pl.

daisy ['deizi] *n* margarita *f*.
dam [dam] *n* (*barrier*) dique *m*; (*reservoir*)
embalse *m*; (*zool*) madre *f*. *v* construir un
dique; embalsar.
damage ['damidʒ] *n* daño *m*; (*fig*)
perjuicio *m*. **damages** *pl n* (*law*) daños y
perjuicios *m pl*. *v* dañar; perjudicar;
(*spoil*) estropear.
damn [dam] *v* (*condemn*) condenar;
(*curse*) maldecir. **damn!** (*interj*)
¡mechacis! **damnable** *adj* condenable;
detestable. **damnation** *n* condenación *f*;
(*interj*) ¡maldición! **damned** *adj* condenado; (*coll*) maldito; tremendo. *adv*
sumamente.
damp [damp] *adj* húmedo. *n* humedad *f*.
damp course aislante hidráfugo *m*. *v* (*also*
dampen) humedecer; (*extinguish*) apagar,
sofocar; (*discourage*) desanimar; (*sound*)
amortiguar. **damper** *n* humedecedor *m*;
(*chimney*) regulador *m*. **put a damper on**
caer como un jarro de agua fría en.
damson ['damzən] *n* (*fruit*) ciruela damas-
cena *f*; (*tree*) ciruelo damsceno *m*.
dance [daɪns] *n* baile *m*; (*ritual*) danza *f*.
dance band orquesta de baile *f*. **dance
floor** pista de baile *f*. **dance hall** sala de
baile *f*. *v* bailar. **dancer** *n* bailarín, -ina
m, f.
dandelion ['dandiˌlaiən] *n* diente de león
m.
dandruff ['dandrəf] *n* caspa *f*.
Dane [dein] *n* danés, -esa *m, f*. **Danish**
nm, adj danés. **Great Dane** perro danés
m.
danger ['deindʒə] *n* peligro *m*. **danger
zone** área de peligro. **dangerous** *adj*
peligroso.
dangle ['dangl] *v* (*hang*) colgar, dejar col-
gado; (*swing*) balancear en el aire.
dare [deə] *v* (*challenge*) desafiar; (*have the
impudence to*) atreverse a. **I dare say**
quizás. *n* desafío *m*, reto *m*. **daredevil** *n*
temerario, -a *m, f*. **daring** *adj* atrevido;
osado. *n* osadía *f*.
dark [daɪk] *adj* oscuro; (*hair, complexion*)
moreno; (*sombre*) triste; (*menacing*)
amenazador; (*mysterious*) misterioso.
Dark Ages edad de las tinieblas *f*. **dark
room** cámara oscura *f*. **grow dark**
anochecer. *n* oscuridad *f*. **after dark**
después del anochecer. **be in the dark**
estar a oscuras. **darken** *v* oscurecer;
entristecer. **darkness** *n* oscuridad *f*.

darling ['dɑːlɪŋ] *n, adj* querido, -a *m, f.*
darn [dɑːn] *v* zurcir. *n* zurcido *m.* **darning needle** aguja de zurcir *f.*
dart [dɑːt] *n (missile)* dardo *m; (movement)* movimiento rápido *m. v* lanzar. **dartboard** *n* blanco *m.* **darts** *pl n (sport)* dardos *m pl.*
dash [daʃ] *n (rush)* carrera *f; (printing)* guión *m; (cookery)* poco *m,* gotas *f pl; (verve)* brío *m. v (rush)* precipitarse, ir de prisa; *(hopes)* defraudar. **dash off** *(letter, etc.)* escribir deprisa. **dashboard** *n* salpicadero *m.* **dashing** *adj* gallardo.
data ['deɪtə] *pl n* datos *m pl.* **data processing** proceso de datos *m.*
date[1] [deɪt] *n (calendar)* fecha *f;* época *f.* **be up to date** estar al día. **out of date** anticuado. **to date** hasta la fecha. **date line** meridiano de cambio de fecha *m. v* fechar.
date[2] [deɪt] *n (fruit)* dátil *m.* **date palm** palmera datilera *f.*
dative ['deɪtɪv] *nm, adj* dativo.
daughter ['dɔːtə] *n* hija *f.* **daughter-in-law** *n* nuera *f,* hija política *f.*
daunt [dɔːnt] *v (dishearten)* desanimar; *(intimidate)* intimidar. **dauntless** *adj* intrépido.
dawdle ['dɔːdl] *v (loiter)* holgazanear; *(waste time)* malgastar; *(walk slowly)* andar despacio.
dawn [dɔːn] *n* alba *m,* amanecer *m; (fig)* alborear *m.* **from dawn to dusk** de sol a sol. *v* alborear, amanecer.
day [deɪ] *n* día *m; (of work)* jornada *f.* **all day** todo el día. **every day** todos los días. **the day after tomorrow** pasado mañana. **the day before yesterday** anteayer. **from day to day** de día en día. **daybreak** *n* amanecer *m.* **daydream** *n* ensueño *m; v* soñar despierto. **daylight** *n* luz del día *f.* **in broad daylight** en pleno día. **good day!** ¡buenos días!
daze [deɪz] *n* aturdimiento *m. v* aturdir. **be in a daze** estar aturdido.
dazzle ['dazl] *n* brillo *m. v* deslumbrar. **dazzling** *adj* deslumbrante, deslumbrador.
dead [ded] *adj* muerto; *(absolute)* absoluto; *(insensible)* insensible; *(battery)* descargado; *(extinguished)* apagado. **deadline** *n* fecha *f.* **deadly** *adj* mortal; *(unerring)* absoluto; *(habit)* pernicioso.
deaden ['dedn] *v (sound, etc.)* amortiguar; *(pain)* calmar; *(feeling)* embotar. **deadening** *adj (tech)* aislante.
deaf [def] *adj* sordo. **turn a deaf ear** hacerse el sordo. **deaf-and-dumb** *adj* sordomudo. **deafen** *v* ensordecer. **deafening** *adj* ensordecedor. **deafness** *n* sordera *f.*
*****deal** [diːl] *v* repartir, distribuir. **deal in** comercir en. *n* transacción *f,* negocio *m; (treatment)* trato *m; (agreement)* convenio *m; (amount)* cantidad *f; (cards)* reparto *m; (wood)* abeto *m.* **it's a deal!** ¡trato hecho! **your deal** te toca. **dealer** *m* comerciante *m, f; (cards)* mano *f.* **dealing** *n* trato *m; (behaviour)* conducta *f.* **dealings** *pl n* relaciones *f pl.*
dean [diːn] *n (rel)* deán *m; (academic)* decano *m.*
dear [dɪə] *adj* querido; *(costly)* caro, costoso. **dear me!** ¡Dios mío! **dear sir** estimado señor. **dearly** *adv (affectionately)* cariñosamente; *(costly)* caro.
death [deθ] *n* muerte *f; (formal)* fallecimiento *m.* **death certificate** certificado de defunción *m.* **death duty** derechos de sucesión *m pl.* **deathless** *adj* inmortal. **deathly** *adj (appearance)* cadavérico; *(silence)* sepulcral. **death penalty** pena de muerte *f.* **death rate** mortalidad *f.*
debase [di'beɪs] *v* degradar; *(coins)* alterar. **debasement** *n* degradación *f;* alteración *f.*
debate [di'beɪt] *n* debate *m,* discusión *f;* controversia *f. v* discutir; controvertir; considerar. **debatable** *adj* discutible. **debating society** asociación que organiza debates *f.*
debit ['debɪt] *n (entry of debt)* débito *m; (left-hand side of account)* debe *m. v* cargar en cuenta.
debris ['deɪbriː] *n* escombros *m pl.*
debt [det] *n* deuda *f.* **run into debt** contraer deudas. **debtor** *n* deudor, -a *m, f.*
decade ['dekeɪd] *n* decenio *m.*
decadent ['dekədənt] *n(m+f), adj* decadente. **decadence** decadencia *f.*
decant [di'kant] *v* decantar. **decanter** *n* garrafa *f,* jarra *f.*
decapitate [di'kapiˌteɪt] *v* decapitar. **decapitation** *n* decapitación *f.*
decay [di'keɪ] *n* decomposición *f; (teeth)* caries *f invar;* decadencia *f; (physics)* desintegración progresiva *f. v* descomponerse; cariarse; decaer.

decease [di'siːs] n fallecimiento m. v fallecer. **deceased** n, adj difunto, -a.

deceit [di'siːt] n (cheating) engaño m; fraude m; decepción; (lying) mentira f. **deceitful** adj engañoso; fraudulento; mentiroso. **deceitfulness** n lo engañoso m; falsedad f.

deceive [di'siːv] v engañar; defraudar. **deceiver** n embustero, -a m, f.

December [di'sembə] n diciembre m.

decent ['diːsənt] adj decente; (satisfactory) razonable; (coll) bueno, simpático. **decency** n decencia f, decoro m.

deceptive [di'septiv] adj engañoso. **deceptiveness** n apariencia engañosa f.

decibel ['desiˌbel] n decibel m, decibelio m.

decide [di'said] v decidir; (line of action) determinar; (conflict) resolver; (choose) optar por. **decided** adj decidido; determinado; resuelto; (difference) marcado.

deciduous [di'sidjuəs] adj de hoja caduca.

decimal ['desiməl] nf, adj decimal. **decimal point** coma de decimales f.

decipher [di'saifə] v descifrar.

decision [di'siʒən] n decisión f. **decisive** adj decisivo; concluyente; (manner) decidido; (tone) tajante. **decisively** adv con decisión.

deck [dek] n (ship) cubierta f; (bus) piso m. **deck chair** tumbona f.

declare [di'kleə] v declarar; proclamar. **declaration** n declaración f; proclamación f. **declaratory** adj declaratorio.

decline [di'klain] n (decrease) disminución f; (life) ocaso m; (decay) decaimiento; (number) baja f. v (to act) negarse (a); (an offer) rehusar; (gramm) declinar; bajar; (med) debilitarse. **declining** adj declinante.

decompose [ˌdiːkəm'pouz] v (break up) descomponer; (rot) pudrir. **decomposition** n descomposición f; putrefacción f.

decorate ['dekəˌreit] v decorar, adornar; (medal) condecorar; (paint) pintar. **decoration** n (medal) condecoración f; (ornament) adorno m; (décor) decoración f. **decorative** adj decorativo. **decorator** n decorador, -a m, f.

decoy ['diːkoi] n señuelo m.

decrease [di'kriːs] v disminuir, reducir. n disminución f, reducción f. **decreasing** adj decreciente.

decree [di'kriː] n decreto m. v decretar; pronunciar.

decrepit [di'krepit] adj decrépito.

dedicate ['dediˌkeit] v (book, life, etc.) dedicar; (church) consagrar. **dedication** n (devotion) dedicación f; (inscription) dedicatoria f. **dedicatory** adj dedicatorio.

deduce [di'djuːs] v deducir.

deduct [di'dʌkt] v descontar. **deductible** adj deducible. **deduction** n (discount) deducción f, rebaja f; descuento m; (conclusion) conclusión f, deducción f.

deed [diːd] n acto m, acción f; (something done) hecho m; (feat) hazaña f; (law) escritura f.

deep [diːp] adj profundo, hondo. **a hole a metre deep** un pozo de un metro de hondo. **deep in debt** cargado de deudas. **go off the deep end** perder los estribos. n (sea) piélago m. **deepfreeze** n congelador m.

deer [diə] n ciervo m.

deface [di'feis] v desfigurar; mutilar. **defacement** n desfiguración f; mutilación f.

default [di'fɔːlt] n (debt) falta de pago; (absence) falta f; (law) contumacia f, rebeldía f. **judgment by default** sentencia en rebeldía f. **win by default** ganar por incomparecencia del adversario. v dejar de pagar; condenar en rebeldía; (a contest) perder por incomparecencia.

defeat [di'fiːt] n derrota f. v derrotar, vencer. **defeatism** n derrotismo m. **defeatist** n(m+f), adj derrotista.

defect ['diːfekt; v di'fekt] n defecto m. v desertar. **defection** n deserción f. **defective** adj defectuoso; incompleto; (gramm) defectivo. **defectiveness** n imperfección f.

defend [di'fend] v defender. **defence** n defensa f. **self-defence** n autodefensa f. **defenceless** adj indefenso. **defendant** n (civil) demandado, -a m, f; (criminal) acusado, -a m, f. **defender** n defensor, -a m, f. **defensible** adj defensible; justificable. **defensive** adj defensivo. **on the defensive** a la defensiva.

defer [di'fɜː] v (postpone) diferir; (submit) someter; (delay) tardar. **deference** n deferencia f. **in deference to** por respeto a. **deferential** adj deferente, respetuoso. **deferment** n aplazamiento m; (mil) prórroga f. **deferrable** adj diferible. **deferred** adj diferido; aplazado.

defiant [di'faiənt] *adj* provocativo; (*challenging*) desafiante. **defiance** *n* desafío *m*. **in defiance of** con desprecio de.
deficient [di'fiʃənt] *adj* deficiente; (*med*) atrasado.
deficit ['defisit] *n* déficit. *adj* deficitario.
define [di'fain] *v* definir; caracterizar; formular; determinar. **definition** *n* definición *f*; (*phot*) claridad *f*.
definite ['definit] *adj* definido; determinado; claro; definitivo; seguro. **definitely** *adv* claramente; categóricamente; (*without doubt*) seguramente.
deflate [di'fleit] *v* desinflar; (*comm*) provocar la deflación de; (*hopes*) reducir. **deflation** *n* desinflado *m*; (*comm*) deflación *f*.
deform [di'fɔːm] *v* deformar, desfigurar. **deformation** *n* deformación *f*.
defraud [di'frɔːd] *v* defraudar, estafar.
defrost [diː'frɔst] *v* deshelar.
deft [deft] *adj* hábil, diestro. **deftness** *n* habilidad *f*, destreza *f*.
defunct [di'fʌŋkt] *adj* difunto.
defy [di'fai] *v* (*challenge*) desafiar, retar; (*resist*) resistir a.
degenerate [di'dʒenə,reit] *n*, *adj* di'dʒenərit] *v* degenerar. *n*, *adj* degenerado, -a. **degeneration** *n* degeneración *f*. **degenerative** *adj* degenerativo.
degrade [di'greid] *v* (*humiliate, reduce in rank*) degradar; (*quality*) rebajar; (*morals*) envilecer. **degradation** *n* degradación *f*. **degrading** *adj* degradante.
degree [di'griː] *v* (*stop*) grado *m*; categoría *f*; (*university*) título *m*. **bachelor's degree** licenciatura *f*. **by degrees** poco a poco. **doctor's degree** doctorado *m*. **to some degree** hasta cierto punto.
dehydrate [diː'haidreit] *v* deshidratar. **dehydration** *n* deshidratación *f*.
de-icer [diː'aisə] *n* descongelador *m*.
deity ['diːəti] *n* deidad *f*.
dejected [di'dʒektid] *adj* descorazonado, desanimado. **dejection** *n* desaliento *m*, abatimiento *m*.
delay [di'lei] *n* dilación *f*, retraso *m*; (*wait*) demora *f*. *v* retrasar; (*postpone*) aplazar. **delaying** *adj* dilatorio.
delegate ['deləgit] *v* 'deləgeit] *n* delegado, -a *m, f*. *v* delegar. **delegation** *n* delegación *f*.
delete [di'liːt] *v* tachar, borrar. **deletion** *n* supresión *f*.
deliberate [di'libərət] *v* di'libəreit] *adj*

(*intentional*) deliberado; (*unhurried*) lento; (*premeditated*) premeditado; (*cautious*) prudente. *v* deliberar; (*ponder*) reflexionar. **deliberately** *adv* (*on purpose*) a propósito; prudentemente; lentamente.
deliberation *n* deliberación *f*; lentitud *f*; reflexión *f*.
delicate ['delikət] *adj* delicado; (*food*) exquisito; refinado; escrupuloso; (*touch*) ligero; (*health*) frágile. **delicacy** *n* delicadeza *f*, fragilidad *f*.
delicious [di'liʃəs] *adj* delicioso.
delight [di'lait] *n* deleite *m*; encanto *m*. *v* deleitar; encantar. **delightful** *adj* delicioso; encantador.
delinquency [di'liŋkwənsi] *n* delincuencia *f*. **delinquent** *n*(*m+f*), *adj* delincuente.
delirious [di'liriəs] *adj* delirante. **be delirious** delirar. **delirium** *n* delirio *m*.
deliver [di'livə] *v* (*hand over*) entregar; (*goods, post*) repartir; (*message*) dar; (*opinion*) expresar; (*speech*) pronunciar; (*baby*) asistir para dar a luz; (*free*) liberar. **deliverance** *n* liberación *f*. **delivery** *n* entrega *f*; reparto *m*; pronunciación *f*; lanzamiento *m*; (*med*) parto *m*; manera de expresarse *f*. **delivery service** servicio a domicilio *m*. **delivery van** furgoneta de reparto *f*. **take delivery of** recibir.
delta ['deltə] *n* delta *m*.
delude [di'luːd] *v* engañar. **delusion** *n* engaño, *m*, error *m*, ilusión *f*.
deluge ['deljuːdʒ] *n* diluvio *m*. *v* inundar; (*fig*) abrumar.
delve [delv] *v* cavar. **delve into** ahondar.
demand [di'maːnd] *n* (*comm*) demanda *f*; (*request*) petición *f*; (*for payment*) reclamación *f*. *v* (*require*) requerir; (*ask urgently*) exigir; reclamar. **demanding** *adj* (*tiring*) agotador; (*absorbing*) aborbente; (*person*) exigente.
demented [di'mentid] *adj* demente, loco. **dementia** *n* demencia *f*.
democracy [di'mokrəsi] *n* democracia *f*. **democrat** *n* demócrata *m, f*. **democratic** *adj* democrático.
demolish [di'moliʃ] *v* (*building*) demoler, derribar; (*fig*) destruir. **demolition** *n* demolición *f*, derribo *m*; destrucción *f*.
demon ['diːmən] *n* demonio *m*, diablo *m*.
demonstrate ['demən,streit] *v* demostrar, probar; (*show how something operates*) mostrar; (*pol*) hacer la manifestación. **demonstration** *n* demostración *f*, prueba *f*; manifestación *f*. **demonstrative** *adj*

demostrativo. **demonstrator** *n* ayudante
m, f; (*protester*) manifestante *m, f.*
demoralize [di'morəˌlaiz] *v* desmoralizar.
demoralization *n* desmoralización *f.*
demoralizing *adj* desmoralizador,
desmoralizante.
demure [di'mjuə] *adj* recatado.
den [den] *n* (*of animals, etc.*) guarida *f;*
(*study*) estudio *m.*
denial [di'naiəl] *n* (*refusal*) negativa *f;*
(*disavowal*) negación *f;* (*rejection*)
rechazamiento *m.* **self-denial** abnegación
f.
denim ['denim] *n* mahón *m.*
Denmark ['denmaık] *n* Dinamarca *f.*
denomination [diˌnomi'neiʃən] *n* (*measure*) denominación *f;* (*rel*) secta *f,* confesión *f;* (*coins*) valor *m;* (*type*) clase *f,* tipo
m. **denominational** *adj* sectario. **denomi-
nator** *n* (*math*) denominador *m.*
denote [di'nout] *v* denotar.
denounce [di'nauns] *v* denunciar.
dense [dens] *adj* (*thick*) denso; (*coll: person*) torpe. **densely** *adv* densamente. **density** *n* densidad *f;* torpeza *f.*
dent [dent] *n* abolladura *f. v* abollar.
dental [dentl] *adj* dental.
dentist ['dentist] *n* dentista *m, f.* **dentistry**
n odolontogia *f.*
denture ['dentʃə] *n* dentadura *f,* postiza *f.*
denude [di'njuːd] *v* desnudar.
denunciation [dinʌnsi'eiʃən] *n* denuncia
f; (*condemnation*) condena *f;* (*criticism*)
censura *f.*
deny [di'nai] *v* (*refuse, dispute*) negar;
(*request*) denegar; (*give the lie to*)
desmentir; (*repudiate*) repudiar.
deodorant [diː'oudərənt] *n* desodorante
m.
depart [di'paːt] *v* (*go away*) marcharse;
(*set off*) salir; (*deviate*) apartarse. **depart-
ed** *adj* pasado; (*dead*) difunto. **departure**
n marcha *f;* salida *f;* desviación *f.*
department [di'paːtmənt] *n* (*in a shop*)
departamento *m;* (*in a business*) servicio
m; (*college, university*) sección *f;* (*ministry*) negociado *m;* (*branch*) ramo *m;* (*fig:
sphere*) esfera *f.* **department store** gran
almacén *m.* **departmental** *adj* departa-
mental.
depend [di'pend] *v* depender. **dependence**
n dependencia *f.* **dependent** *adj*
dependiente; subordinado.
depict [di'pikt] *v* (*art*) pintar; (*fig*)

describir. **depiction** *n* pintura *f;* descripción *f.*
deplete [di'pliːt] *v* vaciar, agotar. **deple-
tion** *n* agotamiento *m.*
deplore [di'ploː] *v* deplorar, lamentar.
deplorable *adj* deplorable, lamentable.
deport [di'poːt] *v* expulsar. **deport oneself**
comportarse. **deportation** *n* expulsión *f.*
deportment *n* porte *m;* conducta *f.*
depose [di'pouz] *v* deponer.
deposit [di'pozit] *n* (*bank*) depósito *m;*
(*substance*) sedimento *m,* poso *m;*
(*pledge*) señal *f;* (*on accommodation*)
entrada *f. v* depositar; (*money in
account*) ingresar; dar de señal. **deposit
account** cuenta de depósitos a plazo *f.*
depot ['depou] *n* (*store*) almacén *m;* (*bus-
es*) cochera *f;* (*mil*) depósito *m.*
deprave [di'preiv] *v* depravar. **depravity** *n*
depravación *f.*
depreciate [di'priːʃiˌeit] *v* (*belittle, money*)
despreciar; (*goods*) abaratar; (*price*)
bajar. **depreciation** *n* depreciación *f;*
abaratamiento *m;* (*fig*) desprecio *m.*
depress [di'pres] *v* (*dishearten*) deprimir;
(*weaken*) debilitar; (*lessen*) disminuir;
(*lower*) bajar; (*push down*) presionar;
(*pedal*) pisar. **depressed** *adj* deprimido;
(*indigent*) necesitado; (*comm*) de depresión. **depressing** *adj* deprimente. **depression** *n* (*dejection*) abatimiento *m;* (*geog,
med, comm*) depresión *f.*
deprive [di'praiv] *v* privar, desposeer. **deprivation** *n* privación *f;* (*loss*) pérdida *f.*
depth [depθ] *n* profundidad *f;* (*colour*)
intensidad *f;* (*sound*) gravedad *f.* **out of
one's depth** perder pie; (*fig*) no entender
nada.
deputy ['depjuti] *n* delegado *m;* (*substitute*) suplente *m;* (*politician*) diputado *m.*
deputation *n* delegación *f.* **deputize** *v*
diputar; delegar; sustituir.
derail [di'reil] *v* hacer descarrilar. **derail-
ment** *n* descarrilamiento *m.*
derelict ['derilikt] *adj* abandonado. *n*
(*neut*) derrelicto *m;* (*person*) deshecho *m.*
dereliction *n* abandono *m;* (*negligence*)
negligencia *f.*
deride [di'raid] *v* ridicular. **derision** *n*
mofas *f pl.* **derisive** or **derisory** *adj*
(*mocking*) mofador; (*petty*) irrisorio.
derive [di'raiv] *v* derivar; (*profit*) sacar.
derivation *n* derivación *f.* **derivative** *nm,
adj* derivado.

derogatory [di'rogətəri] *adj* despectivo, rebajante.

descend [di'send] *v* descender, bajar. **descendant** *n(m+f)*, *adj* descendiente. **descent** *n* descenso *m*, bajada *f*; (*slope*) declive *m*; (*lineage*) descendencia *f*.

describe [di'skraib] *v* describir; (*draw*) trazar. **describe oneself as** presentarse como. **description** *n* descripción *f*; (*sort*) clase *f*. **descriptive** *adj* descriptivo.

desert¹ ['dezət] *n* (*land*) desierto *m*.

desert² [di'zəːt] *v* abandonar; (*mil*) desertar de. **deserter** *n* desertor *m*. **desertion** *n* (*mil*) deserción *f*; abandono *m*.

deserts [di'zəːts] *pl n* **get one's deserts** llevarse su merecido.

deserve [di'zəːv] *v* merecer; ser digno de. **deserving** *adj* digno; (*deed*) meritorio.

design [di'zain] *n* (*intention*) propósito *m*; (*plan*) proyecto *m*; (*drawing*) dibujo *m*; (*style*) estilo *m*. **have designs on** haber puesto sus miras en. *v* (*prepare plans for*) diseñar; dibujar; proyectar; inventar; (*create*) crear; imaginar. **designer** *n* diseñador, -a *m, f*; (*draughtsman*) delineante *m*. **dress designer** modista *m*. **designing** *adj* intrigante.

designate ['dezigneit] *v* (*name for a duty*) designar; (*name*) denominar; (*appoint*) nombrar; (*point out*) señalar. *adj* designado; nombrado. **designation** *n* designación *f*; denominación *f*; nombramiento *m*.

desire [di'zaiə] *n* deseo *m*; (*request*) petición *f*. *v* desear; pedir; (*want*) querer. **desirable** *adj* deseable; atractivo. **desirability** *n* lo atractivo; conveniencia *f*. **desirous** *adj* deseoso.

desk [desk] *n* (*office*) escritorio *m*; (*school*) pupitre *m*.

desolate ['desələt] *adj* (*waste*) desolado; solitario; desierto; disconsolado. *v* (*lay waste*) asolar; abandonar; desconsolar. **desolating** *adj* desolador. **desolation** *n* desolación *f*; soledad *f*.

despair [di'speə] *n* desesperación *f*, desesperanza *f*. *v* desesperar.

desperate ['despərət] *adj* desesperado; (*resistance*) enérgico; (*urgent*) apremiante. **desperation** *n* desesperación *f*.

despise [di'spaiz] *v* despreciar. **despicable** *adj* despreciable. **despicableness** *n* bajeza *f*.

despite [di'spait] *prep* a pesar de.

despondent [di'spondənt] *adj* desanimado, desalentado. **despondency** *n* desánimo *m*, desaliento *m*.

despot ['despot] *n* déspota *m*. **despotic** *adj* despótico. **despotism** *n* despotismo *m*.

dessert [di'zəːt] *n* postre *m*. **dessertspoon** *n* cuchara de postre *f*.

destine ['destin] *v* destinar. **destination** *n* destinación *f*. **destiny** *n* destino *m*.

destitute ['destitjuːt] *adj* indigente, menesteroso. **be destitute** estar en la miseria. **destitution** *n* indigencia *f*, miseria *f*.

destroy [di'stroi] *v* destruir, destrozar. **destroyer** *n* (*naut*) destructor *m*. **destruction** *n* destrucción *f*; ruina *f*. **destructive** *adj* destructivo.

detach [di'tatʃ] *v* despegar; separar. **detachable** *adj* separable; (*collar*) postizo. **detached** *adj* independiente; (*untroubled*) indiferente. **detachment** *n* separación *f*; indiferencia *f*; (*mil*) destacamento *m*.

detail ['diːteil] *n* detalle *m*. *v* detallar; (*itemize*) enumerar; (*mil*) destacar.

detain [di'tein] *v* retener; (*law*) detener. **detention** *n* detención *f*, arresto *m*.

detect [di'tekt] *v* (*discover*) descubrir; (*perceive*) percibir; (*note*) advertir; (*tech*) detectar. **detection** *n* descubrimiento *m*; detección *f*. **detective** *n* detective *m*. **detective story** novela policíaca *f*. **detector** *n* detector *m*. **lie detector** detector de mentiras *m*.

deter [di'təː] *v* desuadir. **deterrent** *adj* disuasivo. *n* fuerza de disuasión *f*.

detergent [di'təːdʒənt] *nm*, *adj* detergente.

deteriorate [di'tiəriə,reit] *v* (*wear out*) deteriorar; (*become worse*) empeorar; (*in value*) depreciar. **deterioration** *n* deterioro *m*; empeoramiento *m*; (*decline*) decadencia *f*.

determine [di'təːmin] *v* (*fix*) determinar; (*cause*) provocar; (*limits*) definir; (*decide*) decidir; resolver. **determination** *n* determinación *f*; resolución *f*; decisión *f*. **determined** *adj* resuelto; decidido; determinado.

detest [di'test] *v* destestar, odiar. **detestable** *adj* detestable, odioso. **detestation** *n* odio *m*.

detonate ['detə,neit] *v* detonar. **detonating** *adj* detonante. **detonation** *n* detonación *f*.

detour ['diːtuə] *n* desvío *m*, desviación *f*; vuelta *f*. **make a detour** dar un rodeo.

detract [di'trakt] v (take away) quitar, reducir; (denigrate) denigrar. **detraction** n denigración f.

detriment ['detrimənt] n detrimento m, perjuicio m. **detrimental** adj perjudicial.

devalue [diː'valjuː] v devaluar, desvalorizar. **devaluation** n devaluación f.

devastate ['devəsteit] v devastar. **devastating** adj devastador. **devastation** n devastación f.

develop [di'veləp] v (expand) desarrollar; (business) explotar; (land) urbanizar; (resources) aprovechar; (promote) fomentar; (taste) adquirir; (ailment) contraer; (tendency) manifestar; (talent) mostrar; (phot) revelar. **developer** n (phot) revelador m. **development** n desarrollo m; evolución f; progreso m.

deviate ['diːviˌeit] v desviarse. **deviation** n desviación f; (from truth) alejamiento m; (sexual) inversión f. **deviationism** n desviacionismo m. **deviationist** n desviacionista m, f.

device [di'vais] n (tech) mecanismo; ingenio; (scheme) ardid m; estratagema f.

devil ['devl] n diablo. **devilish** adj diabólico. **devil's advocate** abogado del diablo m.

devise [di'vaiz] v inventar; (plan) concebir; (plot) tramar.

devoid [di'void] adj desprovisto.

devolution [ˌdiːvə'luːʃən] n (powers) delegación f. **devolve** v delegar; transmitir.

devote [di'vout] v dedicar. **devoted** adj dedicado; (loyal) leal; (devout) devoto. **devotion** n dedicación f; lealtad f; devoción f. **devotional** adj piadoso.

devour [di'vauə] v devorar. **devouring** adj devorador.

devout [di'vaut] adj devoto; sincero. **devoutness** n devoción f.

dew [djuː] n rocío m.

dexterous ['dekstrəs] adj diestro, hábil. **dexterity** n destreza f, habilidad f.

diabetes [ˌdaiə'biːtiz] n diabetes f. **diabetic** n, adj diabético, -a.

diagnose [ˌdaiəg'nouz] v diagnosticar. **diagnosis** n diagnóstico m.

diagonal [dai'agənəl] nf, adj diagonal. **diagonally** adv diagonalmente.

diagram ['daiəˌgram] n (math) figura; (chart) gráfico m; (sketch) esquema; (explanatory) diagrama m. **diagrammatic** adj esquemático.

dial ['daiəl] n (clock) esfera f; (selector) botón m; (telephone) disco m. v marcar. **dialling tone** señal para marcar f.

dialect ['daiəlekt] n dialecto m.

dialogue ['daiəlog] n diálogo m.

diameter [dai'amitə] n diámetro m. **diametrically** adv diametralmente.

diamond ['daiəmənd] n diamante m. **diamond-shaped** adj romboidal.

diaper ['daiəpə] n (US) pañal m.

diaphragm ['daiəfram] n diafragma m.

diarrhoea [ˌdaiə'riə] n diarrea f.

diary ['daiəri] n diario m; (for appointments) agenda f.

dice [dais] n pl dados m pl. v jugar a los dados. **dice with death** jugar con la muerte.

dictate [dik'teit] v dictar; (order) mandar; (impose) imponer. n mandato m. **dictation** n dictado m. **dictator** n dictador m. **dictatorial** adj dictatorial. **dictatorship** n dictadura f.

dictionary ['dikʃənəri] n diccionario m.

did [did] V **do**.

die [dai] v morrir, fallecer. **die away** (sound) desvanecer. **die down** (fire) apagarse; (wind) amainar; (conversation) decaer. **die out** desaparecer.

diesel ['diːzəl] nm, adj diesel. **diesel engine** motor diesel m. **diesel oil** gasoil m.

diet ['daiət] n dieta f, régimen m. v poner a dieta or régimen. **dietary** adj dietético. **dietetics** n dietética f. **dietician** n dietético m.

differ ['difə] v ser diferente, ser distinto. **difference** n diferencia f; (disagreement) desacuerdo m. **different** adj diferente, distinto. **differential** nf, adj diferencial. **differentiate** v diferenciar, distinguir.

difficult ['difikəlt] adj difícil. **difficulty** n dificultad f.

*dig [dig] v cavar; excavar; (coal, etc.) extraer. **dig in** enterrar. **dig into** clavar. **dig up** desenterrar. n (in the ribs) golpe m; excavación arquelógica f; (fig) pinchazo m.

digest [dai'dʒest] n resumen m. v digerir; (summarize) resumir; (fig) asimilar. **digestible** adj digerible. **digestion** n digestión f. **digestive** adj digestivo. **digestive system** aparato digestivo m.

digit ['didʒit] n (finger, toe) dedo m; (math) dígito m. **digital** adj digital.

dignified ['digni,faid] *adj* digno; solemne.
dignify *v* dignificar.
dignity ['dignəti] *n* dignidad *f*. **dignitary** *n* dignatorio *m*.
digress [dai'gres] *v* desviarse, apartarse.
digression *n* digresión *f*.
digs [digz] *n pl* (*coll*) pensión *f sing*.
dilapidated [di'læpi,deitid] *adj* (*building*) ruinoso; (*clothes*) muy estropeado. **dilapidate** *v* deteriorar; estropear. **dilapidation** *n* estado ruinoso *m*.
dilate [dai'leit] *v* dilatar.
dilemma [di'lemə] *n* dilema *m*.
diligent ['dilidʒent] *adj* diligente. **diligence** *n* diligencia *f*.
dilute [dai'luːt] *v* diluir, aguar; (*fig*) atenuar. *adj* diluido; atenuado. **dilution** *n* dilución *f*.
dim [dim] *adj* oscuro; (*memory*) lejano; (*sound*) sordo; (*sight*) turbio; (*light*) débil; (*vague*) borroso; (*colour*) apagado; (*slang*) tonto. **take a dim view of** ver con malos ojos. *v* (*light*) bajar; (*sight*) nublar.
dimly *adv* vagamente; poco iluminado.
dimension [di'menʃən] *n* dimensión *f*.
diminish [di'miniʃ] *v* disminuir.
diminutive [di'minjutiv] *adj* diminuto. *nm*. *adj* (*gramm*) diminutivo.
dimple ['dimpl] *n* hoyuelo *m*. *v* formar hoyuelos en.
din [din] *n* estrépito *m*, alboroto *m*.
dine [dain] *v* cenar. **dining car** coche restaurante *m*. **diningroom** *n* comedor *m*.
dinghy ['diŋgi] *n* bote *m*.
dingy ['dindʒi] *adj* sucio, sórdido.
dinner ['dinə] *n* (*evening*) cena *f*; (*midday*) comida *f*. **dinner jacket** esmoquin *m*. **dinner party** cena *f*. **dinner table** mesa de comedor *f*.
dinosaur ['dainə,soː] *n* dinosaurio *m*.
diocese ['daiəsis] *n* diócesis *f*. **diocesan** *n*, *adj* diocesano, -a.
dip [dip] *v* (*wet*) mojar; (*immerse*) sumergir; (*someone*) zambullir; (*scoop*) sacar; (*put a hand in*) meter; (*flag*) inclinar; (*headlights*) poner luz de cruce; (*road*) bajar; *n* baño *m*; (*slope*) declive *m*.
diphthong ['difθoŋ] *n* diptongo *m*.
diploma [di'ploumə] *n* diploma *m*.
diplomacy [di'plouməsi] *n* diplomacia *f*.
diplomat *n* diplomático *m*. **diplomatic** *adj* diplomático. **diplomatic corps** cuerpo diplomático *m*. **diplomatic immunity** inmunidad diplomática *f*.

dipstick ['dipstik] *n* varilla graduada *f*.
dire [daiə] *adj* extremo; terrible.
direct [di'rekt] *adj* (*straight*) directo; (*blunt*) tajante; (*frank*) franco. **direct current** corriente continua *f*. *v* dirigir; (*order*) mandar; (*show the way*) indicar; (*gaze, attention*) señalar. **direction** *n* dirección *f*. **directions** *n pl* instrucciones *f pl*. **directive** *n* instrucción *f*. **directly** *adv* directamente; (*at once*) en seguida. **directness** *n* franqueza *f*. **director** *m* director *m*. **board of directors** consejo de administración *n*. **managing director** director gerente *m*.
dirt [dəːt] *n* suciedad *f*; (*filth*) mugre *f*; (*rubbish*) basura *f*. **dirt-cheap** *adj* baratísimo. **dirty** *adj* sucio; (*obscene: person*) verde; (*language*) grosero. **dirty trick** mala pasada *f*.
disability [disə'biləti] *n* incapacidad *f*. **disable** *v* incapacitar; (*cripple*) lisiar. **disabled** *adj* inválido. **disablement** *n* incapacidad *f*.
disadvantage [,disəd'vaintidʒ] *n* desventaja *f*. **be at a disadvantage** estar en situación desventajosa.
disagree [,disə'griː] *v* discrepar; no estar de acuerdo. **disagreeable** *adj* desagradable. **disagreement** *n* desacuerdo *m*.
disappear [,disə'piə] *v* desaparecer. **disappearance** *n* desaparición *f*.
disappoint [,disə'point] *v* decepcionar; defraudar. **disappointing** *adj* decepcionante. **disappointment** *n* decepción *f*; disgusto *m*.
disapprove [,disə'pruːv] *v* desaprobar; estar en contra. **disapproval** *n* desaprobación *f*. **disapproving** *adj* desaprobador. **disapprovingly** *adv* con desaprobación.
disarm [dis'aim] *v* desarmar. **disarmament** *n* desarme *m*.
disaster [di'zaistə] *n* desastre *m*. **disastrous** *adj* desastroso.
disband [dis'band] *v* disolver; (*mil*) licenciar.
disc or *US* **disk** [disk] *n* disco *m*. **disc jockey** presentador de discos *m*.
discard [dis'kaid; *n* 'diskaid] *v* (*cast away*) desechar; (*cards*) descartar; (*fig*) renunciar. *n* descarte *m*.
discern [di'səin] *v* discernir. **discernible** *adj* perceptible. **discerning** *adj* perspicaz.
discharge [dis'tʃaidʒ] *v* descargar; (*debt*) saldar; (*gun*) disparar; (*sack*) despedir;

(*law*) absolver; (*duty*) desempeñar; (*prisoner*) liberar; (*patient*) dar de alta; (*bankrupt*) rehabilitar. *n* descarga *f*; (*debt*) descargo; (*gas*) escape *m*; liberación *f*; rehabilitación *f*; absolución *f*; desempeño *m*; alta *f*; disparo *m*.

disciple [di'saipl] *n* discípulo, -a *m, f*.

discipline ['disiplin] *n* disciplina *f. v* castigar. **disciplinarian** *n* disciplinario, -a *m, f*.

disciplinary *adj* disciplinario.

disclaim [dis'kleim] *v* rechazar; (*law*) renunciar. **disclaimer** *n* (*denial*) denegación *f*; (*law*) renuncia *f*.

disclose [dis'klouz] *v* revelar. **disclosure** *n* revelación *f*; descubrimiento *m*.

discolour [dis'kʌlə] *v* descolorar; (*stain*) manchar. **discolouration** *n* descoloración *f*.

discomfort [dis'kʌmfət] *n* molestia *f*; incomodidad *f*; malestar. *v* molestar.

disconcert [diskən'səːt] *v* desconcertar, perturbar. **disconcerting** *adj* desconcertante.

disconnect [diskə'nekt] *v* (*elec*) desconectar; (*separate*) separar. **disconnection** *n* desconexión *f*; separación *f*.

disconsolate [dis'konsələt] *adj* desconsolado. **disconsolateness** *n* desconsuelo *m*.

discontinue [diskən'tinjuː] *v* discontinuar, interrumpir; suspender. **discontinuance** *or* **discontinuation** *n* cesación *f*; suspensión *f*. **discontinuity** *n* discontinuidad *f*; interrupción *f*. **discontinuous** *adj* discontinuo.

discord ['diskoːd] *n* discordia *f*; (*music*) disonancia *f*. **discordant** *adj* discordante; (*music*) discorde.

discotheque ['diskətek] *n* discoteca *f*.

discount ['diskaunt] *n* descuento *m*; (*reduction*) rebaja *f. v* descontar; rabajar; (*disregard*) no hacer caso de.

discourage [dis'kʌridʒ] *v* desanimar. **discourage from** recomendar que no. **discouragement** *n* desánimo *m*. **discouraging** *adj* desalentador.

discover [dis'kʌvə] *v* descubrir; (*realize*) darse cuenta de. **discoverer** *n* descubridor, -a *m, f*. **discovery** *n* descubrimiento *m*.

discredit [dis'kredit] *v* desacreditar; (*disbelieve*) dudar de; (*dishonour*) deshonrar. *n* descrédito *m*; duda *f*. **discreditable** *adj* indigno; vergonzoso.

discreet [di'skriːt] *adj* discreto; prudente.

discretion *n* discreción; circunspección *f*. **at your discretion** a su gusto. **discretionary** *adj* discrecional.

discrepancy [di'skrepənsi] *n* discrepancia *f*; diferencia *f*. **discrepant** *adj* discrepante; diferente.

discrete [di'skriːt] *adj* discreto.

discriminate [di'skrimineit] *v* distinguir. **discriminate against** discriminar contra. **discriminating** *adj* (*law*) discriminatorio; (*taste*) muy bueno. **discrimination** *n* discriminación *f*; discernimiento *m*; buen gusto *m*. **discriminatory** *adj* discriminatorio.

discus ['diskəs] *n* disco *m*.

discuss [di'skʌs] *v* discutir; hablar de. **discussion** *n* discusión *f*.

disease [di'ziːz] *n* enfermedad *f*. **diseased** *adj* enfermo.

disembark [disim'baːk] *v* desembarcar. **disembarkation** *n* (*people*) desembarco *m*; (*cargo*) desembarque *m*.

disengage [disin'geidʒ] *v* (*detach*) soltar; (*unhook*) desenganchar; (*free*) liberar; (*mil*) retirar; (*gears*) desengranar; (*clutch*) desembragar. **disengagement** *n* liberación *f*; retirada *f*; desembrague *m*.

disfigure [dis'figə] *v* desfigurar; (*spoil*) afear. **disfigurement** *n* desfiguración *f*; afeamiento *m*.

disgrace [dis'greis] *n* (*disfavour*) desgracia *f*; (*cause of shame*) vergüenza *f*; deshonra *f*; ignominia *f. v* deshonrar. **disgraceful** *adj* deshonroso; vergonzoso.

disgruntled [dis'grʌntld] *adj* malhumorado.

disguise [dis'gaiz] *v* disfrazar. *n* disfraz *m*.

disgust [dis'gʌst] *n* repugnancia *f. v* repugnar.

dish [diʃ] *n* plato *m*; (*serving vessel*) fuente *f. v* servir. **dish out** dar. **dishwasher** *n* lavaplatos *m*.

dishearten [dis'haːtn] *v* descorazonar, desanimar. **disheartening** *adj* descorazonador.

dishevelled [di'ʃevəld] *adj* despeinado; desarreglado.

dishonest [dis'onist] *adj* fraudulento.

dishonour [dis'onə] *n* deshonra *f*. deshonor *m. v* deshonrar.

disillusion [disi'luːʒən] *v* desilusionar. *n* desilusión *f*.

disinfect [disin'fekt] *v* desinfectar. **disinfectant** *nm, adj* desinfectante.

disinherit [disin'herit] v desheredar. **disinheritance** n desheradamiento m.
disintegrate [dis'inti,greit] v desintegrar. **disintegration** n desintegración f.
disinterested [dis'intristid] adj desinteresado; imparcial. **disinterest** n desinterés m.
disjointed [dis'dʒɔintid] adj desarticulado; (incoherent) inconexo.
disk V **disc.**
dislike [dis'laik] v aborrecer, tener aversión a. n aversión f, antipatía f.
dislocate ['dislǝ,keit] v (joint) dislocar; (plans) desarreglar. **dislocation** n dislocación f; desarreglo m.
dislodge [dis'lodʒ] v desalojar. **dislodgement** n desalojamiento.
disloyal [dis'lɔiǝl] adj desleal. **disloyalty** n deslealtad f.
dismal ['dizmǝl] adj triste; (face) sombrío; (voice) lúgubre.
dismantle [dis'mantl] v desmantelar; desmontar.
dismay [dis'mei] n consternación f; (fright) espanto m. v consternar; espantar; (discourage) desalentar.
dismiss [dis'mis] v despedir; (discharge) licenciar; (assembly) disolver; (mil) romper filas; (idea) descartar. **dismissal** n (employee) despido m; abandono m.
dismount [dis'maunt] v desmontar.
disobey [disǝ'bei] v desobedecer. **disobedience** n desobediencia f. **disobedient** adj desobediente.
disorder [dis'ɔɪdǝ] n desorden m; (riot) disturbio m; (illness) trastorno m. v desordenar. **disorderliness** n desorden m. **disorderly** adj (person) desordenado; (place) desarreglado; (meeting) alborotado.
disorganize [dis'ɔɪgǝnaiz] v desorganizar. **disorganization** n desorganización f.
disown [dis'oun] v repudiar; (deny) negar; no reconocer.
disparage [di'sparidʒ] v desacreditar; (belittle) menospreciar; (denigrate) denigrar. **disparagement** n descrédito m; menosprecio m; denigración f. adj despectivo; menospreciativo; denigrante. **disparagingly** adv con desprecio.
disparity [dis'pariti] n disparidad f. **disparate** adj dispar.
dispassionate [dis'paʃǝnit] adj desapasionado; imparcial.
dispatch [di'spatʃ] n (message) despacho

m, expedición f; (messenger, parcels) envío m; (promptness) diligencia f. v despachar; enviar; matar.
dispel [di'spel] v disipar.
dispense [di'spens] v (drugs) preparar; (justice) administrar; (distribute) distribuir; (laws) aplicar. **dispense with** prescindir de. **dispensable** adj prescindible. **dispensary** n dispensario m; farmacia f. **dispensation** n distribución f; administración f; (exemption) dispensa f.
disperse [di'spɔɪs] v dispersar. **dispersal** n dispersión f.
displace [dis'pleis] v desplazar; (oust) quitar el puesto; (remove from office) destituir. **displacement** n desplazamiento m; destituición f; reemplazo m.
display [di'splei] v exhibir; demostrar. n exhibición f; demostración f; despliegue m; (emotion) alarde m; (show) exposición f; (parade) desfile m; (tech) representación visual f.
displease [dis'plizz] v desagradar, disgustar. **displeasing** adj desagradable. **displeasure** n desagrado m, disgusto m.
dispose [di'spouz] v (arrange) disponer; determinar; inclinar; mover. **dispose of** tirar; (transfer) traspasar; (argument) echar por tierra; (kill) liquidar; (sell) vender; (consume) consumir. **disposable** adj disponible; (to be thrown away) para tirar. **disposal** (arrangement) desposición f; eliminación f; resolución f; traspaso m; venta f. **disposition** n disposición f; traspaso m; predisposición f.
disprove [dis'pruv] v refutar.
dispute [di'spjut] n disputa f; discusión f; controversia f; (law) litigio m. v disputar; discutir; (question) poner en duda. **disputation** n discusión f; controversia f.
disqualify [dis'kwoli,fai] v (render unfit) incapacitar; (competitor) descalificar. **disqualification** n incapacidad f; descalificación f.
disregard [disrǝ'gaɪd] v (neglect) descuidar; desatender. n descuido m; indiferencia f.
disreputable [dis'repjutǝbl] adj (shabby) lamentable; (not respectable) de mala fama. **disrepute** n descrédito m.
disrespect [disrǝ'spekt] n falta de respeto f. **disrespectful** adj irrespetuoso.
disrupt [dis'rʌpt] v (upset) trastornar; (interrupt) interrumpir; (break up) romper; desorganizar. **disruption** n trastorno

m; ruptura *f;* interrupción *f;* desorganización *f.* **disruptive** *adj* perjudicial.

dissatisfy [di'satisfai] *v* no satisfacer. **dissatisfaction** *n* descontento *m.*

dissect [di'sekt] *v* disecar. **dissection** *n* disección *f.*

dissent [di'sent] *n* disensión *f;* (*disagreement*) disentimiento *m. v* (*disagree*) disentir. **dissension** *n* disensión *f.*

dissident ['disidənt] *n(m+f),* *adj* disidente. **dissidence** *n* disidencia *f.*

dissimilar [di'similə] *adj* desigual; distinto. **dissimilarity** *n* desigualdad *f.*

dissociate [di'sousieit] *v* disociar. **dissociation** *n* disociación *f.*

dissolute ['disəluːt] *adj* disoluto. **dissolution** *n* (*society, marriage, melting*) disolución *f.*

dissolve [di'zolv] *v* disolver; (*disintegrate*) descomponer; disipar; (*law; contract*) rescindir.

dissuade [di'sweid] *v* disuadir. **dissuasion** *n* disuasión *f.* **dissuasive** *adj* disuasivo.

distance ['distəns] *n* distancia *f. v* distanciar. **distant** *adj* distante, lejano.

distaste [dis'teist] *n* disgusto *m,* aversión *f.* **distasteful** *adj* desagradable.

distemper [di'stempə] *n* (*dogs*) moquillo *m;* (*paint*) temple *m.*

distend [di'stend] *v* distender. **distension** *n* distensión *f.*

distil [di'stil] *v* destilar. **distillation** *n* destilación *f.* **distillery** *n* destilería *f.*

distinct [di'stiŋkt] *adj* (*clear*) claro; (*different*) distinto; (*definite*) bien determinado. **distinction** *n* distinción *f.* **distinctive** *adj* distintivo. **distinctness** *n* claridad *f;* diferencia *f.*

distinguish [di'stiŋgwiʃ] *v* distinguir. **distinguishable** *adj* distinguible. **distinguished** *adj* (*elegant*) distinguido; (*eminent*) eminente.

distort [di'stoːt] *v* torcer; (*fig*) desvirtuar. **distortion** *n* torcimiento *m;* desvirtuación *f.*

distract [di'strakt] *v* (*divert attention*) distraer; (*confuse*) aturdir; (*madden*) enloquecer. **distraction** *n* distracción *f;* aturdimiento *m;* locura *f.*

distraught [di'stroːt] *adj* distraido; enloquecido.

distress [di'stres] *n* aflicción *f;* (*poverty*) miseria *f;* (*danger*) peligro *m. v* afligir; angustiar. **distressed** *adj* afligido; en la miseria; en peligro. **distressing** *adj* angustioso.

distribute [di'stribjut] *v* distribuir, repartir. **distribution** *n* distribución *f;* reparto *m.* **distributor** *n* distribuidor, -a *m, f;* (*mot*) distribuidor *m.*

district ['distrikt] *n* (*pol*) distrito *m;* (*town*) barrio *m;* (*region*) región *f.* **district manager** representante regional *m.*

distrust [dis'trast] *n* desconfianza *f. v* desconfiar. **distrustful** *adj* desconfiado.

disturb [di'stəːb] *v* molestar; perturbar; agitar; preocupar. **disturbance** *n* molestia *f;* perturbación *f;* agitación *f;* preocupación *f;* (*row*) alboroto *m;* (*public disorder*) disturbio *m.* **disturbing** *adv* molesto; perturbador; preocupante.

disuse [dis'juːs] *n* desuso *m;* abandono *m.*

ditch [ditʃ] *n* (*trench*) zanja *f;* (*roadside*) cuneta *f;* (*irrigation*) acequia *f;* (*drainage*) canal *m. v* (*coll: get rid of*) tirar; (*coll: abandon*) abandonar.

ditto ['ditou] *n* idem *m.*

divan [di'van] *n* diván *m.*

dive [daiv] *n* zambullida *f. v* zambullirse; saltar; bajar en picado; sumergirse. **diver** *n* buzo *m;* saltador, -a *m, f.*

diverge [dai'vəːdʒ] *v* divergir; desviar. **divergence** *n* divergencia *f.* **divergent** *adj* divergente.

diverse [dai'vəːs] *adj* diverso; distinto; diferente; variado. **diversity** *n* diversidad *f.*

divert [dai'vəːt] *v* (*reroute*) desviar; (*distract*) distraer; (*amuse*) divertir. **diversion** *n* desviación *f;* diversión *f.*

divide [di'vaid] *v* dividir. **division** *n* división *f;* separación *f;* distribución *f;* sección *f;* (*fig: opinions*) discrepancia *f;* (*fig: discord*) desunión *f.*

dividend ['dividend] *n* dividendo *m.*

divine [di'vain] *adj* divino. *v* adivinar. **divinity** *n* divinidad *f;* teología *f.*

divorce [di'vɔːs] *n* divorcio *m.* **sue for a divorce** pedir el divorcio. *v* divorciar; divorciarse de. **divorcee** *n* divorciado, -a *m, f.*

divulge [dai'vʌldʒ] *v* divulgar.

dizzy ['dizi] *adj* mareado; (*height, speed*) vertiginoso. **dizziness** *n* mareo *m,* vértigo *m.*

*do [duː] *v* (*act*) hacer; (*deal with*) ocuparse de; (*fulfil*) cumplir con; (*serve*) venir bien; (*feel*) estar, sentirse; (*be suitable*) valer; (*work*) trabajar; **do away with**

suprimir. **do for** llevar la casa a; **do up**
(buttons, belt, etc.) abrocharse; (laces)
atarse; (renovate) renovar. **do well** ir
bien, salir bien; recuperarse. **do without**
prescindir de. **doesn't do** to no conviene.
how do you do? (after being introduced)
encantado; (how are you?) ¿cómo está
usted? **make do with** arreglárselas con.
please do por supuesto, por favor.

docile ['dousail] adj dócil. **docility** n
docilidad f.

dock¹ [dok] n (wharf) dársena f; v (ship)
atracar al muelle; (arrive) llegar.

dock² [dok] n (law) banquillo de los
acusados m.

dock³ [dok] v (cut, shorten) cortar;
reducir; (coll: deduct) descontar; (coll:
fine) multar.

doctor ['doktə] n médico, -a m, f; (university title) doctor, -a m, f. v atender;
adulterar; falsificar. **doctorate** n
doctorado m.

doctrine ['doktrin] n doctrina f. **doctri-
naire** doctrinario. **doctrinal** adj doctrinal.

document ['dokjumənt] n documento m.
v documentar. **documentary** nm, adj doc-
umental.

dodge [dodʒ] v esquivarse; eludir; (bide)
echarse; (avoid) evitar. n (manoeuvre)
regate m; (trick) truco m. **dodgy** (coll) adj
astuto; (unreliable) incierto.

dog [dog] n perro m. **beware of the dog**
cuidado con el perro. v seguir; perseguir.

dog biscuit n galleta de perro f.

dog days n pl canícula f sing.

dog-eared adj sobado.

dogged ['dogid] adj tenaz. **doggedness** n
tenacidad f.

doggerel ['dogərəl] n aleluyas f pl.

dogma ['dogmə] n dogma m. **dogmatic** adj
dogmático.

do-it-yourself [,duritjor'self] adj hágalo
usted mismo.

dole [doul] n (alms) limosna f; (unemployment pay) subsidio de paro m. **be on the
dole** estar parado. **dole out** repartir.

doleful ['doulful] adj triste. **dolefulness** n
tristeza f.

doll [dol] n muñeca f.

dollar ['dolə] n dólar m.

dolphin ['dolfin] n delfín m.

domain [də'mein] n dominio m; (fig)
campo m.

dome [doum] n (arch) cúpula f, domo m.

domestic [də'mestik] adj doméstico;
(home-loving) hogareño; (market)
nacional. **domestic animal** animal doméstico m. **domestic help** doméstico, -a m, f.
domesticate domesticar. **domestication** n
domesticación f. **domesticity** n domesticidad f.

dominate ['domi,neit] v dominar. **dominant** adj dominante. **domineering** adj
dominante.

dominion [də'minjən] n dominio m.

domino ['dominou] n dominó m. **play
dominoes** jugar al dominó.

don [don] v ponerse. n catedrático m.

donate [də'neit] v donar. **donation** n
donativo m.

done [dʌn] V **do.**

donkey ['donki] n burro m.

donor ['dounə] n donante m, f.

doom [duːm] n perdición f. v condenar.

doomsday n día del juicio final m.

door [doː] n puerta f. **next door** en la casa
de al lado.

doorbell ['doːbel] n timbre m.

door-keeper n portero m; conserje m.

door-handle n mano de la puerta f.

doorknob ['doːnob] n tirador de puerta
m.

door-knocker n llamador m.

doormat ['doːmat] n felpudo m.

doorstep ['doːstep] n peldaño m; (threshold) umbral m.

doorway ['doːwei] n portal m.

dope [doup] n (coll: drug) droga f; (coll:
varnish) barniz m; (coll: information)
informes m pl. v drogar.

dormant ['doːmənt] adj letárgico; inactivo; latente.

dormitory ['doːmitəri] n dormitorio m.

dormouse ['doː,maus] n lirón m.

dose [dous] n dosis f invar. v dar la dosis.
dosage n dosis f invar.

dot [dot] n punto m. **on the dot** puntual-
mente. v poner el punto a; (scatter)
salpicar.

dote [dout] v chochear. **dote on** estar
chocho por. **dotage** n chochez f. **doting**
adj chocho.

double ['dʌbl] nm, adj, adv doble. v
doblar.

double bass n contrabajo m.

double bed n cama de matrimonio f.

double-breasted [,dʌbl'brestid] adj cruzado.

double-cross [ˌdʌbl'kros] *n* traición *f*. *v* traicionar.

double-edged [ˌdʌbl'edʒd] *adj* de dos filos.

double-entendre [duːblã'tãdr] *n* expresión con doble sentido *f*.

double entry *n* (*comm*) partida doble *f*.

doubt [daut] *n* duda *f*. **no doubt** sin duda. *v* dudar. **doubtful** *adj* dudozo; sospechoso. **doubtless** *adv* indudablemente.

dough [dou] *n* masa *f*. **doughnut** *n* buñuelo *m*.

dove [dʌv] *n* paloma *f*.

dowdy ['daudi] *adj* desaliñado. **dowdiness** *n* desaliño *m*.

down[1] [daun] *adv* hacia abajo. *prep* abajo. *adj* descendente, bajo. **down payment** al contado. *v* derribar; tirar al suelo; (*food*) tragar; (*drink*) vaciar de un trago.

down[2] [daun] *n* plumón *m*; (*fine hair*) vello *m*; (*upland*) loma *f*.

downcast ['daunˌkaɪst] *adj* (*sad*) abatido; (*in a downward direction*) bajo.

downfall ['daunˌfoːl] *n* ruina *f*; perdición *f*; caída *f*; (*rain*) chaparrón *m*.

downhearted [ˌdaun'haɪtid] *adj* descorazonado.

downhill [ˌdaun'hil] *adj* en pendiente. *adv* cuesta abajo.

downpour ['daunˌpoɪ] *n* aguacero *m*, chaparrón *m*.

downright ['daunˌrait] *adj* categórico; sincero; evidente; verdadero. *adv* categóricamente; verdaderamente; completamente.

downstairs. ['daunˌsteəz; *adv* ˌdaun'steəz] *adj* de abajo. *adv* abajo.

downstream [ˌdaun'striːm] *adj*, *adv* río abajo.

downtrodden ['daunˌtrodn] *adj* (*fig*) oprimido.

downward ['daunwəd] *adj* descendente. *adv* hacia abajo.

downwards ['daunwədz] *adv* hacia abajo.

dowry ['dauəri] *n* dote *f*.

doze [douz] *v* dormitar. *n* cabezada *f*.

dozen ['dʌzn] *n* docena *f*. **baker's dozen** docena del fraile *f*.

drab [drab] *adj* pardo; monótono.

draft [draɪft] *n* (*version*) redacción *f*; (*drawing*) esbozo *m*; (*plan*) bosquejo *m*; (*payment*) libramiento *m*; (*bill*) letra de cambio *f*; (*naut*) calado *m*; (*conscription*) quinta *f*. *v* hacer un proyecto; (*draw up*) redactar; esbozar; (*conscript*) reclutar.

drag [drag] *v* arrastrar; (*river, etc.*) dragar. **drag down** hundir. *n* (*tow*) arrastre *m*; (*that which hinders*) estorbo *m*; (*device for dragging rivers, etc.*) rastra *f*; (*theatre*) disfraz de mujer *m*; (*aero*) resistencia aerodinámica; (*tech: brake*) galga *f*. **what a drag!** ¡qué lata!

dragon ['dragən] *n* dragón *m*. **dragonfly** *n* libélula *f*.

drain [drein] *n* desaguadero *m*; (*sewer inlet*) sumidero *m*; (*strength*) pérdida *f*. *v* desaguar; (*drink empty*) vaciar; (*marshes*) desecar; (*strength*) agotar. **drainage** *n* desagüe *m*; desecación *f*. **drawing board** escurridero *m*. **drainpipe** *n* tubo de desagüe *m*.

drama ['draɪmə] *n* drama *m*. **dramatic** *adj* dramático. **dramatics** *n pl* teatro *m*. **dramatist** *n* dramaturgo, -a *m*, *f*. **dramatize** *v* adaptar al teatro.

drape [dreip] *v* cubrir con ropa, adornar con colgaduras. *n* colgadura *f*. **draper** *n* pañero, -a *m*, *f*. **drapery** *n* telas *f pl*.

drastic ['drastik] *adj* drástico.

draught [draɪft] *n* (*air*) corriente de aire *f*; (*plan*) bosquejo *m*; (*drink*) trago *m*. *adj* (*animals*) de tiro. **draughtboard** *n* tablero de damas *m*. **draughtsman** *n* delineante *m*. **draughtsmanship** *n* dibujo lineal *m*.

*draw [droɪ] *n* (*sport*) empate *m*; (*lots*) sorteo *m*; (*lottery*) lotería *f*. *v* (*pull*) tirar de; (*extract*) extraer; (*attract*) atraer; (*art*) dibujar; (*a line*) trazar; (*nail, water, confession, profits, etc.*) sacar; (*comparisons*) hacer; (*breath*) tomar; (*earn*) cobrar; (*cheque*) librar; (*prize*) ganar; sortear; (*close curtains*) descorrer; (*blinds*) bajar; (*cards*) robar. **draw attention** llamar la atención. **draw up** (*document*) redactar a.

drawback ['droɪbak] *n* (*disadvantage*) desventaja *f*; (*shortcoming*) inconveniente *m*.

drawer ['droɪə] *n* (*container*) cajón *m*; (*art*) dibujante *m*, *f*.

drawing ['droɪiŋ] *n* (*art*) dibujo *m*; (*extraction*) extracción *f*. **drawing board** tablero de dibujo *m*. **drawing pin** chincheta *f*. **drawing room** salón *m*.

drawl [droɪl] *n* voz lenta *f*. *v* arrastrar las palabras.

drawn [droɪn] *adj* (*weary*) cansado. **drawn to** atraído por.

dread [dred] *n* miedo; terror. *v* temer.
dreadful *adj* terrible; espantoso.
*dream [driːm] *v* soñar; imaginarse. *n* sueño *m*. **bad dream** pesadilla *f*. **daydream** *n* ensueño *m*. **dream up** inventar.
dreary ['driəri] *adj* triote; monótono; (*boring*) aburrido. **dreariness** *n* tristeza *f*; monotonía *f*.
dredge [dredʒ] *v* dragar. *n* draga *f*.
dregs [dregz] *n pl* heces *f pl*.
drench [drentʃ] *v* empapar, mojar. **drenched to the skin** estar mojada hasta los huesos.
dress [dres] *n* (*frock*) vestido *m*; (*clothing*) ropa; (*evening dress: men*) traje de etiqueta *m*, (*women*) traje de noche *m*; (*wedding*) traje de novia *m*. *v* vestir. **dress up** poner de tiros largos. **dress up as** disfrazarse de.
dress circle *n* piso principal *m*.
dress coat *n* frac *m*.
dress designer *n* modelista *m, f*.
dresser ['dresə] *n* aparador *m*.
dressing ['dresiŋ] *n* (*act*) vestir *m*; (*clothes*) ropa *f*; (*med*) vendaje *m*; (*cookery*) aliño *m*; (*agriculture*) abono *m*. **dressing gown** bata *f*.
dressmaker ['dresmeikə] *n* modista *m, f*. **dressmaking** *n* costura *f*.
dress rehearsal *n* ensayo general *m*.
dress shirt *n* camisa de frac *f*.
dressy ['dresi] *adj* elegante.
dribble ['dribl] *n* goteo *m*. *v* gotear.
drier ['draiə] *n* secador *m*; (*for clothes*) secadora *f*.
drift [drift] *n* arrastramiento *m*; (*snow*) ventisquero *m*; (*sand*) montón *m*; (*naut, aero*) deriva *f*. *v* ser arrastrado; amontonarse; derivar; (*fig*) vivir sin rumbo. **drift along** vagar. **drifter** *n* (*vagrant*) vagabundo *m*; (*boat*) trainera *f*.
drill [dril] *n* (*tech*) taladro *m*; (*dental*) fresa *f*; (*mil*) instrucción *f*. *v* (*mil*) ejercitar; (*bore*) taladrar, perforar. **drilling** *n* instruccion *f*; perforación *f*.
*drink [driŋk] *v* beber; tomar; (*toast*) brindar por. **drink down** beber de um trago. **drink in** beberse. **drink up** bebérselo todo. *n* bebida *f*; (*alcoholic*) copa; (*water, milk*) vaso *m*; algo de beber. **soft drink** bebida no alcohólica *f*. **have a drink** tomar algo.
drinkable ['driŋkəbl] *adj* potable.
drinker ['driŋkə] *n* bebedor, -a *m, f*.

drinking ['driŋkiŋ] *n* beber *m*; bebida *f*. **drinking fountain** fuente de agua potable *f*. **drinking water** agua potable *f*.
drip [drip] *n* goteo *m*; (*drop*) gota *f*. *v* gotear. **drip-dry** *adj* de lava y pon.
*drive [draiv] *v* (*push onwards*) empujar; (*control a vehicle*) conducir; (*carry in a vehicle*) llevar; (*some distance*) recorrer; (*force someone out*) echar; (*compel*) obligar. **drive at** (*physically*) dirigirse hacia; (*fig*) insinuar. **drive away** irse; alejar. **drive by** passar (por). **drive in** entrar; clavar. **drive into** chocar contra. **drive on** seguir su camino. **drive up** llegar. *n* paseo *m*; excursión *f*; (*journey*) viaje *m*; (*fig*) vigor *m*; (*mil*) ofensiva *f*; (*tennis, golf*) drive *m*; (*mot*) tracción *f*; transmisión *f*; propulsión *f*; (*instinct*) instinto *m*. **driver** *n* conductor, -a *m, f*; chófer *m*; (*taxi*) taxista *m, f*; (*train*) maquinista *m*. **driveway** *n* camino de entrada *m*.
drivel ['drivl] *n* tonterías *f pl*. *v* decir tonterías.
driving ['draiviŋ] *n* conducción *f*. **driving licence** carnet de conducir *m*. **driving school** autoescuela *f*. **driving test** examen para sacar el carnet de conducir *m*.
drizzle ['drizl] *n* llovizna *f*. *v* lloviznar.
drone [droun] *n* (*noise*) zumbido *m*; (*voices*) murmullo *m*; (*bee*) zángano *m*; (*aero*) teledirigido *m*. *v* zumbar; murmurar.
droop [druːp] *n* (*shoulders*) encorvamiento *m*; (*head*) inclinación *f*. *v* estar encorvado; inclinarse; (*flowers*) marchitarse; (*eyelids*) caerse; (*fig*) desanimarse; debilitarse.
drop [drop] *n* gota *f*; (*sweet*) pastilla *f*; (*bit*) pizca *f*; (*fall*) caida *f*; (*in value*) disminución *f*; (*in prices*) baja *f*; (*in temperature*) descenso *m*. *v* (*release*) soltar; (*let fall*) dejar caer; (*tears*) derramar; (*a friend*) dejar; (*prices, eyes, voice*) bajar; (*give up a habit*) dejar de; (*leave behind*) despegarse de. **drop behind** quedarse atrás. **drop dead** caerse muerto. **drop in on** pasar por casa de. **drop off** dormirse.
dropout ['dropaut] *n* abandono *m*; marginado, -a *m, f*.
dropsy ['dropsi] *n* hidropesía *f*.
drought [draut] *n* sequia *f*.
drown [draun] *v* ahogar.
drowsy ['drauzi] *adj* soñoliento. **be drowsy** tener sueño. **drowse** *v* dormitar.

dwindle

drudge [drʌdʒ] *n* esclavo *m*. *v* currelar.
drudgery *n* trabajo penoso *m*.
drug [drʌg] *n* droga *f*; medicamento *m*. *v* drogar. **drug addict** drogadicto, -a *m, f*. **drug addiction** toxicomanía *f*.
drum [drʌm] *n* (*music*) tambor *m*; (*container*) bidón *m*; (*ear*) timpano *m*. *v* tocar el tambor; (*fingers*) tamborilear. **drummer** *n* tambor *m*; batería *f*. **drumstick** *n* palillo de tambor *m*.
drunk [drʌŋk] *adj* borracho; (*fig*) ebrio. **get drunk** emborracharse. **drunkard** *n* borracho, -a *m, f*. **drunkenness** *n* embriaguez *f*.
dry [drai] *adj* seco; (*measure*) para áridos; (*boring*) aburrido; (*thirsty*) sediento; (*wit*) agudo; (*subject*) árido. *v* secar. **dry-clean** *v* limpiar en seco. **dry cleaner** tintorero, -a *m, f*.
dual ['djuəl] *adj* doble. **dual carriageway** pista doble *f*. **dual-purpose** *adj* de dos usos.
dubbed ['dʌbd] *adj* (*named*) apodado; (*knighted*) armado; (*film*) doblado. *v* apodar; armar; doblar.
dubious ['djuːbiəs] *adj* dudoso; ambiguo; indeciso; discutible; sospechoso.
duchess ['dʌtʃis] *n* duquesa *f*.
duck[1] [dʌk] *n* (*bird*) pata *f*; (*drake*) pato *m*; (*dodging*) esquiva *f*; (*in water*) zambullida *f*.
duck[2] [dʌk] *v* (*crouch*) agachar; zambullir.
duckling ['dʌkliŋ] *n* patito *m*.
duct [dʌkt] *n* (*anat*) canal *m*; (*gas*) conducto *m*; (*elec*) tubo *m*.
dud [dʌd] *n* (*coll*) desastre *m*; (*mil*) projectil fallido *m*. *adj* falso; inútil; defectuoso; (*cheque*) sin fondos.
due [djuː] *adj* (*care, time*) debido; (*payable*) pagadero. **due date** vencimiento *m*. **be due** to deberse a. *n* merecido *m*. *adv* derecho hacia. **dues** *pl n* derechos *m pl*.
duly *adv* debidamente; a su debido tiempo.
duel ['djuəl] *n* duelo *m*. *v* batirse en duelo. **duellist** *n* duelista *f*.
duet [djuˈet] *n* dúo *m*.
duke [djuːk] *n* duque *m*.
dull [dʌl] *adj* monótono; (*obtuse*) torpe; (*slow*) tardo; (*tedious*) pesado; (*colour*) apagado; (*surface*) mate; (*weather*) gris; (*sullen*) sombrío; (*blunt*) embotado. *v* (*emotions*) enfriarse; (*pain*) aliviar; (*sound*) apagar. **dullness** *n* monotonía *f*;

torpeza *f*; pesadez *f*. **dully** *adv* torpemente; lentamente.
dumb [dʌm] *adj* mudo; (*coll*) estúpido. **dumbbell** *n* pesa *f*. **dumbfound** *v* dejar sin habla. **dumbfounded** *adj* confuso, atónito. **dumbwaiter** *n* carrito *m*.
dummy ['dʌmi] *n* (*teat*) chupete *m*; (*tailor's*) maniquí *m*; (*puppet*) muñeco *m*; (*cards*) muerto *m*; (*coll*) lobo. -a *m, f*. *adj* ficticio, falso. *v* (*sport*) fintar.
dump [dʌmp] *n* (*rubbish dump*) depósito de basura *m*; (*heap*) montón *m*; (*scrapheap*) vertedero *m*; (*coll: wretched place*) tugurio *m*. *v* (*throw away*) tirar; (*get rid of*) deshacerse de; (*unload*) descargar. **dumping** *n* descarga *f*. **dumpy** *adj* regordete.
dumpling ['dʌmpliŋ] *n* masa hervida *f*.
dunce [dʌns] *n* tonto *m*, burro *m*.
dune [djuːn] *n* duna *f*.
dung [dʌŋ] *n* excrementos *m pl*; (*manure*) estiércol *m*.
dungarees [ˌdʌŋgəˈriːz] *n pl* mono *m sing*.
dungeon ['dʌndʒən] *n* calabozo *m*, mazmorra *f*.
duplicate ['djuːplikət; *v* 'djuːplikeit] *n* copia *f*, doble *m*, duplicado *m*. *adj* duplicado. *v* duplicar; multicopiar. **duplicating machine** multicopista *f*. **duplication** *n* duplicación *f*; copia *f*.
durable ['djuərəbl] *adj* duradero. **durability** *n* durabilidad *f*.
duration [djuˈreiʃən] *n* duración *f*.
during ['djuriŋ] *prep* durante.
dusk [dʌsk] *n* crepúsculo *m*. **dusky** *adj* oscuro; (*complexion*) moreno.
dust [dʌst] *n* polvo *m*. *v* (*clean*) limpiar el polvo; (*powder*) espolvorear. **dustbin** *n* cajón de basura *m*. **duster** (*cloth*) trapo *m*; (*feather*) plumero *m*. **dustman** *n* basurero *m*. **dustpan** *n* recogedor *m*. **dusty** *adj* polvoriento; cubierto de polvo.
duty ['djuːti] *n* deber *m*, obligación *f*; (*tax*) impuesto *m*. (*at customs*) derechos de aduana *m pl*. **off duty** estar libre. **on duty** de servicio. **dutiful** *adj* obediente; deferente. **duty-free** *adj* libre de derechos de aduana.
duvet ['duːvei] *n* colcha de plumón *f*.
dwarf [dwɔːf] *n, adj* enano, -a. *v* achicar.
*dwell [dwel] *v* vivir. **dwell on** (*emphasize*) insistir en; (*a subject*) extenderse en. **dwelling** *n* vivienda *f*.
dwindle ['dwindl] *v* disminuir, menguar.

dye [dai] *n* (*colouring substance*) tinte *m*; (*colour*) fast dye color sólido *m*. *v* teñir.

dyke [daik] *n* (*ditch*) zanja *f*; (*bank*) dique *m*.

dynamic [dai'namik] *adj* dinámico.

dynamite ['dainǝ,mait] *n* dinamita *f*. *v* dinamitar.

dynamo ['dainǝ,mou] *n* dínamo *f*.

dynasty ['dinǝsti] *n* dinastía *f*. **dynastic** *adj* dinástico.

dysentery ['disǝntri] *n* disentería *f*.

dyslexia [dis'leksiǝ] *n* dislexia *f*.

dyspepsia [dis'pepsiǝ] *n* dispepsia *f*. **dyspeptic** *adj* dispéptico.

E

each [iitʃ] *adj* cada. *pron* cada uno, cada una. **each other** el uno al otro.

eager ['iigǝ] *adj* ávido; ansioso; impaciente. **eagerness** *n* ansia *f*; impaciencia *f*.

eagle ['iigl] *n* águila *f*. **eagle-eyed** *adj* tener ojos de lince.

ear[1] [iǝ] *n* oreja *f*; (*fig*) oído *m*. **earache** dolor de oído *m*. **eardrum** *n* tímpano *m*. **earmark** *v* reservar; destinar. **earring** *n* pendiente *m*; **earshot** *n* alcance del oído *m*.

ear[2] [iǝ] *n* (*grain*) espiga *f*.

earl [ǝil] *n* conde *m*.

early ['ǝili] *adv* temprano; pronto; al principio. *adj* temprano; próximo; pronto.

earn [ǝin] *v* ganar; merecer. **earnings** *pl n* (*income*) ingresos *m pl*; (*salary*) sueldo *m sing*.

earnest ['ǝinist] *adj* sincero; aplicado; serio. **in earnest** en serio.

earth [ǝiθ] *n* tierra *f*. **earthenware** *n* alfarería *f*.

earwig ['iǝwig] *n* tijereta *f*.

ease [iiz] *n* facilidad *f*; naturalidad *f*; (*comfort*) comodidad *f*; (*from pain*) alivio *m*. *v* facilitar; aliviar; tranquilizar; (*tension*) relajar.

easel ['iizl] *n* caballete *m*.

east [iist] *n* este *m*. *adj also* **easterly**, **eastern** oriental; del este; *adv* al este, hacia el este. **eastward** *adj*, *adv* hacia el este.

Easter ['iistǝ] *n* Pascua de Resurrección *f*. **Easter egg** huevo de Pascua *m*.

easy ['iizi] *adj* fácil. **easy chair** sillón *m*. **easy-going** *adj* acomodadizo; indolente. **take it easy!** ¡tómatelo con calma! **easiness** *n* facilidad *f*.

*eat [iit] *v* comer. **eat up** comerse. **eatable** *adj also* **edible** comestible.

eavesdrop ['iivzdrop] *v* fisgonear. **eavesdropper** *n* fisgón, -era *m*, *f*.

ebb [eb] *n* reflujo *m*, menguante *m*. *v* menguar; decaer. **ebb tide** marea menguante *f*.

ebony ['ebǝni] *n* ébano *m*.

eccentric [ik'sentrik] *n*, *adj* excéntrico, -a. **eccentricity** *n* excentricidad *f*.

ecclesiastical [iklizzi'astikl] *adj also* **ecclesiastic** eclesiástico.

echo ['ekou] *n* eco *m*; resonancia *f*; repetición *f*. *v* resonar; repetir; imitar.

eclair [ei'kleǝ] *n* relámpago *m*.

eclipse [i'klips] *n* eclipse *m*. *v* eclipsar.

ecology [i'kolǝdʒi] *n* ecología *f*. **ecological** *adj* ecológico. **ecologist** *n* ecólogo *m*.

economy [i'konǝmi] *n* economía *f*. **economic** *adj also* **economical** económico. **economics** *n* economía *f*. **economist** *n* economista *m*, *f*. **economize** *v* economizar.

ecstasy ['ekstǝsi] *n* éxtasis *m*. **ecstatic** *adj* extático. **go into ecstasies over** extasiarse ante.

Ecuador ['ekwǝdoi] *n* Ecuador *m*. **Ecuadoran**, **Ecuadorean**, *or* **Ecuadorian** *n*, *adj* ecuatoriano, -a.

eczema ['eksimǝ] *n* eczema *m*.

edge [edʒ] *n* borde *m*; (*blade*) filo *m*, corte *m*. **have the edge on** llevar ventaja a. **be on edge** tener los nervios de punta. *v* bordear; mover poco a poco. **edging** *n* (*sewing*) orla *f*; (*path*) borde *m*. **edgy** *adj* nervioso.

edible ['edǝbl] *adj* comestible.

Edinburgh ['edinbǝrǝ] *n* Edimburgo *m*.

edit ['edit] *v* (*text*) redactar; (*film*) montar; (*direct a paper*, *magazine*) dirigir. **editor** *n* radactor *m*; director *m*. **editorial** *n* editorial *m*; artículo de fondo *m*. **editorial staff** redacción *f*.

edition [i'diʃǝn] *n* edición *f*; tirada *f*.

educate ['edju,keit] *v* educar. **educated** *adj* culto. **education** *n* educación *f*; (*teaching*) enseñanza *f*; (*specific*) instrucción *f*. **educational** *adj* educativo; (*teaching*) docente.

eel [iːl] *n* anguila *f.*

eerie ['iəri] *adj* misterioso; espantoso.

effect [i'fekt] *n* efecto *m*; resultado *m*; impresión *f*; (*meaning*) significado *m*. **side effect** efecto secundario. **take effect** (*drugs, etc.*) surtir efecto; (*law, etc.*) tener efecto. *v* efectuar. **effective** *adj* (*efficient*) eficaz; (*real*) efectivo; (*in force*) vigente. **effectiveness** *n* eficacia *f*; efecto *m*; vigencia *f.*

effeminate [i'feminət] *adj* afeminado.

effervescent [‚efə'vesənt] *adj* efervescente. **effervesce** *v* estar en efervescencia.

efficient [i'fiʃənt] *adj* eficaz, eficiente. **efficiency** *n* eficacia *f*, eficiencia *f.*

effigy ['efidʒi] *n* efigie *f.*

effort ['efət] *n* esfuenzo *m*. **effortless** *adj* sin esfuerzo.

egg [eg] *n* huevo *m*. **bad egg** huevo podrido. **boiled egg** huevo pasado por agua. **hard-boiled egg** huevo duro. **new-laid egg** huevo fresco. **poached egg** huevo escalfado. **scrambled eggs** huevos revueltos *m pl*. **eggcup** *n* huevera *f.* **egg-shaped** *adj* oviforme. **eggshell** *n* cascarón de huevo *m*. **egg on** incitar.

egotism ['egətizm] *n* egotismo *m*. **egotist** *n* (*self-important person*) egotista *m, f*; (*selfish person*) egoísta *m, f.*

Egypt ['iːdʒipt] *n* Egipto *m*. **Egyptian** *n, adj* egipcio, -a.

eiderdown ['aidədaun] *n* edredón *m.*

eight [eit] *nm, adj* ocho. **eighth** *n, adj* octavo, -a.

eighteen [ei'tiːn] *nm, adj* dieciocho. **eighteenth** *n, adj* decimoctavo, -a.

eighty ['eiti] *nm, adj* ochenta. **eightieth** *n, adj* octogésimo, -a.

either ['aiðə] *adj* cada, ambos. *pron* uno u otro; cualquiera de los dos. *adv* tampoco. *conj* o. **either ... or ...** o ... o....

ejaculate [i'dʒakjuleit] *v* exclamar; (*med*) eyacular. **ejaculation** *n* exclamación *f*; eyaculación *f.*

eject [i'dʒekt] *v* expulsar; echar; (*tenant*) desahuciar. **ejection** *n* expulsión *f*; desahucio *m*. **ejector seat** asiento eyectable *m.*

eke [iːk] *v* **eke out** (*add to*) complementar; (*make last*) escatimar.

elaborate [i'labərət; *v* i'labəreit] *adj* complicado; detallado. *v* elaborar. **elaborate**

on ampliar. **elaborately** *adv* cuidadosamente; complicadamente; detalladamente. **elaboration** *n* elaboración *f*; explicación *f*; complicación *f.*

elapse [i'laps] *v* transcurrir.

elastic [i'lastik] *nm, adj* elástico. **elastic band** goma elástica *f*. **elasticity** *n* elasticidad *f.*

elated [i'leitid] *adj* jubiloso; exaltado. **elation** *n* júbilo *m*; exaltación *f.*

elbow ['elbou] *n* codo *m*. **elbow grease** fuerza de puños *f*. **elbow room** espacio suficiente *m.*

elder[1] ['eldə] *nm, adj* mayor. **elderly** *adj* mayor de edad. **eldest** *adj* mayor.

elder[2] ['eldə] *n* (*bot*) saúco *m*. **elderberry** *n* baya del saúco.

elect [i'lekt] *v* elegir. *adj* elegido. **election** *n* elección *f*. **electoral** *adj* electoral. **electorate** *n* electorado *m.*

electric [ə'lektrik] *adj also* **electrical** eléctrico. **electric blanket** manta eléctrica *f*. **electric fire** estufa eléctrica *f*. **electric shock** electrochoque *m*. **electrician** *n* electricista *m, f*. **electricity** *n* electricidad *f*. **electrify** *v* (*rail, industry*) electrificar; (*produce electricity*) electrizar; (*fig*) entusiasmar.

electrocute [i'lektrəkjuːt] *v* electrocutar. **electrocution** *n* electrocución *f.*

electrode [i'lektroud] *n* electrodo *m.*

electronic [elək'tronik] *adj* electrónico. **electronics** *n* electrónica *f.*

elegant ['eligənt] *adj* elegante; bello. **elegance** *n* elegancia *f.*

elegy ['elidʒi] *n* elegía *f.*

element ['eləmənt] *n* elemento *m*; factor *m*. **elementary** *adj* elemental; fundamental.

elephant ['elifənt] *n* elefante *m.*

elevate ['eliveit] *v* elevar; (*voice, eyes*) levantar; (*honour*) enaltecer. **elevation** *n* elevación *f*; (*hill*) altura *f*; (*thought*) nobleza *f.*

elevator ['eliveitor] *n* ascensor *m.*

eleven [i'levn] *nm, adj* once. **eleventh** *n* undécimo, -a *m, f*; *adj* onceavo.

elf [elf] *n* duende *m.*

eligible ['elidʒəbl] *adj* elegible; atractivo.

eliminate [i'limineit] *v* eliminar. **elimination** *n* eliminación *f.*

elite [ei'liːt] *n* élite *f.*

ellipse [i'lips] *n* elipse *f*. **elliptical** *adj* elíptico.

elm [elm] *n* olmo *m.*

elocution [elǝ'kjuːʃǝn] *n* elocución *f*; declamación *f*.

elope [i'loup] *v* fugarse. **elopement** *n* fuga *f*.

eloquent ['elǝkwǝnt] *adj* elocuente. **eloquence** *n* elocuencia *f*.

else [els] *adv* más, de otra manera. **or else** si no. **elsewhere** *adv* otro sitio.

elude [i'luːd] *v* eludir, escapar; (*a blow*) evitar. **elusive** *adj* escurridizo.

emaciated [i'meiʃieitid] *adj* demacrado. **emaciation** *n* demacración *f*.

emanate ['emǝneit] *v* emanar. **emanation** *n* emanación *f*.

emancipate [i'mansipeit] *v* emancipar. **emancipation** *n* emancipación *f*.

embalm [im'baːm] *v* embalsamar.

embankment [im'baŋkmǝnt] *n* (*road, rail*) terraplén *m*; (*river*) dique *m*.

embargo [im'baːgou] *n* prohibición *f*.

embark [im'baːk] *v* embarcar. **embark on** emprender. **embarkation** *n* (*people*) embarco *m*; (*cargo*) embarque *m*.

embarrass [im'barǝs] *v* desconcertar; molestar. **embarrassment** *n* desconcierto *m*; molestia *f*. **financial embarrassment** apuros de dinero *m pl*.

embassy ['embǝsi] *n* embajada *f*.

embellish [im'beliʃ] *v* embellecer; adornar. **embellishment** *n* embellicimiento *m*; adorno *m*.

ember ['embǝ] *n* ascua *f*.

embezzle [im'bezl] *v* malversar. **embezzlement** *n* malversación *f*. **embezzler** *n* malversador, -a *m*, *f*.

embitter [im'bitǝ] *v* (*person*) amargar. **embittered** *adj* amargado; rencoroso.

emblem ['emblǝm] *n* emblema *m*. **emblematic** *adj* emblemático.

embody [im'bodi] *v* personificar; materializar; incluir. **embodiment** *n* personificación *f*; incorporación *f*.

emboss [im'bos] *v* grabar en relieve; (*paper*) gofrar; (*leather, silver*) repujar. **embossed** *adj* (*letterhead*) gofrado.

embrace [im'breis] *v* abrazar; (*encompass*) abarcar; (*opportunity*) aprovecharse de. *n* abrazo *m*.

embroider [im'broidǝ] *v* bordar; (*fig*) adornar. **embroidery** *n* bordado *m*; adorno *m*.

embryo ['embriou] *n* embrión *m*. **in embryo** en embrión. **embryonic** *adj* embrionario.

emerald ['emǝrǝld] *n* esmeralda *f*.

emerge [i'mǝːdʒ] *v* salir; sacarse. **emergence** *n* salida *f*.

emergency [i'mǝːdʒǝnsi] *n* emergencia *f*; (*med*) urgencia *f*. **emergency exit** salida de emergencia *f*. **emergency landing** aterrizaje forzoso *m*. **in case of emergency** en caso de emergencia.

emigrate ['emigreit] *v* emigrar. **emigrant** (*m+f*), *adj* emigrante. **emigration** *n* emigración *f*.

eminent ['eminǝnt] *adj* eminente. **eminence** *n* eminencia *f*.

emit [i'mit] *v* (*light, sound*) emitir; (*cry*) dar; (*heat*) desprender; (*smoke*) echar; (*smell*) despedir. **emission** *n* emisión *f*.

emotion [i'mouʃǝn] *n* emoción *f*. **emotional** *adj* (*concerning the emotions*) emocional; (*occasion, person*) emotivo. **emotionally** *adv* con emoción.

empathy ['empǝθi] *n* empatía *f*.

emperor ['empǝrǝ] *n* emperador *m*. **empress** *n* emperatriz *f*.

emphasis ['emfǝsis] *n*, *pl* -ses (*fig*) énfasis *m*; importancia *f*; (*stress*) acento *m*. **emphasize** *v* subrayar; (*stress*) acentuar. **emphatic** *adj* enfático; enérgico; categórico.

empire ['empaiǝ] *n* imperio *m*.

empirical [im'pirikǝl] *adj* empírico. **empiricism** *n* empirismo *m*.

employ [im'ploi] *v* emplear. *n* also **employment** empleo *m*. **employee** *n* empleado, -a *m*, *f*. **employer** *n* empresario, -a *m*, *f*; empleador, -a *m*, *f*. **employment agency** agencia de colocaciones *f*.

empower [im'pauǝ] *v* autorizar, habilitar.

empty ['empti] *adj* vacío; vacante; desocupado; desierto. **empty-handed** *adj* con las manos vacías. **empty-headed** *adj* casquivano. *v* vaciar; (*river*) desaguar. **emptiness** *n* vacío *m*; vacuidad *f*.

emu ['iːmjuː] *n* emú *m*.

emulate ['emjuːleit] *v* emular. **emulation** *n* emulación *f*.

emulsion [i'mʌlʃǝn] *n* emulsión *f*. **emulsify** *v* emulsionar.

enable [i'neibl] *v* permitir; capacitar.

enact [i'nakt] *v* (*represent*) representar; (*a law*) promulgar; (*decree*) decretar; (*do*) hacer. **enactment** *n* promulgación *f*; decreto *m*.

enamel [i'namǝl] *n* esmalte *m*. *v* esmaltar.

enamour [i'namə] v enamorar. **be enamoured of** estar enamorado de.

encase [in'keis] v (enclose) encerrar; (box) encajonar.

enchant [in'tʃaɪnt] v encantar. **enchanter** n (magician) hechicero m; encanto m. **enchanting** adj encantador. **enchantment** n (charm) encanto m; (magic) hechizo m. **enchantress** n hechicera f; encanto m.

encircle [in'sɜːkl] v cercar, rodear.

enclose [in'klouz] v (shut in) encerrar; (surround) rodear; (in a letter) adjuntar. **enclosed** adj adjunto. **enclosure** n encierro m; carta adjunta f.

encore ['oŋkɔɪ] interj ¡bis! ¡otra vez! n repetición f. v pedir la repetición; repetir.

encounter [in'kauntə] v encontrarse con; enfrentarse a. n encuentro m.

encourage [in'kʌridʒ] v animar, alentar; estimular; incitar. **encouragement** n ánimo m, aliento m; estimulación f; incitación f. **encouraging** adj alentador; prometedor.

encroach [in'kroutʃ] v invadir; usurpar. **encroachment** n invasión f; usurpación f.

encumber [in'kʌmbə] v (humper) estorbar; (load) cargar; (block) obstruir. **encumbrance** n estorbo m; obstáculo m.

encyclopaedia [insaiklə'piːdiə] n enciclopedia f.

end [end] n (tip) punta f; (tail end) cabo m; (finish) fin m, final m. **end product** (comm) producto final m; (result) resultado m. **make ends meet** pasar con lo que se tiene. v acabar, terminar. **ending** n fin m, final m. **endless** adj interminable.

endanger [in'deindʒə] v arriesgar, poner en peligro.

endeavour [in'devə] n esfuerzo m, empeño m. v esforzarse, procurar.

endemic [en'demik] adj endémico.

endive ['endiv] n escarola f, endibia f.

endorse [in'dɔɪs] v (cheque, etc.) endosar; (approve) aprobar. **endorsement** n endoso m; aprobación f; (mot) nota de inhabilitación f.

endow [in'dau] v dotar; (prize, etc.) fundar. **endowment** n dotación f; fundación f.

endure [in'djuə] v (support) aguantar; (last) durar. **endurable** adj soportable. **endurance** n aguante m; resistencia f. **enduring** adj resistente; duradero.

enemy ['enəmi] n enemigo, -a m, f.

energy ['enədʒi] n energía f. **energetic** adj enérgico.

enfold [in'fould] v envolver; abrazar.

enforce [in'fɔɪs] v (discipline) imponer; (law) hacer cumplir.

engage [in'geidʒ] v (employ) ajustar; (pledge) comprometer; (attention) llamar; (keep busy) ocupar; (clutch) embragar. **engaged** adj prometido; ocupado. **get engaged** comprometerse. **engagement** n compromiso m; (appointment) cita f; (encounter) encuentro m. **engagement ring** sortija de pedida f.

engine ['endʒin] n motor m; máquina f. **engine driver** maquinista m. **engine room** sala de máquinas f.

engineer [endʒi'niə] n ingeniero m; (workman) mecánico m. **engineering** n ingeniería f.

England ['iŋɡlənd] n Inglaterra f. **English** nm, adj inglés. **the English** los ingleses.

English Channel n Canal de la Mancha m.

engrave [in'greiv] v grabar. **engraver** n grabador, -a m, f. **engraving** n grabado m.

engross [in'grous] v absorber. **engrossing** adj absorbente.

engulf [in'gʌlf] v tragarse; (sink) hundir.

enhance [in'hains] v (prices, etc.) aumentar; (beauty) realzar. **enhancement** n aumento m; realce m.

enigma [i'nigmə] n enigma m. **enigmatic** adj enigmático.

enjoy [in'dʒoi] v (like) gustar; (delight in, have the use of) gozar de, disfrutar de; (party) divertirse en. **enjoyable** adj agradable; divertido. **enjoyment** n placer m; diversión f.

enlarge [in'laidʒ] v ampliar, agrandar; (expand) extender. **enlargement** n aumento m; extensión f; (phot) ampliación f. **enlarger** n (phot) ampliadora f.

enlighten [in'laitn] v iluminar; (inform) informar; aclarar. **enlightenment** n aclaración f.

enlist [in'list] v alistar; alistarse; (obtain support) conseguir. **enlistment** n alistamiento m.

enmity ['enmɒti] n enemistad f.

enormous [i'nɔɪməs] adj enorme. **enormity** n enormidad f. **enormously** adv enormemente.

enough [i'nʌf] *adj, adv* bastante. *n* lo bastante. **enough is enough** basta y sobra. **curiously enough** por extraño que parezca. **sure enough** más que seguro. **that's enough** con eso basta.

enquire [in'kwaiə] *V* **inquire**.

enrage [in'reidʒ] *v* enfurecer.

enrich [in'ritʃ] *v* enriquecer; (*soil*) fertilizar. **enrichment** *n* enriquecimiento *m*; fertilización *f*.

enrol [in'roul] *v* inscribir; registrar; matricular; (*mil*) alistar. **enrolment** *n* inscripción *f*; registro *m*; matriculación *f*; alistamiento *m*.

ensign ['ensain] *n* (*flag*) enseña *f*; (*badge*) insignia *f*; (*naut*) bandera de popa *f*.

enslave [in'sleiv] *v* esclavizar. **enslavement** *n* esclavitud *f*.

ensue [in'sjuː] *v* seguir; resultar. **ensuing** *adj* siguiente; resultante.

ensure [in'ʃuə] *v* asegurar.

entail [in'teil] *v* (*involve*) suponer; (*follow as a result of*) acarrear; (*law*) vincular. **entailment** *n* vinculación *f*.

entangle [in'taŋgl] *v* enredar; complicar. **entanglement** *n* enredo *m*; (*fig*) lio *m*.

enter ['entə] *v* entrar en; penetrar; meterse en; registrar; matricular; presentar. **enter for** tomar parte en. **enter into** empezar; establecer; comprender.

enterprise ['entəpraiz] *n* empresa *f*; iniciativa *f*. **enterprising** *adj* emprendedor.

entertain [,entə'tein] *v* (*host*) recibir; (*amuse*) divertir; (*ideas*) abrigar. **entertainer** *n* artista *m*, *f*. **entertaining** *adj* divertido, entretenido. **entertainment** *n* entretenimiento *m*.

enthral [in'θroːl] *v* encantar. **enthralling** *adj* cautivador.

enthusiasm [in'θuːziˌazəm] *n* entusiasmo *m*. **enthusiast** *n* entusiasta *m*, *f*. **enthusiastic** *adj* (*person*) entusiasta; (*praise*, *etc.*) entusiástico.

entice [in'tais] *v* tentar, seducir. **enticing** *adj* tentador; atractivo. **enticement** *n* atracción *f*; seducción *f*.

entire [in'taiə] *adj* entero, completo. **entirety** *n* totalidad *f*.

entitle [in'taitl] *v* (*authorize*) dar derecho a; (*written work*) titular. **be entitled** tener derecho.

entity ['entəti] *n* entidad *f*, ente *m*.

entrails ['entreilz] *pl n* entrañas *f pl*.

entrance¹ ['entrəns] *n* entrada *f*; ingreso *m*. **entrance examination** examen de ingreso *m*. **entrance hall** vestíbulo *m*. **tradesmen's entrance** entrada de servicio *f*.

entrance² [in'trains] *v* arrebatar. **entrancing** *adj* encantador.

entrant ['entrənt] *n* participante *m*, *f*.

entreat [in'triːt] *v* suplicar, implorar. **entreaty** *n* súplica *f*, imploración *f*.

entrée ['ontrei] *n* entrada *f*.

entrench [in'trentʃ] *v* atrincherar. **entrenchment** *n* atrincheramiento *m*; (*encroachment*) invasión *f*.

entrepreneur [,ontrəprə'nəi] *n* empresario *m*; intermediario *m*.

entrust [in'trʌst] *v* (*commit*) confiar; (*someone*) encargar.

entry ['entri] *n* (*entrance*) entrada *f*; (*into profession*) ingreso *m*; (*in a book*) anotación *f*; (*book-keeping*) asiento *m*. **no entry** dirección prohibida *f*.

entwine [in'twain] *v* entrelazar.

enunciate [i'nʌnsiˌeit] *v* enunciar. **enunciation** *n* enunciación *f*.

envelop [in'veləp] *v* envolver. **enveloping** *adj* envolvente.

envelope ['envəˌloup] *n* sobre *m*.

environment [in'vaiərənmənt] *n* ambiente *m*. **environmental** *adj* ambiental.

envisage [in'vizidʒ] *v* (*imagine*) imaginarse; (*foresee*) prever.

envoy ['envoi] *n* enviado *m*.

envy ['envi] *n* envidia *f*. *v* envidiar. **enviable** *adj* envidiable. **envious** *adj* envidioso. **enviously** *adv* con envidia.

enzyme ['enzaim] *n* enzima *f*.

epaulet ['epəlet] *n* charretera *f*.

ephemeral [i'femərəl] *adj* efímero.

epic ['epik] *n* poema épica *f*. *adj* épico.

epidemic [epi'demik] *n* epidemia. *adj* epidémico.

epilepsy ['epilepsi] *n* epilepsia *f*. **epileptic** *n*, *adj* epiléptico, -a. **epileptic fit** ataque epiléptico *m*.

Epiphany [i'pifəni] *n* Epifanía *f*.

episcopal [i'piskəpəl] *adj* episcopal.

episode ['episoud] *n* episodio *m*. **episodic** *adj* episódico.

epitaph ['epiˌtaif] *n* epitafio *m*.

epitome [i'pitəmi] *n* epítome *m*; (*fig*) personificación *f*. **epitomize** *v* compendiar; ser la personificación de.

epoch ['iːpok] *n* época *f*.

equable ['ekwəbl] *adj* uniforme; (*calm*) tranquilo.

equal ['iːkwəl] *n* (*m*+*f*), *adj* igual. *v* igualar. **equality** *n* igualdad *f*. **equalize** *v* igualar; (*draw*) empatar.

equanimity [ekwə'niməti] *n* ecuanimidad *f*.

equate [i'kweit] *v* igualar; comparar; poner en ecuación. **equation** *n* ecuación *f*.

equator [i'kweitə] *n* ecuador *m*. **equatorial** *adj* ecuatorial.

equestrian [i'kwestriən] *adj* ecuestre. *n* caballista *m*.

equilateral [iːkwi'latərəl] *n* figura equilátera *f*. *adj* equilátero.

equilibrium [iːkwi'libriəm] *n* equilibrio *m*.

equinox ['ekwinoks] *n* equinoccio *m*. **equinoctial** *adj* equinoccial.

equip [i'kwip] *v* equipar. **equipment** *n* equipo *m*; (*tools*) herramientas *f pl*.

equity ['ekwəti] *n* equidad *f*, justicia *f*.

equivalent [i'kwivələnt] *nm*, *adj* equivalente.

era ['iərə] *n* era *f*.

eradicate [i'radiˌkeit] *v* erradicar. **eradication** *n* erradicación *f*.

erase [i'reiz] *v* borrar. **eraser** *n* goma de borrar. **erasure** *n* borradura *f*.

erect [i'rekt] *adj* erguido. *v* erigir; (*assemble*) montar. **erection** *n* erección *f*; (*building*) construcción *f*; montaje *m*.

ermine ['əːmin] *n* armiño *m*.

erode [i'roud] *v* corroer; (*wear away*) erosionar. **erosion** *n* corrosión *f*; erosión *f*. **erosive** *adj* erosivo.

erotic [i'rotik] *adj* erótico. **eroticism** *n* erotismo *m*.

err [əː] *v* errar, desviarse; (*sin*) pecar. **erring** *adj* extraviado; pecaminoso.

errand ['erənd] *n* recado *m*. **run an errand** hacer un recado. **errand boy** recadero *m*.

erratic [i'ratik] *adj* desigual; errático.

error ['erə] *n* (*mistake*) error *m*; (*wrongdoing*) extravío *m*.

erudite ['erudait] *adj* erudito. **erudition** *n* erudición *f*.

erupt [i'rupt] *v* estar en erupción, salir con fuerza. **eruption** *n* erupción *f*. **eruptive** *adj* eruptivo.

escalate ['eskəleit] *v* intensificar, agravar. **escalation** *n* intensificación *f*. **escalator** *n* escalera mecánica *f*.

escalope ['eskəlop] *n* escalope *m*.

escape [is'keip] *n* (*flight*) fuga *f*; (*liquid*) salida *f*; (*gas*) escape *m*; (*responsibilities*, *etc*.) evasión *f*. **escape hatch** escotilla de salvamento *f*. **fire escape** escalera de incendios *f*. *v* escapar de; evadir; eludir. **escape notice** pasar inadvertido. **escapism** *n* evasión *f*.

escort ['eskoɪt; *v* i'skoɪt] *n* acompañante *m*; (*mil*) escolta *f*. *v* acompañar; (*mil*) escoltar.

esoteric [esə'terik] *adj* esotérico.

especial [i'speʃəl] *adj* especial, particular; excepcional. **especially** *adv* especialmente, sobre todo.

espionage ['espiəˌnaɪʒ] *n* espionaje *m*.

esplanade [ˌesplə'neid] *n* explanada *f*, bulevar *m*, pasco *m*.

essay ['esei] *n* ensayo *m*; composición *f*; (*attempt*) intento *m*. *v* probar; intentar. **essayist** *n* ensayista *m*, *f*.

essence ['esns] *n* esencia *f*. **essential** *adj* esencial, imprescindible; fundamental. *n* lo esencial. **essentials** *pl n* elementos esenciales *m pl*.

establish [i'stabliʃ] *v* establecer. **establishment** *n* establecimiento *m*. **The Establishment** clase dirigente *f*.

estate [i'steit] *n* (*property*) propiedad *f*; (*land*) finca *f*; (*S. Am.*) hacienda *f*; estancia *f*; (*inheritance*) herencia *f*; (*fortune*) fortuna *f*; (*social class*) estado *m*; (*of the deceased*) testamentaría *f*. **estate agency** agencia inmobiliaria *f*. **estate agent** agente inmobiliario *m*. **estate car** furgoneta *f*.

esteem [i'stiːm] *v* estimar, apreciar. *n* estima *f*, aprecio *m*.

estimate ['estimət; *v* 'estiˌmeit] *n* (*valuation*) estimación *f*; (*statement of cost*) presupuesto *m*. *v* estimar; hacer un presupuesto de. **estimation** *n* juicio *m*; (*esteem*) aprecio *m*.

estuary ['estjuəri] *n* estuario *m*.

eternal [i'təːnl] *adj* eterno. **eternity** *n* eternidad *f*.

ether ['iːθə] *n* éter *m*. **ethereal** *adj* etéreo.

ethical ['eθikl] *adj* ético. **ethics** *pl n* ética *f sing*.

ethnic ['eθnik] *adj* étnico.

etiquette ['etiˌket] *n* etiqueta *f*.

etymology [etiˈmolədʒi] *n* etimología *f*. **etymologist** *n* etimólogo, -a *m*, *f*.

Eucharist ['juːkərist] *n* Eucaristía *f*.

eunuch ['juːnək] *n* eunuco *m*.

euphemism ['juːfə‚mizəm] *n* eufemismo *m*. **euphemistic** *adj* eufemístico.
euphoria [ju'fɔːriə] *n* euforia *f*. **euphoric** *adj* eufórico.
Europe ['juərəp] *n* Europa *f*. **European** *n*, *adj* europeo, -a.
European Economic Community (EEC) *n* Comunidad Económica Europea (CEE) *f*.
euthanasia [juːθəˈneiziə] *n* eutanasia *f*.
evacuate [i'vakjuˌeit] *v* evacuar. **evacuation** *n* evacuación *f*. **evacuee** *n* evacuado, -a *m, f*.
evade [i'veid] *v* evadir, eludir. **evasion** *n* evasión *f*. **evasive** evasivo.
evaluate [i'valjuˌeit] *v* evaluar. **evaluation** *n* evaluación *f*.
evangelical [‚iːvanˈdʒelikəl] *adj* evangélico. **evangelist** *n* evangelizador, -a *m, f*.
evaporate [i'vapəˌreit] *v* evaporar; deshidratar. **evaporated milk** leche evaporada *f*. **evaporation** *n* evaporación *f*; deshidratación *f*.
eve [iːv] *n* víspera *f*. **Christmas Eve** Nochebuena *f*. **New Year's Eve** Noche Vieja *f*. **on the eve of** en vísperas de.
even ['iːvən] *adj* (*surface*) uniforme; (*smooth*) suave; (*calm*) ecuánime; (*fair*) justo; (*same level*) a nivel; (*equal*) igual; (*number*) par. **break even** quedar igual. **get even** desquitarse. *adv* siquiera; incluso. **even if** incluso si. **even so** aun así. **even though** aunque. **even-tempered** *adj* sereno. *v* nivelar; igualar. **evenly** *adv* uniformemente; imparcialmente.
evening ['iːvniŋ] *n* tarde *f*; anochecer *m*. **evening class** clase nocturna *f*. **evening dress** (*man*) traje de etiqueta *m*; (*woman*) traje de noche *m*. **good evening!** (*early*) ¡buenas tardes! (*late*) ¡buenas noches!
event [i'vent] *n* (*occurrence*) acontecimiento *m*; (*case*) caso *m*; (*outcome*) consecuencia *f*; (*in a programme*) número *m*; (*sport*) prueba *f*. **in the event of** en caso de. **eventful** *adj* agitado; memorable. **eventual** *adj* final; consiguiente. **eventuality** *n* eventualidad *f*. **eventually** *adv* finalmente; con el tiempo.
ever ['evə] *adv* (*always*) siempre; nunca, jamás. **we hardly ever go out** casi nunca salimos. **not ever** nunca jamás. **ever after** desde (que).
evergreen ['evəɡriːn] *adj* de hoja perenne.

everlasting [‚evəˈlaːstiŋ] *adj* eterno; perpetuo.
every ['evri] *adj* (*all*) todo; (*each*) cada. **everybody** *also* **everyone** *pron* todo el mundo. **everyday** *adj* diario. **every other day** cada dos días. **everything** *pron* todo. **everywhere** *adv* por *also* en todas partes.
evict [i'vikt] *v* desahuciar. **eviction** *n* desahucio *m*.
evidence ['evidəns] *n* evidencia *f*; (*sign*) indicio *m*; (*law: proof*) prueba *f*; (*law: testimony*) testimonio *m*. *v* evidenciar. **give evidence** declarar como testigo. **evident** *adj* evidente, patente.
evil ['iːvl] *adj* malo; perverso; maligno. *n* mal *m*; desgracia *f*. **evildoer** *n* malhechor, -a *m, f*. **evil-minded** *adj* malpensado.
evoke [i'vouk] *v* evocar. **evocation** *n* evocación *f*. **evocative** *adj* evocador.
evolve [i'volv] *v* evolucinar; (*develop*) desarrollarse. **evolution** *n* evolución *f*; desarrollo *m*. **evolutionary** *adj* evolutivo.
ewe [juː] *n* oveja *f*.
exacerbate [ig'zasə‚beit] *v* exacerbar. **exacerbation** *n* exacerbación *f*.
exact [ig'zakt] *adj* exacto. *v* exigir. **exacting** *adj* (*person*) exigente; (*condition*) severo; (*work*) duro. **exactly** *adv* exactamente; precisamente.
exaggerate [ig'zadʒə‚reit] *v* exagerar; acentuar. **exaggerated** *adj* exagerado. **exaggeration** *n* exageración *f*.
exalt [ig'zolt] *v* exaltar, elevar; (*praise*) glorificar. **exaltation** *n* exaltación *f*; (*ecstasy*) arrobamiento. **exalted** *adj* exaltado, eminente.
examine [ig'zamin] *v* examinar; (*search*) reconocer; (*by touch*) analizar; (*law*) interrogar. **examination** examen *m*; (*law*) interrogatorio *m*. **sit an exam** examinarse. **written exam** prueba escrita *f*. **examiner** *n* examinador, -a *m, f*; inspector, -a *m, f*.
example [ig'zaːmpl] *n* ejemplo *m*. **follow someone's example** tomar ejemplo de uno. **for example** por ejemplo. **set an example** dar ejemplo.
exasperate [ig'zaːspə‚reit] *v* exasperar. **exasperation** *n* exasperación *f*.
excavate ['ekskə‚veit] *v* excavar. **excavation** *n* excavación *f*. **excavator** (*person*) excavador *m*; (*tech*) excavadora *f*.
exceed [ik'siːd] *v* exceder. **exceedingly** *adv* sumamente.

excel [ik'sel] v superar, sobresalir. **excellence** n excelencia f. **His Excellency** su Excelencia m. **excellent** adj excelente.

except [ik'sept] prep excepto, salvo, con excepción de. **except for** excepto. v excluir, exceptuar. **exception** n exclusión f; excepción f. **take exception to** ofenderse por. **exceptional** adj excepcional.

excerpt ['eksərpt] n extracto m. v extractar.

excess [ik'ses] n exceso m. adj excedente. **excess fare** suplemento m. **excess luggage** exceso de equipaje also peso m. **excessive** adj excesivo. **excessively** adv excesivamente.

exchange [iks'tʃeindʒ] v (change) cambiar; (interchange) intercambiar; (courtesies) hacerse; (prisoners) canjear; (blows) darse. n cambio m; intercambio m. **exchange control** control de divisas. **exchange rate** tipo de cambio m. **Stock Exchange** bolsa de valores f. **telephone exchange** central telefónica f.

exchequer [iks'tʃekə] n (finances) hacienda f; tesoro público m. **Chancellor of the Exchequer** Ministro de Hacienda m.

excise ['eksaiz] n impuestos sobre el consumo m pl.

excite [ik'sait] v (stimulate) excitar; emocionar; entusiasmar; (irritate) poner nervioso; (urge) incitar; (imagination) despertar; (admiration, etc.) provocar. **get excited** emocionarse; entusiasmarse. **excitement** n excitación f; emoción f; entusiasmo m; agitación f. **exciting** adj excitante; emocionante; apasionante.

exclaim [ik'skleim] v exclamar. **exclamation** n exclamación f. **exclamation mark** punto de admiración m.

exclude [ik'skluːd] v excluir. **exclusion** n exclusión f. **exclusive** adj (policy) exclusivista; (sole) exclusivo; (select) selecto.

excommunicate [ekskə'mjuːniˌkeit] v excomulgar. **excommunication** n excomunión f.

excrete [ik'skriːt] v excretar. **excrement** n excremento m. **excretion** n excreción f.

excruciating [ik'skruːʃieitiŋ] adj (noise) intolerable; (pain) atroz.

excursion [ik'skəːʃən] n excursión f.

excuse [ik'skjuːz] n excusa f, disculpa f. v excusar, disculpar, perdonar; (duty) dispensar de. **excuse me!** ¡perdón! ¡discúlpeme! **excusable** adj excusable, disculpable, perdonable.

execute ['eksiˌkjuːt] v (order, will, criminal) ejecutar; (carry out) llevar a cabo. **execution** n ejecución f; (of order) cumplimiento m. **executioner** n verdugo m.

executive [ig'zekjutiv] adj (power) ejecutivo; (function) dirigente; (ability) de ejecución. n (government branch) poder ejecutivo m; (person) ejecutivo m.

exemplify [ig'zempliˌfai] v ilustrar con ejemplos. **exemplification** n ejemplificación f.

exempt [ig'zempt] adj exento. v exentar, dispensar. **exemption** n exención f.

exercise ['eksəˌsaiz] n ejercicio m; gimnasia f. **exercise book** n cuaderno m. **take exercise** hacer ejercicio. v (rights, etc.) ejercer; (physically) ejercitarse; (patience) usar de.

exert [ig'zəːt] v ejercer. **exert oneself** esforzarse. **exertion** n esfuerzo m; (of strength) empleo m.

exhale [eks'heil] v exhalar; (breathe out) espirar. **exhalation** n exhalación f; espiración f.

exhaust [ig'zoːst] v agotar. n (system) escape m. **exhaust pipe** tubo de escape m. **exhausting** adj agotador. **exhaustion** n agotamiento m. **exhaustive** adj exhaustivo. **exhaustively** adv exhaustivamente.

exhibit [ig'zibit] v (display) mostrar; (paintings, etc.) exponer; (documents) presentar. n objeto expuesto m. **exhibition** n exposición f. **make an exhibition of oneself** ponerse en ridículo. **exhibitor** n expositor m.

exhilarate [ig'ziləˌreit] v alegrar, animar. **exhilarating** adj estimulante. **exhilaration** n alegría f, regocijo m.

exile ['eksail] n exilio m, destierro m; (person) exiliado, -a m, f; desterrado, -a m, f. **go into exile** exiliarse, exilarse. v exiliar, exilar, desterrar.

exist [ig'zist] v existir; (live) vivir. **existence** n existencia f. **existent** also **existing** adj existente; (present) actual. **existentialism** n existencialismo m. **existentialist** n (m+f), adj existencialista.

exit ['egzit] n salida f; (theatre) mutis m. v (theatre) hacer mutio.

exonerate [ig'zonəˌreit] v (from blame)

disculpar; (*from obligation*) dispensar de.
exoneration *n* disculpa *f*; dispensa *f*.
exorbitant [ig'zoːbitənt] *adj* exorbitante.
exorcize ['eksoːsaiz] *v* exorcizar. **exorcism**
n exorcismo *m*. **exorcist** *n* exorcista *m*, *f*.
exotic [ig'zotik] *adj* exótico. **exoticism** *n*
exotismo *m*.
expand [ik'spand] *v* (*cause to increase*)
desarrollar; (*make larger*) dilatar; (*add
to*) ampliar. **expansion** *n* expansión *f*;
desarollo *m*; dilatación *f*; ampliación *f*.
expansive *adj* (*person*) expansivo; (*wide*)
extenso. **expansiveness** *n* expansibilidad
f.
expanse [ik'spans] *n* extensión *f*; (*wings*)
envergadura *f*.
expatriate [eks'peitriət; *v* eks'peitrieit] *n*,
adj expatriado, -a. *v* desterrar. **expatriation** *n* expatriación *f*.
expect [ik'spekt] *v* (*anticipate, hope for,
require*) esperar; (*suppose*) suponer.
expectant *adj* expectante. **expectant
mother** futura madre *f*. **expectation** *n*
expectación *f*; (*hope*) esperanza *f*; (*anticipation*) previsión *f*.
expedient [ik'spiːdiənt] *adj* expeditivo,
oportuno. *n* expediente. **expedience** *also*
expediency *n* conveniencia *f*.
expedition [ˌekspi'diʃən] *n* expedición *f*.
expel [ik'spel] *v* expulsar.
expenditure [ik'spenditʃə] *n* gasto *m*.
expend *v* gastar; (*effort*) dedicar. **expendable** *adj* (*objects*) gastable; (*people*)
prescindible.
expense [ik'spens] *n* gasto *m*. **at the
expense of** a costa de. **expense account**
cuenta de gastos de representación *f*.
expensive *adj* caro, costoso.
experience [ik'spiəriəns] *n* experiencia *f*.
v experimentar; (*difficulty*) tener. **experienced** *adj* experimentado; experto.
experiment [ik'sperimənt] *n* experimento
m. *v* hacer experimentos, experimentar.
experimental *adj* experimental.
expert ['ekspoːt] *n*, *adj* experto, -a.
expertise [ˌekspoː'tiːz] *n* pericia *f*.
expire [ik'spaiə] *v* (*finish, die*) expirar;
(*become void*) caducar; (*expel air*)
espirar. **expiration** *also* **expiry** *n* expiración *f*; (*comm*) vencimiento *m*.
explain [ik'splein] *v* explicar. **explanation**
n explicación *f*. **explanatory** *adj* explicativo.
expletive [ek'spliːtiv] *n* (*gramm*) expletiva
f; (*oath*) taco *m*.

explicit [ik'splisit] *adj* explícito.
explode [ik'sploud] *v* estallar, hacer
explotar; (*myth*) refutar; (*rumour*)
desmentir. **explosion** *n* explosión *f*.
explosive *nm*, *adj* explosivo.
exploit[1] ['eksploit] *n* hazaña *f*.
exploit[2] [ik'sploit] *v* explotar. **exploitation**
n explotación *f*.
explore [ik'sploː] *v* explorar. **exploration** *n*
exploración *f*. **exploratory** *adj*
exploratorio. **explorer** *n* explorador, -a
m, *f*.
exponent [ik'spounənt] *n* exponente *m*, *f*.
export ['ekspoːt; *v* ik'spoːt] *n* exportación
f. *v* exportar. **exporter** *n* exportador, -a
m, *f*.
expose [ik'spouz] *v* (*leave uncovered*)
exponer; (*reveal*) revelar; (*plot, etc.*)
descubrir; (*phot*) exponer. **exposure** *n*
exposición *f*; revelación *f*;
descubrimiento *m*; (*denunciation*)
denuncia *f*; (*phot*) fotografía *f*. **exposure
meter** exposímetro *m*. **indecent exposure**
exhibicionismo *m*.
expound [ik'spaund] *v* exponer;
comentar.
express [ik'spres] *v* expresar; (*press*)
exprimir. *n* (*train*) rápido *m*; (*mail*) correo urgente *m*. *adj*, *adv* expreso; rápido.
expression *n* expressión *f*. **expressive** *adj*
expresivo; (*mot*) **expressway** autopista
expulsion [ik'spʌlʃən] *n* expulsión *f*.
exquisite ['ekswizit] *adj* exquisito;
intenso.
extend [ik'stend] *v* extender, aumentar;
(*widen*) ampliar; (*lengthen*) prolongar;
(*stretch*) estirar; (*invitation*) enviar; (*aid*)
ofrecer; (*hand*) tender; (*time-limit*)
proragar. **extension** extensión *f*; prolongación *f*; aumento *m*; prórroga *f*. **telephone extension** extensión *f*. **extensive**
adj extenso.
extent [ik'stent] *n* (*length*) extensión *f*;
(*degree*) punto *m*; (*scope*) alcance *m*.
exterior [ik'stiəriə] *nm*, *adj* exterior.
exterminate [ik'stəːmiˌneit] *v* exterminar.
extermination *n* exterminio *m*.
external [ik'stəːnl] *adj* externo. **for external
use only** sólo para uso externo.
extinct [ik'stiŋkt] *adj* extinto; (*fire, volcano*) extinguido. **extinction** *n* extinción *f*.
extinguish [ik'stiŋgwiʃ] *v* extinguir; apagar; (*hope*) destruir. **extinguisher** *n* (*fire*)
extintor.

extort [ik'stɔɪt] v arrancar, sacar por fuerza. **extortion** n extorsión f. **extortionate** adj exorbitante.

extra ['ekstrə] adj extra; de más; adicional; extraordinario; no incluido. n (extra charge) recargo m; (actor) extra m, f. adv extraordinariamente.

extract [ik'strakt; n 'ekstrakt] v extraer; (obtain, parts of books, etc.) sacar. n extracto m. **extraction** n extracción f; (descent) origen m.

extradite ['ekstrədait] v conceder la extradición de; obtener la extradición de. **extradition** n extradición f.

extramural [ˌekstrə'mjuərəl] adj para estudiantes libres.

extraordinary [ik'strɔɪdənəri] adj extraordinario; raro.

extravagant [ik'stravəgənt] adj (lavish) pródigo; (wasteful) despilfarrador; (taste) dispendioso; (language, ideas) extravagante. **extravagance** n prodigalidad f; despilfarro m; extravagancia f.

extreme [ik'striɪm] nm, adj extremo. **go to extremes** llegar a extremos. **extremist** n (m + f), adj extremista. **extremity** n (end) extremidad f; (necessity) apuro m.

extrovert ['ekstrəvɜɪt] n, adj extrovertido, -a.

exuberant [ig'zjuɪbərənt] adj exuberante; enfórico. **exuberance** n exuberancia f; enforia f.

exude [ig'zjuɪd] v exudar.

exult [ig'zʌlt] v exultar. **exult over** triunfar sobre. **exultant** adj exultante. **exultation** n exultación f.

eye [ai] n ojo m. **an eye for an eye** ojo por ojo. **private eye** detective m. **make eyes at** echar miradas a. **see eye to eye with** ver con los mismos ojos que. **turn a blind eye** cerrar los ojos. **up to one's eyes in work** estar hasta aquí en trabajo. **with an eye to** con miras a. **with the naked eye** a simple vista. v mirar.

eyeball ['aibɔɪl] n globo del ojo m.

eyebrow ['aibrau] n ceja f.

eye-catching ['aikatʃin] adj llamativo.

eyelash ['ailaʃ] n pestaña f.

eyelid ['ailid] n párpado m.

eye shadow n sombreador de ojos m.

eyesight ['aisait] n vista f.

eyesore ['aisɔɪ] n algo que ofende la vista.

eyewitness ['aiˌwitnis] n testigo ocular m.

F

fable ['feibl] n fábula f.

fabric ['fabrik] n (cloth) tejido m; estructura f, construcción f. **fabricate** v (invent) fingir. **fabrication** n fabricación f; invención f.

fabulous ['fabjuləs] adj fabuloso; (coll) macanudo.

façade [fə'saɪd] n fachada f.

face [feis] n cara f, rostro m; (side) lado m; (aspect) aspecto m; (grimace) mueca f; (surface) superficie f; (clock) esfera f. **face down** boca abajo. **face up** boca arriba. **face to face** cara a cara. **on the face of it** a primera vista. **fly in the face of** burlarse de. **in the face of** frente a. **keep a straight face** mantenerse impávido. **lose face** quedar mal. **pull faces** hacer muecas. **save face** salvar las apariencias. v mirar hacia, dar a; estar en frente de; enfrentarse con; presentarse ante; (consequences) arrostrar; (stand) aguantar; (resurface) revestir.

face cloth n paño m.

facelift ['feislift] n (coll) lavado m.

face pack n mascarilla de belleza f.

face powder n polvos para la cara m pl.

facet ['fasit] n faceta f.

facetious [fə'siɪʃəs] adj chistoso; gracioso.

face value n (bill) valor nominal m; (stamps) valor facial. **take something at face value** creer algo a pie juntillas.

facing ['feisin] n (sewing) guarnición f; (building) revestimiento m. adj de enfrente.

facsimile [fak'siməli] nm, adj facsímil.

fact [fakt] n hecho m; realidad f. **as a matter of fact** en realidad. **in fact** en verdad. **factual** adj objetivo.

faction ['fakʃən] n facción f. **factious** adj faccioso.

factor ['faktə] n factor m, elemento m; (comm) agente m.

factory ['faktəri] n fábrica f.

faculty ['fakəlti] n (university) facultad f; (gift) facilidad f.

fad [fad] n manía f; novedad f. **faddish** adj maniático.

fade [feid] v (colour) descolorarse; (light) apagarse; (sound) desvanecerse; (interest) decaer. **faded** adj descolorido; marchito.

fag [fag] *n* (*coll: cigarette*) pitillo *m*. **fag end** sobras *f pl*; (*cigarette*) colilla *f*. **fagged out** rendido.

fail [feil] *v* fallar; (*not succeed*) fracasar, no lograr; (*hopes*) frustrarse; (*run out*) acabarse; (*weaken*) decaer; (*exams*) ser suspendido; (*neglect*) dejar (de). **without fail** sin falta. **failing** *n* defecto *m*. **failure** *n* fracaso *m*; fallo *m*; suspenso *m*; (*breakdown*) avería *f*.

faint [feint] *adj* (*near collapse*) mareado; (*weak*) débil; (*colour*) pálido; (*timid*) timorato; (*slight*) ligero; vago; indistinto. *v* desmayarse. *n* desmayo *m*.

fair[1] [feə] *adj* bello; hermoso; (*skin*) blanco; (*hair*) rubio; (*just*) justo; (*reputation, weather*) bueno; (*prospects*) favorable; (*play*) limpio; (*price*) razonable; (*comment*) acertado; (*average*) mediano. **by fair means or foul** por las buenas o por las malas. **fairly** *adv* con justicia; (*reasonably*) bastante. **fairness** *n* belleza *f*; justicia *f*.

fair[2] [feə] *n* (*amusements*) verbena *f*; (*market*) feria *f*. **fun fair** parque de atracciones *m*. **fairground** *n* real *m*.

fairy [ˈfeəri] *n* hada *f*. *adj* de hada. **fairy lights** bombillas de colores *f pl*.

faith [feiθ] *n* confianza *f*. **have faith in** fiarse de. **religious faith** fe religiosa *f*. **faithful** *adj* fiel; exacto. **faithfulness** *n* fidelidad *f*; exactitud *f*. **faithless** *adj* desleal; infiel.

fake [feik] *n* falsificación *f*; impostor *m*. *adj* falso; falsificado; (*feigned*) fingido. *v* falsificar; fingir.

falcon [ˈfɔːlkən] *n* halcón *m*.

*****fall** [fɔːl] *v* caer; (*prices, temperature, water*) bajar; (*wind*) amainar; (*decay*) decaer; (*task, duty, privilege*) tocar; (*accent*) recaer. **fall apart** caerse a pedazos. **fall back on** echar mano a. **fall behind** retrasarse. **fall in love** enamorarse. **fall out** (*quarrel*) reñir. **fall through** venirse abajo. *n* (*body, earth, leaves*) caída *f*; (*prices*) baja *f*; (*slope*) declive *m*; (*US: season*) otoño *m*.

fallacy [ˈfaləsi] *n* falacia *f*; (*deception*) engaño *m*. **fallacious** *adj* erróneo.

fallible [ˈfaləbl] *adj* falible. **fallibility** *n* falibilidad *f*.

fallow [ˈfalou] *adj* (*land*) en barbecho; inculto.

false [fɔːls] *adj* falso; erróneo. **false alarm** falsa alarma *f*. **false pretences** estafa *f*.

false teeth dientes postizos *m pl*. **falsehood** *n* falsedad *f*; mentira *f*. **falseness** *n* falsedad *f*; inexactitud *f*; perfidia *f*. **falsify** *v* falsificar; desvirtuar. **falsification** *n* falsificación *f*.

falsetto [fɔlˈsetou] *n* falsete *m*. *adj* de falsete.

falter [ˈfɔːltə] *v* (*action*) vacilar; (*voice*) titubear. **faltering** *adj* vacilante; titubeante. **falteringly** *adv* con paso vacilante; con voz titubeante.

fame [feim] *n* fama *f*.

familiar [fəˈmiljə] *adj* familiar, conocido. **be familiar with** estar familiarizado con. **familiarity** *n* familiaridad *f*. **familiarize** *v* familiarizar.

family [ˈfaməli] *n* familia *f*. **family allowance** subsidio familiar *m*. **family doctor** médico de cabecera *m*. **family planning** planificación familiar *f*. **family tree** árbol genealógico *m*.

famine [ˈfamin] *n* (*general scarcity*) escasez *f*; (*food*) hambre *f*.

famished [ˈfamiʃt] *adj* famélico. **be famished** estar muerto de hambre.

famous [ˈfeiməs] *adj* famoso, célebre.

fan[1] [fan] *n* (*hand*) abanico *m*; (*tech*) ventilador *m*. **fan belt** correa del ventilador *f*. *v* abanicar; agitar.

fan[2] [fan] *n* aficionado, -a *m*, *f*; admirador, -a *m*, *f*. **fan club** club de admiradores *m*. **fan mail** correspondencia de los admiradores *f*.

fanatic [fəˈnatik] *n*, *adj* fanático, -a. **fanaticism** *n* fanatismo *m*.

fancy [ˈfansi] *adj* de adorno; de fantasía. *n* fantasía *f*; (*whim*) capricho *m*; (*desire*) afición *f*; (*delusion*) ilusión *f*; (*taste*) gusto *m*. *v* imaginarse; suponer; gustar; (*suspect*) parecerle(a); (*desire*) apetecer. **fancy oneself** ser un creido. **fancy that!** ¡imagínate! **fancy dress** disfraz *m*. **fancied** *adj* favorito; imaginario. **fanciful** *adj* imaginario; caprichoso.

fanfare [ˈfanfeə] *n* fanfarria *f*.

fang [faŋ] *n* colmillo *m*; (*snake*) diente *m*.

fantastic [fanˈtastik] *adj* fantástico.

fantasy [ˈfantəsi] *n* fantasía *f*; capricho *m*.

far [faː] *adv* lejos; (*much*) mucho; muy. *adj* lejano; distante. **as far as** hasta; por lo que. **far and wide** por todas partes. **far away** lejos. **far-away** *adj* remoto. **Far East** Extremo Oriente *m*. **far-fetched** *adj* inverosímil. **far-reaching** *adj* de mucho alcance. **so far so good** hasta ahora todo va bien.

farce [faɪs] n farsa f. **farcical** adj ridículo, absurdo.

fare [feə] n precio del billete m, tarifa f; (boat) pasaje m; (passenger) pasajero, -a; (in a taxi) cliente m, f; (in a bus) viajero, -a m, f; (food) comida f. v (get on) irle bien (a uno).

farewell [feə'wel] (interj) ¡adiós! **say farewell** decir adiós, despedirse de. adj de despedida.

farm [faɪm] n also **farmhouse** granja f, finca f; (S. Am.) estancia f, hacienda f. **farmhand** n peón m. **farmland** n tierras de labrantío f pl. **farmyard** n corral m. v cultivar. **farm out** mandar hacer fuera. **farmer** n agricultor m; granjero m. **farming** n labranza f; agricultura f.

fart [faɪt] (impol) n pedo m. v peerse.

farther ['faɪðə] adv (space) más lejos; (time) más adelante. adj (space, time) más lejano.

farthest ['faɪðist] adv más lejos. adj (most distant) más lejano; (longest) más largo.

fascinate ['fasɪˌneit] v fascinar. **fascinating** adj fascinador. **fascination** n fascinación f.

fascism ['faʃizəm] n fascismo m. **fascist** n(m+f), adj fascista.

fashion ['faʃən] n manera f, modo m; moda f. **after a fashion** en cierto modo. **fashion show** desfile de modas m. **in fashion** de moda. **out of fashion** pasado de moda. v hacer; formar; (mould) moldear.

fast¹ [faɪst] adj rápido, veloz; (colour) sólido; (clock, etc.) adelantado; (secure) seguro; firme. **fast asleep** profundamente dormido. **make fast** sujetar, atar. **pull a fast one** jugar una mala jugada. **stuck fast** (in mud) completamente atascado.

fast² [faɪst] n ayuno m. v ayunar.

fasten ['faɪsn] v (fix) fijar; (attach) sujetar; (dress) abrochar; (close) cerrar. **fastener** or **fastening** n corchete m; fijación f.

fastidious [fa'stidiəs] adj quisquilloso; (demanding) exigente. **fastidiousness** n melindre m.

fat [fat] n grasa f; (on meat) gordo m. adj grueso; gordo. **fatten** v (person) engordar; (animal) cebar. **fattening** adj que engorda.

fatal ['feitl] adj fatal, mortal. **fatality** n fatalidad f.

fate [feit] n destino m; suerte f. **fated** adj predestinado; condenado. **fateful** adj profético; fatal.

father ['faɪðə] n padre m. **Father Christmas** Papa Noel m. **father-in-law** n suegro m. **fatherland** n patria f. **fatherless** adj huérfano de padre m. **fatherly** adj paternal.

fathom ['faðəm] n braza f. v (water depth) sondar, sondear; (unravel) desentrañar. **fathomless** adj insondable.

fatigue [fə'tiːg] n fatiga f. v fatigar.

fatuous ['fatjuəs] adj fatuo; necio. **fatuity** or **fatuousness** n fatuidad f; necedad f.

fault [fɔːlt] n culpa f; defecto m; error m; falta f; (geol) falla f. **be at fault** tener la culpa. **faultiness** n imperfección f. **faultless** adj perfecto. **faulty** adj malo; erróneo; defectuoso.

fauna ['fɔːnə] n fauna f.

favour ['feivə] n favor m; favoritismo m; (gift) obsequio m; (comm) carta f, atenta f. **be in favour of** estar a favor de. v favorecer. **favourable** adj favorable. **favourite** n, adj favorito, -a.

fawn [fɔːn] n cervato m. adj color de gamuza m. **fawn on** or **upon** adular.

fear [fiə] n miedo m; temor m. v temer; tener miedo de or a. **fearful** adj (frightening) espantoso; (frightened) temeroso. **fearless** adj intrépido, audaz.

feasible ['fiːzəbl] adj factible. **feasibility** n viabilidad f.

feast [fiːst] n fiesta f; banquete m. **feast day** día festivo m.

feat [fiːt] n hazaña f.

feather ['feðə] n pluma f. **feather bed** colchón de plumas m.

feature ['fiːtʃə] n característica f; (shape) figura f; (face) rasgo m; (written article) artículo principal m. **feature film** película principal f. v presentar; representar; (emphasize) destacar.

February ['februəri] n febrero m.

fed [fed] V **feed**.

federal ['fedərəl] adj federal.

federate ['fedəˌreit] v federar. **federation** n federación f.

fee [fiː] n (professional) honorarios m pl; (club) cuota f. **entrance fee** entrada f.

feeble ['fiːbl] adj débil; (unconvincing) de poco peso. **feebleness** n debilidad f.

*feed [fiːd] v alimentar; dar de comer; (eat) comer. **be fed up with** (coll) estar harto de. **feed on** alimentarse con. n (for babies) comida f; (fodder) foraje m;

(*tech*) alimentación *f*. **feedback** *n* reaprovechamiento *m*; (*tech*) realimentación *f*.

*feel [fiːl] *v* tocar; mirar; sentir; (*realize*) darse cuenta de; (*caress*) sobar; (*think*) pensar. *n* tacto *m*; sensación *f*; atmósfera *f*; sentido *m*. **feeler** *n* antena *f*; tentáculo *m*. **feeling** *n* sentimiento *m*; sentido *m*; sensación *f*; opinión *f*; impresión *f*.

feet [fiːt] *V* **foot**.

feign [fein] *v* fingir; inventar.

feline ['fiːlain] *nm, adj* felino.

fell[1] [fel] *V* **fall**.

fell[2] [fel] *v* derribar; (*trees*) talar.

fellow ['felou] *n* hombre *m*; compañero; (*coll*) tipo *m*; (*of a society*) miembro *m*. **fellowship** *n* comunidad *f*; asociación *f*.

felony ['feləni] *n* delito grave *m*. **felon** *n* criminal *m*.

felt[1] [felt] *V* **feel**.

felt[2] [felt] *n* fieltro *m*. **felt-tip pen** rotulador *m*.

female ['fiːmeil] *adj* hembra; femenino. *n* (*animal*) hembra *f*; (*person*) mujer *f*.

feminine ['feminin] *nm, adj* femenino. **femininity** *n* feminidad *f*. **feminism** *n* feminismo *m*. **feminist** *n*(*m*+*f*), *adj* feminista.

fence [fens] *n* cerca *f*, valla *f*. *v* cercar, vallar; (*sport*) practicar la esgrima. **fencing** *n* (*sport*) esgrima *f*.

fend [fend] *v* **fend for oneself** arreglárselas. **fend off** desviar.

fender ['fendə] *n* guardafuegos *m invar*; (*US: car*) guardabarros *m invar*.

fennel ['fenl] *n* hinojo *m*.

ferment [fə'ment; *n* 'fɔːment] *v* fermentar. *n* fermento *m*; agitación *f*. **fermentation** *n* fermentación *f*.

fern [fəːn] *n* helecho *m*.

ferocious [fə'rouʃəs] *adj* feroz. **ferocity** *n* ferocidad *f*.

ferret ['ferit] *n* hurón *m*. **ferret out** conseguir, descubrir.

ferry ['feri] *n* transbordador *m*. *v* transportar.

fertile ['fəːtail] *adj* fértil; (*person*) fecundo. **fertility** *n* fertilidad *f*; fecundidad *f*. **fertilization** *n* fertilización *f*; fecundación *f*. **fertilize** *v* abonar; fecundar. **fertilizer** *n* abono *m*.

fervent ['fəːvənt] *adj* ferviente. **fervour** *n* fervor *m*.

fester ['festə] *v* supurar; (*fig*) enconarse.

festival ['festəvəl] *n* fiesta *f*.

festoon [fə'stuːn] *v* festonear. *n* guirnalda *f*.

fetch [fetʃ] *v* (*bring*) traer; (*procure*) buscar; (*reach*) alcanzar. **fetching** *adj* atractivo.

fête [feit] *n* fiesta *f*. *v* festejar.

fetid ['fetid] *adj* fétido.

fetish ['fetiʃ] *n* fetiche *m*.

fetter ['fetə] *v* encadenar. **fetters** *pl n* grilletes *m pl*; (*fig*) trabas *f pl*.

feud [fjuːd] *n* enemistad hereditaria *f*. *v* pelear, reñir.

feudal ['fjuːdl] *adj* feudal. **feudalism** *n* feudalismo *m*.

fever ['fiːvə] *n* fiebre *f*. **feverish** *adj* febril.

few [fjuː] *adj* poco. *n* pocos, -as *pl*. **a few** algunos, unos, unos pocos. **quite a few** bastante. **fewer** *adj* menos. **the fewer the better** cuantos menos mejor. **fewest** *adj* menos.

fiancé [fi'onsei] *n* novio *m*. **fiancée** *n* novia *f*.

fiasco [fi'askou] *n* fiasco *m*.

fib [fib] *n* mentirijilla *f*. *v* decir una mentirijilla.

fibre ['faibə] *n* fibra *f*. **fibreglass** *n* fibra de vidrio *f*.

fickle ['fikl] *adj* inconstante, veleidoso.

fiction ['fikʃən] *n* (*stories*) novela *f*; (*invention*) ficción *f*. **fictional** *or* **fictitious** *adj* novelesco; ficticio.

fiddle ['fidl] *n* violín *m*; (*coll: trick*) trampa *f*. *v* tocar el violín; (*coll: cheat*) camelar; (*coll: falsify*) amañar. **fiddle with** juguetear con. **fiddling** *adj* trivial; fútil.

fidelity [fi'deləti] *n* fidelidad *f*.

fidget ['fidʒit] *v* agitar nerviosamente. **fidgety** *adj* nervioso, agitado.

field [fiːld] *n* campo *m*; (*fig*) esfera *f*. **field glasses** gemelos *m pl*. **field marshal** mariscal de campo *m*. **fieldwork** *n* trabajo en el terreno *m*.

fiend [fiːnd] *n* demonio *m*, diablo *m*; (*coll*) fanático, -a *m*, *f*. **fiendish** *adj* diabólico.

fierce [fiəs] *adj* feroz, fiero; (*person*) violento; (*heat*) intenso; (*battle*) encarnizado. **fierceness** *or* **ferocity** *n* ferocidad *f*; violencia *f*; furia *f*; intensidad *f*.

fiery ['faiəri] *adj* (*burning*) ardiente; (*flaming*) llameante; (*passionate*) apasionado; (*temper*) fogoso.

fifteen [fif'tiːn] *nm, adj* quince. **fifteenth** *n, adj* decimoquinto, -a.

fifth [fifθ] *n, adj* quinto, -a.

fifty ['fifti] *nm, adj* cincuenta. **go fifty-fifty** ir a medias. **fiftieth** *n, adj* quincuagésimo, -a. **fiftyish** *adj* cincuentón.

fig [fig] *n (fruit)* higo *m; (tree)* higuera *f*.

fight [fait] *v* luchar contra, combatir. *n* lucha *f*, pelea *f*.

figment ['figmənt] *n* invención *f*.

figure ['figə] *n (number)* número *m*, cifra *f; (price)* precio *m; (statue, design, personage)* figura *f; (human)* línea *f*. **figurehead** *n* mascarón de proa *m; (fig)* testaferro *m*. **figure skating** patinaje artístico *m*. *v (math)* poner en cifras; *(calculate)* calcular. **figure out** comprender; resolver.

filament ['filəmənt] *n* filamento *m*.

file¹ [fail] *n (folder)* carpeta *f; (card index)* fichero *m; (document holder)* archivador *m; (dossier)* expediente *m*. *v* archivar; *(a claim)* presentar. **file in/out** entrar/salir en fila. **file past** desfilar ante. **in single file** en fila de a uno. **filing** *n* clasificación *f*. **filing cabinet** archivo *m*. **filing clerk** archivero, -a *m, f*, archivista *m, f*.

file² [fail] *n (tool)* lima *f*. *v* limar. **filings** *pl n* limaduras *f pl*.

filial ['filiəl] *adj* filial.

fill [fil] *v* llenar; *(space, time)* ocupar; *(vacancy)* cubrir; *(tooth)* empastar; *(hole)* tapar; *(cookery)* rellenar; *(requirements)* satisfacer. **fill in** *(form)* rellenar. **fill up** llenar. **filling** *n* relleno *m*; empaste *m*. **filling station** estación de servicio *f*.

fillet ['filit] *n* filete *m*. *v* cortar en filetes.

film [film] *n (phot, cinema)* película *f; (layer)* capa *f; (eye)* nube *f; (mist, etc.)* velo *m*. **roll of film** rollo de película *m*. **filmgoer** *n* aficionado al cine *m*. **film star** astro de cine *m*, estrella de cine *f*.

filter ['filtə] *n* filtro *m*. *v* filtrar. **filtering** *n* filtración *f*. **filter-tipped** *adj* con filtro, emboquillado.

filth [filθ] *n* inmundicia *f*, suciedad *f; (fig)* obscenidades *f pl*. **filthy** *adj* asqueroso, inmundo; obsceno.

fin [fin] *n* aleta *f*.

final ['fainl] *adj (last)* último; decisivo; definitivo. *n* final *f*. **finalist** *n* finalista *m, f*. **finalize** *v* finalizar. **finally** *adv* finalmente.

finance [fai'nans] *n* finanzas *f pl*. *v*

finanzar. **financial** *adj* financiero. **financial year** año económico *m*. **financier** *n* financiero *m*.

finch [fintʃ] *n* pinzón *m*.

find [faind] *v* encontrar, hallar. **find out** averiguar; descubrir. *n* hallazgo *m*. **findings** *pl n* hallazgos *m pl*; resultados *m pl*.

fine¹ [fain] *adj* excelente; elegante; *(pleasant)* agradable; bueno; fino; delicado. **that's fine!** ¡muy bien! *adv* en trozos pequeños; fino; muy bien. **fine arts** bellas artes *f pl*. **finely** *adv (small)* finamente; *(well)* primorosamente. **finery** *n* galas *f pl*.

fine² [fain] *n* multa *f*. *v* multar.

finesse [fi'nes] *n* fineza *f*, delicadeza *f*; tácto *m; (bridge)* impás *m*.

finger ['fingə] *n* dedo *m*. **little finger** mañique *m*. *v* tocar. **fingernail** *n* uña *f*. **fingerprint** *n* huella dactilar *f*. **fingertip** *n* punta del dedo *f*. **have at one's fingertips** saberse al dedillo.

finish ['finiʃ] *v* terminar, acabar; *(sport)* llegar. **finish off** rematar. *n* fin *m*, conclusión *f; (surface)* acabado *m; (sport)* llegada *f*. **finishing line** meta *f*. **finishing touch** última mano *f*.

finite ['fainait] *adj* finito.

Finland ['finlənd] *n* Finlandia *f*. **Finn** *n* finlandés, -esa *m, f*. **Finnish** *nm, adj* finlandés.

fir [fəː] *n* abeto *m*. **fir cone** piña *f*.

fire ['faiə] *n* fuego *m; (uncontrolled)* incendio *m; (electric or gas)* estufa *f*. **be on fire** estar ardiendo. **catch fire** encenderse. **set on fire, set fire to** pegar fuego, incendiar. *v (with enthusiasm, etc.)* infundir (a); *(gun)* disparar; *(salute)* tirar; *(missile)* lanzar; *(sack)* echar. **fire on** hacer fuego sobre.

fire alarm *n* alarma de incendios *f*.

firearm ['faiəˌɑːm] *n* arma de fuego *f*.

fire brigade *n* cuerpo de bomberos *m*.

fire door *n* puerta incombustible *f*.

fire drill *n* ejercicios para casos de incendio *m pl*.

fire engine *n* bomba de incendios *f*.

fire-escape *n* escalera de incendios *f*.

fire-extinguisher *n* extintor *m*.

firefly ['faiəˌflai] *n* luciérnaga *f*.

fire-guard *n* guardafuego *m*.

firelight ['faiəˌlait] *n* lumbre *m*.

fireman ['faiəmən] *n* bombero *m*.

fireplace ['faiǝ,pleis] *n* chimenea *f*.
fireproof ['faiǝ,pruːf] *adj* ininflamable, incombustible.
fireside ['faiǝ,said] *n* hogar *m*.
fire station *n* parque de bomberos *m*.
firewood ['faiǝ,wud] *n* leña *f*.
firework ['faiǝ,wɔːk] *n* fuego de artificio *m*.
firing squad *n* pelotón de ejecución *m*.
firm¹ [fǝːm] *adj* firme, sólido; estable.
firmness *n* firmeza *f*.
firm² [fǝːm] *n* empresa *f*, firma *f*.
first¹ [fǝːst] *adj* primero; básico; elemental. **first aid** primeros auxilios *m pl*. **first-class** *adj* de primera clase. **first cousin** primo hermano *m*. **first edition** edición príncipe *m*. **first floor** primer piso *m*. **first name** nombre de pila *m*. **first-rate** *adj* de primera calidad. **in the first place** en primer lugar.
first² [fǝːst] *adv* antes, primero. **first and foremost** antes que nada. **first and last** en todos los aspectos. **travel first** viajar en primera. **you go first** usted primero.
first³ [fǝːst] *n* primero, -a *m*, *f*; sobresaliente *m*. **at first** al principio. **be the first to** ser el primero en. **get a first** sacar sobresaliente.
fiscal ['fiskǝl] *adj* fiscal.
fish [fiʃ] *n* (*food*) pescado *m*; (*in water*) pez *m*. **fish and chips** pescado frito con patatas fritas. *v* pescar. **fishy** *adj* (*coll*) sospechoso.
fishbone ['fiʃ,boun] *n* espina *f*.
fish-bowl *n* pecera *f*.
fisherman ['fiʃǝmǝn] *n* pescador *m*.
fish fingers *n* filete de pescado empanado *m*.
fish hook *n* anzuelo *m*.
fishing ['fiʃiŋ] *n* pesca *f*. **fishing line** sedal *m*. **fishing net** red de pesca *f*. **fishing rod** caña de pescar *f*. **fishing tackle** aparejo de pescar *m*. **go fishing** ir de pesca.
fish market *n* mercado de pescado.
fishmonger ['fiʃ,mʌŋgǝ] *n* pescadero *m*. **fishmonger's** *n* pescadería *f*.
fission ['fiʃǝn] *n* fisión *f*, escisión *f*.
fissure ['fiʃǝ] *n* grieta *f*.
fist [fist] *n* puño *m*. **fistful** *n* puñado *m*.
fit¹ [fit] *adj* conveniente; apto; adecuado; (*qualified*) capacitado; (*competent*) capaz; (*worthy*) digno; (*healthy*) sano. **not fit to eat** no se puede comer. **see fit** juzgar conveniente. *v* (*try on*) probar; (*qualify*) capacitar; (*tally with*) cuadrar

con; adaptar; preparar; unir; (*supply with*) equipar con; (*clothes*) sentar bien a; (*tailor*) entallar. **fitness** *n* conveniencia *f*; salud *f*; aptitud *f*. **fitter** *n* (*tailor*) probador, -a *m*, *f*; (*tech*) ajustador *m*. **fitting** *adj* oportuno; digno; apropiado; propio. **fitting room** cuarto de pruebas *m*. **fittings** *pl n* muebles *m pl*; accesorios *m pl*.
fit² [fit] *n* (*med*) ataque *m*.
five [faiv] *nm*, *adj* cinco.
fix [fiks] *v* fijar; sujetar; (*decide*) establecer; (*date*) señalar; (*hopes*) poner; (*coll: put right*) arreglar. *n* aprieto *m*; (*coll*) una dosis de froga *f*. **fixation** *n* obsesión *f*. **fixed** *adj* fijo; (*coll: rigged*) amañado. **fixture** *n* instalación *f*; (*sport*) partido *m*; (*coll*) permanencia *f*.
fizz [fiz] *n* burbujeo *m*; (*coll*) gaseosa *f*. *v* burbujear.
flabbergasted ['flæbe,gɑːstid] *adj* pasmado.
flabby ['flæbi] *adj* fláccido; (*spineless*) blandengue. **flabbiness** *n* flaccidez *f*; blandura *f*.
flag¹ [flæg] *n* bandera *f*; (*stone*) baldosa *f*. **flag down** detener haciendo señales. **flagpole** *n* asta de bandera *f*. **flagship** *n* buque insignia *m*.
flag² [flæg] *v* (*weaken*) flaquear; (*interest*) decaer. **flagging** *adj* flogo; desmadejado.
flagon ['flægǝn] *n* (*jug*) jarra *f*; (*bottle*) botella (de dos litros) *f*.
flagrant ['fleigrǝnt] *adj* flagrante; escandaloso.
flair [fleǝ] *n* don *m*; instinto *m*; talento *m*.
flake [fleik] *n* (*snow*) copo *m*; (*soap*) escama *f*; (*paint*) desconchón *m*. *v* caer en copos; desconchar. **flaky** *adj* escamoso. **flaky pastry** hojaldre *m*.
flamboyant [flæm,boiǝnt] *adj* llamativo. **flamboyance** *n* extravagancia *f*.
flame [fleim] *n* llama *f*. **burst into flames** incendiarse. *v* llamear. **flammable** *adj* inflamable.
flamingo [flǝ'miŋgou] *n* flamenco *m*.
flan [flæn] *n* flan *m*.
flank [flæŋk] *n* (*animal*) ijada *f*; (*person*) costado *m*; (*mil*) flanco *m*. *v* bordear.
flannel ['flænl] *n* (*fabric*) franela *f*; (*face cloth*) pañito para lavarse la cara *m*. **flannels** *pl n* pantalones de franela *m pl*.
flap [flæp] *v* (*shake*) sacudir; (*arms*) agitar; (*wings*) batir. *n* (*pocket*) carterita *f*; (*envelope*, *etc.*) solapa *f*; (*table*) ala

abatible *f*; (*coat*) faldón *m*; (*aero*) alerón *m*; (*coll*) crisis *f*.

flare [fleə] *n* (*blaze*) llamarada *f*; (*signal*) cohete de señales *m*; (*widening*) ensanchamiento *m*. *v* llamear; ensanchar; (*clothes*) acampanar. **flare up** (*anger*) ponerse furioso.

flash [flaʃ] *n* destello *m*; (*sparkle*) centelleo *m*; (*phot*) flash *m*; (*moment*) instante *m*; (*inspiration*) ráfaga *f*; (*genius*) rasgo *m*; (*hope*) resquicio *m*. **flashback** *n* escena retrospectiva *f*. **flash bulb** bombilla de magnesio *f*. **flashlight** *n* linterna *f*. *v* despedir; lanzar; encender; destellar; centellear. **flashing** *adj* intermitente.

flask [flatsk] *n* frasco *m*; (*vacuum*) termo *m*.

flat[1] [flat] *adj* plano, llano, chato; horizontal; (*fig*) categórico; monótono; (*boring*) pesado; (*rate*) fijo; (*below pitch*) desafinado; (*tyre*) desinflado; (*battery*) descargado; (*horse racing*) sin obstáculos. **flat beer** cerveza muerta *f*. **flat-footed** *adj* de pies planos. **be flat broke** estar sin blanca. **go flat out** ir a todo gas. **flatly** *adv* categóricamente; completamente. *n* (*music*) bemol *m*; (*land*) llano *m*; (*tyre*) pinchazo *m*. **flatten** *v* (*make flat*) aplanar; (*crush*) aplastar; (*smooth*) alisar.

flat[2] [flat] *n* apartamento *m*. **flatlet** *n* piso pequeño *m*.

flatter ['flatə] *v* adular, halagar; favorecer. **flatterer** *n* adulador, -a *m, f*. **flattering** *adj* (*words*) halagüeño; (*person*) halagador; (*clothes*) favorecedor. **flattery** *n* halago *m*, adulación *f*.

flatulence ['flatjuləns] *n* flatulencia *f*.

flaunt [flɔɪnt] *v* ostentar. **flaunt oneself** pavonearse.

flautist ['flɔttist] *n* flautista *m, f*.

flavour ['fleivə] *n* sabor *m*, gusto *m*; (*cookery*) sazón *m*, sainete *m*. *v* saborear; condimentar. **flavouring** *n* condimento *m*, sainete *m*.

flaw [flɔɪ] *n* defecto *m*; (*error*) fallo *m*. *v* (*crack*) agrietar; (*spoil*) estropear. **flawed** *adj* falto; imperfecto. **flawless** *adj* sin tacha; perfecto.

flax [flaks] *n* lino *m*. **flaxen** *adj* de lino; (*hair*) rubio.

flea [fliɪ] *n* pulga *f*. **fleabite** *n* picadura de pulga *f*.

fleck [flek] *n* (*speck*) mota *f*; (*colour*)

mancha *f*; (*dust*) partícula *f*. *v* motear; (*paint*) salpicar.

fled [fled] *V* **flee**.

*****flee** [fliɪ] *v* evitar; escapar de.

fleece [fliɪs] *n* (*wool*) lana *f*; (*sheared wool*) velón *m*. *v* (*coll*) pelar. **fleecy** *adj* (*woolly*) lanoso.

fleet [fliɪt] *n* flota *f*; (*navy*) armada *f*. *adj* veloz. **fleeting** *adj* fugaz, breve.

Flemish ['flemiʃ] *nm, adj* flamenco. **Fleming** *n* flamenco, -a *m, f*.

flesh [fleʃ] *n* carne *f*. **flesh-coloured** *adj* de color carne. **flesh-eating** *adj* carnivoro. **flesh wound** herida superficial *f*. **in the flesh** en carne y hueso. **fleshy** *adj* gordo.

flew [fluɪ] *V* **fly**.

flex [fleks] *n* flexible *m*. *v* doblar. **flexibility** *n* flexibilidad *f*. **flexible** *adj* (*pliable*) flexible; (*fig*) elástico.

flick [flik] *v* dar un golpecito a. **flick through** (*book*) hojear. *n* (*whip*) latigazo suave *m*; (*light stroke*) golpecito *m*; (*duster*) pasada *f*; (*wrist*) movimiento rápido *m*. **the flicks** (*coll*) el cine *m*.

flicker ['flikə] *v* (*light*) parpadear; (*flames*) vacilar. *n* parpadeo *m*; (*flame*) llama vacilante *f*; (*hope, etc.*) requicio *m*.

flight[1] [flait] *n* (*birds*) bandada *f*; (*aircraft*) escuadrilla *f*; (*act of flying*) vuelo *m*; (*distance flown*) recorrido *m*. **flight crew** tripulación *f*. **flight deck** cubierta de aterrizaje *f*. **flight of stairs** tramo de escalera *m*. **flight path** trayectoria de vuelo *f*. **in flight** en vuelo. **flightiness** *n* ligereza *f*. **flightless** *adj* incapacitado para volar. **flighty** *adj* volátil; caprichoso.

flight[2] [flait] *n* (*escape*) huida *f*, fuga *f*.

flimsy ['flimzi] *adj* (*lacking substance*) poco sólido; (*fragile*) frágil; (*weak*) débil; (*paper*) fino; (*cloth*) ligero; (*excuse*) flojo. **flimsiness** *n* fragilidad *f*; debilidad *f*; finura *f*; ligereza *f*.

flinch [flintʃ] *v* (*draw back*) retroceder; (*hesitate*) vacilar; (*muscular movement*) encogerse.

*****fling** [fliŋ] *v* arrojar, tirar; (*dash*) precipitarse. **fling aside** dejar de lado. *n* (*throw*) lanzamiento; (*wild tune*) juerga *f*.

flint [flint] *n* pedernal *m*; (*of lighter*) piedra de mechero *f*.

flip [flip] *v* (*flick*) dar un capirotazo; (*coin*) echar a cara o cruz. *n* capirotazo *m*. **flipper** *n* aleta *f*.

flippant ['flipənt] *adj* frívolo. **flippancy** *n* ligereza *f*.

flirt [fləɪt] n (*female*) coqueta f; (*male*) mariposón m. v flirtear, coquetear. **flirtation** n coqueteo m.

flit [flit] v revolotear.

float [flout] v flotar; (*support*) hacer flotar. n flotador m; (*angling*) corcho m; (*carnival*) carroza f.

flock[1] [flok] n (*sheep, goats*) rebaño m; (*birds*) bandada f; (*people*) muchedumbre f. v congregarse.

flock[2] [flok] n (*filling*) borra f.

flog [flog] v (*beat*) azotar; (*coll: sell*) vender. **flogging** n paliza f; flagelación f.

flood [flʌd] v inundar; irrigar; (*overflow*) desbordar. n inundación f; flujo m; diluvio m. **in flood** crecido.

*floodlight [ˈflʌdlait] n foco m. v iluminar con focos. **floodlighting** n iluminación con focos f.

floor [floɪ] n suelo m, piso m; (*ocean*) fondo m; (*dance*) pista f. **first floor** primer piso m. **ground floor** planta baja f. **take the floor** (*speak*) tomar la palabra. v (*knock down*) echar al suelo. **floorboard** n tabla del suelo f. **floorcloth** n trapo m. **flooring** n solado m. **floor polish** cera para el suelo f. floor show espectáculo de cabaret m. **floorwalker** n supervisor de división m.

flop [flop] v desplomarse; (*fail*) fracasar. n (*coll*) fracaso m. **floppy** adj flojo; colgante.

flora [ˈfloɪrə] n flora f.

florist [ˈfloirist] n florista m, f. **florist's shop** florería f.

flounce[1] [flauns] v **flounce in/out** entrar/salir enfadado. n movimiento brusco m.

flounce[2] [flauns] n (*of dress*) volante m.

flounder [ˈflaundə] v forcejear; confundirse.

flour [ˈflauə] n harina f. v enharinar. **flour mill** molino harinero m. **floury** adj (*covered with flour*) enharinado; (*like flour*) harinoso.

flourish [ˈflʌriʃ] v (*prosper*) florecer; (*wave*) agitar; (*brandish*) esgrimir. n ostentación f; (*gesture*) ademán m; (*writing*) rasgo m. **flourishing** adj floreciente.

flout [flaut] v burlarse de.

flow [flou] v (*liquid*) fluir; (*tears*) correr; (*blood in the body*) circular; (*blood from the body*) derramarse; (*tide*) subir. **flow away** irse. **flow from** salir de. **flow in/out** entrar/salir a raudales. **flow into** desembocar. n circulación f; movimiento m. **flow chart** organigrama m. **flowing** adj (*river*) fluente; (*style*) fluido; (*hair*) suelto; (*beard*) largo.

flower [ˈflauə] n flor f. **flower arrangement** ramillete m. **flower bed** arriate m. **flowerpot** n maceta f. **flower shop** florería f. **flower show** exposición de flores f. v florecer. **flowering** adj floreciente; n florecimiento m. **flowery** adj florido.

flown [floun] V **fly.**

flu [fluɪ] n gripe f.

fluctuate [ˈflʌktjuˌeit] v fluctuar; vacilar. **fluctuation** n fluctuación f.

flue [fluɪ] n chimenea f; conducto de humo m.

fluent [ˈfluənt] adj (*language*) bueno; (*writing*) fluido. **fluency** n facilidad f; dominio m. **fluently** adv (*speech*) con soltura; (*writing*) con fluidez.

fluff [flʌf] n pelusa f; mota f; masa esponjosa f. **fluffy** adj (*pillow, cushion*) mullido; (*downy*) velloso; (*cloth*) que tiene pelusa.

fluid [ˈfluid] nm, adj fluido.

fluke [fluɪk] n chiripa f. **fluky** adj de suerte.

flung [flʌŋ] V **fling.**

fluorescent [fluəˈresnt] adj fluorescente. **fluorescence** n fluorescencia f.

fluoride [ˈfluəraid] n fluoruro m. **fluoridation** n fluoración f.

flurry [ˈflʌri] n (*excitement*) agitación f; (*snow*) borrasca f; (*rain*) chaparrón m; (*wind*) ráfaga f.

flush[1] [flʌʃ] n (*blush*) rubor m; (*fever*) sofoco m; (*lavatory*) cisterna f. v ruborizarse; tener sofocos; (*light*) resplandecer. **flush the toilet** tirar de la cadena. **flushed** adj rebosante.

flush[2] [flʌʃ] adj (*abundant*) copioso; (*lavish*) liberal; (*coll: well off*) adinerado. **flush with** (*level*) a nivel con.

fluster [ˈflʌstə] v poner nervioso. n agitación f.

flute [fluɪt] n flauta f.

flutter [ˈflʌtə] v (*leaves, etc.*) revolotear; (*wings*) batir; (*curtains, flags*) ondular; (*heart*) palpitar; (*flap*) agitar. n ondulación f; (*wings*) aleteo m; agitación f; (*eyelids*) parpadeo m; palpitación f.

flux [flʌks] n (*flow*) flujo m; (*changes*) cambios frecuentes m pl. **be in a state of flux** estar siempre cambiando.

*fly¹ [flai] *v* volar; (*escape*) huir; (*time*) pasar volando; (*kite*) echar a volar; (*aircraft*) pilotar; (*flag*) izar, enarbolar; (*go across*) atravesar; (*mileage*) recorrer. **fly away** emprender el vuelo. **fly over** sobrevolar. **fly past** desfilar. **flies** *pl n* (*trousers*) bragueta *f*.

fly² [flai] *n* mosca *f*.

fly-blown *adj* cochambroso.

fly-fishing *n* pesca con moscas *f*.

flying ['flaiiŋ] *adj* volador; volante. *n* aviación *f*.

flying colours *pl n* éxito rotundo *m*.

flying field *n* campo de aviación *m*.

flying fish *n* pez volador *m*.

flying saucer *n* platillo volante *m*.

flying squirrel *n* ardilla volante *f*.

flying start *n* salida lanzada *f*; (*fig*) principio feliz *m*.

flyleaf ['flailif] *n* guarda *f*.

flyover ['flai,ouvə] *n* paso elevado *m*.

fly-paper *n* papel matamoscas *m*.

fly swatter *n* matamoscas *m invar*.

flyweight ['flaiweit] *n* peso mosca *m*.

flywheel ['flaiwiːl] *n* volante *m*.

foal [foul] *n* potro, -a *m*, *f*. *v* parir.

foam [foum] *n* espuma *f*. *v* espumar; (*animal*) espumajear. **foam rubber** gomespuma *f*. **foaming** *adj* espumoso.

focal ['foukəl] *adj* focal. **focal point** punto focal.

focus ['foukəs] *n* foco *m*. **in focus** enfocado. **out of focus** fuera de foco. *v* enfocar; concentrar.

fodder ['fodə] *n* forraje *m*.

foe [fou] *n* enemigo, -a *m*, *f*.

foetus ['fiːtəs] *n* feto *m*. **foetal** *adj* fetal.

fog [fog] *n* niebla *f*, bruma *f*. **fogbound** *adj* (*foggy*) cubierto de niebla; (*immobilized*) detenido por la niebla. **foghorn** *n* sirena de niebla *f*. **foglamp** *or* **foglight** (*mot*) faro antiniebla *m*. **fogginess** *n* nebulosidad *f*. **foggy** *adj* nebuloso, brumoso.

foible ['foibl] *n* extravagancia *f*; (*fad*) manía *f*.

foil¹ [foil] *v* frustrar.

foil² [foil] *n* hoja fina de metal *f*; (*fig*) contraste *m*.

foil³ [foil] *n* (*fencing*) florete *m*.

foist [foist] *v* colar; meter.

fold¹ [fould] *n* (*crease*) pliegue *m*; (*wrinkle*) arruga *f*. *v* doblar, plegar; (*surround*) envolver; (*coll: close down*) liquidarse. **fold one's arms** cruzar los brazos. **folder**

n carpeta *f*. **folding** *adj* plegable. **folding door** puerta de fuelle *f*.

fold² [fould] *n* (*sheep*) redil *m*; (*religion*) grey *f*.

foliage ['fouliidʒ] *n* follaje *m*.

folk [fouk] *pl n* gente *f sing*; pueblo *m*. **folks** *pl n* (*coll*) familia *f sing*. **folk art** arte popular. **folk dance** baile folklórico *m*. **folklore** *n* folklore *m*. **folk music** música popular *f*. **folk singer** cantante de canciones populares. **folk song** canción popular *f*.

follicle ['folikl] *n* folículo *m*.

follow ['folou] *v* seguir; (*pursue*) perseguir; (*practise*) ejercer; (*ensue*) resultar. **follow up** investigar sobre; reforzar. **follower** *n* seguidor, -a *m*, *f*; discípulo *m*; aficionado, -a *m*, *f*. **following** *adj* siguiente. *n* partidarios *m pl*.

folly ['foli] *n* locura *f*.

fond [fond] *adj* cariñoso; indulgente. **be fond of** tenerle cariño a. **fondly** *adj* cariñosamente. **fondness** *n* cariño *m*.

fondle ['fondl] *v* acariciar; mimar.

font [font] *n* (*baptismal*) pila *f*; (*printing*) fundición *f*.

food [fuːd] *n* comida *f*, alimento *m*; comestibles *m pl*. **food and drink** comida y bebida *f*. **food poisoning** intoxicación alimenticia *f*. **food shop** tienda de comestibles *f*. **foodstuff** *n* producto alimenticio *m*.

fool [fuːl] *n* tonto, -a *m*, *f*; bobo, -a *m*, *f*; idiota *m*, *f*; (*jester*) bufón *m*. **foolproof** *adj* infalible. *v* (*deceive*) engañar; (*joke*) bromear. **fool about** *or* **around** juguetear. **foolhardy** *adj* temerario. **foolhardiness** *n* temeridad *f*. **foolish** *adj* insensato; tonto. **foolishly** *adv* neciamente. **foolishness** *n* insensatez *f*; tontería *f*.

foolscap ['fuːlskap] *n* papel de barba *m*.

foot [fut] *n, pl* **feet** pie *m*; (*animal*) pata *f*. **from head to foot** de pies a cabeza. **on foot** a pie. **get cold feet** tener miedo.

football ['fut,boːl] *n* fútbol *m*; (*ball*) pelotá *f*. **football pools** *pl n* quinielas *f pl*.

foot brake *n* freno de pedal *m*.

footbridge ['fut,bridʒ] *n* pasarela *f*.

foothills ['futhilz] *pl n* estribaciones *f pl*.

foothold ['fut,hould] *n* punto de apoyo para el pie *m*; (*fig*) posición *f*.

footing ['futiŋ] *n* pie *m*, equilibrio *m*; condición *f*; posición *f*. **on an equal footing** en un pie de igual.

footlights ['fut,laits] *pl n* candilejas *f pl.*

footloose ['futluːs] *adj* libre.

footnote ['fut,nout] *n* nota *f.*

footpath ['fut,paːθ] *n* senda *f; (pavement)* acera *f.*

footprint ['fut,print] *n* pisada *f.*

footstep ['fut,step] *n* paso *m.*

for [fɔː] *prep* para; por; de; *(time)* desde; durante; *(in favour of)* en favor de; *(in honour of)* en honor de; *(in place of)* en lugar de; *(as regards)* en cuanto a; *(against)* contra; *(in order that)* para que. *conj* pues, puesto que, ya que.

forage ['foridʒ] *v* forrajear; *(fig: seek)* buscar. *n* forraje *m.*

*forbear [fɔː'beə] *v* contenerse; abstenerse. **forbearance** *n* abstención *f;* indulgencia *f;* paciencia *f.*

*forbid [fɔː'bid] *v* prohibir; *(prevent)* impedir. **forbidding** *adj* impresionante; inhóspito; severo; *(threatening)* amenazador.

force [fɔːs] *n* fuerza *f; (mil)* cuerpo *m.* **in force** en vigor. **sales force** vendedores *m pl.* **join forces** unirse. *v* forzar; obligar; *(tech)* inyectar. **be forced to** verse obligado a. **forceful** *adj* fuerte; contundente.

forceps ['fɔːseps] *pl n* fórceps *m sing.*

ford [fɔːd] *n* vado *m. v* vadear.

fore [fɔː] *adj* delantero; anterior. *adv* delante. *n (naut)* proa *f.* **come to the fore** empezar a destacar. *interj (golf)* ¡cuidado!

forearm ['fɔːraːm] *n* antebrazo *m. v* prevenir.

forebears ['fɔːbeəz] *pl n* antepasados *m pl.*

foreboding [fɔː'boudiŋ] *n* presentimiento *m.*

*forecast ['fɔːkaːst] *n* previsión *f;* pronóstico *m;* plan *m. v* pronosticar. **weather forecast** pronóstico meteorológico *m.*

forecourt ['fɔːkɔːt] *n* antepatio *m.*

forefather ['fɔːfaːðə] *n* antepasado *m.*

forefinger ['fɔːfiŋgə] *n* dedo índice *m.*

forefront ['fɔːfrʌnt] *n* delantera *f;* sitio de mayor importancia *m.*

foregone ['fɔːgon] *adj* conocido de antemano. **foregone conclusion** conclusión inevitable *f.*

foreground ['fɔːgraund] *n* primer plano *m;* primer término *m.*

forehand ['fɔːhand] *n (tennis)* golpe derecho *m.*

forehead ['forid] *n* frente *f.*

foreign ['forən] *adj* extranjero; ajeno. **foreign affairs** asuntos exteriores *m pl.* **foreign trade** comercio exterior *m.* **foreign exchange** cambio exterior *m.* **foreign legion** legión extranjera *f.* **foreigner** *n* extranjero, -a *m, f.*

foreleg ['fɔːleg] *n* pata delantera *f.*

foreman ['fɔːmən] *n* capataz *m.*

foremost ['fɔːmoust] *adj* delantero; principal. **first and foremost** ante todo.

forename ['fɔːneim] *n* nombre de pila *m.*

forensic [fə'rensik] *adj* forense. **forensic medicine** medicina legal *f.*

forerunner ['fɔːrʌnə] *n* precursor, -a *m, f; (herald)* anunciador, -a *m, f.*

*foresee [fɔː'siː] *v* prever. **foreseeable** *adj* previsible.

foreshadow [fɔː'ʃadou] *v* presagiar; prefigurar.

foresight ['fɔːsait] *n* previsión *f.*

foreskin ['fɔːskin] *n* prepucio *m.*

forest ['forist] *n* selva *f;* bosque *m.* **forester** *n* guardabosque *m.* **forestry** *n* silvicultura *f.* **Forestry Commission** administración de montes *f.*

forestall [fɔː'stɔːl] *v* prevenir; impedir; anticiparse a.

foretaste ['fɔːteist] *n* anticipación *f.*

*foretell [fɔː'tel] *v* predecir; presagiar.

forethought ['fɔːθɔːt] *n* premeditación *f.*

forever [fɔː'evə] *adv* siempre, para siempre. **forever more** por siempre jamás.

forewarn [fɔː'wɔːn] *v* avisar, adventir. **forewarning** *n* aviso *m,* advertencia *f.*

foreword ['fɔːwɔːd] *n* prefacio *m;* prólogo *m.*

forfeit ['fɔːfit] *v (right)* perder; *(property)* comisar.

forge[1] [fɔːdʒ] *v (counterfeit)* falsificar; *(metal)* fraguar. *n* fragua *f.* **forger** *n* falsificador *m; (metal)* herrero *m.* **forgery** *n* falsificación *f; (things forged)* documento falsificado *m;* moneda falsificada *f.*

forge[2] [fɔːdʒ] *v* **forge ahead** hacer grandes progresos.

*forget [fə'get] *v* olvidar, olvidarse de. **forget-me-not** *n* nomeolvides *f.* **forgetful** *adj* olvidadizo; descuidado. **forgetfulness** *n* olvido *m;* descuido *m.*

*forgive [fə'giv] *v* perdonar; dispensar. **forgiveness** *n* perdón *m;* remisión *f.* **forgiving** *adj* indulgente, clemente.

*forgo [fɔː'gou] *v* abstenerse; renunciar.

fork [fɔɪk] *n* (*cutlery*) tenedor *m*; (*gardening*) horca *f*; (*tree*) horcadura *f*; (*road*) bifurcación *f*; (*river*) horcajo *m*. **tuning fork** diapasón *m*. *v* bifurcarse. **forked** *adj* bifurcado.

forlorn [fəˈlɔɪn] *adj* desamparado; triste.

form [fɔɪm] *n* (*shape*) forma *f*; (*figure*) figura *f*; (*type*) tipo *m*; (*document*) formulario *m*; (*school year*) curso *m*. *v* (*make*) hacer; (*model*) modelar; (*habit*) crear; (*constitute*) constituir; (*put together*) formar. **form a queue** ponerse en cola. **formation** *n* formación *f*. **formative** *adj* de formación, formativo.

formal [ˈfɔɪməl] *adj* formal; solemne; (*person*) formalista; ceremonioso; de cortesía; en debida forma. **formality** *n* (*requirement*) formalidad *f*; ceremonia *f*; rigidez *f*.

format [ˈfɔɪmat] *n* formato *m*.

former [ˈfɔɪmə] *adj* (*previous*) anterior; (*ex-*) antiguo, pasado. *pron* ése, ésa, aquél, equélla. el primero, la primera. **formerly** *adv* anteriormente; antiguamente.

formidable [ˈfɔɪmidəbl] *adj* formidable.

formula [ˈfɔɪmjulə] *n*, *pl* **-ae** fórmula *f*.

formulate [ˈfɔɪmjuleit] *v* formular. **formulation** *n* formulación *f*.

*****forsake** [fəˈseik] *v* abandonar.

fort [fɔɪt] *n* fuerte *m*, fortaleza *f*.

forte [ˈfɔɪtei] *n* fuerte *m*.

forth [fɔɪθ] *adv* en adelante. **and so forth** y así sucesivamente. **forthcoming** *adj* próximo; (*approaching*) venidero; (*person*) abierto. **forthright** *adj* franco. **forthwith** *adv* en seguida; en el acto.

fortify [ˈfɔɪtifai] *v* (*health, moral strength*) fortalecer; (*town*) fortificar; (*wine*) encabezar; (*argument*) reforzar. **fortification** *n* fortalecimiento *m*; fortificación *f*; reforzamiento *m*.

fortitude [ˈfɔɪtitjuɪd] *n* fortaleza *f*; firmeza *f*.

fortnight [ˈfɔɪtnait] *n* quincena *f*. **fortnightly** *adj* quincenal. *adv* quincenalmente.

fortress [ˈfɔɪtris] *n* fortaleza *f*.

fortuitous [fəˈtjuɪitəs] *adj, adv* casual.

fortunate [ˈfɔɪtʃənət] *adj* afortunado; oportuno. **fortunately** *adv* afortunadamente.

fortune [ˈfɔɪtʃən] *n* (*fate*) fortuna *f*; (*luck*) suerte *f*. **cost a fortune** costar un dineral. **stroke of fortune** golpe de suerte *m*. **fortune-teller** *n* adivino, -a *m, f*.

forty [ˈfɔɪti] *nm, adj* cuarenta. **fortieth** *nm, adj* cuarentavo.

forum [ˈfɔɪrəm] *n* foro *m*; (*meeting*) tribuna *f*.

forward [ˈfɔɪwəd] *adj* (*front*) delantero; (*movement*) hacia adelante; (*progressive*) avanzado; (*impertinent*) impertinente. *v* (*send*) expedir; (*promote*) promover. **please forward** remítase al destinario. *n* (*football*) delantero *m*. **forwards** *adv* adelante.

fossil [ˈfosl] *nm, adj* fósil. **fossilized** *adj* fosilizado.

foster [ˈfostə] *v* (*child*) criar; (*idea*) abrigar; (*project*) patrocinar; (*favour*) favorecer. *adj* adoptivo.

fought [fɔɪt] *V* **fight**.

foul [faul] *adj* asqueroso; (*dirty*) sucio; (*air*) viciado; (*language*) grosero; (*smell*) fétido. **foul play** jugada sucia *f*. *n* falta *f*. *v* ensuciar; (*reputation*) manchar; (*sport*) cometer una falta

found[1] [faund] *V* **find**.

found[2] [faund] *v* fundar; construir; (*opinion*) fundamentar. **foundation** *n* (*establishment*) fundación *f*; (*building*) cimientos *m pl*; (*fig*) fundamento *m*. **founder** *n* fundador, -a *m, f*.

founder [ˈfaundə] *v* (*ship*) hundirse; (*fall*) derrumbarse.

foundry [ˈfaundri] *n* fundición *f*.

fountain [ˈfauntin] *n* fuente *f*. **fountain-head** *n* manantial *m*. **fountain pen** pluma estilográfica *f*.

four [fɔɪ] *nm, adj* cuatro. **fourth** *m, adj* cuarto, -a *m, f*.

fourteen [fɔɪˈtiɪn] *nm, adj* catorce. **fourteenth** *n, adj* decimocuarto, -a *m, f*.

fowl [faul] *n* aves de corral *f pl*; (*cock*) gallo *m*; (*hen*) gallina *f*; (*chicken*) pollo *m*.

fox [foks] *n* zorro, -a *m, f*. *v* (*baffle*) desconcertar; (*trick*) engañar. **foxglove** *n* digital *f*. **foxhound** *n* perro raposero *m*. **foxhunting** *n* caza de zorros *f*.

foyer [ˈfoiei] *n* foyer *m*.

fraction [ˈfrakʃən] *n* fracción *f*; pequeña parte *f*. **fractional** *adj* fraccionario.

fracture [ˈfraktʃə] *n* fractura *f*. *v* fracturarse.

fragile [ˈfradʒail] *adj* frágil. **fragility** *n* fragilidad.

fragment ['fragmənt] *n* fragmento *m.* *v* fragmentar.

fragrant ['freigrənt] *adj* fragante. **fragrance** *n* fragancia *f.*

frail [freil] *adj* frágil; débil; delicado. **frailty** *n* fragilidad *f*; debilidad *f*; delicadez *f.*

frame [freim] *n* (*building*) armazón *f*; (*picture*) marco *m*; (*bicycle*) cuadro *m*; (*spectacles*) montura *f*; (*film*) imagen *f*. **frame of mind** estado de ánimo *m. v* (*enclose*) enmarcar; (*devise*) elaborar; (*shape*) formar; hacer la armazón de.

France [frains] *n* Francia *f.*

franchise ['frantʃaiz] *n* derecho de voto *m.*

frank [fraŋk] *adj* franco; abierto. **frankness** *n* franqueza *f.*

frankfurter ['fraŋkfɔitə] *n* salchicha alemana *f.*

frantic ['frantik] *adj* frenético; loco.

fraternal [frə'təinl] *adj* fraternal. **fraternity** *n* (*brotherhood*) fraternidad *f*; (*association*) asociación *f*; (*religious*) hermandad *f.* **fraternize** *v* fraternizar.

fraud [froid] *n* (*law*) fraude *m*; (*deception*) engaño *m*; (*person*) impostor *m.* **fraudulent** *adj* fraudulento.

fraught [froit] *adj* **fraught with** cargado de.

fray[1] [frei] *v* raer, desgastar.

fray[2] [frei] *n* (*brawl*) riña *f*; (*fight*) combate *m.*

freak [friik] *n* capricho *m*; fantasís *f*; monstruosidad *f. adj* imprevisto; extraño.

freckle ['frekl] *n* peca *f.* **freckled** *adj* pecoso.

free [frii] *adj* libre; gratis; (*loose*) suelto; generoso; sincero; (*manner*) desenvuelto. **free and easy** *adj* poco ceremonioso.

freedom ['friidəm] *n* libertad *f*; soltura *f.* **free-for-all** *n* refriega *f.*

freehand ['friihand] *adj* a pulso.

freehold ['friihould] *n* propiedad absoluta *f.*

freelance ['friilains] *n* persona que trabaja independientemente *f.*

freely ['friili] *adj* libremente; voluntariamente; gratuitamente.

freemason ['friimeisn] *n* francmasón. **freemasonry** *n* francmasonería *f.*

freesia ['friiziə] *n* fresia *f.*

freestyle ['friistail] *n* estilo libre *m.*

free trade *n* librecambio *m.*

free will *n* libre albedrío *m.*

***freeze** [friiz] *v* (*preserve*) congelar; (*chill*) refrigerar; (*from cold*) helarse; (*prices, etc.*) bloquear; (*turn to ice*) helar; (*stand still*) quedarse inmóvil. *n* helada *f*; bloqueo *m.* **freezer** *n* congelador *m.* **freezing** *adj* glacial. **freezing point** punto de congelación.

freight [freit] *n* (*load*) carga *f*; (*transportation*) transporte *m*; (*by ship, plane*) flete *m*; (*other*) mercancías *f pl.* **freight train** tren de mercancías *m.* **freighter** *n* (*ship*) buque de carga *m*; (*aircraft*) avión de carga *m.*

French [frentʃ] *nm, adj* francés. **the French** los franceses. **French bean** judía verde *f.* **French horn** trompa de llaves *f.* **French polish** barniz de muebles *m.* **french fries** patata frita *f. v*

frenzy ['frenzi] *n* frenesí *m*, delirio *m.* **frenzied** *adj* frenético.

frequent ['friikwənt; *v* fri'kwent] *adj* frecuente; (*usual*) común. *v* frecuentar. **frequency** *n* frecuencia *f.* **frequently** *adv* frecuentemente.

fresco ['freskou] *n* fresco *m.*

fresh [freʃ] *adj* fresco; (*bread*) tierno; (*water*) dulce; (*air*) puro; (*complexion*) de buen color; (*new*) nuevo. *adv* recientemente. **freshwater** *adj* (*fish*) de aqua dulce. **freshen up** refrescarse. **freshness** *n* frescura *f*; novedad *f.*

fret[1] [fret] *v* irritar; (*complain*) quejarse. **fretful** *adj* mal humorado; (*upset*) apenado.

fret[2] [fret] *n* (*music*) traste *m. v* adornar con calados. **fretsaw** *n* sierra de calar *f.* **fretwork** *n* calado *m.*

friar ['fraiə] *n* fraile *m*, monje *m.* **friary** *n* monasterio *m.*

friction ['frikʃən] *n* fricción *f.*

Friday ['fraidei] *n* viernes *m.* **Good Friday** Viernes Santo *m.*

fridge [fridʒ] *n* (*coll*) nevera *f.*

fried [fraid] *adj* frito.

friend [frend] *n* amigo, -a *m, f.* **make friends with** hacerse amigo de. **the best of friends** muy amigos. **friendliness** *n* simpatía *f.* **friendly** *adj* simpático; amistoso. **friendship** *n* amistad *f.*

frieze [friiz] *n* friso *m.*

frigate ['frigit] *n* fragata *f.*

fright [frait] *n* susto *m*; miedo *m*; terror *m.* **frighten** *v* asustar. **be frightened** tener miedo. **frightening** adj espantoso. **frightful** adj horrible; (fig) tremendo.

frigid ['fridʒid] adj glacial; (manner) frío; (med) frígido. **frigidity** n frialdad f; (med) frigidez f.

frill [fril] n (shirt) pechera f; (fluting) encañonado m; (flared edge) volante m; (ruff) gorguera f. **frilly** adj con volantes.

fringe [frindʒ] n franja f; (edge) borde m. **fringe benefits** beneficios complementarios m pl. v franjar.

frisk [frisk] v brincar; (coll: search) cachear. **friskiness** n viveza f. **frisky** adj juguetón.

fritter¹ ['fritə] v **fritter away** malgastar.

fritter² ['fritə] n (cookery) buñuelo m.

frivolity [fri'voliti] n frivolidad f. **frivolous** adj frívolo; trivial.

frizz [friz] v (hair) rizar. **frizzy** adj crespo.

fro [frou] adv **to and fro** de un lado a otro. **go to and fro** ir y venir.

frock [frok] n vestido m.

frog [frog] n rana f. **frogman** n hombre rana m. **frogs' legs** ancas de rana f pl. **have a frog in one's throat** tener carraspera.

frolic ['frolik] n juego m; diversión f. v juguetar; divertirse. **frolicsome** adj juguetón.

from [from] prep de; desde; (made from) con; (steal, buy, take, etc.) a; (drink, learn) en; (speak, act) por; (according to) según.

front [frʌnt] n (building) fachada f; (shop) escaparate m; parte delantera f; principio m; (face) cara f; (weather) frente m. **in front of** delante de. adj delantero; principal; primero.

frontier ['frʌntiə] n frontera f. adj fronterizo.

frost [frost] n escarcha f; helada f. **frostbite** n congelación f. **frostbitten** adj congelado. v cubrir de escarcha. **frosted glass** vidrio deslustrado m. **frosty** adj escarchado; helado.

froth [froθ] n espuma f; (fig) frivolidad f. v espumar. **frothy** adj espumoso; frívolo.

frown [fraun] n ceño m. v fruncir el entrecejo. **frown on** or **upon** desaprobar. **frowning** adj severo; amenazador.

froze [frouz] V **freeze**.

frozen ['frouzn] adj congelado, helado. **frozen food** comestibles congelados m pl.

frugal ['fruːɡəl] adj frugal; sobrio. **frugality** n frugalidad f; sobriedad f.

fruit [fruːt] n (on tree) fruto m, (as food) fruta f. **fruit cake** pastel de fruta m. **fruit machine** máquina tragaperras f. **fruit salad** ensalada de frutas f. v dar fruto. **fruitful** adj fructífero; (fig) fructuoso. **fruition** n fruición f; realización f; (bot) fructificación f.

frustrate [frʌ'streit] v (plans, etc.) frustrar; impedir.

*****fry** [frai] v freír. **frying pan** sartén f.

fuchsia ['fjuːʃə] n fucsia f.

fuck [fʌk] v (impol) joder.

fudge [fʌdʒ] v fallar; inventar.

fuel ['fjuəl] n combustible m; gasolina f; (mot) carburante f. **fuel gauge** indicador del nivel de gasolina m. **fuel pump** gasolinera f. v (mot) echar gasolina a; (furnace) alimentar; (ship) abastecer de combustible.

fugitive ['fjuːdʒitiv] n, adj fugativo, -a.

fulcrum ['fulkrəm] n fulcro m.

fulfil [ful'fil] v (promise, obligation) cumplir; (ambition) realizar; (purpose) servir; (wishes) satisfacer; (function) desempeñar; (plan) llevar a cabo. **fulfilment** n cumplimiento m; realización f; satisfacción f; (instructions) ejecución f.

full [ful] adj lleno; completo; (text) íntegro; (whole) entero; (price) sin descuento; (extensive) extenso; (daylight, development) pleno; (speed) todo; (capacity) máximo; (measure, weight) exacto; (flavour) mucho. **full employment** pleno empleo m. **full up** completamente lleno. **I'm full** no puedo más. **in full colour** a todo color.

full-blooded adj (thoroughbred) de pura sangre; (robust) vigoroso; (true blue) verdadero.

full-bodied adj (wine) de mucho cuerpo.

full-dress adj de etiqueta; de gala.

full-grown adj crecido; adulto.

full-hearted adj completo.

full house n (theatre or cinema notice) no hay localidades.

full-length adj de cuerpo entero.

full-scale adj de tamaño natural.

full stop n punto m.

full-time adj de jornada completa.

fumble ['fʌmbl] v tojetear; (drop) dejar caer; (feel) hurgar; (search) buscar.

fume [fjuːm] v (fig) bufar de cólera. **fumes** pl n numo m.

fun [fʌn] *n* alegría *f*; gracia *f*; diversión *f*. **for fun** en broma. **funfair** *n* parque de atracciones *m*. **have fun** divertirse. **make fun of** reírse de. **what fun!** ¡qué divertido!

function ['fʌŋkʃən] *n* función *f*; acto *m*; recepción *f*. *v* funcionar. **functional** *adj* funcional.

fund [fʌnd] *n* fondo *m*; (*source*) fuente *f*.

fundamental [fʌndə'mentl] *adj* fundamental.

funeral ['fjuːnərəl] *n* funeral *m*; (*state*) exequias nacionales *f pl*. **funeral parlour** funeraria *f*. **funeral procession** cortejo fúnebre *m*. **funeral service** misa de cuerpo presente *f*.

fungus ['fʌŋgəs] *n, pl* -i (*bot*) hongo *m*; (*med*) fungo *m*.

funnel ['fʌnl] *n* (*pourer*) embudo; (*smokestack*) chimenea *f*. *v* verter por un embudo; (*direct*) encauzar.

funny ['fʌni] *adj* divertido; gracioso; (*curious*) extraño. **taste funny** tener un sabor extraño. **funny business** cosas varas *f pl*. **funny-bone** hueso de la alegría *m*. **funnily** *adv* graciosamente.

fur [fəː] *n* pelo *m*; (*pelt*) piel *f*; (*kettle*) sarro *m*; (*tongue*) saburra *f*. **fur coat** abrigo de pieles *m*. *v* forrar con pieles; incrustar; cubrir de sarro. **furrier** *n* peletero *m*; (*shop*) peletería *f*. **furry** *adj* peludo; sarroso.

furious ['fjuəriəs] *adj* furioso; violento.

furnace ['fəːnis] *n* horno *m*; (*domestic*) estufa *f*; (*boiler*) hogar *m*.

furnish ['fəːniʃ] *v* (*house*) amueblar; (*supply*) suministrar; (*give*) facilitar; (*opportunity*) dar; (*proof*) aducir. **furnishings** *pl n* muebles *m pl*; mobiliario *m*.

furniture ['fəːnitʃə] *n* muebles *m pl*. **furniture van** camión de mudanzas *m*.

furrow ['fʌrou] *n* (*ploughing*) surco *m*; (*forehead*) arruga *f*; (*groove*) ranura *f*. *v* surcar; arrugar.

further ['fəːðə] *adj* (*distant, additional*) otro; (*another*) nuevo; (*later*) posterior; (*education*) superior. *adv* más; más lejos, más allá; (*moreover*) además. *v* favorecer. **furtherance** *n* adelantamiento *m*; formento *m*. **furthermore** *adv* además. **furthermost** *adj* más lejano. **furthest** *adj* más lejano; extremo.

furtive ['fəːtiv] *adj* furtivo.

fury ['fjuəri] *n* furia *f*, furor *m*.

fuse¹ [fjuːz] *n* (*elec*) fusible *m*. **fuse box** caja de fusibles *f*. *v* (*join*) fusionar; (*melt*) fundir.

fuse² [fjuːz] *n* (*explosives*) mecha *f*; (*detonator*) espoleta *f*.

fuselage ['fjuːzə,laːʒ] *n* fuselaje *m*.

fusion ['fjuːʒən] *n* fusión *f*.

fuss [fʌs] *n* (*trouble*) lío *m*; (*commotion*) alboroto *m*; (*complaints*) quejas *f pl*. **a lot of fuss about nothing** mucho ruido y pocas nueces. *v* agitarse; quejarse; preocuparse; molestar. **fussiness** *n* agitación *f*. **fussy** *adj* escrupuloso; exigente; melindroso.

futile ['fjuːtail] *adj* vano; frívolo.

future ['fjuːtʃə] *n* futuro *m*; porvenir *m*. *adj* futuro; venidero.

fuzz [fʌz] *n* (*on face*) vello *m*; (*fluff*) pelusa *f*. **fuzzy** *adj* velloso; (*blurred*) borroso.

G

gabble ['gabl] *v* chacharear. *n* cháchara *f*. **gabbler** *n* chacharero, -a *m, f*.

gable ['geibl] *n* gablete *m*.

gadget ['gadʒit] *n* aparato *m*; accesorio *m*.

gag¹ [gag] *v* amordazar. *n* mordaza *f*.

gag² [gag] *n* (*joke*) broma *f*; chiste *m*.

gaiety ['geiəti] *n* alegría *f*; jovialidad *f*.

gain [gein] *n* ganancia *f*; provecho *m*; aumento *m*. *v* ganar; avanzar.

gait [geit] *n* modo de andar *m*.

gala ['gaːlə] *n* fiesta *f*, gala *f*.

galaxy ['galəksi] *n* galaxia *f*.

gale [geil] *n* vendaval *m*.

gallant ['galənt] *adj* (*to women*) galante; (*brave*) valiente; (*stately*) elegante. **gallantry** *n* galantería *f*; valor *m*; (*courtesy*) cortesía *f*.

gall-bladder ['goːl,bladə] *n* vesícula biliar *f*.

galleon ['galiən] *n* galeón *m*.

gallery ['galəri] *n* galería *f*; (*spectators*) tribuna *f*; (*theatre*) gallinero *m*.

galley ['gali] *n* (*ship*) galera *f*; (*kitchen*) cocina *f*.

gallon ['galən] *n* galón *m*.

gallop ['galəp] *n* galope *m*. *v* galopar.

gallows ['galouz] *pl n* cadalso *m sing*.

gallstone ['gɔːlstoun] n cálculo biliar m.

galore [gə'lɔː] adj, adv en cantidad.

galvanize ['galvənaiz] v galvanizar.

gamble ['gambl] v (bet) apostar; (risk) arriesgar. **gamble on** contar con. n (risky enterprise) empresa arriesgada f; (game) jugada f. **gambler** n jugador, -a m, f. **gambling** n juego m. **gambling den** garito m.

game [geim] n juego m; (sport) deporte m; (of football, tennis, etc.) partido m; (cards, chess, etc.) partida f; (hunting) caza f. **game bird** ave de caza f. **gamekeeper** n guardabosque m. **play the game** jugar limpio. adj (coll) valiente.

gammon ['gamən] n jamón ahumado m.

gang [gaŋ] n (band) cuadrilla f; (of gangsters) banda f. v **gang up on** conspirar contra. **gangster** n gángster m.

gangrene ['gaŋgriːn] n gangrena f. **gangrenous** adj gangrenoso.

gangway ['gaŋwei] n (passage) pasillo m; (naut) pasarela f.

gaol V jail.

gap [gap] n (empty space) vacío m; (breach) brecha f; (cavity) hueco m; (in a wall) portillo m; (between hills) quebrada f; (in education) laguna f; (crack) resquicio m; (in a wood) claro m.

gape [geip] v (stare) quedarse boquiabierto; (open wide) abrirse mucho.

garage ['garɑːdʒ] n garaje m.

garbage ['gɑːbidʒ] n basura f. **garbage can** cubo de la basura m. **garbage disposal** vertedero de basuras m. **garbage man** basurero m.

garble ['gɑːbl] v amañar; mutilar. **garbled** adj amañado; mutilado.

garden ['gɑːdn] n jardín m; huerto m. v cultivar un huerto. **garden city** ciudad jardín f. **garden party** recepción al aire libre f. **garden produce** hortalizas f pl. **gardener** n jardinero, -a m, f. **gardening** n jardinería f.

gargle ['gɑːgl] v hacer gárgaras. n gárgaras f pl.

garland ['gɑːlənd] n guirnalda f. v enguirnaldar.

garlic ['gɑːlik] n ajo m.

garment ['gaːmənt] n prenda f, traje m, vestido m.

garnish ['gɑːniʃ] v adornar, embellecer; (cookery) aderezar. n adorno m; aderezo m.

garrison ['garisn] n guarnición f. v guarnecer.

garter ['gɑːtə] n liga f. **Order of the Garter** orden de la jarretera f.

gas [gas] n gas m; (petrol) gasolina f, bencina f. **step on the gas** (coll) acelerar. v asfixiar con gas. **gaseous** adj gaseoso. **gas burner** n mechero de gas m. **gas fire** n estufa de gas f. **gas main** n cañería maestra de gas f. **gasmask** n máscara para gases f. **gas meter** n contador de gas m. **gaspipe** n cañería de gas f. **gas-ring** n fogón de gas m. **gas stove** n cocina de gas f. **gasworks** n fábrica de gas f.

gash [gaʃ] n herida f; cuchillada f. v acuchillar.

gasket ['gaskit] n junta de culata f.

gasoline ['gasəliːn] n gasolina f.

gasp [gaːsp] n (breathing difficulty) jadeo m; (surprise) boqueada f. v jadear; boquear.

gastric ['gastrik] adj gástrico. **gastric fever** fiebre gástrica f. **gastric juice** jugo gástrico. **gastric ulcer** úlcera gástrica f. **gastritis** n gastritis f. **gastroenteritis** n gastroenteritis f.

gastronomic [gastrə'nomik] adj gastronómico. **gastronomy** n gastronomía f.

gate [geit] n puerta f, entrada f; (metal) verja f; (level-crossing) barrera f. **gatecrash** v asistir sin invitación. **gatekeeper** n portero, -a m, f. **gatepost** n soporte de la puerta m. **gateway** n entrada f, paso m.

gateau ['gatou] n tarta f.

gather ['gaðə] v coger, amontonar; (strength) cobrar; (harvest) cosechar; (understand) colegir; (money) recaudar; (sewing) fruncir. **gather together** reunirse, congregarse. **gathering** n reunión f, afluencia f.

gaudy ['gɔːdi] adj chillón, cursi.

gauge [geidʒ] n (rail) entrevía f; (gun) calibre m; (measure) indicador m; (fig) medida f. v medir, juzgar; calibrar. **broad/narrow gauge railway** ferrocarril de vía ancha/estrecha m. **pressure gauge** manómetro m.

gaunt [gɔːnt] adj demacrado; (grim) feroz; (fig) lúgubre.

gauze [gɔːz] n gasa f.

gave [geiv] V give.

gay [gei] adj alegre; gozoso; (dress) guapo; (event) festivo; (coll) homosexual. n (coll: homosexual) maricón m.

gaze [geiz] *v* mirar fijamente. *n* mirada fija *f*.

gazelle [gə'zel] *n* gacela *f*.

gazetteer [gazə'tiə] *n* gacetero *m*.

gear [giə] *n* (*mech*) engranaje *m*, juego *m*, marcha *f*; (*dress*) traje *m*; (*tackle*) utensilios *m pl*; (*naut*) aparejo *m*. **gearbox** caja de velocidades *f*. **gear lever** palanca de cambio de velocidad. **in gear** engranado. *v* aparejar; engranar; adaptar.

geese [giːs] *V* **goose**.

gelatine ['dʒelə,tiin] *n* gelatina *f*.

gelignite ['dʒelig,nait] *n* gelignita *f*.

gem [dʒem] *n* joya *f*, gema *f*; (*delight*) preciosidad *f*.

Gemini ['dʒemini] *pl n* Géminis *m*.

gender ['dʒendə] *n* género *m*; sexo *m*.

gene [dʒiin] *n* gene *m*.

genealogy [dʒiini,alədʒi] *n* genealogía *f*. **genealogical** *adj* genealógico.

general ['dʒenərəl] *nm*, *adj* general. **general election** elección general *f*. **general opinion** voz común *f*. **general practitioner** médico, -a general *m*, *f*. **in general** generalmente. **generalization** *n* generalización *f*. **generalize** *v* generalizar.

generate ['dʒenəreit] *v* producir; (*elec*) generar. **generation** *n* generación *f*. **generator** *n* generador *m*; dínamo *f*.

generic [dʒi'nerik] *adj* genérico.

generous ['dʒenərəs] *adj* generoso; magnánimo. **generosity** *n* generosidad *f*; liberalidad *f*.

genetic [dʒi'netik] *adj* genético. **genetics** *n* genética *f*.

Geneva [dʒi'niivə] *n* Ginebra. **Lake Geneva** Lago de Ginebra.

genial ['dʒiiniəl] *adj* genial, cordial.

genital ['dʒenitl] *adj* genital. **genitals** *pl n* genitales *m pl*.

genitive ['dʒenitiv] *nm*, *adj* genitivo.

genius ['dʒiinjəs] *n* genio *m*.

genteel [dʒen'tiil] *adj* fino; melindroso.

gentle ['dʒentl] *adj* (*light*) lijero; (*mild*) suave; (*slow*) lento; (*tame*) manso; (*moderate*) moderado; (*friendly*) amable; (*kind*) bondadoso. **gentleman** *n* caballero *m*, señor *m*. **gentlemen** *pl n* (*in correspondence*) muy señores míos, muy señores nuestros *m pl*. **gentleness** *n* amabilidad *f*; bondad *f*; suavidad *f*.

gentry ['dʒentri] *n* pequeña nobleza *f*.

gents [dʒents] *n* (*sign*) caballeros *m pl*.

genuine ['dʒenjuin] *adj* puro; genuino; verdadero; auténtico.

genus ['dʒiinəs] *n* género *m*.

geography [dʒi'ogrəfi] *n* geografía *f*. **geographer** *n* geógrafo *m*. **geographic** *adj also* **geographical** geográfico.

geology [dʒi'olədʒi] *n* geología *f*. **geological** *adj* geológico. **geologist** *n* geólogo *m*.

geometry [dʒi'omətri] *n* geometría *f*. **geometrical** *adj* geométrico.

geranium [dʒə'reiniəm] *n* geranio *m*.

geriatric [dʒeri'atrik] *adj* geriátrico. **geriatrics** *n* geriatría *f*.

germ [dʒəim] *n* (*med*) bacilo *m*; microbio *m*; (*fig*) germen *m*.

Germany ['dʒəiməni] *n* Alemania *f*. **German** *n*, *adj* alemán, -ana *m*, *f*. **German measles** rubéola *f*. **Germanic** *adj* germánico.

germinate ['dʒəimineit] *v* germinar, brotar. **germination** *n* germinación *f*.

gerund ['dʒerənd] *n* gerundio *m*.

gesticulate [dʒe'stikju,leit] *v* gesticular. **gesticulation** *n* gesticulación *f*.

gesture ['dʒestʃə] *v* gesticular. *n* gesto *m*.

*get [get] *v* obtener; tener; recibir; (*fetch*) buscar; (*buy*) comprar; (*call*) llamar; (*find*) encontrar; (*catch, reproduce*) coger; (*bring*) llevar; (*extract*) sacar; (*succeed*) conseguir; (*coll: understand*) llegar a comprender; (*coll: kill*) matar. **get about** desplazarse. **get across** (*cross*) atravesar; hacer comprender. **getaway** *n* huida *f*. **get at** (*reach*) alcanzar; (*tease*) meterse con. **get back** (*return*) volver; (*recover*) récobrar. **get by** (*manage*) arreglárselas. **get down** (*descend*) bajar; (*write*) poner por escrito. **get down to** ponerse a. **get off** bajarse de; escapar. **get on** (*mount*) subir a; (*progress*) progresar; (*agree*) llevarse bien; (*grow old*) envejecer. **get out** salir; (*fig*) sacar. **get up** (*arise*) levantarse; (*climb*) subirse.

geyser ['giizə] *n* (*hot spring*) géiser *m*; (*water-heater*) calentador de agua *m*.

ghastly ['gaistli] *adj* horroroso; (*pale*) de una palidez mortal.

gherkin ['gəikin] *n* cohombrillo *m*.

ghetto ['getou] *n* judería *f*.

ghost [goust] *n* fantasma *m*; espectro; (*spirit*) alma *f*. **ghost writer** escritor fantasma *m*. **Holy Ghost** Espíritu Santo *m*. **give up the ghost** entregar el alma. **ghostly** *adj* espectral. **ghostliness** *n* espiritualidad *f*.

giant ['dʒaiənt] *nm, adj* gigante.

gibberish ['dʒibəriʃ] *n* galimatías *m invar*.

gibe [dʒaib] *n* mofa *f*. *v* **jibe at** mofarse de.

giblets ['dʒiblits] *pl n* menudillos *m pl*.

giddy ['gidi] *adj* (*dizzy*) mareado; (*height*) vertiginoso; (*scatter-brained*) frívolo. **giddiness** *n* mareo *m*, vértigo *m*.

gift [gift] *n* regalo *m*; (*talent*) don *m*; (*offering*) ofrenda *f*. **gift-token** vale para comprar un regalo *m*. **gifted** *adj* dotado; talentoso.

gigantic [dʒai'gantik] *adj* gigantesco.

giggle ['gigl] *v* reírse tontamente. *n* risita *f*. **the giggles** la risa tonta *f sing*.

gill [gil] *n* (*fish*) branquia *f*; (*plant*) laminilla *f*; (*measure*) medida de líquidos *f*.

gilt [gilt] *nm, adj* dorado. **gilt-edged** (*book*) con cantos dorados. **gilt-edged securities** valores de máxima garantía *m pl*.

gimmick ['gimik] *n* (*coll: gadget*) artefact *m*; (*coll: trick*) truco *m*.

gin [dʒin] *n* ginebra *f*.

ginger ['dʒindʒə] *n* jengibre *m*. **ginger beer** gaseosa *f*. **gingerbread** *n* pan de jengibre *m*. *adj* (*hair*) rojizo. *v* (*coll*) animar.

gingerly ['dʒindʒəli] *adv* delicadamente.

gipsy ['dʒipsi] *n* gitano, -a *m, f*.

giraffe [dʒi'raif] *n* jirafa *f*.

girder ['gəidə] *n* viga *f*.

girdle ['gəidl] *n* (*belt*) cinturón *m*; (*corset*) faja *f*. *v* ceñir; (*fig*) rodear.

girl [gəil] *n* niña *f*, chica *f*; muchacha *f*; señorita *f*. **girlfriend** *n* amiguita *f*, novia *f*. **girlhood** *n* niñez *f*; juventud *f*. **girlish** *adj* de niña; (*of boys*) afeminado.

girth [gəiθ] *n* circumferencia *f*; (*waist, etc.*) gordura *f*; (*saddle*) cincha *f*.

gist [dʒist] *n* esencia *f*, importe *m*.

*give [giv] *v* dar; (*offer as a present*) regalar; (*deliver*) entregar; (*hand over*) pasar; (*provide with*) proveer de; (*grant*) conceder; (*infect*) contagiar; (*communicate*) comunicar; (*a speech*) pronunciar; (*med: administer*) poner; (*telephone: connect with*) poner con. **give-and-take** *n* toma y daca *m*. **give away** distribuir; regalar; revelar. **giveaway** *n* revelación *f*. **give back** devolver. **give in** darse por vencido; ceder; (*hand in*) entregar. **give off** despedir. **give out** distribuir; emitir; anunciar; divulgar; (*run out*) agotarse.

give up abandonar; renunciar a; rendirse; entregar; ceder. **give way to** retirarse ante; abandonarse a.

glacier ['glasiə] *n* glaciar *m*. **glaciation** *n* glaciación *f*.

glad [glad] *adj* feliz, alegre. **be glad** alegrarse. **gladden** *v* regocijar. **gladly** *adv* alegremente.

glamour [glamə] *n* encanto *m*. **glamorous** *adj* encantador.

glance [glains] *n* (*look*) vistazo *m*, ojeada *f*; (*light*) vislumbre *f*; (*projectile*) desviación *f*. *v* echar un vistazo, ojear; relumbrar; desviarse.

gland [gland] *n* glándula *f*. **glandular** *adj* glandular. **glandular fever** fiebre glandular *f*.

glare [gleə] *n* (*look*) mirada feroz *f*; (*dazzle*) deslumbramiento *m*. *v* mirar con ferocidad; deslumbrar. **glaring** *adj* feroz; deslumbrante; (*conspicuous*) manifiesto.

glass [glais] *n* vidrio *m*; cristal *m*; (*for drinking*) vaso *m*; (*mirror*) espejo *m*; (*lens*) lente *f*. **glasses** *pl n* gafas *f pl*. **glassware** *n* cristalería *f*. **glassworks** *n* fábrica de cristal y vidrio *f*. **glassy** *adj* vitreo; (*eyes*) vidrioso; (*smooth*) liso.

glaze [gleiz] *v* (*pottery*) vidriar; (*window*) poner cristales a; (*cookery*) glasear. *n* vidriado *m*; brillo *m*. **glazier** *n* vidriero *m*.

gleam [gliim] *n* rayo *m*. *v* relucir. **gleaming** reluciente.

glean [gliin] *v* espigar.

glee [glii] *n* alegría *f*. **gleeful** *adj* alegre.

glib [glib] *adj* locuaz; fácil. **glibly** *adv* con labia.

glide [glaid] *v* (*aero*) planear; (*slide*) resbalar. **glide away** escurrirse. *n* planeo *m*; (*slide*) deslizamiento *m*. **glider** *n* planeador *m*.

glimmer ['glimə] *n* luz trémula *f*; (*fig*) vislumbre *m*. *v* brillar con luz trémula.

glimpse [glimps] *v* entrever. *n* vistazo *m*. **catch a glimpse of** vislumbrar.

glint [glint] *n* destello *m*. *v* destellar.

glisten ['glisn] *v* relucir. **glistening** *adj* reluciente.

glitter ['glitə] *v* brillar. *n* brillo *m*. **glittering** *adj* brillante.

gloat [glout] *v* recrearse con.

globe [gloub] *n* globo *m*. **globe artichoke** alcachofa *f*. **globe-trotter** *n* trotamundos *m invar*. **global** *adj* global; mundial.

gloom [gluːm] *n* obscuridad *f*; (*fig*) melancolía *f*. **gloomy** *adj* obscuro; melancólico.

glory ['gloːri] *n* gloria *f*; esplendor. **glorify** *v* glorificar. **glorious** *adj* glorioso; espléndido.

gloss [glos] *n* brillo *m*; lustre *m*; (*fig*) apariencia *f*. *v* **gloss over** disculpar.

glossary ['glosəri] *n* glosario *m*.

glove [glʌv] *n* guante *m*. **boxing gloves** *pl n* guantes de boxeo *m pl*. **glovecompartment** guantera *f*. **fit like a glove** sentar como anillo al dedo. **hand in glove with** juntar diestra con diestra. *v* enguantar.

glow [glou] *v* (*shine*) brillar.

glucose ['gluːkous] *n* glucosa *f*.

glue [gluː] *n* cola *f*. *v* pegar.

glum [glʌm] *adj* deprimido, sombrío.

glut [glʌt] *n* exceso *m*. *v* hartar.

glutton ['glʌtən] *n* glotón, -ona *m, f*. **gluttonous** *adj* glotón. **gluttony** *n* glotonería *f*.

gnarled [naːld] *adj* nudoso; (*persons*) curtido.

gnash [naʃ] *v* **gnash one's teeth** crujir los dientes.

gnat [nat] *n* mosquito *m*.

gnaw [noː] *v* roer. **gnawing** *adj* roedor.

gnome [noum] *n* gnomo *m*.

***go** [gou] *v* ir; (*depart*) irse; (*lead to*) conducir a; (*go towards*) dirigirse a; (*leave*) dejar; (*vanish*) desaparecer; (*be removed*) quitarse; (*turn, become*) ponerse; (*function*) funcionar. **go off** (*leave*) marcharse; (*rot*) estropearse; (*gun*) dispararse. **go out** salir; (*lights, fire, etc.*) apagarse. **go round** dar la vuelta. **go with** acompañar; (*harmonize*) hacer juego con. **go without** (*manage*) arreglárselas. *n* (*coll*) energía *f*. **it's your go** te toca a ti. **on the go** ocupado. **go-between** *n* intermediario, -a *m, f*.

goad [goud] *v* aguijar; (*fig*) incitar; *n* garrocha *f*; (*fig*) estímulo *m*.

goal [goul] *n* (*structure*) meta *f*; (*score*) gol *m*; (*destination*) destinación *f*; (*purpose*) objeto *m*. **goalkeeper** *n* portero *m*; **goalpost** *n* poste *m*.

goat [gout] *n* (*nanny*) cabra *f*; (*billy*) cabrón *m*.

gobble ['gobl] *v* engullir.

goblin ['goblin] *n* trasgo *m*, duende *m*.

god [god] *n* dios *m*. **by God!** ¡vive Dios! **for God's sake** por el amor de dios. **goddaughter** *n* ahijada *f*. **godfather** padrino

m. **godmother** *n* madrina *f*. **godsend** *n* don del cielo *m*. **godson** *n* ahijado *m*. **goddess** *n* diosa *f*.

goggles ['goglz] *pl n* anteojos *m pl*.

goings-on [,gouiŋz'on] *pl n* (*coll*) tejemanejes *m pl*.

gold [gould] *n* oro *m*. **golden** *adj* dorado; de oro.

goldfinch ['gouldfintʃ] *n* jilguero *m*.

goldfish ['gouldfiʃ] *n* pez de colores *m*. **goldfish bowl** pecera *f*.

goldsmith ['gouldsmiθ] *n* orfebre *m*.

golf [golf] *n* golf *m*. **golf course** campo de golf *m*. **golfer** *n* golfista *m, f*.

gondola ['gondələ] *n* góndola *f*. **gondolier** *n* gondolero *m*.

gone [gon] *V* go.

gong [goŋ] *n* gong *m*.

gonorrhoea [,gonə'riə] *n* gonorrea *f*.

good [gud] *adj* bueno; (*before m sing nouns*) buen; (*wholesome*) sano; (*pleasant*) amable; (*genuine*) legítimo; (*virtuous*) virtuoso. *n* bien *m*. **no good** inútil. **for good** para siempre. **goodness** *n* bondad *f*. **good-looking** *adj* guapo.

good afternoon *interj* buenas tardes *f pl*.

goodbye [gud'bai] *interj* ¡adios!

good evening *interj* buenas tardes *f pl*.

good-for-nothing *n*(*m*+*f*), *adj* inútil.

Good Friday *n* Viernes Santo *m*.

good morning *interj* buenos días *m pl*.

good night *interj* buenas noches *f pl*.

goods [gudz] *pl n* (*comm*) artículos *m pl*; (*possessions*) bienes *m pl*. **goods and chattels** muebles y enseres *m pl*. **goods train** tren de mercancías *m*.

goose [guːs] *n, pl* **geese** ganso *m*, oca *f*.

gooseberry ['guzbəri] *n* (*fruit*) grosella espinosa *f*; (*bush*) grosellero espinoso *m*.

gore[1] [goː] *v* cornear.

gore[2] [goː] *n* sangre *f*.

gorge [goːdʒ] *n* cañón *m*. *v* hartarse.

gorgeous ['goːdʒəs] *adj* magnífico.

gorilla [gə'rilə] *n* gorila *m*.

gorse [goːs] *n* tojo *m*.

gory [goːri] *adj* ensangrentado.

gospel ['gospəl] *n* evangelio *m*.

gossip ['gosip] *n* (*chat*) charla *f*; (*unkind*) chisme; (*person*) murmurador, -a *m, f*; chismoso, -a *m, f*. **gossip column** ecos de sociedad *m pl*. *v* (*talk scandal*) cotillear; (*chatter*) charlar.

got [gɒt] V **get**.
Gothic ['gɒθik] adj gótico.
goulash ['guːlaʃ] n estofado húngaro m.
gourd [guəd] n calabaza f.
gourmet ['guəmei] n gastrónomo m.
gout [gaut] n gota f.
govern ['gʌvən] v (rule) gobernar; (administer) dirigir; (determine) guiar; (restrain) dominar; (prevail) prevalecer. **governess** n aya f. **government** n gobierno m. **governor** n gobernador m; administrador m; (coll: boss) jefe m.
gown [gaun] n traje largo m; (law, university) toga f. **dressing gown** bata f.
grab [grab] v agarrar, arrebatar. n asimiento m, presa f; (mech) gancho m.
grace [greis] n gracia f, elegancia; (courtesy) cortesía f; (kindness) bondad f; (forgiveness) perdón m; (before meals) bendición mesa f; (favour) favor; (delay) plazo m. **graceful** adj elegante; gracioso; cortés. **gracious** adj gracioso; grato.
grade [greid] n grado m; (persons, things) clase f; (mark) nota f; (gradient) pendiente f. v graduar; (goods) clasificar.
gradient ['greidiənt] n (declivity) decline m; (slope) cuesta f.
gradual ['gradjuəl] adj gradual.
graduate ['gradjuət; v 'gradjueit] n, adj graduado, -a. v graduarse; diplomarse.
graft [graːft] n injerto m. v injertarse.
grain [grein] n grano m; (wood) fibra f.
gram [gram] n gramo m.
grammar ['gramə] n gramática f. **grammar school** instituto de segunda enseñanza m. **grammatical** adj gramático.
gramophone ['graməfoun] n gramófono m; tocadiscos m invar.
granary ['granəri] n granero m.
grand [grand] adj magnífico; grande; importante; espléndido. **grandiose** adj grandioso.
grand-dad n also **grandpa** (coll) abuelito m.
grandchild ['grantʃaild] n nieto, -a m, f.
grandfather ['gran,faːðə] n abuelo m.
grandma ['granmaː] n also **granny** (coll) abuelita f.
grandmother ['gran,mʌðə] n abuela f.
grandparent ['gran,peərənt] n abuelo, -a m, f.
grand piano n piano de cola m.
grandstand ['granstand] n tribuna f.
granite ['granit] n granito m. adj granítico.

grant [graːnt] v conceder; (agree to) acceder; (bestow) otorgar; (assume) suponer. n concesión f; otorgamiento m; (student) beca f.
granule ['granjuːl] n gránulo m. **granulated sugar** azúcar en polvo m.
grape [greip] n uva f. **grapevine** n vid f; (coll) rumores m pl.
grapefruit ['greipfruːt] n pomelo m.
graph [graf] n gráfica f. **graph paper** papel cuadriculado m. **graphic** adj gráfico.
grapple ['grapl] v **grapple with** (fight) luchar cuerpo a cuerpo; (fig) intentar a resolver.
grasp [graːsp] v agarrar; (fig) comprender. n agarro m; (reach) alcance m. **grasping** adj avaro.
grass [graːs] n hierba f; (pasture) pasto m; (lawn) césped m. **grasshopper** n saltamontes m. **grass snake** culebra f. **grassy** adj cubierto de hierba; (like grass) herbáceo.
grate[1] [greit] n parrilla f. **grating** n rejilla f.
grate[2] [greit] v rallar; (teeth) hacer rechinar. **grater** n rallador m.
grateful ['greitful] adj agradecido.
gratify ['gratifai] v satisfacer; (please) agradar. **gratifying** adj satisfactorio; agradable.
gratitude ['gratitjuːd] n agradecimiento m.
gratuity [grə'tjuəti] n propina f.
grave[1] [greiv] n sepultura f; (monument) tumba f. **gravedigger** n sepulturero m. **gravestone** n lápida sepulcral. **graveyard** n cementerio m.
grave[2] [greiv] adj grave, serio.
gravel ['gravəl] n grava f.
gravity ['graviti] n (force) gravedad f; (seriousness) solemnidad f.
gravy ['greivi] n salsa f.
graze[1] [greiz] v (scrape) raspar; (rub) rozar. n rozadura f.
graze[2] [greiz] v pastar.
grease [griːs] n grasa f. **greasepaint** n maquillaje m. **greaseproof paper** papel vegetal m. v engrasar. **greasy** adj grasiento; (slippery) resbaladizo.
great [greit] adj gran, grande; famoso; poderoso; magnífico. **greatly** adv grandemente, enormemente. **greatness** n grandeza f.
great-aunt n tía abuela f.

Great Britain n Gran Bretaña f.
Great Dane n perro danés m.
great-grandchild n biznieto, -a m, f.
great-grandfather n bisabuelo m.
great-grandmother n bisabuela f.
great-uncle n tío abuelo m.
Greece [griːs] n Grecia f. **Greek** n, adj griego, -a m, f.
greed [griːd] n avaricia f; (for food) glotonería f. **adj** avaro; glotón.
green [griːn] adj verde; (inexperienced) novato; (fresh) fresco; (recent) nuevo. n (colour) verde m; (meadow) prado m; (lawn) césped m. **greens** pl n verduras f pl. **greenery** n verdor m.
greenfly ['griːnflai] n pulgón m.
greengage ['griːngeidʒ] n ciruela claudia f.
greengrocer ['griːngrousə] n verdulero m. **greengrocery** n verdulería f.
greenhouse ['griːnhaus] n invernadero m.
Greenland ['griːnlənd] n Groenlandia f. **Greenlander** n groenlandés, -esa m, f.
greet [griːt] v saludar. **greeting** n salutación f. **greetings** pl n recuerdos m pl.
gregarious [griˈgeəriəs] adj gregario.
grew [gruː] V grow.
grey [grei] nm, adj gris; (hair) cano. **grey-haired** adj canoso. **greyhound** n galgo m. **go grey** (hair) encanecer.
grid [grid] n rejilla f; (elec) red f.
grief [griːf] n pena f, dolor m. **grief-stricken** adj desconsolado.
grieve [griːv] v afligir; lamentar. **grieve for** echar de menos. **grievous** adj doloroso; grave; apenado; lamentable. **grievous bodily harm** daños corporales m pl.
grill [gril] v (cook) asar a la parrilla; (interrogate) interrogar. n arrilla f; (meal) asado a la parrilla m. **grillroom** n parrilla f.
grille [gril] n reja f; rejilla f.
grim [grim] adj feroz; severo; horrible; (coll) desagradable. **grimly** adv severamente; horriblemente.
grimace [griˈmeis] n mueca f. v hacer muecas.
grime [graim] n mugre f. **grimy** adj mugriento.
*__grind__ [graind] v (coffee, etc.) moler; (sharpen) afilar; (teeth) crujir. n (coll) trabajo pesado m. **grinder** n afilador m. **grindstone** n muela f. **keep one's nose to the grindstone** batir al yunque.

grip [grip] n (of hand) mano f; (hold) agarro m; (bag) maleta f; (understanding) comprensión f. v asir; (wheels) agarrarse; (press) apretar; (the attention) atraer. **gripping** adj impresionante.
gripe [graip] v retortijón m. v (coll) quejarse.
grisly ['grizli] adj espantoso; horroroso; repugnante.
gristle ['grisl] n cartílago m.
grit [grit] n cascajo m; polvo m; (coll: courage) valor m. v (teeth) rechinar.
groan [groun] n gemido m; (dismay) gruñido m. v gemir; gruñir.
grocer ['grousə] n tendero, -a m, f. **groceries** pl n comestibles m pl. **grocery** n tienda de comestibles f.
groin [groin] n ingle f.
groom [gruːm] n (horse) mozo de caballos m; (of bride) novio m. v (horse) almohazar; (smarten) arreglar.
groove [gruːv] n ranura f, muesca f; (record) surco m; (fig) rutina f. v hacer ranuras en; estriar. **grooved** adj acanalado; estriado. **groovy** adj (coll) fenómeno.
grope [group] v andar a tientas. **grope for** buscar a tientas. **gropingly** adv a tientas.
gross [grous] adj (not net) bruto; (coarse) grosero; grueso, denso. n gruesa f.
grotesque [grəˈtesk] nm, adj grotesco.
grotto ['grotou] n gruta f.
ground[1] [graund] V grind.
ground[2] [graund] n suelo m; (earth) tierra f; (sport) campo m; (basis) base f; (background) fondo m; (fig) terreno m. v poner en tierra; (teach) enseñar los rudimentos de. **grounds** pl n jardines m pl; (sediment) sedimento m sing; (reason) causa f sing.
ground control n control desde tierra m.
ground floor n planta baja f.
grounding ['graundiŋ] n **have a good grounding in** tener una buena base en.
groundless ['graundlis] adj sin fundamento.
ground level n nivel del suelo m.
ground rent n alquiler del terreno m.
groundsheet ['graundʃiːt] n tela impermeable f.
groundwork ['graundwɔːk] n base f.
group [gruːp] n grupo m. v agrupar.
grouse[1] [graus] n ortega f.
grouse[2] [graus] v (coll) quejarse.

grove [grouv] *n* boscaje *m*.
grovel ['grovl] *v* arrastrarse; (*fig*) humi-
llarse.
*grow [grou] *v* crecer; (*increase*)
aumentar; (*become*) hacerse; (*turn*)
ponerse; (*develop*) desarrollarse; (*cultivate*) cultivar. **grown-up** *n* adulto, -a *m*, *f*.
growth *n* crecimiento *m*; aumento *m*;
desarrollo *m*; (*med*) bulto *m*; vegetación
f.
growl [graul] *v* gruñir. *n* gruñido *m*.
grub [grʌb] *n* larva *f*; (*coll: food*) comida
f. *v* cavar. **grubby** *adj* sucio.
grudge [grʌdʒ] *v* envidiar. *n* rencor *m*.
bear a grudge tener ojeriza. **grudging** *adj*
mezquino. **grudgingly** *adv* de mala gana.
gruelling ['gruəliŋ] *adj* penoso; agotador.
gruesome ['gruːsəm] *adj* pavoroso,
macabro.
gruff [grʌf] *adj* (*manner*) brusco; (*voice*)
bronco. **gruffness** *n* brusquedad *f*; bron-
quedad *f*.
grumble ['grʌmbl] *v* quejarse. *n* queja *f*.
grumpy ['grʌmpi] *adj* malhumorado.
grumpiness *n* malhumor *m*.
grunt [grʌnt] *v* gruñir. *n* gruñido *m*.
guarantee [garən'tiː] *n* garantía *f*. *v*
garantizar. **guarantor** *n* garante *m*, *f*.
guard [gaɪd] *n* (*soldier*) guardia *m*; (*sentry*) centinela *m*; (*escort*) escolta *f*; (*keeper*) guardián *m*; (*train*) jefe de tren *m*;
(*protection*) defensa *f*; (*watchfulness*) vigilancia *f*. **be on guard** estar de guardia.
guard dog perro de guardia *m*. **guard's
van** furgón de equipajes *m*. *v* guardar;
proteger. **guard against** protegerse contra. **guarded** *adj* (*cautious*) cauteloso.
guardian *n* (*custodian*) guardián; (*of an
orphan*) tutor, -a *m*, *f*. **guardian angel**
ángel de la Guardia *m*.
guerrilla [gə'rilə] *n* guerrillero *m*. **guerrilla
warfare** guerrilla *f*.
guess [ges] *n* cálculo *m*; conjetura *f*;
suposición *f*. **at a guess** a primera vista.
guesswork *n* conjetura *f*. *v* adivinar;
suponer; acertar.
guest [gest] *n* invitado, -a *m*, *f*; (*hotel*)
huésped, -a *m*, *f*. **be my guest** yo invito.
guest of honour invitado de honor *m*.
guest-house *n* casa de huéspedes *f*. **guest-
room** cuarto de huéspedes *m*.
guide [gaɪd] *n* guía *m*, *f*; (*counsellor*) consejero, -a *m*, *f*. **girl guide** exploradora *f*.
guidebook *n* guía turística *f*. *v* guiar; conducir; dirigir. **guidance** *n* consejo *m*.

guided missile projectil teledirigido *m*.
guided tour visita acompañada *f*.
guild [gild] *v* (*association*) gremio *m*;
(*craftsmen, etc.*) guilda *f*.
guillotine ['gilətiːn] *n* guillotina *f*. *v* guillotinar.
guilt [gilt] *n* culpabilidad *f*. **guilty** *adj* culpable. **plead guilty** confesarse culpable.
guinea pig ['ginipig] *n* conejillo de Indias
m.
guitar [gi'taɪ] *n* guitarra *f*. **guitarist** *n*
guitarrista *m*, *f*.
gulf [gʌlf] *n* golfo *m*; (*abyss*) abismo *m*.
gull [gʌl] *n* gaviota *f*.
gullet ['gʌlit] *n* esófago *m*; (*throat*) garganta *f*.
gullible ['gʌləbl] *adj* crédulo. **gullibility** *n*
credulidad *f*.
gully ['gʌli] *n* hondonada *f*.
gulp [gʌlp] *v* tragar. *n* (*drink*) trago *m*;
(*food*) bocado *m*.
gum[1] [gʌm] *n* goma *f*. *v* engomar.
gum[2] [gʌm] *n* (*mouth*) encía *f*.
gun [gʌn] *n* (*weapon*) arma *f*; revólver *m*;
pistola *f*; (*hunting*) escopeta *f*; rifle *m*;
cañón *m*. **gunfire** *n* cañonazos *m pl*. **gunman** *n* pistolero *m*. **gunpowder** pólvora *f*.
gun-running *n* contrabanda de armas *f*.
gunshot *n* disparo *m*.
gurgle ['gəɪgl] *n* (*water*) borboteo *m*;
(*child*) gorjeo *m*. *v* borbotear; gorjear.
gush [gʌʃ] *v* derramar. *n* chorro *m*; (*fig*)
efusión *f*. **gushing** *adj* (*person*) efusivo.
gust [gʌst] *n* (*wind*) ráfaga *f*; (*smoke*)
bocanada *f*; (*rain*) aguacero *m*; (*laughter,
anger*) accesión *f*. **gusty** *adj* borrascoso.
gusto ['gʌstou] *n* placer *m*; brío *m*; entusiasmo *m*.
gut [gʌt] *n* (*anat*) intestino *m*, tripa *f*. **guts**
pl n (*coll*) agallas *f pl*. *v* destripar; vaciar.
gutter ['gʌtə] *n* (*roof*) canal *m*; (*street*)
arroyo *m*.
guy[1] [gai] *n* (*coll*) tipo *m*.
guy[2] [gai] *n* (*rope*) tirante *m*.
gymnasium [dʒim'neiziəm] *n* gimnasio *m*.
gymnast *n* gimnasta *m*, *f*. **gymnastic** *adj*
gimnástico. **gymnastics** *n* gimnasia *f*.
gynaecology [gainə'kolədʒi] *n* ginecología
f. **gynaecological** *adj* ginecológico.
gynaecologist *n* ginecólogo, -a *m*, *f*.
gypsum ['dʒipsəm] *n* yeso *m*.
gyrate [,dʒai'reit] *v* girar. **gyration** *n* giro
m.

gyroscope ['dʒairəˌskoup] giroscopio m.

H

haberdasher ['habədaʃə] n mercero, -a m,
f. **haberdashery** n mercería f.
habit ['habit] n costumbre f; (clothes)
traje m. **habitual** adj acostumbrado.
habitable ['habitəbl] adj habitable.
habitat ['habitat] n medio m, habitación f.
hack[1] [hak] v acuchillar, cortar; (kick) dar
un puntapié. n corte m; puntapié m.
hacking adj (cough) seco.
hack[2] [hak] n (horse) rocín m; (writer)
escritorzuelo m.
hackneyed ['haknid] adj usado, trillado.
had [had] V **have**.
haddock ['hadək] n eglefino m.
haemorrhage ['heməridʒ] n hemorragia f.
haemorrhoids ['heməroidz] pl n hemorri-
odes f pl.
hag [hag] n (coll) bruja f.
haggard ['hagəd] adj ojeroso; extraviado.
haggle ['hagl] v regatear. n regateo m.
Hague, The [heig] n La Haya.
hail[1] [heil] n granizo m. **hailstone** n
granizo m, piedra f. **hailstorm** n
granizada f.
hail[2] [heil] v (salute) saludar; (coll) llamar.
hail from proceder de.
hair [heə] n pelo m; (human head) cabello
m. **comb one's hair** peinarse. **have one's
hair done** ir a la peluquería. **let one's hair
down** (coll) soltarse el pelo. **split hairs**
hilar muy fino. **tear one's hair out** tirarse
de los pelos. **hairy** adj peludo.
hairbrush ['heəbrʌʃ] n cepillo (para el
pelo) m.
haircut ['heəkʌt] n corte de pelo m. **have
a haircut** cortarse el pelo.
hairdresser ['heəˌdresə] n peluquero, -a
m, f. **hairdresser's** n peluquería f. **hair-
dressing** n peluquería f.
hair dryer n secador (para el pelo) m.
hairnet ['heənet] n redecilla f.
hairpiece ['heəpiːs] n postizo m.
hairpin ['heəpin] n horquilla f.
hair-remover n depilatorio m.
hairspray ['heəsprei] n fijador (para el
pelo) m.
hairstyle ['heəstail] n peinado m.

Haiti ['heiti] n Haití m. **Haitian** n, adj
haitiano, -a.
half [haɪf] n mitad f; medio m; (division
of a match) tiempo m. **by half** con
mucho. **half-and-half** mitad y mitad. **in
half** por la mitad. **go halves with** ir a
medias con. adj medio. **half an hour**
media hora. **half a dozen** media docena.
adv a medias; media. **half as many** or
much la mitad. **half as much again** la
mitad más. **not half!** (coll) ¡no poco!
half-baked [ˌhaɪfˈbeikt] adj (coll: idea) mal
concebido; (coll: person) disparatado.
half-breed ['haɪfbriːd] n mestizo, -a m, f.
half-brother ['haɪfˌbrʌðə] n hermanastro
m.
half-hearted [ˌhaɪfˈhaɪtid] adj poco entusiasta.
half-mast [ˌhaɪfˈmaɪst] n **at half-mast** a
media asta.
half-price [ˌhaɪfˈprais] adj, adv a mitad de
precio.
half-sister ['haɪfˌsistə] n hermanastra f.
half-time [ˌhaɪfˈtaim] n (sport) descanso
m. adj (work) de media jornada.
halfway [ˌhaɪfˈwei] adv a medio camino.
meet halfway (compromise) partir la
diferencia (con). adj medio.
half-wit ['haɪfwit] n tonto, -a m, f.
halibut ['halibət] n halibut m.
hall [hoɪl] n (entrance) vestíbulo m;
(room) sala f. **hall porter** conserje m. **hall-
stand** n perchero m.
hallmark ['hoɪlmaɪk] n contraste m; (fig)
sello m. v contrastar.
hallowed ['haloud] adj santo. **hallow** santificar.
Hallowe'en [halouˈiːn] n víspera del Día
de todos los Santos f.
hallucination [həˌluːsiˈneiʃən] n alucinación f.
halo ['heilou] n halo m; (rel) aureola f.
halt [hoɪlt] n alto m, parada f. v parar;
interrumpir.
halter ['hoɪltə] n cabestro m.
halve [haɪv] v compartir; partir en dos;
reducir a la mitad.
ham [ham] n jamón m.
hamburger ['hambɔɪgə] n hamburguesa f.
hammer ['hamə] n martillo m; (firearm)
percursor m. **come under the hammer**
salir a subasta. v martillar, martillear;
(nail) clavar; (iron) batir. **hammer out**
(disputes, etc.) elaborar.

hammock ['hamək] *n* hamaca *f*.
hamper¹ ['hampə] *v* impedir; embarazar.
hamper² ['hampə] *n* canasta *f*.
hamster ['hamstə] *n* hámster *m*.
hamstring ['hamstriŋ] *v* (*coll*) paralizar.
hand [hand] *n* mano *f*; (*watch, etc.*) aguja *f*; (*worker*) trabajador *m*; (*writing*) escritura *f*; (*applause*) ovación *f*; (*measure*) palmo *m*; (*naut*) marinero *m*. **at first hand** de primera mano. **at hand** a mano. **by hand** en mano. **hand and foot** de pies y manos. **hand in hand** de la mano. **hands up!** ¡arriba las manos! **hand to hand** cuerpo a cuerpo. **keep one's hand in** no perder la práctica. **on the other hand** por otra parte. *v* dar. **hand down** transmitir. **hand in** entregar. **hand over** ceder. **handful** *n* puñado *m*.
handbag ['handbag] *n* bolso *m*.
handbook ['handbuk] *n* manual *m*; guía *f*.
handbrake ['handbreik] *n* freno de mano *m*.
handcuff ['handkʌf] *v* poner las esposas a. **handcuffs** *pl n* esposas *f pl*.
handicap ['handikap] *n* desventaja *f*; (*sport*) handicap *m*. *v* perjudicar.
handicraft ['handikraift] *n* mano de obra *f*.
handiwork ['handiwəik] *n* obra *f*.
handkerchief ['haŋkətʃif] *n* pañuelo *m*.
handle ['handl] *n* (*cup, bag, etc.*) asa *f*; (*grip of a tool*) mango *m*; (*stick, door knob*) pomo *m*; (*door lever*) tirador *m*; (*lever*) brazo *m*. *v* tocar; (*naut*) dirigir; (*mot*) conducir; (*tool*) manejar; (*lift, shift*) manipular; (*cope*) poder con; (*deal with*) ocuparse de. **handle with care** frágil. **handlebars** *pl n* manillar *m sing*.
handmade [,hand'meid] *adj* hecho a mano.
hand-out ['handaut] *n* (*leaflet*) prospecto *m*; (*charity*) limosna *f*. **hand out** dar; distribuir.
hand-pick [hand'pik] *v* (*people*) escoger a dedo; (*objects*) escoger con sumo cuidado.
handrail ['handreil] *n* pasamano *m*.
handshake ['handʃeik] *n* apretón de manos *m*.
handsome ['hansəm] *adj* hermoso, bello; guapo.
handstand ['hand,stand] *n* pino *m*.
handwriting ['hand,raitiŋ] *n* escritura *f*. **handwritten** *adj* escrito a mano.

handy ['handi] *adj* (*near*) a mano; (*skilful*) mañoso; diestro; (*convenient*) cómodo; (*manageable*) manejable; (*useful*) útil. **come in handy** venir bien.
*hang [haŋ] *v* colgar, suspender; (*execute*) ahorcar; (*head*) bajar; (*wallpaper*) empapelar; (*of clothes*) caer. **hang about** *or* **around** vagar. **hang fire** estar en suspenso. **hang-gliding** *n* vuelo libre *m*.
hangman *n* verdugo *m*. **hang on** mantenerse firme; (*remain*) quedarse; (*hold on*) agarrarse; (*depend upon*) depender de. **hangover** *n* (*slang*) resaca *f*. **hang-up** *n* (*coll*) complejo *m*.
hangar ['haŋə] *n* hangar *m*.
hanker ['haŋkə] *v* **hanker for** *or* **after** anhelar. **hankering** *n* anhelo *m*.
haphazard [,hap'hazəd] *adj* fortuito.
happen ['hapən] *v* acontecer, suceder; (*take place*) tener lugar; (*arise*) sobrevenir. **happening** *n* suceso *m*, ocurrencia *f*.
happy ['hapi:] *adj* feliz, alegre. **happy birthday!** ¡feliz cumpleaños! **happy Christmas!** ¡felices Pascuas! **happy-go-lucky** *adj* descuidado. **happiness** *n* alegría *f*. **happily** *adv* felizmente.
harass ['harəs] *v* hostigar. **harassment** *n* hostigamiento *m*.
harbour ['haibə] *n* puerto *m*; (*haven*) asilo *m*. *v* dar refugio a; (*cherish*) abrigar.
hard [haid] *adj* duro; firme; violento; inflexible; cruel; (*unjust*) opresivo; (*weather*) severo; (*stiff*) tieso. *adv* duro; de firme; vigorosamente; (*raining*) a cántaros; (*closely*) de cerca; (*badly*) mal; (*heavily*) pesadamente. **hard-and-fast** *adj* (*rule*) inalterable. **hard-bitten** *adj also* **hard-boiled** (*fig*) duro, tenaz. **hard-hearted** *adj* insensible. **hard labour** trabajos forzados *m pl*. **hard up** (*coll*) apurado. **hardware** *n* ferretería *n*. **harden** *v* endurecer; (*make callous*) hacer insensible. **hardness** *n* dureza *f*; inhumanidad *f*; tiesura *f*; dificultad *f*. **hardship** *n* penas *f pl*; sufrimiento *m*; privación *f*.
hardy ['haidi] *adj* audaz; fuerte; (*bot*) resistente.
hare [heə] *n* liebre *f*. **hare-brained** *adj* casquivano. **hare-lip** *n* labio leporino *m*.
haricot ['harikou] *n* judía *f*.
harm [haim] *n* mal *m*; daño *m*. **harmful** *adj* malo; dañino. **harmless** *adj* inofensivo; inocuo.

harmonic [haɪˈmɒnik] *nm, adj* armónico.
harmonica [haɪˈmɒnikə] *n* armónica *f.*
harmonize [ˈhaɪmənaiz] *v* armonizar.
harmony [ˈhaɪməni] *n* armonía *f.* **harmonious** *adj* armonioso.
harness [ˈhaɪnis] *n* guarniciones *f pl.* *v* enjaezar; (*power, etc.*) represar.
harp [haɪp] *n* arpa *f.* *v* **harp on** volver a repetir. **harpist** *n* arpista *m, f.*
harpoon [haɪˈpuɪn] *n* arpón *m.* *v* arponear.
harpsichord [ˈhaɪpsi̩kɔɪd] *n* arpicordio *m,* clavicémbalo *m.*
harrowing [ˈharouiŋ] *adj* atormentador, patibulario.
harsh [haɪʃ] *adj* (*features*) duro; (*voice*) ronco; (*sound*) discordante; (*texture*) áspero.
harvest [ˈhaɪvist] *n* cosecha *f.* *v* cosechar.
has [haz] *V* **have.**
hash [haʃ] *n* (*food*) picadillo *m;* (*coll*) lío *m.* **make a hash of** estropear por completo. *v* (*food*) picar.
hashish [ˈhaʃiːʃ] *n* hachís *m invar.*
haste [heist] *n* prisa *f.* **hasten** *v* dar prisa a; apresurar. **hastily** *adv* de prisa; (*rashly*) a la ligera. **hasty** *adj* precipitado; (*rash*) apresurado.
hat [hat] *n* sombrero *m.* **bowler hat** sombrero hongo *m.* **Panama hat** jipijapa *m.* **top hat** sombrero de copa *m.* **take one's hat off to** descubrirse ante.
hatch[1] [hatʃ] *v* hacer salir del cascarón; (*coll: plot*) maquinar.
hatch[2] [hatʃ] *n* (*serving*) ventanilla *f;* (*naut*) escotilla *f;* (*trapdoor*) trampa *f.*
hatchet [ˈhatʃit] *n* hacha *f.*
hate [heit] *v* odiar, aborrecer. *n also* **hatred** odio *m.* **pet hate** pesadilla *f.* **hateful** *adj* odioso.
haughty [ˈhɔɪti] *adj* altanero. **haughtiness** *n* altanería *f.*
haul [hɔɪl] *v* (*drag*) arrastrar; (*transport*) acarrear. *n* (*pull*) tirón *m;* (*journey*) recorrido *m;* (*fish*) redada *f;* (*loot*) botín *m.* **haulage** *n* acarreo *m,* transporte *m.*
haunt [hɔɪnt] *v* (*ghost*) aparecer en; (*follow*) perseguir; (*frequent*) frecuentar; (*memories*) obsesionar. *n* lugar predilecto *m.* **haunting** *adj* obsesionante.
***have** [hav] *v* tener; (*receive*) recibir; (*drink, food*) tomar; (*get*) conseguir; (*coll: deceive*) engañar. **have on** (*wear*) llevar; (*coll: tease*) tomar el pelo a. **have to** tener que.

haven [ˈheivn] *n* abrigo *m;* (*fig*) refugio *m.*
haversack [ˈhavəsak] *n* mochila *f.*
havoc [ˈhavək] *n* estragos *m pl.* **play havoc with** hacer estragos en.
hawk [hɔɪk] *n* halcón *m.*
hawthorn [ˈhɔɪθɔɪn] *n* espino *m.*
hay [hei] *n* heno *m.* **make hay while the sun shines** hacer su agosto. **hay fever** fiebre del heno *f.* **haystack** *n* almiar *m.* **go haywire** (*machine*) estropearse; (*plans*) desorganizarse.
hazard [ˈhazəd] *n* peligro *m;* (*chance*) azar *m.* *v* arriesgar; (*guess*) aventurar. **hazardous** *adj* arriesgado, peligroso.
haze [heiz] *n* neblina *f;* (*fig*) confusión *f.* **hazy** *adj* nebuloso; (*fig*) confuso.
hazel [ˈheizl] *n* avellano *m.* **hazel-nut** *n* avellana *f.* *adj* de avellano.
he [hiː] *pron* él.
head [hed] *n* cabeza *f;* (*chief*) jefe *m;* (*school*) director, -a *m, f;* (*bed, table, river*) cabecera *f;* (*coin*) cara *f;* (*spear, arrows*) punta *f;* (*steam*) presión *f;* (*hammer*) cotillo *m.* *v* (*demonstration, list, etc.*) encabezar; (*lead*) estar a la cabeza de; dirigir; conducir; (*goal*) meter de cabeza. **head off** cortar el paso a. **head for** dirigirse hacia. **headed** *adj* (*notepaper*) con membrete. **heading** *n* título *m.* **heady** *adj* embriagador.
headache [ˈhedeik] *n* dolor de cabeza *m.*
headfirst [ˌhedˈfɔɪst] *adv* de cabeza.
headlamp [ˈhedlamp] *or* **headlight** *n* (*mot*) faro *m.*
headland [ˈhedlənd] *n* punta *f,* promontorio *m.*
headline [ˈhedlain] *n* (*book*) título *m;* (*newspaper*) titular *m.* **make the headlines** estar en primera plana.
headlong [ˈhedloŋ] *adv* (*headfirst*) de cabeza; (*rush*) precipitado.
headmaster [ˌhedˈmaɪstə] *n* director *m.* **headmistress** *n* directora *f.*
head-on [ˌhedˈon] *adj, adv* de frente.
headphones [ˈhedfounz] *pl n* auriculares *m pl.*
headquarters [ˌhedˈkwɔɪtəz] *n* (*mil*) cuartel general *m;* (*firm*) domicilio social *m;* (*organization*) sede *f.*
headrest [ˈhedrest] *n* cabecero *m,* cabezal *m.*
headscarf [ˈhedskaɪf] *n* pañuelo *m.*
headstrong [ˈhedstroŋ] *adj* testarudo.

headway ['hedweɪ] n progreso m.

heal [hiːl] v (disease) curar, sanar; (wound) cicatrizar.

health [helθ] n salud f. **health certificate** certificado médico m. **health food** alimentos naturales m pl. **health officer** inspector de sanidad m. **health resort** balneario m. **Ministry of Health** Dirección General de Sanidad f. **public health** sanidad pública f. **your health!** ¡a su salud! **healthy** adj sano, saludable; salubre. **healthy appetite** buen apetito m.

heap [hiːp] n montón m, pila f; (people) muchedumbre f. v amontonar, apilar.

***hear** [hɪə] v oír; (listen) escuchar; (attend) asistir a; (give audience) dar audiencia; (news) enterarse de. **hear from** enterarse de. **hear hear!** ¡i muy bien! **hear about** or **of** oír hablar de. **hearing** n (sense) oído m; (act of hearing) audición f. **hearing aid** aparato para sordos m. **hearsay** n rumor m.

hearse [hɜːs] n coche fúnebre m.

heart [haɪt] n (anat) corazón m; (feelings) entrañas f pl; (courage) ánimo m; (soul) alma f; (cards) copas f pl; (lettuce) repollo m. **by heart** de memoria. **set one's heart on** poner el corazón en. **to one's heart's content** hasta quedarse satisfecho. **a man after my own heart** un hombre de los que me gustan. **hearten** v animar. **heartless** adj cruel. **hearty** adj (welcome) cordial; (meal) abundante.

heart attack n ataque cardíaco m.

heartbeat ['haɪtbiːt] n latido del corazón m.

heart-breaking ['haɪtbreɪkiŋ] adj desgarrador. **heart-broken** adj acongojado.

heartburn ['haɪtbɜːn] n acedía f.

heart failure n colapso cardíaco m.

heartfelt ['haɪtfelt] adj de todo corazón.

hearth [haɪθ] n hogar m. **hearthrug** n alfombra f.

heart-throb ['haɪtθrob] n ídolo m.

heart-to-heart adj franco, sincero. **have a heart-to-heart talk** tener una conversación íntima.

heartwarming ['haɪtwɔːmiŋ] adj caluroso.

heat [hiːt] n calor m; (animals) celo m; (fig) vehemencia f; (passion) ardor m; (of a race) carrera eliminatoria f. v calentar; excitar; (annoy) irritar. **heatstroke** n insolación f. **heatwave** n onda de calor f. **in the heat of the moment** en el calor del momento. **heated** adj calentado; (argument) apasionado. **heater** n calentador m. **heating** n calefacción f. **central heating** calefacción central f.

heath [hiːθ] n (plant) brezo m; (land) brezal m.

heathen ['hiːðn] n, adj pagano, -a.

heather ['heðə] n brezo m.

heave [hiːv] n (lift) gran esfuerzo m; (pull) tirón m; (sea) movimiento m; (breast) palpitación f; (retching) náusea f. v (pull) tirar de; (lift) levantar; (sigh) exhalar; (waves) subir y bajar; (retch) tener náusea; (breast) palpitar. **heave to** ponerse al pairo.

heaven ['hevn] n cielo m, paraíso m. **heavenly** adj celeste; (fig) delicioso.

heavy ['hevi] adj pesado, torpe; (slow) lento; (thick) grueso; (hard) duro; (strong) fuerte; (oppressive) opresivo; (cold) malo; (sky) anublado; (meal) abundante; (food) indigesto; (soil) recio. **heavyweight** nm, adj peso pesado. **heaviness** n peso m; torpor m; tristeza f; ponderosidad f.

Hebrew ['hiːbruː] n (people) hebreo, -a m, f; (language) hebreo m. adj hebreo.

heckle ['hekl] v interrumpir. **heckler** n perturbador, -a m, f. **heckling** n interrupción f.

hectare ['hektaɪ] n hectárea f.

hectic ['hektik] adj agitado.

hedge [hedʒ] n seto m. v cercar con un seto; (fig) vacilar; (a bet) compensar.

hedgehog ['hedʒhog] n erizo m.

heed [hiːd] v atender. n atención f, cuidado m. **heedless** adj desatento; negligente.

heel [hiːl] n (anat) talón m; (shoe) tacón m. v poner tacón a.

hefty ['hefti] adj (heavy) pesado; (robust) robusto.

heifer ['hefə] n novilla f.

height [haɪt] n altura f; (people) estatura f; (hill) colina f; (fig) colmo m; cumbre f. **heighten** v elevar; (fig) aumentar.

heir [eə] n heredero m; **heiress** n heredera f. **heirloom** n reliquia de familia f.

held [held] V **hold**.

helicopter ['helikoptə] n helicóptero m.

hell [hel] n infierno m. **go to hell!** (impol) ¡vete al infierno! **go hell for leather** ir como si se llevara al diablo. **to hell with it!** ¡qué diablos! **hellish** adj infernal; (fig) horrible.

hello [həˈlou] *interj* (*greeting*) ¡hola!; (*attract attention*) ¡oye!; (*phone*) ¡oiga!; (*answering the phone*) ¡diga!

helm [helm] *n* caña del timón *f.* **be at the helm** empuñar el timón.

helmet [ˈhelmit] *n* casco *m*; (*of motorcyclist, labourer, etc.*) careta *f.*

help [help] *n* ayuda *f*; socorro *m*; auxilio *m*; remedio *m*; (*employee*) empleado *m*; (*servant*) criado, -a *m, f. interj* ¡socorro! *v* ayudar; auxiliar; socorrer; (*relieve*) aliviar; (*serve*) servir; (*avoid*) evitar; (*facilitate*) facilitar; (*prevent oneself from*) no poder menos que. **help yourself!** ¡sírvese! **it can't be helped!** ¡no hay más remedio! **helper** *n* ayudante *m.* **helpful** *adj* útil; provechoso; amable. **helping** *n* porción *f.* **helpless** *adj* desamparado.

hem [hem] *n* dobladillo *m. v* hacer un dobladillo en. **hem in** (*fig*) rodear. **hemline** *n* bajo *m.*

hemisphere [ˈhemiˌsfiə] *n* hemisferio *m.*

hemp [hemp] *n* cáñamo *m.*

hen [hen] *n* (*chicken*) gallina *f*; (*female of other birds*) hembra *f.* **henhouse** *n* gallinero *m.* **hen party** (*coll*) reunión de mujeres *f.* **henpecked** *adj* dominado por su mujer.

hence [hens] *adv* por eso, por lo consiguiente; (*time*) de ahora; (*place*) de aquí. **henceforth** *adv* desde aquí en adelante.

henna [ˈhenə] *n* alheña *f.*

her [hər] *pron* ella; (*direct object*) la; (*indirect object*) le, a ella. *adj* su (*pl* sus).

herald [ˈherəld] *n* heraldo *m. v* proclamar. **heraldic** *adj* heráldico. **heraldry** *n* heráldica *f.*

herb [həːb] *n* hierba *f.* **herbal** *adj* herbario.

herd [həːd] *n* rebaño *m*, manada *f. v* (*round up*) reunir en manada; (*drive*) conducir; (*fig*) agrupar.

here [hiə] *adv* aquí. **hereafter** *adv* en lo futuro; en adelante. **here and now** ahora mismo. **here and there** aquí y allá. **here goes!** ¡vamos a ver! **here is/are** aquí está/están.

hereditary [hiˈredətəri] *adj* hereditario.

heredity [hiˈredəti] *n* herencia *f.*

heresy [ˈherəsi] *n* herejía *f.* **heretic** *n* hereje *m, f.* **heretical** *adj* herético.

heritage [ˈheritidʒ] *n* herencia *f.*

hermit [ˈhəːmit] *n* ermitaño *m.*

hernia [ˈhəːniə] *n* hernia *f.*

hero [ˈhiərou] *n* héroe *m.* **heroine** *n* heroína *f.* **hero-worship** *n* culto a los héroes *m.* **heroic** *adj* heroico. **heroism** *n* heroísmo *m.*

heroin [ˈherouin] *n* heroína *f.*

heron [ˈherən] *n* garza *f.*

herring [ˈheriŋ] *n* arenque *m.* **red herring** (*coll*) pista falsa *f.*

hers [həːz] *pron* suyo, suya.

herself [həːˈself] *pron* (*reflexive*) se; (*emphatic*) ella misma. **by herself** a solas.

hesitate [ˈheziteit] *v* vacilar. **hesitant** *adj* vacilante. **hesitation** *n* vacilación *f.*

heterosexual [hetərəˈsekʃuəl] *n*(*m+f*), *adj* heterosexual.

hexagon [ˈheksəgən] *n* hexágono *m.* **hexagonal** *adj* hexagonal.

heyday [ˈheidei] *n* auge *m*, apogeo *m.*

hiatus [haiˈeitəs] *n* laguna *f.*

hibernate [ˈhaibəneit] *v* hibernar. **hibernation** *n* hibernación *f.*

hiccup [ˈhikʌp] *n* hipo *m.* **have the hiccups** tener hipo. *v* hipar.

hide[1] [haid] *v* esconder. **hide something from someone** ocultar algo a alguien. **hide-and-seek** *n* escondite *m.* **hide-out** *n* escondrijo *m.*

hide[2] [haid] *n* piel *f*; (*leather*) cuero *m.*

hideous [ˈhidiəs] *adj* horroroso.

hiding[1] [ˈhaidiŋ] *n* **be in hiding** estar escondido. **go into hiding** esconderse. **hiding place** escondite *m.*

hiding[2] [ˈhaidiŋ] *n* (*beating*) paliza *f.*

hierarchy [ˈhaiərɑːki] *n* jerarquía *f.* **hierarchical** *adj* jerárquico.

hi-fi [ˈhaiˌfai] *n* alta fidelidad *f.*

high [hai] *adj* alto; de alto; (*speed, hopes, number*) grande; (*post*) importante; (*wind*) fuerte; (*altar, Mass*) mayor; (*voice*) agudo; (*quality*) superior; (*river*) crecido; (*noon*) pleno; (*game*) manido; (*shine, polish*) brillante; (*colour*) subido.

highbrow [ˈhaibrau] *n*(*m+f*), *adj* intelectual.

high chair *n* silla alta para niño *f.*

high frequency *adj* de alta frecuencia.

high-heeled *adj* de tacón alto.

high jump *n* salto de altura *m.*

highland [ˈhailənd] *n* tierras altas *f pl. adj* montañoso.

highlight [ˈhailait] *v* destacar. *n* (*art*) toque de luz *m*; (*fig*) atracción principal *f.*

Highness ['hainis] n Alteza f.
high-pitched adj de tono alto.
high-rise block n torre f.
high-speed adj de gran velocidad.
high-spirited adj brioso.
high street n calle principal f.
highway ['haiwei] n camino real m, carretera f. **highway code** código de la circulación m. **highwayman** n salteador de caminos m.
hijack ['haidʒak] v (aircraft) secuestrar; (people) asaltar; (goods) robar. n secuestro m; asalto m.
hike [haik] n excursión a pie f. v ir de excursión. **hiker** n excursionista m, f. **hiking** n excursionismo m.
hilarious [hi'leəriəs] adj (funny) hilarante; (merry) alegre. **hilarity** n hilaridad f.
hill [hil] n colina f, cerro m; (slope) cuesta f. **hillside** n ladera f. **hilly** adj montañoso.
him [him] pron él; (direct object) le, lo.
himself [him'self] pron (reflexive) se; sí, sí mismo; (emphatic) él mismo. **by himself** a solas.
hind [haind] adj trasero, posterior. **hindquarters** pl n cuarto trasero m sing. **hindsight** n percepción retrospectiva f.
hinder ['hində] v impedir; interrumpir. **hindrance** n impedimento m; obstáculo m.
Hindu [hin'duː] n(m+f), adj hindú. **Hinduism** n hinduismo m.
hinge [hindʒ] n bisagra f; (stamps) fijasellos m invar. v **hinge on** depender de.
hint [hint] n indirecta f; (tip) consejo m; (clue) pista f; indicación f; (trace) pizca f. **broad hint** una insinuación muy clara. **take the hint** (pejorative) darse por aludido; (follow advice) aprovechar el consejo. v insinuar; soltar indirectas.
hip [hip] n cadera f.
hippopotamus [hipə'potəməs] n hipopótamo m.
hire [haiə] v alquilar; (person) contratar. **hire out** alquilar. n (house, etc.) alquiler m; (engagement) contratación f; (wages) sueldo m. **for hire** de alquiler; (taxi) libre. **hire purchase** compra a plazos f.
his [hiz] adj su (pl sus); de él. pron suyo, suya.
hiss [his] n silbido m. v silbar.
history ['histəri] n historia f. **historian** n historiador, -a m, f. **historic** adj histórico.
***hit** [hit] v golpear, pegar a; (target) dar

en; (wound) herir; (collide) chocar con. **hit home** dar en el blanco. **hit it off with** hacer buenas migas con. n golpe m; (mil) impacto m; (success) exito m. **hit-or-miss** adv a la buena de Dios.
hitch [hitʃ] n obstáculo m; problema m; (knot) vuelta de cabo m. v (travel) hacerse llevar en coche; (tie) atar; (link) enganchar. **hitch-hike** v hacer autostop. **hitch-hiker** n autostopista m, f. **hitch-hiking** n autostop m.
hitherto [hiðə'tuː] adv hasta ahora.
hive [haiv] n colmena f.
hoard [hoːd] n acumulación f; tesoro m. v acumular, amasar.
hoarding ['hoːdiŋ] n (fence) valla f; (advertising) cartelera f.
hoarse [hoːs] adj ronco. **hoarsely** adv roncamente. **hoarseness** n ronquera f.
hoax [houks] n estafa f; engaño m; burla f. v estafar; engañar; burlar.
hobble ['hobl] v cojear. n (gait) cojera f.
hobby ['hobi] n pasatiempo m.
hock[1] [hok] n (pork, etc.) pernil m.
hock[2] [hok] n vino del Rin m.
hockey ['hoki] n hockey m. **hockey stick** bastón de hockey m.
hoe [hou] n azadón m. v azadonar.
hog [hog] n cerdo m, puerco m. v (coll) acaparar.
hoist [hoist] v (heavy objects) levantar; (sails, flag) izar. n (lifting) levantamiento m; (crane) grúa f; (lift) montacargas m invar; (lifting mechanism) cabria f.
***hold**[1] [hould] v tener; mantener; agarrar; (believe) creer; (keep) guarder; (sustain) sostener; (opinion) defender. **hold back** reprimir. **hold forth** perorar. **hold on** sujetar; (wait) aguantar; (grip) agarrarse. **hold out** (hand) tender, ofrecer; (last) durar; (resist) resistir. **hold up** (raise) levantar; (support) sostener; (delay) retrasar. n (grip) asimiento m, agarro m; (handhold) asidero m; (control) autoridad f; dominio m. **get hold of** coger, agarrar. **hold-up** n interrupción f; (robbery) atraco a mano armada m; (traffic jam) embotellamiento m. **holder** n (person) poseedor, -a m, f; (object) receptáculo m.
hold[2] [hould] n (naut) bodega f.
hole [houl] n agujero m; (from digging) hoyo m; (in garments) boquete m; (mouse) ratonera f; (rabbit) madriguera f.

holiday ['holədi] *n* (*day*) fiesta *f*; (*several days*) vacaciones *f pl*. **holiday resort** centro de turismo *m*.

Holland ['holənd] *n* Holanda *f*.

hollow ['holou] *n* hueco *m*; (*in ground*) hondonada *f*. *adj*, *adv* hueco. *v* ahuecar.

holly ['holi] *n* acebo *m*.

hollyhock ['holihok] *n* malva loca *f*.

holster ['houlstə] *n* pistolera *f*.

holy ['houli] *adj* santo; sacro; sagrado; (*bread*, *water*) bendito. **holiness** *n* santidad *f*.

homage ['homidʒ] *n* homenaje *m*. **pay homage** rendir homenaje.

home [houm] *n* casa *f*; hogar *m*; domicilio *m*; (*fig*) morada *f*. **at home** en casa. **make yourself at home** está usted en su casa. *adv* a casa. **go home** volver a casa. **homeless** *adj* sin casa ni hogar. **home address** dirección privada *f*. **homesick** *adj* nostálgico.

homicide ['homisaid] *n* (*act*) homicidio *m*; (*person*) homicida *m*, *f*. **homicidal** *adj* homicida.

homogeneous [homə'dʒiːniəs] *adj* homogéneo.

homosexual [homə'sekʃuəl] *n*(*m+f*). *adj* homosexual. **homosexuality** *n* homosexualidad *f*.

honest ['onist] *adj* honrado; sincero; franco. **honesty** *n* honradez *f*; sinceridad *f*; rectitud *f*.

honey ['hʌni] *n* miel *f*. **honeycomb** *n* panal *m*. **honeymoon** *n* luna de miel *f*. **honeysuckle** *n* madreselva *f*.

honour ['onə] *n* honor *m*; rectitud *f*. *v* honrar. **honorary** *adj* honorario. **honourable** *adj* honorable.

hood [hud] *n* capucha *f*; (*car*, *pram*) capota *f*.

hoof [huːf] *n* casco *m*; (*cloven*) pezuña *f*.

hook [huk] *n* gancho *m*; (*fish*) anzuelo *m*; (*dress*) corchete *m*; (*hanger*) colgadero *m*. *v* enganchar; (*fish*) pescar; (*dress*) abrochar; colgar. **hooked** *adj* (*shaped*) ganchudo. **get hooked on** (*coll*) enviciarse en.

hooligan ['huːligən] *n* rufián *m*. **hooliganism** *n* rufianería *f*.

hoop [huːp] *n* (*toy*) aro *m*; (*barrel*) fleje *m*.

hoot [huːt] *n* (*owl*) ululato *m*; (*person*) silbato *m*; (*shout*) grito *m*; (*boat*, *factory*) toque de sirena *m*. *v* ulular; silbar; dar

un bocinazo; gritar; dar un toque de sirena; (*boo*) abuchear.

hop[1] [hop] *v* saltar; brincar; saltar con un pie. *n* salto *m*; brinco *m*; (*coll: dance*) baile *m*; (*coll: stage in a journey*) etapa *f*.

hop[2] [hop] *n* (*bot*) lúpulo *m*.

hope [houp] *n* esperanza *f*. *v* esperar. **hopeful** *adj* lleno de esperanzas; confiado. **hopeless** *adj* desesperado; (*coll*) inútil.

horde [hoːd] *n* horda *f*.

horizon [hə'raizn] *n* horizonte *m*.

horizontal [hori'zontl] *adj* horizontal.

hormone ['hoːmoun] *n* hormona *f*.

horn [hoːn] *n* cuerno *m*; (*mot*) bocina *f*.

hornet ['hoːnit] *n* avispón *m*.

horoscope ['horəskoup] *n* horóscopo *m*.

horrible ['horibl] *adj* horrible, espantoso.

horrid ['horid] *adj* horroroso, odioso.

horrify ['horifai] *v* horrorizar. **horrific** *adj* horrífico, horrendo.

horror ['horə] *n* horror *m*. *adj* (*film*, *story*, *etc*.) de miedo.

hors d'œuvres [oː'dəːvr] *pl n* entremeses *m pl*.

horse [hoːs] *n* caballo *m*. **on horseback** a caballo. **horsepower** *n* caballo de vapor *m*. **horseradish** *n* rábano picante *m*. **horse show** concurso hípico *m*.

horticulture ['hoːtikʌltʃə] *n* horticultura *f*. **horticultural** *adj* horticultural.

hose [houz] *n* manga *f*; manguera *f*; (*stockings*) medias *f pl*. *v* regar con una manga.

hosiery ['houziəri] *n* medias *f pl*; (*business*) calcetería *f*.

hospitable [ho'spitəbl] *adj* hospitalario.

hospital ['hospitl] *n* hospital *m*. **hospitalize** *v* hospitalizar.

hospitality [hospi'taliti] *n* hospitalidad *f*.

host[1] [houst] *n* huésped *m*. **hostess** *n* huéspeda *f*.

host[2] [houst] *n* (*crowd*) muchedumbre *f*.

hostage ['hostidʒ] *n* rehén *m*.

hostel ['hostəl] *n* hostería *f*; residencia *f*. **youth hostel** albergue juvenil *m*.

hostile ['hostail] *adj* hostil; enemigo. **hostility** *n* hostilidad *f*; enemistad *f*.

hot [hot] *adj* caliente; (*climate*) cálido; (*sun*) abrasador; (*day*) caluroso; (*spicy*) picante; (*temper*) vivo; (*issue*) controvertido; (*pursuit*) porfiado. **be hot** (*person*) tener calor; (*weather*) hacer calor. **hot dog** perro caliente *m*. **hot-house** *n* invernadero *m*. **hotplate** *n* calientaplato

m invar. **hot-tempered** *adj* enfadadizo.
hot-water bottle bolsa de agua caliente *f.*
hotel [houˈtel] *n* hotel *m.*
hound [haund] *n* perro de caza *m.* *v* (*fig*) perseguir.
hour [ˈauə] *n* hora *f.* **after hours** fuera de horas. **by the hour** por horas. **hour by hour** de hora en hora. **peak hours** horas de mayor consumo. **rush hour** hora punta. **small hours** altas horas. **zero hour** hora H. **hourly** *adv* de cada hora.
house [haus; *v* hauz] *n* casa *f*; (*theatre*) sala *f*; (*audience*) público *m.* *v* (*hold*) alojar; (*put up*) albergar.
houseboat [ˈhausbout] *n* casa flotante *f.*
housecoat [ˈhauskout] *n* bata *f.*
household [ˈhaushould] *n* casa *f*, familia *f.* *adj* casero.
housekeeper [ˈhausˌkiːpə] *n* (*paid*) ama de llaves *f*; (*housewife*) ama de casa *f.*
housekeeping *n* (*work*) quehaceres domésticos *m pl*; (*money*) dinero para gastos domésticos *m.*
housemaid [ˈhausmeid] *n* criada *f.*
house-to-house *adj, adv* de casa en casa.
house-trained [ˈhaustreind] *adj* enseñado.
house-warming [ˈhausˌwoːmiŋ] *n* **have a house-warming party** inaugurar la casa.
housewife [ˈhauswaif] *n* ama de casa *f.*
housing [ˈhauziŋ] *n* alojamiento *m.* **housing estate** urbanización *f.*
hovel [ˈhovəl] *n* casucha *f.*
hover [ˈhovə] *v* cernerse; (*fig*) rondar.
hovercraft *n* aerodeslizador *m.*
how [hau] *adv* (*as*) como; (*in what way*) cómo; (*in exclamation before adv or adj*) qué. **how are you?** *or* **how do you do?** ¿cómo está usted? **how much?** ¿cuánto?
however [hauˈevə] *conj* sin embargo. *adv* de cualquier manera que.
howl [haul] *v* (*dog, wolf*) aullar; (*wind*) bramar; (*pain*) dar alaridos; (*child*) berrear. *n* aullido *m*; bramido *m*; alarido *m*; grito *m*; berrido *m.*
hub [hʌb] *n* (*wheel*) cubo *m*; (*fig*) centro *m.* **hubcap** *n* (*mot*) tapacubos *m invar.*
huddle [ˈhʌdl] *v* amontonar. *n* grupo *m.*
hue [hjuː] *n* color *m.*
huff [hʌf] *n* **in a huff** enojado.
hug [hʌg] *v* abrazar. *n* abrazo *m.*
huge [hjuːdʒ] *adj* enorme.
hulk [hʌlk] *n* (*ship*) carraca *f*; (*derog: person*) armatoste *m.* **hulking** *adj* voluminoso.
hull [hʌl] *n* (*naut*) casco *m.*

hum [hʌm] *n* (*bees, engines*) zumbido *m*; (*a tune*) canturreo *m.* *v* zumbar; canturrear; (*fig: with activity*) hervir. **humming-bird** *n* colibrí *m.*
human [ˈhjuːmən] *nm, adj* humano. **human being** ser humano *m.* **human nature** naturaleza humana *f.*
humane [hjuːˈmein] *adj* humano.
humanity [hjuːˈmanəti] *n* humanidad *f.* **humanitarian** *adj* humanitario.
humble [ˈhʌmbl] *adj* humilde. *v* humillar.
humdrum [ˈhʌmdrʌm] *adj* monótono.
humid [ˈhjuːmid] *adj* húmedo. **humidity** *n* humedad *f.*
humiliate [hjuːˈmilieit] *v* humillar. **humiliation** *n* humillación *f.*
humility [hjuːˈmiləti] *n* humildad *f.*
humour [ˈhjuːmə] *n* humor *m*; (*temperament*) disposición *f.* *v* complacer. **humorist** *n* humorista *m, f.* **humorous** *adj* humorístico.
hump [hʌmp] *n* horoba *f.* *v* (*coll: carry*) cargar con.
hunch [hʌntʃ] *v* encorvarse. *n* (*coll*) presentimiento *m.* **hunchback** *n* jorobado, -a *m, f.*
hundred [ˈhʌndrəd] *n* ciento *m*; centenar *m*; centena *f.* *adj* cien, ciento. **hundredth** *nm, adj* centésimo.
hung [hʌŋ] *V* **hang.**
Hungary [ˈhʌŋgəri] *n* Hungría *f.* **Hungarian** *n, adj* húngaro, -a.
hunger [ˈhʌŋgə] *n* hambre *f.* *v also* **be hungry** tener hambre, estar hambriento. **hunger for** desear. **hungrily** *adv* hambrientamente.
hunt [hʌnt] *n* caza *f*; (*search*) busca *f.* *v* cazar; buscar. **hunting** *n* caza *f.* **huntsman** *n* cazador *m.*
hurdle [ˈhəːdl] *n* (*sport*) valla *f*; (*fig*) obstáculo *m.* *v* vallar.
hurl [həːl] *v* lanzar, arrojar; (*abuse*) soltar.
hurricane [ˈhʌrikən] *n* huracán *m.*
hurry [ˈhʌri] *n* prisa *f.* **be in a hurry** llevar prisa. *v* dar prisa (a), apresurar. **hurried** *adj* apresurdado. **hurriedly** *adj* apresuradamente.
***hurt** [həːt] *v* (*cause pain*) doler; (*wound*) herir; (*damage*) hacer daño (a); ofender; (*feelings*) mortificar. *n* herida *f*; daño *m*; mal *m.* *adj* lastimado; herido. **hurtful** *adj* dañoso; perjudicial; (*words*) hiriente.
husband [ˈhʌzbənd] *n* marido *m*, esposo *m.*

hush [hʌʃ] n silencio m. interj ¡calla! v silenciar. **hush up** echar tierra a. **hushed** adj callado.

husk [hʌsk] n (cereals) cáscara f; (peas and beans) vaina f; (chestnut) erizo m. v descascarar; desvainar; pelar.

husky ['hʌski] n (dog) perro esquimal m. adj (hoarse) ronco; (strong) fuerte. **huskily** adv con voz ronca. **huskiness** n ronquera f.

hussar [hə'zaɪ] n húsar m.

hustle ['hʌsl] v empujar; (fig) precipitar. n (energy) empuje m; (hurry) prisa f; (push) empujón m. **hustle and bustle** vaivén m.

hut [hʌt] n choza f, cabaña f.

hutch [hʌtʃ] n (rabbit) conejera f.

hyacinth ['haiəsinθ] n jacinto m.

hybrid ['haibrid] nm, adj híbrido. **hybridization** n hibridación f.

hydraulic [hai'drɔːlik] adj hidráulico.

hydrocarbon [ˌhaidrə'kaɪbən] n hidrocarburo m.

hydro-electric adj hidroeléctrico.

hydrofoil ['haidrəfoil] n aerodeslizador m.

hydrogen ['haidrədʒən] n hidrógeno m.

hyena [hai'iːnə] n hiena f.

hygiene ['haidʒiːn] n higiene f. **hygienic** adj higiénico.

hymn [him] n himno m. **hymn-book** or **hymnal** n himnario m.

hyphen ['haifən] n guión m.

hypnosis [hip'nousis] n hipnosis f. **hypnotic** adj hipnótico. **hynotism** n hipnotismo m. **hypnotist** n hipnotizador, -a m, f. **hypnotize** v hipnotizar.

hypochondria [haipə'kondriə] n hipocondría f. **hypochondriac** n, adj hipocondríaco, -a m, f.

hypocrisy [hi'pokrəsi] n hipocresía f. **hypocrite** n hipócrita m, f. **hypocritical** adj hipócrita.

hypodermic [haipə'dəɪmik] adj hipodérmico. n jeringa hipodérmica f.

hypothesis [hai'poθəsis] n, pl -ses hipótesis f. **hypothetical** adj hipotético.

hysterectomy [ˌhistə'rektəmi] n histerectomía f.

hysteria [hi'stiəriə] n histeria f. **hysterical** adj histérico. **hysterics** n histerismo m; ataque histérico m.

I

I [ai] pron yo.

Iberian [ai'biəriən] adj ibérico. n ibero, -a m, f.

ice [ais] n hielo m. **iceberg** n iceberg m. **icebreaker** n rompehielos m invar. **ice-cold** adj helado. **ice cream** helado m. **ice-skate** n patín de cuchilla m. v (turn into ice) helar; (chill) enfriar. **icing** n escarchado m. **icing sugar** azúcar en polvo m, f. **icy** adj (wind, place) glacial; (hand, foot) helado.

Iceland ['aisland] n Islandia f. **Icelander** n islandés, -esa m, f. **Icelandic** adj islandés.

icicle ['aisikl] n carámbano m.

icon ['aikon] n icono m.

idea [ai'diə] n idea f.

ideal [ai'diəl] nm, adj ideal. **idealist** n idealista m, f. **idealistic** adj idealista.

identical [ai'dentikəl] adj idéntico. **identical twins** gemelos homólogos m pl.

identify [ai'dentifai] v identificar. **identify with** identificarse con. **identification** n identificación f; (papers) documentos de identidad m pl.

identity [ai'dentiti] n identidad f. **identity card** carnet de identidad m.

ideology [aidi'olədʒi] n ideología f.

idiom ['idiəm] n (expression) idiotismo m; (language) idioma m. **idiomatic** adj idiomático.

idiosyncrasy [ˌidiə'siŋkrəsi] n idiosincrasia f.

idiot ['idiət] n imbécil m, f, idiota m, f. **idiotic** adj idiota.

idle ['aidl] adj (lazy) perezoso; (at leisure) ocioso; (unemployed) desocupado; (machine) parado; (talk) frívolo; (fears) infundado. v (waste time) perder el tiempo; (be lazy) holgazanear; (mechanism) girar loco. **idleness** n (laziness) holgazanería f; (leisure) ociosidad f; (unemployment) paro m.

idol ['aidl] n ídolo m. **idolatry** n idolatría f. **idolize** v idolatrar.

idyllic [i'dilik] adj idílico.

if [if] conj si. **as if** como si. **if not** si no. **if only** ¡ojalá que! **if so** si es así.

ignite [ig'nait] v encender, prender fuego a.

ignition [ig'niʃən] n ignición f; (mot)

encendido *m*. **ignition key** llave de contacto *f*. **ignition switch** interruptor del encendido *m*.

ignorant ['ignərənt] *adj* ignorante. **ignorance** *n* ignorancia *f*.

ignore [ig'nɔː] *v* (*warning*) no hacer caso de; (*person*) no hacer caso a; (*leave out*) pasar por alto.

ill [il] *adj* (*sick*) enfermo; (*bad*) malo. *nm*, *adv* mal. **ill-advised** *adj* malaconsejado. **ill-at-ease** *adj* molesto. **ill-mannered** *adj* mal educado. **ill health** mala salud *f*. **ill-treat** *v* maltratar. **ill will** mala voluntad *f*. **illness** *n* enfermedad *f*.

illegal [i'liːgəl] *adj* ilegal.

illegible [i'ledʒəbl] *adj* ilegible.

illegitimate [ˌili'dʒitimit] *adj* ilegítimo. **illegitimacy** *n* ilegitimidad *f*.

illicit [i'lisit] *adj* ilícito.

illiterate [i'litərit] *n*, *adj* analfabeto, -a. **illiteracy** *n* analfabetismo *m*.

illogical [i'lodʒikəl] *adj* ilógico.

illuminate [i'luːmiˌneit] *v* (*light up*) iluminar; (*clear*) aclarar. **illumination** *n* iluminación *f*; aclaración *f*.

illusion [i'luːʒən] *n* ilusión *f*.

illustrate ['iləˌstreit] *v* ilustrar; (*demonstrate*) demostrar. **illustration** *n* ilustración *f*; ejemplo *m*. **illustrator** *n* ilustrador, -a *m*, *f*.

illustrious [i'lʌstriəs] *adj* ilustre.

image ['imidʒ] *n* imagen *f*; (*fig*) reputación *f*. **be the image of** ser el retrato de. **imagery** *n* imágenes *f pl*.

imagine [i'madʒin] *v* imaginar. **imaginary** *adj* imaginario. **imagination** *n* imaginación *f*. **imaginative** *adj* imaginativo.

imbalance [im'baləns] *n* desequilibrio *m*.

imbecile ['imbəˌsiːl] *n* imbécil *m*, *f*.

imitate ['imiˌteit] *v* imitar. **imitation** *n* imitación *f*.

immaculate [i'makjulit] *adj* inmaculado.

immaterial [ˌimə'tiəriəl] *adj* indiferente; no importa.

immature [ˌimə'tjuə] *adj* inmaduro. **immaturity** *n* inmadurez *f*.

immediate [i'miːdiət] *adj* inmediato; (*near*) cercano. **immediately** *adv* inmediatamente; directamente.

immense [i'mens] *adj* inmenso, enorme.

immerse [i'məːs] *v* sumergir. **immersion** *n* sumersión *f*. **immersion heater** calentador de inmersión *m*.

immigrate ['imiˌgreit] *v* inmigrar. **immigrant** *n*(*m*+*f*), *adj* inmigrante. **immigration** *n* inmigración *f*.

imminent ['iminənt] *adj* inminente.

immobile [i'moubail] *adj* inmóvil. **immobilize** *v* inmovilizar.

immoral [i'morəl] *adj* inmoral. **immorality** *n* inmoralidad *f*.

immortal [i'mɔːtl] *adj* inmortal. **immortality** *n* inmortalidad *f*. **immortalize** *v* inmortalizar.

immovable [i'muːvəbl] *adj* inmóvil; (*steadfast*) inflexible.

immune [i'mjuːn] *adj* inmune. **immunity** *n* inmunidad *f*. **immunization** *n* inmunización *f*. **immunize** *v* inmunizar.

imp [imp] *n* diablillo *m*.

impact ['impakt] *n* impacto *m*.

impair [im'peə] *v* dañar. **impairment** *n* daño *m*.

impale [im'peil] *v* atravesar.

impart [im'paːt] *v* (*give*) impartir; (*grant*) conceder; (*make known*) comunicar.

impartial [im'paːʃəl] *adj* imparcial. **impartiality** *n* imparcialidad *f*.

impasse [am'paːs] *n* callejón *m*.

impassive [im'pasiv] *adj* impasible.

impatient [im'peiʃənt] *adj* impaciente. **become impatient** perder la paciencia. **impatience** *n* impaciencia *f*.

impeach [im'piːtʃ] *v* acusar; (*prosecute*) encausar; (*a witness*) recusar. **impeachment** *n* acusación *f*; (*prosecution*) enjuiciamiento *m*; recusación *f*.

impeccable [im'pekəbl] *adj* impecable.

impede [im'piːd] *v* estorbar; impedir. **impediment** [im'pedimənt] *n* estorbo *m*; obstáculo *m*; defecto *m*.

impel [im'pel] *v* impeler; mover; (*push*) empujar; obligar.

impending [im'pendiŋ] *adj* inminente; próximo.

imperative [im'perətiv] *adj* (*peremptory*) perentorio; (*urgent*) imperioso; (*necessary*) indispensable.

imperfect [im'pəːfikt] *adj* imperfecto; incompleto. *n* (*gramm*) imperfecto *m*.

imperial [im'piəriəl] *adj* imperial; (*fig*) señorial. **imperialism** *n* imperialismo *m*.

impersonal [im'pəːsənl] *adj* impersonal.

impersonate [im'pəːsəˌneit] *v* hacerse pasar por; (*theatre*) imitar. **impersonation** *n* imitación *f*.

impertinent [im'pəːtinənt] *adj* impertinente. **impertinence** *n* impertinencia *f*.

impervious [im'pɔɪvɪəs] *adj* impenetrable; (*to criticism, pain, etc.*) insensible.

impetuous [im'petjuəs] *adj* impetuoso.

impetus ['impətəs] *n* (*force*) ímpetu *m*; (*fig*) impulso *m*; estímulo *m*.

impinge [im'pindʒ] *v* **impinge on** tropezar con; usurpar.

implement ['implimənt; *v* 'impliment] *n* (*tool*) herramienta *f*; (*utensil*) utensilio; **implements** *pl n* (*writing*) artículos *m pl*; (*agr*) aperos *m pl*. *v* llevar a cabo; (*law*) aplicar.

implication [impli'keiʃən] *n* implicación *f*; complicidad *f*; consecuencia *f*. **implicate** *v* implicar; comprometer.

implicit [im'plisit] *adj* implícito; absoluto.

implore [im'plɔɪ] *v* suplicar. **imploring** *adj* suplicante.

imply [im'plai] *v* implicar; presuponer; significar; dar a entender. **implied** *adj* implícito.

impolite [impə'lait] *adj* descortés.

import [im'pɔɪt] *n* (*comm*) artículo importado *m*; (*meaning*) sentido *m*; importancia *f*. *v* (*comm*) importar; significar.

importance [im'pɔɪtəns] *n* importancia *f*. **important** *adj* importante.

impose [im'pouz] *v* imponer; (*tax*) gravar con. **impose on** abusar de. **imposing** *adj* imponente. **imposition** *n* imposición *f*; abuso *m*; (*tax*) impuesto *m*.

impossible [im'posəbl] *adj* imposible.

impostor [im'postə] *n* impostor, -a *m, f*.

impotent ['impətənt] *adj* impotente. **impotence** *n* impotencia *f*.

impound [im'paund] *v* confiscar.

impoverish [im'povəriʃ] *v* (*people*) empobrecer; (*land*) agotar.

impregnate [im'preg,neit] *v* fecundar; (*saturate*) empapar. **impregnable** *adj* inexpugnable. **impregnation** *n* fecundación *f*; impregnación *f*.

impress [im'pres] *v* impresionar; (*print*) imprimir. **impression** *n* impresión *f*. **impressive** *adj* impresionante.

imprint ['imprint; *v* im'print] *n* impresión *f*. *v* imprimir.

imprison [im'prizn] *v* encarcelar. **imprisonment** *n* encarcelamiento *m*.

improbable [im'probəbl] *adj* improbable; (*story, etc.*) inverosímil.

impromptu [im'promptjuɪ] *adv* improvisadamente. *adj* improvisado.

improper [im'propə] *adj* indecente; indecoroso; incorrecto.

improve [im'pruɪv] *v* mejorar; favorecer; perfeccionar. **improvement** *n* mejora *f*; progreso *m*; reforma *f*.

improvise ['imprə,vaiz] *v* improvisar. **improvisation** *n* improvisación *f*.

impudent ['impjudənt] *adj* impudente. **impudence** *n* impudencia *f*.

impulse ['impʌls] *n* impulso *m*. **impulsive** *adj* impulsivo.

impure [im'pjuə] *adj* impuro. **impurity** *n* impureza *f*.

in [in] *prep* en; de; durante; a. *adv* dentro. **be in** (*at home*) estar en casa. **be in on** estar enterado de.

inability [inə'biləti] *n* incapacidad *f*.

inaccessible [inak'sesəbl] *adj* inaccesible. **inaccessibility** *n* inaccesibilidad *f*.

inaccurate [in'akjurit] *adj* inexacto. **inaccuracy** *n* inexactitud *f*.

inactive [in'aktiv] *adj* inactivo. **inaction** *n* inacción *f*. **inactivity** *n* inactividad *f*.

inadequate [in'adikwit] *adj* insuficiente. **inadequacy** *n* insuficiencia *f*.

inadvertent [inəd'vɔɪtənt] *adj* inadvertido; descuidado. **inadvertently** *adv* por inadvertencia.

inane [in'ein] *adj* (*futile*) inane; (*silly*) necio. **inanity** *n* inanidad *f*; necedad *f*.

inanimate [in'animit] *adj* inanimado.

inarticulate [inaɪ'tikjulit] *adj* (*sound*) inarticulado; (*person*) incapaz de expresarse.

inasmuch [inəz'mʌtʃ] *adv* **inasmuch as** puesto que, visto que.

inaudible [in'ɔɪdəbl] *adj* inaudible.

inaugurate [i'nɔɪgju,reit] *v* inaugurar. **inaugural** *adj* inaugural. **inauguration** *n* inauguración *f*.

inborn [in'bɔɪn] *adj* innato; (*med*) congénito.

incapable [in'keipəbl] *adj* incapaz.

incendiary [in'sendiəri] *adj* incendiario. **incendiary bomb** bomba incendiaria *f*.

incense[1] ['insens] *n* incienso *m*.

incense[2] [in'sens] *v* encolerizar.

incentive [in'sentiv] *n* incentivo *m*, estímulo *m*.

incessant [in'sesənt] *adj* incesante, continuo.

incest ['insest] *n* incesto *m*. **incestuous** *adj* incestuoso.

inch [intʃ] *n* pulgada *f*. **inch by inch** poco a poco. **within an inch of** a dos pasos de. *v* **inch forward** avanzar poco a poco.

incident ['insidənt] n incidente m; (in a story) episodio m. **incidental** adj incidente; incidental; imprevisto; (expense) accesorio m; (music) de fondo; (secondary) secundario; (casual) fortuito. **incidentally** adv (by the way) a propósito.
incinerator [in'sinə,reitə] n quemador de basuras m. **incinerate** v quemar. **incineration** n incineración f.
incite [in'sait] v incitar; provocar. **incitement** n incitamiento m; estímulo m.
incline [in'klain] v inclinar. **be inclined to** inclinarse a. n pendiente f. **inclination** n (tilt) inclinación f; (slope) pendiente f; (leaning) tendencia f.
include [in'kluːd] v incluir; (enclose in a letter) adjuntar. **including** adj incluso. **inclusion** n inclusión f. **inclusive** adj inclusivo.
incognito [,inkog'niːtou] adv de incógnito.
incoherent [,inkə'hiərənt] adj incoherente. **incoherence** n incoherencia f. **incoherently** adv de modo incoherente.
income ['inkʌm] n ingresos m pl. **income tax** impuesto de utilidades m.
incomparable [in'kompərəbl] adj incomparable. **incomparably** adv incomparablemente.
incompatible [inkəm'patəbl] adj incompatible. **incompatibility** n incompatibilidad f.
incompetent [in'kompitənt] adj incompetente. **incompetence** n incompetencia f.
incomplete [,inkəm'pliːt] adj incompleto; sin terminar.
incomprehensible [in,kompri'hensəbl] adj incomprensible.
inconceivable [inkən'siːvəbl] adj inconcebible.
incongruous [in'kongruəs] adj incongruo; incompatible. **incongruity** n incongruidad f.
inconsiderate [,inkən'sidərit] adj (thoughtless) inconsiderado; (lacking consideration for others) desconsiderado.
inconsistent [,inkən'sistənt] adj (substance) inconsistente; (actions, thoughts) inconsecuente. **inconsistency** n inconsistencia f; inconsecuencia f.
incontinence [in'kontinəns] n incontinencia f. **incontinent** adj incontinente.
inconvenient [inkən'viːnjənt] adj (place) incómodo; (time) inoportuno. **inconvenience** n inconvenientes m pl, molestia f. v incomodar, molestar.

incorporate [in'koːpə,reit] v incorporar, incluir; (contain) contener; (comm) constituir en sociedad.
incorrect [inkə'rekt] adj incorrecto; erróneo.
increase [in'kriːs] v aumentar. n aumento m. **increasing** adj creciente. **increasingly** adv cada vez más.
incredible [in'kredəbl] adj increíble.
incredulous [in'kredjuləs] adj incrédulo. **incredulity** n incredulidad f.
increment ['inkrəmənt] n aumento m.
incriminate [in'krimineit] v incriminar. **incriminating** adj acriminador.
incubate ['inkju,beit] v incubar. **incubation** n incubación f. **incubator** n incubadora f.
incur [in'kəː] v incurrir; (debt) contraer; (loss) sufrir.
incurable [in'kjuərəbl] adj incurable.
indebted [in'detid] adj (owing money) endeudado (con); (fig) agradecido. **indebtedness** n deuda f; agradecimiento m.
indecent [in'diːsnt] adj indecente. **indecency** n indecencia f.
indeed [in'diːd] adv en efecto; realmente. **yes indeed!** ¡ya lo creo!
indefinite [in'definit] adj indefinido; impreciso.
indelible [in'deləbl] adj indeleble.
indemnity [in'demnəti] n (security) indemnidad f; reparación f.
indent [in'dent] v (dent) abollar; (notch) dentar; (comm) pedir; (print) sangrar. **indentation** n (notch) muesca f; (print) sangría f.
independent [,indi'pendənt] adj independiente. **independence** n independencia f.
index ['indeks] n índice m; (math) exponente m. **index finger** dedo índice m. **cost-of-living index** el índice del coste de la vida. v (file) clasificar; (a book) poner un índice a.
India ['indjə] n India f. **Indian** n indio, -a m, f; (language) indio m. adj indio. **Indian ink** tinta china f. **Indian summer** veranillo de San Martín m. **india paper** papel de China m. **india rubber** goma de borrar f.
indicate ['indikeit] v indicar, señalar. **indication** n indicación f, señal f. **indicative** nm, adj indicativo. **indicator** n indicador m.

indict [in'dait] v acusar. **indictment** n acusación f.

indifferent [in'difrənt] adj indiferente; insignificante; (mediocre) regular. **indifference** n indiferencia f.

indigenous [in'didʒinəs] adj indígena.

indigestion [,indi'dʒestʃən] n indigestión f. **indigestible** adj indigesto.

indignant [in'dignənt] adj indignado. **get indignant** indignarse. **indignantly** adv con indignación. **indignation** n indignación f.

indignity [in'dignəti] n (lack of dignity) indignidad f; (outrage) afrenta f.

indirect [,indi'rekt] adj indirecto.

indiscreet [,indi'skriːt] adj indiscreto. **indiscretion** n indiscreción f.

indiscriminate [,indi'skriminit] adj indistinto; universal; (person) sin criterio.

indispensable [,indi'spensəbl] adj indispensable.

indisposed [,indi'spouzd] adj (ill) indispuesto, enfermo; (reluctant) maldispuesto. **indisposition** n indisposición f; aversión f.

individual [,indi'vidjuəl] adj individual; personal. n individuo m. **individuality** n individualidad f.

indoctrinate [in'doktri,neit] v adoctrinar. **indoctrination** n adoctrinamiento m.

indolent ['indələnt] adj indolente. **indolence** n indolencia f.

indoor ['indoː] adj interior. **indoor pool** piscina cubierta f. **indoors** adv dentro; en casa.

induce [in'djuːs] v (convince) inducir, persuadir; (cause) causar, provocar. **inducement** n incentivo m; (motive) móvil m.

indulge [in'dʌldʒ] v (pamper) mimar; (give way to) ceder a. **indulge in** entregarse a. **indulgence** n indulgencia f; satisfacción f; tolerancia f; (self-indulgence) desenfreno m. **indulgent** adj indulgente.

industry ['indəstri] n industria f; diligencia f. **industrial** adj industrial. **industrial relations** relaciones profesionales f pl. **industrialist** n industrial m. **industrialize** v industrializar. **industrious** adj trabajador.

inebriated [i'niːbrieitid] adj ebrio.

inedible [in'edibl] adj incomible.

inefficient [,ini'fiʃnt] adj ineficaz; incompetente. **inefficiency** n ineficacia f; incompetencia f.

inept [i'nept] adj inepto.

inequality [,ini'kwoləti] n desigualdad f; injusticia f.

inert [i'nəːt] adj inerte. **inertia** n inercia f.

inevitable [in'evitəbl] adj inevitable. **inevitability** n inevitabilidad f.

inexpensive [,inik'spensiv] adj poco costoso, barato.

inexperienced [,inik'spiəriənst] adj inexperto.

infallible [in'faləbl] adj infalible.

infamous ['infəməs] adj de mala fama; odioso. **infamy** n infamia f.

infancy ['infənsi] n infancia f, niñez f.

infant ['infənt] n niño, -a m, f. adj naciente. **infantile** adj infantil.

infantry ['infəntri] n infantería f.

infatuate [in'fatjueit] v **be infatuated with** (person) estar chiflado por; (idea) estar encaprichado por. **infatuation** n enamoramiento m.

infect [in'fekt] v infectar; contaminar. **infection** n infección f; contaminación f. **infectious** adj infeccioso; contagioso.

infer [in'fəː] v deducir. **inference** n deducción f.

inferior [in'fiəriə] nm, adj inferior. **inferiority** n inferioridad f. **inferiority complex** complejo de inferioridad m.

infernal [in'fəːnl] adj infernal; (coll) maldito.

infest [in'fest] v infestar. **infestation** n infestación f.

infidelity [,infi'deliti] n infidelidad f.

infiltrate [in'fil,treit] v infiltrarse. **infiltration** n infiltración f.

infinite ['infinit] nm, adj infinito. **infinity** n infinidad f; (math) infinito m.

infinitive [in'finitiv] nm, adj infinitivo.

infirm [in'fəːm] adj débil. **infirmity** n debilidad f; (illness) enfermedad f.

infirmary [in'fəːməri] n enfermería f; hospital m.

inflame [in'fleim] v (set on fire) inflamar; (passion) avivar; (anger) encender. **inflammable** adj inflamable. **inflammation** n inflamación f. **inflammatory** adj incendiario.

inflate [in'fleit] v hinchar; (prices) provocar la inflación de. **inflation** n (air) inflado m; (comm) inflación f. **inflationary** adj inflacionista.

inflection [in'flekʃən] n inflexión f.

inflict [in'flikt] v infligir, imponer. **infliction** n (punishment) castigo m.

influence ['influəns] n influencia f. **under the influence of** bajo los efectos de. v (person) influenciar; (decision) influir en. **influential** adj influyente.

influenza [,influ'enzə] n gripe f.

influx ['inflʌks] n (gas, etc.) entrada f; (people) afluencia f.

inform [in'fɔːm] v informar. **informative** adj informativo. **informer** n denunciante m, f.

informal [in'fɔːml] adj sin ceremonia; (person) sencillo; (tone) familiar; (unofficial) no oficial. **informality** n ausencia de ceremonia f; sencillez f.

information [,infə'meiʃən] n información f. **information bureau** centro de informaciones m. **information desk** informaciones f pl.

infra-red [,infrə'red] adj infrarrojo.

infringe [in'frindʒ] v infringir, violar. **infringe on** usurpar. **infringement** n infracción f; usurpación f.

infuriate [in'fjuəri,eit] v enfurecer; exasperar. **infuriating** adj exasperante.

ingenious [in'dʒiːnjəs] adj ingenioso. **ingenuity** n ingeniosidad f.

ingot ['iŋgət] n lingote m.

ingredient [in'griːdjənt] n ingrediente m.

inhabit [in'habit] v (occupy) habitar; (live in) vivir en. **inhabitant** n habitante m.

inhale [in'heil] v inhalar; (smoke) tragar.

inherent [in'hiərənt] adj inherente.

inherit [in'herit] v heredar. **inheritance** n herencia f; sucesión f.

inhibit [in'hibit] v (restrain) inhibir; (prevent) impedir. **inhibition** n inhibición f.

inhuman [in'hjuːmən] adj inhumano; insensible. **inhumanity** n inhumanidad f.

iniquity [i'nikwəti] n iniquidad f. **iniquitous** adj inicuo.

initial [i'niʃl] adj inicial, primero. n inicial f; (used as abbreviation) siglas f pl. v poner iniciales a. **initially** adv al principio.

initiate [i'niʃi,eit] v iniciar; (proceedings) entablar; (membership) admitir. **initiation** n iniciación f.

initiative [i'niʃiətiv] n iniciativa f.

inject [in'dʒekt] v inyectar. **injection** n inyección f.

injure ['indʒə] v herir; lastimar; ofender. **injury** n herida f; daño m; ofensa f. **injurious** adj injurioso; ofensivo.

injustice [in'dʒʌstis] n injusticia f.

ink [iŋk] n tinta f. **ink-well** n tintero m. v entintar.

inkling ['iŋkliŋ] n idea f; algo m; sospecha f; indicio m.

inland ['inlənd; adv in'land] adj interior. **Inland Revenue** fisco m. adv hacia el interior.

in-laws ['in,lɔːs] pl n (coll) familia política f sing.

*inlay [in'lei; n 'inlei] v incrustar; adornar con marquetería. n incrustación f; (with coloured woods) taracea f.

inlet ['inlet] n cala f; brazo de mar m; (tech) entrada f.

inmate ['inmeit] n (prison) preso m; (asylum) internado, -a m, f; (hospital) enfermo, -a m, f.

inn [in] n posada f; taberna f. **innkeeper** n posadero, -a m, f; tabernero, -a m, f.

innate [,i'neit] adj innato.

inner ['inə] adj interior; íntimo. **inner tube** cámara de neumático f.

innocent ['inəsnt] adj inocente. **innocence** n inocencia f.

innocuous [i'nokjuəs] adj inocuo; inofensivo.

innovation [inə'veiʃən] n innovación f.

innuendo [,inju'endou] n insinuación f.

innumerable [i'njuːmərəbl] adj innumerable.

inoculate [i'nokju,leit] v inocular. **inoculation** n inoculación f.

inorganic [,inor'ganik] adj inorgánico.

input ['input] n entrada f; (computer) input m.

inquest ['inkwest] n encuesta f.

inquire [in'kwaiə] v informarse de; preguntar. **inquire into** investigar. **inquiring** adj (mind) curioso; (look) inquisidor. **inquiry** n pregunta f; (official) investigación f; (request for information) petición de información f. **inquiry office** oficina de informaciones f. **inquiries** pl n (sign) información f sing.

inquisition [,inkwi'ziʃən] n investigación f. **the Inquisition** la Inquisición f.

inquisitive [in'kwizətiv] adj preguntón; curioso. **inquisitiveness** n curiosidad f.

insane [in'sein] adj loco. **insane asylum** manicomio m. **insanity** n locura f.

insatiable [in'seiʃəbl] adj insaciable.

inscribe [in'skraib] v inscribir; (engrave) grabar. **inscription** n inscripción f.

insect ['insekt] n insecto m; (coll) bicho m. **insecticide** n insecticida f.

insecure [ˌinsi'kjuə] *adj* inseguro; *(unstable)* inestable. **insecurity** *n* inseguridad *f.*
inseminate [in'semineit] *v* inseminar. **insemination** *n* inseminación *f.*
insensitive [in'sensətiv] *adj* insensible. **insensitivity** *n* insensibilidad *f.*
inseparable [in'sepərəbl] *adj* inseparable.
insert [in'səːt; *n* 'insəːt] *v* introducir; *(advert)* insertar; *(between pages)* intercalar. *n (in a book)* encarte *m.* **insertion** *n* inserción *f;* encarte *m; (advert)* anuncio *m.*
inshore [ˌin'ʃoː] *adj* cercano a la orilla.
inside [ˌin'said] *adv* dentro, adentro. *prep* dentro de. *adj* interior; confidencial. *n* interior *m;* parte de adentro *f.* **inside out** al revés.
insidious [in'sidiəs] *adj* insidioso. **insidiousness** *n* insidia *f.*
insight ['insait] *n* perspicacia *f.*
insignificant [ˌinsig'nifikənt] *adj* insignificante. **insignificance** *n* insignificancia *f.*
insincere [ˌinsin'siə] *adj* insincero; hipócrita. **insincerity** *n* insinceridad *f;* hipocresía *f.*
insinuate [in'sinjueit] *v* insinuar. **insinuation** *n* insinuación *f.*
insipid [in'sipid] *adj* insípido, soso.
insist [in'sist] *v* insistir, empeñarse. **insistence** *n* insistencia *f,* empeño *m.* **insistent** *adj* insistente. **insistently** *adv* insistentemente.
insolent ['insələnt] *adj* insolente. **insolence** *n* insolencia *f.*
insoluble [in'soljubl] *adj* insoluble.
insomnia [in'somniə] *n* insomnio *m.* **insomniac** *n(m+f),* *adj* insomne.
inspect [in'spekt] *v* inspeccionar, examinar. **inspection** *n* inspección *f,* examen *m.* **inspector** *n* inspector *m, f.*
inspire [in'spaiə] *v* inspirar. **inspiration** *n* inspiración *f.* **inspirational** *adj* inspirador.
instability [ˌinstə'biləti] *n* inestabilidad *f,* instabilidad *f.*
install [in'stoːl] *v* instalar. **installation** *n* instalación *f.*
instalment [in'stoːlmənt] *n (payment)* plazo *m; (serial)* fascículo *m.* **monthly instalment** mensualidad *f.*
instance ['instəns] *n* ejemplo *m.* **for instance** por ejemplo.
instant ['instənt] *n* instante *m,* momento *m. adj (coffee, soup, etc.)* instantáneo; urgente; inmediato; inminente; *(this*

month) corriente. **instantaneous** *adj* instantáneo. **instantly** *adv* al instante.
instead [in'sted] *adv* en su lugar. **instead of** en vez de.
instep ['instep] *n* empeine *m.*
instigate ['instigeit] *v* instigar, incitar; fomentar. **instigation** *n* instigación *f.* **instigator** *n* instigador, -a *m, f.*
instil [in'stil] *v* instilar; inculcar.
instinct ['instiŋkt] *n* instinto *m.* **instinctive** *adj* instintivo.
institute ['institjuːt] *n* instituto *m. v* instituir, establecer; *(start)* empezar. **institution** *n* institución *f;* establecimiento *m.*
instruct [in'strʌkt] *v (teach)* instruir; *(order)* mandar. **instruction** *n* instrucción *f.* **instructive** *adj* instructivo. **instructor** *n* instructor *m;* profesor *m;* maestro *m.*
instrument ['instrəmənt] *n* instrumento *m.* **instrumental** *adj* instrumental. **be instrumental in** contribuir a.
insubordinate [ˌinsə'boːdənət] *adj* insubordinado. **insubordination** *n* insubordinación *f.*
insufficient [ˌinsə'fiʃənt] *adj* insuficiente. **insufficiency** *n* insuficiencia *f.*
insular ['insjulə] *adj* insular; *(outlook)* estrecho de miras.
insulate ['insjuleit] *v* aislar. **insulation** *n* aislamiento *m; (material)* aislador *m.*
insulin ['insjulin] *n* insulina *f.*
insult [in'sʌlt; *n* 'insʌlt] *v* insultar. *n* insulto *m.*
insure [in'ʃuə] *v* asegurar. **insurance** *n* seguro *m.* **insurance broker** corredor de seguros *m.* **insurance policy** póliza de seguro *f.* **fully comprehensive insurance** seguro a todo riesgo *m.* **third party insurance** seguro contra terceros *m.* **national insurance** seguros sociales *m pl.* **take out insurance** hacerse un seguro.
intact [in'takt] *adj* intacto.
intake ['inteik] *n (air, water)* toma *f; (mot)* entrada *f; (fuel, steam)* válvula de admisión *f; (food)* ración *f; (school)* número de personas admitidas *m; (thing taken in)* consumo *m.*
intangible [in'tandʒəbl] *adj* intangible. **intangibility** *n* intangibilidad *f.*
integral ['intigrəl] *adj (part)* integrante; *(complete)* integral. *n* integral *f.*
integrate ['intigreit] *v* integrar. **integration** *n* integración *f.*

integrity [in'tegrəti] *n* integridad *f.*

intellect ['intilekt] *n* intelecto *m,* inteligencia *f.* **intellectual** *n(m+f),* *adj* intelectual.

intelligent [in'telidʒənt] *adj* inteligente. **intelligence** *n* inteligencia *f*; (*information*) noticia *f*; (*secret information*) información *f.*

intelligible [in'telidʒəbl] *adj* inteligible.

intend [in'tend] *v* proponerse.

intense [in'tens] *adj* intenso; fuerte; profundo; ardiente; enorme. **intensify** *v* intensificar; aumentar. **intensity** *n* intensidad *f.* **intensive** *adj* intensivo. **intensive care** asistencia intensiva *f.*

intent[1] [in'tent] *n* intención *f*, propósito *m.*

intent[2] [in'tent] *adj* atento; profundo; constante.

intention [in'tenʃən] *n* intención *f.* **intentional** *adj* intencional.

inter [in'tər] *v* enterrar. **interment** *n* entierro *m.*

interact [,intər'akt] *v* actuar recíprocamente. **interaction** *n* interacción *f.*

intercede [,intə'siːd] *v* interceder. **intercession** *n* intercesión *f.*

intercept [,intə'sept] *v* (*message*) interceptar; (*stop someone*) parar. **interception** *n* intercepción *f,* interceptación *f.*

interchange [,intə'tʃəindʒ] *n* intercambio *m*; cambio *m.* **interchangeable** *adj* intercambiable.

intercom ['intə,kom] *n* interfono *m.*

intercourse ['intəkɔɪs] *n* (*social*) trato *m*; (*pol, comm*) relaciones *f pl*; (*sexual*) contacto sexual *m.*

interest ['intrist] *n* interés *m*; (*advantage*) beneficio *m.* **business interests** negocios *m pl. v* interesar. **be interested** interesarse en.

interfere [,intə'fiə] *v* entrometerse. **interfere with** (*hinder*) estorbar; (*touch*) tocar; (*interests*) oponerse a. **interference** *n* intromisión *f*; obstrucción *f*; (*radio*) parásitos *m pl.* **interfering** *adj* (*person*) entrometido; interferente.

interim ['intərim] *n* ínterin *m. adj* provisional.

interior [in'tiəriə] *nm, adj* interior.

interjection [,intə'dʒekʃən] *n* interjección *f.*

interlude ['intəluːd] *n* intervalo *m*; (*theatre*) entremés *m*; (*music*) interludio *m.*

intermediate [,intə'miːdiət] *adj* intermedio. **intermediary** *n* intermediario, -a *m, f.*

interminable [in'təɪminəbl] *adj* interminable.

intermission [,intə'miʃən] *n* (*interruption*) intermisión *f*; (*theatre*) entreacto *m*; (*cinema*) descanso *m.*

intermittent [,intə'mitənt] *adj* intermitente. **intermittently** *adv* a intervalos.

intern [in'təɪn] *n* interno *m. v* internar. **internment** *n* internamiento *m.*

internal [in'təɪnl] *adj* interno. **internal combustion engine** motor de combustión interna *m.*

international [,intə'naʃənl] *adj* internacional. **international date line** línea de cambio de fecha *f.*

interpose [,intə'pouz] *v* interponer; intervenir. **interposition** *n* interposición *f.*

interpret [in'təɪprit] *v* interpretar. **interpretation** *n* interpretación *f.* **interpreter** *n* intérprete *m, f.*

interrogate [in'terəgeit] *v* interrogar. **interrogation** *n* interrogatorio *m.* **interrogator** *n* interrogador, -a *m, f.*

interrogative [,intə'rogətiv] *adj* (*sentence*) interrogativo; (*look*) interrogador. *n* palabra interrogativa *f.*

interrupt [,intə'rʌpt] *v* interrumpir. **interruption** *n* interrupción *f.*

intersect [,intə'sekt] *v* cruzar; (*math*) cortar. **intersection** *n* (*mot*) cruce *m*; (*math*) intersección *f.*

intersperse [,intə'spəɪs] *v* esparcir.

interval ['intəvəl] *n* (*time, space, music*) intervalo *m*; (*theatre*) entreacto *m*; (*cinema*) descanso *m.*

intervene [,intə'viːn] *v* intervenir; (*happen*) ocurrir; (*time*) transcurrir; (*distance*) mediar. **intervention** *n* intervención *f.*

interview ['intəvjuɪ] *n* entrevista *f,* interviú *f. v* entrevistar. **interviewer** *n* entrevistador, -a *m, f.*

intestine [in'testin] *n* intestino *m.* **intestinal** *adj* intestinal.

intimate[1] ['intimət] *adj* íntimo; (*individual*) personal; (*loving*) amoroso; (*detailed*) profundo. **intimacy** *n* relaciones íntimas *f pl.*

intimate[2] ['intimeit] *v* insinuar; anunciar. **intimation** *n* insinuación *f*; indicación *f*; indicio *m.*

intimidate [in'timideit] v intimidar. **intim-idation** n intimidación f.
into ['intu] prep en; a; hacia; contra; dentro.
intolerable [in'tolərəbl] adj intolerable.
intolerant [in'tolərənt] adj intolerante. **intolerance** n intolerancia f.
intonation [.intə'neiʃən] n entonación f. **intone** v entonar.
intoxicate [in'toksikeit] v embriagar, emborrachar. **intoxicated** adj borracho, ebrio. **intoxication** n embriaguez f, borrachera f.
intransitive [in'transitiv] nm, adj intransitivo.
intravenous [.intrə'viːnəs] adj intravenoso.
intrepid [in'trepid] adj intrépido.
intricate ['intriket] adj intrincado; complejo. **intricacy** n intrincamiento m; complejidad f.
intrigue ['intriːg; v in'triːg] n intriga f. v intrigar.
intrinsic [in'trinsik] adj intrínseco.
introduce [.intrə'djuːs] v presentar; introducir; (acquaint) iniciar. **introduction** n presentación f; introducción f. **introductory** adj introductorio.
introspective [.intrə'spektiv] adj introspectivo. **introspection** n introspección f.
introvert ['intrə.vɜːt] n. introvertido, -a m, f. **introverted** adj introvertido.
intrude [in'truːd] v imponer; meter por fuerza. **intruder** n intruso, -a m, f. **intrusion** n entremetimiento m.
intuition [.intjuː'iʃən] n intuición f. **intuitive** adj intuitivo.
inundate ['inʌndeit] v inundar. **inundation** n inundación f.
invade [in'veid] v invadir. **invader** n invasor, -a m, f. **invasion** n invasión f.
invalid¹ ['invəlid] nm, adj (disabled) inválido; (sick) enfermo.
invalid² [in'valid] adj (not valid) nulo.
invaluable [in'valjuəbl] adj inestimable.
invariable [in'veəriəbl] adj invariable. **invariably** adv invariablemente; constantemente.
invective [in'vektiv] n invectiva f.
invent [in'vent] v inventar. **invention** n invención f. **inventive** adj inventivo. **inventor** n inventor, -a m, f.
inventory ['invəntri] n inventario m.
invert [in'vɜːt] v invertir. **inverted commas** comillas f pl. **inversion** n inversión f.

invertebrate [in'vɜːtibrət] nm, adj invertebrado.
invest [in'vest] v invertir; (install) investir. **invest in** (fig) comprarse. **invest with** (fig) envolver en. **investment** n inversión f. **investor** n inversionista m, f.
investigate [in'vestigeit] v investigar, examinar; estudiar. **investigation** n investigación f; estudio m.
invigorating [in'vigəreitiŋ] adj tónico, estimulante. **invigorate** v vigorizar, estimular.
invincible [in'vinsəbl] adj invencible.
invisible [in'vizəbl] adj invisible. **invisibility** n invisibilidad f.
invite [in'vait] v invitar, convidar; (questions) solicitar; (ask for) pedir; (cause) provocar. **invitation** n invitación f. **inviting** adj atractivo; seductor; tentador; apetitoso.
invoice ['invois] n factura f. v facturar.
invoke [in'vouk] v invocar; (ask for) pedir; (fall back on) recurrir. **invocation** n invocación f.
involuntary [in'voləntəri] adj involuntario. **involuntarily** adv sin querer.
involve [in'volv] v (concern) concernir; (imply) suponer; (affect) afectar; (entail) ocasionar; (draw somebody in) comprometer; mezclar; (require) exigir; (complicate) complicar. **involved** adj complicado. **involvement** n envolvimiento m; participación f; compromiso m.
inward ['inwəd] adj interior, interno; (thoughts) íntimo. **inwardly** adv interiormente. **inwards** adv hacia dentro.
iodine ['aiədiːn] n yodo m.
ion ['aiən] n ion m.
irate [ai'reit] adj furioso.
Ireland ['aiələnd] n Irlanda f. **Irish** nm, adj irlandés. **the Irish** los irlandeses m pl.
iris ['aiəris] n lirio m.
irk [ɜːk] v molestar. **irksome** adj molesto.
iron ['aiən] n (metal) hierro m; (for pressing) plancha f. (golf) palo de golf m. **cast iron** hierro colado m. **Iron Curtain** telón de acero m. **wrought iron** hierro forjado m. **ironmonger** n quincallería f. v planchar. **iron out** (fig) allanar. **ironing** n planchado m. **ironing board** tabla de planchar.
irony ['aiərəni] n ironía f. **ironic** adj irónico.
irrational [i'raʃənl] adj irracional. n (math) número irracional m.

irregular [i'regjulə] *adj* irregular. **irregularity** *n* irregularidad *f*.

irrelevant [i'reləvənt] *adj* (*remark*) fuera de propósito; (*beside the point*) no pertinente.

irreparable [i'repərəbl] *adj* irreparable.

irresistible [ˌiri'zistəbl] *adj* irresistible.

irrespective [ˌiri'spektiv] *adj* **irrespective of** sin tener en cuenta.

irresponsible [ˌiri'sponsəbl] *adj* irresponsable; irreflexivo.

irrevocable [i'revəkəbl] *adj* irrevocable.

irrigate ['irigeit] *v* irrigar. **irrigation** *n* irrigación *f*.

irritate ['iriteit] *v* irritar. **irritable** *adj* irritable. **irritation** *n* irritación *f*.

is [iz] *V* be.

island ['ailənd] *n* isla; (*traffic*) refugio *m*.

isolate ['aisəleit] *v* aislar. **isolation** *n* aislamiento *m*.

issue ['iʃuː] *n* (*stamps, shares, etc.*) emisión *f*; (*publication*) publicación *f*; (*edition*) tirada *f*; (*copy*) número *m*; (*passport*) expedición *f*; (*distribution*) reparto *m*; (*outcome*) resultado *m*; (*question*) cuestión *f*; (*affair*) asunto *m*; (*offspring*) progenie *f*. **take issue with** estar en desacuerdo con. *v* salir; resultar; publicar; distribuir; (*give*) dar; emitir; (*decree*) promulgar; (*warrant, cheque*) extender; (*tickets*) expender; (*licence*) facilitar.

isthmus ['isməs] *n* istmo *m*.

it [it] *pron* él, ella ello; (*direct object*) lo, la; (*indirect object*) le.

italic [i'talik] *adj* itálico. **italics** *pl n* bastardilla *f sing*.

Italy ['itəli] *n* Italia *f*. **Italian** *n, adj* italiano, -a.

itch [itʃ] *n* picazón *f*; (*desire*) ganas *f pl*. *v* picar.

item ['aitəm] *n* artículo *m*; noticia *f*; detalle *m*; punto *m*. **itemize** *v* detallar.

itinerary [ai'tinərəri] *n* itinerario *m*.

its [its] *adj* su (*pl* sus).

itself [it'self] *pron* se; él/ello mismo, ella misma; (*after prep*) sí mismo, -a. **by itself** aislado; (*alone*) solo.

ivory ['aivəri] *n* marfil *m*.

ivy ['aivi] *n* hiedra *f*, yedra *f*.

J

jab [dʒab] *v* (*stab*) pinchar; (*elbow*) dar un codazo a. *n* pinchazo *m*; codazo *m*; (*blow*) golpe seco *m*; (*coll: injection*) injección *f*.

jack [dʒak] *n* (*mot*) gato *m*; (*cards*) valet *m*, jota *f*; (*Spanish cards*) sota *f*. *v* **jack up** levantar con el gato.

jackal ['dʒakoɪl] *n* chacal *m*.

jackdaw ['dʒakdoɪ] *n* grajilla *f*.

jacket ['dʒakit] *n* chaqueta *f*; (*book*) sobrecubierta *f*; (*tech: cylinder, pipe, etc.*) camisa *f*.

jackpot ['dʒakpot] *n* premio gordo *m*.

jade [dʒeid] *nm, adj* jade *m*.

jaded ['dʒeidid] *adj* cansado.

jagged ['dʒagid] *adj* dentado.

jaguar ['dʒagjuə] *n* jaguar *m*.

jail [dʒeil] *n* cárcel *f*. *v* encarcelar. **jailer** *n* carcelero *m*.

jam[1] [dʒam] *v* (*force in*) meter a la fuerza; (*squash*) apretar; (*catch*) pillar; (*pack*) atestar; (*clog*) atorar; (*block*) bloquear; (*moving part*) atascar; (*radio*) interferir; (*become wedged*) atrancarse. *n* atasco *m*; (*people*) agolpamiento *m*; (*traffic*) embotellamiento *m*. **be in a jam** (*coll*) estar en un apuro.

jam[2] [dʒam] *n* mermelada *f*.

janitor ['dʒanitə] *n* portero *m*.

January ['dʒanjuəri] *n* enero *m*.

Japan [dʒə'pan] *n* Japón *m*. **Japanese** *nm, adj* japonés.

jar[1] [dʒaɪ] *n* (*vessel*) vasija *f*; (*jam pot*) tarro *m*; (*large pot*) tinaja *f*.

jar[2] [dʒaɪ] *v* (*sound*) chirriar; (*shake*) sacudir; (*colours*) chocar; (*music*) sonar mal; (*nerves*) irritar.

jargon ['dʒaɪgən] *n* jerga *f*.

jasmine ['dʒazmin] *n* jazmín *m*.

jaundice ['dʒoɪndis] *n* ictericia *f*; (*fig*) celos *m pl*.

jaunt [dʒoɪnt] *n* paseo *m*.

jaunty ['dʒoɪnti] *adj* vivaz; desenvuelto.

javelin ['dʒavəlin] *n* jabalina *f*.

jaw [dʒoɪ] *n* (*person*) mandíbula *f*; (*animal*) quijada *f*. **jawbone** *n* mandíbula *f*; quijada *f*.

jazz [dʒaz] *n* jazz *m*. **jazz band** orquesta de jazz *f*.

jealous ['dʒeləs] *adj* celoso; envidioso. **jealousy** *n* celos *m pl*; envidia *f*.

jeans [dʒiːns] *pl n* pantalones vaqueros *m pl.*

jeep [dʒiːp] *n* jeep *m.*

jeer [dʒiə] *v* (*boo*) abuchear; (*mock*) mofarse de. *n* abucheo *m*; mofa *f.*

jelly ['dʒeli] *n* jalea *f*. **jellyfish** *n* medusa *f.*

jeopardize ['dʒepədaiz] *v* arriesgar. **jeopardy** *n* riesgo *m*, peligro *m.*

jerk [dʒɜːk] *n* sacudida *f*; (*shove*) empujón *m*; (*pull*) tirón. *v* sacudir; mover a tirones. **jerkily** *adv* con sacudidas. **jerky** *adj* espasmódico.

jersey ['dʒɜːzi] *n* jersey *m.*

jest [dʒest] *v* bromear. *n* broma *f*. **jester** *n* bromista *m, f.*

jet [dʒet] *n* (*liquid*) chorro *m*; (*flame*) llama *f*; (*plane*) avión de reactor *m*. **jet-propelled** *adj* de reacción.

jetty ['dʒeti] *n* muelle *m.*

Jew [dʒuː] *n* judío, -a *m, f*. **Jewish** *adj* judío.

jewel ['dʒuːəl] *n* joya *f*, piedra preciosa *f*; (*in a watch*) rubí *m*. **jeweller** *n* joyero *m*. **jeweller's** *n* joyería *f*. **jewellery** *n* joyería *f.*

jig [dʒig] *n* giga *f*. *v* bailar la giga; dar saltitos.

jigsaw ['dʒigsɔː] *n* (*puzzle*) rompecabezas *m invar*; (*saw*) sierra de vaivén *f.*

jilt [dʒilt] *v* dejar plantado a.

jingle ['dʒiŋgl] *n* tintineo *m*; (*verse*) copla *f*. *v* tintinear.

jinx [dʒiŋks] *n* (*coll*) maleficio *m*. **put a jinx on** echar mal de ojo a.

job [dʒob] *n* trabajo *m*, empleo *m*. **job lot** colección miscelánea *f*. **make a good job of** (**something**) hacer (algo) bien. **odd-job man** factótum *m.*

jockey ['dʒoki] *n* jinete *m*; jockey *m.*

jocular ['dʒokjulə] *adj* jocoso; bromista.

jodhpurs ['dʒodpəz] *pl n* pantalones de montar *m pl.*

jog [dʒog] *n* sacudida *f*; (*with elbow*) codazo *m*. **jogtrot** *n* trote corto *m*. *v* sacudir; (*memory*) refrescar. **jog someone's elbow** darle en el codo a uno. **jogging** *n* jogging *m.*

join [dʒoin] *v* juntar, unir; (*roads*) ir a dar a; (*friends*) reunirse con; (*a company*) ingresar en; (*a club*) hacerse socio de; (*a political party*) afiliarse a; (*hands*) darse la mano; (*two pieces*) ensamblar; (*rivers*) confluir. **join in** participar en. **join up** (*mil*) alistarse. **joiner** carpintero *m.*

joint [dʒoint] *n* juntura *f*, unión *f*; (*anat*) articulación *f*; (*meat*) corte para asar; (*slang: place*) antro *m*. *adj* unido; colectivo; conjunto; mutuo. **jointly** *adv* en común.

joist [dʒoist] *n* vigueta *f.*

joke [dʒouk] *n* chiste *m*; (*prank*) broma *f*. *v* contar chistes; bromear. **joker** *n* chistoso, -a *m, f*; bromista *m, f*; (*fool*) payaso, -a *m, f*; (*cards*) comodín *m.*

jolly ['dʒoli] *adj* alegre, jovial; divertido. *adv* (*coll: emphatic*) muy. **jollity** *n* alegría *f*, jovialidad *f.*

jolt [dʒoult] *v* sacudir; (*vehicle*) traquetear. *n* sacudida *f*; choque *m*; (*fig: shock*) susto *m.*

jostle ['dʒosl] *v* (*push*) empujar; (*elbow*) codear. *n* empujones *m pl.*

jot [dʒot] *n* jota *f*. *v* **jot down** apuntar.

journal ['dʒɜːnl] *n* (*newspaper*) periódico *m*; (*magazine*) revista *f*; (*diary*) diario *m*; (*of a learned society*) boletín *m*. **journalism** *n* periodismo *m*. **journalist** *n* periodista *m, f.*

journey ['dʒɜːni] *n* viaje *m*. *v* viajar.

jovial ['dʒouviəl] *adj* jovial. **joviality** *n* jovialidad *f.*

joy [dʒoi] *n* alegría *f*, placer *m*. **joyful** *or* **joyous** *adj* alegre, gozoso.

jubilant ['dʒuːbilənt] *adj* jubiloso. **jubilation** *n* júbilo *m.*

jubilee ['dʒuːbiliː] *n* jubileo *m.*

Judaism ['dʒuːdeiˌizəm] *n* judaísmo *m.*

judge [dʒʌdʒ] *n* juez *m*; árbitro *m*. *v* juzgar; arbitrar. **judging by** a juzgar por. **judgement** *n* (*trial*) juicio; (*legal sentence*) sentencia *f*; apreciación *f.*

judicial [dʒuːˈdiʃəl] *adj* judicial.

judicious [dʒuːˈdiʃəs] *adj* juicioso.

judo ['dʒuːdou] *n* judo *m.*

jug [dʒʌg] *n* jarra *f*; (*slang: prison*) chirona *f.*

juggernaut ['dʒʌgənɔːt] *n* camión grande *m.*

juggle ['dʒʌgl] *v* hacer juegos malabares. **juggler** *n* malabarista *m, f*. **juggling** *n* juegos malabares *m pl.*

jugular ['dʒʌgjulə] *nf, adj* yugular.

juice [dʒuːs] *n* jugo *m*. **juicy** *adj* jugoso.

jukebox ['dʒuːkboks] *n* máquina de discos *f.*

July [dʒuˈlai] *n* julio *m.*

jumble ['dʒʌmbl] *v* embrollar; mezclar. *n* embrollo *m*; mezcolanza *f*. **jumble sale** venta de caridad *f.*

kill

jump [dʒʌmp] *n* salto *m*. *v* saltar. **jump at** (*offer, etc.*) aprovechar. **make someone jump** sobresaltar a uno. **jumpy** *adj* (*coll*) nervioso.

jumper [ˈdʒʌmpə] *n* (*garment*) jersey *m*.

junction [ˈdʒʌŋktʃən] *n* (*join*) unión *f*; (*rail*) empalme *m*; (*road*) cruce *f*.

juncture [ˈdʒʌŋkʃə] *n* coyuntura *f*. **at this juncture** en esta coyuntura.

June [dʒuːn] *n* junio *m*.

jungle [ˈdʒʌŋgl] *n* selva *f*.

junior [ˈdʒuːnjə] *adj* (*younger*) hijo; (*lower rank*) subalterno. *n* menor *m, f*; subalterno, -a *m, f*; (*in school*) pequeño, -a *m, f*.

juniper [ˈdʒuːnipə] *n* enebro *m*. **juniper berry** enebrina *f*.

junk¹ [dʒʌŋk] *n* trastos viejos *m pl*; (*coll*: *rubbish*) porquería *f*. **junk-shop** *n* baratillo *m*.

junk² [dʒʌŋk] *n* (*naut*) junco *m*.

jurisdiction [dʒuərisˈdikʃən] *n* jurisdicción *f*.

jury [ˈdʒuəri] *n* jurado *m*. **juror** *n* jurado, -a *m, f*.

just [dʒʌst] *adv* justo; justamente; precisamente. **have just** acabar de. *adj* justo; exacto.

justice [ˈdʒʌstis] *n* justicia *f*. **Justice of the Peace** juez de paz *m*.

justify [ˈdʒʌstifai] *v* justificar. **justifiable** *adj* justificable. **justification** *n* justificación *f*.

jut [dʒʌt] *v* **jut out** sobresalir.

jute [dʒuːt] *n* yute *m*.

juvenile [ˈdʒuːvənail] *n* joven *m, f*, adolescente *m, f*, menor *m, f*. *adj* juvenil; infantil. **juvenile delinquent** delincuente juvenil *m, f*.

juxtapose [ˌdʒʌkstəˈpouz] *v* yuxtaponer. **juxtaposition** *n* yuxtaposición *f*.

K

kaftan [ˈkaftan] *n* caftán *m*.

kaleidoscope [kəˈlaidəskoup] *n* calidoscopio *m*.

kangaroo [kaŋgəˈruː] *n* canguro *m*.

karate [kəˈraːti] *n* karate *m*.

kebab [kiˈbab] *n* pincho *m*.

keel [kiːl] *n* quilla *f*. **keel over** (*naut*) zozobrar; (*coll: faint*) desplomarse.

keen [kiːn] *adj* entusiasta; fuerte, vivo; penetrante; (*prices*) competitivo; (*mind*) agudo; (*sharp*) afilado. **keenly** *adv* con entusiasmo; profundamente. **keenness** *n* entusiasmo *m*; deseo *m*; profundidad *f*; agudeza *f*; finura *f*.

*keep [kiːp] *v* guardar; tener. (*promise*) cumplir; (*appointment*) acudir a; (*hang on to*) quedarse; (*support*) mantener; (*hold*) reservar; (*detain*) detener; (*look after*) cuidar; (*continue*) seguir. **keep at** seguir con. **keep away** mantener a distancia. **keep down** contener. **keep fit** mantenerse en forma. **keep out** ¡prohibida la entrada! **keep up with** seguir. **keeper** *n* guarda *m*.

keg [keg] *n* barril *m*.

kennel [ˈkenl] *n* perrera *f*.

kerb [kəːb] *n* bordillo *m*.

kernel [ˈkəːnl] *n* (*nut*) pepita *f*; (*seed*) grano.

kerosene [ˈkerəsiːn] *n* queroseno *m*.

ketchup [ˈketʃəp] *n* salsa de tomate *f*.

kettle [ˈketl] *n* hervidor *m*. **kettledrum** *n* timbal *m*.

key [kiː] *n* llave *f*; (*for a code*) clave *f*; (*music*) tono *m*; (*piano, typewriter*) tecla *f*. **keyboard** *n* teclado *m*. **keyhold** *n* ojo de la cerradura *m*. **key-ring** *n* llavero *m*. *adj* clave.

khaki [ˈkaːki] *nm, adj* caqui.

kick [kik] *n* patada *f*, puntapié *m*; (*animal*) coz *f*; (*recoil*) culatazo *m*; (*fig: energy*) fuerza *f*. *v* dar una patada a; dar una coza. **kick off** (*football*) hacer el saque del centro; (*fig*) comenzar. **kick-off** *n* saque del centro *m*; (*coll*) comienzo *m*. **kick out** (*coll*) poner de patitas en la calle.

kid¹ [kid] *n* (*goat*) cabrito *m*; (*leather*) cabritilla *f*; (*coll: child*) niño, -a *m, f*.

kid² [kid] *v* (*coll*) tomar el pelo.

kidnap [ˈkidnap] *v* secuestrar, raptar. **kidnapper** *n* secuestrador, -a *m, f*, raptor, -ora *m, f*. **kidnapping** *n* secuestro *m*, rapto *m*.

kidney [ˈkidni] *n* riñón *m*.

kill [kil] *v* matar; (*fig: hopes*) arruinar. *n* muerte *f*; caza *f*. **killjoy** *n* aguafiestas *m, f invar*. **killer** *n* asesino, -a *m, f*. **killing** *n* (*murder*) asesinato *m*; (*slaughter*) matanza *f*.

kiln [kiln] *n* horno *m*.
kilo ['kiːlou] *n* kilo *m*.
kilogram ['kiləgram] *n* kilogramo *m*.
kilometre ['kiləmiːtə] *n* kilómetro *m*.
kin [kin] *n* parientes *m pl*. **kinship** *n* parentesco *m*.
kind[1] [kaind] *adj* amable; bueno. **kindhearted** *adj* bondadoso. **kindness** *n* amabilidad *f*; bondad *f*.
kind[2] [kaind] *n* clase *f*, tipo *m*; género *m*; especie *f*. **in kind** en especie.
kindergarten ['kindəgaːtn] *n* jardín de la infancia *m*.
kindle ['kindl] *v* encender; despertar.
kindred ['kindrid] *n* parientes *m pl*. *adj* (*related*) emparentado; (*similar*) semejante. **kindred spirits** almas gemelas *f pl*.
kinetic [kin'etik] *adj* cinético.
king [kiŋ] *n* rey *m*; (*draughts*) dama *f*. **kingfisher** *n* martín pescador *m*. **kingdom** *n* reino *m*. **king-size** *adj* enorme, gigante.
kink [kiŋk] *n* (*rope*) retorcimiento *m*; (*hair*) rizo *m*. *v* retorcer. **kinky** *adj* retorcido; (*coll*) extraño.
kiosk ['kiːosk] *n* quiosko *m*, kiosko *m*.
kipper ['kipə] *n* arenque ahumado *m*.
kiss [kis] *v* besar. *n* beso *m*. **kiss of life** respiración boca a boca *f*.
kit [kit] *n* (*tools*) herramientas *f pl*; (*sport*) equipo *m*; (*first aid*) botiquín *m*; (*model for assembling*) maqueta *f*. **kit out** equipar.
kitchen ['kitʃin] *n* cocina *f*. **kitchen sink** fregadero *m*.
kite [kait] *n* cometa *f*; (*bird*) milano *m*.
kitten ['kitn] *n* gatito *m*.
kitty ['kiti] *n* plato *m*, platillo *m*.
kleptomania [kleptə'meiniə] *n* cleptomanía *f*. **kleptomaniac** *n*(*m*+*f*), *adj* cleptómano.
knack [nak] *n* facilidad *f*; tino *m*; habilidad *f*. **get the knack of** coger el tino de.
knapsack ['napsak] *n* mochila *f*.
knead [niːd] *v* amasar.
knee [niː] *n* rodilla *f*. **kneecap** *n* rótula *f*.
***kneel** [niːl] *v* arrodillarse.
knew [njuː] *V* **know**.
knickers ['nikəz] *pl n* bragas *f pl*.
knife [naif] *n* cuchillo *m*. *v* (*stab*) apuñalar.
knight [nait] *n* caballero *m*. *v* armar caballero. **knighthood** *n* título de caballero *m*.
knit [nit] *v* tejer. **knit together** juntar;

(*bones*) soldarse. **knitting** *n* tejido de punto *m*. **knitting machine** máquina de hacer punto *f*. **knitting needle** aguja de hacer punto *f*.
knob [nob] *n* bulto *m*; (*door*) pomo *m*; (*radio, etc.*) botón *m*; (*drawer*) tirador *m*; (*butter*) pedazo *m*.
knobbly ['nobli] *adj* nudoso.
knock [nok] *n* golpe *m*, toque *m*. *v* golpear, pegar; (*fig: criticize*) meterse con. **knock down** (*price*) rebajar; (*person*) atropellar; (*object*) derribar. **knock-kneed** *adj* patizambo. **knock out** (*stun*) dejar K.O.; (*from contest*) eliminar. **knockout** *n* (*boxing*) knock out *m*, K.O. *m*. **knock over** tirar. **knocker** *n* aldaba *f*, aldabón *m*.
knot [not] *n* nudo *m*. *v* anudar. **knotty** (*problem*) espinoso.
***know** [nou] *v* (*facts*) saber; (*people, places*) conocer; (*recognize*) reconocer; (*distinguish*) distinguir. **know-all** *n* (*coll*) sabelotodo *m*, *f*. **know-how** *n* (*coll*) habilidad *f*; conocimientos *m pl*. **knowing** *adj* astuto; (*look*) de entendimiento.
knowledge ['nolidʒ] *n* conocimiento *m*. **knowledgeable** *adj* informado; erudito.
knuckle ['nʌkl] *n* nudillo *m*. **knuckle down to** ponerse seriamente a. **knuckle under** someterse.

L

label ['leibl] *n* etiqueta *f*. *v* poner etiqueta a.
laboratory [lə'borətəri] *n* laboratorio *m*.
labour ['leibə] *n* (*work*) trabajo *m*; (*task*) tarea *f*; (*effort*) esfuerzo *m*; (*childbirth*) parto *m*; (*manpower*) trabajadores *m pl*. **labour-saving** *adj* que ahorra trabajo. *v* trabajar; esforzarse. **laborious** *adj* laborioso. **labourer** *n* obrero *m*; peón *m*.
labyrinth ['labərinθ] *n* laberinto *m*.
lace [leis] *n* (*fabric*) encaje *m*. (*shoe*) cordón *m*. *v* atar; (*drink*) rociar.
lacerate ['lasəreit] *v* lacerar. **laceration** *n* laceración *f*.
lack [lak] *n* falta *f*, carencia *f*. **for lack of** por falta de. *v* carecer de, faltar a; necesitar.

lackadaisical [ˌlakəˈdeizikəl] *adj* apático; descuidado; tardo.

lacquer [ˈlakə] *n* (*hair*) laca *f*; (*paint*) pintura al duco *f*. *v* echar laca a; pintar al duco.

lad [lad] *n* (*coll*) chico *m*, muchacho *m*.

ladder [ˈladə] *n* escalera de mano *f*; (*stocking*) carrera *f*. **ladderproof** *adj* indesmallable.

laden [ˈleidn] *adj* cargado.

ladle [ˈleidl] *n* cucharón *m*.

lady [ˈleidi] *n* señora *f*. **ladies** (*sign*) servicios de señoras *m pl*. **ladies and gentlemen!** ¡señoras y señores! **ladybird** *n* mariquita *f*. **lady-in-waiting** *n* dama de honor *f*. **ladylike** *adj* distinguida.

lag¹ [lag] *v* (*be behind time*) retrasarse; (*trail*) quedarse atrás. *n* intervalo *m*; (*delay*) retraso *m*.

lag² [lag] *v* poner un revestimiento calorífugo a. **lagging** *n* revestimiento calorífugo *m*.

lager [ˈlaːgə] *n* cerveza dorada *f*.

lagoon [ləˈguːn] *n* laguna *f*.

laid [leid] *V* **lay¹**.

lain [lein] *V* **lie¹**.

lair [leə] *n* guarida *f*.

laity [ˈleiəti] *n* laicado *m*.

lake [leik] *n* lago *m*.

lamb [lam] *n* cordero *m*. **lamb chop** chuleta de cordero *f*.

lame [leim] *adj* cojo; (*excuse, etc.*) malo. **lame duck** incapaz *m*, *f*. *v* dejar cojo. **lamely** *adv* cojeando. **lameness** *n* cojera *f*; debilidad *f*.

lament [ləˈment] *n* lamento *m*. *v* lamentar, llorar. **lamentable** *adj* lamentable. **lamentation** *n* lamentación *f*.

laminate [ˈlamineit] *v* laminar. **laminated** *adj* laminado.

lamp [lamp] *n* lámpara *f*; (*street*) farol *m*; (*mot*) faro *m*. **lamppost** *n* poste de alumbrado *m*. **lampshade** *n* pantalla *f*.

lance [lains] *n* lanza *f*. *v* (*med*) abrir.

land [land] *n* tierra *f*; (*country*) país *m*. **landlady** *n* patrona *f*, dueña *f*. **landlord** *n* patrón *m*, dueño *m*. **landmark** *n* señal *f*. **landscape** *n* paisaje *m*. *v* desembarcar; (*aircraft*) aterrizar; (*fall*) caer; (*arrive*) llegar. **landing** *n* (*passengers*) desembarco *m*; (*cargo*) desembarque *m*; aterrizaje *m*. (*staircase*) rellano *m*. **landing stage** desembarcadero *m*.

lane [lein] *n* camino *m*; (*motorway*) banda *f*; (*running, swimming*) calle *f*.

language [ˈlaŋgwidʒ] *n* (*means of expression*) lenguaje *m*; (*of a nation*) lengua *f*. **bad** *or* **foul language** palabrotas *f pl*.

languish [ˈlaŋgwiʃ] *v* languidecer.

lanky [ˈlaŋki] *adj* larguirucho.

lantern [ˈlantən] *n* farol *m*, linterna *f*.

lap¹ [lap] *n* (*sport*) vuelta *f*. *v* dar una vuelta; (*fold*) doblar; (*wrap*) envolver.

lap² [lap] *v* (*drink*) chapotear; beber a lengüetadas.

lap³ [lap] *n* rodillas *f pl*.

lapel [ləˈpel] *n* solapa *f*.

lapse [laps] *n* (*time*) lapso *m*; (*failure*) fallo *m*; (*moral error*) desliz *m*; (*fall*) caída *f*. *v* (*time*) transcurrir; cometer un desliz; caer.

larceny [ˈlaːsəni] *n* ratería *f*.

larch [laːtʃ] *n* alerce *m*.

lard [laːd] *n* manteca de cerdo *f*.

larder [ˈlaːdə] *n* despensa *f*.

large [laːdʒ] *adj* grande, amplio. **at large** libre. **large-scale** *adj* en escala grande. **largely** *adv* en gran parte.

lark¹ [laːk] *n* (*zool*) alondra *f*.

lark² [laːk] *n* (*coll*) *n* juerga *f*; (*joke*) broma *f*. **lark about** hacer el tonto.

larva [ˈlaːvə] *n*, *pl* **larvae** larva *f*.

larynx [ˈlariŋks] *n* laringe *f*. **laryngitis** *n* laringitis *f*.

laser [ˈleizə] *n* laser *m*.

lash [laʃ] *n* (*whip*) azote *m*; (*tail*) coletazo *m*; (*waves*) embate *m*; (*eyelash*) pestaña *f*. *v* azotar; (*wind*) sacudir; (*bind*) atar. **lash out** repartir golpes a diestro y siniestro; (*coll: money*) gastar. **lashing** *n* flagelación *f*; **lashings** *pl n* (*coll*) montones *m pl*.

lass [las] *n* chica *f*, muchacha *f*.

lassitude [ˈlasitjuːd] *n* lasitud *f*.

lasso [laˈsuː] *n* lazo *m*. *v* coger con el lazo.

last [laist] *adj* último. **last-minute** *adj* de última hora. **last night** anoche. *adv* el último, la última, lo último; por última vez; finalmente. *n* último, -a *m*, *f*; final *m*. **at least** por fin. **lastly** *adv* por último. *v* durar; permanecer; aguantar. **last out** resistir. **lasting** *adj* duradero.

latch [latʃ] *n* picaporte *m*. *v* cerrar.

late [leit] *adj* tardío; (*recent*) reciente; (*last*) último; (*delayed*) retrasado; (*former*) antiguo; (*dead*) fallecid. *adv* (*not on time*) tarde; (*after the appointed time*) con retraso; recientemente; anteriormente. **lately** *adv* hace poco. **lateness** *n* retraso *m*. **later** *adj* más tarde. **see you**

later! ¡hasta luego! **latest** adj (most recent) último. **at the latest** a más tardar.

latent ['leitənt] adj latente.

lateral ['latərəl] adj lateral.

lathe [leið] n torno m.

lather ['laːðə] n (soap) espuma f; (horse) sudor m. v enjabonar.

Latin ['latin] n, adj latino, -a. n (language) latín m.

Latin America n América Latina f. **Latin American** n, adj latinoamericano, -a m, f.

latitude ['latitjuːd] n latitud f.

latrine [lə'triːn] n letrina f; retrete m.

latter ['latə] adj último. **the latter** éste, ésta.

lattice ['latis] n celosía f; enrejado m.

laugh [laːf] v reír, reírse. **laugh at** reírse de. n risa f. **laughable** adj ridículo. **it's no laughing matter** no es cosa de risa. **laughing-stock** n hazmerreir m invar. **laughter** n risa f. risas f pl.

launch¹ [loːntʃ] v (ship) botar; (lifeboat) echar al mar; (missile) lanzar; (issue) emitir; (an attack) emprender; (a company) fundar; (film, play) estrenar. **launching** n botadura f; lanzamiento m; fundación f; iniciación f.

launch² [loːntʃ] n lancha f. **motor launch** lancha motora f.

launder ['loːndə] v lavar. **launderette** n lavandería automática f. **laundry** n (place) lavandería f.

laurel ['lorəl] n laurel m.

lava ['laːvə] n lava f.

lavatory ['lavətəri] n retrete m; servicios m pl.

lavender ['lavində] n espliego m.

lavish ['laviʃ] adj pródigo; generoso; abundante; lujoso. v prodigar.

law [loː] n ley f; (profession) derecho m. leyes f pl. **law-abiding** adj respetuoso de las leyes. **lawsuit** n proceso m. **lawful** adj legal; lícito. **lawyer** n jurista m. f; abogado m.

lawn [loːn] n césped m. **lawn-mower** n cortacéspedes m invar.

lax [laks] adj flojo; elástico; negligente. **laxity** n laxitud f; elasticidad f; negligencia f; flojedad f.

laxative ['laksətiv] nm, adj laxante.

*lay¹ [lei] v (place) poner; (table) cubrir. **layabout** n holgazán, -ana m, f. **lay-by** n área de aparcamiento f. **lay off** (workers) despedir. **lay on** (provide) proveer de. **layout** n (arrangement) disposición f; (printing) composición f; (money) gasto m.

lay² [lei] adj laico. **layman** n seglar m.

lay³ [lei] V **lie**.

layer ['leiə] n capa f.

lazy ['leizi] adj perezoso. **laze around** holgazanear. **laziness** n pereza f.

*lead¹ [liːd] v llevar, conducir; remitir; (orchestra) dirigir; ir a la cabeza. **lead on** (encourage) animar; (seduce) seducir a. **lead up to** conducir a; preparar el terreno para. n (role) primer papel m; supremacía f; (clue) pista f; ejemplo; primer lugar; (advantage) ventaja f; (elec) cable m; (newspaper) noticia más importante f. **leader** n guía m, f; jefe m. f; caudillo m; editorial m. **leadership** n dirección f; mando m; jefatura f. **leading** adj primero principal; que encabeza.

lead² [led] n plomo m; (pencil) mina f.

leaf [liːf] n hoja f; página f; (table) hoja abatible f. v **leaf through** hojear. **leaflet** n (pamphlet) folleto m.

league [liːg] n liga f; **in league with** asociado con.

leak [liːk] n gotera f; (hole) agujero m; (gas, liquid) fuga f, salida f; (information) filtración f. v gotear; (boat) hacer agua; salirse; perder; filtrarse.

*lean¹ [liːn] v inclinarse. **lean back** reclinarse. **lean on** apoyarse. **lean over backwards to** (coll) no escatinar esfuerzos para. **leaning** (liking) predilección f; (tendency) tendencia f.

lean² [liːn] adj magro, sin grasa; (person) flaco. n carne magra f. **leanness** n magrez f; flaqueza f.

*leap [liːp] v saltar; lanzarse. n salto m, brinco m. **by leaps and bounds** a pasos agigantados. **leapfrog** n pídola f. **leap year** año bisiesto m.

*learn [ləːn] v aprender. **learn of** enterarse de. **learned** adj instruido; erudito. **learner** n principiante m, f; (driver) aprendiz, -a m, f. **learning** n erudición f; saber m.

lease [liːs] n arrendamiento m. v arrendar. **leasehold** adj arrendado.

leash [liːʃ] n correa f.

least [liːst] adj menor. pron lo menos. adv menos. **at least** por lo menos.

leather ['leðə] n cuero m, piel f. **patent leather** charol m. **leathery** adj (meat) correoso; (skin) curtido.

*leave¹ [liːv] v irse, marcharse; *(abandon)* dejar; *(go out of)* salir de. **be left** quedar. **leave off** dejar de. **leave out** omitir. **left-luggage office** consigna *f.* **left-overs** *pl n* sobras *f pl.*

leave² [liːv] *n* permiso *m.* **be on leave** estar de permiso. **take leave of** despedirse de.

lecherous ['letʃərəs] *adj* lascivo. **lecher** *n* lascivo, -a *m, f.* **lechery** *n* lascivia *f.*

lectern ['lektən] *n* atril *m.*

lecture ['lektʃə] *n* conferencia *f.* **lecture hall** sala de conferencias *f.* *v* dar una conferencia; dar clase. **lecturer** *n* conferenciante *m, f;* *(university)* profesor, -a *m, f.*

led [led] *V* **lead¹.**

ledge [ledʒ] *n* saliente *m;* *(window)* antepecho *m;* *(shelf)* repisa *f.*

ledger ['ledʒə] *n* libro mayor *m.*

lee [liː] *n* *(shelter)* abrigo *m;* *(naut)* sotavento *m.* **leeward** *adj, adv* a sotavento.

leech [liːtʃ] *n* sanguijuela *f;* *(person)* lapa *f.*

leek [liːk] *n* puerro *m.*

leer [liə] *v* mirar de soslayo. *n* mirada de soslayo *f.* **leering** *adj* de soslayo.

leeway ['liːwei] *n* *(naut)* deriva *f;* *(fig)* campo *m.*

left¹ [left] *V* **leave¹.**

left² [left] *adj* izquierdo. *n* izquierda *f.* *adv* a *or* hacia la izquierda. **left-handed** *adj* zurdo. **left-wing** *adj* izquierdista.

leg [leg] *n* *(person)* pierna *f;* *(animal)* pata *f;* *(furniture)* pie; *(trousers)* pernera *f;* *(cookery: lamb)* pierna *f;* *(chicken)* muslo *m;* *(pork, venison)* pernil *m;* *(sport, journey)* etapa *f.*

legacy ['legəsi] *n* legado *m,* herencia *f.*

legal ['liːgəl] *adj* jurídico; legal; legítimo; lícito. **legality** *n* legalidad *f.* **legalize** *v* legalizar.

legend ['ledʒənd] *n* leyenda *f.* **legendary** *adj* legendario.

legible ['ledʒəbl] *adj* legible. **legibility** *n* legibilidad *f.*

legion ['liːdʒən] *n* legión *f.*

legislate ['ledʒisleit] *v* legislar; establecer por ley. **legislation** *n* legislación *f.* **legislature** *n* legislatura *f.*

legitimate [lə'dʒitimət] *adj* legítimo; válido; auténtico. **legitimacy** *n* legitimidad *f.*

leisure ['leʒə] *n* ocio *n;* tiempo libre *m.*

lemon ['lemən] *n* *(fruit)* limón *m;* *(tree)* limonero *m;* *(colour)* amarillo limón *m.* **lemonade** *n* limonada *f.* **lemon squeezer** exprimelimones *m invar.*

*lend [lend] *v* prestar. **lending library** biblioteca de préstamo *f.*

length [leŋθ] *n* longitud *f,* largo *m;* *(distance)* distancia *f;* *(space)* espacio *m;* *(piece)* pedazo *m;* **lengthen** *v* alargar; prolongar. **lengthy** *adj* largo; prolongado.

lenient ['liːniənt] *adj* indulgente, clemente. **leniency** *n* indulgencia *f,* clemencia *f.*

lens [lenz] *n* lente *f;* *(magnifying glass)* lupa *f;* *(photo)* objetivo *m;* *(eye)* cristalino *m.* **contact-lens** lente de contacto *f.*

lent [lent] *V* **lend.**

Lent [lent] *n* Cuaresma *f.*

lentil ['lentil] *n* lenteja *f.*

Leo ['liːou] *n* *(astrol)* León *m.*

leopard ['lepəd] *n* leopardo *m.*

leotard ['liːətaɪd] *n* leotardo *m.*

leper ['lepə] *n* leproso, -a *m, f.* **leprosy** *n* lepra *f.* **leprous** *adj* leproso.

lesbian ['lezbiən] *nf, adj* lesbiana. **lesbianism** *n* lesbianismo *m.*

less [les] *adj* menos; menor; inferior. *adv,* *prep* menos. *n* menor *m, f.* **less and less** cada vez menos. **lessen** *v* disminuir, reducir. **lesser** *adj* menor.

lesson ['lesn] *n* lección *f;* clase *f.*

lest [lest] *conj* de miedo que; para no.

*let [let] *v* permitir, dejar; *(rent)* alquilar. **let down** *(lower)* bajar, descender; *(disappoint)* fallar. **let-down** *n* decepción *f.* **let in** dejar entrar; hacer entrar. **let out** dejar salir; *(clothes)* ensanchar;

lethal ['liːθəl] *adj* mortífero.

lethargy ['leθədʒi] *n* letargo *m.* **lethargic** *adj* letárgico.

letter ['letə] *n* *(character)* letra *f;* *(message)* carta *f.* **letter-box** *n* buzón *m.*

lettuce ['letis] *n* lechuga *f.*

leukaemia [luːˈkiːmiə] *n* leucemia *f.*

level ['levl] *adj* horizontal; *(flat)* llano; *(even)* a nivel; *(equal)* igual; *(spoonful)* raso; uniforme. **be level with** al nivel de. **level crossing** paso a nivel *m.* **level-headed** *adj* juicioso. *n* nivel *m.* **on the level** *(coll)* honrado. *v* nivelar, allanar.

lever ['liːvə] *n* palanca *f.* **leverage** *n* apalancamiento *m.*

levy ['levi] *n* exacción *f;* impuesto *m.* *v* exigir; imponer.

lewd [luːd] *adj* lascivo.
liable ['laiəbl] *adj* sujeto; (*law*) responsable. **liable to** capaz de. **liability** *n* responsabilidad *f*; inconveniente *m*; (*nuisance*) estorbo *m*.
liaison [liˈeizon] *n* enlace *m*.
liar ['laiə] *n* mentiroso, -a *m, f*.
libel ['laibəl] *n* (*act*) difamación *f*; (*writing*) escrito difanatorio *m*. *v* difamar. **libellous** *adj* difamatorio.
liberal ['libərəl] *adj* liberal; libre; generoso.
liberate ['libəreit] *v* liberar. **liberation** *n* liberación *f*.
liberty ['libəti] *n* libertad *f*. **at liberty** libre.
Libra ['liːbrə] *n* Libra *f*.
library ['laibrəri] *n* biblioteca *f*. **librarian** *n* bibliotecario, -a *m, f*.
libretto [liˈbretou] *n* libreto *m*.
lice [lais] *V* **louse.**
licence ['laisəns] *n* licencia *f*, permiso *m*, autorización *f*; (*driving*) carnet de conducir *m*. **licence number** matrícula *f*. *v* conceder una licencia; autorizar. **licensed** *adj* autorizado. **licensee** *n* concesionario *m*.
lichen ['laikən] *n* liquen *m*.
lick [lik] *v* lamer. *n* lamedura *f*, lamido *m*.
lid [lid] *n* tapa *f*, tapadera *f*.
***lie*[1]** [lai] *v* acostarse; echarse. **lie around** estar tirado. **lie down** acostarse. **lie in** quedarse en la cama.
lie[2] [lai] *n* mentira *f*. *v* mentir.
lieutenant [ləfˈtenənt] *n* (*mil*) teniente *m*; (*deputy*) lugarteniente *m*.
life [laif] *n* vida *f*. **lifeless** *adj* sin vida, muerto.
lifebelt ['laifbelt] *n* cinturón salvavidas *m*.
lifeboat ['laifbout] *n* bote salvavidas *m*.
lifebuoy ['laifboi] *n* boya salvavidas *f*.
lifeguard ['laifgaːd] *n* vigilante *m*.
life insurance *n* seguro de vida *m*.
life-jacket *n* chaleco salvavidas *m*.
lifelike ['laiflaik] *adj* natural; parecido.
lifeline ['laiflain] *n* (*diver's*) cordel de señales *m*; (*fig*) cordón umbilical *m*.
lifelong ['laifloŋ] *adj* de toda la vida.
life-size *adj* de tamaño natural.
lifetime ['laiftaim] *n* vida *f*.
lift [lift] *n* ascensor *m*; (*act of lifting*) levantamiento *m*; (*upward support*) empuje *m*. **give someone a lift** llevar en coche. *v* levantar; alzar; coger; elevar.
ligament ['ligəmənt] *n* ligamento *m*.

***light*[1]** [lait] *v* (*set fire to*) encender; (*room, etc.*) iluminar. *n* luz *f*; lámpara *f*; (*mot*) faro *m*. *adj* claro; luminoso. **light bulb** bombilla *f*. **lighthouse** *n* faro *m*. **light meter** fotómetro *m*. **light-year** *n* año luz *m*. **lighten** *v* aclarar. **lighter** (*cigarette*) *n* mechero *m*. **lighting** *n* alumbrado *m*; iluminación *f*.
light[2] [lait] *adj* liviano; ligero. **light-headed** *adj* mareado; delirante. **light-hearted** *adj* alegre. **lightweight** *adj* ligero, de poco peso. **lighten** *v* alijerar; aliviar. **lightness** *n* ligereza *f*.
***light*[3]** [lait] *v* **light upon** posarse.
lightning ['laitniŋ] *n* relámpago *m*. **lightning conductor** pararrayos *m invar*.
like[1] [laik] *adj* parecido; semejante; igual; mismo. *prep* como, igual que. **be** or **look like** parecerse a. **liken** *v* comparar. **likeness** *n* semejanza *f*; forma *f*; retrato *m*. **likewise** *adv* del mismo modo.
like[2] [laik] *v* gustarle (a uno); querer a; (*want*) querer. **likeable** *adj* amable, simpático. **liking** *n* cariño *m*; simpatía *f*; gusto *m*.
likely ['laikli] *adj* probable; posible; plausible. **be likely to** ser probable que. *adv* probablemente. **likelihood** *n* probabilidad *f*.
lilac ['lailək] *n* lila *f*; (*colour*) lila *m*. *adj* de color lila.
lily ['lili] *n* azucena *f*. **lily-of-the-valley** *n* lirio de los valles *m*.
limb [lim] *n* miembro *m*.
limbo ['limbou] *n* (*rel*) limbo *m*; (*fig*) olvido *m*.
lime[1] [laim] *n* cal *f*. **limestone** *n* piedra caliza *f*.
lime[2] [laim] *n* (*fruit*) lima *f*; (*tree*) limero *m*. **lime juice** jugo de lima *m*.
limelight ['laim,lait] *n* **in the limelight** en el candelero.
limerick ['limərik] *n* quintilla humorística *f*.
limit ['limit] *n* límite *m*. *v* limitar. **limitation** *n* limitación *f*. **limitless** *adj* ilimitado.
limousine ['liməˌziːn] *n* limusina *f*.
limp[1] [limp] *v* cojear.
limp[2] [limp] *adj* flácido. **limpness** *n* flojedad *f*.
limpet ['limpit] *n* lapa *f*.
line [lain] *n* línea *f*, rayo *m*, trazo *m*; (*wrinkle*) arruga *f*; (*row*) fila *f*; (*wire*) cable *m*; (*people*) cola *f*; (*of poem*) verso

m; (*rope*) cuerda *f*; (*flex*) cordón *m*; (*of communication*) vía *f*; (*shipping*) compañía *f*. *v* rayar; arrugar; alinearse por; bordear; (*provide an inner layer*) forrar; (*brakes*) guarnecer. **line up** poner en fila.
linear *adj* lineal.
linen ['linin] *n* hilo *m*, lino *m*; (*sheets, etc.*) ropa blanca *f*. **linen basket** canasta de la ropa *f*.
liner ['lainə] *n* transatlántico *m*.
linger ['liŋgə] *v* (*person*) quedarse; (*memory, etc.*) persistir; (*dawdle*) rezagarse; (*loiter*) callejear.
lingerie ['lãʒəriː] *n* ropa interior *f*.
linguist ['liŋgwist] *n* lingüista *m*, *f*. **linguistic** *adj* lingüístico. **linguistics** *n* lingüística *f*.
lining ['lainiŋ] *n* (*clothes*) forro *m*; (*brakes*) guarnición *f*.
link [liŋk] *n* (*chain*) eslabón *m*; (*cuff*) gemelos *m pl*; (*fig*) vínculo *m*. *v* unir; acoplar; conectar.
linoleum [li'nouliəm] *n* *also* **lino** linóleo *m*.
linseed ['lin,siːd] *n* linaza *f*. **linseed oil** aceite de linaza *m*.
lint [lint] *n* hilas *f pl*.
lion ['laiən] *n* león *m*. **lioness** *n* leona *f*.
lip [lip] *n* labio *m*; (*jug*) pico *m*; (*cup*) borde *m*. **lip-read** *v* leer en los labios.
lipstick *n* barra de labios *f*.
liqueur [li'kjuə] *n* licor *m*.
liquid ['likwid] *nm, adj* líquido. **liquidate** *v* liquidar. **liquidation** *n* liquidación *f*.
liquor ['likə] *n* bebida alcohólica *f*.
liquorice ['likəris] *n* regaliz *m*.
Lisbon ['lizbən] *n* Lisboa. *f*.
lisp [lisp] *n* ceceo *m*. *v* decir ceceando.
list[1] [list] *v* hacer una lista de; enumerar. *n* lista *f*; catálogo *m*.
list[2] [list] *v* (*naut*) escorar. *n* escora *f*.
listen ['lisn] *v* escuchar, oír. **listener** *n* oyente *m*, *f*.
listless ['listlis] *adj* decaído, apático.
lit [lit] *V* **light**.
litany ['litəni] *n* letanía *f*.
literacy ['litərəsi] *n* capacidad de leer y escribir *f*. **be literate** saber leer y escribir.
literal ['litərəl] *adj* literal.
literary ['litərəri] *adj* literario.
literature ['litrətʃə] *n* literatura *f*; (*advertising matter*) folletos publicitarios *m pl*.
litigation [liti'geiʃən] *n* litigio *m*.
litre ['liːtə] *n* litro *m*.
litter ['litə] *n* basura *f*; desorden *m*; (*zool*)

camada *f*; (*bedding for animals*) pajaza *f*; (*stretcher*) camilla *f*. **litter-bin** *n* papelera *f*. *v* ensuciar; cubrir; desordenar.
little ['litl] *adj* (*small*) pequeño; (*quantity*) poco. *nm, adv* poco. **little by little** poco a poco.
liturgy ['litədʒi] *n* liturgia *f*. **liturgical** *adj* litúrgico.
live[1] [liv] *v* vivir. **live down** conseguir que se olvide. **live up to** cumplir con.
live[2] [laiv] *adj* vivo; (*broadcast*) en directo; (*coal*) en ascuas; (*elec*) cargado. *adv* en directo.
livelihood ['laivlihud] *n* sustento *m*.
lively ['laivli] *adj* vivo; enérgico; activo. **liveliness** *n* viveza *f*; animación *f*.
liven ['laivn] *v* **liven up** animar.
liver ['livə] *n* hígado *m*.
livestock ['laivstok] *n* ganado *m*.
livid ['livid] *adj* lívido; (*coll*) furioso.
living ['liviŋ] *adj* vivo, viviente. *n* vida *f*; vivos *m pl*. **living room** sala de estar *f*.
lizard ['lizəd] *n* lagarto *m*.
load [loud] *n* (*burden*) carga *f*; (*animals, vehicles*) cargamento *m*; (*fig*) peso *m*. *v* cargar. **loaded** *adj* cargado; (*coll: rich*) podrido de dinero.
loaf[1] [louf] *n* pan *m*.
loaf[2] [louf] *v* **loaf around** callejear. **loafer** *n* (*coll*) holgazán, -ana *m*, *f*.
loan [loun] *n* préstamo *m*. *v* prestar.
loathe [louð] *v* aborrecer. **loathing** *n* aborrecimiento *m*. **loathsome** *adj* asqueroso.
lob [lob] *v* volear. *n* volea alta *f*, lob *m*.
lobby ['lobi] *n* pasillo *m*; vestíbulo *m*; grupo de presión *m*. *v* ejercer presiones sobre.
lobe [loub] *n* lóbulo *m*.
lobster ['lobstə] *n* langosta *f*.
local ['loukəl] *adj* local; vecinal. *n* (*coll: pub*) bar del barrio *m*. **the locals** (*coll: people*) la gente del lugar *f*. **locality** *n* (*neighbourhood*) localidad *f*; (*place*) lugar *m*. **localize** *v* localizar. **locally** *adv* localmente; en el sitio.
locate [lə'keit] *v* (*find*) encontrar; (*look for and discover*) localizar; situar. **location** *n* localización *f*; colocación *f*; situación *f*; (*cinema*) exteriores *m pl*. **film on location** *v* rodar.
lock[1] [lok] *n* (*on door, box, etc.*) cerradura *f*; (*canal*) esclusa *f*. *v* cerrarse con llave; (*mech*) bloquearse. **lock away** guardar bajo llave. **lock in** encerrar. **lock out** cerrar la puerta. **lock up** (*house*) cerrar;

(*money*) dejar bajo llave; (*imprison*) encarcelar.

lock² [lok] *n* (*of hair*) mecha *f*, mechón *m*.

locker ['lokə] *n* (*shelf*) casillero *m*, (*cupboard*) armario *m*.

locket ['lokit] *n* relicario *m*.

locomotive [ˌloukə'moutiv] *n* locomotiva *f*. *adj* locomotor. **locomotion** *n* locomoción *f*.

locust ['loukəst] *n* langosta *f*.

lodge [lodʒ] *n* (*porter's*) portería *f*; (*caretaker's*) casa del guarda *f*; (*hunting*) pabellón *m*. *v* alojar; (*place*) colocar; presentar; (*appeal*) interponer. **lodger** *n* huésped, -a *m, f*. **lodgings** *pl n* habitación *f*. **board and lodging** pensión completa *f*.

loft [loft] *n* (*for hay*) pajar *m*; (*attic*) desván. **lofty** *adj* (*high*) alto; (*principles*) elevado; (*haughty*) arrogante.

log [log] *n* tronco *m*. **logbook** *n* (*naut*) cuaderno de bitácora *m*; (*aero*) diario de vuelo *m*. *v* anotar, apuntar.

logarithm ['logəriðəm] *n* logaritmo *m*.

loggerheads ['logəhedz] *pl n* **be at loggerheads** estar a mal.

logic ['lodʒik] *n* lógica *f*. **logical** *adj* lógico.

loins [loins] *pl n* lomos *m pl*.

loiter ['loitə] *v* callejear.

lollipop ['loliˌpop] *n* chupón *m*.

London ['lʌndən] *n* Londres.

lonely ['lounli] *adj* solo; aislado; solitario. **loneliness** *n* soledad *f*.

long¹ [loŋ] *adj* (*length*) largo; (*memory*) bueno; (*time*) mucho; (*long-lasting*) viejo. **as long as** mientras. **long-range** *adj* de larga distancia. **long-sighted** *adj* hipermétrope; (*having foresight*) previsor. **long-sleeved** *adj* de mangas largas. **long-standing** *adj* de muchos años. **long-term** *adj* a largo plazo. **long-winded** *adj* (*person*) prolijo; (*speech*) interminable.

long² [loŋ] *v* **long for** desear con ansia. **long to** tener muchas ganas de. **longing** *n* anhelo *m*.

longevity [lon'dʒevəti] *n* longevidad *f*.

longitude ['londʒitjuːd] *n* longitud *f*. **longitudinal** *adj* longitudinal.

loo [luː] *n* (*coll*) retrete *m*.

look [luk] *n* (*glance*) mirada *f*; (*inspection*) ojeada *f*; aspecto *m*. *v* mirar; parecer; representar. **look after** cuidar a, cuidar de; (*watch over*) vigilar. **look at** mirar. **look down on** mirar despectivamente.

look for buscar. **look forward to** esperar. **look out** tener cuidado. **look up** levantar los ojos; (*improve*) ponerse mejor; (*research*) consultar, buscar. **look up to** apreciar.

loom¹ [luːm] *v* perfilarse; surgir.

loom² [luːm] *n* telar *m*.

loop [luːp] *n* lazo *m*; (*belt*) presilla *f*. *v* hacer un lazo en.

loophole ['luːphoul] *v* (*fig*) escapatoria *f*.

loose [luːs] *adj* suelto; (*fitting*) holgado; (*knot*) flojo; (*translation*) libre; (*tooth*) que se mueve; **get loose** escaparse. **let loose** soltar. **loose change** dinero suelto *m*. **loose-leaf** *adj* de hojas sueltas. *v* (*free*) soltar; (*untie*) desatar. **loosely** *adv* sin apretar; aproximadamente; vagamente. **loosen** *v* aflojar, soltar.

loot [luːt] *n* botín *m*. **looter** *n* saqueador, -a *m, f*. **looting** saqueo *m*.

lop [lop] *v* cortar.

lopsided [ˌlop'saidid] *adj* ladeado; desequilibrado.

lord [loːd] *n* señor *m*.

lorry ['lori] *n* camión *m*. **lorry-driver** *n* camionero *m*.

*lose [luːz] *v* perder; (*watch, clock*) atrasar. **loser** *n* perdedor, -a *m, f*. **lost property** objetos perdidos *m pl*.

loss [los] *n* pérdida *f*; (*damage*) daño *m*. (*defeat*) derrota *f*. **be at a loss** estar perdido. **sell at a loss** vender con pérdida.

lost [lost] *V* **lose**.

lot [lot] *n* destino *m*; porción *f*; (*auction*) lote *m*; (*ground*) parcela *f*. **a lot** mucho. **lots of** cantidades de. **quite a lot of** bastante.

lotion ['loufən] *n* loción *f*.

lottery ['lotəri] *n* lotería *f*.

lotus ['loutəs] *n* loto *m*.

loud [laud] *adj* fuerte; alto; ruidoso; sonoro; (*colours*) chillón; vulgar. *adv* (*laugh*) estrepitosamente. **loud-hailer** *n* megáfono *m*. **loud-mouthed** *adj* fanfarrón, -ona *m, f*. **loudspeaker** *n* altavoz *m*. **loudly** *adv* en voz alta. **loudness** *n* fuerza *f*.

lounge [laundʒ] *n* salón *m*. **lounge suit** traje de calle *m*. *v* (*lazy posture*) repantigarse; (*idle*) gandulear. **lounger** *n* tumbona *f*.

louse [laus] *n*, *pl* **lice** piojo *m*. **lousy** *adj* piojoso; (*slang*) malísimo.

lout [laut] *n* bruto *m*. **loutish** *adj* bruto.
love [lʌv] *n* amor *m*; cariño *m*; pasión *f*; (*tennis*) cero *m*. **fall in love with** enamorarse de. **love affair** amorío *m*. **make love** hacer el amor con. **with love from** (*in letter*) abrazos *m pl*. *v* amar, querer. **lovable** *adj* adorable. **lover** *n* amante *m*, *f*; (*enthusiast*) aficionado, -a *m*, *f*. **loving** *adj* cariñoso; amoroso.
lovely ['lʌvli] *adj* encantador; delicioso; precioso.
low [lou] *adj* bajo; pequeño; (*scarce*) escaso; (*weak*) débil; (*downhearted*) desanimado. **lowland** *n* tierra baja *f*. **low-lying** *adj* bajo. **low-paid** *adj* mal pagado. **low-priced** *adj* barato. **lowly** *adj* humilde.
lower ['louə] *adj* inferior; más bajo. *v* bajar. **lower oneself** rebajarse.
loyal ['lɔiəl] *adj* leal; fiel. **loyalty** *n* lealtad *f*; fidelidad *f*.
lozenge ['lozindʒ] *n* pastilla *f*.
lubricate ['luːbrikeit] *v* lubrificar, lubricar. **lubricant** *n* lubrificante *m*, lubricante *m*. **lubrication** *n* lubrificación *f*, lubricación *f*, engrase *m*.
lucid ['luːsid] *adj* lúcido; claro. **lucidity** *n* lucidez *f*; claridad *f*.
luck [lʌk] *n* suerte *f*; destino *m*. **bad luck** mala suerte *f*. **good luck** buena suerte *f*. **lucky** *adj* afortunado; oportuno. **be lucky** tener mucha suerte.
lucrative ['luːkrətiv] *adj* lucrativo.
ludicrous ['luːdikrəs] *adj* ridículo, absurdo.
lug [lʌg] *v* arrastrar.
luggage ['lʌgidʒ] *n* equipaje *m*; maletas *f pl*. **luggage label** etiqueta *f*. **luggage rack** portaequipajes *m invar*. **luggage van** furgón de equipajes *m*.
lukewarm ['luːkwɔːm] *adj* tibio.
lull [lʌl] *n* (*in storm*) calma *f*; (*fig*) tregua *f*. *v* sosegar.
lullaby ['lʌlə,bai] *n* canción de cuna *f*.
lumbago [lʌm'beigou] *n* lumbago *m*.
lumber¹ ['lʌmbə] *n* (*wood*) maderos *m pl*; (*junk*) trastos viejos *m pl*. **lumberjack** *n* leñador *m*. **lumber yard** depósito de madera *m*. *v*. **lumber with** (*coll*) hacer que cargue con.
lumber² ['lʌmbə] *v* moverse pesadamente.
luminous ['luːminəs] *adj* luminoso.
lump [lʌmp] *n* pedazo *m*, trozo *m*; (*mass*) masa *f*; (*clay*) pella *f*; (*stone*) bloque *m*; (*earth, sugar*) terrón *m*; (*med*) chichón.

lump sum cantidad total *f*. **lumpy** *adj* lleno de bultos.
lunar ['luːnə] *adj* lunar.
lunatic ['luːnətik] *n*, *adj* loco, -a *m*, *f*. **lunacy** *n* locura *f*.
lunch [lʌntʃ] *n* almuerzo *m*. *v* almorzar. **lunchtime** *n* hora de comer *f*.
lung [lʌŋ] *n* pulmón *m*.
lunge [lʌndʒ] *v* embestir, lanzarse. *n* embestida *f*.
lurch¹ [ləːtʃ] *v* dar bandazos. **lurch along** ir dando bandazos. *n* bandazo *m*.
lurch² [ləːtʃ] *n* **leave in the lurch** dejar en la estacada.
lure [luə] *v* atraer. *n* aliciente *m*; encanto *m*; (*decoy*) cebo *m*.
lurid ['luərid] *adj* espeluznante; sensacional.
lurk [ləːk] *v* (*lie in wait*) estar al acecho; (*be hidden*) esconderse; (*fig: be always around*) rondar. **lurking** *adj* vago; oculto.
luscious ['lʌʃəs] *adj* exquisito; apetitoso; voluptuoso.
lush [lʌʃ] *adj* lozano, exuberante.
lust [lʌst] *n* (*sexual*) lascivia *f*; (*for power, etc.*) anhelo *m*. *v* **lust after** (*object*) codiciar; (*person*) desear. **lusty** *adj* robusto, fuerte.
lustre ['lʌstə] *n* lustre *m*.
lute [luːt] *n* laúd *m*.
Luxembourg ['lʌksəm,bəːg] *n* Luxemburgo *m*.
luxury ['lʌkʃəri] *n* lujo *m*. **luxuriant** *adj* exuberante. **luxurious** *adj* lujoso.
lynch [lintʃ] *v* linchar.
lynx [links] *n* lince *m*.
lyre [laiə] *n* lira *f*.
lyrical ['lirikəl] *adj* lírico.
lyrics ['liriks] *pl n* letra *f sing*. **lyricist** *n* autor de la letra de una canción *m*.

M

mac [mak] *n* (*coll*) impermeable *m*.
macabre [mə'kaːbr] *adj* macabro.
macaroni [makə'rouni] *n* macarrones *m pl*.
mace¹ [meis] *n* (*staff*) maza *f*.
mace² [meis] *n* (*spice*) macis *f*.
machine [mə'ʃiːn] *n* máquina *f*. **machine-**

gun *n* ametralladora *f*. **machinery** *n* maquinaria *f*; mecanismo *m*.

mackerel ['makrəl] *n* caballa *f*.

mackintosh ['makin,toʃ] *n* impermeable *m*.

mad [mad] *adj* loco, demente; rabioso; (*angry*) furioso. **madden** *v* enloquecer; enfurecer. **maddening** *adj* desesperante. **madly** *adv* locamente; furiosamente. **madness** *n* locura *f*; rabia *f*; furia *f*. **madam** ['madəm] *n* señora *f*.

made [meid] *V* **make**.

Madeira [mə'diərə] *n* (*island*) Madera *f*; (*wine*) madera *m*.

magazine [,magə'ziːn] *n* (*publication*) revista *f*; (*warehouse*) almacén *m*; (*explosives store*) polvorín *m*; (*rifle*) recámara *f*.

maggot ['magət] *n* gusano *m*, cresa *f*. **maggoty** *adj* gusanoso.

magic ['madʒik] *n* magia *f*. *adj also* **magical** mágico. **magician** *n* ilusionista *m*, *f*.

magistrate ['madʒistreit] *n* magistrado *m*; juez municipal *m*.

magnanimous [mag'nanimas] *adj* magnánimo. **magnanimity** *n* magnanimidad *f*.

magnate ['magneit] *n* magnate *m*.

magnet ['magnət] *n* imán *m*. **magnetic** magnético; atractivo. **magnetism** *n* magnetismo *m*. **magnetize** *v* magnetizar; atraer.

magnificent [mag'nifisnt] *adj* magnífico. **magnificence** *n* magnificencia *f*.

magnify ['magnifai] *v* magnificar; aumentar; exagerar. **magnifying glass** lupa *f*. **magnification** *n* aumento *m*; exageración *f*.

magnitude ['magnitjuːd] *n* magnitud *f*.

magnolia [mag'noulia] *n* magnolia *f*.

magpie ['magpai] *n* urraca *f*.

mahogany [mə'hogəni] *n* caoba *f*.

maid [meid] *n* (*servant*) criada *f*; muchacha *f*. **old maid** solterona *f*.

maiden ['meidən] *n* doncella *f*. *adj* virgen; soltera; inaugural. **maiden name** apellido de soltera *m*.

mail [meil] *n* (*letters*) correspondencia *f*; (*service*) correo *m*. **mailbag** *n* saca de correspondencia *f*. **mail order** pedido hecho por correo *m*.

maim [meim] *v* mutilar.

main [mein] *adj* principal. **main course** plato principal *m*. **mainland** *n* continente *m*. **main line** línea principal *f*. **main road** carretera general *f*. **mainstay** *n* estay

mayor *m*. *n* (*gas, water*) cañería principal *f*. **in the main** por lo general. **mains** *n* (*elec*) la red eléctrica *f*.

maintain [mein'tein] *v* mantener; conservar. **maintenance** *n* mantenimiento *m*; conservación *f*. **maintenance allowance** pensión alimenticia *f*.

maisonette [meizə'net] *n* casita *f*.

maize [meiz] *n* maíz *m*.

majesty ['madʒəsti] *n* majestad *f*. **majestic** *adj* majestuoso.

major ['meidʒə] *adj* mayor; principal. *n* (*mil*) comandante *m*.

majority [mə'dʒoriti] *n* mayoría *f*. **overwhelming majority** mayoría abrumadora *f*.

*make [meik] *v* hacer, efectuar; servir de; llegar a. *n* marca *f*; hechura *f*. **make-believe** *n* simulación *f*. **make out** (*draw up*) hacer; (*cheque*) extender. **make do with** arreglárselas con. **makeshift** *adj* improvisado. **make up** inventar; completar; recuperar; (*face*) maquillarse. **make-up** *n* maquillaje *m*; carácter *m*. **make up for** compensar. **maker** *n* fabricante *m*. **making** *n* fabricación *f*.

maladjusted [malə'dʒʌstid] *adj* inadaptado. **maladjustment** *n* inadaptación *f*.

malaria [mə'leəriə] *n* malaria *f*, paludismo *m*.

male [meil] *nm*, *adj* macho.

malevolent [mə'levələnt] *adj* malévolo. **malevolence** *n* malevolencia *f*.

malfunction [mal'fʌŋkʃən] *n* funcionamiento defectuoso *m*. *v* funcionar defectuosamente.

malice ['malis] *n* malicia *f*. **malicious** *adj* malicioso.

malignant [mə'lignənt] *adj* malvado; malo; (*med*) maligno. **malignancy** *n* maldad *f*; malignidad *f*.

malinger [mə'liŋgə] *v* fingirse enfermo.

mallet ['malit] *n* mazo *m*.

malnutrition [malnju'triʃən] *n* desnutrición *f*.

malt [moilt] *n* malta *f*.

Malta ['moiltə] *n* Malta. **Maltese** *n*, *adj* maltés, -esa.

maltreat [mal'triːt] *v* maltratar. **maltreatment** *n* maltrato *m*.

mammal ['maməl] *n* mamífero *m*.

mammoth ['maməθ] *n* mamut *m*. *adj* gigantesco.

man [man] *n, pl* **men** hombre *m*. *v* armar; ocupar. **manhood** *n* virilidad *f*. **manly** *adj* masculino.

manage ['manidʒ] *v* (*business, affairs, etc.*) dirigir; (*instrument*) manejar; (*property*) administrar. **manage to** conseguir, arreglárselas. **manageable** *adj* manejable; (*undertaking*) factible; (*animal, person*) dócil. **management** *n* gestión *f*, administración *f*, dirección *f*; (*board of directors*) junta directiva *f*. **manager** *n* gerente *m*, director *m*. **managerial** *adj* directorial. **managing director** director gerente *m*.

mandarin ['mandərin] *n* mandarín *m*. *adj* mandarino. **mandarin orange** mandarina *f*; (*tree*) mandarino *m*.

mandate ['mandeit] *n* mandato *m*. **mandatory** *adj* obligatorio.

mandolin ['mandəlin] *n* mandolina *f*.

mane [mein] *n* crin *f*, crines *f pl*.

mange [meindʒ] *n* sarna *f*. **mangy** *adj* sarnoso; (*coll*) asqueroso.

manger ['meindʒə] *n* pesebre *m*.

mangle¹ ['maŋgl] *n* (*wringer*) escurridor *m*. *v* pasar por el escurridor.

mangle² ['maŋgl] *v* despedazar; (*fig*) deformar.

mango ['maŋgou] *n* mango *m*.

manhandle [man'handl] *v* (*person*) maltratar; (*goods*) manipular.

manhole ['manhoul] *n* registro *m*.

mania ['meiniə] *n* mania *f*. **maniac** *n* maníaco, -a *m, f*; (*fig*) fanático, -a *m, f*.

manicure ['manikjuə] *n* manicura *f*. *v* hacer la manicura a. **manicurist** *n* manicuro, -a *m, f*.

manifest ['manifest] *adj* manifiesto, evidente. *v* mostrar, manifestarse. **manifestation** *n* manifestación *f*.

manifesto [mani'festou] *n* manifiesto *m*.

manifold ['manifould] *adj* múltiple; diverso. *n* **exhaust manifold** (*mot*) colector de escape *m*.

manipulate [mə'nipjuleit] *v* manipular. **manipulation** *n* manipulación *f*.

mankind [man'kaind] *n* raza humana *f*, humanidad *f*.

man-made [man'meid] *adj* sintético, artificial.

manner ['manə] *n* manera *f*, modo *m*; clase *f*; aire *m*. **manners** *pl n* modales *m pl*.

mannerism ['manə,rizəm] *n* amaneramiento *m*.

manoeuvre [mə'nuɪvə] *n* maniobra *f*. *v* maniobrar.

manor ['manə] *n* señorío *m*. **manor house** casa solariega *f*.

manpower ['man,pauə] *n* mano de obra *f*.

mansion ['manʃən] *n* (*country*) gran casa de campo *f*; (*town*) palacete *m*.

manslaughter ['man,slɔɪtə] *n* homicidio sin premeditación *m*.

mantelpiece ['mantlpiɪs] *n* repisa de chimenea *f*.

mantle ['mantl] *n* (*cloak*) capa *f*; (*gaslamp*) manguito *m*.

manual ['manjuəl] *nm, adj* manual. **manually** *adv* a mano.

manufacture [manju'faktʃə] *n* (*product*) producto manufacturado; (*act*) fabricación *f*. *v* manufacturar, fabricar. **manufacturer** *n* fabricante *m*.

manure [mə'njuə] *n* estiércol *m*, abono. *v* estercolar, abonar.

manuscript ['manjuskript] *nm* manuscrito.

many ['meni] *adj* muchos, mucho, un gran número de. *pron* muchos. **as many as** hasta. **how many?** ¿cuántos? ¿cuántas? **so many** tantos, tantas. **too many** demasiado.

map [map] *n* mapa *m*; (*town*) plano *m*. *v* levantar un mapa de. **map out** proyectar.

maple ['meipl] *n* arce *m*.

mar [maɪ] *v* estropear; frustrar.

marathon ['marəθɔn] *nm, adj* maratón.

marble ['maɪbl] *n* mármol *m*; (*toy*) bola *f*. *v* jaspear.

march [maɪtʃ] *v* marchar. *n* marcha *f*.

March [maɪtʃ] *n* marzo *m*.

marchioness [,maɪʃə'nes] *n* marquesa *f*.

mare [meə] *n* yegua *f*.

margarine [,maɪdʒə'riɪn] *n* margarina *f*.

margin ['maɪdʒin] *n* borde *m*, lado *m*; orilla *f*; margen *m*. **marginal** *adj* marginal. **marginally** *adv* por muy poco.

marguerite [,maɪgə'riɪt] *n* margarita *f*.

marigold ['marigould] *n* caléndula *f*.

marijuana [mari'waɪnə] *n* marijuana *f*, marihuana *f*.

marina [mə'riɪnə] *n* puerto deportivo *m*.

marinade [,mari'neid] *n* adobo *m*. *v* adobar.

marine [mə'riɪn] *adj* marino. *n* (*mil*) soldado de infantería de marina. **merchant marine** marina mercante *f*.

marital ['maritl] *adj* marital, matrimonial.

maritime ['maritaim] *adj* marítimo.
marjoram ['maidӡərəm] *n* mejorana *f.*
mark[1] [maik] *n* marca *f.* señal *f.* mancha *f*; (*school*) nota *f*; calificación *f*; (*trace*) huella *f.* **marksman** *n* tirador *m. v* marcar, señalar; calificar. **marked** *adj* marcado; pronunciado; sensible.
mark[2] [maik] *n* (*currency*) marco *m.*
market ['maikit] *n* mercado *m*; (*demand*) salida *f.* **market day** día de mercado *m.* **market place** plaza de mercado *f.* **market research** estudio de mercados *m.* **market value** valor corriente *m. v* poner en venta, vender. **marketing** *n* comercialización.
marmalade ['maiməleid] *n* mermelada de naranja *f.*
maroon[1] [mə'ruin] *adj* castaño.
maroon[2] [mə'ruin] *v* abandonar.
marquee [mai'kii] *n* gran tienda de campaña *f.*
marquess ['maikwis] *n* marqués *m.*
marquetry ['maikətri] *n* marquetería *f.*
marriage ['maridӡ] *n* matrimonio *m*; (*wedding*) boda *f.* **marriage certificate** partida de casamiento *f.*
marrow ['marou] *n* (*bone*) médula *f.* **vegetable marrow** calabacín *m.*
marry ['mari] *v* casar; (*get married*) casarse. **married** *adj* casado. **married couple** matrimonio *m.* **married name** apellido de casada *m.*
Mars [maiz] *n* Marte *m.* **Martian** *n, adj* marciano, -a.
marsh [maiʃ] *n* pantano *m.* **marshmallow** *n* (*bot*) malvavisco *m*; (*cookery*) melcocha *f.* **marshy** *adj* pantanoso.
marshal ['maiʃəl] *n* (*mil*) mariscal *m*; (*organizer*) maestro de ceremonias *m. v* poner en orden; (*mil*) formar.
martial ['maiʃəl] *adj* marcial.
martin ['maitin] *n* avión *m.*
martyr ['maitə] *n* mártir *m, f. v* martinizar. **martyrdom** *n* martirio *m.*
marvel ['maivəl] *n* maravilla *f. v* maravillarse. **marvellous** *adj* maravilloso.
marzipan ['maizi'pan] *n* mazapán *m.*
mascara [ma'skairə] *n* rimel *m.*
mascot ['maskət] *n* mascota *f.*
masculine ['maskjulin] *adj* masculino. **masculinity** *n* masculinidad *f.*
mash [maʃ] *v* machacar. *n* (*animal feed*) afrecho remojado *m.*
mask [maisk] *n* máscara *f.* careta *f. v* enmascarar.

masochist ['masəkist] *n* masoquista *m, f.* **masochism** *n* masoquismo *m.* **masochistic** *adj* masoquista.
mason ['meisn] *n* albañil *m.* **masonry** *n* albañilería.
masquerade [maskə'reid] *n* (*pretence*) mascarada *f. v* **masquerade as** hacerse pasar por.
mass[1] [mas] *n* masa *f.* **mass media** medios informativos *m pl.* **mass meeting** mitin popular *m.* **mass-produce** *v* fabricar en serie. **mass production** fabricación en serie *f. v* agrupar.
mass[2] [mas] *n* (*rel*) misa *f.*
massacre ['masəkə] *n* matanza *f. v* matar en masa.
massage ['masaiӡ] *n* masaje *m. v* dar un masaje. **masseur, masseuse** *n* masajista *m, f.*
massive ['masiv] *adj* sólido; masivo.
mast [maist] *n* (*naut*) palo *m,* mástil *m*; (*radio, etc.*) poste *m.*
master ['maistə] *n* (*owner*) dueño *m*; (*college*) director *m*; (*secondary school*) profesor *m*; (*primary school*) maestro; (*graduate*) licenciado, -a *m, f*; (*household*) señor *m*; (*work force*) patrón *m*; (*ship*) capitán *m.* **master copy** original *m.* **master key** llave maestra *f.* **master of ceremonies** maestro de ceremonias *m.* **masterpiece** *n* obra maestra *f. v* (*passions, language*) dominar; (*an animal*) domar; (*difficulties*) vencer. **mastery** *n* dominio *m*; maestría *f.*
masturbate ['mastəbeit] *v* masturbarse. **masturbation** *n* masturbación *f.*
mat [mat] *n* (*floor*) estera *f*; (*door*) esterilla *f*; (*table*) salvamanteles *m invar*; (*doily*) tapete *m.* **matted** *adj* (*hair*) enmarañado.
match[1] [matʃ] *n* fósforo *m,* cerilla *f.* **matchbox** *n* caja de fósforos *or* cerillas *f.*
match[2] [matʃ] *n* (*sport*) partido *m*; (*equal*) igual *m*; (*pair*) pareja *f. v* igualar; (*colours*) casar; (*gloves, etc.*) parear; (*clothes, furnishings*) hacer juego con; (*fit*) encajar; corresponder. **matchless** *adj* sin igual.
mate [meit] *n* (*animals*) macho, hembra *m, f*; amigo, -a *m, f*; camarada *m, f*; (*spouse*) compañero, -a *m, f. v* acoplar; casar; (*chess*) dar jaque mate a.
material [mə'tiəriəl] *n* material *m*; (*cloth*) tela *f.* **materials** *pl n* (*building*) materiales *m pl*; (*teaching*) material *m*; artículos *m*

pl. adj material; esencial. **materialist**
n(m+f), *adj* materialista. **materialize** *v*
materializar; realizar.
maternal [mə'tɜɪnl] *adj* maternal; *(relation)* materno.
maternity [mə'tɜɪnəti] *n* maternidad *f*.
maternity hospital casa de maternidad *f*.
mathematics [maθə'matiks] *n* matemáticas *f pl*. **mathematical** *adj* matemático.
mathematician *n* matemático, -a *m*, *f*.
matinée ['matinei] *n* *(cinema)* primera
sesión *f*; *(theatre)* función de la tarde *f*.
matinée idol ídolo del público *m*.
matins ['matinz] *n* maitines *m pl*.
matriarch ['meitriaɪk] *n* mujer que manda
f. **matriarchal** *adj* matriarcal.
matrimony ['matriməni] *n* matrimonio *m*.
matrimonial *adj* matrimonial.
matrix ['meitriks] *n* matriz *f*.
matron ['meitrən] *n* matrona *f*; *(hospital)*
enfermera jefe *f*; *(school)* ama de llaves *f*.
matt [mat] *adj* mate.
matter ['matə] *n* materia *f*; material *m*;
asunto *m*; cuestión *f*; tema *m*. **as a matter of fact** en realidad. **matter-of-fact** *adj*
prosaico. **what's the matter?** ¿qué pasa? *v*
importar. **it doesn't matter** no importa.
mattress ['matris] *n* colchón *m*. **spring-
mattress** *n* colchón de muelles *m*.
mature [mə'tjuə] *adj* maduro. *v* madurar.
maturity *n* madurez *f*.
maudlin ['mɔɪdlin] *adj* sensiblero.
maul [mɔɪl] *v* maltratar; herir gravemente.
mausoleum [mɔɪsə'liəm] *n* mausoleo *m*.
mauve [mouv] *nm*, *adj* malva.
maxim ['maksim] *n* máxima *f*.
maximum ['maksiməm] *nm*, *adj* máximo.
***may** [mei] *v* poder.
May [mei] *n* mayo *m*. **May Day** primero
de mayo *m*.
maybe ['meibiɪ] *adv* quizás, quizá.
mayday ['meidei] *n* señal de socorro *f*.
mayonnaise [ˌmeiə'neiz] *n* mayonesa *f*.
mayor [meə] *n* alcalde *m*. **mayoress** *n*
alcaldesa *f*.
maze [meiz] *n* laberinto *m*.
me [miɪ] *pron* me; *(after prep)* mí.
mead [miɪd] *n* *(drink)* aguamiel *f*.
meadow ['medou] *n* prado *m*.
meagre ['miɪgə] *adj* escaso, pobre.
meal¹ [miɪl] *n* *(food)* comida *f*.
meal² [miɪl] *n* *(flour)* harina *f*.
***mean¹** [miɪn] *v* *(signify)* tener la inten-
ción de, querer decir.

mean² [miɪn] *adj* *(humble)* humilde; *(petty)* mezquino; *(stingy)* agarrado; *(character)* vil; *(unkind)* malo. **meanness** *n*
humildad *f*; mezquindad *f*; *(stinginess)*
tacañería *f*; vileza *f*; maldad *f*.
mean³ [miɪn] *n* *(average)* promedio;
(math) media *f*. *adj* medio; mediano.
meander [mi'andə] *v* *(river)* serpentear;
(person) vagar. *n* meandro *m*.
meaning ['miɪniŋ] *n* significación *f*; sentido *m*; pensamiento *m*. **meaningful** *adj*
significativo. **meaningless** *adj* sin sentido; insignificante.
means [miɪnz] *n* *(way)* medio *m*, manera
f; *(wealth)* fondos *m pl*. **by all means!**
¡por supuesto! **by means of** por medio
de. **by no means** de ningún modo.
meanwhile ['miɪnwail] *adv* mientras tanto.
measles ['miɪzlz] *n* sarampión *m*.
measure ['meʒə] *v* medir. *n* medida *f*.
made to measure hecho a medida. **measurement** *n* medida *f*.
meat [miɪt] *v* carne *f*. **cold meat** fiambre
m. **meatball** *n* albóndiga *f*. **meat pie**
empanada *f*.
mechanic [mi'kanik] *n* mecánico *m*.
mechanical *adj* mecánico. **mechanics** *n*
mecánica *f sing*. **mechanism** *n* mecanismo *m*. **mechanize** *v* mecanizar.
medal ['medl] *n* medalla *f*. **medallion** *n*
medallón *m*. **medallist** *n* condecorado
con una medalla.
meddle ['medl] *v* **meddle in** meterse en;
meddle with toquetear. **meddlesome** *adj*
entremetido.
media ['miɪdiə] *pl n* medios *m pl*.
mediate ['miɪdieit] *v* ser mediador en;
mediar. **mediation** *n* mediación *f*. **media-
tor** *n* mediador, -a *m*, *f*.
medical ['medikəl] *adj* médico; de
medicina. **medical consultant** médico
consultor *m*. **medical school** facultad de
medicina *f*. **medicate** *v* medicinar. **medi-
cated** *adj* medicinal.
medicine ['medsən] *n* *(art and drug)*
medicina *f*; *(coll)* purga *f*. **medicine cabinet** botiquín *m*. **medicinal** *adj* medicinal.
medieval [medi'iɪvəl] *adj* medieval.
mediocre [miɪdi'oukə] *adj* mediocre.
mediocrity *n* mediocridad *f*.
meditate ['mediteit] *v* meditar. **meditation**
n meditación *f*. **meditative** *adj* medita-
tivo.

Mediterranean [ˌmeditəˈreiniən] adj mediterráneo. n Mediterráneo m.

medium [ˈmiːdiəm] n (environment) medio ambiente m; (means) medio m; (spiritualism) médium m, f. **happy medium** justo medio m. adj mediano. **medium wave** (radio) onda media f.

medley [ˈmedli] n mezcla f; (music) popurrí m.

meek [miːk] adj dócil, manso; humilde. **meekness** n docilidad f, mansedumbre f.

*meet [miːt] v (encounter) encontrar, encontrarse a; (come together) entrevistarse con; (come across) cruzarse con; (roads) desembocar en; (correspond to) empalmar con; satisfacer; (requirement, engagement) cumplir con; (expenses) costear; (claims) acceder a. **meet someone half-way** llegar a un arreglo con alguien. **pleased to meet you!** ¡mucho gusto!

meeting n encuentro m; reunión f; sesión f; (interview) cita f; (official) entrevista f.

megaphone [ˈmegəfoun] n megáfono m.

melancholy [ˈmelənkəli] n melancolía f. adj also **melancholic** melancólico.

mellow [ˈmelou] adj (ripe) maduro; (wine) añejo; (voice) suave. v madurar; suavizar.

melodrama [ˈmelədraːmə] n melodrama m. **melodramatic** adj melodramático.

melody [ˈmelədi] n melodía f. **melodious** adj melodioso.

melon [ˈmelən] n melón m.

melt [melt] v fundir; derretir; (fig) ablandar. **melting** n fusión f, fundición f.

member [ˈmembə] n miembro m. **membership** n calidad de miembro f. **membership fee** cuota de socio f.

membrane [ˈmembrein] n membrana f. **membranous** adj membranoso.

memento [məˈmentou] n recuerdo m.

memo [ˈmemou] n (coll) memorándum m.

memoirs [ˈmemwaːz] pl n memorias f pl.

memorable [ˈmemərəbl] adj memorable.

memorandum [meməˈrandəm] n memorándum m.

memory [ˈmeməri] n memoria f; (thing remembered) recuerdo m. **memorize** v memorizar, aprender de memoria.

men [men] V **man**.

menace [ˈmenis] n amenaza f. v amenazar.

menagerie [miˈnadʒəri] n casa de fieras f.

mend [mend] v remendar; reparar; (improve) mejorar. **be on the mend** (coll) estar mejorando.

menial [ˈmiːniəl] adj (of a servant) doméstico; (mean) bajo. n (servant) criado, -a m, f.

meningitis [ˌmeninˈdʒaitis] n meningitis f.

menopause [ˈmenəpɔːz] n menopausia f.

menstrual [ˈmenstruəl] adj menstrual. **menstruate** v menstruar. **menstruation** n menstruación f.

mental [ˈmentl] adj mental; (coll: mad) chiflado. **mental arithmetic** cálculo mental m. **mental deficiency** deficiencia mental f. **mental home** or **hospital** manicomio m. **mentality** n mentalidad f. **mentally** adj mentalmente. **mentally handicapped** anormal.

menthol [ˈmenθəl] n mentol m.

mention [ˈmenʃən] v mencionar, hablar de. **don't mention it!** ¡de nada! ¡no hay de qué! **not to mention** por no decir nada de. n mención f.

menu [ˈmenjuː] n carta f, lista de platos f.

mercantile [ˈmɜːkənˌtail] adj mercantil; mercante.

mercenary [ˈmɜːsinəri] nm, adj mercenario.

merchandise [ˈmɜːtʃəndaiz] n mercancías f pl. **merchandizing** n comercio mercantil m.

merchant [ˈmɜːtʃənt] n comerciante m, f, negociante m, f; (shopkeeper) tendero, -a m, f. **merchant navy** marina mercante f.

mercury [ˈmɜːkjuri] n mercurio m.

mercy [ˈmɜːsi] n misericordia f, merced f. **at the mercy of** a merced de. **merciful** adj clemente; misericordioso. **merciless** adj despiadado.

mere [miə] adj mero.

merge [mɜːdʒ] v (parties, companies) fusionar; (join) unir; (colours) fundir. **merger** n fusión f; unión f.

meridian [məˈridiən] nm, adj meridiano.

meringue [məˈraŋ] n merengue f.

merit [ˈmerit] n mérito m. v merecer.

mermaid [ˈmɜːmeid] n sirena f.

merry [ˈmeri] adj alegre; divertido; (coll: slightly drunk) achispado. **merry-go-round** n tiovivo m. **merriment** n alegría f; diversión f.

mesh [meʃ] n mella f; (gears) engranaje m. v engranar (con).

mesmerize [ˈmezməraiz] v hipnotizar.

mess [mes] n confusión f, desorden m; (dirt) porquería f, suciedad f; (awkward situation) lío m; (mil) comedor de la tropa m. **make a mess of** desordenar;

ensuciar. **what a mess!** ¡qué asco! ¡qué
porquería! ¡qué lío! **mess up** desordenar;
ensuciar. **messy** *adj* confuso;
desordenado; sucio.
message ['mesidʒ] *n* recado *m*; (*official
communication*) mensaje *m*; (*errand*)
encargo *m*. **messenger** *n* mensajero, -a *m*,
f.
met [met] *V* **meet**.
metal ['metl] *n* metal *m*. *adj* de metal.
metallic *adj* metálico. **metallurgist** *n*
metalúrgico *m*. **metallurgy** *n* metalurgia
f.
metamorphosis [metə'mɔɪfəsis] *n*
metamorfosis *f*.
metaphor ['metəfə] *n* metáfora *f*. **metaphorical** *adj* metafórico.
metaphysics [,metə'fiziks] *n* metafísica *f*.
metaphysical *adj* metafísico. **metaphysi-
cian** *n* metafísico *m*.
meteor ['miɪtiə] *n* meteoro. **meteoric** *adj*
meteórico. **meteorite** *n* meteorito *m*.
meteorology [,miɪtiə'rolədʒi] *n* meteorología *f*. **meteorological** *adj* meteorológico.
meteorologist *n* meteorologista *m*, *f*.
meter ['miɪtə] *n* contador *m*.
methane ['miɪθein] *n* metano *m*.
method ['meθəd] *n* método *m*; técnica *f*.
methodical *adj* metódico.
Methodist ['meθədist] *n* metodista *m*, *f*.
Methodism *n* metodismo *m*.
methylated spirits ['meθileitid] *pl n* alcohol desnaturalizado *m*.
meticulous [mi'tikjuləs] *adj* meticuloso.
metre ['miɪtə] *n* metro *m*. **metric** *adj*
métrico.
metronome ['metrənoum] *n* metrónomo
m.
metropolis [mə'tropəlis] *n* metrópoli *f*.
metropolitan *adj* metropolitano.
Mexico ['meksikou] *n* Méjico, México.
Mexican *n*, *adj* mejicano, -a, mexicano,
-a.
mice [mais] *V* **mouse**.
microbe ['maikroub] *n* microbio *m*.
microfilm ['maikrəfilm] *n* microfilm *m*.
microphone ['maikrəfoun] *n* micrófono
m.
microscope ['maikrəskoup] *n* microscopio
m. **microscopic** *adj* microscópico.
microwave ['maikrəweiv] *n* microonda *f*.
mid [mid] *adj* medio; mediados.
mid-air [,mid'eə] *n* **in mid-air** entre cielo y
tierra.
midday [,mid'dei] *n* mediodía *m*.

middle ['midl] *n* medio *m*, centro *m*;
mitad *f*. **in the middle** en el centro. *adj*
central; mediano; de en medio; medio;
intermedio. **middle-aged** *adj* de mediano
edad. **the Middle Ages** Edad Media *f*
sing. **middle-class** *adj* de la clase media;
burgués. **Middle East** Oriente Medio *m*.
middleman *n* intermediario *m*. **middle-of-
the-road** *adj* centrista, moderado. **middle-
weight** *n* peso medio *m*. **middling** *adj* regular, mediano.
midge [midʒ] *n* mosca enana *f*.
midget ['midʒit] *n* enano, -a *m*, *f*.
midnight ['midnait] *n* medianoche *f*.
midriff ['midrif] *n* diafragua *m*.
midst [midst] *n* **in our midst** entre nosotros. **in the midst of** en medio de.
midstream [,mid'striɪm] *n* **in midstream** en
medio del río.
midsummer ['mid,sʌmə] *n* pleno verano
m. **Midsummer Day** el día de San Juan
m.
midway [,mid'wei] *adv*, *adj* a medio camino.
midweek [,mid'wiɪk] *n* medio de la
semana *m*.
midwife ['midwaif] *n* comadrona *f*,
partera *f*. **midwifery** *n* obstetricia *f*.
midwinter [,mid'wintə] *n* pleno invierno
m.
might¹ [mait] *V* **may**.
might² [mait] *n* poder *m*; fuerza *f*.
mighty ['maiti] *adj* poderoso; fuerte;
enorme. *adv* (*coll*) muy.
migraine ['miɪgrein] *n* migraña *f*.
migrate [mai'greit] *v* emigrar. **migration** *n*
migración. *adj* migratoria.
mike [maik] *n* (*coll: microphone*) micro *m*.
mild [maild] *adj* (*person*) dulce, apacible;
(*weather*) templado; (*wind*) suave; (*disease*) benigno. **mildness** *n* dulzura *f*;
suavidad *f*; benignidad *f*.
mildew ['mildjuɪ] *n* moho *m*; (*vine*)
mildeu *m*; (*plants*) tizón *m*.
mile [mail] *n* milla *f*. **mileage** recorrido en
millas *m*. **milestone** *n* mojón *m*; (*fig*)
jalón *m*.
militant ['militənt] *adj* belicoso; (*pol*)
militante. *n* militante *m*, *f*.
military ['militəri] *adj* militar.
milk [milk] *n* leche *f*. **milk chocolate** *n*
chocolate con leche *m*. **milkman** *n*
lechero *m*. **milk of magnesia** *n* leche de
magnesia *f*. *v* ordeñar; (*fig*) exprimir.

milkiness *n* aspecto lechoso *m.* **milking** *n* ordeño *m.* **milky** *adj* lechoso.

Milky Way *n* Vía Láctea *f.*

mill [mil] *n* molino *m*; (*grinder*) molinillo *m*; (*factory*) fábrica *f.* **millstone** *n* muela *f*; (*burden*) cruz *f.* *v* moler. **miller** *n* molinero, -a *m, f.*

millennium [mi'leniəm] *n* milenario *m.*

millet ['milit] *n* mijo *m.*

milligram ['mili,gram] *n* miligramo *m.*

millimetre ['mili,miitə] *n* milímetro *m.*

milliner ['milinə] *n* sombrerero, -a *m, f.* **milliner's** *n* sombrerería *f.* **millinery** *n* sombreros de señora *m pl.*

million ['miljən] *n* millón *m.* **millionaire** *n* millonario, -a *m. f.* **millionth** *n, adj* millonésimo, -a *m, f.*

mime [maim] *n* mimo *m*, pantomima *f.* *v* actuar de mimo.

mimic ['mimik] *adj* mímico; imitativo. *n* mimo *m*; imitador, -a *m, f.* *v* imitar, remedar. **mimicry** *n* mímica *f*; (*zool*) mimetismo *m.*

minaret [minə'ret] *n* minarete *m.*

mince [mins] *n* (*meat*) carne picada *f.* **mincemeat** *n* conserva de fruta picada y especias *f.* **mince pie** pastel con frutas picadas *m.* *v* picar; (*walk*) andar con pasos menuditos. **mince words** tener pelos en la lengua. **mincer** *n* máquina de picar carne *f.* **mincing** *adj* afectado.

mind [maind] *n* mente *f.* **bear in mind** tener en cuenta. **go out of one's mind** perder el juicio. **have a good mind to** tener ganas de. **keep in mind** acordarse de. **make up one's mind** decidirse. **read someone's mind** adivinar el pensamiento de alguien. **to my mind** a mi parecer. *v* (*look out*) tener cuidado; (*guard*) cuidar; (*rules*) cumplir; (*pay attention*) prestar atención. **do you mind?** ¿le importa? **I don't mind** a mí no me importa. **never mind** no se precocupe.

mine[1] [main] *pron* (el) mío, (la) mía, (lo) mío.

mine[2] [main] *n* mina *f.* **minefield** *n* campo de minas *m.* **mineshaft** *n* pozo de extracción *m.* **minesweeper** *n* dragaminas *m invar.* *v* minar; (*mil*) sembrar minas en. **miner** *n* minero *m.* **mining** *n* minería *f.* **mining engineer** ingeniero de minas *m.*

mineral ['minərəl] *nm, adj* mineral. **minerals** (*coll: drinks*) *pl n* gaseosas *f pl.*

mingle ['miŋgl] *v* mezclar.

miniature ['minitʃə] *nf, adj* miniatura.

minim ['minim] *n* mínima *f*, blanca *f.*

minimum ['miniməm] *nm, adj* mínimo. **minimal** *adj* mínimo. **minimize** *v* minimizar.

minister ['ministə] *n* ministro *m.* *v* **minister to** atender a. **ministerial** *adj* ministerial. **ministry** *n* ministerio *m.*

mink [miŋk] *n* visón *m.*

minor ['mainə] *adj* menor, más pequeño; secundario; de poca importancia. *n* menor de edad *m, f.*

minority [mai'noriti] *n* minoría *f.* **in the minority** en la minoría. *adj* minoritario.

minstrel ['minstrəl] *n* trovador *m.*

mint[1] [mint] *n* (*bot*) menta *f.*

mint[2] [mint] *n* casa de la moneda *f. adj* nuevo. *v* acuñar.

minuet [minju'et] *n* minué *m.*

minus ['mainəs] *prep* menos. *adj* negativo. **minus sign** signo menos *m.*

minute[1] ['minit] *n* minuto *m.* **minutes** *pl n* actas *f pl.*

minute[2] [mai'njuɪt] *adj* (*tiny*) diminuto; (*detailed*) minucioso.

miracle ['mirəkl] *n* milagro *m.* **miraculous** *adj* milagroso.

mirage ['miraɪʒ] *n* espejismo *m.*

mirror ['mirə] *n* espejo *m*; (*mot*) retrovisor *m.* *v* reflejar.

mirth [məɪθ] *n* alegría *f*; hilaridad *f.*

misadventure [misəd'ventʃə] *n* desgracia *f.*

misanthropist [miz'anθrəpist] *n* misántropo *m.* **misanthropic** *adj* misantrópico. **misanthropy** *n* misantropía *f.*

misapprehension [misapri'henʃən] *n* malentendido *m.*

misbehave [misbi'heiv] *v* portarse mal. **misbehaviour** *n* mala conducta *f.*

miscalculate [mis'kalkjuleit] *v* calcular mal. **miscalculation** *n* cálculo erróneo *m.*

miscarriage [mis'karidʒ] *n* (*med*) aborto *m*; (*plans, etc.*) fracaso *m.* **miscarriage of justice** error judicial *m.*

miscellaneous [misə'leiniəs] *adj* diverso.

mischief ['mistʃif] *n* (*evil*) maldad *f*; (*of child*) travesura *f*; (*damage*) daño *m.* **get into mischief** hacer tonterías. **make mischief** sembrar la discordia. **mischievous** *adj* malo; travieso; dañino.

misconception [miskən'sepʃən] *n* concepto falso *m.*

misconduct [mis'kondʌkt] *n* (*misbehaviour*) mala conducta *f*; (*mismanagement*) mala administración *f.*

misconstrue [miskən'struː] v interpretar mal.

misdeed [mis'diːd] n delito m.

misdemeanour [misdi'miːnə] n (law) infracción f; (misbehaviour) mala conducta f.

miser ['maizə] n avaro, -a m, f. **miserly** adj mezquino.

miserable ['mizərəbl] adj (sad) triste; (sick) mal; (unfortunate) desgraciado; (wretched) miserable; (distressing) de pena.

misery ['mizəri] n tristeza f; (pain) dolor m; desgracia f; miseria f; (coll: person) aguafiestas m, f.

misfire [mis'faiə] v fallar; (mot) tener fallos. n fallo m.

misfit ['misfit] n inadaptado, -a m, f.

misfortune [mis'fɔːtʃən] n desgracia f.

misgiving [mis'giviŋ] n recelo m; inquietud f.

misguided [mis'gaidid] adj descaminado; poco afortunado.

mishap ['mishap] n contratiempo m.

misinterpret [misin'təːprit] v interpretar mal. **misinterpretation** n interpretación errónea f.

misjudge [mis'dʒʌdʒ] v juzgar mal. **misjudgment** n estimación errónea f.

*****mislay** [mis'lei] v extraviar.

*****mislead** [mis'liːd] v engañar; equivocar. **misleading** adj engañoso.

misnomer [mis'noumə] n nombre inapropiado m.

misogynist [mi'sodʒənist] n misógino m.

misplace [mis'pleis] v colocar mal; (lose) extraviar.

misprint ['misprint] n errata f.

miss¹ [mis] v fallar; no dar en; (train, bus, etc.) perder; (a meeting) no asistir a; (long for) echar de menos. **miss out** omitir. n tiro errado m; (failure) fracaso m. **missing** adj (lacking) que falta; perdido; ausente; desaparecido.

miss² [mis] n señorita.

misshapen [miʃ'ʃeipən] adj (object) deformado; (person) deforme.

missile ['misail] n proyectil m. **guided missile** proyectil teledirigido m.

mission ['miʃən] n misión f. **missionary** n, adj misionero, -a.

mist [mist] n (haze) calina f; (fog) neblina f; (at sea) bruma f; (on glasses) vaho m. **mist over** or **up** empañar. **misty** adj de niebla; brumoso; vago; empañado.

*****mistake** [mi'steik] v (be wrong) equivocarse en; (the way) equivocarse de; (misunderstand) entender mal. n error m; equivocación f; falta f. **by mistake** sin querer. **make a mistake** equivocarse. **mistaken** adj equivocado; erróneo; mal comprendido. **be mistaken** estar equivocado.

mistletoe ['misltou] n muérdago m.

mistress ['mistris] n (of the house) señora f; (owner) dueña f; (lover) amante f; (teacher) profesora f.

mistrust [mis'trʌst] n desconfianza f; (suspicion) recelo m. v desconfiar de; recelar de. **mistrustful** adj desconfiado; receloso.

*****misunderstand** [misʌndə'stand] v entender mal. **misunderstanding** n malentendido m.

misuse [mis'juːs; v mis'juːz] n mal uso m; abuso m; maltrato m; mal empleo m. v abusar de; maltratar; emplear mal.

mitigate ['mitigeit] v mitigar; aliviar; atemar. **mitigation** n mitigación f; alivio m; atenuación f.

mitre ['maitə] n (rel) mitra f; (carpentry) inglete m. v unir con ingletes.

mitten ['mitn] n mitón m.

mix [miks] v mezclar; (drinks) preparar; (salad) aliñar; (flour, cement, etc.) amasar. **mix up** mezclar; confundir. **mix-up** n lío m; confusión f. **mixed feelings** sentimientos contradictorios m pl. **mixed grill** plato combinado m. **mixer** n (elec) mezclador m; (cement) mezcladora f. **mixture** n mezcla f; (med) mixturia f.

moan [moun] v gemir; (coll: complain) quejarse. n gemido m; queja f.

moat [mout] n foso m.

mob [mob] n multitud f; (rabble) chusma f. v acosar.

mobile ['moubail] nm, adj móvil. **mobility** n movilidad f. **mobilize** v movilizar.

moccasin ['mokəsin] n mocasín m.

mock [mok] v burlarse de; ridiculizar. adj simulado; falso; imitado. **mockery** n burla f; simulacro m; imitación f. **mocking** adj burlón.

mode [moud] n modo m, manera f; (fashion) moda f.

model ['modl] n modelo m; (of a statue) maqueta f; (fashion) maniquí m; (dressmaking pattern) patrón m. v modelar; (dress) presentar.

moderate ['modərət; v 'modəreit] n, adj moderado, -a. v moderar; aplacar. **moderately** adv moderadamente; (fairly) mediocremente. **in moderation** con moderación.

modern ['modən] adj moderno. **modern languages** lenguas vivas f pl. **modernization** n modernisación f. **modernize** v modernizar.

modest ['modist] adj modesto; discreto. **modesty** n modestia f.

modify ['modifai] v modificar. **modification** n modificación f.

modulate ['modjuleit] v modular. **modulation** n modulación f.

module ['modjuːl] n módulo m.

mohair ['mouheə] n moer m.

moist [moist] adj húmedo. **moisten** v numedecer, mojar. **moisture** n humedad f. **moisturize** v humedecer. **moisturizing cream** crema hidratante f.

molasses [mə'lasiz] n melaza f.

mole[1] [moul] n (on skin) lunar m.

mole[2] [moul] n (zool) topo m. **molehill** n topera f.

molecule ['molikjuːl] n molécula f. **molecular** adj molecular.

molest [mə'lest] v molestar, importunar.

mollusc ['moləsk] n molusco m.

molten ['moultən] adj fundido.

moment ['moumənt] n momento m. **at the moment** de momento. **momentary** adj momentáneo. **momentarily** adv momentáneamente. **momentous** adj de gran importancia.

momentum [mə'mentəm] n momento m; ímpetu m; impulso m.

monarch ['monək] n monarca m. **monarchist** n, adj monárquico, -a. **monarchy** n monarquía f.

monastery ['monəstəri] n monasterio m. **monastic** adj monacal.

Monday ['mʌndi] n lunes m.

money ['mʌni] n dinero m. **get one's money's worth** sacar jugo al dinero. **moneylender** n prestamista m, f.

mongol ['moŋgəl] n, adj (med) mongol, -a. **mongolism** n mongolismo m.

mongrel ['mʌŋgrəl] n (dog) perro mestizo m.

monitor ['monitə] n monitor m; instructor m; (tech) radioescucha m. v controlar.

monk [mʌŋk] n monje m.

monkey ['mʌŋki] n mono m. **monkey around** entretenerse, perder el tiempo.

monogamy [mə'nogəmi] n monogamia f. **monogamous** adj monógamo.

monogram ['monəgram] n monograma m.

monologue ['monəlog] n monólogo m.

monopolize [mə'nopəlaiz] v monopolizar. **monopoly** n monopolio m.

monosyllable ['monəsiləbl] n monosílabo m. **monosyllabic** adj (word) monosílabo; (statement) monosilábico.

monotone ['monətoun] n monotonía f. **monotonous** adj monótono. **monotony** n monotonía f.

monsoon [mon'suːn] n monzón m.

monster ['monstə] n monstruo m. **monstrosity** n monstruosidad f. **monstrous** adj monstruoso.

month [mʌnθ] n mes m. **calendar month** mes civil m. **monthly** n, adj mensual. adv mensualmente.

monument ['monjument] n monumento m. **monumental** adj monumental; enorme.

mood[1] [muːd] n humor m. **moody** adj malhumorado; caprichoso.

mood[2] [muːd] n (gramm) modo m.

moon [muːn] n luna f. **crescent moon** media luna f. **full moon** luna llena f. **new moon** luna nueva f. **moonbeam** n rayo de luna m. **moonlight** n claro de luna m. **moonlighting** n (coll) pluriempleo m.

moor[1] [muə] n páramo m.

moor[2] [muə] v marrrar.

mop [mop] n (floor) fregona f; (hair) pelambrera f. v fregar. **mop up** limpiar.

mope [moup] v tener ideas negras.

moped ['mouped] n ciclomotor m.

moral ['morəl] adj moral; virtuoso. **moral support** apoyo moral m. n (fable) moraleja f. **morals** pl n moralidad f sing. **moralist** n moralista m, f. **moralize** v moralizar.

morale [mə'raːl] n moral f.

morbid ['moːbid] adj mórbido.

more [moː] adj más; superior; mayor. pron, adv más. **all the more** aún más. **and what's more** y lo que es más. **even more** más aún. **more and more** cada vez más. **more than ever** más que nunca. **once more** una vez más.

moreover [moː'rouvə] adv además, también; por otra parte.

morgue [moːg] n depósito de cadáveres m.

morning ['mɔɪnɪŋ] *n* mañana *f. adj* de la mañana. **morning coat** chaqué *m.* **morning sickness** náuseas *f pl.*

moron ['mɔɪrɒn] *n* retrasado mental *m*; (*coll*) imbécil *m, f.* **moronic** *adj* retrasado mental; (*coll*) idiota.

morose [mə'rous] *adj* malhumorado.

morphine ['mɔɪfiɪn] *n* morfina *f.*

Morse code [mɔɪs] *n* morse *m.*

morsel ['mɔɪsəl] *n* bocado *m.*

mortal ['mɔɪtl] *nm, adj* mortal. **mortality** *n* mortalidad *f.*

mortar ['mɔɪtə] *n* mortero *m.*

mortgage ['mɔɪgɪdʒ] *n* hipoteca *f.*

mortify ['mɔɪtifai] *v* mortificar. **mortification** *n* mortificación *f.*

mortuary ['mɔɪtjuəri] *n* depósito de cadáveres *m.*

mosaic [mə'zeiik] *n* mosaico *m. adj* de mosaico.

Moscow ['mɒskou] *n* Moscú.

mosque [mɒsk] *n* mezquita *f.*

mosquito [mə'skiːtou] *n* mosquito *m.* **mosquito bite** picadura de mosquito *f.* **mosquito net** mosquitero *m.*

moss [mɒs] *n* musgo *m.* **mossy** *adj* musgoso.

most [moust] *adj* más; la mayoría de. *pron* la mayoría; la mayor parte; lo máximo. *adv* más; (*very*) de lo más. **at most** a lo sumo. **make the most of** sacar el mayor provecho de. **mostly** *adv* principalmente, sobre todo; en general.

motel [mou'tel] *n* motel *m.*

moth [mɒθ] *n* mariposa nocturna *f.* **clothes moth** polilla *f.* **mothball** bola de naftalina *f.* **moth-eaten** *adj* apohillado; (*fig*) anticuado.

mother ['mʌðə] *n* madre *f.* **mother-in-law** *n* suegra *f.* **mother-of-pearl** *n* madreperla *f.* **Mothers' Day** día de la Madre *m.* **mother-to-be** futura madre *f.* **motherhood** *n* maternidad *f.* **motherly** *adj* maternal.

motion ['mouʃən] *n* movimiento *m*; (*signal*) señas *f pl*; (*indication*) ademán *m*; (*of a machine*) mecanismo *m*; (*med*) deposición *f*; (*at a meeting*) moción *f.* **set in motion** poner en marcha. *v* indicar con la mano; hacer señas. **motionless** *adj* inmóvil.

motivate ['moutiveit] *v* motivar. **motivation** *n* motivo *m.*

motive ['moutiv] *n* (*reason*) motivo *m*; (*law*) móvil *m. adj* motor, motriz.

motor ['moutə] *n* motor *m.* **motorbike** *n*

(*coll*) moto *f.* **motorboat** *n* lancha motora *f.* **motorcar** *n* automóvil *m*, coche *m.* **motorcyclist** *n* motociclista *m, f.* **motoring** *n* automovilismo *m.* **motorist** *n* automovilista *m, f.* **motorway** *n* autopista *f.*

mottled ['mɒtld] *adj* abigarrado.

motto ['mɒtou] *n* lema *m.*

mould[1] [mould] *n* (*container*) molde *m*; (*shape*) forma *f*; (*pattern*) modelo *m. v* moldear; formar.

mould[2] [mould] *n* (*fungus*) moho *m.* **mouldy** *adj* mohoso. **go mouldy** enmohecerse.

moult [moult] *v* mudar. *n* muda *f.*

mound [maund] *n* (*natural*) montículo *m*; (*artificial*) terraplén *m*; (*heap*) montón *m*; (*burial*) túmulo *m.*

mount[1] [maunt] *v* subir; montar a caballo. **mount up** aumentar. *n* (*horse*) montura *f*; (*base*) soporte *m*; (*phot*) borde *m*; (*drawing*) fondo *m.*

mount[2] [maunt] *n* monte *m.*

mountain ['mauntən] *n* montaña *f.* **mountaineer** *n* montañero, -a *m, f.* **mountaineering** *n* montañismo *m.* **mountainous** *adj* montañoso.

mourn [mɔɪn] *v* lamentar. **mournful** *adj* triste; afligido. **mourning** *n* luto *m*, duelo *m.*

mouse [maus] *n, pl* **mice** ratón *m.* **mousetrap** *n* ratonera *f.* **mousy** *adj* (*coll: hair*) pardusco; (*coll: shy*) tímido.

mousse [muːs] *n* crema batida *f.*

moustache [mə'stɑːʃ] *n* bigote *m.*

mouth [mauθ] *n* boca *f*; (*opening*) abertura *f*; (*entrance*) entrada *f*; (*bottle*) gollete *m*; (*river*) desembocadura *f.* **mouthpiece** *n* (*music*) boquita *f*; (*phone*) micrófono *m*; (*spokesman*) portavoz *m.* **mouthwash** *n* enjuague *m.* **mouth-watering** *adj* muy apetitoso. *v* articular.

move [muːv] *v* cambiar de; mudarse de; mover; transportar; (*from one place to another*) trasladar; poner en marcha; (*emotionally*) emocionar; (*in debate*) proponer. *n* (*fig*) paso *m*; marcha *f*; medida *f*; (*house*) mudanza *f*; (*turn*) turno *m*; (*chess*, *etc*.) jugada *f.* **movable** *adj* movible, móvil. **movement** *n* movimiento *m*; (*gesture*) ademán *m*; acto *m*; tendencia *f*; transporte *m*; traslado *m*; (*vehicles*) tráfico *m*; (*tech*) mecanismo *m*; (*mil*) maniobra *f.* **moving** *adj* móvil; en movimiento; (*emotional*) conmovedor.

movie ['muːvi] n (US) película f. **go to the movies** ir al cine.

***mow** [mou] v (lawn) cortar, segar. **mow down** barrer.

Mr ['mistə] n señor m; Sr.

Mrs ['misiz] n señora f; Sra.

much [mʌtʃ] adj, adv, pron mucho. **as much** tanto (como). **how much?** ¿cuánto? **much as** por mucho que. **so much** tanto. **too much** demasiado.

muck [mʌk] n (manure) estiércol m; (dirt) suciedad f. v **muck about** (coll) perder el tiempo. **mucky** adj asqueroso.

mucus ['mjuːkəs] n mucosidad f. **mucous** adj mucoso.

mud [mʌd] n barro m; (thick mud) fango m. **mudguard** n guardabarros m invar. **muddy** adj fangoso.

muddle ['mʌdl] n desorden m; confusión f. v confundir, embrollar. **muddle through** salir del paso. **muddleheaded** adj atontado.

muff [mʌf] n manguito m.

muffle ['mʌfl] v amortiguar. **muffle up** embozar. **muffler** n bufanda f.

mug [mʌg] n tazón m; (slang: face) jeta f; (slang: fool) primo, -a m, f. v asaltar. **mugging** n asalto m.

muggy ['mʌgi] adj bochornoso.

mulberry ['mʌlbəri] n (fruit) mora f; (tree) morera f, moral m.

mule[1] [mjuːl] n (animal) mulo, -a m, f. **mulish** adj testarudo.

mule[2] [mjuːl] n (slipper) babucha f.

multicoloured [,mʌlti'kʌləd] adj multicolor.

multilingual [,mʌlti'liŋgwəl] adj poligloto.

multiple ['mʌltipl] adj múltiple. n múltiplo m. **multiple sclerosis** esclerosis en placas f.

multiply ['mʌltiplai] v multiplicar. **multiplication** n multiplicación f. **multiplication table** tabla de multiplicar f.

multiracial [,mʌlti'reiʃəl] adj multiracial.

multitude ['mʌltitjuːd] n multitud f, muchedumbre f.

mumble ['mʌmbl] v mascullar. n refunfuño m.

mummy[1] ['mʌmi] n momia f. **mummification** n momificación f. **mummify** v momificar.

mummy[2] ['mʌmi] n (coll: mother) mamá f.

mumps [mʌmps] n paperas f pl.

munch [mʌntʃ] v mascar.

mundane [mʌn'dein] adj mundano.

municipal [mju'nisipəl] adj municipal. **municipality** n municipio m.

mural ['mjuərəl] nm, adj mural.

murder ['məːdə] n homicidio m, asesinato m. **murderer** n asesino m. **murderess** n asesina f. **murderous** adj homicida, asesino.

murky ['məːki] adj oscuro; lóbrego.

murmur ['məːmə] v murmurar. n murmullo m.

muscle ['mʌsl] n músculo m. v **muscle in** (coll) meterse por fuerza en. **muscular** adj muscular; (person) musculoso.

muse [mjuːz] n musa f. v meditar, contemplar.

museum [mju'ziəm] n museo m.

mushroom ['mʌʃrum] n hongo m, seta f; (food) champiñón m. v crecer como hongos.

music ['mjuːzik] n música f. **music hall** music-hall m. **music stand** atril m. **musical** adj de música; (ear) musical; (person) aficionado a la música. **musical (comedy)** n comedia musical f. **musical instrument** instrumento de música m. **musician** n músico, -a m, f.

musk [mʌsk] n almizcle m.

musket ['mʌskit] n mosquete m. **musketeer** n mosquetero m.

Muslim ['mʌzlim] n, adj musulmán, -ana.

muslin ['mʌzlin] n muselina f.

mussel ['mʌsl] n mejillón m.

***must** [mʌst] v deber; tener que.

mustard ['mʌstəd] n mostaza f. **mustard pot** mostacera f.

muster ['mʌstə] v reunir; (mil) formar. n reunión f; asamblea f; (mil) revista f. **pass muster** ser aceptable.

musty ['mʌsti] adj mohoso. **smell musty** oler a cerrado.

mute [mjuːt] n, adj mudo, -a; (music) sordina f. v apagar; poner sordina a. **muted** adj sordo.

mutilate ['mjuːtileit] v mutilar. **mutilation** n mutilación f.

mutiny ['mjuːtini] n motín m, rebelión f. v amotinarse, rebelarse. **mutinous** adj amotinado; (fig) rebelde.

mutter ['mʌtə] v murmurar. n murmullo m. **muttering** n refunfuño m.

mutton ['mʌtn] n cordero m.

mutual ['mjuːtʃuəl] adj mutuo; común.

muzzle ['mʌzl] n (nose) hocico m; (device) bozal m; (gun) boca f. v abozalar.

my [mai] *adj* mi (*pl* mis), mío, mía (*pl* míos, mías).
myself [mai'self] *pron* (*reflexive*) me; (*emphatic*) yo mismo, -a; (*after prep*) mí. **by myself** (completamente) solo, -a.
mystery ['mistəri] *n* misterio *m*. **mysterious** *adj* misterioso.
mystic ['mistik] *n* iniciado, -a *m*, *f*; místico, -a *m*, *f*. *adj also* **mystical** místico; esotérico; oculto; sobrenatural.
mystify ['mistifai] *v* oscurecer; desconcertar; desorientar; (*deceive*) engañar. **mystification** *n* mistificación *f*; complejidad *f*; confusión *f*.
mystique [mi'stiːk] *n* mística *f*.
myth [miθ] *n* mito *m*. **mythical** *adj* mítico. **mythological** *adj* mitológico. **mythology** *n* mitología *f*.

N

nag [nag] *v* regañar. *n* (*horse*) rocín *m*.
nail [neil] *n* (*metal*) clavo *m*; (*anat*) uña *f*; (*claw*) garra *f*. **nailbrush** *n* cepillo de uñas *m*. **nail-file** *n* lima de uñas *f*. **nail polish** esmalte de uñas *m*. **nail-scissors** *n* tijeras para las uñas *f pl*. *v* clavar.
naive [nai'iːv] *adj* ingenuo. **naivety** *n* ingenuidad *f*.
naked ['neikid] *adj* desnudo. **nakedness** *n* desnudez *f*.
name [neim] *n* nombre *m*; (*surname*) apellido *m*; *fama f*; título *m*. **my name is ...** me llamo .... **namesake** *n* tocayo, -a *m*, *f*. **what's your name?** ¿cómo se llama? *v* llamar; nombrar. **nameless** *adj* sin nombre; anónimo. **namely** *adv* a saber.
nanny ['nani] *n* niñera *f*.
nap¹ [nap] *n* sueño ligero *m*. *v* dormitar. **be caught napping** estar desprevenido.
nap² [nap] *n* (*of cloth*) lanilla *f*.
nape [neip] *n* nuca *f*.
napkin ['napkin] *n* servilleta *f*.
nappy ['napi] *n* pañal *m*.
narcotic [naɪ'kotic] *nm*, *adj* narcótico.
narrate [nə'reit] *v* contar. **narration** *n* narración *f*. **narrator** *n* narrador, -a *m*, *f*.
narrative ['narətiv] *n* narrativa *f*. *adj* narrativo.
narrow ['narou] *adj* estrecho. **narrow-**gauge *adj* de vía estrecha. **narrow-minded** *adj* de miras estrechas. *v* estrechar. **narrow down** reducir. **narrowly** *adv* (*only just*) por muy poco; estrechamente. **narrowness** *n* estrechez *f*.
nasal ['neizəl] *adj* nasal. **nasalize** *v* nasalizar.
nasturtium [nə'stəɪʃəm] *n* capuchina *f*.
nasty ['naɪsti] *adj* sucio; repugnante; (*unfriendly*) antipático; grosero; desagradable.
nation ['neiʃən] *n* nación *f*. **national** *nm*, *adj* nacional. **national anthem** himno nacional *m*. **nationalism** *n* nacionalismo *m*. **nationalist** *n*(*m*+*f*), *adj* nacionalista. **nationality** *n* nacionalidad *f*. **nationalization** *n* nacionalización *f*. **nationalize** *v* nacionalizar.
native ['neitiv] *adj* (*country*, *town*) natal; (*inhabitant*) nativo; (*language*) materno; (*product*) del país. *n* natural *m*, *f*; nativo, -a *m*, *f*.
nativity [nə'tivəti] *n* nacimiento *m*.
natural ['natʃərəl] *adj* natural. **naturalism** *n* naturalismo *m*. **naturalist** *n* naturalista *m*, *f*. **naturally** *adv* naturalmente; por naturaleza.
nature ['neitʃə] *n* naturaleza *f*; (*character*) natural *m*; esencia *f*.
naughty ['noiti] *adj* travieso; malvado. **naughtiness** *n* travesura *f*.
nausea ['noiziə] *n* náusea *f*. **nauseate** *v* dar asco.
nautical ['noitikəl] *adj* marítimo, náutico.
naval ['neivəl] *adj* naval; de marina. **naval officer** oficial de marina *m*.
navel ['neivəl] *n* ombligo *m*. **navel orange** naranja navel *f*.
navigate ['navigeit] *v* navegar; (*steer*) gobernar. **navigable** *adj* navegable. **navigation** *n* navegación *f*. **navigator** *n* navegante *m*.
navy ['neivi] *n* marina *f*. **navy blue** azul marino *m*.
near [niə] *adv* cerca. *prep* cerca de. *adj* cercano. *v* acercarse a; aproximarse a. **the near future** el futuro próximo. **nearby** *adv* cerca. **nearly** *adv* casi. **not nearly** ni con mucho. **very nearly** casi casi.
neat [niːt] *adj* limpio; bien cuidado; ordenado; (*drink*) solo. **neaten** *v* limpiar; ordenar. **neatly** *adv* con cuidado; (*dress*) con gusto; (*skilfully*) hábilmente. **neatness** *n* limpieza *f*; orden *m*; gusto *m*.

necessary ['nesisəri] *adj* necesario. **if necessary** si es preciso. **it is necessary** es preciso. **necessitate** *v* necesitar. **necessity** *n* necesidad *f.*

neck [nek] *n* (*human, garment*) cuello *m;* (*animal*) pescuezo *m;* (*bottle*) gollete *m.* **neck and neck** parejos. **necklace** *n* collar *m.*

nectar ['nektə] *n* néctar *m.*

need [niid] *n* necesidad *f;* (*lack*) carencia *f. v* necesitar; hacer falta a uno. **needless** *adj* innecesario; inútil. **needy** *adj* necesitado. *n* **the needy** los necesitados *m pl.*

needle ['niidl] *n* aguja *f.* **darning needle** aguja de zurcir. **knitting needle** aguja de hacer punto. **needlework** *n* costura *f. v* (*coll*) pinchar.

negative ['negətiv] *adj* negativo. *n* (*gramm*) negación *f;* (*phot*) negativo *m;* (*reply*) contestación negativa *f.*

neglect [ni'glekt] *v* no cumplir con; dejar de; no observar; descuidar; abandonar. *n* negligencia *f;* abandono *m;* inobservancia *f;* dejadez *f.* **neglected** *adj* descuidado; abandonado.

negligée ['negliʒei] *n* negligé *m.*

negligence ['neglidʒəns] *n* negligencia *f;* descuido *m.* **negligent** *adj* negligente; descuidado.

negotiate [ni'gouʃieit] *v* negociar; (*obstacle*) franquear; (*hill*) subir; (*bend*) tomar. **negotiable** *adj* negociable; franqueable. **negotiation** *n* negociación *f.*

Negro ['niigrou] *nm, adj* negro.

neigh [nei] *v* relinchar. *n* relincho *m.*

neighbour ['neibə] *n* vecino, -a *m, f.* **neighbourhood** *n* vecindad *f;* (*district*) barrio *m.* **neighbouring** *adj* vecino; (*near*) cercano. **neighbourly** *adj* de buena vecindad.

neither ['naiðə] *adv* tampoco. **neither ... nor ...** ni ... ni .... *conj* ni, tampoco. *pron* ninguno, -a *m, f. adj* ninguno de los dos.

neon ['niion] *n* neón *m.*

nephew ['nefjuɪ] *n* sobrino *m.*

nepotism ['nepɔtizəm] *n* nepotismo *m.*

nerve [nəɪv] *n* nervio *m;* valor *m;* (*coll: cheek*) cara *f.* **get on someone's nerves** crisparle los nervios a uno. **lose one's nerve** (*coll*) rajarse. **nerve-wracking** *adj* crispante; horribilante. **nerves** *pl* (*coll*) nerviosismo *m.* **nervous** *adj* nervioso;

(*apprehensive*) miedoso. **nervous breakdown** depresión nerviosa *f.*

nest [nest] *n* nido *m. v* anidar.

nestle ['nesl] *v* arrellanarse; acurrucarse.

net¹ [net] *n* red *f.* **net curtains** visillo *m sing.* **network** *n* red *f. v* coger.

net² [net] *adj* neto. **net weight** peso neto *m.*

Netherlands ['neðələndz] *pl n* Países Bajos *m pl.*

nettle ['netl] *n* ortiga *f.* **nettle rash** urticaria *f. v* irritar.

neuralgia [nju'raldʒə] *n* neuralgia *f.* **neuralgic** *adj* neurálgico.

neurosis [nju'rousis] *n* neurosis *f.* **neurotic** *n, adj* neurótico, -a.

neuter ['njuɪtə] *nm, adj* neutro.

neutral ['njuɪtrəl] *adj* neutro. *n* (*mot*) punto muerto *m.* **neutrality** *n* neutralidad *f.* **neutralize** *v* neutralizar.

never ['nevə] *adv* nunca, jamás. **neverending** *adj* sin fin. **nevermore** *adv* nunca más.

nevertheless [nevəðə'les] *adv* sin embargo, no obstante.

new [njuɪ] *adj* nuevo; fresco.

newcomer ['njuɪkʌmə] *n* recién llegado, -a *m, f.*

new-born ['njuɪbɔɪn] *adj* recién nacido, -a *m, f.*

new-fangled ['njuɪ,faŋɡəld] *adj* recién inventado.

new-laid [njuɪ'leid] *adj* (*egg*) recién puesto.

newly-wed ['njuɪli,wed] *adj* recién casado, -a *m, f.*

news [njuɪz] *n* noticias *f pl;* actualidad *f;* (*radio*) diario hablado *m;* (*TV*) telediario *m;* (*film*) noticiario *m.* **news agency** agencia de información *f.* **news flash** noticia de última hora *f.* **news item** noticia *f.* **newsletter** *n* boletín *m.* **newspaper** *n* periódico *m,* diario *m.* **newsstand** *n* quiosco de periódicos *m.*

newt [njuɪt] *n* tritón *m.*

New Testament *n* Nuevo Testamento *m.*

New Year *n* Año Nuevo *m.* **Happy New Year!** ¡feliz Año Nuevo! **New Year's Eve** nochevieja *f.*

New Zealand [njuɪ'ziilənd] *n* Nueva Zelanda *f,* Nueva Zelandia *f.* **New Zealander** neocelandés, -esa *m, f,* neozelandés, -esa *m, f.*

next [nekst] *adj* próximo; siguiente; que
viene; (*adjoining*) vecino. *adv* luego,
después; la proxima vez; ahora. *prep*
junto a, cerca de. **the next day** el día
siguiente *m*. **next-door** *adj* de al lado.
next to al lado de. **next-of-kin** *n* pariente
más cercano *m*. **who's next?** ¿a quién le
toca?

nib [nib] *n* plumilla *f.*

nibble ['nibl] *v* mordiscar, mordisquear. *n*
mordisqueo *m.*

nice [nais] *adj* (*kind*) amable; (*agreeable*)
agradable; (*likeable*) simpático; (*pretty*)
bonito; (*pleasant*) ameno; precioso;
escrupuloso; (*weather*) bueno; (*point*)
delicado. **nicely** *adv* amablemente;
agradablemente; bien. **nicety** *n* precisión
f; delicadeza *f.*

niche [nitʃ] *n* nicho *m*, hornacina *f.*

nick [nik] *n* (*notch*) muesca *f.* (*cut*) rasguño *m.* **in the nick of time** justo a tiempo.
v hacer muescas; cortar; (*slang: steal*)
birlar; (*slang: arrest*) pescar.

nickel ['nikl] *n* níquel *m.*

nickname ['nikneim] *n* apodo *m. v*
apodar.

nicotine ['nikətiːn] *n* nicotina *f.*

niece [niːs] *n* sobrina *f.*

niggle ['nigl] *v* ocuparse de menudencias.
niggling *adj* de poca monta; molesto.

night [nait] *n* noche *f.* **good night!**
¡buenas noches! **last night** anoche *f.*
tomorrow night mañana por la noche *f.*

night cap *n* (*garment*) gorro de dormir;
(*coll: drink*) bebida tomada antes de
acostarse *f.*

nightclub ['naitklʌb] *n* night club *m.*

nightdress ['naitdres] *n* camisón *m*, camisa de dormir *f.*

nightfall ['naitfoːl] *n* anochecer *m.*

nightingale ['naitiŋgeil] *n* ruiseñor *m.*

night-life ['naitlaif] *n* vida nocturna *f.*

night-light ['naitlait] *n* lamparilla *f.*

nightly ['naitli] *adj* nocturno. *adv* por las
noches; todas las noches.

nightmare ['naitmeə] *n* pesadilla *f.*

night-school ['naitˌskuːl] *n* escuela nocturna *f.*

nightshade ['naitʃeid] *n* **deadly nightshade**
belladona *f.*

night shift *n* turno de noche *m.*

night-watchman [ˌnait'wotʃmən] *n* guarda
nocturno *m*; sereno *m.*

nil [nil] *n* nada *f*; ninguno, -a *m, f*; (*sport*)
cero *m.*

nimble ['nimbl] *adj* ágil; (*mind*) vivo. **nim-
bleness** *n* agilidad *f*; vivacidad *f.*

nine [nain] *nm, adj* nueve. **dressed up to
the nines** de punta en blanco. **ninth** *n,
adj* noveno, -a.

nineteen [nain'tiːn] *nm, adj* diecinueve.
nineteenth *n, adj* decimonoveno, -a.

ninety ['nainti] *nm, adj* noventa. **ninetieth**
n, adj nonagésimo, -a.

nip[1] [nip] *v* (*pinch*) pellizcar; (*bite*)
morder; (*coll: go quickly*) pegar un salto.
nip in the bud cortar de raíz. *n* pellizco
m; mordisco *m.* **nippy** *adj* rápido; (*chilly*)
fresquito.

nip[2] [nip] *n* (*drop*) gota *f*; (*drink*) trago *m.*

nipple ['nipl] *n* (*female*) pezón *m*; (*male*)
tetilla *f*; (*bottle*) tetina *f.*

nit [nit] *n* liendre *f*; (*coll*) papanatas *m
invar.*

nitrogen ['naitrədʒən] *n* nitrógeno *m.*

no [nou] *adv* no. *adj* ninguno. **no longer**
or more ya no. **no parking** prohibido
aparcar. **no smoking** prohibido fumar. **no
thoroughfare** calle sin salida.

noble ['noubl] *n(m+f), adj* noble. **nobility**
n nobleza *f.*

nobody ['noubodi] *pron* nadie.

nocturnal [nok'təːnəl] *adj* nocturno.

nod [nod] *v* inclinar; asentir con la
cabeza; saludar con la cabeza; (*sleepily*)
dar cabezadas. *n* inclinación de cabeza *f*;
saludo con, la cabeza *m*; cabezada *f.*

noise [noiz] *n* ruido *m.* **noiseless** *adj*
silencioso. **noisy** *adj* ruidoso.

nomad ['noumad] *n* nómada *m, f.* **nomadic** *adj* nómada.

nominal ['nominl] *adj* nominal.

nominate ['nomineit] *v* (*appoint*) nombrar; (*propose*) designar. **nomination** *n*
nombramiento *m*, designación *f.*

nonchalant ['nonʃələnt] *adj* imperturbable; indiferente. **nonchalance** *n* imperturbabilidad *f*; indiferencia *f.*

nonconformist [nonkən'foːmist] *n(m+f),
adj* disidente.

nondescript   ['nondiskript]   *adj*
indescriptible.

none [nʌn] *pron* nadie; ninguno, -a. *adv*
de ningún modo, de ninguna manera.

nonentity [non'entəti] *n* nulidad *f.*

nonetheless [ˌnʌnðə'les] *adv* sin embargo,
no obstante.

non-existent [nonig'zistənt] *adj* inexis-
tente.

non-fiction [nonˈfikʃən] n literatura no novelesca f.

non-resident [nonˈrezidənt] n(m+f), adj no residente.

nonsense [ˈnonsəns] n tonterías f pl. **nonsensical** adj disparatado.

non-stop [nonˈstop] adj directo; continuo; sin escalas. adv sin parar; directamente.

noodles [ˈnuːdlz] pl n fideos m pl.

noon [nuːn] n mediodía m.

no-one [ˈnouwʌn] pron nadie.

noose [nuːs] n nudo corredizo m; lazo m; (hangman's) soga f.

nor [noː] conj ni; tampoco.

norm [noːm] n norma f.

normal [ˈnoːməl] adj normal. n lo normal m.

north [noːθ] n norte m. adj also **northerly, northern** del norte, norteño; (facing north) que da al norte. adv hacia el norte. **northbound** adj de dirección norte. **north-east** nm, adj nordeste. **north-west** nm, adj noroeste.

Norway [ˈnoːwei] n Noruega f. **Norwegian** n, adj noruego, -a.

nose [nouz] n nariz f; (sense of smell) olfato m; (aircraft, car) morro m. **blow one's nose** sonarse. **have a nosebleed** sangrar por la nariz. **nosey** adj (coll) entremetido.

nostalgia [noˈstaldʒə] n nostalgia f. **nostalgic** adj nostálgico.

nostril [ˈnostrəl] n ventanilla de la nariz f; (horse) ollar m. **nostrils** pl n narices f pl.

not [not] adv no; ni; como no; sin. **certainly not!** ¡de ninguna manera! **not at all** (acknowledging thanks) no hay de qué.

notable [ˈnoutəbl] adj notable. **notably** adv notablemente, señaladamente.

notary [ˈnoutəri] n notario m.

notch [notʃ] n (cut) muesca f; (degree) grado m. v hacer una muesca en.

note [nout] n nota f; (key of piano, organ) tecla f; (sound) sonido m; (money) billete m; (music) tono m; (renown) renombre m; marca. **notebook** n cuaderno m. **notepaper** papel de escribir m. **noteworthy** adj notable. v tomar nota de; darse cuenta de; anotar, apuntar. **noted** adj notable; célebre.

nothing [ˈnʌθiŋ] pron nada; no . . . nada. n cero m. **nothing but** sólo.

notice [ˈnoutis] n (advert) anuncio m; (poster) cartel m; (sign) letrero m; atención f; (warning) aviso m; (dismissal) despido m; (resignation) dimisión f. **notice-board** n tablón de anuncios m. **at short notice** a corto plazo. **notice to quit** desahucio m. v darse cuenta de; fijarse en; observar; ver; prestar atención. **noticeable** adj notable; evidente.

notify [ˈnoutifai] v avisar, notificar.

notion [ˈnouʃən] n idea f, concepto m.

notorious [nouˈtoːriəs] adj notorio. **notoriety** n notoriedad f.

notwithstanding [notwiðˈstandiŋ] prep a pesar de. adv sin embargo. conj por más que.

nougat [ˈnuːgaː] n turrón de almendras m.

nought [noːt] n cero m.

noun [naun] n nombre m, sustantivo m.

nourish [ˈnʌriʃ] v alimentar. **nourishing** adj alimenticio. **nourishment** n alimento m.

novel[1] [ˈnovəl] n novela f. **novelist** n novelista m, f.

novel[2] [ˈnovəl] adj nuevo; original. **novelty** n novedad f.

November [nəˈvembə] n noviembre m.

novice [ˈnovis] n novicio, -a m, f.

now [nau] adv ahora; ya; ya ahora; actualmente; inmediatamente. **from now on** de ahora en adelante. **nowadays** adv hoy día. **now and again** de vez en cuando. **up to now** hasta ahora.

nowhere [ˈnouweə] adv por ninguna parte; en ninguna parte; a ninguna parte.

noxious [ˈnokʃəs] adj nocivo.

nozzle [ˈnozl] n boca f, boquilla f.

nuance [ˈnjuːãs] n matiz m.

nuclear [ˈnjuːkliə] adj nuclear.

nucleus [ˈnjuːkliəs] n núcleo m.

nude [ˈnjuːd] nm, adj desnudo. **nudism** n nudismo m. **nudist** n(m+f), adj nudista. **nudity** n desnudez f.

nudge [nʌdʒ] v dar un codazo a. n codazo m.

nugget [ˈnʌgit] n pepita f.

nuisance [ˈnjuːsns] n (thing) molestia f; (person) molesta f. **be a nuisance** ponerse pesado. **what a nuisance!** (coll) ¡qué pesadez!

null [nʌl] adj nulo. **null and void** nulo y sin valor.

numb [nʌm] adj entumecido; (with fear) petrificado. v entumecer; dejar helado.

numbness *n* entumecimiento *m*; parálisis *f*.

number ['nʌmbə] *n* número *m*. **number plate** (*mot*) matrícula *f*. *v* numerar; contar.

numeral ['njuːmərəl] *n* número *m*, cifra *f*.

numeration [ˌnjuːmə'reiʃn] *n* numeración *f*. **numerator** *n* numerador *m*.

numerical [njuː'merikl] *adj* numérico.

numerous ['njuːmərəs] *adj* numeroso.

nun [nʌn] *n* monja *f*.

nurse [nəːs] *n* enfermera *f*; (*nanny*) niñera *f*. *v* (*the sick*) cuidar; (*suckle*) criar; (*cradle*) mecer; (*hopes*) abrigar; (*plans*) acariciar. **nursing home** clínica *f*.

nursery ['nəːsəri] *n* (*room*) habitación de los niños *f*; (*day nursery*) guardería infantil *f*; (*plants*) vivero *m*. **nursery rhyme** poesía infantil *f*. **nursery school** escuela de párvulos *f*.

nurture ['nəːtʃə] *v* nutrir, alimentar; (*rear*) criar.

nut [nʌt] *n* (*bot*) nuez *f*; (*tech*) tuerca *f*; (*person*) loco, -a *m, f*. **in a nutshell** en pocas palabras. **nutcracker** *n* cascanueces *m* *invar*. **nutmeg** *n* nuez moscada *f*.

nutrient ['njuːtriənt] *n* alimento nutritivo *m*.

nutrition [nju'triʃən] *n* nutrición *f*. **nutritious** *adj* nutritivo.

nuzzle ['nʌzl] *v* hocicar.

nylon ['nailon] *n* nilón *m*.

nymph [nimf] *n* ninfa *f*.

O

oak [ouk] *n* roble *m*.

oar [oː] *n* remo *m*. **oarsman** *n* remero *m*.

oasis [ou'eisis] *n* oasis *m* *invar*.

oath [ouθ] *n* (*law*) juramento *m*; (*expletive*) blasfemia *f*. **take the oath** prestar juramento.

oats [outs] *pl n* avena *f* *sing*. **oatmeal** *n* harina de avena *f*.

obedient [ə'biːdiənt] *adj* obediente. **obedience** *n* obediencia *f*.

obese [ə'biːs] *adj* obeso. **obesity** *n* obesidad *f*.

obey [ə'bei] *v* obedecer.

obituary [ə'bitjuəri] *n* necrología *f*.

object ['obʒikt; *v* əb'ʒekt] *n* objeto *m*;

(*gramm*) complemento *m*; (*aim*) meta *f*. *v* oponerse; objetar; protestar. **objection** *n* objeción *m*; reparo *m*. **objectionable** *adj* censurable; desagradable. **objective** *nm, adj* objetivo.

oblige [ə'blaidʒ] *v* (*compel*) obligar; (*please*) complacer; (*assist*) hacer un favor. **be obliged to** (*have to*) verse obligado a; (*be grateful*) estar agradecido a. **obligation** *n* obligación *f*; (*comm*) compromiso *m*. **obligatory** *adj* obligatorio.

oblique [ə'bliːk] *adj* sesgado; indirecto.

obliterate [ə'blitəreit] *v* borrar; cancelar. **obliteration** *n* borrado *m*; cancelación *f*.

oblivion [ə'bliviən] *n* olvido *m*. **oblivious** *adj* olvidadizo; ignorante.

oblong ['oblon] *adj* oblongo. *n* cuadrilongo *m*.

obnoxious [əb'nokʃəs] *adj* ofensivo; execrable.

oboe ['oubou] *n* oboe *m*. **oboist** *n* oboe *m*, oboísta *m, f*.

obscene [əb'siːn] *adj* obsceno. **obscenity** *n* obscenidad *f*.

obscure [əb'skjuə] *adj* oscuro; confuso. *v* oscurecer; (*hide*) esconder. **obscurity** *n* oscuridad *f*.

observe [əb'zəːv] *v* observar; ver; decir. **observant** *adj* observador; atento. **observation** *n* (*remark*) observación *f*; (*of rules*) observancia *f*. **observatory** *n* observatorio *m*.

obsess [əb'ses] *v* obsesionar. **obsession** *n* obsesión *f*.

obsolescent [obsə'lesnt] *adj* que cae en desuso. **obsolescence** *n* caída en desuso *f*.

obsolete ['obsəliːt] *adj* anticuado.

obstacle ['obstəkl] *n* obstáculo *m*.

obstetrics [ob'stetriks] *n* obstetricia *f*. **obstetrician** *n* tocólogo *m*.

obstinate ['obstinət] *adj* obstinado; terco; rebelde. **obstinacy** *n* obstinación *f*; terquedad *f*.

obstruct [əb'strʌkt] *v* obstruir; (*hinder*) estorbar. **obstruction** *n* obstrucción *f*; estorbo *m*.

obtain [əb'tein] *v* obtener, lograr; (*acquire*) adquirir; (*extract*) sacar.

obtrusive [əb'truːsiv] *adj* importuno, molesto; (*meddlesome*) entrometido. **obtrusion** *n* intrusión *f*.

obtuse [əb'tjuːs] *adj* obtuso.

obverse ['obvəːs] *n* anverso *m*. *adj* del anverso.

obvious ['obviəs] *adj* obvio.

occasion [ə'keiʒən] *n* ocasión *f*, oportunidad *f*; (*cause*) motivo *m*; circunstancia *f*. *v* ocasionar; incitar. **occasional** *adj* ocasional. **occasionally** *adv* de vez en cuando.

occult ['okʌlt] *adj* oculto. *n* **the occult** ciencias ocultas *f pl*.

occupy ['okjupai] *v* ocupar; emplear. **occupant** *n* (*place*) ocupante *m, f*; (*position*) posesor, -a *m, f*. **occupation** *n* ocupación *f*; profesión *f*; trabajo *m*. **occupational** *adj* profesional. **occupational hazard** gajes del oficio *m pl*.

occur [ə'kəi] *v* (*happen*) ocurrir, acontecer; producirse; (*opportunity*) presentarse; (*take place*) tener lugar. **occurrence** *n* acontecimiento *m*; caso *m*.

ocean ['ouʃən] *n* océano *m*. **oceanic** *adj* oceánico.

ochre ['oukə] *n* ocre *m*.

o'clock [ə'klok] *adv* **one o'clock** la una. **two/three/etc**. **o'clock** las dos/tres/etc.

octagon ['oktəgən] *n* octágono *m*. **octagonal** *adj* octagonal.

octane ['oktein] *n* octano *m*.

octave ['oktiv] *n* octava *f*.

October [ok'toubə] *n* octubre *m*.

octopus ['oktəpəs] *n* pulpo *m*.

oculist ['okjulist] *n* oculista *m, f*.

odd [od] *adj* extraño, raro; (*number*) impar; (*left over*) sobrante; (*occasional*) alguno. **odd jobs** pequeños arreglos *m pl*. **oddity** *n* (*thing*) curiosidad *f*; (*quality*) singularidad *f*. **oddment** *n* saldo *m*. **odds** *pl n* (*betting*) apuesta *f sing*; (*chances*) posibilidades *f pl*. **be at odds with** estar peleado con uno. **it makes no odds** no importa. **odds and ends** pedazos *m pl*.

ode [oud] *n* oda *f*.

odious ['oudiəs] *adj* odioso.

odour ['oudə] *n* olor *m*; perfume *m*. **odourless** *adj* inodoro.

oesophagus [iː'sofəgəs] *n* esófago *m*.

of [ov] *prep* de.

off [of] *adj* (*substandard*) malo; (*fruit, vegetables, meat, fish*) pasado; (*wine*) agriado; (*cancelled*) suspendido; (*elec*) apagado; (*water*) cortado; (*brake*) suelto. *prep* de; fuera de; a . . . de; desde; en.

offal ['ofəl] *n* asadura *f*.

off-chance [,of'tʃaɪns] *n* **on the off-chance** (*coll*) por si acaso.

off-colour [of'kʌlə] *adj* **be off-colour** (*coll*) encontrarse indispuesto.

offend [ə'fend] *v* ofender; escandalizar; (*eyes, ears*) herir. **offence** *n* ofensa *f*; escándalo *m*; (*law*) delito *m*. **take offence** ofenderse por. **offender** *n* ofensor, -a *m, f*; delincuente *m, f*. **offensive** *adj* ofensivo; chocante; insultante.

offer ['ofə] *v* ofrecer; (*proposal*) proponer; presentarse. *n* oferta *f*; propuesta *f*. **offering** *n* (*action*) oferta *f*; (*gift*) regalo *m*.

offhand [of'hand] *adj* improvisado; brusco. *adv* sin pensarlo; bruscamente.

office ['ofis] *n* (*place*) oficina *f*; (*public office*) cargo *m*; (*function*) funciones *f pl*. **take office** entrar en funciones. **officer** *n* (*mil*) oficial *m*; (*public appointee*) funcionario, -a *m, f*; (*police*) policía *f*.

official [ə'fiʃəl] *adj* oficial. *n* funcionario, -a *m, f*.

officious [ə'fiʃəs] *adj* oficioso.

offing ['ofiŋ] *n* **in the offing** en perspectiva.

off-licence ['oflaisns] *n* bodega *f*.

off-peak [of'piːk] *adj, adv* de menos tráfico; (*elec*) de menor consumo.

off-season [of'siːzn] *n* estación muerta *f*. *adv, adj* fuera de temporada.

offset [of'set; *n* 'ofset] *v* compensar; desviar. *n* (*printing*) offset *m*.

offshore ['offoi] *adj* de la costa.

offside [of'said] *n* (*mot: right*) lado derecho *m*; (*mot: left*) lado izquierdo *m*; (*sport*) fuera de juego *m*.

offspring ['ofspriŋ] *n* progenitura *f*; (*fig*) fruto *m*.

offstage [of'steidʒ] *adv, adj* entre bastidores.

off-the-cuff [ofðə'kʌf] *adj* espontáneo. *adv* de proviso.

off-white [of'wait] *adj* blancuzco.

often ['ofn] *adv* a menudo. **as often as not** la mitad de las veces. **every so often** alguna que otra vez.

ogre ['ougə] *n* ogro *m*.

oil [oil] *n* aceite *m*; petróleo *m*; (*painting*) óleo *m*; fuel *m*. **oily** *adj* (*tech*) grasiento; (*food*) aceitoso; (*skin*) graso; (*fig: manner*) zalamero.

oilcan ['oilkan] *n* aceitera *f*; (*for storage*) bidón de aceite *m*.

oilcloth ['oilkloθ] *n* hule *m*.

oil colour *n* óleo *m*.

oilfield ['oilfiːld] *n* yacimiento petrolífero *m.*

oil-fired [oil'faiəd] *adj* alimentado con mazut.

oilskin ['oilˌskin] *n* impermeable de hule *m.*

oil stove *n* estufa de mazut *f.*

oil tanker *n* petrolero *m.*

oil well *n* pozo de petróleo *m.*

ointment ['ointmənt] *n* ungüento *m.*

O.K. [ou'kei] *interj* ¡de acuerdo!

old [ould] *adj* viejo; antiguo; (*adult*) mayor; (*clothes*) usado; (*wine*) añejo; (*other food*) pasado; (*familiar*) conocido. **I am six years old** tengo seis años. **how old is he?** ¿cuántos años tiene? **old age** vejez *f.* **old-age pensioner** pensionista *m, f.* **old-fashioned** *adj* chapado a la antigua; pasado de moda. **old maid** solterona *f.*

olive ['oliv] *n* (*fruit*) aceituna *f,* oliva *f;* (*tree*) olivo *m.* **olive green** *nm, adj* verde oliva *m.* **olive oil** aceite de oliva *m.*

Olympic [ə'limpik] *adj* olímpico. **Olympic Games** juegos olímpicos *m pl.*

omelette ['omlit] *n* tortilla *f.*

omen ['oumən] *n* presagio *m,* augurio *m.*

ominous ['ominəs] *adj* amenazador.

omit [ou'mit] *v* omitir; suprimir. **omission** *n* omisión *f;* olvido *m.*

omnipotent [om'nipətənt] *adj* omnipotente. **omnipotence** *n* omnipotencia *f.*

on [on] *pron* en, sobre; a. **oncoming** *adj* venidero. **onlooker** *n* espectador, -a *m, f.* **onset** *n* principio *m;* ataque *m.* **onshore** *adj* hacia la tierra. **onslaught** *n* ataque violento *m.* **onward(s)** *adj, adv* hacia adelante. **from now onwards** de ahora en adelante.

once [wʌns] *adv* una vez; (*formerly*) antes, hace tiempo. *conj* una vez que. **at once** en seguida. **once again** una vez más. **once and for all** de una vez para siempre.

one [wʌn] *n, pron, adj* uno, -a *m, f.* **be one up on** marcar un tanto a costa de. **one by one** uno por uno. **one-sided** *adj* parcial; desigual. **one-way** *adj* de dirección única. **that one** ése *or* aquél, ésa *or* aquélla. **this one** éste, ésta. **which one?** ¿cuál?

oneself [wʌn'self] *pron* se; sí; sí mismo, -a; (*emphatic*) uno mismo, una misma. **by oneself** solo, -a.

onion ['ʌnjən] *n* cebolla *f.*

only ['ounli] *adj* solo; único. *adv* sólo, solamente. *conj* pero, sólo que.

onus ['ounəs] *n* responsabilidad *f.*

onyx ['oniks] *n* ónice *m, f.*

ooze [uːz] *v* rezumar; exudar.

opal ['oupəl] *n* ópalo *m.*

opaque [ə'paik] *adj* opaco; oscuro. **opacity** *n* opacidad *f;* oscuridad *f.*

open ['oupən] *v* abrir; (*exhibition*) inaugurar; iniciar. *adj* abierto; (*unfolded*) desplegado; (*frank*) franco; (*meeting*) público; (*unsolved*) pendiente; (*post*) vacante; (*free*) libre; (*sea*) alta. **open-air** *adj* al aire libre. **open-handed** *adj* generoso. **open-minded** *adj* imparcial. **open-mouthed** *adj, adv* boquiabierto.

opening ['oupəniŋ] *n* abertura *f;* inauguración *f;* oportunidad *f;* vacante *f;* principio *m;* (*act of opening*) apertura *f;* (*breach*) brecha *f. adj* inaugural. **opening night** noche de estreno *f.*

opera ['opərə] *n* ópera *f.* **opera glasses** *pl* prismáticos *m pl.* **opera house** ópera *f.* **opera singer** cantante de ópera *m, f.* **operatic** *adj* operístico. **operetta** *n* opereta *f,* zarzuela *f.*

operate ['opəreit] *v* (*machine*) manjar; (hacer) funcionar; (*direct*) dirigir; (*med*) operar. **operable** *adj* operable. **operating table** quirófano *m.* **operation** *n* funcionamiento *m;* manejo *m;* maniobra *f;* aplicación *f;* actividad *f.* **in operation** en vigor; en funcionamiento. **operational** *adj* operacional. **operative** *adj* en vigor; operativo; eficaz. **operator** *n* operario, -a *m, f;* maquinista *m, f;* telefonista *m, f;* (*tour*) agente de viajes; (*wireless*) radiotelegrafista *m.*

ophthalmic [of'θalmik] *adj* oftálmico.

opinion [ə'pinjən] *n* opinión *f.* **in my opinion** a mi parecer. **public opinion poll** sondeo de la opinión pública *m.*

opium ['oupiəm] *n* opio *m.*

opponent [ə'pounənt] *n* adversario, -a *m, f;* contrario, -a *m, f.*

opportune [opə'tjuɪn] *adj* oportuno. **opportunism** *n* oportunismo *m.* **opportunist** *n(m + f),* adj oportunista.

opportunity [opə'tjuɪnəti] *n* oportunidad *f.*

oppose [ə'pouz] *v* oponerse a. **opposed** *adj* opuesto. **be opposed to** oponerse a. **opposition** *n* oposición *f;* resistencia *f.*

opposite ['opəzit] *adj* opuesto; contrario. **the opposite sex** el otro sexo. *prep* enfrente de, frente a. *n* lo opuesto, lo contrario.

oppress [ə'pres] *v* oprimir. **oppression** *n* opresión *f*. **oppressive** *adj* opresor, opresivo; (*heat*) sofocante; (*mentally*) agobiante. **oppressor** *n* opresor, -a *m, f*.

opt [opt] *v* **opt out of** no meterse. **opt to** optar por.

optical ['optikl] *adj* óptico. **optical illusion** ilusión óptica *f*. **optician** *n* óptico *m*.

optimism ['optimizəm] *n* optimismo *m*. **optimist** *n* optimista *m, f*. **optimistic** *adj* optimista.

optimum ['optiməm] *adj* óptimo. *n* lo óptimo.

option ['opʃən] *n* opción *f*; posibilidad *f*; elección *f*. **optional** *adj* facultativo.

opulent ['opjulənt] *adj* opulento; abundante. **opulence** *n* opulencia *f*.

or [oɪ] *conj* o; (*negative*) ni. **or else** si no. **or not** o no.

oracle ['orəkl] *n* oráculo *m*.

oral ['oɪrəl] *nm, adj* oral.

orange ['orindʒ] *n* (*fruit*) naranja *f*; (*tree*) naranjo *m*; (*colour*) naranja *m*. *adj* naranja. **orangeade** *n* naranjada *f*.

orator ['orətə] *n* orador, -a *m, f*. **orate** *v* perorar. **oration** *n* oración *f*. **oratory** *n* oratoria *f*.

orbit ['oɪbit] *n* órbita *f*. *v* estar en órbita; dar vueltas.

orchard ['oɪtʃəd] *n* huerto *m*; (*apple*) manzanal *m*; (*pear*) peral *m*.

orchestra ['oɪkəstrə] *n* orquesta *f*. **orchestral** *adj* orquestal. **orchestrate** *v* orquestar. **orchestration** *n* orquestación *f*.

orchid ['oɪkid] *n* orquídea *f*.

ordain [oɪ'dein] *v* (*rel*) ordenar; (*fate*) destinar. **ordination** *n* ordenación *f*.

ordeal [oɪ'diɪl] *n* sufrimiento *m*.

order ['oɪdə] *n* orden *m*; (*rel*) orden *f*; (*comm*) pedido *m*; (*medal*) condecoración *f*. **in order** (*correct*) en regla. **in order to** para. **out of order** no funcionar. *v* ordenar; organizar; clasificar; pedir; mandar.

orderly ['oɪdəli] *adj* ordenado; metódico; disciplinado. *n* (*mil*) ordenanza *m*.

ordinal ['oɪdinl] *adj* ordinal.

ordinary ['oɪdənəri] *adj* corriente, usual; (*mediocre*) ordinario; simple; (*average*) medio. *n* lo corriente, lo ordinario. **out of the ordinary** extraordinario, excepcional.

ore [oɪ] *n* mineral *m*.

oregano [ori'gaɪnou] *n* orégano *m*.

organ ['oɪgən] *n* órgano *m*. **organist** *n* organista *m, f*.

organic [oɪ'ganik] *adj* orgánico.

organism ['oɪgənizəm] *n* organismo *m*.

organize ['oɪgənaiz] *v* organizar. **organization** *n* organización *f*. **organizer** *n* organizador, -a *m, f*.

orgasm ['oɪgazəm] *n* orgasmo *m*.

orgy ['oɪdʒi] *n* orgía *f*.

oriental [oɪri'entl] *n*(*m*+*f*), *adj* oriental. **orientate** ['oɪriənteit] *v* orientar. **orientation** *n* orientación *f*.

orifice ['orifis] *n* orificio *m*.

origin ['oridʒin] *n* origen *m*. **originate** *v* originar, provocar; comenzar. **originate from** ser descendiente de. **originator** *n* autor, -a *m, f*; creador, -a *m, f*.

original [ə'ridʒinl] *adj* original; (*first*) primero. *n* original *m*. **originally** *adv* al principio; con originalidad.

ornament ['oɪnəmənt] *n* ornamento *m*, adorno *m*. *v* ornamentar, adornar. **ornamental** *adj* ornamental, de adorno.

ornate [oɪ'neit] *adj* recargado.

ornithology [oɪni'θolədʒi] *n* ornitología *f*. **ornithological** *adj* ornitológico. **ornithologist** *n* ornitólogo *m*.

orphan ['oɪfən] *n, adj* huérfano, -a. *v* dejar huérfano. **orphanage** *n* orfanato *m*.

orthodox ['oɪθədoks] *adj* ortodoxo. **orthodoxy** *n* ortodoxia *f*.

orthopaedic [oɪθə'piɪdik] *adj* ortopédico.

oscillate ['osileit] *v* oscilar; fluctuar. **oscillation** *n* oscilación *f*; fluctuación *f*.

ostensible [o'stensəbl] *adj* aparente. **ostensibly** *adv* aparentemente.

ostentatious [osten'teiʃəs] *adj* ostentoso. **ostentation** *n* ostentación *f*.

osteopath ['ostiəpaθ] *n* osteópata *m, f*.

ostracize ['ostrəsaiz] *v* condenar al ostracismo. **ostracism** *n* ostracismo *m*.

ostrich ['ostritʃ] *n* avestruz *m*.

other ['ʌðə] *pron, adj* otro, -a. **other than** de otra manera que.

otherwise ['ʌðəwaiz] *adj* distinto. *adv* de otra manera; a parte de eso.

otter ['otə] *n* nutria *f*.

***ought** [oɪt] *v* deber; tener que.

our [auə] *pron* nuestro, -a; el nuestro, la nuestra. *adj* nuestro.

ours [auəz] *pron* nuestro, -a; el nuestro, la nuestra.

ourselves [auə'selvz] *pron* nos; nosotros, nosotras; (*emphatic*) nosotros mismos, nosotras mismas. **by ourselves** solos, solas.

oust [aust] v expulsar, echar.

out [aut] adj fuera; (light, fire, etc.) apagado; (games) eliminado. **out loud** en voz alta. **out of** fuera de; (through) por; (from) de; (without) no tener, sin.

outboard ['autbɔɪd] adj fuera borda, fuera bordo.

outbreak ['autbreik] n (start) comienzo m; (disease) epidemia f; (spots) erupción f; (violence, crime) ola f; (revolution) motín m; (temper) arrebato m.

outbuilding ['autbildiŋ] n dependencia f.

outburst ['autbɔɪst] n explosión f; (applause) salvo m; (temper) arrebato m.

outcast ['autkaɪst] n proscrito, -a m, f; paria m, f.

outcome ['autkʌm] n resultado m; consecuencias f pl.

outcry ['autkrai] n (noise) alboroto m; protesta f.

*****outdo** [aut'duɪ] v superar.

outdoor ['autdɔɪ] adj al aire libre; (clothes) de calle. **outdoors** adv fuera; al aire libre.

outer ['autə] adj externo, exterior. **outer space** espacio exterior m.

outfit ['autfit] n (gear) equipo m; (clothes) ropa f; (lady's costume) conjunto m.

outgoing [aut'gouiŋ] adj saliente; (manner) sociable. **outgoings** pl n gastos m pl.

*****outgrow** [aut'grou] v crecer más que; (lose) perder con la edad. **outgrowth** n excrecencia f.

outing ['autiŋ] n excursión f; paseo m.

outlandish [aut'landiʃ] adj extraño; apartado.

outlaw ['autlɔ] n proscrito, -a m, f. v proscribir; declarar ilegal.

outlay ['autlei] n gastos m pl.

outlet ['autlit] n salida f; (drain) desaguadero m; (elec) toma f; (comm) mercado m.

outline ['autlain] n contorno m; perfil m; silueta f; (draft) bosquejo m; (summary) resumen m; (map) trazado m; (sketch) esbozo m. v perfilar; bosquejar; resumir; trazar.

outlive [aut'liv] v sobrevivir.

outlook ['autluk] n vista f; punto de vista m.

outlying ['autlaiiŋ] adj exterior; remoto.

outnumber [aut'nʌmbə] v exceder en número.

out-of-date [autəv'deit] adj anticuado; pasado de moda.

outpatient ['autpeiʃənt] n paciente no internado m.

outpost ['autpoust] n puesto avanzado m.

output ['autput] n producción f; (tech) rendimiento m; (power) potencia f.

outrage ['autreidʒ] n ultraje m; desafuero m. v ultrajar.

outrageous [aut'reidʒəs] adj ultrajante; escandaloso.

outright [aut'rait; adj 'autrait] adv francamente; (entirely) en su totalidad; (at once) en el acto. adj completo; absoluto; categórico; franco.

outset ['autset] n principio m. **at the outset** al principio.

outside [aut'said; adj 'autsaid] adv fuera, afuera. prep fuera de; más allá de. n exterior m. adj exterior, externo; al aire libre; remoto; independiente. **outsider** n (to a group) intruso, -a m, f; (to a place) forastero, -a m, f; (horse racing) caballo no favorito m.

outsize ['autsaiz] adj de talla muy grande.

outskirts ['autskɔɪts] pl n afueras f pl; cercanías f pl.

outspoken [aut'spoukən] adj franco. **outspokenness** n franqueza f.

outstanding [aut'standiŋ] adj destacado, notable; (features) sobresaliente; (success) excepcional; (debt) pendiente; (still to be done) por hacer.

outstrip [aut'strip] v dejar atrás.

outward ['autwəd] adj exterior; (journey) de ida. **outward bound** que sale. **outwardly** adv exteriormente; aparentemente. **outwards** adv hacia fuera.

outweigh [aut'wei] v pesar más que; (value) valer más que.

outwit [aut'wit] v burlar.

oval ['ouvəl] adj oval, ovalado. n óvalo m.

ovary ['ouvəri] n ovario m.

ovation [ou'veiʃən] n ovación f.

oven ['ʌvn] n horno m. **ovenproof** adj de horno.

over ['ouvə] adv encima, por encima; (too much) demasiado; al otro lado. adj (finished) terminado. prep sobre, encima de; al otro lado de; superior a; durante.

overall ['ouvərɔ:l] adj de conjunto; total. adv en conjunto; por todas partes. **overalls** pl n guardapolvo m sing.

overbalance [ouvə'baləns] v (hacer) perder el equilibrio.

overbearing [ouvə'beəriŋ] adj dominante, autoritario.

overboard ['ouvəbɔːd] adv (fall) por la borda. **go overboard** (coll) pasarse de la raya. **man overboard!** ¡hombre al agua!

overcast [ouvə'kɑːst] adj nublado.

overcharge [ouvə'tʃɑːdʒ] v cobrar un precio excesivo; (overload) sobrecargar.

overcoat ['ouvəkout] n abrigo m, sobretodo m.

***overcome** [ouvə'kʌm] v vencer; triunfar. **be overcome by** estar muerto de.

overcrowded [ouvə'kraudid] adj atestado; superpoblado. **overcrowding** n atestamiento m; superpoblación f.

***overdo** [ouvə'duː] v exagerar; (exhaust) fatigarse demasiado.

overdose ['ouvədous] n dosis excesiva f.

overdraft ['ouvədrɑːft] n giro en descubierto m.

***overdraw** [ouvə'drɔː] v girar en descubierto. **be overdrawn** adj tener un descubierto en su cuenta.

overdue [ouvə'djuː] adj (train, etc.) atrasado; (comm) vencido y sin pagar.

overestimate [ouvə'estimeit] v sobreestimar.

overexpose [ouvəik'spouz] v (phot) sobreexponer.

overflow [ouvə'flou; n 'ouvəflou] v (flow over) derramarse; (flood) inundar. n desbordamiento m; derrame m; inundación f; (pipe) cañería de desagüe f.

overgrown [ouvə'groun] adj cubierto de hierba; (too big) demasiado crecido para su edad.

***overhang** [ouvə'haŋ; n 'ouvəhaŋ] v sobresalir. n saliente m. **overhanging** adj saliente, sobresaliente.

overhaul [ouvə'hɔːl] v investigar; revisar. n examen m, revisión f; arreglo m.

overhead [ouvə'hed] adv arriba. adj de arriba. **overheads** pl n gastos generales m pl.

***overhear** [ouvə'hiə] v oir (por casualidad); sorprender.

overheat [ouvə'hiːt] v recalorar; (fig) acalorar.

overjoyed [ouvə'dʒɔid] adj contentísimo.

overland [ouvə'land] adv por vía terrestre. adj terrestre.

overlap [ouvə'lap; n 'ouvəlap] v traslapar. n traslapo m.

***overlay** [ouvə'lei; n 'ouvəlei] v revestir. n revestimiento m; cubierta f.

overleaf [ouvə'liːf] adv a la vuelta.

overload [ouvə'loud; n 'ouvəloud] v sobrecargar. n sobrecarga f.

overlook [ouvə'luk] v (miss) no notar; (ignore) no darse cuenta de; (excuse) perdonar; (command a view) dar a; dominar.

overnight [ouvə'nait] adv (during the night) por la noche; (suddenly) de la noche a la mañana. **stay overnight** pasar la noche. adj (journey) de noche; (stay) por una noche.

overpower [ouvə'pauə] v subyugar; (smell, etc.) trastornar; dominar. **overpowering** adj (desire) irresistible; abrumador.

overrated [ouvə'reitid] adj sobreestimado.

***override** [ouvə'raid] v (ride over) pasar por encima de; dominar; (fig) anular, rechazar. **overriding** adj principal.

overrule [ouvə'ruːl] v denegar, no admitir.

***overrun** [ouvə'rʌn] v (exceed) rebasar; (overflow) derramarse; (invade) invadir; (flood) inundar; (infest) plagar.

overseas [ouvə'siːz] adv en ultramar. adj de ultramar; (foreign) extranjero; (comm) exterior.

overseer [ouvə'siə] n capataz m; inspector, -a m, f.

overshadow [ouvə'ʃadou] v sombrear; (fig) eclipsar.

***overshoot** [ouvə'ʃuːt] v ir más allá de.

oversight ['ouvəsait] n descuido m; omisión f. **through an oversight** por descuido.

***oversleep** [ouvə'sliːp] v dormir demasiado.

overspill ['ouvəspil] n exceso m.

overt [ou'vɜːt] adj abierto; manifiesto. **overtly** adv evidentemente.

***overtake** [ouvə'teik] v (pass) adelantar; (catch up) alcanzar.

***overthrow** [ouvə'θrou; n 'ouvəθrou] v (overturn) volcar; (plans) desbaratar; (government) derrocar; (empire) derrumbar. n desbaratamiento m; derrocamiento m; derrumbamiento m.

overtime ['ouvətaim] n horas extraordinarias f pl.

overtone ['ouvətoun] n (music) armónico m; (fig) alusión f.

overture ['ouvətjuə] n (music) obertura f; (proposal) propuesta f.

overturn [ouvə'tɜɪn] v (car) volcar; (government, etc.) derrocar.
overweight [ouvə'weit] adj be **overweight** pesar demasiado.
overwhelm [ouvə'welm] v (conquer) vencer; (with grief) postrar; (work) inundar; (in argument) confundir; (joy) rebosar. **overwhelming** adj (desire) irresistible; (defeat) aplastante; (work) abrumador.
overwork [ouvə'wɜɪk] v usar demasiado; hacer trabajar demasiado. n exceso de trabajo m.
overwrought [ouvə'rɔɪt] adj sobreexcitado, neviosisimo.
ovulation [ovju'leiʃn] n ovulación f.
owe [ou] v deber; tener deudas. **owing** adj que se debe. **owing to** debido a.
owl [aul] n lechuza f.
own [oun] v tener, poseer; (acknowledge) reconocer. **own up** confesar. adj propio. **get one's own back** desquitarse. **on one's own** solo, sola. **owner** n dueño, -a m, f; poseedor, -a m, f. **ownership** n propiedad f; posesión f.
ox [oks] n, pl **oxen** buey m. **oxtail** n rabo de buey m.
oxygen ['oksidʒən] n oxigeno m. **oxygen tent** cámara de oxigeno f.
oyster ['oistə] n ostra f.

P

pace [peis] n paso m; (gait) andar m; (horse) andadura f; (speed) velocidad f. **keep pace with** ajustarse al paso de; (events) mantenerse al corriente de. v andar; recorrer. **pace up and down** dar vueltas.
pacific [pə'sifik] adj pacifico.
Pacific Ocean n Océano Pacifico m.
pacifism ['pasifizəm] n pacifismo m. **pacifist** n(m+f), adj pacifista.
pacify ['pasifai] v pacificar; calmar.
pack [pak] n (gang) partida f; (hounds) jauría f; (cards) baraja f; (bundle) bulto m; (med) paño m, compresa f. **packhorse** n caballo de carga m. v embalar; envasar; (suitcase) hacer; (cram) apretar. **pack it in** (coll) dejarlo. **packing** n embalaje m; envase m.

package ['pakidʒ] n paquete m; (bundle) fardo m. adj (deal) acuerdo global m; (holiday, tour) viaje todo comprendido m. v embalar; envasar.
packet ['pakit] n paquete m; (tea, etc.) sobre m; (cigarettes) cajetilla f.
pact [pakt] n pacto m.
pad¹ [pad] n (paper) bloc m; (blotting) carpeta f; (ink) tampón m; (cushion) almohadilla f; (launching) plataforma de lanzamiento f. v acolchar; rellenar. **pad out** (coll) meter paja en. **padding** n acolchado m; relleno m; (fig) paja f.
pad² [pad] v andar a pasos quedos.
paddle¹ ['padl] n (oar) canalete m; (waterwheel) álabe m. **paddle boat** or **steamer** vapor de ruedas m. v remar con canalete.
paddle² ['padl] n (wade) chapotear.
paddock ['padək] n paddock m.
padlock ['padlok] n candado m. v cerrar con candado.
paediatric [piɪdi'atrik] adj pediátrico. **paediatrician** n pediatra m, pediatra m. **paediatrics** n pediatria f.
pagan ['peigən] n, adj pagano, -a.
page¹ [peidʒ] n (book) página f.
page² [peidʒ] n also **page-boy** (hotel) botones m invar; (court, wedding) paje m. v (person) hacer llamar por un paje.
pageant ['padʒənt] n desfile histórico m. **pageantry** n aparato m, pompa f.
paid [peid] V **pay**.
pail [peil] n cubo m.
pain [pein] n dolor m. **painkiller** n calmante m. **pains** pl n (effort) esfuerzo m. **painstaking** adj concienzudo; cuidadoso. v doler; afligir. **painful** adj doloroso; (embarrassing) difícil. **painless** adj sin dolor; (easy) fácil.
paint [peint] n pintura f. **paintbox** n caja de pinturas f. **paintbrush** (artist) pincel m; (house painter) brocha f. **paint roller** rodillo m. v pintar; (fig) describir. **painter** n pintor, -a m, f. **painting** n pintura f; (picture) cuadro m.
pair [peə] n (objects) par m; (people, animals) pareja f; (oxen) yunta f; (horses) tronco m. v (socks, etc.) emparejar; (mate) aparearse. **pair off** (people) formar pareja.
pal [pal] n (coll) amigote m; camarada m, f.
palace ['paləs] n palacio m. **palatial** adj magnifico; suntuoso.

palate ['palit] *n* paladar *m*. **palatable** *adj* sabroso; *(fig)* agradable.
pale [peil] *adj* pálido. *v* palidecer. **paleness** *n* palidez *f*.
palette ['palit] *n* paleta *f*.
pall¹ [poːl] *v* perder el sabor; aburrirse (de).
pall² [poːl] *n* paño mortuorio *m*; *(smoke)* cortina *f*; *(snow)* capa *f*.
pallid ['palid] *adj* pálido.
palm¹ [paɪm] *n (hand)* palma *f*. **palm off** *(coll)* colar. **palmist** *n* quiromántico, -a *m*, *f*. **palmistry** *n* quiromancia *f*.
palm² [paɪm] *n (tree)* palma *f*, palmera *f*.
palpitate ['palpiteit] *v* palpitar. **palpitation** *n* palpitación *f*.
paltry ['poːltri] *adj* miserable.
pamper ['pampə] *v* mimar.
pamphlet ['pamflit] *n* folleto *m*.
pan [pan] *n* cacerola *f*.
Panama [panə'maɪ] *n* Panamá *m*. **Panama City** *n* Panamá.
pancake ['pankeik] *n* pancake *m*. **Pancake Tuesday** martes de carnaval.
pancreas ['paŋkriəs] *n* páncreas *m*. **pancreatic** *adj* pancreático.
panda ['pandə] *n* panda *m*.
pandemonium [pandi'mouniəm] *n* pandemonio *m*.
pander ['pandə] *v* **pander to** complacer.
pane [pein] *n* vidrio *m*, cristal *m*.
panel ['panl] *n (door)* panel *m*; *(wall)* lienzo *m*; *(dress)* paño *m*; *(control)* tablero *m*; *(experts)* grupo *m*; *(judges)* jurado *m*. *v* revestir con paneles; artesonar. **panelist** *n* miembro del jurado *m*. **panelling** *n* revestimiento de madera *m*; artesonado *m*.
pang [paŋ] *n (pain, hunger)* punzada *f*; *(jealousy)* angustia *f*; *(love)* herida *f*; *(conscience)* remordimiento *m*.
panic ['panik] *n* pánico *m*. **panic-stricken** *adj* preso de pánico. *v* asustarse.
panorama [panə'raɪmə] *n* panorama *m*. **panoramic** *adj* panorámico.
pansy ['panzi] *n* pensamiento *m*.
pant [pant] *v* jadear. *n* jadeo *m*.
panther ['panθə] *n* pantera *f*.
pantomime ['pantəmaim] *n (mime)* pantomima *f*.
pantry ['pantri] *n* despensa *f*.
pants [pants] *pl n (underpants)* calzoncillos *m pl*; *(coll: trousers)* pantalones *m pl*.
papal ['peipl] *adj* papal.

paper ['peipə] *n* papel *m*; *(news)* periódico *m*, diario *m*; *(blotting)* papel secante *m*; *(brown)* papel de estraza *m*; *(carbon)* papel carbón *m*; *(drawing)* papel de dibujo *m*; *(greaseproof)* papel vegetal *m*; *(tissue)* papel de seda *m*; *(toilet)* papel higiénico *m*; *(writing)* papel de escribir *m*; *(identity)* documentación *f*. *v (walls)* empapelar.
paperback ['peipəbak] *n* libro en rústica *m*.
paper bag *n* saco de papel *m*.
paper-boy *n* repartidor de periódicos *m*.
paper-clip *n* sujetapapeles *m invar*.
paper-knife *n* cortapapeles *m invar*.
paper-mill *n* fábrica de papel *f*.
paper shop *n (coll)* vendedor de periódicos *m*.
paperweight ['peipəweit] *n* pisapapeles *m invar*.
paperwork ['peipəwəɪk] *n* papeleo *m*.
paprika ['paprikə] *n* paprika *f*.
par [paɪ] *n* igualdad *f*; *(comm)* par *f*; *(golf)* recorrido normal *m*. **be on a par with** correr parejas con. **feel below par** *(coll)* no sentirse bien.
parable ['parəbl] *n* parábola *f*.
parachute ['parəʃuɪt] *n* paracaídas *m invar*. *v* saltar con paracaídas. **parachutist** *n* paracaidista *m*, *f*.
parade [pə'reid] *n* alarde *m*; *(mil)* desfile *m*; *(promenade)* paseo público *m*. *v (display)* hacer alarde de; hacer desfilar; *(placard)* pasear.
paradise ['parədais] *n* paraíso *m*.
paradox ['parədoks] *n* paradoja *f*. **paradoxical** *adj* paradójico.
paraffin ['parəfin] *n (solid)* parafina *f*; *(fuel)* petróleo *m*.
paragraph ['parəgraɪf] *m* párrafo *m*. **new paragraph** punto y aparte.
parallel ['parəlel] *adj* paralelo. *n* paralela *f*. **parallelogram** *n* paralelogramo *m*.
paralyse ['parəlaiz] *v* paralizar. **paralysis** *n* parálisis *f*. **paralytic** *n*, *adj* paralítico, -a. *adj (coll: drunk)* como una cuba.
paramilitary [parə'militəri] *adj* paramilitar.
paramount ['parəmaunt] *adj* supremo.
paranoia [parə'noiə] *n* paranoia *f*. **paranoid** *n*, *adj* paranoico, -a.
parapet ['parəpit] *n* parapeto *m*.
paraphernalia [parəfə'neiliə] *n* avíos *m pl*.

paraphrase ['parəfreiz] *n* paráfrasis *f*. *v* parafrasear.

paraplegic [ˌparə'pliːdʒik] *n*, *adj* parapléjico, -a.

parasite ['parəsait] *n* parásito *m*. **parasitic** *adj* parasito.

parasol ['parəsol] *n* parasol *m*.

paratrooper ['parəˌtruːpə] *n* soldado paracaidista *m*.

parcel ['paːsəl] *n* paquete *m*; (*portion*) parcela *f*. **parcel office** despacho de paquetes *m*. **parcel post** servicio de paquetes *m*. *v also* **parcel up** empaquetar.

parch [paːtʃ] *v* (*land*) resecar; (*person*) abrasar; **be parched with thirst** abrasarse de sed.

parchment ['paːtʃmənt] *n* pergamino *m*.

pardon ['paːdn] *n* perdón *m*; (*law*) indulto *m*; (*rel*) indulgencia *f*. *v* perdonar; disculpar; indultar. **pardon?** ¿cómo? **I beg your pardon** dispénseme.

pare [peə] *v* reducir; (*vegetables*) pelar; (*fruit*) mondar.

parent ['peərənt] *n* padre, madre *m*, *f*. **parents** *pl n* padres *m pl*. **parental** *adj* de los padres. **parenthood** *n* paternidad *f*, maternidad *f*.

parenthesis [pə'renθəsis] *n* paréntesis *m invar*. **in parentheses** entre paréntesis.

Paris ['paris] *n* París.

parish ['pariʃ] *n* parroquia *f*; (*civil*) municipio *m*. **parish church** iglesia parroquial *f*. **parishioner** *n* parroquiano, -a *m*, *f*.

parity ['pariti] *n* paridad *f*.

park [paːk] *n* parque (público) *m*. **car park** aparcamiento de coches *m*. *v* aparcar. **parking** *n* estacionamiento *m*. **parking meter** parcómetro *m*. **parking ticket** multa por aparcamiento indebido *f*.

parliament ['paːləmənt] *n* parlamento *m*. **parliamentary** *adj* parlamentario.

parlour ['paːlə] *n* salón *m*; sala de recibir *f*.

parochial [pə'roukiəl] *adj* parroquial; (*derog*) pueblerino.

parody ['parədi] *n* parodia *f*. *v* parodiar.

parole [pə'roul] *n* libertad bajo palabra *f*.

paroxysm ['parəksizəm] *n* paroxismo *m*; (*joy*, *anger*, *etc*.) ataque *m*.

parrot ['parət] *n* loro *m*. **parrot fashion** como un loro.

parsley ['paːsli] *n* perejil *m*.

parsnip ['paːsnip] *n* pastinaca *f*.

parson ['paːsn] *n* (*priest*) cura *m*; (*Protestant*) pastor *m*. **parsonage** *n* casa del cura *f*.

part [paːt] *n* parte *f*; (*role*) papel *m*; (*tech*) pieza *f*. **on my part** di mi parte. **part exchange** cambio de un objeto por otro pagando la diferencia. **part-time** *adv* a media jornada; *adj* de media jornada. *v* dividir; separar; (*leave*) despedirse. **part one's hair** hacerse la raya. **part with** tener que separarse de. **parting** *n* separación *f*; despedida *f*; (*hair*) raya *f*. **partly** *adv* en parte.

*partake** [paːteik] *v* **partake of** compartir.

partial ['paːʃəl] *adj* parcial. **be partial to** ser aficionado a. **partiality** *n* parcialidad *f*; inclinación *f*.

participate [paː'tisipeit] *v* participar. **participant** *n* partícipe *m*, *f*. **participation** *n* participación *f*.

participle ['paːtisipl] *n* participio *m*.

particle ['paːtikl] *n* partícula *f*; (*dust*, *etc*.) grano *m*; (*fig*) pizca *f*.

particular [pə'tikjulə] *adj* particular; detallado; exigente. *n* detalle *m*. **in particular** particularmente. **I'm not particular** me da igual. **full particulars** información completa *f*.

partisan [paːti'zan] *n* partidario, -a *m*, *f*; (*mil*) guerrillero *m*. **partisanship** *n* partidismo *m*.

partition [paː'tiʃən] *n* división *f*; (*section*) parte *f*. *v* dividir; repartir.

partner ['paːtnə] *n* (*comm*) asociado, -a *m*, *f*, socio, -a *m*, *f*; (*dancing*) pareja *f*; (*cards*, *etc*.) compañero, -a *m*, *f*; (*marriage*) cónyuge *m*, *f*. *v* asociarse con; ser pareja de. **partnership** *n* asociación *f*; (*firm*) sociedad *f*. **go into partnership with** asociarse con.

partridge ['paːtridʒ] *n* perdiz *f*.

party ['paːti] *n* (*pol*) partido *m*; (*law*) parte *f*; (*reception*) fiesta *f*; (*gathering*) reunión *f*. **party line** (*phone*) línea telefónica compartida *f*; (*pol*) línea política del partido *f*.

pass [paːs] *v* pasar; (*exam*) aprobar; (*be acceptable*) aceptarse; **pass away** *or* **on** (*die*) pasar a mejor vida. **pass out** (*faint*) desmayarse. **pass round** (*detour*) dar la vuelta a; (*distribute*) pasar de mano en mano. **pass up** (*decline*) rechazar. *n* (*permit*) pase *m*; (*exam*) aprobado *m*; (*mountain*) desfiladero *m*; (*sport*) pase *m*.

passage ['pasidʒ] *n* (*way*) pasaje *m*; (*alley*) callejón *m*; (*house*) corredor *m*; (*time*) paso *m*; (*literature*) trozo *m*; (*bill*) aprobación *f*; (*sea voyage*) travesía *f*.
passenger ['pasindʒə] *n* pasajero, -a *m, f*.
passer-by [,paisə'bai] *n* transeúnte *m, f*.
passion ['paʃən] *n* pasión *f*; (*anger*) cólera *f*. **passionate** *adj* apasionado; colérico.
passive ['pasiv] *adj* pasivo. *n* (*gramm*) voz pasiva *f*. **passiveness** *also* **passivity** *n* pasividad *f*.
Passover ['paisouvə] *n* pascua (de los Judíos) *f*.
passport ['paispoit] *n* pasaporte *m*.
password ['paiswəid] *n* contraseña *f*.
past [paist] *nm, adj* pasado. *prep* por delante de; (*beyond*) más allá de; (*time*) más de. **twenty past nine** las nueve y veinte. **go past** pasar.
pasta ['pastə] *n* pastas *f pl*.
paste [peist] *n* (*meat*) .pasta *f*; (*glue*) engrudo *m*; (*jewellery*) estrás *m*. *v* pegar.
pastel ['pastəl] *n* pastel *m*.
pasteurize ['pastʃəraiz] *v* pasteurizar. **pasteurization** *n* pasteurización *f*.
pastime ['paistaim] *n* pasatiempo *m*.
pastoral ['paistərəl] *adj* pastoril; (*rel*) pastoral.
pastry ['peistri] *n* (*dough*) pasta *f*; (*cakes*) pasteles *m pl*. **puff pastry** hojaldre *m*. **pastry-cook** *n* pastelero *m*.
pasture ['paistʃə] *n* (*grass*) pasto *m*; (*field*) prado *m*. *v* apacentar.
pasty[1] ['peisti] *adj* pastoso; (*face*) pálido.
pasty[2] ['pasti] *n* empanada *f*.
pat [pat] *v* dar palmaditas; (*a pet*) acariciar. *n* palmadita *f*; caricia *f*; (*of butter*) porción *f*. *adj* adecuado. *adv* oportunamente.
patch [patʃ] *n* (*clothes*) pieza *f*, remiendo *m*; (*for puncture, wound, etc.*) parche *m*; (*land*) parcela *f*. **patchwork** *n* labor de retazos *m*. *v* remendar; poner un parche. **patchy** *adj* desigual.
patent ['peitənt] *adj* patente, evidente; patentado. **patent leather** charol *m*. *v* patentar. *n* patente *f*. **patently** *adv* evidentemente.
paternal [pə'təinl] *adj* paterno, paternal. **paternity** *n* paternidad *f*.
path [paiθ] *n* (*way*) camino *m*, sendero *m*; (*star, sun*) curso *m*.
pathetic [pə'θetik] *adj* patético.

pathology [pə'θolədʒi] *n* patología *f*. **pathological** *adj* patológico. **pathologist** *n* patólogo *m*.
patient ['peiʃənt] *adj* paciente. *n* enfermo, -a *m, f*. **patience** *n* paciencia *f*; (*game*) solitario *m*.
patio ['patiou] *n* patio *m*.
patriarchal ['peitriaikəl] *adj* patriarcal.
patriot ['patriət] *n* patriota *m, f*. **patriotic** *adj* patriótico. **patriotism** *n* patriotismo *m*.
patrol [pə'troul] *n* patrulla *f*. **patrol car** coche patrulla *m*. *v* patrullar.
patron ['peitrən] *n* patrocinador, -a *m, f*; (*saint*) patrón, -ona *m, f*, patrono *m*; (*arts*) mecenas *m*; (*customer*) cliente *m, f*. **patronage** *n* (*sponsorship*) patrocinio *m*; (*royal*) patronato *m*. **patronize** *v* (*comm*) patrocinar; (*arts*) fomentar; (*artist*) proteger; (*be condescending*) tratar con condescencia. **patronizing** *adj* de superioridad.
patter[1] ['patə] *v* (*rain*) repiquetear; (*footsteps*) corretear. *n* golpecitos *m pl*; repiqueteo *m*.
patter[2] ['patə] *n* (*salesman*) charlatanería *f*. *v* chapurrear.
pattern ['patən] *n* (*design*) dibujo *m*; (*needlework*) patrón *m*; (*sample*) muestra *f*; (*example*) ejemplo *m*. *v* diseñar; (*cloth*) estampar. **patterned** *adj* adornado con dibujos.
paunch [pointʃ] *n* panza *f*, barriga *f*.
pauper ['poipə] *n* pobre *m, f*.
pause [poiz] *n* pausa *f*; silencio *m*. *v* hacer una pausa; descansar; vacilar; pararse.
pave [peiv] *v* empedrar, enlosar. **pave the way for** facilitar el paso de. **pavement** *n* acera *f*. **paving** *n* pavimento *m*. **paving stone** adoquín *m*.
pavilion [pə'viljən] *n* pabellón *m*.
paw [poi] *n* pata *f*; (*cat*) garra *f*. *v* tocar con la pata; (*coll*) manosear.
pawn[1] [poin] *v* empeñar. *n* prenda *f*. **pawnbroker** *n* prestanista *m, f*. **pawnshop** *n* casa de empeños *f*.
pawn[2] [poin] *n* peón *m*.
*****pay** [pei] *v* pagar; dar; (*compliment, visit*) hacer; (*attention*) prestar. **pay back** (*money*) reembolsar; (*avenge*) devolver. **pay in** ingresar. **pay off** (*debt*) saldar; (*creditor*) reembolsar; (*mortgage*) redimir; (*be worthwhile*) merecer la pena; (*be fruitful*) dar resultado. *n* paga *f*;

salario *m*. **pay-as-you-earn** *n* deducción del sueldo para los impuestos *f*. **payday** *n* día de paga *m*. **pay rise** aumento de sueldo *m*. **pay-roll** *n* nómina *f*. **pay-slip** *n* hoja de paga *f*. **payable** *adj* pagadero. **payee** *n* beneficiario, -a *m*, *f*. **payment** *n* pago *m*; recompensa *f*.

pea [piː] *n* guisante *m*.

peace [piːs] *n* paz *f*. **peacemaker** *n* pacificador, -a *m*, *f*. **peace offering** sacrificio propiciatorio *m*. **peaceful** *adj* pacífico.

peach [piːtʃ] *n* (*fruit*) melocotón *m*; (*tree*) melocotonero *m*.

peacock ['piːkok] *n* pavo real *m*.

peak [piːk] *n* punta *f*; peñasco *m*; (*cap*) visera *f*. **peak hours** horas punta *f pl*.

peal [piːl] *n* (*bells*) ripiqueteo *m*; (*laughter*) carcajada *f*; (*thunder*) trueno *m*. *v* repiquetear; (*thunder*) retumbar; (*laugh*) resonar.

peanut ['piːnʌt] *n* cacahuete *m*.

pear [peə] *n* (*fruit*) pera *f*; (*tree*) peral *m*.

pearl [pəːl] *n* perla *f*. **pearly** *adj* nacarado.

peasant ['peznt] *n*, *adj* campesino, -a.

peat [piːt] *n* turba *f*.

pebble ['pebl] *n* guijarro *m*. **pebbly** *adj* guijarroso.

peck [pek] *v* picotear; picar. *n* picotazo *m*; (*coll*: *kiss*) besito *m*.

peckish ['pekiʃ] *adj* **feel peckish** (*coll*) tener gazuza.

peculiar [pi'kjuːljə] *adj* raro; extraño; característico; propio; especial. **peculiarity** *n* particularidad *f*; rareza *f*; característica *f*.

pedal ['pedl] *n* pedal *m*. *v* pedalear.

pedantic [pi'dantik] *adj* pedante.

peddle ['pedl] *v* vender de puerta en puerta.

pedestal ['pedistil] *n* pedestal *m*.

pedestrian [pi'destriən] *n* peatón *m*. **pedestrian crossing** paso de peatones *m*. **pedestrian precinct** zona reservada para peatones *f*. *adj* (*style*) prosaico.

pedigree ['pedigriː] *n* (*ancestry*) linaje *m*; (*animals*) pedigrí *m*. **pedigree animal** animal de raza *m*.

pedlar ['pedlə] *n* vendedor ambulante *m*.

peel [piːl] *v* pelar. **peel off** quitar, despegar. *n* (*potatoes*, *oranges*) monda *f*, cáscara *f*; (*candied*) piel confitada *f*. **potato-peeler** *n* pelapatatas *m invar*. **peelings** *pl* *n* peladuras *f pl*.

peep [piːp] *n* ojeada *f*. *v* echar una ojeada

(a). **peeping Tom** mirón *m*. **peep out** asomar.

peer[1] [piə] *v* entornar los ojos. **peer into** mirar dentro de.

peer[2] [piə] *n* (*nobility*) par *m*; (*equal*) igual *m*. **peerage** *n* pares *m pl*. **peerless** *adj* sin par.

peevish ['piːviʃ] *adj* displicente; enojadizo.

peg [peg] *n* (*hats*, *coats*) percha *f*; (*clothes*) pinza *f*; (*tent*) estaca *f*. **off the peg** *adj* de confección. *v* enclavijar; (*prices*) estabilizar.

pejorative [pə'dʒorətiv] *adj* pejorativo.

Peking [ˌpiː'kin] *n* Pekín, Pequín.

pelican ['pelikən] *n* pelicano *m*.

pellet ['pelit] *n* bolita *f*; (*gun*) perdigón *m*; (*med*) píldora *f*.

pelmet ['pelmit] *n* galería *f*.

pelt[1] [pelt] *v* tirar, arrojar; (*with questions*) acribillar; (*rain*) llover a cántaros; (*coll*: *run*) ir a todo correr. **at full pelt** a toda mecha.

pelt[2] [pelt] *n* pellejo *m*, piel *f*.

pelvis ['pelvis] *n* pelvis *f*. **pelvic** *adj* pélvico.

pen[1] [pen] *n* pluma *f*. **penknife** *n* cortaplumas *m invar*. **pen-name** *n* seudónimo *m*.

pen[2] [pen] *n* (*farm animals*) corral *m*; (*sheep*) redil *m*; (*pigs*) pocilga *f*. *v* scorralar.

penal ['piːnl] *adj* penal. **penal colony** penal *m*. **penalize** *v* penar, castigar. **penalty** *n* pena *f*; (*football*) penalty *m*; (*fig*) castigo *m*.

penance ['penəns] *n* penitencia *f*.

pencil ['pensl] *n* lápiz *m*. **pencil-sharpener** *n* sacapuntas *m invar*. *v* escribir con lápiz.

pendant ['pendənt] *n* colgante *m*.

pending ['pendin] *adj* pendiente. *prep* hasta; durante.

pendulum ['pendjuləm] *n* péndulo *m*.

penetrate ['penitreit] *v* penetrar. **penetrable** *adj* penetrable. **penetration** *n* penetración *f*.

penguin ['pengwin] *n* pingüino *m*.

penicillin [peni'silin] *n* penicilina *f*.

peninsula [pə'ninsjulə] *n* península *f*. **peninsular** *adj* peninsular.

penis ['piːnis] *n* pene *m*.

penitent ['penitənt] *n*(*m*+*f*), *adj* penitente. **penitence** *n* penitencia *f*.

pennant ['penənt] *n* (*small flag*) banderín *m*; (*naut*) gallardete *m*.
penniless ['penilis] *adj* sin dinero.
pension ['penʃən] *n* (*old age, retirement*) jubilación *f*; (*allowance*) pensión *f*. **pension fund** caja de jubilaciones *f*. *v* pensionar. **pension off** jubilar. **pensioner** *n* pensionista *m, f*.
pensive ['pensiv] *adj* pensativo.
pentagon ['pentəgən] *n* pentágono *m*. **pentagonal** *adj* pentagonal.
penthouse ['penthaus] *n* ático *m*.
pent-up [pent'ʌp] *adj* reprimido.
penultimate [pi'nʌltimət] *adj* penúltimo.
people ['piːpl] *n* personas *f pl*; gente *f sing*; (*nation*) nación *f sing*; pueblo *m sing*; habitantes *m pl*; (*coll*) familia *f sing*. *v* poblar.
pepper ['pepə] *n* (*spice*) pimienta *f*; (*vegetable*) pimiento *m*. **peppercorn** *n* grano de pimiento *m*. **peppermint** *n* (*plant*) hierbabuena *f*; (*flavour*) menta *f*; (*sweet*) pastilla de menta *f*. **pepper-pot** *n* pimentero *m*. *v* sazonar con pimienta. **peppery** *adj* picante.
per [pəː] *prep* por. **per cent** por ciento. **percentage** *n* porcentaje *m*.
perceive [pə'siːv] *v* percibir; (*notice*) notar.
perceptible [pə'septibl] *adj* perceptible; sensible. **perceptibly** *adv* sensiblemente.
perception [pə'sepʃən] *n* percepción *f*; sensibilidad *f*. **perceptive** *adj* perceptivo; perspicaz.
perch [pəːtʃ] *n* percha *f*. *v* (*bird*) posarse; encaramar.
percolate ['pəːkəleit] *v* filtrar. **percolator** *n* cafetera de filtro *f*.
percussion [pə'kʌʃən] *n* percusión *f*.
perennial [pə'reniəl] *adj* perenne. *n* planta perenne.
perfect ['pəːfikt; *v* pə'fekt] *adj* perfecto; absoluto. *n* (*gramm*) pretérito perfecto *m*. *v* perfeccionar. **perfection** *n* perfección *f*; (*perfecting*) perfeccionamiento *m*. **perfectionist** *n*(*m+f*), *adj* perfeccionista.
perforate ['pəːfəreit] *v* perforar. **perforation** *n* perforación *f*.
perform [pə'fɔːm] *v* llevar a cabo, ejecutar; (*duty*) cumplir; (*functions*) desempeñar; (*act*) representar. **performance** *n* ejecución *f*; cumplimiento *m*; desempeño *m*; representación *f*; (*machine*) funcionamiento *m*; *m*; celebración *f*; (*sport*) actuación *f*.

perfume ['pəːfjuːm] *n* perfume *m*. *v* perfumar.
perhaps [pə'haps] *adv* quizá, quizás, tal vez.
peril ['peril] *n* peligro *m*. **perilous** *adj* peligroso.
perimeter [pə'rimitə] *n* perímetro *m*.
period ['piəriəd] *n* período *m*; época *f*; edad *f*; tiempo *m*; (*school*) clase *f*; (*menstrual*) regla *f*. **periodic** *adj* periódico. **periodical** *nm, adj* periódico.
peripheral [pə'rifərəl] *adj* periférico. **periphery** *n* periferia *f*.
periscope ['periskoup] *n* periscopio *m*.
perish ['periʃ] *v* perecer. **perishable** *adj* perecedero.
perjure ['pəːdʒə] *v* **perjure oneself** perjurarse. **perjurer** *n* perjuro, -a *m, f*. **perjury** *n* perjurio *m*. **commit perjury** jurar en falso.
perk [pəːk] *v* **perk up** animarse. **perky** *adj* descarado; fresco.
perm [pəːm] *n* (*coll*) permanente *f*. **have a perm** hacerse la permanente.
permanent ['pəːmənənt] *adj* permanente. **permanence** *n* permanencia *f*. **permanently** *adv* permanentemente, para siempre.
permeate ['pəːmieit] *v* penetrar; (*soak*) impregnar. **permeable** *adj* permeable.
permit [pə'mit; *n* 'pəːmit] *v* permitir; dar permiso; tolerar. *n* permiso *m*; licencia *f*; pase *m*. **permissible** *adj* permisible. **permission** *n* permiso *m*; licencia *f*. **permissive** *adj* permisivo; tolerante.
permutation [pəːmju'teiʃən] *n* permutación *f*.
pernicious [pə'niʃəs] *adj* (*med*) pernicioso; (*evil*) funesto.
perpendicular [ˌpəːpen'dikjulə] *nf, adj* perpendicular.
perpetrate ['pəːpitreit] *v* perpetrar; cometer. **perpetration** *n* perpetración *f*; comisión *f*. **perpetrator** *n* (*law*) perpetrador, -a *m, f*; (*author*) autor, -a *m, f*.
perpetual [pə'petʃuəl] *adj* perpetuo.
perpetuate [pə'petʃueit] *v* perpetuar. **perpetuation** *n* perpetuación *f*.
perplex [pə'pleks] *v* dejar perplejo, confundir. **perplexed** *adj* perplejo; confuso. **perplexing** *adj* confuso; complicado; difícil. **perplexity** *n* perplejidad *f*; confusión *f*.
persecute ['pəːsikjuːt] *v* perseguir; molestar. **persecution** *n* persecución *f*.

persevere [,pɔːsi'viə] *v* perseverar. **perseverance** *n* perseverancia *f.* **persevering** *adj* perseverante.

persist [pɔ'sist] *v* persistir. **persistence** *n* persistencia *f.* **persistent** *adj* persistente; continuo.

person ['pɔːsn] *n* persona *f.* **personal** *adj* personal; en persona. **personality** *n* personalidad *f.* **personally** *adv* personalmente.

personify [pɔ'sonifai] *v* personificar. **personification** *n* personificación *f.*

personnel [pɔːsɔ'nel] *n* personal *m.*

perspective [pɔ'spektiv] *n* perspectiva *f.*

perspire [pɔ'spaiə] *v* transpirar, sudar. **perspiration** *n* transpiración *f*, sudor *m.*

persuade [pɔ'sweid] *v* persuadir. **persuasion** *n* persuasión *f.* **persuasive** *adj* persuasivo; convincente.

pert [pɔːt] *adj* impertinente; alegre; animado.

pertain [pɔ'tein] *v* pertenecer; ser propio de. **pertinent** *adj* pertinente. **pertinent to** relacionado con.

perturb [pɔ'tɔːb] *v* perturbar. **perturbation** perturbación *f.*

Peru [pɔ'ruː] *n* Perú *m.*

peruse [pɔ'ruːz] *v* leer atentamente; examinar. **perusal** *n* lectura atenta *f*; examen *m.*

pervade [pɔ'veid] *v* penetrar; saturar.

perverse [pɔ'vɔːs] *adj* obstinado; contrario; (*wicked*) perverso. **perversity** *n* obstinación *f*; perversidad *f.*

pervert [pɔ'vɔːt; *n* 'pɔːvɔːt] *v* (*person*) pervertir; (*facts*) desnaturalizar. *n* pervertido (-a) sexual *m, f.* **perversion** *n* perversión *f*; desnaturalización *f.*

pessimism ['pesimizɔm] *n* pesimismo *m.* **pessimist** *n* pesimista *m, f.* **pessimistic** *adj* pesimista.

pest [pest] *n* animal *or* insecto mocivo *m*; (*coll: person*) lata *f.* **pesticide** *n* pesticida *m.*

pester ['pestɔ] *v* importunar, molestar.

pet [pet] *n* animal doméstico *m*; (*person*) preferido, -a *m, f.* **my pet!** ¡mi cielo! *adj* mimado. **pet hate** pesadilla *f.* **pet name** nombre cariñoso *m.* **pet subject** tema preferido *m. v* minar; (*caress*) acariciar.

petal ['petl] *n* pétalo *m.*

petition [pɔ'tiʃɔn] *n* petición *f. v* suplicar; pedir.

petrify ['petrifai] *v* petrificarse; quedarse seco.

petrol ['petrɔl] *n* gasolina *f*; (*S.Am.*) nafta *f.* **petrol pump** surtidor de gasolina *m.* **petrol station** gasolinera *f.* **petrol tank** depósito de gasolina *m.*

petroleum [pɔ'trouliəm] *n* petróleo *m.*

petticoat ['petikout] *n* enaguas *f pl*, enagua *f.*

petty ['peti] *adj* pequeño; insignificante. **petty cash** dinero suelto *m.* **petty-minded** mezquino. **petty officer** contramaestre *m.* **pettiness** *n* pequeñez *f*; insignificancia *f.*

petulant ['petjulɔnt] *adj* malhumorado, irritable. **petulance** *n* mal humor *m*, irritabilidad *f.*

pew [pjuː] *n* banco de iglesia *m.*

pewter ['pjuːtɔ] *n* estaño *m*, peltre *m.*

phantom ['fantɔm] *n* fantasma *m.*

pharmacy ['faːmɔsi] *n* farmacia *f.* **pharmaceutical** *adj* farmacéutico. **pharmacist** *n* farmacéutico, -a *m, f.*

pharynx ['fariŋks] *n* faringe *f.* **pharyngitis** *n* faringitis *f.*

phase [feiz] *n* fase *f.* **phase in** introducir progresivamente. **phase out** reducir progresivamente.

pheasant ['feznt] *n* faisán *m.*

phenomenon [fɔ'nomɔnɔn] *n, pl* **-ena** fenómeno *m.* **phenomenal** *adj* fenomenal.

phial ['faiəl] *n* frasco *m.*

philanthropy [fi'lanθrɔpi] *n* filantropía *f.* **philanthropic** *adj* filantrópico. **philanthropist** *n* filántropo, -a *m, f.*

philately [fi'latɔli] *n* filatelia *f.* **philatelic** *adj* filatélico. **philatelist** *n* filatelista *m, f.*

philosophy [fi'losɔfi] *n* filosofía *f.* **philosopher** *n* filósofo, -a *m, f.* **philosophical** *adj* filosófico. **philosophize** *v* filosofar.

phlegm [flem] *n* flema *f.* **phlegmatic** *adj* flemático.

phobia ['foubiə] *n* fobia *f.*

phone [foun] *n* (*coll*) teléfono *m. v* telefonear.

phonetic [fɔ'netik] *adj* fonético. **phonetics** *n* fonética *f.*

phoney ['founi] *adj* (*coll*) falso, espurio.

phosphate ['fosfeit] *n* fosfato *m.*

phosphorescence [fosfɔ'resɔns] *n* fosforescencia *f.* **phosphorescent** *adj* fosforescente.

phosphorus ['fosfɔrɔs] *n* fósforo *m.* **phosphorous** *adj* fosforoso.

photo ['foutou] *n* (*coll*) foto *f.*

photocopy ['foutou,kopi] *n* fotocopia *f. v* fotocopiar. **photocopier** *n* fotocopiadora *f.* **photocopying** *n* fotocopiaje *m.*

photogenic [ˌfoutou'dʒenik] *adj* fotogénico.

photograph ['foutəgraɪf] *n* fotografía *f*. **photograph album** álbum de fotografías *m*. *v* fotografiar. **photographer** *n* fotógrafo, -a *m,f*. **photographic** *adj* fotográfico. **photography** *n* fotografía *f*.

phrase [freiz] *n* frase *f*, expresión *f*; (*gramm*) locusión *f*. **phrase-book** *n* repertorio de expresiones *m*. *v* expresar.

physical ['fizikəl] *adj* físico; *n* (*coll*) reconocimiento médico *m*.

physician [fi'ziʃən] *n* médico *m*.

physics ['fiziks] *n* física *f*. **physicist** *n* físico *m*.

physiology [ˌfizi'olədʒi] *n* fisiología *f*. **physiological** *adj* fisiológico. **physiologist** *n* fisiólogo, -a *m, f*.

physiotherapy [ˌfiziou'θerəpi] *n* fisioterapia *f*. **physiotherapist** *n* fisioterapeuta *m, f*.

physique [fi'ziːk] *n* constitución *f*; (*appearance*) físico *m*.

piano [pi'anou] *n* piano *m*. **pianist** *n* pianista *m, f*.

pick¹ [pik] *n* elección *f*, selección *f*. **take one's pick** elegir a su gusto. *v* escoger; seleccionar; (*fruit*) recoger; (*flowers*) coger; (*lock*) abrir con ganzúa. **pick at** (*food*) picar (la comida). **pick-me-up** *n* (*coll*) tónico. *m*. **pick out** escoger; distinguir; (*highlight*) hacer resaltar. **pickpocket** *n* ratero, -a *m, f*. **pick up** levantar; recoger; (*improve*) mejorarse; (*learn*) aprender; (*arrest*) detener.

pick² [pik] *n* (*tool*) piqueta *f*; (*music*) plectro *m*.

picket ['pikit] *n* piquete *m*; (*person*) huelguista *m, f*. *v* estar de guardia.

pickle ['pikl] *v* conservar en vinagre. *n* encurtido *m*.

picnic ['piknik] *n* merienda campestre *f*. *v* merendar en el campo.

pictorial [pik'tɔːriəl] *adj* pictórico, ilustrado.

picture ['piktʃə] *n* ilustración *f*; (*portrait*) retrato *m*; (*painting*) cuadro *m*; (*film*) película *f*. **picture frame** marco *m*. **picture gallery** museo de pintura *m*. **pictures** *n* (*coll*) cine *m*. *v* describir; imaginarse.

picturesque [piktʃə'resk] *adj* pintoresco.

pidgin ['pidʒən] *n* lengua macarrónica *f*.

pie [pai] *n* (*fruit*) pastel *m*; (*meat*) pastel de carne *m*.

piece [piːs] *n* pedazo *m*, trozo *m*; parte *f*; (*material*) pieza *f*. **piecemeal** *adv* hecho por partes. **piecework** *n* trabajo a destajo *m*. *v* **piece together** juntar.

pier [piə] *n* malecón *m*; (*landing-stage*) muelle *m*.

pierce [piəs] *v* penetrar; perforar; (*go through*) traspasar. **piercing** *adj* penetrante; (*wind*) cortante.

piety ['paiəti] *n* piedad *f*.

pig [pig] *n* puerco *m*, cerdo *m*. **pigskin** *n* piel de cerdo *f*. **pigsty** *n* pocilga *f*. **pigtail** *n* coleta *f*.

pigeon ['pidʒən] *n* paloma *f*. **pigeonhole** *n* casilla *f*.

pigment ['pigmənt] *n* pigmento *m*.

pike [paik] *n* (*fish*) lucio *m*.

pilchard ['piltʃəd] *n* sardina arenque *f*.

pile¹ [pail] *n* (*heap*) pila *f*, montón *m*. *v* amontonar. **pile up** acumular. **pile-up** *n* accidente múltiple *m*.

pile² [pail] *n* (*post*) poste *m*.

pile³ [pail] *n* (*of carpet, etc.*) pelo *m*.

piles [pailz] *pl n* (*med*) hemorroides *f pl*.

pilfer ['pilfə] *v* (*coll*) sisar. **pilferage** *n* sisa *f*.

pilgrim ['pilgrim] *n* peregrino, -a *m, f*. **pilgrimage** *n* peregrinación *f*.

pill [pil] *n* píldora *f*.

pillage ['pilidʒ] *n* saqueo *m*. *v* saquear.

pillar ['pilə] *n* pilar *m*, columna *f*. **pillar-box** *n* buzón *m*.

pillion ['piljən] *n* grupa *f*. **ride pillion** ir a la grupa.

pillow ['pilou] *n* almohada *f*. **pillowcase** *n* funda de almohada *f*.

pilot ['pailət] *n* piloto *m*. **pilot-light** *n* piloto *m*. *v* guiar; conducir.

pimento [pi'mentou] *n* pimienta de Jamaica *f*.

pimp [pimp] *n* chulo *m*.

pimple ['pimpl] *n* espinilla *f*. **pimply** *adj* espinilloso.

pin [pin] *n* alfiler *m*; (*hairpin*) horquilla *f*; (*safety pin*) imperdible *m*; (*tech*) pezonera *f*; (*bolt*) perno *m*. **pincushion** *n* almohadilla *f*. **pin-money** *n* alfileres *m pl*; **pinpoint** *v* localizar con toda precisión. **pins and needles** hormigueo *m*. **pinstripe** *n* raya muy fina *f*. *v* prender con alfileres. **pin down** (*fix*) sujetar; (*find*) encontrar; (*enemy*) inmovilizar. **pin up** (*notice*) fijar.

pinafore ['pinəfɔː] *n* (*apron*) delantal *m*. **pinafore dress** falda con peto *f*.

pincers ['pinsəz] *pl n* (*tool*) tenazas *f pl*; (*zool*) pinzas *f pl.*
pinch [pintʃ] *n* pellizco *m*; (*salt, etc.*) pizca *f.* **at a pinch** en caso de necesidad. **feel the pinch** empezar a pasar apuros. *v* pellizcar; (*shoes, etc.*) apretar; (*coll: steal*) mangar.
pine[1] [pain] *n* pino. *m.* **pine-cone** *n* piña *f.*
pine[2] [pain] *v* languidecer. **pine for** anhelar.
pineapple ['painapl] *n* ananás *m,* piña *f.*
ping-pong ['piŋpoŋ] *n* ping-pong *m,* tenis de mesa *m.*
pinion ['pinjən] *n* ala *f. v* maniatar.
pink [piŋk] *n* (*colour*) rosa *m*; (*flower*) clavel *m. adj* rosa.
pinnacle ['pinəkl] *n* pináculo *m.*
pioneer [,paiə'niə] *n* pionero *m,* iniciador *m.*
pious ['paiəs] *adj* pío, devoto.
pip[1] [pip] *n* (*seed*) pepita *f.*
pip[2] [pip] *n* (*phone, etc.*) señal *f.*
pipe [paip] *n* (*gas, water, etc.*) tubo *m,* tubería *f,* cañería *f*; (*tobacco*) pipa *f*; (*music*) caramillo *m.* **pipe-cleaner** limpiapipas *m invar.* **pipeline** *n* (*oil*) oleoducto *m*; (*gas*) gasoducto *m*; (*water*) tubería *f. v* conducir por tubería; transportar por oleoducto. **pipe down** (*coll*) callarse. **piping** *n* (*music*) sonido de la gaite *m*; (*sewing*) ribete; tubería *f.*
piquant ['piːkənt] *adj* picante. **piquancy** *n* picante *m.*
pique [piːk] *n* pique *m. v* picar; herir.
pirate ['paiərət] *n* pirata *m. v* piratear. **piracy** *n* piratería *f.*
pirouette [piru'et] *n* pirueta *f. v* hacer piruetas.
Pisces ['paisiːz] *n* Piscis *m.*
piss [pis] *n* (*impol*) meada *f. v* mear. **piss off!** ¡vete al cuerno! **pissed** *adj* (*drunk*) trompa. **be pissed off** estar furioso (con).
pistachio [pi'staɪʃiou] *n* pistacho *m.*
pistol ['pistl] *n* pistola *f.*
piston ['pistən] *n* émbolo *m,* pistón *m.*
pit [pit] *n* (*hole*) pozo *m,* hoyo; mina; (*orchestra*) foso de la orquesta *m*; (*of the stomach*) boca *f*; *v* llenar de hojitos; (*oppose*) oponer. **pit oneself against** medirse con.
pitch[1] [pitʃ] *n* (*throw*) lanzamiento *m*; (*sport*) campo *m*; (*music*) tono *m*; (*gradient*) grado de inclinación *m*; (*of a ship*) cabezada *f. v* lanzar, echar; entonar; (*of a ship*) cabecear; (*tent*) armar; (*fall*)

caerse. **pitchfork** *n* horca *f. v* (*fig*) catapultar.
pitch[2] [pitʃ] *n* pez *f,* brea *f.* **pitch-black** *adj* negro como el carbón.
pitfall ['pitfɔil] *n* escollo *m*; trampa *f.*
pith [piθ] *n* médula *f*; (*fig*) meollo *m.* **pithy** *adj* conciso, expresivo.
pittance ['pitəns] *n* miseria *f.*
pituitary [pi'tjuːitəri] *n* glándula pituitaria *f.*
pity ['piti] *n* compasión *f*; lástima *f.* **take pity on** tener lástima de. **what a pity!** ¡qué lástima! *v* compadecese de. **pitiful** *adj* lastimoso; (*bad*) lamentable. **pitiless** *adj* despiadado.
pivot ['pivət] *n* pivote *m*; eje *m. v* girar sobre su eje.
placard ['plakaɪd] *n* cartel *m. v* fijar carteles.
placate [plə'keit] *v* aplacar. **placatory** *adj* placativo.
place [pleis] *n* sitio *m,* lugar *m*; (*post*) puesto *m*; local *m*; posición *f.* **all over the place** por todas partes. **in place** en su sitio. **in place of** en lugar de. **out of place** fuera de lugar. **take place** suceder, ocurrir. **take the place of** sustituir a. *v* colocar; poner; situar; (*an order*) hacer. **be well placed** estar en buena posición.
placenta [plə'sentə] *n* placenta *f.*
placid ['plasid] *adj* plácido. **placidity** *n* placidez *f.*
plagiarize ['pleidʒəraiz] *v* plagiar. **plagiarism** *n* plagio *m.* **plagiarist** *n* plagiario, -a *m, f.*
plague [pleig] *n* (*disease*) peste *f*; (*social scourge*) plaga *f*; (*nuisance*) molestia *f. v* importunar.
plaice [pleis] *n* platija *f.*
plaid [plad] *n* tartán *m. adj* escocés.
plain [plein] *adj* (*clear*) claro; simple; puro; completo; (*frank*) franco; natural; (*unattractive*) sin atractivo. **plain-clothes** *adj* en traje de calle. **make plain** poner de manifiesto. *n* llanura *f.*
plaintiff ['pleintif] *n* demandante *m, f.*
plaintive ['pleintiv] *adj* quejumbroso.
plait [plat] *n* (*fold*) pliegue *m*; (*hair*) trenza *f. v* plisar; trenzar.
plan [plan] *n* (*map*) plano *m*; (*scheme*) plan *m,* proyecto *m. v* (*for the future*) hacer planes para; (*holidays*) hacer plan de; (*design*) hacer el plano de; (*action*) planear; (*production*) planificar. **planning** *n* planificación *f.*

plane¹ [plein] *n* plano *m*; (*coll*: *aeroplane*) avión *m*. *adj* plano.

plane² [plein] *n* (*tool*) cepillo *m*. *v* cepillar.

plank [plaŋk] *n* tabla *n*.

plankton ['plaŋktən] *n* plancton *m*.

plant [plaɪnt] *n* (*bot*) planta *f*; (*tech*) maquinaria *f*; (*factory*) fábrica *f*; (*installation*) instalación *f*. *v* plantar. **plantation** *n* plantación *f*; hacienda *f*.

plaque [plaɪk] *n* placa *f*.

plasma ['plazmə] *n* plasma *m*.

plaster ['plaɪstə] *n* (*walls*) yeso *m*; (*for wounds*) emplasto *m*. **plaster of Paris** yeso blanco *m*. *v* enyesar; cubrir. **plasterer** yesero *m*.

plastic ['plastik] *nm*, *adj* plástico. **plastic surgery** cirugía plástica *f*.

plate [pleit] *n* (*dish*) plato *m*; (*of metal*) chapa *f*; (*tableware*) vajilla *f*; (*in book*) lámina *f*. *v* chapar; (*silver*) platear; (*gold*) dorar. **plateful** *n* plato *m*.

plateau ['platou] *n* meseta *f*.

platform ['platfoɪm] *n* plataforma *f*; (*rail*) andén *m*; (*stage*) estrado *m*; (*builders*) andamio *m*; (*pol*) programa *m*. **platform ticket** billete de andén *m*.

platinum ['platinəm] *n* platino *m*.

platonic [plə'tonik] *adj* platónico.

platoon [plə'tuɪn] *n* (*mil*) pelotón *m*.

plausible ['plɔɪzəbl] *adj* plausible; (*person*) convincente. **plausibility** *n* plausibilidad *f*.

play [plei] *n* juego *m*, diversión *f*. (*theatre*) obra de teatro *f*; (*manoeuvre*) jugada *f*. *v* jugar. **player** *n* jugador, -a *m*, *f*; (*music*) intérprete *m*, *f*; (*theatre*) actor, actriz *m*, *f*. **playful** *adj* juguetón. **playfulness** *n* carácter juguetón *m*.

playback ['pleibak] *n* reproducción *f*. **play back** *v* volver a poner.

playground ['pleigraund] *n* campo de juegos *m*.

playhouse ['pleihaus] *n* teatro *m*.

playing card *n* carta *f*, naipe *m*.

playing field *n* campo de deportes *m*.

plaything ['pleiθiŋ] *n* juguete *m*.

playwright ['pleirait] *n* autor de teatro *m*.

plea [pliɪ] *n* súplica *f*; petición *f*; (*law*) alegato *m*.

plead [pliɪd] *v* suplicar; implorar; intervenir; tomar un alegato.

pleasant ['pleznt] *adj* agradable.

please [pliɪz] *v* gustar, agradar. **if you please** por favor. **pleased** *adj* contento. **pleasing** *adj* agradable.

pleasure ['pleʒə] *n* placer *m*, gusto *m*. **pleasurable** *adj* grato.

pleat [pliɪt] *n* pliegue *m*. *v* plisar.

plectrum ['plektrəm] *n* plectro *m*.

pledge [pledʒ] *n* prenda *f*; promesa *f*. *v* dar en prenda; prometer.

plenty ['plenti] *n* abundancia *f*; cantidad *f*. **plenty of** bastante. **plentiful** *adj* abundante, copioso.

pleurisy ['pluərisi] *n* pleuresía *f*.

pliable ['plaiəbl] *adj* flexible; (*person*) dócil. **pliability** *n* flexibilidad *f*; docilidad *f*.

pliers ['plaiəz] *pl n* alicates *m pl*.

plight [plait] *n* aprieto *m*; crisis *f*.

plimsolls ['plimsəlz] *pl n* zapatos de tenis *m pl*.

plod [plod] *v* andar con paso pesado; (*coll*: *work*) trabajar con ahinco. **plodder** *n* empollón, -ona *m*, *f*.

plonk [ploŋk] *n* (*coll*) pirriaque *m*.

plop [plop] *n* plaf *m*. *v* hacer plaf.

plot¹ [plot] *n* (*story*, *etc*.) argumento *m*; (*conspiracy*) conspiración *f*; *v* tramar, maquinar; (*route*) trazar.

plot² [plot] *n* (*land*) terreno *m*; (*garden*) cuadro *m*.

plough [plau] *n* arado *m*. *v* arar. **plough one's way through** abrirse paso. **ploughman** *n* arador.

pluck [plʌk] *n* valor *m*; (*music*) plectro *m*; (*pull*) tirón *m*. *v* (*pull*) arrancar; (*music*) puntear; (*fruit*) coger; (*fowl*) desplumar; (*eyebrows*) despilarse. **pluck out** arrancar. **pluck up courage** armarse de valor. **plucky** *adj* valiente.

plug [plʌg] *n* (*stopper*) taco *m*; (*sink*, *bath*) tapón *m*; (*elec*) enchufe *m*; (*mot*) bujía *f*. *v* taponar; tapar; enchufar; (*block up*) atascar; (*coll*: *advertise*) dar publicidad a. **plug away at** perseverar en. **plug in** enchufar.

plum [plʌm] *n* (*fruit*) ciruela *f*; (*tree*) ciruelo *m*.

plumage ['pluɪmidʒ] *n* plumaje *m*.

plumb [plʌm] *n* plomada *f*, plomo *m*. **plumbline** *n* cuerda de plomada *f*; (*in water*) sonda *f*. *adj* vertical. *adv* a plomo. *v* aplomar; sondar. **plumber** *n* fontanero *m*. **plumbing** *n* fontanería *f*; instalación de cañerías *f*.

plume [pluɪm] *n* (*feather*) pluma *f*; (*smoke*) penacho *m*. *v* emplumar.

plummet ['plʌmit] *n* plomo *m*. *v* (*bird, aircraft*) caer en picado; (*person, thing*) caer a plomo; (*prices*) caer verticalmente.

plump[1] [plʌmp] *adj* (*person*) rellenito; (*animal*) gordo. **plumpness** *n* gordura *f*.

plump[2] [plʌmp] *v* caer de golpe. **plump for** decidirse por.

plunder ['plʌndə] *v* saquear; robar. *n* saqueo *m*; (*loot*) botín *m*. **plunderer** *n* saqueador *m*. **plundering** *n* saqueo *m*.

plunge [plʌndʒ] *n* (*fall*) caída *f*; (*short dive*) zambullida *f*; (*high dive*) salto *m*. **take the plunge** aventurarse. *v* (*knife, etc*.) meter; sumergir; (*into despair*) hundirse; (*launch oneself*) lanzarse; (*fall*) caer.

pluperfect [plur'pəfikt] *n* pluscuamperfecto *m*.

plural ['pluərəl] *nm*, *adj* plural.

plus [plʌs] *prep* más. *n* cantidad positiva *f*; (*sign*) signo más *m*. *adj* positivo.

plush [plʌʃ] *adj* afelpado; (*fig*) lujoso. *n* felpa *f*.

ply[1] [plai] '*v* (*tool*) manejar; (*trade*) ejercer; (*questions*) acosar; (*ship, etc*.) hacer el trayecto de. **ply between** hacer el servicio entre.

ply[2] [plai] *n* (*wood*) chapa *f*; (*wool*) cabo *m*; (*fabric*) capa *f*. **plywood** *n* contrapachado *m*.

pneumatic [nju'matik] *adj* neumático. **pneumatic drill** barreno neumático *m*.

pneumonia [nju'mouniə] *n* pulmonía *f*.

poach[1] [poutʃ] *v* cazar *or* pescar en vedado. **poacher** *n* cazador *or* pescador furtivo *m*. **poaching** *n* caza *or* pesca furtiva *f*.

poach[2] [poutʃ] *v* (*egg*) escalfar.

pocket ['pokit] *n* bolsillo *m*. **pocket-money** *n* dinero de bolsillo *m*. *v* embolsarse.

pod [pod] *n* vaina *f*.

podgy ['podʒi] *adj* (*coll*) gordo.

poem ['pouim] *n* poema *m*.

poet ['pouit] *n* poeta *m*. **poetess** *n* poetisa *f*. **poetic** *adj* poético. **poetry** *n* poesía *f*.

poignant ['poinjənt] *adj* conmovedor.

point [point] *n* punto *m*; (*sharp end*) punta *f*; (*decimal*) coma *f*; (*elec*) contacto *m*; (*meaning*) sentido *m*; motivo; (*headland*) cabo *m*. **points** *pl n* (*railway*) agujas *f pl*. **beside the point** que no viene al caso. **come** *or* **get to the point** ir al grano. **make a point of** insistir en. **point-blank** *adv* (*shoot*) a quema ropa;

(*demand*) sin rodeos; (*refuse*) categóricamente. **what's the point?** ¿para qué sirve? *v* señalar; (*a weapon*) apuntar. **point out** señalar; advertir. **pointed** *adj* (*sharpened*) afilado; (*shape*) puntiagudo; (*remark*) directo. **pointless** *adj* inútil.

poise [poiz] *n* equilibrio *m*; (*bearing*) porte *m*; elegancia *f*; serenidad *f*. *v* poner en equilibrio; preparar. **be poised** estar en equilibrio; estar preparado.

poison ['poizən] *n* veneno *m*. *v* envenenar. **poisoning** *n* envenenamiento *m*. **poisonous** *adj* venenoso; tóxico.

poke [pouk] *n* empujón con el dedo; (*with elbow*) codazo *m*; (*fig*) hurgonada *f*. *v* dar con la punta del dedo; dar un codazo; hurgar. **poker** *n* hurgón *m*.

poker ['poukə] *n* (*cards*) póker *m*. **poker-faced** *adj* de cara inmutable.

Poland ['poulənd] *n* Polonia *f*. **Pole** *n* polaco, -a *m*, *f*. **Polish** *nm*, *adj* polaco.

polar ['poulə] *adj* polar. **polar bear** oso blanco. **polarize** *v* polarizar.

pole[1] [poul] *n* (*wood*) palo *m*; (*metal*) barra *f*; (*telegraphs*) poste *m*; (*flag*) asta *f*. **pole-vault** *n* salto de pértiga *m*.

pole[2] [poul] *n* (*geog, elec*) polo *m*. **pole star** estrella polar *f*.

police [pə'liːs] *n* policía *f*. **the police force** el cuerpo de policía *m*. **policeman** *n* policía *m*, guardia *m*. **police station** comisaría de policía *f*. **policewoman** *n* mujer policía *f*.

policy[1] ['polisi] *n* (*government*) política *f*; principio *m*; táctica *f*.

policy[2] ['polisi] *n* (*insurance*) póliza *f*.

polio ['pouliou] *n* polio *f*.

polish ['poliʃ] *n* (*shine*) brillo *m*; (*act*) pulimento *m*; (*furniture*) cera *f*; (*shoes*) betún *m*; (*nails*) esmalte *m*; (*fig*) elegancia *f*. *v* (*shoes*) limpiar; (*metal*) pulir; (*floors*) encerar. **polish off** zampar. **polish up** dar brillo a; (*improve*) perfeccionar.

polite [pə'lait] *adj* cortés. **politeness** *n* cortesía *f*.

politics ['politiks] *n* polítca *f*. **political** *adj* político. **politician** *n* político.

polka ['polkə] *n* polca *f*.

poll [poul] *n* votación *f*; elecciones *f pl*; (*survey*) sondeo *m*. *v* obtener; sondear. **polling booth** cabina electoral *f*; **polling day** día de elecciones *m*. **polling station** central electoral *m*.

pollen ['polən] *n* polen *m*. **pollen count**

índice de polen *m*. **pollinate** *v* polinizar.
pollination *n* polinización *f*.
pollute [pəˈluːt] *v* contaminar. **pollution** *n*
contaminación *f*.
polo [ˈpoulou] *n* polo *m*. **water polo** polo
acuático *m*. **polo-neck** *n* cuello vuelto *m*.
polyester [ˌpoliˈestə] *n* poliéster *m*.
polygamy [pəˈligəmi] *n* poligamia *f*.
polygon [ˈpoligən] *n* polígono *m*.
polystyrene [ˌpoliˈstaiəriːn] *n* poliestireno
m.
polytechnic [ˌpoliˈteknik] *n* escuela
politécnica *f*.
polythene [ˈpoliθiːn] *n* polietileno *m*.
pomegranate [ˈpomigranit] *n* (*fruit*) granada *f*; (*tree*) granado *m*.
pomp [pomp] *n* pompa *f*. **pompous** *adj*
pomposo.
pond [pond] *n* charca *f*; (*artificial*) estanque *m*.
ponder [ˈpondə] *v* considerar; meditar.
pony [ˈpouni] *n* poney *m*. **pony-tail** *n* cola
de caballo *f*.
poodle [ˈpuːdl] *n* perro de lanas *m*.
poof [puːf] *n* (*derog*) marica *m*.
pool¹ [puːl] *n* (*liquid*) charco *m*; (*swimming*) piscina *f*.
pool² [puːl] *n* (*money*) banca *f*; (*things*)
recursos comunes *m pl*; (*reserve*) reserva
f; (*comm*) fondos comunes *m pl*; (*typing*)
servicio de mecanografía *m*. **pools** *pl n*
(*football*) quinielas *f pl*. *v* aunar; reunir;
poner en un fondo común.
poor [puə] *adj* pobre; mediocre.
poorly [ˈpuəli] *adj* pobremente; mal. **be
poorly** estar malo.
pop¹ [pop] *n* taponazo *m*; (*drink*) gaseosa
f. **popcorn** *n* rosetas de maíz *f pl*. *v*
pinchar; (*cork*) hacer saltar; (*put*) meter.
pop in entrar un momento.
pop² [pop] *adj* popular. **pop music** música
pop *f*.
pope [poup] *n* papa *m*.
poplar [ˈpoplə] *n* álamo *m*.
poplin [ˈpoplin] *n* popelina *f*.
poppy [ˈpopi] *n* amapola *f*.
popular [ˈpopjulə] *adj* popular. **popularity**
n popularidad *f*. **popularize** *v* popularizar.
population [ˌpopjuˈleiʃən] *n* población *f*.
populate *v* poblar.
porcelain [ˈpoːslin] *n* porcelana *f*.
porch [poːtʃ] *n* pórtico *m*.
porcupine [ˈpoːkjupain] *n* puerco espú *m*.

pore¹ [poː] *n* (*anat*) poro *m*.
pore² [poː] *v* **pore over** estar absorto en.
pork [poːk] *n* cerdo *m*.
pornography [poːˈnogrəfi] *n* pornografía
f. **pornographic** *adj* pornográfico.
porous [ˈpoːrəs] *adj* poroso.
porpoise [ˈpoːpəs] *n* marsopa *f*.
porridge [ˈporidʒ] *n* gachas de avena *f pl*.
port¹ [poːt] *n* (*harbour*) puerto *m*.
port² [poːt] *n* (*naut: left*) babor *m*.
port³ [poːt] *n* (*wine*) oporto *m*.
portable [ˈpoːtəbl] *adj* portátil.
portent [ˈpoːtent] *n* presagio *m*.
porter [ˈpoːtə] *n* (*attendant*) mozo *m*;
(*doorman*) portero; (*in government build-
ings*) conserje *m*.
portfolio [poːtˈfouliou] *n* (*folder*) carpeta
f; (*pol*) cartera *f*.
porthole [ˈpoːthoul] *n* portilla *f*.
portion [ˈpoːʃən] *n* porción *f*; parte *f*.
portrait [ˈpoːtrət] *n* retrato *m*.
portray [poːˈtrei] *v* retratar; representar.
portrayal *n* retrato *m*; representación *f*.
Portugal [ˈpoːtjugl] *n* Portugal *m*. **Portuguese** *nm, adj* portugués. **the Portuguese**
los portugueses.
pose [pouz] *n* postura *f*; afectación *f*. *v*
colocar; (*question*) formular; (*problem*)
plantear. **pose as** dárselas de.
posh [poʃ] *adj* elegante, de lujo; afectado.
position [pəˈziʃən] *n* posición *f*; sitio *m*;
situación *f*; opinión *f*; (*job*) empleo *m*. *v*
situar, disponer.
positive [ˈpozitiv] *adj* seguro; categórico;
verdadero; afirmativo; positivo.
possess [pəˈzes] *v* poseer. **possession** *n*
posesión *f*. **possessive** *nm, adj* posesivo.
possible [ˈposəbl] *adj* posible. **possibility** *n*
posibilidad *f*. **possibly** *adv* (*perhaps*) tal
vez.
post¹ [poust] *n* (*pole*) poste *m*. *v* pegar.
post² [poust] *n* (*sentry, job*) puesto *m*. *v* (*a
sentry*) apostar; (*mil: send*) destinar.
post³ [poust] *n* (*mail*) correo *m*; (*letters*)
cartas *f pl*. *v* mandar, enviar; echar. **postage** *n* franqueo *m*. **postage stamp** sello *m*.
postal *adj* postal. **postal order** giro postal
m.
postbox [ˈpousboks] *n* buzón *m*.
postcard [ˈpouskaːd] *n* tarjeta postal *f*.
post-code *n* código postal *m*.
poster [ˈpoustə] *n* cartel *m*.
poste restante [poustˈrestãt] *n* lista de
correos *f*.

posterior [po'stɪərɪə] *adj* posterior. *n* (*coll*) trasero *m*.

posterity [po'sterəti] *n* posteridad *f*.

postgraduate [poust'gradjuit] *n, adj* postgraduado, -a.

post-haste *adv* a toda prisa.

posthumous ['postjuməs] *adj* póstumo.

postman ['pousmən] *n* cartero *m*.

postmark ['pousmaɪk] *n* matasellos *m invar. v* matasellar.

postmaster ['pousmaɪstə] *n* administrador de correos *m*. **postmistress** *n* administradora de correos *f*.

post-mortem *n* autopsia *f*.

post office *n* correos *m pl*.

postpone [pous'poun] *v* aplazar. **postponement** *n* aplazamiento *m*.

postscript ['pousskript] *n* posdata *f*.

postulate ['postjuleit; *n* 'postjulət] *v* postular. *n* postulado *m*.

posture ['postʃə] *n* postura *f*, actitud *f*.

pot [pot] *n* (*cooking*) olla *f*; (*flowers*) tiesto *m*; (*preserves*) tarro *m*. **pot roast** carne asada *f*. **pots and pans** batería de cocina *f*. *v* (*plant*) poner en tiesto.

potassium [pə'tasjəm] *n* potasio *m*.

potato [pə'teitou] *n* patata *f*.

potent ['poutənt] *adj* poderoso; (*drink*) fuerte.

potential [pə'tenʃəl] *adj* posible; (*phys*) potencial. *n* posibilidad *f*; (*phys*) potencial *m*; (*elec*) voltaje *m*.

pot-hole ['pothoul] *n* (*in road*) bache *m*; (*underground*) cueva *f*. **pot-holer** *n* espeleólogo *m*. **pot-holing** *n* espeleología *f*.

potion ['pouʃən] *n* dosis *f*, poción *f*.

potter[1] ['potə] *v* (*coll*) **potter about** or **around** no hacer nada de particular.

potter[2] ['potə] *n* alfarero *m*. **potter's wheel** torno de alfarero *m*.

pottery ['potəri] *n* (*shop, craft*) alfarería *f*; (*pots*) cacharros de barro *m pl*.

potty ['poti] *n* (*coll: baby's*) orinal *m*. *adj* (*coll: crazy*) chiflado.

pouch [pautʃ] *n* bolsa *f*; (*tobacco*) petaca *f*.

poultice ['poultis] *n* cataplasma *f*.

poultry ['poultri] *n* aves de corral *f pl*.

pounce [pauns] *v* saltar. *n* salto *m*, ataque *m*.

pound[1] [paund] *v* aporrear; martillear; azotar.

pound[2] [paund] *n* libra *f*.

pour [poɪ] *v* verter; echar; servir; (*rain*) diluviar; (*flow*) fluir; (*people*) salir en tropel.

pout [paut] *n* mala cara *f*. *v* poner mala cara.

poverty ['povəti] *n* pobreza *f*.

powder ['paudə] *n* polvo *m*; (*cosmetic*) polvos *m pl*; (*gun*) pólvora *f*. **powder puff** borla *f*. **powder room** cuarto tocador *m*. *v* pulverizar. **powdery** *adj* en polvo; pulverizado.

power ['pauə] *n* poder *m*; (*elec*) potencia *f*; (*tech*) fuerza *f*; (*energy*) energía *f*. **power station** central eléctrica *f*. *v* accionar, impulsar. **powerful** *adj* poderoso; potente. **powerless** *adj* impotente; sin autoridad.

practicable ['praktikəbl] *adj* practicable; utilizable; realizable. **practicability** *n* practicabilidad *f*.

practical ['praktikəl] *adj* práctico. **practical joke** broma pesada *f*.

practice ['praktis] *n* práctica *f*; (*music*) ejercicios *m pl*; (*training*) entrenamiento *m*; (*profession*) ejercicio *m*.

practise ['praktis] *v* practicar; (*professionally*) ejercer; (*exercise*) ejercitarse; (*patience, etc.*) tener; (*music*) hacer ejercicios en.

practitioner [prak'tiʃənə] *n* (*med*) médico *m*. **general practitioner** internista *m*.

pragmatic [prag'matik] *adj* pragmático; dogmático.

Prague [praɪg] *n* Praga.

prairie ['preəri] *n* llanura *f*, pradera *f*.

praise [preiz] *n* alabanza *f*, elogio *m*. *v* alabar, elogiar. **praiseworthy** *adj* laudable.

pram [pram] *n* cochecito de niño *m*.

prance [praɪns] *v* caracolear, encabritarse.

prank [praŋk] *n* (*joke*) broma *f*; (*mischief*) travesura *f*.

prattle ['pratl] *v* (*chatter*) charlar; (*of a child*) balbucear. *n* cháchara *f*; balbuceo *m*.

prawn [proɪn] *n* gamba *f*.

pray [prei] *v* orar, rezar. **prayer** *n* oración *f*, rezo *m*. **prayer book** devocionario *m*.

preach [priɪtʃ] *v* predicar. **preacher** *n* predicador, -a *m, f*. **preaching** *n* predicación *f*.

precarious [pri'keəriəs] *adj* precario.

precaution [pri'koɪʃən] *n* precaución *f*. **take precautions** tomar precauciones.

precede [pri'siɪd] *v* preceder, anteceder.

precedence n precedencia f; prioridad f.
precedent n precedente m.
precinct ['priːsiŋkt] n recinto m; frontera f; zona f. **shopping precinct** zona comercial f.
precious ['preʃəs] adj precioso.
precipice ['presipis] n precipicio m.
precipitate [pri'sipiteit; adj pri'sipitət] v (throw) precipitar, arrojar; (hasten) acelerar; (cause) causar. adj precipitado.
precipitation n precipitación f.
précis ['preisi] n resumen m.
precise [pri'sais] adj preciso; exacto. **precision** n precisión f; exactitud f.
preclude [pri'kluːd] v excluir; evitar; impedir.
precocious [pri'kouʃəs] adj precoz. **precociousness** or **precocity** n precocidad f.
preconceive [,priːkən'siːv] v preconcebir. **preconception** n preconcepción f.
precursor [,priː'kəːsə] n precursor, -a m, f.
predator ['predətə] n animal de rapiña m; (person) depredador, -a m, f.
predecessor ['priːdisesə] n predecesor, -a m, f.
predestine [pri'destin] v predestinar. **predestination** n predestinación f.
predicament [pri'dikəmənt] n situación difícil f.
predicate ['predikət] n predicado m. v afirmar; implicar.
predict [pri'dikt] v predecir. **predictable** adj previsible. **prediction** n predicción f.
predominate [pri'domineit] v predominar. **predominance** n predominio m. **predominant** adj predominante.
pre-eminent [priː'eminənt] adj preeminente. **pre-eminence** n preeminencia f.
preen [priːn] v limpiar. **preen oneself** pavonearse.
prefabricate [priː'fabrikeit] v prefabricar. **prefabrication** n prefabricación f. **prefab** n (coll) casa prefabricada f.
preface ['prefis] n prólogo m. v (introduce) introducir.
prefect ['priːfekt] n (school) alumno/alumna responsable de disciplina m, f.
prefer [pri'fəː] v preferir. **preferable** adj preferible. **preference** n preferencia f. **preferential** adj preferente.
prefix ['priːfiks] n prefijo m. v poner un prefijo; anteponer.
pregnant ['pregnənt] adj (woman)

embarazada, encinta; (animal) preñada. **pregnancy** n embarazo m.
prehistoric [,priːhi'storik] adj prehistórico.
prejudice ['predʒədis] n prejuicio m; parcialidad f. v predisponer; (damage) perjudicar. **prejudiced** adj predispuesto; parcial. **prejudicial** adj perjudicial.
preliminary [pri'liminəri] adj preliminar. **preliminaries** pl n preliminares m pl.
prelude ['preljuːd] n preludio m.
premarital [priː'maritl] adj premarital.
premature [premə'tʃuə] adj prematuro.
premeditate [priː'mediteit] v premeditar. **premeditation** n premeditación f.
premier ['premiə] adj primero. n primer ministro m.
première ['premieə] n estreno m.
premise ['premis] n premisa f. **premises** pl n local m sing; edificio m sing.
premium ['priːmiəm] n (comm) prima f; (award) premio m. **at a premium** a premio.
premonition [,premə'niʃən] n premonición f.
preoccupied [priː'okjupaid] adj preocupado. **preoccupation** n preocupación f.
prepare [pri'peə] v preparar, disponer. **preparation** n preparación f. **preparations** pl n preparativos m pl. **preparatory** adj preparatorio; preliminar. **preparatory school** escuela preparatoria f.
preposition [,prepə'ziʃən] n preposición f.
preposterous [pri'postərəs] adj ridículo, absurdo.
prerogative [pri'rogətiv] n prerrogativa f.
prescribe [pri'skraib] v prescribir; (med) recetar. **prescription** n (med) receta f, prescripción f.
presence ['prezns] n presencia f.
present[1] ['preznt] adj presente. n presente m, actualidad f. **at present** ahora, en la actualidad. **those present** los presentes. **presently** adv luego.
present[2] [pri'zent; n 'preznt] v presentar; regalar; (a problem) plantear; (an argument) exponer. n regalo m. **presentable** adj presentable. **presentation** n presentación f; (gift) regalo m; (ceremony) entrega f.
preserve [pri'zəːv] v (food) conservar; (protect) preservar. **preserved** adj en conserva. **preserves** pl n conservas f pl; (jam) confitura f. **preservation** n conservación

f; (*protection*) preservación *f*. **preservative** *n* producto de conservación *m*.

preside [pri'zaid] *v* presidir.

president ['prezidənt] *n* presidente, -a *m*, *f*. **presidency** *n* presidencia *f*. **presidential** *adj* presidencial.

press [pres] *n* (*newspapers*) prensa *f*; (*printing*) imprenta *f*. **press conference** rueda de prensa *f*. **press cutting** recorte de periódico *m*. *v* (*mechanical*) prensar; (*push*) apretar; (*iron*) planchar; (*button*) dar a; (*squeeze*) estrucar; (*urge*) urgir. **press for** pedir con insistencia. **pressing** *adj* urgente.

pressure ['preʃə] *n* presión *f*; (*weight*) peso *m*; (*strength*) fuerza *f*; (*elec, med*) tensión *f*. **pressure cooker** olla de presión *f*. **pressure gauge** manómetro *m*. **pressurize** *v* (*cabin, etc.*) presurizar; (*coll: force*) acozar.

prestige [pre'stiːʒ] *n* prestigio *m*.

presume [pri'zjuːm] *v* suponer; permitirse. **presumption** *n* presunción *f*; (*daring*) atrevimiento *m*. **presumptuous** *adj* presuntuoso; atrevido.

pretend [pri'tend] *v* fingir; (*claim*) pretender; (*imagine*) suponer. **pretence** *n* fingimiento *m*; pretensión *f*; pretexto *m*; apariencia *f*. **pretension** *n* pretensión *f*. **pretentious** *adj* pretencioso; (*showy*) presumido.

pretext ['priːtekst] *n* pretexto *m*.

pretty ['priti] *adj* bonito, lindo. *adv* bastante.

prevail [pri'veil] *v* prevalecer, triunfar; predominar. **prevail upon** convencer. **prevailing** *adj* (*wind*) predominante, reinante; (*present*) actual. **prevalent** *adj* predominante; (*present-day*) actual; (*common*) común; extendido.

prevent [pri'vent] *v* impedir; (*avoid*) evitar. **prevention** *n* prevención *f*; impedimento *m*. **preventive** *adj* preventivo.

preview ['priːvjuː] *n* preestreno *m*. *v* ver antes que los demás.

previous ['priːviəs] *adj* anterior. **previously** *adv* antes.

prey [prei] *n* presa *f*; víctima *f*. **be a prey to** ser víctima de. *v* **prey on** (*animals*) alimentarse de. **prey on one's mind** preocupar mucho.

price [prais] *n* precio *m*. **fixed price** precio fijo *m*. **full price** precio fuerte *m*. **price list** tarifa *f*. **sale price** precio de venta *m*.

v poner precio a; valorar. **priceless** *adj* inestimable.

prick [prik] *n* pinchazo *m*. *v* pinchar. **prick up one's ears** aguzar el oído.

prickle ['prikl] *n* espina. *v* picar. **prickly** *adj* espinoso.

pride [praid] *n* orgullo *m*; dignidad *f*. **pride oneself on** enorgullecerse de.

priest [priːst] *n* sacerdote *m*. **priesthood** *n* (*office*) sacerdocio *m*; (*clergy*) clero *m*.

prim [prim] *adj* (*fussy*) remilgado; (*demure*) recatado.

primary ['praiməri] *adj* primario; básico; primero.

primate ['praimət] *n* (*zool*) primate *m*; (*rel*) primado *m*.

prime [praim] *adj* primero; principal; original; selecto; (*math*) primo. **prime minister** primer ministro *m*. *v* preparar; (*person*) informar. **primer** *n* (*book*) cartilla *f*. **primer coat** primera mano *f*.

primitive ['primitiv] *adj* primitivo.

primrose ['primrouz] *n* primavera *f*.

prince [prins] *n* príncipe *m*. **princely** *adj* principesco. **princess** *n* princesa *f*.

principal ['prinsəpəl] *adj* principal. *n* (*school*) director, -a *m*, *f*.

principle ['prinsəpl] *n* principio *m*. **on principle** por principio.

print [print] *n* (*finger*) huella *f*; (*impression*) marca *f*; (*phot*) prueba *f*; (*edition*) tirada *f*; (*type*) tipo *m*; (*picture*) grabado *m*. **out of print** agotado. *v* imprimir; (*phot*) sacar. **printed matter** impresos *m pl*. **printer** *n* impresor *m*. **printing** *n* impresión *f*; (*phot*) tiraje *m*. **printing press** prensa *f*.

prior ['praiə] *adj* anterior; preferente. **prior to** antes de. **priority** *n* prioridad *f*.

prise [praiz] *v* **prise off/open** abrir; levantar por fuerza.

prism ['prizm] *n* prisma *m*.

prison ['prizn] *n* cárcel *f*. **prisoner** *n* preso, -a *m*, *f*.

private ['praivət] *adj* privado; personal; reservado; (*house, car, lessons, etc.*) particular; confidencial. *n* soldado raso *m*. **privacy** *n* intimidad *f*; aislamiento *m*. **privately** *adv* en privado; personalmente.

privet ['privət] *n* alheña *f*.

privilege ['privəlidʒ] *n* privilegio *m*. **privileged** *adj* privilegiado.

privy ['privi] *n* letrina *f*.

prize [praiz] *n* premio *m*. **prizewinner** *n*

premiado, -a *m, f. adj* premiado. *v* estimar.

probable ['probǝbl] *adj* probable; *(credible)* verosímil. **probability** *n* probabilidad *f*. **probably** *adv* probablemente.

probation [prǝ'beifǝn] *n (law)* libertad vigilada *f*; *(trial period)* período de prueba *m*. **on probation** a prueba. **probationary** *adj* de prueba.

probe [proub] *n (act)* sondeo *m*; *(med)* sonda *f. v* sondear; explorar.

problem ['problǝm] *n* problema *m*. **problematic** *adj* problemático.

proceed [prǝ'siːd] *v* seguir; proceder; avanzar. **proceed to** ponerse a. **procedure** *n* procedimiento *m*. **proceedings** *pl n* debates *m pl*; *(law)* proceso *m sing*.

process ['prouses] *n* proceso *m*; procedimiento *m*; método *m*. **in the process of** en curso de. *v* tratar; *(phot)* revelar.

procession [prǝ'sefǝn] *n* procesión *f*, desfile *m*.

proclaim [prǝ'kleim] *v* proclamar; declarar. **proclamation** *n* proclamación *f*; declaración *f*.

procreate ['proukrieit] *v* procrear. **procreation** *n* procreación *f*.

procure [prǝ'kjuǝ] *v* conseguir.

prod [prod] *n* golpecito *m. v* punzar; *(urge)* estimular.

prodigal ['prodigǝl] *adj* pródigo.

prodigy ['prodiʒi] *n* prodigio *m*. **prodigious** *adj* prodigioso.

produce [prǝ'djuːs; *n* 'prodjuːs] *v* producir; *(manufacture)* fabricar; causar. *n* productos *m pl*. **producer** *n* productor, -a *m, f*; *(theatre)* escenógrafo *m*. **product** *m* producto *m*. **production** *n* producción *f*; fabricación *f*; presentación *f*; *(theatre)* dirección *f*. **productive** *adj* productivo; fecundo. **productivity** *n* productividad *f*.

profane [prǝ'fein] *adj* profano. *v* profanar. **profanity** *n* lo profano; impiedad *f*.

profess [prǝ'fes] *v (state)* declarar; *(claim)* pretender; *(affirm)* afirmar.

profession [prǝ'fefǝn] *n* profesión *f*. **professional** *n(m+f)*, *adj* profesional.

professor [prǝ'fesǝ] *n* catedrático, -a *m, f*. **professorship** *n* cátedra *f*.

proficient [prǝ'fifǝnt] *adj* competente; experto. **proficiency** *n* competencia *f*; pericia *f*.

profile ['proufail] *n* perfil *m*; *(biography)* reseña *f*.

profit ['profit] *n (financial)* ganancia *f*; *(fig)* provecho *m*. **profit-making** *adj* productivo. *v* **profit by** *or* **from** beneficiarse de. **profitable** *adj* provechoso.

profound [prǝ'faund] *adj* profundo. **profoundly** *adv* profundamente.

profuse [prǝ'fjuːs] *adj* profuso; abundante. **profusely** *adv* profusamente. **profusion** *n* profusión *f*; abundancia *f*.

programme ['prougram] *n* programa *m. v* programar. **programmer** *n* programador, -a *m, f*. **programming** *n* programación *f*.

progress ['prougres] *n* progreso *m*. **in progress** en curso. **make progress** hacer progresos. *v* progresar, avanzar, hacer progresos. **progression** *n* progresión *f*. **progressive** *adj* progresivo; *(political, social)* progresista.

prohibit [prǝ'hibit] *v* prohibir; impedir. **prohibition** *n* prohibición *f*.

project ['prodʒekt; *v* prǝ'dʒekt] *n* proyecto *m. v* proyectar; *(protrude)* hacer resaltar. **projectile** *n* proyectil *m*. **projecting** *adj* saliente. **projection** *n* proyección *f*; saliente *m*. **projector** *n* proyector *m*; *(planner)* proyectista *m, f*.

proletarian [proulǝ'teǝriǝn] *n, adj* proletario, -a. **proletariat** *n* proletariado *m*.

proliferate [prǝ'lifǝreit] *v* proliferar. **proliferation** *n* proliferación *f*.

prolific [prǝ'lifik] *adj* prolífico.

prologue ['proulog] *n* prólogo *m*.

prolong [prǝ'lon] *v* prolongar. **prolongation** *n* prolongación *f*.

promenade [promǝ'naid] *n* paseo *m. v* pasear, pasearse.

prominent ['prominǝnt] *adj* prominente; saliente; preeminente. **prominence** *n* prominencia *f*; importancia *f*.

promiscuous [prǝ'miskjuǝs] *adj* promiscuo; *(person)* libertino. **promiscuity** *n* promiscuidad *f*.

promise ['promis] *n* promesa *f. v* prometer. **promising** *adj* que promete.

promontory ['promǝntǝri] *n* promontorio *m*.

promote [prǝ'mout] *v* promover, ascender; *(comm)* promocionar; *(encourage, stir up)* fomentar; financiar. **promotion** *n* ascenso *m*; promoción *f*; fomento *m*.

prompt [prompt] *adj* pronto; rápido; inmediato; puntual. *v* incitar; inspirar;

provision

sugerir; (*theatre*) apuntar. **prompter** *n*
apuntador, -a *m, f.*
prone [proun] *adj* propenso; (*lying*) boca
abajo.
prong [prɒŋ] *n* diente *m*, púa *f.*
pronoun ['prounaun] *n* pronombre *m.*
pronounce [prə'nauns] *v* pronunciar;
declarar. **pronouncement** *n* declaración *f.*
pronunciation *n* pronunciación *f.*
proof [pruːf] *n* prueba *f*; (*alcohol*) graduación normal *f. adj* resistente (a); al
abrigo de. **proof-read** *v* corregir pruebas.
proof-reading *n* corrección de pruebas *f.*
prop[1] [prop] *n* puntal *m*; (*fig*) sostén *m*,
apoyo *m. v* (*lean*) apoyar; (*support*)
mantener.
prop[2] [prop] *n* (*coll: theatre*) accesorio *m.*
propaganda [propə'gandə] *n* propaganda
f.
propagate ['propəgeit] *v* propagar. **propagation** *n* propagación *f.*
propel [prə'pel] *v* propulsar, impulsar.
propeller *n* propulsor *m*; (*aircraft, ship*)
hélice *f.* **propelling pencil** portaminas *m*
invar.
proper ['propə] *adj* propio; correcto;
decente; formal; justo; (*suitable*) apto;
(*true*) verdadero; (*characteristic*) peculiar. **proper noun** nombre propio *m.*
properly *adv* propiamente; bien;
decentemente; correctamente.
property ['propəti] *n* (*estate*) hacienda *f*;
(*possessions*) bienes *m pl*, propiedad *f.*
(*quality*) cualidad *f.*
prophecy ['profəsi] *n* profecía *f.* **prophesy**
v profetizar. **prophet** *n* profeta *m.* **prophetic** *adj* profético.
proportion [prə'pɔːʃən] *n* proporción *f*;
parte *f.* out of proportion desproporcionado. *v* proporcionar; distribuir. **proportional** *adj* proporcional, en proporción.
propose [prə'pouz] *v* proponer; (*marriage*) declararse; (*toast*) brindar;
(*intend*) intentar. **proposal** *n* proposición
f; (*marriage*) oferta de matrimonio *f*;
(*plan*) proyecto *m.* **proposition** *n* proposición *f*; proyecto *m.*
proprietor [prə'praiətə] *n* propietario, -a
m, f; dueño *m, f.*
propriety [prə'praiəti] *n* decoro *m*; conveniencia *f*; oportunidad *f*; corrección *f.*
propulsion [prə'pʌlʃən] *n* propulsión *f.*
prose [prouz] *n* prosa *f.*
prosecute ['prosikjuːt] *v* proseguir; (*law*)

procesar. **prosecution** *n* (*of duty*) cumplimiento *m*; (*continuation*) continuación
f; (*action of prosecuting*) procesamiento
m; (*trial*) proceso *m*; (*party*) parte
acusadora *f.*
prospect ['prospekt] *v* prə'spekt] *n* perspectiva *f*; vista *f.* **prospects** *pl n* (*of a
job, etc.*) perspectivas *f pl. v* prospectar.
prospective *adj* eventual; futuro.
prospectus [prə'spektəs] *n* prospecto *m.*
prosper ['prospə] *v* prosperar. **prosperity**
n prosperidad *f.* **prosperous** *adj* próspero.
prostitute ['prostitjuːt] *n* prostituta *f. v*
prostituir. **prostitution** *n* prostitución *f.*
prostrate ['prostreit] *v* pro'streit] *adj*
(*lying down*) boca abajo; (*exhausted*)
postrado. *v* postrar. **prostrate oneself**
postrarse. **prostration** *n* prostración *f*;
prosternación *f.*
protagonist [prou'tagənist] *n* protagonista
m, f
protect [prə'tekt] *v* proteger. **protection** *n*
protección *f.* **protective** *adj* protector.
protégé ['protəʒei] *n* protegido *m.* **protégée** *n* protegida *f.*
protein ['proutiːn] *n* proteína *f.*
protest ['proutest] *v* prə'test] *n* protesta *f.*
v protestar. **protester** *n* (*on march*)
manifestador, -a *m, f.*
Protestant ['protistənt] *n*(*m+f*), *adj*
protestante.
protocol ['proutəkol] *n* protocolo *m.*
prototype ['proutətaip] *n* prototipo *m.*
protractor [prə'traktə] *n* transportador *m.*
protrude [prə'truːd] *v* sacar; sobresalir.
protruding *adj* saliente, sobresaliente.
proud [praud] *adj* orgulloso; soberbio.
prove [pruːv] *v* probar; demostrar; (*show*)
mostrar.
proverb ['provɜːb] *n* proverbio *m.* **proverbial** *adj* proverbial.
provide [prə'vaid] *v* proveer; dar;
preparar (por); proporcionar medios de
vida (a). **provided that** si siempre que.
provident ['providənt] *adj* próvido. **providence** *n* providencia *f.* **providential** providencial.
province ['provins] *n* provincia *f*; esfera *f.*
the provinces la provincia *f.* **provincial**
adj provincial.
provision [prə'viʒən] *n* (*supply*) suministro *m*; (*providing*) provisión *f*; (*of treaty,
law, etc.*) disposición *f.* **make provision
for** prever. **provisions** *pl n* provisiones *f*
pl. **provisional** *adj* provisional.

proviso [prəˈvaizou] *n* condición *f*; estipulación *f*.
provoke [prəˈvouk] *v* provocar. **provocation** *n* provocación *f*. **provocative** *adj* provocador.
prow [prau] *n* proa *f*.
prowess [ˈprauis] *n* valor *m*; proeza *f*.
prowl [praul] *v* rondar. **prowler** *n* rondador, -a *m*, *f*.
proximity [prokˈsimɪti] *n* proximidad *f*.
proxy [ˈproksi] *n* poder *m*, procuración *f*. **by proxy** por poderes.
prude [pruːd] *n* mojigato, -a *m*, *f*. **prudish** *adj* mojigato.
prudent [ˈpruːdənt] *adj* prudente. **prudence** *n* prudencia *f*.
prune[1] [pruːn] *n* (*fruit*) ciruela pasa *f*.
prune[2] [pruːn] *v* podar; cortar; reducir.
pry [prai] *v* fisgar, fisgonear. **pry into** entrometerse en. **prying** *adj* fisgón.
psalm [saɪm] *n* salmo *m*.
pseudonym [ˈsjuːdənim] *n* pseudónimo *m*.
psychedelic [ˌsaikəˈdelik] *adj* psiquedélico.
psychiatry [saiˈkaiətri] *n* psiquiatría *f*.
psychic [ˈsaikik] *adj* psíquico. *n* medium *m*.
psychoanalysis [ˌsaikouəˈnaləsis] *n* psicoanálisis *m*. **psychoanalyse** *v* psicoanalizar. **psychoanalyst** *n* psicoanalista *m*, *f*.
psychology [saiˈkolədʒi] *n* psicología *f*. **psychological** *adj* psicológico. **psychologist** *n* psicólogo, -a *m*, *f*.
psychopath [ˈsaikəpaθ] *n* psicópata *m*, *f*. **psychopathic** *adj* psicopático.
psychosis [saiˈkousis] *n* psicosis *f*. **psychotic** *adj* psicopático. *n* psicópata *m*, *f*.
psychosomatic [ˌsaikəsəˈmatik] *adj* psicosomático.
psychotherapy [ˌsaikəˈθerəpi] *n* psicoterapia *f*.
pub [pʌb] *n* taberna *f*. **pub crawl** chateo *m*.
puberty [ˈpjuːbəti] *n* pubertad *f*.
pubic [ˈpjuːbik] *adj* púbico.
public [ˈpʌblik] *nm*, *adj* público.
publication [ˌpʌbliˈkeiʃən] *n* publicación *f*.
publicity [pʌbˈlisəti] *n* publicidad *f*.
publicize [ˈpʌblisaiz] *v* publicar.
public library *n* biblioteca de préstamo *f*.
public relations *n* colegio privado de enseñanza media *m*.

public-spirited *adj* de espíritu cívico.
public transport *n* servicio de transportes *m*.
publish [ˈpʌbliʃ] *v* publicar. **publisher** *n* editor, -a *m*, *f*. **publishing** *n* publicación *f*. **publishing house** casa editora *f*.
pucker [ˈpʌkə] *v* (*wrinkle*) arrugar; (*pleat*) fruncir. *n* (*pleat*) frunce *m*.
pudding [ˈpudin] *n* pudín *m*, budín *m*.
puddle [ˈpʌdl] *n* charco *m*.
puerile [ˈpjuərail] *adj* pueril.
Puerto Rico [ˌpwəːtouˈriːkou] *n* Puerto Rico.
puff [pʌf] *n* (*breath*) resoplido *m*; (*air*) soplo *m*; (*wind*) ráfaga *f*; (*smoke*) bocanada *f*; *v* (*blow*) soplar; (*pant*) jadear; (*smoke*) echar bocanadas. **puff out** *or* **up** hinchar. **puffy** *adj* hinchado.
pull [pul] *n* tracción *f*; (*tide*) arrastre *m*; esfuerzo *m*; (*influence*) enchufe *m*; atracción *f*. *v* (*open*) tirar de; (*drag*) arrastrar; (*uproot*) arrancar; (*tooth*) sacar; (*trigger*) apretar; (*attract*) atraer. **pull ahead** destacarse. **pull away** separar, apartar. **pull down** bajar; echar abajo. **pull in** entrar; llegar. **pull oneself together** serenarse. **pull out** (*mot*) salirse; sacar; arrancar; (*mil*) retirarse. **pull through** sacar de un apuro. **pull together** aunar sus esfuerzos. **pull up** (*mot*) parar; (*socks*) subirse; (*a chair*) acercar.
pulley [ˈpuli] *n* polea *f*.
pullover [ˈpulˌouvə] *n* jersey *m*.
pulp [pʌlp] *n* pulpa *f*. *v* reducir a pulpa.
pulpit [ˈpulpit] *n* púlpito *m*.
pulsate [pʌlˈseit] *v* palpitar; vibrar; brillar. **pulsation** *n* pulsación *f*; vibración *f*.
pulse [pʌls] *n* (*med*) pulso *m*; (*phys*) pulsación *f*. *v* latir; vibrar.
pulverize [ˈpʌlvəraiz] *v* pulverizar. **pulverization** *n* pulverización *f*.
pump [pʌmp] *n* bomba *f*; (*petrol*) surtidor *m*; (*plimsoll*) zapato de lona *m*. *v* bombear; sacar. **pump up** inflar.
pumpkin [ˈpʌmpkin] *n* calabaza *f*.
pun [pʌn] *n* retruécano *m*.
punch[1] [pʌntʃ] *n* puñetazo *m*; golpe *m*. *v* dar um puñetazo.
punch[2] [pʌntʃ] *n* (*drink*) ponche *m*.
punch[3] [pʌntʃ] *n* (*tool*) sacabocados *m* invar; perforadora *f*. *v* taladrar; perforar; picar.
punctual [ˈpʌŋktʃuəl] *adj* puntual. **punctuality** *n* puntualidad *f*.

punctuate ['pʌŋktʃueit] v puntuar. **punctuation** n puntuación f.

puncture ['pʌŋktʃə] n (tyre) pinchazo m; (leather, skin) perforación f. **have a puncture** tener un pinchazo. v pinchar; perforar.

pungent ['pʌndʒənt] adj (smell) acre; (taste) picante. **pungency** n acritud f; lo picante; mordazidad f.

punish ['pʌniʃ] v castigar. **punishment** n castigo m.

punt¹ [pʌnt] n (boat) batea f.

punt² [pʌnt] v (bet) apostar. **punter** n jugador m.

puny ['pjuːni] adj escuchimizado.

pupil¹ ['pjuːpl] n alumno, -a m, f.

pupil² ['pjuːpl] n (eye) pupila f.

puppet ['pʌpit] n títere m; marioneta f.

puppy ['pʌpi] m cachorro m.

purchase ['pəːtʃəs] n compra f. **purchase tax** impuesto sobre la venta m. v comprar.

pure ['pjuə] adj puro. **purify** v purificar. **purist** n purista m, f. **purity** n pureza f.

purée ['pjuərei] n puré m.

purgatory ['pəːgətəri] n purgatorio m.

purge [pəːdʒ] v purgar; purificar. n purga f. **purgative** nm, adj purgante.

puritan ['pjuəritən] n, adj puritano, -a. **puritanical** adj puritano.

purl [pəːl] v ribetear; hacer al revés. n (on lace) puntilla f; (thread) hilo de oro o de plata m.

purple ['pəːpl] nm, adj morado.

purpose ['pəːpəs] n propósito m, objetivo m; destino m; determinación f; uso m; utilidad f. **on purpose** a propósito. **purposeful** adj decidido; (person) resuelto; útil.

purr [pəː] v ronronear. n ronroneo m.

purse [pəːs] n monedero m, portamonedas m invar; (prize) premio m. v **purse one's lips** apretar los labios.

purser ['pəːsə] n contador m.

pursue [pə'sjuː] v perseguir. **pursuer** n perseguidor, -a m, f. **pursuit** n persecución f; profesión f; ocupación f; pasatiempo m.

pus [pʌs] n pus m.

push [puʃ] n empujón m; (force) empuje m. v empujar; presionar; (notice on doors) empujen. **be pushed for time** tener prisa. **pushing** adj ambicioso.

*put [put] v poner; meter; echar; (question) hacer; (state) decir. **put away**

guardar; (money) ahorrar. **put back** volver a poner; (clock) atrasar. **put down** bajar; (in writing) apuntar; (repress) reprimir; (kill) sacrificar. **put off** (postpone) aplazar; (disgust) censar; (revolt) asquear; disuadir. **put on** (clothes) ponerse; (a show) representar; (pretend) fingir. **put up** levantar; (hang) colgar; (resistance) oponer; (build) construir. **put up with** aguantar; conformarse con. **put upon** engañar.

putrid ['pjuːtrid] adj pútrido; podrido.

putt [pʌt] n put m. v tirar al hoyo. **putter** n putter m.

putty ['pʌti] n masilla f.

puzzle ['pʌzl] n enigma f; (game) rompecabezas m invar. v dejar perplejo. **puzzle out** resolver; descifrar. **puzzling** adj enigmático; misterioso.

pyjamas [pə'dʒaiməz] pl n pijama m sing.

pylon ['pailən] n poste m.

pyramid ['pirəmid] n pirámide f.

python ['paiθən] n pitón m.

Q

quack¹ [kwak] n (duck) graznido m. v graznar.

quack² [kwak] n charlatán m.

quadrangle ['kwodraŋgl] n (courtyard) patio m; (math) cuadrángulo m.

quadrant ['kwodrənt] n cuadrante m.

quadrilateral [kwodrə'latərəl] nm, adj cuadrilátero.

quadruped ['kwodruped] nm, adj cuadrúpedo.

quadruple [kwod'ruːpl] adj cuádruple.

quadruplets [kwo'druːplits] pl n cuatrillizos, -as m, f pl.

quagmire ['kwagmaiə] n pantano m.

quail¹ [kweil] n (zool) codorniz f.

quail² [kweil] v acobardarse.

quaint [kweint] adj pintoresco; excéntrico.

quake [kweik] v estremecerse. n estremecimiento. **quake with fear** temblar de miedo.

qualify ['kwolifai] v (entitle) capacitar; calificar; modificar; limitar. **qualification** n reserva f; aptitud f; requisito m. **qualifications** pl n títulos m pl. **qualified** adj competente; capacitado; titulado; con reservas.

quality ['kwolǝti] n (*attribute*) cualidad f; calidad f.

qualm [kwaɪm] n escrúpulo m.

quandary ['kwondǝri] n incertidumbre f, dilema m.

quantify ['kwontɪfaɪ] v determinar la cantidad de.

quantity ['kwontǝti] n cantidad f.

quarantine ['kworǝntiɪn] n cuarentena f. v someter a cuarentena.

quarrel ['kworǝl] n disputa f, pelea f. v disputar, pelear. **quarrelsome** adj peleador.

quarry[1] ['kwori] n (*stone, etc.*) cantera f. v explotar una cantera.

quarry[2] ['kwori] n presa f.

quarter ['kwoɪtǝ] n cuarto m; cuarta parte f; (*of year*) trimestre m; (*district*) barrio m. **quartermaster** n (*naut*) cabo de la marina m. **quarter past four** las cuatro y quince. **quarters** pl n (*mil*) cuartel m sing. **at close quarters** de cerca. **quarter to four** las cuatro menos cuarto. v dividir en cuatros; (*mil*) acuartelar. **quarterly** adj trimestral.

quartet [kwoɪ'tet] n cuarteto m.

quartz [kwoɪts] n cuarzo m.

quash [kwoʃ] v amular; ahogar; (*rebellion*) reprimir.

quaver ['kweivǝ] n (*music*) corchea f; temblor m. v temblar.

quay [kiɪ] n muelle m.

queasy ['kwiɪzi] adj (*sick*) mareado; (*upset*) delicado. **queasiness** n náuseas f pl.

queen [kwiɪn] n reina f; (*cards*) dama f. **Queen Mother** reina madre f.

queer [kwiǝ] adj raro; curioso; (*unwell*) indispuesto; (*slang: homosexual*) maricón. n (*slang*) maricón m, marica f.

quell [kwel] v reprimir.

quench [kwentʃ] v (*flames*) apagar; (*thirst*) aplacar; (*desire*) sofocar.

query ['kwiǝri] n pregunta f; duda f. v preguntar; dudar (de).

quest [kwest] n búsqueda f.

question ['kwestʃǝn] n pregunta f; cuestión f; problema m. **begging the question** petición de principio f. **beside the question** que no viene al caso. **out of the question** imposible. **question mark** signo de interrogación m. **without question** sin

duda. v preguntar; interrogar; poner en duda. **questionable** adj dudoso; discutible. **questioning** n interrogatorio m. **questionnaire** n cuestionario m.

queue [kjuɪ] n cola f. v hacer cola.

quibble ['kwibl] n pega f; subterfugio m. v sutilizar; (*find fault*) ser quisquilloso.

quick [kwik] adj rápido; (*reply*) pronto; (*lively*) vivo; (*clever*) agudo; (*on feet*) ligero. **quicksand** n avena movediza f. **quick-tempered** adj irascible. **quick-witted** adj agudo. **quicken** v acelerar; estimular. **quickly** adv rápidamente.

quid [kwid] n (*coll*) libra f.

quiet ['kwaiǝt] adj silencioso; callado; (*step*) ligero; tranquilo; (*dress*) sobrio. n also **quietness** tranquilidad f; silencio m; reposo m. **quieten** v callar; calmar. **quietly** adv silenciosamente; tranquilamente.

quill [kwil] n (*feather*) pluma f; (*pen*) cálamo m; (*porcupine*) púa f.

quilt [kwilt] n colcha f; (*eiderdown*) edredón m. v acolchar.

quince [kwins] n membrillo m.

quinine [kwi'niɪn] n quinina f.

quinsy ['kwinzi] n angina f.

quintet [kwin'tet] n quinteto m.

quirk [kwɔɪk] n peculiaridad f.

quit [kwit] v (*job*) abandonar; (*place*) dejar; (*leave*) irse de.

quite [kwait] adv completamente, enteramente; exactamente; verdaderamente; (*fairly*) bastante.

quiver[1] ['kwivǝ] v temblar; estremecerse. n temblor m; estremecimiento m.

quiver[2] ['kwivǝ] n (*for arrows*) aljaba f.

quiz [kwiz] n (*inquiry*) encuesta f; (*questioning*) interrogatorio m; examen m. v interrogar.

quizzical ['kwizikl] adj curioso; (*bantering*) burlón.

quota ['kwoutǝ] n cupo m; (*share*) cuota f.

quote [kwout] v citar; dar; (*comm*) cotizar. **quotation** n cita f; (*comm*) cotización f. **quotation marks** comillas f pl.

R

rabbi ['rabai] n rabino m.

rabbit ['rabit] n conejo m.

rabble ['rabl] n gentío m; (derog) populacho m.

rabies ['reibitz] n rabia f. **rabid** adj rabioso.

race[1] [reis] n carrera f; (yacht) regata f. **racehorse** n caballo de carreras m. v (person) competir con; (horse) hacer correr; (pulse) latir a ritmo acelerado.

race[2] [reis] n raza f; familia f. **racial** adj racial. **racialism** n also **racism** racismo m. **racialist** n(m+f), adj also **racist** racista.

rack [rak] n (shelf) estante m; (coats, etc.) percha f; (plates) escurreplatos m invar; (car roof) baca f; (torture) potre m. v atormentar. **rack one's brains** devanarse los sesos.

racket[1] ['rakit] n (sport) raqueta f.

racket[2] ['rakit] n (noise) alboroto m, barullo m; (coll: crime) tráfico m; timo m.

radar ['reidai] n radar m.

radial ['reidiəl] adj radial. **radial tyre** neumático radial m.

radiant ['reidiənt] adj resplandeciente. **radiance** n resplandor m.

radiate ['reidieit] v (heat) irradiar; (rays) emitir; (spread) difundir. **radiation** n radiación f. **radiator** n radiador m.

radical ['radikəl] nm, adj radical.

radio ['reidiou] n radio f. **radio beacon** radiofaro m. **radio contact** radiocomunicación f. **radio control** teledirección f. **radio station** emisora f. **radio wave** onda f. v transmitir por radio.

radioactive [reidiou'aktiv] adj radioactivo. **radioactivity** n radioactividad f.

radiography [reidi'ogrəfi] n radiografía f. **radiographer** n radiógrafo m.

radiology [reidi'olədʒi] n radiología f. **radiologist** n radiólogo m.

radiotherapy [reidiou'θerəpi] n radioterapia f.

radish ['radiʃ] n rábano m.

radium ['reidiəm] n radio m.

radius ['reidiəs] n radio m.

raffia ['rafiə] n rafia f.

raffle ['rafl] n rifa f. v rifar.

raft [raift] n balsa f.

rafter ['raiftə] n viga f.

rag[1] [rag] n (waste piece) harapo m; (cleaning) trapo m; (derog: newspaper) periodicucho m. **ragamuffin** n golfo m.

ragged adj (clothes) hecho jirones; (edge) mellado.

rag[2] [rag] v (coll) tomar el pelo a. n payasadas f pl. **ragtime** n música sincopada f.

rage [reidʒ] n (anger) cólera f, rabia f; (of elements) furia f; (fashion) moda f. **be all the rage** hacer furor. v (be angry) estar furioso; (wind, fire, beasts) bramar; (sea) alborotarse. **raging** adj (person) furioso; (pain) muy fuerte; (storm) encrespado.

raid [reid] n (mil) correria f; (aerial) ataque m; (police) redada f; (robbery) asalto m. v hacer una redada; asaltar. **raider** n invasor m; (thief) ladrón m.

rail [reil] n (stairs) barandilla f; (bridge) antepecho m; (balcony) baranda f; (bar) barra f; (fence) cerco m; (train, tram) via férrea f. **by rail** por ferrocarril. **railway** or US **railroad** n ferrocarril m.

railings ['reiliŋz] pl n barandilla f sing.

rain [rein] n lluvia f. **rainbow** n arco iris m. **raincoat** n impermeable m. **raindrop** n gota de lluvia f. **rainfall** n precipitación f; **rainwater** n agua de lluvia f. v llover. **rainy** adj lluvioso.

raise [reiz] v alzar, levantar; (increase) aumentar; provocar; (problem) plantar; (animals) criar.

raisin ['reizən] n pasa f.

rake [reik] n rastro m. v rastrillar. **rake together** reunir a duras penas.

rally ['rali] n reunión f; (pol) mitin político m; (mot) rallye m; (tennis) peloteo m. v reunir; (recover) recuperarse. **rally round** tomar el partido de.

ram [ram] n carnero m; (battering ram) ariete m. v (earth, etc.) apisonar; (fist, head) dar con; (pack) meter a la fuerza.

ramble ['rambl] n excursión f. v pasear; (fig) divagar.

ramp [ramp] n rampa f.

rampage ['rampeidʒ] n **be on the rampage** alborotar.

rampant ['rampənt] adj (plant) exuberante; (heraldry) rampante; (aggressive) violento. **be rampant** estar difundido.

rampart ['rampait] n terraplén m, muralla f.

ramshackle ['ramʃakl] adj desvenajado.

ran [ran] V **run**.

ranch [raintʃ] n rancho m; hacienda f.

rancid ['ransid] adj rancio.

rancour ['raŋkə] n rencor m.

random ['randəm] *n* **at random** al azar. *adj* hecho al azar. **random sample** muestra cogida al azar *f.*

rang [raŋ] *V* **ring**.

range [reɪndʒ] *n* (*row*) fila *f*; (*mountains*) sierra *f*; (*area*) extensión *f*; (*distance*) alcance *m*; (*of an aircraft*) autonomía *f*. (*mil: firing*) campo de tiro *m*; (*voice*) registro *m*; (*colours, prices*) gama *f*; (*subjects*) variedad *f*; (*grazing land*) dehesa *f*; (*cooking stove*) cocina económica *f. v* (*place*) colocar; (*put in a row*) alinear; clasificar; (*wander*) recorrer.

rank[1] [raŋk] *n* fila *f*; grado *m*; categoría *f*. **the rank and file** la tropa *f*; (*ordinary people*) gente del montón *f. v* (*estimate*) situar, poner; figurar; (*mil*) alinear.

rank[2] [raŋk] *adj* lozano; rancio.

rankle ['raŋkl] *v* escocer.

ransack ['ransak] *v* saquear; (*search*) registrar.

ransom ['ransəm] *n* rescate *m*. **hold to ransom** exigir rescate. *v* rescatar.

rap [rap] *v* golpear. *n* golpecito *m*.

rape [reɪp] *n* violación *f. v* violar. **rapist** *n* violador *m*.

rapid ['rapid] *adj* rápido. **rapids** *pl n* rápidos *m pl*. **rapidity** *n* rapidez *f.*

rapier ['reɪpiə] *n* estoque *m.*

rapport [ra'poɪ] *n* relación *f*; armonía *f.*

rapture ['raptʃə] *n* éxtasis *m invar*. **go into raptures over** extasiarse por.

rare[1] ['reə] *adj* raro. **rarity** *n* rareza *f.*

rare[2] ['reə] *adj* (*cookery*) poco hecho.

rascal ['raɪskəl] *n* bribón *m*, pícaro *m.*

rash[1] [raʃ] *adj* temerario. **rashness** *n* temeridad *f.*

rash[2] [raʃ] *n* (*med*) erupción *f.*

rasher ['raʃə] *n* loncha *f.*

raspberry ['raɪzbəri] *n* (*fruit*) frambuesa *f*; (*bush*) frambueso *m.*

rat [rat] *n* rata *f*. **rat poison** matarratas *m invar*. **rat race** competencia *f.*

rate [reɪt] *n* proporción *f*; índice *m*; velocidad *f*; ritmo *m*; precio; (*discount, interest*) tipo *m*; (*pulse*) frecuencia *f*. **at any rate** de todos modos. **ratepayer** *n* contribuyente *m, f*. **rates** *pl n* contribución municipal *f sing. v* valorar; considerar; clasificar; estimar. **rateable** *adj* valorable.

rather ['raɪðə] *adv* más bien; bastante; (*fairly*) algo. **I would rather ...** prefiero ....

ratify ['ratifai] *v* ratificar. **ratification** *n* ratificación *f.*

ratio ['reɪʃiou] *n* razón *f*, relación *f.*

ration ['raʃən] *n* ración *f. v* racionar. **rationing** *n* racionamiento *m.*

rational ['raʃnl] *adj* racional; razonable; lógico. **rationale** *n* razón fundamental *f*. **rationalize** *v* racionalizar.

rattle ['ratl] *n* (*toy*) sonajero *m*; (*football fan's*) carraca *f*; ruido de sonajero; (*train noise*) traqueteo *m*; (*chains*) ruido metálico *m*; (*door, window*) golpe *m*; (*teeth*) castañeteo *m*; (*machine gun*) tableteo *m; v* hacer sonar; traquetear; hacer un ruido metálico; golpetear; castañetear; tabletear; (*put off*) desconcertar.

raucous ['roɪkəs] *adj* ronco.

ravage ['ravidʒ] *n* estrago *m. v* asolar.

rave [reɪv] *v* delirar, desvariar. **rave over** entusiasmarse por. **raving** *adj* delirante.

raven ['reɪvən] *n* cuervo *m.*

ravenous ['ravənəs] *adj* hambriento. **be ravenous** tener um hambre canina.

ravine [rə'viɪn] *n* desfiladero *m.*

ravish ['raviʃ] *v* violar; raptar. **ravishing** *adj* encantador.

raw [roɪ] *adj* (*uncooked*) crudo; (*unrefined*) bruto; (*inexperienced*) novato; (*nerves*) a flor de piel; (*flesh*) vivo; (*weather*) frío y húmedo. **raw deal** (*coll*) injusticia *f*. **raw materials** materias primas *f pl*. **rawness** *n* crudeza *f.*

ray [reɪ] *n* rayo *m*; (*line, fish*) raya *f.*

rayon ['reɪon] *n* rayón *m.*

razor ['reɪzə] *n* navaja *f*; (*safety*) maquinilla de afeitar *f*; (*elec*) máquina de afeitar eléctrica *f*. **razor blade** hoja de afeitar *f.*

reach [riɪtʃ] *v* (*arrive at*) llegar a; (*achieve*) lograr; (*stretch out*) extender; alcanzar. *n* alcance *m*; poder *m*; capacidad *f*. **out of reach** fuera del alcance. **within reach** al alcance.

react [ri'akt] *v* reaccionar. **reaction** *n* reacción *f*. **reactionary** *n, adj* reaccionario, -a. **reactor** *n* reactor *m.*

*read [riɪd] *v* leer; estudiar; (*public address*) decir; (*riddle*) interpretar; (*meter, etc.*) marcar. **reader** *n* lector, -a *m, f*; (*university*) profesor, -a *m, f*; (*book*) libro de lectura *m*. **reading** *n* lectura *f*; estudio *m*; interpretación *f*. **reading-glass** *n* lente para leer *m*. **reading-lamp** lámpara de sobremesa *f.*

readjust [riːəˈdʒʌst] v reajustar. **readjustment** n reajuste m.

ready [ˈredi] adj listo; pronto; a mano. **get ready** prepararse. **ready cash** dinero contante m. **ready-made** adj hecho. **readily** adv fácilmente; en seguida. **readiness** n prontitud f; facilidad f.

real [riəl] adj real, verdadero. **realism** n realismo m. **realist** n realista m, f. **reality** n realidad f, verdad f. **really** adv realmente, en verdad. **really?** ¿de veras?

realize [ˈriəlaiz] v (understand) darse cuenta de; (achieve) llevar a cabo; (make real) realizar. **realization** n comprensión f; realización f.

realm [relm] n reino m; (fig) esfera f.

reap [riːp] v segar; (fig) cosechar. **reaping** n siega f; cosecha f. **reaping machine** segadora mecánica f.

reappear [riːəˈpiə] v reaparecer. **reappearance** n reaparición f.

rear¹ [riə] adj posterior, de atrás. **rear-admiral** n contraalmirante m. **rearguard** n retaguardia f. **rear-view mirror** retrovisor m. n parte posterior f, parte de atrás f; (of a column) cola f. **bring up the rear** cerrar la marcha.

rear² [riə] v (family) criar; (lift up) alzar, levantar; (horse, etc.) empinarse.

rearrange [riːəˈreindʒ] v arreglar de otra manera; volver a arreglar. **rearrangement** n nuevo arreglo m.

reason [ˈriːzn] n razón f. v razonar. **reasonable** adj razonable. **reasoning** n razonamiento m.

reassure [riːəˈʃuə] v asegurar de nuevo; confortar. **reassurance** n confianza restablecida f. **reassuring** adj tranquilizador.

rebate [ˈriːbeit] n rebaja f, descuento m.

rebel [ˈrebl] n(m+f), adj rebelde. v rebelarse. **rebellion** n rebelión f. **rebellious** adj rebelde.

rebound [riˈbaund; n ˈriːbaund] v rebotar. n rebote m.

rebuff [riˈbʌf] v rechazar. n desaire m.

*rebuild [riːˈbild] v reedificar.

rebuke [riˈbjuk] n censura f, reproche m. v censurar, reprochar.

recall [riˈkoil] v llamar; recordar. n llamada f; (dismissal) destitución f.

recant [riˈkant] v retractar.

recap [ˈriːkap] v (coll) recapitular. n recapitulación f.

recapture [riˈkaptʃə] v reconquistar; (recreate) hacer revivir. n reconquista f.

recede [riˈsiːd] v retroceder; (tide) descender.

receipt [rəˈsiːt] n (act of receiving) recepción f; (slip of paper) recibo m.

receive [rəˈsiːv] v recibir; aceptar. **receiver** n (of loot) recibidor, -a m, f; (law) síndico m; (phone) auricular m.

recent [ˈriːsnt] adj reciente. **recently** adv recientemente.

receptacle [rəˈseptəkl] n receptáculo m.

reception [rəˈsepʃən] n recepción f; acogida f. **receptionist** n recepcionista m, f. **receptive** adj receptivo.

recess [riˈses] n (hollow) hueco m; (niche) nicho m; (parliament) periodo de clausura m; (rest) descanso m.

recession [rəˈseʃən] n (comm) recesión f; (retreat) retroceso m.

recharge [riˈtʃɑːdʒ] v recargar.

recipe [ˈresəpi] n receta f.

recipient [rəˈsipiənt] n (receiver) receptor, -a m, f; (cheque, letter, etc.) destinatario, -a m, f.

reciprocate [rəˈsiprəkeit] v corresponder; intercambiar. **reciprocating engine** motor alternativo m. **reciprocal** adj recíproco.

recite [rəˈsait] v recitar. **recital** n (a relating) relato m; (music) recital m. **recitation** n relato m; recitación f.

reckless [ˈrekləs] adj temerario; audaz. **recklessness** n temeridad f; audacia f.

reckon [ˈrekən] v calcular; contar; considerar; (coll) creer. **reckoning** n cálculo m; cuenta f; (fig) retribución f.

reclaim [riˈkleim] v (land) ganar; (reform) reformar; (by-product) regenerar. **reclamation** n (claiming back) reclamación f; (moral) enmienda f; (land) aprovechamiento m; regeneración f.

recline [rəˈklain] v apoyar; recostar.

recluse [rəˈkluːs] n recluso, -a m, f.

recognize [ˈrekəgnaiz] v reconocer; confesar. **recognition** n reconocimiento m. **recognizable** adj identificable.

recoil [rəˈkoil; n ˈriːkoil] v echarse atrás; (gun) dar culatazo; (spring) aflojarse. n culatazo m; aflojamiento m; (repugnance) asco m.

recollect [rekəˈlekt] v acordarse de. **recollection** n recuerdo m.

recommence [rekəˈmens] v empezar de nuevo.

recommend [rekəˈmend] v recomendar; aconsejar. **recommendation** n recomendación f.

recompense ['rekəmpens] *n* recompensa *f*; (*law*) compensación *f*. *v* recompensar; compensar.

reconcile ['rekənsail] *v* (*dispute*) arreglar; (*individuals*) reconciliar; (*ideas*) conciliar. **reconcile oneself to** resignarse a. **reconciliation** *n* arreglo *m*; reconciliación *f*; conciliación *f*.

reconstruct [riːkən'strʌkt] *v* (*building*) reconstruir; (*crime*) reconstituir. **reconstruction** *n* reconstrucción *f*; reconstitución *f*.

record [rə'kɔid; *n* 'rekɔid] *v* registrar; tomar nota de; (*sound*) grabar. *n* registro *m*; anotación *f*; grabación *f*; disco *m*; (*account*) relación *f*; (*minutes*) actas *f pl*; (*personal history*) historial *m*; (*sport*) récord *m*. **long-playing record** disco de larga duración *m*. **record-player** *n* tocadiscos *m invar*. **recorded** *adj* grabado; registrado. **recorded delivery** entrega registrada *f*. **recorder** *n* archivista *m, f*; (*music*) flauta *f*. **recording** *n* (*music*) grabación *f*.

recount [ri'kaunt; *n* 'riːkaunt] *v* contar. *n* recuento *m*.

recoup [ri'kuːp] *v* (*recover*) recuperar; (*compensate*) indemnizar.

recover [rə'kʌvə] *v* (*get back*) recuperar; (*get well*) recobrar; ganar; obtener. **recovery** *n* recuperación *f*; (*med*) restablecimiento *m*.

recreation [rekri'eiʃən] *n* recreación *f*; (*school break*) recreo *m*.

recrimination [rəkrimi'neiʃən] *n* recriminación *f*. **recriminate** *v* recriminar.

recruit [rə'kruːt] *n* recluta *m*. *v* reclutar. **recruitment** *n* reclutamiento *m*.

rectangle ['rektaŋgl] *n* rectángulo *m*. **rectangular** *adj* rectangular.

rectify ['rektifai] *v* rectificar.

rectum ['rektəm] *n* recto *m*.

recuperate [rə'kjuːpəreit] *v* recuperar; (*health*) recobrar. **recuperation** *n* recuperación *f*; (*health*) restablecimiento *m*.

recur [ri'kəɪ] *v* volver; repetirse. **recurrence** *n* vuelta *f*; repetición *f*; reaparición *f*. **recurrent** *adj also* **recurring** periódico; que vuelve; (*med*) recurrente.

red [red] *n* rojo *m*, colorado *m*. **in the red** deber dinero. *adj* rojo, colorado. **go red** ruborizarse. **Red Cross** Cruz Roja *f*. **redcurrant** grosella *f*. **red-handed** *adv* con las manos en la masa. **redhead** *n* pelirrojo, -a *m, f*. **red-hot** *adj* al rojo; ardiente. **red-letter day** día memorable *m*. **red-light district** barrio de mala fama *m*. **red tape** (*coll*) papeleo *m*. **redness** *n* color rojo *m*.

redeem [rə'diːm] *v* (*promise*) cumplir; (*mortgage*) amortizar; (*pawn*) desempeñar; (*fault*) expiar; (*rescue*) rescatar. **redemption** *n* cumplimiento *m*; amortización *f*; desempeño *m*; expiación *f*; rescate *m*; (*rel*) redención *f*. **beyond redemption** sin redención, irremediable.

redirect [riːdai'rekt] *v* (*letter, etc.*) remitir al destinatario.

redress [rə'dres] *v* rectificar. *n* reparación *f*.

reduce [rə'djuːs] *v* reducir; rebajar; (*slim*) adelgazar. **reduction** *n* reducción *f*; (*length*) acortamiento *m*; (*width*) estrechamiento *m*; (*weight*) adelgazamiento *m*; (*rank*) degradación *f*; (*prices*) disminución *f*; (*discount*) rebaja *f*; (*temperature*) baja *f*.

redundant [rə'dʌndənt] *adj* excesivo, superfluo. **be made redundant** perder su empleo. **redundancy** *n* desempleo *m*.

reed [riːd] *n* caña *f*; (*of wind instrument*) lengüeta *f*.

reef [riːf] *n* arrecife *m*.

reek [riːk] *v* apestar. *n* tufo *m*.

reel¹ [riːl] *n* (*cotton*) carrete *m*, bobina *f*; (*film*) cinta; (*fishing*) carretel *m*. **reel off** (*recite*) recitar de un tirón.

reel² [riːl] *v* (*sway*) hacer eses, dar vueltas.

refectory [rə'fektəri] *n* refectorio *m*.

refer [rə'fəɪ] *v* remitir; enviar; (*date, event*) situar; atribuir. **reference** *n* referencia *f*; alusión *f*; relación *f*; (*source of information*) fuente *f*; (*person*) fiador *m*. **reference book** libro de consulta *m*. **reference library** biblioteca de consulta *f*. **reference number** número de referencia *m*. **terms of reference** mandato *m*. **make reference to** referirse a. **without reference to** sin consultar. **with reference to** en cuanto a.

referee [refə'riː] *n* árbitro *m*; (*guarantor of character*) garante *m*. *v* arbitrar.

referendum [refə'rendəm] *n* referéndum *m*.

refill [riː'fil; *n* 'riːfil] *v* rellenar. *n* recambio *m*; carga *f*.

refine [rə'fain] *v* refinar; purificar; (*technique*) perfeccionar; (*style*) pulir. **refinement** *n* (*person*) refinamiento *m*; (*manners*) finura *f*; (*sugar, oil*) refinado *m*;

(*metal*) purificación *f*; (*technique*) perfeccionamiento *m*; (*style*) elegancia *f*. **refinery** *n* refinería *f*.
reflect [rə'flekt] *v* reflejar; (*think*) reflexionar. **reflection** *n* (*image*) reflejo *m*; (*act*) reflexión; meditación *f*; crítica *f*.
reflex ['riːfleks] *nm, adj* reflejo. **reflexive** *adj* reflexivo.
reform [rə'fɔːm] *v* reformar; formar de nuevo. *n* reforma *f*. **reformation** *n* reformación *f*. **reformed** *adj* reformado.
refract [rə'frakt] *v* refractar. **refraction** *n* refracción *f*.
refrain[1] [rə'frein] *v* abstenerse.
refrain[2] [rə'frein] *n* estribillo *m*.
refresh [rə'freʃ] *v* refrescar. **refresher course** cursillo de repaso *m*. **refreshing** *adj* refrescante. **refreshments** *pl n* refrescos *m pl*.
refrigerator [rə'fridʒəreitə] *n* refrigerador *m*, nevera *f*. **refrigerate** *v* refrigerar. **refrigeration** *n* refrigeración *f*.
refuel [riː'fjuːəl] *v* repostar(se).
refuge ['refjuːdʒ] *n* refugio *m*; asilo *m*. **take refuge** refugiarse en. **refugee** *n* refugiado, -a *m, f*.
refund [ri'fʌnd; *n* 'riːfʌnd] *v* reembolsar. *n* reembolso *m*.
refuse[1] [rə'fjuːz] *v* negar. **refusal** *n* negativa *f*; (*rejection*) rechazo *m*.
refuse[2] ['refjuːs] *n* basura *f*, desecho *m*, desperdicios *m pl*.
refute [ri'fjuːt] *v* refutar.
regain [ri'gein] *v* recobrar; (*return to*) volver a.
regal ['riːgəl] *adj* real, regio.
regard [rə'gaːd] *v* mirar; observar; considerar. **as regards** con respecto a. *n* mirada *f*; atención *f*; respeto *m*; aprecio *m*. **regards** *pl n* (*in a letter*) saludos *m pl*. **regarding** *prep* con respecto a. **regardless** *adv* a pesar de todo. **regardless of** sin tener en cuenta.
regatta [rə'gatə] *n* regata *f*.
regent ['riːdʒənt] *n* regente *m, f*. **regency** *n* regencia *f*.
regime [rei'ʒiːm] *n* régimen *m*.
regiment ['redʒimənt] *n* regimiento *m*. **regimental** *adj* del regimiento.
region ['riːdʒən] *n* región *f*. **regional** *adj* regional.
register ['redʒistə] *n* registro *m*; lista *f*. *v* registrar; (*a complaint*) presentar; (*luggage*) facturar; (*letter*) certificar; (*birth,*

death) declarar. **registrar** *n* registrador *m*; (*med*) doctor, -a *m, f*. **registration** *n* (*trademark*) registro *m*; inscripción *f*; declaración *f*; certificación *f*; facturación *f*; matrícula *f*. **registration number** número de matrícula *m*. **registration plate** placa de matrícula *f*. **registry office** registro civil *m*.
regress [ri'gres] *v* retroceder. **regression** *n* regresión *f*.
regret [rə'gret] *v* sentir, lamentar. *n* sentimiento *m*; pesar *m*; arrepentimiento *m*; excusas *f pl*. **regrettable** *adj* lamentable; doloroso.
regular ['regjulə] *adj* regular; normal; habituado. *n* (*mil*) regular; (*bar*) asiduo, -a *m, f*. **regularity** *n* regularidad *f*.
regulate ['regjuleit] *v* regular; ajustar.
regulation [regju'leiʃən] *n* regulación *f*; regla *f*. *adj* reglamentario.
rehabilitate [riːhə'biliteit] *v* (*reputation*) rehabilitar; (*for work*) restaurar. **rehabilitation** *n* reconstrucción *f*; (*med*) reeducación *f*.
rehearse [rə'həːs] *v* ensayar. **rehearsal** *n* ensayo *m*.
reign [rein] *n* reinado *m*; dominio *m*. *v* reinar.
reimburse [riːim'bəːs] *v* reembolsar. **reimbursement** *n* reembolso *m*.
rein [rein] *n* rienda *f*; (*fig*) riendas *f pl*.
reincarnation [riːinkaː'neiʃən] *n* reencarnación *f*.
reindeer ['reindiə] *n* reno *m*.
reinforce [riːin'fɔːs] *v* reforzar. **reinforcement** *n* refuerzo *m*. **reinforced concrete** hormigón armado *m*.
reinstate [riːin'steit] *v* reinstalar; restablecer. **reinstatement** *n* reintegración *f*, restablecimiento *m*.
reinvest [riːin'vest] *v* reinvertir. **reinvestment** *n* reinversión *f*.
reissue [riː'iʃuː] *v* (*book*) reeditar; (*shares, stamps*) volver a emitir.
reject [rə'dʒekt; *n* 'riːdʒekt] *v* rechazar. *n* cosa defectuosa *f*. **rejection** *n* rechazamiento *m*; (*a reject*) cosa rechazada *f*.
rejoice [rə'dʒois] *v* alegrar, regocijar. **rejoicing** *n* alegría *f*, regocijo *m*.
rejoin [rə'dʒoin] *v* (*reply*) replicar; (*club, society, etc.*) reincorporarse a; (*friends*) reunirse con; (*two objects*) volver a unirse a.

rejuvenate [rə'dʒuɪvəneit] *v* rejuvenecer. **rejuvenation** *n* rejuvenecimiento *m*.

relapse [rə'laps] *n* recaída *f*; (*med*) recidiva *f*. *v* recaer; reincidir.

relate [rə'leit] *v* (*tell*) contar; (*be connected*) relacionar. **related** *adj* (*subjects*) relacionado; (*by birth or marriage*) emparentado. **relating to** lo que tiene que ver con.

relation [rə'leiʃn] *n* (*account*) narración *f*; (*relative*) pariente, -a *m, f*; (*connection*) relación *f*. **relationship** *n* relación *f*; (*kinship*) parentesco *m*.

relative ['relətiv] *adj* relativo. *n* pariente, -a *m, f*. **relatively** *adv* relativamente. **relativity** *n* relatividad *f*.

relax [rə'laks] *v* relajar; (*loosen*) aflojar. **relaxation** *n* relajación *f*; descanso *m*; distracción *f*. **relaxing** *adj* relajante.

relay [ri'lei; *n* 'riːlei] *v* transmitir. *n* relevo *m*. **relay race** carrera de relevos *f*.

release [rə'liːs] *n* liberación *f*; (*exemption*) exención *f*; (*film, record*) salida *f*; (*information*) anuncio *m*; (*gas, steam*) escape *m*. *v* liberar; (*film, record*) estrenar; anunciar; (*let go*) soltar; (*mechanism*) disparar.

relegate ['religeit] *v* relegar. **relegation** *n* relegación *f*.

relent [rə'lent] *v* ceder; enternecerse. **relentless** *adj* inexorable.

relevant ['reləvənt] *adj* pertinente; relativo; aplicable. **relevance** *n* pertinencia *f*; aplicabilidad *f*.

reliable [ri'laiəbl] *adj* de confianza; seguro. **reliability** *n* seguridad *f*; formalidad *f*.

reliance [rə'laiəns] *n* dependencia *f*; (*trust*) confianza *f*.

relic ['relik] *n* reliquia *f*; vestigio *m*.

relief [rə'liːf] *n* alivio *m*; (*aid*) socorro *m*; (*for the poor*) auxilio *m*; (*substitute worker*) relevo *m*; (*geog, art*) relieve *m*. *adj* suplementario.

relieve [rə'liːv] *v* aliviar; liberar; (*replace*) relevar; (*help*) socorrer.

religion [rə'lidʒən] *n* religión *f*. **religious** *adj* religioso.

relinquish [rə'liŋkwiʃ] *v* renunciar.

relish ['reliʃ] *v* (*food*) saborear; (*enjoy*) disfrutar. *n* gusto *m*; atracción *f*; entusiasmo *m*; (*food*) condimento *m*.

relive [riː'liv] *v* volver a vivir, revivir.

reluctant [rə'lʌktənt] *adj* maldispuesto.

reluctance *n* resistencia *f*. **reluctantly** *adv* de mala gana.

rely [rə'lai] *v* **rely on** contar con, confiar en.

remain [rə'mein] *v* quedarse. **remainder** *n* residuo *m*; resto *m*. **remains** *pl n* restos *m pl*; ruinas *f pl*.

remand [rə'maind] *v* reencarcelar. *n* reencarcelamiento *m*. **be on remand** estar detenido.

remark [rə'maik] *n* observación *f*; comentario *m*. *v* observar, notar; hacer una observación. **remarkable** *adj* notable.

remarry [riː'mari] *v* volver a casarse. **remarriage** *n* segundas nupcias *f pl*.

remedy ['remədi] *n* remedio *m*. *v* remediar. **remedial** *adj* remediador; reparador.

remember [ri'membə] *v* recordar, acordarse de. **remembrance** *n* recuerdo *m*.

remind [rə'maind] *v* recordar. **reminder** *n* advertencia *f*; (*comm*) notificación *f*.

reminiscence [remə'nisens] *n* reminiscencia *f*. **reminisce** *v* recordar el pasado. **reminiscent** *adj* evocador. **be reminiscent of** recordar.

remiss [rə'mis] *adj* descuidado.

remission [rə'miʃn] *n* remisión *f*, perdón *m*; exoneración *f*.

remit [rə'mit] *v* (*send*) remitir; (*forgive*) perdonar; (*return to a lower court*) devolver a un tribunal inferior. **remittance** *n* remesa *f*.

remnant ['remnənt] *n* resto *m*; (*fabric*) retal *m*.

remorse [rə'mois] *n* remordimiento *m*. **remorseful** *adj* arrepentido. **remorseless** *adj* sin remordimientos.

remote [rə'mout] *adj* (*distant*) lejano; (*in time or space*) remoto; (*slight*) ligero; (*out-of-the-way*) retirado; (*stand-offish*) distante. **remote control** mando a distancia *m*.

remove [rə'muiv] *v* quitar; sacar; separar; (*move house*) mudar. **removal** *n* mudanza *f*; (*transfer*) traslado *m*; (*from office*) despido *m*.

remunerate [rə'mjuinəreit] *v* remunerar. **remuneration** *n* remuneración *f*. **remunerative** *adj* remunerador.

renaissance [rə'neisəns] *n* renacimiento *m*.

rename [riː'neim] *v* poner un nuevo nombre a.

render ['rendə] v (*comm*) rendir; dar; (*a service*) hacer; (*assistance*) prestar; interpretar; (*fat*) derretir. **rendering** n *also* **rendition** interpretación f.
rendezvous ['rondivu:] n cita f. v reunir.
renegade ['renigeid] n, adj renegado, -a.
renew [rə'nju:] v renovar; (*extend*) prorogar; (*efforts*) reanudar. **renewal** n renovación f; prórroga f; (*continuation after interruption*) reanudación f.
renounce [ri'nauns] v renunciar. **renunciation** n renunciación f.
renovate ['renəveit] v renovar; reformar. **renovation** n renovación f; reforma f.
renown [rə'naun] n renombre m, fama f. **renowned** adj renombrado, afamado.
rent [rent] n alquiler m. **rent-free** sin pagar alquiler. v alquilar. **rental** n alquiler m.
reopen [ri:'oupən] v volver a abrir. **reopening** n reapertura f.
reorganize [ri:'o:gənaiz] v reorganizar. **reorganization** n reorganización f.
rep [rep] n (*coll*) viajante m.
repair [ri'peə] v reparar; componer. n reparación f; compostura f; arreglo m. **beyond repair** no tener arreglo. **closed for repairs** cerrado por reformas.
repartee [repɑ'ti:] n respuesta aguda f; (*coll*) dimes y diretes m pl.
repatriate [ri:'patrieit] v repatriar. **repatriation** n repatriación f.
*repay [ri'pei] v (*money*) devolver; (*debt*) liquidar; (*a person*) compensar; (*return*) corresponder a. **repayment** n devolución f. pago m; (*reward*) recompensa f.
repeal [rə'pi:l] v revocar, abrogar. n revocación f, abrogación f.
repeat [rə'pi:t] v repitir; recitar. n repetición f.
repel [rə'pel] v repeler; rechazar. **repellent** adj repelente.
repent [rə'pent] v arrepentirse de. **repentance** n arrepentimiento m. **repentant** adj arrepentido.
repercussion [ri:pə'kʌʃən] n repercusión f.
repertoire ['repətwɑ:] n *also* **repertory** repertorio m.
repetition [repə'tiʃn] n repetición f. **repetitive** adj reiterativo.
replace [rə'pleis] v (*substitute*) sustituir; (*put back*) reponer. **replacement** n repuesto m; (*person*) sustituto, -a m, f.
replay [ri:'plei; n 'ri:plei] v (*sport*) volver a

jugar; (*music*) volver a tocar. n (*sport*) repetición de un partido f; (*television*) repetición f.
replenish [rə'pleniʃ] v rellenar. **replenishment** n relleno m.
replica ['replikə] n réplica f, copia f.
reply [rə'plai] v responder, contestar. n respuesta f, contestación f.
report [rə'po:t] n (*spoken account*) relato m; (*piece of news*) noticia f; (*official*) informe m; (*newspaper or broadcast story*) reportaje m; (*reputation*) fama f; (*school*) boletin m; (*explosion*) estampido m. v relatar; (*for a newspaper*) hacer la crónica de; (*message*) repetir; (*denounce*) denunciar; presentar un informe. **reporter** n reportero m, periodista m, f.
repose [rə'pouz] n reposo m, descanso m. v reposar, descansar.
represent [reprə'zent] v representar. **representation** n representación f.
representative [reprə'zentətiv] adj representativo. n representante m, f.
repress [rə'pres] v reprimir. **repression** n represión f. **repressive** adj represivo.
reprieve [rə'pri:v] n (*law*) indulto m; (*fig*: *relief*) alivio m. v indultar; aliviar.
reprimand ['reprimɑ:nd] n reprimenda f. v reprender.
reprint ['ri:print; v ri:'print] n reimpresión f. v reimprimir.
reprisal [rə'praizəl] n represalia f.
reproach [rə'proutʃ] v reprochar. n reproche m. **reproachful** adj represor, acusador.
reproduce [ri:prə'dju:s] v reproducir. **reproduction** n reproducción f. **reproductive** adj reproductor.
reprove [rə'pru:v] v reprobar, censurar. **reproof** n reprobación f, censura f.
reptile ['reptail] n reptil m.
republic [rə'pʌblik] n república f. **republican** n, adj republicano, -a.
repudiate [rə'pju:dieit] v (*person*) repudiar; (*reject*) rechazar; (*contract*) negarse a cumplir. **repudiation** n repudiación f; rechazo m; desconocimiento m.
repugnant [rə'pʌgnənt] adj repugnante. **repugnance** n repugnancia f.
repulsion [rə'pʌlʃn] n repulsión f. **repulsive** adj repulsivo. **repulsiveness** n carácter repulsivo m.
repute [rə'pju:t] n reputación f. **reputable** adj acreditado. **reputation** n reputación f. **reputed** adj supuesto.

request [ri'kwest] *n* ruego *m*; demanda *f*. **at the request of** a petición de. *v* rogar, pedir. **request stop** parada discrecional *f*.
requiem ['rekwiəm] *n* requiem *m*.
require [rə'kwaiə] *v* (*need*) requerir; (*demand*) exigir; (*desire*) desear. **requirement** *n* requisito *m*; necesidad *f*.
requisite ['rekwizit] *adj* necesario, indispensable.
requisition [,rekwi'ziʃən] *n* demanda *f*; pedido *m*. *v* requisar.
***reread** [rii'riid] *v* releer.
re-route [rii'ruit] *v* cambiar el itinerario de.
***rerun** [rii'rʌn; *n* 'riirʌn] *v* (*film*) reestrenar; (*race*) correr de nuevo. *n* reestreno *m*.
resale [rii'seil] *n* reventa *f*.
rescue ['reskjui] *n* rescate *m*. **rescue operations** operaciones de salvamento *f pl*. **go to the rescue of** ir en auxilio de. *v* rescatar, salvar. **rescuer** *n* rescatador, -a *m*, *f*; salvador, -a *m*, *f*.
research [ri'səitʃ] *n* investigación *f*. *v* investigar. **researcher** *n* investigador, -a *m*, *f*.
***resell** [rii'sel] *v* revender.
resemble [rə'zembl] *v* parecerse a. **resemblance** *n* parecido *m*.
resent [ri'zent] *v* tomar a mal; ofenderse por. **resentful** *adj* resentido; ofendido. **resentment** *n* resentimiento *m*.
reserve [rə'zəiv] *v* reservar. *n* reserva *f*; (*mil*) reservista *m*. **reservation** *n* reserva *f*. **reserved** *adj* reservado.
reservoir ['rezəvwai] *n* represa *f*, embalse *m*.
reside [rə'zaid] *v* residir. **residence** *n* (*building*) residencia *f*; (*stay*) permanencia *f*. **resident** *n*(*m*+*f*), *adj* residente. **residential** *adj* residencial.
residue ['rezidjui] *n* residuo *m*. **residual** *adj* residual.
resign [rə'zain] *v* renunciar; (*hand over*) ceder. **resign oneself to** resignarse a. **resignation** *n* renuncia *f*; (*from a post*) dimisión *f*; resignación *f*. **resigned** *adj* resignado.
resilient [rə'ziliənt] *adj* elástico; (*human body*) resistente; (*person*) de carácter fuerte. **resilience** *n* elasticidad *f*; resistencia *f*; fuerza moral *f*.
resin ['rezin] *n* resina *f*.
resist [rə'zist] *v* resistir; (*bear*) aguantar;

(*impede*) impedir. **resistance** *n* resistencia *f*; aguante *f*. **resistant** *adj* resistente.
***resit** [rii'sit] *v* (*exam*) representarse.
resolute ['rezəluit] *adj* resuelto.
resolve [rə'zolv] *v* resolverse. **resolution** *n* resolución *f*.
resonant ['rezənənt] *adj* resonante. **resonance** *n* resonancia *f*. **resonate** *v* resonar.
resort [rə'zoit] *n* estación *f*; centro *m*; recurso *m*. **as a last resort** como último recurso. *v* **resort to** recurrir a.
resound [rə'zaund] *v* resonar; (*fig*) tener resonancias. **resounding** *adj* resonante; sonoro; (*fig*) tremendo.
resource [rə'zois] *n* recurso *m*; expediente *m*. **resourceful** *adj* ingenioso, inventivo. **resourcefulness** *n* ingenio *m*, inventiva *f*.
respect [rə'spekt] *n* respeto *m*; consideración *f*; (*aspect*) aspecto *m*. **pay one's respects** presentar sus respetos a. **with respect to** con respecto a. *v* respetar. **respectable** *adj* respetable; decente. **respectful** *adj* respetuoso. **respective** *adj* respectivo.
respiration [respə'reiʃn] *n* respiración *f*.
respite ['respait] *n* respiro *m*.
respond [rə'spond] *v* contestar; responder; reaccionar. **response** *n* respuesta *f*. **responsive** *adj* sensible.
responsible [rə'sponsəbl] *adj* responsable. **responsibility** *n* responsabilidad *f*.
rest¹ [rest] *n* descanso *m*; reposo *m*; (*music*) pausa *f*; tranquilidad *f*; (*support*) apoyo *m*. *v* descansar; (*stop*) pararse; (*stay*) quedar; (*decision*) depender de; (*lean*) apoyar. **restful** *adj* descansado; tranquilo. **restive** *adj* inquieto. **restless** *adj* desasosegado.
rest² [rest] *n* (*remainder*) resto *m*. **the rest** lo demás.
restaurant ['restront] *n* restaurant(e) *m*, restorán *m*. **restaurant car** coche restaurante *m*.
restore [rə'stoi] *v* restaurar; restablecer; (*return*) restituir; (*repair*) reformar; (*to former rank*) rehabilitar. **restoration** *n* restauración *f*; restablecimiento *m*; (*returning*) restituición *f*.
restrain [rə'strein] *v* impedir; limitar; (*repress*) contener. **restraint** *n* restricción *f*; limitación *f*; (*feelings*) represión *f*; moderación *f*.
restrict [rə'strikt] *v* restringir. **restricted** *adj* restringido; (*outlook*) estrecho.

restriction *n* restricción *f*. **restrictive** *adj* restrictivo.

result [rə'zʌlt] *n* resultado *m*. *v* resultar. **result from** derivarse de. **result in** tener por resultado. **resultant** *adj* resultante.

resume [rə'zjuɪm] *v* reanudar. **resumption** *n* reanudación *f*.

résumé ['reizumei] *n* resumen *m*.

resurgence [ri'səɪdʒəns] *n* resurgimiento *m*.

resurrect [rezə'rekt] *v* resucitar. **resurrection** *n* resurrección *f*.

resuscitate [rə'sʌsəteit] *v* resucitar. **resuscitation** *n* resucitación *f*.

retail ['riːteil] *n* venta al por menor. *adj, adv* al por menor. *v* vender al por menor; (*relate*) contar. **retailer** *n* vendedor al por menor.

retain [rə'tein] *v* (*keep*) quedarse con; conservar; retener.

retaliate [rə'talieit] *v* vengarse. **retaliation** *n* venganza *f*. **in retaliation** para vengarse.

retard [rə'taɪd] *v* retardar, retrasar. **retarded** *adj* atrasado.

reticent ['retisənt] *adj* reservado. **reticence** *n* reserva *f*.

retina ['retinə] *n* retina *f*.

retinue ['retinjuː] *n* comitiva *f*.

retire [rə'taiə] *v* (*from work*) jubilarse; (*draw back*) retirarse; (*go to bed*) cogerse. **retired** *adj* (*trader, soldier*) retirado; (*civilian*) jubilado. **retirement** *n* retiro *m*; jubilación *f*.

retort[1] [rə'tort] *v* replicar. *n* réplica *f*.

retort[2] [rə'tort] *n* (*chem*) retorta *f*.

retrace [ri'treis] *v* volver a trazar; repasar. **retrace one's steps** desandar lo andado.

retract [rə'trakt] *v* retractar. **retraction** *n* retractación *f*, retracción *f*.

retreat [rə'triːt] *v* retirarse; retroceder. *n* retirada *f*; (*place*) retiro *m*.

retrial [riː'traiəl] *n* nuevo juicio *m*.

retrieve [rə'triːv] *v* recuperar; (*from ruin*) salvar; (*hunting*) cobrar. **retrieval** *n* recuperación *f*. **retriever** *n* (*dog*) perro cobrador *m*.

retrograde ['retrəgreid] *adj* a retrógrado.

retrospect ['retrəspekt] *n* **in retrospect** retrospectivamente. **retrospective** *adj* retrospectivo.

return [rə'təɪn] *v* devolver; (*refund*) reembolsar; (*lost or stolen property*) restituir; (*investment*) dar; (*elect*) elegir; (*come back*) volver. **return a call** devolver una visita. *n* vuelta *f*, retorno *m*; (*reward*) recompensa *f*; restitución *f*; (*profit*) ganancias *f pl*; (*interest*) interés *m*; (*tax*) declaración *f*; (*ballot*) resultados *m pl*. **many happy returns!** ¡feliz cumpleaños! **return ticket** billete de ida y vuelta *m*. **in return** en recompensa. **on sale or return** en depósito.

reunite [riːju'nait] *v* reunir. **reunion** *n* reunión *f*.

rev [rev] (*mot*) *n* revolución *f*. **rev counter** cuentarrevoluciones *m invar*. **rev up** acelerar.

reveal [rə'viːl] *v* revelar, descubrir. **revealing** *adj* revelador. **revelation** *n* revelación *f*.

revel ['revl] *v* jaranear, ir de juerga. *n* jarana *f*, juerga *f*. **revelry** *n* jolgorio *m*.

revenge [rə'vendʒ] *n* venganza *f*. *v* vengar. **take revenge for** vengarse de.

revenue ['revinjuː] *n* (*from taxes*) rentas públicas *f pl*; (*income*) entrada *f*.

reverberate [rə'vɔɪbəreit] *v* reverberar, reflejar. **reverberation** *n* reverberación *f*.

reverence ['revərəns] *n* reverencia *f*, veneración *f*. **revere** *v* reverenciar, venerar. **reverent** *adj* reverente, respetuoso.

reverse [rə'vɔɪs] *n* lo contrario; (*cloth*) revés *m*; (*coin*) cruz *f*; (*printed form*) dorso *m*; (*mot: gear*) marcha atrás *f*. *adj* opuesto; contrario; inverso. *v* invertir; (*turn the other way round*) volver al revés; (*decision*) revocar; (*car*) dar marcha atrás. **reverse the charges** (*phone*) poner una conferencia a cobro revertido. **reversal** *n* inversión *f*. **reversible** *adj* reversible.

revert [rə'vɔɪt] *v* volver; revertir.

review [rə'vjuː] *n* examen *m*; crítica *f*; (*mil, theatre*) revista *f*. *v* examinar; volver a examinar; hacer una crítica de. **reviewer** *n* crítico, -a *m, f*.

revise [rə'vaiz] *v* revisar; corregir. **revision** *n* repaso *m*; corrección *f*.

revive [rə'vaiv] *v* (*med*) reanimar, resucitar; (*trade*) reactivar; (*play*) reponer; (*custom*) restablecer; (*interest*) renovar; (*hopes*) despertar. **revival** *n* reanimación *f*; resucitación *f*; reactivación *f*; restablecimiento *m*; (*interest*) renacimiento *m*.

revoke [rə'vouk] *v* revocar; (*withdraw*) suspender.

revolt [rə'voult] *n* rebelión *f*. *v* (*offend*) dar asco a; rebelarse. **revolting** *adj* asqueroso.

revolution [revə'luːʃən] *n* revolución *f*. **revolutionary** *n, adj* revolucionario, -a. **revolutionize** *v* revolucionar.

revolve [rə'volv] *v* girar. **revolver** *n* revólver *m*. **revolving door** puerta giratoria *f*.

revue [rə'vjuː] *n* revista *f*.

revulsion [rə'vʌlʃən] *n* repulsión *f*.

reward [rə'woːd] *n* premio *m*, recompensa *f*. *v* premiar, recompensar.

***rewind** [riː'waind] *v* (*film, tape*) rebobinar. **rewinding** *n* rebobinado *m*.

***rewrite** [riː'rait] *v* volver a escribir; volver a redactar.

rhesus ['riːsəs] *n* macaco de la India *m*. **rhesus factor** factor Rhesus *m*.

rhetoric ['retərik] *n* retórica *f*. **rhetorical** *adj* retórico.

rheumatism ['ruːmətizəm] *n* reumatismo *m*, reúma *m*. **rheumatic** *adj* reumático.

rhinoceros [rai'nosərəs] *n* rinoceronte *m*.

rhododendron [roudə'dendrən] *n* rododendro *m*.

rhubarb ['ruːbaːb] *n* ruibarbo *m*.

rhyme [raim] *n* rima *f*. *v* rimar.

rhythm ['riðəm] *n* ritmo *m*. **rhythmic** *adj* rítmico.

rib [rib] *n* costilla *f*; (*umbrella*) varilla *f*; (*knitting*) cordoncillo *m*.

ribbon ['ribən] *n* cinta *f*. **in ribbons** hecho jirones.

rice [rais] *n* arroz *m*.

rich [ritʃ] *adj* rico. **riches** *pl n* riqueza *f sing*. **richness** *n* abundancia *f*; fertilidad *f*.

rickety ['rikəti] *adj* tambaleante.

***rid** [rid] *v* librar, desembarazar. **get rid of** deshacerse de. **riddance** *n* libramiento *m*. **good riddance!** ¡menudo alivio!

riddle[1] ['ridl] *n* enigma *m*; acertijo *m*.

riddle[2] ['ridl] *v* cribar.

***ride** [raid] *v* montar; (*horse*) montar a caballo. **ride a bicycle/motorbike** montar en bicicleta/motocicleta. *n* vuelta *f*, paseo *m*; (*journey*) viaje *m*. **rider** *n* (*horse*) jinete *m*; (*addition*) cláusula adicional *f*. **riding** *n* equitación *f*.

ridge [ridʒ] *n* (*hills*) cadena *f*; (*crest*) cumbre *f*; (*surface*) ondulación *f*; (*roof*) caballete *m*.

ridicule ['ridikjuːl] *n* ridículo *m*. *v* ridiculizar. **ridiculous** *adj* ridículo.

rife [raif] *adj* abundante.

rifle[1] ['raifl] *n* fusil *m*. **rifle range** campo de tiro *m*.

rifle[2] ['raifl] *v* saquear.

rift [rift] *n* (*fissure*) grieta *f*; (*in clouds*) claro *m*; (*fig*) ruptura *f*.

rig [rig] *n* (*naut*) aparejo *m*. *v* (*mast*) enjarciar; preparar; arreglar; equipar; (*election*) amañar. **rig out** ataviar. **rig up** improvisar. **rigging** *n* aparejo *m*; montaje *m*; equipo *m*.

right [rait] *adj* (*not left*) derecho; bueno; bien; justo; correcto; exacto. **be right** tener razón. *adv* a la derecha; (*straight*) derecho; bien; correctamente; exactamente; inmediatamente. *n* bien *m*; justicia *f*; (*divine, to the throne, etc.*) derecho *m*; (*right hand*) derecha *f*. **civil rights** *pl n* derechos civiles *m pl*. **right angle** ángulo recto *m*. **right-handed** *adj* que usa la mano derecha. **right-of-way** *n* (*public*) servidumbre de paso *m*; (*roads*) prioridad *f*. **right-wing** *adj* (*pol*) derechista.

righteous ['raitʃəs] *adj* justo, honrado.

rightful ['raitfəl] *adj* legítimo.

rigid ['ridʒid] *adj* rígido; severo. **rigidity** *n* rigidez *f*; severidad *f*.

rigmarole ['rigməroul] *n* (*coll*) galimatías *m invar*.

rigour ['rigə] *n* rigor *m*; severidad *f*. **rigorous** *adj* riguroso; severo.

rim [rim] *m* (*cup*) borde *m*; (*wheel*) llanta *f*.

rind [raind] *n* (*fruit*) cáscara *f*; (*cheese, bacon*) corteza *f*.

ring[1] [riŋ] *n* (*finger*) anillo *m*, sortija *f*; círculo *m*; (*napkin*) aro *m*; (*keys*) llavero *m*. *v* formar círculo. **ringleader** *n* cabecilla *m*. **ring road** carretera de circunvalación *f*.

***ring**[2] [riŋ] *v* (*bell*) sonar; llamar (por teléfono); (*ears*) zumbar. **ring off** (*phone*) colgar. **ring up** (*phone*) llamar (por teléfono); (*curtain*) subir. *n* (*phone*) llamada *f*; (*sound*) sonido *m*; (*large bell*) campaneo *m*; (*electric bell*) toque *m*; (*alarm clock*) timbre *m*; (*laughter*) cascabeleo *m*.

rink [riŋk] *n* (*ice-skating*) pista de hielo *f*; (*roller-skating*) pista de patinaje *f*.

rinse [rins] *v* aclarar. *n* aclarado *m*.

riot ['raiət] *n* revuelta *f*. **run riot** desmandarse. *v* alborotarse. **rioter** *n* alborotador, -a *m, f*. **riotous** *adj* alborotado.

rip [rip] v rasgar. **rip off** or **out** arrancar. n rasgón m, rasgadura f.

ripe [raip] adj maduro. **ripen** v madurar. **ripeness** n madurez f.

ripple ['ripl] n rizo m; (sound of water) chapoteo m; (conversation) murmullo m. v rizar.

*rise [raiz] v (get up) levantarse; (in the air) elevarse; (temperature, slope) subir; (in rank) ascender; salir; crecer; desarrollarse; (revolt) sublevarse. **rising** adj naciente; ascendente; creciente. n (sun, moon) salida f; (tide) flujo m; (water level) crecida f; (slope, temperature, curtain) subida f; (hill) elevación f; (development) desarrollo m; (prices, rate, pressure) aumento m. **give rise to** provocar.

risk [risk] n riesgo m, peligro m. **at risk** a riesgo. v arriesgar. **risky** adj arriesgado.

rissole ['risoul] n croqueta f.

rite [rait] n rito m.

ritual ['ritʃuəl] nm, adj ritual.

rival ['raivəl] n(m+f), adj rival. v competir con. **rivalry** n rivalidad f, competencia f.

river ['rivə] n río m. **riverside** n ribera f. **River Plate** n Río de la Plata m.

rivet ['rivit] n remache m, roblón m. v (tech) remachar; (fig) fijar; (fig) cautivar. **rivetting** adj cautivador.

road [roud] n camino m; carretera f; (in town) calle f. **road-block** n barricada f. **road-side** n borde de la carretera m. **road sign** señal de tráfico f. **roadway** n calzada f. **roadworks** pl n obras f pl.

roam [roum] v rondar, vagar por.

roar [rɔɪ] v (lion) rugir; (bull, sea, wind) bramar; (engine) zumbar; (shout) vociferar. **roar with anger** rugir de cólera. **roar with laughter** reírse a carcajadas. n rugido m; bramido m; zumbido m; (crowd) clamor m; vociferaciones f pl.

roast [roust] v (meat) asar; (coffee) tostar. nm, adj asado.

rob [rob] v robar, hurtar. **robber** n ladrón, -ona m, f. **robbery** n robo m, hurto m.

robe [roub] n (judge's) toga f; (dressing gown) bata f; (costume) traje m; (monk's) hábito m. v vestir.

robin ['robin] n petirrojo m.

robot ['roubot] n robot m.

robust [rə'bʌst] adj robusto, vigoroso.

rock¹ [rok] n roca f; (in the sea) peña f; (stone) piedra f; (sweet) pirulí m.

rock² [rok] v (cradle) mecer; (move)

balancear; (shake) sacudir. n (music) rock m. **rocking chair** mecedora f. **rocking-horse** n caballito de balancín m.

rocket ['rokit] n cohete m. v (prices) subir vertiginosamente.

rod [rod] n (pole) barra f; (fishing) caña f; (curtain) varilla f.

rode [roud] V **ride**.

rodent ['roudənt] n roedor m.

roe [rou] n (fish eggs) hueva f. **soft roe** lechas f pl.

rogue [roug] n granuja m, pícaro m. **roguish** adj pícaro, picaresco. **roguishness** n picardía f.

role [roul] n papel m.

roll [roul] n (paper, film, butter, tobacco) rollo m; (bread) panecillo m; (cloth) pieza f; (register) registro m; (list of names) nómina f; (thunder) fragor m; (drum) redoble m. **roll-call** n lista f. **roll of honour** lista de honor f. v hacer rodar; (cigarettes) liar; (waves) arrastrar. **roll along** rodar por. **roll over** dar una vuelta. **roller** n (lawn) rodillo m. **roller-coaster** n montaña rusa f. **roller-skate** n patín de ruedas m. **rolling-pin** n rodillo m.

romance [rou'mans] n (love) amores m pl; aventura amorosa f; (story) novela romántica f. adj (language) romance. v fantasear. **romantic** n, adj romántico, -a.

Rome [roum] n Roma. **Roman** n, adj romano, -a. **Roman Catholic** n, adj católico romano, católica romana. **Roman numeral** número romano m.

romp [romp] n retozo m. v retozar.

roof [ruːf] n, pl **roofs** (building) tejado m; (cave, car, etc.) techo m. **roof of the mouth** cielo de la boca m. **roof rack** baca f.

rook [ruk] n (bird) grajo m; (chess) torre f.

room [ruːm] n cuarto m; (public) sala f; (hotel) habitación de hotel f; (space) sitio m; (accommodation) alojamiento m. **double room** habitación de matrimonio f. **make room for** dejar sitio. **room and board** cama y comida f, pensión completa f. **room-mate** n compañero/compañera de habitación m, f. **room service** servicio de habitaciones m. **single room** habitación individual f. **roomy** adj espacioso.

roost [ruːst] n percha f; gallinero m. v posarse. **rooster** n gallo m.

root¹ [ruːt] n raíz f; origen m. v echar raíces; (become fixed) arraigar.

root² [ruːt] v (pigs) hozar.

rope [roup] n cuerda f; (pearls) sarta f. **know the ropes** estar al tanto. **learn the ropes** ponerse al tanto. v (tie) amarrar; (lasso) coger con lazo. **rope off** acordonar. **ropy** adj (coll) malo.

rosary ['rouzəri] n rosario m.

rose¹ [rouz] n rosa f. **rose-bush** n rosal m. **rose garden** rosaleda f. **rosewood** n palisandro m. **rosy** adj rosado.

rose² [rouz] V **rise**.

rosemary ['rouzməri] n romero m.

rosette [rou'zet] n escarapela f.

*rot [rot] v pudrirse. n putrefacción f; (substance) podredumbre f; (coll: rubbish) bobadas f pl. **rotten** adj podrido; (coll: bad) pésimo; (coll: ill) fatal.

rota ['routə] n lista f.

rotate [rou'teit] v (hacer) girar, (hacer) dar vueltas; (crops) alternar. **rotary** adj rotatorio, rotativo. **rotation** n giro m; revolución f.

rouge [ruːʒ] n colorete m.

rough [rʌf] adj (surface) áspero; (coarse) tosco; duro; brutal; (draft) aproximado. **rough-and-ready** adj improvisado. **rough copy** or **draft** borrador m. v **rough it** (coll) vivir sin comodidades. **roughly** adv más o menos. **roughness** n aspereza f; tosquedad f; brutalidad f; dureza f.

roulette [ruːˈlet] n ruleta f.

round [raund] adj redondo. prep alrededor de. n círculo m; esfera f; (slice) rodaja f; (patrol, drinks) ronda f; (ammunition) andanada f; (applause) salva f. v redondear; dar la vuelta; doblar. **round off** acabar. **round up** acorralar; reunir; (figure) redondear.

roundabout ['raundəbaut] n (mot) plaza circular f; (fair) tiovivo m. adj indirecto.

rouse [rauz] v despertar; animar.

route [ruːt] n ruta f, itinerario m.

routine [ruːˈtiːn] adj rutinario. n rutina f.

rove [rouv] v vagar, errar.

row¹ [rou] n (file) fila f; (knitting) vuelta f.

row² [rou] v (boat) remar; (a person) llevar a remo. **rowing** n remo m. **rowing boat** n bote de remos m.

row³ [rau] n (quarrel) bronca f; (fuss) jaleo m; (noise) alboroto m. v reñir.

rowdy ['raudi] n(m+f), adj camorrista. **rowdiness** n alboroto m; ruido m.

royal ['roiəl] adj real, regio. **royalist** n

monárquico, -a m, f. **royalties** pl n derechos de autor m pl. **royalty** n realeza f.

rub [rʌb] n frotamiento m. v frotar. **rubbing** n (brass, etc.) frotamiento m.

rubber ['rʌbə] n caucho m, goma f; (eraser) goma de borrar f. **rubber band** goma f. **rubber stamp** sello de goma m. **rubber tree** gomero m. **rubbery** adj parecido a la goma.

rubbish ['rʌbiʃ] n (refuse) basura f; (waste) desperdicios m pl; (derog) porquería f; (nonsense) tonterías f pl.

rubble ['rʌbl] n escombros m pl.

ruby ['ruːbi] n rubí m.

rucksack ['rʌksak] n mochila f.

rudder ['rʌdə] n timón m.

rude [ruːd] adj (coarse) grosero; (impolite) descortés; (rough) tosco; (hard) duro; (painful) penoso; (health) robusto. **rudeness** n grosería f; descortesía f; indecencia f.

rudiment ['ruːdimənt] n rudimento m. **rudimentary** adj rudimentario.

rueful ['ruːfəl] adj contrito; vergonzoso; triste. **ruefully** adv tristemente. **ruefulness** n tristera f, aflicción f.

ruff [rʌf] n (dress) gorguera f; (on animals) collarín m.

ruffian ['rʌfiən] n rufián m.

ruffle ['rʌfl] v (disturb) agitar; (hair) desgreñar; (feathers) erizar; (cloth) fruncir; (wrinkle) arrugar; (worry) perturbar.

rug [rʌg] n (carpet) alfombra f; (small carpet) tapete m; (blanket) manta de viaje f.

rugged ['rʌgid] adj (rock) escarpado; (ground) accidentado; (character) desabrido; (face) duro; (climate) riguroso. **ruggedness** n lo escarpado; lo accidentado; desabrimiento m; dureza f.

ruin ['ruːin] n ruina f. v arruinar. **ruinous** adj ruinoso.

rule [ruːl] n regla f; mando m, gobierno m. **as a rule** por regla general. **rule of the road** reglamento del tráfico. **rules and regulations** reglamento m sing. v mandar, gobernar; (lines) tirar (una línea). **rule out** excluir. **ruler** n gobernante m, f; soberano, -a m, f; (measuring) regla f. **ruling** n (law) decisión f.

rum [rʌm] n ron m.

rumble ['rʌmbl] n ruido sordo m; (stomach) borborigmo m. v retumbar; (stomach) sonar.

rummage ['rʌmidʒ] v revolver. **rummage sale** venta de prendas usadas f.

rumour ['ruːmə] n rumor m. **it is rumoured (that)** se rumorea (que).

rump [rʌmp] n (quadruped) ancas f pl; (person) trasero m; (cookery) cuarto trasero m.

***run** [rʌn] v correr; circular; (theatre) estar en cartel; (leak) salirse; (car) marchar; (machine) funcionar; (melt) derretirse; (colours) desteñirse; (road) pasar; (stockings) hacerse una carrerilla. n (race) carrera f; (short trip) paseo m; (of a train, etc.) trayecto m; (series) serie f; (ski) pista f; (print) tirada f. **in the long run** a la larga.

run away v escaparse. **runaway** nm, adj fugitivo.

run down v (knock over) atropellar; (criticize) poner por los suelos. **run-down** adj (exhausted) agotado. **rundown** n informe detallado m.

rung[1] [rʌŋ] V **ring**.

rung[2] [rʌŋ] n peldaño m.

run in v (mot) rodar; (arrest) detener.

runner ['rʌnə] n (athlete) corredor, -a m, f; (sledge) patín m. **runner bean** judía escarlata f. **runner-up** n subcampeón, -ona m, f.

run out v acabarse.

run over v (hit) pillar; (rehearse) volver a ensayar; (text) echar un vistazo a; (overflow) rebosar.

run up v (make quickly) hacer rápidamente; (flag) izar. **run up against** tropezar con.

runway ['rʌnwei] n pista f.

rupture ['rʌptʃə] n ruptura f; (med) hernia f. v romper.

rural ['ruərəl] adj rural, campestre.

ruse [ruːz] n ardid m.

rush[1] [rʌʃ] n ímpetu m; prisa f; carrera precipitada f. v hacer precipitadamente; meter prisa. **rush hour** hora punta f.

rush[2] [rʌʃ] n (bot) junco m.

rusk [rʌsk] n galleta dura f.

Russia ['rʌʃə] n Rusia f. **Russian** n, adj ruso, -a.

rust [rʌst] n orín m, herrumbre f. v oxidar. **rusty** adj oxidado.

rustic ['rʌstik] adj rústico.

rustle ['rʌsl] v (leaves) susurrar; (paper) crujir. n susurro m; crujido m.

rut [rʌt] n rodera f.

ruthless ['ruːθlis] adj despiadado, implacable.

rye [rai] n centeno m.

S

sabbatical [sə'batikəl] adj sabático. **sabbatical year** año de permiso m.

sable ['seibl] n cebellina f.

sabotage ['sabətaːʒ] n sabotaje m. v sabotear. **saboteur** n saboteador, -a m, f.

sabre ['seibə] n sable m.

saccharin ['sakərin] n sacarina f. adj sacarino.

sachet ['saʃei] n saquito m.

sack [sak] n saco m. **get the sack** (coll) recibir el pasaporte. v (coll) despedir.

sacrament ['sakrəmənt] n sacramento m.

sacred ['seikrid] adj sagrado.

sacrifice ['sakrifais] n sacrificio m. v sacrificar.

sacrilege ['sakrəlidʒ] n sacrilegio m. **sacrilegious** adj sacrilego.

sad [sad] adj triste. **sadden** v entristecer. **sadly** adv tristemente; (unfortunately) desgraciadamente. **sadness** n tristeza f.

saddle ['sadl] n (horse) silla f; (bicycle) sillín m. **saddle-bag** n (horse) alforja f; (bicycle) cartera f. **saddle with** cargar con. **saddler** n guarnicionero m. **saddlery** n guarnicones f pl.

sadism ['seidizəm] n sadismo m. **sadist** n sádico, -a m, f. **sadistic** adj sádico.

safari [sə'faːri] n safari m. **safari park** reserva f.

safe [seif] adj (unhurt) sano y salvo; (undamaged) intacto; (secure) seguro; (harmless) inofensivo; (trustworthy) de fiar. n caja de caudales f. **safekeeping** n custodia f. **be on the safe side** para mayor seguridad. **safely** adv a buen puerto; sin peligro. **safety** n seguridad f; salvamento m. **safety belt** cinturón de seguridad m. **safety pin** imperdible m.

safeguard ['seifgaːd] n salvaguardia f. v salvaguardar.

saffron ['safrən] n azafrán m. adj azafranado.

sag [sag] v doblegarse; flaquear. n hundimiento m; flexión f.

saga ['saɪgə] *n* saga *f.*
sage¹ [seɪdʒ] *nm, adj* sabio.
sage² [seɪdʒ] *n* (*bot*) salvia *f.*
Sagittarius [sadʒɪ'teərɪəs] *n* Sagitario *m.*
said [sed] *V* say.
sail [seɪl] *n* vela *f;* (*trip*) paseo *m;* (*windmill*) brazo *m.* **sailcloth** *n* lona *f.* **set sail** hacerse a la mar. *v* (*leave*) salir; (*cross*) atravesar; (*boat*) navegar. **sail through** (*coll*) hacer muy fácilmente. **sailing** *n* (*navigation*) navegación *f;* (*departure*) salida *f.* **sailing boat** barco de vela *m.* **sailor** *n* marinero *m.*
saint [seɪnt] *n* santo, -a *m, f.*
sake [seɪk] *n* **for the sake of** por; para; por amor de.
salad ['saləd] *n* ensalada *f.* **salad cream** mayonesa *f.* **salad dressing** vinagreta *f.*
salami [sə'laɪmɪ] *n* salchichón *m.*
salary ['salərɪ] *n* sueldo *m.*
sale [seɪl] *n* venta *f;* (*reductions*) liquidación *f.* **for** *or* **on sale** en venta. **sale-room** *n* sala de subasta *f.* **salesman** *n* (*shop*) dependiente *m;* (*rep*) representante *m.* **salesmanship** *n* arte de vender *m.*
saline ['seɪlaɪn] *adj* salino. **salinity** *n* salinidad *f.*
saliva [sə'laɪvə] *n* saliva *f.* **salivary** *adj* salival. **salivate** *v* salivar.
sallow ['salou] *adj* cetrino.
salmon ['samən] *n* salmón *m.*
salon ['salon] *n* salón *m.*
saloon [sə'luɪn] *n* salón *m;* sala *f.* **saloon bar** salón interior *m.* **saloon car** coche salón *m.*
salt [soɪlt] *n* sal *f.* **salt-cellar** *n* salero *m. v* salar. **salty** *adj* salado.
salute [sə'luɪt] *n* saludo *m;* (*gun*) salva *f. v* saludar.
salvage ['salvɪdʒ] *n* salvamento *m;* objetos salvados *m pl. v* salvar.
salvation [sal'veɪʃən] *n* salvación *f.*
same [seɪm] *adj* mismo; igual. *pron* el mismo, la misma. *adv* de la misma forma. **all the same** sin embargo. **at the same time** al mismo tiempo.
sample ['saɪmpl] *n* muestra *f;* prueba *f;* ejemplo *m. v* probar; (*drinks*) catar.
sanatorium [sanə'toɪrɪəm] *n* sanatorio *m.*
sanctify ['saŋktɪfaɪ] *v* santificar. **sanctification** *n* santificación *f.*
sanctimonious [saŋktɪ'mounɪəs] *adj* santurrón.
sanction ['saŋkʃən] *n* sanción *f. v* sancionar; autorizar.

sanctity ['saŋktətɪ] *n* santidad *f;* inviolabilidad *f.*
sanctuary ['saŋktʃuərɪ] *n* santuario *m;* (*refuge*) refugio *m;* (*animal*) reserva *f.*
sand [sand] *n* arena *f.* **sandbag** *n* saco terrero *m.* **sand dune** duna *f.* **sandpaper** *n* papel de lija *m. v* (*with sandpaper*) lijar.
sandy *adj* (*beach*) arenoso; (*hair*) rubio rojizo.
sandal ['sandl] *n* sandalia *f.*
sandwich ['sanwɪdʒ] *n* bocadillo *m. v* intercalar.
sane [seɪn] *adj* sano; razonable. **sanity** *n* juicio *m;* (*sensibleness*) sensatez *f.*
sang [saŋ] *V* sing.
sanitary ['sanɪtərɪ] *adj* sanitario; higiénico. **sanitary towel** paño higiénico *m.*
sank [saŋk] *V* sink.
sap [sap] *n* savia *f.*
sapphire ['safaɪə] *n* zafiro *m.*
sarcasm ['saɪkazəm] *n* sarcasmo *m.*
sardine [saɪ'diɪn] *n* sardina *f.*
Sardinia [saɪ'dɪnjə] *n* Cerdeña *f.* **Sardinian** *n, adj* sardo, -a *m, f.*
sardonic [saɪ'donɪk] *adj* sardónico.
sash¹ [saʃ] *n* faja *f;* (*chest ribbon*) banda *f;* (*waist*) fajín *m.*
sash² [saʃ] *n* (*frame*) marco *m.* **sash window** ventana de guillotina *f.*
sat [sat] *V* sit.
Satan ['seɪtən] *n* Satán *m,* Satanás *m.* **satanic** *adj* satánico.
satchel ['satʃəl] *n* cartera *f.*
satellite ['satəlaɪt] *n* satélite *m.*
satin ['satɪn] *n* raso *m.*
satire ['sataɪə] *n* sátira *f.* **satirical** *adj* satírico. **satirize** *v* satirizar.
satisfy ['satɪsfaɪ] *v* satisfacer; convencer. **satisfaction** *n* satisfacción *f.* **satisfactory** *adj* satisfactorio.
saturate ['satʃəreɪt] *v* saturar; (*soak*) empapar. **saturation** *n* saturación *f.* **reach saturation point** llegar al punto de saturación.
Saturday ['satədɪ] *n* sábado *m.*
sauce [soɪs] *n* salsa *f;* (*slang*) insolencia *f.* **saucy** *adj* descarado; coquetón.
saucepan ['soɪspən] *n* cacerola *f.*
saucer ['soɪsə] *n* platillo *m.* **flying saucer** platillo volante *m.*
sauerkraut ['sauəkraut] *n* sauerkraut *m.*
sauna ['soɪnə] *n* sauna *f.*
saunter ['soɪntə] *v* pasearse. *n* paso lento *m;* paseo *m.*

sausage ['sɔsidʒ] *n* salchicha *f.* **sausage-meat** *n* carne de salchicha *f.* **sausage roll** empanadilla de salchicha *f.*

savage ['savidʒ] *adj* (*fierce*) feroz; (*primitive*) salvaje; cruel; violento. *n* salvaje *m, f. v* embestir. **savagery** *n* salvajada *f*; ferocidad *f.*

save[1] [seiv] *v* salvar; (*put aside*) ahorrar; (*keep till later*) quardar; (*protect*) proteger; (*goal*) parar. **savings** *pl n* ahorros *m pl.* **savings bank** caja de ahorros *f.*

save[2] [seiv] *prep* salvo, excepto. *conj* a no ser que.

saviour ['seivjə] *n* salvador, -a *m, f.*

savoir-faire [,savwaˈfeə] *n* desparpajo *m*; sentido común *m.*

savour ['seivə] *v* saborear; tener sabor de. *n* sabor *m*, gusto *m.* **savoury** *adj* sabroso; salado. *n* entremés salado *m.*

saw[1] [sɔ] *V* see.

*saw[2] [sɔ] *n* (*tool*) sierra *f*; (*proverb*) refrán *m.* **sawdust** *n* aserrín *m.* **sawmill** *n* aserradero *m. v* aserrar.

saxophone ['saksəfoun] *n* saxofón *m.*

*say [sei] *v* decir; recitar. *n* **have no say** no tener ni voz ni voto. **saying** *n* (*act*) decir *m*; (*maxim*) refrán *m.*

scab [skab] *n* costra *f*, postilla *f*; (*derog: blackleg*) esquirol *m.*

scaffold ['skafəld] *n* (*platform*) tarina *f*; (*gallows*) cadalso *m.* **scaffolding** *n* andamio *m.*

scald [skɔild] *v* escaldar; (*instruments*) esterilizar. *n* escaldadura *f.* **scalding** *adj* hirviendo, hirviente.

scale[1] [skeil] *n* (*fish, etc.*) escama *f*; (*tartar*) sarro *m.* **scaly** *adj* escamoso; sarroso.

scale[2] [skeil] *n* (*music, measurement*) escala *f*; (*damage, etc.*) amplitud *f.* **scale drawing** dibujo hecho a escala *m. v* (*climb*) escalar. **scale down** reducir a escala.

scales [skeilz] *pl n* balanza *f sing.*

scallop ['skaləp] *n* (*zool*) venera *f*; (*cookery*) escalope *m*; (*sewing*) festón *m.* **scallop shell** concha *f. v* festonear.

scalp [skalp] *n* cuero cabelludo *m. v* escalpar.

scalpel ['skalpəl] *n* escalpelo *m.*

scamper ['skampə] *v* corretear.

scampi ['skampi] *n* gamba grande *f.*

scan [skan] *v* recorrer con la mirada; escrutar; (*tech*) explorar; (*poetry*) escandir.

scandal ['skandl] *n* escándalo *m*; (*gossip*)

chismorreo *m*; (*law*) difamación *f.* **scandalize** *v* escandalizar. **scandalous** *adj* escandaloso.

Scandinavia [,skandiˈneivjə] *n* Escandinavia *f.* **Scandinavian** *n, adj* escandinavo, -a.

scant [skant] *adj also* **scanty** insuficiente. **scantily** *adv* muy ligeramente.

scapegoat ['skeipgout] *n* cabeza de turco *f.*

scar [skai] *n* cicatriz *f. v* cicatrizar; (*fig*) marcar.

scarce [skeəs] *adj* escaso; insuficiente; raro. **scarcely** *adv* apenas; casi. **scarcity** *n* escasez *f.*

scare [skeə] *n* susto *m*; alarma *f. v* asustar, espantar. **be scared** tener miedo. **scarecrow** *n* espantapájaros *m invar.*

scarf [skaif] *m* (*woollen*) bufanda *f*; (*light*) pañuelo *m.*

scarlet ['skailit] *adj* escarlato. **scarlet fever** escarlatina *f.*

scathing ['skeiðiŋ] *adj* cáustico, mordaz.

scatter ['skatə] *v* esparcir; (*sprinkle*) salpicar; (*put to flight*) derrotar; dispersar; (*squander*) desparramar. **scatter-brained** *adj* atolondrado.

scavenge ['skavindʒ] *v* recoger; buscar entre. **scavenger** *n* barrendero *m*; animal que se alimenta de carroña *m.*

scene [siin] *n* escena *f*; (*place*) lugar *m*; espectáculo *m*; vista *f.* **scenic** *adj* escénico; pintoresco.

scenery ['siinəri] *n* (*landscape*) paisaje *m*; (*theatre*) decorado *m.*

scent [sent] *n* perfume *m*; (*smell*) olor *m*; (*track*) rastro *m. v* perfumar; (*smell*) oler.

sceptic ['skeptik] *n* escéptico, -a *m, f.* **sceptical** *adj* escéptico. **scepticism** *n* esceptisismo *m.*

sceptre ['septə] *n* cetro *m.*

schedule ['fedjuil] *n* programa *m*; (*timetable*) horario *m. v* programar; fijar.

scheme [skiim] *n* plan *m*; proyecto *m*, esquema *m*; (*plot*) intriga *f. v* proyectar; intrigar, conspirar.

schizophrenia [,skitsəˈfriiniə] *n* esquizofrenia *f.* **schizophrenic** *n, adj* esquizofrénico, -a.

scholar ['skolə] *n* (*learned person*) erudito, -a *m, f*; (*schoolchild*) colegial, -a *m, f*, alumno, -a *m, f*; (*student*) estudiante *m, f.* **scholarly** *adj* erudito. **scholarship** *n* (*award*) beca *f*; erudición *f.*

scholastic [skə'lastik] *adj* escolar, escolástico.

school[1] [skuːl] *n* escuela *f*; (*private or secondary*) colegio *m*. **schoolboy** *n* alumno *m*, colegial *m*. **schoolgirl** *n* alumna *f*, colegiala *f*. **schooling** *n* educación *f*, enseñanza *f*. **schoolmaster** *n* (*primary*) maestro *m*; (*secondary*) profesor *m*. **schoolmistress** *n* maestra *f*; profesora *f*. **school-room** *n* clase *f*; sala de clase *f*.

school[2] [skuːl] *n* (*of fish*) banco *m*.

schooner ['skuːnə] *n* goleta *f*.

sciatica [sai'atikə] *n* ciática *f*. **sciatic** *adj* ciático.

science ['saiəns] *n* ciencia *f*. **science fiction** ciencia ficción *f*. **scientific** *adj* científico. **scientist** *n* científico, -a *m*, *f*.

scintillating ['sintileitiŋ] *adj* relumbrante; (*fig*) brillante.

scissors ['sizəz] *pl n* tijeras *f pl*.

scoff[1] [skof] *v* burlarse.

scoff[2] [skof] *v* (*coll: eat*) zamparse.

scold [skould] *v* reñir, reprender. *n* virago *f*. **scolding** *n* reprensión *f*.

scone [skon] *n* bollo *m*.

scoop [skuːp] *n* pala de mano *f*; (*press*) éxito periodístico *m*. *v* sacar con pala; (*dig*) excavar.

scooter ['skuːtə] *n* (*motor*) scooter *m*; (*child's*) patinete *m*.

scope [skoup] *n* (*range*) alcance *m*; (*opportunity*) libertad *f*; (*field of action*) esfera *f*.

scorch [skɔːtʃ] *n* quemadura *f*. *v* quemar; (*singe*) chamuscar.

score [skɔː] *n* (*number of points*) tanteo *m*; (*result*) resultado *m*; (*test marks*) calificación *f*; (*twenty*) veintena *f*; (*music*) partitura *f*; (*notch*) muesca *f*. **scoreboard** *n* marcador *m*. *v* (*point, goal*) marcar; orquestar; hacer una muesca en. **scorer** *n* (*scorekeeper*) tanteador *m*; (*football*) goleador *m*.

scorn [skɔːn] *n* desdén *m*, desprecio *m*. *v* desdeñar, despreciar. **scornful** *adj* desdeñoso, despreciativo.

Scorpio ['skɔːpiou] *n* Escorpión *m*.

scorpion ['skɔːpiən] *n* escorpión *m*.

Scotland ['skotlənd] *n* Escocia *f*. **Scot** *n* escocés, -esa *m*, *f*. **Scotch** *n* whisky escocés *m*. **Scots** *nm*, *adj* escocés. **Scottish** *adj* escocés.

scoundrel ['skaundrəl] *n* sinvergüenza *m*.

scour[1] [skauə] *v* (*clean*) fregar. **scourer** *n* (*pad*) estropajo *m*.

scour[2] [skauə] *v* (*search*) recorrer, batir.

scout [skaut] *n* explorador *m*. **scoutmaster** *n* jefe de exploradores *m*.

scowl [skaul] *v* fruncir el entrecejo. *n* ceño *m*.

scramble ['skrambl] *v* (*climb*) trepar; (*struggle*) pelearse; (*mix*) mezclar; (*eggs*) revolver. *n* lucha *f*, pelea *f*.

scrap [skrap] *n* (*piece*) trozo *m*; (*metal*) chatarra *f*; (*coll: fight*) pelea *f*. **scrapbook** *n* álbum de recortes *m*. papel para apuntes *m*. **scraps** *pl n* restos *m pl*, sobras *f pl*. *v* desechar; (*coll*) pelear.

scrape [skreip] *n* (*noise*) chirrido *m*; (*act*) raspado *m*; (*mark*) arañazo *m*; (*graze*) rasguño *m*; (*coll: trouble*) apuro *m*. *v* raspar; (*graze*) arañar; (*drag*) arrastrar.

scratch [skratʃ] *n* arañazo *m*; raya *f*; rasguño *m*; cero *m*.

scrawl [skrɔːl] *v* garabatear. *n* garabato *m*.

scream [skriːm] *n* grito *m*, chillido *m*. *v* gritar, chillar.

screech [skriːtʃ] *v* chillar, gritar; (*brakes*) chirriar. *n* chillido *m*, grito *m*; chirrido *m*.

screen [skriːn] *n* (*TV, film*) pantalla *f*; (*folding*) biombo *m*; (*fig*) cortina *f*. **screen-play** *n* guión *m*. **screen test** prueba cinematográfica *f*. *v* (*film*) proyectar; (*shelter*) proteger; (*sift*) tamizar.

screw [skruː] *n* tornillo *m*; (*propeller*) hélice *f*. **screwdriver** *n* destornillador *m*. *v* atornillar. **screw up** (*paper*) arrugar.

scribble ['skribl] *v* garabatear. *n* garabato *m*.

script [skript] *n* (*film*) guión *m*; (*theatre*) argumento *m*; (*writing*) escritura *f*.

scripture ['skriptʃə] *n* (*school*) religión *f*; (*holy*) Sagrada Escritura *f*.

scroll [skroul] *n* rollo *m*; (*arch*) voluta *f*.

scrounge [skraundʒ] *(coll) v* sablear; gorronear. **scrounger** *n* sablista *m*, *f*; gorrón, -ona *m*, *f*.

scrub[1] [skrʌb] *n* fregado *m*; fricción *f*. *v* fregar; restregar; (*coll: cancel*) cancelar. **scrubbing brush** cepillo de fregar *m*.

scrub[2] [skrʌb] *n* matorral *m*; maleza *f*.

scruff [skrʌf] *n* **by the scruff of the neck** por el cogote.

scruffy ['skrʌfi] *adj* desaliñado. **scruffiness** *n* desaliño *m*.

scrum [skrʌm] *n* melée *f.*
scruple ['skruːpl] *n* escrúpulo *m.* **scrupulous** *adj* escrupuloso.
scrutiny ['skruːtəni] *n* escrutinio *m.* **scrutinize** *v* escudriñar.
scuffle ['skʌfl] *n* pelea *f.* refriega *f.* *v* pelear, reñir.
scull [skʌl] *n* remo *m.*
scullery ['skʌləri] *n* trascocina *f.*
sculpt [skʌlpt] *v* esculpir. **sculptor** *n* escultor, -a *m, f.* **sculpture** *n* escultura *f.*
scum [skʌm] *n* espuma *f;* (*derog*) escoria *f.*
scurf [skɔːf] *n* caspa *f.*
scurvy ['skəːvi] *n* escorbuto *m.*
scuttle[1] ['skʌtl] *n* (*coal*) cubo del carbón *m.*
scuttle[2] ['skʌtl] *v* (*naut*) barrenar.
scuttle[3] ['skʌtl] *v* escabullirse.
scythe [saið] *n* guadaña *f.* *v* guadañar.
sea [siː] *n* mar *m, f.*
sea-bed *n* fondo del mar *m.*
seaborne ['siːbɔɪn] *adj* transportado por mar.
seafood ['siːfuːd] *n* mariscos *m pl.*
seafront ['siːfrʌnt] *n* paseo marítimo *m.*
seagoing ['siːˌgouiŋ] *adj* (*ship*) de alta mar; (*person*) marinero.
seagull ['siːgʌl] *n* gaviota *f.*
seahorse ['siːhɔɪs] *n* caballo de mar *m.*
seal[1] [siːl] *n* sello *m.* *v* sellar; (*close*) cerrar; (*fate*) decidir. **sealing wax** lacre *m.*
seal[2] [siːl] *n* (*zool*) foca *f.* **sealskin** *n* piel de foca *f.*
sea-level *n* nivel del mar *m.*
sea-lion *n* león marino *m.*
seam [siːm] *n* (*sewing*) costura *f;* (*coal*) vena *f;* (*geol*) capa *f.* **seamy** *adj* (*fig*) sórdido.
seaman ['siːmən] *n pl* **seamen** marinero *m.*
séance ['seiãs] *n* sesión de espiritismo *f.*
sear [siə] *v* (*scorch*) abrasar; (*wither*) marchitar. **searing** *adj* (*pain*) punzante.
search [sɔːtʃ] *n* investigación *f;* (*to find something*) búsqueda *f;* (*house, car*) registro *m.* **searchlight** *n* reflector *m.* **search-party** *n* equipo de salvamento *m.* **search warrant** *n* mandamiento de registro *m.* *v* buscar; registrar; investigar. **searching** *adj* (*look*) penetrante; (*examination*) minucioso.
sea shell *n* concha marina *f.*
seashore ['siːʃɔɪ] *n* playa *f;* costa *f.*

seasick ['siːsik] *adj* **be seasick** marearse. **sea sickness** mareo *m.*
seaside ['siːsaid] *n* playa *f;* costa *f.* **seaside resort** estación balnearia *f.*
season ['siːzn] *n* estación *f;* temporada *f;* época *f.* **season ticket** abono *m.* *v* (*food*) sazonar; (*wood*) secar. **seasonal** *adj* estacional; (*work*) temporal. **seasoning** *n* condimento *m.*
seat [siːt] *n* asiento *m;* silla *f;* localidad *f;* centro *m.* **seat-belt** *n* cinturón de seguridad *m.* *v* sentar; colocar; tener cabida para.
seawater ['siːˌwɔɪtə] *n* agua de mar *f.*
seaweed ['siːwiːd] *n* alga *f.*
seaworthy ['siːwɔːði] *adj* marinero. **seaworthiness** *n* navegabilidad *f.*
secluded [siˈkluːdid] *adj* retirado; aislado. **seclusion** *n* reclusión *f;* soledad *f.*
second[1] ['sekənd] *n* (*time*) segundo *m.* **second hand** segundero *m.*
second[2] ['sekənd] *n* segundo, -a *m, f.* (*gear*) segunda *f.* **seconds** *pl n* articulos de segunda clase *m pl. adj* segundo. **on second thoughts** pensándolo bien. **second-class** *adj* de segunda clase. **travel second-class** viajar en segunda. **secondhand** *adj* de segunda mano, usado. **second-rate** *adj* de segunda categoria. *v* (*in debate*) apoyar. **secondly** *adv* en segundo lugar.
secondary ['sekəndəri] *adj* secundario. **secondary school** instituto de enseñanza media *m.*
secret ['siːkrit] *nm, adj* secreto. **secrecy** *n* secreto *m.* **secretive** *adj* reservado; callado. **secretly** *adv* en secreto.
secretary ['sekrətəri] *n* secretario, -a *m, f.* **secretarial** *adj* de secretario.
secrete [siˈkriːt] *v* (*hide*) esconder; (*med*) secretar. **secretion** *n* secreción *f.*
sect [sekt] *n* secta *f.* **sectarian** *adj* sectario.
section ['sekʃən] *n* sección *f;* parte *f.*
sector ['sektə] *n* sector *m.*
secular ['sekjulə] *adj* profano; secular; laico.
secure [siˈkjuə] *adj* seguro. *v* asegurar; cerrar firmemente; garantizar; conseguir; reservar; consolidar. **security** *n* seguridad *f;* (*for loan*) garantía *f.*
sedate [siˈdeit] *adj* sosegado; tranquilo. **sedation** *n* sedación *f.* **sedative** *nm, adj* sedante.

sediment ['sedimənt] n (*geol*) sedimento m; (*liquid*) poso m.
seduce [si'djuːs] v seducir. **seduction** n seducción f. **seductive** adj seductor.
*see¹ [siː] v ver; comprender; mirar; visitar; recibir. **see off** ir a despedir. **see through** (*not be deceived*) calar. **see to** ocuparse de. **see you later!** ¡hasta luego!
see² [siː] n (*rel*) obispado m.
seed [siːd] n semilla f; (*fruit*) pepita f; (*sperm*) semen m. **seedless** adj sin semillas; sin pepitas. **seedling** n plantón m. **seedy** adj granado; (*coll: ill*) pachucho.
*seek [siːk] v buscar; tratar; solicitar.
seem [siːm] v parecer. **seeming** adj aparente. **seemingly** adv al parecer, por lo visto.
seep [siːp] v rezumarse. **seepage** n filtración f.
seesaw ['siːsɔː] n columpio m, subibaja m. v columpiarse.
seethe [siːð] v borbotar. **seething** adj (*coll*) bufando de cólera.
segment ['segmənt] n segmento m; (*orange, etc.*) gajo m.
segregate ['segrigeit] v segregar. **segregation** n segregación f.
seize [siːz] v tomar; (*grab firmly*) agarrar; (*a person*) detener. **seize up** (*tech*) agarrotarse. **seizure** n asimiento m; detención f; (*property*) embargo m; (*in war*) toma f; (*med*) ataque m.
seldom ['seldəm] adv raramente.
select [sə'lekt] v escoger, elegir. adj escogido; (*exclusive*) selecto. **selection** n selección f. **selective** adj selectivo.
self [self] n sí mismo m, sí misma f; personalidad f.
self-addressed adj con su propia dirección.
self-adhesive adj autoadhesivo.
self-assured adj seguro de sí mismo. **self-assurance** n confianza en sí mismo f.
self-centred adj egocéntrico.
self-confident adj seguro de sí mismo. **self-confidence** n seguridad en sí mismo f.
self-conscious adj cohibido. **self-consciousness** n turbación f.
self-contained adj independiente.
self-control n dominio de sí mismo m. **self-controlled** adj sereno.
self-defence n (*technique*) autodefensa f; (*law*) legítima defensa f.

self-determination n autodeterminación f.
self-discipline n autodisciplina f.
self-educated adj autodidacto.
self-employed adj que trabaja por cuenta propia.
self-esteem n amor propio m.
self-evidence adj patente, manifiesto.
self-explanatory adj que se explica por sí mismo.
self-expression n expresión de la propia personalidad f.
self-interest n interés propio m.
selfish ['selfiʃ] adj egoísta. **selfishness** n egoísmo m.
selfless ['selflis] adj desinteresado.
self-made adj **self-made man** hijo de sus propias obras m.
self-opinionated adj obstinado.
self-pity n lástima de sí mismo f.
self-portrait n autorretrato m.
self-possessed adj seguro de sí mismo.
self-respect n dignidad f.
self-righteous adj farisaico. **self-righteousness** n fariseísmo m.
self-rule n autonomía f.
self-sacrifice n sacrificio de sí mismo m.
selfsame ['selfseim] adj mismísimo m.
self-satisfied adj satisfecho de sí mismo.
self-service n autoservicio m.
self-sufficient adj independiente. **self-sufficiency** n independencia f.
self-willed adj obstinado.
self-winding adj de cuerda automática.
*sell [sel] v vender(se); hacer vender. **sell off** liquidar. **seller** n vendedor, -a m, f; (*dealer*) comerciante m.
semantic [sə'mantik] adj semántico. **semantics** n semántica f.
semaphore ['seməfɔː] n semáforo m.
semblance ['sembləns] n apariencia f.
semen ['siːmən] n semen m.
semibreve ['semibriːv] n semibreve f.
semicircle ['semisəːkl] n semicírculo m. **semicircular** adj semicircular.
semicolon [ˌsemi'koulən] n punto y coma m.
semiconscious [semi'konʃəs] adj semiconsciente.
semi-detached house n casa doble f.
semifinal [semi'fainl] n semifinal f.
seminar ['seminaː] n seminario m.
semi-precious adj fino; semiprecioso.
semiquaver ['semikweivə] n semicorchea f.

semitone ['semitoun] n semitono m.

semolina [,semə'liinə] n sémola f.

senate ['senit] n senado m. **senator** n senador m.

*send [send] v enviar, mandar; remitir; echar; transmitir. **send back** devolver. **send for** llamar a; (mail-order) escribir pidiendo.

senile ['siːnail] adj senil. **senility** n senilidad f.

senior ['siːnjə] adj (age) mayor; (rank) superior. n (school) mayor m, f. **seniority** n antigüedad f.

sensation [sen'seifən] n sensación f. **sensational** adj sensacional.

sense [sens] n sentido m; significado m; sensación f; sentimiento m; (consensus) sentir m. **senses** pl n (reason) juicio m sing; (consciousness) sentido m. v sentir. **senseless** adj (unconscious) sin sentido; (silly) insensato.

sensible ['sensəbl] adj sensato; razonable; (clothes) práctico.

sensitive ['sensitiv] adj sensible; (easily hurt) susceptible. **sensitivity** n sensibilidad f; susceptibilidad f.

sensual ['sensjuəl] adj sensual. **sensuality** n sensualidad f.

sensuous ['sensjuəs] adj sensual.

sent [sent] V **send**.

sentence ['sentəns] n (gramm) frase f; (law) sentencia f. v sentenciar, condenar.

sentiment ['sentimənt] n sentimiento m; (sentimentality) sentimentalismo m; opinión f. **sentimental** adj sentimental.

sentry ['sentri] n centinela m.

separate ['sepərət; v 'sepəreit] adj separado; distinto; independiente; (room) particular. v separar; dividir; distinguir entre. **separation** n separación f.

September [sep'tembə] n septiembre m, setiembre m.

septic ['septik] adj séptico.

sequel ['siːkwəl] n consecuencia f; secuela f.

sequence ['siːkwəns] n sucesión f; serie f; orden m.

sequin ['siːkwin] n lentejuela f.

serenade [serə'neid] n serenata f. v dar una serenata a.

serene [sə'riːn] adj sereno. **serenity** n serenidad f.

serf [səːf] n siervo, -a m, f.

sergeant ['saːdʒənt] n (mil) sargento m; (police) cabo m. **sergeant-major** n sargento mayor m.

serial ['siəriəl] n serial m. adj de serie; seriado. **serialize** v publicar por entregas.

series ['siəriːz] n serie f.

serious ['siəriəs] adj serio; grave. **seriousness** n seriedad f; gravedad f.

sermon ['səːmən] n sermón m.

serpent ['səːpənt] n serpiente f.

serrated [sə'reitid] adj serrado; dentado.

servant ['səːvənt] n criado, -a m, f; sirviente, -a m, f; empleado, -a m, f; funcionario, -a m, f.

serve [səːv] v servir; atender. **it serves you right** te está bien empleado. n (tennis) saque m.

service ['səːvis] n servicio m; favor m; (mot) revisión f; (tea) juego m; (tennis) saque m. **service charge** servicio m. **serviceman** n militar m. **service station** (mot) estación de servicio f. v (check) revisar; (maintain) mantener. **serviceable** adj utilizable; práctico.

serviette [,səːvi'et] n servilleta f.

servile ['səːvail] adj servil. **servility** n servilismo m.

session ['sefən] n sesión f; junta f.

*set [set] v poner; colocar; fijar; (clock) regular; (bones) reducir; (type) componer; (to music) poner en música; (sun) ponerse. **set about** ponerse (a). **setback** n revés m; contratiempo m. **set off** (leave) partir; (explode) hacer estallar; (cause) hacer. **set out** partir; disponer. **set up** erigir; montar; establecer. n grupo m; (tools, china, etc.) batería f; (books) colección f; (people) clase f; (clothes) caída f; (sun, etc.) puesta f; (radio, etc.) aparato m; (tennis) set m; (theatre) decorado m. adj fijo; inmóvil; asignado; establecido. **setting** n (adjustment) ajuste m; (theatre) decorado m.

settee [se'tiː] n canapé m.

settle ['setl] v (solve) resolver; calmar; (country) colonizar. **settle down** instalarse; calmarse. **settle up** (bill) pagar. **settlement** n colonización f; arreglo m; liquidicación f; satisfacción f.

seven ['sevn] nm, adj siete. **seventh** n, adj séptimo, -a..

seventeen [sevn'tiːn] nm, adj diecisiete. **seventeenth** n, adj decimoséptimo, -a.

seventy ['sevnti] *nm, adj* setenta. **seventieth** *n, adj* septuagésimo, -a.
sever ['sevə] *v* cortar.
several ['sevrəl] *adj, pron* varios.
severe [sə'viə] *adj* severo; duro; (*pain*) agudo; (*illness*) grave. **severity** *n* severidad *f*; gravedad *f*; (*weather*) inclemencia *f*.
*sew [sou] *v* coser. **sewing** *n* costura *f*. **sewing machine** máquina de coser *f*.
sewage ['sjuidʒ] *n* aguas residuales *f pl*.
sewer ['sjuə] *n* alcantarilla *f*, albañal *m*.
sex [seks] *n* sexo *m*. **sexual** *adj* sexual. **sexual intercourse** relaciones sexuales *f pl*. **sexuality** *n* sexualidad *f*. **sexy** *adj* provocativo.
sextet [seks'tet] *n* sexteto *m*.
shabby ['ʃabi] *adj* andrajoso; (*behaviour*) mezquino.
shack [ʃak] *n* choza *f*.
shade [ʃeid] *n* sombra *f*; (*lamp*) pantalla *f*; (*colour*) tono *m*; (*meaning*) matiz *m*. *v* dar sombra; (*art*) sombrear. **shady** *adj* sombreado; (*person*) dudoso.
shadow ['ʃadou] *n* sombra *f*. **shadow cabinet** gabinete fantasma *m*. *v* (*follow*) seguir. **shadowy** *adj* indistinto; misterioso.
shaft [ʃaɪft] *n* (*handle*) mango *m*; (*lift*) hueco *m*; (*light*) rayo *m*; (*ventilation*) pozo de ventilación *m*; (*mine*) pozo *m*; (*spear*) asta *f*.
shaggy ['ʃagi] *adj* peludo.
*shake [ʃeik] *v* sacudir; (*bottle*) agitar; (*head*) menear; (*brandish*) esgrimir. **shake hands** darse la mano. **shake off** librarse de. *n* sacudida *f*; meneo *m*; movimiento *m*; temblor *m*. **shaky** *adj* tembloroso; (*weak*) poco sólido.
shall [ʃal] *aux translated by future tense.*
shallot [ʃə'lot] *n* chalote *m*.
shallow ['ʃalou] *adj* poco profundo; superficial.
sham [ʃam] *adj* fingido, simulado; falso. *n* (*person*) impostor, -a *m, f*; (*object*) impostura *f*. *v* fingir, simular.
shame [ʃeim] *n* vergüenza *f*; deshonra *f*; pena *f*. *v* avergonzar; deshonrar. **shamefaced** *adj* avergonzado; tímido. **shameful** *adj* vergonzoso. **shameless** *adj* desvergonzado; sinvergüenza.
shampoo [ʃam'puɪ] *n* champú *m*. *v* dar un champú a.
shamrock ['ʃamrok] *n* trébol *m*.
shandy ['ʃandi] *n* cerveza con gaseosa *f*.

shanty[1] ['ʃanti] *n* (*hut*) chabola *f*. **shanty town** barrio de las latas *m*.
shanty[2] ['ʃanti] *n* (*music*) saloma *f*.
shape [ʃeip] *n* forma *f*; figura *f*; aspecto *m*. *v* dar forma a; labrar; cortar; (*idea*) formular. **shapeless** *adj* informe. **shapely** *adj* bien proporcionado.
share [ʃeə] *n* parte *f*; (*comm*) acción *f*. **shareholder** *n* accionista *m, f*. *v* compartir.
shark [ʃaɪk] *n* tiburón *m*.
sharp [ʃaɪp] *adj* (*edge*) afilado; (*point*) punzante; (*bend*) brusco; (*phot*) nítido; (*outline*) definido; (*pain*) agudo; (*taste*) picante; (*clever*) vivo. *n* (*music*) sostenido *m*. **sharpen** *v* (*knife*) afilar; (*pencil*) sacar punta a. **sharpness** *n* lo afilado; agudeza *f*; (*clarity*) nitidez *f*.
shatter ['ʃatə] *v* destrozar; (*health*) quebrantar; (*fig*) echar por tierra. **shattered** *adj* destrozado; roto; quebrantado. **shattering** *adj* demoledor; fulgurante.
shave [ʃeiv] *v* afeitarse. **shaving** *n* (*of wood, metal*) viruta *f*. **shaving brush** brocha de afeitar *f*. **shaving cream** crema de afeitar *f*.
shawl [ʃoɪl] *n* chal *m*.
she [ʃiɪ] *pron* ella. **she who** la que, aquella que, quien.
sheaf [ʃiɪf] *n* (*corn*) gavilla *f*; (*arrows*) haz *m*; (*papers*) fajo *m*.
*shear [ʃiə] *v* esquilar. **shears** *pl n* tijeras *f pl*.
sheath [ʃiɪθ] *n* (*umbrella, knife, etc.*) funda *f*; (*sword*) vaina *f*. **sheathe** *v* envainar; cubrir.
*shed[1] [ʃed] *v* (*drop*) deshacerse de.
shed[2] [ʃed] *n* cobertizo *m*; barraca *f*.
sheen [ʃiɪn] *n* brillo *m*; (*silk*) viso *m*.
sheep [ʃiɪp] *n* oveja *f*. **sheepdog** *n* perro pastor *m*. **sheepskin** *n* piel de carnero *f*. **sheepish** *adj* vergonzoso.
sheer[1] [ʃiə] *adj* completo; total; puro; (*cliff*) cortado a pico; (*stockings*) diáfano.
sheer[2] [ʃiə] *v* (*naut*) guiñar.
sheet [ʃiɪt] *n* (*bed*) sábana *f*; (*paper, glass*) hoja *f*; (*ice*) capa *f*; (*metal*) chapa; (*water*) extensión *f*. **sheet lightning** fucilazo *m*. **sheet music** música en hojas sueltas *f*.
sheikh [ʃeik] *n* jeque *m*.
shelf [ʃelf] *n* estante *m*.
shell [ʃel] *n* concha *f*; (*crustacean*) caparazón *m*; (*egg, nut*) cáscara *f*; (*pea*) vaina *f*; (*cannon*) proyectil *m*. **shellfish** *pl*

n mariscos *m pl. v* (*mil*) bombardear;
(*peas, shrimps*) pelar; (*nuts*) descascarar.
shelter ['ʃeltə] *n* abrigo *m*; asilo *m. v*
abrigar; proteger; dar asilo.
shelve [ʃelv] *v* (*project*) dar carpetazo a.
shelving *n* estantería *f.*
shepherd ['ʃepəd] *n* pastor *m.*
sheriff ['ʃerif] *n* sheriff *m.*
sherry ['ʃeri] *n* jerez *m.*
shield [ʃiːld] *n* escudo *m*; (*fig*) defensa *f. v*
escudar; proteger.
shift [ʃift] *n* cambio *m*; movimiento *m*;
(*work*) turno *m.* **shift key** tecla de mayús-
culas *f.* **shift work** trabajo por turnos *m.*
v cambiar; mover. **shifty** *adj* furtivo.
shimmer ['ʃimə] *v* relucir. *n* luz trémula *f.*
shin [ʃin] *n* espinilla *f.*
*****shine** [ʃain] *v* brillar. *n* brillo *m*, lustre
m. **shiny** *adj* lustroso, brillante.
shingle ['ʃiŋgl] *n* (*pebbles*) guijarros *m pl.*
shingles *n* (*med*) herpes *m, f pl.*
ship [ʃip] *n* barco *m*, navío *m*, buque *m.*
shipshape *adj* en buen orden. **shipwreck**
n naufragio *m. v* embarcar; transportar;
(*send*) enviar. **shipment** *n* cargamento *m.*
shipping *n* barcos *m pl*, buques *m pl.*
shirk [ʃəːk] *v* esquivar. **shirker** *n* gandul,
-a *m, f.*
shirt [ʃəːt] *n* camisa *f.* **in one's shirt
sleeves** en mangas de camisa. **shirt-tail** *n*
faldón *m.*
shit [ʃit] *nf, interj* (*vulgar*) mierda. *v*
cagar.
shiver ['ʃivə] *v* temblar; estremecerse. *n*
temblor *m*; estremecimiento *m.*
shoal [ʃoul] *n* (*fish*) banco *m.*
shock [ʃok] *n* choque *m*; (*elec*) descarga *f.*
shock absorber amortiguador *m.* **shock-
proof** *adj* a prueba de choques. *v* conmocionar; escandalizar. **shocking** *adj*
escandaloso; espantoso; (*news*) aterrador.
shoddy ['ʃodi] *adj* inferior. **shoddiness** *n*
fabricación inferior *f.*
*****shoe** [ʃuː] *v* (*horse*) herrar. *n* zapato *m.*
shoelace *n* cordón *m.* **shoemaker** *n*
zapatero *m.* **shoe repairer's** zapatería de
viejo *f.* **shoe shop** zapatería *f.*
shone [ʃon] *V* **shine**.
shook [ʃuk] *V* **shake**.
*****shoot** [ʃuːt] *v* (*fire*) lanzar, tirar; (*kill*)
matar; (*wound*) herir; (*film*) filmar;
(*hunt*) cazar. *n* (*bot*) brote *m.* **shooting** *n*
tiro *m pl*; (*hunting*) caza *f.*
shop [ʃop] *n* tienda *f*; (*larger*) almacén *m.*

shop assistant *n* dependiente, -a *m, f.*
shopkeeper ['ʃopkiːpə] *n* comerciante *m,
f.*
shoplifter ['ʃopliftə] *n* ratero, -a *m, f.*
shoplifting *n* ratería *f.*
shopper ['ʃopə] *n* comprador, -a *m, f.*
shopping ['ʃopiŋ] *n* compras *f pl.* **go shopping** ir de compras. **shopping bag** bolsa
de la compra *f.* **shopping centre** centro
comercial *m.* **shopping trolley** carrito *m.*
shop steward *n* enlace sindical *m.*
shore [ʃoː] *n* (*beach*) playa *f*; (*edge of sea*)
orilla *f*; (*coast*) costa *f.*
short [ʃoːt] *adj* corto; pequeño; (*not tall*)
bajo; (*brusque*) seco; (*temper*) vivo. **in
short** en resumen. **shortage** *n* falta *f.*
escasez *f.* **shorten** *v* acortar; disminuir;
abreviar. **shortly** *adv* dentro de poco.
shortbread ['ʃoːtbred] *n* mantecada *f.*
short-circuit *n* cortocircuito. *v* ponerse en
cortocircuito.
shortcoming ['ʃoːtkʌmiŋ] *n* defecto *m.*
short cut *n* atajo *m.*
shorthand ['ʃoːthand] *n* taquigrafía *f.*
shorthand typist taquimecanógrafo, -a *m.
f.*
short list *n* lista de los posibles *f.*
short-lived *adj* efímero.
shorts [ʃoːts] *pl n* pantalones cortos *m pl.*
short-sighted *adj* miope.
short story *n* novela corta *f.*
short-tempered *adj* de mal genio.
short-term *adj* de corto plazo.
short wave *n* onda corta *f. adj* de onda
corta.
shot¹ [ʃot] *V* **shoot**.
shot² [ʃot] *n* bala *f*; tiro *m*; tirador, -a *m,
f*; (*sport*) peso *m*; (*med*) inyección *f.* **shotgun** *n* escopeta *f.*
should¹ [ʃud] *v* deber, tener que.
should² [ʃud] *aux translated by conditional
tense.*
shoulder ['ʃouldə] *n* hombro *m.* **shoulder-
blade** *n* omóplato *m*; (*animal*) paletilla *f.
v* llevar al hombro.
shout [ʃaut] *n* grito *m. v* gritar.
shove [ʃʌv] *n* empujón *m. v* empujar.
shovel ['ʃʌvl] *n* pala *f. v* traspalar.
*****show** [ʃou] *v* mostrar; descubrir; reve-
lar; exhibir; indicar; demostrar; probar.
n exposición *f*; espectáculo *m*; (*appearance*) apariencia *f*; (*ostentation*) pompa *f.*
show business *n* mundo del espectáculo
m.

shower ['ʃauə] *n* (*rain*) chubasco *m*; (*bath*) ducha *f*. *v* llover; ducharse; (*pour*) derramar.
show in *v* hacer pasar.
show jumping *n* concurso hípico *m*.
show off *v* (*coll*) darse pisto.
showpiece ['ʃoupiːs] *n* modelo *m*; obra maestra *f*.
showroom ['ʃourum] *n* sala de muestras *f*.
show up *v* (*coll*: *arrive*) aparecer; (*embarrass*) poner en evidencia.
showy ['ʃoui] *adj* ostentoso.
shrimp [ʃrimp] *n* camarón *m*.
shrine [ʃrain] *n* capilla *f*; santuario *m*; altar *m*.
*****shrink** [ʃriŋk] *v* (*clothes*) encoger. **shrink from** repugnarse de. **shrinkage** *n* encogimiento *m*.
shrivel ['ʃrivl] *v* secar, marchitar. **shrivel up** apergaminarse.
shroud [ʃraud] *n* sudario *m*, mortaja *f*; (*fig*) velo *m*. *v* amortajar; (*fig*) envolver.
Shrove Tuesday [ʃrouv] *n* martes de carnaval *m*.
shrub [ʃrʌb] *n* arbusto *m*. **shrubbery** *n* arbustos *m pl*, matorrales *m pl*.
shrug [ʃrʌg] *v* encogimiento de hombros *m*. *v* encogerse de hombros.
shudder ['ʃʌdə] *n* repeluzno *m*; (*engine*) vibración *f*. *v* estremecerse.
shuffle ['ʃʌfl] *n* arrastramiento de los pies *m*; (*cards*) barajada *f*. *v* arrastrar; barajar.
shun [ʃʌn] *v* evitar, rehuir.
shunt [ʃʌnt] *v* (*trains*) desviar.
*****shut** [ʃʌt] *v* cerrar. **shut in** encerrar. **shut out** no admitir. **shut up** (*coll*) callarse; hacer callar.
shutter ['ʃʌtə] *n* (*window*) postigo *m*; (*phot*) obturador *m*.
shuttle ['ʃʌtl] *n* lanzadera *f*. **shuttlecock** *n* volante *m*. **shuttle service** servicio regular de ida y vuelta *m*.
shy [ʃai] *adj* tímido. *v* (*horse*) espantarse. **shyness** *n* timidez *f*.
Siamese [ˌsaiə'miːz] *adj* (*cat*, *twin*) siamés.
sick [sik] *adj* enfermo. **be sick** vomitar. **be sick of** (*coll*) estar harto de. **feel sick** tener náuseas. **sickbed** *n* lecho de enfermo *m*. **sick benefit** subidio de enfermedad *m*. **sicken** *v* poner enfermo. **sickening** *adj* nauseabundo; (*distressing*) deprimente. **sickly** *adj* (*person*) enfermizo; (*taste*) empalagoso. **sickness** *n* enfermedad *f*; (*sea*, *air*) mareo *m*.

sickle ['sikl] *n* hoz *f*.
side [said] *n* lado *m*; (*edge*) borde; (*team*) equipo *m*. **side with** ponerse de parte de. *adj* lateral; secundario; indirecto.
sideboard ['saidbord] *n* aparador *m*.
sideburns ['saidbərnz] *pl n* patillas *f pl*.
sidecar ['saidkar] *n* sidecar *m*.
side effects *pl n* efectos secundarios *m pl*.
sidelight ['saidlait] *n* (*mot*) luz de posición *f*.
sideline ['saidlain] *n* negocio accesorio *m*; (*sport*) banquillo *m*.
sidelong ['saidloŋ] *adj*, *adv* de reojo.
side-splitting *adj* divertidísimo.
side-step *v* evitar.
side street *n* calle lateral *f*.
side-track *v* despistar.
sideways ['saidweiz] *adv* oblicuamente. *adj* de lado.
siding ['saidiŋ] *n* (*rail*) vía muerta *f*.
sidle ['saidl] *v* avanzar furtivamente. **sidle up to** acercarse furtivamente.
siege [siːdʒ] *n* sitio *m*, asedio *m*.
sieve [siv] *n* tamiz *m*, scolador *m*. *v* tamizar.
sift [sift] *v* tamizar; (*sprinkle*) espolvorear; (*evidence*) examinar cuidadosamente. **sift out** encontrar; seleccionar. **sifter** cedazo *m*.
sigh [sai] *n* suspiro *m*. *v* suspirar.
sight [sait] *n* vista *f*; espectáculo *m*. **sightseeing** *n* turismo *m*. *v* avistar; (*aim*) apuntar.
sign [sain] *n* señal *f*; indicio *m*; (*notice*) anuncio *m*; muestra *f*. **signpost** *n* letrero *m*. *v* firmar.
signal ['signəl] *n* señal *f*. *v* hacer señales; indicar.
signature ['signətʃə] *n* firma *f*.
signify ['signifai] *v* significar. **significance** *n* significado *m*. **significant** *adj* significativo.
silence ['sailəns] *n* silencio *m*. *v* callar; hacer callar. **silencer** (*mot*, *gun*) *n* silenciador *m*. **silent** *adj* silencioso; callado.
silhouette [silu'et] *n* silueta *f*. **be silhouetted against** destacarse contra.
silk [silk] *n* seda *f*. **silkworm** *n* gusano de seda *m*. **silky** *adj* (*fabric*) sedoso; (*voice*, *manner*) suave.
sill [sil] *n* antepecho *m*, alféizar *m*.
silly ['sili] *adj* tonto, bobo. **silliness** *n* tontería *f*, bobería *f*.

silt [silt] *n* cieno *m*, limo *m*. **silt up** encenagar.

silver ['silvə] *n* plata *f*; (*coll: change*) suelto *m*. *adj* de plata; (*like silver*) plateado. **silver plate** baño de plata *m*. **silversmith** *n* platero *m*. *v* platear. **silvery** *adj* plateado; (*voice*) argentino.

similar ['similə] *adj* semejante, parecido. **similarity** *n* semejanza *f*.

simile ['siməli] *n* símil *m*.

simmer ['simə] *v* hervir a fuego lento; (*fig*) germentar. **simmer down** calmarse.

simple ['simpl] *adj* sencillo; natural; fácil; simple; puro; inocente; (*simple-minded*) necio. **simpleton** *n* simplón, -ona *m*, *f*. **simplicity** *n* sencillez *f*; simpleza *f*. **simplify** *v* simplificar. **simply** *adv* sencillamente; meramente.

simulate ['simjuleit] *v* similar. **simulation** *n* simulación *f*.

simultaneous [‚siməl'teinjəs] *adj* simultáneo.

sin [sin] *n* pecado *m*. *v* pecar. **sinful** *adj* (*person*) pecador; pecaminoso. **sinner** *n* pecador, -a *m*, *f*.

since [sins] *adv* desde entonces. *prep* desde. *conj* desde que; (*because*) ya que.

sincere [sin'siə] *adj* sincero. **sincerity** *n* sinceridad *f*.

sinew ['sinjuː] *n* tendón *m*.

***sing** [siŋ] *v* cantar. **singer** *n* cantor, -a *m*, *f*, cantante *m*, *f*. **singing** *n* canto *m*.

singe [sindʒ] *v* chamuscar. *n* chamusquina *f*.

single ['siŋgl] *adj* solo; único; (*copy*) suelto; (*not double*) individual; (*unmarried*) soltero. **single bed** cama individual *f*. **single file** fila de a uno *f*. **single-handed** *adv* sin ayuda. **single-minded** *adj* resuelto. **single room** habitación individual *f*. **single (ticket)** billete de ida *m*. **singles** *n* (*sport*) individual *m*. **single out** separar, distinguir.

singular ['siŋgjulə] *nm*, *adj* singular.

sinister ['sinistə] *adj* siniestro.

***sink** [siŋk] *v* hundir, sumergir; (*mine*) cavar; (*voice*) bajar; (*collapse*) dejarse caer; (*go down*) descender. **sink in** (*idea, etc.*) darse cuenta de. *n* (*kitchen*) fregadero; (*bathroom, bedroom*) lavabo *m*.

sinuous ['sinjuəs] *adj* sinuoso.

sinus ['sainəs] *n* seno *m*. **sinusitis** *n* sinusitis *f*.

sip [sip] *n* sorbo *m*. *v* sorber, beber a sorbos.

siphon ['saifən] *n* sifón *m*. *v* trasegar con sifón. **siphon off** sacar con un sifón.

sir [səi] *n* señor *m*, caballero *m*.

siren ['saiərən] *n* sirena *f*.

sirloin ['səːloin] *n* solomillo *m*.

sister ['sistə] *n* hermana *f*; (*hospital*) enfermera *f*; (*nun*) monja *f*; (*religious title*) sor *f*. **sister-in-law** *n* cuñada *f*.

***sit** [sit] *v* sentar; (*exam*) presentarse a; (*committee*) ser miembro. **baby-sit** *v* cuidar niños. **sit down** sentarse. **sit up** incorporarse; (*stay up*) no acostarse. **sitting** *n* sentada *f*; sesión *f*; (*meal*) servicio *m*. **sittingroom** *n* sala de estar *f*.

site [sait] *n* lugar *m*, sitio *m*; (*building*) solar *m*; camping *m*.

situation [sitju'eifən] *n* situación *f*; (*job*) empleo *m*. **situate** *v* situar.

six [siks] *nm*, *adj* seis. **sixth** *n*, *adj* sexto, -a; (*date*) seis *m*.

sixteen [siks'tiin] *nm*, *adj* dieciséis. **sixteenth** *n*, *adj* decimosexto, -a.

sixty ['siksti] *nm*, *adj* sesenta. **sixtieth** *n*, *adj* sexagésimo, -a.

size [saiz] *n* tamaño *m*; (*person, clothes*) talla *f*; (*gloves, shoes*) número *m*. **size up** evaluar, juzgar. **sizeable** *adj* grande; considerable.

sizzle ['sizl] *v* chisporrotear. *n* chisporroteo *m*.

skate[1] [skeit] *n* patín *m*. *v* patinar. **skateboard** *n* skateboard *m*. **skater** *n* patinador, -a *m*, *f*. **skating** *n* patinaje *m*. **skating-rink** *n* pista de patinaje *f*.

skate[2] [skeit] *n* (*fish*) raya *f*.

skeleton ['skelitn] *n* esqueleto *m*. *adj* (*staff, etc.*) muy reducido. **skeleton key** *n* llave maestra *f*.

sketch [sketʃ] *n* dibujo *m*; (*rough*) croquis *m*; (*theatre*) sketch *m*. *v* dibujar; hacer un croquis de. **sketch-book** *n* bloc de dibujo *m*. **sketchy** *adj* incompleto; impreciso.

skewer ['skjuə] *n* brocheta *f*. *v* espetar.

ski [skiː] *n* esquí *m*. **ski-lift** telesquí *m*. *v* esquiar. **skier** *n* esquiador, -a *m*, *f*. **skiing** *n* esquí *m*.

skid [skid] *n* patinazo *m*. *v* patinar.

skill [skil] *n* habilidad *f*; destreza *f*. **skilful** *adj* hábil; diestro. **skilled** diestro; experto; (*worker*) cualificado.

skim [skim] *v* (*milk*) desnatar; (*surface*) rozar. **skim through** hojear.

skimp [skimp] *v* escatimar; chapucear.
skimpy *adj* escaso; pequeño; corto.
skin [skin] *n* piel *f*; (*face*) cutis *m*; (*milk*)
nata *f*. **skin-diving** *n* natación submarina
f. **skin-tight** *adj* muy ajustado. *v* (*an
animal*) despellejar. **skinny** *adj* flaco,
descarnado.
skip [skip] *n* pequeño salto *m*, brinco *m*.
v saltar, brincar; saltar a la comba;
(*miss*) saltarse.
skipper ['skipə] *n* capitán *m*.
skirmish ['skəɪmiʃ] *n* escaramuza *f*. *v*
escaramuzar.
skirt [skəɪt] *n* falda *f*. *v* dar la vuelta a.
skirting board zócalo *m*.
skittle ['skitl] *n* bolo *m*. **skittles** *n* juego
de bolos *m*.
skull [skʌl] *n* cráneo *m*. **skull and cross-
bones** calavera *f*.
skunk [skʌŋk] *n* mofeta *f*.
sky [skai] *n* cielo *m*. **sky-blue** *nm, adj* azul
celeste. **skylark** *n* alondra *f*. **skylight** *n*
claraboya *f*. **skyline** *n* horizonte *m*. **skyscraper** *n* rascacielos *m invar*.
slab [slab] *n* (*lump*) trozo *m*; (*cake*) porción *f*; (*block*) bloque *m*; (*stone*) losa *f*;
(*metal*) plancha *f*; (*chocolate*) tableta *f*.
slack [slak] *adj* (*loose*) flojo; (*lazy*) perezoso; (*trade*) encalmado. **slacken** *v*
aflojar; disminuir.
slacks [slaks] *pl n* pantalones *m pl*.
slag [slag] *n* escoria *f*. **slag heap** escorial
m.
slam [slam] *n* golpe *m*; (*door*) portazo *m*;
(*bridge*) slam *m*. *v* hacer golpear; cerrar
de un golpe. **slam on the brakes** dar un
frenazo.
slander ['slaɪndə] *n* calumnia *f*; (*law*)
difamación *f*. *v* calumniar; difamar. **slan-
derous** *adj* calumnioso; difamatorio.
slang [slaŋ] *n* germanía *f*, argot *m*; jerga
f.
slant [slaɪnt] *n* inclinación *f*, sesgo *m*. *v*
inclinar. **slanting** *adj* inclinado, al sesgo.
slap [slap] *n* palmada *f*; (*on face*)
bofetada *f*. *v* pegar con la mano; (*put*)
poner violentamente. **slapdash** *adj* (*person*) descuidado; (*work*) chapucero. **slap-
stick** *n* payasada *f*.
slash [slaʃ] *n* (*knife*) cuchillada *f*; (*whip*)
latigazo *m*. *v* acuchillar; dar latigazos a;
(*coll: prices*) sacrificar.
slat [slat] *n* tablilla *f*.
slate [sleit] *n* pizarra *f*. *v* empizarrar.

slaughter [sloitə] *n* matanza *f*. **slaughter-
house** *n* matadero *m*. *v* matar;
exterminar.
slave [sleiv] *n* esclavo, -a *m, f*. *v* trabajar
como un negro. **slavery** *n* esclavitud *f*.
sledge [sledʒ] *n* trineo *m*.
sledgehammer ['sledʒhamə] *n* almádena
f.
sleek [sliːk] *adj* liso; pulcro.
*sleep [sliːp] *v* dormir; (*spend the night*)
pasar la noche. *n* sueño *m*. **go to sleep**
dormirse. **sleeper** (*rail*) traviesa *f*.
sleeping-bag *n* saco de dormir *m*. **sleep-
ing-pill** *n* somnífero *m*. **sleepless night**
noche en blanco *f*. **sleepy** *adj* soñoliento.
sleet [sliːt] *n* aguanieve *f*. *v* caer
aguanieve.
sleeve [sliːv] *n* manga *f*; (*record*) funda *f*.
sleeveless *adj* sin manga.
sleigh [slei] *n* trineo *m*.
slender ['slendə] *adj* (*thin*) delgado, fino;
(*light and graceful*) esbelto; (*resources*)
escaso; (*excuse*) pobre; (*hopes*) ligero.
slice [slais] *n* tajada *f*; (*bread*) rebanada *f*;
(*fruit*) raja *f*; (*implement*) pala *f*. *v* cortar;
partir en tajadas/rebanadas/rajas.
slick [slik] *adj* (*derog*) astuto; resbaladizo.
n (*oil*) capa de aceite *f*.
*slide [slaid] *v* deslizar; hacer resbalar. *n*
(*children's*) tobogán *m*; (*act of sliding*)
deslizamiento *m*; (*microscope*)
portaobjeto *m*; (*phot*) diapositiva *f*. **slide-
rule** *n* regla de cálculo *f*. **sliding** *adj*
(*door*) corredera; (*roof*) corredizo; (*scale*)
móvil.
slight [slait] *adj* pequeño; insignificante;
(*person*) débil; frágil. *v* despreciar. *n*
desprecio *m*. **slightest** *adj* lo más
mínimo. **slightly** *adv* ligeramente.
slim [slim] *adj* delgado; esbelto. *v* adelgazar. **slimming** *adj* (*diet, etc.*) que no
engorda, para adelgazar.
slime [slaim] *n* limo *m*; (*fig*) cieno *m*.
slimy *adj* limoso; (*person*) rastrero.
*sling [sliŋ] *v* lanzar; suspender. *n* (*med*)
cabestrillo *m*; (*weapon*) honda *f*.
*slink [sliŋk] *v* **slink away** escurrirse.
slip [slip] *n* (*error*) falta *f*; (*oversight*)
inadvertencia *f*; (*skid*) patinazo *m*;
(*stumble*) traspiés *m*; (*moral lapse*) desliz
m; (*petticoat*) combinación *f*; (*pillow*)
funda *f*; (*paper*) trozo. **slip of the tongue**
or **pen** lapsus *m*. *v* resbalar; pasar;
poner; descorrer; escurrirse.

slipper ['slipə] n zapatilla f.

slippery ['slipəri] adj resbaladizo; (person) escurridizo.

*slit [slit] v cortar; rasgar. n cortadura f; resquicio m.

slither ['sliðə] v resbalar; deslizarse.

slobber ['slobə] v babosear. n baba f.

sloe [slou] n endrina f.

slog [slog] n (coll) pesadez f. v (coll) sudar tinta.

slogan ['slougən] n slogan m.

slop [slop] v (splash) salpicar; (pour) derramar.

slope [sloup] n inclinación f; (hill) falda f. v inclinarse. **sloping** adj inclinado; (shoulders) caídos.

sloppy ['slopi] adj (food) aguoso; (garment) muy ancho; (careless) capucero; (sentimental) sensiblero. **sloppiness** n (sentiment) sensiblería f.

slot [slot] n ranura f, muesca f. v encajar; hacer una ranura.

slouch [slautʃ] v andar cabizbajo.

slovenly ['slʌvnli] adj desaliñado.

slow [slou] adj despacio; lento; (clock) atrasado; (stupid) tardo; (boring) aburrido. **in slow motion** a cámara lenta. **slow down** ir más despacio.

slug [slʌg] n (zool) babosa f; (bullet) posta f.

sluggish ['slʌgiʃ] adj perezoso; lento.

sluice [sluːs] n esclusa f. v regar; lavar.

slum [slʌm] n barrio bajo m. **the slums** tugurios m pl.

slumber ['slʌmbə] n sueño tranquilo m. v dormir tranquilo.

slump [slʌmp] n (fig) baja f; (comm) baja repentina f; depresión económica f. v desplomarse.

slung [slʌŋ] V sling.

slunk [slʌŋk] V slink.

slur [sləɪ] n baldón m; borrón m; (music) ligado m. v articular mal.

slush [slʌʃ] n nieve sucia y deshecha f.

slut [slʌt] n marrana f.

sly [slai] adj astuto; disimulado.

smack¹ [smak] n golpe m; bofetada f; (sound) chasquido m; v dar una bofetada; dar una palmada; pegar con la mano.

smack² [smak] v **smack of** saber a; (fig) oler a.

small [smɔil] adj pequeño; poco; chico; escaso. **small change** dinero suelto m.

smallpox n viruela f. **small talk** charla f. n **the small of the back** región lumbar f.

smart [smaɪt] adj vivo; rápido; (clever) listo; de moda; majo. v picar. **smarten up** ponerse elegante. **smartness** n viveza f; elegancia f.

smash [smaʃ] n (sound) estrépito m; accidente m; (blow) puñetazo m; ruina f. v quebrar, romper; destruir; aplastar; chocar con. **smashing** adj (slang) estupendo.

smear [smiə] n mancha f; (med) frotis m; (fig) calumnia f. v manchar; (bread) untar; calumniar.

*smell [smel] v oler; tener olor. n olor m; (sense) olfato m. **smelly** adj maloliente.

smile [smail] n sonrisa f. v sonreír.

smirk [sməɪk] n sonrisa afectada f. v sonreír afectadamente.

smock [smok] n blusa f.

smog [smog] n niebla espesa con humo f.

smoke [smouk] n humo m. **smoke-screen** n cortina de humo f. v humear; (tobacco) fumar. **smoker** n fumador, -a m, f. **no smoking** se prohibe fumar. **smoky** adj que huele a humo.

smooth [smuːð] adj liso; suave; llano; uniforme; (person) suavón. v alisar; suavizar. **smooth over** exculpar. **smoothly** adv lisamente; con suavidad.

smother ['smʌðə] v sofocar; apagar.

smoulder ['smouldə] v arder sin llama.

smudge [smʌdʒ] n mancha f; tiznón m. v manchar; tiznar.

smug [smʌg] adj pagado de sí mismo.

smuggle ['smʌgl] v pasar de contrabando; matutear. **smuggler** n contrabandista m, f. **smuggling** n contrabando m.

snack [snak] n bocado m, tentempié m. **snack bar** cafetería f.

snag [snag] n pega f, obstáculo m. v enganchar; estorbar.

snail [sneil] n caracol m.

snap [snap] n (fingers) castañeteo m; (bones, teeth, mouth) crujido m; (breaking wood) chasquido m; (bite) mordisco m; (phot) instantánea f. adj instantáneo; rápido. **snapdragon** n dragón m. **snapshot** n instantánea f. v (bones) romper; (branch) partir; (joints) hacer crujir; (dog) intentar morder; (person) regañar.

snare [sneə] n trampa f, lazo m. v atrapar.

snarl [snaɪl] n gruñido m. v gruñir.

snatch [snatʃ] *n* fragmento *m*; (*theft*) robo *m*. *v* agarrar; tomar.

sneak [sniːk] *v* hacer furtivamente. **sneak in/out** entrar/salir furtivamente. *n* (*slang*) chivato, -a *m, f*.

sneer [snɪə] *v* decir con desprecio. *n* desprecio *m*. **sneering** *adj* burlón.

sneeze [sniːz] *n* estornudo *m*. *v* estornudar.

sniff [snif] *n* aspiración *f*; inhalación *f*. *v* (*smell*) oler; aspirar.

snigger ['snigə] *n* risa disimulada *f*. reírse por lo bajo.

snip [snip] *v* cortar de un tijeretazo. *n* (*coll: bargain*) ganga *f*.

snipe [snaip] *n* agachadiza *f*. *v* **snipe at** (*mil*) tirotear. **sniper** *n* paco *m*.

snivel ['snivl] *v* lloriquear. **snivelling** *adj* llorón; mocoso.

snob [snob] *n* snob *m*, esnob *m*. **snobbish** *adj* snob, esnob.

snooker ['snuːkə] *n* snooker *m*.

snoop [snuːp] *v* fisgonear; entrometerse.

snooty ['snuːti] *adj* (*coll*) presumido.

snooze [snuːz] *n* siesta *f*; sueñecito *m*. *v* dormitar.

snore [snoɪ] *n* ronquido *m*. *v* roncar. **snoring** *n* ronquido *m*.

snorkel ['snoɪkəl] *n* (*swimmer's*) tubo de respiración *m*; (*submarine's*) esnórquel *m*.

snort [snoɪt] *n* resoplido *m*. *v* resoplar.

snout [snaut] *n* hocico *m*.

snow [snou] *n* nieve *f*. *v* nevar. **be snowed under with** estar abrumado de. **snowy** *adj* nevoso.

snowball ['snoubɔɪl] *n* bola de nieve *f*. *v* tirar bolas de nieve; acumularse.

snowbound ['snoubaund] *adj* bloqueado por la nieve.

snowdrift ['snoudrift] *n* ventisquero *m*.

snowdrop ['snoudrop] *n* campanilla blanca *f*.

snowfall ['snoufɔɪl] *n* nevada *f*.

snowflake ['snoufleik] *n* copo de nieve *m*.

snowstorm ['snoustoɪm] *n* tormenta de nieve *f*.

snub [snʌb] *n* repulsa *f*. *v* repulsar.

snuff [snʌf] *n* rapé *m*. **snuff-box** *n* tabaquera *f*. *v* (*extinguish*) despabilar.

snug [snʌg] *adj* cómodo; abrigadito.

snuggle ['snʌgl] *v* arrimarse; apretarse.

so [sou] *adv* así; tan; también; tanto; por lo tanto. *conj* así que, de modo que, de manera que. **and so on** y así sucesivamente. **if so** de ser así. **is that so?** ¿de veras? **... or so** a poco más o menos ... **. so as to** de manera que. **so-called** *adj* llamado. **so much** *or* **many** tanto, tantos. **so-so** *adj* (*coll*) así así. **so that** para que. **so what?** ¿y qué?

soak [souk] *v* empapar. **soak in** penetrar en. **soak up** absorber. **soaking** *n* remojo *m*. **soaking wet** calado hasta los huesos.

soap [soup] *n* jabón *m*. **soap dish** jabonera *f*. **soap powder** jabón en polvo *m*. **soapsuds** *pl n* jabonaduras *f pl*. *v* jabonar. **soapy** *adj* jabonoso.

soar [soɪ] *v* remontarse; (*fig*) elevarse.

sob [sob] *n* sollozo *m*. *v* sollozar.

sober ['soubə] *adj* moderado; serio; (*not drunk*) sobrio. *v* **sober up** serenarse.

soccer ['sokə] *n* fútbol *m*.

sociable ['souʃəbl] *adj* sociable.

social ['souʃəl] *adj* social; (*friendly*) amistoso. **social science** sociología *f*. **social security** seguridad social *f*. **socialism** *n* socialismo *m*. **socialist** *n(m+f)*, *adj* socialista. **socialize** *v* socializar.

society [sə'saiəti] *n* sociedad *f*.

sociology [sousi'olədʒi] *n* sociología *f*. **sociological** *adj* sociológico. **sociologist** *n* sociólogo, -a *m, f*.

sock [sok] *n* calcetín *m*.

socket ['sokit] *n* hueco *m*; (*elec*) enchufe *m*.

soda ['soudə] *n* (*chem*) sosa *f*; (*water*) agua de seltz *f*.

sodden ['sodn] *adj* empapado, saturado.

sofa ['soufə] *n* sofá *m*.

soft [soft] *adj* blando; suave; (*low*) bajo. **soft-boiled** *adj* (*egg*) pasado por agua. **soften** *v* ablandar; suavizar; bajar; **softness** *n* blandura *f*; suavidad *f*; dulzura *f*; debilidad *f*; estupidez *f*.

soggy ['sogi] *adj* empapado; (*bread*) pastoso.

soil¹ [soil] *n* tierra *f*.

soil² [soil] *v* ensuciar.

solar ['soulə] *adj* solar.

sold [sould] *V* **sell**.

solder ['soldə] *n* soldadura *f*. *v* soldar. **soldering-iron** *n* soldador *m*.

soldier ['souldʒə] *n* soldado *m*.

sole¹ [soul] *adj* solo, único.

sole² [soul] *n* (*of shoe*) suela *f*; (*of foot*) planta *f*. *v* solar.

sole³ [soul] *n* (*fish*) lenguado *m*.

solemn ['soləm] *adj* solemne. **solemnity** *n* solemnidad *f.*

solicitor [sə'lisitə] *n* abogado, -a *m, f.* **solicitude** [sə'lisitjuːd] *n* solicitud *f.*

solid ['solid] *adj* sólido; firme; continuo. *n* sólido *m.* **solids** *pl n* alimentos sólidos *m pl.* **solidarity** *n* solidaridad *f.* **solidify** *v* solidificarse; congelarse.

solitary ['solitəri] *adj* solitario; solo, único.

solitude ['solitjuːd] *n* soledad *f.*

solo ['soulou] *nm, adj* solo. **soloist** *n.* solista *m, f.*

solstice ['solstis] *n* solsticio *m.*

soluble ['soljubl] *adj* soluble.

solution [sə'luːʃən] *n* solución *f.*

solve [solv] *v* resolver; acertar.

solvent ['solvənt] *adj* (*finance*) solvente. *n* (*chem*) disolvente *m.* **solvency** *n* solvencia *f.*

sombre ['sombə] *adj* sombrío.

some [sʌm] *adj* algún, alguno, algunos; unos, varios. *pron* algunos; unos; un poco; parte. *adv* bestante; unos. **somebody** *or* **someone** *pron* alguien. **somehow** *adv* de algún modo; por alguna razón. **something** *pron* algo. **sometime** *adv* alguna vez, algún día. **sometimes** *adv* a veces, de vez en cuando. **somewhat** *adv* algo, algún tanto. **somewhere** *adv* en alguna parte. **somewhere else** en alguna otra parte.

somersault ['sʌməsoːlt] *n* salto mortal *m.* *v* dar un salto mortal.

son [sʌn] *n* hijo *m.* **son-in-law** *n* yerno *m.*

sonata [sə'naːtə] *n* sonata *f.*

song [soŋ] *n* (*art*) canto *m*; (*composition*) canción *f.*

sonic ['sonik] *adj* sónico.

sonnet ['sonit] *n* soneta *m.*

soon [suːn] *adv* pronto, dentro de poco; (*early*) temprano. **as soon as** tan pronto como. **sooner or later** tarde o temprano.

soot [sut] *n* hollín *m.*

soothe [suːð] *v* tranquilizar, calmar. **soothing** *adj* tranquilizador, calmante.

sophisticated [sə'fistikeitid] *adj* sofisticado; mundano; (*machinery*) complejo.

sopping ['sopiŋ] *adj* empapadísimo.

soprano [sə'praːnou] *n* soprano *m, f.*

sordid ['soːdid] *adj* sórdido.

sore [soː] *adj* malo; dolorido; (*fig*) doloroso. **sore point** tema delicado *m.* **sorely** *adv* (*bitterly*) profundamente; (*very*) muy. **soreness** *n* dolor *m.*

sorrow ['sorou] *n* pesar *m*; tristeza *f.* *v* afligirse. **sorrowful** *adj* afligido; triste.

sorry ['sori] *adj* afligido; triste; apenado; lastimoso. **feel sorry for** compadecer. *interj* ¡perdóneme! ¡disculpe!

sort [soːt] *n* clase *f*; especie *f*; tipo *m*; modo *m*; persona *f.* *v* separar de; clasificar. **sort out** apartar; (*problems*) arreglar. **sorting office** sala de batalla *f.*

soufflé ['suːflei] *n* soufflé *m.*

sought [soːt] *V* seek.

soul [soul] *n* alma *f.* **soulful** *adj* expresivo; conmovedor.

sound[1] [saund] *n* (*noise*) sonido *m*, ruido *m.* **sound barrier** barrera del sonido *f.* **sound effects** efectos sonoros *m pl.* **soundproof** *adj* insonoro. **sound-track** *n* pista sonora *f.* *v* sonar, resonar; (*seem*) parecer.

sound[2] [saund] *adj* sano; (*reasonable*) lógico; (*argument*) válido; (*policy*) prudente; (*investment*) seguro; (*comm*) solvente. **be sound asleep** estar profundamente dormido.

sound[3] [saund] *v* (*depth*) sondar; (*opinion*) sondear.

soup [suːp] *n* sopa *f.* **clear soup** consomé *m.* **thick soup** puré *m.* **soup plate** plato sopero *m.* **soup spoon** cuchara sopera *f.*

sour [sauə] *adj* ácido, agrio. *v* agriar. **sourness** *n* acidez *f*, agrura *f.*

source [soːs] *n* fuente *f*; origen *m.*

south [sauθ] *n* sur *m.* *adj* also **southerly**, **southern** del sur. *adv* hacia el sur. **southbound** *adj* con rumbo al sur. **south-east** *nm, adj* sudeste. **south-west** *nm, adj* sudoeste.

South America *n* Sudamérica *f*, América del Sur *f.* **South American** sudamericano, -a *m, f.*

souvenir [suːvə'niə] *n* recuerdo *m.*

sovereign ['sovrin] *n, adj* soberano, -a.

***sow**[1] [sou] *v* sembrar; esparcir.

sow[2] [sau] *n* cerda *f*, puerca *f.*

soya ['soiə] *n* soja *f.* **soya bean** soja *f.* **soy sauce** salsa picante de soja *f.*

spa [spaː] *n* balneario *m*; manantial mineral *m.*

space [speis] *n* espacio *m*; (*place*) sitio *m*; (*time*) temporada *f.* **spaceman** *n* astronauta *m*, cosmonauta *m.* **spaceship** *n* nave espacial *f.* *v* espaciar. **spacious** *adj* espacioso; amplio.

spade [speid] *n* pala *f*.
spades [speidz] *pl n* (*cards*) picos *m pl*; (*Spanish cards*) espadas *f pl*.
spaghetti [spə'geti] *n* espaguetis *m pl*.
Spain [spein] *n* España *f*. **Spaniard** *n* español, -a *m, f*. **Spanish** *nm, adj* español.
span [span] *n* (*time*) espacio *m*, duración *f*; (*wings*) envergadura *f*; (*space*) distancia *f*; (*bridge*) tramo *m*. *v* atravesar; medir.
spaniel ['spanjəl] *n* perro de aguas *m*; (*cocker*) sabueso *m*.
spank [spaŋk] *v* dar una azotaina. **spanking** *n* azotaina *f*.
spanner ['spanə] *n* llave *f*.
spare [speə] *adj* de reserva; de sobra; disponible. **spare part** (*mot*) recambio *m*. **spare-ribs** *pl n* (*cookery*) costillas de cerdo *f pl*. **spare room** cuarto de los invitados *m*. **spare time** ratos libres *m pl*. **spare tyre** neumático de repuesto *m*. *v* (*do without*) pasarse sin; (*avoid*) evitar; (*expense*) escatimar. **sparing** *adj* (*words*) parco; limitado; escaso; frugal.
spark [spaɪk] *n* chispa *f*. *v* chispear. **spark off** provocar. **sparking-plug** *n* bujía *f*.
sparkle ['spaɪkl] *n* centelleo *m*; (*fig*) brillo *m*. *v* centellear; (*fig*) brillar. **sparkling** *adj* (*drink*) espumoso.
sparrow ['sparou] *n* gorrión *m*.
sparse [spaɪs] *adj* escaso, poco denso. **sparsely** *adv* escasamente.
spasm ['spazəm] *n* espasmo *m*; (*fit*) ataque *m*. **spasmodic** *adj* espasmódico.
spastic ['spastik] *n, adj* espástico, -a.
spat [spat] *V* **spit**.
spatial ['speiʃl] *adj* espacial.
spatula ['spatjulə] *n* espátula *f*.
spawn [spoɪn] *n* (*fish*) freza *f*, hueva *f*; (*frog*) huevos *m pl*. *v* frezar; depositar.
***speak** [spiɪk] *v* decir; hablar. **speak up** hablar más fuerte. **speak up for** hablar en favor de. **speaker** *n* orador, -a *m, f*; (*loudspeaker*) altavoz *m*.
spear [spiə] *n* lanza *f*. *v* traspasar. **spearhead** *n* vanguardia *f*.
special ['speʃəl] *adj* especial; particular; extraordinario. **specialist** *n* especialista *m, f*. **speciality** *n* especialidad *f*. **specialize** *v* especializar.
species ['spiɪʃiɪz] *n* especie *f*.
specify ['spesifai] *v* especeficar. **specific** *adj* específico. **specification** *n* especificación *f*; estipulación *f*; requisito *m*.

specimen ['spesimin] *n* (*biol*) espécimen *m*; modelo *m*; (*sample*) muestra *f*; (*example*) ejemplar *m*.
speck [spek] *n* manchita *f*; pizca *f*. **speckle** *v* motear.
spectacle ['spektəkl] *n* espectáculo *m*. **spectacles** *pl n* gafas *f pl*. **spectacular** *adj* espectacular.
spectator [spek'teitə] *n* espectador, -a *m, f*.
spectrum ['spektrəm] *n* espectro *m*.
speculate ['spekjuleit] *v* especular; conjeturar. **speculation** *n* especulación *f*; conjetura *f*. **speculative** *adj* especulativo; conjetural.
speech [spiɪtʃ] *n* (*address*) discurso *m*; (*faculty*) habla *f*; (*lecture*) conferencia *f*; conversación *f*; pronunciación *f*. **speechless** *adj* mudo.
***speed** [spiɪd] *v* (*mot*) ir a toda velocidad. **speed along** apresurarse. **speed up** acelerar. **speeding** *n* exces de velocidad *m*. **speedy** *adj* veloz. *n* prisa *f*; velocidad *f*; rapidez *f*. **speedboat** *n* lancha motora *f*. **speed limit** velocidad máxima *f*. **speedometer** *n* velocímetro *m*.
***spell[1]** [spel] *v* escribir; deletrear; significar. **spelling** *n* ortografía *f*.
spell[2] [spel] *n* (*magic*) hechizo *m*, encanto *m*. **spellbound** *adj* encantado.
spell[3] [spel] *n* período *m*; turno *m*.
***spend** [spend] *v* (*money*) gastar; (*time*) pasar. **spending** *n* gasto *m*. **spending money** dinero para gastos menudos *m*.
sperm [spəɪm] *n* esperma *f*.
spew [spjuɪ] *v* vomitar.
sphere [sfiə] *n* esfera *f*; (*province*) competencia *f*. **spherical** *adj* esférico.
spice [spais] *n* especia *f*. *v* especiar. **spicy** *adj* especiado, picante; (*fig*) sabroso.
spider ['spaidə] *n* araña *f*. **spider's web** telaraña *f*.
spike [spaik] *n* escarpia *f*.
***spill** [spil] *v* derramar. *n* (*coll: fall*) caida *f*.
***spin** [spin] *v* girar, dar vueltas; dar efecto a; (*cotton, silk, etc.*) hilar; (*web*) tejer; (*fig: a yarn*) contar. **spin-dryer** *n* secador centrífugo *m*. **spin out** prolongar. **spinning** *n* hilado *m*. **spinning wheel** rueca *f*. *n* giro *m*.
spinach ['spinidʒ] *n* espinaca *f*.
spindle ['spindl] *n* (*axle, shaft*) eje *m*; (*of a lathe*) mandril *m*; (*of a spinning wheel*) huso *m*. **spindly** *adj* largirucho.

spine [spain] *n* (*anat*) espina dorsal *f*; (*zool*) púa *f*; (*book*) lomo *m*. **spinal** *adj* espinal. **spiny** *adj* espinoso.

spinster ['spinstə] *n* soltera *f*.

spiral ['spaiərəl] *adj* espiral. *n* espiral *f*. *v* dar vueltas en espiral.

spire ['spaiə] *n* aguja *f*.

spirit ['spirit] *n* espíritu *m*, alma *f*; (*ghost*) fantasma *m*; (*courage*) valor *m*; (*liveliness*) ánimo *m*; (*mood*) humor *m*; alcohol *m*. **spirited** *adj* animado, vigoroso. **spirited** *adj* espiritual. **spiritualism** *n* espiritualismo *m*. **spiritualist** *n*(*m*+*f*), *adj* espiritualista.

*spit[1] [spit] *v* escupir. *n* saliva *f*, escupitajo *m*.

spit[2] [spit] *n* (*cookery*) espetón *m*, asador *m*; (*geog*) lengua de tierra *f*.

spite [spait] *n* rencor *m*, malevolencia *f*. **in spite of** a pesar de. *v* mortificar. **spiteful** *adj* rencoroso.

splash [splaʃ] *n* salpicadura *f*; (*sound*) chapoteo; (*mark*) mancha *f*. *v* salpicar.

spleen [splitn] *n* (*anat*) bazo *m*; (*fig*) mal humor *m*.

splendid ['splendid] *adj* espléndido; excelente. **splendour** *n* resplandor *m*.

splice [splais] *v* empalmar; (*coll: marry*) unir, casar.

splint [splint] *n* férula *f*.

splinter ['splintə] *n* (*wood*) astilla *f*; (*bomb*) casco *m*; (*bone*) esquirla *f*; (*piece*) fragmento *m*. *v* astillar.

*split [split] *v* hender, partir; rajar; dividir; separar; (*atom*) desintegrar. *n* partido *m*, hendido *m*; división *f*; (*in cloth*) rasgón *m*; (*quarrel*) ruptura *f*. **split second** fracción de segundo *f*.

splutter ['splʌtə] *v* (*person*) farfullar; (*flame*) chisporrotear. *n* farfulla *f*; chisporroteo *m*.

*spoil [spoil] *v* estropear, echar a perder; (*child*) minar; (*damage*) dañar. **spoilsport** *n* aguafiestas *m*, *f invar*. **spoils** *pl n* botín *m sing*.

spoke[1] [spouk] *V* **speak**.

spoke[2] [spouk] *n* reyo *m*.

spokesman ['spouksmən] *n* portavoz *m*.

sponge [spʌndʒ] *n* esponja *f*; (*cake*) bizcocho esponjoso *m*. **sponge bag** esponjera *f*. *v* limpiar con esponja; (*coll: cadge*) sacar de gorra. **spongy** *adj* esponjoso.

sponsor ['sponsə] *n* (*for financial support*) patrocinador, -a *m*, *f*; (*warrantor*) fiador,

-a *m*, *f*; (*for club membership*) padrino, -a *m*, *f*. *v* patrocinar; fiar; apadrinar. **sponsorship** *n* patrocinio *m*.

spontaneous [spon'teinjəs] *adj* espontáneo. **spontaneity** *n* espontaneidad *f*.

spool [spuɪl] *n* bobina *f*.

spoon [spuɪn] *n* cuchara *f*. **spoonful** *n* cucharada *f*.

sporadic [spə'radik] *adj* esporádico.

sport [spoɪt] *n* deporte *m*; (*plaything*) juguete *m*; (*amusement*) bula *f*. **sports car** coche deportivo *m*. **sports jacket** chaqueta de sport *f*. **sportsman/woman** *n* deportista *m*, *f*. *v* llevar; ostentar. **sporting** *adj* deportista; caballeroso. **sportive** *adj* juguetón; bromista.

spot [spot] *n* (*med*) grano *m*; espinilla *f*; (*mark*) mancha *f*; (*pattern*) lunar *m*; (*place*) sitio *m*; (*liquid*) gota *f*; parte *f*; punto *m*; (*coll*) poco *m*. **on the spot** en el momento; en el acto. **spot check** inspección repentina *f*. **spotlight** *n* foco *m*. *v* manchar; reconocer; notar. **spotless** *adj* inmaculado. **spotted** *adj* (*speckled*) moteado; con manchas; de lunares. **spotty** *adj* espinilloso.

spouse [spaus] *n* esposo, -a *m*, *f*.

spout [spaut] *n* (*teapot*) pitorro *m*; (*jug*) pico *m*; (*rainwater pipe*) caño *m*; (*jet*) chorro *m*; (*waterspout*) tromba *f*. *v* echar; (*coll*) soltar.

sprain [sprein] *n* torcedura *f*. *v* torcer.

sprawl [sproɪl] *n* postura desgarbada *f*. *v* extender.

spray[1] [sprei] *n* (*water*) rociada *f*; (*sea*) espuma *f*; (*sprayer*) pulverizador *m*. *v* (*sprinkle*) rociar; pulverizar; (*crops*) fumigar; vaporizarse.

spray[2] [sprei] *n* (*flowers*) ramo *m*, ramillete *m*.

*spread [spred] *v* extender; (*on the ground*) exponer; (*marmalade, butter, etc.*) untar; propagar; difundir; (*wings*) desplegar. **spread out** esparcir. *n* propagación *f*, difusión *f*; (*town*) extensión *f*; (*span*) envergadura *f*; (*range*) gama *f*.

spree [spriɪ] *n* juerga *f*.

sprig [sprig] *n* ramito *m*.

sprightly ['spraitli] *adj* despierto, vivo.

*spring [spriŋ] *v* saltar. **spring up** brotar; surgir. *n* (*season*) primavera *f*; (*leap*) salto *m*, brinco *m*; (*water*) fuente *f*; (*coil*) muelle *m*. **springboard** *n* trampolín *m*. **spring-cleaning** *n* limpieza general *f*.

spring onion cebolleta *f*. **springy** *adj* elástico.

sprinkle ['spriŋkl] *v* (*water*) rociar; (*sugar, salt, etc.*) salpicar. **sprinkler** *n* regadera *f*; (*fire*) extintor *m*.

sprint [sprint] *n* sprint *m*, esprint *m*. *v* sprintar, esprintar.

sprout [spraut] *n* brote *m*, retoño *m*. **Brussels sprouts** coles de Bruselas *f pl*.

spruce [spruːs] *n* (*bot*) pícea *f*. *adj* elegante. **spruce up** acicalar.

spun [spʌn] *V* **spin.**

spur [spəː] *n* espuela *f*; (*fig*) estímulo *m*. **on the spur of the moment** sin pensarlo. *v* espolear. **spur on** estimular.

spurious ['spjuəriəs] *adj* espurio, falso.

spurn [spəːn] *v* desdeñar, rechazar.

spurt [spəːt] *n* (*water*) chorro *m*; (*energy*) gran esfuerzo *m*. *v* chorrear; hacer un gran esfuerzo; acelerar.

spy [spai] *n* espía *m, f*. *v* espiar; observar. **spying** *n* espionaje *m*.

squabble ['skwobl] *n* riña *f*. *v* disputar.

squad [skwod] *n* escuadra *f*; (*mil*) pelotón *m*.

squadron ['skwodrən] *n* (*mil*) escuadrón *m*; (*naut*) escuadra *f*; (*aero*) escuadrilla *f*.

squalid ['skwolid] *adj* mugriento; escuálido; miserable. **squalor** *n* mugre *f*; miseria *f*.

squall [skwoːl] *n* ráfaga *f*.

squander ['skwondə] *v* malgastar.

square [skweə] *n* (*shape*) cuadrado *m*; (*pattern*) cuadro *m*; (*chessboard*) casilla *f*; (*in a town*) plaza *f*. *adj* cuadrado; rectangular; (*coll: old-fashioned*) anticuado. *v* cuadrar; (*settle*) arreglar.

squash [skwoʃ] *n* (*sport*) juego de pelota *m*; (*drink*) limonada *f*, naranjada *f*; (*crushing*) aplastamiento *m*. *v* (*crush*) aplastar; (*squeeze*) apretar.

squat [skwot] *n* posición en cuclillas *f*. *adj* rechoncho. *v* agacharse. **squatter** *n* persona que ocupe ilegalmente un sitio *f*.

squawk [skwoːk] *n* graznido *m*. *v* graznar.

squeak [skwiːk] *n* (*mice, etc.*) chillido *m*; (*hinge*) chirrido *m*. *v* chillar; chirriar.

squeal [skwiːl] *n* chillido *m*. *v* chillar.

squeamish ['skwiːmiʃ] *adj* remilgado; delicado.

squeeze [skwiːz] *n* presión *f*; (*hug*) abrazo *m*; (*hand*) apretón *m*; (*crowd*) gentío *m*. *v* abrazar; apretar; (*extract*) exprimir.

squid [skwid] *n* calamar *m*.

squint [skwint] *n* (*med*) estrabismo *m*;

(*coll: glance*) ojeada *f*. *v* entrecerrar los ojos.

squirm [skwəːm] *v* retorcerse.

squirrel ['skwirəl] *n* ardilla *f*.

squirt [skwəːt] *n* chorro *m*. *v* lanzar; chorrear.

stab [stab] *n* puñalada. *v* apuñalar.

stabilize ['steibilaiz] *v* estabilizar. **stabilizer** *n* estabilizador *m*.

stable¹ ['steibl] *n* cuadra *f*.

stable² ['steibl] *adj* estable; fijo. **stability** *n* estabilidad *f*; firmeza *f*.

staccato [stə'kaːtou] *adv* staccato. *adj* (*voice, style, etc.*) entrecortado.

stack [stak] *n* (*hay, etc.*) almiar *m*; (*pile*) montón *m*; (*chimney*) cañón *m*. **stacks of** (*coll*) un montón de *m sing*. *v* hacinar; amontonar.

stadium ['steidiəm] *n* estadio *m*.

staff [staːf] *n* vara *f*; palo *m*; (*flag*) asta *f*; personal *m*. **staff-room** *n* (*school*) sala de profesores *f*. *v* proveer de personal.

stag [stag] *n* venado *m*, ciervo *m*. **stag party** reunión de hombres *f*.

stage [steidʒ] *n* (*theatre*) escenario *m*; (*platform*) estrado *m*; (*point*) etapa *f*; (*phase*) fase *f*. **stage manager** regidor de escena *m*. *v* representar; efectuar; organizar.

stagger ['stagə] *n* tambaleo *m*. *v* tambalearse; (*amaze*) asombrar; (*payments, etc.*) escalonar. **staggering** *adj* asombroso.

stagnant ['stagnənt] *adj* estancado. **stagnate** *v* estancarse. **stagnation** *n* estancamiento *m*.

staid [steid] *adj* serio; formal.

stain [stein] *n* mancha *f*; tinte *m*. **stain remover** quitamanchas *m invar*. *v* manchar; (*wood*) teñir. **stained-glass window** vidriera *f*.

stair [steə] *n* escalón *m*. **staircase** *n also* **stairs** *pl n* escalera *f sing*.

stake¹ [steik] *n* (*post*) poste *m*; estaca *f*; (*for plants*) rodrigón *m*; (*for execution*) hoguera *f*. *v* estacar.

stake² [steik] *n* (*bet*) apuesta *f*; (*investment*) intereses *m pl*. **at stake** en juego. *v* apostar.

stale [steil] *adj* (*bread*) duro; (*egg*) poco fresco; (*food*) rancio; (*air*) viciado. **staleness** *n* ranciedad *f*.

stalemate ['steilmeit] *n* (*chess*) ahogado *m*; (*fig*) punto muerto *m*.

stalk¹ [stɔːk] *n* (*stem*) tallo *m*.
stalk² [stɔːk] *v* acechar. **stalk in/out** entrar/salir con paso airado.
stall¹ [stɔːl] *n* (*market*) puesto *m*; (*theatre*) butaca *f*; (*exhibition*) caseta *f*. *v* (*engine*) parar.
stall² [stɔːl] *v* (*delay*) andar con rodeos. **stall off** dar largas a.
stallion ['staljən] *n* semental *m*.
stamina ['staminə] *n* vigor *m*; aguante *m*.
stammer ['stamə] *n* tartamudez *f*. *v* tartamudear.
stamp [stamp] *n* sello *m*, timbre *m*; marca *f*; impresión *f*; (*with foot*) zapatazo *m*. **stamp-collecting** *n* filatelia *f*. *v* estampar; sellar; imprimir; (*one's foot*) patear.
stampede [stam'piːd] *n* desbocamiento *m*; desbandada *f*. *v* provocar la desbandada de.
***stand** [stand] *v* (*on feet*) estar de pie; (*place*) poner; resistir; soportar; (*trial*) someterse a; (*remain*) permanecer; (*pay for*) sufragar. *n* posición *f*; plataforma *f*; (*coats, hats*) percha *f*; (*fig*) postura *f*. **stand for** significar; representar. **stand out** sobresalir. **standstill** *n* parada *f*. **come to a standstill** pararse. **stand up for** defender.
standard ['standəd] *n* (*weight, length, money*) patrón *m*; (*of living*) nivel *m*; modelo *m*; criterio *m*. *adj* normal; oficial; legal; (*comm*) standard. **standard lamp** lámpara de pie *f*. **standardize** *v* estandardizar; normalizar.
standing ['standiŋ] *adj* de pie; vertical; clásico; fijo. **standing order** (*bank*) pedido regular *m*. *n* posición *f*; situación *f*; reputación *f*; duración *f*.
stank [staŋk] *V* **stink**.
stanza ['stanzə] *n* estancia *f*, estrofa *f*.
staple¹ [steipl] *n* (*papers*) grapa *f*; (*of wool, cotton*) fibra *f*. *v* sujetar con una grapa.
staple² [steipl] *adj* básico; principal.
star [staɪ] *n* (*astron, cinema*) estrella *f*; asterisco *m*. **stars** *pl n* (*astrol*) astros *m pl*. **starfish** *n* estrella de mar *f*. *v* estrellar; ser protagonista. **stardom** *n* estrellato *m*. **starry** *adj* estrellado.
starboard ['staɪbəd] *n* estribor *m*.
starch [staɪtʃ] *n* almidón *m*. *v* almidonar. **starchy** *adj* almidonado.
stare [steə] *n* mirada fija *f*. *v* mirar fijamente.
stark [staɪk] *adj* (*bleak*) desolado; (*stiff*)

rígido; completo; puro; absoluto. **stark naked** completamente desnudo.
starling ['staɪliŋ] *n* estornino *m*.
start [staɪt] *n* comienzo *m*; (*of a race*) salida *f*; (*jump*) sobresalto *m*; (*fright*) susto *m*. *v* comenzar, empezar; (*clock*) poner en marcha; (*car*) arrancar; (*establish*) fundar; (*rumour*) lanzar; provocar; sobresaltar. **starter** *n* (*mot*) arranque *m*; (*meal*) entremés *m*.
startle ['staɪtl] *v* asustar. **startling** *adj* sorprendente; alarmante.
state [steit] *n* estado *m*; condición *f*; (*luxury*) lujo *m*; gran pompa *f*. **statesman** *n* estadista *m*. *v* afirmar, declarar; dar; decir; consignar; exponer. **stately** *adj* majestuoso. **statement** *n* declaración *f*; informe *m*; comunicado *m*; (*bank*) balance mensual *m*.
static ['statik] *adj* estático. *n* (*radio*) parásitos *m pl*.
station ['steiʃən] *n* (*rail, radio*) estación *f*; (*position*) puesto *m*; (*place*) lugar *m*; (*social*) posición *f*. *v* apostar; estacionar.
stationary ['steiʃənəri] *adj* estacionario; inmóvil.
stationer ['steiʃənə] *n* papelero *m*. **stationer's** *n* papelería *f*. **stationery** *n* objetos de escritorio *m pl*; papel de escribir y sobres *m*.
statistics [stə'tistiks] *n* (*science*) estadística *f*. *pl n* (*data*) estadísticas *f pl*. **statistical** *adj* estadístico.
statue ['statjuɪ] *n* estatua *f*.
stature ['statʃə] *n* estatura *f*; (*fig*) talla *f*.
status ['steitəs] *n* (*standing*) categoría *f*; (*state*) condición *f*; (*social standing*) posición *f*.
statute ['statjuɪt] *n* estatuo *m*. **statutory** *adj* establecido por la ley.
staunch¹ [stɔːntʃ] *adj* fiel; inquebrantable.
staunch² [stɔːntʃ] *v* restañar.
stay [stei] *n* estancia *f*; (*support*) apoyo *m*. *v* (*remain*) quedarse; (*postpone*) aplazar; (*endure*) resistir; (*support*) apoyar.
steadfast ['stedfaɪst] *adj* constante; fijo.
steady ['stedi] *adj* constante; firme; regular; continuo. *v* estabilizar; calmar; sostener. **steadily** *adv* firmemente; regularmente; sin parar. **steadiness** *n* firmeza *f*; estabilidad *f*; uniformidad *f*; regularidad *f*.
steak [steik] *n* (*beefsteak*) bistec *m*; (*of other meat or fish*) filete *m*.

*steal [stiːl] v robar. **stealing** n robo m.
stealthy ['stelθi] adj furtivo.
steam [stiːm] n vapor m. **let off steam**
(coll) desahogarse. v echar vapor;
(cookery) cocinar al vapor.
steel [stiːl] n acero m. **steel wool**
estropajo m. **steelworks** pl n aceria f sing.
steely adj acerado; inflexible.
steep¹ [stiːp] adj escarpado.
steep² [stiːp] v empapar.
steeple ['stiːpl] n aguja f. **steeplechase** n
carrera de obstáculos f. **steeplejack** n
reparador de chimeneas m.
steer [stiə] v (ship) gobernar; (vehicle)
dirigir; (bicycle) llevar; (course) seguir;
(car) manejar. **steering** n (naut) gobierno
m; (mot) conducción f. **steering-wheel** n
volante m.
stem¹ [stem] n tallo m; (glass) pie m.
stem from derivarse de.
stem² [stem] v (stop) detener, contener.
stench [stentʃ] n tufo m.
stencil ['stensl] n estarcido m. v (typing)
cliché de multicopista m.
step [step] n paso m; (stairs, ladder)
peldaño m; (doorway) umbral m;
(degree) escalón m; (measure) medida f.
stepladder n escalera de tijera f. v dar un
paso; ir. **step up** subir; aumentar.
stepbrother ['stepbrʌðə] n hermanastro
m.
stepdaughter ['stepdɔːtə] n hijastra f.
stepfather ['stepfaːðə] n padrastro m.
stepmother ['stepmʌðə] n madrastra f.
stepsister ['stepsistə] n hermanastra f.
stepson ['stepsʌn] n hijastro m.
stereo ['steriou] nf, adj estéreo. **stereophonic** adj estereofónico.
stereotype ['steriətaip] n estereotipo m. v
estereotipar.
sterile ['sterail] adj estéril. **sterility** n
esterilidad f. **sterilization** esterilización f.
sterilize v esterilizar.
sterling ['stəːliŋ] n libra esterlina f. adj
(silver) plata de ley f; (character)
excelente.
stern¹ [stəːn] adj severo.
stern² [stəːn] n (naut) popa f.
stethoscope ['steθəskoup] n estetoscopio
m.
stew [stjuː] n estofado m. v (meat)
estofar; guisar; (fruit) cocer.
steward ['stjuəd] n camarero m; despen-
sero m. **shop steward** enlace sindical m.

stewardess n (ship) camarera f; (air)
azafata f.
stick¹ [stik] n madero m; estaca f; palo
m; (club) garrote m; (walking) bastón m.
*stick² [stik] v fijar; (thrust) clavar; (penetrate) pinchar; (glue) pegar; (stay)
quedarse. **stick out** sacar; sobresalir.
stick up for (coll) defender. **sticky** adj
pegajoso; (coll) difícil.
stickler ['stiklə] n **be a stickler for** dar
mucha importancia a.
stiff [stif] adj rígido; (manner) distante;
(person) severo. **stiffen** v atiesarse;
endurecerse. **stiffness** n rigidez f; frialdad
f; obstinación f.
stifle ['staifl] v ahogar, sofocar; (smile,
etc.) suprimir. **stifling** adj sofocante.
stigma ['stigmə] n estigma m.
stile [stail] n portilla con escalones f.
still¹ [stil] adv todavía, aún; (always)
siempre; (nevertheless) sin embargo; (sit,
stand) quieto. adj tranquilo; inmóvil;
silencioso. **stillborn** adj nacido muerto.
still life bodegón m. n calma f; (phot)
vista fija f.
still² [stil] n alambique m; destilería f.
stilt [stilt] n zanco m. **stilted** adj
campanudo.
stimulus ['stimjuləs] n, pl -li estímulo m;
incentivo m. **stimulant** nm, adj estimulante. **stimulate** v estimular. **stimulation** n
estímulo m.
*sting [stiŋ] v picar; herir; (coll: overcharge) clavar. n (insect) aguijón m;
(wound) picadura f; (pain) escozor m.
*stink [stiŋk] v heder, oler mal. n hedor
m.
stint [stint] n sesión de trabajo f. v escatimar; limitar.
stipulate ['stipjuleit] v estipular. **stipulation** n estipulación f.
stir [stəː] n agitación f; sensación f; conmoción f. v (tea, etc.) revolver; mezclar;
(move) mover; excitar. **stir up** provocar;
fomentar.
stirrup ['stirəp] n estribo m.
stitch [stitʃ] n (sewing) puntada f; (knitting) punto m; (med) punto de sutura m;
(pain) dolor de costado m. v coser; (med)
suturar.
stoat [stout] n armiño m.
stock [stok] n (supply) reserva f; (farm)
ganado m; (cookery) caldo m; (lineage)
linaje m; (race) raza f; (tree) tronco m.
stockbroker n corredor de Bolsa m. **stock**

exchange Bolsa f. **stockpile** n reservas f pl. **stocktaking** n inventario m. v surtir, abastecer.

Stockholm ['stokhoum] n Estocolmo.

stocking ['stokiŋ] n media f.

stocky ['stoki] adj rechoncho.

stodge [stodʒ] n (coll) comida indigesta f. **stodgy** adj indigesto.

stoical ['stouikl] adj estoico.

stoke [stouk] v alimentar.

stole[1] [stoul] V **steal.**

stole[2] [stoul] n estola f.

stomach ['stʌmək] n estómago m. **stomach-ache** n dolor de estómago m. v soportar.

stone [stoun] n piedra f; (fruit) hueso m; (med) cálculo m. **stone-cold** adj helado. v (throw) apedrear. **stony** adj pedregoso.

stood [stud] V **stand.**

stool [stuil] n taburete m.

stoop [stuip] n espaldas encorvadas f pl. v encorvarse; agacharse. **stoop to** rebajarse a.

stop [stop] n parada f; cesación f; suspensión f; (stay) estancia f; (gramm) punto m. v parar; impedir; interrumpir; evitar; dejar de; (a hole) tapar; (a gap) rellenar; cesar. **stop-watch** n cronómetro m. **stoppage** n (blockage) obstrucción f; (strike) huelga f. **stopper** n tapón m.

store [stoi] n (supply) provisión f; (warehouse) depósito m; (large shop) almacén m; (smaller shop) tienda f. v (keep) guardar; almacenar; (supply) suministrar. **storage** n almacenaje m.

storey ['stoiri] n piso m.

stork [stoik] n cigüeña f.

storm [stoim] n tempestad f; (thunderstorm) tormenta f. v (mil) asaltar; (wind) ser tempestuoso; (fig) fabiar. **stormy** adj tempestuoso; violento.

story ['stoiri] n historia f; cuento m.

stout [staut] adj fuerte; intrépido; gordo; grueso. n cerveza negra f.

stove [stouv] n (cooker) cocina f; (heater) estufa f.

stow [stou] v colocar, meter. **stow away** guardar; esconder. **stowaway** n polizón m.

straddle ['stradl] v estar a caballo sobre; montar a horcajadas.

straggle ['stragl] v (leg) rezagarse; (spread) desparramarse. **straggler** n rezagado, -a m, f.

straight [streit] adj derecho; recto; en orden; (hair) lacio. adv derecho; directamente. **straight ahead** todo recto. **straight away** en seguida. **straightforward** adj sincero; (simple) sencillo. **straighten** v enderezar; arreglar.

strain[1] [strein] n tensión f; esfuerzo m; (med) torcedura f. v (stretch) estirar; forzar; (sprain) torcer; (filter) filtrar; (cookery) colar. **strainer** n colador m.

strain[2] [strein] n raza f; tendencia f.

strait [streit] n estrecho m.

strand[1] [strand] n (hair) trenza f; (rope) cabo m; (thread) hebra f.

strand[2] [strand] n (shore) playa f; (river) ribera f. v (ship) encallar. **be stranded** hallarse abandonado.

strange [streindʒ] adj extraño; raro; inesperado; (unknown) desconocido. **stranger** n desconocido, -a m, f.

strangle ['straŋgl] v estrangular. **stranglehold** n collar de fuerza m. **strangler** n estrangulador, -a m, f.

strap [strap] n correa f; (on garment) tirante m. v atar con correa; (med) vendar. **strapping** adj robusto.

strategy ['stratədʒi] n estrategia f. **strategic** adj estratégico.

stratum ['straitəm] n, pl -ta estrato m, capa f.

straw [stroi] n paja f. **it's the last straw!** ¡es el colmo!

strawberry ['stroibəri] n (plant and fruit) fresa f.

stray [strei] n animal extraviado m. adj perdido; extraviado; aislado. v errar; desviarse; perderse.

streak [striik] n raya f; vena f; (light) rayo m. v rayar; ir como un rayo. **streaky** adj rayado.

stream [striim] n río m; arroyo m; corriente f. **streamlined** adj aerodinámico; (mot) carenado; (efficient) eficaz. v correr, fluir. **streamer** n serpentina f.

street [striit] n calle f.

strength [streŋθ] n fuerza f. **strengthen** v fortalecer; reforzar; confirmar.

strenuous ['strenjuəs] adj arduo; enérgico.

stress [stres] n tensión f; presión f; (gramm) acento tónico m. v (emphasize) subrayar; insistir en; acentuar.

stretch [stretʃ] n (scope) alcance m; (of arms, distance) extensión f; (time) período m; (of road) trecho m. **home**

stretch última etapa *f. v* estirar; tender; extender. **stretcher** *n* camilla *f.*

stricken ['strikən] *adj* afligido.

strict [strikt] *adj* severo; exacto. **strictly** *adv* severamente; exactamente. **strictly speaking** en realidad. **strictness** *n* severidad *f*; exactitud *f.*

***stride** [straid] *v* dar zancadas; andar a pasos largos. *n* zancada *f*; tranco *m.*

strident ['straidənt] *adj* estridente; llamativo.

strife [straif] *n* disputa *f*, lucha *f.*

***strike** [straik] *n* (*industry*) huelga *f*; (*hit*) golpe *m*; (*oil, etc.*) descubrimiento *m. v* (*hit*) golpear; pegar; declararse en huelga; (*clock*) sonar; (*a bargain*) cerrar; descubrir; (*a match*) encender. **striker** *n* huelguista *m, f.* **striking** *adj* impresionante; en huelga.

***string** [striŋ] *v* (*beads*) ensartar; (*hang*) enristrar. *n* cuerda *f*; (*of cars*) fila *f.* **string bean** judía verde *f.* **string quartet** cuarteto de cuerdas *m.* **stringy** *adj* fibroso.

stringent ['strindʒənt] *adj* estricto, riguroso.

strip¹ [strip] *v* quitar; (*undress*) desnudar; (*bed*) deshacer.

strip² [strip] *n* (*of land*) zona *f*; (*of wood*) listón *m*; (*tatter, scrap*) tira *f.*

stripe [straip] *n* raya *f*; azote *m.* **striped** *adj* con rayas.

***strive** [straiv] *v* esforzarse (a).

strode [stroud] *V* stride.

stroke¹ [strouk] *n* golpe *m*, choque *m*; (*swimming*) braza *f*; (*clock*) campanada *f*; (*mark*) trazo *m*; (*med*) ataque *m*; (*lightning*) rayo *m.*

stroke² [strouk] *v* acariciar. *n* caricia *f.*

stroll [stroul] *n* vuelta *f*, paseo *m. v* dar un paseo, pasearse.

strong [stroŋ] *adj* fuerte; robusto. *adv* muy bien. **stronghold** *n* fortaleza *f*; (*fig*) baluarte *m.* **strong-minded** *adj* resuelto. **strong-room** *n* cámara acorazada *f.*

struck [strʌk] *V* strike.

structure ['strʌktʃə] *n* estructura *f*; construcción *f.* **structural** *adj* estructural; de construcción.

struggle ['strʌgl] *n* lucha *f. v* luchar; (*to escape*) forcejear. *struggle in/out* entrar/salir penosamente.

strum [strʌm] *v* (*guitar*) rasguear; (*other instruments*) rascar. *n* (*guitar*) rasgueo *m.*

strung [strʌŋ] *V* string.

strut¹ [strʌt] *v* pavonearse.

strut² [strʌt] *n* (*arch*) puntal *m*; (*aero*) montante *m.*

stub [stʌb] *n* (*tree*) tocón *m*; (*cigarette*) colilla *f*; (*cheque*) talón *m*; (*ticket*) resguardo *m*; (*pencil, candle*) cabo *m. v* (*toe*) tropezar con. **stub out** apagar.

stubble ['stʌbl] *n* rastrojo *m*; (*chin*) barba *f.*

stubborn ['stʌbən] *adj* terco; inflexible. **stubbornness** *n* terquedad *f*; tenacidad *f.*

stuck [stʌk] *V* stick.

stud¹ [stʌd] *n* (*collar*) botón de camisa *m*; (*boot*) taco *m*; (*nail, rivet*) tachón *m. v* tachonar. **studded with** sembrado de, lleno de.

stud² [stʌd] *n* (*place*) cuadra *f*; (*animal*) semental *m.* **stud horse** caballo padre *m.*

student ['stjuːdənt] *n* estudiante *m, f*; (*pupil*) alumno, -a *m, f.*

studio ['stjuːdiou] *n* estudio *m.*

study ['stʌdi] *n* estudio *m*; (*room*) gabinete *m. v* estudiar; examinar. **studious** *adj* estudioso; solícito.

stuff [stʌf] *n* material *m*, materia *f*; cosas *f pl*; (*cloth*) tejido *m. v* llenar; (*cram*) atestar; (*cookery*) rellenar. **stuffing** *n* (*furniture*) rehenchimiento *m*; (*cookery*) relleno *m*; (*padding*) paja *f.* **stuffy** *adj* mal ventilado; (*person*) pomposo.

stumble ['stʌmbl] *v* tropezar.

stump [stʌmp] *n* (*tree*) tocón *m*; (*limb*) muñón *m*; (*pencil, etc.*) cabo *m*; (*cricket*) poste *m. v* (*fig*) dejar perplejo.

stun [stʌn] *v* aturdir; (*amaze*) pasmar. **stunning** *adj* aturdidor; (*coll*) fenomenal.

stung [stʌŋ] *V* sting.

stunk [stʌŋk] *V* stink.

stunt¹ [stʌnt] *v* impedir el crecimiento de. **stunted** *adj* atrofiado.

stunt² [stʌnt] *n* hazaña *f*; truco publicitario *m.* **stunt man** doble especial *m.*

stupid ['stjuːpid] *adj* estúpido. **stupidity** *n* estupidez *f.*

stupor ['stjuːpə] *n* estupor *m.*

sturdy ['stəːdi] *adj* robusto, vigoroso. **sturdiness** *n* robustez *f*; vigor *m.*

sturgeon ['stəːdʒən] *n* esturión *m.*

stutter ['stʌtə] *n* tartamudeo *m. v* tartamudear.

sty [stai] *n* (*pig*) pocilga *f*; (*med*) orzuelo *m.*

style [stail] *n* estilo *m*; (*kind*) tipo *m*; manera *f*; (*fashion*) moda *f*; (*clothes*) hechura *f*; (*hair*) peinado *m*. *v* (*design*) diseñar. **stylish** *adj* elegante.

stylus ['stailəs] *n* (*tool*) estilete *m*; (*record player*) aguja *f*.

suave [swɑɪv] *adj* afable, urbano.

subconscious [sʌb'kɒnʃəs] *nm, adj* subconsciente.

subcontract [sʌbkən'trakt] *v* subcontratar. **subcontractor** *n* subcontratista *m*.

subdivide [sʌbdi'vaid] *v* subdividir(se). **subdivision** *n* subdivisión *f*.

subdue [səb'djuː] *v* (*riot, etc.*) sojuzgar; (*sound, light*) atenuar; (*voice*) bajar; (*pain*) aliviar; (*feelings*) contener. **subdued** *adj* sojuzgado; atenuado; bajo; aliviado; contenido.

subject ['sʌbdʒikt; *v* səb'dʒekt] *n* sujeto *m*; (*school*) asignatura *f*; (*theme*) tema *m*; motivo *m*; (*people*) súbdito, -a *m, f*. **subject to** sujeto a; propenso a. *v* sojuzgar; (*to an examination*) someter. **subjection** *n* sujeción *f*. **subjective** *adj* subjetivo.

subjunctive [səb'dʒʌŋktiv] *nm, adj* subjuntivo.

sublet [sʌb'let] *v* subarrendar.

sublime [sə'blaim] *adj* sublime. *n* lo sublime.

submarine ['sʌbməriːn] *n* submarino *m*.

submerge [səb'mɜːdʒ] *v* sumergir. *n* sumersión *f*.

submit [səb'mit] *v* someter. **submission** *n* sumisión *f*. **submissive** *adj* sumiso.

subnormal [sʌb'nɔːməl] *adj* subnormal.

subordinate [sə'bɔːdinət] *adj* (*gramm*) subordinado; subalterno. *n* subordinado, -a *m, f*; subalterno, -a *m, f*. *v* subordinar. **subordination** *n* subordinación *f*.

subscribe [səb'skraib] *v* subscribe to aprobar; (*newspaper*) subscribirse a. **subscriber** *n* suscriptor, -a *m, f*; abonado, -a *m, f*. **subscription** *n* suscripción *f*; abono *m*; (*membership fee*) cuota *f*.

subsequent ['sʌbsikwənt] *adj* subsiguiente; posterior.

subservient [səb'sɜːviənt] *adj* subordinado; servil.

subside [səb'said] *v* (*land*) hundirse; (*flood*) bajar; (*excitement*) calmarse; (*wind*) amainar. **subsidence** *n* hundimiento *m*.

subsidiary [səb'sidiəri] *adj* subsidiario; secundario; (*comm*) afiliado. *n* (*comm*) filial *f*.

subsidize ['sʌbsidaiz] *v* subvencionar. **subsidy** *n* subvención *f*.

subsist [səb'sist] *v* subsistir. **subsistence** *n* subsistencia *f*.

substance ['sʌbstəns] *n* sustancia *f*. **substantial** *adj* sustancial; sustancioso; importante.

substandard [sʌb'standəd] *adj* inferior.

substitute ['sʌbstitjuːt] *n* (*person*) sustituto, -a *m, f*, substituto, -a *m, f*; (*thing*) sucedáneo *m*. *v* sustituir, reemplazar. **substitution** *n* sustitución *f*.

subtitle ['sʌbtaitl] *n* subtítulo *m*. *v* subtitular.

subtle ['sʌtl] *adj* sutil; delicado. **subtlety** *n* sutileza f; delicadeza *f*.

subtract [səb'trakt] *v* restar, sustraer. **subtraction** *n* resta *f*, sustracción *f*.

suburb ['sʌbɜːb] *n* suburbio *m*. **the suburbs** las afueras *f pl*. **suburban** *adj* suburbano.

subvert [səb'vɜːt] *v* derribar; corromper. **subversion** *n* subversión *f*. **subversive** *adj* subversivo.

subway ['sʌbwei] *n* pasaje subterráneo *m*; (*US*) metro *m*.

succeed [sək'siːd] *v* triunfar; (*follow*) suceder; (*inherit*) heredar. **succeeding** *adj* sucesivo; venidero. **success** *n* éxito *m*; triunfo *m*. **successful** *adj* que tiene éxito; próspero. **successfully** *adv* con éxito. **succession** *n* sucesión *f*; herencia *f*. **successive** *adj* sucesivo. **successor** *n* sucesor, -a *m, f*.

succinct [sək'siŋkt] *adj* sucinto.

succulent ['sʌkjulənt] *adj* suculento; (*plant*) carnoso. *n* planta carnosa *f*.

succumb [sə'kʌm] *v* sucumbir.

such [sʌtʃ] *adj* tal; semejante, parecido; tan, tanto. **such as** como. *adv* tan, tanto. *pron* los que, las que; lo que; todo lo que; esto, éste, ésta. **as such** en sí.

suck [sʌk] *v* chupar; (*baby*) mamar. **suck up to** (*slang*) dar coba a.

sucker ['sʌkə] *n* (*bot*) chupón *m*; (*device*) émbolo *m*; (*slang: simpleton*) primo *m*.

suction ['sʌkʃən] *n* succión *f*.

sudden ['sʌdən] *adj* súbito; inesperado; repentino. **all of a sudden** de repente.

suds [sʌdz] *pl n* jabonaduras *f pl*.

sue [suː] *v* proceder contra.

suede [sweid] *n* ante *m*.

suet ['suːit] *n* sebo *m*.

suffer ['sʌfə] *v* sufrir, padecer; tolerar; dejar; (*undergo*) aguantar. **suffering** *n* sufrimiento *m*, padecimiento *m*; dolor *m*.

sufficient [sə'fiʃənt] *adj* suficiente; bastante. **suffice** *v* ser suficiente, bastar. **sufficiently** *adv* suficientemente, bastante.

suffix ['sʌfiks] *n* sufijo *m*.

suffocate ['sʌfəkeit] *v* ahogar, sofocar. **suffocation** *n* ahogo *m*; asfixia *f*.

sugar ['ʃugə] *n* azúcar *m*. **sugar bowl** azucarero *m*. **sugar cane** caña de azúcar *f*. **sugar lump** terrón de azúcar *m*.

suggest [sə'dʒest] *v* sugerir; indicar. **suggestion** *n* sugerencia *f*; indicación *f*. **suggestive** *adj* sugestivo; evocador.

suicide ['suisaid] *n* (*act*) suicidio *m*; (*person*) suicida *m*, *f*. **commit suicide** suicidarse. **suicidal** *adj* suicida.

suit [suit] *n* traje *m*; (*woman's*) conjunto *m*; (*law*) pleito *m*; (*cards*) palo *m*. **suitcase** *n* maleta *f*. *v* convenir; venir bien a. **suitable** *adj* conveniente; apropiado.

suite [swit] *n* (*in hotel*) suite *f*; (*furniture*) juego *m*.

sulk [sʌlk] *v* enfurruñarse. *n* enfurruñamiento *m*. **sulky** *adj* enfurruñado.

sullen ['sʌlən] *adj* taciturno; malhumorado. **sullenness** *n* taciturnidad *f*; mal humor *m*.

sulphur ['sʌlfə] *n* azufre *m*. **sulphuric** *adj* sulfúrico.

sultan ['sʌltən] *n* sultán *m*.

sultana [sʌl'taːnə] *n* pasa de Esmirna *f*.

sultry ['sʌltri] *adj* (*weather*) sofocante; (*person*) sensual.

sum [sʌm] *n* suma *f*; cantidad *f*; cálculo *m*. *v* **sum up** recapitular; resumir; (*person*) evaluar.

summarize ['sʌməraiz] *v* resumir, recapitular. **summary** *n* resumen *m*; *adj* sumario.

summer ['sʌmə] *n* verano *m*. **summer holidays** vacaciones de verano *f pl*. **summerhouse** *n* cenador *m*.

summit ['sʌmit] *n* cumbre *f*, cima *f*; (*fig*) apogeo *m*.

summon ['sʌmən] *v* llamar, convocar; mandar; hacer venir. **summon up** evocar.

summons ['sʌmənz] *pl n* llamamiento *m*; (*law*) citación *f*. *v* citar.

sumptuous ['sʌmptʃuəs] *adj* suntuoso.

sun [sʌn] *n* sol *m*. **sunny** *adj* bañado de sol.

sunbathe ['sʌnbeið] *v* tomar el sol. **sunbathing** *n* baños de sol *m pl*.

sunbeam ['sʌnbiːm] *n* rayo de sol *m*.

sunburn ['sʌnbəːn] *n* (*tan*) bronceado *m*; (*pain*) quemadura del sol *f*. **sunburnt** *adj* bronceado; quemado por el sol.

Sunday ['sʌndi] *n* domingo *m*.

sundial ['sʌndaiəl] *n* reloj de sol *m*.

sundry ['sʌndri] *adj* varios. **all and sundry** todo el mundo. **sundries** *pl n* artículos diversos *m pl*.

sunflower ['sʌnflauə] *n* girasol *m*.

sun-glasses ['sʌnglaːsiz] *pl n* gafas de sol *f pl*.

sunk [sʌŋk] *V* sink.

sunlight ['sʌnlait] *n* luz del sol *f*.

sunrise ['sʌnraiz] *n* salida del sol *f*.

sunset ['sʌnset] *n* puesta del sol *f*.

sunshine ['sʌnʃain] *n* sol *m*.

sunstroke ['sʌnstrouk] *n* insolación *f*.

sun-tan ['sʌntan] *n* bronceado *m*. **sun-tan lotion** loción bronceadora *f*.

super ['suːpə] *adj* (*coll*) estupendo; formidable.

superannuation [,suːpərənju'eiʃən] *n* jubilación *f*.

superb [suː'pəːb] *adj* soberbio; magnífico.

supercilious [,suːpə'siliəs] *adj* altanero; desdeñoso.

superficial [,suːpə'fiʃəl] *adj* superficial.

superfluous [su'pəːfluəs] *adj* superfluo.

superhuman [suːpə'hjuːmən] *adj* sobrehumano.

superimpose [,suːpərim'pouz] *v* sobreponer. **superimposed** *adj* (*photo, etc.*) superpuesto.

superintendent [,suːpərin'tendənt] *n* superintendente *m*, *f*; director, -a *m*, *f*; (*police*) subjefe de la policía *m*.

superior [suː'piəriə] *n*, *adj* superior, -a. **superiority** *n* superioridad *f*.

superlative [suː'pəːlativ] *adj* superlativo; supremo. (*gramm*) *nm*, *adj* superlativo.

supermarket ['suːpə,maːkit] *n* supermercado *m*.

supernatural [,suːpə'natʃərəl] *adj* sobrenatural. *n* lo sobrenatural.

supersede [,suːpə'siːd] *v* sustituir, reemplazar.

supersonic [,suːpə'sonik] *adj* supersónico.

superstition [suːpə'stiʃən] *n* superstición *f*. **superstitious** *adj* supersticioso.

supervise ['suːpəvaiz] *v* supervisar; vigilar. **supervision** *n* superintendencia *f*. **supervisor** *n* supervisor, -a *m*, *f*; director, -a *m*, *f*.

supper ['sʌpə] *n* cena *f*.

supple ['sʌpl] *adj* flexible, elástico. **suppleness** *n* flexibilidad *f*.

supplement ['sʌpləmənt] *n* suplemento *m*. *v* suplir, complementar. **supplementary** *adj* suplementario.

supply [sə'plai] *n* (*stock*) surtido *m*; provisión *f*; (*act of supplying*) suministro *m*. **supplies** *pl n* material *m sing*; provisiones *f pl*; (*stores*) víveres *m pl*. *v* alimentar; proveer; abastecer; presentar.

support [sə'poɹt] *n* apoyo *m*; sostén *m*; soporte *m*. *v* apoyar; sostener; defender; (*financially*) mantener. **supporter** *n* partidario, -a *m, f*; (*sport*) aficionado, -a.

suppose [sə'pouz] *v* suponer. **supposed** *adj* supuesto. **be supposed to** deber. **supposedly** *adv* según se supone. **supposing** *conj* si, suponiendo (que). **supposition** *n* suposición *f*.

suppress [sə'pres] *v* suprimir; (*yawn, laugh, etc.*) contener; (*passion*) dominar; (*fact*) disimular; (*revolt*) sofocar; (*publication*) prohibir; (*news*) ocultar. **suppression** *n* supresión *f*; dominio *m*; represión *f*; prohibición *f*; ocultación *f*.

supreme [su'priːm] *adj* supremo. **supremacy** *n* supremacía *f*.

surcharge ['səɹtʃaɹdʒ] *n* sobrecarga *f*.

sure [ʃuə] *adj* seguro, cierto. **sure enough** efectivamente. **sure-footed** *adj* de pie firme. **surely** *adv* seguramente; sin duda.

surety ['ʃuərəti] *n* garantía *f*, fianza *f*.

surf [səɹf] *n* resaca *f*; (*foam*) espuma *f*. **surf-board** *n* tabla hawaiana *f*. **surfing** *n* surf *m*.

surface ['səɹfis] *n* superficie *f*. **on the surface** en apariencia. *v* (*road*) revestir; (*swimmer*) salir a la superficie; (*submarine*) sacar a la superficie.

surfeit ['səɹfit] *n* exceso *m*.

surge [səɹdʒ] *n* oleada *f*; (*anger*) ola *f*. *v* (*sea*) levantarse; (*crowd*) bullir.

surgeon ['səɹdʒən] *n* cirujano *m*. **surgery** *n* (*skill*) cirugía *f*; (*place*) consultorio *m*. **surgical** *adj* quirúrgico.

surly ['səɹli] *adj* malhumorado.

surmount [sə'maunt] *v* vencer, superar.

surname ['səɹneim] *n* apellido *m*.

surpass [sə'paɹs] *v* superar, sobrepasar.

surplus ['səɹpləs] *n* excedente *m*. *adj* sobrante.

surprise [sə'praiz] *n* sorpresa *f*. *adj* de sorpresa. *v* sorprender.

surrealism [sə'riəlizəm] *n* surrealismo *m*. **surrealist** *n*(*m*+*f*). *adj* surrealista. **surrealistic** *adj* surrealista.

surrender [sə'rendə] *v* rendir; (*give up*) ceder; entregar. *n* rendición *f*; capitulación *f*.

surreptitious [ˌsʌrəp'tiʃəs] *adj* subrepticio.

surround [sə'raund] *v* cercar, rodear. *n* borde *m*. **surrounding** *adj* circundante. **surroundings** *pl n* (*environment*) medio ambiente *m*; (*environs*) alrededores *m pl*.

survey ['səɹvei; *v* sə'vei] *n* inspección *f*; (*report*) informe *m*; (*of a question*) examen *m*; panorama *m*; (*land*) medición *f*. *v* inspeccionar; estudiar; examinar; contemplar; medir. **surveying** *n* inspección *f*; agrimensura *f*. **surveyor** *n* (*land*) agrimensor *m*; (*house*) inspector *m*.

survive [sə'vaiv] *v* sobrevivir a. **survival** *n* supervivencia *f*. **survivor** *n* sobreviviente *m, f*.

susceptible [sə'septəbl] *adj* susceptible; sensible.

suspect ['sʌspekt; *v* sə'spekt] *n, adj* sospechoso, -a. *v* sospechar.

suspend [sə'spend] *v* suspender. **suspender** *n* liga *f*. **suspense** *n* incertidumbre *f*; (*book, film*) suspense *m*. **in suspense** pendiente. **suspension** *n* suspensión *f*. **suspension bridge** puente colgante *m*.

suspicion [sə'spiʃən] *n* sospecha *f*. **suspicious** *adj* (*suspecting*) suspicaz; (*suspected*) sospechoso.

sustain [sə'stein] *v* sostener; mantener; apoyar; (*suffer*) sufrir.

swab [swob] *n* (*mop*) estropajo *m*; (*med: pad*) tapón *m*. *v* fregar con estropajo; limpiar con tapón.

swagger ['swagə] *n* pavoneo *m*. *v* pavonearse; darse importancia.

swallow[1] ['swolou] *v* tragar. **swallow up** tragarse. *n* trago *m*; (*amount*) bocado *m*.

swallow[2] ['swolou] *n* (*bird*) golondrina *f*.

swam [swam] *V* swim.

swamp [swomp] *n* pantano *m*; marisma *f*. *v* sumergir; inundar. **swampy** *adj* pantanoso.

swan [swon] *n* cisne *m*.

swank [swaŋk] (*coll*) *n* fanfarronada *f*; (*person*) fanfarrón, -ona *m, f*. *v* fanfarronear. **swanky** *adj* fanfarrón.

swap *or* **swop** [swop] *n* cambio *m*, trueque *m*. *v* cambiar, trocar.

swarm [swoɹm] *n* (*bees*) enjambre *m*; (*fig*) multitud *f*. *v* enjambrar; (*fig*) pulular.

swarthy ['swoɹði] *adj* moreno.

swat [swot] *v* aplastar.

sway [swei] *n* balanceo *m*; oscilación *f*; dominio *m*. *v* balancearse; oscilar; (*influence*) influir.

***swear** [sweə] *v* jurar. **swear in** tomar juramento a. **swear-word** *n* palabrota *f*.

sweat [swet] *n* sudor *m*. *v* sudar.

sweater *n* suéter *m*.

swede [swiːd] *n* naba *f*.

Sweden ['swiːdn] *n* Suecia *f*. **Swede** *n* sueco, -a *m*, *f*. **Swedish** *nm*, *adj* sueco.

***sweep** [swiːp] *v* deshollinar; barrer; explorar. **sweep in/out** entrar/salir rápidamente. **sweep through** difundirse. *n* (*chimney*) deshollinador *m*; (*a cleaning*) barrido *m*; (*curve*) curva *f*. **make a clean sweep** llevárselo todo. **sweeping** *adj* aplastante; demasiado general. **sweeping statement** declaración demasiado general *f*.

sweet [swiːt] *adj* (*taste*) dulce; (*air, breath, etc.*) fresco; (*smell*) bueno; (*friendly*) encantador; (*kind*) bondadoso. *n* (*toffee*) caramelo *m*; (*dessert*) postre *m*. **sweetbread** *n* mollejas *f pl*. **sweet corn** maiz tierno *m*. **sweetheart** *n* novio, -a *m*, *f*. **sweet potato** patata boniato *f*. **sweetshop** *n* confitería *f*. **sweeten** *v* azucarar, endulzar. **sweetly** *adv* dulcemente; (*sound*) melodiosamente. **sweetness** *n* dulzor *m*; (*character*) dulzura *f*.

***swell** [swel] *v* hinchar; inflarse. *n* inflado *m*; hinchazón *m*; curvatura *f*. **swelling** *n* inflamiento *m*.

swelter ['sweltə] *v* sofocarse de calor. **sweltering** *adj* sofocante.

swerve [swəːv] *v* desviar; (*vehicle*) dar un viraje. *n* viraje *m*.

swift [swift] *adj* rápido; pronto. *n* (*bird*) vencejo *m*. **swiftness** rapidez *f*; prontitud *f*.

swill [swil] *v* lavar con much agua; (*drink*) beber a tragos. *n* (*for pigs*) bazofia *f*.

***swim** [swim] *v* nadar. *n* baño *m*. **swimmer** *n* nadador, -a *m*, *f*. **swimming** *n* natación *f*. **swimming baths** *or* **pool** piscina *f*. **swimming costume** traje de baño *m*.

swindle ['swindl] *n* estafa *f*. *v* estafar. **swindler** *n* estafador, -a *m*, *f*.

swine [swain] *n* cerdo *m*, puerco *m*; (*impol*) canalla *m*, *f*.

***swing** [swiŋ] *v* hacer girar; balancear; oscilar; virar. *n* (*amusement*) columpio *m*; oscilación *f*; impulso *m*; (*pol*) viraje *m*. **in full swing** a toda velocidad.

swipe [swaip] (*coll*) *n* golpetazo *m*. *v* golpear con fuerza; (*steal*) afanar.

swirl [swəːl] *n* remolino *m*. *v* arremolinarse.

swish [swiʃ] *n* silbo *m*; (*of water*) susurro *m*; (*of garment*) crujido *m*. *v* (*cane*) blandir; (*tail*) menear.

Swiss [swis] *n*, *adj* suizo, -a. **Swiss roll** brazo de gitano *m*.

switch [switʃ] *n* (*elec*) interruptor *m*, conmutador *m*; (*change*) paso *m*; (*stick*) varilla *f*. **switchboard** *n* centralita de teléfonos *f*. *v* (*opinion, policy*) cambiar de; (*places*) cambiar; (*a train*) desviar. **switch off** desconectar. **switch on** encender.

Switzerland ['switsələnd] *n* Suiza *f*.

swivel ['swivl] *n* pivote *m*. *v* girar sobre un eje; dar una vuelta.

swollen ['swoulən] *V* **swell**.

swoop [swuːp] *n* calada *f*; redada *f*. **at one fell swoop** de un solo golpe. *v* calarse, abatirse.

swop *V* **swap**.

sword [soːd] *n* espada *f*. **swordfish** *n* pez espada *m*.

sworn [swoːn] *V* **swear**.

swot [swot] (*coll*) *n* empollón, -ona *m*, *f*. *v* empollar **swotting** *n* estudio *m*.

swum [swʌm] *V* **swim**.

swung [swʌŋ] *V* **swing**.

sycamore ['sikəmoː] *n* sicomoro *m*.

syllable ['siləbl] *n* sílaba *f*. **syllabic** *adj* silábico.

syllabus ['siləbəs] *n* programa *m*.

symbol ['simbl] *n* símbolo *m*, emblema *m*. **symbolic** *adj* simbólico. **symbolism** *n* simbolismo *m*. **symbolize** *v* simbolizar.

symmetry ['simitri] *n* simetría *f*. **symmetrical** *adj* simétrico.

sympathy ['simpəθi] *n* pésame *m*; compasión *f*. **sympathetic** *adj* compasivo; comprensivo; favorable. **sympathize with** compadecerse de.

symphony ['simfəni] *n* sinfonía *f*. **symphonic** *adj* sinfónico.

symposium [sim'pouziəm] *n* simposio *m*.

symptom ['simptəm] *n* síntoma *m*. **symptomatic** *adj* sintomático.

synagogue ['sinəgog] *n* sinagoga *f*.

synchromesh ['siŋkroumeʃ] *n* sincronizador.

synchronize ['siŋkrənaiz] *v* sincronizar. **synchronization** *n* sincronización *f*.

syncopate ['siŋkəpeit] *n* sincopar. **syncopation** *n* síncopa *f*.

syndicate ['sindikit] *n* sindicato *m*.

syndrome ['sindroum] *n* síndrome *m*.

synonym ['sinənim] *n* sinónimo *m*. **synonymous** *adj* sinónimo.

synopsis [si'nopsis] *n*, *pl* -ses sinopsis *f invar*.

syntax ['sintaks] *n* sintaxis *f*.

synthesis ['sinθisis] *n*, *pl* -ses síntesis *f invar*. **synthesize** *v* sintetizar.

syphilis ['sifilis] *n* sífilis *f*.

syringe [si'rindʒ] *n* jeringa *f*. *v* jeringar.

syrup ['sirəp] *n* (*med*) jarabe *m*; (*fruit*) almíbar *m*. **syrupy** *adj* almibarado.

system ['sistəm] *n* sistema *m*; método *m*. **systematic** *adj* sistemático.

T

tab [tab] *n* etiqueta *f*. **keep tabs on** (*coll*) tener controlado.

tabby ['tabi] *n* gato atigrador *m*.

table ['teibl] *n* mesa *f*. **table-cloth** *n* mantel *m*. **table-mat** *n* salvamanteleo *m invar*. **table-napkin** *n* servilleta *f*. **tablespoon** *n* cucharón *m*. **tablespoonful** cucharada *f*. **table tennis** tenis de mesa *m*. **clear the table** levantar la mesa. **set the table** poner la mesa.

table d'hôte [taiblə'dout] *n* menú *m*.

tablet ['tablit] *n* (*med*, *soap*) pastilla *f*; (*stone*, *chocolate*) tableta *f*; (*writing-paper*) bloc *m*.

taboo [ta'buɪ] *nm*, *adj* tabú.

tabulate ['tabjuleit] *v* tabular.

tacit ['tasit] *adj* tácito.

taciturn ['tasitəɪn] *adj* taciturno.

tack [tak] *n* (*nail*) tachuela *f*; (*sewing*) hilván *m*; (*naut: change of direction*) virada *f*; (*distance sailed*) bordada *f*. *v* clavar con tachuelas; hilvanar; virar de bordo.

tackle ['takl] *n* (*ropes*) jarcias *f pl*; (*rigging*) aparejo *m*; (*equipment*) trastos *m pl*; (*sport*) placaje *m*. *v* placar; (*seize*) agarrar; (*fig*) abordar, emprender.

tact [takt] *n* tacto *m*. **tactful** *adj* con tacto, discreto. **tactless** *adj* falto de tacto, indiscreto.

tactics ['taktiks] *pl n* táctica *f sing*. **tactical** *adj* táctico.

tadpole ['tadpoul] *n* renacuajo *m*.

taffeta ['tafitə] *n* tafetán *m*.

tag [tag] *n* etiqueta *f*; (*shoelace*) herrete *m*; (*game*) pillapilla *m*. **tag along** (*coll*) seguir.

tail [teil] *n* cola *f*; rabo *m*; (*coat*, *shirt*) faldón *m*. **tail-end** *n* zaga *f*, rabera *f*. **tails** *pl n* (*coin*) cruz *f sing*. *v* (*coll*) seguir.

tailor ['teilə] *n* sastre *m*. *v* entallar; (*fig*) adaptar.

taint [teint] *v* (*stain*) manchar; (*food*) corromper; (*air*) viciar; (*fig*) mancillar. *n* mancha *f*; corrupción *f*; contaminación *f*.

*****take** [teik] *v* tomar; llevarse; (*carry*) cargarse; (*phot*) sacar; (*shoe size*) calzar; (*occupy*) ocupar; (*responsibility*) asumir; (*bear*) aguantar; (*suppose*) suponer. **take after** parecerse a. **take along** llevarse. **take away** quitar; (*subtract*) restar. **take back** (*return*) devolver; (*retract*) retirar. **take down** (*pictures*, *curtains*) descolgar; (*from a shelf*) bajar; (*write*) apuntar. **take someone down a peg** (*coll*) bajarle los humos a alguien. **take in** acoger; (*situation*) entender; (*clothes*) achicar; (*coll: deceive*) engañar. **take off** (*clothes*) quitarse; (*aero*) despegar. **take-off** *n* despegue *m*; (*coll*) imitamonos *m invar*. **take on** (*employ*) contratar; (*challenge*) competir con. **take-over** (*comm*) adquisición *f*.

talcum powder ['talkəm] *n* talco *m*.

tale [teil] *n* cuento *m*. **fairy tales** cuentos de hadas *m pl*. **tell tales** (*coll*) contar chismes.

talent ['talənt] *n* talento *m*. **talented** *adj* talentoso, talentudo.

talk [toɪk] *n* conversación *f*; charla *f*; (*lecture*) conferencia *f*; (*speech*) discurso *m*. *v* decir; hablar. **talk back** replicar. **talk down to** ponerse al alcance de. **talk into** convencer para que. **talk over** discutir. **talkative** *adj* hablador. **talking** *n* conversación *f*. **talking point** tema de conversación *m*.

tall [toɪl] *adj* alto; grande. **tallboy** *n* cómoda alta *f*. **tallness** *n* altura *f*; lo alto.

tally ['tali] *n* tarja *f*; cuenta *f*. *v* tarjar; cuadrar.

talon ['talən] *n* garra *f*.

tambourine [tambə'riɪn] *n* pandereta *f*, pandero *m*.

tame [teim] *adj* manso; domesticado; (*not exciting*) aburrido. *v* domesticar; amansar.

tamper ['tampə] *v* **tamper with** (*text*) amañar; (*spoil*) estropear.

tampon ['tampon] *n* tapón *m*.

tan [tan] *n* bronceado *m*, color tostado *m*. *adj* bronceado, tostado. (*hide*) curtir; (*sun*) broncear, tostar.

tandem ['tandəm] *n* tándem *m*.

tangent ['tandʒənt] *nf*, *adj* tangente. **go off at a tangent** salirse por la tangente.

tangerine [tandʒə'riːn] *n* (*fruit*) mandarina *f*.

tangible ['tandʒəbl] *adj* tangible.

tangle ['taŋgl] *v* enmarañar; enredar. *n* maraña *f*; enredo *m*.

tank [taŋk] *n* tanque *m*, cisterna *f*, depósito *m*; (*mil*) tanque *m*. **tanker** *n* (*lorry*) camión cisterna *m*; (*ship*) petrolero *m*.

tankard ['taŋkəd] *n* jarro *m*.

tantalize ['tantəlaiz] *v* atormentar. **tantalizing** *adj* que atormenta.

tantamount ['tantəmaunt] *adj* **be tantamount to** ser equivalente a.

tantrum ['tantrəm] *n* berrinche *m*, rabieta *f*. **fly into a tantrum** coger una rabieta.

tap[1] [tap] *n* golpecito *m*. **tap-dance** *n* zapateado *m*. *v* golpear ligeramente.

tap[2] [tap] *n* (*water*) grifo *m*; (*barrel*) espita *f*. *v* poner una espita a; (*phone*) interceptar; (*fig: draw on*) utilizar.

tape [teip] *n* cinta *f*; (*recording*) cinta magnetofónica *f*. **tape-measure** *n* cinta métrica *f*. **tape-recorder** *n* magnetófono *m*. **tapeworm** *n* tenia *f*. *v* (*record*) grabar; (*fasten*) atar con cinta.

taper ['teipə] *n* (*candle*) vela *f*; (*narrowing*) estrachamiento *m*. *v* estrechar. **tapering** *adj* cónico.

tapestry ['tapəstri] *n* tapiz *m*.

tapioca [tapi'oukə] *n* tapioca *f*.

tar [taː] *n* alquitrán *m*. *v* alquitranar.

tarantula [tə'rantjulə] *n* tarántula *f*.

target ['taːgit] *n* blanco *m*; (*fig*) objeto *m*.

tariff ['tarif] *n* tarifa *f*.

tarmac ['taːmak] *n* superficie alquitranada *f*.

tarnish ['taːniʃ] *v* deslustrar. *n* deslustre *m*.

tarpaulin [taː'poːlin] *n* lona alquitranada *f*.

tarragon ['tarəgən] *n* estragón *m*.

tart[1] [taːt] *adj* agrio; ácido.

tart[2] [taːt] *n* tarta *f*; (*slang*) fulana *f*.

tartar ['taːtə] *n* (*chem*) tártaro *m*; (*on teeth*) sarro *m*.

task [taːsk] *n* tarea *f*. **taskmaster** *n* capataz *m*.

tassel ['tasəl] *n* borla *f*.

taste [teist] *n* (*sense*) gusto *m*; sabor *m*. *v* probar; saber. **taste of** saber a. **tasteful** *adj* de buen gusto. **tasteless** *adj* insípido; (*in bad taste*) de mal gusto. **tasty** *adj* sabroso.

tattered ['tatəd] *adj* andrajoso.

tattoo[1] [tə'tuː] *n* (*on skin*) tatuaje *m*. *v* tatuar.

tattoo[2] [tə'tuː] *n* (*mil*) desfile militar *m*; (*drumming*) repiqueteo *m*.

tatty ['tati] *adj* (*coll*) en mal estado.

taunt [toːnt] *v* mofarse de. *n* mofa *f*. **taunting** *adj* burlón; provocante.

Taurus ['toːrəs] *n* Tauro *m*.

taut [toːt] *adj* tenso, tirante. **tautness** *n* tensión *f*, tirantez *f*.

tavern ['tavən] *n* (*bar*) taberna *f*; (*inn*) venta *f*.

tawny ['toːni] *adj* leonado.

tax [taks] *n* impuesto *m*, contribución *f*. **tax-free** *adj* exento de impuestos. **tax evasion** evasión fiscal *f*. **tax haven** refugio fiscal *m*. **taxpayer** *n* contribuyente *m*, *f*. **tax return** declaración de renta *f*. *v* gravar con un impuesto; imponer contribuciones; (*try*) poner a prueba. **taxable** *adj* imponible. **taxation** *n* impuestos *m pl*; (*system*) sistema tributario *m*.

taxi ['taksi] *n* taxi *m*. **taxi-driver** *n* taxista *m*, *f*. **taximeter** *n* taxímetro *m*. **taxi rank** parada de taxis *f*. *v* (*aero*) rodar por la pista.

tea [tiː] *n* té *m*; (*snack*) merienda *f*. **teacup** *n* tasa de té *f*. **teapot** *n* tetera *f*. **teaspoon** *n* cucharilla *f*. **teaspoonful** *n* cucharadita *f*. **tea towel** trapo de cocina *m*.

*teach [tiːtʃ] *v* enseñar. **teacher** *n* (*primary*) maestro, -a *m*, *f*; (*secondary*) profesor, -a *m*, *f*. **teaching** *n* enseñanza *f*.

teak [tiːk] *n* teca *f*.

team [tiːm] *n* (*yoked animals*) yunta *f*; (*horses*) tronco *m*; (*people*) equipo *m*. **team-mate** *n* compañero de equipo *m*. **team spirit** espíritu de equipo *m*. **teamwork** *n* trabajo de equipo *m*. *v* **team up** agruparse.

tense

*tear¹ [teə] v desgarrar; (snatch) arrancar. **tear along/out** ir a toda velocidad. **tear down** demoler. **tear off** (coupon) cortar. n rasgón m.

tear² [tiə] n lágrima f. **tear gas** gas lacrimógeno m. **tear-jerker** (coll) n obra sentimental f. **tearful** adj lloroso.

tease [tiːz] v provocar. n broma f; (person) bromista m, f. **teasing** n bromas f pl.

teat [tiːt] n pezón m; (animals) teta f.

technique [tek'niːk] n técnica f. **technical** adj técnico. **technicality** n detalle técnico m. **technician** n técnico, -a m, f. **technological** adj tecnológico. **technology** n tecnología f.

teddy bear ['tedi͵beə] n osito de felpa m.

tedious ['tiːdiəs] adj latoso. **tediousness** n also **tedium** pesadez f, tedio m.

tee [tiː] n tee m. v **tee off** dar el primer golpe.

teem [tiːm] v pulular, hormiguear.

teenage ['tiːneidʒ] adj adolescente. **teenager** n adolescente m, f. **teens** pl n adolescencia f sing.

teeth [tiːθ] V **tooth**.

teethe [tiːð] v echar los dientes. **teething** n dentición f.

teetotaller [tiː'toutələ] n abstemio, -a m, f.

telecommunications [͵telikəmjuːni'keiʃənz] pl n telecomunicaciones f pl.

telegram ['teligram] n telegrama m.

telegraph ['teligraːf] n telégrafo m. **telegraph pole** poste telegráfico m. v telegrafiar. **telegraphic** adj telegráfico.

telepathy [tə'lepəθi] n telepatía f. **telepathic** adj telepático.

telephone ['telifoun] n teléfono m. **telephone box** or **kiosk** cabina telefónica f. **telephone call** llamada telefónica f. **telephone directory** guía de teléfonos f. **telephone exchange** central telefónica f. **telephone number** número de teléfono m. **telephone operator** or **telephonist** telefonista m, f. v telefonear a.

telescope ['teliskoup] n telescopio m. **telescopic** adj telescópico.

television ['telivi3ən] n televisión f. **television set** televisor m. **televise** v televisar.

telex ['teleks] n télex m.

*tell [tel] v decir; (story) contar; comunicar; mandar; (identify) reconocer; (distinguish) distinguir; (deduce) deducir;

(observe) notar. **tell against** perjudicar. **tell of** hablar de. **tell off** (coll) regañar. **tell on** afectar a. **telltale** adj revelador.

temper ['tempə] n (anger) cólera f; temperamento m; humor m. **lose one's temper** enfadarse. v templar.

temperament ['tempərəmənt] n temperamento m. **temperamental** adj caprichoso.

temperate ['tempərət] adj templado.

temperature ['temprətʃə] n temperatura f; (med) fiebre f.

tempestuous [tem'pestjuəs] adj tempestuoso.

temple¹ ['templ] n (rel) templo m.

temple² ['templ] n (anat) sien f.

tempo ['tempou] n (music) tiempo m; (fig) ritmo m.

temporary ['tempərəri] adj temporal, provisional. **temporary worker** temporario, -a m, f.

tempt [tempt] v tentar; seducir. **temptation** n tentación f.

ten [ten] nm, adj diez. **tenth** n, adj décimo, -a.

tenacious [tə'neiʃəs] adj tenaz. **tenaciousness** also **tenacity** n tenacidad f.

tenant ['tenənt] n habitante m, f, ocupante m, f. **tenancy** n alquiler m, arrendamiento m.

tend¹ [tend] v tender, tener tendencia a. **tendency** n tendencia f.

tend² [tend] v (look after) cuidar; manejar.

tender¹ ['tendə] adj tierno; delicado; (kind) cariñoso; compasivo; (sensitive) sensible; (painful) dolorido. **tenderize** v ablandar. **tenderness** n (affection) ternura f; (meat) lo tierno.

tender² ['tendə] v ofertar, hacer una oferta. n oferta f. **legal tender** moneda corriente f.

tendon ['tendən] n tendón m.

tendril ['tendril] n zarcillo m.

tenement ['tenəmənt] n casa de vecindad f.

tennis ['tenis] n tenis m. **tennis ball** pelota de tenis f. **tennis court** campo de tenis m. **tennis player** tenista m, f. **tennis shoes** zapatos de tenis m pl.

tenor ['tenə] n (music) tenor m; (sense) significado m; (course) curso m.

tense¹ [tens] adj tenso; estirado. v tensar. **tension** n tensión f.

tense² [tens] n tiempo m.

tent [tent] *n* tienda de campaña *f*. **pitch a tent** armar una tienda de campaña.

tentacle ['tentəkl] *n* tentáculo *m*.

tentative ['tentətiv] *adj* provisional; de tanteo; indeciso.

tenterhooks ['tentəhuks] *pl n* **be on tenterhooks** estar sobre ascuas.

tenuous ['tenjuəs] *adj* tenue; delgado.

tepid ['tepid] *adj* templaducho; (*fig*) tibio.
tepidness *n* *also* **tepidity** tibieza *f*.

term [tɜːm] *n* período *m*; (*comm*) plazo *m*; (*school*) trimestre *m*; curso *m*; (*end*) término *m*. **terms** *pl n* condiciones *f pl*; (*terminology*) términos *m pl*; (*comm*) tarifa *f sing*; (*relationship*) relaciones *f pl*. **come to terms with** llegar a un acuerdo con. **on good/bad terms with** en buenas/malas relaciones con. **terms of reference** mandato *m sing*. *v* llamar, calificar.

terminal ['tɜːminl] *adj* terminal, final. *n* final de línea *m*; (*extremity*) extremidad *f*; (*elec*) borne *m*.

terminate ['tɜːmineit] *v* terminar, concluir. **termination** *n* terminación *f*.

terminology [tɜːmiˈnolədʒi] *n* terminología *f*.

terminus ['tɜːminəs] *n* término *m*.

terrace ['terəs] *n* terraza *f*; (*houses*) hilera de casas *f*.

terrain [təˈrein] *n* terreno *m*.

terrestrial [təˈrestriəl] *adj* terrestre.

terrible ['terəbl] *adj* terrible; atroz; horrible. **terribly** *adv* terriblemente. **terribly bad** malísimo. **terribly good** buenísimo.

terrier ['teriə] *n* terrier *m*.

terrify ['terifai] *v* aterrorizar. **terrific** *adj* (*coll: excellent*) estupendo; (*coll: extreme*) terrible; enorme.

territory ['teritəri] *n* territorio *m*. **territorial** *adj* territorial.

terror ['terə] *n* terror *m*. **terrorism** *n* terrorismo *m*. **terrorist** *n*(*m+f*), *adj* terrorista. **terrorize** *v* aterrorizar, aterrar.

terse [tɜːs] *adj* conciso.

terylene ® ['terəliːn] *n* terylene ® *m*.

test [test] *n* prueba *f*; examen *m*; (*med*) análisis *m*. **test case** (*law*) juicio que hace jurisprudencia *m*. **test match** partido internacional *m*. **test paper** examen *m*. **test pilot** piloto de pruebas *m*. **test tube** tubo de ensayo *m*. *v* probar; poner un examen a; analizar; (*sight*) graduar; (*weight*) comprobar.

testament ['testəmənt] *n* testamento *m*.

the New Testament el Nuevo Testamento *m*. **the Old Testament** el Antiguo Testamento *m*.

testicle ['testikl] *n* testículo *m*.

testify ['testifai] *v* testificar; dar testimonio.

testimony ['testiməni] *n* testimonio *m*. **testimonial** *n* testimonio *m*; recomendación *f*.

tetanus ['tetənəs] *n* tétanos *m*.

tether ['teðə] *n* traba *f*, atadura *f*. **at the end of one's tether** hartísimo. *v* trabar, atar.

text [tekst] *n* texto *m*. **textbook** *n* libro de texto *m*. **textual** *adj* textual.

textile ['tekstail] *nm*, *adj* textil.

texture ['tekstjuə] *n* textura *f*.

than [ðən] *conj* que; de; cuando; del que.

thank [θaŋk] *v* agradecer. **thank you** gracias. **thanksgiving** *n* acción de gracias *f*. **thanks to** gracias a. **thankful** *adj* agradecido. **thankless** *adj* desagradecido; ingrato.

that [ðat] *adj* ese, esa; aquel, aquella; el, la. *pron* ése, ésa; aquél, aquélla; (*neuter*) eso; (*neuter: farther away*) aquello; (*before relative pron or of*) el, la, lo; (*who, which*) que; el que, la que; quien; el cual, la cual; (*neuter*) lo que. *adv* así de; tan; tanto. *conj* que; de que; para que; porque.

thatch [θatʃ] *n* (*straw*) paja *f*; (*roof*) techo de paja *m*. *v* cubrir con un tejado de paja.

thaw [θɔː] *n* (*ice*) deshielo *m*; (*snow*) derretimento *m*. *v* deshelar; derretir.

the [ðə] *art* el, la (*pl* los, las); (*neuter*) lo.

theatre ['θiətə] *n* teatro *m*. **theatrical** *adj* teatral, de teatro.

theft [θeft] *n* hurto, robo.

their [ðeə] *adj* su, sus; suyo, suya.

theirs [ðeəz] *pron* el suyo, la suya.

them [ðem] *pron* ellos, ellas; (*direct object*) los, las; (*indirect object*) les.

theme [θiːm] *n* tema *m*. **thematic** *adj* temático.

themselves [ðəmˈselvz] *pl pron* se; ellos mismos, ellas mismas; sí mismos, sí mismas. **by themselves** solos.

then [ðen] *adv* (*that time*) entonces; (*afterwards*) después; luego; (*furthermore*) además; (*despite that*) a pesar de eso; (*consequently*) por lo tanto. *n* entonces; ese momento. *conj* en ese caso; entonces.

theology [θɪ'olədʒɪ] *n* teología *f*. **theologi-an** *n* teólogo, -a *m*, *f*. **theological** *adj* teológico.

theorem [θɪərəm] *n* teorema *m*.

theory ['θɪərɪ] *n* teoría *f*. **theoretical** *adj* teórico.

therapy ['θerəpɪ] *n* terapia *f*. **therapeutic** *adj* terapéutico. **therapist** *n* terapeuta *m*, *f*.

there [ðeə] *adv* ahí; allí; allá. **thereabouts** *adv* (*place*) por ahí, por allí; (*degree*) más o menos. **thereafter** *adv* después, más tarde. **thereby** *adv* por eso, por ello. **therefore** *adv* por lo tanto. **therein** *adv* allí dentro; en eso. **there is** *or* **are** hay. **thereof** *adv* de eso; su. **thereto** *adv* a eso, a ello. **thereupon** *adv* immediatamente después; sobre eso. **therewith** *adv* con eso. **there you are** eso es.

thermal ['θəɪməl] *adj* termal; (*tech*) térmico. *n* corriente de aire caliente que sube.

thermodynamics [θəɪmoudai'namiks] *n* termodinámica *f*.

thermometer [θə'momitə] *n* termómetro *m*.

thermonuclear [θəɪmou'njuklɪə] *adj* termonuclear.

Thermos ® ['θəɪməs] *n* termo ® *m*, termos ® *m*.

thermostat ['θəɪməstat] *n* termostato *m*. **thermostatic** *adj* termostático.

these [ðiɪz] *pl adj* estos, estas. *pl pron* éstos, éstas.

thesis ['θiɪsis] *n*, *pl* **-ses** tesis *f invar*.

they [ðeɪ] *pl pron* ellos, ellas.

thick [θɪk] *adj* grueso; espeso; denso; (*coll*) torpe. **thick-skinned** *adj* (*fig*) insensible. **thicken** *v* espesar(se). **thickness** *n* espesor *m*.

thief [θiɪf] *n* ladrón, -ona *m*, *f*.

thigh [θai] *n* muslo *m*.

thimble ['θimbl] *n* dedal *m*.

thin [θin] *adj* (*person*) flaco; delgado; fino; (*hair*) ralo; (*audience*) escaso; (*air*) enrarecido; (*beer*) aguado; (*voice*) débil; (*liquid*) claro; (*excuse*) flojo. *v* adelgazar; (*dilute*) diluir. **thinness** *n* delgadez *f*, flaqueza *f*.

thing [θiŋ] *n* cosa *f*; objeto *m*; artículo *m*; (*coll*) chisme *m*. **things** *pl n* (*affairs*, *belongings*) cosas *f pl*.

*****think** [θiŋk] *v* pensar; meditar; imaginar. **I think so** creo que sí. **think about** pensar en. **think over** pensar bien.

third [θəɪd] *adj* tercero. *n* tercero, -a *m*, *f*; (*fraction*) tercio *m*; (*music*) tercera *f*. **third-party insurance** seguro contra tercera persona *m*. **third-rate** *adj* de poca calidad.

thirst [θəɪst] *n* sed *f*. *v* tener sed. **be thirsty** tener sed.

thirteen [θəɪ'tiɪn] *nm*, *adj* trece. **thirteenth** *n*, *adj* decimotercero, -a *m*, *f*.

thirty ['θəɪtɪ] *nm*, *adj* treinta. **thirtieth** *n*, *adj* trigesimo, -a *m*, *f*.

this [ðis] *adj* este, esta. *pron* éste, ésta. *adv* tan; así de.

thistle ['θisl] *n* cardo *m*.

thong [θoŋ] *n* correa *f*.

thorn [θoɪn] *n* espina *f*. **thorny** *adj* espinoso.

thorough ['θʌrə] *adj* (*search*, *etc.*) minucioso; (*person*) concienzudo; a fondo; completo. **thoroughbred** *n* pura sangre *m*, *f*. **thoroughfare** *n* vía pública *f*. **thoroughly** *adv* a fondo; completamente. **thoroughness** *n* minuciosidad *f*.

those [ðouz] *adj* esos, esas; aquellos, aquellas. *pron* ésos, ésas; aquéllos, aquéllas.

though [ðou] *conj* aunque. *adv* sin embargo. **as though** como si.

thought [θoɪt] *n* pensamiento *m*; idea *f*; consideración *f*; intención *f*; opinión *f*. **thoughtful** *adj* pensativo; serio; (*mindful*) cuidadoso; (*considerate*) solícito. **thoughtless** *adj* irreflexivo; descuidado; desconsiderado.

thousand ['θauzənd] *nm*, *adj* mil. **thousandth** *adj* milésimo. *n* (*fraction*) milésima parte *f*; (*position*) número mil *m*.

thrash [θraʃ] *v* dar una paliza a. **thrash about** revolcarse. **thrash out** discutir a fondo. **thrashing** *n* paliza *f*.

thread [θred] *n* hilo *m*; (*screw*) rosca *f*, filete *m*. *v* ensartar, enhebrar. **threadbare** *adj* raído, gastado.

threat [θret] *n* amenaza *f*. **threaten** *v* amenazar.

three [θriɪ] *nm*, *adj* tres. **three-cornered** *adj* triangular. **three-dimensional** *adj* tridimensional. **threefold** *adj* triple. **three-legged** *adj* de tres patas. **three-piece suite** tresillo *m*. **three-ply** *adj* contrapachado. **three-quarter** *adj* tres cuartos.

thresh [θreʃ] *v* trillar. **threshing machine** *n* trilladora *f*.

threshold ['θreʃould] *n* umbral *m*.

threw [θruː] *V* throw.

thrift [θrift] *n* economía *f*. **thrifty** *adj* económico.

thrill [θril] *n* emoción *f*; (*quiver*) estremecimiento *m*. *v* estremecer. **thriller** *n* novela *or* película escalofriante *f*. **thrilling** *adj* emocionante; escalofriante.

thrive [θraiv] *v* crecer; desarrollarse; tener buena salud; prosperar. **thriving** *adj* lozano; próspero.

throat [θrout] *n* garganta *f*. **clear one's throat** aclararse la voz. **throaty** *adj* gutural.

throb [θrob] *n* (*heart*) latido *m*, palpitación *f*; (*engine*) zumbido *m*; (*pulse*) pulsación *f*; (*pain*) punzada *f*. *v* latir; pulsar; zumbar; dar punzadas.

thrombosis [θrom'bousis] *n* trombosis *f* invar.

throne [θroun] *n* trono *m*.

throng [θroŋ] *n* multitud *f*, muchedumbre *f*. *v* atestar; afluir.

throttle ['θrotl] *v* estrangular. *n* (*tech*) regulador *m*; (*mot*) acelerador.

through [θruː] *adj* directo; continuo. *adv* de parte a parte; completamente. *prep* (*via*) por; (*time*) durante; (*place*) a través de. **no through road** calle sin salida *f*. **through traffic** tránsito *m*. **throughout** *prep* (*place*) por todo, en todo; (*time*) durante todo. *adv* hasta el final.

*throw [θrou] *n* tiro *m*, lanzamiento *m*; (*wrestling*) tumbado *m*. *v* lanzar, tirar, arrojar; (*a blow*) dar; (*light*) proyectar. **throw away** tirar; (*get rid of*) desechar; (*money*) despilfarrar. **throw off** (*a habit*) renunciar a; (*the scent*) despistar. **throw out** expulsar, echar; rechazar. **throw up** (*job*) dejar; (*vomit*) devolver.

thrush [θrʌʃ] *n* tordo *m*.

*thrust [θrʌst] *v* empujar; clavar; meter; poner. *n* empujón *m*; (*stab*) estocada *f*.

thud [θʌd] *n* ruido sordo *m*. *v* caer con un ruido sordo.

thumb [θʌm] *n* pulgar *m*. *v also* **thumb through** hojear. **thumb a lift** (*coll*) hacer autostop. **thumb index** uñeros *m pl*.

thump [θʌmp] *n* (*blow*) porrazo *m*; (*noise*) ruido sordo *m*. *v* (*strike*) golpear; (*heart*) latir con fuerza.

thunder ['θʌndə] *n* trueno *m*; (*fig*) estruendo *m*. **thunderstorm** *n* tormenta *f*. **thunderstruck** *adj* atónito. *v* tronar.

Thursday ['θəːzdi] *n* jueves *m*.

thus [ðʌs] *adv* así; de este modo.

thwart [θwoːt] *v* frustrar, impedir.

thyme [taim] *n* tomillo *m*.

thyroid ['θairoid] *n* tiroides *f* invar. *adj* tiroideo.

tiara [ti'aːrə] *n* tiara *f*.

tick¹ [tik] *n* (*mark*) marca *f*; (*sound*) tictac *m*. **tick off** (*coll*) reprender.

tick² [tik] *n* (*zool*) garrapata *f*.

ticket ['tikit] *n* (*price*) etiqueta *f*; (*entrance*) entrada *f*; (*transport*) billete *m*; (*permit*) pase *m*. **cloakroom ticket** número del guardarropa *m*. **complimentary ticket** entrada de favor *f*. **parking ticket** multa por aparcamiento indebido *f*. **return ticket** billete de ida y vuelta *m*. **single ticket** billete de ida *m*. **ticket agency** agencia de venta de billetes *f*. **ticket office** taquilla *f*.

tickle ['tikl] *v* hacer cosquillas a. *n* cosquilleo *m*. **ticklish** *adj* cosquilloso.

tide [taid] *n* marea *f*. **tide-mark** *n* línea de la marea alta *f*; (*coll*) lengua del agua *f*. *v* **tide over** sacar de apuro.

tidy ['taidi] *adj* ordenado; (*appearance*) arreglado; (*clean*) limpio. *v* ordenar; limpiar. **tidily** *adv* bien; aseadamente. **tidiness** *n* orden *m*; aseo *m*.

tie [tai] *v* atar; (*lace*) lacear; (*knot*) hacer; (*unite*) unir; (*link*) ligar; (*sport*) empatar. *n* (*neck*) corbata *f*; (*knot*) nudo *m*; (*bond*) lazo *m*; (*sport*) empate *m*; (*fig*) atadura *f*.

tier [tiə] *n* grada *f*; (*row*) fila *f*; (*cake*) piso *m*.

tiger ['taigə] *n* tigre *m*.

tight [tait] *adj* (*bolt, knot, etc.*) apretado; (*clothes*) ajustado; (*taut*) tirante; (*control*) estricto; (*seal*) hermético; (*bend*) cerrado; (*coll: drunk*) borracho; (*coll: mean*) agarrado. **tight-fisted** *adj* tacaño. **tight-lipped** *adj* callado. **tightrope** *n* cuerda de volatinero *f*. *v adv also* **tightly** bien; herméticamente. **hold tight!** ¡agárrense bien! **tighten** (*screw, etc.*) apretar; (*rope, etc.*) tensar; (*control*) estrechar. **tighten one's belt** (*coll*) apretarse el cinturón.

tights *pl n* mallas *f pl*.

tile [tail] *n* (*roof*) teja *f*; (*floor*) baldosa *f*. *v* tejar; embaldosar.

till¹ [til] *V* until.

till² [til] *n* caja *f*.

till³ [til] *v* labrar, cultivar.

tiller ['tilə] n (naut) caña del timón f.

tilt [tilt] n inclinación f. **at full tilt** en toda mecha. v inclinar. **tilt at** arremeter contra.

timber ['timbə] n madera de construcción f. **timbered** (house) enmaderado.

time [taim] n tiempo m, momento m; época f; período m; (season) estación f; (clock) hora f; (occasion) vez f; (fixed time period) plazo m; (music) duración f; (music: tempo) compás m; (sport) final m. **a long time** mucho tiempo. **a short time** poco tiempo. **at the same time** al mismo tiempo. **from time to time** de vez en cuando. **in time** a tiempo. **on time** a la hora. **timeless** adj eternal. **timely** adj oportuno.

time exposure n exposición f.

time limit n límite de tiempo m.

timepiece ['taimpiːs] n reloj m.

timesaving ['taimˌseiviŋ] adj que ahorra tiempo.

time signal n señal horaria f.

timetable ['taimteibl] n horario m; (transport) guía f.

time zone n huso horario m.

timid ['timid] adj tímido. **timidity** n timidez f.

tin [tin] n estaño m; (tinplate) hojalata f; (can) lata f; (baking) molde m. **tinfoil** n papel de estaño m. **tin-opener** n abrelatas m invar. **tinny** adj (sound, taste) metálico.

tinge [tindʒ] n tinte m. v teñir.

tingle ['tiŋgl] v sentir hormigueo. n hormigueo m.

tinker ['tiŋkə] n calderero m. v componer, arreglar. **tinker with** jugar con.

tinkle ['tiŋkl] n tintineo m. v hacer tintinear.

tinsel ['tinsəl] n oropel m.

tint [tint] n (hair) tinte m; tono m; matiz m. v teñir; matizar.

tiny ['taini] adj diminuto.

tip[1] [tip] n punta f; (cigarette) filtro m. **on tiptoe** de puntillas.

tip[2] [tip] v (tilt) inclinar; (pour) verter; (upset) volcar.

tip[3] [tip] n (hint) consejo m, información f; (money) propina f. v dar una propina a. **tip-off** n (coll) información f.

tipsy ['tipsi] adj (coll) achispado.

tire[1] [taiə] v cansar(se). **tire out** agotar. **tired** adj cansado. **be tired of** estar harto de. **tiredness** n cansancio m. **tiresome** adj pesado.

tire[2] V tyre.

tissue ['tiʃuː] n (anat) tejido m; (cloth) tisú m; (handkerchief) pañuelo de papel m. **tissue paper** papel de seda m.

title ['taitl] n título m; derecho m. **title deed** título de propiedad m. **title page** portada f. v titular. **titled** adj con título de nobleza.

titter ['titə] n risita f. v reírse nerviosamente.

to [tu] prep a; (direction) hacia; (as far as) hasta; (time) menos; (destination, purpose) para; (according to) según; (in juxtaposition) contra; (compared with) en comparación con; (in) por; (in memory of) en honor a. **to-do** n (coll) follón m.

toad [toud] n sapo m. **toadstool** n hongo venenoso m.

toast [toust] n pan tostado m; (speech) brindis m invar. **toast-rack** n portatostadas m invar. v tostar. **toaster** n tostador m.

tobacco [tə'bakou] n tabaco m. **tobacconist's** n estanco m.

toboggan [tə'bogən] n tobogán m. v deslizarse en tobogán.

today [tə'dei] nm, adj hoy.

toddler ['todlə] n niño pequeño m; niña pequeña f.

toe [tou] n dedo del pie. **big toe** dedo gordo m. **toenail** n uña (del dedo del pie) f. **toe the line** (coll) conformarse.

toffee ['tofi] n caramelo m. **toffee-apple** n manzana garrapiñada f.

together [tə'geðə] adv juntos; (at the same time) a la vez; (agreed) de acuerdo. **togetherness** n solidaridad f.

toil [toil] n trabajo agotador m. v trabajar duro.

toilet ['toilit] n (lavatory) retrete m; (washing, etc.) arreglo m. **toilet paper** papel higiénico m. **toilet soap** jabón de tocador m. **toilet water** agua de Colonia f.

token ['toukən] n (sign) muestra f, prueba f; (symbol) símbolo m; (keepsake) recuerdo m; (disc) ficha f; (book, record) vale m. **as a token of** como prueba de. adj simbólico.

told [tould] V tell.

tolerate ['toləreit] v tolerar, soportar; admitir; respetar. **tolerable** adj tolerable; (fair) mediano. **tolerance** n also **toleration** tolerancia f. **tolerant** adj tolerante.

toll¹ [toul] *n* (*road*) peaje *m*; (*bridge*) pontaje *m*; (*victims*) bajas *f pl*. **toll-gate** *n* barrera de peaje *f*.

toll² [toul] *v* tocar, tañar.

tomato [tə'maɪtou] *n* tomate *m*.

tomb [tuɪm] *n* tumba *f*. **tombstone** *n* piedra sepulcral *f*.

tomorrow [tə'morou] *nm, adv* mañana. **the day after tomorrow** pasado mañana *m*.

ton [tʌn] *n* tonelada *f*.

tone [toun] *n* tono *m*; estilo *m*. *v* (*colour*) matizar. **tone down** atenuarse.

tongs [toŋz] *pl n* (*coal*) tenazas *f pl*; (*sugar*) tenacillas *f pl*.

tongue [tʌŋ] *n* lengua *f*. **tongue-tied** *adj* mudo.

tonic ['tonik] *adj* tónico. *n* (*med*) tónico *m*; (*music*) tónica *f*.

tonight [tə'nait] *n, adv* esta noche.

tonsil ['tonsil] *n* amígdala *f*. **tonsillitis** *n* amigdalitis *f*.

too [tuɪ] *adv* demasiado; (*also*) también; (*moreover*) además.

took [tuk] *V* **take**.

tool [tuɪl] *n* herramienta *f*; utensilio *m*. **toolshed** *n* cobertizo para herramientas *m*.

tooth [tuɪθ] *n, pl* **teeth** diente *m*; (*back tooth*) muela *f*. **toothache** *n* dolor de muelas *m*. **tooth-brush** *n* cepillo de dientes *m*. **toothpaste** *n* pasta dentífrica *f*. **toothpick** *n* palillo de dientes *m*. **toothless** *adj* desdentado.

top¹ [top] *n* parte de arriba *f*, lo alto *m*; (*of mountain*) cima *f*; (*of tin, pan, bottle, etc.*) tapa *f*; (*of page*) cabeza *f*; (*of the head*) coronilla *f*; (*surface*) superficie *f*. *adj* de arriba; (*best*) mejor; (*first*) primero. *v* (*cover*) cubrir; (*exceed*) superar. **top up** llenar completamente.

top² [top] *n* (*toy*) peón *m*, trompo *m*.

topaz ['toupaz] *n* topacio *m*.

topcoat ['topkout] *n* abrigo *m*.

topdressing ['top,dresiŋ] *n* abono *m*.

top hat *n* chistera *f*.

top-heavy *adj* inestable.

topic ['topik] *n* tema *m*, asunto *m*. **topical** *adj* de actualidad.

topography [tə'pogrəfi] *n* topografía *f*. **topographical** *adj* topográfico.

topple ['topl] *v* derribar, volcar, hacer caer.

top-secret *adj* confidencial.

topsoil ['topsoil] *n* tierra vegetal *f*.

topsy-turvy [topsi'təɪvi] *adj* revuelto.

torch [toɪtʃ] *n* (*electric*) linterna *f*; (*burning*) antorcha *f*.

tore [toɪ] *V* **tear**.

torment ['toɪment; *v* toɪ'ment] *n* tormento *m*, suplicio *m*. *v* atormentar.

tornado [toɪ'neidou] *n* tornado *m*.

torpedo [toɪ'piɪdou] *n* torpedo *m*. *v* torpedear.

torrent ['torənt] *n* torrente *m*. **torrential** *adj* torrencial.

torso ['toɪsou] *n* torso *m*.

tortoise ['toɪtəs] *n* tortuga *f*. **tortoise-shell** *n* carey *m*.

tortuous ['toɪtʃuəs] *adj* tortuoso.

torture ['toɪtʃə] *n* tortura *f*. *v* torturar. **torturer** *n* torcionario *m*.

toss [tos] *v* (*throw*) lanzamiento *m*; (*fall*) caída *f*; (*head*) sacudida *f*; (*coin*) sorteo a cara o cruz *m*; (*bull*) cogida *f*. *v* lanzar; sacudir; (*coin*) echar a cara o cruz; (*salad*) dar vueltas a.

tot¹ [tot] *n* (*child*) nene *m*; (*drink*) trago *m*.

tot² [tot] *v* **tot up** sumar.

total ['toutəl] *nm, adj* total. *v* (*add up*) sumar; (*add up to*) totalizar. **totalitarian** *n, adj* totalitario, -a.

totter ['totə] *v* bambolearse.

touch [tʌtʃ] *n* (*sense*) tacto *m*; (*contact*) contacto *m*; (*light stroke*) toque *m*; (*tap*) golpe ligero *m*; (*brush*) roce *m*. *v* tocar; rozar; (*reach*) alcanzar; (*affect*) afectar; (*move*) enternecer; (*food*) tomar. **touchy** *adj* susceptible.

tough [tʌf] *adj* (*hard*) duro; resistente; (*character*) tenaz; (*job*) difícil. **toughen** *v* endurecer. **toughness** *n* dureza *f*; resistencia *f*; dificultad *f*.

toupee ['tuɪpei] *n* tupé *m*.

tour [tuə] *n* excursión *f*; visita *f*; viaje *m*; (*theatre*) gira *f*. **package tour** viaje todo comprendido *m*. **tour of duty** turno de servicio *m*. *v* recorrer. **touring** *n* also **tourism** turismo *m*. **tourist** *n* turista *m, f*. **tourist agency** agencia de viajes *f*.

tournament ['tuənəmənt] *n* torneo *m*.

tousled ['tauzld] *adj* (*hair*) despeinado.

tow [tou] *n* remolque *m*. *v* remolear; (*from towpath*) sirgar. **towpath** *n* camino de sirga *m*. **tow-rope** *n* remolque *m*.

towards [tə'woɪdz] *prep* hacia; (*for*) para; (*with*) con; (*with regard to*) con respecto a.

towel ['tauəl] *n* toalla *f*; (*bath*) toalla de baño *f*; (*sanitary*) paño higiénico *m*. **towel-rail** *n* toallero *m*. **towelling** *n* felpa *f*.

tower ['tauə] *n* torre *f*. **control tower** torre de control *f*. **tower over** dominar. **towering** *adj* sobresaliente.

town [taun] *n* (*large*) ciudad *f*; (*small*) pueblo *m*. **new town** pueblo nuevo *m*. **town hall** ayuntamiento *m*. **town planning** urbanismo *m*.

toxic ['toksik] *adj* tóxico.

toy [toi] *n* juguete *m*. *adj* de juguete. *v* **toy with** toquetear; (*idea*) acariciar.

trace [treis] *n* (*trail*) rastro *m*; (*indication*) indicio *m*; (*a little*) pizca *f*. *v* (*plan*) trazar; (*through paper*) calcar; (*trail*) rastrear; (*find*) encontrar. **tracing** *n* calco *m*. **tracing paper** papel de calcar *m*.

track [trak] *n* (*of animals, people*) huella *f*; (*of things*) rastro *m*; (*path*) sendero *m*; (*rail*) vía *f*; (*course*) curso *m*; (*racing*) pista *f*; (*tank, tractor*) oruga *f*. **tracksuit** *n* mono de entrenamiento *m*. *v* (*hunt*) rastrear; (*pursue*) seguir la pista de. **track down** acorralar. **tracker** *n* perseguidor *m*.

tract[1] [trakt] *n* (*region*) trecho *m*; (*anat*) aparato *m*.

tract[2] [trakt] *n* (*pamphlet*) folleto *m*.

tractor ['traktə] *n* tractor *m*.

trade [treid] *n* comercio *m*; (*job*) ramo *m*. **trademark** *n* marca de fábrica *f*. **tradesman** *n* comerciante *m*. **trade union** sindicato *m*. **trade unionist** sindicalista *m*, *f*. *v* comerciar; negociar; cambiar. **trade in** tomar como entrada. **trader** *n* comerciante *m*, *f*; negociante *m*, *f*.

tradition [trə'diʃən] *n* tradición *f*. **traditional** *adj* tradicional.

traffic ['trafik] *n* (*mot*) circulación *f*, tráfico *m*; (*tourist*) tránsito *m*; (*trade*) comercio *m*. **traffic jam** embotellamiento *m*. **traffic-light** *n* semáforo *m*. **traffic warden** guardián del tráfico *m*.

tragedy ['tradʒədi] *n* tragedia *f*. **tragic** *adj* trágico.

trail [treil] *n* (*path*) camino *m*, sendero; (*person or animal*) huellas *f pl*; (*smoke*) estela *f*; (*blood*) reguero *m*. *v* (*drag*) arrastrar; (*chase*) perseguir; (*an animal*) rastrear; (*lag*) ir detrás de; (*hang down*) colgar. **trailer** *n* (*mot*) remolque *m*; (*film*) trailer *m*.

train [trein] *n* (*railway*) tren *m*; (*procession*) desfile *m*; (*series*) serie *f*; (*dress*) cola *f*. *v* (*teach*) educar; (*someone for a job*) formar, capacitar; (*animal*) amaestrar; (*horse*) domar; (*sport*) entrenar. **trainee** *n* aprendiz, -a *m*, *f*. **trainer** *n* (*sport*) entrenador, -a *m*, *f*; (*boxing*) cuidador *m*; (*animals*) amaestrador, -a *m*, *f*; (*horses*) domador, -a *m*, *f*.

trait [treit] *n* rasgo *m*.

traitor ['treitə] *n* traidor, -a *m*, *f*.

tram [tram] *n* tranvía *m*.

tramp [tramp] *n* (*person*) vagabundo, -a *m*, *f*; (*hike*) caminata *f*; (*sound*) ruido de pasos *m*. *v* patear; vagabundear.

trample ['trampl] *v* pisotear, pisar.

trampoline ['trampəliːn] *n* cama elástica *f*.

trance [trains] *n* trance *m*.

tranquil ['traŋkwil] *adj* tranquilo. **tranquillity** *n* tranquilidad *f*. **tranquillize** *v* tranquilizar. **tranquillizer** *n* tranquilizante *m*.

transact [tran'zakt] *v* (*negotiate*) tratar; (*perform*) llevar a cabo. **transaction** *n* (*business*) negociación *f*; (*deal*) transacción *f*.

transcend [tran'send] *v* exceder, superar. **transcendental** *adj* trascedental.

transcribe [tran'skraib] *v* transcribir. **transcription** *n* transcripción *f*.

transept ['transept] *n* transepto *m*.

transfer [trans'fəː; *n* 'transfəː] *v* trasladar; transferir. *n* traslado *m*; (*law*) cesión *f*; (*picture*) calcomanía *f*. **transferable** *adj* transferible. **not transferable** (*right*) inalienable; (*ticket*) intransferible.

transfix [trans'fiks] *v* traspasar.

transform [trans'foːm] *v* transformar. **transformation** *n* transformación *f*. **transformer** *n* (*elec*) transformador *m*.

transfuse [trans'fjuːz] *v* transfundir. **transfusion** *n* transfusión *f*.

transient ['tranziənt] *adj* transitorio.

transistor [tran'zistə] *n* transistor *m*. **transistorize** *v* transistorizar.

transit ['transit] *n* tránsito *m*. **in transit** de tránsito.

transition [tran'ziʃən] *n* transición *f*. **transitional** *adj* transitorio.

transitive ['transitiv] *adj* transitivo.

transitory ['transitəri] *adj* transitorio.

translate [trans'leit] *v* traducir. **translation** *n* traducción *f*. **translator** *n* traductor, -a *m*, *f*.

translucent [trans'luːsnt] *adj* translúcido. **translucence** *n* translucidez *f*.

transmit [tranz'mit] *v* transmitir, trasmitir. **transmission** *n* transmisión *f*, trasmisión *f*. **transmitter** *n* (*apparatus*) transmisor *m*; (*station*) emisora *f*.

transparent [trans'peərənt] *adj* transparente. **transparency** *n* transparencia *f*; (*phot*) transparente *m*.

transplant [trans'plaint; *n* 'transplaint] *v* trasplantar. *n* trasplante *m*.

transport ['transpoit; *v* trans'poit] *n* transporte *m*. *v* transportar. **transportation** *n* transporte *m*; (*convicts*) deportación *f*.

transpose [trans'pouz] *v* transponer; (*music*) transportar. **transposition** *n* transposición *f*; transporte *m*.

transverse ['tranzvɔis] *adj* transverso.

transvestite [tranz'vestait] *n* travestido *m*.

trap [trap] *n* trampa *f*; (*mice, rats*) ratonera *f*; (*vehicle*) cabriolé *m*; (*tech*) sifón de depósito *m*; (*theatre*) escotillón *m*. **trapdoor** *n* trampa *f*. *v* coger; coger en una trampa; rodear; pillar; bloquear.

trapeze [trə'piiz] *n* trapecio *m*. **trapeze artist** trapecista *m, f*.

trash [traʃ] *n* basura *f*; (*coll*) cachivaches *m pl*.

trauma ['troimə] *n* trauma *f*. **traumatic** *adj* traumático.

travel ['travl] *v* recorrer; viajar por. **travels** *pl n* viajes *m pl*. **travel agency** agencia de viajes *f*. **travel-sickness** *n* mareo *m*. **traveller** *n* viajero, -a *m, f*; (*comm*) viajante de comercio *m*. **traveller's cheque** cheque de viaje *m*.

travesty ['travəsti] *n* parodia *f*.

trawler ['troilə] *n* barco rastreador *m*. **trawling** *n* pesca a la rastrea *f*.

tray [trei] *n* bandeja *f*.

treachery ['tretʃəri] *n* traición *f*. **treacherous** *adj* (*person*) traidor; (*action*) traicionero.

treacle ['triikl] *n* melaza *f*.

*****tread** [tred] *v* pisar; (*walk*) andar por. **tread on** (*crush*) pisotear. *n* paso *m*; (*step of a staircase*) huella *f*; (*tyre*) banda de rodadura *f*.

treason ['triizn] *n* traición *f*.

treasure ['treʒə] *n* tesoro *m*. *v* valorar; guardar en la memoria. **treasurer** *n* tesorero, -a *m, f*. **treasury** *n* tesorería *f*.

treat [triit] *v* tratar; tomar; (*a patient*) atender; (*pay for*) invitar, comprar. *n* invitación *f*; placer *m*. **treatment** *n* trato *m*; (*med*) tratamiento *m*.

treatise ['triitiz] *n* tratado *m*.

treaty ['triiti] *n* tratado *m*; acuerdo *m*.

treble ['trebl] *n* (*music*) tiple *m*, soprano *m*. *adj* triple; (*music*) de tiple. *v* triplicar. *adv* tres veces.

tree [trii] *n* árbol *m*.

trek [trek] *v* caminar trabajosamente. *n* expedición *f*; caminata *f*.

trellis ['trelis] *n* enrejado *m*; espaldera *f*. *v* poner un enrejado.

tremble ['trembl] *v* temblar. *n* temblor *m*.

tremendous [trə'mendəs] *adj* tremendo, enorme; extraordinario; (*coll: excellent*) formidable.

tremor ['tremə] *n* temblor *m*.

trench [trentʃ] *n* zanja *f*; (*mil*) trinchera *f*.

trend [trend] *n* tendencia *f*; dirección *f*; orientación *f*. **trendy** *adj* (*coll*) modernísimo.

trespass ['trespəs] *n* entrada ilegal *f*. *v* violar; abusar; invadir. **trespasser** *n* intruso, -a *m, f*. **trespassers will be prosecuted** prohibido el paso.

trestle ['tresl] *n* caballete *m*. **trestle table** mesa de caballete *f*.

trial ['traiəl] *n* (*law*) juicio *m*; (*experiment*) prueba *f*, ensayo *m*; (*annoyance*) molestia *f*; (*hardship*) dificultad *f*. *adj* de prueba.

triangle ['traiaŋgl] *n* triángulo *m*. **triangular** *adj* triangular.

tribe [traib] *n* tribu *f*. **tribal** *adj* tribal. **tribesman** *n* miembro de una tribu *m*.

tribunal [trai'bjuinl] *n* tribunal *m*.

tributary ['tribjutəri] *n* afluente *m*. *adj* tributario.

tribute ['tribjuit] *n* tributo *m*.

trick [trik] *n* (*stratagem*) truco *m*; (*ruse*) astucia *f*; (*practical joke*) broma *f*; (*cards*) baza *f*. **trick photography** trucaje *m*. **trick question** pega *f*. *v* engañar. **trickery** *n* engaño *m*; astucia *f*. **tricky** *adj* difícil; delicado.

trickle ['trikl] *n* hilo *m*, chorrito *m*. *v* verter poco a poco; gotear.

tricycle ['traisikl] *n* triciclo *m*.

trifle ['traifl] *n* nadería *f*. *v* **trifle with** jugar con. **trifling** *adj* insignificante.

trigger ['trigə] *n* gatillo *m*. *v* accionar. **trigger off** provocar.

trigonometry [trigə'nomətri] *n* trigonometría *f*.

trill [tril] *n* trino *m*. *v* trinar.

trim [trim] *adj* aseado; (*neat*) arreglado; elegante. *v* arreglar; (*reduce*) cercenar; (*hair*) entresacar; (*nails*) recortar; (*hedge*) podar; (sails) orientar. **trimmings** pl n recortes m pl; accesorios m pl.

trinket ['trɪŋkɪt] n dije m.

trio ['trɪou] n trío m.

trip [trɪp] n (voyage, effect of drugs) viaje m; (stumble) tropezón m. v dar un traspié; tropezar; (make someone fall) echar la zancadilla.

tripe [traɪp] n callos m pl; (coll) bobadas f pl.

triple ['trɪpl] nm, adj triple. v triplicar. adv tres veces.

triplet ['trɪplɪt] n (music) tresillo m; (poetry) terceto m; (person) trillizo, -a m, f.

tripod ['traɪpod] n trípode m.

trite [traɪt] adj trillado, trivial. **triteness** n lo trillado; trivialidad f.

triumph ['traɪʌmf] n triunfo m. v triunfar. **triumphant** adj triunfante. **triumphantly** adv triunfantemente.

trivial ['trɪvɪəl] adj trivial. **trivia** pl n also **trivialities** trivialidades f pl.

trod [trod] V **tread**.

trolley ['trolɪ] n (shopping) carretilla f; (tea) carrito m; (in mines) vagoneta f.

trombone [trom'boun] n trombón m.

troop [truːp] n (people) banda f, grupo m; (animals) manada f. **troops** pl n (mil) tropas f pl. v **troop in/out** entrar/salir en tropel.

trophy ['troufɪ] n trofeo m.

tropic ['tropɪk] n trópico m. **Tropic of Cancer** Trópico de Cáncer. **Tropic of Capricorn** Trópico de Capricornio. **tropical** adj tropical.

trot [trot] n trote m. **on the trot** (coll) seguidos, seguidas. v trotar. **trotter** n mano f.

trouble ['trʌbl] n (worry) preocupación f; apuro m; pena f; (misfortune) desgracia f; problema m; disturbios m pl. **be in trouble** estar en un apuro. **look for trouble** buscar camorra. **what's the trouble?** ¿qué pasa? **troublemaker** n alborotador, -a m, f. **troublesome** adj molesto. v preocupar; pertubar; afectar; molestar.

trough [trof] n (food) pesebre m; (drinking) abrevadero m; (depression) depresión f.

trousers ['trauzəz] pl n pantalón m sing.

trout [traut] n trucha f.

trowel ['trauəl] n palustre m; (gardening) desplantador m.

truant ['truːənt] n **play truant** hacer novillos. **truancy** n rabona f.

truce [truːs] n tregua f. **call a truce** acordar una tregua.

truck [trʌk] n camión m; (rail) batea f. **truck driver** conductor de camión m.

trudge [trʌdʒ] v andar con dificultad.

true [truː] adj verdadero; (faithful) fiel; legítimo; (real) auténtico; (accurate) exacto. **true to life** conforme a la realidad. **truly** adv verdaderamente.

truffle ['trʌfl] n trufa f.

trump [trʌmp] n (cards) triunfo m. v fallar. **trump up** inventar.

trumpet ['trʌmpɪt] n trompeta f. v (elephant) barritar. **trumpeter** n trompetista m, f.

truncate [trʌŋ'keɪt] v truncar.

truncheon ['trʌntʃən] n matraca f; (police) porra f.

trunk [trʌŋk] n (anat, bot) tronco m; (elephant) trompa f; (case) baúl m. **trunk call** conferencia telefónica f. **trunk road** carretera principal f. **trunks** pl n calzoncillos cortos m pl ; (mot) maleta

truss [trʌs] n (hay) haz m; (fruit) racimo m; (med) braguero m. v atar.

trust [trʌst] n confianza f; (law) fideicomiso m; (comm) trust m; (expectation) esperanza f. **trustworthy** adj digno de confianza; fidedigno. v tener confianza en; confiar; esperar; creer. **trustee** n guardián m; (law) fideicomisario, -a m, f. **trusting** adj confiado. **trusty** adj leal, seguro.

truth [truːθ] n verdad f. **truthful** adj veraz; verdadero. **truthfulness** n veracidad f.

try [traɪ] n tentativa f, prueba f; (rugby) ensayo m. v probar; intentar; ensayar; (law) ver; (strain) poner a prueba; (annoy) molestar; (tire) cansar; (afflict) hacer sufrir. **try on** (garment) probarse. **try it on** (coll) intentar dar el pego. **trying** adj molesto.

tsar [zaɪ] n zar m.

T-shirt ['tiːʃəɪt] n camiseta f.

tub [tʌb] n tina f; (bath) bañera f.

tuba ['tjuːbə] n tuba f.

tube [tjuːb] n tubo m; (coll: underground) metro m. **tubeless** adj (tyre) sin cámara.

tuber ['tjuːbə] n tubérculo m.

tuberculosis [tjubəɪkju'lousis] n tuberculosis f.

tuck [tʌk] n (sewing) alforza f; (food) comida f; (sweets) cucherías f pl. v meter; (sheets) remeter; (fold) alforzar. **tuck up** (in bed) arropar.

Tuesday ['tjuːzdi] *n* martes *m*.

tuft [tʌft] *n* (*plants*) mata *f*; (*feathers*) penacho *m*; (*hair*) mechón *m*.

tug [tʌg] *n* tirón *m*; (*boat*) remolcador *m*. **tug-of-war** *n* juego de la cuerda *m*. *v* (*pull*) tirar; (*tow*) remolcar; (*drag*) arrastrar.

tuition [tjuˈiʃən] *n* enseñanza *f*.

tulip ['tjuːlip] *n* tulipán *m*.

tumble ['tʌmbl] *n* caída *f*; (*acrobatics*) voltereta *f*. *v* caerse; dar volteretas; (*knock over*) derribar. **tumbledown** *adj* ruinoso. **tumble-dryer** *n* secadora al aire caliente *f*. **tumbler** *n* (*glass*) vaso *m*; (*acrobat*) voltalinero, -a *m*, *f*.

tummy ['tʌmi] *n* (*coll*) barriga *f*.

tumour ['tjuːmə] *n* tumor *m*.

tumult ['tjuːmʌlt] *n* tumulto *m*. **tumultuous** *adj* tumultuoso.

tuna ['tjuːnə] *n* atún *m*.

tune [tjuːn] *n* aire *m*. **in tune** afinado. **out of tune** desafinado. *v* (*music*) afinar; (*mot*) poner a punto. **tune in to** (*radio*) sintonizar con. **tuneful** *adj* melodioso. **tuneless** *adj* discordante. **tuner** *n* (*person*) afinador *m*; (*radio*) sintonizador *m*. **tuning** afinación *f*; sintonización *f*; puesta a punto *f*. **tuning fork** diapasón *m*.

tunic ['tjuːnik] *n* túnica *f*.

tunnel ['tʌnl] *n* túnel *m*. *v* hacer un túnel en; (*dig*) cavar.

turban ['təːbən] *n* turbante *m*.

turbine ['təːbain] *n* turbina *f*.

turbot ['təːbət] *n* rodaballo *m*.

turbulent ['təːbjulənt] *adj* turbulento. **turbulence** *n* turbulencia *f*.

tureen [təˈriːn] *n* sopera *f*.

turf [təːf] *n* cesped *m*; (*sport*) turf *m*. *v* encespedar. **turf out** (*coll*) echar.

turkey ['təːki] *n* pavo *m*.

Turkish ['təːkiʃ] *nm*, *adj* turco. **Turkish bath** baño turco *m*.

turmeric ['təːmərik] *n* cúrcuma *f*.

turmoil ['təːmoil] *n* desorden *m*; agitación *f*; alboroto *m*.

turn [təːn] *n* vuelta *f*; (*road*) curva *f*; (*body*) movimiento *m*; (*opportunity*) turno *m*; (*change*) cambio *m*; (*change in situation*) viraje *m*; (*fright*) susto *m*. **take turns at** turnarse en. *v* dar vueltas; dar la vuelta a; (*body*) volver; (*corner*) doblar; (*page*) pasar; cambiar. **turn down** (*lower*) bajar; (*reject*) rechazar. **turn off** cerrar; (*light*) apagar; (*engine*) parar. **turn on** (*light*, *radio*) encender; (*current*) conectar; (*coll: excite*) excitar. **turn out** (*end up*) resultar; (*light*) apagar. **turnover** *n* (*comm*) volumen de negocios *m*. **turnstile** *n* torniquete *m*. **turntable** *n* (*record-player*) plato giratorio *m*. **turn up** presentarse; (*appear*) aparecer. **turning** *n* vuelta *f*; curva *f*; (*side road*) bocacalle *f*. **turning point** momento crucial *m*.

turnip ['təːnip] *n* nabo *m*.

turpentine ['təːpəntain] *n* trementina *f*.

turquoise ['təːkwoiz] *n* (*stone*) turquesa *f*; (*colour*) azul turquesa *m*.

turret ['tʌrit] *n* torreón *m*; (*mil*) torreta *f*.

turtle ['təːtl] *n* tortuga de mar *f*. **turtleneck** *n* (*jumper collar*) cuello que sube ligeramente *m*.

tusk [tʌsk] *n* defensa *f*.

tussle ['tʌsl] *n* pelea *f*; lucha *f*. *v* pelearse.

tutor ['tjuːtə] *n* (*private*) profesor particular *m*; (*university*) tutor *m*. *v* dar clases privadas.

tuxedo [tʌkˈsiːdou] *n* smoking *m*.

tweed [twiːd] *n* tweed *m*.

tweezers ['twiːzəz] *pl n* pinzas *f pl*.

twelve [twelv] *nm*, *adj* doce. **twelfth** *n*, *adj* duodécimo, -a.

twenty ['twenti] *nm*, *adj* veinte. **twentieth** *n*, *adj* vigésimo, -a.

twice [twais] *adv* dos veces.

twiddle ['twidl] *v* dar vueltas a. **twiddle one's thumbs** estar mano sobre mano.

twig [twig] *n* ramita *f*.

twilight ['twailait] *n* crepúsculo *m*.

twin [twin] *n*, *adj* gemelo, -a. **twin beds** camas gemelas *f pl*.

twine [twain] *n* bramante *m*. *v* (*twist*) retorcer; (*interlace*) trenzar; (*embrace*) rodear con.

twinge [twindʒ] *n* (*pain*) punzada *f*; (*fig*) arrebato *m*.

twinkle ['twiŋkl] *n* centelleo *m*; (*brightness*) brillo *m*. *v* centellear; (*eyes*) brillar.

twirl [twəːl] *v* dar vueltas a. *n* vuelta *f*.

twist [twist] *v* torcer; retorcer. *n* torcimiento *m*, torsión *f*; (*tobacco*) rollo *m*; vuelta *f*; deformación *f*; contorsión *f*; inclinación *f*; (*warp*) abarquillamiento *m*; (*ankle*) torcedura *f*; (*swindle*) trampa *f*.

twit [twit] *n* (*slang*) imbécil *m*, *f*.

twitch [twitʃ] *n* (*pull*) tirón *m*; (*med*) tic *m*. *v* tirar bruscamente de; (*nervously*) crispar.

twitter ['twitə] v gorjear. n gorjeo m.

two [tuɪ] nm, adj dos. **two-faced** adj falso.

two-legged adj bípedo.

tycoon [tai'kuɪn] n magnate m.

type [taip] n (sort) tipo m, clase f; (print) carácter m, tipo m. **typesetting** n composición f. **typewriter** n máquina de escribir f. v escribir a máquina. **typical** adj típico. **typing** n mecanografía f. **typist** n mecanógrafo, -a m, f.

typhoid ['taifoid] n fiebre tifoidea f.

typhoon [tai'fuɪn] n tifón m.

tyrant ['tairənt] n tirano m. **tyrannical** adj tiránico. **tyranny** n tiranía f.

tyre or US **tire** ['taiə] n neumático m.

U

ubiquitous [ju'bikwitəs] adj ubicuo.

udder ['ʌdə] n ubre f.

ugly ['ʌgli] adj feo; repugnante. **ugliness** n fealdad f.

ulcer ['ʌlsə] n úlcera f.

ulterior [ʌl'tiəriə] adj ulterior. **ulterior motive** segunda intención f.

ultimate ['ʌltimət] adj último; fundamental. **ultimately** adv por fin, al final; esencialmente. **ultimatum** n ultimátum m.

ultraviolet [ʌltrə'vaiələt] adj ultravioleta.

umbilical [ʌm'bilikəl] adj umbilical. **umbilical cord** cordón umbilical m.

umbrage ['ʌmbridʒ] n resentimiento m, enfado m. **take umbrage at** ofenderse por.

umbrella [ʌm'brelə] n paraguas m invar.

umpire ['ʌmpaiə] n árbitro m. v arbitrar.

umpteen [ʌmp'tiɪn] adj (coll) muchísimos. **umpteenth** adj enésimo.

unable [ʌn'eibl] adj incapaz. **be unable to** (physical) ser incapaz de; (due to circumstances) no poder hacer.

unabridged [ʌnə'bridʒd] adj íntegro.

unacceptable [ʌnək'septəbl] adj inaceptable.

unaccompanied [ʌnə'kumpənid] adj solo, sin compañía; (music) sin acompañamiento.

unaided [ʌn'eidid] adj sin ayuda, solo.

unadulterated [ʌnə'dʌltəreitid] adj no adulterado, sin mezcla.

unanimous [ju'naniməs] adj unánime. **unanimity** n unanimidad f.

unarmed [ʌn'aɪmd] adj (person) sin armas; desarmado.

unattached [ʌnə'tatʃt] adj (loose) suelto; libre; independiente.

unattractive [ʌnə'traktiv] adj poco atrayente, desagradable.

unauthorized [ʌn'ɔɪθəraizd] adj no autorizado.

unavoidable [ʌnə'voidəbl] adj inevitable.

unaware [ʌnə'weə] adj inconsciente; ignorante. **be unaware of** ignorar. **unawares** adv sin querer; de improviso.

unbalanced [ʌn'balənst] adj desequilibrado; (mentally) trastornado.

unbearable [ʌn'beərəbl] adj insoportable, intolerable, insufrible.

unbelievable [ʌnbi'liɪvəbl] adj increíble.

***unbend** [ʌn'bend] v (straighten) desencorvar; (fig) relajar. **unbending** adj inflexible.

unbiased [ʌn'baiəst] adj imparcial.

unbreakable [ʌn'breikəbl] adj irrompible.

unbridled [ʌn'braidld] adj (fig) desenfrenado.

unbutton [ʌn'butn] v desabrochar; (fig) desahogarse.

uncalled-for [ʌn'kɔɪldfoɪ] adj innecesario; injustificado; gratuito.

uncanny [ʌn'kani] adj extraño; misterioso.

uncertain [ʌn'səɪtn] adj incierto. **uncertainty** n incertidumbre f.

uncle ['ʌŋkl] n tío m.

uncomfortable [ʌn'kʌmfətəbl] adj incómodo; (anxious) inquieto; (awkward) difícil.

uncommon [ʌn'komən] adj poco común, raro.

uncompromising [ʌn'komprəmaiziŋ] adj inflexible; irreconciliable.

unconditional [ʌnkən'diʃənl] adj incondicional.

unconscious [ʌn'konʃəs] adj (med) inconsciente; (unaware) ignorante.

unconventional [ʌnkən'venʃənl] adj poco convencional.

uncooked [ʌn'kukt] adj no cocido, crudo.

uncouth [ʌn'kuɪθ] adj grosero.

uncover [ʌn'kʌvə] v descubrir; (reveal) revelar; (take the lid off) destapar.

uncut [ʌn'kʌt] adj no cortado.

undecided [ʌndi'saidid] *adj* indeciso;
irresoluto.
undeniable [ʌndi'naiəbl] *adj* incontestable.
under ['ʌndə] *adv* debajo; abajo; más
abajo; (*insufficient*) insuficiente; (*for less*)
para menos. *prep* debajo de; bajo; por
debajo de; menos de; (*age*) menor de;
(*lower in rank*) por debajo de; (*repair,
construction, etc.*) en; (*according to*)
según; conforme a.
underarm ['ʌndəraim] *adj, adv* por debajo
del brazo; sobacal.
undercharge [ʌndə'tʃaidʒ] *v* cobrar
menos de lo debido.
underclothes ['ʌndəklouðz] *pl n* ropa
interior *f sing.*
undercoat ['ʌndəkout] *n* (*paint*) primera
capa *f.*
undercover [ʌndə'kʌvə] *adj* secreto;
clandestino.
undercut [ʌndə'kʌt] *v* vender más barato
que.
underdeveloped [ʌndədi'veləpt] *adj* de
desarrollo atrasado; (*phot*) no revelado
lo suficiente.
underdog ['ʌndədog] *n* desvalido *m.*
underdone [ʌndə'dʌn] *adj* (*meat*) poco
hecho.
underestimate [ʌndə'estimeit] *v* tasar en
menos; menospreciar. *n also* **underesti-
mation** infravaloración *f*; menosprecio
m.
underfoot [ʌndə'fut] *adv* debajo de los
pies.
***undergo** [ʌndə'gou] *v* sufrir, pasar por.
undergraduate [ʌndə'gradjuət] *n* estudiante no licenciado, -a *m, f.*
underground ['ʌndəgraund] *adv*
ʌndə'graund] *adj* subterráneo; oculto,
secreto. *adv* bajo tierra; clandestina-
mente.
undergrowth ['ʌndəgrouθ] *n* maleza *f.*
underhand [ʌndə'hand] *adj* bajo mano;
secreto.
***underlie** [ʌndə'lai] *v* estar debajo de;
servir de base a. **underlying** *adj* básico,
fundamental.
underline [ʌndə'lain] *v* subrayar. **underlining** *n* subrayado *m.*
undermine [ʌndə'main] *v* socavar, minar.
underneath [ʌndə'niiθ] *prep* bajo, debajo
de. *adv* debajo, por debajo. *adj* inferior,
de abajo.

underpaid [ʌndə'peid] *adj* mal pagado.
underpants ['ʌndəpants] *pl n* calzoncillos
m pl.
underpass ['ʌndəpais] *n* paso subterráneo
m.
underprivileged [ʌndə'privilidʒd] *adj*
menesteroso.
underrate [ʌndə'reit] *v* subestimar.
underskirt ['ʌndəskəit] *n* enaguas *f pl.*
understaffed [ʌndə'staift] *adj* falto de
personal.
***understand** [ʌndə'stand] *v* entender, com-
prender; (*believe*) creer. **understandable**
adj comprensible. **understanding** *n*
entendimiento *m*; comprensión *f*; (*reason*) razón *f*; interpretación *f*;
(*knowledge*) conocimientos *m pl*; (*agreement*) acuerdo *m.*
understate *v* quitar importancia a. **make
an understatement** describir sin énfasis.
that's an understatement! ¡y usted que lo
diga!
understudy ['ʌndəstʌdi] *n* suplente *m, f. v*
suplir, doblar.
***undertake** [ʌndə'teik] *v* emprender;
prometer. **undertaker** *n* empresario de
pompas funebres *m.* **undertaking** *n*
empresa *f*; compromiso *m.*
undertone ['ʌndətoun] *n* **in an undertone**
en voz baja.
underwater [ʌndə'wotə] *adj* submarino.
underwear ['ʌndəweə] *n* ropa interior *f.*
underweight [ʌndə'weit] *adj* de peso
insuficiente.
underworld ['ʌndəwəild] *n* (*criminal*)
hampa *f*; (*hell*) infierno *m.*
***underwrite** [ʌndə'rait] *v* (*sign, bonds*)
subscribir; (*guarantee*) garantizar;
(*insure*) asegurar.
undesirable [ʌndi'zaiərəbl] *adj* no deseable; pernicioso. *n* indeseable *m, f.*
***undo** [ʌn'dui] *v* (*open*) abrir; (*knot*)
desatar; (*a tie*) desanudar; (*button*)
desabrochar; (*parcel*) deshacer; (*zip*)
bajar; (*ruin*) arruinar. **undoing** *n* ruina *f.*
come undone desatarse.
undoubted [ʌn'dautid] *adj* indudable.
undress [ʌn'dres] *v* desnudar(se).
undue [ʌn'djui] *adj* excesivo; impropio.
unduly *adv* excesivamente; impropiamente.
undulate ['ʌndjuleit] *v* ondular. **undulating**
adj ondulante. **undulation** *n* ondulación
f.

unearth [ʌn'ɔːθ] v desenterrar; descubrir.
unearthly adj sobrenatural; misterioso; espantoso. **unearthly hour** (coll) hora intempestiva f.
uneasy [ʌn'iːzi] adj inquieto; molesto; agitado; preocupado.
uneducated [ʌn'edjukeitid] adj ineducado.
unemployed [ʌnem'ploid] adj parado, desempleado. **the unemployed** los parados m pl. **unemployment** n paro m, desempleo m.
unenthusiastic [ʌnenθjuːzi'astik] adj sin entusiasmo.
unequal [ʌn'iːkwəl] adj desigual; (inadequate) inadecuado; (med) irregular.
uneven [ʌn'iːvn] adj accidentado; (unequal) designal; (number) impar.
uneventful [ʌni'ventfəl] adj sin acontecimientos.
unexpected [ʌneks'pektid] adj inesperado.
unfailing [ʌn'feiliŋ] adj infalible; (inexhaustible) inagotable; (unceasing) constante.
unfair [ʌn'feə] adj injusto. **unfairness** n injusticia f.
unfaithful [ʌn'feiθfəl] adj infiel. **unfaithfulness** n infidelidad f.
unfamiliar [ʌnfə'miljə] adj desconocido; extraño.
unfasten [ʌn'faːsn] v (open) abrir; (dress, button) desabrochar; (knot) desatar; (set free) soltar; (loosen) aflojar.
unfavourable [ʌn'feivərəbl] adj desfavorable, adverso.
unfinished [ʌn'finiʃt] adj inacabado, no terminado.
unfit [ʌn'fit] adj incapaz; no apto; incompetente; impropio; (ill) enfermo, malo.
unfold [ʌn'fould] v desplegar; (plans) revelar; (thoughts) desarrollarse.
unforeseen [ʌnfoː'siːn] adj imprevisto.
unforgivable [ʌnfə'givəbl] adj imperdonable.
unfortunate [ʌn'foːtʃənət] adj desafortunado; desgraciado.
unfounded [ʌn'faundid] adj infundado, sin fundamento.
unfriendly [ʌn'frendli] adj hostil; desfavorable.
unfurnished [ʌn'fɔːniʃd] adj desamueblado.
ungainly [ʌn'geinli] adj desgarbado.

ungrateful [ʌn'greitfəl] adj ingrato.
unhappy [ʌn'hapi] adj infeliz; triste. **unhappiness** n infelicidad f.
unhealthy [ʌn'helθi] adj (person) enfermo; (place) malsano.
unheard-of [ʌn'hɔːdov] adj inaudito; sin precedente.
unhoped-for [ʌn'houptfoː] adj inesperado.
unhurt [ʌn'hɔːt] adj indemne, ileso.
unhygienic [ʌnhai'dʒiːnik] adj antihigiénico.
unicorn ['juːnikoːn] n unicornio m.
unidentified flying object [ʌnai'dentifaid] n also **UFO** objeto volador no identificado m, OVNI m.
uniform ['juːnifoːm] nm, adj uniforme. **uniformity** n uniformidad f.
unify ['juːnifai] v unificar. **unification** n unificación f.
unilateral [juːni'latərəl] adj unilateral.
unimaginative [ʌni'madʒinətiv] adj poco imaginativo.
unimportant [ʌnim'poːtnt] adj poco importante.
uninhabited [ʌnin'habitid] adj inhabitado.
uninhibited [ʌnin'hibitid] adj sin inhibición.
unintentional [ʌnin'tenʃnl] adj involuntario.
uninterested [ʌn'intristid] adj indiferente; desinteresado. **uninteresting** adj poco interesante.
union ['juːnjən] n unión f; (trade) sindicato m.
unique [juː'niːk] adj único.
unisex ['juːni,seks] adj (coll) unisexo invar.
unison ['juːnisn] n unisonancia. **in unison** al unisono.
unite [juː'nait] v unir; reunir; juntarse. **united** adj unido. **United Kingdom** Reino Unido m. **United Nations** Naciones Unidas f pl. **United States of America** Estados Unidos de América m pl.
unity ['juːniti] m unidad f.
universe ['juːnivəːs] m universo m. **universal** adj universal.
university [juːni'vəːsəti] n universidad f. adj universitario.
unjust [ʌn'dʒʌst] adj injusto.
unkempt [ʌn'kempt] adj descuidado; (hair) despeinado.
unkind [ʌn'kaind] adj poco amable; severo; cruel. **unkindness** n falta de amabilidad f; severidad f; crueldad f.

unknown [ʌn'noun] *n, adj* desconocido, -a.

unlawful [ʌn'lɔɪfəl] *adj* ilegal; ilegítimo.

unless [ʌn'les] *conj* a no ser que, a menos que.

unlike [ʌn'laik] *adj* diferente, distinto. *prep* a diferencia de.

unlikely [ʌn'laikli] *adj* improbable; (*unexpected*) inverosímil.

unlimited [ʌn'limitid] *adj* ilimitado.

unload [ʌn'loud] *v* descargar; (*get rid of*) deshacerse de.

unlock [ʌn'lok] *v* abrir.

unlucky [ʌn'lʌki] *adj* desgraciado; (*day, number, etc.*) funesto.

unmarried [ʌn'marid] *adj* soltero.

unnatural [ʌn'natʃərəl] *adj* antinatural; anormal; artificial.

unnecessary [ʌn'nesəsəri] *adj* innecesario, inútil.

unnerving [ʌn'nərviŋ] *adj* desconcertante.

unnoticed [ʌn'noutist] *adv* inadvertido; desapercibido. **go** *or* **pass unnoticed** pasar desapercibido.

unobtainable [ʌnəb'teinəbl] *adj* que no se puede conseguir.

unobtrusive [ʌnəb'truːsiv] *adj* discreto, modesto.

unoccupied [ʌn'okjupaid] *adj* (*at leisure*) desocupado; (*untenanted*) deshabitado; (*seat*) libre.

unofficial [ʌnə'fiʃəl] *adj* no oficial.

unorthodox [ʌn'ɔɪθədoks] *adj* poco ortodoxo.

unpack [ʌn'pak] *v* (*box*) desembalar; (*suitcase*) deshacer.

unpaid [ʌn'peid] *adj* impagado; (*bill*) por pagar; (*worker*) no retribuido.

unpleasant [ʌn'pleznt] *adj* (*weather*) desagradable; (*unfriendly*) antipático; (*annoying*) molesto.

unpopular [ʌn'popjulə] *adj* impopular.

unprecedented [ʌn'presidentid] *adj* sin precedentes.

unpredictable [ʌnprə'diktəbl] *adj* que no se puede prever; (*capricious*) antojadizo.

unqualified [ʌn'kwolifaid] *adj* sin título; (*without reservation*) sin reserva.

unravel [ʌn'ravəl] *v* (*wool*) deshacer; (*untangle*) desenredar; (*mystery*) desembrollar.

unreal [ʌn'riəl] *adj* irreal.

unreasonable [ʌn'riːzənəbl] *adj* irrazonable; extravagante; excesivo.

unrelenting [ʌnri'lentiŋ] *adj* implacable.

unreliable [ʌnri'laiəbl] *adj* (*character*) inconstante; (*person*) poco seguro; (*machine*) poco fiable; (*service*) dudoso.

unrest [ʌn'rest] *n* desasosiego *m*, agitación *f*.

unruly [ʌn'ruːli] *adj* ingobernable; rebelde.

unsafe [ʌn'seif] *adj* inseguro; peligroso.

unsatisfactory [ʌnsatis'faktəri] *adj* poco satisfactorio.

unscrew [ʌn'skruː] *v* destornillar.

unscrupulous [ʌn'skruːpjuləs] *adj* poco escrupuloso.

unselfish [ʌn'selfiʃ] *adj* desinteresado; generoso.

unsettle [ʌn'setl] *v* pertubar; (*mentally*) desequilibrar. **unsettled** *adj* perturbado; agitado; desequilibrado; (*weather*) incierto.

unsightly [ʌn'saitli] *adj* feo, repugnante.

unskilled [ʌn'skild] *adj* no cualificado; no especializado. **unskilled worker** obrero no cualificado *m*.

unsound [ʌn'saund] *adj* (*unhealthy*) enfermizo; (*mentally*) demente; (*morally*) corrompido; (*goods*) imperfecto; (*foundations*) poco sólido; (*business*) poco seguro; (*argument, opinion*) falso.

unspeakable [ʌn'spiːkəbl] *adj* indecible.

unspecified [ʌn'spesifaid] *adj* no especificado.

unstable [ʌn'steibl] *adj* inestable.

unsteady [ʌn'stedi] *adj* inestable; inconstante.

unstuck [ʌn'stʌk] *adj* **come unstuck** despegarse; (*hopes, plans*) fracasar.

unsuccessful [ʌnsək'sesfəl] *adj* sin éxito; (*person, attempt, etc.*) fracasado; (*candidate*) suspendido. **be unsuccessful** fracasar. **unsuccessfully** *adv* sin éxito; infructuosamente.

unsuitable [ʌn'suːtəbl] *adj* inapropiado; inconveniente; inoportuno.

untangle [ʌn'taŋgl] *v* desenmarañar.

untidy [ʌn'taidi] *adj* desarreglado; (*person*) desordenado. **untidiness** *n* desorden *m*.

untie [ʌn'tai] *v* desatar.

until [ən'til] *prep* hasta. *conj* hasta que.

untoward [ʌntə'wɔɪd] *adj* insumiso; adverso; desafortunado.

untrue [ʌn'truː] *adj* falso, mentiroso; imaginario; infiel.

unusual [ʌnˈjuːʒuəl] *adj* desacostumbrado; extraño; excepcional.

unwanted [ʌnˈwɒntid] *adj* no deseado; superfluo.

unwell [ʌnˈwel] *adj* indispuesto, enfermo.

*unwind [ʌnˈwaind] *v* desenrollar; *(relax)* descansar.

unwise [ʌnˈwaiz] *adj* imprudente; indiscreto.

unworthy [ʌnˈwɜːði] *adj* indigno.

unwrap [ʌnˈrap] *v* desenvolver; *(parcel)* deshacer.

up [ʌp] *adv* arriba; hacia arriba; al aire; en el aire; *(louder)* más fuerte; *(out of bed)* levantado; *(standing)* de pie, en pie. **be up to** ser capaz de. *prep* arriba; en; contra; en el fondo de. **walk up and down** pasearse a lo largo y a lo ancho. **ups and downs** los altibajos *m pl.* **up-and-coming** *adj* joven y prometedor.

upbringing [ˈʌpbriŋiŋ] *n* educación *f.*

update [ʌpˈdeit] *v (bring up to date)* poner al día; *(modernize)* modernizar.

upheaval [ʌpˈhiːvl] *n (geol)* levantamiento *m;* *(fig)* agitación *f.*

uphill [ʌpˈhil] *adj* ascendente; *(struggle)* arduo.

*uphold [ʌpˈhould] *v* sostener; defender; confirmar.

upholster [ʌpˈhoulstə] *v* entapizar. **upholstery** *n (material)* tapicería *f;* *(filling)* relleno *m.*

upkeep [ˈʌpkiːp] *n* mantenimiento *m.*

uplift [ʌpˈlift] *n (geol)* elevación *f;* *(fig)* inspiración *f.*

upon [əˈpɒn] *prep* sobre, encima de.

upper [ˈʌpə] *adj* alto; superior. **upperclass** *adj* de la clase alta. **upper hand** dominio *m.* **uppermost** *adj* más alto; predominante.

upright [ˈʌprait] *adj* vertical; derecho; *(fig)* recto. *adv* en posición vertical.

uprising [ˈʌpraiziŋ] *n* sublevación *f.*

uproar [ˈʌprɔː] *n* alboroto *m,* tumulto *m.* **uproarious** *adj* tumultuoso; ruidoso.

uproot [ʌpˈruːt] *v* desarraigar; *(fig)* arrancar.

*upset [ʌpˈset; *n* ˈʌpset] *v (knock over)* volcar; *(spill)* derramar; *(plans, etc.)* trastornar; desconcertar; *(displease)* enfadar. *adj (worried)* preocupado; *(ill)* indispuesto; *(nerves)* desquiciado; enfadado; *(stomach)* trastornado. *n* vuelco *m;* trastorno *m;* *(illness)* malestar *m;* dificultad *f;* *(trouble)* molestia *f.*

upshot [ˈʌpʃot] *n* resultado *m.*

upside down [ʌpsaiˈdaun] *adv, adj* al revés.

upstairs [ʌpˈsteəz] *adv* arriba. **go upstairs** subir. *adj* de arriba.

upstream [ʌpˈstriːm] *adv* río arriba, aguas arriba; *(swim)* a contracorriente.

up-to-date *adj* moderno.

upward [ˈʌpwəd] *adj* ascendente. **upwards** *adv* hacia arriba.

uranium [juˈreiniəm] *n* uranio *m.*

urban [ˈɜːbən] *adj* urbano.

urchin [ˈɜːtʃin] *n* pilluelo *m.*

urge [ɜːdʒ] *v* incitar; exhortar; requerir. *n* vivo deseo *m;* impulso *m.*

urgent [ˈɜːdʒənt] *adj* urgente; insistente. **urgency** *n* urgencia *f;* insistencia *f.*

urine [ˈjuːrin] *n* orina *f.* **urinate** *v* orinar.

urn [ɜːn] *n* urna *f.*

Uruguay [ˈjuərəgwai] *n* Uruguay *m.* **Uruguayan** *n, adj* uruguayo, -a.

us [ʌs] *pron* nos; nosotros.

usage [ˈjuːzidʒ] *n (custom)* usanza *f;* *(treatment)* tratos *m pl;* *(gramm)* uso *m.*

use [juːs; *v* juːz] *n* uso *m;* empleo *m;* *(tool)* manejo *m.* **it's no use** es inútil. **what's the use?** ¿para qué? *v* usar, emplear; consumir; tomar; utilizar. **use up** agotar. **used** de segunda mano. **be used for** servir para. **be used to** estar acostumbrado a. **get used to** habituarse a. **useful** *adj* útil. **useless** *adj* inútil. **user** *n* usuario, -a *m, f.*

usher [ˈʌʃə] *n (law)* ujier *m;* (theatre) acomodador *m.* *v* **usher in** anunciar; hacer pasar. **usherette** *n* acomodadora *f.*

usual [ˈjuːzuəl] *adj* normal; habitual; acostumbrado. **as usual** como siempre. **usually** *adv* normalmente.

usurp [juˈzɜːp] *v* usurpar.

utensil [juˈtensl] *n* utensilio *m.*

uterus [ˈjuːtərəs] *n* útero *m.*

utility [juˈtiləti] *n* utilidad *f.* *adj* utilitario.

utilize [ˈjuːtilaiz] *v* utilizar.

utmost [ˈʌtmoust] *adj* mayor; supremo; extremo; más lejano. *n* máximo *m.* **do one's utmost** hacer todo lo posible.

utter¹ [ˈʌtə] *v* decir; *(cries)* lanzar; *(sigh)* dar; *(sentiments)* expresar.

utter² [ˈʌtə] *adj* absoluto; completo.

U-turn [ˈjuːtɜːn] *n* media vuelta *f.*

V

vacant *adj* (*empty*) vacío; deshabitado; (*free*) libre; (*absent-minded*) distraído; vago; estúpido. **vacancy** (*job*) vacante *f*; (*room*) habitación libre *f*. **no vacancies** completo.

vacate *v* dejar vacío.

vacation *n* vacaciones *f pl*.

vaccine *n* vacuna *f*. **vaccinate** *v* vacunar. **vaccination** *n* vacunación *f*.

vacillate *v* vacilar; oscilar. **vacillation** *n* vacilación *f*.

vacuum *n* vacío *m*. **vacuum cleaner** aspiradora *f*. **vacuum flask** termo *m*. *v* pasar la aspiradora en.

vagina *n* vagina *f*.

vagrant *n*, *adj* vagabundo, -a. **vagrancy** *n* vagabundeo *m*.

vague *adj* vago, indistinto; incierto.

vain *adj* vano, inútil; (*conceited*) vanidoso. **in vain** en vano.

valiant *adj* valeroso.

valid *adj* válido. **validity** *n* validez *f*.

valley *n* valle *m*.

value *n* valor *m*; precio *m*; importancia *f*. *v* (*appraise*) valorar, tasar; estimar; apreciar. **valuable** *adj* valioso; precioso; costoso. **valuables** *pl n* objetos de valor *m pl*. **valuation** *n* valuación *f*; estimación *f*.

valve *n* válvula *f*.

vampire *n* vampiro *m*.

van *n* (*road*) camión *m*; (*removal*) carro de mudanzas *m*; (*guard's*) furgón de equipajes *m*; (*leading section*) vanguardia *f*.

vandal *n* vándalo, -a *m*, *f*. **vandalism** *n* vandalismo *m*. **vandalize** *v* destrozar.

vanilla *n* vainilla *f*.

vanish *v* desaparecer.

vanity *n* vanidad *f*. **vanity case** neceser *m*.

vapour *n* vapor *m*. **vapourize** *v* vaporizar.

varicose veins *pl n* varices *f pl*.

variety *n* variedad *f*; diversidad *f*. **variety show** función de variedades *f*.

various *adj* diverso; vario.

varnish *n* barniz *m*. *v* barnizar.

vary *v* variar; cambiar; modificar. **vary from** diferenciarse de. **variable** *nf*, *adj* variable. **variant** *nf*, *adj* variante. **variation** *n* variación *f*.

vase *n* vaso *m*; jarrón *m*.

vasectomy *n* vasectomía *f*.

vast *adj* vasto. **vastness** *n* inmensidad *f*.

vat *n* tinaja *f*.

Vatican *n* Vaticano *m*. **Vatican City** Ciudad del Vaticano *f*.

vault[1] *n* (*cellar*) sótano *m*; (*arch*) bóveda *f*; (*tomb*) panteón *m*; (*bank*) cámara acorzada *f*.

vault[2] *v* saltar. *n* salto *m*. **vaulting horse** potro *m*.

veal *n* ternera *f*.

veer *v* (*wind*) girar; (*ship*) virar; (*fig*) cambiar.

vegetable *n* (*bot*) vegetal *m*; (*cookery*) verdura *f*, legumbre *f*. *adj* vegetal. **vegetable garden** huerto *m*, huerta *f*. **vegetarian** *n*, *adj* vegetariano, -a. **vegetation** *n* vegetación *f*.

vehement *adj* vehemente; violento. **vehemence** *n* vehemencia *f*; violencia *f*. **vehemently** *adj* con vehemencia.

vehicle *n* vehículo *m*.

veil *n* velo *m*. *v* velar.

vein *n* vena *f*.

velocity *n* velocidad *f*.

velvet *n* terciopelo *m*. *adj* de terciopelo. **velvety** *adj* aterciopelado.

vending machine *n* distribuidor automático *m*.

veneer *n* chapa *f*; (*fig*: *gloss*) barniz *m*. *v* chapear.

venerate *v* veneral. **venerable** *adj* venerable. **veneration** *n* veneración *f*.

venereal disease *n* enfermedad venérea *f*.

Venetian blind *n* persiana veneciana *f*.

Venezuela [,veniˈzweilə] *n* Venezuela *f*. **Venezuelan** *n*, *adj* venezolano, -a.

vengeance *n* venganza *f*. **with a vengeance** (*coll*) de verdad.

venison *n* venado *m*.

venom *n* veneno *m*. **venomous** *adj* venenoso.

vent *n* (*hole*) agujero *m*, abertura *f*; (*air-hole*) respiradero *m*; (*tube*) conducto de ventilación *m*. **give vent to** dar libre curso a. *v* desahogar.

ventilate *v* ventilar. **ventilation** *n* ventilación *f*.

ventriloquist *n* ventrílocuo, -a *m*, *f*. **ventriloquism** *n* ventriloquia *f*.

venture *n* aventura *f*, empresa arriesgada *f*. *v* aventurar; arriesgar.

venue *n* lugar de reunión *m*.

veranda *n also* **verandah** veranda *f*, galería *f*.
verb *n* verbo. **verbal** *adj* verbal.
verdict *n* veredicto *m*.
verge *n* margen *m*, borde *m*; (*lake*) orilla *f*. **on the verge of** (*fig*) a punto de, a dos dedos de. *v* **verge on** rayar en.
verify *v* verificar. **verification** *n* verificación *f*.
vermin *n* (*rats, mice, etc.*) bichos *m pl*; (*fleas, people*) sabandijas *f pl*. **verminous** *adj* (*lousy*) piojoso.
vermouth *n* vermut *m*.
vernacular *adj* vernáculo. *n* lenguaje vulgar *m*.
versatile *adj* de talentos variados; (*mind*) flexible. **versatility** *n* diversos talentos *m pl*; flexibilidad *f*.
verse *n* (*poetry*) poesía *f*; (*stanza*) estrofa *f*; (*Bible*) versículo *m*.
version *n* versión *f*.
versus *prep* contra.
vertebra *n, pl* -**brae** vértebra *f*. **vertebral** *adj* vertebral. **vertebrate** *nm, adj* vertebrado.
vertical *nf, adj* vertical.
vertigo *n* vértigo *m*.
very *adv* muy; mucho, mucha. **very much** mucho, muchísimo. *adj* mismo; propio; (*real*) verdadero; puro.
vessel *n* (*container*) vasija *f*; (*ship*) nave *f*.
vest *n* camiseta *f*.
vestibule *n* vestíbulo *m*.
vestige *n* vestigio *m*, rastro *m*.
vestry *n* vestuario *m*, sacristía *f*.
vet *n* (*coll*) veterinario *m*. *v* (*coll*) corregir, revisar.
veteran *nm, adj* veterano. **veteran troops** tropas aguerridas *f pl*.
veterinary surgeon *n* veterinario *m*.
veto *n* veto *m*. *v* vetar, poner el veto.
vex *v* molestar; enfadar. **vexation** *n* molestia *f*; disgusto *m*.
via *prep* por, por la vía de.
viable *adj* viable. **viability** *n* viabilidad *f*.
viaduct *n* viaducto *m*.
vibrate *v* vibrar. **vibration** *n* vibración *f*.
vicar *n* vicario *m*; (*of a parish*) cura *m*. **vicarage** *n* casa del cura *f*.
vicarious *adj* vicario.
vice¹ *n* (*evil*) vicio *m*; (*defect*) defecto *m*.
vice² *n* (*tool*) tornillo de banco *m*.
vice-chancellor *n* rector *m*.
vice-consul *n* vicecónsul *m*.

vice-president *n* vicepresidente *m*.
vice versa *adv* viceversa.
vicinity *n* vecindad *f*; (*nearness*) cercanía *f*.
vicious *adj* (*of vice*) vicioso; (*bad*) malo; (*depraved*) pervertido; (*taste*) corrompido; (*life*) disoluto; (*crime*) atroz. **vicious circle** círculo vicioso *m*. **viciousness** *n* lo vicioso; maldad *f*; perversidad *f*.
victim *n* víctima *f*. **victimize** *v* perseguir; tomar como víctima. **victimization** *n* persecución *f*.
victory *n* victoria *f*. **victorious** *adj* victorioso.
video-tape *n* cinta magnética video *f*. *v* grabar programas de televisión.
vie *v* competir, rivalizar.
Vienna *n* Viena *f*.
view *n* vista *f*; panorama *m*; inspección *f*; idea *f*. **viewfinder** *n* visor *m*. **viewpoint** punto de vista *m*. *v* mirar; visitar; considerar. **viewer** *n* (*TV*) telespectador, -a *m, f*; (*onlooker*) espectador, -a *m, f*; (*for slides*) visionadora *f*.
vigil *n* vela *f*, vigilia *f*. **vigilance** *n* vigilancia *f*. **vigilant** *adj* vigilante.
vigour *n* vigor *m*. **vigorous** *adj* vigoroso.
vile *adj* vil; horrible.
villa *n* chalet *m*; (*country house*) casa de campo *f*.
village *n* aldea *f*, pueblo *m*. **villager** *n* aldeano, -a *m, f*.
villain *n* canalla *m*. **villainy** *n* villanía *f*.
vindictive *adj* vengativo.
vine *n* vid *f*; parra *f*. **vineyard** *n* viña *f*.
vinegar *n* vinagre *m*.
vintage *adj* (*season*) vendimia *f*; (*crop*) cosecha *f*. **vintage wine** vino añejo *m*.
vinyl *n* vinilo *m*.
viola *n* (*music*) viola *f*.
violate *v* (*ravish*) violar; (*desecrate*) profanar; (*infringe*) contravenir. **violation** *n* violación *f*; profanación *f*; contravención *f*.
violence *n* violencia *f*. **violent** *adj* violento.
violet *n* (*flower, colour*) violeta *f*. *adj* violado.
violin *n* violín *m*. **violinist** *n* violinista *m, f*.
viper *n* víbora *f*.
virgin *nf, adj* virgen. **virginity** *n* virginidad *f*.

Virgo n Virgo m.
virile adj viril. **virility** n virilidad f.
virtually adv virtualmente; prácticamente.
virtue n virtud f; (advantage) ventaja f. **by virtue of** debido a. **virtuous** adj virtuoso.
virus n virus m.
visa n visado m.
viscount n vizconde m. **viscountess** vizcondesa f.
visible adj visible. **visibility** n visibilidad f.
vision n (sight, apparition) visión f; (capacity to see) vista f; (dream) sueño m.
visionary n, adj visionario, -a m, f.
visit n visita f. v (go to, call on) visitar; (stay in) pasar una temporada en. **visitor** n visitante m, f; visita f.
visor n visera f.
visual adj visual. **visualize** v imaginarse.
vital adj vital. **vitality** n vitalidad f. **vitally** adv vitalmente.
vitamin n vitamina f.
vivacious adj vivo; vivaracho. **vivaciousness** n also **vivacity** viveza f, vivacidad f.
vivid adj vivo; (description) gráfico. **vividness** n (colour) viveza f, intensidad f; (style) fuerza f.
vivisection n vivisección f.
vixen n zorra f, raposa f.
vocabulary n vocabulario m.
vocal adj vocal; (fig) ruidoso. **vocalist** n cantante m, f.
vocation n vocación f. **vocational** adj profesional.
vociferous adj ruidoso.
vodka n vodca m.
voice n voz f. v hablar; expresar.
void n vacío m. adj (empty) vacío; (job) vacante; (law) nulo.
volatile adj (chem) volátil; (fig) voluble.
volcano n volcán m. **volcanic** adj volcánico.
volley n (bullets) andanada f; (arrows, stones) lluvia f; (applause) salva f; (sport) voleo m. v (missile) lanzar; (sport) volear.
volt n voltio m. **voltage** n voltaje m.
volume n (space, sound) volumen m; (book) tomo m, volumen m. **voluminous** adj voluminoso; abundante.
volunteer nm, adj voluntario. v ofrecer; (remark) hacer; (information) dar.
voluptuous adj voluptuoso. **voluptuousness** n voluptuosidad f.
vomit n vómito m. v vomitar.

voodoo n vodú m.
voracious adj voraz. **voraciousness** n also **voracity** voracidad f.
vote n voto m; (action) votación f. **vote of confidence** voto de confianza f. **vote of thanks** voto de gracias m. v votar; elegir; proponer; declarar. **voter** n votante m, f; elector, -a m, f.
vouch v **vouch for** (thing) responder de, garantizar; (person) responder por.
voucher n (comm) bono m, vale m. **luncheon voucher** vale de comida m.
vow n voto m; promesa solemne f. v jurar; prometer.
vowel n vocal f.
voyage n viaje m. v viajar (por mar).
vulgar adj común; ordinario; grosero. **vulgarity** n vulgaridad f; grosería f.
vulnerable adj vulnerable.
vulture n buitre m.

W

wad n (bung) tapón m; (notes) rollo m; (cotton wool) bolita f. **wadding** n (cotton wool) guata f; (filling) relleno m.
waddle v anadear. n anadeo m.
wade v vadear. **wade through** (book, etc.) estudiar detenidamente.
wafer n (for ices) barquillo m. **wafer-thin** adj finísimo.
waft v llevar por el aire; flotar. n ráfaga f.
wag v agitar; (tail) menear. n (tail) coleada f; movimiento m; (joker) bromista m, f.
wage n salario m, paga f. v **wage war** hacer guerra.
wager n apuesta f. v apostar.
waggle v menear, agitar. n meneo m.
wagon n carro m; carreta f; (rail) vagón m.
waif n niño abandonado m.
wail n lamento m, gemido. v lamentarse, gemir.
waist n cintura f, talle m. **waistband** n pretina f. **waistcoat** n chaleco m. **waistline** n cintura f.
wait n espera f. **lie in wait for** acechar. v esperar; (at table) atender. **waiter** n mozo m, camarero m. **waiting** n espera f; servicio m. **waiting-list** n lista de espera f.

waiting-room *n* sala de espera *f.* **waitress** *n* camarera *f.*

waive *v* renunciar a; desitir de.

wake[1] *n* velatorio *m.*

*wake[2] *v also* **wake up** despertar(se).

Wales *n* el País de Gales.

walk *n* paseo *m*; camino *m*; (*gait*) andar *m*; (*pace*) paso *m. v* (*go on foot*) recorrer a pie; (*distance*) hacer a pie; (*take out*) pasear; (*escort*) acompañar. **walkout** *n* huelga *f.* **walkover** *n* victoria fácil *f.* **walker** *n* paseante *m, f.* **walking** *n* andar *m.* **walking-stick** *n* bastón *m.*

wall *n* pared *f*; muro *m. v* murar; amurallar.

wallet *n* cartera *f.*

wallflower *n* alhelí *m.* **be a wallflower** quedarse en el poyete.

wallop (*coll*) *n* golpazo *m*, trompazo *m. v* zurrar. **walloping** *n* paliza *f.*

wallow *v* revolcarse.

wallpaper *n* papel pintado *m. v* empapelar.

walnut *n* (*nut*) nuez *f*; (*tree, wood*) nogal *m.*

walrus *n* morsa *f.*

waltz *n* vals *m. v* valsar.

wan *adj* macilento.

wand *n* (*magic*) varita *f*; vara *f.*

wander *v* vagar por; (*stroll*) pasearse; (*mentally*) desvariar.

wane *v* (*moon*) menguar; (*fig*) decaer.

wangle *v* conseguir con trampas. (*coll*) *n* trampa *f.*

want *n* (*lack*) falta *f*; (*need*) necesidad *f*; (*poverty*) miseria *f*; (*wish*) deseo *m*; (*gap*) vacío *m.* **for want of** por falta de. *v* querer; desear; necesitar; (*ask*) pedir; (*look for*) buscar. **wanted** *adj* buscado (por la policía). **wanting** *adj* (*absent*) ausente; (*lacking*) deficiente.

wanton *adj* lascivo; (*promiscuous*) libertino; (*senseless*) sin sentido. **wantonness** *n* libertinaje *f*; crueldad *f*; exuberancia *f*; (*lack of moderation*) desenfreno *m.*

war *n* guerra *f.* **be on the warpath** (*coll*) estar buscando guerra. **warfare** *n* guerra *f.* **warhead** *n* cabeza de guerra *f.* **war memorial** monumento a los Caídos *m.* **War Office** Ministerio de la Guerra *m.* **warship** *n* buque de guerra *m.* **wartime** *n* tiempo de guerra *m.*

warble *v* gorjear, trinar. *n* gorjeo *m*, trino *m.*

ward *n* (*hospital*) sala *f*; (*pol*) distrito electoral *m*; (*law: guardianship*) custodia *f*; (*minor*) pupilo *m. v* **ward off** evitar.

warden *n* guarda *m*; vigilante *m*; director *m.*

warder *n* carcelero *m*; guardián *m.*

wardrobe *n* guardarropa *m*; (*theatre*) vestuario *m.*

warehouse *n* almacén *m. v* almacenar.

warm *adj* tibio; caliente; (*climate*) cálido; (*fire*) acogedor; (*welcome*) caluroso; (*kind*) cariñoso. *v* calentar; acalorar. **warm up** calentar; (*reheat*) recalentar. **warming-pan** *n* calentador de cama *m.* **warmth** *n* calor *m*; cordialidad *f.*

warn *v* advertir; aconsejar; (*rebuke*) amonestar. **warning** *n* advertencia *f*, aviso *m*; alarma *f*; ejemplo *m*; amonestación *f.* **warning light** lámpara indicadora *f.*

warp *v* (*wood*) alabear; (*yarn*) urdir; (*fig*) deformar. *n* alabeo *m*; urdimbre *f*; deformación *f.*

warrant *n* (*police*) orden *f*; (*law*) autorización legal *f*; justificación *f*; garantía *f. v* autorizar; justificar; garantizar. **warranty** *n* garantía *f.*

warren *n* (*rabbit*) conejal *m*; (*fig*) colmena *f.*

warrior *n* guerrero *m.*

Warsaw ['woisoi] *n* Varsovia.

wart [woit] *n* verruga *f.*

wary ['weəri] *adj* cauto, precavido.

was [woz] *V* **be.**

wash [woʃ] *v* lavar; (*dishes*) fregar. **wash away** quitar. **wash down** (*swallow*) tragar. **wash up** fregar. **washable** *adj* lavable. **wash-and-wear** *adj* de lava y pon. **washbasin** *n* lavabo *m.* **washboard** *n* tabla de lavar *f.* **washer** *n* arandela *f.* **washing** *n* lavado *m*; colada *f*; fregado *m.* **washing machine** lavadora *f.* **washing powder** jabón en polvo *m.* **washing-up bowl** barreño *m.* **washout** *n* (*slang*) desastre *m.*

wasp [wosp] *n* avispa *f.*

waste [weist] *n* pérdida *f*; (*food*) desperdicios *m pl*; (*rubbish*) basura *f.* **waste disposal unit** vertedero de basuras *m.* **waste land** yermo *m*; erial *m.* **waste paper** papel usado *m.* **waste-paper basket** papelera *f. v* malgastar; despilfarrar; perder; (*use up*) consumir; (*by disuse*) desperdiciar. **waste away** consumirse. **wasteful** *adj* (*person*) despilfarrador, -a *m. f;* ruinoso. **waster** *n also* **wastrel** derrochador, -a *m, f.*

watch [wotʃ] *n (wrist)* reloj de la pulsera *m; (pocket)* reloj de bolsillo *m; (naut)* guardia *f;* vigilancia *f.* **keep watch** estar de guardia. **watch chain** cadena de reloj *f.* **watchdog** *n* perro guardián *m.* **watchmaker** *n* relojero *m.* **watchman** *n* vigilante *m.* **watch spring** muelle *m.* **watch strap** correa de reloj *f.* **watchword** *n* consigna *f.* *v* mirar, ver, observar; *(pay attention to)* fijarse en; *(keep an eye on)* vigilar. **watchful** *adj* atento; vigilante.

water ['wɔɪtə] *n* agua *f.* *v (wet)* humedecer; *(soak)* mojar; *(plants)* regar; *(eyes)* llorar. **water down** moderar. **watery** *adj* acuoso; aguado, insípido.

water-biscuit *n* galleta de harina y agua *f.*

water-closet *n* retrete *m,* wáter *m.*

water-colour *n* acuarela *f.*

watercress ['wɔɪtəkres] *n* berro *m.*

waterfall ['wɔɪtəfɔɪl] *n* cascada *f;* catarata *f.*

water-ice *n* sorbete *m.*

watering-can *n* regadera *f.*

water lily *n* nenúfar *m.*

waterline ['wɔɪtəlain] *n* linea de flotación *f.*

waterlogged ['wɔɪtəlogd] *adj (wood)* empapado; *(med)* inundado.

water main *n* cañería principal *f.*

watermark ['wɔɪtəmaɪk] *n* filigrana *f;* *(tide)* marca del nivel de agua *f.*

watermelon ['wɔɪtəmelən] *n* sandía *f.*

waterproof ['wɔɪtəpruf] *nm, adj* impermeable. *v* impermeabilizar.

watershed ['wɔɪtəfed] *n (fig)* momento decisivo *m; (geog)* línea divisoria de las aguas *f.*

water-ski *v* hacer esqui acuático. **water-skiing** *n* esquí acuático *m.*

water softener *n* ablandador del agua *m.*

watertight ['wɔɪtətait] *adj* estanco; hermético; *(fig)* perfecto.

waterway ['wɔɪtəwei] *n* vía navegable *f.*

waterworks ['wɔɪtəwɔɪks] *n* sistema de abastecimiento de agua *m.*

watt [wot] *n* vatio *m.*

wave [weiv] *n (sea)* ola *f; (hair)* ondulación *f; (physics, radio, etc.)*onda *f; (hand)* señal *f.* **permanent wave** permanente *f.* **waveband** *n* banda de ondas *f.* **wavelength** *n* longitud de onda *f.* *v* agitar; *(hair)* ondular. **wavy** *adj* ondulado.

waver ['weivə] *v* vacilar; *(falter)* flaquear; *(totter)* titubear. **wavering** *adj* vacilante; tembloroso.

wax[1] [waks] *n* cera *f.* **waxwork** *n* figura de cera *f.* **waxworks** *n* museo de figuras de cera *m.* *v* encerar. **waxy** *adj* ceroso.

wax[2] [waks] *v* crecer.

way [wei] *n* camino *m;* paso *m;* ruta *f;* senda *f;* dirección *f;* rumbo *m;* distancia *f; (journey)* viaje *m;* progreso *m;* modo *m,* manera *f; (means)* medio *m.* **be in the way** estar de por medio. **by the way** a propósito. **give way** ceder. **on the way** en camino. **this way** por aquí. **under way** en marcha; en preparación. **way in** entrada *f.* **way out** salida *f.*

*****waylay** [wei'lei] *v* abordar.

wayside ['weisaid] *n* borde del camino *m.* *adj* al borde del camino.

wayward ['weiwəd] *adj* voluntarioso; díscolo.

we [wiɪ] *pron* nosotros, -as.

weak [wiɪk] *adj* débil; flaco; flojo. **weaken** *v* debilitar. **weakling** *n* persona débil *f;* cobarde *m.* **weakness** *n* debilidad *f; (point)* punto flaco *m.*

wealth [welθ] *n* riqueza *f;* abundancia *f.* **wealthy** *adj* rico.

wean [wiɪn] *v (baby)* destetar. **wean from** apartar de.

weapon ['wepən] *n* arma *f.*

*****wear** [weə] *v* llevar; poner; gastar. **wear off** pasar(se). **wear out** usarse, consumirse. *n* uso *m;* gasto *m;* deterioro *m.* **wear and tear** desgaste *m.*

weary ['wiəri] *adj* fatigado, cansado, aburrido. *v* fatigar, causar; aburrir. **wearily** *adv* cansadamente. **weariness** *n* fatiga *f.*

weasel ['wiɪzl] *n* comadreja *f.*

weather ['weðə] *n* tiempo *m.* **weatherbeaten** *adj* curtido. **weather chart** mapa meteorológico *m.* **weathercock** *n* veleta *f.* **weather forecast** boletin meteorológico *m.* *v (survive)* superar.

*****weave** [wiɪv] *v* tejer; entrelazar; *(through traffic, etc.)* zigzaguear.

web [web] *n (spider)* tela de araña *f; (fabric)* tejido *m; (on feet)* membrana *f; (network)* red *f; (fig)* sarta *f.* **web-footed** *adj* palmipedo.

wed [wed] *v* casarse con; casar. **wedding** *n* boda *f,* casamiento *m.* **wedding dress** traje de novia *m.* **wedding ring** alianza *f.*

wedge [wedʒ] *n* cuña *f*, calzo *m*. *v* encajar; (*jam*) apretar.

Wednesday ['wenzdi] *n* miércoles *m*.

weed [wiːd] *n* mala hierba *f*. **weed-killer** *n* herbicida *m*. *v* desherbar. **weeding** *n* escarda *f*.

week [wiːk] *n* semana *f*. **a week today/tomorrow** hoy/mañana en ocho. **weekday** *n* día de trabajo *m*. **weekend** *n* fin de semana *m*. **weekly** *adv* semanal. **weekly** *n* semanario *m*.

***weep** [wiːp] *v* llorar, lamentar. **weeping willow** sauce llorón *m*.

weigh [wei] *v* pesar. **weigh down** doblar bajo un peso. **weight** *n* peso *m*. **pull one's weight** poner de su parte. **weightlifting** *n* halterofilia *f*. **weightlessness** *n* ingravidez *f*.

weird [wiəd] *adj* extraño; misterioso; fantástico. **weirdness** *n* misterio *m*; lo sobrenatural.

welcome ['welkəm] *adj* bienvenido; grato. **be welcome** ser oportuno. **you're welcome!** ¡eres el bienvenido!; (*after thanks*) ¡no hay de qué! *n* bienvenida *f*. *v* dar la bienvenida a; recibir; alegrarse por.

weld [weld] *v* soldar. **welder** *n* soldador *m*. **welding** *n* soldadura *f*.

welfare ['welfeə] *n* bienestar *m*, bien *m*. **welfare state** estado benefactor *m*.

well[1] [wel] *n* pozo *m*. **well up** brotar.

well[2] [wel] *adj, adv* bien. **as well** también.

well-advised *adj* juicioso.

well-behaved *adj* bien educado.

well-being *n* bienestar *m*.

well-born *adj* de buena familia.

well-bred *adj* (*person*) bien educado; (*animal*) de raza pura.

well-built *adj* bien hecho.

well-dressed *adj* bien vestido.

well-informed *adj* muy documentado.

wellington ['weliŋtən] *n* bota de agua *f*.

well-kept *adj* (*secret*) bien guardado; (*garden*) bien cuidado.

well-known *adj* bien conocido.

well-made *adj* bien hecho.

well-off *adj* rico.

well-paid *adj* bien pagado.

well-read *adj* leído.

well-spent *adj* (*time*) bien empleado.

well-spoken *adj* bienhablado.

well-timed *adj* oportuno.

well-to-do *adj* rico.

well-trodden *adj* trillado.

well-worn *adj* gastado.

Welsh [welʃ] *adj* galés. *n* (*language*) galés *m*; (*person*) galés, -esa *m*, *f*.

went [went] *V* **go**.

wept [wept] *V* **weep**.

were [wəː] *V* **be**.

west [west] *n* oeste *m*. **the West** el Mundo Occidental *m*. *adj also* **westerly** del oeste, occidental. *adv* al oeste, hacia el oeste. **westbound** *adj* con rumbo al oeste. **western** *adj* occidental, del oeste. *n* (*film*) western *m*.

wet [wet] *adj* mojado; húmedo; (*weather*) lluvioso; (*paint*) fresco. **wet blanket** aguafiestas *m, f invar*. **wet suit** traje de buzo *m*. *n* lluvia *f*. *v* mojar; humedecer.

whack [wak] *n* golpe *m*. *v* golpear, pegar.

whale [weil] *n* ballena *f*.

wharf [woːf] *n* muelle *m*.

what [wot] *pron* lo que; (*interrog, interj*) qué, cuál, cómo, cúanto. *adj* el que la que, lo que; qué.

whatever [wot'evə] *pron* todo lo que; lo que; cualquier cosa que. *adj* cualquiera. **nothing/whatever** nada en absoluto.

wheat [wiːt] *n* trigo *m*.

wheel [wiːl] *n* rueda *f*; (*steering*) volante *m*. **wheelbarrow** *n* carretilla *f*. **wheelchair** *n* sillón de ruedas *m*. *v* hacer rodar; empujar; dar una vuelta.

wheeze [wiːz] *n* respiración dificultosa *f*. *v* respirar con dificultad. **wheezy** *adj* asmático.

whelk [welk] *n* buccino *m*.

when [wen] *adv* cuándo, a qué hora. *conj* cuando; en que; (*as soon as*) en cuanto.

whenever *conj* cuando; cada vez que.

where [weə] *interrog adv* dónde; adónde; de dónde; por dónde; (*in what respect*) en qué. *relative adv* donde; en donde, en que, en el cual, en la cual; adonde, a donde, al que, al cual, **a la cual**. *conj* donde. **whereabouts** *adv* dónde, por dónde; *n* paradero *m*. **whereas** *conj* mientras, en tanto que. **whereupon** *adv* después de lo cual. **wherever** *conj* dondequiera que; a dondequiera que.

whether ['weðə] *conj* si.

which [witʃ] *interrog pron* cuál; qué. **relative pron** que; el cual, la cual, el que, la que; lo cual, lo que. *adj* qué; cuál; cuyo; cómo. **of which** del que, de la que; del cual; de la cual. **whichever** *pron* el que, la que; cualquiera que; *adj* cualquier.

whiff [wɪf] n soplo m; olorcillo m.

while [waɪl] conj mientras; (although) aunque. n rato m, tiempo m. **while away** pasar.

whim [wɪm] n capricho m.

whimper ['wɪmpə] n quejido m, gemido m. v quejarse, gemir.

whimsical ['wɪmzɪkl] adj caprichoso; fantástico.

whine [waɪn] n (animal) gañido m; (complaint) queja f; (pain) quejido m; (engine) zumbido m. v gañir; quejarse; zumbar.

whip [wɪp] n azote m; (riding) látigo m. **whiplash** n latigazo m. **whip-round** n (coll) colecta f. v azotar; (cookery) batir. **whip up** avivar. **whipping** n azotamiento m.

whippet ['wɪpɪt] n lebrel m.

whirl [wəːl] n vuelta f, giro m; (fig) torbellino m. v dar vueltas, girar. **whirlpool** n remolino m.

whirr [wəː] n (wings) batir m; (engine) zumbido m. v girar; zumbar.

whisk [wɪsk] n (cookery) batidor. v batir.

whisker ['wɪskə] n pelo del bigote m. **whiskers** pl n bigotes m pl.

whisky ['wɪski] n whisky m.

whisper ['wɪspə] n cuchicheo m. v cuchichear.

whistle ['wɪsl] n pito m; (sound) silbido m; pitido m. v silbar.

white [waɪt] adj blanco. **white elephant** (fig) objeto costoso e inútil m. n blanco m; (person) blanco, -a m, f. **whiten** v blanquear. **whiteness** n blancura f.

whitewash ['waɪtwɒʃ] n cal f. v encalar; (fig: cover up) encubrir.

whiting ['waɪtɪŋ] n pescadilla f.

whittle ['wɪtl] v tallar. **whittle down** reducir poco a poco.

whizz [wɪz] n zumbido m. **whizz-kid** n (coll) promesa f. **whizz past** pasar como un rayo.

who [huː] relative pron quien, el quel la que; que, el cual, la cual; que, a quien. interrog pron quién. **whoever** pron quienquiera que, cualquiera que, el que, la que, quien.

whole [houl] adj todo, completo, entero, total; íntegro, intacto. n todo m, total m, totalidad f. **on the whole** en general. **wholehearted** adj sin reservas. **wholeheartedly** adv incondicionalmente. **wholemeal** adj integral. **wholesome** adj saludable.

wholesale ['houlseɪl] n venta al por mayor f. adj, adv al por mayor; en masa.

whom [huːm] relative pron que, quien, a quien. interrog pron quién, a quién. **of whom** del cual, de la cual, de quien.

whooping cough ['huːpɪŋ] n tos ferina f.

whore [hɔː] n (derog) puta f.

whose [huːz] relative pron cuyo, cuya. interrog pron de quién.

why [waɪ] adv (interrog) por qué; (on account of which) por el cual, por la cual, por lo cual. interj ¡vaya! ¡toma! ¡pues bien!

wick [wɪk] n mecha f.

wicked ['wɪkɪd] adj malo, perverso, malicioso. **wickedness** n maldad f, perversidad f.

wicker ['wɪkə] n mimbre m. **wickerwork** n cestería f.

wicket ['wɪkɪt] n (cricket) palos m pl.

wide [waɪd] adj ancho; vasto; grande. adv lejos; mucho. **wide awake** completamente despierto. **widespread** adj general. **widely** adv muy; mucho; generalmente.

widow ['wɪdou] n viuda f. **be widowed** quedar viuda. **widower** n viudo m.

width [wɪdθ] n anchura f.

wield [wiːld] v (tool) manejar; (weapon) blandir; (power) ejercer.

wife [waɪf] n mujer f, esposa f.

wig [wɪg] n peluca f.

wiggle ['wɪgl] v menear. n meneo m. **wiggly** adj (line) ondulante.

wild [waɪld] adj (animal, person) salvaje; (plant) silvestre; (bull) bravo; (character) violento. **like wildfire** como un reguero de pólvora. **wildlife** n fauna f. **wildly** adv violentamente; locamente; frenéticamente; disolutamente.

wilderness ['wɪldənəs] n desierto m; soledad f.

wilful ['wɪlfəl] adj (stubborn) obstinado; (headstrong) voluntarioso; deliberado.

will[1] [wɪl] aux translated by future tense.

will[2] [wɪl] n voluntad f; testamento m. v disponer; desear; (bequeath) legar. **against one's will** de mal grado. **willpower** n fuerza de voluntad f. **willing** adj de buena voluntad; (obliging) complaciente. **be willing to** estar dispuesto a. **willingly** adv de buena gana. **willingness** n buena voluntad f.

willow ['wɪlou] n sauce m. **willowy** adj esbelto.

wilt [wilt] *v* marchitar(se); *(person)* languidecer.

wily ['waili] *adj* astuto, chuzón.

***win** [win] *n* victoria *f*; *(amount won)* ganancia *f*. *v* ganar; conquistar; triunfar. **winner** *n* ganador, -a *m, f*; vencedor, -a *m, f*. **winning** *adj* ganador; *(smile, etc.)* encantador. **winnings** *pl n* ganancias *f pl*.

wince [wins] *v* hacer muecas. *n* mueca de dolor *f*.

winch [wintʃ] *n* torno *m*. *v* guindar.

wind[1] [wind] *n* viento *m*; *(breath)* aliento *m*; respiración *f*; *(med)* gases *m pl*. *v* dejar sin aliento. **windy** *adj (place)* expuesto al viento; *(day, night)* ventoso.

***wind**[2] [waind] *v* devanar; envolver; enrollar; *(bend)* torcer; *(road)* serpentear; *(watch)* dar cuerda a. **wind up** terminar; *(comm)* liquidar. **winding** *adj* sinuoso; tortuoso.

wind-break *n* protección contra el viento *f*.

windfall ['windfoil] *n* fruta caída *f*; *(fig)* ganancia inesperada *f*.

wind instrument *n* instrumento de viento *m*.

windlass ['windləs] *n* torno *m*.

windmill ['wind.mil] *n* molino de viento *m*.

window ['windou] *n* ventana *f*; *(car)* ventanilla *f*; *(cashier's)* taquilla *f*; *(shop)* escaparate *m*. **window blind** persiana *f*. **window-box** *n* jardinera *f*. **window cleaner** limpiacristales *m invar*. **window-sill** *n* antepecho *m*. **window-shopping** *n* contemplación de escaparates *f*.

windpipe ['windpaip] *n* tráquea *f*.

windproof ['windpruif] *adj* a prueba de viento.

windshield ['windʃiild] *n* parabrisas *m invar*. **windshield wiper** limpiaparabrisas *m invar*.

wind-sock *n* manga de aire *f*.

windswept ['windswept] *adj (hair)* despeinado.

wind tunnel *n* túnel aerodinámico *m*.

wine [wain] *n* vino *m*. **wineglass** *n* copa *f*. **wine list** lista de vinos *f*. **wine-taster** *n* catavinos *m invar*. **wine waiter** bodeguero *m*.

wing [wiŋ] *n* ala *f*. **wing chair** sillón de orejas *m*. **wing commander** teniente coronel *m*. **wing-mirror** *n* retrovisor *m*. **wing nut** palometa *f*. **wings** *pl n (theatre)* bastidores *m pl*. **wingspan** *n* envergadura *f*.

wink [wiŋk] *n* guiño *m*; *(light)* parpadeo *m*. *v* guiñar; (light) parpadear.

winkle ['wiŋkl] *n* bígaro *m*. *v* **winkle out** sacar con dificultad.

winter ['wintə] *n* invierno *m*. *v* invernar. **wintry** *adj* de invierno; *(fig)* frío.

wipe [waip] *v* limpiar; *(mop)* enjugar; *(dry)* secar. **wipe out** destruir. *n* limpieza *f*.

wire [waiə] *n* alambre *m*; *(elec)* cordón *m*, cable *m*; hilo *m*; *(piano)* cuerda *f*; telegrama *m*. **barbed wire** alambrada *f*. **wire-brush** *n* cepillo metálico *m*. **wire-cutters** *pl n* cortaalambres *m invar*. **wireless** *n* radio *f*. *v* telegrafiar; *(a house)* poner la instalación eléctrica de. **wiry** *adj (hair)* tieso; *(person)* enjuto y fuerte.

wise [waiz] *adj* sabio; juicioso; *(informed)* enterado. **wisdom** *n* sabiduría *f*; juicio *m*. **wisdom tooth** muela del juicio *f*.

wish [wiʃ] *v* querer; desear; gustar. *n* deseo *m*. **wishbone** *n* espoleta *f*. **wishful** *adj* deseroso. **wishful thinking** ilusiones *f pl*.

wisp [wisp] *n (straw)* manojo *m*; *(hair)* mechón *m*; *(smoke)* voluta *f*; *(trace)* vestigio *m*. **wispy** *adj* fino.

wistful ['wistfəl] *adj* triste; ansioso; pensativo. **wistfully** *adv* tristemente; con ansia.

wit [wit] *n* inteligencia *f*; agudeza *f*; *(humour)* gracia *f*; *(person)* persona aguda *f*. **be at one's wits' end** no saber qué hacer.

witch [witʃ] *n* bruja *f*. **witchcraft** *n* brujería *f*. **witch-doctor** *n* hechicero *m*. **witch-hunt** *n* persecución *f*.

with [wið] *prep* con; junto con; en manos de; más; en compañía de; *(because of)* de.

***withdraw** [wið'droi] *v* quitar; apartar; retirar; sacar. **withdrawal** *n* retirada *f*; *(bank)* salida *f*; renuncia *f*; retractación *f*; abandono *m*. **withdrawn** *adj* ensimismado.

wither ['wiðə] *v (plant)* marchitar(se); *(weaken)* debilitar. **withered** *adj* marchito; seco. **withering** *adj (look)* fulminante; *(remark)* mordaz.

***withhold** [wið'hould] *v (refuse)* negar; *(hold back)* retener; *(hide)* ocultar.

within [wi'ðin] *adv* dentro; *(at home)* en casa. *prep* dentro de; en; al alcance de; *(less than)* a menos de.

without [wi'ðaut] *prep* sin: (*outside*) fuera de. *adv* fuera.

***withstand** [wið'stand] *v* resistir. aguantar: oponerse a.

witness ['witnis] *n* (*person*) testigo *m*; (*evidence*) prueba *f*; (*testimony*) testimonio *m*. *v* (*be present at*) asistir a; (*document*) firmar como testigo. **witness to** atestiguar.

witty ['witi] *adj* salado, gracioso. **witticism** *n* rasgo de ingenio *m*. agudeza *f*.

wizard ['wizəd] *n* mago *m*.

wobble ['wobl] *v* tambalearse. *n* tambaleo *m*. **wobbly** *adj* tambaleante.

woke [wouk] *V* **wake**.

wolf [wulf] *n* lobo *m*. **wolfhound** *n* perro lobo *m*. **wolf-whistle** *n* silbido de admiración *m*. *v* **wolf down** (*coll*) zamparse.

woman ['wumən] *n*, *pl* **women** mujer *f*. **Women's Lib** (*coll*) Movimiento de la Liberación de la Mujer *m*. **womanhood** *n* mujeres *f pl*; femenidad *f*. **womanly** *adj* femenino.

womb [wuːm] *n* matriz *f*, útero *m*.

won [wʌn] *V* **win**.

wonder ['wʌndə] *n* maravilla *f*; milagro *m*; admiración *f*. **no wonder** no es de extrañar. *v* preguntarse; pensar; asombrarse. **wonderful** *adj* maravilloso; (*astonishing*) asombroso.

woo [wuː] *v* cortejar; (*fig*) solicitar. **wooing** *nm*, *adj* galanteo.

wood [wud] *n* (*forest*) bosque *m*; (*material*) madera *f*; (*stick*) palo *m*; (*firewood*) leña *f*. **wooden** *adj* de madera; (*stiff*) estirado. **woody** *adj* arbolado; (*stem*) leñoso.

woodcock ['wudkok] *n* chocha *f*, becada *f*.

woodcut ['wudkʌt] *n* grabado en madera *m*. **woodcutter** *n* (*forester*) leñador *m*.

woodland ['wudlənd] *n* bosque *m*.

woodpecker ['wudpekə] *n* pájaro carpintero *m*.

wood-pigeon *n* paloma torcaz *f*.

woodshed ['wudʃed] *n* leñera *f*.

woodwind ['wudwind] *n* (*music*) instrumentos de viento de madera *m pl*.

woodwork ['wudwɔːk] *n* carpintería *f*.

woodworm ['wudwɔːm] *n* carcoma *f*.

wool [wul] *n* lana *f*. **woollen** *adj* de lana. **woolly** *adj* lanoso; de lana; (*ideas*) borroso.

word [wɔːd] *n* palabra *f*; (*gramm*) vocablo *m*. **in other words** en otras palabras; es

decir. *v* expresar; redactar. **wording** *n* redacción *f*; términos *m pl*. **wordy** *adj* verboso.

wore [wɔː] *V* **wear**.

work [wɔːk] *n* trabajo *m*, obra *f*. **men at work** obras *f pl*. **out of work** parado, -a. *v* trabajar. **work out** resolver. **workable** *adj* (*plan*) realizable.

worker ['wɔːkə] *n* trabajador, -a *m*, *f*; obrero, -a *m*, *f*.

work-force *n* mano de obra *f*.

working ['wɔːkiŋ] *n* trabajo *m*; funcionamiento *m*; manejo *m*; cultivo *m*. **working-class** *adj* de la clase obrera. **workings** *pl n* excavaciones *f pl*.

workman ['wɔːkmən] *n* trabajador *m*; obrero *m*. **workmanship** *n* (*skill*) artesanía *f*; ejecución *f*.

work permit *n* permiso de trabajo *m*.

workshop ['wɔːkʃop] *n* taller *m*.

work-to-rule *n* trabajo a ritmo lento *m*.

world [wɔːld] *n* mundo *m*. **world-wide** *adj* mundial. **worldly** *adj* mundano; material.

worm [wɔːm] *n* guzano *m*; (*earthworm*) lombriz *f*.

worn [wɔːn] *V* **wear**.

worry ['wʌri] *n* preocupación *f*. *v* preocupar(se); molestar. **don't worry!** ¡no te ocupes! **worried** *adj* preocupado.

worse [wɔːs] *adj*, *adv* peor. **get worse** or **worsen** empeorar. **to make matters worse** para empeorar las cosas. *n* lo peor.

worship ['wɔːʃip] *n* culto *m*; (*fig*) adoración *f*. *v* venerar; (*fig*) adorar.

worst [wɔːst] *adj*, *adv* peor. *n* el peor *m*. la peor *f*. lo peor. **at worst** en el peor de los casos.

worsted ['wustid] *n* estambre *m*.

worth [wɔːθ] *n* valor *m*; mérito *m*; valía *f*; fortuna *f*. **be worth** valer. **be worth it** merecer la pena. **worthless** *adj* sin valor; inútil. **worthwhile** *adj* que vale la pena; útil.

would [wud] *aux translated by conditional or imperfect tense*.

wound[1] [waund] *V* **wind**[2].

wound[2] [wuːnd] *n* herida *f*. *v* herir.

wove [wouv] *V* **weave**.

wrangle ['raŋgl] *n* disputa *f*. *v* discutir.

wrap [rap] *v* envolver; cubrir. **wrap up** abrigarse. *n* (*shawl*) chal *m*. **wrapper** *n* envoltura *f*; (*book*) sobrecubierta *f*. **wrapping** *n* envoltura *f*. **wrapping-paper** *n* papel de envolver *m*.

wreath [riːθ] *n* guirnalda *f*; (*funeral*) corona *f*. **wreathe** *v* enguirnaldar; (*wind*) enroscar.

wreck [rek] *n* (*ship*) naufragio *m*; (*train, car, plane*) restos *m pl*; (*accident*) accidente *m*; (*person*) ruina *f*. *v* (*ship*) hundir; (*building*) destruir; destrozar; (*hopes*) estropear. **wreckage** *n* restos *m pl*; (*building*) escombros *m pl*.

wren [ren] *n* reyezuelo *m*.

wrench [rentʃ] *n* (*tool*) llave inglesa *f*; (*pull*) tirón *m*; (*emotional*) dolor *m*. *v* arrancar; (*med*) torcer.

wrestle ['resl] *v* luchar con *or* contra. **wrestler** *n* luchador, -a *m, f*. **wrestling** *n* lucha *f*.

wretch [retʃ] *n* desgraciado, -a *m, f*; miserable *m, f*. **wretched** *adj* desgraciado; (*weather*) miserable; horrible.

wriggle ['rigl] *v* menear; agitar; (*fish*) colear. *n* meneo *m*; serpenteo *m*.

*****wring** [riŋ] *v* retorcer. **wringer** *n* escurridor *m*. **wringing wet** chorreando.

wrinkle ['riŋkl] *n* arruga *f*. *v* arrugar.

wrist [rist] *n* muñeca *f*.

writ [rit] *n* (*law*) orden *f*, mandato *m*. **issue a writ against someone** demandar a alguien en juicio.

*****write** [rait] *v* escribir; redactar. **writer** *n* escritor, -a *m, f*; autor, -a *m, f*. **writing** *n* el escribir *m*; (*handwriting*) escritura *f*; (*something written*) escrito *m*. **in writing** por escrito. **writing-pad** *n* bloc de papel de escribir *m*. **writing-paper** *n* papel de escribir *m*.

writhe [raið] *v* retorcerse; angustiarse.

wrong [roŋ] *adj* malo; mal; (*incorrect*) equivocado; impropio; falso; erróneo. **be wrong** tener la culpa; (*mistaken*) estar equivocado. *adv* mal. *n* mal *m*; error *m*; daño *m*; injusticia *f*. **wrongful** *adj* injusto; ilegal.

wrote [rout] *V* write.

wrought iron [ˌrɔːtˈaiən] *n* hierro forjado *m*.

wry [rai] *adj* torcido; doblado; (*smile*) forzado.

X

xenophobia *n* xenofobia *f*. **xenophobic** *adj* xenófobo.

Xerox ® *n* (*machine*) Xérox ® *m*, fotocopiadora *f*; (*copy*) xerografía *f*. *v* fotocopiar.

Xmas *V* Christmas.

X-ray *n* (*photo*) radiografía *f*. **X-rays** *pl n* rayos X *m pl*. *v* radiografiar.

xylophone *n* xilófono *m*.

Y

yacht *n* yate *m*. **yachting** *n* navegación a vela *f*.

yank *n* tirón *m*. *v* dar un tirón.

yap *n* ladrido *m*. *v* ladrar.

yard *n* patio *m*; (*site*) depósito *m*; (*repair*) taller *m*; (*rail*) estación *f*.

yarn *n* hilo *m*; (*tale*) cuento *m*.

yawn *v* bostezar; (*hole*) abrirse. *n* bostezo *m*.

year *n* año *m*. **yearbook** *n* anuario *m*. **yearly** *adj* anual.

yearn *v* anhelar, ansiar. **yearning** *n* anhelo *m*, ansia *f*.

yeast *n* levadura *f*; (*fig*) fermento *m*.

yell *n* grito *m*. *v* gritar.

yellow *nm, adj* amarillo. *v* volver amarillo.

yelp *n* gañido *m*. *v* gañir.

yes *nm, adv* sí.

yesterday *nm, adv* ayer. **the day before yesterday** anteayer.

yet *adv* todavía, aún; (*already*) ya. *conj* sin embargo, no obstante; (*but*) pero.

yew *n* tejo *m*.

yield *v* producir; entregar; dar; ceder; (*interest*) devengar. *n* producción *f*; (*crop*) cosecha *f*; (*interest*) rédito *m*.

yodel *n* canción tirolesa *f*. *v* cantar a la tirolesa.

yoga *n* yoga *m*.

yoghurt *n* yogur *m*.

yoke *n* (*animals*) yugo *m*; (*oxen*) yunta *f*; (*dress*) canesú *m*. *v* **yoke together** trabajar juntos.

yolk *n* yema *f*.

yonder *adv* allá, a lo lejos.

you *pron* (*subject: fam*) tú *sing*; (*subject: fam*) vosotros, vosotras *pl*; (*after prep*) ti; (*direct and indirect object*) te *sing*; (*direct and indirect object*) os *pl*; (*subject and after prep: polite*) usted, ustedes; (*direct object*) le, la; (*indirect object*) le; (*indirect object with direct object pron*) se *sing, pl*.

young *adj* joven. *pl n* (*people*) los jóvenes *m pl*; (*of an animal*) cría *f sing*. **youngster** *n* joven *m, f*.

your *adj* (*fam*) tu *sing*, vuestro *pl*; (*polite*) su, sus, de usted, de ustedes. **yours** *pron* (*fam*) el tuyo, la tuya, los tuyos, las tuyas, el vuestro, la vuestra, los vuestros, las vuestras; (*polite*) el suyo, la suya, el de usted, la de usted.

yourself *pron* (*fam*) tú mismo *m*, tú misma *f*; (*after prep*) ti *m, f*; (*polite*) usted mismo *m*, usted misma *f*. **by yourself** tú solo, usted solo. **yourselves** *pl pron* (*fam*) vosotros mismos *m pl*; vosotras mismas *f pl*; (*polite*) ustedes mismos *m pl*, ustedes mismas *f pl*.

youth *n* juventud *f*; (*boy*) joven *m*. **youth hostel** albergue de juventud *m*.

Yugogslavia [juːgə'slaɪviə] *n* Yugoslavia *f*.

Yugoslav *n, adj* yugoslavo, -a. **Yugoslavian** *n, adj* yugoslavo, -a.

Z

zany *adj* (*coll*) estrafalario.

zeal *n* celo *m*. **zealous** *adj* celoso.

zebra *n* cebra *f*. **zebra crossing** paso de peatones *m*.

zero *n* cero *m*. **zero hour** hora H *f*, momento decisivo *m*.

zest *n* ánimo *m*; brío *m*; sabor *m*. **zestful** *adj* animado; sabroso.

zigzag *n* zigzag *m*. *v* zigzaguear.

zinc *n* cinc *m*, zinc *m*.

zip *n* cremallera *f*. **zip code** (*US*) código postal *m*. *v* **zip up** subir la cremallera de.

zodiac *n* zodiaco *m*.

zone *n* zona *f*. *v* dividir en zonas.

zoo *n* zoo *m*, parque zoológico *m*.

zoology *n* zoología *f*. **zoological** *adj* zoológico. **zoologist** *n* zoólogo, -a *m, f*.

zoom *n* zumbido *m*. **zoom lens** zoom *m*. *v* zumbar. **zoom past** (*coll*) pasar zumbando.

Spanish—Inglés

A

a [a] *prep* to, at; on, in; by, by means of.
abacero [aβa'θero] *sm* grocer. **abacería** *sf* grocery.
abad [a'βað] *sm* abbot. **abadesa** *sf* abbess. **abadía** *sf* abbey.
abadejo [aβa'ðexo] *sm* codfish.
abajo [a'βaxo] *adv* underneath, below, down. ¡**abajo** ... ! *interj* down with ... ! **de abajo** *adj* lower.
abalanzar [aβalan'θar] *v* balance; hurl. **abalanzarse a** rush at.
abandonar [aβando'nar] *v* abandon; leave. **abandonarse** *v* give way; lose heart. **abandonado** *adj* abandoned; slovenly. **abandono** *sm* abandonment; neglect.
abanicar [aβani'kar] *v* fan. **abanico** *sm* fan.
abarcar [aβar'kar] *v* take in; comprise; undertake.
abarrotar [aβarro'tar] *v* stow; fill up; overload.
*****abastecer** [aβaste'θer] *v* supply, provide with. **abastecimiento** *sm* supply. **abasto** *sm* supply of provisions.
abatir [aβa'tir] *v* knock down; kill; humble. **abatido** *adj* dejected; depressed; dismayed. **abatimiento** *sm* depression; discouragement.
abdicar [aβði'kar] *v* abdicate. **abdicación** *sf* abdication.
abdomen [aβ'ðomen] *sm* abdomen.
abedul [aβe'ðul] *sm* birch-tree.
abeja [a'βexa] *sf* bee. **abeja machiega** honey bee.
aberración [aβerra'θjon] *sf* aberration.
abertura [aβer'tura] *sf* aperture, opening; gap.
abeto [a'βeto] *sm* fir.

abierto [a'βjerto] *adj* open; candid.
abigarrar [aβigar'rar] *v* variegate; fleck. **abigarrado** *adj* flecked; mottled; variegated.
abismo [a'βismo] *sm* abyss. **abismal** *adj* abysmal.
abjurar [aβxu'rar] *v* abjure, forswear. **abjuración** *sf* abjuration.
ablandar [aβlan'dar] *v* soften. **ablandarse** *v* mellow; relent.
*****abnegarse** [aβne'garse] *v* deny oneself; renounce.
abobado [aβo'βaðo] *adj* stupid, silly; stupefied.
abocarse [aβo'karse] *v* approach; meet by appointment.
abochornar [aβotʃor'nar] *v* overheat; (*fig*) shame. **abochornarse** *v* blush.
abofetear [aβofete'ar] *v* slap.
abogar [aβo'gar] *v* plead; advocate.
abolengo [aβo'lengo] *sm* ancestry; inheritance.
abolir [aβo'lir] *v* abolish.
abollar [aβo'ʎar] *v* dent. **abolladura** *sf* dent. **abollonar** *v* emboss.
abominar [aβomi'nar] *v* abominate. **abominable** *adj* abominable. **abominación** *sf* abomination.
abonar [aβo'nar] *v* guarantee; stand surety for; subscribe to; improve; (*agr*) manure. **abonado** *adj* safe; sure; trustworthy. *sm* subscriber; season-ticket holder. **abono** *sm* guarantee; subscription; fertilizer.
abordar [aβor'ðar] *v* approach; (*mar*) board ship; (*mar*) put into port.
aborigen [aβo'rixen] *s(m+f), adj* aborigine, aboriginal.
*****aborrecer** [aβorre'θer] *v* hate. **aborrecimiento** *sm* hatred.
abortar [aβor'tar] *v* abort. **aborto** *sm* (*med*) abortion; (*fig*) failure.

abotonar [aβotoˈnar] v button up.
abovedado [aβoβeˈðaðo] adj arched.
abovedar v arch.
abrasar [aβraˈsar] v burn; dry up.
abrasarse (de, en) v (de, en amor) burn with. **abrasivo** adj abrasive.
abrazar [aβraˈθar] v embrace, hug. **abrazo** sm embrace.
abrelatas [aβreˈlatas] sm invar tin-opener.
abreviar [aβreˈβjar] v abbreviate; speed up. **abreviatura** sf abbreviation.
abrigar [aβriˈgar] v shelter; wrap up. **abrigo** sm shelter; overcoat.
abril [aˈβril] sm April.
abrir [aˈβrir] v open; extend; unfold; reveal.
abrochar [aβroˈtʃar] v fasten; button.
abrogar [aβroˈgar] v repeal. **abrogación** sf repeal.
abrumar [aβruˈmar] v oppress; weigh down; overwhelm; annoy. **abrumarse** v become foggy. **abrumador** adj overwhelming; annoying.
abrupto [aˈβrupto] adj rugged; steep; abrupt.
absceso [aβsˈθeso] sm abscess.
ábside [ˈaβsiðe] sm apse.
absolución [aβsoluˈθjon] sf (rel) absolution; (jur) acquittal.
absoluto [aβsoˈluto] adj absolute; complete; (fig) overbearing. **en absoluto** absolutely.
*absolver [aβsolˈβer] v absolve; acquit.
absorber [aβsorˈβer] v absorb. **absorbente** adj absorbent. **absorción** sf absorption.
absorto adj absorbed; amazed.
abstemio [aβsˈtemjo] adj abstemious.
*abstenerse [aβsteˈnerse] v abstain. **abstinencia** sf abstinence.
abstracto [aβsˈtrakto] adj abstract. **abstracción** sf abstraction. ***abstraer** v abstract; refrain from; become thoughtful. **abstraer de** exclude; do without. **abstraído** adj retired; preoccupied; absent-minded.
absurdo [aβsurðo] adj absurd.
abuelo [aˈβuelo] sm grandfather. **abuela** sf grandmother.
abultar [aβulˈtar] v enlarge; increase; be bulky. **abultado** adj bulky; exaggerated. **abultamiento** sm bulkiness; exaggeration.
abundar [aβunˈdar] v abound. **abundancia** sf abundance. **abundante** adj abundant.
aburrir [aβuˈrrir] v bore; (fam) spend time/money; grow bored; grow weary.

aburrido adj boring; weary. **aburrimiento** sm boredom; wearisomeness.
abusar [aβuˈsar] v abuse; impose upon; go too far. **abuso** sm abuse; misuse.
abyecto [aˈβjecto] adj abject. **abyección** sf degradation; misery.
acá [aˈka] adv here; now. **acá y allá** here and there.
acabar [akaˈβar] v end; complete; kill; be destroyed. **acabar de** have just. **acabarse** v run out. **acabado** adj finished; perfect. sm finish.
academia [akaˈðemja] sf academy. **académico** adj academic.
*acaecer [akaeˈθer] v happen. **acaecimiento** sm happening.
acalorar [akaloˈrar] v make warm; (fig) excite. **acalorarse** v become heated. **acalorado** adj hot.
acallar [akaˈʎar] v quieten; silence; (fig) ease.
acampar [akamˈpar] v camp.
acantilado [akantiˈlaðo] adj steep; rocky. sm cliff.
acaparar [akapaˈrar] v monopolize; hoard. **acaparador** adj monopolistic; (fig) acquisitive.
acariciar [akariˈθjar] v caress, fondle, stroke; (fig) cherish. **acariciador** adj caressing.
acarrear [akarreˈar] v transport; carry; (fig) cause; bring about.
acaso [aˈkaso] sm chance. adv perhaps. **por si acaso** just in case.
acatar [akaˈtar] v respect; heed; observe. **acatable** adj worthy of respect. **acatador** adj respectful. **acatamiento** sm respect.
acaudalar [akauðaˈlar] v accumulate, hoard. **acaudalado** adj wealthy.
acaudillar [akauðiˈʎar] v lead, command. **acaudillamiento** sm leadership.
acceder [akθeˈðer] v accede, consent. **acceder a** agree to. **accesión** sf agreement.
acceso [akˈθeso] sm access; (med) fit.
accidente [akθiˈðente] sm accident. **accidental** adj accidental.
acción [akˈθjon] sf action. **acciones** s pl shares pl, stock sing. **accionar** v work, actuate. **accionista** s(m+f) shareholder.
acebo [aˈθeβo] sm holly.
acechar [aθeˈtʃar] v spy on; watch; ambush; stalk. **acecho** sm observation; lying in wait.

aceite [a'θeite] *sm* oil. **aceite de motor** engine oil. **aceitoso** *adj* oily. **aceituna** *sf* olive.

acelerar [aθele'rar] *v* accelerate; quicken. **acelerarse** *v* hurry. **acelerador** *sm* accelerator.

acendrar [aθen'drar] *v* (*metales*) refine; (*fig*) purify.

acentuar [aθen'twar] *v* accentuate; stress. **acento** *sm* accent; stress.

aceptar [aθep'tar] *v* accept. **aceptable** *adj* acceptable, passable. **aceptación** *sf* acceptance.

acequia [a'θekja] *sf* irrigation ditch; drain.

acera [a'θera] *sf* pavement.

acerbo [a'θerβo] *adj* harsh; sharp; sour; (*fig*) severe.

acerar [aθe'rar] *v* harden with steel; strengthen; (*fig*) fortify.

acerca de [a'θerka ðe] *adv* about.

acercar [aθer'kar] *v* approach; bring near. **acercarse** *v* approach, draw near. **acercamiento** *sm* approach; approximation; reconciliation.

acero [a'θero] *sm* steel.

acérrimo [a'θerrimo] *adj* very strong; extremely tenacious; stalwart.

*****acertar** [aθer'tar] *v* (*el blanco*) hit; guess; be right; find; succeed. **acertado** *adj* correct; apt.

acertijo [aθer'tixo] *sm* riddle.

aciago [a'θjago] *adj* unlucky; ill-fated.

acicalar [aθika'lar] *v* polish; bedeck; groom; (*fam*) spruce oneself up. **acicalado** *adj* spruce; dapper; polished. **acicaladura** *sf also* **acicalamiento** *sm* polishing; grooming; dressing up.

ácido ['aθiðo] *sm, adj* acid.

acierto [a'θjerto] *sm* success; good idea; skill.

aclamar [akla'mar] *v* acclaim; applaud. **aclamación** *sf* acclamation.

aclarar [akla'rar] *v* explain, clarify; (*color*) lighten; thin out; (*dudas*) remove; (*la ropa*) rinse. **aclaración** *sf* explanation. **aclarado** *sm* rinse.

aclimatizar [aklimati'θar] *v* acclimatize.

acné [ak'ne] *sm* acne.

acobardar [akoβar'ðar] *v* frighten; discourage.

acoger [ako'xer] *v* welcome; receive; shelter; accept. **acogerse** *v* take refuge. **acogedor** *adj* (*persona*) welcoming; (*ambiente*) friendly. **acogida** *sf* welcome.

acolchar [akol'tʃar] *v* pad; upholster; (*fig*) muffle. **acolchado** *adj* padded.

acólito [a'kolito] *sm* acolyte.

acometer [akome'ter] *v* attack; undertake; fill; occur to. **acometida** *sf* attack.

acomodar [akomo'ðar] *v* arrange; settle; accommodate; adjust; adapt; prepare; (*fig*) reconcile. **acomodación** *sf* arrangement; preparation. **acomodamente** *adv* conveniently; easily. **acomodadizo** *adj* accommodating; adaptable. **acomodado** *adj* convenient; prepared; well-to-do. **acomodador** *sm* usher. **acomodamiento** *sm* convenience; arrangement; preparation.

acompañar [akompa'nar] *v* accompany; escort. **acompañamiento** *sm* accompaniment; escort; (*cortejo*) funeral procession.

acondicionar [akondiθjo'nar] *v* set up; fix; prepare; improve. **acondicionarse** *v* condition oneself. **acondicionado** *adj* equipped. **aire acondicionado** air-conditioning.

acongojar [akongo'xar] *v* sadden; distress.

aconsejar [akonse'xar] *v* advise. **aconsejarse** *v* seek advice.

*****acontecer** [akonte'θer] *v* happen. **acontecimiento** *sm* event.

acopiar [ako'pjar] *v* store; collect. **acopiamiento** *sm* stock.

acoplar [ako'plar] *v* fit; connect; couple; (*animales*) mate. **acoplarse** *v* become friends again. **acoplado** *adj* well-matched. **acoplamiento** *sm* connection; coordination.

acorazar [akora'θar] *v* armour. **acorazado** *adj* armoured; (*fig*) hardened.

*****acordar** [akor'ðar] *v* agree; decide; remind. **acordarse** *v* remember; agree. **acordado** *adj* agreed to; wise.

acordeón [akorðe'on] *sm* accordion.

acordonar [akorðo'nar] *v* cordon off; (*los zapatos*) lace. **acordonado** *adj* cordoned off; ribbed.

acorralar [akorra'lar] *v* enclose; corner; round up.

acortar [akor'tar] *v* shorten; reduce. **acortarse** *v* become shorter; (*intimidarse*) be shy. **acortamiento** *sm* shortening; reduction.

acosar [ako'sar] *v* hound; pursue; harass; pester. **acoso** *sm* pursuit.

*acostar [akos'tar] *v* lay down; put to bed. **acostarse** *v* lie down; go to bed.

acostumbrar [akostum'brar] *v* accustom; be in the habit of. **acostumbrarse a** *v* become used to. **acostumbrado** *adj* usual.

acotar [ako'tar] *v* (*terreno*) demarcate; enclose; delimit; outline; accept. **acotado** *adj* enclosed. **acotamiento** *sm* demarcation; boundary mark; outline.

acre[1] ['akre] *adj* acrid; bitter.

acre[2] ['akre] *sm* acre.

*acrecentar [akreθen'tar] *v* increase. **acrecentamiento** *sm* increase; growth.

acreditar [akreði'tar] *v* accredit; prove; vouch for; authorize; (*com*) credit. **acreditado** *adj* reputable.

acreedor [akree'ðor] *s(m+f)* creditor. *adj* worthy.

acribillar [akriβi'ʎar] *v* riddle with holes.

acróbata [a'kroβata] *s(m+f)* acrobat.

acta ['akta] *sf* minutes of a meeting; official document.

actitud [akti'tud] *sf* posture, attitude.

activar [akti'βar] *v* speed up; stimulate; (*quím*) activate. **actividad** *sf* activity.

activo [ak'tiβo] *adj* active. *sm* (*com*) assets *pl*.

acto ['akto] *n* act, deed; ceremony; (*teatro*) act. **salón de actos** *sm* assembly hall.

actor *sm* actor. **actriz** *sf* actress. **actual** *adj* present; topical; of this month. **actualmente** *adv* at present; nowadays.

actuar [ak'twar] *v* act; perform; behave. **actuación** *sf* action; performance; conduct. **actuario** *sm* (*jur*) clerk of the court.

acuarela [akwa'rela] *sf* watercolour.

acuario [a'kwario] *sm* aquarium.

acuático [a'kwatiko] *adj* aquatic.

acuciar [aku'θjar] *v* urge; pester; (*anhelar*) long for. **acucioso** *adj* urgent; diligent; desirous.

acuclillarse [akukli'ʎarse] *v* crouch, squat.

acuchillar [akutʃi'ʎar] *v* knife, stab, hack. **acuchillado** *adj* knifed; (*fig*) experienced.

acudir [aku'ðir] *v* come; go; (*a una cita*) keep; answer; attend; help; (*al médico*) consult.

acueducto [akwe'ðukto] *sm* aqueduct.

acuerdo [a'kwerðo] *sm* agreement. **¡de acuerdo!** O.K.! **ponerse de acuerdo** come to an agreement.

acumular [akumu'lar] *v* accumulate; pile; store. **acumulación** *sf* accumulation.

acuñar [aku'ɲar] *v* (*monedas*) mint; (*poner cuñas*) wedge.

acuoso [aku'oso] *adj* watery. **acuosidad** *sf* wateriness.

acurrucarse [akurru'karse] *v* curl up.

acusar [aku'sar] *v* (*jur*) accuse; charge; blame; denounce; reveal; (*com*) acknowledge. **acusación** *sf* accusation. **acusado** *sm* (*jur*) defendant.

acústico [a'kustiko] *adj* acoustic. **acústica** *sf* acoustics.

achacar [atʃa'kar] *v* attribute.

achatar [atʃa'tar] *v* flatten.

achicar [atʃi'kar] *v* reduce; (*mar*) bale; (*fig*) humiliate. **achicado** *adj* childish.

achicoria [atʃi'korja] *sf* chicory.

achicharrar [atʃitʃar'rar] *v* burn; (*molestar*) annoy. **achicharradero** *sm* furnace.

achispado [atʃis'paðo] *adj* tipsy. **achispar** *v* make tipsy.

adalid [aða'lið] *sm* leader.

adaptar [aðap'tar] *v* adapt; adjust. **adaptabilidad** *sf* adaptability. **adaptable** *adj* adaptable. **adaptación** *sf* adaptation; (*tecn*) fitting.

adecuado [aðe'kwaðo] *adj* adequate; suitable.

adefesio [aðe'fesjo] (*fam*) *sm* nonsense; (*traje*) ridiculous garment; (*persona*) ridiculously dressed person.

adelantar [aðelan'tar] *v* advance; (*reloj*) put forward; speed up; gain; (*auto*) overtake. **prohibido adelantar** no overtaking. **adelantarse** *v* go forward. **adelantado** *adj* advanced. **adelantamiento** *sm* also **adelanto** advance. **adelante** *adv* ahead, forward. **¡adelante!** come in! **de hoy en adelante** in future.

adelgazar [aðelga'θar] *v* make thin; slim. **adelgazador** *adj* slimming. **adelgazamiento** *sm* slimming. **régimen de adelgazamiento** diet.

ademán [aðe'man] *sm* expression; gesture. **ademanes** *s pl* manners.

además [aðe'mas] *adv* besides, furthermore. **además de** as well as.

adentro [a'ðentro] *adv* within, inside. **¡adentro!** come in! **mar adentro** out to sea. **tierra adentro** inland.

adepto [a'ðepto] *s(m+f)* adept; supporter.

adestrar *V* **adiestrar**.

aderezar [aðere'θar] *v* adorn; (*culin*) prepare; guide. **aderezo** *sm* adornment; cooking; seasoning; (*de ensalada*) dressing.

adeudar [aðeu'ðar] *v* owe; (*com*) charge; run into debt. **adeudado** *adj* owing; (*persona*) in debt. **adeudo** *sm* (*deuda*) debt; (*com*) charge.

*adherir [aðe'rir] *v* adhere, stick. **adherirse** adhere to. **adherencia** *sf* (*acción de pegar*) adherence. **adhesión** *sf* adhesion; (*apoyo*) support. **adhesivo** *sm*, *adj* adhesive.

adición [aði'θyon] *sf* addition. **adicional** *adj* additional. **adicionar** *v* add.

adicto [a'ðikto] *adj* devoted. *s*(*m*+*f*) supporter; addict.

adiestrar [aðjes'trar] *v* train, teach. **adiestrador, -a** *sm*, *sf* trainer. **adiestramiento** *sm* training.

adinerado [aðine'raðo] *adj* wealthy. **adinerado, -a** *sm*, *sf* rich person. **adinerarse** *v* (*fam*) make one's fortune.

adiós [a'ðjos] *interj*, *sm* goodbye.

adivinar [aðiβi'nar] *v* foretell; guess; (*el pensamiento*) read. **adivinable** *adj* foreseeable. **adivinación** *sf also* **adivinamiento** *sm* divination; guessing. **adivinador, -a** *sm*, *sf* fortune-teller.

adjetivo [aðxe'tiβo] *sm* adjective.

adjudicar [aðxuði'kar] *v* award; adjudicate.

adjuntar [aðxun'tar] *v* attach; enclose; give.

adjunto [að'xunto] *adj* attached; enclosed. *sm* assistant.

administrar [aðminis'trar] *v* administer, control; (*fam*) hand out. **administración** *sf* administration. **administrativo** *adj* administrative.

admirar [aðmi'rar] *v* admire. **admirarse** *v* surprise, astonish. **admirable** *adj* admirable. **admiración** *sf* admiration.

admirador [aðmiraðor], **-a** *sm*, *sf* admirer. *adj* admiring.

admitir [aðmi'tir] *v* admit; accept; allow; acknowledge. **admisible** *adj* admissible. acceptable. **admisión** *sf* admission; acceptance.

adobar [aðo'βar] *v* pickle; season; cook.

*adolecer [aðole'θer] *v* fall ill. **adolecer de** suffer from.

adolescencia [aðoles'θenθja] *sf* adolescence. **adolescente** *s*(*m*+*f*), *adj* adolescent.

adonde ['aðonde] *adv* where. **¿adónde?** where?

adoptar [aðop'tar] *v* adopt; assume. **adopción** *sf* adoption. **adoptivo** *adj* adoptive.

adoquín [aðo'kin] *sm* paving-stone; (*fam*) dunce. **adoquinar** *v* pave.

adorar [aðo'rar] *v* adore; worship; pray. **adorable** *adj* adorable. **adoración** *sf* adoration; worship.

*adormecer [aðorme'θer] *v* make sleepy. **adormecerse** fall asleep. **adormecerse en** give oneself up to.

adormidera [aðormi'ðera] *sf* poppy.

adornar [aðor'nar] *v* adorn, decorate; (*trajes*) trim; (*coc*) garnish; (*fig*) embellish. **adornarse** *v* dress up. **adorno** *sm* decoration; trimming; garnish.

*adquirir [aðki'rir] *v* acquire, obtain. **adquisición** *sf* acquisition; (*compra*) purchase. **adquisitivo** *adj* acquisitive.

adrede [að'rede] *adv* on purpose.

adscribir [aðskri'βir] *v* attribute, ascribe; assign. **adscripción** *sf* attribution; assignment. **adscripto** *adj* attributed; assigned.

aduana [a'ðwana] *sf* customs *pl*. **derechos de aduana** *sm pl* customs duty *sing*. **aduanero** *sm* customs officer.

*aducir [aðu'θir] *v* (*razones*) allege; (*un texto*) quote; (*pruebas*) offer as proof.

adueñarse [aðwe'narse] *v* appropriate.

adular [aðu'lar] *v* flatter. **adulación** *sf* flattery.

adulterar [aðulte'rar] *v* adulterate; commit adultery. **adulterio** *sm* adultery. **adúltero, -a** *sm*, *sf* adulterer, adulteress.

adulto [a'ðulto], **-a** *s*, *adj* adult.

adusto [a'ðusto] *adj* very hot; (*fig*) harsh.

advenedizo [aðβene'ðiθo], **-a** *s*, *adj* upstart.

advenimiento [aðβeni'mjento] *sm* advent; coming.

adverbio [að'βerβjo] *sm* adverb.

adversario [aðβer'sarjo] *sm* adversary. **adversidad** *sf* adversity. **adverso** *adj* adverse; opposing.

*advertir [aðβer'tir] *v* warn; recommend; (*señalar*) point out; tell; (*comprender*) realize. **advertido** *adj* informed; experienced. **advertencia** *sf also* **advertimiento** *sm* warning.

adyacente [aðja'θente] *adj* adjacent.

aéreo [a'ereo] *adj* aerial.

aerodinámica [aeroði'namika] *sf* aerodynamics. **aerodinámico** *adj* aerodynamic.

aeronáutica [aero'nautika] *sf* aeronautics. **aeronáutico** *adj* aeronautical.

aeroplano [aero'plano] *sm* aeroplane.

aeropuerto [aero'pwerto] *sm* airport.
aerosol [aero'sol] *sm* aerosol.
afable [a'faβle] *adj* pleasant; genial.
afabilidad *sf* affability.
afamado [afa'maðo] *adj* famous.
afán [a'fan] *sm* (*trabajo penoso*) toil; (*deseo*) desire; (*entusiasmo*) zeal; (*preocupación*) anxiety. **afanador** *adj* enthusiastic. **afanar** *v* work hard; (*fig: robar*) steal. **afanarse** *v* exert oneself. **afanoso** *adj* laborious; hectic.
afección [afek'θjon] *sf* (*cariño*) affection; (*med*) complaint. **afeccionarse** *v* grow fond.
afectar [afek'tar] *v* affect; pretend; adopt; (*atañer*) concern; (*dañar*) damage. **afectado** *adj* spoiled; unnatural; upset.
afecto [a'fekto] *adj* dear. **afecto a** fond of. *sm* affection.
afeitar [afei'tar] *v* shave. **afeitarse** *v* shave; make up one's face. **afeite** *sm* make-up, cosmetics *pl*.
afeminado [afemi'naðo] *adj* effeminate. *sm* effeminate person.
*aferrar [afer'rar] *v* seize; (*mar*) moor. **aferrarse** *v* cling.
afianzar [afjan'θar] *v* reinforce; establish; restore; guarantee; seize; support. **afianzarse** *v* steady oneself; become strong. **afianzamiento** *sm* surety; guarantee; establishment.
afición [afi'θjon] *sf* inclination; fondness; (*interés*) hobby. **la afición** *sf* the fans *pl*. **aficionado, -a** *sm*, *sf* fan. *adj* amateur; keen.
afilar [afi'lar] *v* sharpen; grind. **afilado** *adj* sharp. **afilador** *sm* (*persona*) knife-grinder; (*correa*) strop. **afilamiento** *sm* (*la nariz*) pointedness; (*los dedos*) slenderness.
afiliar [afi'ljar] *v* affiliate. **afiliación** *sf* affiliation.
afín [a'fin] *adj* adjacent; similar; related. **afinidad** *sf* similarity, affinity.
afinar [afi'nar] *v* polish; perfect; (*música*) tune. **afinarse** *v* become slimmer. **afinadura** *sf also* **afinamiento** *sm* tuning; (*fig*) refinement.
afirmar [afir'mar] *v* affirm; strengthen. **afirmarse** *v* steady oneself. **afirmación** *sf* statement; strengthening. **afirmativo** *adj* affirmative.
aflicción [aflik'θjon] *sf* affliction, grief. **afligido** *adj* distressed; (*por una muerte*) bereaved. **afligir** *v* grieve; distress; afflict.

aflojar [aflo'xar] *v* loosen, slacken; relax; (*fiebre*) abate; (*fam*) fork out, cough up. **aflojamiento** *sm* loosening, slackening; abatement; relaxation.
afluencia [aflu'enθja] *sf* crowd; (*tropel*) rush; influx; abundance.
*afluir [aflu'ir] *v* flow.
afónico [afo'niko] *adj* hoarse, voiceless. **afonía** *sf* loss of voice.
*aforar [afo'rar] *v* gauge, measure; appraise. **aforo** *sm* measurement; appraisal.
aforrar [afor'rar] *v* (*ropa, etc.*) line. **aforrarse** *v* wrap oneself up.
afortunado [afortu'naðo] *adj* fortunate; happy.
afrenta [a'frenta] *sf* insult; disgrace. **afrentar** *v* insult. **afrentarse** *v* be ashamed. **afrentador** *adj also* **afrentoso** insulting; offensive.
África ['afrika] *sf* Africa. **africano, -a** *s*, *adj* African.
afrontar [afron'tar] *v* confront; bring face to face. **afrontamiento** *sm* confrontation.
afuera [a'fwera] *adv* out, outside. ¡**afuera**! get out! **afueras** *s pl* suburbs *pl*.
agachar [aga'tʃar] *v* lower, bend. **agacharse** *v* bend over; crouch; (*para evitar algo*) duck. **agachada** *sf* (*fam*) trick.
agalla [a'gaʎa] *sf* gill; (*fam*) pluck. **agallas** *s pl* tonsils *pl*.
agarrar [agar'rar] *v* seize, clutch; (*comprender*) grasp; get; take; win; (*fam*) stick. **agarro** *sm* hold, grasp. **agarradero** *sm* handle.
agarrotar [agarro'tar] *v* tighten; strangle. **agarrotarse** *v* (*motor*) seize up; (*músculo*) go numb. **agarrotado** *adj* bound; stiff; seized up.
agasajar [agasa'xar] *v* welcome warmly; entertain. **agasajo** *sm* gift; welcome. **agasajos** *sm pl* hospitality *sing*.
agazapar [agaθa'par] *v* (*fam*) nab, catch. **agazaparse** *v* crouch; duck.
agencia [a'xenθja] *sf* agency; office. **agencia de prensa** news agency. **agencia de turismo** *or* **viajes** travel agency. **agenciar** *v* get; (*fam*) wangle. **agente** *sm* agent; policeman. **agente de bolsa** stockbroker. **agente inmobiliario** estate agent.
agenda [a'xenda] *sf* diary.
ágil ['axil] *adj* agile. **agilidad** *sf* agility.
agitar [axi'tar] *v* wave; shake; upset; stir up. **agitarse** *v* sway; fidget. **agitación** *sf* waving; shaking; movement; excitement.

agitado *adj* agitated; rough. **agitador, -a** *sm, sf* agitator.

aglomerar [aglome'rar] *v* form a crowd; amass. **aglomeración** *sf* mass. **aglomeración de tráfico** traffic jam.

agobiar [ago'βjar] *v* weigh down; overwhelm; humiliate; depress. **agobiado** *v* bent down; overwhelmed; exhausted. **agobio** *sm* burden.

agolparse [agol'parse] *v* crowd together; amass. **agolpamiento** *sm* crowd; (*cosas*) pile.

agonía [ago'nia] *sf* (*muerte*) death; desire; agony. **agonizar** *v* be dying; suffer; annoy.

*agorar [ago'rar] *v* predict. **agorero, -a** *sm, sf* fortune-teller.

agosto [a'gosto] *sm* August.

agotar [ago'tar] *v* drain; exhaust. **agotador** *adj* exhausting. **agotamiento** *sm* exhaustion.

agraciar [agra'θjar] *v* adorn; award; pardon. **agraciado** *adj* pretty; graceful.

agradar [agra'ðar] *v* please. **agradable** *adj* pleasant.

*agradecer [agraðe'θer] *v* thank; be grateful for; be welcome. **agradecido** *adj* grateful. **¡muy agradecido!** much obliged! **agradecimiento** *sm* gratitude.

agrado [agra'ðo] *sm* pleasure; liking.

agrandar [agran'ðar] *v* make larger; exaggerate. **agrandamiento** *sm* enlargement.

agravar [agra'βar] *v* aggravate; worsen. **agravación** *sf* also **agravamiento** *sm* aggravation. **agravante** *adj* aggravating.

agraviar [agra'βjar] *v* offend; insult; wrong; take offence. **agravio** *sm* insult; affront; wrong.

*agredir [agre'ðir] *v* assault.

agregado [agre'gaðo] *sm* aggregate; assistant; attaché; addition. **agregar** join; incorporate. **agregarse** *v* be added; be incorporated.

agricultura [agrikul'tura] *sf* agriculture. **agrícola** *adj* agricultural.

agrietar [agrje'tar] *v* crack; chap.

agrio ['agrjo] *adj* sour; (*carácter*) bitter. *sm* (*sabor*) sourness.

agrupar [agru'par] *v* group; gather together. **agruparse** *v* come together.

agua [a'gwa] *sf* water. **agua abajo/arriba** down-/upstream. **agua dulce** fresh water. **entre dos aguas** sitting on the fence. **hacer agua** leak. **irse al agua** fall through.

aguacate [agwa'kate] *sm* avocado pear.

aguacero [agwa'θero] *sm* shower, downpour.

aguantar [agwan'tar] *v* tolerate, bear; (*sostener*) support; (*esperar*) wait, await; (*durar*) last. **aguante** *sm* patience; endurance.

aguar [a'gwar] *v* dilute; spoil. **aguarse** be ruined. **aguado** *adj* watered down.

aguardar [agwar'ðar] *v* wait for.

aguardiente [agwar'ðjente] *sm* liquor.

aguarrás [agwar'ras] *sm* turpentine.

aguazal [agwa'θal] *sm* mire.

agudeza [agu'deθa] *sf* (*de los sentidos*) sharpness; (*del dolor*) acuteness; (*ingenio*) wit. **agudizar** *v* sharpen; worsen. **agudo** *adj* sharp; acute; witty.

agüero [a'gwero] *sm* omen. **de buen agüero** lucky.

aguijar [agi'xar] *v* goad; hurry. **aguijón** *sm* (*de un insecto*) sting; stimulus. **aguijonada** *sf* sting; prick. **aguijonear** *v* goad; spur on.

águila ['agila] *sf* eagle. **águila ratonera** buzzard.

aguinaldo [agi'naldo] *sm* Christmas present.

aguja [a'guxa] *sf* needle; (*reloj*) hand; (*arq*) spire. **agujas** *s pl* points *pl*.

agujero [agu'xero] *sm* hole; (*alfiletero*) pincushion.

agujetas [agu'xetas] *sf pl* stiffness *sing*. **lleno de agujetas** stiff all over.

aguzar [agu'θar] *v* sharpen; (*estimular*) encourage; (*el apetito*) whet. **aguzado** *adj* sharp; sharpened. **aguzadar** *adj* sharpening.

ahí [a'i] *adv* there. **de ahí** thus, so. **por ahí** that way; thereabouts. **¡ahí es nada!** fancy that!

ahijada [ai'xaða] *sf* goddaughter; protégée. **ahijado** *sm* godson; protégé.

ahincar [ain'kar] *v* urge. **ahincarse** *v* hurry. **ahincadamente** *adv* tenaciously. **ahincado** *adj* insistent; eager. **ahínco** *sm* effort.

ahogar [ao'gar] *v* drown; flood; stifle; overwhelm. **ahogarse** *v* drown, be drowned. **ahogadero** *sm* Turkish bath. **ahogado** *adj* drowned; (*por el gas*) asphyxiated; strangled; (*grito*) muffled. **ahogador** *adj* suffocating. **ahogo** *sm* breathlessness; (*angustia*) distress.

ahora [a'ora] *adv* now. *conj* now, now then. **ahora bien** come now. **ahora mismo** right away.

ahorcar [aor'kar] v hang. **ahorcarse** v hang oneself. **ahorcadura** sf hanging.

ahorrar [aor'rar] v save; free; avoid. **ahorrador** adj thrifty. **ahorro** sm saving; thrift.

ahuecar [awe'kar] v hollow. **¡ahueca!** (fam) scram!

ahumar [au'mar] v (culin) smoke; (llenar de humo) fill with smoke. **ahumarse** v taste smoky; (fam: emborracharse) become tipsy. **ahumado** adj smoky; smoked; (fam) tipsy.

ahuyentar [aujen'tar] v frighten off; keep at bay; (fig) dismiss. **ahuyentarse** v flee.

airado [ai'raðo] adj vexed; immoral.

aire ['aire] sm air; (parecido) likeness; (aspecto) appearance; (porte) bearing; (música) time; (auto: estrangulador) choke. **hace aire** it's windy. **aire acondicionado** air conditioning. **aireación** sf ventilation. **airear** v ventilate. **airoso** adj ventilated; windy; (fig) graceful.

aislar [ai'slar] v isolate; (elec) insulate. **aislado** adj alone; remote; insulated. **aislador** adj insulating. **cinta aisladora** sf insulating tape. **aislamiento** sm isolation; insulation.

ajar [a'xar] v crumple; wrinkle; fade; (fig) age.

ajedrez [axe'ðreθ] sm chess.

ajeno [a'xeno] adj of other people; alien; free; detached; irrelevant.

ajetreo [axe'treo] sm rush; activity; bustle; exhaustion. **ajetreado** adj busy. **ajetrearse** v be busy; rush; exhaust oneself.

ajo ['axo] sm garlic. **ajo cebollino** chive. **ajo porro** leek. **diente de ajo** clove of garlic. **soltar ajos** swear.

ajuar [a'xwar] sm (de novia) trousseau; (de casa) furnishings pl.

ajustar [axus'tar] v adjust; arrange; tighten. **ajuste** sm adjustment; fitting.

ajusticiar [axusti'θjar] v execute.

al [al] contraction of **a el**.

ala ['ala] sf wing; hat brim.

alabar [ala'βar] v praise. **alabarse** v (jactarse) boast. **alabanza** sf praise.

alabastro [ala'βastro] sm alabaster.

alacena [ala'θena] sf larder; cupboard.

alacrán [ala'kran] sm scorpion.

alambicar [alambi'kar] v distil; complicate; (precio) minimize. **alambicado** adj elaborate; (estilo) subtle; affected; minimized. **alambique** sm still. **pasar algo por**

el alambique examine something very carefully.

alambre [a'lambre] sm wire. **alambrada** sf (de la guerra) barbed wire; (reja) wire netting.

alameda [ala'meða] sf (avenida) tree-lined walk; (de álamos) poplar grove.

álamo ['alamo] sm poplar. **álamo temblón** aspen.

alano [a'lano] sm mastiff.

alarde [a'larðe] sm parade; display. **alardear** v boast. **alardeo** sm boasting.

alargar [alar'gar] v lengthen, increase, enlarge; (posponer) defer; (dar) reach, hand; (la mano) stretch. **alargarse** v get longer. **alargado** adj elongated. **alargamiento** sm lengthening; extension.

alarido [ala'riðo] sm yell, shriek.

alarmar [alar'mar] v alarm; alert. **alarmarse** v be frightened. **alarma** sf alarm.

alba ['alβa] sf dawn.

albañil [alβa'ɲil] sm bricklayer.

albaricoque [alβari'koke] sm apricot.

albatros [alβa'tros] sm albatross.

albedrío [alβe'ðrio] sm will; (capricho) whim; custom. **libre albedrío** free will.

albergar [alβer'gar] v shelter; accommodate; (fig) cherish. **albergue** sm lodgings pl; (refugio) shelter; (posada) hostel.

albóndiga [al'βonðiga] sf rissole.

albor [al'βor] sm dawn; (blancura) whiteness.

albornoz [alβor'noθ] sm bathrobe.

alborotar [alβoro'tar] v make a noise; disturb. **alborotarse** v (perturbarse) become upset; get excited; (una muchedumbre) riot. **alborotado** adj excited; (fig) eventful. **alborotador** adj noisy; rebellious. **alboroto** sm disturbance, uproar.

alborozar [alβoro'θar] v gladden; produce laughter. **alborozarse** v rejoice. **alborozado** adj overjoyed.

álbum ['alβum] sm album.

alcachofa [alka'tʃofa] sf artichoke.

alcahuete [alka'wete] sm pimp; (chismoso) gossip. **alcahueta** sf procuress; gossip.

alcalde [al'kalðe] sm mayor. **alcaldesa** sf mayoress. **alcaldía** sf mayorship; (oficina) mayor's office.

alcance [al'kanθe] sm reach; (sonido, arma de fuego, etc.) range; scope; importance. **al alcance** within reach. **dar alcance a** catch up with. **alcanzar** v reach; catch up; understand; hit; affect; succeed; be enough; (*durar*) last.

alcantarilla [alkanta'riʎa] *sf* sewer; drain.

alcázar [al'kaθar] *sm* palace; fortress; (*mar*) quarterdeck.

alcoba [al'koβa] *sf* bedroom.

alcohol [alko'ol] *sm* alcohol. **alcohólico, -a** *s, adj* alcoholic.

alcornoque [alkor'noke] *sm* cork tree; (*fig*) nitwit.

aldaba [al'ðaβa] *sf* door knocker; (*pestillo*) latch, bolt. **tener buenas aldabas** (*fam*) have influential friends.

aldea [al'ðea] *sf* village.

aleación [alea'θjon] *sf* alloy.

alegar [ale'gar] *v* allege; state; emphasize; quote; (*jur*) plead, claim. **alegato** *sm* declaration; plea.

alegoría [alego'ria] *sf* allegory. **alegórico** *adj* allegorical.

alegrar [ale'grar] *v* gladden; make merry; be pleasing to; excite. **alegrarse** *v* be happy; (*fam*) become tipsy. **alegre** *adj* happy; bright; good; (*fam*) tipsy; (*atrevido*) daring. **alegría** *sf* joy; happiness. **¡qué alegría!** great!

alejar [ale'xar] *v* move away; keep away; avert. **alejarse** *v* go away. **alejado** *adj* far away; aloof. **alejamiento** *sm* removal; absence.

Alemania [ale'manja] *sf* Germany. **alemán, -ana** *sm, sf* German (person). **alemán** *sm* (*idioma*) German (language).

***alentar** [alen'tar] *v* breathe; (*fig*) glow; (*animar*) encourage. **alentado** *adj* encouraged; (*orgulloso*) proud; (*valiente*) brave. **alentador** *adj* encouraging.

alerce [a'lerθe] *sm* larch.

alergia [a'lerxja] *sf* allergy. **alérgico** *adj* allergic.

alero [a'lero] *sm* eaves *pl*. **estar en el alero** hang in the balance.

alerta [a'lerta] *sm* alert. *adv* on the alert. **¡alerta!** look out! **alertar** *v* alert, warn. **alerto** *adj* alert.

aleta [a'leta] *sf* (*peces*) fin; (*foca*) flipper.

aleve [a'leβe] *adj also* **alevoso** treacherous. **alevosía** *sf* treachery. **alevoso, -a** *sm, sf* traitor.

alfabeto [alfa'βeto] *sm* alphabet. **alfabético** *adj* alphabetical. **por orden alfabético** in alphabetical order. **alfabetizado** *adj* literate.

alfarero [alfa'rero] *sm* potter. **alfarería** *sf* pottery (art and workshop).

alférez [al'fereθ] *sm* (*mil*) second lieutenant.

alfil [al'fil] *sm* (*ajedrez*) bishop.

alfiler [alfi'ler] *sm* pin; brooch. **alfiler de la ropa** clothes-peg. **alfilerar** *v* pin. **alfilerazo** *sm* pinprick.

alfombra [al'fombra] *sf* carpet; rug. **alfombrar** *v* carpet.

alforja [al'forxa] *sf* rucksack.

alga ['alga] *sf* seaweed.

algarabía [algara'βia] *sf* Arabic; (*fig*) gibberish; (*ruido*) noise, row.

algazara [alga'θara] *sf* hubbub, uproar.

álgebra ['alxebra] *sf* algebra. **algebráico** *adj also* **algébrico** algebraic.

álgido [al'xiðo] *adj* icy cold; (*fig*) decisive.

algo ['algo] *pron* something; anything. *adv* rather, quite. *sm* something; (*comida*) snack.

algodón [algo'ðon] *sm* cotton. **algodón hidrófilo** cotton wool.

alguacil [algwa'θil] *sm* sheriff; city governor.

alguien ['algjen] *pron* someone, somebody; (*interrog*) anybody.

algún [al'gun] *adj* some, any. **algún tanto** a little.

alguno [al'guno] *adj* some, any. *pron* one, some; someone. **algunos** *ms pl* some, a few.

alhaja [al'axa] *sf* jewel; treasure.

alhelí [ale'li] *sm, pl* **-líes** wallflower.

alheña [a'leɲa] *sf* privet; blight, mildew. **alheñar** *v* (*secarse*) wither; become mildewed.

alhucema [alu'θema] *sf* lavender.

aliaga [ali'aga] *sf* gorse.

aliar [ali'ar] *v* ally. **aliado, -a** *sm, sf* ally. **alianza** *sf* alliance.

alicaído [alika'iðo] *adj* depressed; weak.

alicates [ali'kates] *sm pl* pliers, pincers *pl*.

aliciente [ali'θjente] *sm* lure; interest; encouragement.

alienar [alje'nar] *v* alienate. **alienación** *sf* alienation. **alienado** *adj* insane.

aliento [a'ljento] *sm* breath; (*fig*) courage. **cobrar aliento** catch one's breath.

aligerar [alixe'rar] *v* lighten; shorten; alleviate. **aligerarse** *v* get a move on.

alimentar [alimen'tar] *v* feed; supply; (*promover*) foster. **alimentación** *sf* food; feeding. **alimenticio** *adj* nourishing. **alimiento** *sm* food.

alinear [aline'ar] v line up. **alinearse en** join. **alineación** sf also **alineamiento** sm alignment.

aliñar [ali'ɲar] v adorn; (culin) season; prepare. **aliño** sm adornment; seasoning; preparation.

alisar [ali'sar] v smooth; polish; level. **alisaduras** sf pl shavings pl.

alistar [alis'tar] v list; recruit; prepare. **alistado** adj enlisted. **alistamiento** sm enlistment.

aliviar [ali'βjar] v lighten; alleviate; help; console. **aliviarse** v feel better, recover. **alivio** sm lightening; relief. **... de alivio** (fam) a hell of a ....

alma ['alma] sf soul; spirit; person. **con el alma en la boca** at death's door.

almacén [alma'θen] sm warehouse; department store. **almacenaje** sm storage. **almacenero** sm storekeeper.

almanaque [alma'nake] sm almanac; diary.

almeja [al'mexa] sf clam.

almendra [al'mendra] sf almond. **almendro** sm almond tree.

almiar [al'mjar] sm haystack.

almíbar [al'miβar] sm syrup.

almidón [almi'ðon] sm starch.

almirante [almi'rante] sm admiral. **almirantazgo** sm admiralty.

almohada [almo'aða] sf pillow; cushion; (funda) pillowslip.

almoneda [almo'neða] sf auction; (a bajo precio) clearance sale.

almorranas [almor'ranas] sf pl haemorrhoids pl, piles pl.

*****almorzar** [almor'θar] v lunch. **almuerzo** sm lunch.

alojar [alo'xar] v lodge, accommodate. **alojarse** v put up, stay. **alojamiento** sm accommodation, lodgings pl.

alondra [a'londra] sf lark.

alpargata [alpar'gata] sf rope-soled shoe. **alpargatería** sf shoe factory or shop.

Alpes ['alpes] sm pl Alps pl.

alpinismo [alpi'nismo] sm mountaineering. **alpinista** s(m+f) climber.

alpiste [al'piste] sm canary seed; (fam) drink; (fam) money.

alquería [alke'ria] sf farm; (aldea) village.

alquilar [alki'lar] v rent; hire; charter. **alquilarse** v be for hire; to be let. **se alquila** (casa) to rent; (coche) for hire.

alquiler sm renting; letting; hiring.

alquileres sm pl rent sing. **exento de alquiler** rent-free.

alquimia [al'kimja] sf alchemy.

alquitrán [alki'tran] sm tar. **alquitranado** adj tarred.

alrededor [alreðe'ðor] adv round, around. **alrededor de** about, around. **alrededores** sm pl environs pl, outskirts pl.

alta ['alta] sf (del hospital) discharge; (ingreso) enrolment. **dar de alta** pass as fit. **darse de alta** enrol.

altanero [alta'nero] adj haughty, arrogant.

altar [al'tar] sm altar.

altavoz [alta'βoθ] sm loudspeaker.

alterar [alte'rar] v change, alter; disturb; (estropear) spoil. **alterarse** v go sour; change; be disturbed; get excited. **alteración** sf alteration; (altercado) quarrel.

altercar [alter'kar] v argue, quarrel. **altercación** sf argument, quarrel.

alternar [alter'nar] v alternate; be sociable. **alterno** adj alternating; alternate.

alternativa [alterna'tiβa] sf alternative choice; (trabajo) shift-work; (rotación de cosechas) rotation. **tomar la alternativa** qualify as a bullfighter.

alto[1] ['alto] adj tall; high; upper; (fuerte) loud; advanced; noble. **lo alto** the top. adv high; high up; out loud. sm (elevación) hill; (altura) height. **alteza** sf height; (título) highness; grandeur. **altitud** sf altitude; (geog) elevation.

alto[2] sm, interj halt. **hacer alto** stop.

alubia [a'luβja] sf French bean.

alucinación [aluθina'θjon] sf hallucination.

alud [a'luð] sm avalanche.

aludir [alu'ðir] v allude, mention. **aludido** adj in question. **no darse por aludido** turn a deaf ear.

alumbrar [alum'brar] v light; illuminate; give light; (descubrir) find; (parir) give birth; (brillar) shine. **alumbrarse** v (fam) become tipsy. **alumbramiento** sm lighting; illumination. **alumbrante** adj illuminating; (fig) enlightening.

aluminio [alu'minjo] sm aluminium.

alumno [a'lumno] sm pupil, student.

alzar [al'θar] v raise; lift. **alzarse** v rise; stand out. **alza** sf raise. **¡alza!** bravo! **alzamiento** sm increase; uprising.

allá [a'ʎa] adv there; long ago. **más allá** farther on. **vamos allá** let's go.

allanar [aʎa'nar] v level, flatten, smooth. **allanar el terreno** clear the way.

allegar [aʎeˈɣar] v collect, reap; add; unite. **allegar fondos** raise funds. **allegarse** v arrive; approach. **allegarse a** become attached to.

allegado [aʎeˈɣaðo], **-a** sm, sf relative; close friend. adj related, close.

allegamiento sm collection; gathering; union; friendship; relationship.

allende [aˈʎende] adv beyond; besides. **allende el mar** overseas.

allí [aˈʎi] adv there; then. **aquí y allí** here and there. **por allí** over there.

ama [ˈama] sf mistress of the house; (patrona) landlady.

amable [aˈmaβle] adj kind. **amabilidad** sf kindness.

amaestrar [amaesˈtrar] v train.

amagar [amaˈɣar] v threaten; show signs of. **amagarse** v (fam) hide.

amainar [amaiˈnar] v lessen; moderate. **amainarse** v yield.

amalgamar [amalɣaˈmar] v amalgamate. **amalgamación** sf amalgamation.

amamantar [amamanˈtar] v suckle, nurse. **amamantador** adj suckling. **amamantamiento** sm suckling.

*amanecer [amaneˈθer] v dawn; arrive at break of day. sm dawn, daybreak.

amansar [amanˈsar] v break in; tame; (fig: dolor) ease.

amante [aˈmante] sm, sf lover. adj fond.

amañado [amaˈɲaðo] adj skilful; (falso) fake. **amañar** v fix; fake.

amapola [amaˈpola] sf poppy.

amar [aˈmar] v love.

amargar [amarˈɣar] v embitter; be or taste bitter. **amargo** adj bitter. **amargor** sm also **amargura** sf bitterness.

amarillo [amaˈriʎo] adj yellow.

amarrar [amaˈrrar] v fasten; tie; moor. **amarradero** sm moorings pl. **amarro** sm fastening.

amartelar [amarteˈlar] v (enamorar) make lovesick; (dar celos) make jealous. **amartelarse de** (fam) get a crush on.

amartillar [amartiˈʎar] v hammer.

amasar [amaˈsar] v knead; mix; prepare; (med) massage; (fam) cook up; (fig) amass. **amasijo** sm (harina) dough; (fam) mixture, hotchpotch; plot.

amatista [amaˈtista] sf amethyst.

ámbar [ˈambar] sm amber.

ambición [ambiˈθjon] sf ambition. **ambicioso** adj ambitious.

ambiente [amˈbjente] sm atmosphere; environment. adj surrounding.

ambiguo [amˈbiɣwo] adj ambiguous. **ambigüedad** sf ambiguity.

ámbito [ˈambito] sm (recinto) enclosure; (alcance) scope; sphere; (extensión) expanse.

ambos [ˈambos] adj, pron both.

ambulancia [ambuˈlanθja] sf ambulance.

ambulante [ambuˈlante] adj travelling; walking.

amedrentar [ameðrenˈtar] v frighten.

amenazar [amenaˈθar] v threaten. **amenaza** sf threat. **amenazador** adj threatening.

amenguar [amenˈgwar] v lessen; (deshonrar) dishonour.

amenizar [ameniˈθar] v make pleasant. **amenidad** sf pleasantness; amenity. **ameno** adj pleasant, delightful.

América [aˈmerika] sf America. **América del Norte/Sur** North/South America. **América Latina** Latin America. **americano, -a** s, adj American.

ametralladora [ametraʎaˈðora] sf machine gun.

amianto [aˈmjanto] sm asbestos.

amígdala [aˈmiɣðala] sf tonsil. **amigdalitis** sf tonsillitis.

amigo [aˈmiɣo] sm friend; boyfriend. **amiga** sf friend; girlfriend; mistress. **amigo por correspondencia** pen friend. **amigo** adj friendly.

amilanar [amilaˈnar] v frighten, terrify. **amilanarse** v become terrified.

aminorar [aminoˈrar] v lessen, reduce. **aminoración** sf lessening.

amistad [amisˈtað] sf friendship. **amistades** sf pl friends pl. **hacer las amistades** make up. **amistar** v reconcile. **amistoso** adj friendly.

amnesia [amˈnesja] sf amnesia.

amnistía [amnisˈtia] sf amnesty. **amnistiar** v grant an amnesty to.

amo [ˈamo] sm master; overseer; employer; proprietor; (fam) boss.

amodorrarse [amoðoˈrrarse] v become drowsy. **amodorrado** adj drowsy.

amohinar [amoiˈnar] v irritate; fret. **amohinarse** v become irritated or peevish.

*amolar [amoˈlar] v (cuchillo) grind, sharpen; (fam: fastidiar) annoy.

amoldar [amolˈðar] v mould; fit; shape. **amoldarse** v adapt oneself.

amonestar [amones'tar] *v* warn; advise; admonish; (*anuncio de bodas*) publish the banns of. **amonestación** *sf* warning, admonition. **correr las amonestaciones** publish the banns.

amontonar [amonto'nar] *v* pile up; accumulate. **amontonarse** *v* crowd together; heap up; (*fam*) become angry.

amor [a'mor] *sm* love; devotion. **amor interesado** love of money. **amor propio** self-esteem. **amoroso** *adj* affectionate.

amoratar [amora'tar] *v* (*frío*) make purple; (*golpes*) bruise. **amoratado** *adj* purple; black and blue.

amordazar [amorða'θar] *v* gag; (*un perro*) muzzle; (*fig*) gag, silence.

amorfo [a'morfo] *adj* amorphous.

amortiguar [amorti'gwar] *v* (*luz*) dim; (*ruido*) deaden; (*fuego*) damp; (*golpe*) cushion; (*fig*) mitigate. **amortiguación** *sf* also **amortiguamiento** *sm* dimming; deadening; mitigation.

amortiguador [amortigwa'ðor] *sm* (*auto*) shock absorber. *adj* dimming; deadening; mitigating.

amortizar [amorti'θar] *v* amortize; (*una máquina*) depreciate.

amotinar [amoti'nar] *v* incite to revolt; (*fig*) disturb. **amotinarse** *v* mutiny. **amotinado** *adj* also **amotinador** mutinous, rebellious. **amotinamiento** *sm* mutiny.

amparar [ampa'rar] *v* shelter; protect; (*ayudar*) help. **ampararse** *v* seek help *or* protection. **amparo** *sm* aid; protection; refuge.

ampliar [am'pljar] *v* enlarge; lengthen; expand; increase. **amplio** *adj* wide, full; spacious. **amplitud** *sf* width; fullness; spaciousness; extent.

amplificar [amplifi'kar] *v* amplify. **amplificación** *sf* amplification. **amplificador** *sm* amplifier; *adj* amplifying.

ampolla [am'poʎa] *sf* blister; (*redoma*) phial; (*frasco*) flask. **ampollar** *v* blister.

amputar [ampu'tar] *v* amputate. **amputación** *sf* amputation.

amueblar [amwe'βlar] *v* furnish.

amuleto [amu'leto] *sm* amulet.

anacronismo [anakro'nismo] *sm* anachronism.

anales [a'nales] *sm pl* annals *pl*. **analista** *s*(*m* + *f*) annalist.

analfabeto [anafa'βeto], **-a** *s*, *adj* illiterate.

análisis [a'nalisis] *sm invar* analysis. **analista** *s*(*m* + *f*) analyst. **analítico** *adj* analytical. **analizar** *v* analyse.

analogía [analo'xia] *sf* analogy. **análogo** *adj* analogous, similar.

ananás [ana'nas] *sm* pineapple.

anaquel [ana'kel] *sm* shelf. **anaquelería** *sf* shelving.

anarquía [anar'kia] *sf* anarchy. **anarquismo** *sm* anarchism. **anarquista** *s*(*m* + *f*) *adj* anarchist.

anatomía [anato'mia] *sf* anatomy. **anatómico** *adj* anatomical.

anca ['anka] *sf* haunch; rump. **ancas** *sf pl* (*fam*) bottom *sing*.

anciano [an'θjano] *adj* old. *sm* old man. **ancianidad** *sf* old age.

ancla ['ankla] *sf* anchor. **anclar** *v* also **echar anclas** anchor.

ancho ['antʃo] *adj* wide, broad; thick; (*fig*) relieved. *sm* width. **a sus anchas** at ease. **anchura** *sf* width; fullness; (*media*) measurement; (*fig: frescura*) cheek.

anchoa [an'tʃoa] *sf* anchovy.

Andalucía [andalu'θia] *sf* Andalusia. **andaluz, -a** *s*, *adj* Andalusian.

andamio [an'damjo] *sm* scaffold; platform. **andamios** *sm pl* scaffolding *sing*.

*andar [an'dar] *v* walk; go; come; (*máquina*) work; (*correr*) run. ¡**anda!** go on! **andar en** be engaged in; rummage in. *sm* walk, gait.

andas ['andas] *sf pl* (*para una imagen*) portable platform *sing*; (*féretro*) bier *sing*; (*para enfermo*) stretcher *sing*.

andén [an'den] *sm* station platform; (*de autopista*) hard shoulder.

Andorra [an'dorra] *sf* Andorra. **andorrano, -a** *s*, *adj* Andorran.

andrajo [an'draxo] *sm* rag. **estar hecho un andrajo** be in rags. **andrajoso** *adj* ragged, tattered.

anécdota [a'nekðota] *sf* anecdote. **anecdótico** *adj* anecdotal.

anegar [ane'gar] *v* flood; drown. **anegación** *sf* drowning; flooding.

anejo [a'nexo] *adj* joined, attached. *sm* annexe.

anemia [a'nemja] *sf* anaemia. **anémico** *adj* anaemic.

anestésico [anes'tesiko] *sm*, *adj* anaesthetic. **anestesista** *s*(*m* + *f*) anaesthetist.

anexar [anek'sar] *v* annex. **anexión** *sf* annexation.

anfibio [an'fiβjo] *sm* amphibian. *adj* amphibious.

anfiteatro [anfite'atro] *sm* amphitheatre; (*universidad*) lecture theatre; (*teatro*) gallery.

anfitrión [anfitri'on], **-ona** *sm, sf* host, hostess.

ángel ['anxel] *sm* angel. **tener ángel** be charming. **angelical** *adj also* **angélico** angelic. **angelito** *sm* cherub.

angina [an'xina] *sf* angina.

anglicano [angli'kano], **-a** *s, adj* Anglican.

angosto [an'gosto] *adj* narrow. **angostura** *sf* narrowness.

anguila [an'gila] *sf* eel.

ángulo ['angulo] *sm* angle; bend. **anguloso** *adj* angular.

angustiar [angus'tjar] *v* distress; worry. **angustia** *sf* anguish. **angustiado** *adj* distressed; miserable. **angustioso** *adj* distressing; anguished.

anhelar [ane'lar] *v* pant, gasp; (*desear*) yearn for, crave. **anhelo** *sm* panting; desire.

anidar [ani'ðar] *v* nest; (*fig*) shelter.

anillo [a'niʎo] *sm* ring. **anillo de boda** wedding ring. **anillo de compromiso** *or* **pedida** engagement ring. **anillar** *v* ring.

ánima ['anima] *sf* soul.

animal [ani'mal] *sm* animal, beast. *adj* animal. **animalada** *sf* stupid thing to do *or* say; (*grosería*) bad language.

animar [ani'mar] *v* animate; entertain; encourage; comfort. **animarse** *v* cheer up. **animación** *sf* animation. **animado** *adj* lively. **animador, -a** *sm, sf* entertainer; master of ceremonies; *adj* entertaining; encouraging.

ánimo ['animo] *sm* soul; spirit; mind; courage; intention. **¡ánimo!** come on! **animoso** *adj* spirited; courageous.

aniquilar [aniki'lar] *v* annihilate.

anís [a'nis] *sm* aniseed.

aniversario [aniβer'sarjo] *sm* anniversary.

ano ['ano] *sm* anus.

anoche [a'notʃe] *adv* last night.

***anochecer** [anotʃe'θer] *v* grow dark. *sm* nightfall.

anomalía [anoma'lia] *sf* anomaly. **anómalo** *adj* anomalous.

anónimo [a'nonimo] *adj* anonymous. *sm* anonymous person.

anormal [anor'mal] *adj* abnormal. **anormalidad** *sf* abnormality.

anotar [ano'tar] *v* note, jot down. **anotación** *sf* note.

ansiar [an'sjar] *v* long for. **ansia** *sf* longing; (*pena*) anguish; (*fervor*) eagerness. **ansias** *sf pl* retching *sing*. **ansiedad** *sf* longing; anxiety; eagerness. **ansioso** *adj* anxious; eager; longing.

antagonismo [antago'nismo] *sm* antagonism. **antagonista** *adj* antagonistic. **antagonizar** *v* antagonize.

antaño [an'taɲo] *adv* last year; formerly.

antártico [an'tartiko] *adj* antarctic. *sm* the Antarctic. **Antártica** *sf* Antarctica.

ante¹ ['ante] *prep* before; in the presence of; with regard to. **ante todo** to begin with.

ante² ['ante] *sm* suede.

anteanoche [antea'notʃe] *adv* the night before last.

anteayer [antea'jer] *adv* the day before yesterday.

antecedente [anteθe'ðente] *sm* antecedent. *adj* previous. **antecedencia** *sf* lineage. **anteceder** *v* precede.

antecesor [anteθe'sor], **-a** *sm, sf* predecessor; ancestor. *adj* antecedent.

antelación [antela'θjon] *sf* preference. **con antelación** in advance.

antemano [ante'mano] *adv* **de antemano** beforehand.

antena [an'tena] *sf* (*radio*) aerial; (*insecto*) antenna.

antenatal [antena'tal] *adj* antenatal.

anteojo [ante'oxo] *sm* small telescope. **anteojos** *sm pl* spectacles *pl*.

antepasado [antepa'saðo] *adj* previous. *sm* ancestor.

antepecho [ante'petʃo] *sm* (*de escalera*) handrail; (*de ventana*) window sill.

***anteponer** [antepo'ner] *v* prefer. **anteponerse** *v* push forward.

anterior [ante'rjor] *adj* preceding, former; front.

antes ['antes] *adv* before, formerly; first; rather. **antes de** before. **antes que** rather than. **cuanto antes** as soon as possible.

antiaéreo [antja'ereo] *adj* anti-aircraft.

antibiótico [anti'bjotiko] *sm, adj* antibiotic.

anticiclón [antiθi'klon] *sm* anticyclone.

anticipar [antiθi'par] *v* anticipate; advance. **anticiparse a** (*con infinitivo*) to ... before. **anticipación** *sf* anticipation. **con anticipación** in advance. **anticipado**

adj early, premature. **anticipo** *sm* advance payment; foretaste.

anticoncepcional [antikonθepθjo'nal] *sm*, *adj* contraceptive. **anticonceptivo** *adj* contraceptive.

anticuado [anti'kwaðo] *adj* out of date; old-fashioned.

anticuario [anti'kwarjo], **-a** *sm*, *sf* antiquarian.

antídoto [an'tiðoto] *sm* antidote.

antieconómico [antieko'nomiko] *adj* uneconomic.

antiguo [an'tigwo] *adj* ancient, antique; senior; former. **de antiguo** of old. **antigualla** *sf* antique; (*persona*) old fogey; (*noticia*) stale news. **antiguamente** *adv* formerly. **antigüedad** *sf* antiquity; seniority.

antílope [an'tilope] *sm* antelope.

Antillas [an'tiʎas] *sf pl* West Indies.

antipatía [antipa'tia] *sf* antipathy; dislike; unfriendliness. **antipático** *adj* disagreeable; unfriendly; nasty.

antisemítico [antise'mitiko] *adj* anti-Semitic. **antisemitismo** *sm* anti-Semitism.

antiséptico [anti'septiko] *sm*, *adj* antiseptic.

antisocial [antiso'θjal] *adj* antisocial.

antítesis [an'titesis] *sf* antithesis.

antojarse [anto'xarse] *v* seem; imagine; fancy; take a fancy to. **antojarsele a uno** take it into one's head to.

antojo [an'toxo] *sm* whim; (*lunar*) birthmark. **antojos** *sm pl* craving *sing*. **antajadizo** *adj* capricious.

antología [antolo'xia] *sf* anthology.

antorcha [an'tortʃa] *sf* torch.

antro ['antro] *sm* cave, den; (*fam: tasca*) low dive.

antropófago [antro'pofago], **-a** *sm*, *sf* cannibal. *adj* cannibalistic. **antropofagia** *sf* cannibalism.

antropología [antropolo'xia] *sf* anthropology. **antropológico** *adj* anthropological. **antropólogo**, **-a** *sm*, *sf* anthropologist.

anual [a'nwal] *adj* annual. **anualidad** *sf* annuity. **anuario** *sm* yearbook.

anublar [anu'βlar] *v* cloud over, obscure. **anublarse** *v* become cloudy; fade away.

anudar [anu'ðar] *v* knot; join; tie; (*empezar*) begin. **anudarse** become knotted; (*plantas*) wither. **anudadura** *sf also* **anudamiento** *sm* knotting; withering.

anular [anu'lar] *v* (*cheque*) cancel; (*ley*)

repeal; (*fig: dominar*) overshadow. **anularse** *v* (*fig: renunciar*) give up everything. **anulación** *sf* cancellation; abrogation; repeal. **anulador** *adj* repealing.

anunciar [anun'θjar] *v* announce, proclaim; notify; (*hacer publicidad*) advertise; (*predecir*) foretell. **anunciador, -a** *sm*, *sf* announcer; advertiser; *adj* announcing; advertising. **anuncio** *sm* announcement; advertisement; omen; sign.

anzuelo [an'θwelo] *sm* fish-hook; (*fig: aliciente*) lure.

añadir [aɲa'ðir] *v* add; increase. **añadido** *sm* addition. **añadidura** *sf* addition; extra. **por añadidura** furthermore, besides.

añejo [a'ɲexo] *adj* mature; (*carne*) cured; very old.

añicos [a'ɲikos] *sm pl* pieces, bits. **hacerse añicos** wear oneself out.

añil [a'ɲil] *sm* indigo plant; indigo dye.

año ['aɲo] *sm* year. **al año** yearly. **tener ... años** be ... years old. **todos los años** every year.

añorar [aɲo'rar] *v* long for; be homesick. **añoranza** *sf* homesickness; nostalgia; yearning.

***apacentar** [apaθen'tar] *v* graze. **apacentadero** *sm* pasture. **apacentador, -a** *sm*, *sf* herdsman/woman.

apacible [apa'θiβle] *adj* mild; gentle; peaceful. **apacibilidad** *sf* mildness; peacefulness.

apaciguar [apaθi'gwar] *v* pacify; appease. **apaciguarse** *v* calm down. **apaciguador, -a** *sm*, *sf* peace-maker. **apaciguamiento** *sm* pacification; appeasement.

apagar [apa'gar] *v* (*fuego*) extinguish; switch off; muffle; (*sed*) quench; (*dolor*) soothe; (*disturbio*) calm down. **apagado** *adj* extinguished; dull; lifeless; muffled. **apagaincendios** *sm invar* fire-extinguisher.

apalear [apale'ar] *v* beat; (*grano*) thresh; (*maltratar*) thrash. **apaleo** *sm* beating; winnowing; thrashing.

apañar [apa'ɲar] *v* fix; arrange; repair; (*ataviar*) dress up; (*coger*) grab; (*fam: robar*) swipe; (*fam: preparar*) get ready. **apañado** *adj* handy; dressed up.

aparador [apara'ðor] *sm* sideboard; (*escaparate*) shop window.

aparato [apa'rato] *sm* apparatus; machine; ceremony.

*aparecer [apare'θer] *v* appear. **aparecido** *sm* ghost.

aparejar [apare'xar] *v* prepare; (*caballos*) harness, saddle; (*cuadro*) prime. **aparejador** *sm* quantity surveyor. **aparejo** *sm* preparation; equipment; harness.

aparentar [aparen'tar] *v* pretend; feign.

aparente [apa'rente] *adj* apparent; evident; (*adecuado*) suitable.

aparición [apari'θjon] *sf* appearance; (*visión*) apparition; publication.

apariencia [apari'enθja] *sf* appearance; aspect; probability.

apartamento [aparta'mento] *sm* flat.

apartar [apar'tar] *v* separate; (*quitar*) remove; (*clasificar*) sort; (*poner a un lado*) put aside. **apartarse** *v* turn aside; (*irse*) leave. **apartado** *adj* separated; distant; *sm* paragraph; (*habitación*) spare room. **apartado de correos** post-office box. **apartamiento** *sm* separation; remoteness. **aparte** *adv* apart (from); aside.

apasionar [apasjo'nar] *v* rouse, stir. **apasionarse** *v* become excited. **apasionado** *adj* madly in love; passionate; (*ardiente*) fervent. **apasionamiento** *sm* passion.

apatía [apa'tia] *sf* apathy. **apático** *adj* apathetic.

apear [ape'ar] *v* get down; dismount. **apearse** *v* alight, get off.

apedrear [apeðre'ar] *v* stone. **apedrearse** *v* hail. **apedreo** *sm* stoning.

apelar [ape'lar] *v* appeal. **apelar a** appeal to. **apelar de** appeal against.

apellido [ape'ʎiðo] *sm* surname; (*apodo*) nickname. **apellido de soltera** maiden name.

apenar [ape'nar] *v* grieve.

apenas [a'penas] *adv* scarcely; no sooner than.

apéndice [a'penðiθe] *sm* appendix; supplement. **apendicitis** *sf* appendicitis.

apercibir [aperθi'βir] *v* prepare; (*proveer*) equip; (*advertir*) warn. **apercibirse de** equip oneself with. **apercibimiento** *sm* preparation; advice; (*jur*) summons.

aperitivo [aperi'tiβo] *sm* appetizer; apéritif. *adj* appetizing.

apero [a'pero] *sm* equipment; tools *pl*.

apertura [aper'tura] *sf* opening.

apesadumbrar [apesadum'brar] *v* grieve, afflict. **apesadumbrarse** *v* be upset.

apestar [apes'tar] *v* infect; (*fig*) vex; (*fam*) stink. **apestado** *adj* (*olor*) foul; (*que tiene peste*) plague-ridden; infested.

*apetecer [apete'θer] *v* have a hankering for, fancy; (*bienvenido*) be welcome. **apetecible** *adj* desirable, tempting. **apetencia** *sf* desire; appetite.

apetito [ape'tito] *sm* appetite.

apiadarse [apja'ðarse] *v* have pity on.

ápice ['apiθe] *sm* apex; jot, iota.

apiñar [api'ɲar] *v* squeeze together. **apiñarse** *v* crowd, throng. **apiñadura** *sf* also **apiñamiento** *sm* congestion; throng.

apio ['apjo] *sm* celery.

apisonadora [apisona'ðora] *sf* steam roller. **apisonar** *v* flatten. **apisonamiento** *sm* flattening.

aplacar [apla'kar] *v* appease; calm. **aplacable** *adj* appeasable. **aplacamiento** *sm* appeasement. **aplacador** *adj* appeasing.

aplanar [apla'nar] *v* level, flatten; (*fam*) make dejected. **aplanador** *adj* levelling. **aplanadora** *sf* leveller. **aplanamiento** *sm* levelling, flattening; (*fam*) dejection.

aplastar [aplas'tar] *v* crush, flatten.

aplaudir [aplau'ðir] *v* applaud. **aplauso** *sm* applause.

aplazar [apla'θar] *v* postpone; (*convocar*) summon. **aplazamiento** *sm* postponement; summons.

aplicar [apli'kar] *v* apply; attach; (*recursos, dinero*) assign. **aplicarse** *v* apply oneself; be applicable. **aplicación** *sf* application. **aplicado** *adj* studious.

aplomo [a'plomo] *sm* aplomb, self-confidence. **aplomado** *adj* self-assured.

apocar [apo'kar] *v* lessen; belittle. **apocarse** *v* become cowed. **apocado** *adj* spineless, timid. **apocamiento** *sm* timidity.

apodar [apo'ðar] *v* nickname. **apodo** *sm* nickname.

apoderar [apoðe'rar] *v* authorize. **apoderarse de** take possession of. **apoderado** *sm* agent; sports manager.

apogeo [apo'xeo] *sm* climax; summit.

apolillarse [apoli'ʎarse] *v* become moth-eaten. **apolilladura** *sf* moth-hole.

apoplejía [apople'xia] *sf* apoplexy. **apoplético, -a** *s, adj* apoplectic.

aportar [apor'tar] *v* bring, contribute; arrive. **aportación** *sf* contribution.

aposentar [aposen'tar] *v* lodge; give lodging to. **aposentarse** *v* take lodgings. **aposentamiento** *sm* lodging. **aposento** *sm* room; lodging.

*apostar [apos'tar] *v* bet. **apostarse** *v* bet; take up one's post. **apostador, -a** *sm, sf* punter.

apóstol [a'postol] *sm* apostle. **apostólico** *adj* apostolic.

apóstrofo [a'postrofo] *sm* (*gram*) apostrophe.

apoyar [apo'jar] *v* support; back up; lean; rest. **apoyar en** lean against. **apoyarse en** lean on. **apoyo** *sm* support.

apreciar [apre'θjar] *v* appreciate; value. **apreciar en mucho** value highly. **apreciable** *adj* appreciable; estimable; (*ruido*) audible. **apreciación** *sf* appreciation; (*valoración*) appraisal. **apreciativo** *adj* appreciative. **aprecio** *sm* appraisal; esteem.

aprehender [apreen'der] *v* seize; understand. **aprehensible** *adj* understandable. **aprehensión** *sf* capture, arrest; understanding.

apremiar [apre'mjar] *v* press, urge; (*obligar*) force; (*dar prisa*) hurry. **apremiador** *adj* urgent. **apremio** *sm* urgency; compulsion.

aprender [apren'der] *v* learn. **aprendiz, -a** *sm, sf* apprentice. **aprendizaje** *sm* apprenticeship.

aprensión [apren'sjon] *sf* apprehension, fear. **aprensivo** *adj* apprehensive.

apresar [apre'sar] *v* seize, arrest. **apresamiento** *sm* seizure.

aprestar [apres'tar] *v* prepare; (*telas*) size. **aprestarse** *v* get ready. **apresto** *sm* preparation.

apresurar [apresu'rar] *v* hurry, quicken. **apresuradamente** *adv* hastily. **apresurado** *adj* hurried. **apresuramiento** *sm* haste.

*apretar [apre'tar] *v* squeeze; grip; tighten; (*botón*) press; (*la mano*) shake; (*dolor*) get worse; (*comprimir*) press down. **apretarse** *v* crowd together; huddle together. **apretado** *adj* tight; (*colchón*) hard; cramped; cluttered; difficult; (*tacaño*) miserly. **apretón** *sm* squeeze; (*fam: aprieto*) tight spot; (*fam: accesidad natural*) call of nature. **aprieto** *sm* awkward situation.

aprisa [a'prisa] *adv* quickly.

aprisionar [aprisjon'ar] *v* imprison.

*aprobar [apro'βar] *v* approve; approve of; (*examen*) pass. **aprobación** *sf* approval; pass. **aprobado** *adj* approved. *sm* pass.

apropiar [apro'pjar] *v* appropriate; adapt.

apropiarse de algo appropriate something. **apropiado** *adj* appropriate, suitable.

aprovechar [aproβe'tʃar] *v* profit by; be useful; make progress. **aprovecharse de** take advantage of. **aprovechado** *adj* thrifty; (*apañado*) resourceful; studious; (*egoísta*) selfish. **aprovechamiento** *sm* profit; exploitation; benefit.

aproximar [aproksi'mar] *v* bring nearer. **aproximarse** *v* approach. **aproximación** *sf* approximation; nearness. **aproximado** *adj* approximate.

aptitud [apti'tuð] *sf* aptitude; capacity. **apto** *adj* apt; suitable.

apuesta [a'pwesta] *sf* bet.

apuesto [a'pwesto] *adj* smart, spruce.

apuntar [apun'tar] *v* (*señalar*) point at; (*arma*) aim; (*sugerir*) point out; (*anotar*) make a note of; (*demostrar*) display; (*sacar punta*) sharpen; (*jugar*) bet; (*teatro*) prompt. **apuntarse** *v* put one's name down; (*fam*) enrol. **apuntado** *adj* pointed. **apunte** *sm* (*nota*) note; (*puesta*) stake; prompter; (*teatro*) cue; (*dibujo*) sketch.

apuñalar [apuɲa'lar] *v* stab.

apurar [apu'rar] *v* purify; (*acabar*) exhaust; (*vaciar*) drain; examine in detail; (*dar prisa*) rush, hurry. **apurarse** *v* (*preocuparse*) worry; hurry up. **apuradamente** *adv* with difficulty; (*ser indigente*) in want; (*fam*) exactly. **apurado** *adj* (*pobre*) hard up; (*agotado*) worn out; (*avergonzado*) embarrassed. **apuro** *sm* (*dificultad*) tight spot; embarrassment.

aquejar [ake'xar] *v* afflict. **aquejoso** *adj* afflicted.

aquel, aquella [a'kel, a'keʎa] *adj* that. **aquellos, aquellas** *pl* those. **aquél, aquélla** *pron* that; the one; the former.

aquí [a'ki] *adv* here. **de aquí en adelante** from now on. **heme aquí** here I am. **por aquí** this way.

aquietar [akje'tar] *v* quieten.

aquilatar [akila'tar] *v* test, examine closely.

Arabia [a'raβja] *sf* Arabia. **árabe** *adj* Arab, Arabian, Arabic; *sm, sf* Arab, Arabian; *sm* (*lengua*) Arabic. **arábico** *adj* *also* **arábigo** Arabic.

arancel [aran'θel] *sm* tariff, duty.

araña [a'raɲa] *sf* spider; (*luz*) chandelier. **arañar** [ara'ɲar] *v* scratch. **arañada** *sf* scratch. **arañador** *adj* scratching, scraping. **arañazo** *sm* scratch.

arar [a'rar] v plough. **arado** sm plough.
arbitrar [arβi'trar] v arbitrate; referee.
arbitraje sm arbitration. **arbitrario** adj
arbitrary. **árbitro** sm referee, umpire.
arbitrio [ar'βitrjo] sm (voluntad) will;
(recurso) means; (jur) judgment. **arbitrios**
sm pl taxes pl.
árbol [ar'βol] sm tree; (tecn) shaft; (palo)
mast. **árbol de Navidad** Christmas tree.
arboleda sf wood, spinney.
arbusto [ar'βusto] sm bush.
arca ['arka] sf box, chest. **arca de agua**
reservoir.
arcada [ar'kaða] sf arcade. **arcadas** sf pl
nausea sing.
arcaico [ar'kaiko] adj archaic. **arcaísmo**
sm archaism.
arce ['arθe] sm maple.
arcilla [ar'θiʎa] sf clay.
arco [arko] sm arc; arch; (arma, música)
bow. **arco iris** rainbow.
archiduque [artʃi'ðuke] sm archduke.
archiduquesa sf archduchess.
archipiélago [artʃi'pjelago] sm archipelago.
archivo [ar'tʃiβo] sm file; archives pl.
archivador sm filing cabinet. **archivar** v
file. **archivero, -a** sm, sf also **archivista**
s(m+f) archivist.
arder [ar'ðer] v burn; (estiércol) rot; (fig)
seethe. **arderse** v burn up. **ardiente** adj
ardent, burning; feverish.
ardid [ar'ðið] sm trick, ruse.
ardilla [ar'ðiʎa] sf squirrel.
ardor [ar'ðor] sm ardour; (quemazón)
burn; (fig) enthusiasm. **ardorosamente**
adv ardently. **ardoroso** adj burning;
feverish; fervent.
arduo ['arðuo] adj arduous, difficult.
área ['area] sf area.
arena [a'rena] sf sand; (en el circo) arena;
(ruedo) bullring. **arena movediza** quicksand. **arenal** sm stretch of sand. **arenar** v
sand.
arengar [aren'gar] v harangue. **arenga** sf
harangue.
arenque [a'renke] sm herring.
argamasa [arga'masa] sf mortar.
argamasar v mortar.
Argentina [arxen'tina] sf Argentina.
argentino adj (de plata) silvery; Argentinian. **argentino, -a** sm, sf Argentine,
Argentinian.
argolla [ar'goʎa] sf large metal ring,
hoop.

argucia [ar'guθja] sf fallacy; subtlety.
*****argüir** [ar'gwir] v (alegar) argue; indi-
cate; demonstrate; (delatar) accuse;
infer.
aria ['arja] sf aria.
argumento [argu'mento] sm argument;
(cuento) plot. **argumentador** adj argumentative.
aridez [ari'ðeθ] sf dryness. **aridecer** v dry
up. **aridecerse** v become dry. **árido** adj
arid. **medida de áridos** sf dry measure.
arisco [a'risko] adj (tímido) shy; (huraño)
unfriendly; (animales) wild.
aristocracia [aristo'kraθja] sf aristocracy.
aristócrata s(m+f) aristocrat. **aristocrático** adj aristocratic.
aritmética [arit'metika] sf arithmetic.
aritmético adj arithmetic, arithmetical.
armada [ar'maða] sf navy, fleet.
armar [ar'mar] v arm; prepare; reinforce;
(proveer) provide; organize. **armarse** v
arm oneself; prepare oneself; (estallar)
break out. **arma** sf weapon. **armado** adj
armed. **armadura** sf armour; framework.
armamento sm armament.
armario [ar'marjo] sm cupboard; (para
ropa) wardrobe.
armazón [arma'θon] sm (anat) skeleton. sf
(conjunto de piezas) framework.
armería [arme'ria] sf gunsmiths; (heráldica) heraldry.
armisticio [armis'tiθjo] sm armistice.
armonía [armo'nia] sf harmony. **armónic**
adj also **armonioso** harmonious.
armónica [ar'monika] sf harmonica.
aro ['aro] sm (argolla) iron ring; (de tonel)
hoop.
aroma [a'roma] sm aroma. **aromático** adj
aromatic, fragrant. **aromatizante** adj
flavouring. **aromatizar** v flavour.
arpa ['arpa] sf harp. **arpista** s(m+f) harpist.
arpón [ar'pon] sm harpoon.
arquear [arke'ar] v arch, curve. **arqueo** sm
arching.
arqueología [arkeolo'xia] sf archaeology.
arqueológico adj archaeological. **arqueólogo** sm archaeologist.
arquero [ar'kero] sm archer; (com) cashier.
arquitectura [arkitek'tura] sf architecture.
arquitecto sm architect.
arrabal [arra'βal] sm suburb. **arrabales** sm
pl outskirts pl.

arraigar [arrai'gar] v take root. **arraigarse** v settle down. **arraigado** adj deep-rooted. **arraigo** sm roots pl; influence.

arrancar [arran'kar] v root up, tear out, force out; (las flemas) expectorate; (suspiro) heave; (agarrar) snatch; (auto) start. **arrancarse** v begin. **arrancada** sf sudden start; jerk. **arrancado** adj uprooted; (fam) broke. **arrancadura** sf pulling; uprooting; (dientes) extraction. **arranque** sm (auto) starting; (carretera) beginning; (energía) burst; origin.

arrasar [arra'sar] v (llenar) fill to the brim; (edificio) demolish; (allanar) level. **arrasarse** v clear up. **arrasadura** sf levelling. **arrasamiento** sm levelling; demolition.

arrastrar [arras'trar] v pull, haul, drag; (viento) blow away; (provocar) give rise to; attract. **arrastrarse** v crawl, creep. **arrastre** sm dragging; haulage. **ser de mucho arrastre** be highly influential.

arrebatar [arreβa'tar] v snatch; (viento) blow away; carry away; (arrancar) rip off; enrage; captivate. **arrebatarse** v get overcooked. **arrebatadamente** adv hurriedly. **arrebatadizo** adj short-tempered. **arrebatamiento** sm seizure; (éxtasis) rapture. **arrebato** sm (furor) rage; rapture.

arrebujarse [arreβu'xarse] v wrap oneself up.

arreciar [arre'θjar] v grow worse or stronger; increase in intensity.

arrecife [arre'θife] sm reef.

arreglar [arre'glar] v organize, regulate; (poner en orden) tidy; (disponer) arrange; (componer) mend; get ready; (rectificar) put right. **arreglarse** v be content; (vestirse) dress; (ponerse de acuerdo) agree; (ir tirando) get by. **arreglado** adj regulated; tidy; (bien vestido) smart; reasonable; (conducta) good. **arreglo** sm agreement; arrangement; repair.

arremeter [arreme'ter] v attack. **arremetida** sf assault.

*__arrendar__ [arren'dar] v let; (alquilar) rent. **arrendador** sm landlord; (que toma en alquiler) tenant. **arrendadora** sf landlady; tenant. **arrendamiento** sm letting; rent.

arreo [ar'reo] sm adornment. **arreos** sm pl harness sing.

*__arrepentirse__ [arrepen'tirse] v repent. **arrepentimiento** sm repentance.

arrestar [arres'tar] v arrest. **arrestarse** v rush boldly. **arrestado** adj imprisoned; (audaz) bold. **arresto** sm arrest; imprisonment. **arrestos** sm pl boldness sing.

arriar [ar'rjar] v (vela, bandera) strike, lower; (cable) slacken. **arriarse** v (inundarse) be flooded.

arriba [ar'riβa] adv up; upstairs; above. **de arriba abajo** from head to foot. **¡mano arriba!** hands up! **arriba** prep above.

arribar [arri'βar] v arrive. **arribar a** reach. **arribada** sf arrival.

arriendo [ar'rjendo] sm letting; renting; hiring.

arriesgar [arrjes'gar] v risk. **arriesgarse** v take a risk. **arriesgarse en** venture on. **arriesgado** adj dangerous.

arrimar [arri'mar] v (acercar) get near or close; put away. **arrimarse** v draw up; gather together; live together.

arrinconar [arrinko'nar] v corner; (desechar) discard; (fam: vivir solo) live in isolation. **arrinconado** adj (olvidado) forgotten; (abandonado) forsaken.

arroba [ar'roβa] sf weight of 11.5 kg.

arrobar [arro'βar] v entrance. **arrobado** adj in ecstasy. **arrobador** adj bewitching. **arrobamiento** sm also **arrobo** ecstasy, rapture.

arrodillarse [arroði'ʎarse] v kneel. **arrodillamiento** sm kneeling.

arrogancia [arro'ganθja] sf arrogance. **arrogante** adj arrogant.

arrojar [arro'xar] v throw, hurl; emit. **arrojarse** v hurl oneself. **arrojado** adj bold. **arrojo** sm boldness, daring.

arrollar [arro'ʎar] v (enrollar) roll up; (llevarse) sweep away; (atropellar) run over; (aniquilar) crush.

arropar [arro'par] v (abrigarse) wrap up; (en una cama) tuck up; cover.

arrostrar [arros'trar] v face up to, confront.

arroyo [ar'roʎo] sm stream; (calle) gutter.

arroz [ar'roθ] sm rice.

arrugar [arru'gar] v wrinkle; (ropa) crease. **arruga** sf wrinkle; crease.

arruinar [arrui'nar] v ruin; destroy.

arrullar [arru'ʎar] v lull to sleep; (paloma) coo. **arrullo** sm cooing.

arrumbar [arrum'bar] v discard; (fig) ignore.

arrurruz [arrur'ruθ] sm arrowroot.

arsenal [arse'nal] sm arsenal; (astillero) shipyard.

arsénico [ar'seniko] *sm* arsenic.

arte ['arte] *sm*, *sf* art; (*hechura*) workmanship; (*astucia*) cunning. **no tener arte ni parte en** have nothing to do with. **por buenas o malas artes** by fair means or foul.

artefacto [arte'fakto] *sm* device, appliance.

artejo [ar'texo] *sm* knuckle.

arteria [ar'terja] *sf* artery.

artesano [arte'sano] *sm* craftsman. **artesanía** *sf* craftsmanship.

ártico ['artiko] *adj* arctic. **Ártico** *sm* the Arctic. **Círculo Polar Ártico** *sm* Arctic Circle.

articular [artiku'lar] *v* articulate, join together. **articulación** *sf* articulation.

artículo [ar'tikulo] *sm* article; item; (dictionary) entry. **artículos** *sm pl* goods *pl*.

artificial [artifi'θjal] *adj* artificial.

artificio [arti'fiθjo] *sm* device; skill; (*truco*) trick.

artillería [artiʎe'ria] *sf* artillery. **artillero** *sm* gunner.

artimaña [arti'maɲa] *sf* (*trampa*) trap; (*astucia*) trick.

artista [ar'tista] *s(m+f)* artist; actor, actress. **artístico** *adj* artistic.

artritis [ar'tritis] *sf* arthritis.

arzobispo [arθo'βispo] *sm* archbishop.

as [as] *sm* ace.

asa ['asa] *sf* handle.

asado [a'saðo] *sm* (*culin*) roast (meat). *adj* roast, roasted. **asador** *sm* spit. **asar** *v* roast; (*fam*) pester.

asalariado [asala'rjaðo], **-a** *sm*, *sf* wage-earner. *adj* paid, wage-earning.

asaltar [asal'tar] *v* assault, attack; (*banco*) raid; (*fig: idea*) cross one's mind. **asalto** *sm* attack; (*boxeo*) round.

asamblea [asam'blea] *sf* assembly, meeting.

asbesto [as'βesto] *sm* asbestos.

ascendencia [asθen'denθja] *sf* ancestry; origin; (*predominio*) influence.

*ascender [asθen'der] *v* ascend; (*subir a*) add up; (*empleo*) be promoted; promote. **ascendiente** *sm* influence. **ascendientes** *sm pl* ancestors *pl*, ancestry *sing*. **ascensión** *sf* ascent; promotion. **ascensor** *sm* elevator.

asco ['asko] *sm* disgust, loathing. **dar asco** disgust. **hacer asco** turn one's nose up.

ascua ['askwa] *sf* ember. **estar sobre ascuas** be on tenterhooks.

asear [ase'ar] *v* clean; wash; decorate; (*arreglar*) tidy up. **asearse** *v* have a wash; spruce oneself up. **aseado** *adj* clean; tidy. **aseo** *sm* cleanliness; tidiness.

asechar [ase'tʃar] *v* ambush. **asecho** *sm* trap.

asediar [ase'ðjar] *v* besiege; (*fig*) bother. **asedio** *sm* siege.

asegurar [asegu'rar] *v* secure; safeguard; (*consolidar*) strengthen; (*confortar*) reassure; insure; assure. **asegurarse** *v* make sure. **asegurado** *adj* insured; assured. **asegurador** *sm* underwriter. **aseguramiento** *sm* securing; insurance; assurance.

asemejarse [aseme'xarse] *v* resemble, be alike.

*asentar [asen'tar] *v* place; seat; (*cimientos*) lay; (*polvo*) settle; (*campamento*) pitch; (*establecer*) found; (*afilar*) sharpen; (*convenir*) agree; (*acalmar*) calm down; (*ir bien*) be suitable. **asentarse** *v* sit down; settle down.

*asentir [asen'tir] *v* agree, assent. **asentimiento** *sm* assent.

asequible [ase'kiβle] *adj* reasonable; (*alcanzable*) obtainable; affable.

*aserrar [aser'rar] *v* saw. **aserradero** *sm* sawmill. **aserrado** *adj* serrated. **aserrín** *sm* sawdust.

aserto [a'serto] *sm* assertion.

asesinar [asesi'nar] *v* murder; assassinate. **asesinato** *sm* murder; assassination. **asesino** *adj* murderous.

asesorar [aseso'rar] *v* advise; take advice. **asesoramiento** *sm* advising; opinion.

asestar [ases'tar] *v* (*arma*) aim; (*golpe*) strike. **asestadura** *sf* aiming.

asfalto [as'falto] *sm* asphalt. **asfaltado** *adj* covered with asphalt. **asfaltar** *v* asphalt.

asfixiar [asfik'sjar] *v* suffocate. **asfixia** *sf* suffocation.

así [a'si] *adv* so, thus, in this way, in that way. **así así** so-so. **así como** just as; as well as. **así que** as soon as; therefore. **así sea** so be it.

Asia ['asja] *sf* Asia. **asiático**, **-a** *s*, *adj* Asiatic, Asian.

asidero [asi'ðero] *sm* handle; (*fig*) excuse.

asiduo [a'siðwo] *adj* assiduous, hard-working; frequent.

asiento [a'sjento] *sm* seat, chair; place; (*de botellas, etc.*) base, bottom; (*tratado*) treaty; note; stability; (*sentido común*) common sense. **asientos** *sm pl* seat *sing*, bottom *sing.* **asiento de estómago** attack of indigestion. **tomar asiento** sit down.

asignar [asig'nar] *v* assign; attribute; allocate. **asignación** *sf* (*atribución*) allocation; (*cita*) appointment; (*subsidio*) grant; (*sueldo*) wages.

asignatura [asigna'tura] *sf* (scholastic) subject.

asilo [a'silo] *sm* asylum; refuge; home; shelter.

asimilar [asimi'lar] *v* assimilate; compare. **asimilarse** *v* be assimilated; (*asemejarse*) resemble. **asimilación** *sf* assimilation; comparison.

asimismo [asi'mismo] *adv* in like manner, in the same way.

***asir** [a'sir] *v* grasp; grip; (*plantas*) take root. **asirse de** hang on to.

asistir [asis'tir] *v* help; attend; be present; (*testigo*) witness. **asistencia** *sf* assistance; attendance; (*teatro, etc.*) audience; (*muchedumbre*) crowd; (*médica*) care; presence. **asistencias** *sf pl* maintenance *sing.* **asistenta** *sf* charlady; (*hotel*) chambermaid. **asistente** *sm* assistant; (*mil*) orderly; member of an audience.

asma ['asma] *sf* asthma.

asno ['asno] *sm* donkey, ass; (*fig*) idiot.

asociar [aso'θjar] *v* associate; (*com*) enter into partnership. **asociarse** *v* associate oneself; share. **asociación** *sf* association; (*com*) partnership. **asociado** *sm* member.

asolar [aso'lar] *v* destroy; (*arrasar*) flatten; (*calor*) parch. **asalador** *adj* devastating. **asolamiento** *sm* devastation.

asolear [asole'ar] *v* put in the sun. **asolearse** *v* sunbathe.

asomar [aso'mar] *v* show, appear. **asomarse** *v* lean out; (*fam: archisparse*) become tipsy. **asomada** *sf* brief appearance. **asomo** *sm* appearance; (*sombra*) shadow; (*indicio*) hint.

asombrar [asom'brar] *v* astonish; (*dar sombra*) shade; (*color*) darken. **asombrador** *adj* astonishing. **asombramiento** *sm also* **asombro** *sm* astonishment; (*fam: aparecido*) ghost. **asombroso** *adj* astonishing; stupefying.

aspecto [as'pekto] *sm* aspect; appearance.

áspero ['aspero] *adj* (*tosco*) rough; (*agrio*) sour; (*persona*) gruff; (*voz*) harsh; (*clima*) hard; (*terreno*) rugged. **aspereza** *sf* roughness; sourness; harshness.

aspersión [asper'sjon] *sf* sprinkling; spraying. **asperjar** *v* sprinkle.

aspirar [aspi'rar] *v* inhale; (*fig*) aspire. **aspiración** *sf* inhalation; aspiration. **aspiradora** *sf* vacuum cleaner.

aspirina [aspi'rina] *sf* aspirin.

asqueroso [aske'roso] *adj* disgusting; vile; dirty; repulsive. **asquerosidad** *sf* filth; obscenity.

asta ['asta] *sf* (*arma*) spear; (*palo*) shaft; (*de la bandera*) staff; (*cuerno*) horn. **a media asta** at half mast.

asterisco [aste'risko] *sm* asterisk.

astil [as'til] *sm* handle; (*pluma*) quill.

astillar [asti'ʎar] *v* splinter; smash.

astillero [asti'ʎero] *sm* shipyard.

astringir [astrin'xir] *v* constrict; (*sujetar*) blind. **astringente** *sm, adj* astringent.

astro ['astro] *sm* star.

astrología [astrolo'xia] *sf* astrology. **astrólogo** *sm* astrologer.

astronauta [astro'nauta] *s(m+f)* astronaut. **astronáutica** *sf* astronautics.

astronomía [astrono'mia] *sf* astronomy. **astronómico** *adj* astronomical. **astrónomo** *sm* astronomer.

astucia [as'tuθja] *sf* (*habilidad*) cleverness; (*ingenio*) cunning. **astuto** *adj* clever; cunning.

asumir [asu'mir] *v* assume.

asunto [a'sunto] *sm* (*tema*) subject; (*cosa*) affair; (*negocio*) business; (*caso*) fact; (*cuestión*) matter. **asuntos a tratar** *pl* agenda *sing.* **asuntos exteriores** foreign affairs.

asustar [asus'tar] *v* frighten.

atacar [ata'kar] *v* attack; (*recalcar*) stuff; (*un botón*) fasten. **atacador, -a** *sm, sf* assailant. **ataque** *sm* attack; (*med*) fit. **ataque cardíaco** heart attack. **ataque fulminante** (*med*) stroke.

atado [a'taðo] *sm* bundle. *adj* shy.

atajar [ata'xar] *v* intercept; (*detener*) check; (*impedir*) obstruct; (*tomar el camino más corto*) take a short cut. **atajador, -a** *sm, sf* interceptor. **atajo** *sm* short cut.

atar [a'tar] *v* tie; lace; bind. **loco de atar** raving mad. **atarse** *v* become confused. **atador** *adj* binding. **atadura** *sf* binding; (*cuerda*) rope; (*fig: vínculo*) bond.

***atardecer** [ataɾðe'θer] *v* get late; grow dark. *sm* dusk.

atareado [atare'aðo] *adj* very busy. **atarear** *v* load with work.

atascar [atas'kar] *v* plug, stop (a leak); obstruct. **atascadero** *sm* mire; (*fig*) stumbling-block. **atasco** *sm* obstruction.

ataúd [ata'uð] *sm* coffin.

ataviar [ata'βjar] *v* dress up, adorn. **ataviarse en** *or* **de** dress oneself up in. **atavío** *sm* attire.

ateísmo [ate'ismo] *sm* atheism. **ateísta** *s*(*m*+*f*) atheist. **ateo, -a** *sm, sf* atheist.

atemorizar [atemori'θar] *v* frighten.

atención [aten'θjon] *sf* attention; courtesy; interest; (*cariño*) kindness. **prestar atención** pay attention. **atenciones** *sf pl* business affairs. **atento** *adj* attentive; kind; careful; special; (*consciente*) aware.

*atender [aten'der] *v* attend to; (*cuidar*) look after; serve; (*una máquina*) service; (*un aviso*) listen to.

*atenerse [ate'nerse] *v* abide, adhere; (*a una persona*) rely on.

atentar [aten'tar] *v* attempt; offend.

atenuar [ate'nwar] *v* attenuate; lessen; (*la luz*) dim. **atenuación** *sf* attenuation.

*aterrar¹ [ater'rar] *v* demolish.

aterrar² [ater'rar] *v* frighten, terrify. **aterrador** *adj* terrifying.

aterrizar [aterri'θar] *v* (*aviac*) land. **aterrizaje** *sm* landing.

aterrorizar [aterrori'θar] *v* terrify; terrorize. **aterrorizador** *adj* terrifying.

atesorar [ateso'rar] *v* hoard; (*fig*) possess. **atesoramiento** *sm* hoarding.

*atestar [ates'tar] *v* (*llenar*) stuff; (*un tren*) crowd, pack; (*desordenar*) clutter up. **atestado** *adj* full up; packed.

atestiguar [atesti'gwar] *v* testify.

ático ['atiko] *sm* attic.

atisbar [atis'βar] *v* (*mirar*) spy on; (*vislumbrar*) distinguish; (*vigilar*) watch for. **atisbo** *sm* spying; (*fig*) hint.

atizar [ati'θar] *v* (*el fuego*) poke, stir; (*fig*) stir up, incite. **atizador** *sm* poker.

Atlántico [at'lantiko] *sm* Atlantic. **atlántico** *adj* Atlantic.

atlas ['atlas] *sm* atlas.

atleta [at'leta] *s*(*m*+*f*) athlete. **atlético** *adj* athletic. **atletismo** *sm* athletics.

atmósfera [at'mosfera] *sf* atmosphere. **mala atmósfera** atmospherics *pl*. **atmosférico** *adj* atmospheric.

atolondrar [atolon'drar] *v* confuse; (*aturdir*) stun. **atolondrarse** *v* lose one's head. **atolondradamente** *adv* recklessly. **atolondramiento** *sm* recklessness; confusion.

atolladero [atoʎa'ðero] *sm* bog; (*fig*) impasse. **atollarse** *v* get bogged down.

átomo ['atomo] *sm* atom. **atómico** *adj* atomic.

atónito [a'tonito] *adj* astonished.

atontar [aton'tar] *v* (*golpe*) stun, daze; (*dejar sin habla*) dumbfound; (*embrutecer*) deaden; (*drogas*) make stupid. **atontado** *adj* stunned; bewildered; dumbfounded; stupid.

atormentar [atormen'tar] *v* torment; torture. **atormentador** *sm* tormentor; torturer.

atornillar [atorni'ʎar] *v* screw in/on/down.

atosigar [atosi'gar] *v* poison; (*molestar*) pester. **atosigarse** *v* toil. **atosigador** *adj* poisoning; pestering. **atosigamiento** *sm* poisoning; pestering.

atracar [atra'kar] *v* (*robar*) hold up; moor; (*fam*) gorge. **atracarse** *v* gorge oneself. **atracada** *sf* docking; (*pelea*) scuffle. **atracador** *sm* bandit.

atracción [atrak'θjon] *sf* attraction. **atracciones** *sf pl* entertainment *sing*. **atractivo** *adj* attractive.

*atraer [atra'er] *v* attract. **attracción** *sf* attraction. **atracciones** *sf pl* entertainment *sing*.

atrancar [atran'kar] *v* (*puerta*) bar; block up. **atrancarse** *v* become blocked/stuck/jammed.

atrapar [atra'par] *v* catch, trap.

atrás [a'tras] *adv* behind; in the rear; back; backwards; previously; **¡atrás!** get back! **atrasado** *adj* late; behind; in arrears; (*reloj*) slow; backward; in debt. **atrasar** *v* (*diferir*) postpone; put back; slow down; lose (time). **atrasarse** lag behind; be late; be slow. **atraso** *sm* delay; backwardness; slowness.

*atravesar [atraβe'sar] *v* (*poner*) place *or* put across; (*traspasar*) pierce; penetrate; cross; (*apostar*) bet. **atravesarse** *v* stand *or* lie across; get stuck; interfere; quarrel. **atravesado** *adj* lying across; pierced; (*fig*) wicked.

atreverse [atre'βerse] *v* dare; venture; be insolent. **atrevido, -a** *sm, sf* daredevil; cheeky person. **atrevimiento** *sm* boldness; effrontery.

*atribuir [atriβu'ir] *v* attribute. **atribución** *sf* attribution. **atributo** *sm* attribute.

atrocidad [atroθi'ðað] *sf* atrocity. **atroz** *adj* atrocious. **atrozmente** *adv* atrociously.

atrófia [a'trofja] *sf* atrophy. **atrofiar** *v* atrophy.

atropellar [atrope'ʎar] *v* knock down; (*pisotear*) trample on; (*ultrajar*) offend; (*agraviar*) bully; (*trabajo*) rush. **atropellar por** ignore. **atropellarse** *v* hurry. **atropelladamente** *adv* hurriedly. **atropellado** *adj* hasty. **atropellador** *adj* precipitate. **atropello** *sm* jostling, pushing; accident; outrage.

atún [a'tun] *sm* tunny, tuna.

aturdir [atur'ðir] *v* stun, daze; (*marear*) make dizzy; bewilder. **aturdido** *adj* dazed; (*imprudente*) thoughtless. **aturdidor** *adj* deafening. **aturdimiento** *sm* daze; giddiness; amazement.

aturrullar [aturru'ʎar] *v* confuse, bewilder. **aturrullarse** *v* become confused; panic.

atusar [atu'sar] *v* (*cortar*) trim; (*alisar*) smooth; (*acariciar*) stroke. **atusarse** *v* spruce oneself up.

audacia [au'ðaθja] *sf* audacity. **audaz** *adj* audacious.

audible [au'ðiβle] *adj* audible. **audibilidad** *sf* audibility.

audición [auði'θjon] *sf* hearing; (*prueba*) audition.

audiencia [au'ðjenθja] *sf* audience; hearing; (*tribunal*) court.

audífono [au'ðifono] *sm* hearing aid.

audiovisual [auðjoβi'swal] *adj* audiovisual.

auge ['auxe] *sm* peak; progress.

augurar [augu'rar] *v* predict. **augurio** *sm* augury, omen.

aula ['aula] *sf* lecture hall; (*escuela*) classroom. **aula magna** assembly hall.

aullar [au'ʎar] *v* howl. **aullido** *sm* howl.

aumentar [aumen'tar] *v* increase; (*sueldo*) raise; magnify; (*mejorar*) get better; (*empeorar*) get worse. **aumento** *sm* increase; rise; magnification.

aun [a'un] *adv* even. **aun así** even so. **aun cuando** although. **aún** *adv* still, yet. **aún no** not yet.

aunque [a'unke] *conj* even though, although.

áureo ['aureo] *adj* gold(en).

aureola [aure'ola] *sf* halo.

auricular [auriku'lar] *adj* of the ear, aural.

sm (*dedo*) little finger; (*teléfono*) telephone receiver. **auriculares** *sm pl* headphones *pl*.

aurora [au'rora] *sf* dawn.

ausencia [au'senθja] *sf* absence. **ausente** *adj* absent; missing.

auspicio [aus'piθjo] *sm* auspice, omen; (*patrocinio*) patronage.

austero [aus'tero] *adj* austere. **austeridad** *sf* austerity.

austral [aus'tral] *adj* southern.

Australia [aus'tralja] *sf* Australia. **australiano, -a** *s, adj* Australian.

Austria ['austrja] *sf* Austria. **austriaco, -a** *s, adj* Austrian.

auténtico [au'tentiko] *adj* authentic. **autenticar** *v* authenticate. **autenticidad** *sf* authenticity.

autístico [au'tistiko] *adj* autistic.

auto¹ ['auto] *sm* (*fam*) car. **auto de choque** dodgem car.

auto² *sm* (*jur*) sentence; (*de un pleito*) judgment. **autos** *sm pl* proceedings *pl*.

autobiografía [autoβjogra'fia] *sf* autobiography. **autobiográfico** *adj* autobiographical.

autobús [auto'βus] *sm* bus.

autocar [auto'kar] *sm* motor coach.

autodominio [autoðo'minjo] *sm* self-control.

autoescuela [autoes'kwela] *sf* driving school.

autoexpresión [autoekspre'sjon] *sf* self-expression.

autógrafo [au'tografo] *sm, adj* autograph.

automata [au'tomata] *sm* robot.

automático [auto'matiko] *adj* automatic. **automización** *sf* automation.

automóvil [auto'moβil] *sm* motorcar. **automovilista** *s(m+f)* motorist.

autonomía [autono'mia] *sf* autonomy. **autónomo** *adj* autonomous.

autopista [auto'pista] *sf* expressway.

autopsia [au'topsja] *sf* autopsy, postmortem.

autor [au'tor], **-a** *sm, sf* author; creator.

autorizar [autori'θar] *v* authorize; approve. **autoridad** *sf* authority. **autoritario** *adj* authoritarian. **autorización** *sf* authorization. **autorizado** *adj* authorized, official; (*seguro*) reliable.

autorretrato [autorre'trato] *sm* self-portrait.

autoservicio [autoser'βiθjo] *sm* self-service restaurant; supermarket.

autostop [auto'stop] *sm* hitchhiking. **hacer el autostop** hitchhike. **autostopista** *s(m+f)* hitchhiker.

auxiliar [auksi'ljar] *v* help; attend. *sm, adj* assistant; auxiliary.

avalancha [aβa'lantʃa] *sf* avalanche.

avalorar [aβalo'rar] *v* (*realzar*) enhance; (*fig*) inspire.

avaluar [aβalu'ar] *v* value, appraise.

avanzar [aβan'θar] *v* advance, progress. **avance** *sm* advance; (*com*) balance. **avanzada** *sf* (*mil*) outpost.

avaricia [aβa'riθja] *sf* avarice. **avaricioso** *adj* greedy; miserly. **avaro** *adj* miserly, mean.

avasallar [aβasa'ʎar] *v* subjugate; dominate. **avasallarse** *v* submit.

ave ['aβe] *sf* bird. **aves de corral** *pl* poultry *sing*.

avecinarse [aβeθi'narse] *v* approach.

avellana [aβe'ʎana] *sf* hazelnut.

avena [a'βena] *sf sing* oats *pl*.

avenencia [aβe'nenθja] *sf* agreement; (*arreglo*) compromise.

avenida [aβe'niða] *sf* avenue.

*avenir [aβe'nir] *v* reconcile, bring together; (*suceder*) happen. **avenirse** *v* agree; adapt; correspond to. **avenimiento** *sm* agreement.

aveñtajar [aβenta'xar] *v* lead; come in front of; (*sobresalir*) surpass; prefer. **aventajado** *adj* outstanding; favourable.

aventura [aβen'tura] *sf* adventure; (*riesgo*) risk; (*amor*) affair. **aventurado** *adj* risky. **aventurar** *v* risk; venture. **aventurero** *adj* adventurous.

*avergonzar [aβergon'θar] *v* shame; (*poner en un apuro*) embarrass. **avergonzarse** *v* be ashamed. **avergonzado** *adj* ashamed; embarrassed.

avería[1] [aβe'ria] *sf* aviary.

avería[2] [aβe'ria] *sf* (*coche*) breakdown; (*daño*) damage. **averiar** *v* damage; break down.

averiguar [aβeri'gwar] *v* investigate; (*examinar*) verify. **averiguación** *sf* investigation; verification. **averiguador** *adj* investigating; inquiring.

aversión [aβer'sjon] *sf* aversion.

avestruz [aβes'truθ] *sm* ostrich.

aviación [aβja'θjon] *sf* aviation; air force. **aviador, -a** *sm, sf* aviator.

ávido ['aβiðo] *adj* avid; (*con ganas*) eager. **avidez** *sf* avidity; eagerness.

avinagrar [aβina'grar] *v* sour, make bitter. **avinagrado** *adj* sour; (*fam*) peevish.

avión[1] [a'βjon] *sm* aircraft. **avión a reacción** jet plane. **por avión** by airmail.

avión[2] *sm* swift; martin.

avisar [aβi'sar] *v* inform; advise; admonish. **avisado** *adj* prudent. **mal avisado** rash. **avisador, -a** *sm, sf* adviser; informer; messenger. **aviso** *sm* notice; announcement; advice; (*advertencia*) warning; prudence.

avispa [a'βispa] *sf* wasp.

avivar [aβi'βar] *v* enliven; (*acelerar*) hasten; revive. **avivador** *adj* hastening; enlivening.

ay ['ai] *interj* alas!

aya ['aja] *sf* governess.

ayer [a'jer] *adv* yesterday; (*fig*) formerly, lately. *sm* the recent past. **de ayer acá** since yesterday.

ayo ['ajo] *sm* tutor.

ayudar [aju'ðar] *v* help. **ayudarse** *v* help each other; make use of. **ayuda** *sf* help. **ayudante, -a** *sm, sf* assistant.

ayunar [aju'nar] *v* fast. **ayuno** *sm* fast, fasting.

ayuntamiento [ajunta'mjento] *sm* union; joint; (*cópula*) copulation; (*institución*) town council; (*edificio*) town hall.

azada [a'θaða] *sf* hoe; spade.

azafata [aθa'fata] *sf* air hostess.

azafrán [aθa'fran] *sm* saffron.

azahar [aθa'ar] *sm* orange blossom; lemon blossom.

azar [a'θar] *sm* chance, accident; (*desgracia*) misfortune. **al azar** at random.

azogue [a'θoge] *sm* mercury.

azorar [aθo'rar] *v* upset, embarrass. **azorarse** *v* become flustered. **azoramiento** *sm* embarrassment; (*miedo*) fear.

azotar [aθo'tar] *v* beat; (*a un niño*) spank; (*látigo*) whip. **azote** *sm* whip; spanking; (*fig: verdugo*) scourge.

azotea [aθo'tea] *sf* flat roof.

azúcar [a'θukar] *sm or sf* sugar. **azúcar en terrón** lump sugar. **azúcar extra fina** castor sugar. **azúcar morena** brown sugar. **azucarado** *adj* sugary. **azucarero, -a** *sm, sf* sugar bowl.

azucena [aθu'θena] *sf* white lily.

azufre [a'θufre] *sm* sulphur.

azul [a'θul] *sm, adj* blue. **azul marino** navy blue. **azulado** *adj* blue, bluish.

azulejo [aθu'lexo] *sm* tile.
azuzar [aθu'θar] *v* (*fig*) incite; urge; cause trouble. **azuzador, -a** *sm, sf* trouble-maker.

B

baba ['baβa] *sf* saliva, spit. **babero** *sm* bib.
Babia ['baβja] *sf* **estar en Babia** have one's head in the clouds.
babor [ba'βor] *sm* (*mar*) port side.
babosa [ba'βosa] *sf* slug.
bacalao [baka'lao] *sm* cod.
bacía [ba'θia] *sf* (*de barbero*) shaving-bowl; (*recipiente*) metal basin.
bacteria [bak'teria] *sf* germ. **bacterias** *sf pl* bacteria *pl*.
bache ['batʃe] *sm* pothole.
bachiller [batʃi'ʎer] *s*(*m+f*) holder of a school-leaving certificate; (*universidad*) holder of a bachelor's degree. **bachillerato** *sm* school-leaving certificate; bachelor's degree.
bagaje [ba'gaxe] *sm* (*mil*) baggage; (*animal*) beast of burden.
bahía [ba'ia] *sf* bay.
bailar [bai'lar] *v* dance. **bailarín, -ina** *sm, sf* ballet dancer. **baile** *sm* dancing; dance; ball. **baile de disfraces** *or* **trajes** fancy-dress ball.
bajamar [baxa'mar] *sf* low tide.
bajar [ba'xar] *v* get down; lower; let down; take *or* bring down. **baja** *sf* fall, drop. **bajada** *sf* (*caída*) drop; (*pendiente*) slope; (*descendimiento*) descent.
bajo ['baxo] *adj* (*estatura*) short; low; lowered; (*sonido*) soft; (*conducta*) disgraceful. *adv* low; below; quietly, softly. *prep* under. **bajeza** *sf* base act; lowness.
bajón [ba'xon] *sm* (*música*) bassoon; (*bajada*) fall.
bala ['bala] *sf* (*proyectil*) bullet; (*algodón*) bale. **balazo** *sm* (*tiro*) shot; (*herida*) wound.
balada [ba'laða] *sf* ballad.
baladí [bala'ði] *adj* trivial, unimportant.
baladrón [bala'ðron], **-ona** *sm, sf* boaster, braggart. *adj* boastful.
balancear [balanθe'ar] *v* balance; (*barco*)

roll; (*vacilar*) hesitate. **balancearse** *v* roll; (*en un columpio*) swing. **balance** *sm* (*com*) balance sheet; (*inventario*) stocktaking. **balanceo** *sm* balancing; (*oscilación*) swaying. **balanza** *sf* scales *pl*.
balar [ba'lar] *v* bleat.
balaustrada [balau'straða] *sf* balustrade.
balbucear [balβuθe'ar] *v* stammer, stutter. **balbuceo** *sm* stammer.
balcón [bal'kon] *sm* balcony.
baldar [bal'ðar] *v* cripple; (*naipes*) trump; (*molestar*) inconvenience. **baldarse** *v* wear oneself out. **baldado, -a** *sm, sf* cripple.
baldadura *sf* infirmity.
balde¹ ['balðe] *sm* bucket.
balde² *adv* **de balde** free of charge. **en balde** in vain.
baldío [bal'ðio] *sm* wasteland. *adj* uncultivated; (*fig*) useless.
baldón [bal'ðon] *sm* (*afrenta*) affront; (*deshonra*) disgrace.
baldosa [bal'ðosa] *sf* paving tile.
balneario [balne'arjo] *sm* spa.
balón [ba'lon] *sm* ball, football; (*com*) bale. **baloncesto** *sm* basketball. **balonvolea** *sm* volleyball.
balsa¹ ['balsa] *sf* balsa.
balsa² *sf* raft.
balsa³ *sf* (*agua*) pond.
bálsamo ['balsamo] *sm* balsam; (*fig*) balm.
Báltico ['baltiko] *sm* Baltic Sea. **báltico** *adj* Baltic.
ballena [ba'ʎena] *sf* whale.
ballesta [ba'ʎesta] *sf* crossbow. **ballestero** *sm* archer.
ballet [ba'le] *sm* ballet.
bambolear [bambole'ar] *v* sway.
bambolla [bam'boʎa] *sf* show, ostentation. **darse bambolla** show off.
bambú [bam'bu] *sm* bamboo.
banana [ba'nana] *sf* banana. **banano** *sm* banana tree.
banasta [ba'nasta] *sf* large basket.
banca ['banka] *sf* (*asiento*) bench; (*com*) banking.
bancarrota [bankar'rota] *sf* bankruptcy. **hacer bancarrota** go bankrupt.
banco ['banko] *sm* bench; (*iglesia*) pew; (*colegio*) desk; (*com*) bank.
banda ['banda] *sf* group; (*pandilla*) gang; (*faja*) sash; (*cinta*) ribbon; (*lado*) side; (*orilla*) river bank. **bandada** *sf* flock.
bandeja [ban'dexa] *sf* tray.

bandera [ban'dera] *sf* flag, banner. **a banderas desplegadas** openly. **banderilla** *sf* bullfighter's dart. **banderillero** *sm* one who thrusts banderillas into the bull.

bandido [ban'diðo] *sm* bandit.

bando ['bando] *sm* proclamation; (*facción*) faction; party; (*pez*) shoal (of fish).

bandolero [bando'lero], **-a** *sm, sf* bandit.

banjo ['banxo] *sm* banjo.

banquete [ban'kete] *sm* banquet, feast.

bañar [ba'ɲar] *v* bathe. **bañarse** *v* (*en la bañera*) have a bath; (*en el mar*) bathe. **bañera** *sf* bathtub. **bañero** *sm* lifeguard. **bañista** *s(m+f)* bather. **baño** *sm* bath; (*en el agua*) dip, swim; (*cubierta*) coating. **cuarto de baño** bathroom.

baquetear [bakete'ar] *v* (*incomodar*) bother; (*maltratar*) treat harshly. **baquetazo** *sm* blow, knock. **baqueteo** *sm* (*traqueteo*) jolting; (*molestia*) bother.

bar [bar] *sm* bar.

baraja [ba'raxa] *sf* pack of cards. **barajar** *v* shuffle.

barandilla [baran'diʎa] *sf* rail, railing.

barato [ba'rato] *adj* cheap. **dar de barato** take for granted. **baratear** *v* undersell. **baratija** *sf* trinket. **baratijas** *sf pl* junk *sing*. **baratura** *sf* cheapness.

baraúnda [bara'unda] *sf* (*alboroto*) uproar; (*confusión*) chaos.

barba ['barβa] *sf* beard. **barba a barba** face to face. **barbado** *adj* bearded. **barbería** *sf* barber's shop. **barbero** *sm* barber. **barbudo** *adj* having a full beard.

bárbaro ['barβaro], **-a** *sm, sf* barbarian; (*fig*) lout. *adj* barbarous, barbaric; (*bruto*) rough; (*fam*) fantastic. **barbaridad** *sf* barbarity; (*ultraje*) outrage. **¡qué barbaridad!** fancy that! how terrible!

barbecho [bar'βetʃo] *sm* fallow land. **barbechar** *v* leave fallow.

barbilla [bar'βiʎa] *sf* chin.

barca ['barka] *sf* boat. **barca de pasaje** ferry boat.

barco ['barko] *sm* ship, boat. **ir en barco** go by boat.

barnizar [barni'θar] *v* (*madera*) varnish; (*cerámica*) glaze. **barniz** *sm* varnish; glaze.

barómetro [ba'rometro] *sm* barometer. **barométrico** *adj* barometric.

barón [ba'ron] *sm* baron. **baronesa** *sf* baroness. **baronet** *sm* baronet.

barquillo [bar'kiʎo] *sm* thin sweet wafer.

barra ['barra] *sf* (*metal, madera, chocolate, jabón, etc.*) bar; (*vara*) rod; (*joya*) pin; (*palanca*) lever; (*pan*) loaf; (*jur*) dock; (*mar*) tiller.

barraca [bar'raka] *sf* cabin, hut; (*feria*) stall.

barranco [bar'ranko] *sm* ravine, gully; (*fig*) obstacle.

barrenar [barre'nar] *v* drill, bore; (*leyes*) violate; (*una empresa*) foil. **barrena** *sf* drill.

barrer [bar'rer] *v* sweep.

barrera [bar'rera] *sf* barrier; obstacle; gate. **barrera de peaje** tollgate.

barricada [barri'kada] *sf* barricade.

barriga [bar'riga] *sf* belly.

barril [bar'ril] *sm* barrel.

barrio ['barrjo] *sm* district, quarter.

barro ['barro] *sm* mud. **barroso** *adj* muddy.

barroco [bar'roko] *sm* baroque period. *adj* baroque.

barruntar [barrun'tar] *v* have a feeling; (*suponer*) suppose. **barruntador** *adj* prophetic. **barrunte** *or* **barrunto** *sm* feeling; supposition; (*indicio*) sign.

bártulos ['bartulos] *sm pl* belongings, odds and ends. **liar los bártulos** pack one's bags.

barullo [ba'ruʎo] *sm* confusion; (*alboroto*) row. **a barullo** galore.

basar [ba'sar] *v* found; base. **basarse en** be based on. **base** *sf* base, basis. **a base de** by. **alimento base** staple food. **básico** *adj* basic, essential.

bastante [bas'tante] *adj* enough. *adv* enough, sufficiently; (*algo*) rather, fairly. **bastar** *v* suffice. **¡basta!** that's enough!

bastardo [bas'tardo], **-a** *s, adj* bastard. **bastardear** *v* degenerate. **bastardilla** *sf* italics *pl*. **bastardillo** *adj* italic.

bastidor [basti'ðor] *sm* frame; (*ventana*) sash. **entre bastidores** behind the scenes.

basto¹ ['basto] *adj* coarse, crude.

basto² *sm* (*arnés*) pack-saddle.

basto³ *sm* (*naipes*) ace of clubs. **bastos** *sm pl* clubs.

bastón [bas'ton] *sm* cane, stick.

basura [ba'sura] *sf* rubbish, litter. **basurero** *sm* dustman.

bata ['bata] *sm* (*de cama*) dressing gown; (*de médico, etc.*) overall.

batalla [ba'taʎa] *sf* battle. **campo de batalla** battlefield.

batata [ba'tata] *sf* sweet potato.

batea [ba'tea] *sf* (*barco*) punt; (*bandeja*) tray; (*vagón*) open wagon.

batería [bate'ria] *sf* battery; (*teatro*) footlights; (*música*) percussion. **batería de cocina** kitchen utensils *pl*.

batir [ba'tir] *v* (*huevos*) beat; (*las manos*) clap; (*vencer*) defeat; (*derribar*) knock down; (*culin*) whisk. **batirse** *v* fight.

batido *sm* (*leche*) milk shake; (*culin*) batter. **batidor** *sm* whisk.

batuta [ba'tuta] *sf* (*música*) baton. **llevar la batuta** rule the roost.

baúl [ba'ul] *sm* trunk.

bautizar [bauti'θar] *v* baptize, christen; (*fam*: *vino*, *etc*.) water down. **bautismo** *sm* baptism, christening. **bautista** *sm* Baptist.

baya ['baja] *sf* berry.

bayeta [ba'jeta] *sf* baize; floorcloth; rag.

bayoneta [bajo'neta] *sf* bayonet.

baza ['baθa] *sf* (*naipes*) trick. **meter baza** intervene.

bazar [ba'θar] *sm* bazaar.

bazo ['baθo] *sm* spleen. *adj* brownish yellow.

beato [be'ato] *adj* pious; blessed; (*fam*) sanctimonious.

beber [be'βer] *v* drink. **beberse** *v* drink up. **bebida** *sf* drink.

beca ['beka] *sf* grant; scholarship.

becerro [be'θerro] *sm* yearling calf.

bedel [be'ðel] *sm* porter; beadle.

befar [be'far] *v* mock, taunt. **befa** *sf* jeer, taunt.

béisbol ['beisβol] *sm* baseball.

Belén [be'len] *s* Bethlehem. **belén** *sm* Nativity scene; (*fam*) bedlam.

Bélgica ['belxika] *sf* Belgium. **belga** *s*(*m*+*f*). *adj* Belgian.

bélico ['beliko] *adj* warlike. **belicosidad** *sf* bellicosity. **belicoso** *adj* bellicose.

beligerante [belixe'rante] *s*(*m*+*f*). *adj* belligerent. **beligerancia** *sf* belligerence.

bellaco [be'ʎako], **-a** *sm, sf* rogue. *adj* cunning; wicked.

belleza [be'ʎeθa] *sf* beauty. **bellísimo** *adj* gorgeous. **bello** *adj* beautiful; noble.

bellota [be'ʎota] *sf* acorn.

bemol [be'mol] *sm, adj* (*música*) flat.

bencina [ben'θina] *sf* benzine.

***bendecir** [bende'θir] *v* bless; praise. **bendición** *sf* benediction; grace. **bendito** *adj* blessed; saintly; (*fam*) wretched.

beneficiar [benefi'θjar] *v* benefit; profit. **benefactor**, **-a** *sm, sf also* **beneficiador**, **-a** benefactor. **beneficencia** *sf* charity; welfare. **beneficiado**, **-a** *sm, sf also* **beneficiario**, **-a** beneficiary. **beneficio** *sm* benefit; gain. **beneficioso** *adj* beneficial.

benemérito [bene'merito] *adj* worthy, well-deserving.

beneplácito [bene'plaθito] *sm* consent, approval.

benevolencia [benevo'lenθja] *sf* benevolence. **benevolente** *or* **benévolo** *adj* benevolent.

benignidad [benigni'dað] *sf* kindness; (*clima*) mildness. **benigno** *adj* kind; mild.

beodo [be'oðo], **-a** *sm, sf* drunkard. *adj* drunk.

berberecho [berβe'retʃo] *sm* cockle.

berenjena [beren'xena] *sf* eggplant.

bermejo [ber'mexo] *adj* vermilion; (*cabellos*) ginger.

bermellón [berme'ʎon] *sm* vermilion.

berrear [berre'ar] *v* bellow; yell. **berrearse** *v* (*fam*) spill the beans. **berrido** *sm* bellow; yell.

berrinche [ber'rintʃe] *sm* (*fam*) tantrum.

berro ['berro] *sm* watercress.

berza ['berθa] *sf* cabbage.

besar [be'sar] *v* kiss. **beso** *sm* kiss.

bestia ['bestja] *sf* beast, animal. *sm, sf* (*persona*) beast; idiot. **bestial** *adj* bestial; beastly; (*fam*) smashing; enormous. **bestialidad** *sf* bestiality; beastliness.

betún [be'tun] *sm* shoe polish; bitumen.

biblia ['biβlia] *sf* Bible. **bíblico** *adj* biblical.

bibliografía [biβliogra'fia] *sf* bibliography. **bibliográfico** *adj* bibliographic(al). **bibliógrafo**, **-a** *sm, sf* bibliographer.

biblioteca [biβlio'teka] *sf* library. **bibliotecario**, **-a** *sm, sf* librarian.

bíceps ['biθeps] *sm invar* biceps.

bicicleta [biθi'kleta] *sf* bicycle.

bicho ['bitʃo] *sm* small animal; insect; (*fam*) odd character; (*fam*) ugly person.

bieldo ['bjelðo] *sm* pitchfork.

bien [bjen] *adv* well; right; properly; very; fully; easily; gladly. **ahora bien** nevertheless. **o bien** or else. **¿y bien?** so what? *sm* good; welfare; advantage; gain; darling. **bien que** *conj* also **si bien** although. **no bien** no sooner. **bienes** *sm pl* property *sing*, riches. **bienes inmuebles** real estate *sing*.

bienal [bje'nal] *sf, adj* biennial.

bienaventurado [bjenaβentu'raðo] *adj* happy; blessed; (*fig*) naïve.

bienestar [bjenes'tar] *sm* well-being; comfort.

bienhechor [bjene'tʃor], **-a** *sm, sf* benefactor.

bienio ['bjenjo] *sm* period of two years.

bienvenida [bjenβe'niða] *sf* welcome. **dar la bienvenida a** welcome.

biftec [bif'tek] *sm* steak.

bifurcarse [bifur'karse] *v* fork; branch off. **bifurcación** *sf* fork; junction.

bigamia [bi'gamja] *sf* bigamy. **bígamo**, **-a** *sm, sf* bigamist.

bigote [bi'gote] *sm* moustache.

bilingüe [bi'lingwe] *adj* bilingual.

bilis ['bilis] *sf* bile; (*fig*) bad temper.

billar [bi'ʎar] *sm* billiards. **billar ruso** snooker.

billete [bi'ʎete] *sm* ticket; (*dinero*) banknote; (*carta*) letter. **billete de abono** season ticket. **billete de ida** single ticket. **billete de ida y vuelta** return ticket. **sacar un billete** buy a ticket.

billón [bi'ʎon] *sm* billion.

binóculo [bi'nokulo] *sm* binoculars *pl*.

biografía [biogra'fia] *sf* biography. **biográfico** *adj* biographical. **biógrafo**, **-a** *sm, sf* biographer.

biología [biolo'xia] *sf* biology. **biológico** *adj* biological. **biólogo** *sm* biologist.

biombo ['bjombo] *sm* folding screen.

bióxido [bi'oksido] *sm* dioxide. **bioxido de carbono** carbon dioxide.

biplano [bi'plano] *sm* biplane.

birlar [bir'lar] *v* (*fam: robar*) pinch, swipe; (*fam: matar*) bump off.

bisabuela [bisa'βwela] *sf* great-grandmother. **bisabuelo** *sm* great-grandfather.

bisagra [bi'sagra] *sf* hinge.

bisiesto [bi'sjesto] *adj* **año bisiesto** leap year.

bisoño [bi'soɲo], **-a** *sm, sf* greenhorn, novice; (*mil*) rookie.

bizarría [biθar'ria] *sf* (*valor*) bravery; generosity.

bizcar [biθ'kar] *v* squint. **bizco** *adj* cross-eyed. **dejar bizco** (*fam*) dumbfound.

bizcocho [biθ'kotʃo] *sm* sponge cake. **bizcocho borracho** rum baba.

bizma ['biθma] *sf* poultice.

blanco ['blanko], **-a** *adj* white; blank; (*fam*) cowardly. *sm, sf* white man/woman; white colour; *sm* (*de tiro*)

target. **blanca** *sf* (*música*) minim. **no tener blanca** be completely broke. **blancura** *sf* whiteness. **dar en el blanco** be on target. **quedarse en blanco** be disappointed. **blanquear** *v* whiten; whitewash. **blanquecer** *v* whitewash; bleach.

blandir [blan'dir] *v* flourish, brandish.

blando ['blando] *adj* soft; mild; gentle. *adv* softly; gently. **blandura** *sf* softness; tenderness; (*carácter*) weakness.

blasfemar [blasfe'mar] *v* blaspheme; (*fig*) curse. **blasfemia** *sf* blasphemy; curse. **blasfemo**, **-a** *sm, sf* blasphemer.

blasón [bla'son] *sm* heraldry; (*escudo*) coat of arms. **hacer blasón de** boast about.

blindaje [blin'daxe] *sm* armour. **blindado** *adj* armoured; armour-plated.

bloquear [bloke'ar] *v* block; obstruct; (*mil*) blockade. **bloque** *sm* block; bloc. **bloqueo** *sm* blockade.

blusa ['blusa] *sf* blouse; (*guardapolvo*) overall.

boa ['boa] *sf* boa constrictor.

boato [bo'ato] *sm* pomp; show.

bobada [bo'baða] *sf* nonsense; foolish thing. **bobería** *sf* stupidity. **bobo**, **-a** *sm, sf* fool, idiot.

bobina [bo'bina] *sf* reel, spool.

boca ['boka] *sf* mouth; opening. **a boca de jarro** point-blank. **a boca de noche** at dusk. **boca abajo/arriba** face down/up. **¡punto en boca!** mum's the word!

bocacalle [boka'kaʎe] *sf* intersection.

bocadillo [boka'ðiʎo] *sm* sandwich; snack. **bocado** *sm* mouthful; bite.

boceto [bo'θeto] *sm* (*dibujo*) sketch; (*escrito*) draft.

bocina [bo'θina] *sf* trumpet; (*aut*) horn, hooter.

bochorno [bo'tʃorno] *sm* sultry weather; (*vergüenza*) embarrassment; (*mareo*) giddiness. **sufrir un bochorno** feel embarrassed. **bochornoso** *adj* sultry; thundery; embarrassing.

boda ['boða] *sf* wedding, marriage.

bodega [bo'ðega] *sf* wine cellar; wine shop; bar.

bofetada [bofe'taða] *sf* slap; blow.

boga ['boga] *sf* (*mar*) rowing; (*fig*) vogue. **estar en boga** be in fashion. **bogador**, **-a** *sm, sf* rower.

bohemio [bo'emjo], **-a** *s, adj* Bohemian; (*gitano*) gipsy.

boicotear [boikote'ar] v boycott. **boicot** or **boicoteo** sm boycott.

boina ['boina] sf beret.

bola ['bola] sf ball; (*canica*) marble; (*betún*) shoe polish; (*del mundo*) globe; (*fig*) fib. **bola de naftalina** mothball.

bolear v fib; throw.

boleta [bo'leta] sf ticket; pass; (*vale*) voucher; (*votación*) ballot paper.

boleto [bo'leto] sm lottery ticket; betting slip; (*fam*) fib. **boletín** sm bulletin. **boletín de noticias** news bulletin. **boletín de precios** price list. **boletín meteorológico** weather forecast.

bolígrafo [bo'ligrafo] sm ballpoint pen.

Bolivia [bo'liβja] sf Bolivia. **boliviano, -a** s, adj Bolivian.

bolsa ['bolsa] sf bag; purse. **bolsillo** sm pocket.

bollo ['boʎo] sm roll, bun, small loaf.

bomba ['bomba] sf pump, bomb. **bomba de gasolina** petrol pump.

bombardear [bombarðe'ar] v bombard.

bombilla [bom'biʎa] sf (*elec*) light bulb; (*tecn*) small pump; glass tube.

bombo ['bombo] sm big drum; great praise. adj surprised.

bombón [bom'bon] sm sweet, chocolate.

bonachón [bona'tʃon] adj (*fam*) genial.

bondad [bon'dað] sf goodness; kindness. **tenga la bondad de ...** please ... . **bondadoso** adj warm-hearted; good.

bonete [bo'nete] sm academic cap. **gran bonete** important person.

bonito [bo'nito] adj pretty, nice, graceful.

bono ['bono] sm voucher; certificate; bond. **bono postal** money-order.

boquear [boke'ar] v gasp; utter; be dying. **boqueada** sf gasp.

boquerón [boke'ron] sm large opening; anchovy; whitebait. **boquete** sm small hole; gap.

boquiabierto [bokja'βjerto] adj open-mouthed; gaping.

boquilla [bo'kiʎa] sf mouthpiece; nozzle; pipe stem.

borboll(e)ar [borβo'ʎar] v bubble. **borbolleo** sm bubbling. **borbollón** sm bubble.

borbotar [borβo'tar] v bubble; boil; gush. **borbotón** sm bubbling; boiling.

bordar [bor'ðar] v embroider. **bordado** sm embroidery.

borde ['borðe] sm border, edge; rim. **bordear** v skirt, edge round.

bordillo [bor'ðiʎo] sm kerb.

bordo ['borðo] sm (*mar*) side of a ship; tack. **a bordo** on board. **de alto bordo** ocean-going.

boreal [bore'al] adj northern.

bornear [borne'ar] v bend, turn, twist; warp.

borra ['borra] sf coarse wool; nap; waste; (*fam*) idle chatter.

borracho [bor'ratʃo] adj drunk; (*fam*) crazy. **borrachera** or **borrachería** sf drunkenness; drunken spree.

borrador [borra'ðor] sm rough copy; blotter; scribbling pad.

borrar [bor'rar] v cross out; erase; blot. **goma de borrar** rubber. **borrable** adj erasable.

borrasca [bor'raska] sf storm; squall. **borrascoso** adj stormy; squally; (*fig*) boisterous.

borrico [bor'riko] sm ass. **puesto en el borrico** hellbent.

borrón [bor'ron] sm blot, smudge; blemish; stain. **borronear** v scribble (on). **borroso** adj blurred; smudged; stained; illegible.

bosque ['boske] sm forest, wood.

bosquejar [boske'xar] v make a rough sketch of. **bosquejo** sm outline; sketch.

bostezar [boste'θar] v yawn. **bostezo** sm yawn.

bota[1] ['bota] sf boot. **ponerse las botas a** do justice to (something).

bota[2] sf wineskin.

botánica [bo'tanika] sf botany. **botánico** adj botanical. **botanista** s(m+f) botanist.

botar [bo'tar] v throw, fling; launch.

bote[1] ['bote] sm thrust; blow; jump; bounce.

bote[2] sm jar; can.

bote[3] sm boat. **bote salvavidas** lifeboat.

botella [bo'teʎa] sf bottle.

botica [bo'tika] sf chemist's shop; medicine chest; medicines pl; shop, store. **hay de todo como en botica** there is everything under the sun. **boticario** sm chemist.

botija [bo'tixa] sf earthenware pot. **botijo** sm earthenware jug.

botín [bo'tin] sm booty, loot.

botón [bo'ton] sm button; (*flor*) bud; (*puerta*) knob. **botonar** v bud.

bóveda ['boβeða] sf vault. **bóveda de jardín** bower.

bucle

bovino [bo'βino] adj bovine.
boxear [bokse'ar] v box. **boxeador** sm boxer. **boxeo** sm boxing.
boya ['boja] sf buoy. **boyante** adj buoyant.
bozal [bo'θal] sm muzzle. s(m+f) (fam) greenhorn. adj (fam) stupid; foolish; untamed.
bracero [bra'θero], **-a** sm, sf hired hand; labourer.
braga ['braga] sf (cuerda) guy-rope; (de mujer) knickers pl; (de niño) nappy. **calzarse las bragas** wear the trousers.
bramar [bra'mar] v roar, bellow. **bramido** sm roar, bellow.
brasa ['brasa] sf live coal. **estar en brasas** be on edge. **brasero** sm brazier.
Brasil [bra'sil] sm Brazil. **brasileño, -a** s, adj Brazilian.
bravío [bra'βio] adj wild; fierce. sm fierceness.
bravo ['braβo] adj brave; fierce; (fam) rough; (fam) rude; (fam) luxurious. **mar bravo** rough sea. **¡bravo!** interj bravo! well done! **bravura** sf ferocity; courage; manliness.
brazada [bra'θaða] sf arm movement; stroke. **brazado** sm armful.
brazalete [braθa'lete] sm bracelet.
brazo ['braθo] sm arm; branch; (fig) strength, power. **brazo a brazo** hand to hand. **a brazo partido** with bare fists. **brazo derecho** right-hand man. **tener brazo** be tough.
brea ['brea] sf pitch, tar.
brebaje [bre'βaxe] sm concoction, potion.
brecol ['brekol] sm broccoli.
brecha ['bretʃa] sf breach, opening.
bregar¹ [bre'gar] v struggle; fight. **brega** sf struggle; quarrel. **andar a la brega** (fig) slog away.
bregar² v (amasar) knead.
Bretaña [bre'taɲa] sf Britain; Brittany. **Gran Bretaña** Great Britain. **bretón, -ona** s, adj Breton.
breve ['breβe] adj brief, short. **en breve** before long. sf (música) breve. **brevedad** sf brevity.
brezal [bre'θal] sm heath. **brezo** sm heather.
bribón [bri'βon], **-ona** sm, sf rascal; rogue; vagabond. adj rascally.
brida ['briða] sf bridle; rein; horsemanship. **a toda brida** hell for leather.

brigada [bri'gaða] sf brigade; gang; squad. sm sergeant-major.
brillar [bri'ʎar] v shine; sparkle; gleam. **brillante** adj brilliant; shining; glossy. **brillo** sm brilliance; brightness; glitter.
brincar [brin'kar] v bounce; jump; hop. **brinco** sm jump; hop; skip; bounce.
brindar [brin'ðar] v offer; drink someone's health. **brindis** sm invar toast.
brío ['brio] sm spirit; vigour; determination. **brioso** adj spirited; vigorous; determined; elegant.
brisa ['brisa] sf breeze.
británico [bri'taniko], **-a** sm, sf Briton. adj British. **los británicos** the British.
brocha ['brotʃa] sf paintbrush; (afeitar) shaving brush.
broche ['brotʃe] sm brooch; clasp, clip. **broche de oro** finishing touch.
broma ['broma] sf joke; fun; trick. **broma pesada** practical joke. **en broma** as a joke. **sin broma** joking apart. **bromear** v joke. **bromista** s(m+f) practical joker; funny person.
bromuro [bro'muro] sm bromide.
bronca ['bronka] sf (fam) row; brawl; ticking off. **echar una bronca** tick off.
bronce ['bronθe] sm bronze. **bronceado** adj bronzed; sun-tanned.
bronco ['bronko] adj rough; brittle; (voz) harsh; (carácter) hard, rude.
bronquial [bronki'al] adj bronchial. **bronquitis** sf bronchitis.
brotar [bro'tar] v grow; bud; germinate; spring forth. **brote** sm bud; shoot; (agua) gushing; (fiebre) rise; (fig) outbreak.
bruja ['bruxa] sf witch. **brujo** sm sorcerer.
brújula ['bruxula] sf compass. **perder la brújula** lose one's grip.
bruma ['bruma] sf mist. **brumoso** adj misty.
bruno ['bruno] adj dark brown.
bruñir [bru'ɲir] v polish. **bruñido** sm shine, polish. **bruñidor** sm polisher.
brusco ['brusko] adj brusque; abrupt; rough.
Bruselas [bru'selas] sf Brussels.
bruto ['bruto] adj coarse; brutish; rough; gross. sm brute; beast. **en bruto** gross; rough; uncut. **brutal** adj brutal; savage. **brutalidad** sf brutality; brutishness.
bucear [buθe'ar] v dive; swim underwater. **buceo** sm dive; diving; skin diving.
bucle ['bukle] sm curl; ringlet.

buche ['butʃe] *sm* craw; crop; stomach; (*fam*) belly; (*fam*) bosom, breast.

budismo [bu'ðismo] *sm* Buddhism. **budista** *s*(*m+f*), *adj* Buddhist.

buenaventura [bwenaβen'tura] *sf* good luck, fortune.

bueno ['bweno] *adj also* **buen** good; right; sound; fine; (*fam*) funny; (*fam*) amazing. *interj, conj* well; all right. **a buenas** of one's own accord. **buena voluntad** goodwill. **de buena gana** willingly. **¡buenas!** hello! **buenas noches** good night. **buenas tardes** good afternoon; good evening. **buenos días** good morning. **de buenas a primeras** without warning; at first sight; straight away. **estar de buenas** be in a good mood.

buey [bwej] *sm* ox. **a paso de buey** at a snail's pace.

búfalo ['bufalo] *sm* buffalo.

bufanda [bu'fanda] *sf* scarf, muffler.

bufar [bu'far] *v* spit; snort; puff and blow.

bufete [bu'fete] *sm* (*mesa*) writing-desk; (*despacho*) solicitor's office; clientele.

buhardilla [bwar'ðiʎa] *sf* attic, garret; skylight.

búho ['buo] *sm* owl; (*fam*) recluse.

buhonero [bwo'nero] *sm* pedlar, hawker. **buhonería** *sf* hawking, peddling.

buitre ['bwitre] *sm* vulture.

bujía [bu'xia] *sf* candle; candlepower; (*aut*) sparking-plug.

bulbo ['bulβo] *sm* (*bot*) bulb. **bulboso** *adj* bulbous.

Bulgaria [bul'garja] *sf* Bulgaria. **búlgaro, -a** *s, adj* Bulgarian.

bulto ['bulto] *sm* bulk, size; shape; form; bale, package; piece of luggage; (*med*) lump, swelling. **a bulto** approximately. **de bulto** obvious. **escoger a bulto** pick at random.

bulla ['buʎa] *sf* noise; bustle. **meter bulla** kick up a racket.

bullir [bu'ʎir] *v* boil; swarm; stir; bustle; abound; itch. **bullicio** *sm* bustle; uproar. **bullicioso** *adj* lively; noisy; bustling.

buñuelo [bu'ɲwelo] *sm* fritter; doughnut; (*fam*) mess.

buque ['buke] *sm* ship, vessel. **buque de guerra** warship. **buque cargero** freighter.

burbujear [burβuxe'ar] *v* bubble. **burbuja** *sf* bubble.

burdel [bur'ðel] *sm* brothel.

burdo ['burðo] *adj* clumsy; coarse; crude.

burgués [bur'ges] *adj* bourgeois, middle-class. **burguesía** *sf* bourgeoisie, middle class.

burla ['burla] *sf* hoax; joke; trick; taunt. **burlar** *v* hoax; trick; mock. **burlarse de** make fun of. **burlería** *sf* fun; artifice; deceit; ridicule.

burocracia [buro'kraθja] *sf* bureaucracy. **burócrata** *s*(*m+f*) bureaucrat. **burocrático** *adj* bureaucratic.

burro ['burro] *sm* donkey; (*fam*) fool. **burro cargado de letras** pompous ass.

buscar [bus'kar] *v* search for, look for. **busca** *sf* search. **en busca de** in search of. **buscador, -a** *sm, sf* seeker. **búsqueda** *sf* search.

busto ['busto] *sm* bust.

butaca [bu'taka] *sf* theatre seat; armchair.

buzo ['buθo] *sm* diver. **campana de buzo** diving-bell.

buzón [bu'θon] *sm* pillar box, letter box; plug, bung.

C

cabal [ka'βal] *adj* exact; complete; perfect. *adv* exactly; perfectly.

cábala ['kaβala] *sf* (*fig*) intrigue; divination.

cabalgar [kaβal'gar] *v* ride. **cabalgada** *sf* raid; cavalcade. **cabalgador** *sm* horseman.

caballa [ka'βaʎa] *sf* mackerel.

caballero [kaβa'ʎero] *sm* horseman; gentleman; knight. **caballeresco** *adj* chivalrous. **caballería** *sf* cavalry.

caballete [kaβa'ʎete] *sm* ridge; trestle; easel; bridge of the nose.

caballo [ka'βaʎo] *sm* horse; (*ajedrez*) knight; (*naipes*) queen. **a caballo** on horseback. **caballo de vapor** horsepower. **caballo entero** stallion. **caballito** *sm* pony.

cabaña [ka'βaɲa] *sf* cabin; herd, flock.

cabaret [kaβa're] *sm* cabaret; nightclub.

cabecear [kaβeθe'ar] *v* nod; shake one's head. **cabecera** *sf* (*de mesa, cama, etc.*) head; river's source.

cabello [ka'βeʎo] *sm* hair. **traído por los cabellos** far-fetched. **cabelludo** *adj* hairy; shaggy; downy.

*caber [ka'βer] v fit, find room; befall; be possible. **no cabe duda** there is no doubt.

cabestro [ka'βestro] sm halter; leading ox. **llevar del cabestro** lead by the nose.

cabestrillo sm arm sling.

cabeza [ka'βeθa] sf head; chief; summit; capital. **cabeza de turco** scapegoat. **cabeza torcida** hypocrite. **cabezudo** adj big-headed.

cabida [ka'βiða] sf capacity, space. **dar cabida a** make room for. **tener cabida** be appropriate.

cabildo [ka'βilðo] sm town council; (rel) chapter.

cabina [ka'βina] sf cabin; telephone kiosk.

cabizbajo [kaβiθ'βaxo] adj downcast.

cable ['kaβle] sm cable, rope; cable(gram). **cablegrafiar** v cable. **cablegrama** sm cable(gram).

cabo ['kaβo] sm cape, headland; end; stump; handle; rope; corporal; bit, piece. **al cabo de** at the end of. **llevar a cabo** carry out.

cabotaje [kaβo'taxe] sm coastal navigation.

cabra ['kaβra] sf goat.

cabria ['kaβrja] sf crane, hoist.

cabriola [ka'βrjola] sf gambol; hop; jump. **cabriolar** v jump; caper.

cacahuete [kaka'wete] sm peanut.

cacao [ka'kao] sm cocoa; cacao.

cacarear [kakare'ar] v crow, cackle; boast. **cacareo** sm crowing, cackling; boasting.

cacería [kaθe'ria] sf hunting; hunt.

cacerola [kaθe'rola] sf saucepan.

cacique [ka'θike] sm political boss; tyrant.

caco ['kako] sm pickpocket; thief; (fam) coward.

cacto ['kakto] sm cactus.

cacharrería [katʃarre'ria] sf crockery.

cacharro sm earthenware vessel; thing; piece of junk. **lavar los cacharros** do the washing-up.

cachemir [katʃe'mir] sm cashmere.

cachete [ka'tʃete] sm blow, slap; cheek; swollen cheek. **cachetear** v slap.

cachivache [katʃi'βatʃe] sm pot; thing; utensil; bauble.

cacho ['katʃo] sm piece, chunk, slice.

cachorro [ka'tʃorro], **-a** sm, sf pup; cub; kitten.

cada ['kaða] adj invar each, every. **cada vez más** more and more.

cadáver [ka'ðaβer] sm corpse.

cadena [ka'ðena] sf chain. **cadena perpetua** life imprisonment. **estar en cadena** be in prison.

cadencia [ka'ðenθja] sf cadence, rhythm.

cadera [ka'ðera] sf hip.

cadete [ka'ðete] sm cadet.

caducar [kaðu'kar] v expire, lapse; become senile. **caduco** adj senile; in decline.

*caer [ka'er] v fall, drop, tumble; decline; fall due; fade; fit, suit; realize, understand; be located, lie. **caer en** or **sobre** fall upon. **caer en la cuenta** understand. **caer en saco roto** fall on deaf ears. **caída** sf fall; downfall; lapse.

café [ka'fe] sm coffee; café. **café con leche** white coffee. **café solo** black coffee. **cafeína** sf caffeine. **cafetera** sf coffee pot. **cafetería** sf coffee bar.

caimán [kai'man] sm alligator.

caja ['kaxa] sf box, case; safe; coffin; frame; hole, slot; cash box; cashier's office; cash; (música) drum; (auto) body. **caja de ahorros** savings bank. **cajero, -a** sm, sf cashier. **cajetilla** sf packet; small box. **cajón** sm large box; crate, chest; drawer; coffin.

cal [kal] sm lime.

calabaza [kala'βaθa] sf pumpkin; gourd; (fam) fool. **dar calabazas a** (examen) fail; jilt. **llevar calabazas** be jilted. **calabazada** sf (fam) blow on the head.

calabozo [kala'βoθo] sm prison cell; pruning knife.

calamar [kala'mar] sm squid.

calambre [ka'lambre] sm cramp.

calamidad [kalami'ðað] sf calamity.

calar [ka'lar] v soak; perforate; slice; size up; (fam) pick pockets. **calarse hasta los huesos** get soaked to the skin.

calavera [kala'βera] sf skull. **calaverada** sf wild escapade, tomfoolery. **calaverear** v act recklessly; live it up.

calcar [kal'kar] v trace; copy; trample upon. **calco** sm tracing; copy.

calce ['kalθe] sm (de rueda) rim; wedge.

calceta [kal'θeta] sf stocking; fetter. **hacer calceta** knit. **calcetero, -a** sm, sf hosier. **calcetín** sm sock.

calcinar [kalθi'nar] v burn, blacken.

calcio ['kalθjo] sm calcium.

calcular [kalku'lar] v calculate. **calcula-ción** sf calculation. **calculadora** sf calculating machine. **cálculo** sm calculation; estimate; (med) gallstone.

calda ['kalða] sf heating. **caldas** sf pl thermal springs pl.

caldera [kal'ðera] sf cauldron, boiling pan. **calderilla** sf small change.

caldo ['kalðo] sm broth; soup; salad dressing. **caldos** sm pl liquid foodstuffs pl; wines pl.

calefacción [kalefak'θjon] sf heating. **calefacción central** central heating.

calendario [kalen'darjo] sm calendar.

✝calentar [kalen'tar] v heat, warm; (fam) thrash. **calentarse** v warm oneself; become excited. **calentador** sm heater. **calentura** sf fever. **caliente** adj hot, warm.

caletre [ka'letre] sm (fam) good sense, sound judgment.

calibrar [kali'βrar] v calibrate; gauge, measure. **calibre** sm calibre; gauge; (fig) importance.

calidad [kali'ðað] sf quality; (med) fever. **calidades** sf pl conditions pl; rules pl. **a calidad de que** on condition that. **en calidad de** in the capacity of.

cálido ['kaliðo] adj hot, warm.

calificar [kalifi'kar] v qualify; judge; distinguish; prove worthy. **calificarse** v give proof of nobility. **calificación** sf appreciation; distinction; judgment. **calificado** adj distinguished; suitable.

calina [ka'lina] sf mist, fog.

cáliz ['kaliθ] sm chalice, cup.

calmante [kal'mante] adj soothing. sm sedative.

calmar [kal'mar] v calm; be calm. **calmarse** v quieten down. **calma** sf calm, lull. **calmoso** adj calm.

calor [ka'lor] sm heat, warmth; fervour; fever. **hacer calor** (temperatura) be hot. **tener calor** (persona) be hot. **caluroso** adj hot, warm; (fig) ardent.

caloría [kalo'ria] sf calorie.

calvo ['kalβo] adj bald; bare; threadbare. **calvez** sf also **calvicie** baldness.

calzar [kal'θar] v put shoes on; wear (shoes, gloves, spurs); wedge. **calza** sf chock; (fam) stocking. **calzada** sf roadway.

calzón [kal'θon] sm trousers pl; safety belt. **calzones** sm pl trousers pl. **calzoncillos** sm pl underpants pl.

callar [ka'ʎar] v be silent; shut up. **callado** adj silent; reserved; secret. **de callado** quietly.

calle ['kaʎe] sf street, road. **dejar en la calle** leave penniless. **hacer calle** clear the way. **callejón** sm alley. **callejón sin salida** cul-de-sac. **callejuela** sf back street; (fig) loophole.

callo ['kaʎo] sm (med) corn, callus. **callos** sm pl tripe sing. **calloso** adj hard, callous.

cama ['kama] sf bed; litter; floor. **caer en cama** fall ill. **cama de campaña/matrimonio/soltero** camp/double/single bed.

camafeo [kama'feo] sm cameo.

camaleón [kamale'on] sm chameleon.

camandulero [kamandu'lero] adj (fam) sly; hypocritical.

cámara ['kamara] sf room; loft; chamber; cine or TV camera; inner tube. **ayuda de cámara** sf valet. **música de cámara** sf chamber music.

camarada [kama'raða] sm comrade; colleague.

camarero [kama'rero] sm waiter; steward. **camarera** sf waitress; stewardess; chambermaid.

camarilla [kama'riʎa] sf clique; parliamentary lobby.

camarón [kama'ron] sm shrimp.

camarote [kama'rote] sm cabin.

cambiar [kam'bjar] v change; exchange. **cambiante** sm moneychanger. **cambio** sm change; alteration; small change. **a cambio de** in exchange for. **en cambio** on the other hand.

camelar [kame'lar] v (fam) flatter; woo. **cameleo** sm (fam) flattery.

camello [ka'meʎo] sm camel.

camilla [ka'miʎa] sf stretcher; litter; couch.

caminar [kami'nar] v walk; travel; move along. **caminante** s(m+f) traveller. **camino** sm path; road; route; way. **abrirse camino** make one's way. **camino adelante** straight on. **ponerse en camino** set out.

camión [ka'mjon] sm truck. **camión de bomberos** fire engine.

camisa [ka'misa] sf shirt; fruit skin; casing; lining; dust jacket; paper wrapper. **camisa de dormir** nightdress. **camisa de fuerza** straightjacket. **dejar sin camisa** ruin (someone). **camiseta** sf vest. **camisón** sm nightdress; nightshirt.

camorra [ka'morra] *sf* (*fam*) quarrel, fight. **buscar camorra** look for trouble.
campamento [kampa'mento] *sm* camp.
campar *v* camp; excel.
campana [kam'pana] *sf* bell; mantelpiece; parish (church); curfew.
campante [kam'pante] *adj* proud; pleased; (*fam*) relaxed, cool.
campaña [kam'paɲa] *sf* plain; campaign.
campechano [kampe'tʃano] *adj* (*fam*) genial; frank. **campechanía** *sf* good nature; frankness.
campeón [kampe'on], **-ona** *sm*, *sf* champion. **campeón de venta** bestseller. **campeonato** *sm* championship. **de campeonato** (*fig*, *fam*) fantastic.
campo ['kampo] *sm* field; countryside; camp; pitch; background. **campo de aviación** airfield. **campo raso** open country. **campesino**, **-a** *s*, *adj* peasant, rustic.
can [kan] *sm* dog; trigger.
cana ['kana] *sf* white *or* grey hair. **peinar canas** be getting old.
Canadá [kana'ða] *sm* Canada. **canadiense** *s(m+f)*, *adj* Canadian.
canal [ka'nal] *sm* canal; channel; ditch; tube. *sf* carcass. **canalón** *sm* drainpipe; gutter.
canalla [ka'naʎa] *sf* rabble, mob. *sm* swine, scoundrel.
canapé [kana'pe] *sm* couch, sofa; (*culin*) canapé.
Canarias [ka'narjas] *sf pl* Canary Islands *pl*. **canario**, **-a** *sm*, *sf* inhabitant of the Canary Islands.
canario [ka'narjo] *sm* canary.
canasta [ka'nasta] *sf* basket.
cancelar [kanθe'lar] *v* cancel, annul. **cancelación** *sf* cancellation.
cáncer ['kanθer] *sm* (*med*) cancer.
Cáncer *sm* (*astron*) Cancer.
canciller [kanθi'ʎer] *sm* chancellor.
canción [kan'θjon] *sf* song; tune; rhyme. **mudar de canción** change one's tune. **cancionero** *sm* song-book.
cancha ['kantʃa] *sf* football ground; tennis court; racecourse.
candado [kan'daðo] *sm* padlock.
candela [kan'dela] *sf* candle; candlestick; fire; blossom; (*fam*) light. **candelero** *sm* candlestick; oil lamp. **poner en el candelero** make popular.
candente [kan'dente] *adj* red-hot, burning.

candidato [kandi'ðato] *sm* candidate. **candidatura** *sf* candidature.
cándido ['kandiðo] *adj* innocent, pure; gullible; candid. **candidez** *sf* candour; gullibility; stupid remark.
candil [kan'ðil] *sm* oil lamp.
candor [kan'dor] *sm* innocence; candour; simplicity. **candoroso** *adj* ingenuous; innocent; frank.
canela [ka'nela] *sf* cinnamon.
canelón [kane'lon] *sm* gutter; spout; icicle.
cangrejo [kan'grexo] *sm* crab.
canguro [kan'guro] *sm* kangaroo.
caníbal [ka'niβal] *s(m+f)*, *adj* cannibal. **canibalismo** *sm* cannibalism.
canilla [ka'niʎa] *sf* (*tecn*) bobbin, spool; (*med*) shinbone; tap, spout.
canino [ka'nino] *adj* canine. **hambre canina** ravenous hunger.
canjear [kanxe'ar] *v* exchange. **canje** *sm* exchange.
cano ['kano] *adj* white-haired, grey-haired; (*fig*) ancient.
canoa [ka'noa] *sf* canoe.
canon ['kanon] *sm* rule; levy; perfect example; (*rel*, *música*) canon.
canónigo [ka'nonigo] *sm* (*rel*) canon. **canónico** *adj* canonical. **canonización** *sf* canonization. **canonizar** *v* canonize.
cansar [kan'sar] *v* tire, fatigue. **cansado** *adj* tired, weary; tiresome. **vista cansada** weak eyesight. **cansancio** *sm* weariness, fatigue.
cantar [kan'tar] *v* sing; chant; praise; (*fam*) squeal, confess. *sm* song; tune; poem. **cantante** *s(m+f)* singer.
cántara ['kantara] *sf* pitcher; liquid measure.
cántaro ['kantaro] *sm* pitcher. **llover a cántaros** rain cats and dogs.
cantera [kan'tera] *sf* quarry; (*fig*) breeding ground, source. **cantería** *sf* masonry; building made of hewn stone. **cantero** *sm* stonemason; crust of bread; strip of land.
cantidad [kanti'ðað] *sf* quantity, amount.
cantimplora [kantim'plora] *sf* siphon; water bottle.
cantina [kan'tina] *sf* buffet; canteen; wine cellar; picnic basket.
canto[1] ['kanto] *sm* song; singing. **cantor**, **-a** *sm*, *sf* singer.
canto[2] *sm* edge; border; crust; corner;

pebble. **al canto** (*fam*) in support. **de canto** edgeways.

caña ['kaɲa] *sf* cane; reed; walking stick; beer glass; shin bone. **caña de azúcar** sugar-cane. **caña de pescar** fishing-rod.

cañada [ka'ɲaða] *sf* glen, ravine.

cáñamo ['kaɲamo] *sm* hemp.

caño ['kaɲo] *sm* pipe; sewer. **cañería** *sf* drain; piping.

cañón [ka'ɲon] *sm* canyon; cannon, gun; gun barrel; pipe, tube.

caoba [ka'oβa] *sf* mahogany.

caos ['kaos] *sm* chaos. **caótico** *adj* chaotic.

capa ['kapa] *sf* cloak; cape; covering; lid.

capacidad [kapaθi'ðað] *sf* capacity; ability; opportunity.

capacha [ka'patʃa] *sf* also **capacho** *sm* shopping basket.

capar [ka'par] *v* castrate; (*fam*) reduce.

capataz [kapa'taθ] *sm* foreman; overseer.

capaz [ka'paθ] *adj* capable; able; spacious.

capellán [kape'ʎan] *sm* chaplain.

capilar [kapi'lar] *sm, adj* capillary.

capilla [ka'piʎa] *sf* chapel; choir; hood. **estar en capilla** (*fam*) in suspense.

capital [kapi'tal] *sm* (*com*) capital. *sf* capital city. *adj* principal.

capitán [kapi'tan] *sm* captain, leader. **capitanear** *v* command; lead.

capitular [kapitu'lar] *v* capitulate; make an agreement. **capitulación** *sf* capitulation; agreement.

capítulo [ka'pitulo] *sm* (*libro*) chapter; town council meeting; (*rel*) chapter.

capón [ka'pon] *sm* capon; eunuch; gelding; bundle of sticks.

capote [ka'pote] *sm* cape; greatcoat. **capotear** *v* (*fig, fam*) shirk.

capricho [ka'pritʃo] *sm* caprice, whim. **caprichoso** *adj* capricious.

cápsula ['kapsula] *sf* capsule; cartridge case; metal cap.

captar [kap'tar] *v* win over; gain; grasp.

capturar [kaptu'rar] *v* capture; arrest. **captura** *sf* capture.

capucha [ka'putʃa] *sf* hood; circumflex accent.

capuchina [kapu'tʃina] *sf* nasturtium.

capullo [ka'puʎo] *sm* cocoon; bud. **en capullo** in embryo.

cara ['kara] *sf* face; appearance; surface. **cara adelante/atrás** forwards/backwards. **cara o cruz** heads or tails. **dar la cara** face the music. **hacer cara a** face up to. **tener cara de** look like.

carabina [kara'βina] *sf* carbine; rifle. **carabinero** *sm* rifleman.

caracol [kara'kol] *sm* snail; spiral.

carácter [ka'rakter] *sm* character; nature; condition; sign, mark. **característica** *sf* characteristic. **característico** *adj* characteristic. **caracterización** *sf* characterization; (*teatro*) make-up. **caracterizar** *v* characterize; confer an honour on; (*teatro*) make up.

¡caramba! [ka'ramba] *interj* damn it!

caramelo [kara'melo] *sm* sweet, toffee; caramel.

carapacho [kara'patʃo] *sm* shell, carapace.

carátula [ka'ratula] *sf* mask; (*fam*) theatre, stage.

caravana [kara'βana] *sf* caravan; group, crowd.

carbohidrato [karβoi'ðrato] *sm* carbohydrate.

carbón [kar'βon] *sm* coal; charcoal; carbon; carbon paper. **carbonera** *sf* coal cellar; coal scuttle; charcoal burner. **carbonería** *sf* coalyard. **carbono** *sm* carbon.

carbunclo [kar'βunklo] *sm* also **carbunco** (*med*) carbuncle.

carburador [karβura'ðor] *sm* carburettor.

carcajada [karka'xaða] *sf* burst of laughter.

cárcel ['karθel] *sf* prison. **carcelero, -a** *sm, sf* jailer, warder.

carcomer [karko'mer] *v* corrode, eat away; undermine.

cardar [kar'ðar] *v* (*tecn*) card, comb. **carda** *sf* (*tecn*) card, carding; (*fam*) reprimand.

cardenal [karðe'nal] *sm* cardinal; bruise.

cardíaco [kar'ðiako] *adj* cardiac.

cardinal [karði'nal] *adj* principal; cardinal.

cardo ['karðo] *sm* thistle.

carear [kare'ar] *v* confront; compare; come face to face. **carearse** *v* meet.

*carecer [kare'θer] *v* lack, need. **carencia** *sf* lack, shortage; deficiency.

carestía [kares'tia] *sf* shortage, scarcity; high price.

careta [ka'reta] *sf* mask. **careta antigás** gasmask.

carey [ka'rej] *sm* turtle; tortoiseshell.

cargar [kar'gar] *v* load; burden; charge; tax; blame; attack; (*fam*) vex; lean, incline. **cargarse de** become full; be overburdened; *(fam)* be fed up; *(cielo)* become dark. **carga** *sf* load, burden; charge; tax; pressure. **cargadero** *sm* loading bay. **cargador** *sm* freighter; loader; carrier. **cargamento** *sm* cargo, load.

cargo ['kargo] *sm* post; accusation; responsibility; *(com)* charge; freighter. **cuenta a cargo** *sf* charge account.

cariarse [ka'rjarse] *v* decay. **caries** *sf invar* caries.

caribe [ka'riβe] *s(m+f)*, *adj* Caribbean. **Mar Caribe** *sm* Caribbean Sea.

caricatura [karika'tura] *sf* caricature.

caricia [ka'riθja] *sf* caress. **caricioso** *adj* caressing.

caridad [kari'ðað] *sf* charity. **caritativo** *adj* charitable.

cariño [ka'riɲo] *sm* love, affection. **cariñoso** *adj* affectionate, loving.

cariz [ka'riθ] *sm* appearance, aspect.

carmesí [karme'si] *sm*, *adj* crimson.

carmín [kar'min] *sm*, *adj* carmine.

carnada [kar'naða] *sf* bait.

carnaval [karna'βal] *sm* carnival.

carne ['karne] *sf* meat, flesh. **carne magra** lean meat. **carnal** *adj* carnal. **carnicería** *sf* butcher's shop. **carnicero** *sm* butcher.

carnero [kar'nero] *sm* sheep; ram; mutton; cemetery.

carpa ['karpa] *sf* carp.

caro ['karo] *adj* expensive; dear, beloved.

carpeta [kar'peta] *sf* folder, file; portfolio; briefcase; tablecloth. **dar carpetazo a** shelve.

carpintería [karpinte'ria] *sf* carpentry; carpenter's shop. **carpintero** *sm* carpenter, joiner.

carrera [kar'rera] *sf* race; road; career; course; line; *(media)* ladder. **de carrera** swiftly. **hacer carrera** succeed.

carreta [kar'reta] *sf* cart, wagon. **carretear** *v* cart, haul.

carrete [kar'rete] *sm* reel, spool, bobbin.

carretera [karre'tera] *sf* road, highway. **carretera de circunvalación** by-pass.

carril [kar'ril] *sm* furrow, rut; narrow road; rail.

carro ['karro] *sm* cart; car; typewriter carriage. **carro blindado** armoured car. **carro de mudanzas** removal van.

carroña [kar'roɲa] *sf* carrion.

carroza [kar'roθa] *sf* carriage; state coach; float.

carta ['karta] *sf* letter; chart; map; playing card; charter, document. **carta certificada** registered letter. **carta de venta** bill of sale. **tomar cartas en** *(fam)* take part in.

cartel [kar'tel] *sm* placard, poster. **cartelera** *sf* hoarding.

cartera [kar'tera] *sf* wallet; purse; briefcase; notebook; portfolio; office of a cabinet minister.

cartero [kar'tero] *sm* postman.

cartílago [kar'tilago] *sm* cartilage.

cartón [kar'ton] *sm* cardboard; carton; cartoon.

cartucho [kar'tutʃo] *sm* cartridge; paper cone.

casa ['kasa] *sf* house, home; household; business; building; flat. **casa de empeños** pawnshop. **casa de huéspedes** boarding-house. **casa pública** brothel. **casa y comida** board and lodging. **en casa** at home. **un amigo de casa** a friend of the family.

casar [ka'sar] *v* give in marriage; join. **casarse con** marry, get married. **casamiento** *sm* marriage.

cascabel [kaska'βel] *sm* small bell. **serpiente de cascabel** *sf* rattlesnake. **cascabelada** *sf* *(fam)* foolish action.

cascada [kas'kaða] *sf* waterfall.

cascar [kas'kar] *v* crack; burst; split; break; *(fam)* beat up; *(fam)* cough up; *(fam)* chatter; *(fam)* kick the bucket.

cáscara ['kaskara] *sf* shell; peel; rind; husk; bark.

cascarón [kaska'ron] *sm* egg-shell.

casco ['kasko] *sm* skull; helmet; skin; segment; shrapnel. **cascotes** *sm pl* rubble *sing.*

caserío [kase'rio] *sm* group of houses; settlement; country house.

casero [ka'sero] *adj* home-made; familiar; informal; *(fam)* domestic. *sm* landlord; tenant; caretaker.

casi ['kasi] *adv* nearly, almost.

casilla [ka'siʎa] *sf* hut, cabin; lodge; pigeonhole; section.

caso ['kaso] *sm* case, matter; event; chance; occasion. **el caso es** the fact is. **en tal caso** in such a case. **en todo caso** in any case. **hacer caso a** pay attention to.

caspa ['kaspa] *sf* dandruff.

casta ['kasta] *sf* caste; breed; class.

castaño [kas'taɲo] *sm* chestnut-tree;

chestnut brown. *adj* chestnut. **castaña** *sf* chestnut; hair bun.

castañuela [kasta'ɲwela] *sf* castanet.

castellano [kaste'ʎano], **-a** *s, adj* Castilian. *sm* (*lengua*) Castilian.

castidad [kasti'ðað] *sf* chastity.

castigar [kasti'gar] *v* punish, chastise. **castigo** *sm* punishment.

Castilla [kas'tiʎa] *sf* Castile.

castillo [kas'tiʎo] *sm* castle.

castizo [kas'tiθo] *adj* pure; pure-blooded; traditional.

casto ['kasto] *adj* chaste, pure.

castor [kas'tor] *sm* beaver.

castrar [kas'trar] *v* castrate; (*agr*) prune. **castrado** *sm* eunuch.

castrense [kas'trense] *adj* military.

casual [ka'swal] *adj* chance, coincidental. **casualidad** *sf* chance; coincidence; accident. **por casualidad** by chance.

casucha [ka'sutʃa] *sf also* **casuca** hovel.

cataclismo [kata'klismo] *sm* cataclysm.

catacumbas [kata'cumbas] *sf pl* catacombs *pl*.

catadura[1] [kata'ðura] *sf* tasting. **catador** *sm* taster, sampler. **catar** *v* taste, sample.

catadura[2] *sf* (*fam*) expression, look.

catalejo [kata'lexo] *sm* telescope.

catálogo [ka'talogo] *sm* catalogue. **catalogar** *v* catalogue; classify.

Cataluña [kata'luɲa] *sf* Catalonia.

cataplasma [kata'plasma] *sf* poultice.

catarata [kata'rata] *sf* waterfall; (*med*) cataract.

catarro [ka'tarro] *sm* catarrh, common cold. **catarro pradial** hay fever. **coger un catarro** catch cold.

catástrofe [ka'tastrofe] *sf* catastrophe.

catastrófico *adj* catastrophic.

catecismo [kate'θismo] *sm* catechism.

cátedra ['kateðra] *sf* lecture room; senior teaching post; (*puesto*) chair.

catedral [kate'ðral] *sf* cathedral.

categoría [katego'ria] *sf* category; class; rank. **categórico** *adj* categorical; strict.

caterva [ka'terβa] *sf* crowd; heap.

cátodo ['katoðo] *sm* cathode.

católico [ka'toliko], **-a** *s, adj* (Roman) Catholic. **catolicismo** *sm* (Roman) Catholicism.

catorce [ka'torθe] *sm, adj* fourteen. **catorceno** *adj* fourteenth.

catre ['katre] *sm* camp-bed; cot.

cauce ['kauθe] *sm* river bed; ditch.

caución [kau'θjon] *sf* caution; pledge; bail.

caucho ['kautʃo] *sm* rubber.

caudal [kau'ðal] *sm* wealth; abundance.

caudillo [kau'ðiʎo] *sm* leader, chief.

causar [kau'sar] *v* cause, create, occasion. **causa** *sf* cause, reason, motive; (*jur*) trial. **a causa de** owing to. **causa pública** public welfare.

cáustico ['kaustiko] *adj* caustic, burning; scathing.

cautela [kau'tela] *sf* care, caution; cunning. **cauteloso** *adj* cautious; cunning. **cauto** *adj* cautious, wary.

cautivar [kauti'βar] *v* capture; captivate; charm. **cautividad** *sf* captivity. **cautivo, -a** *sm, sf* captive.

cavar [ka'βar] *v* dig; excavate; (*agr*) dress; ponder. **cava** *sf* cultivation. **cavadura** *sf* digging; dressing.

caverna [ka'βerna] *sf* cavern, cave. **cavernoso** *adj* cavernous; (*fig*) deep.

cavidad [kaβi'ðað] *sf* cavity.

cavilar [kaβi'lar] *v* think deeply, meditate. **caviloso** *adj* pensive; worried.

cayado [ka'jaðo] *sm* shepherd's crook; walking-stick.

cazar [ka'θar] *v* hunt; chase; shoot; catch. **caza** *sf* hunt; chase; game. **cazador, -a** *sm, sf* hunter.

cazo ['kaθo] *sm* ladle; saucepan; gluepot. **cazo eléctrico** electric kettle.

cazoleta [kaθo'leta] *sf* small pan; pipe bowl.

cazuela [ka'θwela] *sf* casserole; (*teatro*) the gods.

cebada [θe'βaða] *sf* barley. **cebadar** *v* feed (animals).

cebar [θe'βar] *v* feed, fatten up; prime, charge; penetrate; long for. **cebarse en** vent one's rage on; glut over.

cebolla [θe'βoʎa] *sf* onion; flower bulb. **cebollana** *sf* chive. **cebolleta** *sf* leek.

cebra ['θeβra] *sf* zebra. **paso de cebra** *sm* zebra crossing.

cecear [θeθe'ar] *v* lisp. **ceceo** *sm* lisp. **ceceoso** *adj* lisping.

ceder [θe'ðer] *v* give up; yield; sag.

cedro ['θeðro] *sm* cedar.

cédula ['θeðula] *sf* charter; certificate; form; patent.

***cegar** [θe'gar] *v* blind; go blind; block up; cover. **cegador** *adj* blinding. **cegarra** *adj* (*fam*) short-sighted. **cegarrita** *adj* (*fam*) peering. **ceguedad** *or* **ceguera** *sf* blindness.

ceja ['θexa] *sf* eyebrow; mountain top; rim; cloud-cap. **fruncir las cejas** knit one's brows. **quemarse las cejas** burn the midnight oil. **tener entre ceja y ceja** (*fam*) concentrate on.

celada [θe'laða] *sf* helmet; trick; ambush.

celar [θe'lar] *v* check on; watch; conceal; protect. **celador** *sm* watchman.

celda ['θelða] *sf* cell.

celebrar [θele'βrar] *v* celebrate; praise; acclaim; conduct; (*rel*) say mass. **celebrarse** *v* take place. **celebración** *sf* celebration; acclamation. **celebrante** *sm* celebrant priest. **célebre** *adj* famous. **celebridad** *sf* fame; celebration.

celeridad [θeleri'ðað] *sf* speed.

celeste [θe'leste] *adj* heavenly.

celibato [θeli'βato] *sm* celibacy; (*fam*) bachelor. **célibe** *s(m+f)* single person; bachelor; spinster.

celo ['θelo] *sm* zeal; heat, rut. **celos** *sm pl* jealousy *sing*. **dar celos a** make jealous. **tener celos** be jealous. **celosía** *sf* window lattice; venetian blind; jealousy. **celoso** *adj* zealous; jealous.

celta ['θelta] *s(m+f)* Celt. *sm* (*lengua*) Celtic.

célula ['θelula] *sf* cell.

celuloide [θelu'lojðe] *sm* celluloid.

celulosa [θelu'losa] *sf* cellulose.

cementerio [θemen'terjo] *sm* cemetery.

cemento [θe'mento] *sm* cement. **cemento armado** reinforced concrete.

cenagal [θena'gal] *sm* marsh, swamp; (*fam*) tight spot, mess.

cenar [θe'nar] *v* dine on, have for supper/dinner. **cena** *sf* evening meal, supper, dinner.

cenefa [θe'nefa] *sf* border; edging; frieze.

ceniza [θe'niθa] *sf* ash, cinder. **convertir en cenizas** reduce to ashes. **cenicero** *sm* ashtray.

censo ['θenso] *sm* census; tax; annuity; pension; ground rent; (*fig*) burden. **censar** *v* take a census of. **censor** *sm* censor; auditor.

censurar [θensu'rar] *v* censor; censure; condemn. **censura** *sf* censoring; censorship. **censurable** *adj* blameworthy. **censurador** *sm* censor. **censurista** *s(m+f)* critic; fault-finder.

centellear [θenteʎe'ar] *v also* **centellar**

sparkle; flash; twinkle; flicker. **centella** *sf* flash; spark. **centelleo** *sm* gleam; glitter; sparkle.

centavo [θen'taβo] *sm* cent.

centena [θen'tena] *sf* hundred. **centenada** *sf also* **centenar** *sm* hundred. **a** *or* **por centenares** by the hundred. **centenario** *sm* centenary.

centeno[1] [θen'teno] *sm* rye.

centeno[2] *adj* hundred.

centésimo [θen'tesimo] *adj* hundredth. *sm* cent.

centígrado [θen'tigraðo] *adj* centigrade.

centímetro [θen'timetro] *sm* centimetre.

céntimo ['θentimo] *adj* hundredth. *sm* cent.

centinela [θenti'nela] *s(m+f)* guard, sentry.

centrar [θen'trar] *v* centre. **central** *adj* central. **central** *sf* head office; headquarters; power station; switchboard. **centro** *sm* centre, middle; aim, goal, objective.

centrífugo [θen'trifugo] *adj* centrifugal.

centroamérica [θentroa'merika] *sf* Central America. **centroamericano** *adj* Central American.

centuria [θen'turja] *sf* century.

***ceñir** [θe'ɲir] *v* gird, surround, encircle; crown; frame; shorten, take in; be a tight fit for. **ceñirse** *v* limit; adapt oneself to; cling. **ceñido** *adj* tight-fitting. **ceñidor** *sm* belt.

ceño ['θeɲo] *sm* frown. **fruncir el ceño** frown. **ceñudo** *adj* frowning.

cepa ['θepa] *sf* tree stump; stock; root; origin.

cepillar [θepi'ʎar] *v* brush; plane. **cepillarse** *v* (*fam*) fail an exam; (*fam*) polish off. **cepillo** *sm* brush; plane.

cepo ['θepo] *sm* branch; stocks *pl*; collecting box; (*tecn*) clamp, socket.

cera ['θera] *sf* wax.

cerámico [θe'ramiko] *adj* ceramic. **cerámica** *sf* ceramics; pottery.

cerca ['θerka] *adv* near, close, nearby. **cerca de** close by; almost; about. **de cerca** closely. **cercanía** *sf* nearness. **cercamás** *sf pl* vicinity *sing*, neighbourhood *sing*. **cercano** *adj* near, close.

cercar [θer'kar] *v* enclose; fence; surround. **cerca** *sf* enclosure, wall, fence. **cercado** *sm* enclosure.

cerco ['θerko] *sm* ring; circle; enclosure; frame; siege.

cerda [ˈθerda] *sf* (*zool*) sow; bristle.
cerdear *v* (*animales*) be lame, limp. **cerdo**
vm pig; pork. **cerdoso** *adj* bristly.

Cerdeña [θerˈðeɲa] *sf* Sardinia.

cereal [θereˈal] *sm, adj* cereal.

cerebro [θeˈreβro] *sm* brain. **cerebral** *adj*
cerebral.

ceremonia [θereˈmonja] *sf* ceremony. **ceremonial** *adj* ceremonial. **ceremonioso** *adj*
ceremonious.

cereza [θeˈreθa] *sf* cherry. **cerezo** *sm* cherry tree.

cerilla [θeˈriʎa] *sf* match.

*cerner [θerˈner] *v* sift; sieve; examine
carefully; drizzle. **cernerse** *v* sway; waddle; hover; threaten.

cero [ˈθero] *sm* zero, nothing.

*cerrar [θerˈrar] *v* shut, close. **cerrarse** *v*
close up; stand firm; heal; cloud over.
cerrar con llave lock. **cerrar la boca** shut
up. **cerrar la marcha** bring up the rear.
cerrado *adj* closed; secretive; obtuse;
overcast. **cerradura** *sf* lock; locking up.
cerraje *sm* lock.

cerril [θerˈril] *adj* rough, rocky; wild; illbred.

cerro [ˈθerro] *sm* hill, ridge; animal's
neck.

cerrojo [θerˈroxo] *sm* bolt.

certeza [θerˈteθa] *sf also* **certidumbre** certainty.

certificar [θertifiˈkar] *v* certify; register;
guarantee. **certificado** *sm* certificate; registered letter.

cervato [θerˈβato] *sm* (*zool*) fawn.

cerveza [θerˈβeθa] *sf* beer.

cerviz [θerˈβiθ] *sf* nape of the neck, cervix. **bajar la cerviz** bow one's head.

cesar [θeˈsar] *v* cease, stop; leave one's
job. **cesación** *sf* cessation, stoppage.
cesante *adj* out of office, unemployed.
cesantía *sf* suspension from office.

cesión [θeˈsjon] *sf* transfer; assignment;
conveyance; resignation.

césped [ˈθespeð] *sf* turf, lawn. **césped
inglés** lawn.

cesta [ˈθesta] *sf* basket, hamper. **cestería**
sf basketwork, wickerwork. **cesto** *sm*
basket.

cetro [ˈθetro] *sm* sceptre; (*fig*) power.

cheque [tʃek] *s* check

cianuro [θjaˈnuro] *sm* cyanide.

ciática [θiˈatika] *sf* sciatica. **ciático** *adj* sciatic.

cicatería [θikateˈria] *sf* stinginess.

cicatriz [θikaˈtriθ] *sf* scar.

ciclismo [θiˈklismo] *sm* cycling. **ciclista**
s(m + f) cyclist.

ciclo [ˈθiklo] *sm* cycle. **cíclico** *adj* cyclical.

ciclón [θiˈklon] *sm* cyclone.

cidra [ˈθiðra] *sf* citron. **cidro** *sm* citron
tree.

ciego [ˈθjego], **-a** *sm, sf* blind person. *adj*
blind.

cielo [ˈθjelo] *sm* sky; heaven; ceiling; climate. **¡cielos!** good heavens!

ciempiés [θjemˈpjes] *sm invar* centipede.

ciénaga [θiˈenaga] *sf* bog, marsh, swamp.

ciencia [ˈθjenθja] *sf* science; knowledge,
learning. **ciencia ficción** science fiction.

científico [θjenˈtifiko], **-a** *sm, sf* scientist.
adj scientific.

cieno [ˈθjeno] *sm* mud. **cienoso** *adj* muddy.

ciento [ˈθjento] *sm, adj also* **cien** hundred.

cierre [ˈθjerre] *sm* closing; fastening; lock.

cierto [ˈθjerto] *adj* certain. *adv* certainly.
de cierto certainly. **por cierto** of course.

ciervo [ˈθjerβo] *sm* deer; stag. **cierva** *sf*
hind.

cierzo [ˈθjerθo] *sm* north wind.

cifra [ˈθifra] *sf* number, figure; cipher;
code; abbreviation. **en cifra** in short.
cifrar *v* summarize; cipher; enclose.
cifrar las esperanzas en set one's hopes
on.

cigarro [θiˈgarro] *sm* cigar. **cigarrillo** *sm*
cigarette.

cigüeña [θiˈgweɲa] *sf* stork.

cilindro [θiˈlindro] *sm* cylinder. **cilíndrico**
adj cylindrical.

cima [ˈθima] *sf* top; summit. **dar cima a**
finish off. **por cima** at the top; superficially.

címbalo [ˈθimbalo] *sm* cymbal.

cimbrar [θimˈbrar] *v also* **cimbrear**
vibrate; bend; sway.

*cimentar [θimenˈtar] *v* found; establish.
cimiento *sm* foundation.

cinc [θink] *sm* zinc.

cincel [θinˈθel] *sm* chisel. **cincelador** *sm*
engraver; stonecutter.

cinco [ˈθinko] *sm, adj* five.

cincuenta [θinˈkwenta] *sm, adj* fifty.

cinchar [θinˈtʃar] *v* girth; fasten with
hoops. **cincha** *sf* girth, cinch. **cincho** *sm*
belt; hoop.

cine [ˈθine] *sm* cinema.

cínico ['θinico], **-a** *sm*, *sf* cynic. *adj* cynical; shameless. **cinismo** *sm* cynicism.

cínife ['θinife] *sm* mosquito.

cinta ['θinta] *sf* ribbon; strip; tape; tape-measure. **cinteado** *adj* beribboned.

cintura [θin'tura] *sf* waist; belt. **meter a uno en cintura** make someone behave. **cinturón** *sm* belt; zone; circle. **cinturón de seguridad** safety belt.

ciprés [θi'pres] *sm* cypress.

circo ['θirko] *sm* circus.

circuito [θir'kwito] *sm* circuit.

circular [θirku'lar] *v* circulate; circularize; move. *adj* round, circular. **circulación** *sf* circulation; traffic.

circuncidar [θirkunθi'ðar] *v* circumcise. **circuncisión** *sf* circumcision. **circunciso** *adj* circumcised.

circundar [θirkun'dar] *v* surround, encircle.

circunferencia [θirkunfe'renθja] *sf* circumference.

circunflejo [θirkun'flexo] *sm* circumflex.

circunscribir [θirkunskri'βir] *v* circumscribe.

circunspecto [θirkun'spekto] *adj* circumspect. **circunspección** *sf* circumspection.

circunstancia [θirkun'stanθja] *sf* circumstance; condition; incident. **circunstancial** *adj* circumstantial. **circunstante** *adj* surrounding; present.

circunvecino [θirkunβe'θino] *adj* neighbouring.

ciruela [θi'rwela] *sf* plum. **ciruelo** *sm* plum-tree.

cirugía [θiru'xia] *sf* surgery. **cirujano** *sm* surgeon.

cisco ['θisko] *sm* coal dust; (*fam*) hubbub.

cisma ['θisma] *sm* schism; discord.

cisne ['θisne] *sm* swan.

cisterna [θis'terna] *sf* cistern, water tank.

cita ['θita] *sf* citation; appointment; quotation. **citar** *v* make an appointment; quote; (*jur*) summons.

ciudad [θju'ðað] *sf* city. **ciudadanía** *sf* citizenship. **ciudadano, -a** *sm*, *sf* citizen. **ciudadela** *sf* citadel.

cívico ['θiβiko] *adj* civic; patriotic.

civilizar [θiβili'θar] *v* civilize. **civil** *adj* civil. **civilización** *sf* civilization.

cizalla [θi'θaʎa] *sf* shears *pl*; metal shavings *pl*.

clamar [kla'mar] *v* cry out; beseech.

clamor [kla'mor] *sm* shout; cry. **clamorear** *v* cry out for; beseech. **clamoroso** *adj* noisy.

clandestino [klandes'tino] *adj* secret.

clara ['klara] *sf* white of egg; bald patch.

claraboya [klara'βoja] *sf* skylight.

clarear [klare'ar] *v* clear; dawn; grow light; be transparent; (*fam*) reveal secrets.

clarete [kla'rete] *sm* claret.

clarificar [klarifi'kar] *v* clarify. **clarificación** *sf* clarification.

clarín [kla'rin] *sm* bugle.

clarinete [klari'nete] *sm* clarinet.

claro ['klaro] *adj* light; clear; distinct. *adv* clearly. *sm* opening; space; clearing. **claro que** of course. **claro que sí** certainly. **claridad** *sf* clarity; light; brightness.

clase ['klase] *sf* class, type; lesson; classroom. **clase media** middle class. **clase particular** private lesson.

clásico ['klasiko] *adj* classic(al). *sm* classic.

clasificar [klasifi'kar] *v* classify. **clasificación** *sf* classification.

claudicar [klauði'kar] *v* limp; (*fam*) yield; (*fig*) shirk; (*fig*) falter. **claudicación** *sf* limping; yielding; shirking.

claustro ['klaustro] *sm* cloister; teaching staff. **claustral** *adj* cloistered.

claustrofobia [klaustro'foβja] *sf* claustrophobia.

cláusula ['klausula] *sf* clause.

clavar [kla'βar] *v* nail; fasten, fix; (*fam*) cheat. **clava** *sf* club, cudgel. **clavado en la cama** bed-ridden. **clavija** *sf* peg, pin. **clavo** *sm* nail; spike.

clave ['klaβe] *sf* key; clue; clef. *sm* harpsichord.

clavel [kla'βel] *sm* carnation.

clavícula [kla'βikula] *sf* collar bone.

clemencia [kle'menθja] *sf* mercy. **clemente** *adj* merciful.

clérigo ['klerigo] *sm* clergyman, priest. **clerical** *adj* clerical. **clericato** *sm* also **clero** clergy.

cliente ['kljente], **-a** *sm*, *sf* client, customer; patient. **clientela** *sf* clients *pl*, customers *pl*; practice.

clima ['klima] *sm* climate. **climático** *adj* climatic.

clínica ['klinika] *sf* clinic. **clínico** *adj* clinical.

clisé [kli'se] *sm* (*foto*) negative; (*fig*) cliché.

cloaca [klo'aka] *sf* sewer, drain.

cloro ['kloro] *sm* chlorine.

clorofila [kloro'fila] *sf* chlorophyll.

cloroformo [kloro'formo] *sm* chloroform. **cloroformar** *v* chloroform.

club [kluβ] *sm* club. **club de noche** nightclub.

coacción [koak'θjon] *sf* coercion. **coactivo** *adj* coercive.

coagular [koagu'lar] *v* coagulate; curdle; clot. **coagulación** *sf* coagulation; clotting.

coalición [koali'θjon] *sf* coalition.

coartada [koar'taða] *sf* alibi.

coartar [koar'tar] *v* hinder; prevent; limit; restrict.

cobarde [ko'βarðe] *s(m+f)* coward. *adj* cowardly. **cobardía** *sf* cowardice.

cobertizo [koβer'tiθo] *sm* garage; shed.

cobertura [koβer'tura] *sf* covering.

cobijar [koβi'xar] *v* cover, shelter. **cobijo** *sm* shelter.

cobrar [ko'βrar] *v* charge; earn; gain. **cobrarse** *v* (*med*) recover. **cobradero** *adj* recoverable. **cobrador, -a** *sf* collector; conductor; receiver. **cobranza** *sf* collection; receipt.

cobre [ko'βre] *sm* copper. **batirse el cobre** (*fam*) get on with it. **cobres** *sm pl* (*música*) brass.

***cocer** [ko'θer] *v* cook. **cocido** *sm* stew.

cocinar [koθi'nar] *v* cook. **cocina** *sf* kitchen; cookery. **cocinero, -a** *sm, sf* cook.

coco ['koko] *sm* coconut; coconut palm; grub, larva; (*fam*) face; (*fam*) head. **hacer cocos** make faces.

cocodrilo [koko'ðrilo] *sm* crocodile.

cóctel ['koktel] *sm* cocktail.

coche ['kotʃe] *sm* car; coach; carriage. **coche cama** sleeper. **coche de alquiler** self-drive car. **coche fúnebre** hearse.

cochino [ko'tʃino] **, -a** *sm, sf* pig, swine. *adj* (*fam*) rotten; filthy; disgusting. **cochinada** *sf* filth; filthy thing. **cochinera** *sf* pigsty.

codear [koðe'ar] *v* nudge, elbow. **codearse** *v* rub shoulders with. **codazo** *sm* nudge. **codo** *sm* elbow; bend.

codeína [koðe'ina] *sf* codeine.

codelincuente [koðelin'kwente] *s(m+f)* accomplice. **codelincuencia** *sf* complicity.

códice ['koðiθe] *sm* codex.

codiciar [koði'θjar] *v* covet. **codicia** *sf* greed. **codicioso** *adj* greedy.

codificar [koðifi'kar] *v* codify. **codificación** *sf* codification.

código ['koðigo] *sm* code. **código de carreteras** highway code.

codillo [ko'ðiʎo] *sm* forearm; (*culin*) shoulder.

codorniz [koðor'niθ] *sf* quail.

coercer [koer'θer] *v* coerce. **coerción** *sf* coercion.

coexistir [koeksis'tir] *v* coexist. **coexistencia** *sf* coexistence.

cofia ['kofja] *sf* coif; hair-net.

cofradía [kofra'ðia] *sf* fraternity; society.

cofre ['kofre] *sm* chest.

coger [ko'xer] *v* get; take; catch; seize; fit; collect. **cogida** *sf* gathering; (*tauromaquia*) goring. **cogido** *sm* fold, pleat.

cogote [ko'gote] *sm* nape of the neck. **ser tieso de cogote** be stiff-necked.

cohete [ko'ete] *sm* rocket.

cohibir [koi'βir] *v* inhibit; embarrass. **cohibidor** *adj* inhibiting. **cohibición** *sf* inhibition. **cohibido** *adj* restricted.

cohombrillo [koom'briʎo] *sm* gherkin. **cohombro** *sm* cucumber.

coincidencia [koinθi'ðenθja] *sf* coincidence. **coincidente** *adj* coincidental.

cojear [koxe'ar] *v* limp; hobble; (*fig*) waver; (*fig*) lapse. **cojera** *sf* lameness. **cojo** *adj* lame; lopsided.

cojín [ko'xin] *sm* cushion. **cojinete** *sm* small pillow; pad; (*tecn*) bearing. **cojinete de bolas** ball-bearing.

cok [kok] *sm* coke.

col [kol] *sf* cabbage. **coles de Bruselas** Brussels sprouts *pl*.

cola ['kola] *sf* tail; end; (*vestido*) train; queue; glue. **hacer cola** form a queue.

colaborar [kolaβo'rar] *v* collaborate. **colaboración** *sf* collaboration. **colaborador, -a** *sm, sf* collaborator.

colapso [ko'lapso] *sm* collapse, breakdown.

***colar** [ko'lar] *v* strain; filter; wash; confer; (*fig, fam*) slip through. **colarse** *v* slip; gatecrash; jump the queue; err. **colada** *sf* washing. **coladero** *sm* colander, sieve.

colcha ['koltʃa] *sf* bedspread.

colchón [kol'tʃon] *sm* mattress.

colear [kole'ar] *v* wag the tail.

colección [kolek'θjon] *sf* collection. **colectivo** *adj* collective. **colectividad** *sf* collectivity; community.

colega [ko'lega] *sm* colleague.

colegio [ko'lexjo] *sm* college, school. **colegial** *sm* schoolboy.

colegir [kole'xir] *v* infer, conclude.

cólera ['kolera] *sf* anger. *sm* cholera.

colérico *adj* angry.

coleta [ko'leta] *sf* pigtail; postscript.

*colgar [kol'gar] *v* hang, hang up, hang out. **colgadero** *sm* hook; peg; hanger. **puente colgante** *sm* suspension bridge.

coliflor [koli'flor] *sf* cauliflower.

colilla [ko'liʎa] *sf* cigarette stub.

colina [ko'lina] *sf* hill.

colindar [kolin'dar] *v* adjoin. **colindante** *adj* adjacent.

colisión [koli'sjon] *sf* collision.

colmar [kol'mar] *v* fill to overflowing. **colmado** *adj* plentiful.

colmena [kol'mena] *sf* beehive.

colmillo [kol'miʎo] *sm* tooth; fang; tusk. **enseñar los colmillos** (*fam*) threaten.

colmo ['kolmo] *sm* highest point; limit.

colocar [kolo'kar] *v* place; put in position; arrange; find employment for. **colocarse** *v* get a job. **colocación** *sf* employment; position; investment.

Colombia [ko'lombja] *sf* Colombia. **colombiano, -a** *s, adj* Colombian.

colonia [ko'lonja] *sf* colony. **colonial** *adj* colonial; imported. **colonialismo** *sm* colonialism. **colonización** *sf* colonization. **colonizar** *v* colonize. **colono** *sm* colonist, colonial.

coloquio [ko'lokjo] *sm* conversation.

color [ko'lor] *sm* colour; dye; paint; complexion. **colorado** *sm, adj* coloured; red. **ponerse colorado** blush. **colorar** *v* colour, dye. **colorear** *v* colour, dye; grow red; ripen. **colorete** *sm* rouge. **colorido** *sm* colour, colouring. **colorín** *sm* goldfinch; (*fam*) measles.

colosal [kolo'sal] *adj* colossal.

columbrar [kolum'brar] *v* glimpse; (*fig*) suspect.

columna [ko'lumna] *sf* column, pillar.

columpiar [kolum'pjar] *v* swing. **columpiarse** *v* sway; (*fam*) waddle; blunder. **columpio** *sm* swing.

collado [ko'ʎaðo] *sm* hill; fell.

collar [ko'ʎar] *sm* necklace; collar.

coma¹ ['koma] *sf* (*gram*) comma.

coma² *sm* (*med*) coma.

comadre [ko'maðre] *sf* midwife; godmother; (*fam*) neighbour, friend. **comadrear** *v* gossip. **comadreo** *sm* gossip.

comadreja [koma'ðrexa] *sf* weasel.

comadrona [koma'ðrona] *sf* midwife.

comandante [koman'dante] *sm* commander. **comandar** *v* command.

comandita [koman'dita] *sf* sleeping partnership. **socio comanditario** *sm* sleeping partner.

comarca [ko'marka] *sf* region, district.

comba ['komba] *sf* bend, curve; camber; sag. **combadura** *sf* curvature; camber.

combatir [komba'tir] *v* combat, fight. **combate** *sm* combat, battle, struggle. **combatiente** *sm* fighter; soldier.

combinar [kombi'nar] *v* combine; plan, arrange. **combinación** *sf* combination; project; permutation. **combinatorio** *adj* combining.

combustible [kombus'tiβle] *adj* combustible. *sm* fuel.

comedero [kome'ðero] *adj* edible. *sm* dining-room; feeding-trough.

comedia [ko'meðja] *sf* play; comedy; theatre. **comediante, -a** *sm, sf* actor/actress.

comediar [kome'ðjar] *v* divide into equal shares.

comedido [kome'ðiðo] *adj* polite, courteous; moderate. **comedir** *v* prepare. **comedirse** *v* restrain oneself.

comedor [kome'ðor] *sm* dining-room.

comensal [komen'sal] *sm* table companion.

comentar [komen'tar] *v* comment on; discuss. **comentario** *sm* commentary. **comentarista** *s(m+f)* commentator. **comento** *sm* comment.

*comenzar [komen'θar] *v* commence. **comienzo** *sm* beginning.

comer [ko'mer] *v* eat; corrode; erode. **no tener qué comer** have nothing to eat. **ser de buen comer** have a good appetite. **comerse** *v* swallow; eat up. **comestible** *adj* edible. **comestibles** *sm pl* food *sing*; groceries *pl*. **comida** *sf* food; meal; lunch.

comercio [ko'merθjo] *sm* commerce; trade; shop. **comercio al por mayor/menor** wholesale/retail trade. **comerciante** *sm* shopkeeper; merchant; tradesman. **comerciar** *v* trade.

cometa [ko'meta] *sf* kite. *sm* comet.

cometer [kome'ter] *v* commit. **cometido** *sm* task; assignment; mission.

comezón [kome'θon] *sf* itch; itching.

cómico ['komiko] *adj* comic(al). *sm* comedian.

comilón [komi'lon], **-ona** *sm, sf* glutton. *adj* gluttonous. *sf* feast.

comillas [ko'miʎas] *sf pl* inverted commas *pl.*

comisaría [komisa'ria] *sf* police station. **comisario** *sm* commissary; commissioner; police inspector.

comisión [komi'sjon] *sf* commission; mission; committee.

comiso [ko'miso] *sm (jur)* confiscation.

comité [komi'te] *sm* committee.

comitiva [komi'tiβa] *sf* retinue.

como ['komo] *adv* how; as; as if; why; when; so that; about, approximately. *conj* as, since, because; if. **así como** as soon as; in the same way that. **como quiera que sea** in one way or another. **tan pronto como** as soon as. **¿cómo?** *adv* how? why? in what way? **¡cómo!** *interj* what! why! eh! **el cómo y el porqué** the how and the why.

cómoda ['komoða] *sf* chest of drawers.

cómodo ['komoðo] *adj* convenient; comfortable. **comodidad** *sf* convenience, comfort. **a su comodidad** at your earliest convenience.

compacto [kom'pakto] *adj* compact, close.

*****compadecer** [kompaðe'θer] *v* pity. **compadecerse** *v* sympathize; agree.

compadre [kom'paðre] *sm* godfather; pal, crony.

compaginar [kompaxi'nar] *v* arrange; combine; join; match; agree.

compañero [kompa'ɲero], **-a** *sm, sf* companion, partner; one of a pair. **compañerismo** *sm* fellowship. **compañiá** *sf* company, society.

comparar [kompa'rar] *v* compare. **comparación** *sf* comparison. **comparativo** *adj* comparative.

*****comparecer** [kompare'θer] *v* appear in court. **orden de comparecer** *sm* summons.

compartimiento [komparti'mjento] *sm* compartment; section; division. **compartir** *v* divide; share.

compás [kom'pas] *sm (mar)* compass; *(mat)* pair of compasses; rhythm; pattern, standard. **llevar el compás** beat time. **compasado** *adj* orderly, moderate. **compasar** *v* measure; regulate.

compasión [kompa'sjon] *sf* compassion. **compasivo** *adj* compassionate.

compatible [kompa'tiβle] *adj* compatible. **compatibilidad** *sf* compatibility.

compatriota [kompa'trjota] *s(m+f)* compatriot.

compeler [kompe'ler] *v* compel.

compendio [kom'pendjo] *sm* compendium; summary, précis. **en compendio** briefly. **compendir** *v* summarize.

compensar [kompen'sar] *v* compensate; offset; make amends. **compensación** *sf* compensation. **compensatorio** *adj* compensatory.

*****competir** [kompe'tir] *v* compete; contest. **competencia** *sf* competition; concern; competence. **competente** *adj* competent; able. **competición** *sf* competition. **competidor, -a** *sm, sf* competitor.

compilar [kompi'lar] *v* compile. **compilación** *sf* compilation.

compinche [kom'pintʃe] *s(m+f)* pal, chum; accomplice.

*****complacer** [kompla'θer] *v* please; oblige; humour. **complacerse** *v* be pleased, be glad (to). **complacencia** *sf* pleasure; indulgence. **complaciente** *adj* helpful; obliging.

complejo [kom'plexo] *adj, sm* complex. **complejidad** *sf* complexity.

complementario [komplemen'tarjo] *adj* complementary. **complemento** *sm* complement.

completar [komple'tar] *v* complete. **completo** *adj* complete.

complicar [kompli'kar] *v* complicate; be complicated *or* confused. **complicarse** *v* become confused *or* complicated. **complicación** *sf* complication. **complicado** *adj* complicated.

cómplice ['kompliθe] *s(m+f)* accomplice. **complicidad** *sf* complicity.

complot [kom'plot] *sm* plot; intrigue; *(fam)* understanding.

*****componer** [kompo'ner] *v* compose; form; repair; adjust; write. **componerse** *v* compose oneself; tidy oneself up; dress up; agree. **componerse de** consist of. **componedor, -a** *sm, sf* compositor; repairer; arbitrator. **componente** *sm* component; ingredient. **componible** *adj* adjustable.

comportar [kompor'tar] *v* tolerate; involve. **comportarse** *v* behave. **comportamiento** *sm* behaviour. **comporte** *sm* behaviour; bearing.

composición [komposi'θjon] *sf* composition; mixture; agreement; settlement. **compositor, -a** *sm, sf* composer.

compostura [kompos'tura] *sf* composition, structure; repair; neatness; adornment; agreement; composure; adjustment.

compota [kom'pota] *sf* (*culin*) compote.

comprar [kom'prar] *v* buy; bribe. **compra** *sf* purchase. **comprador, -a** *sm, sf* shopper.

comprender [kompren'der] *v* understand; include. **comprensibilidad** *sf* intelligibility. **comprensible** *adj* understandable. **comprensión** *sf* understanding; inclusion. **comprensivo** *adj* understanding; comprising.

comprimir [kompri'mir] *v* squeeze, compress. **comprimirse** *v* control oneself. **compresa** *sf* compress; sanitary towel. **compresión** *sf* compression.

***comprobar** [kompro'βar] *v* verify, check. **comprobación** *sf* verification. **comprobante** *adj* verifying. *sm* voucher; receipt.

comprometer [komprome'ter] *v* risk; compromise; commit. **comprometido** *adj* embarrassing; committed; implicated. **compromiso** *sm* commitment; agreement; compromise.

compuesto [kom'pwesto] *sm* compound. *adj* compound; repaired; dressed-up.

compunción [kompun'θjon] *sf* compunction; contrition.

computar [kompu'tar] *v* compute, calculate. **computadora** *sf* computer.

comulgar [komul'gar] *v* give/take communion; (*fig*) share.

común [ko'mun] *adj* common; ordinary; vulgar. *sm* community, public toilet. **por lo común** generally. **comunal** *adj* communal.

comunicar [komuni'kar] *v* communicate; convey; transmit; (*dos cuartos*) connect. **comunicarse** *v* spread; keep in touch with; exchange. **comunicación** *sf* communication; message. **comunicativo** *adj* talkative; catching.

comunidad [komuni'ðað] *sf* community.

comunión [komu'njon] *sf* communion.

comunismo [komu'nismo] *sm* communism. **comunista** *s(m+f)*, *adj* communist.

con [kon] *prep* with; by; in spite of; to, towards. **con que** *conj* whereupon; and so. **con tal que** provided that.

cóncavo ['konkaβo] *adj* concave. **concavidad** *sf* hollow, cavity.

***concebir** [konθe'βir] *v* conceive; imagine; understand; take; (*med*) conceive.

concebible *adj* conceivable, imaginable. **concepción** *sf* conception, idea; (*med*) conception. **concepto** *sm* concept; idea; opinion; witticism.

conceder [konθe'ðer] *v* concede, grant; allow; spare; award. **concesión** *sf* concession; grant.

concejo [kon'θexo] *sm* council. **concejal** *sm* councillor. **concejil** *adj* municipal.

concentrar [konθen'trar] *v* concentrate. **concentración** *sf* concentration.

concerniente [konθer'njente] *adj* concerning, regarding. **concernir** *v* concern.

***concertar** [konθer'tar] *v* harmonize; agree; adjust; compare. **concertado** *adj* concerted.

conciencia [kon'θjenθja] *sf* conscience; consciousness; mind; conscientiousness. **concienzudo** *adj* conscientious.

concierto [kon'θjerto] *sm* concert; concerto; agreement; (*fig*) harmony. **de concierto** in agreement.

conciliar [konθi'ljar] *v* conciliate; reconcile; gain. *adj* of a council. *sm* councillor. **concilio** *sm* councillor; council.

conciso [kon'θiso] *adj* concise.

concitar [konθi'tar] *v* stir up.

***concluir** [konklu'ir] *v* conclude; deduce; settle; convince. **conclusión** *sf* conclusion.

***concordar** [konkor'ðar] *v* agree. **concordancia** *sf* agreement. **concorde** *adj* in agreement. **concordia** *sf* harmony.

concretar [konkre'tar] *v* bring together; limit; specify; state explicitly. **concretarse** *v* confine oneself; be definite; keep; take shape. **concreto** *adj* concrete, specific. **en concreto** in brief.

concubina [konku'βina] *sf* concubine.

concurrir [konkur'rir] *v* meet; attend; go; coincide; contribute; concur; compete. **concurrido** *adj* popular; crowded. **concurso** *sm* meeting; cooperation; help; competition.

concusión [konku'sjon] *sf* concussion.

concha ['kontʃa] *sf* shell.

condado [kon'daðo] *sm* earldom; county. **conde** *sm* earl. **condesa** *sf* countess.

condecorar [kondeko'rar] *v* (*persona*) decorate. **condecoración** *sf* medal, decoration.

condenar [konde'nar] *v* condemn; sentence; block up. **condena** *sf* sentence; conviction. **cumplir condena** serve a sentence. **condenación** *sf* condemnation;

damnation. **condenado, -a** *sm, sf* condemned person; wretch.

condensar [konden'sar] *v* condense. **condensación** *sf* condensation. **condensador** *sm* condenser.

*condescender [kondesθen'der] *v* condescend; yield; comply. **condescendencia** *sf* condescension; compliance. **condescendiente** *adj* condescending; obliging.

condicionar [kondiθjo'nar] *v* condition; determine. **condición** *sf* condition; quality; temperament.

condimentar [kondimen'tar] *v* season. **condimento** *sm* seasoning, condiment.

condolerse [kondo'lerse] *v* condole, sympathize. **condolencia** *sf* condolence.

condonar [kondo'nar] *v* pardon, condone; *(deuda)* cancel. **condonación** *sf* pardon.

*conducir [kondu'θir] *v* conduct; transport; guide; manage; *(auto)* drive; be suitable. **conducirse** *v* behave. **conducción** *sf* transport; guidance; direction, management. **conducción a izquierda** left-hand drive. **permiso de conducción** *sm* driving licence. **conducta** *sf* transport; conduct; direction; behaviour.

conducto [kon'dukto] *sm* conduit; pipe. **conductor** *sm (tecn)* conductor.

conectar [konek'tar] *v* connect; switch on. **conectador** *sm* connector. **conexión** *sf* connection.

conejo [ko'nexo] *sm* rabbit.

confabularse [konfaβu'larse] *v* plot. **confabulación** *sf* conspiracy.

confeccionar [konfekθjon'ar] *v* make, make up. **confección** *sf* making; tailoring; clothing. **confeccionado** *adj* ready-made, ready-to-wear.

confederar [konfeδe'rar] *v* confederate. **confederación** *sf* confederation, confederacy.

conferenciar [konferen'θjar] *v* talk, discuss. **conferencia** *sf* conference; lecture; telephone call. **conferencia a cobro revertido** reverse-charge call. **conferencia en la cumbre** summit conference. **conferencia interurbana** trunk call.

*conferir [konfe'rir] *v* confer, consult; award, grant.

*confesar [konfe'sar] *v* confess, admit. **confesar de plano** own up. **confesión** *sf* confession.

confeti [kon'feti] *sm pl* confetti *sing*.

confiar [kon'fjar] *v* entrust; trust; rely. **confiable** *adj* trustworthy. **confiado** *adj* confident; trusting. **confianza** *sf* confidence; reliability; informality.

confidencia [konfi'δenθja] *sf* secret; confidence. **confidencial** *adj* confidential. **confidente** *adj* faithful.

confinar [konfi'nar] *v* confine; banish. **confinar con** border on. **confin** *sm* border, limit.

confirmar [konfir'mar] *v* confirm. **confirmarse** *v* be confirmed. **confirmación** *sf* confirmation.

confiscar [konfis'kar] *v* confiscate. **confiscación** *sf* confiscation.

confitar [konfi'tar] *v* coat with sugar; preserve in syrup. **confite** *sm* sweet. **confitería** *sf* sweet-shop. **confitura** *sf* candied fruit.

conflicto [kon'flikto] *sm* conflict.

*confluir [konflu'ir] *v* converge, meet.

conformar [konfor'mar] *v* conform. **conformarse** *v* resign oneself. **conforme** *adj* in agreement; alike; according. **conforme a** in accordance with. **según y conforme** it all depends.

confortar [konfor'tar] *v* comfort; encourage. **confortable** *adj* comfortable. **conforte** *sm* solace, comfort.

confrontar [konfron'tar] *v* confront; compare. **confrontar con** border on; confront. **confrontación** *sf* confrontation.

confundir [konfun'dir] *v* confuse; mistake. **confusión** *sf* confusion. **confuso** *adj* confused; embarrassed.

congelar [konxe'lar] *v* freeze; congeal. **congelación** *sf* freezing. **congelación de salarios** wage freeze. **congelador** *sm* freezer.

congénito [kon'xenito] *adj* congenital.

congestionar [konxestjo'nar] *v* congest. **congestión** *sf* congestion.

conglomerarse [konglome'rarse] *v* conglomerate. **conglomeración** *sf* conglomeration.

congoja [kon'goxa] *sf* agony; distress.

congratular [kongratu'lar] *v* congratulate. **congratularse** *v* be delighted. **congratulación** *sf* congratulation; delight.

congregar [kongre'gar] *v* congregate. **congregación** *sf* congregation.

congreso [kon'greso] *sm* congress; assembly; conference.

congrio ['kongrjo] *sm* conger eel.

congruente [kongru'ente] *adj* congruent; suitable. **congruencia** *sf* congruence; suitability.

cónico ['koniko] *adj* conical.

conífero [ko'nifero] *adj* coniferous. **conífera** *sf* conifer.

conjeturar [konxetu'rar] *v* conjecture, guess. **conjetura** *sf* conjecture, guess.

conjugar [konxu'gar] *v* combine; (*gram*) conjugate. **conjugación** *sf* conjugation.

conjunto [kon'xunto] *sm* whole. *adj* joint. **en conjunto** as a whole. **conjunción** *sf* (*gram*) conjunction.

conjurar [konxu'rar] *v* bind by oath; implore; ward off; conspire; exorcise. **cónjura** *sf also* **conjuración** conspiracy. **conjurador** *sm* exorcist. **conjuro** *sm* exorcism; entreaty.

conmemorar [konmemo'rar] *v* commemorate. **conmemoración** *sf* commemoration. **conmemorativo** *adj* commemorative.

conmigo [kon'migo] *pron* with me, with myself.

conminar [konmi'nar] *v* threaten; warn. **conminativo** *adj* threatening; compulsory.

conmiseración [konmisera'θjon] *sf* commiseration.

conmoción [konmo'θjon] *sf* commotion; upheaval; shock. **conmoción cerebral** concussion.

conmover [konmo'βer] *v* disturb; touch. **conmoverse** *v* be moved. **conmovedor** *adj* moving, touching.

conmutar [konmu'tar] *v* exchange. **conmutador** *sm* switch.

connivencia [konni'βenθja] *sf* connivance.

connotar [konno'tar] *v* imply. **connotación** *sf* connotation.

cono ['kono] *sm* cone.

*****conocer** [kono'θer] *v* know; understand; recognize. **conocer de** know about. **conocer de** *or* **en** (*jur*) try (a case). **conocer de nombre** know by name. **conocerse** *v* meet; be acquainted with. **se conoce que** it is clear that. **conocedor, -a** *s, adj* expert. **conocido, -a** *sm, sf* acquaintance. **conocimiento** *sm* knowledge; good sense; consciousness; (*com*) bill of lading; proof of identity. **perder el conocimiento** lose consciousness.

conque ['konke] *conj* so. *sm* (*fam*) condition. **conqué** *sm* (*fam*) means.

conquistar [konkis'tar] *v* conquer; win;

win over. **conquista** *sf* conquest. **conquistador, -a** *sm, sf* conqueror.

consabido [konsa'βiðo] *adj* traditional; well known; aforementioned.

consagrar [konsa'grar] *v* consecrate; dedicate. **consagración** *sf* consecration; dedication.

consanguíneo [konsan'gineo] *adj* related by blood. **consanguinidad** *sf* blood relationship.

consciente [kons'θjente] *adj* conscious.

consecuencia [konse'kwenθja] *sf* consequence; outcome; consistency. **en** *or* **por consecuencia** consequently. **ser de consecuencia** be of importance. **traer como consecuencia** result in. **consecuente** *adj* consequent; consistent.

consecutivo [konseku'tiβo] *adj* consecutive.

*****conseguir** [konse'gir] *v* get; attain; procure; bring about; manage. **dar por conseguido** take for granted.

consejo [kon'sexo] *sm* advice, counsel; council. **consejo de guerra** court-martial. **entrar en consejo** begin consultation. **consejero** *sm* adviser; member of board of directors.

*****consentir** [konsen'tir] *v* allow; believe; tolerate; spoil; agree. **consentir en** consent to. **consentirse** *v* begin to crack; come loose. **consentido** *adj* pampered.

conserje [kon'serxe] *sm* porter, doorkeeper.

conservar [konser'βar] *v* conserve; preserve. **conservarse** *v* last, wear well. **conserva** *sf* preserved food; jam; pickles *pl*. **conservación** *sf* conservation; preserving. **conservador, -a** *sm, sf* (*pol*) Conservative; (*museo*) curator.

considerar [konsiðe'rar] *v* consider. **considerable** *adj* considerable; substantial. **consideración** *sf* consideration. **por consideración a** out of respect for. **ser de consideración** be important. **tener** *or* **guardar consideraciones** show consideration.

consignar [konsig'nar] *v* consign; assign; deposit; send. **consignación** *sf* consignment. **consigna** *sf* left-luggage office; password; slogan.

consigo [kon'sigo] *pron* with him/her/you/one.

consiguiente [konsi'gjente] *adj* consequent.

consistir [konsis'tir] *v* consist. **consistir en** consist of. **consistencia** *sf* consistency. **consistente** *adj* consistent.

***consolar** [konso'lar] *v* console. **consolación** *sf* consolation.

consolidar [konsoli'ðar] *v* consolidate; strengthen. **consolidación** *sf* consolidation.

consonante [konso'nante] *sm* consonant. *adj* rhyming; harmonious. **consonancia** *sf* rhyme; harmony. **consonar** *v* rhyme; harmonize.

consorte [kon'sorte] *s(m+f)* consort; accomplice; companion. **consorcio** *sm* association; fellowship; consortium.

conspicuo [kons'pikwo] *adj* conspicuous.

conspirar [konspi'rar] *v* conspire, plot. **conspiración** *sf* conspiracy, plot.

constante [kons'tante] *adj* constant. **constancia** *sf* constancy.

constar [kons'tar] *v* be clear; be evident; be on record. **constar de** consist of. **constar en** appear; be recorded.

constelación [konstela'θjon] *sf* constellation; climate.

consternarse [konster'narse] *v* be dismayed. **consternación** *sf* consternation, dismay.

constiparse [konsti'parse] *v* catch a cold. **constipación** *sf* cold. **estar constipado** have a cold.

***constituir** [konstitu'ir] *v* constitute; establish; compose. **constitución** *sf* constitution.

constreñir [konstre'ɲir] *v* constrain; force; constipate. **constreñimiento** *sm* constraint. **constricción** *sf* constriction.

***construir** [konstru'ir] *v* construct. **construcción** *sf* construction. **constructor, -a** *sm, sf* builder, constructor.

consuelo [kon'swelo] *sm* consolation.

cónsul ['konsul] *sm* consul. **consulado** *sm* consulate.

consultar [konsul'tar] *v* consult. **consulta** *sf* consultation.

consumado [konsu'maðo] *adj* consummate; accomplished. **consumación** *sf* consummation; completion. **consumar** *v* accomplish; complete.

consumir [konsu'mir] *v* consume. **consumirse** *v* languish; be uneasy. **consumido** *adj* consumed; (*fam*) lean; (*fam*) timid. **consumo** *sm* consumption.

contabilidad [kontaβili'ðað] *sf* accounting; bookkeeping. **contable** *sm* bookkeeper; accountant.

contacto [kon'takto] *sm* contact.

contagiar [konta'xjar] *v* infect, contaminate; corrupt. **contagio** *sm* contagion. **contagioso** *adj* contagious.

contaminar [kontami'nar] *v* contaminate. **contaminación** *sf* contamination.

***contar** [kon'tar] *v* count; relate. **contar con** count on; expect; possess. **contado** *adj* counted, limited. **al contado** cash down. **de contado** immediately. **por de contado** certainly. **contador** *sm* counter; cashier; (*tecn*) meter. **contador de aparcamiento** parking meter.

contemplar [kontem'plar] *v* contemplate. **contemplación** *sf* contemplation. **contemplativo** *adj* contemplative.

contemporáneo [kontempo'raneo], **-a** *s, adj* contemporary.

***contender** [konten'der] *v* contend; struggle; argue. **contención** *sf* contention. **contencioso** *adj* contentious. **contendedor** *sm* contender, antagonist. **contendiente** *s(m+f)* litigant. **contienda** *sf* contest; dispute.

***contener** [konte'ner] *v* contain; control; suppress; stop.

contenido [konte'niðo] *adj* reserved; moderate; contained. *sm* contents *pl*.

contentar [konten'tar] *v* satisfy, content. **contentarse** *v* be pleased. **contentamiento** *sm* contentment. **contento** *adj* content, satisfied.

contestar [kontes'tar] *v* answer; confirm; agree. **contestable** *adj* questionable. **contestación** *sf* reply; dispute.

contexto [kon'teksto] *sm* context.

contigo [kon'tigo] *pron* (*fam*) with you.

contiguo [kon'tigwo] *adj* contiguous; adjoining. **contigüidad** *sf* contiguity.

continente [konti'nente] *sm* continent; bearing; container. *adj* containing; continent. **continencia** *sf* continence. **continental** *adj* continental.

contingente [kontin'xente] *adj* contingent, accidental. *sm* contingent. **contingencia** *sf* contingency.

continuar [konti'nwar] *v* continue; remain; endure. **continuación** *sf* continuation. **a continuación de** following. **continuo** *adj* continuous.

contorno [kon'torno] *sm* contour, outline.

contornos sm pl environs pl. **en contorno** round about.

contra ['kontra] prep against; opposite; facing. **el pro y el contra** the pros and cons. **en contra de** in opposition to.

contrabajo [kontra'βaxo] sm double bass.

contrabando [kontra'βando] sm contraband; smuggling.

contracción [kontrak'θjon] sf contraction.

*contradecir [kontraðe'θir] v contradict. **contradicción** sf contradiction.

*contraer [kontra'er] v contract; enter into; be infected with. **contraer matrimonio con** marry.

contrafuerte [kontra'fwerte] sm buttress.

*contrahacer [kontraa'θer] v counterfeit; copy. **contrahacerse** v feign.

contrahecho [kontra'etʃo] adj deformed.

contramaestre [kontrama'estre] sm foreman; (mar) boatswain.

contramandar [kontraman'dar] v countermand.

contrapelo [kontra'pelo] adv **a contrapelo** against the grain.

contrapesar [kontrape'sar] v counterpoise, counterbalance; offset. **contrapeso** sm counterpoise.

contraponer [kontrapo'ner] v set against; oppose; contrast.

contrapunto [kontra'punto] sm counterpoint.

contrariar [kontra'rjar] v oppose. **contrariedad** sf opposition; setback; annoyance.

contrario [kon'trarjo], -a sm, sf opponent. **al contrario** on the contrary. **de lo contrario** otherwise. adj contrary, opposite.

contrarrestar [kontrarres'tar] v counteract; oppose; resist; (la pelota) return.

contrarrevolución [kontrarreβolu'θjon] sf counter-revolution. **contrarrevolucionario**, -a s, adj counter-revolutionary.

contrasentido [kontrasen'tiðo] sm contradiction; nonsense; mistranslation; misinterpretation.

contraseña [kontra'seɲa] sf countersign; password.

contrastar [kontras'tar] v contrast; resist; inspect. **contraste** sm contrast; opposition; hallmark; inspector. **en contraste con** in contrast to.

contrato [kon'trato] sm contract; covenant.

contraveneno [kontraβe'neno] sm antidote.

*contravenir [kontraβe'nir] v contravene. **contravención** sf contravention.

*contribuir [kontri'βwir] v contribute; pay tax. **contribución** sf contribution; tax. **contribuyente** s(m + f) tax-payer.

contrición [kontri'θjon] sf contrition.

contrincante [kontrin'kante] sm competitor; rival.

controversia [kontro'βersja] sf controversy. **controvertible** adj controversial. **controvertir** v dispute, argue.

contumacia [kontu'maθja] sf stubbornness, obstinacy; (jur) contempt of court. **contumaz** adj stubborn; perverse.

conturbar [kontur'βar] v perturb; disturb. **conturbación** sf perturbation.

contusión [kontu'sjon] sf contusion, bruise. **contusionar** v bruise.

*convalecer [konβale'θer] v convalesce. **convalecencia** sf convalescence.

convecino [konβe'θino] adj neighbouring.

convencer [konβen'θer] v convince. **convencedor** adj convincing. **convencimiento** sm conviction.

*convenir [konβe'nir] v agree, be agreed; arrange; be convenient; be advisable. **me conviene** it suits me. **convención** sf convention; agreement; assembly. **convencional** adj conventional. **convenible** adj docile. **conveniencia** sf convenience; conformity; usefulness; advantage. **conveniente** adj convenient; expedient; proper. **convenio** sm agreement; compact.

convento [kon'βento] sm convent.

converger [konβer'xer] v also **convergir** converge; (fig) agree. **convergencia** sf convergence. **convergente** adj convergent.

conversar [konβer'sar] v converse. **conversar con** talk to. **conversar sobre** talk about. **conversador** adj sociable. **conversación** sf conversation.

*convertir [konβer'tir] v convert. **convertirse** v become, turn into. **conversión** sf conversion. **convertible** adj convertible.

convexo [kon'βekso] adj convex. **convexidad** sf convexity.

convicción [konβik'θjon] sf conviction. **convicto** adj convicted.

convidar [konβi'ðar] v invite. **convidarse** v offer one's services. **convidada** sf (fam) invitation to a drink. **pagar la convidada** (fam) treat to a drink. **convidado**, -a sm, *sf* guest. **convidador, -a** *sm, sf* host/hostess.

convincente [konβin'θente] *adj* convincing.

convivir [konβi'βir] *v* coexist. **convivencia** *sf* coexistence.

convocar [konβo'kar] *v* convoke. **convocación** *sf* convocation. **convocador, -a** *sm, sf* convener. **convocatoria** *sf* summons.

convoy [kon'βoj] *sm* convoy. **convoyar** *v* convoy.

convulsión [konβul'sjon] *sf* convulsion. **convulsivo** *adj* convulsive.

conyugal [konju'gal] *adj* conjugal. **cónyuge** *s(m+f)* spouse.

coñac [ko'nak] *sm* cognac, brandy.

cooperar [koope'rar] *v* cooperate. **cooperación** *sf* cooperation. **cooperativa** *sf* cooperative.

coordinar [koorði'nar] *v* coordinate. **coordinación** *sf* coordination.

copa ['kopa] *sf* glass; cup; goblet. **sombrero de copa** top-hat. **tomar una copa** have a drink. **copas** *sf pl* (*naipes*) hearts. **copado** *adj* (*árbol*) bushy. **copera** *sf* cupboard; sideboard.

Copenhague [kope'nage] *sf* Copenhagen.

copete [ko'pete] *sm* tuft of hair; bun; (*pájaro*) crest; summit; (*fig*) haughtiness. **de alto copete** aristocratic.

copiar [ko'pjar] *v* copy; record. **copia** *sf* copy; duplicate; image; abundance. **copiador, -a** *sm, sf* copier. **copiante** *s(m+f)* copyist.

copla ['kopla] *sf* verse; song; ballad. **coplas de ciego** doggerel.

copo ['kopo] *sm* flake; ball of wool; clot; lump.

coque ['koke] *sm* coke.

coquetear [kokete'ar] *v* flirt. **coqueta** *sf* flirt. **coqueteo** *sm* flirtation. **coquetón** (*fam*) philanderer.

coraje [ko'raxe] *sm* courage; anger. **corajinoso** *adj* irate.

coral [ko'ral] *sm* coral. *adj* choral.

coraza [ko'raθa] *sf* armour.

corazón [kora'θon] *sm* heart. **de corazón** sincerely.

corbata [kor'βata] *sf* necktie.

corcovado [korko'βaðo], **-a** *sm, sf* hunchback. *adj* hunchbacked.

corchea [kor'tʃea] *sf* (*música*) quaver.

corchete [kor'tʃete] *sm* clasp.

corcho ['kortʃo] *sm* cork.

cordel [kor'ðel] *sm* thin rope, line. **a cordel** in a straight line.

cordero [kor'ðero] *sm* lamb.

cordial [kor'ðjal] *adj* invigorating, stimulating; cordial, friendly. **dedo cordial** *sm* middle finger. **cordialidad** *sf* cordiality.

cordillera [korði'ʎera] *sf* mountain range.

cordón [kor'ðon] *sm* string; cord; braid.

cordura [kor'ðura] *sf* prudence; discretion.

coreografía [koreogra'fia] *sf* choreography.

cornada [kor'nada] *sf* goring. **cornear** *v* gore.

corneja [kor'nexa] *sf* crow.

corneta [kor'neta] *sf* bugle; hunting horn. **corneta de llaves** cornet.

cornudo [kor'nuðo] *adj* horned; cuckolded. *sm* cuckold.

coro ['koro] *sm* chorus.

coronar [koro'nar] *v* crown. **corona** *sf* crown. **coronación** *sf* coronation.

coronel [koro'nel] *sm* colonel.

coronilla [koro'niʎa] *sf* crown of the head.

corporal [korpo'ral] *adj* corporal. **corporación** *sf* corporation. **corpóreo** *adj* corporeal. **corpulencia** *sf* corpulence. **corpulento** *adj* corpulent.

corpúsculo [kor'pusculo] *sm* corpuscle.

corral [kor'ral] *sm* yard; courtyard; corral; enclosure.

correa [kor'rea] *sf* leather strap; belt. **correa de ventilador** fan belt.

corredor [korre'ðor] *sm* corridor: runner; (*com*) broker.

*corregir** [korre'xir] *v* correct. **corregirse** *v* reform oneself. **corrección** *sf* correction; punishment. **correccional** *adj* reformatory. **correctivo** *sm, adj* corrective. **correcto** *adj* correct; well-bred.

correo [kor'reo] *sm* mail, post; post office; courier. **correo certificado** registered post. **a vuelta de correo** by return of post.

correr [kor'rer] *v* run; flow; pass; sail; cover; travel over. **correrse** *v* move; (*fam*) talk too much.

corresponder [korrespon'der] *v* correspond; concern; reply; repay; be grateful; belong to; match; suit; fit. **a quien corresponda** to whom it may concern. **corresponderse** *v* correspond; agree; like each other. **correspondencia** *sf* correspondence, letters *pl*; agreement; reciprocation. **corresponsal** *s(m + f)* newspaper correspondent.

corrida [kor'riða] *sf* sprint. **corrida de toros** bullfight.

corrido [kor'riðo] *adj* abashed; experienced; over the specified weight.

corriente [kor'rjente] *sf* current, flow. *adj* current; running; everyday; standard; fluent. **agua corriente** running water. **al corriente** informed, up-to-date. **corriente alterna/continua** alternating/direct current. **corriente de aire** draught.

corroborar [korroβo'rar] *v* corroborate; strengthen. **corroboración** *sf* corroboration.

*****corroer** [korro'er] *v* corrode. **corrosión** *sf* corrosion.

corromper [korrom'per] *v* corrupt; ruin; bribe. **corromperse** *v* putrefy; be corrupted. **corrupción** *sf* corruption; stink; bribery.

corsé [kor'se] *sm* corset.

cortabolsas [korta'bolsas] *sm invar* (*fam*) pickpocket.

cortaplumas [korta'plumas] *sm invar* penknife.

cortar [kor'tar] *v* cut; cut short; break in on; stop; switch off. **cortarse** *v* cut oneself; become embarrassed. **cortante** *adj* cutting; sharp. **corte** *sm* cut; cutting edge.

corte ['korte] *sf* (royal) court.

cortejar [korte'xar] *v* court; accompany. **cortejo** *sm* courtship; accompaniment; homage.

cortesía [korte'sia] *sf* courtesy. **cortés** *adj* courteous.

corteza [kor'teθa] *sf* bark; rind; crust.

cortijo [kor'tixo] *sm* farmhouse and farm.

cortina [kor'tina] *sf* curtain; screen; dregs *pl*. **cortina de hierro** iron curtain. **cortina de humo** smokescreen.

corto ['korto] *adj* short; defective; stupid; timid. **corto circuito** *sm* short circuit. **corto de vista** short-sighted.

corvo ['korβo] *adj* curved; bent; crooked.

cosa ['kosa] *sf* thing; something; affair. **cosa de oir/ver** something worth listening to/seeing. **no sea cosa que** lest.

cosecha [ko'setʃa] *sf* harvest. **cosechar** *v* reap, harvest.

coser [ko'ser] *v* sew; stitch; join. **coserse la boca** (*fam*) keep mum.

cosquillas [kos'kiʎas] *sf* tickling; ticklishness. **hacer cosquillas a** tickle. **cosquillear** *v* tickle. **cosquilloso** *adj* ticklish.

costa[1] ['kosta] *sf* coast. **costear** *v* sail along the coast. **costera** *sf* slope, hill. **costero** *adj* coastal.

costa[2] *sf* cost; expense. **a toda costa** at all costs. **costar** *v* cost; cause. **coste** *sm* cost, price.

costado [kos'taðo] *sm* side. **costados** *sm pl* lineage *sing*.

costilla [kos'tiʎa] *sf* rib; chop, cutlet. **costillas** *sf pl* shoulders *pl*.

costra ['kostra] *sf* scab; crust; (*fam*) filthiness.

costumbre [kos'tumbre] *sf* custom. **de costumbre** usual; usually.

costura [kos'tura] *sf* sewing; seam; dressmaking. **costurera** *sf* seamstress.

cotejar [kote'xar] *v* compare. **cotejo** *sm* comparison.

cotidiano [koti'ðjano] *adj* daily.

coto ['koto] *sm* enclosure; reserve; limit. **coto de caza** hunting reserve.

cotorra [ko'torra] *sf* parrot; magpie; (*fam*) chatterbox.

coyuntura [konjun'tura] *sf* joint; opportunity.

coz [koθ] *sf* recoil; kick.

cráneo ['kraneo] *sm* skull.

cráter ['krater] *sm* crater.

crear [kre'ar] *v* create; make; invent; found. **creación** *sf* creation. **creador, -a** *sm, sf* creator; inventor. **creativo** *adj also* **creador** creative.

*****crecer** [kre'θer] *v* grow. **crecerse** *v* become conceited; take courage. **creces** *sf pl* increase *sing*. **con creces** amply, with interest. **crecido** *adj* grown; high; large; in flood. **crecimiento** *sm* growth; increase; flooding.

credenciales [kreðen'θjales] *sf pl* credentials *pl*.

crédito ['kreðito] *sm* credit; credence; reputation. **carta de crédito** *sf* credit card.

credo ['kreðo] *sm* creed.

crédulo ['kreðulo] *adj* credulous.

*****creer** [kre'er] *v* believe; think. ¡**créamelo!** believe me! ¡**ya lo creo!** of course! **creíble** *adj* credible.

crema ['krema] *sf* cream; custard.

cremación [krema'θjon] *sf* cremation.

cremallera [krema'ʎera] *sf* zip-fastener.
crepúsculo [kre'puskulo] *sm* twilight.
crespo ['krespo] *adj* crispy; fuzzy; crinkled; (*fig*) obscure; (*fig*) angry.
cresta ['kresta] *sf* crest; comb; tuft.
creta ['kreta] *sf* chalk.
criar [kri'ar] *v* breed; create; beget. **criarse** *v* grow up; be raised *or* reared. **cría** *sf* act of breeding; litter; brood; young. **criada** *sf* maid. **criadero** *sm* (*plants*) nursery. **criado** *sm* manservant. **crianza** *sf* breeding; nursing. **buena/mala crianza** good/bad upbringing. **criatura** *sf* creature; infant.
cribar [kri'βar] *v* sieve; sift. **criba** *sf* sieve; screen.
crimen ['krimen] *sm* crime. **criminal** *sm*, *adj* criminal.
criollo [kri'oʎo], **-a** *s*, *adj* Creole.
cripta ['kripta] *sf* crypt.
crisálida [kri'saliða] *sf* chrysalis.
crisantemo [krisan'temo] *sm* chrysanthemum.
crisis ['krisis] *sf invar* crisis (*pl* -ses).
crisol [kri'sol] *sm* crucible.
crispar [kris'par] *v* cause to contract *or* twitch; contort; irritate. **crisparse** *v* twitch.
cristal [kirs'tal] *sm* crystal; glass; window; mirror. **cristal de contacto** contact lens. **cristal tallado** cut glass. **cristal trasero** (*auto*) rear window. **cristalería** *sf* glassworks; glassware. **cristalero, -a** *sm*, *sf* glazier; glassblower. **cristalino** *adj* crystalline; (*fig*) limpid.
Cristo ['kristo] *sm* Christ. **cristiandad** *sf* Christianity. **cristianismo** *sm* Christianity. **cristiano, -a** *s*, *adj* Christian.
criterio [kri'terjo] *sm* criterion (*pl* -a); point of view; opinion.
criticar [kriti'kar] *v* criticize. **crítica** *sf* criticism; review.
crítico ['kritiko] *sm* critic. *adj* critical.
cromo ['kromo] *sm* chromium, chrome; picture card.
crónica ['kronika] *sf* chronicle; report. **cronista** *sm* chronicler; correspondent.
crónico ['kroniko] *adj* chronic.
cronología [kronolo'xia] *sf* chronology. **cronológico** *adj* chronological.
cronómetro [kro'nometro] *sm* chronometer; stopwatch.
croqueta [kro'keta] *sf* croquette.
croquis ['krokis] *sm invar* sketch, rough draft.

crucero [kru'θero] *sm* cruiser; cruise; crossroads *pl*.
crucificar [kruθifi'kar] *v* crucify. **crucifijo** *sm* crucifix. **crucifixión** *sf* crucifixion.
crucigrama [kruθi'grama] *sm* crossword puzzle.
crudo ['kruðo] *adj* crude; raw; immature; (*fam*) boastful.
cruel [kru'el] *adj* cruel. **crueldad** *sf* cruelty.
cruento [kru'ento] *adj* bloody.
crujir [kru'xir] *v* creak; rustle; crackle. **crujido** *sm* creak; rustle; crackle.
crustáceo [krus'taθeo] *sm*, *adj* crustacean.
cruz [kruθ] *sf* cross. **en cruz** crosswise. **cruzada** *sf* crusade; crossroads *pl*. **cruzado** *sm* crusader; knight. **cruzar** *v* cross; cross oneself; pass *or* place across; dub. **cruzarse** *v* pass each other; exchange.
cuaderno [kwa'ðerno] *sm* notebook; exercise book; (*fam*) pack of cards.
cuadra ['kwaðra] *sf* stable; hut; large hall; hospital ward.
cuadragésimo [kwaðra'xesimo] *adj* fortieth.
cuadrante [kwa'ðrante] *adj* squaring. *sm* quadrant.
cuadrar [kwa'ðrar] *v* square. **cuadrado** *adj* square; stocky; perfect.
cuadrilla [kwa'ðriʎa] *sf* gang. **cuadrillero** *sm* foreman.
cuadro ['kwaðro] *sm* square; picture; sight, scene. **en cuadro** in a square.
cuadrúpedo [kwa'ðrupeðo] *sm*, *adj* quadruped.
cuajar [kwa'xar] *v* coagulate; congeal; clot; settle; fill with; (*fam*) catch on. **cuajado** *adj* curdled; congealed; (*fig*) dumbfounded. **cuajadura** *sf* curdling; congealing; coagulation.
cual [kwal] *pron* which; who. *adv* such as. **a cual más** equally. **¿cuál?** *pron interrog* which? what?
cualidad [kwali'ðað] *sf* quality.
cualquier [kwal'kjer] *adj* (*con sustantivo*) any. **cualquiera** *pron, pl* **cualesquiera** any; anyone; anybody.
cuan [kwan] *adv* how; as.
cuando ['kwando] *adv* when. **de vez en cuando** from time to time. **hasta cuando** until. **¿cuándo?** *adv interrog* when?
cuantía [kwan'tia] *sf* quantity.
cuanto ['kwanto] *adj* as much as; all; whatever. *adv* **en cuanto** as soon as. **en**

cumplir

cuanto a as to. **¿cuánto?** *pron interrog* how much? how long?

cuarenta [kwa'renta] *sm, adj* forty.

cuaresma [kwa'resma] *sf* Lent.

cuartear [kwarte'ar] *v* quarter; cut into joints. **cuartearse** *v* crack.

cuartel [kwar'tel] *sm* quarter; barracks.

cuarto ['kwarto] *adj* fourth. *sm* quarter; room. **cuarto de baño** bathroom. **cuarto de estar** livingroom.

cuarzo ['kwarθo] *sm* quartz.

cuatro ['kwatro] *sm, adj* four.

cuba ['kuba] *sf* barrel; tub; drunkard. **estar como una cuba** (*fam*) be drunk.

Cuba *sf* Cuba. **cubano, -a** *s, adj* Cuban.

cúbico ['kuβiko] *adj* cubic. **raíz cúbica** *sf* cube root.

cubículo [ku'βikulo] *sm* cubicle.

cubo ['kuβo] *sm* bucket.

cubrir [ku'βrir] *v* cover; drown; repay. **cubrirse** *v* cover oneself; put on one's hat; cloud over. **cubierta** *sf* cover; roof; tyre; bedspread; (*mar*) deck. **cubierto** *sm* cover; place-setting; menu. **bajo cubierto** under cover. **precio del cubierto** *sm* cover charge.

cucaracha [kuka'ratʃa] *sf* cockroach.

cuclillas [ku'kliʎas] *adv* **en cuclillas** squatting, on one's haunches.

cuclillo [ku'kliʎo] *sm* cuckoo; cuckold.

cuchara [ku'tʃara] *sf* spoon; ladle; trowel. **cucharada** *sf* spoonful. **cucharadita** *sf* teaspoonful. **cucharita** *sf* teaspoon; coffeespoon. **cucharón** *sm* ladle; scoop.

cuchichear [kutʃitʃe'ar] *v* whisper. **cuchicheo** *sm* whisper; whispering.

cuchilla [ku'tʃiʎa] *sf* kitchen knife; chopper; razor blade; range of mountains. **patines de cuchilla** *sm pl* ice skates *pl*. **cuchillada** *sf* slash; stab; knifing. **andar a cuchilladas** be at daggers drawn. **cuchillería** *sf* cutlery; cutlery shop. **cuchillo** *sm* knife.

cuello ['kweʎo] *sm* collar; neck; throat. **cuello de pico** V-neck. **cuello vuelto** polo neck.

cuenca ['kwenka] *sf* wooden bowl; eye socket; (*geog*) basin.

cuenta ['kwenta] *sf* account; bill; count; report. **a cuenta** on account. **¿a cuenta de qué?** why? **tener en cuenta** bear in mind.

cuento ['kwento] *sm* tale; fib; fuss. **cuento chino** nonsense.

cuerda ['kwerða] *sf* cord; rope; string;

chain; (*anat*) chord. **cuerdas vocales** vocal chords *pl*.

cuerdo ['kwerðo], **-a** *sm, sf* sane person. *adj* sane.

cuerno ['kwerno] *sm* horn; antler; feeler.

cuero ['kwero] *sm* skin; hide; leather.

cuerpo ['kwerpo] *sm* body; piece, section; stage; corps. **cuerpo de casa** housework. **cuerpo entero** full-length. **cuerpo muerto** (*mar*) mooring buoy.

cuervo ['kwerβo] *sm* raven.

cuesta ['kwesta] *sf* slope; hill. **a cuestas** on one's back. **cuesta abajo/arriba** down/uphill.

cuestión [kwes'tjon] *sf* question, issue; dispute. **cuestionar** *v* question; argue.

cueva ['kweβa] *sf* cave; cellar; den.

cuidar [kwi'ðar] *v* take care of; pay attention to. **cuidar de que** take care that. **no cuidarse de** take no notice of. **cuidado** *sm* care; carefulness; affair; worry. **¡cuidado!** beware! **cuidador** *adj* careful.

cuita ['kwita] *sf* worry; sorrow. **cuitado** *adj* worried; bashful.

culebra [ku'leβra] *sf* snake; (*fam*) practical joke. **culebrear** *v* wriggle; zigzag.

culinario [kuli'narjo] *adj* culinary.

culminar [kulmi'nar] *v* culminate. **culminación** *sf* culmination. **culminante** *adj* culminating.

culo ['kulo] *sm* (*fam*) bottom, arse. **ir de culo** go downhill.

culpar [kul'par] *v* blame. **culparse** *v* take the blame. **culpa** *sm* blame; fault; guilt. **echar la culpa** a lay the blame on. **culpabilidad** *sf* culpability. **culpable** *adj* guilty.

cultivar [kulti'βar] *v* cultivate; grow; develop. **cultivador, -a** *sm, sf* farmer; grower; *sf* (*máquina*) cultivator. **cultivación** *sf* cultivation; culture. **cultivo** *sm* cultivation; culture.

culto ['kulto] *adj* cultivated; cultured; civilized. *sm* worship; cult. **rendir culto a** worship. **cultura** *sf* culture, learning.

cumbre ['kumbre] *sf* peak, summit.

cumpleaños [kumple'aɲos] *sm invar* birthday. **feliz cumpleaños** happy birthday.

cumplir [kum'plir] *v* fulfil; reach; end; do one's duty. **cumplirse** *v* be realized. **cumplir años** have a birthday. **por cumplir** as a matter of form. **cumplido** *adj* plentiful;

faultless; polite. **cumplimentar** v compliment; fulfil. **cumplimentero** adj excessively formal. **cumplimiento** sm compliment; fulfilment; politeness.

cúmulo ['kumulo] sm heap; large amount; (*nube*) cumulus.

cuna ['kuna] sf cradle; (*fig*) origin; birthplace.

cundir [kun'dir] v spread; increase; grow.

cuneta [ku'neta] sf ditch; gutter; hard shoulder.

cuña ['kuɲa] sf wedge; chock. **tener cuña** (*fam*) have friends at court.

cuñado [ku'ɲado] sm brother-in-law

cuño ['kuɲo] sm die; die-stamp; (*fig*) impression.

cuota ['kwota] sf quota; contribution; dues pl.

cupón [ku'pon] sm coupon; ticket.

cúpula ['kupula] sf dome.

cura¹ ['kura] sm priest. **cura párroco** parish priest.

cura² sf cure; healing; remedy; treatment; dressing. **primera cura** first aid. **curación** sf cure. **curador, -a** sm, sf guardian; tutor; curator. **curativo** adj healing.

curioso [ku'rjoso] adj curious; neat; attentive. sm bystander. **curiosidad** sf curiosity.

cursar [kur'sar] v attend; study; frequent. **cursado** adj skilled. **cursante** s(m+f) student.

cursi ['kursi] adj pretentious; affected; vulgar. s(m+f) pretentious person; snob.

curso ['kurso] sm course; direction; school year. **curso acelerado** crash course.

curtir [kur'tir] v tan; harden. **curtirse** v become tanned; become hardened; accustom oneself. **curtidor** sm tanner. **curtiduría** sf tannery. **curtimiento** sm tanning.

curva ['kurβa] sf curve, bend. **curvar** v curve, bend. **curvatura** sf curvature. **curvo** adj curved, bent.

cúspide ['kuspiðe] sf peak, summit.

custodiar [kusto'ðjar] v take care of; guard; defend. **custodia** sf custody. **custodio** sm custodian.

cutis ['kutis] sm invar skin, complexion.

cuyo ['kujo] pron whose; of which; of whom.

CH

chabacano [tʃaβa'kano] adj vulgar, common. **chabacanería** sf vulgarity; vulgar remark.

chacal [tʃa'kal] sm jackal.

chafar [sʃa'far] v flatten; crush; crease; (*en una discusión*) stump.

chal [tʃal] sm shawl.

chalado [tʃa'laðo] adj (*fam*) crazy, dotty.

chalán [tʃa'lan] sm horse dealer; shady businessman.

chaleco [tʃa'leko] sm waistcoat.

chalupa [tʃa'lupa] sf canoe; launch.

chambelán [tʃambe'lan] sm chamberlain.

champaña [tʃam'paɲa] sm champagne.

champú [tʃam'pu] sm shampoo.

chamuscar [tʃamus'kar] v singe, scorch.

chancear [tʃanθe'ar] v joke. **chancearse** v make fun of. **chanza** sf joke.

chanchullo [tʃan'tʃuʎo] sm (*fam*) crooked deal.

chantaje [tʃan'taxe] sm blackmail. **chantajista** s(m+f) blackmailer.

chapa ['tʃapa] sf metal sheet; rouge; (*fam*) common sense.

chaparro [tʃa'parro] adj (*fam*) tubby.

chaparrón [tʃapar'ron] sm downpour, cloudburst.

chapón [tʃa'pon] sm ink blot.

chapotear [tʃapote'ar] v sponge; moisten; splash. **chapoteo** sm sponging; moistening; splashing.

chapucero [tʃapu'θero], -a sm, sf bungler; liar. adj crude, clumsy. **chapucear** v botch, bungle.

chapuzar [tʃapu'θar] v duck, plunge into water.

chaqueta [tʃa'keta] sf jacket.

charca ['tʃarka] sf pool.

charco ['tʃarko] sm puddle.

charlar [tʃar'lar] v (*fam*) chat, chatter; gossip. **charla** sf chatter, talk. **charlador, -a** sm, sf also **charlatán, -ana** sm, sf chatterbox. **charladuría** sf chatter; gossip.

charol [tʃa'rol] sm varnish; patent leather. **darse charol** boast. **charolar** v varnish.

charro ['tʃarro] adj (*fam*) churlish; illbred; tawdry. **charrada** sf boorishness.

chasquear [tʃaske'ar] v trick; disappoint. **chasco** sm trick; disappointment.
chato ['tʃato] adj flat-nosed; flat. sm small glass.
chaval [tʃa'βal] sm (fam) lad; kid. **chavala** sf (fam) lass; girl.
Checoslovaquia [tʃekoslo'βakja] sf Czechoslovakia. **checoslovaco, -a** s, adj Czechoslovak(ian).
cheque ['tʃeke] sm cheque. **cheque de viajero** traveller's cheque.
chicle ['tʃikle] sm chewing gum.
chico ['tʃiko] adj small. sm boy. **chica** sf girl.
chichón [tʃi'tʃon] sm lump, bump.
chiflar [tʃi'flar] v whistle; hiss; (fam) swig. **chiflarse por** be crazy about. **chifla** sf whistle; hissing. **chiflado, -a** sm, sf (fam) crackpot; (fam: aficionado) fan; adj (fam) crazy.
chile ['tʃile] sm chili, chilli.
Chile ['tʃile] sm Chile. **chileno, -a** s, adj Chilean.
chillar [tʃi'ʎar] v scream; howl; squeak; blare. **chillador** adj screaming; shrieking. **chillería** sf screaming; scolding. **chillido** sm scream; howl; squeak.
chimenea [tʃime'nea] sf chimney; fireplace.
chimpancé [tʃimpan'θe] sm chimpanzee.
china ['tʃina] sf porcelain; china.
China sf China. **chino, -a** s, adj Chinese.
chinche ['tʃintʃe] sf bedbug.
chingar [tʃin'gar] v (fam) drink; (fam) pester.
Chipre ['tʃipre] sm Cyprus. **chipriota** s(m+f), adj Cypriot.
chiripa [tʃi'ripa] sf fluke, lucky accident.
chirriar [tʃirri'ar] v creak; squeak; chatter. **chirrido** sm creaking; squeaking; chattering.
chisme ['tʃisme] sm gadget; contrivance; knick-knack. **chismes** sm pl gossip sing. **chismear** v gossip. **chismería** sf tittle-tattle. **chismoso** adj gossiping.
chispear [tʃispe'ar] v spark; sparkle; drizzle. **chispa** sf spark; little bit. **chispeante** adj sparkling.
chisporrotear [tʃisporrote'ar] v spark; sizzle. **chisporroteo** sm sparking; sizzling.
chistar [tʃis'tar] v speak; open one's lips. **no chistar** say not a word. **¡chite!** interj hush!
chiste ['tʃiste] sf joke. **tener chiste** be funny. **chistoso** adj funny; joking.

chivo ['tʃiβo], **-a** sm, sf (zool) kid.
chocar [tʃo'kar] v surprise; shock; collide. **choque** sm shock; jolt; crash; dispute.
chocolate [tʃoko'late] sm chocolate. **chocolatería** chocolate shop.
chochear [tʃotʃe'ar] v be in one's dotage. **chochera** sf dotage. **chocho** adj doddering.
chofer ['tʃofer] sm chauffeur.
chorizo [tʃo'riθo] sm spicy sausage.
chorrear [tʃorre'ar] v gush; spout; drip. **chorreo** sm gushing; spouting; dripping. **chorro** sm jet; gush; flow; stream.
choza ['tʃoθa] sf hut, hovel.
chubasco [tʃu'βasko] sm shower; squall; (fig) setback.
chuleta [tʃu'leta] sf chop, cutlet; (fam) slap.
chulo ['tʃulo] sm pimp; (fam) ruffian; (fam) spiv. adj cheeky; flashy; insolent. **chulada** sf cheek; vulgar thing; funny thing. **chulear** v get cheeky with.
chungar [tʃun'gar] v (fam) tease; tell jokes. **chunga** sf banter, fun.
chupar [tʃu'par] v suck; absorb. **chuparse** v become worn to a shadow. **chupada** sf suck, sucking. **chupadero** also **chupador** adj sucking; absorbent. **chupete** sm (para niños) dummy. **chupetear** v suck at.
churro ['tʃurro] sm deep-fried batter; (fam) dead loss.
chusco ['tʃusko], **-a** sm, sf wag, wit. adj funny.
chusma ['tʃusma] sf rabble, riffraff.
chuzo ['tʃuθo] sm (arma) pike. **llover a chuzos** pour down.

D

dactilógrafo [dakti'lografo], **-a** sm, sf typist. **dactilografía** sf typing.
dádiva ['daðiβa] sf gift. **dadivoso** adj generous.
dado ['daðo] sm die (pl dice).
daga ['daga] sf dagger.
dama ['dama] sf lady; mistress; (ajedrez) queen; (juego de damas) king. **damas** sf pl draughts.
damasco [da'masko] sm damask.

damnificar [damnifiˈkar] v injure, harm.

danés [daˈnes], **-esa** sm, sf Dane. sm (lengua) Danish. adj Danish.

danzar [danˈθar] v dance. **danza** sf dance, dancing. **danzante**, **-a** sm, sf dancer.

dañar [daˈnar] v harm; damage; spoil. **dañino** adj destructive. **daño** sm injury; damage; loss.

***dar** [dar] v give; grant; yield; (reloj) strike; (naipes) deal. **dar a** face; overlook. **dar como** or **por** declare; consider. **dar con** meet. **lo mismo da** it makes no difference. **darse** v regard oneself; devote oneself; matter; occur. **darse cuenta** realize.

dardo [ˈdarðo] sm dart.

dársena [ˈdarsena] sf dock.

dátil [ˈdatil] sm (fruto) date.

dato [ˈdato] sm fact; piece of information.

de [de] prep of; from.

debajo [deˈβaxo] adv underneath. **debajo de** prep under, beneath, below.

debatir [deβaˈtir] v debate, discuss. **debate** sm debate.

deber [deˈβer] v owe; must; ought. sm duty; debt. **debidamente** adv fittingly. **debido** adj fitting; just. **debido a** due to. **débito** sm debt.

debilitar [deβiliˈtar] v weaken. **débil** adj weak. **debildad** sf weakness.

***decaer** [dekaˈer] v decline; decay. **decadencia** sf decadence; decline. **decadente** adj decadent.

decano [deˈkano] sm dean.

decapitar [dekapiˈtar] v decapitate. **decapitación** sf decapitation.

decena [deˈθena] sf unit of ten.

decencia [deˈθenθja] sf decency; modesty; cleanliness. **decente** adj decent; modest; clean.

decenio [deˈθenjo] sm decade.

decepción [deθepˈθjon] sf disappointment.

decidir [deθiˈðir] v decide. **decidirse** v make up one's mind. **decisión** sf decision. **decisivo** adj decisive.

décima [ˈdeθima] sf tenth; tithe. **decimal** adj decimal. **décimo** adj tenth. **decimoctavo** adj eighteenth. **decimocuarto** adj fourteenth. **decimonono** or **decimonoveno** adj nineteenth. **decimoquinto** adj fifteenth. **decimoséptimo** adj seventeenth. **decimosexto** adj sixteenth. **decimotercio** adj thirteenth.

***decir** [deˈθir] v say; tell; speak; call. **¿diga?** (teléfono) hello!

declamar [deklaˈmar] v declaim; speak out; recite. **declamación** sf declamation; oration. **declamador**, **-a** sm, sf orator.

declarar [deklaˈrar] v declare; state; explain. **declararse** v declare oneself; (fuego, etc.) break out; (amor) propose. **declaración** sf declaration.

declinar [dekliˈnar] v decay; fade; depart; (gram) decline. **declinación** sf decline; (gram) declension.

declive [deˈkliβe] sm slope; (com) slump.

decorar [dekoˈrar] v decorate. **decoración** sf decoration. **decorador**, **-a** sm, sf decorator. **decorativo** adj decorative.

decoro [deˈkoro] sm decorum; dignity; respect.

***decrecer** [dekreˈθer] v decrease. **decremento** sm diminution.

decrépito [deˈkrepito] adj decrepit.

decretar [dekreˈtar] v decree. **decreto** sm decree.

dedal [deˈðal] sm thimble.

dédalo [ˈdeðalo] sm maze.

dedicar [deðiˈkar] v dedicate, devote. **dedicación** sf dedication. **dedicatoria** sf (libro) dedication.

dedillo [deˈðiʎo] sm **al dedillo** at one's fingertips.

dedo [ˈdeðo] sm finger; toe. **dedo del corazón** middle finger. **dedo índice** forefinger. **dedo meñique** little finger. **dedo pulgar** thumb.

***deducir** [deðuˈθir] v deduce; allege; deduct. **deducción** sf deduction. **deductivo** adj deductive.

defectible [defekˈtiβle] adj fallible; defective. **defecto** sm defect. **defectuoso** adj defective.

***defender** [defenˈder] v defend; prohibit; oppose. **defendible** adj defensible. **defendido**, **-a** sm, sf (jur) defendant. **defensa** sf defence; shelter. **defensa pasiva** civil defence. **defensivo** adj defensive. **defensor**, **-a** sm, sf protector; counsel.

deferencia [defeˈrenθja] sf deference. **deferente** adj deferential.

***deferir** [defeˈrir] v defer; delegate.

deficiencia [defiˈθjenθja] sf deficiency. **deficiente** adj deficient.

definir [defiˈnir] v define. **definición** sf definition. **definido** adj definite. **definitivo** adj definitive. **en definitiva** in short.

deformar [defor'mar] v deform; disfigure.
deformación sf deformation; distortion.
deforme adj deformed; abnormal.
deformidad sf deformity; (fig) perversion.
defraudar [defrau'dar] v defraud; evade; disappoint; frustrate. **defraudar al fisco** evade taxes. **defraudación** sf fraud; deceit. **defraudador, -a** sm, sf tax evader; swindler.
defunción [defun'θjon] sf decease.
degenerar [dexene'rar] v degenerate. **degeneración** sf degeneration.
deglutir [deglu'tir] v swallow. **deglución** sf swallowing.
***degollar** [dego'ʎar] v cut the throat of; behead; (fig) ruin. **degollación** sf throat-cutting; decapitation. **degolladero** sm slaughter-house; scaffold. **degollador, -a** sm, sf executioner.
degradar [degra'ðar] v degrade. **degradación** sf degradation.
degustación [degusta'θion] sf tasting; sampling.
dehesa [de'esa] sf pasture.
deificar [deifi'kar] v deify. **deidad** sf deity. **deificación** sf deification.
dejar [de'xar] v leave; yield; drop; let, allow. **dejar de** leave off, stop; fail to. **dejarse** v neglect oneself. **dejarse vencer** give in to. **dejarse de** cease to.
del [del] contraction of **de el**.
delantal [delan'tal] sm apron.
delante [de'lante] adv before, in front, ahead. **delante de** before, in front of.
delantera sf front; advantage; lead.
delantero adj front; foremost.
delatar [dela'tar] v denounce; betray. **delator, -a** sm, sf informer.
delegar [dele'gar] v delegate. **delegación** sf delegation. **delegado** adj delegated.
deleitar [delei'tar] v delight; please. **deleitarse** v take delight. **deleite** sm delight; pleasure. **deleitoso** adj delightful.
deletrear [deletre'ar] v spell out; interpret. **deletreo** sm spelling out; decipherment.
deleznable [deleθ'naβle] adj brittle; fragile; frail.
delfín [del'fin] sm dolphin.
delgado [del'gaðo] adj thin; delicate; ingenious. **delgadez** sf thinness.
deliberar [deliβe'rar] v deliberate, consider. **deliberación** sf deliberation. **deliberado** adj deliberate.

delicado [deli'kaðo] adj delicate; tender; touchy. **delicadez** sf delicacy; tenderness; touchiness; frailty; squeamishness.
delicioso [deli'θjoso] adj delicious; delightful. **delicia** sf delight.
delimitar [delimi'tar] v delimit. **delimitación** sf delimitation.
delincuencia [delin'kwenθja] sf delinquency. **delincuente** s(m+f) delinquent; criminal.
delinear [deline'ar] v delineate; outline; sketch. **delineación** sf delineation. **delineante** sm draughtsman.
delirar [deli'rar] v be delirious; rave. **delirio** sm delirium.
delito [de'lito] sm crime.
delta ['delta] sm delta.
demacrarse [demaˈkrarse] v waste away. **demacración** sf emaciation. **demacrado** adj emaciated.
demagogia [demaˈgoxja] sf demagogy. **demagogo** sm demagogue.
demandar [deman'dar] v request; desire; (jur) sue. **demanda** sf demand; appeal; petition; question. **demandado, -a** sm, sf (jur) defendant. **demandante** s(m+f) (jur) plaintiff.
demarcar [demar'kar] v demarcate. **demarcación** sf demarcation.
demás [de'mas] adj other; rest; remaining. **los demás, las demás** the others. **estar demás** be unwanted. **y demás** etcetera. **demasía** sf excess; outrage; insolence. **demasiado** adj, adv too much.
demencia [de'menθja] sf insanity. **demente** adj insane.
democracia [demoˈkraθja] sf democracy. **demócrata** adj democratic. s(m+f) democrat. **democrático** adj democratic.
***demoler** [demo'ler] v demolish. **demolición** sf demolition.
demonio [de'monjo] sm demon. **demoniaco** adj demoniac.
demorar [demo'rar] v delay; remain. **demora** sf delay.
***demostrar** [demos'trar] v demonstrate; prove. **demostrable** adj demonstrable. **demostración** sf demonstration. **demostrativo** adj demonstrative.
***denegar** [dene'gar] v deny, refuse. **denegación** sf denial, refusal.
denigrar [deni'grar] v denigrate; slander; insult. **denigración** sf denigration; disgrace.

denominar [denomi'nar] *v* name. **denominación** *sf* denomination.

denotar [deno'tar] *v* denote; indicate.

denso ['denso] *adj* dense. **densidad** *sf* density.

dentado [den'taðo] *adj* toothed; jagged; (*tecn*) cogged. **dentadura** *sf* set of teeth. **dental** *adj* dental. **dentar** *v* furnish with teeth; cut one's teeth. **dentellar** *v* (*dientes*) chatter. **dentellear** *v* bite. **dentífrico** *sm* toothpaste. **dentista** *s(m+f)* dentist.

dentro ['dentro] *adv* inside, within. **dentro de poco** shortly.

denudar [denu'ðar] *v* denude.

denunciar [denun'θjar] *v* denounce; inform; accuse. **denuncia** *sf* denunciation; accusation.

departamento [departa'mento] *sm* department.

depender [depen'der] *v* depend. **dependencia** *sf* dependence; reliance. **dependiente, -a** *sm, sf* shop assistant. **dependiente de** dependent on.

deplorar [deplo'rar] *v* deplore; regret. **deplorable** *adj* deplorable.

***deponer** [depo'ner] *v* lay down; lay aside; remove from office; depose; (*jur*) give evidence; defecate. **deponente** *s(m+f)* witness.

deportar [depor'tar] *v* deport. **deportación** *sf* deportation.

deporte [de'porte] *sm* sport. **deportismo** *sm* sport; enthusiasm for sport. **deportista** *s(m+f)* sportsman/woman. **coche deportivo** sports car.

depositar [deposi'tar] *v* deposit. **depósito** *sm* deposit; store; tank; tip.

depravar [depra'βar] *v* deprave; corrupt. **depravación** *sf* depravity. **depravado** *adj* depraved.

depreciar [depre'θjar] *v* depreciate, lessen in value. **depreciación** *sf* depreciation.

deprimir [depri'mir] *v* depress. **depresión** *sf* depression. **depresivo** *adj* depressing.

depurar [depu'rar] *v* purify. **depuración** *sf* purification.

derecha [de'retʃa] *sf* right; right hand. **a la derecha** on the right. **derecho** *sm* law; *adj* right; straight; upright.

derivar [deri'βar] *v* derive. **derivación** *sf* derivation.

derogar [dero'gar] *v* repeal; abolish; cancel. **derogación** *sf* repeal; abolition.

derramar [derra'mar] *v* spill; overflow; scatter; spread. **derramarse** *v* be scattered; overflow. **derrame** *sm* spilling; leakage; overflow; slope.

***derretir** [derre'tir] *v* melt; dissipate. **derretirse** *v* be deeply in love; (*fam*) be impatient. **derretimiento** *sm* melting; (*fam*) consuming passion.

derribar [derri'βar] *v* tear down; knock down; throw down. **derribarse** *v* fall down. **derribo** *sm* demolition. **derribos** *sm pl* rubble *sing*.

derrocar [derro'kar] *v* hurl down; ruin.

derrochar [derro'tʃar] *v* squander. **derrochador, -a** *s, adj* prodigal; spendthrift.

derrotar [derro'tar] *v* defeat; ruin; put to flight. **derrota** *sf* defeat; failure. **derrotado** *adj* defeated; shabby.

derrumbar [derrum'bar] *v* knock down, hurl down, pull down. **derrumbarse** *v* collapse. **derrumbo** *sm* collapse; overthrow; demolition.

desabotonar [desaβoto'nar] *v* unbutton; blossom. **desabotonarse** *v* come undone.

desabrigar [desaβri'gar] *v* uncover; leave without shelter; take off clothing. **desabrigado** *adj* uncovered; unprotected; exposed. **desabrigo** *sm* uncovering; exposure.

desabrochar [desaβro'tʃar] *v* unfasten; undo. **desabrocharse** *v* come undone.

desacatar [desaka'tar] *v* be disrespectful; disobey. **desacato** *sm* disrespect; contempt.

***desacertar** [desaθer'tar] *v* be wrong; act foolishly. **desacertado** *adj* mistaken; illadvised; unsuccessful; unfortunate; clumsy. **desacierto** *sm* mistake, blunder.

desacomodar [desakomo'ðar] *v* inconvenience; dismiss. **desacomodarse** *v* lose one's job. **desacomodado** *adj* poor; inconvenient; unemployed. **desacomodamiento** *sm also* **desacomodo** *sm* discomfort; inconvenience.

desaconsejado [desakonse'xaðo] *adj* illadvised. **desaconsejar** *v* advise against.

***desacordar** [desakor'ðar] *v* put out of tune. **desacordarse** *v* get out of tune; be forgetful. **desacordado** *adj* discordant.

desacostumbrar [desakostum'brar] *v* break a habit. **desacostumbrado** *adj* unusual.

desacreditar [desakreði'tar] *v* discredit.

desacuerdo [desa'kwerðo] *sm* discord; disagreement; unconsciousness.

desafecto [desa'fekto] *adj* disaffected; indifferent; adverse.

desafinar [desafi'nar] *v* be out of tune; (*fig*) speak out of turn.

desafío [desa'fio] *sm* challenge.

desagradar [desagra'ðar] *v* displease; be unpleasant. **desagradable** *adj* unpleasant.

desagradecido [desagraðe'θiðo], **-a** *sm, sf* ingrate. *adj* ungrateful.

desagraviar [desagra'βjar] *v* make amends for. **desagravio** *sm* indemnity; compensation.

desaguar [desa'gwar] *v* drain. **desaguadero** *sm* drain; channel. **desagüe** *sm* drainage; outlet.

desahogar [desao'gar] *v* ease; console. **desahogarse** *v* recover; free oneself; speak one's mind; get out of debt. **desahogado** *adj* impudent; well-off; spacious; uncluttered. **desahogo** *sm* ease; comfort; relief.

desahuciar [desau'θjar] *v* evict; despair of. **desahucio** *sm* eviction.

desairar [desai'rar] *v* disregard; snub. **desairado** *adj* spurned; unattractive; awkward. **desaire** *sm* snub; rebuff; gracelessness.

desajustar [desaxus'tar] *v* disarrange. **desajustarse** *v* break down. **desajuste** *sm* breakdown.

desalado [desa'laðo] *adj* impatient; hasty; unsalted.

*****desalentar** [desalen'tar] *v* make breathless; discourage. **desalentarse** *v* lose heart.

desaliñar [desali'ɲar] *v* disturb; ruffle. **desaliñado** *adj* slovenly. **desaliño** *sm* slovenliness; uncleanness; negligence.

desalojar [desalo'xar] *v* remove; eject. **desalojarse** *v* move out. **desalojamiento** *sm* ejection.

desalquilado [desalki'laðo] *adj* vacant. **desalquilar** *v* vacate.

desamor [desa'mor] *sm* indifference; ingratitude.

desamparar [desampa'rar] *v* abandon. **desamparo** *sm* abandonment; helplessness.

desangrar [desan'grar] *v* bleed; impoverish. **desangrarse** *v* lose much blood.

desanimar [desani'mar] *v* discourage. **desanimarse** *v* become discouraged. **desánimo** *sm* discouragement.

desanudar [desanu'ðar] *v* untie; disentangle.

desapacible [desapa'θiβle] *adj* disagreeable. **desapacibilidad** *sf* unpleasantness.

*****desaparecer** [desapare'θer] *v* disappear; hide; wear off. **desaparecido** *adj* missing. **desaparecimiento** *sm* disappearance.

desapegarse [desape'garse] *v* lose interest in. **desapego** *sm* lack of interest; coldness.

desapercibido [desaperθi'βiðo] *adj* unnoticed. **coger desapercibido** catch unawares.

desapoderar [desapoðe'rar] *v* dispossess; dismiss.

*****desapretar** [desapre'tar] *v* loosen.

*****desaprobar** [desapro'βar] *v* disapprove of. **desaprobación** *sf* disapproval.

desaprovechar [desaprobe'tʃar] *v* waste; lose ground. **desaprovechado** *adj* unprofitable; backward. **desaprovechamiento** *sm* waste; misuse.

desapuntar [desapun'tar] *v* unstitch.

desarmar [desar'mar] *v* disarm; disband; dismantle; calm. **desarme** *sm* disarmament.

desarraigar [desarrai'gar] *v* uproot. **desarraigado** *adj* uprooted; rootless.

desarreglar [desarre'glar] *v* upset; disarrange. **desarreglado** *adj* slovenly; faulty. **desarreglo** *sm* disorder; untidiness; trouble.

desarrollar [desarro'ʎar] *v* unfold; develop. **desarrollo** *sm* development.

desarrugar [desarru'gar] *v* smooth out.

desasear [desase'ar] *v* soil; disarrange. **desaseo** *sm* dirtiness; disorder.

*****desasir** [desa'sir] *v* loosen, undo. **desasirse** de get rid of.

*****desasosegar** [desasose'gar] *v* disturb. **desasosiego** *sm* disquiet; restlessness.

desastre [de'sastre] *sm* disaster. **desastrado** *adj* unlucky; dirty; disorderly. **desastroso** *adj* disastrous.

desatar [desa'tar] *v* undo; unravel. **desatarse** *v* break out; lose all reserve. **desatadura** *sf* untying.

*****desatender** [desaten'der] *v* ignore; slight. **desatención** *sf* inattention; discourtesy. **desatentado** *adj* absent-minded. **desatento** *adj* discourteous.

desatinar [desati'nar] *v* bewilder; rave; blunder. **desatinado** *adj* silly; rash. **desatino** *sm* absurdity; blunder; tactlessness.

*****desavenir** [desaβe'nir] *v* cause to quarrel. **desavenirse** *v* quarrel. **desavenido** *adj* incompatible.

desaventajado [desaβentaˈxaðo] *adj*
unfavourable; inferior.

desaviar [desaˈβjar] *v* lead astray; deprive
of necessities; inconvenience. **desavío** *sm*
inconvenience; lack of means.

desayunar [desajuˈnar] *v* breakfast.
desayuno *sm* breakfast.

desazonar [desaθoˈnar] *v* render tasteless;
displease. **desazón** *sm* insipidity; displeasure. **desazonado** *adj* tasteless; displeased.

desbandarse [desβanˈdarse] *v* disband;
disperse.

desbarajustar [desβaraxusˈtar] *v* confuse.
desbarajuste *sm* confusion.

desbaratar [desβaraˈtar] *v* ruin; spoil;
waste; talk rubbish. **desbaratarse** *v* fall
apart; get carried away. **desbaratado** *adj*
wrecked; dissipated. **desbaratamiento** *sm*
waste; disorder; wrecking.

desbordar [desβorˈðar] *v* flood; overflow;
(*fig*) lose one's self-control.
desbordamiento *sm* overflow.

descabezar [deskaβeˈθar] *v* behead.
descabezarse *v* rack one's brains.
descabezado *adj* headless; rash.

descalabrar [deskalaˈβrar] *v* wound (in
the head); maltreat; defeat. **descalabro**
sm setback; defeat.

descalificar [deskalifiˈkar] *v* disqualify.
descalificación *sf* disqualification.

descalzar [deskalˈθar] *v* take off one's
shoes. **descalzo** *adj* barefoot.

descamisado [deskamiˈsaðo] *adj* destitute.
sm tramp.

descansar [deskanˈsar] *v* rest; sleep; lean;
depend. **descansado** *adj* rested. **descanso**
sm rest; repose.

descarado [deskaˈraðo] *adj* brazen;
cheeky; blatant.

descargar [deskarˈgar] *v* unload; discharge; free; absolve. **descarga** *sf* discharge; unloading. **descargado** *adj*
(*batería*) flat. **descargo** *sm* unloading;
discharge of debt. **descargue** *sm* unloading of goods.

descartar [deskarˈtar] *v* discard; leave
out. **descartarse** *v* get out of. **descarte** *sm*
discarding; rejection.

*descender [desθenˈder] *v* descend; flow;
lower. **descendencia** *sf* lineage.
descendiente *s*(*m*+*f*) descendant.
descenso *sm* descent; fall; decline.

descentralizar [desθentraliˈθar] *v* decen-
tralize.

descifrar [desθiˈfrar] *v* decipher. **descifrable**
adj decipherable.

*descolgar [deskolˈgar] *v* lower; (*teléfono*)
pick up; take down. **descolgarse** *v* come
down; slip; drop; surprise.

descolorar [deskoloˈrar] *v* discolour.
descolorido *adj* discoloured.

descomedido [deskomeˈðiðo] *adj* immod-
erate; disproportionate; rude.
descomedirse *v* go too far.

*descomponer [deskompoˈner] *v* decompose; disturb. **descomponerse** *v* rot;
become upset. **descomposición** *sf* decomposition. **descompuesto** *adj* broken;
faulty; insolent.

*desconcertar [deskonθerˈtar] *v* disconcert; damage. **desconcierto** *sm* disorder;
confusion.

desconectar [deskonekˈtar] *v* disconnect.

desconfiar [deskonˈfjar] *v* lack confidence.
desconfiar de distrust. **desconfiado** *adj*
distrustful. **desconfianza** *sf* mistrust, suspicion.

desconformar [deskonforˈmar] *v* disagree,
dissent.

*desconocer [deskonoˈθer] *v* fail to recognize; ignore; deny; disown. **desconocido**
adj unknown; unrecognized; ungrateful.
desconocimiento *sm* ignorance; ingratitude; repudiation.

desconsiderado [deskonsideˈraðo] *adj*
inconsiderate.

*desconsolar [deskonsoˈlar] *v* grieve, distress. **desconsolado** *adj* disconsolate.
desconsuelo *sm* grief; affliction.

*descontar [deskonˈtar] *v* discount;
deduct; take for granted.

descontento [deskonˈtento] *adj* dissatis-
fied.

descontinuar [deskontinuˈar] *v* discontinue.

descorazonar [deskoraθoˈnar] *v* discourage.

descorchar [deskorˈtʃar] *v* uncork.
descorchador *sm* corkscrew.

descortés [deskorˈtes] *adj* discourteous.
descortesía *sf* discourtesy.

descreer [deskreˈer] *v* disbelieve; discredit. **descrédito** *sm* discredit.

describir [deskriˈβir] *v* describe. **descripción** *sf* description. **descriptivo** *adj*
descriptive.

descuajar [deskwaˈxar] *v* liquefy; uproot;
dishearten.

descubrir [desku'βrir] v discover; uncover; publish. **descubierto** adj exposed; manifest; hatless. **descubridor, -a** sm, sf discoverer. **descubrimiento** sm discovery.

descuento [des'kwento] sm discount.

descuidar [deskwi'ðar] v neglect; release; distract. **descuidar de** forget to. **¡descuida!** don't worry! **descuidarse** v be careless; neglect one's health. **descuidado** adj neglectful; careless; casual. **descuido** sm negligence; carelessness; thoughtlessness.

desde ['desðe] prep from; since; after. **desde luego** of course; immediately.

***desdecir** [desðe'θir] v gainsay; be unworthy of. **desdecirse** v retract.

desdeñar [desðe'ɲar] v disdain; scorn. **desdén** sm disdain; scorn. **al desdén** nonchalantly. **desdeñoso** adj disdainful.

desdicha [des'ðitʃa] sf misfortune; misery. **desdichado** adj unfortunate; wretched.

desdoblar [desðo'βlar] v unfold; split.

desdorar [desðo'rar] v tarnish. **desdoro** sm stain; dishonour.

desear [dese'ar] v wish, desire. **deseable** adj desirable. **deseo** sm desire. **deseoso** adj desirous.

desecar [dese'kar] v dry up.

desechar [dese'tʃar] v refuse; reject. **desecho** sm residue; rubbish; contempt.

desembalar [desemba'lar] v unpack.

desembarazar [desembara'θar] v clear; extricate; vacate. **desembarazarse** v get rid of. **desembarazo** sm freedom; naturalness.

desembarcar [desembar'kar] v unload; disembark. **desembarcadero** sm landing-stage. **desembarco** sm disembarkation; landing.

desembocar [desembo'kar] v flow; empty. **desembocadura** sf mouth; outlet; opening.

desembolsar [desembol'sar] v pay out. **desembolso** sm payment. **desembolsos** sm pl expenses pl.

desembragar [desembra'gar] v disengage; release; (auto) declutch. **desembrague** sm disengaging; (auto) declutching; (auto) clutch pedal.

desembrollar [desembro'ʎar] v disentangle; sort out.

desempate [desem'pate] sm (fútbol) play-off.

desempeñar [desempe'ɲar] v·(teatro) play a role; release from debt. **desempeño** sm redemption of a pledge; freedom from an obligation.

desempleado [desemple'aðo] adj unemployed. **desempleo** sm unemployment.

desencantar [desenkan'tar] v disillusion. **desencanto** sm disillusionment.

desenfadar [desenfa'ðar] v appease. **desenfadarse** v calm down. **desenfadado** adj free, unencumbered. **desenfado** sm freedom; naturalness.

desenfrenar [desenfre'nar] v unbridle. **desenfrenarse** v give way to passion. **desenfrenado** adj unbridled. **desenfreno** sm licentiousness.

desenganchar [desengan'tʃar] v unfasten, unhook.

desengañar [desenga'ɲar] v disabuse, disillusion. **desengaño** sm disillusionment.

desenlace [desen'laθe] sm dénouement; outcome.

desenredar [desenre'ðar] v disentangle; straighten out. **desenredo** sm disentanglement.

desenrollar [desenro'ʎar] v unroll; unwind.

***desentenderse** [desenten'derse] v pretend to be ignorant (of); take no part in.

***desenterrar** [desenter'rar] v disinter; unearth; recall. **desenterramiento** sm disinterment; recollection.

desentonar [desento'nar] v be out of tune; humiliate; behave badly. **desentono** sm discord; bad behaviour.

desentrañar [desentra'ɲar] v disembowel; (fig) unravel.

desenvainar [desenβai'nar] v unsheath; (fig) bring into the open.

***desenvolver** [desenβol'βer] v unwrap; unwind; develop; expand. **desenvolverse** v become unwrapped; fend for oneself; prosper. **desenvoltura** sf naturalness; cheerfulness; eloquence.

deseo [de'seo] V desear.

desequilibrar [desekili'βrar] v unbalance. **desequilibrado** adj off balance; mentally unbalanced. **desequilibrio** sm imbalance.

desertar [deser'tar] v desert. **desertor, -a** sm, sf deserter.

desesperar [desespe'rar] v (cause to) despair; exasperate. **desesperación** sf desperation; despair; anger. **desesperado** adj desperate; hopeless. **desesperanza** sf despair.

desestimar [desesti'mar] *v* undervalue; reject. **desestima** *sf* lack of esteem.

desfachatado [desfatʃa'taðo] *adj* brazen; shameless. **desfachatez** *sf* brazenness; impudence.

desfalcar [desfal'kar] *v* embezzle. **desfalco** *sm* embezzlement.

***desfallecer** [desfaʎe'θer] *v* faint; weaken. **desfallecido** *adj* faint; weak. **desfallecimiento** *sm* weakness; faintness.

desfavorable [desfaβo'raβle] *adj* unfavourable.

desfigurar [desfigu'rar] *v* disfigure; disguise; distort. **desfiguramiento** *sm* disfigurement; distortion.

desfilar [desfi'lar] *v* parade. **desfiladero** *sm* gorge, defile. **desfile** *sm* parade. **desfile de modas** fashion show.

desgajar [desga'xar] *v* tear off; break off.

desganar [desga'nar] *v* spoil the appetite of. **desganarse** *v* lose one's appetite. **desgana** *sf* loss of appetite; reluctance. **desganado** *adj* lacking appetite; reluctant.

desgarbado [degar'βaðo] *adj* gawky; ungainly.

desgarrar [degar'rar] *v* rend; tear; (*fig: corazón*) break. **desgarrado** *adj* dissolute. **desgarro** *sm* tear; impudence.

desgastar [desgas'tar] *v* wear away; corrode; ruin. **desgaste** *sm* wear; corrosion; ruin.

desgraciar [desgra'θjar] *v* displease; prevent; spoil. **desgraciarse** *v* fail; lose favour. **desgracia** *sf* misfortune; accident; grief; disgrace; unfriendliness. **por desgracia** unfortunately. **desgraciado** *adj* unlucky; unhappy; in disgrace.

deshabitado [desaβi'taðo] *adj* uninhabited.

***deshacer** [desa'θer] *v* undo; cancel; destroy; frustrate. **deshacerse** *v* get rid of; break; go to pieces. **deshacerse por** strive to.

***deshelar** [dese'lar] *v* thaw; melt. **deshelamiento** *sm* de-icing. **deshielo** *sm* thawing; melting.

desheredar [desere'ðar] *v* disinherit. **desheredado** *adj* disinherited; underprivileged. **desheredamiento** *sm* disinheritance.

deshidratar [desiðra'tar] *v* dehydrate. **deshidratación** *sf* dehydration.

deshilar [desi'lar] *v* unravel. **deshilado** *adj* unravelled; frayed.

deshilvanado [desilβa'naðo] *adj* (*fig: discurso*) disjointed; disconnected.

deshinchar [desin'tʃar] *v* deflate; give vent to. **deshincharse** *v* go down; go flat; (*fig*) come off one's high horse. **deshinchado** *adj* flat; deflated. **deshinchadura** *sf* deflation.

deshojar [deso'xar] *v* defoliate.

deshollinar [desoʎi'nar] *v* sweep chimneys. **deshollinador** *sm* chimney-sweep.

deshonesto [deso'nesto] *adj* dishonest; indecent.

deshonrar [deson'rar] *v* dishonour. **deshonra** *sf* dishonour; affront. **deshonroso** *adj* shameful, disgraceful.

deshora [des'ora] *adv* **a deshora** at an inconvenient time.

deshuesar [deswe'sar] *v* (*carne*) bone; (*fruta*) stone.

desidia [de'siðja] *sf* carelessness; inertia. **desidioso** *adj* lazy.

desierto [de'sjerto] *sm* desert. *adj* deserted.

designar [desig'nar] *v* designate. **designación** *sf* designation. **designio** *sm* intention, idea.

desigual [desi'gwal] *adj* unequal; uneven; changeable; different. **desigualdad** *sf* inequality.

desilusionar [desilusjo'nar] *v* disillusion. **desilución** *sf* disillusionment.

desinfectar [desinfek'tar] *v* disinfect. **desinfección** *sf* disinfection. **desinfectante** *sm*, *adj* disinfectant.

desinflar [desin'flar] *v* deflate.

desinterés [desinte'res] *sm* disinterest. **desinteresado** *adj* disinterested.

desistir [desis'tir] *v* desist.

desleal [desle'al] *adj* disloyal. **deslealdad** *sf* disloyalty.

deslenguado [deslen'gwado] *adj* foulmouthed; shameless. **deslenguarse** *v* (*fam*) use foul language.

desligar [desli'gar] *v* loosen; untie; (*fig*) absolve. **desligarse** *v* break away.

deslindar [deslin'dar] *v* define the limits of. **deslinde** *sm* delimitation.

deslizar [desli'θar] *v* slip; glide; slide. **desliz** *sm* skid; (*fig*) indiscretion. **deslizadero** *sm* slippery place.

***deslucir** [deslu'θir] *v* tarnish.

deslumbrar [deslum'βrar] *v* dazzle; (*fig*) bewilder. **deslumbrador** *adj* dazzling. **deslumbramiento** *sm* dazzle; glare.

desmán [des'man] *sm* excess; misconduct; outrage.

desmandar [desman'dar] *v* countermand. **desmandarse** *v* stray; get out of hand.

desmantelar [desmante'lar] *v* dismantle.

desmayar [desma'jar] *v* falter; discourage. **desmayarse** *v* faint. **desmayado** *adj* faint, fainting. **desmayo** *sm* swoon.

*desmedirse [desme'ðirse] *v* forget oneself; lose self-control. **desmedido** *adj* excessive.

desmejorar [desmexo'rar] *v* weaken; impair. **desmejorarse** *v* deteriorate.

*desmembrar [desmem'brar] *v* dismember; divide. **desmembración** *sf* dismemberment.

*desmentir [desmen'tir] *v* contradict; deny; belie. **desmentirse** *v* go back on one's word.

desmenuzar [desmenu'θar] *v* crumble; sift.

desmerecer [desmere'θer] *v* be unworthy of; be inferior. **desmerecimiento** *sm* demerit.

desmesurado [desmesu'raðo] *adj* disproportionate; excessive. **desmesurarse** *v* go too far.

desmontar [desmon'tar] *v* clear; level; (*árbol*) fell; dismantle.

desmoralizar [desmorali'θar] *v* demoralize. **desmoralización** *sf* demoralization.

desmoronar [desmoro'nar] *v* cause to crumble away. **desmoronarse** *v* crumble.

desnatar [desna'tar] *v* (*leche*) skim; (*fig*) take the best of.

desnivel [desni'βel] *sm* unevenness; gradient; difference of level.

desnudar [desnu'ðar] *v* strip, denude. **desnudez** *sf* nakedness. **desnudo** *adj* naked.

*desobedecer [desoβeðe'θer] *v* disobey. **desobediencia** *sf* disobedience. **desobediente** *adj* disobedient.

desocupar [desoku'par] *v* vacate. **desocuparse** *v* leave work; retire. **desocupación** *sf* leisure; unemployment. **desocupado** *adj* idle; unemployed; free.

desolar [deso'lar] *v* lay waste; afflict. **desolarse** *v* grieve. **desolación** *sf* desolation. **desolado** *adj* desolate; disconsolate.

desodorante [desoðo'rante] *sm, adj* deodorant.

desorden [des'orden] *sm* disorder. **desordenado** *adj* disordered.

desorganizar [desorgani'θar] *v* disorganize. **desorganización** *sf* disorganization.

desorientar [desorjen'tar] *v* mislead; (*fig*) confuse. **desorientarse** *v* lose one's bearings. **desorientación** *sf* disorientation; perplexity.

despabilado [despaβi'laðo] *adj* wide awake; alert. **despabilarse** *v* wake up.

despacio [des'paθjo] *adv* slowly; gradually.

despachar [despa'tʃar] *v* dispatch; attend to; dismiss. **despacharse** *v* get rid of; finish; hurry. **despacho** *sm* dispatch; customs clearance; study; office; warrant; telegram.

despachurrar [despatʃur'rar] *v* (*fam*) crush; squash; (*fig*) make a mess of.

desparpajo [despar'paxo] *sm* self-assurance; nonchalance. **desparpajado** *adj* self-assured. **desparpajar** *v* disarrange; (*fam*) prattle.

desparramar [desparra'mar] *v* scatter; squander.

despavorido [despaβori'ðo] *adj* terrified.

despectivo [despek'tiβo] *adj* contemptuous, scornful.

despechar [despe'tʃar] *v* drive to despair; slight; enrage; (*fam*) wean. **despecharse** *v* despair. **despecho** *sm* despair. **a despecho de** in spite of.

despedazar [despeða'θar] *v* tear to pieces; smash.

*despedir [despe'ðir] *v* dismiss; see off; give off; escort. **despedirse** *v* say goodbye. **despedida** *sf* dismissal; farewell.

despegar [despe'gar] *v* unstick. **despegarse** *v* become detached; become indifferent. **despegado** *adj* unstuck; (*fig*) cold.

despeinar [despei'nar] *v* disarrange the hair.

despejar [despe'xar] *v* free from obstructions. **despejarse** *v* be free and easy. **despejado** *adj* bright; clear. **despejo** *sm* brightness; self-confidence.

despellejar [despeʎe'xar] *v* skin, flay.

despensa [des'pensa] *sf* pantry; store of food.

despeñadero [despeɲa'ðero] *sm* precipice; (*fam*) risk. **despeñadizo** *adj* steep. **despeñar** *v* precipitate. **despeño** *sm* fall.

desperdiciar [desperði'θjar] *v* waste. **desperdiciador, -a** *sm, sf* squanderer.

desperezarse [despere'θarse] *v* stretch oneself; rouse oneself.

*despertar [desper'tar] *v* awaken. **despertarse** *v* wake up. **despertador** *sm* alarm clock; warning. **despertamiento** *sm* awakening. **despierto** *adj* awake; watchful.

despiadado [despja'ðaðo] *adj* cruel, pitiless.

despilfarrar [despilfar'rar] *v* squander. **despilfarrado** *adj* wasteful; shabby. **despilfarro** *sm* waste; slovenliness.

despintar [despin'tar] *v* take paint off; fade.

despistar [despis'tar] *v* throw off the scent. **despistarse** *v* get lost. **despiste** *sm* absent-mindedness.

*desplegar [desple'gar] *v* unfold; reveal; display. **desplegadura** *sf* unfolding.

desplomarse [desplo'marse] *v* tilt; collapse; drop. **desplomo** *sm* (*pared, etc.*) bulge.

despojar [despo'xar] *v* deprive; dispossess. **despojarse** *v* divest oneself. **despojo** *sm* plunder. **despojos** *sm pl* scraps *pl*, leavings *pl*.

desposado [despo'saðo] *adj* newly-wed. **desposanda** *sf* bride. **desposando** *sm* bridegroom. **desposar** *v* marry. **desposarse** *v* become engaged; get married.

desposeer [despose'er] *v* dispossess.

déspota ['despota] *sm* despot. **despótico** *adj* despotic. **despotismo** *sm* despotism.

despreciar [despre'θjar] *v* reject; ignore; despise. **despreciarse de** not deign to. **despreciable** *adj* despicable. **desprecio** *sm* scorn; contempt; snub.

desprender [despren'der] *v* separate, remove; give off. **desprenderse** *v* withdraw; renounce; be deduced. **desprendimiento** *sm* disinterestedness; generosity; separation. **desprendimiento de tierras** landslide.

desprevenido [despreβe'niðo] *adj* unprepared. **desprevención** *sf* lack of foresight.

desproporción [despropor'θjon] *sf* disproportion. **desproporcionado** *adj* disproportionate.

después [des'pwes] *adv* afterwards, after, next, later; since. **después de** after. **después que** after.

desquiciar [deski'θjar] *v* unhinge; disconnect. **desquiciarse** *v* lose control. **desquiciado** *adj* off balance; (*fam*) crazy.

desquitar [deski'tar] *v* compensate.

desquitarse *v* recoup; get one's revenge. **desquite** *sm* compensation; revenge.

destacar [desta'kar] *v* (*mil*) detach; stand out. **destacarse** *v* be conspicuous. **destacado** *adj* outstanding.

destajo [des'taxo] *sm* piecework. **destajar** *v* settle the terms for a job.

destapar [desta'par] *v* uncover. **destaparse** *v* reveal oneself.

destartalado [destarta'laðo] *adj* (*casa*) tumbledown; rambling.

destello [des'teʎo] *sm* sparkling. **destellar** *v* sparkle.

destemplar [destem'plar] *v* disconcert. **destemplarse** *v* get out of tune; lose one's temper. **destemplado** *adj* out of tune; inharmonious.

*desteñir [deste'ɲir] *v* discolour; fade.

*desterrar [dester'rar] *v* banish; (*fig*) discard. **desterrarse** *v* go into exile. **destierro** *sm* exile.

destilar [desti'lar] *v* distil; filter; ooze. **destilación** *sf* distillation. **destilador** *sm* still.

destinar [desti'nar] *v* destine; assign. **destino** *sm* destiny; destination; job. **con destino a** bound for. **destinario** *sm* addressee.

*destituir [desti'twir] *v* dismiss; deprive of. **destitución** *sf* removal; dismissal.

destornillar [destorni'ʎar] *v* unscrew. **destornillarse** *v* (*fam*) go crazy. **destornillador** *sm* screwdriver.

destreza [des'treθa] *sf* skill, dexterity.

destronar [destro'nar] *v* dethrone; depose. **destronamiento** *sm* dethronement.

destrozar [destro'θar] *v* destroy; squander. **destrozo** *sm* destruction.

*destruir [destru'ir] *v* destroy. **destruirse** *v* (*mat*) cancel out. **destrucción** *sf* destruction. **destructivo** *adj* destructive. **destructor** *adj* destructive.

desunir [desu'nir] *v* separate; disunite. **desunión** *sf* separation.

desusar [desu'sar] *v* be unaccustomed to. **desusarse** *v* become obsolete. **desusado** *adj* obsolete. **desuso** *sm* disuse.

desvalido [desβa'liðo] *adj* helpless; destitute.

desvalijar [desβali'xar] *v* rifle; rob.

desván [des'βan] *sm* attic.

*desvanecer [desβane'θer] *v* make disappear; remove. **desvanecerse** *v* evaporate; disappear; faint. **desvanecido** *adj* smug;

vain; (*med*) faint. **desvanecimiento** *sm* disappearance; smugness; faint.

desvariar [desβa'rjar] *v* rave. **desvarío** *sm* delirium.

desvelar [desβe'lar] *v* stop from sleeping. **desvelarse** *v* stay awake; (*fig*) dedicate oneself. **desvelo** *sm* insomnia; effort; devotion. **gracias a mis desvelos** thanks to my efforts.

desventaja [desβen'taxa] *sf* disadvantage. **desventajoso** *adj* disadvantageous.

desventura [desβen'tura] *sf* misfortune. **desventurado** *adj* unfortunate; faint-hearted.

desvergonzado [desβergon'θaðo], **-a** *sm*, *sf* shameless person. *adj* shameless.

desviar [des'βjar] *v* deviate; turn aside. **desviarse** *v* branch off. **desvío** *sm* detour; deviation.

desvirtuar [desβir'twar] *v* impair; decrease in strength *or* merit.

desvivirse [desβi'βirse] *v* long for; go out of one's way to.

detallar [deta'ʎar] *v* (*com*) retail; tell in detail. **detalle** *sm* detail; nice gesture. **vender al detalle** sell retail. **detalladamente** *adv* in detail. **detallista** *s(m+f)* retailer.

detective [detek'tiβe] *s(m+f)* detective.

*detener [dete'ner] *v* detain. **detenerse** *v* linger. **detención** *sf* arrest; delay; thoroughness. **detenido** *adj* under arrest; careful.

detergente [deter'xente] *sm*, *adj* detergent.

deteriorar [deterjo'rar] *v* deteriorate; damage. **deterioración** *sf also* **deterioro** *sm* deterioration.

determinar [determi'nar] *v* determine. **determinarse** *v* make up one's mind. **determinación** *sf* determination; decision. **determinado** *adj* determined; decided; definite.

detestar [detes'tar] *v* detest. **detestable** *adj* detestable. **detestación** *sf* detestation.

detonar [deto'nar] *v* detonate. **detonación** *sf* detonation.

detractar [detrak'tar] *v* defame. **detracción** *sf* defamation.

*detraer [detra'er] *v* denigrate; withdraw.

detrás [de'tras] *adv* behind. **detrás de** *prep* behind. **por detrás de uno** behind someone's back.

detrimento [detri'mento] *sm* detriment;

damage. **en detrimento de** to the detriment of.

deuda ['deuða] *sf* debt; trespass. **deudor, -a** *sm*, *sf* debtor.

deudo ['deuðo], **-a** *sm*, *sf* relative. *sm* relationship.

devanar [deβa'nar] *v* wind, coil. **devanarse los sesos** (*fam*) rack one's brains.

devanear [deβane'ar] *v* rave. **devaneo** *sm* delirium; flirtation.

devastar [deβas'tar] *v* devastate. **devastación** *sf* devastation.

devengar [deβen'gar] *v* have due; (*intereses*) yield.

devoción [deβo'θjon] *sf* devotion. **devocionario** *sm* prayer book.

*devolver [deβol'βer] *v* return. **devolución** *sf* return; refund.

devorar [deβo'rar] *v* devour.

devoto [de'βoto], **-a** *sm*, *sf* devotee. *adj* devout; devoted.

día ['dia] *sm* day. **¡buenos días!** good morning! **del día** fresh. **ocho días** a week. **todos los días** every day.

diablo ['djaβlo] *sm* devil. **diabólico** *adj* diabolical.

diafragma [dja'fragma] *sm* diaphragm.

diagnosticar [diagnosti'kar] *v* diagnose. **diagnosis** *sf invar* diagnosis. **diagnóstico** *adj* diagnostic.

diagonal [diago'nal] *sf*, *adj* diagonal.

diagrama [dia'grama] *sm* diagram.

dialecto [dia'lekto] *sm* dialect.

diálogo [di'alogo] *sm* dialogue.

diamante [dia'mante] *sm* diamond.

diámetro [di'ametro] *sm* diameter. **diametral** *adj* diametric.

diario [di'arjo] *sm* daily newspaper; diary. **diario hablado** news bulletin. *adj* daily. **de diario** for everyday use.

diarrea [diar'rea] *sf* diarrhoea.

dibujar [diβu'xar] *v* draw. **dibujante** *s(m+f)* artist; designer; cartoonist; draughtsman. **dibujo** *sm* drawing; sketch; design.

dicción [dik'θjon] *sf* diction; word.

diccionario [dikθjo'narjo] *sm* dictionary.

diciembre [di'θjembre] *sm* December.

dictado [dik'taðo] *sm* dictation; title. **dictados** *sm pl* dictates *pl*. **dictador** *sm* dictator. **dictadura** *sf* dictatorship. **dictar** *v* dictate.

dictamen [dik'tamen] *sm* opinion; advice; report.

dicha ['ditʃa] *sf* happiness; good luck. **por dicha** luckily. **dichoso** *adj* happy; lucky; (*fam*) boring.

dicho ['ditʃo] *V* **decir**. *sm* saying; remark; proverb. **dicho y hecho** no sooner said than done.

diente ['djente] *sm* tooth.

diestra ['djestra] *sf* right hand. **diestro** *adj* right; skilful; sly.

dieta ['djeta] *sf* diet.

diez [djeθ] *sm, adj* ten. **diecinueve** *sm, adj* nineteen. **dieciocho** *sm, adj* eighteen. **dieciséis** *sm, adj* sixteen. **diecisiete** *sm, adj* seventeen. **diezmar** *v* decimate.

difamar [difa'mar] *v* defame, slander. **difamación** *sf* defamation. **difamatorio** *adj* defamatory.

diferencia [dife'renθja] *sf* difference. **a diferencia de** unlike. **diferenciar** *v* differentiate; differ. **diferenciarse** be different. **diferente** *adj* different.

*diferir [dife'rir] *v* defer; differ.

difícil [di'fiθil] *adj* difficult. **dificultad** *sf* difficulty. **dificultar** *v* make difficult; hinder.

difidente [difi'ðente] *adj* mistrustful. **difidencia** *sf* mistrust.

difundir [difun'dir] *v* diffuse; broadcast; divulge; spread. **difusión** *sf* spread; broadcast; diffusion.

difunto [di'funto] *adj* dead. *sm* deceased person.

*digerir [dixe'rir] *v* digest; (*fig*) endure. **digestible** *adj* digestible. **digestión** *sf* digestion.

dignarse [dig'narse] *v* deign, condescend.

dignidad [digni'ðað] *sf* dignity; rank. **dignitario** *sm* dignitary. **digno** *adj* worthy.

digresión [digre'sjon] *sf* digression.

dilación [dila'θjon] *sf* delay.

dilatar [dila'tar] *v* dilate; expand; delay. **dilatarse** *v* speak at great length. **dilatación** *sf* extension; delay. **dilatado** *adj* numerous; long-winded. **dilatorio** *adj* dilatory.

dilema [di'lema] *sm* dilemma.

diligencia [dili'xenθja] *sf* diligence; (*fam*) job.

dilucidar [diluθi'ðar] *v* elucidate; solve.

diluir [dilu'ir] *v* dilute. **dilución** *sf* dilution.

diluvio [di'luβjo] *sm* deluge.

dimanar [dima'nar] *v* arise from; flow.

dimensión [dimen'sjon] *sf* dimension.

diminutivo [diminu'tiβo] *adj* diminutive. **diminuto** *adj* tiny.

dimitir [dimi'tir] *v* resign. **dimisión** *sf* resignation.

Dinamarca [dina'marka] *sf* Denmark. **dinamarqués, -esa** *sm, sf* Dane; *adj* Danish.

dinamita [dina'mita] *sf* dynamite.

dínamo ['dinamo] *sm* dynamo. **dinámico** *adj* dynamic.

dinastía [dinas'tia] *sf* dynasty.

dinero [di'nero] *sm* money. **de dinero** rich. **dinero suelto** loose change. **estar mal de dinero** be hard up.

dintel [din'tel] *sm* lintel.

dio [djo] *V* **dar**.

diócesi(s) [di'oθesi(s)] *sf invar* diocese.

dios [djos] *sm* god, idol. **diosa** *sf* goddess.

diploma [di'ploma] *sf* diploma.

diplomacia [diplo'maθja] *sf* diplomacy. **diplomático** *sm* diplomat; *adj* diplomatic.

diputado [dipu'taðo] *sm* deputy, delegate, representative.

dique ['dike] *sm* dike; dam; dry dock.

dirigir [diri'xir] *v* direct; govern; steer; regulate. **dirigirse** *v* go; speak; write. **dirección** *sf* direction; directorship; management; postal address. **directivo** *adj* directive; guiding. **directo** *adj* direct; straight. **director, -a** *sm, sf* director; editor. **directorio** *sm* directory.

*discernir [disθer'nir] *v* discern. **discernimiento** *sm* discernment.

disciplina [disθip'lina] *sf* discipline; doctrine; obedience. **disciplinar** *v* discipline; train.

discípulo [dis'θipulo], **-a** *sm, sf* disciple; pupil.

disco ['disko] *sm* disc; record; discus.

disconforme [diskon'forme] *adj* in disagreement. **disconformidad** *sf* disagreement.

discontinuar [disconti'nwar] v discontinue. **discontinuación** sf discontinuation. **discontinuo** adj discontinuous.

discordia [dis'korðja] sf discord. **discordante** adj also **discorde** discordant.

discoteca [disko'teka] sf disco; record library.

discreción [diskre'θjon] sf discretion. **a discreción** optional, at will.

discrepancia [diskre'panθja] sf discrepancy.

discreto [dis'kreto] adj discreet; moderate; sober; witty.

disculpar [diskul'par] v excuse; forgive. v apologize. **disculpa** sf excuse; apology.

discurrir [diskur'rir] v ponder; speak; roam; invent.

discurso [dis'kurso] sm discourse; reasoning; passage of time. **discursivo** adj discursive.

discutir [disku'tir] v discuss; debate. **discusión** sf discussion; argument. **discutido** adj controversial.

disecar [dise'kar] v dissect. **disección** sf dissection.

diseminar [disemi'nar] v scatter. **diseminarse** v spread. **diseminación** sf dissemination.

disentería [disente'ria] sf dysentery.

*****disentir** [disen'tir] v dissent; differ. **disensión** sf dissent; disagreement; quarrel.

diseñar [dise'ɲar] v sketch; design. **diseñador, -a** sm, sf designer. **diseño** sm sketch; design.

disfrazar [disfra'θar] v disguise. **disfraz** sm disguise; fancy dress.

disfrutar [disfru'tar] v possess; enjoy; receive. **disfrute** sm enjoyment.

disgregar [disgre'gar] v disintegrate; separate. **disgregación** sf disintegration; separation.

disgustar [disgus'tar] v upset; displease. **disgustarse** v become angry. **disgustado** adj annoyed; displeased; disappointed. **disgusto** sm annoyance; displeasure; repugnance; trouble.

disidente [disi'ðente] s(m+f). adj dissident. **disidir** v dissent.

disimular [disimu'lar] v pretend; dissemble; hide; tolerate. **disimulable** adj excusable. **disimulo** sm concealment; indulgence.

disipar [disi'par] v dissipate. **disiparse** v disperse; vanish; clear up. **disipación** sf dissipation. **disipado** adj dissipated.

dislocar [dislo'kar] v dislocate. **dislocación** sf dislocation.

*****disminuir** [disminu'ir] v diminish. **diminución** sf decrease; reduction.

disociar [diso'θjar] v dissociate. **disociación** sf dissociation.

*****disolver** [disol'βer] v dissolve. **disoluble** adj dissoluble. **disolución** sf dissolution; (fig) dissoluteness. **disoluto** adj dissolute.

*****disonar** [diso'nar] v disagree; be inharmonious. **disonancia** sf discord. **disonante** adj discordant.

disparar [dispa'rar] v fire; shoot; throw. **dispararse** v explode; fly off; race. **disparadamente** adv hurriedly; foolishly. **disparo** sm firing; shot; attack.

disparatado [dispara'taðo] adj absurd. **disparatar** v talk nonsense; act foolishly. **disparate** sm absurdity.

disparidad [dispari'ðað] sf disparity.

dispensar [dispen'sar] v dispense; pardon. **dispense usted** forgive me. **dispensa** sf dispensation; exemption. **dispensable** adj dispensable. **dispensario** sm dispensary.

dispersar [disper'sar] v disperse. **dispersión** sf dispersal. **disperso** adj dispersed, scattered.

*****disponer** [dispo'ner] v dispose; arrange; decide; prepare. **disponer de** dispose of; have. **disponerse a** get ready. **disponible** adj disposable; available. **disposición** sf disposition; instruction; inclination; determination. **tomar disposiciones** take steps. **ultima disposición** last will and testament. **dispuesto** adj arranged; disposed; ready; willing.

disputar [dispu'tar] v dispute; debate. **disputa** sf dispute, argument.

distancia [dis'tanθja] sf distance. **distante** adj distant.

distinguir [distin'gir] v distinguish; esteem. **distinción** sf distinction; politeness. **distinguido** adj distinguished. **distintivo** adj distinctive. **distinto** adj distinct; different.

*****distraer** [distra'er] v distract; entertain. **distracción** sf distraction. **distraído** adj absent-minded; entertaining.

*****distribuir** [distriβu'ir] v distribute; deliver; allot. **distribución** sf distribution. **cuadro de distribución** sm switchboard. **distribuidor** sm (auto) distributor; agent. **distribuidor automático** slot machine.

distrito [dis'trito] *sm* district.
disturbar [distur'βar] *v* disturb. **disturbio** *sm* disturbance.
disuadir [diswa'ðir] *v* dissuade.
diurno [di'urno] *adj* daily.
divagar [diβa'gar] *v* digress; roam. **divagación** *sf* digression.
diván [di'βan] *sm* divan.
divergir [diβer'xir] *v* diverge; disagree. **divergencia** *sf* divergence. **divergente** *adj* divergent.
diverso [di'βerso] *adj* diverse. **diversos** *adj pl* various; many. **diversidad** *sf* diversity.
*divertir [diβer'tir] *v* entertain; divert. **divertido** *adj* amusing; entertaining.
dividir [diβi'ðir] *v* divide; split. **división** *sf* division; (*gram*) hyphen, dash. **divisor** *sm* divider. **divisorio** *adj* dividing.
divino [di'βino] *adj* divine. **divinidad** *sf* divinity.
divisa [di'βisa] *sf* emblem; (*com*) currency. **divisas** *sf pl* (*com*) foreign exchange *sing*. **control de divisas** (*com*) exchange control.
divisar [diβi'sar] *v* distinguish, discern.
divorciar [diβor'θjar] *v* divorce. **divorciarse** *v* get divorced. **divorciado, -a** *sm, sf* divorcee. **divorcio** *sm* divorce.
divulgar [diβul'gar] *v* divulge; circulate; spread. **divulgarse** *v* come out. **divulgación** *sf* disclosure.
doblar [do'βlar] *v* double; fold; bend; (*fig*) persuade; (*fig*) submit. **doblarse** *v* fold; buckle; stoop; yield. **dobladillo** *sm* hem; trouser turn-up. **dobladura** *sf* crease, fold. **doble** *adj also* **doblado** double; dual; stocky; deceitful. **el doble** twice as much.
doce ['doθe] *sm, adj* twelve. **docena** *sf* dozen.
docente [do'θente] *adj* educational. **personal docente** teaching staff.
dócil ['doθil] *adj* docile; obedient. **docilidad** *sf* docility.
doctor [dok'tor], **-a** *sm, sf* doctor. **docto** *adj* learned. **doctorado** *sm* doctorate.
doctrina [dok'trina] *sf* doctrine. **doctrinal** *adj* doctrinal.
documentar [dokumen'tar] *v* document. **documentación** *sf* documentation; identity papers *pl*.
dogal [do'gal] *sm* halter.
dogma ['dogma] *sm* dogma. **dogmático** *adj* dogmatic. **dogmatismo** *sm* dogmatism.

dogo ['dogo] *sm* bulldog.
*doler [do'ler] *v* hurt; ache; grieve. **dolerse de** feel the effects of; regret; pity. **dolor** *sm* pain; grief; repentance. **dolorido** *adj* in pain; grief-stricken. **doloroso** *adj* painful; pitiful; sorrowful.
domar [do'mar] *v* tame; train. **doma** *sf* training.
doméstico [do'mestiko], **-a** *sm, sf* servant. *adj* domestic. **domesticar** *v* domesticate. **domesticidad** *sf* domesticity.
domiciliar [domiθi'ljar] *v* domicile. **domiciliarse** *v* take up residence. **domiciliado** *adj* resident. **domicilio** *sm* home.
dominar [domi'nar] *v* dominate; master. **dominación** *sf* domination; authority. **dominador** *adj* dominating. **dominante** *adj* dominating; dominant. **dominio** *sm* dominion; authority; supremacy.
domingo [do'mingo] *sm* Sunday. **hacer domingo** take a day off.
dominó [domi'no] *sm* (*juego*) dominoes *pl*.
don¹ [don] *sm* (*con nombre de pila*) Mr.
don² *sm* gift; talent. **donación** *sf* donation. **donador, -a** *sm, sf* donor. **donar** *v* give, bestow. **donativo** *sm* offering.
donaire [do'naire] *sm* charm, grace; wit. **donairoso** *adj* graceful; witty.
donde ['donðe] *adv* where. **dondequiera** *adv* wherever. **¿dónde?** where? **¿por dónde?** which way?
doña ['dopa] *sf* (*con el nombre de pila de una señora o una viuda*) Mrs.
dorar [do'rar] *v* gild; (*culin*) brown. **dorado** *adj* gilt; golden.
*dormir [dor'mir] *v* sleep. **dormirse** *v* go to sleep. **dormilón, -ona** *sm, sf* sleepyhead. **dormitorio** *sm* dormitory.
dorso ['dorso] *sm* back. **dorsal** *adj* dorsal.
dos [dos] *sm, adj* two. **dos veces** twice. **las dos** two o'clock. **los dos** both.
dosis ['dosis] *sf invar* dose. **dosificación** *sf* dosage. **dosificar** *v* dose.
dotar [do'tar] *v* endow; equip; staff. **dotación** *sf* endowment; foundation; personnel. **dotado** *adj* endowed; gifted. **dotador, -a** *sm, sf* donor. **dote** *sf* dowry. **dotes** *sf pl* endowments *pl*, talents *pl*.
draga ['draga] *sf* dredge. **dragado** *sm* dredging. **dragar** *v* dredge; (*minas*) sweep.

dragón [dra'gon] *sm* dragon.
drama ['drama] *sm* drama. **dramática** *sf* dramatic art. **dramático** *adj* dramatic. **dramatizar** *v* dramatize. **dramaturgo, -a** *sm, sf* playwright.
drenaje [dre'naxe] *sm* drainage. **drenar** *v* drain.
droga ['droga] *sf* drug. (*fam*, *fig*) trick, practical joke, fib. **drogadicto, -a** *s, adj* drug addict. **drogar** *v* drug, dope.
dual [dwal] *adj* dual. **dualidad** *sf* duality. **dualismo** *sm* dualism.
ducado [du'kaðo] *sm* duchy.
dúctil ['duktil] *adj* ductile; malleable.
ducha ['dutʃa] *sf* shower. **ducharse** *v* have *or* take a shower.
dudar [du'ðar] *v* doubt. **duda** *sf* doubt. **sin duda** doubtless. **dudoso** *adj* doubtful; dubious.
duelo¹ ['dwelo] *sm* sorrow; mourning.
duelo² *sm* duel.
duende ['dwende] *sm* imp; goblin; elf.
dueño ['dweɲo], **-a** *sm*, *sf* owner; master/mistress; landlord/landlady.
dulce ['dulθe] *sm* sweet. *adj* sweet; mild; gentle; soft; (*agua*) fresh. **dulcería** *sf* confectionery. **dulzura** *sf* sweetness; mildness.
dúo ['duo] *sm* duet.
duodécimo [duo'ðeθimo] *sm, adj* twelfth.
duplicar [dupli'kar] *v* duplicate. **duplicarse** *v* double. **duplicación** *sf* duplication; doubling. **duplicado** *sm, adj* duplicate. **duplicador** *sm* duplicator.
duplicidad [dupliθi'ðað] *sf* duplicity.
duque ['duke] *sm* duke. **duquesa** *sf* duchess.
durar [du'rar] *v* last, endure. **durable** *adj* durable. **duración** *sf* duration. **durante** *adv* during.
durazno [du'raθno] *sm* peach; peach tree.
durmiente [dur'mjente] *adj* sleeping.
duro ['duro] *adj* hard; firm. **dureza** *sf* hardness; severity.

E

e [e] *conj* and.
ébano ['eβano] *sm* ebony.
ebrio ['eβrjo] *adj* drunk.

eclesiástico [ekle'sjastiko] *adj, sm* ecclesiastic.
eclipse [e'klipse] *sm* eclipse. **eclipsar** *v* eclipse.
eco ['eko] *sm* echo.
economía [ekono'mia] *sf* economy. **económico** *adj* economical. **economista** *s(m+f)* economist. **economizar** *v* economize.
ecuador [ekwa'ðor] *sm* equator.
ecuestre [e'kwestre] *adj* equestrian.
echar [e'tʃar] *v* throw; emit; (*naipes*) deal/pour out; dismiss; begin; perform. **echar a** start to. **echar abajo** demolish. **echar a perder** spoil. **echar de ver** notice. **echarse** *v* lie down.
edad [e'ðað] *sf* age. **edad madura** middle age.
edicto [e'ðikto] *sm* edict.
edificar [eðifi'kar] *v* build; (*fig*) edify. **edificio** *sm* edifice.
editar [eði'tar] *v* publish. **edición** *sf* edition. **editor, -a** *sm, sf* publisher.
edredón [eðre'ðon] *sm* eiderdown.
educar [eðu'kar] *v* educate; bring up; train. **educación** *sf* education; upbringing. **educado** *adj* educated; well-mannered.
efectivo [efek'tiβo] *adj* effective; real. **dinero efectivo** *sm* cash. **efecto** *sm* effect; result; (*com*) document. **efectos** *sm pl* effects *pl*, assets *pl*. **efectos en cartera** holdings *pl*. **efectuar** *v* carry out.
efervescencia [eferβes'θenθja] *sf* effervescence. **efervescente** *adj* effervescent.
eficacia [efi'kaθja] *sf* efficacy; efficiency. **eficaz** *adj* efficacious; efficient. **eficiencia** *sf* efficiency. **eficiente** *adj* efficient.
efigie [e'fixje] *sf* effigy.
efímero [e'fimero] *adj* ephemeral.
efusión [efu'sjon] *sf* effusion.
Egipto [e'xipto] *sm* Egypt. **egipcio, -a** *s, adj* Egyptian.
egoísmo [ego'ismo] *sm* egoism. **egoísta** *s(m+f)* egoist. **egotismo** *sm* egotism. **egotista** *s(m+f)* egotist.
egregio [e'grexjo] *adj* eminent.
eje ['exe] *sm* axis; axle; (*fig*) core, hub. **eje del mundo** earth's axis.
ejecutar [exeku'tar] *v* execute; put to death; seize; perform. **ejecución** *sf* execution. **ejecutivo** *sm, adj* executive. **ejecutor, -a** *sm, sf* executor; executioner.
ejemplar [exem'plar] *sm* copy; model;

specimen; example. *adj* exemplary. **ejem-plificar** *v* exemplify. **ejemplo** *sm* example. **dar ejemplo** set an example. **sin ejemplo** unprecedented.

ejercer [exer'θer] *v* practise; exercise. **ejercicio** *sm* exercise.

ejército [e'xerθito] *sm* army.

el [el] *art m* the.

él [el] *pron* he. it.

elaborar [elaβo'rar] *v* elaborate; make; manufacture. **elaboración** *sf* elaboration. **elaborado** *adj* elaborate.

elástico [e'lastiko] *sm*, *adj* elastic. **elasticidad** *sf* elasticity.

elección [elek'θjon] *sf* election; choice; selection. **elector, -a** *sm*, *sf* elector. **electorado** *sm* electorate. **electoral** *adj* electoral.

eléctrico [e'lektriko] *adj* electric(al). **electricidad** *sf* electricity. **electrizar** *v* electrify. **electrocutar** *v* electrocute. **electrodo** *sm* electrode. **electrónico** *adj* electronic.

elefante [ele'fante] *sm* elephant.

elegancia [ele'ganθja] *sf* elegance. **elegante** *adj* elegant.

***elegir** [ele'xir] *v* elect. choose. **elegible** *adj* eligible.

elemental [elemen'tal] *adj* elementary. **elemento** *sm* element. **elementos** *sm pl* elements; rudiments.

elevar [ele'βar] *v* elevate. lift. raise. **elevarse** *v* rise; soar; be elated. **elevación** *sf* elevation; rapture; pride. **elevado** *adj* lofty; sublime.

eliminar [elimi'nar] *v* eliminate. **eliminación** *sf* elimination.

elocución [eloku'θjon] *sf* elocution. **elocuencia** *sf* eloquence. **elocuente** *adj* eloquent.

elogiar [elo'xjar] *v* praise. **elogio** *sm* praise. **elogioso** *adj* laudatory.

elucidar [eluθi'ðar] *v* elucidate. **elucidación** *sf* elucidation.

eludir [elu'ðir] *v* elude.

ella ['eʎa] *pron* she. it.

ello ['eʎo] *pron* it.

emanar [ema'nar] *v* emanate. **emanación** *sf* emanation.

emancipar [emanθi'par] *v* emancipate. **emancipación** *sf* emancipation.

embajada [emba'xaða] *sf* embassy; (*fig*) errand. **embajador** *sm* ambassador.

embalar [emba'lar] *v* pack, bale. **embalaje** *sm* packing; bale.

embarazar [embara'θar] *v* embarrass; hinder; make pregnant. **embarazarse** *v* become pregnant. **embarazada** *adj* pregnant. **embarazo** *sm* embarrassment; obstacle; pregnancy. **embarazoso** *adj* embarrassing; awkward.

embarcar [embar'kar] *v* embark; ship; (*fam*) involve. **embarcarse** *v* go on board. **embarcación** *sf* boat; embarkation; voyage. **embarcadero** *sm* landing-stage. **embarco** *sm* embarkation.

embargar [embar'gar] *v* (*jur*) seize; (*fig*) overcome; blunt. **embargo** *sm* embargo. **sin embargo** nevertheless.

embarque [em'barke] *sm* shipment.

embarrar [embar'rar] *v* smear; cover with mud. **embarrarse** *v* get dirty.

embeber [embe'βer] *v* absorb, soak up; shrink. **embeberse** *v* (*fig*) immerse oneself.

***embellecer** [embeʎe'θer] *v* embellish.

***embestir** [embes'tir] *v* attack; charge. **embestida** *sf* onslaught; charge.

emblema [em'blema] *sm* emblem. **emblemático** *adj* emblematic.

embobar [embo'βar] *v* stupefy; fascinate.

embocar [embo'kar] *v* put in the mouth; enter; (*fig*) swallow. **embocadura** *sf* mouth of a river; (*vino*) taste; (*caballo*) bit.

embolsar [embol'sar] *v* pocket.

emborrachar [emborra'tʃar] *v* intoxicate. **emborracharse** *v* get drunk.

emboscar [embos'kar] *v* ambush. **emboscarse** *v* lie in ambush. **emboscada** *sf* ambush.

embotar [embo'tar] *v* blunt, dull; pack in a jar. **embotarse** *v* become enervated. **embotadura** *sf also* **embotamiento** *sm* bluntness, dullness.

embotellar [embote'ʎar] *v* bottle. **embotellarse** *v* learn by heart. **embotellado** *adj* bottled; jammed. **embotellamiento** *sm* bottling; traffic jam.

embozar [embo'θar] *v* muffle; wrap up. **embozadamente** *adv* secretly. **embozo** *sm* fold; (*fig*) disguise. **quitarse el embozo** bare one's face.

embragar [embra'gar] *v* (*auto*) engage the clutch. **embrague** *sm* (*auto*) clutch.

embriagarse [embrja'garse] *v* get drunk. **embriagado** *adj* drunk.

embrión [em'brjon] *sm* embryo. **embriología** *sf* embryology.

embrollar [embro'ʎar] v muddle. confuse. **embrollarse** v get mixed up. **embrollo** sm confusion.

embrujar [embru'xar] v bewitch.

***embrutecer** [embrute'θer] v brutalize; stupefy.

embudo [em'buðo] sm funnel; crater; (fig) trick.

embuste [em'buste] sm lie; trick. **embustear** v lie; cheat. **embustería** sf deceit; imposture. **embustero, -a** sm, sf liar; cheat; adj lying; deceitful.

embutir [embu'tir] v stuff; cram; (tecn) inlay. **embutido** sm sausage.

emergencia [emer'xenθja] sf emergence; emergency. **emergente** adj emergent; resultant. **emerger** v emerge.

emigrar [emi'grar] v emigrate; migrate. **emigración** sf emigration; migration. **emigrado, -a** sm, sf emigrant. **emigrante** s(m+f), adj emigrant.

eminencia [emi'nenθja] sf eminence; height. **eminente** adj eminent.

emisario [emi'sarjo], **-a** sm, sf emissary.

emitir [emi'tir] v emit; broadcast; transmit. **emisión** sf emission; broadcast; programme. **emisor** sm transmitter. **emisora** sf radio station.

emoción [emo'θjon] sf emotion; thrill. **emocionante** adj moving; exciting.

empachar [empa'tʃar] v satiate; give indigestion; sicken; conceal; (fig) hinder. **empacharse** v have indigestion; become confused; get fed up. **empachado** adj clumsy; sick; fed up. **empacho** sm indigestion; (fig) embarrassment.

empadronar [empaðro'nar] v register. **empadronamiento** sm census.

empalagar [empala'gar] v cloy; vex. **empalagarse** v get fed up. **empalagoso** adj cloying.

empalar [empa'lar] v impale.

empalizada [empali'θaða] sf stockade. **empalizar** v fence.

empalmar [empal'mar] v splice; couple, join. **empalme** sm joint; junction.

empanada [empa'naða] sf meat pie.

empañar [empa'par] v tarnish; swathe; obscure. **empañarse** v cloud over. **empañado** adj misty.

empapar [empa'par] v soak; drench. **empapamiento** sm soaking.

empapelar [empape'lar] v paper; wrap in paper.

empaquetar [empake'tar] v pack. package. **empaque** sm packing.

emparejar [empare'xar] v match; pair; draw level; catch up. **emparejadura** sf matching; levelling.

empastar [empas'tar] v paste; fill. **empastado** adj filled; (libro) clothbound.

empatar [empa'tar] v (juegos) tie. draw. **empate** sm tie. draw.

***empedernir** [empeðer'nir] v harden. **empedernido** adj hardened; inveterate.

***empedrar** [empe'ðrar] v pave. **empedrado** adj paved; cobbled.

empeine [em'peine] sm groin; instep; (med) impetigo.

empeñar [empe'par] v pawn. pledge; commit; get involved. **empeñarse** v start; strive; get into debt. **empeñado** adj insistent. **empeño** sm pledge; contract; insistence; yearning. **casa de empeño** sf pawnshop. **en empeño** in pawn.

empeorar [empeo'rar] v make worse; worsen. **empeoramiento** sm deterioration.

***empequeñecer** [empekepe'θer] v dwarf; belittle.

emperador [empera'ðor] sm emperor. **emperatriz** sf empress.

***empezar** [empe'θar] v begin.

empinar [empi'nar] v straighten; exalt. **empinarse** v rear up; stand on tiptoe; tower. **empinado** adj erect; on tiptoe; haughty.

empírico [em'piriko] adj empirical. **empirismo** sm empiricism.

emplazar [empla'θar] v summon; locate. **emplazamiento** sm (jur) summons.

emplear [emple'ar] v employ; use; invest; spend. **empleado, -a** sm, sf employee. **empleador, -a** sm, sf employer. **empleo** sm employment; job; use.

***empobrecer** [empoβre'θer] v impoverish. **empobrecimiento** sm impoverishment.

empollar [empo'ʎar] v hatch; (fam) swot, mug up.

emponzoñar [emponθo'par] v poison. **emponzoñamiento** sm poisoning.

empotrar [empo'trar] v embed. **empotramiento** sm embedding.

emprender [empren'der] v undertake; start; attack. **emprender con** accost. **emprendedor** adj enterprising.

empresa [em'presa] sf enterprise; (com) company; management. **empresario, -a** sm, sf impresario; contractor.

empréstito [em'prestito] *sm* loan.
empujar [empu'xar] *v* push; press; (*fig*) urge. **empuje** *sm* push; enterprise. **a empujes** by fits and starts.
empuñar [empu'ɲar] *v* seize; take up. **empuñadura** *sf* hilt.
emular [emu'lar] *v* emulate.
emulsión [emul'sjon] *sf* emulsion. **emulsionar** *v* emulsify.
en [en] *prep* on; in; into; onto. **en casa** at home. **en donde** where. **en tren** by train.
enaguas [e'nagwas] *sf pl* petticoat *sing.*
enajenar [enaxe'nar] *v* alienate; transfer; drive mad; enrapture. **enajenarse** *v* lose one's self-control. **enajenación** *sf also* **enajenamiento** *sm* alienation; absent-mindedness; rapture; panic.
enamorar [enamo'rar] *v* court; win the love of. **enamorarse** *v* fall in love. **enamorado, -a** *sm*, *sf* sweetheart.
enano [e'nano], **-a** *sm*, *sf* dwarf.
enarbolar [enarβo'lar] *v* hoist. **enarbolarse** *v* rear; lose one's temper.
*****enardecer** [enarðe'θer] *v* inflame. **enardecerse** *v* become excited.
encabestrar [enkaβes'trar] *v* put a halter on.
encabezar [enkaβe'θar] *v* lead; head; take a census of; put a title to. **encabezamiento** *sm* headline; heading; census.
encadenar [enkaðe'nar] *v* chain, shackle. **encadenamiento** *sm* chaining; (*fig*) linking.
encajar [enka'xar] *v* fit; join; bear; pocket; drop; land. **encajarse** *v* get stuck; squeeze in. **encajadura** *sf* (*hueso*) setting; socket. **encaje** *sm* joint; setting; socket; lace.
encallar [enka'ʎar] *v* run aground. **encallarse** *v* harden. **encalladero** *sm* sandbank; reef.
encaminar [enkami'nar] *v* direct; guide. **encaminarse** *v* set out for.
encandilar [enkandi'lar] *v* dazzle; stimulate. **encandilarse** *v* (*ojos*) sparkle.
encantar [enkan'tar] *v* enchant; charm **encantado** *adj* charmed; haunted. **¡encantado!** pleased to meet you! **encantador** *adj* charming. **encanto** *sm* charm; delight.
encapotar [enkapo'tar] *v* cover with a cloak. **encapotarse** *v* cloak oneself; look sullen; cloud over. **encapotado** *adj* overcast.

encapricharse [enkapri'tʃarse] *v* set one's mind on. **encapricharse por** *or* **con** become infatuated with.
encarar [enka'rar] *v* face up to; aim; confront. **encaramiento** *sm* encounter.
encarcelar [enkarθe'lar] *v* imprison. **encarcelamiento** *sm* imprisonment.
*****encarecer** [enkare'θer] *v* raise the price of; praise; urge. **encarecidamente** *adv* earnestly. **encarecido** *adj* highly recommended. **encarecimiento** *sm* price increase; emphasis; recommendation.
encargar [enkar'gar] *v* (*com*) order; commission; entrust; charge; advise. **encargarse de** take charge of. **encargado** *sm* agent. **encargo** *sm* errand; job; order.
encarnar [enkar'nar] *v* personify; heal; pierce the flesh; bait. **encarnarse** *v* mix, join in. **encarnación** *sf* incarnation. **encarnado** *adj* incarnate; red; (*uña*) ingrowing.
encarnizar [enkarni'θar] *v* infuriate. **encarnizarse** *v* devour. **encarnizado** *adj* inflamed; bloody.
encasillar [enkasi'ʎar] *v* classify.
encauzar [enkau'θar] *v* channel; direct. **encauzamiento** *sm* channelling; (*fig*) guidance.
*****encender** [enθen'der] *v* light; set on fire; turn on; arouse. **encendedor** *sm* lighter. **encendido** *adj* lit; burning; flushed. **encendimiento** *sm* burning; ardour.
*****encerrar** [enθer'rar] *v* shut up; enclose; contain. **encerrarse** *v* live in seclusion. **encerramiento** *sm* enclosure; lock-up. **encierro** *sm* enclosure; prison.
encía [en'θia] *sf* (*anat*) gum.
enciclopedia [enθiklo'peðja] *sf* encyclopaedia. **enciclopédico** *adj* encyclopaedic.
encima [en'θima] *adv* above; overhead. **por encima** over; quickly; superficially. **encima de** on top of.
encina [en'θina] *sf* ilex, holm oak.
encinta [en'θinta] *adj* pregnant.
enclavar [enkla'βar] *v* locate; nail; pierce. **enclave** *sm* enclave; situation.
enclenque [en'klenke] *adj* sickly; feeble; skinny.
encoger [enko'xer] *v* shrink. **encogerse de hombros** shrug one's shoulders. **encogido** *adj* shrunk; (*fig*) timid. **encogimiento** *sm* shrinkage; shyness.
encolar [enko'lar] *v* glue. **encolamiento** *sm* gluing.

*encomendar [enkomen'ðar] *v* entrust.
encomendarse *v* commend oneself.
encomienda *sf* assignment; tribute; land
concession.

encomiar [enko'mjar] *v* praise.
encomiador *adj* laudatory.

enconar [enko'nar] *v* inflame; infect.
enconarse *v* become inflamed; become
infected; get angry.

encontrar [enkon'trar] *v* find; meet.
encontrarse *v* find oneself; quarrel.
encontrado *adj* opposed.

encopetado [enkope'taðo] *adj* of noble
birth; aristocratic; presumptuous.

encorvar [enkor'βar] *v* curve. **encorvarse** *v*
become bent; (*caballo*) buck. **encorvado**
adj bent; stooped. **encorvamiento** *sm*
bend; stoop.

encrespar [enkres'par] *v* curl; make
rough; excite; irritate. **encresparse** *v*
curl; become rough; become entangled.

encrucijada [enkruθi'xaða] *sf* crossroads
pl.

encuadernar [enkwaðer'nar] *v* (*libro*)
bind. **encuadernación** *sf* bookbinding.

encuadrar [enkwa'ðrar] *v* frame; insert.
encuadre *sm* frame.

*encubrir [enku'βrir] *v* conceal; (*jur*)
receive stolen goods. **encubierto** *adj* concealed. **encubrimiento** *sm* concealment.

encuentro [en'kwentro] *sm* encounter;
collision.

encumbrar [enkum'brar] *v* raise; ascend;
exalt. **encumbrado** *adj* high, lofty.
encumbramiento *sm* height; praise.

enchufar [entʃu'far] *v* plug in; connect.
enchufado, -a *sm, sf* (*fam*) wirepuller.
enchufe *sm* electric plug; joint; (*fam*)
cushy job. **enchufismo** *sm* (*fam*) wirepulling.

endeble [en'deβle] *adj* frail. **endeblez** *sf*
frailty.

endémico [en'demiko] *adj* endemic.

enderezar [endere'θar] *v* straighten;
guide; put right. **enderezarse** *v* stand up
straight. **enderezado** *adj* favourable.

endeudarse [endeu'ðarse] *v* get into debt.

endiablado [endja'βlaðo] *adj* devilish.
endiablar *v* bedevil.

endiosar [endjo'sar] *v* deify. **endiosarse** *v*
be conceited. **endiosado** *adj* deified; conceited.

endosar [endo'sar] *v* *also* **endorsar**
endorse. **endoso** *sm* *also* **endorso** *sm*
endorsement.

endulzar [endul'θar] *v* sweeten.
endulzadura *sf* sweetening.

*endurecer [endure'θer] *v* harden.
endurecido *adj* hardened. **endurecimiento**
sm hardening.

enebro [e'neβro] *sm* juniper.

enemigo [ene'migo], **-a** *sm, sf* enemy. *adj*
hostile. **enemistar** *v* make an enemy of.

energía [ener'xia] *sf* energy. **enérgico** *adj*
energetic; vigorous; drastic.

enero [e'nero] *sm* January.

enfadar [enfa'ðar] *v* anger. **enfado** *sm*
anger; annoyance. **enfadoso** *adj* annoying.

énfasis ['enfasis] *s(m or f)* emphasis.
enfático *adj* emphatic.

enfermar [enfer'mar] *v* make ill; fall ill.
enfermedad *sf* illness. **enfermedad profesional** occupational disease. **enfermería**
sf infirmary. **enfermera, -o** *sf, sm* nurse.
enfermo *adj* ill.

enfilar [enfi'lar] *v* line up.

*enflaquecer [enflake'θer] *v* weaken;
make thin; grow thin. **enflaquecimiento**
sm weakening; emaciation.

enfocar [enfo'kar] *v* focus; approach,
tackle. **enfoque** *sm* focus; approach.

enfrascar [enfras'kar] *v* bottle. **enfrascarse**
v become involved; become engrossed.

enfrentar [enfren'tar] *v* confront; face;
resist. **enfrentarse** *v* face up to. **enfrente**
adv opposite. **enfrente de** *prep* opposite.

enfriar [enfri'ar] *v* cool. **enfriarse** *v* cool
down. **enfriadero** *sm* coldroom.
enfriamiento *sm* cooling.

*enfurecer [enfure'θer] *v* infuriate.
enfurecerse *v* rage. **enfurecimiento** *sm*
fury.

enganchar [engan'tʃar] *v* hook; hitch;
hang up; harness. **enganche** *sm* hook;
coupling; harnessing; enlistment.

engañar [enga'ɲar] *v* deceive. **engaño** *sm*
deceit. **engañoso** *adj* deceitful.

engatusar [engatu'sar] *v* coax; flatter.
engatusamiento *sm* coaxing.

engendrar [enxen'drar] *v* engender;
breed. **engendrador** *adj* generating.
engendramiento *sm* generating. **engendro**
sm foetus; abortion; monster;
brainchild.

englobar [englo'βar] *v* include; embrace.

engordar [engor'ðar] *v* fatten; gain
weight. **engorde** *sm* (*animales*) fattening
up.

engorro [en'gorro] *sm* nuisance. **engorroso** *adj* troublesome.

engranar [engra'nar] *v* put in gear, mesh, interlock. **engranaje** *sm* gear; cogs; connection.

***engrandecer** [engrande'θer] *v* enlarge; exaggerate; promote. **engrandecimiento** *sm* enlargement; increase; exaggeration.

engrasar [engra'sar] *v* grease. **engrase** *sm* greasing.

engreído [engre'iðo] *adj* conceited. **engreimiento** *sm* conceit. **engreir** *v* make conceited.

***engrosar** [engro'sar] *v* fatten; thicken; increase. **engrosarse** *v* enlarge. **engrosamiento** *sm* fattening; thickening.

***engullir** [engu'ʎir] *v* gobble; gulp down.

enhiesto [e'njesto] *adj* erect; upright. **enhestar** *v* erect. **enhestarse** *v* rise; straighten oneself up.

enhorabuena [enora'βwena] *sf* congratulations *pl.* **dar la enhorabuena** congratulate. **enhoramala** *adv* inopportunely.

enigma [e'nigma] *sm* enigma. **enigmático** *adj* enigmatic.

enjabonar [enxaβo'nar] *v* soap. **enjabonadura** *sf* lathering.

enjambre [en'xambre] *sm* swarm. **enjambrar** *v* swarm.

enjaular [enxau'lar] *v* cage.

enjuagar [enxwa'gar] *v* rinse. **enjuague** *sm* rinse, rinsing; (*fig*) plot.

enjugar [enxu'gar] *v* dry; wipe; cancel. **enjugador** *sm* clothes-drier.

enjuiciar [enxwi'θjar] *v* (*jur*) sue; try; prosecute; judge. **enjuiciamiento** *sm* trial; lawsuit; judgment.

enlace [en'laθe] *sm* link; connection; liaison; marriage. **enlazar** *v* join; connect; relate. **enlazarse** *v* marry.

***enloquecer** [enloke'θer] *v* madden. **enloquecido** *adj* mad. **enloquecimiento** *sm* madness.

enlosar [enlo'sar] *v* tile; pave. **enlosado** *sm* tiling; paving.

***enlucir** [enlu'θir] *v* plaster; polish. **enlucido** *sm* plaster. **enlucimiento** *sm* plastering; polishing.

enlutar [enlu'tar] *v* dress in mourning; (*fig*) sadden. **enlutado** *adj* in mourning.

enmarañar [enmara'ɲar] *v* entangle; muddle; confuse. **enmarañamiento** *sm* tangle; confusion.

enmascarar [enmaska'rar] *v* mask. **enmascararse** *v* go in disguise. **enmascaramiento** *sm* camouflage.

***enmendar** [enmen'dar] *v* amend; correct; reform. **enmendadura** *sf* correction. **enmienda** *sf* rectification; repair; amendment.

***enmohecer** [enmoe'θer] *v* rust; make mouldy. **enmohecerse** *v* get rusty; grow mouldy. **enmohecimiento** *sm* rusting; mouldering.

***enmudecer** [enmuðe'θer] *v* silence. **enmudecerse** *v* fall silent; become dumb.

ennoblecer [ennoβle'θer] *v* ennoble; do honour to. **ennoblecimiento** *sm* ennobling.

enojar [eno'xar] *v* annoy; offend. **enojarse** *v* get cross. **enojado** *adj* angry. **enojo** *sm* annoyance; anger.

***enorgullecer** [enorguʎe'θer] *v* make proud. **enorgullecerse** *v* grow proud. **enorgullecerse de** pride oneself on. **enorgullecimiento** *sm* pride.

enorme [e'norme] *adj* enormous. **enormidad** *sf* hugeness; enormity.

***enrarecer** [enrare'θer] *v* make rare; rarefy. **enrarecerse** *v* become scarce. **enrarecido** *adj* rarefied. **enrarecimiento** *sm* scarcity.

enredar [enre'ðar] *v* catch; entangle; compromise; involve. **enredarse** *v* become involved. **planta enredadera** *sf* climbing plant. **enredador** *adj* mischievous. **enredo** *sm* tangle; mess; love affair. **enredoso** *adj* complicated; mischievous.

enrevesado [enreβe'saðo] *adj* complicated, involved.

***enriquecer** [enrike'θer] *v* enrich.

***enrojecer** [enroxe'θer] *v* redden; cause to blush. **enrojecerse** *v* blush. **enrojecimiento** *sm* glowing; blush.

enrollar [enro'ʎar] *v* coil up. **enrollamiento** *sm* rolling up; coiling.

***enronquecer** [enronke'θer] *v* make hoarse. **enronquecimiento** *sm* hoarseness.

enroscar [enros'kar] *v* twist, curl. **enroscarse** *v* curl up. **enroscadura** *sf* twisting, curling.

ensalada [ensa'laða] *sf* salad.

ensalmar [ensal'mar] *v* (*huesos*) set; cure. **ensalmador, -a** *sm, sf* quack; bonesetter. **ensalmado** *sm* quack remedy.

ensalzar [ensal'θar] *v* praise. **ensalzarse** *v* boast. **ensalzamiento** *sm* praise.

ensamblar [ensam'blar] *v* assemble; join.

ensamblado sm joint. **ensamblador** sm joiner. **ensamblaje** sm joining; joint.

ensanchar [ensan'tʃar] v grow broader; enlarge; stretch. **ensancharse** v put on airs. **ensanche** sm enlargement; extension; new suburb.

ensañar [ensa'ɲar] v infuriate. **ensañarse** v be merciless.

ensayar [ensa'jar] v test; try; rehearse. **ensayarse** v practise; rehearse. **ensayo** sm test; trial; essay; rehearsal. **ensayo general** dress rehearsal.

ensenada [ense'naða] sf cove; inlet.

enseñar [ense'ɲar] v show; teach. **bien/mal enseñado** well/ill-bred. **enseñanza** sf teaching; education.

enseres [en'seres] sm pl goods and chattels; equipment sing.

ensillar [ensi'ʎar] v saddle.

ensimismarse [ensimis'marse] v become lost in thought. **ensimismado** adj lost in thought. **ensimismamiento** sm pensiveness.

*ensordecer [ensorðe'θer] v deafen. **ensordecerse** v grow deaf. **ensordecedor** adj deafening. **ensordecimiento** sm deafness.

ensuciar [ensu'θjar] v dirty. **ensuciador** adj dirtying. **ensuciamiento** sm dirtiness, dirt.

ensueño [en'sweɲo] sm dream; fantasy. **¡ni por ensueño!** not likely!

entablar [enta'βlar] v begin; open; establish; board up; put in a splint; (juegos) set up. **entablado** sm planking; wooden floor.

entallar [enta'ʎar] v carve; notch; engrave; fit to the body. **entalladura** sf notch; mortise; carving.

ente ['ente] sm entity; (fam) fellow.

*entender [enten'der] v understand; believe; mean. **entenderse** v make oneself understood. **entendedor, -a** sm, sf expert. **entendidamente** adv cleverly. **entendido** adj understood; well informed; clever. **¡entendido!** O.K.!

enterar [ente'rar] v inform; instruct. **enterarse** v become aware. **enterado** adj aware.

*enternecer [enterne'θer] v soften. **enternecerse** v be moved; relent.

entero [en'tero] adj entire, whole; perfect; pure; strong. **por entero** completely. **enteramente** adv entirely.

*enterrar [enter'rar] v bury. **entarrador** sm gravedigger. **entierro** sm burial; funeral.

entidad [enti'ðað] sf society; company; significance; entity.

entonar [ento'nar] v tune; intone; sing in tune. **entonación** sf intonation. **entonado** adj in tune; haughty.

entonces [en'tonθes] adv then; in that case; and so.

entornar [entor'nar] v (ojos, puerta) half close; tilt.

*entorpecer [entorpe'θer] v benumb; obstruct. **entorpecimiento** sm numbness; sluggishness; obstruction.

entrada [en'traða] sf entrance; doorway; admission; (deporte) gate; ticket; income; takings pl. **derechos de entrada** sm pl import duty sing. **de entrada** to begin with. **entrar** v enter; flow into; fit; join; introduce; invade. **el año que entra** the coming year.

entrambos [en'trambos] pl adj both.

entraña [en'traɲa] sf essence; core; disposition. **entrañas** sf pl entrails, bowels. **no tener entrañas** be heartless. **entrañable** adj dear, beloved. **entrañar** v bury deep; involve. **entrañarse** v penetrate to the core.

entre ['entre] prep between; among. **entre semana** on weekdays. **entretanto** adv meanwhile.

entreabierto [entrea'βjerto] adj half-open.

entrecejo [entre'θexo] sm frown.

entregar [entre'gar] v deliver; surrender. **entrega** sf delivery; (fascículo) instalment.

entrelazar [entrela'θar] v entwine.

entremés [entre'mes] sm (culin) hors d'oeuvre; (teatro) short farce.

entremeter [entreme'ter] v also **entrometer** mix; insert. **entremeterse** also **entrometerse** v interfere. **entremetido, -a** sm, sf also **entrometido, -a** busybody.

entrenar [entre'nar] v train; coach. **entrenador, -a** sm, sf trainer; coach. **entrenamiento** sm training; coaching.

entresacar [entresa'kar] v select; prune; thin out.

entresuelo [entre'swelo] sm mezzanine.

entretejer [entrete'xer] v interweave.

*entretener [entrete'ner] v entertain; delay; maintain. **entretenerse** v pass the time. **entretenido** adj entertaining; busy. **entretenimiento** sm entertainment; pastime; delaying.

*entrever [entre'βer] v make out; foresee.
entrevista [entre'βista] sf interview.
entrevistar v interview. **entrevistarse** v hold an interview.
*entristecer [entriste'θer] v sadden. **entristecerse** v grow sad. **entristecimiento** sm sadness.
*entumecer [entume'θer] v numb. **entumecerse** v go numb; (mar) surge. **entumecido** adj numb. **entumecimiento** sm numbness.
enturbiar [entur'βjar] v make cloudy; muddy. **enturbiarse** v be in disorder.
entusiasmar [entusjas'mar] v fill with enthusiasm. **entusiasmarse** v be very keen. **entusiasmo** sm enthusiasm. **entusiasta** s(m+f) enthusiast; adj enthusiastic. **entusiástico** adj enthusiastic.
enumerar [enume'rar] v enumerate. **enumeración** sf enumeration.
enunciar [enun'θjar] v enunciate, state. **enunciación** sf statement, enunciation.
envainar [enβai'nar] v sheathe.
*envanecer [enβane'θer] v make vain. **envanecimiento** sm vanity.
envasar [enβa'sar] v pack; wrap; bottle. **envasador** sm packer; large funnel. **envase** sm packing; bottling; container.
*envejecer [enβexe'θer] v age. **envejecerse** v grow old. **envejecido** adj aged. **envejecimiento** sm ageing.
envenenar [enβene'nar] v poison. **envenenador** adj poisonous. **envenenamiento** sm poisoning; pollution.
envergadura [enβerga'ðura] sf wingspan; (fig) scope.
enviar [en'βjar] v send. **enviado, -a** sm, sf messenger; representative; envoy.
envidiar [enβi'ðjar] v envy. **envidia** sf envy. **envidioso** adj envious.
*envilecer [enβile'θer] v debase. **envilecimiento** sm debasement; degradation.
envío [en'βio] sm dispatch; shipment; remittance.
*envolver [enβol'βer] v envelop; wrap up; involve; imply; (mil) encircle. **envoltura** sf wrapping; envelope.
enzarzar [enθar'θar] v cover with brambles; set at odds. **enzarzarse** v get caught up in brambles; (fig) squabble.
enzima [en'θima] sf enzyme.
épico ['epiko] adj epic.
epidemia [epi'ðemja] sf epidemic. **epidémico** adj epidemic.

epígrafe [e'pigrafe] sm epigraph.
epílogo [e'pilogo] sm epilogue.
episcopado [episko'paðo] sm bishopric; episcopate. **episcopal** adj episcopal.
episodio [epi'soðjo] sm episode.
epitafio [epi'tafjo] sm epitaph.
época ['epoka] sf epoch.
equidad [eki'ðað] sf equity; fairness.
equilibrar [ekili'βrar] v balance. **equilibrio** sm equilibrium; balance; poise. **equilibrismo** sm acrobatics. **equilibrista** s(m+f) acrobat.
equinoccio [eki'nokθjo] sm equinox. **equinoccial** adj equinoctial.
equipar [eki'par] v equip. **equipaje** sm luggage; equipment. **equipo** sm team; equipment; trousseau.
equitación [ekita'θjon] sf riding; horsemanship.
equitativo [ekita'tiβo] adj fair, equitable.
equivalencia [ekiβa'lenθja] sf equivalence. **equivalente** adj equivalent. **equivaler** v be equivalent.
equivocar [ekiβo'kar] v mistake. **equivocarse** v be mistaken. **equivocación** sf mistake. **equívoco** adj ambiguous.
era¹ ['era] sf era.
era² ['era] V ser.
eremita [ere'mita] sm also **ermitaño** sm hermit.
eres ['eres] V ser.
*erguir [er'gir] v raise, erect. **erguirse** v straighten up. **erguimiento** sm raising.
erigir [eri'xir] v erect; build; establish. **erigirse** v set oneself up. **erección** sf erection; establishment. **erecto** adj erect.
erizar [eri'θar] v bristle. **erizarse** v bristle; (pelo) stand on end. **erizado** adj bristly. **erizo** [e'riθo] sm hedgehog.
erradicar [erraði'kar] v eradicate; uproot. **erradicación** sf eradication.
*errar [er'rar] v miss; fail; wander. **errarse** v be mistaken. **erradizo** adj wandering. **errado** adj mistaken. **errante** adj wandering; nomadic. **erróneo** adj erroneous, mistaken. **error** sm error.
eructar [eruk'tar] v belch. **eructo** sm belch.
erudición [eruði'θjon] sf erudition. **erudito, -a** sm, sf scholar; adj erudite.
erupción [erup'θjon] sf eruption; (med) rash. **eruptivo** adj eruptive.
esbelto [es'βelto] adj slim. **esbeltez** sf slimness.

esbozar [esβo'θar] v sketch. **esbozo** sm sketch.

escabechar [eskaβe'tʃar] v (culin) pickle; (fam) fail an exam; (fam) bump off. **escabeche** sm pickle.

escabroso [eska'βroso] adj rough; crude; harsh; (fig) difficult. **escabro** sm (med) scab. **escabrosidad** sf roughness; crudity; harshness.

***escabullirse** [eskaβu'ʎirse] v sneak away or out.

escala [es'kala] sf ladder; scale; port of call. **en gran escala** on a large scale. **escala franca** free port. **hacer escala en** put in at. **escalar** v climb; escalate. **escalamiento** sm escalation.

escaldar [eskal'ðar] v scald; make red hot. **escaldado** adj scalded; cautious.

escalera [eska'lera] sf stairs pl. **escalera móvie** escalator.

escalfar [eskal'far] v (culin) poach. **escalfado** adj poached. **escalfador** sm poacher.

escalofrío [eskalo'frio] sm shiver. **escalofriante** adj bloodcurdling.

escalón [eska'lon] sm rung; step. **escalonar** v space; stagger. **escalonado** adj spread out; staggered. **escalonamiento** sm spacing; staggering.

escalonia [eska'lonja] sf also **escaloña** shallot.

escalpelo [eskal'pelo] sm scalpel.

escama [es'kama] sf (jabón) flake; (animal) scale. **escamado** adj (fam) suspicious. **escamar** v scale; (fam) make suspicious. **escamarse** v (fam) become suspicious. **escamoso** adj scaly; (fam) suspicious.

escamot(e)ar [eskamo't(j)ar] v make disappear; shirk. **escamoteo** sm (fam) swindle. **escamoteador, -a** sm, sf conjurer; (fam) swindler.

escampar [eskam'par] v clear out; stop raining. **escampada** sf clear spell.

escándalo [es'kandalo] sm scandal; uproar; viciousness. **dar un escándalo** make a scene. **escandalizar** v scandalize. **escandalizarse** v be shocked. **escandaloso** adj scandalous; turbulent.

escaño [es'kaɲo] sm bench; seat in Parliament.

escapar [eska'par] v escape. **escaparse** v escape; leak. **escapada** sf escape; escapade. **escape** sm escape; leakage. **a**

escape at full speed. **tubo de escape** exhaust pipe.

escaparate [eskapa'rate] sm shop window.

escarabajo [eskara'βaxo] sm beetle; (fam) dwarf.

escaramuza [eskara'muθa] sf skirmish. **escaramucear** v skirmish.

escarbar [eskar'βar] v scratch; scrape; pry into. **escarbo** sm scraping; scratching.

escarcha [es'kartʃa] sf frost.

escarlata [eskar'lata] sf, adj scarlet.

***escarmentar** [eskarmen'tar] v punish; learn from experience; be warned. **escarmiento** sm punishment; warning.

***escarnecer** [eskarne'θer] v mock. **escarnecimiento** sm scorn; derision.

escarola [eska'rola] sf endive.

escarpa [es'karpa] sf slope.

escasear [eskase'ar] v skimp; be scarce. **escasamente** adv scantily. **escasez** sf scarcity. **escaso** adj scarce; skimpy.

escena [es'θena] sf scene; stage. **poner en escena** stage. **escénico** adj scenic.

escéptico [es'θeptiko] s, adj sceptic(al). **escepticismo** sm scepticism.

***esclarecer** [esklare'θer] v brighten; clear; dawn. **esclarecido** adj illustrious. **esclarecimiento** sm illumination; splendour; dawn.

esclavitud [esklaβi'tuð] sf slavery. **esclavizar** v enslave. **esclavo, -a** sm, sf slave.

esclusa [es'klusa] sf lock; floodgate. **esclusa de aire** airlock.

escoba [es'koβa] sf broom, brush. **escobar** v sweep; brush.

***escocer** [esko'θer] v smart, sting. **escocerse** v chafe. **escocedor** adj painful. **escocedura** sf sting.

escoger [esko'xer] v choose. **escogido** adj chosen, choice. **escogimiento** sm choice, selection.

escolar [esko'lar] s(m+f) schoolboy/girl. adj scholastic. **escolástica** sf scholasticism. **escolástico** adj scholastic.

escolta [es'kolta] sf escort. **escoltar** v escort.

escollo [es'koʎo] sm reef; difficulty; danger.

escombro [es'kombro] sm mackerel; débris; rubbish.

esconder [eskon'der] v hide. **esconderse** v conceal oneself. **escondidamente** adv secretly. **escondite** *sm* hiding place; (*juego*) hide-and-seek.

escopeta [esko'peta] *sf* shotgun; rifle. **escopeta de aire comprimido** airgun.

escoplo [es'koplo] *sm* chisel. **escoplear** *v* chisel; gouge.

escoria [es'korja] *sf* slag; dross; (*fig*) scum. **escorial** *sm* slag heap.

escorpión [eskor'pjon] *sf* scorpion.

escotado [esko'taðo] *adj* (*vestido*) low-cut. **escotar** *v* lower the neckline; scoop out.

escotilla [esko'tiʎa] *sf* (*mar*) hatch.

escribano [eskri'βano] *sm* clerk; notary.

*escribir [eskri'βir] *v* write. **escribir a máquina** type. **escribirse** *v* spell. **escribido** *adj* (*fam*) well read. **escribiente** *s(m+f)* clerk. **escrito a mano** handwritten. *sm* writing; document; letter. **escritor, -a** *sm, sf* writer. **escritorio** *sm* bureau; office. **escritura** *sf* writing; script; (*jur*) deed.

escrúpulo [es'krupulo] *sm* scruple; conscientiousness. **escrupuloso** *adj* scrupulous.

escrutinio [eskru'tinjo] *sm* scrutiny. **escrutar** *v* scrutinize.

escuadra [es'kwaðra] *sf* carpenter's square; (*mil*) squad; (*mil*) corporal; (*mar*) squadron; (*fig*) gang. **a escuadra** at right angles. **escuadrar** *v* square.

escuálido [es'kwaliðo] *adj* squalid; weak; skinny. **escualidez** *sf* squalor; weakness; emaciation.

escuchar [esku'tʃar] *v* listen to; hear. **escucharse** *v* pay too much attention to oneself. **escucha** *sf* listening; sentry; chaperone. **a la escucha** on the alert. **escuchador, -a** *sm, sf* listener.

escudero [esku'ðero] *sm* squire, page. **escudar** *v* shield. **escudo** *sm* shield.

escudriñar [eskuðri'nar] *v* scrutinize. **escudriñador** *adj* examining; curious. **escudriñamiento** *sm* investigation; search.

escuela [es'kwela] *sf* school.

esculpir [eskul'pir] *v* sculpture; engrave. **escultor, -a** *sm, sf* sculptor. **escultura** *sf* sculpture.

escupir [esku'pir] *v* spit. **escupidura** *sf* spittle.

escurrir [eskur'rir] *v* drain; wring out; drip; slip; ooze. **escurrirse** *v* drain; sneak off. **escurridizo** *adj* slippery. **escurridor** *sm* plate rack; colander; draining board; wringer. **escurriduras** *sf pl* dregs *pl*. **escurrimiento** *sm* draining; dripping.

ese ['ese] *adj also* **esa** that.

ése ['ese] *pron also* **ésa** that one; the former.

esencia [e'senθja] *sf* essence. **esencial** *adj* essential.

esfera [es'fera] *sf* sphere. **esférico** *adj* spherical.

esfinge [es'finxe] *sf* sphinx.

*esforzar [esfor'θar] *v* invigorate; strengthen; encourage. **esforzarse** *v* make an effort. **esforzado** *adj* vigorous. **esfuerzo** *sm* effort.

esgrimir [esgri'mir] *v* brandish; fence. **esgrima** *sf* fencing. **esgrimidor, -a** *sm, sf* fencer.

eslabón [esla'βon] *sm* link. **eslabonamiento** *sm* linking. **eslabonar** *v* link.

esmaltar [esmal'tar] *v* enamel; (*las uñas*) varnish. **esmalte** *sm* varnish.

esmerado [esme'raðo] *adj* careful, painstaking. **esmerar** *v* polish; take great pains.

esmeralda [esme'ralða] *sf* emerald.

esnórquel [es'norkel] *sm* snorkel.

eso ['eso] *pron* that, that thing. **en eso** at that moment. **eso es** that's right. **eso mismo** just so. **por eso** because of that. **esos** *adj pl also* **esas** those. **ésos** *pron pl also* **ésas** those; the former.

espabilar [espaβi'lar] *v* (*vela*) snuff. **espabilarse** *v* (*fam*) look sharp.

espaciar [espa'θjar] *v* space out; spread. **espaciarse** *v* expatiate; enjoy oneself. **espacial** *adj* space. **nave espacial** spaceship. **espaciamiento** *sm* spacing. **espacio** *sm* space. **espacioso** *adj* spacious.

espada [es'paða] *sf* sword; swordsman. *sm* matador. **pez espada** swordfish.

espalda [es'palða] *sf* shoulder; back. **a espaldas** behind someone's back. **volver las espaldas** turn tail.

espantapájaros [espanta'paxaros] *sm invar* scarecrow.

espantar [espan'tar] *v* scare. **espantarse** *v* take fright. **espanto** *sm* fright; terror. **espantoso** *adj* frightful; amazing.

España [es'paɲa] *sf* Spain.

español [espa'ɲol], **-a** *sm, sf* Spaniard. *sm* (*lengua*) Spanish. *adj* Spanish.

*esparcir [espar'θir] *v* scatter; spread. **esparcirse** *v* amuse oneself. **esparcidamente** *adv* separately. **esparcido** *adj* cheerful; amusing; scattered. **esparcimiento** *sm* scattering; pastime.

espárrago [es'parrago] *sm* asparagus.
espasmo [es'pasmo] *sm* spasm. **espasmódico** *adj* spasmodic.
especia [es'peθja] *sf* spice.
especial [espe'θjal] *adj* special; particular. **en especial** especially. **especialidad** *sf* speciality. **especialista** *s(m+f)*, *adj* specialist. **especializarse** *v* specialize.
especie [es'peθje] *sf* species; kind; affair; appearance.
específico [espe'θifiko] *adj* specific. *sm* (*med*) patent medicine. **especificación** *sf* specification. **especificación normalizada** standard specification. **especificar** *v* specify.
espectáculo [espek'takulo] *sm* spectacle; entertainment. **espectacular** *adj* spectacular. **espectador, -a** *sm, sf* spectator.
espectro [es'pektro] *sm* spectre.
espejo [es'pexo] *sm* mirror. **espejo retrovisor** (*auto*) rear-view mirror. **espejismo** *sm* mirage.
esperar [espe'rar] *v* hope; expect; await. **esperar a que** wait until. **espera** *sf* waiting; expectation; delay. **sala de espera** waiting room. **esperanza** *sf* hope. **esperanzador** *adj* encouraging.
esperpento [esper'pento] *sm* fright; grotesqueness; absurdity.
espesar [espe'sar] *v* thicken; tighten. **espeso** *adj* thick; greasy. **espesamiento** *sm* thickening.
espetar [espe'tar] *v* (*culin*) skewer; pierce. **espetarse** *v* be pompous.
espía [es'pia] *s(m+f)* spy. **espiar** *v* spy upon. **espionaje** *sm* espionage.
espiga [es'piga] *sf* (*bot*) ear. spike. **espigado** *adj* gone to seed. **espigar** *v* glean.
espín [es'pin] *sm* porcupine.
espina [es'pina] *sf* thorn; spine; splinter; fishbone. **espina dorsal** backbone.
espinaca [espi'naka] *sf* spinach.
espiral [espi'ral] *sf*, *adj* spiral.
espíritu [es'piritu] *sm* spirit; soul; ghost; wit; breathing. **espiritado** *adj* possessed; (*fam*) skinny. **espiritismo** *sm* spiritualism. **espiritista** *s(m+f)* spiritualist. **espiritoso** *adj* spirited. **espiritual** *adj* spiritual. **espiritualidad** *sf* spirituality.
espléndido [es'plendiðo] *adj* splendid; magnificent. **esplendor** *sm* splendour.
espliego [es'pljego] *sm* lavender.
esplín [es'plin] *sm* spleen.
espolear [espole'ar] *v* spur. spur on. **espoleo** *sm* spurring.

esponja [es'ponxa] *sf* sponge. **esponjar** *v* make spongy; puff up. **esponjarse** *v* become spongy; (*fig*) become puffed up with pride; glow with health.
esponsales [espon'sales] *sm pl* betrothal sing.
espontáneo [espon'taneo] *adj* spontaneous. **espontaneidad** *sf* spontaneity.
esporádico [espo'raðiko] *adj* sporadic.
esposa [es'posa] *sf* wife. **esposas** *sf pl* handcuffs. **esposado** *adj* newly married; handcuffed.
espuela [es'pwela] *sf* spur. **echar la espuela** have one for the road.
espuma [es'puma] *sf* foam; froth; lather. **espumadera** *sf* strainer. **espumajear** *v* foam at the mouth. **espumajoso** *adj* foaming; frothy. **espumar** *v* skim; froth; lather; sparkle. **espumoso** *adj* frothy; sparkling.
esquela [es'kela] *sf* note; short letter; obituary.
esqueleto [eske'leto] *sm* skeleton.
esquema [es'kema] *sm* scheme. **esquemático** *adj* schematic.
esquí [es'ki] *sm*. *pl* **esquies** *or* **esquis** ski. **esquiador, -a** *sm, sf* skier. **esquiar** *v* ski.
esquilar [eski'lar] *v* shear. clip. **sin esquilar** unshorn.
esquimal [eski'mal] *sm*. *adj* Eskimo.
esquina [es'kina] *sf* (*afuera*) corner. **doblar la esquina** turn the corner. **esquinar** *v* form a corner with.
esquirol [eski'rol] *sm* (*fam*) strike-breaker. blackleg.
esquivar [eski'βar] *v* avoid, shun; disappear. **esquivarse** *v* shy away. **esquivo** *adj* unsociable.
estabilidad [estaβili'ðað] *sf* stability.
*estabilizar *v* stabilize. **estable** *adj* stable.
*establecer [estaβle'θer] *v* establish. **establecerse** *v* settle down; set up. **establecido** *adj* established. **establecimiento** *sm* establishment.
establo [es'taβlo] *sm* cowshed.
estaca [es'taka] *sf* stake. post. **estacada** *sf* fence; stockade. **estacar** *v* fence; stake out.
estación [esta'θjon] *sf* station; season. **estacionamiento** *sm* parking. **estacionar** *v* park.
estadio [es'taðjo] *sm* stadium; (*med*) phase.

estado [es'taðo] *vm* state; status; order; estate; statement. **estado de ánimo** state of mind. **estar en estado** be pregnant. **hombre de estado** statesman.

Estados Unidos [es'taðos u'niðos] *sm pl* United States (of America). **estadounidense** *s(m+f).* *adj* American.

estafa [es'tafa] *sf* swindle. **estafador. -a** *sm. sf* swindler. **estafar** *v* swindle.

estafeta [esta'feta] *sf* courier; sub-post office.

estallar [esta'ʎar] *v* explode; burst; erupt. **estallido** *sm* explosion; crash.

estampar [estam'par] *v* stamp; print; imprint. **estampa** *sf* print; engraving; impression; footprint.

estampida [estam'piða] *sf* stampede; explosion, bang. **estampido** *sm* explosion, bang.

estancar [estan'kar] *v* stem; block; delay; monopolize. **estancarse** *v* stagnate. **estancación** *sf* stagnation. **estancado** *adj* stagnant; blocked. **estanco** *sm* monopoly; state tobacco shop. **estanquero. -a** *sm. sf* tobacconist.

estandarte [estan'darte] *sm* banner.

estanque [es'tanke] *sm* reservoir; ornamental pond.

estante [es'tante] *sm* shelf. **estantería** *sf* shelving; bookcase.

estaño [es'taɲo] *sm* tin. **estañar** *v* solder.

***estar** [es'tar] *v* be. **está bien** (it's) all right. **estar para** be about to. **no está he** *or* she is not at home. **ya que estamos** while we're at it.

estático [es'tatiko] *adj* static.

estatua [es'tatwa] *sf* statue.

estatura [esta'tura] *sf* stature, height.

estatuto [esta'tuto] *sm* statute. **estatuario** *adj* statutory.

este¹ ['este] *adj also* **esta** this; the latter. **este²** *sm. adj* east.

éste ['este] *pron also* **ésta** this.

estela [es'tela] *sf (mar)* wake; trail.

estelar [este'lar] *adj* stellar.

estepa [es'tepa] *sf* steppe.

estera [es'tera] *sf* matting.

estereofónico [estereo'foniko] *adj* stereophonic.

estereotipo [estereo'tipo] *sm* stereotype.

estéril [es'teril] *adj* sterile; pointless. **esterelizar** *v* sterilize.

esterlina [ester'lina] *adj* sterling. **libra esterlina** pound sterling.

estético [es'tetiko] *adj* aesthetic. **estética** *sf* aesthetics.

estetoscopio [esteto'skopjo] *sm* stethoscope.

estiércol [es'tjerkol] *sm* manure.

estigma [es'tigma] *sm* stigma. **estigmatizar** *v* stigmatize.

estilar [esti'lar] *v* be accustomed; (*documento*) draw up; be in use; be in fashion. **estilístico** *adj* stylistic. **estilizado** *adj* stylized. **estilo** *sm* style; type; fashion.

estimar [esti'mar] *v* esteem; estimate. **estima** *sf* esteem. **estimable** *adj* estimable. **estimación** *sf* estimate; estimation.

estimular [estimu'lar] *v* stimulate. **estimulante** *adj* stimulating; *sm (med)* stimulant. **estimulo** *sm* stimulus.

estipular [estipu'lar] *v* stipulate. **estipulación** *sf* stipulation.

estirar [esti'rar] *v* stretch; extend. **estirado** *adj* affected; miserly. **estirón** *sm* jerk.

estirpe [es'tirpe] *sf* lineage; stock.

esto ['esto] *pron* this. **en esto** whereupon.

estofa [es'tofa] *sf (fig)* quality; class; brocade. **estofado** *adj* quilted; (*culin*) stewed. **estofar** *v* quilt; stew.

estoico [es'toiko]. **-a** *s. adj* stoic. **estoicismo** *sm* stoicism.

estómago [es'tomago] *sm* stomach. **estomagar** *v* give indigestion.

estorbar [estor'βar] *v* hinder; be in the way. **estorbo** *sm* hindrance; obstruction.

estornino [estor'nino] *sm* starling.

estornudar [estornu'ðar] *v* sneeze. **estornudo** *sm* sneeze.

estoy [es'toi] *V* estar.

estrafalario [estrafa'larjo] *adj* outlandish; extravagant; slovenly.

estrada [es'traða] *sf* road, highway.

estragar [estra'gar] *v* corrupt; destroy. **estrago** *sm* ruin, havoc. **hacer estragos** wreak havoc.

estrangular [estrangu'lar] *v* strangle. **estrangulación** *sf* strangulation. **estrangulador** *sm* strangler; (*auto*) choke.

estratagema [estrata'xema] *sf* stratagem. **estrategia** *sf* strategy. **estratégico** *adj* strategic.

estrechar [estre'tʃar] *v* make smaller; tighten; bring closer together. **estrecharse** *v* become narrower; squeeze together; shake hands; make economies. **estrechamente** *adv* narrowly. **estrechamiento** *sm* narrowing; taking-in;

tightening; handshake. **estrecho** adj narrow; cramped; tight; strict.

estrella [es'treʎa] sf star. **estrellado** adj starry.

estrellar [estre'ʎar] v smash (to pieces).

***estremecer** [estreme'θer] v shake; startle. **estremecerse** v shudder; tremble. **estremecimiento** sm shake; shudder; tremble.

estrenar [estre'nar] v wear for the first time; (teatro) perform for the first time. **estreno** sm inauguration; first night; dress rehearsal.

estrenuo [es'trenwo] adj strong; courageous.

estreñido [estre'ɲiðo] adj constipated. **estreñimiento** sm constipation.

estrépito [es'trepito] sm noise, din; fuss. **estrepitoso** adj noisy; resounding.

estribo [es'triβo] sm stirrup; step; running-board. **perder los estribos** lose one's head.

estribor [estri'βor] sm (mar) starboard.

estricto [es'trikto] adj strict.

estridente [estri'ðente] adj strident.

estropajo [estro'paxo] sm scourer; rubbish. **estropajoso** adj thick; stringy; slovenly.

estropear [estrope'ar] v spoil; break; maim; age.

estructura [estruk'tura] sf structure; framework. **estructural** adj structural. **estructurar** v organize; construct.

estruendo [estru'endo] sm din; uproar; bustle; pomp. **estruendoso** adj noisy.

estrujar [estru'xar] v squeeze; crush. **estrujadura** sf pressure. **estrujón** sm squeeze.

estuario [es'twarjo] sm estuary.

estuche [es'tutʃe] sm box; case; casket; sheath.

estudiar [estu'ðjar] v study. **estudiante** s(m+f) student. **estudio** sm study; research; studio. **estudioso** adj studious.

estufa [es'tufa] sf stove; fire; hothouse.

estupefacto [estupe'fakto] adj stupefied; astonished. **estupefacción** sf stupefaction; astonishment.

estupefaciente [estupefa'θjente] adj stupefying; astonishing. sm (med) narcotic.

estupendo [estu'pendo] adj stupendous.

estúpido [es'tupiðo] adj stupid. **estupidez** sf stupidity. **estupor** sm stupor.

esturión [estu'rjon] sm sturgeon.

etapa [e'tapa] sf (de un viaje) stage; period.

éter ['eter] sm ether. **etéreo** adj ethereal. **eternidad** [eterni'ðað] sf eternity. **eternal** adj eternal. **eternizar** v perpetuate.

ética ['etika] sf ethics. **ético** adj ethical.

etimología [etimolo'xia] sf etymology. **etimológico** adj etymological.

etiqueta [eti'keta] sf etiquette; label; tag. **etiquetero** adj formal.

eucalipto [euka'lipto] sm eucalyptus.

eufemismo [eufe'mismo] sm euphemism. **eufemístico** adj euphemistic.

eunuco [eu'nuko] sm eunuch.

Europa [eu'ropa] sf Europe. **europeo, -a** s, adj European.

eutanasia [euta'nasja] sf euthanasia.

evacuar [eβa'kwar] v evacuate; fulfil. **evacuación** sf evacuation. **evacuado, -a** sm, sf evacuee.

evadir [eβa'ðir] v evade. **evadirse** v escape. **evadido, -a** sm, sf fugitive. **evasión** sf escape; flight. **evasivo** adj evasive.

evaluar [eβa'lwar] v evaluate; value. **evaluación** sf evaluation.

evangélico [eβan'xeliko] adj evangelical. **evangelio** sm gospel. **evangelista** sm evangelist.

evaporar [evapo'rar] v evaporate. **evaporación** sf evaporation.

evento [e'βento] sm (unforeseen) event. **eventual** [even'twal] adj temporary; possible; accidental. **eventualidad** sf contingency.

evidencia [evi'ðenθja] sf certainty; proof; evidence. **evidenciar** v make evident. **evidente** adj evident.

evitar [eβi'tar] v avoid. **evitable** adj avoidable.

evocar [evo'kar] v evoke. **evocación** sf evocation. **evocativo** adj evocative.

evolución [evolu'θjon] sf evolution. **evolucionar** v evolve. **evolutivo** adj evolutionary.

exacerbar [eksaθer'βar] v exacerbate; exasperate. **exacerbación** sf exacerbation.

exactitud [eksakti'tuð] sf exactitude; accuracy. **exacto** adj exact; correct.

exagerar [eksaxe'rar] v exaggerate. **exagerado** adj exaggerated. **exageración** sf exaggeration.

exaltar [eksal'tar] v exalt; raise; praise. **exaltarse** v get worked up; get heated. **exaltación** sf exaltation. **exaltado** adj hotheaded.

examinar [eksami'nar] *v* examine; inspect; test. **examinarse** *v* take an examination. **examen** *sm* examination; inquiry; investigation. **examen de conductor** driving test. **examinador, -a** *sm, sf* examiner.

exangüe [ek'sangwe] *adj* bloodless; weak.

exánime [ek'sanime] *adj* lifeless; unconscious; weak. **caer exánime** fall in a faint.

exasperar [eksaspe'rar] *v* exasperate; vex. **exasperarse** *v* become annoyed. **exasperación** *sf* exasperation. **exasperante** *adj* exasperating.

excavar [ekska'βar] *v* excavate; dig. **excavación** *sf* excavation.

exceder [eksθe'ðer] *v* exceed. **excederse** *v* forget oneself. **excedente** *adj* exceeding; excessive.

excelencia [eksθe'lenθja] *sf* excellence. **excelente** *adj* excellent; first-rate.

excéntrico [eks'θentriko] *adj, sm* eccentric. **excentricidad** *sf* eccentricity.

excepción [eksθep'θjon] *sf* exception. **a excepción de** with the exception of. **estado de excepción** state of emergency. **excepcional** *adj* exceptional. **excepto** *prep* excepting.

excerpta [ek'θerpta] *sf* excerpt.

excesivo [eksθe'siβo] *adj* excessive. **exceso** *sm* excess; surplus. **exceso de equipaje** excess luggage.

excitar [eksθi'tar] *v* excite; stir up. **excitabilidad** *sf* excitability. **excitable** *adj* excitable. **excitante** *adj* exciting.

exclamar [ekskla'mar] *v* exclaim. **exclamarse contra** protest against. **exclamación** *sf* exclamation. **exclamativo** *adj* exclamatory.

***excluir** [eksklu'ir] *v* exclude. **exclusivo** *adj* exclusive. **exclusión** *sf* exclusion.

excomulgar [ekskomul'gar] *v* excommunicate. **excomulgación** *sf* excommunication. **excomulgado** *adj* excommunicated; (*fam*) accused.

excreción [ekskre'θjon] *sf* excretion. **excremento** *sm* excrement. **excretar** *v* excrete.

excursión [ekskur'sjon] *sf* excursion. **excursión a pie** hike. **ir de excursión** go on an outing. **excursionista** *s(m+f)* tripper; hiker.

excusar [eksku'sar] *v* excuse; avoid; exempt. **excusarse** *v* apologize. **excusa** *sf* excuse; apology. **excusable** *adj* pardonable. **excusadamente** *adv* unnecessarily. **excusado** *adj* excused; unnecessary; exempt; concealed; private. **excusado es decir** needless to say. **excusado** *sm* toilet.

exentar [eksen'tar] *v* exempt. **exención** *sf* exemption. **exento** *adj* exempt.

exequias [ek'sekjas] *sf pl* funeral rites.

exhalar [eksa'lar] *v* exhale; emit; utter. **exhalación** *sf* exhalation; vapour; shooting star; lightning flash.

exhausto [ek'sausto] *adj* exhausted. **exhaustivo** *adj* exhaustive.

exhibir [eksi'βir] *v* exhibit. **exhibición** *sf* exhibition. **exhibicionismo** *sm* exhibitionism. **exhibicionista** *s(m+f)* exhibitionist.

exhortar [eksor'tar] *v* exhort. **exhortación** *sf* exhortation.

exigir [eksi'xir] *v* demand. **exigencia** *sf* demand; requirement. **exigente** *adj* exacting.

exiguo [ek'sigwo] *adj* scanty. **exigüidad** *sf* scantiness.

eximir [eksi'mir] *v* exempt; excuse. **eximente** *adj* exempting.

existir [eksis'tir] *v* exist. **existencia** *sf* existence. **en existencia** in stock. **existente** *adj* existent; extant; in stock.

éxito ['eksito] *sm* success; result. **tener éxito** be successful.

éxodo [ek'soðo] *sm* exodus, emigration.

exonerar [eksone'rar] *v* exonerate; relieve; dismiss. **exoneración** *sf* exoneration; relief.

exorbitante [eksorβi'tante] *adj* exorbitant, excessive.

exorcizar [eksorθi'θar] *v* exorcize. **exorcismo** *sm* exorcism. **exorcista** *sm* exorcist.

exótico [ek'sotiko] *adj* exotic.

expansión [ekspan'sjon] *sf* expansion; recreation. **expansionarse** *v* give vent to one's feelings. **expansivo** *adj* expansive.

expatriar [ekspatri'ar] *v* exile. **expatriación** *sf* banishment.

expectación [ekspekta'θjon] *sf* expectation. **expectante** *adj* expectant.

expedición [ekspeði'θjon] *sf* expedition; party; shipment; dispatch; speed.

***expedir** [ekspe'ðir] *v* send, dispatch; issue. **expediente** *sm* (*jur*) proceedings *pl*; dossier; inquiry; record. **expediente** *adj* expedient.

expendedor [ekspenðe'ðor], **-a** *sm, sf*

dealer; retailer; ticket agent. *adj* spending.

experiencia [ekspe'rjenθja] *sf* experience; experiment.

experimentar [eksperimen'tar] *v* experiment; test; feel. **experimentado** *adj* experienced. **experimental** *adj* experimental. **experimento** *sm* experiment.

experto [eks'perto] *sm, adj* expert.

expiar [eks'pjar] *v* atone for. **expiación** *sf* atonement.

expirar [ekspi'rar] *v* expire; die; die down. **expiración** *sf* expiration.

explanar [ekspla'nar] *v* level; (*fig*) explain. **explanación** *sf* levelling; (*fig*) explanation.

explicar [ekspli'kar] *v* explain; justify; lecture. **explicarse** *v* speak plainly; understand. **explicación** *sf* explanation. **explicativo** *adj* explanatory.

explícito [eks'pliθito] *adj* explicit.

explorar [eksplo'rar] *v* explore, investigate. **exploración** *sf* exploration. **explorador** *sm* explorer; (*mil*) scout; boy scout; *adj* exploratory.

explosión [eksplo'sjon] *sf* explosion. **explosivo** *sm, adj* explosive.

explotar [eksplo'tar] *v* exploit; develop; cultivate; explode. **explotación** *sf* exploitation; operation; development; cultivation.

*exponer [ekspo'ner] *v* expose; set out; explain. **exponerse** *v* lay oneself open. **exponente** *s*(*m*+*f*) exponent; example; proof.

exportar [ekspor'tar] *v* export. **exportación** *sf* export. **exportador, -a** *sm, sf* exporter.

exposición [eksposi'θjon] *sf* exhibition; display; statement; explanation; risk; (*foto*) exposure. **sala de exposición** showroom.

exprés [eks'pres] *sm* (*tren*) express; (*café*) espresso.

expresar [ekspre'sar] *v* express, convey. **expresarse** *v* express oneself; state. **expresamente** *adv* specifically; explicitly. **expresión** *sf* expression. **expresiones** *sf pl* greetings; regards. **expresivamente** *adv* expressively; affectionately. **expresivo** *adj* expressive; affectionate. **expreso** *adj* expressed; express.

exprimir [ekspri'mir] *v* squeeze; exploit. **exprimidor** *sm* squeezer.

expuesto [eks'pwesto] *adj* on display; exposed; explained.

expulsar [ekspul'sar] *v* expel, throw out.

exquisito [ekski'sito] *adj* exquisite; delightful; refined.

éxtasis ['ekstasis] *sm invar* ecstasy.

*extender [eksten'der] *v* extend; spread. **extenderse** *v* spread; range; enlarge. **extendido** *adj* extended; widespread; outstretched. **extensamente** *adv* at length. **extensible** *adj* extending. **extensión** *sf* extension; expanse; extent; area. **extensivo** *adj* extendible. **extenso** *adj* extensive; large; widespread; full.

extenuar [ekste'nwar] *v* weaken; exhaust. **extenuación** *sf* emaciation; extenuation.

exterior [ekste'rjor] *adj* exterior, external; foreign. **asuntos exteriores** *sm pl* foreign affairs. *sm* outside, exterior; appearance. **al exterior** outside. **del exterior** from abroad.

exterminar [ekstermi'nar] *v* exterminate. **exterminación** *sf* extermination. **exterminador, -a** *sm, sf* exterminator.

externo [eks'terno], **-a** *sm, sf* day pupil. *adj* external; outward. **externado** *sm* day school.

extinguir [ekstin'gir] *v* extinguish; wipe out; put down. **extinguirse** *v* die out. **extinción** *sf* extinction. **extinto** *adj* extinct. **extintor** *sm* fire extinguisher.

extirpar [ekstir'par] *v* uproot; remove. **extirpación** *sf* uprooting; extraction.

extra ['ekstra] *adj invar* extra; best-quality. *sm* (*cine, teatro*) extra.

*extraer [ekstra'er] *v* extract; release. **extracción** *sf* extraction; birth. **extracto** *sm* extract; excerpt; abstract.

extranjero [ekstran'xero], **-a** *sm, sf* foreigner; foreign countries *pl. adj* foreign.

extrañar [ekstra'nar] *v* be surprised; surprise; be shy; banish. **extrañarse** *v* go into exile. **extrañamiento** *sm* surprise; banishment. **extrañeza** *sf* strangeness; surprise. **extraño, -a** *sm, sf* stranger. **extraño** *adj* strange; peculiar; foreign.

extraordinario [ekstraorði'narjo] *adj* extraordinary. *sm* (*diario*) special edition.

extravagancia [ekstraβa'ganθja] *sf* extravagance; strangeness. **extravagante** *adj* extravagant; eccentric.

extraviar [ekstra'βjar] *v* lose; mislay; mislead. **extraviarse** *v* get lost; be missing; go astray.

extremar [ekstre'mar] *v* take to extremes.
extremarse *v* do one's best.
extremo [ek'stremo] *adj* extreme. last. **en caso extremo** as a last resort. *sm* extreme; end; point. **al extremo de** to the point of. **de extremo a extremo** from end to end. **Extremo Oriente** Far East.
extremidad *sf* extremity; end; limit.
exuberancia [eksuβe'ranθja] *sf* exuberance; abundance. **exuberante** *adj* exuberant.
exudar [eksu'ðar] *v* exude. **exudación** *sf* exudation.
exultar [eksul'tar] *v* exult. **exultación** *sf* exultation.

F

fábrica ['faβrika] *sf* factory; manufacture. **fabricación** *sf* manufacture. **de fabricación casera** home-made. **fabricación en serie** mass production. **fabricante** *s(m+f)* manufacturer. **fabricar** *v* manufacture; make; build.
fábula ['faβula] *sf* fable; story; gossip. **fabuloso** *adj* fabulous; incredible.
facción [fak'θjon] *sf* faction; gang. **facciones** *sf pl* features.
faceta [fa'θeta] *sf* facet.
facial [fa'θjal] *adj* facial.
fácil ['faθil] *adj* easy; simple; likely; well-behaved. **facilidad** *sf* facility; ease; fluency; gift. **facilitar** *v* facilitate; supply; provide; arrange. **fácilmente** *adv* easily.
facsímil [fak'simil] *sm, adj also* **facsímile** facsimile.
factible [fak'tiβle] *adj* feasible.
factor [fak'tor] *sm* factor; agent.
facturar [faktu'rar] *v* invoice; (*ferrocarril*) register luggage. **factura** *sf* invoice. **facturación** *sf* invoicing.
facultad [fakul'taθ] *sf* faculty; authority; school. **facultar** *v* commission; authorize. **facultativo** *adj* optional.
facha ['fatʃa] *sf* (*fam*) appearance, looks; (*fam*) mess.
fachada [fa'tʃaða] *sf* façade.
faena [fa'ena] *sf* task; (*fam*) dirty trick. **estar de faena** be at work. **faenas domésticas** housework.
fagot [fa'got] *sm* bassoon.

faisán [fai'san] *sm* pheasant.
faja ['faxa] *sf* bandage; sash; belt; wrapper; strip of land. **fajar** *v* wrap; bandage.
falaz [fa'laθ] *adj* fallacious; deceitful.
falda ['falda] *sf* skirt; side of a hill; hat brim; lap.
falsear [false'ar] *v* falsify. **falseador, -a** *sm, sf* forger; counterfeiter. **falseamiento** *sm* misrepresentation. **falsedad** *sf* falsity. **falseo** *sm* bevelling. **falso** *adj* false; treacherous; sham.
falsificar [falsifi'kar] *v* falsify; forge; adulterate. **falsificación** *sf* falsification; adulteration.
falta ['falta] *sf* lack, want, need; shortage; failure; (*deporte*) foul. **faltar** *v* be lacking; fail; be absent; be untrue. **falto** *sm* shortage; deficiency; fault. **falto** *adj* short; deficient; incomplete.
fallar [fa'ʎar] *v* (*jur*) judge; sentence; fail; (*naipes*) trump. **no falla** it's always the same. **sin falla** without fail.
*****fallecer** [faʎe'θer] *v* die. **fallecido** *adj* deceased. **fallecimiento** *sm* death.
fallido [fa'ʎiðo] *sm* bankrupt. *adj* bankrupt; unsuccessful. **fallo** *sm* (*jur*) sentence, judgment; failure; fault; (*naipes*) trump.
fama ['fama] *sf* fame; reputation. **es fama que** it is rumoured that. **famoso** *adj* famous.
familia [fa'milja] *sf* family; household. **familiar** *adj* family; familiar; simple. **familiar** *sm* friend; relative. **familiaridad** *sf* familiarity. **familiarizar** *v* familiarize.
fanático [fa'natiko] *adj, sm* fanatic(al). **fanatismo** *sm* fanaticism.
fanfarrón [fanfar'ron], **-ona** *sm, sf* bully; braggart. *adj* boastful. **fanfarronear** *v* brag.
fango ['fango] *sm* mire, mud. **fangal** *sm* quagmire. **fangoso** *adj* muddy.
fantasía [fanta'sia] *sf* fantasy; fancy; whim. **joyas de fantasía** imitation jewellery.
fantasma [fan'tasma] *sm* ghost. **fantasmal** *adj* ghostly.
fantástico [fan'tastiko] *adj* fantastic; wonderful; vain.
fantoche [fan'totʃe] *sm* puppet; foolish figure.
fardo ['farðo] *sm* bundle, pack; burden.
fariseo [fari'seo] *sm* Pharisee; (*fam*) hypocrite. **farisaico** *adj* (*fam*) hypocritical.

farmacia [far'maθja] *sf* chemist's shop. **farmacia de guardia** all-night chemist's. **farmacéutico** *adj* pharmaceutical.
faro ['faro] *sm* lighthouse; beacon; (*auto*) headlamp.
farol [fa'rol] *sm* lantern; lamp; street lamp; (*fam*) swank.
farsa ['farsa] *sf* farce; humbug. **farsante** *sm* charlatan.
fas [fas] *adv* (*fam*) **por fas o por nefas** rightly or wrongly; by hook or by crook.
fascinar [fasθi'nar] *v* fascinate. **fascinación** *sf* fascination. **fascinador** *adj* fascinating.
fascismo [fas'θismo] *sm* fascism. **fascista** *s, adj* fascist.
fase ['fase] *sf* phase.
fastidiar [fasti'ðjar] *v* annoy; bore; upset. **¡no fastidies!** don't talk rot! **fastidio** *sm* annoyance; nuisance. **fastidioso** *adj* annoying; tedious.
fastuoso [fas'twoso] *adj* magnificent, grand, splendid.
fatal [fa'tal] *adj* fatal; inevitable; (*fam*) awful. **fatalidad** *sf* fatality; bad luck; destiny; disaster. **fatalista** *s(m+f)* fatalist. **fatalismo** *sm* fatalism.
fatigar [fati'gar] *v* weary; annoy. **fatigarse** *v* get tired. **fatiga** *sf* fatigue. **fatigas** *sf pl* troubles. **fatigoso** *adj* tiring; tiresome; laboured.
fatuidad [fatwi'ðað] *sf* fatuity; vanity.
fausto ['fausto] *adj* lucky; happy. *sm* display; pomp.
favor [fa'βor] *sm* favour; gift; grace; help. **a favor de** in favour of. **de favor** complimentary. **hacer el favor de** be so kind as to. **por favor** please. **favorable** *adj* favourable. **favorecer** *v* favour; help. **favoritismo** *sm* favouritism. **favorito, -a** *s, adj* favourite.
faz [faθ] *sf* face; obverse.
fe [fe] *sf* faith; faithfulness; trust; witness; certificate. **a fe de** on the word of. **dar fe de** certify. **prestar fe a** believe in.
fealdad [feal'ðað] *sf* ugliness.
febrero [fe'βrero] *sm* February.
febril [fe'βril] *adj* feverish; (*fig*) anxious.
fecundar [fekun'dar] *v* fertilize. **fecundación** *sf* fertilization. **fecundidad** *sf* fertility; fruitfulness. **fecundizar** *v* fertilize. **fecundo** *adj* fertile; fruitful; prolific. **fecundo en** full of.
fecha ['fetʃa] *sf* date. **hasta la fecha** to date. **fechar** *v* date.
federación [feðera'θjon] *sf* federation.

federal *adj* federal. **federalismo** *sm* federalism. **federar** *v* federate. **federativo** *adj* federative.
fehaciente [fea'θjente] *adj* (*jur*) authentic; irrefutable; reliable.
felicidad [feliθi'ðað] *sf* happiness; success. **¡felicidades!** congratulations! **feliz** *adj* happy; fortunate.
felicitar [feliθi'tar] *v* congratulate. **felicitación** *sf* congratulation; compliment.
feligrés [feli'gres], **-esa** *sm, sf* parishioner. **feligresía** *sf* parish.
felino [fe'lino] *sm, adj* feline.
felpa ['felpa] *sf* plush; towelling; (*fam*) beating. **felpar** *v* cover with plush. **felpudo** *adj* plushy.
femenino [feme'nino] *adj* feminine; female. **feminismo** *sm* feminism. **feminista** *s, adj* feminist.
*fenecer [fene'θer] *v* die; end. **fenecimiento** *sm* death; end.
fenómeno [fe'nomeno] *sm* phenomenon; freak. *adj* fantastic.
feo ['feo] *adj* ugly.
féretro ['feretro] *sm* coffin; bier.
feria ['ferja] *sf* fair; show; festival; holiday. **feria de muestras** trade fair.
fermentar [fermen'tar] *v* ferment; agitate. **fermentación** *sf* fermentation.
ferocidad [feroθi'ðað] *sf* ferocity; fury. **feroz** *adj* savage; wild; fierce.
férreo ['ferreo] *adj* iron; ferrous; (*fig*) stern. **ferretería** *sf* ironmonger's shop; hardware shop. **ferretero** *sm* ironmonger.
ferrocarril [ferrokar'ril] *sm* railway. **ferroviario** *adj* railway.
fértil ['fertil] *adj* fertile; abundant. **fertilidad** *sf* fertility. **fertilizante** *sm* fertilizer. **fertilizar** *v* fertilize.
ferviente [fer'βjente] *adj* fervent. **fervor** *sm* fervour. **fervoroso** *adj* fervid, ardent.
festejar [feste'xar] *v* entertain; feast; celebrate; woo. **festejo** *sm* entertainment; celebration; courtship.
festival [festi'βal] *sm* festival. *adj* festive. **festividad** *sf* festivity. **festivo** *adj* festive.
fétido ['fetiðo] *adj* fetid, stinking.
feto ['feto] *sm* foetus. **fetal** *adj* foetal.
feudal [feu'ðal] *adj* feudal. **feudalismo** *sm* feudalism.
fiado ['fjaðo] *sm* trust. **comprar al fiado** buy on credit. **fiador, -a** *sm, sf* guarantor. **fiador** *sm* press stud; pin; bracket; tumbler; safety catch. **salir fiador de** go bail for. **fianza** *sf* deposit; guarantor; surety.

libertad bajo fianza release on bail. **fiar** v guarantee; go bail for; sell on credit; trust. **no se fía** no credit given.

fiambre ['fjambre] sm cold cooked meat; (coll) corpse.

fiasco [fi'asko] sm fiasco; flop.

fibra ['fiβra] sf fibre; (fig) vigour. **fibra de vidrio** fibreglass.

ficción [fik'θjon] sf fiction; invention. **ficticio** adj fictitious.

ficha ['fitʃa] sf counter, chip; (juegos) piece; filing card.

fidedigno [fiðe'ðigno] adj trustworthy. **fidelidad** sf loyalty, fidelity. **alta fidelidad** hi-fi.

fideos [fi'ðeos] sm pl noodles.

fiebre ['fjeβre] sf fever. **tener fiebre** be feverish.

fiel [fjel] adj faithful; true; accurate; reliable; honourable. sm good Christian; inspector; scale pointer.

fieltro ['fjeltro] sm (tejido) felt; felt hat.

fiera ['fjera] sf wild beast; (persona) brute. **casa de fieras** menagerie. **fiero** adj wild.

fiesta ['fjesta] sf feast day; holiday; party. **estar de fiesta** be in high spirits. **hacer fiestas a uno** make a fuss over someone.

figurar [figu'rar] v shape; adorn; figure; pretend. **figurarse** v imagine, seem. **figura** sf shape; figure; face; (música) note; (naipes) court card; (fig) personality; (fam) unpleasant person. **figurado** adj also **figurativo** figurative.

fijar [fi'xar] v fasten; fix; stick; secure; draw up. **fijarse** v settle; take notice; look. **¡fíjate!** just think! **¡fijamos en esto!** that's settled! **fijación** sf setting; fixing; sticking. **fijador** sm fixative. **fijeza** sf fixity; certainty; firmness. **fijo** adj fixed; permanent; steady.

fila ['fila] sf row; line; file; column. **en fila india** in single file.

filantropía [filantro'pia] sf philanthropy. **filantrópico** adj philanthropic. **filántropo, -a** sm, sf philanthropist.

filete [fi'lete] sm sirloin; fillet; (ropa) edging; (tecn) screw thread.

filiación [filja'θjon] sf filiation; relationship; association; personal description. **filial** [fi'ljal] adj filial. sf subsidiary.

filigrana [fili'grana] sf filigree work; watermark; delicate object.

filo ['filo] sm cutting edge; dividing line. **dar un filo a** sharpen. **por filo** exactly.

filón [fi'lon] sm (mineral) vein, seam; (fam) cushy job.

filosofía [filoso'fia] sf philosophy. **filosofar** v philosophize. **filósofo, -a** sm, sf philosopher. **filósofe** adj philosophic(al).

filtrar [fil'trar] v filter; strain. **filtrarse** v seep through. **filtración** sf filtration; (fig) leak. **filtrador** sm filter. **filtro** sm filter; strainer; love potion.

fin [fin] sm end; death; aim. **a fin de** in order to. **a fines de** at the end of. **al fin y al cabo** when all is said and done. **por fin** at last.

final [fi'nal] adj final. sm end. **al final de** at the end of. **finalidad** sf aim; purpose; finality. **finalizar** v finalize.

financiar [finan'θjar] v finance. **financiero** sm financier. **financiero** adj financial. **finanzas** sf pl finances.

finca ['finka] sf property; estate; farm.

fineza [fi'neθa] sf refinement; kindness; gift.

fingir [fin'xir] v pretend; sham. **fingirse** v pretend to be. **fingimiento** sm pretence; deceit.

Finlandia [fin'landja] sf Finland. **finlandés, -esa** s, adj Finn(ish).

fino ['fino] adj fine; refined; delicate; sharp; shrewd; elegant; precious; select; pure.

firmar [fir'mar] v sign. **firma** sf signature; (negocio) firm.

firme ['firme] adj firm; steady; rigid; hard; settled. sm firm ground; foundation; roadbed. **de firme** steadily. **oferta en firme** firm offer. **¡firmes!** (mil) attention! **firmeza** sf firmness; steadfastness.

fiscal [fis'kal] adj fiscal; tax. sm treasury official; (jur) public prosecutor. **fiscalizar** v control; criticize; pry into. **fisco** sm exchequer.

física ['fisika] sf physics. **físico** sm physician; physique. **físico** adj physical. **físico, -a** sm, sf physicist.

fisiología [fisjolo'xia] sf physiology. **fisiológico** adj physiological. **fisiólogo, -a** sm, sf physiologist.

fisionomía [fisjono'mia] sf physiognomy. **fisioterapia** [fisjote'rapja] sf physiotherapy. **fisioterapeuta** s(m+f) physiotherapist.

flaco ['flako] adj thin; weak; (memoria) short. sm weak point. **flaquear** v weaken; slacken; flag; fail. **flaqueza** sf thinness; frailty.

flagrante [fla'grante] *adj* flagrant, blatant. **en flagrante** in the act.

flamante [fla'mante] *adj* blazing; brand-new.

flamenco[1] [fla'menko] *adj* Flemish; gypsy; flamenco.

flamenco[2] *sm* flamingo.

flanco ['flanko] *sm* flank. **coger por el flanco** catch unawares.

flauta ['flauta] *sf* flute. **flautista** *s(m+f)* flautist.

fleco ['fleko] *sm* fringe.

flecha ['fletʃa] *sf* arrow. **flecha de dirección** traffic indicator. **flecha de mar** squid. **subir en flecha** shoot up. **flechar** *v* shoot with an arrow; (*fam*) inspire love at first sight; (*fam*) rush. **flechero** *sm* archer.

fletar [fle'tar] *v* charter; hire. **fletamento** *also* **fletamiento** *sm* charter. **flete** *sm* freight.

flexible [flek'siβle] *adj* flexible. *sm* flex. **flexibilidad** *sf* flexibility. **flexión** *sf* flexing; (*gram*) inflexion.

flojo ['floxo] *adj* loose; weak; meagre; lazy. **flojear** *v* slacken; grow weak. **flojedad** *sf* slackness; weakness; carelessness.

flor [flor] *sf* flower. **a flor de tierra** at ground level. **echar flores** flatter. **en flor** in bloom. **flor de lis** lily. **floral** *adj* floral. **florar** *v* flower. **florecer** *v* flourish; flower. **florescerse** *v* mildew. **florería** *sf* florist's shop. **florero** *sm* vase. **florido** *adj* flowery; florid. **florista** *s(m+f)* florist.

flotar [flo'tar] *v* float; flutter; stream. **flota** *sf* fleet. **flotable** *adj* buoyant. **flotación** *sf* floatation; fluttering. **flotante** *adj* floating; flowing. **flote** *sm* floatation. **a flote** afloat.

fluctuar [fluk'twar] *v* fluctuate. **fluctuación** *sf* fluctuation.

***fluir** [flu'ir] *v* flow. **fluente** *adj* fluid; flowing. **fluidez** *sf* fluidity; fluency. **flúido** *sm, adj* fluid. **flujo** *sm* stream; flow; rising tide. **flujo de vientre** diarrhoea.

fluorescencia [fluores'θenθ]a] *sf* fluorescence. **fluorescente** *adj* fluorescent.

fluoruro [flwo'ruro] *sm* fluoride.

fobia ['foβja] *sf* phobia.

foca ['foka] *sf* (*zool*) seal.

foco ['foko] *sm* focus; centre; source. **focal** *adj* focal.

fogata [fo'gata] *sf* blaze; bonfire.

fogón [fo'gon] *sm* fireplace; stove.

fogoso [fo'goso] *adj* fiery; impetuous.

follaje [fo'ʎaxe] *sm* foliage; excessive decoration.

folletín [foʎe'tin] *sm* serial story; newspaper article. **folleto** *sm* pamphlet. **folletista** *s(m+f)* pamphleteer.

follón [fo'ʎon] *adj* lazy; arrogant; blustering; cowardly. **follón, -ona** *sm, sf* good-for-nothing; coward; loafer.

fomentar [fomen'tar] *v* foment; warm; incubate; (*fig*) encourage.

fonda ['fonda] *sf* inn, boarding house.

fondear [fonde'ar] *v* anchor; sound; search.

fondo ['fondo] *sm* bottom; depth; essence; capital; fund; character; disposition. **a fondo** thoroughly. **artículo de fondo** leading article. **en el fondo** at heart. **estar en fondos** be well off.

fontanero [fonta'nero] *sm* plumber. **fontanar** *sm* spring. **fontanería** *sf* plumbing.

forajido [fora'xiðo], **-a** *sm, sf* outlaw; fugitive.

forastero [foras'tero], **-a** *sm, sf* stranger; alien. *adj* strange.

forcejear [forθexe'ar] *v* struggle, strive. **forcej(e)o** *sm* struggle.

forense [fo'rense] *adj* forensic; strange.

forjar [for'xar] *v* forge; beat into shape; invent. **forja** *sf* forge; forging.

formal [for'mal] *adj* formal; regular; methodical; serious; steady; reliable. **formalidad** *sf* formality; seriousness; orderliness; propriety. **formalismo** *sm* formalism. **formalizar** *v* formulate; legalize. **formalizarse** *v* take seriously.

formar [for'mar] *v* form; educate; train. **formarse** *v* be trained; develop. **forma** *sf* form; shape; manner; convention; mould. **de forma que** so that. **tener buenas formas** be polite.

formidable [formi'ðaβle] *adj* formidable; tremendous. **¡formidable!** great!

fórmula ['formula] *sf* formula; (*med*) prescription.

fornicar [forni'kar] *v* fornicate. **fornicación** *sf* fornication. **fornicador, -a** *sm, sf* fornicator.

fornido [for'niðo] *adj* robust, husky.

foro ['foro] *sm* forum; legal profession; leasehold; (*teatro*) back.

forraje [fo'rraxe] *sm* fodder; forage; (*fam*) hodgepodge. **forrajeador** *sm* forager. **forrajear** *v* forage.

forrar [for'rar] *v* line; pad; put a cover on. **forrarse** *v* line one's pockets. **forro** *sm* lining; cover.

*__fortalecer__ [fortale'θer] *v* strengthen; encourage. **fortalecimiento** *sm* fortification; strengthening. **fortaleza** *sf* fortress; fortitude; vigour. **fortificación** *sf* fortification. **fortificar** *v* fortify; strengthen. **fortificarse** *v* gain strength.

fortuito [for'twito] *adj* fortuitous; accidental.

fortuna [for'tuna] *sf* fortune, wealth; good luck; happiness; fate. **por fortuna** luckily. **probar fortuna** try one's luck.

*__forzar__ [for'θar] *v* force; rape. **forzadamente** *adv* forcibly. **forzado** *adj* forced; hard; far-fetched. **forzosamente** *adv* unavoidably. **forzoso** *adj* unavoidable; necessary.

fosa ['fosa] *sf* grave; (*anat*) cavity.

fosfato [fos'fato] *sm* phosphate. **fosforescencia** *sf* phosphorescence. **fosforescente** *adj* phosphorescent. **fósforo** *sm* phosphorus; match.

fósil ['fosil] *sm* fossil. **fosilizarse** *v* fossilize.

foso ['foso] *sm* hole; ditch; (*teatro*) pit; (*mil*) trench.

fotocopiar [fotoko'pjar] *v* photocopy. **fotocopia** *sf* photocopy. **fotocopiadora** *sf* copier.

fotografía [fotogra'fia] *sf* photography; photograph. **fotografiar** *v* photograph. **fotográfico** *adj* photographic. **fotógrafo, -a** *sm, sf* photographer.

frac [frak] *sm* dress coat, tails *pl*.

fracasar [fraka'sar] *v* fail. **fracaso** *sm* failure.

fracción [frak'θjon] *sf* (*mat*) fraction; portion; fragment. **fraccionamiento** *sm* breaking-up. **fraccionar** *v* break up; divide.

fractura [frak'tura] *sf* (*med*) fracture. **robo con fractura** *sm* burglary. **fracturar** *v* fracture.

fragancia [fra'ganθja] *sf* fragrance. **fragante** *adj* fragrant; flagrant.

fragata [fra'gata] *sf* frigate.

frágil ['fraxil] *adj* fragile; weak. **fragilidad** *sf* fragility; weakness.

fragmento [frag'mento] *sm* fragment. **fragmentar** *v* fragment. **fragmentario** *adj* fragmentary.

fragor [fra'gor] *sm* row, noise. **fragoroso** *adj* deafening.

fraguar [fra'gwar] *v* (*hierro*) forge; concoct; (*cemento*) harden. **fragua** *sf* forge. **fraguador, -a** *sm, sf* schemer, plotter.

fraile ['fraile] *sm* friar, monk.

frambuesa [fram'bwesa] *sf* raspberry. **frambueso** *sm* raspberry bush.

Francia ['franθja] *sf* France. **francés, -esa** *sm, sf* Frenchman/woman. **francés** *sm, adj* French.

francmasón [frankma'son] *sm* freemason. **francmasonería** *sf* freemasonry.

franco ['franko] *adj* frank, open; generous; free; (*com*) post *or* duty free.

franela [fra'nela] *sf* flannel.

franja ['franxa] *sf* fringe; border. **franjar** *v* fringe, trim.

franquear [franke'ar] *v* free; clear; exempt; grant. **franquearse** *v* open one's heart. **franqueo** *sm* franking, stamping; postage.

franqueza [fran'keθa] *sf* frankness; generosity; freedom.

frasco ['frasko] *sm* flask.

frase ['frase] *sf* (*gram*) sentence; phrase; expression. **frase hecha** cliché. **fraseología** *sf* phraseology.

fraternal [frater'nal] *adj* fraternal. **fraternidad** *sf* fraternity. **fraternizar** *v* fraternize. **fraterno** *adj* fraternal.

fraude ['frauðe] *sm* fraud; deception. **fraudulencia** *sf* dishonesty. **fraudulento** *adj* fraudulent.

fray [fraj] *sm* (*rel*) friar, brother.

frecuencia [fre'kwenθja] *sf* frequency. **con frecuencia** often. **frecuentar** *v* frequent. **frecuente** *adj* frequent.

*__fregar__ [fre'gar] *v* rub; scrub; wash up. **fregadero** *sm* sink. **fregado** *sm* rubbing; scrubbing; washing; (*fam*) intrigue. **fregador, -a** *sm, sf* dishwasher; *sm* sink, dishcloth.

*__freír__ [fre'ir] *v* fry; (*fam*) bother. **freidura** *sf* frying. **freiduría** *sf* fish shop.

fréjol ['frexol] *sm* kidney bean.

frenar [fre'nar] *v* brake; check. **freno** *sm* brake; bridle. **freno de mano** handbrake. **poner/soltar el freno** apply/release the brake.

frenesí [frene'si] *sm* frenzy.

frente ['frente] *sm* front; face; façade. **al frente** at the head. **de frente** forward. **en frente** opposite. *sf* forehead; head. **frente a frente** face to face.

fresa ['fresa] *sf* strawberry.

fresco ['fresko] *adj* cool; fresh; new; calm. **frescura** *sf* coolness; freshness; fertility; calmness; indifference; (*fam*) insolence.

fresno ['fresno] *sm* (*bot*) ash.

fricción [frik'θjon] *sf* friction; (*med*) massage. **friccionar** *v* rub; massage.

frigidez [frixi'ðeθ] *sf* frigidity. **frígido** *adj* frigid. **frigorífico** *sm* refrigerating; refrigerator.

frijón [fri'xon] *sm* bean.

frío ['frio] *adj* cold; cool; indifferent. *sm* cold. **coger frío** catch cold. **tener frío** be cold. **frialdad** *sf* coldness; indifference; impotence.

friolera [frjo'lera] *sf* triviality, trifle.

frisar [fri'sar] *v* frizz, curl. **frisar en** (*edad*) border on.

frito ['frito] *V* freír. *adj* fried. **estar frito** be fed up. **patatas fritas** chips. **quedarse frito** (*fam*) nod off.

frívolo ['friβolo] *adj* frivolous. **frivolidad** *sf* frivolity.

frondoso [fron'doso] *adj* leafy; lush. **frondosidad** *sf* leafiness; lushness.

frontera [fron'tera] *sf* frontier.

frotar [fro'tar] *v* rub; (*cerilla*) strike. **frotación** *sf* rubbing; friction. **frote** *sm* rub.

fructífero [fruk'tifero] *adj* fruit-bearing; fruitful.

frugal [fru'gal] *adj* frugal. **frugalidad** *sf* frugality.

fruncir [frun'θir] *v* wrinkle; gather; pleat. **fruncir el ceño** frown. **fruncido** *adj* gathered; wrinkled. **fruncimiento** *sm* gathering; wrinkling.

frustrar [frus'trar] *v* frustrate. **frustrarse** *v* fail.

fruta ['fruta] *sf* fruit. **fruta de sartén** fritter. **frutal** *adj* fruit. **frutería** *sf* fruiterer's. **frutero, -a** *sm, sf* fruiterer. **fruto** *sm* fruit; product; result; offspring; profit. **frutos civiles** (*jur*) unearned income.

fue¹ ['fue] *V* ir.

fue² ['fue] *V* ser.

fuego ['fwego] *sm* fire; light; burner; heat; rash; passion; zeal. **apagar el fuego** put out the fire. **arma de fuego** firearm. **cocer a fuego lento/vivo** cook slowly/quickly. **fuegos artificiales** fireworks. **prender fuego a** set fire to.

fuelle ['fweʎe] *sm* bellows.

fuente ['fwente] *sf* fountain; spring; source; serving dish.

fuera ['fwera] *adv* outside; out; abroad. **aquí/allí fuera** out here/there. **estar fuera** be away. **¡fuera!** get out! **ir fuera** go outside. **por fuera** on the outside.

fuero ['fwero] *sm* law; code of laws; jurisdiction.

fuerte ['fwerte] *adj* strong; large; heavy; concentrated. **precio fuerte** full price. *sm* (*mil*) fort; stronghold. **fuerza** *sf* strength; loudness; power; effort; electric current. **fuerza pública** police force.

fugarse [fu'garse] *v* run away; escape. **fuga** *sf* escape; elopement; (*gas, etc.*) leak; (*música*) fugue. **ponerse en fuga** take flight. **fugaz** *adj* fleeting. **fugitivo, -a** *s, adj* fugitive.

fulano [fu'lano] *sm* so-and-so, what's-his-name. **fulana** *sf* whore.

fulcro ['fulkro] *sm* fulcrum.

fulgor [ful'gor] *sm* glow; sparkle; brilliance. **fulgente** *also* **fúlgido** *adj* brilliant. **fulgir** *v* shine. **fulgurante** *adj* shining; glowing. **fulgurar** *v* flash; shine; glow.

fulminante [fulmi'nante] *adj* explosive; thundering; (*med*) grave; (*med*) mortal. **fulminar** *v* strike (by lightning); thunder; explode.

fumar [fu'mar] *v* smoke. **prohibido fumar** no smoking. **fumarse** *v* squander. **fumada** *sf* (*de humo*) puff.

fumigar [fumi'gar] *v* fumigate. **fumigación** *sf* fumigation. **fumigador** *sm* fumigator.

funcionar [funθjo'nar] *v* function, work, go. **no funciona** out of order. **función** *sf* function; performance; party; duty. **funcional** *adj* functional. **funcionamiento** *sm* functioning; operation; performance. **funcionario, -a** *sm, sf* public official.

funda ['funda] *sf* case, cover. **funda de almohada** pillowcase.

fundar [fun'dar] *v* found; establish; base. **fundarse** *v* be based. **fundación** *sf* foundation. **fundado** *adj* founded; justified. **fundamental** *adj* fundamental. **fundamento** *sm* foundation; basis; reason; reliability.

fundir [fun'dir] *v* cast; smelt; melt; merge. **fundición** *sf* melting; smelting; foundry.

fúnebre ['funeβre] *adj* funeral; mournful. **coche fúnebre** hearse.

funesto [fu'nesto] *adj* ill-fated; disastrous; fatal.

furgón [fur'gon] *sm* wagon; truck; van. **furgón de cola** guard's van. **furgoneta** *sf* van. **furgoneta familiar** station wagon.

furia ['furja] *sf* fury; violence; frenzy. **furioso** *adj* furious; raging; enormous. **furor** *sm* fury; passion; fever. **con furor** furiously. **hacer furor** be all the rage.

furtivo [fur'tiβo] *adj* furtive; sly.

furúnculo [fu'runkulo] *sm* (*med*) boil.

fusible [fu'siβle] *adj* fusible. *sm* fuse.

fusil [fu'sil] *sm* rifle.

fusión [fu'sjon] *sf* fusion; melting; thawing. **fusionar** *v* fuse; merge. **fusionamiento** *sm* merger.

fuste ['fuste] *sm* wood; (*fig*) importance. **gente de fuste** people of consequence.

fútbol ['futβol] *sm* football. **futbolista** *sm* footballer.

fútil ['futil] *adj* futile, trivial. **futilidad** *sf* futility; triviality.

futuro [fu'turo] *sm*, *adj* future. **futurista** *adj* futuristic.

G

gabán [ga'βan] *sm* overcoat.

gabardina [gaβar'ðina] *sf* raincoat.

gabinete [gaβi'nete] *sm* (*pol*) cabinet; study; studio.

gacela [ga'θela] *sf* gazelle.

gaceta [ga'θeta] *sf* gazette; journal. **gacetero** *sm* journalist; **gacetilla** *sf* gossip column.

gachas ['gatʃas] *sf pl* porridge *sing*; slops *pl*.

gacho ['gatʃo] *adj* drooping.

gafas ['gafas] *sf pl* spectacles. **gafas de sol** sunglasses.

gajo ['gaxo] *sm* (*de horcas*) prong; (*de naranja*) segment; (*de frutas*) cluster.

gala ['gala] *sf* full dress; pomp; elegance. **de gala** in full dress. **hacer gala de** show off. **tener a gala** pride oneself in.

galán [ga'lan] *sm* gallant; suitor; handsome man; (*teatro*) leading man. **galante** *adj* gallant; flirtatious. **galantear** *v* woo; flirt; flatter. **galanteo** *sm* flirtation; courting; flattery. **galantería** *sf* gallantry; elegance.

galardón [galar'ðon] *sm* reward. **galardonar** *v* reward.

galeón [gale'on] *sm* galleon.

galera [ga'lera] *sf* (*mar*) galley; wagon.

galería [gale'ria] *sf* gallery.

Gales ['gales] *sm* Wales. **galés, -esa** *sm, sf* Welshman/woman. **galés** *sm* (*lengua*) Welsh.

galgo ['galgo] *sm* greyhound.

galón[1] [ga'lon] *sm* braid; (*mil*) stripe. **quitar los galones** demote.

galón[2] *sm* gallon.

galopar [galo'par] *v* gallop. **galope** *sm* gallop. **a medio galope** at a canter.

galvanizar [galβani'θar] *v* galvanize.

gallardo [ga'ʎarðo] *adj* elegant; gallant. **gallardía** *sf* elegance; charm. **gallardear** *v* behave gracefully.

galleta [ga'ʎeta] *sf* biscuit.

gallina [ga'ʎina] *sf* hen, chicken. **gallo** *sm* cock, rooster.

gamuza [ga'muθa] *sf* chamois; (*trapo*) duster.

gana ['gana] *sf* desire; wish; appetite. **de buena/mala gana** willingly/unwillingly. **tener ganas de** want to.

ganadería [ganaðe'ria] *sf* cattle-raising; cattle farm; cattle; breed. **ganadero, -a** *sm, sf* cattle-raiser; stockbreeder. **ganado** *sm* cattle; livestock.

ganar [ga'nar] *v* gain, get; earn; take; surpass. **ganar en peso** put on weight. **ganancia** *sf* profit. **ganancias** *sf pl* earnings; winnings.

gancho ['gantʃo] *sm* hook; (*fam*) decoy; (*fam*) pimp; (*fam*) sex appeal.

ganga ['ganga] *sf* (*fam*) bargain; (*fam*) cushy job.

gangrena [gan'grena] *sf* gangrene. **gangrenoso** *adj* gangrenous.

ganso ['ganso] *sm* goose, gander; (*fam*) boor. **gansada** *sf* (*fam*) stupid thing.

garabatear [garaβate'ar] *v* scribble; (*fam*) beat about the bush. **garabateo** *sm* scribbling. **garabato** *sm* scribble.

garaje [ga'raxe] *sm* garage.

garantizar [garanti'θar] *v* guarantee. **garantía** *sf* guarantee.

garbanzo [gar'βanθo] *sm* chickpea.

garbo ['garβo] *sm* grace; generosity; jauntiness. **garboso** *adj* graceful; generous; jaunty.

garganta [gar'ganta] *sf* throat. **tener buena garganta** have a good voice. **gargantear** *v* warble.

gargarizar [gargari'θar] v gargle. **gárgara** sf gargle.

gárgola ['gargola] sf gargoyle.

garita [ga'rita] sf sentry box; lavatory; porter's lodge. **garita de señales** signalbox.

garra ['garra] sf claw.

garrafa [gar'rafa] sf decanter.

garrapata [garra'pata] sf (zool) tick.

garrote [gar'rote] sm stick, club; garotte; (med) tourniquet. **dar garrote a** execute.

garza ['garθa] sf heron.

gas [gas] sm gas. **a todo gas** flat out.

gasa ['gasa] sf gauze.

gaseosa [gase'osa] sf lemonade.

gasolina [gaso'lina] sf gasoline. **gasolinera** sf gasoline pump.

gastar [gas'tar] v spend; waste; wear out or away. **gasto** sm expense; outlay. **gastos** sm pl expenses; costs. **gastos generales** overheads.

gatillo [ga'tiʎo] sm trigger; dentist's forceps; (tecn) jack.

gato ['gato] sm cat; (tecn) jack; (fam) hoard. **a gatas** on all fours. **gatear** v clamber; (fam) crawl. **gatearse** v scratch.

gavilán [gaβi'lan] sm hawk; (pluma) nib; (bot) thistle.

gavilla [ga'βiʎa] sf sheaf; bundle; (fam) gang.

gaviota [ga'βjota] sf seagull.

gazapo [ga'θapo] sm young rabbit; slip of the tongue; blunder; misprint.

gazpacho [gaθ'patʃo] sm cold vegetable soup.

gelatina [xela'tina] sf gelatine.

gelignita [xelig'nita] sf gelignite.

gemelo [xe'melo] sm, adj twin. sm pl cufflinks; opera glasses.

*__gemir__ [xe'mir] v groan. **gemido** sm groan; wail.

genealogía [xenealo'xia] sf genealogy. **genealógico** adj genealogical. **árbol genealógico** family tree.

generación [xenera'θjon] sf generation. **generador** sm (tecn) generator. **generar** v generate.

generalizar [xenerali'θar] v generalize. **general** adj general. **general** sm (mil) general. **generalidad** sf majority. **generalización** sf generalization.

genérico [xe'neriko] adj generic. **género** sm race; kind; style; material; article; gender. **géneros** sm pl goods, merchandise sing.

generoso [xene'roso] adj generous. **generosidad** sf generosity.

genética [xe'netika] sf genetics. **genético** adj genetic.

genial [xe'njal] adj brilliant; outstanding; pleasant. **genio** sm genius; character. **estar de mal genio** be in a bad temper.

genital [xeni'tal] adj genital. **genitales** sm pl genitals.

gente ['xente] sf people. **gente baja** lower classes. **gente menuda** children.

gentil [xen'til] adj charming; genteel; civil; gentile; heathen. sm gentile; heathen; pagan. **gentileza** sf grace; elegance; gentility; civility.

gentío [xen'tio] sm crowd.

genuino [xe'nwino] adj genuine.

geografía [xeogra'fia] sf geography. **geográfico** adj geographic(al). **geógrafo** sm geographer.

geología [xeolo'xia] sf geology. **geológico** adj geological. **geólogo** sm geologist.

geometría [xeome'tria] sf geometry. **geométrico** adj geometric.

geranio [xe'ranjo] sm geranium.

gerencia [xe'renθja] sf management. **gerente** sm manager.

germinar [xermi'nar] v germinate. **germen** sm germ.

gesticular [xestiku'lar] v gesticulate. **gesticulación** sf gesticulation; grimace.

gestión [xes'tjon] sf arrangement; measure; management. **gestionar** v negotiate; get hold of.

gesto ['xesto] sm expression; countenance; gesture.

geyser ['xejser] sm geyser.

gigante [xi'gante] sm giant. adj gigantic.

gimnasia [xim'nasja] sf gymnastics. **gimnasio** sm gymnasium. **gimnasta** s(m + f) gymnast.

ginebra [xi'neβra] sf gin.

ginecología [xinekolo'xia] sf gynaecology. **ginecólogo, -a** sm, sf gynaecologist.

gira ['xira] sf tour; excursion; picnic.

giralda [xi'ralδa] sf weathercock.

girar [xi'rar] v turn; swivel; send; (com) draw. **girar dinero** remit money. **giratorio** adj gyratory. **puerta giratoria** revolving door. **giro** sm turn; (com) draft. **giro postal** sm postal order; money order.

girasol [xira'sol] sm sunflower.

gitano [xi'tano], **-a** s, adj gypsy.

glacial [gla'θjal] *adj* freezing.

glaciar [gla'θjar] *sm* glacier.

gladio ['glaðjo] *sm* (*bot*) gladiolus.

glándula ['glandula] *sf* gland. **glandular** *adj* glandular.

glicerina [gliθe'rina] *sf* glycerine.

global [glo'βal] *adj* global; comprehensive; total. **globo** *sm* globe, sphere. **en globo** all in all. **globo ocular** eyeball. **globular** *adj* globular. **glóbulo** *sm* globule.

gloriarse [glo'rjarse] *v* boast; glory. **gloria** *sf* glory; (*culin*) custard tart. **glorificación** *sf* glorification. **glorificar** *v* glorify. **glorioso** *adj* glorious; conceited.

glosar [glo'sar] *v* annotate. **glosa** *sf* annotation. **glosario** *sm* glossary.

glotón [glo'ton], **-ona** *sm, sf* glutton. *adj* gluttonous.

glucosa [glu'kosa] *sf* glucose.

*gobernar [goβer'nar] *v* govern; control; manage. **gobernación** *sf* government. **gobernador** *sm* governor. **gobierno** *sm* (*pol*) government; guidance.

goce ['goθe] *sm* enjoyment.

gol [gol] *sm* (*deporte*) goal. **golear** *v* score a goal.

golfo ['golfo] *sm* gulf; (*geog*) bay; guttersnipe.

golondrina [golon'drina] *sf* (*zool*) swallow.

golosina [golo'sina] *sf* sweet; delicacy; (*fig*) desire; (*fig*) greed. **goloso** *adj* sweet-toothed; appetizing; greedy.

golpear [golpe'ar] *v* strike, hit. **golpe** *sm* blow; coup; large amount; attack. **golpe de estado** coup d'état. **golpe de gracia** coup de grâce.

goma ['goma] *sf* rubber; gum; rubber band; elastic. **goma de borrar** eraser. **goma espuma** foam rubber.

gordo ['gorðo] *sm, adj* fat. **gordura** *sf* fatness, obesity.

gorila [go'rila] *sm* gorilla.

gorjear [gorxe'ar] *v* chirp, trill; twitter. **gorjeo** *sm* chirping; trilling; twittering.

gorra ['gorra] *sf* peaked cap; bonnet; (*fam*) sponger. **de gorra** free. **vivir de gorra** sponge.

gorrión [gor'rjon] *sf* sparrow.

gorro ['gorro] *sm* cap.

gotear [gote'ar] *v* drip; trickle; leak. **gota** *sf* drop. **gotera** *sf* leak; gutter. **goteras** *sf pl* (*fig*) aches and pains.

gótico ['gotiko] *adj* Gothic.

gozar [go'θar] *v* enjoy; possess. **gozarse** *v* rejoice. **gozo** *sm* joy. **gozoso** *adj* joyful.

gozne ['goθne] *sm* hinge.

grabar [gra'βar] *v* engrave; carve; imprint; record. **grabado** *sm* engraving; picture; recording. **grabador de cinta** *sm* tape recorder.

gracia ['graθja] *sf* grace; favour; charm; joke. **me hace gracia** it amuses me. **tener gracia** be amusing.

gracias ['graθjas] *sf pl* thanks. **acción de gracias** thanksgiving. **dar gracias** thank. **muchas gracias** many thanks.

gracioso [gra'θjoso] *adj* graceful; amusing; gracious. *sm* (*teatro*) buffoon.

grada ['graða] *sf* step; stair. **gradería** *sf* flight of steps; row of seats.

grado ['graðo] *sm* grade; degree; rank; pleasure. **de grado** willingly. **graduación** *sf* graduation. **gradual** *adj* gradual. **graduando, -a** *sm, sf* undergraduate. **graduar** *v* graduate; award a degree to. **graduarse** *v* gain a degree.

gráfico ['grafiko] *adj* graphic. *sm* graph; diagram.

grajo ['graxo] *sm* (*zool*) rook.

gramática [gra'matika] *sf* grammar. **gramático** *adj* grammatical.

gramo ['gramo] *sm* gramme.

gramófono [gra'mofono] *sm* gramophone.

gran [gran] *V* **grande**.

grana[1] ['grana] *sf* small seed; seeding time.

grana[2] *sf, adj* scarlet.

granada [gra'naða] *sf* pomegranate.

grande ['grande] *adj also* **gran** large, big, great. **grandeza** *sf* greatness; size. **grandioso** *adj* grandiose; grand.

granel [gra'nel] *adv* **a granel** in bulk.

granero [gra'nero] *sm* granary.

granito [gra'nito] *sm* granite.

granizar [grani'θar] *v* hail. **granizo** *sm* hail.

granja ['granxa] *sf* farm. **granja avícola** poultry farm. **granjero, -a** *sm, sf* farmer.

grano ['grano] *sm* grain; bean; pimple. **ir al grano** come to the point. **granoso** *adj* granular.

grapa ['grapa] *sf* clamp; staple; dowel.

grasa ['grasa] *sf* grease; fat. **grasera** *sf* dripping pan. **grasiento** *adj* greasy; oily; filthy. **graso** *adj* fatty.

gratificar [gratifi'kar] *v* gratify; reward; tip. **gratificación** *sf* reward; gratuity; bonus; gratification.

gratis ['gratis] *adv* free.

gratitud [grati'tuð] *sf* gratitude.

grato ['grato] *adj* pleasing; pleasant; welcome. **me es grato . . .** I am pleased . . . .

gratuito [gra'twito] *adj* free; gratuitous.

gravamen [gra'βamen] *sm* charge; obligation; burden; tax. **gravar** *v* burden; oppress. **gravar impuéstos a** *or* **sobre** tax.

grave ['graβe] *adj* grave, serious; weighty. **ponerse grave** become gravely ill. **gravedad** *sf* gravity, seriousness.

gravitar [graβi'tar] *v* gravitate. **gravitación** *sf* gravitation, gravity.

graznar [graθ'nar] *v* croak; cackle. **graznido** *sm* croak; cackle.

Grecia ['greθja] *sf* Greece. **griego** *s*, *adj* Greek. **griego** *sm* (*idioma*) Greek; (*fam*) gibberish.

greda ['greða] *sf* clay. **gredoso** *adj* clayey.

gregario [gre'garjo] *adj* gregarious.

gremio ['gremjo] *sm* guild; fraternity; union. **gremio obrero** trade union.

greña ['grenja] *sf* tangled hair. **andar a la greña** (*fam*) squabble.

grey [grej] *sf* congregation; flock, herd.

grieta ['grjeta] *sf* crack.

grifo ['grifo] *sm* tap. **al grifo** on draught.

grillo ['griʎo] *sm* (*zool*) cricket. **grillos** *sm pl* shackles, fetters.

gringo ['gringo], **-a** *sm*, *sf* (*fam*) foreigner.

gripe ['gripe] *sf* (*med*) influenza, flu.

gris [gris] *adj* grey.

gritar [gri'tar] *v* shout, scream, yell. **grito** *sm* shout, scream, yell. **el último grito** the latest fashion.

grosella [gro'seʎa] *sf* currant. **grosella espinosa/negra/roja** gooseberry/blackcurrant/redcurrant.

grosería [grose'ria] *sf* vulgarity. **grosero** *adj* vulgar.

grotesco [gro'tesko] *adj* grotesque; absurd.

grúa ['grua] *sf* (*tecn*) crane.

grueso [gru'eso] *adj* thick; large; heavy; dull; slow; coarse. *sm* thickness; heaviness. **gruesa** *sf* (*número*) gross.

grulla ['gruʎa] *sf* (*zool*) crane.

grumete [gru'mete] *sm* cabin boy.

***gruñir** [gru'ɲir] *v* growl. **gruñido** *sm* growl.

grupo ['grupo] *sm* group. **grupo sanguíneo** blood group.

gruta ['gruta] *sf* grotto; cave.

guadaña [gwa'ðaɲa] *sf* scythe.

guante ['gwante] *sm* glove. **guantear** *v* slap.

guapo ['gwapo] *adj* handsome; pretty; flashy. *sm* boaster; bully; (*fam*) lover.

guardar [gwar'ðar] *v* guard; keep; protect; respect. **guarda** *s(m+f)* guard; keeper. **guarda** *sf* custody; protection. **guardacostas** *sm invar* coastguard. **guardafuego** *sm* hearth fender. **guardapolvo** *sm* dust-cover. **guardarropa** *sm* wardrobe; cloakroom. **guardia** *sf* guard; police force. **guardia civil** Civil Guard.

guardián [gwar'ðjan], **-a** *sm*, *sf* guardian; keeper; caretaker.

guardilla [gwar'ðiʎa] *sf* attic.

guarida [gwa'riða] *sf* den, lair; haunt; shelter.

***guarnecer** [gwarne'θer] *v* equip; provide; furnish; adorn; garnish; plaster. **guarnición** *sf* adornment; provision; (*mil*) garrison. **guarnicionar** *v* garrison.

guasa ['gwasa] *sf* joke. **sin guasa** seriously. **guasearse** *v* (*fam*) joke; tease. **guaseo** *sm* leg-pull.

gubernamental [guβernamen'tal] *adj* governmental.

guerra ['gerra] *sf* war. **guerra mundial** world war. **guerrear** *v* wage war. **guerrero**, **-a** *sm*, *sf* warrior. **guerrilla** *sf* guerrilla band; guerrilla warfare. **guerrillero** *sm* guerrilla fighter.

guiar [gi'ar] *v* guide; steer; drive. **guía** *sm* (*persona*) guide. **guía** *sf* (*libro*) guide, guidebook. **guía sonora** soundtrack.

guija ['gixa] *sf* pebble.

guillotina [giʎo'tina] *sf* guillotine. **guillotinar** *v* guillotine.

guiñar [gi'ɲar] *v* wink. **guiño** *sm* wink.

guión [gi'on] *sm* hyphen; film script; outline; subtitle.

guisa ['gisa] *sf* way, manner. **a guisa de** like. **de tal guisa** in such a manner.

guisado [gi'saðo] *sm* stew. **guisar** *v* cook; prepare. **guiso** *sm* cooked dish; stew.

guisante [gi'sante] *sm* pea. **guisante de olor** sweet pea.

guitarra [gi'tarra] *sf* guitar. **guitarrista** *s(m+f)* guitarist.

gula ['gula] *sf* greed.

gusano [gu'sano] *sm* worm; maggot; caterpillar. **gusano de seda** silkworm.

gustar [gus'tar] *v* please; like; taste; try. **gustar de** enjoy. **¡así me gusta!** that's what I like! **gusto** *sm* pleasure; fancy;

style; taste; flavour. **de buen/mal gusto**
in good/bad taste. **con mucho gusto** with
great pleasure. **¡mucho gusto!** how do
you do? **gustoso** *adj* tasty; pleasant.
gutural [gutu'ral] *adj* guttural.

H

haba ['aβa] *sf* broad bean; swelling;
bruise.
***haber** [a'βer] *v* have. **haber de** have to.
hay que one must. **no hay de que** don't
mention it. **haberes** *sm pl* assets; property *sing*; income *sing*.
habichuela [aβi'tʃwela] *sf* bean. **habichuela verde** French bean.
hábil ['aβil] *adj* clever; able. **habilidad** *sf*
cleverness; ability.
habilitar [aβili'tar] *v* qualify; enable.
habilitación *sf* qualification.
habitar [aβi'tar] *v* inhabit. **habitable** *adj*
habitable. **habitación** *sf* habitation;
room; lodgings *pl*. **habitante** *s(m+f)*
inhabitant.
hábito ['aβito] *sm* habit; attire. **habitual**
adj habitual. **habituar** *v* accustom.
habituarse *v* become accustomed to.
hablar [a'βlar] *v* speak, talk. **¿quién
habla?** (*al teléfono*) who's speaking? **se
habla español** Spanish spoken. **habla** *sf*
language; speech. **hablador, -a** *sm, sf*
chatterbox. **hablilla** *sf* rumour; gossip.
hacedero [aθe'ðero] *adj* feasible. **hacedor,
-a** *sm, sf* creator.
hacendado [aθen'daðo] *sm* landowner.
***hacer** [a'θer] *v* do; make; perform; pro-
duce. **hacer calor/frío** be hot/cold. **hacer
fiesta** take a holiday. **hace mucho tiempo
que** it is a long time since. **hacer para**
make an effort to. **hacerse** *v* become.
hacia ['aθja] *prep* towards; about. **hacia
atrás** backwards.
hacienda [a'θjenda] *sf* estate; ranch.
hacina [a'θina] *sf* stack, rick. **hacinar** *v*
stack; amass.
hacha ['atʃa] *sf* axe.
hada ['aða] *sf* fairy. **hada madrina** fairy
godmother. **cuento de hadas** *sm* fairy
tale.
hado ['aðo] *sm* fate.

halagar [ala'gar] *v* flatter. **halago** *sm*
flattery. **halagüeño** *adj* flattering.
halcón [al'kon] *sm* falcon. **halconería** *sf*
falconry.
hálito ['alito] *sm* breath.
hallar [a'ʎar] *v* find; find out. **hallarse** *v*
be situated. **hallarse bien con** be pleased
with. **hallazgo** *sm* discovery.
hamaca [a'maka] *sf* hammock.
hambre ['ambre] *sf* hunger; starvation.
pasar hambre go hungry. **tener hambre**
be hungry. **hambriento** *adj* hungry.
hamburguesa [ambur'gesa] *sf* hamburger.
haragán [ara'gan] *adj* lazy. **haraganear** *v*
idle.
harapiento [ara'pjento] *adj* ragged.
harapo *sm* rag.
harina [a'rina] *sf* flour. **harinero** *adj* also
harinoso floury.
hartar [ar'tar] *v* stuff; gorge; weary; bore.
harto *adj* satiated. **hartura** *sf* satiety.
hasta ['asta] *prep* until; up to; as much
as; as far as. *adv* even. **hasta ahora** up to
now. **hasta aquí** so far. **hasta luego**
(*interj*) so long. good-bye. **hasta que**
until.
hastío [as'tio] *sm* disgust; weariness. **has-
tiar** *v* disgust; bore.
hato ['ato] *sm* herd; flock; gang.
hay [aj] there is; there are. **hay que** one
must.
haya ['aja] *sf* beech.
haz[1] [aθ] *sm* bunch; bundle; sheaf.
haz[2] *sf* face; surface. **a sobre haz** on the
surface.
hazaña [a'θaɲa] *sf* deed; feat; exploit.
hazmerreír [aθmerre'ir] *sm* laughing-
stock.
hebilla [e'βiʎa] *sf* buckle; clasp.
hebra ['eβra] *sf* fibre; thread; (*de madera*)
grain.
hebreo [e'βreo] *s, adj* Hebrew. *sm*
(*lengua*) Hebrew.
hechicero [etʃi'θero] *sm* sorcerer; wizard.
hechicera *sf* sorceress; witch. **hechicería**
sf witchcraft; sorcery; enchantment.
hechizar *v* bewitch. **hechizo** *sm* magic
spell.
hecho ['etʃo] *V* hacer. *adj* mature;
finished; cooked. **hecho y derecho** in
every sense of the word. **muy/poco
hecho** overdone/underdone. *sm* fact;
deed; feat; matter; event. **de hecho** in
fact. **hechura** *sf* making; making-up;
shape; workmanship.

hediondo [e'ðjondo] adj stinking; repulsive. **heder** v stink; vex. **hedor** sm stink.

*helar [e'lar] v freeze. **helada** sf frost. **helado** sm ice cream.

helecho [e'letʃo] sm fern.

hélice ['eliθe] sf helix; spiral; propeller.

helicóptero [eli'koptero] sm helicopter.

hembra ['embra] sf female; clasp; socket; (de tornillo) nut.

hemisferio [emis'ferjo] sm hemisphere. **hemisférico** adj hemispheric, hemispherical.

hemorragia [emor'raxja] sf haemorrhage.

hemorroides [emor'rojðes] sf pl haemorrhoids.

*henchirse [en'tʃirse] v swell up; stuff oneself. **henchidura** sf filling.

*hender [en'der] v split. **hendidura** sf split; crack.

heno ['eno] sm hay.

heraldo [e'raldo] sm herald. **heráldica** sf heraldry. adj heraldic.

herbaje [er'βaxe] sm pasture. **herbario** adj herbal. **herbicida** sm weedkiller. **herbívoro, -a** sm, sf herbivore. **herbívoro** adj herbivorous. **herbolario** sm herbalist. **herboso** adj grassy.

heredar [ere'ðar] v inherit. **heredad** sf estate. **heredero, -a** sm, sf heir/heiress. **hereditario** adj hereditary.

hereje [e'rexe] s(m+f) heretic. **herejía** sf heresy. **herético** adj heretic.

herencia [e'renθja] sf inheritance; heredity.

*herir [e'rir] v wound. **herida** sf wound. **herido** sm casualty.

hermano [er'mano] sm brother. **hermana** sf sister. **hermandad** sf brotherhood. **hermanastro, -a** sm, sf stepbrother/stepsister.

hermético [er'metiko] adj hermetic.

hermoso [er'moso] adj beautiful; handsome. **hermosura** sf beauty; handsomeness.

héroe ['eroe] sm hero. **heroico** adj heroic. **heroísmo** sm heroism.

heroína [ero'ina] sf heroin.

herramienta [erra'mjenta] sf tool; implement.

*herrar [er'rar] v (caballo) shoe. **herradura** sf horseshoe. **camino de herradura** bridle path. **herrería** sf smithy, forge. **herrero** sm blacksmith.

herrumbre [er'rumbre] sf rust. **herrumbrar** v rust. **herrumbroso** adj rusty.

*hervir [er'βir] v boil. **hervidero** sm boiling; bubbling; (fig) swarm, crowd; hotbed. **hervidor** sm kettle. **hervor** sm boiling; fervour.

hesitar [esi'tar] v hesitate. **hesitación** sf hesitation.

hez [eθ] sf, pl **heces** dregs pl; scum.

hibernar [iβer'nar] v hibernate. **hibernación** sf hibernation.

híbrido ['iβriðo] sm, adj hybrid. **hibridación** sf hybridization. **hibridizar** v hybridize.

hidalgo [i'ðalgo] sm nobleman. adj noble. **hidalguía** sf nobility.

hidráulico [i'ðrauliko] adj hydraulic. **freno hidráulico** sm hydraulic brake.

hidroala [iðro'ala] sf hovercraft.

hidroavión [iðroa'βjon] sm seaplane.

hidroeléctrico [iðroe'lektriko] adj hydroelectric.

hidrofobia [iðro'foβja] sf hydrophobia.

hidrógeno [i'ðroxeno] sm hydrogen.

hidropesía [iðrope'sia] sf dropsy.

hiedra ['jeðra] sf ivy.

hielo ['jelo] sm ice.

hiena ['jena] sf hyena.

hierba ['jerβa] sf grass; herb. **mala hierba** weed.

hierbabuena [jerβa'βwena] sf mint.

hierro ['jerro] sm iron. **hierro colado** cast iron. **hierro forjado** wrought iron.

hígado ['igaðo] sm liver.

higiene [i'xjene] sf hygiene. **higiénico** adj hygienic. **paños higiénicos** sm pl sanitary towels.

higo ['igo] sm fig. **higuera** sf fig-tree.

hijo ['ixo] sm son. **hijos** sm pl children. **hija** sf daughter. **hijo/hija político, -a** son/daughter-in-law.

hilar [i'lar] v spin; infer. **hiladora** sf spinning wheel. **hilandería** sf spinning. **hilandero, -a** sm, sf (persona) spinner.

hilarante [ila'rante] adj hilarious. **hilaridad** sf hilarity.

hilera [i'lera] sf row; rank; file.

hilo ['ilo] sm thread; yarn; wire. **hilo de coser** sewing thread. **hilo de perlas** string of pearls. **telegrafía sin hilos** sf wireless telegraphy.

himno ['imno] sm hymn; anthem. **himno nacional** national anthem. **himnario** sm hymn book.

hincapié [inka'pje] sm foothold; emphasis. **hacer hincapié en** insist on.

hincar [in'kar] v drive in; sink; plunge.
hincarse de rodillas kneel down.

hinchar [in'tʃar] v inflate; swell. **hincharse**
v puff up; (fam) become bigheaded.
hinchazón sm (med) swelling; arrogance.

hinojo [i'noxo] sm fennel. **hinojos** sm pl
knees.

hípico ['ipiko] adj equine. **hipismo** sm
show-jumping. **hipódromo** sm race
course.

hipnosis [ip'nosis] sm hypnosis. **hipnótico**
adj hypnotic. **hipnotismo** sm hypnotism.
hipnotizador, -a sm, sf hypnotist. **hipnotizar** v hypnotize.

hipo ['ipo] sm hiccup; longing; grudge.
tener hipo have the hiccups.

hipocondría [ipokon'dria] sf hypochondria. **hipocondríaco, -a** sm, sf hypochondriac.

hipocresía [ipokre'sia] sf hypocrisy.
hipócrita adj hypocritical. **hipócrita**
s(m+f) hypocrite.

hipodérmico [ipo'ðermiko] adj hypodermic.

hipopótamo [ipo'potamo] sm hippopotamus.

hipotecar [ipote'kar] v mortgage. **hipoteca**
sf mortgage.

hipótesis [i'potesis] sf hypothesis. **hipotético** adj hypothetical.

hirsuto [ir'suto] adj hairy.

hirviente [ir'βjente] adj boiling.

hispánico [is'paniko] adj Hispanic.

hispanoamericano [ispanoameri'kano] s,
adj Spanish American.

histerectomía [isterekto'mia] sf hysterectomy.

histeria [is'terja] sf hysteria. **histérico** adj
hysterical.

historia [is'torja] sf history; story; fib;
gossip; trouble. **armar historias** (fam)
make trouble. **historiador, -a** sm, sf historian. **histórico** adj historical; historic.

hogar [o'gar] sm hearth; home.

hoguera [o'gera] sf bonfire.

hoja ['oxa] sf leaf; petal; sheet; layer;
flake; blade; newspaper; (formulario)
form. **hoja de afeitar** razor blade. **hoja de
paga** payroll.

hojalata [oxa'lata] sf tinplate; tin.

hojear [oxe'ar] v leaf through.

Holanda [o'landa] sf Holland. **holandés**
adj Dutch. **holandés** sm Dutchman;
(lengua) Dutch. **holandesa** sf
Dutchwoman.

*holgar [ol'gar] v rest; be idle; be unnecessary. **holgarse** v enjoy oneself. **holgazán**
adj idle. **holgazanear** v idle. **holgura** sf
roominess; comfort.

*hollar [o'ʎar] v tread; trample down.

hollín [o'ʎin] sm soot. **hollimiento** adj
sooty.

hombre ['ombre] sm man. **hombre bueno**
arbiter. **hombre de negocios** businessman. **¡hombre!** good heavens, man! **hom-
brear** v act the man.

hombro ['ombro] sm (anat) shoulder.
echarse al hombro shoulder.

homenaje [ome'naxe] sm homage.
homenajear v pay homage to.

homeópata [ome'opata] s(m+f) homeo-
path. adj homeopathic. **homeopatía** sf
homeopathy.

homicida [omi'θiða] s(m+f) murderer.
adj homicidal. **homicidio** sm murder.

homogéneo [omo'xeneo] adj homogeneous. **homogeneidad** sf homogeneity,
homogeneousness.

homólogo [o'mologo] adj corresponding;
synonymous.

honda ['onda] sf catapult; sling.

hondo ['ondo] adj deep. sm bottom.
hondonada sf depression; hollow.
hondura sf depth.

honesto [o'nesto] adj honest; modest;
chaste. **honestidad** sf honesty; modesty;
chastity.

hongo ['ongo] sm mushroom; bowler hat.

honor [o'nor] sm honour. **honorable** adj
honourable. **honorario** adj honorary.
honorario sm honorarium. **honra** sf honour; reputation; dignity; respect. **tener a
mucha honra** be very proud of. **honradez**
sf honesty; uprightness. **honrado** adj
honest; upright. **honrar** v honour; be a
credit to. **honrarse** v be honoured.
honroso adj honourable.

hora ['ora] sf hour. **pedir hora** make an
appointment. **¿qué hora es?** what time is
it? **horario** adj hour. **horario** sm hours of
work; timetable.

horca ['orka] sf gallows pl; pitchfork. **hor-
cado** adj forked.

horda ['orða] sf horde.

horizonte [ori'θonte] sm horizon. **horizontal** adj horizontal.

hormiga [or'miga] sf ant; itch. **hormigoso**
adj ant-eaten; itchy. **hormiguear** v
swarm; creep; itch. **hormigueo** sm

itching; swarming. **hormiguero** *sm* ant-hill; swarm.

hormigón [ormi'gon] *sm* concrete. **hormigón armado** reinforced concrete.

hormona [or'mona] *sf* hormone.

hornero [or'nero], **-a** *sm, sf* baker. **hornear** *v* bake. **hornería** *sf* baking.

horno ['orno] *sm* oven; furnace. **hornillo** *sm* stove, cooker; gas or electric ring.

horóscopo [o'roskopo] *sm* horoscope.

horquilla [or'kiʎa] *sf* pitchfork; hairpin; rowlock.

horrible [or'riβle] *adj* horrible.

horror [or'ror] *sm* horror. **horrendo** *adj* hideous; horrible. **horrífico** *adj* horrific, horrifying. **horrorizar** *v* horrify. **horroroso** *adj* horrid, horrible.

hortaliza [orta'liθa] *sf* green vegetable. **hortelano**, **-a** *sm, sf* gardener. **hortelano** *adj* market-gardening.

horticultura [ortikul'tura] *sf* horticulture. **hortícula** *adj* horticultural.

hosco ['osko] *adj* grim; surly; gloomy. **hoscoso** *adj* bristly.

hospedar [ospe'ðar] *v* lodge, put up. **hospedarse** *v* have lodgings. **hospedaje** *sf* lodging. **hospedería** *sf* inn, hostelry.

hospicio [os'piθjo] *sm* orphanage; poorhouse.

hospital [ospi'tal] *sm* hospital. **hospitalario** *adj* hospitable. **hospitalidad** *sf* hospitality. **hospitalización** *sf* hospitalization. **hospitalizar** *v* hospitalize.

hostelero [oste'lero], **-a** *sm, sf* innkeeper. **hostería** *sf* inn.

hostia ['ostja] *sf* (*rel*) wafer; (*fam*) bashing.

hostigar [osti'gar] *v* whip; harass; molest. **hostigamiento** *sm* harassing; molesting; lashing. **hostigo** *sm* lash.

hostil [os'til] *adj* hostile. **hostilidad** *sf* hostility.

hotel [o'tel] *sm* hotel; villa. **hotelería** *sf* hotel-keeping. **hotelero**, **-a** *sm, sf* hotel-keeper.

hoy [oj] *adv* today; now. **de hoy en adelante** from now on. **hoy en día** nowadays. **hoy por hoy** for the time being.

hoya ['oja] *sf* hole; valley.

hoyo ['ojo] *sm* pit; hole; dent; grave. **hoyuelo** *sm* small hole; dimple.

hoz [oθ] *sf* sickle; ravine.

hueco ['weko] *adj* hollow; empty; vain; resonant. *sm* hollow; gap; cavity; vacancy.

huelga ['welga] *sf* (*de obreros*) strike. **huelgista** *s(m + f)* striker.

huelgo ['welgo] *sm* breath; (*tecn*) play.

huella ['weʎa] *sf* footprint; tread; impression. **huella digital** fingerprint. **huella de sonido** soundtrack.

huérfano ['werfano], **-a** *sm, sf* orphan.

huerta ['werta] *sf* vegetable garden; orchard; irrigated land. **huerto** *sm* orchard; kitchen garden.

hueso ['weso] *sm* bone; stone; pip; (*fam*) drudgery. **dar con sus huesos** end up. **estar en los huesos** be very thin. **huesudo** *adj* bony.

huésped ['wespeð], **-a** *sm, sf* guest; lodger. **casa de huéspedes** boarding house.

hueva ['weβa] *sf* roe. **huevas** *sf pl* spawn.

huevo ['weβo] *sm* egg. **huevo de Pascua** Easter egg. **huevo duro** hard-boiled egg. **huevo escalfado** poached egg. **huevo frito** fried egg. **huevo pasado por agua** soft-boiled egg. **huevo revuelto** scrambled egg.

*****huir** [wir] *v* flee. **huida** *sf* flight; escape.

hule[1] ['ule] *sm* oilskin; rubber.

hule[2] *sm* (*cornada*) goring.

hulla ['uʎa] *sf* coal.

humano [u'mano] *adj* human; humane. *sm* human being. **humanar** *v* humanize. **humanidad** *sf* humanity. **humanismo** *sm* humanism. **humanista** *s(m + f)* humanist. **humanitario**, **-a** *s*, *adj* humanitarian.

húmedo ['umeðo] *adj* humid, damp, moist. **humedad** *sf* humidity, dampness. **humedecer** *v* dampen, moisten.

humillar [umi'ʎar] *v* humiliate; shame. **humildad** *sf* humility. **humilde** *adj* humble. **humillación** *sf* humiliation.

humo ['umo] *sm* smoke; fumes *pl*. **vender humos** boast. **humear** *v* smoke. **humoso** *adj* smoky.

humor [u'mor] *sm* humour; temper; mood. **buen/mal humor** good/bad temper. **humorada** *sf* witticism. **humorista** *s(m + f)* humorist. **humorístico** *adj* humorous.

hundir [un'dir] *v* sink; drive in; crush. **hundirse** *v* go under; collapse. **hundimiento** *sm* sinking; collapse.

Hungría [un'gria] *sf* Hungary. **húngaro** *s*, *adj* Hungarian.

huracán [ura'kan] *sm* hurricane.

hurgar [ur'gar] *v* poke; stir; pick. **hurgón** *sm* poker.

hurón [u'ron] *sm* ferret. **huronear** *v* hunt with a ferret; (*fam*) pry.

hurtadillas [urta'ðiʎas] *adv* **a hurtadillas** slyly, stealthily.

hurtar [ur'tar] *v* steal; remove; cheat. **hurtar el cuerpo** dodge. **hurtador**, -**a** *sm*, *sf* thief. **hurto** *sm* theft; thing stolen.

husmear [usme'ar] *v* scent; track; (*fam*) pry; (*fam*: *carne*) smell high. **husmeo** *sm* scenting; smelling; prying.

huso ['uso] *sm* spindle; (*avión*) fuselage.

I

íbice ['iβiθe] *sm* ibex.

ictericia [ikte'riθja] *sf* jaundice.

ida ['iða] *sf* departure; journey. **idas y venidas** coming and going.

idea [i'ðea] *sf* idea; intention. **tener idea de** intend to. **ideal** *adj* ideal; imaginary. **idealismo** *sm* idealism. **idealista** *s*, *adj* idealist. **idealizar** *v* idealize. **idear** *v* imagine; plan.

idéntico [i'ðentiko] *adj* identical. **identidad** *sf* identity. **identificación** *sf* identification. **identificar** *v* identify.

ideología [iðeolo'xia] *sf* ideology. **ideológico** *adj* ideological.

idilio [i'ðiljo] *sm* idyll. **idílico** *adj* idyllic.

idioma [i'ðjoma] *sm* language. **idiomático** *adj* idiomatic; linguistic.

idiosincrasia [iðjosin'krasja] *sf* idiosyncrasy. **idiosincrásico** *adj* idiosyncratic.

idiota [i'ðjota] *s*(*m*+*f*) idiot. *adj* idiotic. **idiotez** *sf* idiocy. **idiótico** *adj* idiotic.

ídolo ['iðolo] *sm* idol. **idólatra** *s*(*m*+*f*) idolater. **idólatra** *adj* idolatrous. **idolatrar** *v* idolize. **idolatría** *sf* idolatry.

idóneo [i'ðoneo] *adj* apt, fit. **idoneidad** *sf* aptness, fitness.

iglesia [i'glesja] *sf* church.

ignición [igni'θjon] *sf* ignition. **ignito** *adj* ignited.

ignominia [igno'minja] *sf* ignominy. **ignominioso** *adj* ignominious.

ignorar [igno'rar] *v* be unaware of; refuse to know. **ignorancia** *sf* ignorance. **ignorante** *adj* ignorant.

igual [i'gwal] *adj* same; equal; even. **por**

igual evenly. **es igual** it makes no difference. **igualar** *v* equalize. **igualación** *sf* equalization. **igualdad** *sf* equality.

íjada [i'xaða] *sf* flank. **ijadear** *v* pant.

ilegal [ile'gal] *adj* illegal. **ilegalidad** *sf* illegality.

ilegible [ile'xiβle] *adj* illegible.

ilegítimo [ile'xitimo] *adj* illegitimate. **ilegitimidad** *sf* illegitimacy.

ileso [i'leso] *adj* unharmed.

ilícito [i'liθito] *adj* illicit.

ilógico [i'loxiko] *adj* illogical.

iluminar [ilumi'nar] *v* illuminate. **iluminación** *sf* illumination.

ilusión [ilu'sjon] *sf* illusion; delusion; expectation. **ilusionado** *adj* eager. **ilusionar** *v* fascinate. **ilusionarse** *v* delude oneself; build up hopes. **ilusionismo** *sm* conjuring trick. **ilusionista** *s*(*m*+*f*) conjurer. **iluso** *adj* deceived; deluded. **ilusorio** *adj* illusory.

ilustrar [ilu'strar] *v* illustrate. **ilustración** *sf* illustration; enlightenment. **ilustrador**, -**a** *sm*, *sf* illustrator.

imaginar [imaxi'nar] *v* imagine. **imagen** *sf* image. **imaginación** *sf* imagination. **imaginario** *adj* imaginary. **imaginativo** *adj* imaginative.

imán [i'man] *sm* magnet **imanar** *v* *also* **imantar** magnetize. **imantación** *sf* magnetization.

imbécil [im'βeθil] *adj* imbecile. **imbecilidad** *sf* imbecility.

imborrable [imbor'raβle] *adj* unforgettable.

*imbuir [imbu'ir] *v* imbue.

imitar [imi'tar] *v* imitate, copy. **imitable** *adj* imitable. **imitación** *sf* imitation. **imitador**, -**a** *sm*, *sf* imitator. **imitativo** *adj* imitative.

impaciente [impa'θjente] *adj* impatient. **impaciencia** *sf* impatience. **impacientarse** *v* become impatient.

impacto [im'pakto] *sm* impact.

impar [im'par] *adj* (*mat*) odd. **número impar** odd number.

imparcial [impar'θjal] *adj* impartial. **imparcialidad** *sf* impartiality.

impartir [impar'tir] *v* impart.

impasible [impa'siβle] *adj* impassive. **impasibilidad** *sf* impassivity.

impávido [im'paβiðo] *adj* fearless, dauntless. **impavidez** *sf* fearlessness, dauntlessness.

impecable [impe'kaβle] *adj* impeccable.
impecabilidad *sf* impeccability.
***impedir** [impe'ðir] *v* impede; prevent.
impediente *adj* obstructing. **impedimento**
sm impediment.
impeler [impe'ler] *v* impel; drive; propel.
impenetrable [impene'traβle] *adj* impenetrable.
impenitente [impeni'tente] *adj* impenitent.
imperar [impe'rar] *v* rule; prevail. **imperativo** *adj* imperative; commanding.
imperceptible [imperθep'tiβle] *adj* imperceptible.
imperdible [imper'ðiβle] *sm* safety pin.
imperdonable [imperðo'naβle] *adj* unforgivable.
imperfecto [imper'fekto] *adj* imperfect.
imperfección *sf* imperfection.
imperio [im'perjo] *sm* empire. **imperial** *adj* imperial. **imperialismo** *sm* imperialism.
imperialista *s, adj* imperialist.
impermeable [imperme'aβle] *adj* waterproof. *sm* mackintosh.
impersonal [imperso'nal] *adj* impersonal.
impertinente [imperti'nente] *adj* impertinent. **impertinencia** *sf* impertinence.
imperturbable [impertur'βaβle] *adj* imperturbable. **imperturbabilidad** *sf* imperturbability.
ímpetu ['impetu] *sm* impetus.
impetuosidad *sf* impetuosity.
impío [im'pio] *adj* godless, impious.
impiedad *sf* impiety.
implacable [impla'kaβle] *adj* implacable.
implacabilidad *sf* implacability.
implantar [implan'tar] *v* implant.
implicar [impli'kar] *v* imply; implicate; entail. **implicación** *sf* implication; contradiction. **implicatorio** *adj* contradictory.
implícito [im'pliθito] *adj* implicit.
implorar [implo'rar] *v* implore, beg.
imploración *sf* entreaty.
***imponer** [impo'ner] *v* impose; inflict; acquaint; inspire; deposit; impute falsely. **imponerse** *v* dominate. **imponente** *adj* imposing; striking; (*fam*) sensational, smashing.
impopular [impopu'lar] *adj* unpopular.
impopularidad *sf* unpopularity.
importante [impor'tante] *adj* important.
importancia *sf* importance. **importar** *v* matter, concern. **no importa** it doesn't matter.
importunar [importu'nar] *v* importune,

pester. **importunidad** *sf* importunity.
importuno *adj* importunate, pestering.
imposible [impo'siβle] *adj* impossible.
imposibilidad *sf* impossibility.
imposibilitar *v* make impossible.
imposición [imposi'θjon] *sf* imposition; tax.
impostor [impos'tor], **-a** *sm, sf* impostor.
impotente [impo'tente] *adj* impotent; powerless. **impotencia** *sf* impotence.
impracticable [imprakti'kaβle] *adj* impracticable.
imprecar [impre'kar] *v* curse. **imprecación** *sf* curse. **imprecatorio** *adj* abusive.
impreciso [impre'θiso] *adj* imprecise.
imprecisión *sf* imprecision.
impregnar [impreg'nar] *v* impregnate; saturate. **impregnable** *adj* absorbent.
impregnación *sf* impregnation.
imprescindible [impresθin'diβle] *adj* indispensable.
impreso [im'preso] *adj* printed. **imprenta** *sf* press; printing. **impresión** *sf* impression; imprint; stamp; print; printing; edition. **impresionable** *adj* impressionable. **impresionar** *v* impress; shock. **impresionarse** *v* be deeply moved. **impresionismo** *sm* impressionism. **impresionista** *s(m+f)* impressionist. **impresor** *sm* printer.
imprevisto [impre'βisto] *adj* unexpected.
imprimir [impri'mir] *v* print; implant.
improbable [impro'βaβle] *adj* improbable. **improbabilidad** *sf* improbability.
ímprobo ['improβo] *adj* wicked; arduous.
improbidad *sf* dishonesty.
improcedente [improθe'ðente] *adj* improper; inappropriate; (*jur*) inadmissible. **improcedencia** *sf* impropriety; inappropriateness; (*jur*) inadmissibility.
improductivo [improduk'tiβo] *adj* unproductive.
impropio [im'propjo] *adj* improper; unbecoming. **impropiedad** *sf* impropriety.
impróvido [im'proβiðo] *adj* improvident.
improvidencia *sf* improvidence.
improvisar [improβi'sar] *v* improvise.
improvisación *sf* improvisation.
improvisto [impro'βisto] *adj* unforeseen.
a la improvista without warning.
imprudente [impru'ðente] *adj* imprudent.
imprudencia *sf* imprudence.
impúdico [im'puðiko] *adj* shameless, immodest.

impuesto [im'pwesto] *sm* tax; duty.

impugnar [impug'nar] *v* impugn; oppose; refute.

impulsar [impul'sar] *v* impel; drive; move. **impulsión** *sf* impulse; impetus. **impulso** *sm* impulse; drive; momentum.

impune [im'pune] *adj* unpunished. **impunidad** *sf* impunity.

impuro [im'puro] *adj* impure; lewd. **impureza** *sf* impurity; lewdness. **impurificación** *sf* defilement. **impurificar** *v* defile.

imputar [impu'tar] *v* impute; ascribe. **imputable** *adj* chargeable. **imputación** *sf* imputation; accusation.

inacabable [inaka'βaβle] *adj* endless.

inaccesible [inakθe'siβle] *adj* inaccessible. **inaccesibilidad** *sf* inaccessibility.

inaceptable [inaθep'taβle] *adj* unacceptable.

inacostumbrado [inakostum'braðo] *adj* unaccustomed.

inactivo [inak'tiβo] *adj* inactive. **inactividad** *sf* inactivity.

inadecuado [inaðe'kwaðo] *adj* inadequate. **inadecuación** *sf* inadequacy.

inadmisible [inaðmi'siβle] *adj* inadmissible.

inadvertido [inaðβer'tiðo] *adj* inadvertent. **inadvertencia** *sf* inadvertence; carelessness.

inagotable [inago'taβle] *adj* inexhaustible.

inaguantable [inagwan'taβle] *adj* unbearable.

inajenable [inaxe'naβle] *adj* inalienable.

inalterable [inalte'raβle] *adj* unalterable; imperturbable. **inalterabilidad** *sf* immutability; imperturbability. **inalterado** *adj* unchanged.

inanición [inani'θjon] *sf* starvation; weakness; exhaustion.

inanimado [inani'maðo] *adj* inanimate; lifeless.

inapagable [inapa'gaβle] *adj* unquenchable.

inaplicable [inapli'kaβle] *adj* inapplicable. **inaplicado** *adj* indolent.

inapreciable [inapre'θjaβle] *adj* priceless; invaluable.

inapto [in'apto] *adj* unsuitable; incapable.

inasequible [inase'kiβle] *adj* unattainable.

inaudible [inau'ðiβle] *adj* inaudible.

inaudito [inau'ðito] *adj* unheard of; outrageous.

inaugurar [inaugu'rar] *v* inaugurate. **inauguración** *sf* inauguration.

incalculable [inkalku'laβle] *adj* incalculable.

incandescente [inkandes'θente] *adj* incandescent. **incandescencia** *sf* incandescence.

incansable [inkan'saβle] *adj* indefatigable; untiring.

incapacitar [inkapaθi'tar] *v* incapacitate; disable; disqualify. **incapacidad** *sf* incapacity; incompetence; disability. **incapaz** *adj* unfit; incompetent.

incautarse [inkau'tarse] *v* (*jur*) confiscate. **incautación** *sf* confiscation.

incauto [in'kauto] *adj* incautious; gullible.

incendiar [inθen'djar] *v* set on fire. **incendiarse** *v* catch fire. **incendiario, -a** *sm, sf* arsonist. **incendiario** *adj* incendiary. **incendio** *sm* fire. **incendio provocado** arson.

incentivo [inθen'tiβo] *sm* incentive. **incentivar** *v* incite.

incertidumbre [inθerti'ðumbre] *sf* uncertainty.

incesante [inθe'sante] *adj* incessant.

incesto [in'θesto] *sm* incest. **incestuoso** *adj* incestuous.

incidente [inθi'ðente] *sm* incident. *adj* incidental. **incidencia** *sf* incident; incidence. **incidental** *adj* incidental.

incienso [in'θjenso] *sm* incense.

incierto [in'θjerto] *adj* uncertain; untrue.

incinerar [inθine'rar] *v* incinerate; cremate. **incineración** *sf* incineration; cremation.

incipiente [inθi'pjente] *adj* incipient.

incisivo [inθi'siβo] *adj* incisive; cutting. *sm* (*diente*) incisor. **incisión** *sf* incision, cut. **inciso** *adj* cut.

incitar [inθi'tar] *v* incite; instigate. **incitación** *sf* incitement; enticement. **incitador, -a** *sm, sf* instigator.

incivil [inθi'βil] *adj* uncivil, impolite.

inclemente [inkle'mente] *adj* inclement; harsh. **inclemencia** *sf* inclemency; harshness.

inclinar [inkli'nar] *v* incline; lean; influence; induce; lower. **inclinarse** *v* feel disposed; bow; stoop. **inclinación** *sf* inclination; leaning; slope; dip. **inclinado** *adj* inclined; sloping.

***incluir** [inklu'ir] *v* include. **inclusión** *sf* inclusion. **inclusivo** *adj* inclusive. **incluso** *adj* included; enclosed. **incluso** *adv* even.

incógnito [in'kognito] *adj* unknown. **de incógnito** incognito.

incoherente [inkoe'rente] *adj* incoherent. **incoherencia** *sf* incoherence.

incoloro [inko'loro] *adj* colourless.

incombustible [inkombus'tiβle] *adj* incombustible, fireproof.

incomodar [inkomo'ðar] *v* disturb, annoy, molest. **incomodidad** *sf* inconvenience; discomfort. **incómodo** *adj* uncomfortable; annoying.

incomparable [inkompa'raβle] *adj* incomparable.

incompatible [inkompa'tiβle] *adj* incompatible. **incompatibilidad** *sf* incompatibility.

incompetente [inkompe'tente] *adj* incompetent. **incompetencia** *sf* incompetence.

incompleto [inkom'pleto] *adj* incomplete. **incompletamente** *adv* incompletely.

incomprensible [inkompren'siβle] *adj* incomprehensible. **incomprensibilidad** *sf* incomprehensibility. **incomprensión** *sf* lack of understanding.

incomunicado [inkomuni'kaðo] *adj* isolated. **incomunicable** *adj* incommunicable. **incomunicación** *sf* isolation. **incomunicar** *v* isolate.

inconcebible [inkonθe'βiβle] *adj* inconceivable.

inconcluso [inkon'kluso] *adj* unfinished; inconclusive.

incondicional [inkondiθjo'nal] *adj* unconditional. *s(m+f)* staunch supporter.

inconfundible [inkonfun'diβle] *adj* unmistakable.

incongruente [inkongru'ente] *adj* incongruous; incongruent. **incongruencia** *sf* incongruousness; incongruity.

inconmensurable [inkonmensu'raβle] *adj* immeasurable.

inconmovible [inkonmo'βiβle] *adj* unshakable; firm.

inconsciente [inkons'θjente] *adj* unconscious; unaware; thoughtless. **inconsciencia** *sf* unconsciousness; unawareness; thoughtlessness.

inconsecuente [inkonse'kwente] *adj* inconsequential; inconsistent. **inconsecuencia** *sf* inconsistency.

inconsiderado [inkonsiðe'raðo] *adj* ill-considered. **inconsideración** *sf* inconsiderateness.

inconstante [inkon'stante] *adj* inconstant, fickle. **inconstancia** *sf* inconstancy, fickleness.

incontable [inkon'taβle] *adj* innumerable.

incontestable [inkontes'taβle] *adj* incontestable, indisputable.

incontinente [inkonti'nente] *adj* incontinent. **incontinencia** *sf* incontinence.

inconveniente [inkonβe'njente] *adj* inconvenient, impolite. *sm* objection; trouble; obstacle. **inconveniencia** *sf* inconvenience; impropriety; unsuitability.

incorporar [inkorpo'rar] *v* incorporate. **incorporarse** *v* sit up; become a member. **incorporación** *sf* incorporation. **incorporado** *adj* incorporated.

incorrecto [inkor'rekto] *adj* incorrect. **incorrección** *sf* inaccuracy. **incorregibilidad** *sf* incorrigibility. **incorregible** *adj* incorrigible.

incorrupto [inkor'rupto] *adj* incorrupt, pure. **incorruptible** *adj* incorruptible.

incrédulo [in'kreðulo] *adj* incredulous, sceptical. **incredulidad** *sf* incredulity, scepticism. **increíble** *adj* incredible.

incremento [inkre'mento] *sm* increase.

increpar [inkre'par] *v* reproach; rebuke. **increpación** *sf* rebuke.

incriminar [inkrimi'nar] *v* incriminate; exaggerate. **incriminación** *sf* incrimination.

incrustar [inkrus'tar] *v* encrust. **incrustación** *sf* encrustation.

incubar [inku'βar] *v* incubate; (*med*) be sickening for. **incubación** *sf* incubation. **incubadora** *sf* incubator.

inculcar [inkul'kar] *v* inculcate. **inculcarse** *v* be obstinate. **inculcación** *sf* inculcation.

inculpable [inkul'paβle] *adj* blameless. **inculpabilidad** *sf* blamelessness.

inculto [in'kulto] *adj* uncouth; uneducated. **incultura** *sf* lack of culture.

incumbencia [inkum'benθja] *sf* responsibility, duty. **incumbir** *v* be incumbent upon.

incurable [inku'raβle] *adj* incurable.

incurrir [inkur'rir] *v* incur; fall; commit.

incursión [inkur'sjon] *sf* incursion, raid.

indagar [inda'gar] *v* investigate. **indagación** *sf* investigation. **indagador, -a** *sm, sf* investigator.

indebido [inde'βiðo] *adj* unjust; improper.

indecente [inde'θente] *adj* indecent; foul; wretched. **indecencia** *sf* indecency; obscenity.

indecible [inde'θiβle] *adj* indescribable; unspeakable.

indecifrable [indeθi'fraβle] *adj* indecipherable.

indecisión [inde'θisjon] *sf* indecision. **indeciso** *adj* indecisive.

indecoroso [indeco'roso] *adj* indecorous. **indecoro** *sm* lack of propriety.

indefectible [indefek'tiβle] *adj* unfailing.

indefenso [inde'fenso] *adj* defenceless. **indefendible** *adj* indefensible.

indefinible [indefi'niβle] *adj* indefinable. **indefinido** *adj* indefinite.

indeleble [inde'leβle] *adj* indelible.

indelicado [indeli'kaðo] *adj* indelicate. **indelicadeza** *sf* indelicacy.

indemne [in'demne] *adj* unhurt. **indemnidad** *sf* indemnity. **indemnización** *sf* compensation. **indemnizar** *v* indemnify, compensate.

independencia [indepen'denθja] *sf* independence. **independiente** *adj* independent.

indescriptible [indescrip'tiβle] *adj* indescribable.

indeseable [indese'aβle] *adj* undesirable.

indestructible [indestruk'tiβle] *adj* indestructible. **indestructibilidad** *sf* indestructibility.

indeterminado [indetermi'naðo] *adj* indeterminate; undetermined.

India ['indja] *sf* India. **indio, -a** *s, adj* Indian.

indicar [indi'kar] *v* indicate; show; suggest. **indicación** *sf* indication. **indicado** *adj* suitable; recommended. **indicador** *sm* pointer; gauge. **indicativo** *adj* indicative. *sm* (*gram*) indicative.

índice ['indiθe] *sm* index.

indicio [in'diθjo] *sm* sign; trace. **indicios** *sm pl* (*jur*) evidence *sing*.

indiferencia [indife'renθja] *sf* indifference. **indiferente** *adj* indifferent.

indígena [in'dixena] *s(m + f), adj* native.

indigestión [indixes'tjon] *sf* indigestion. **indigestible** *adj* indigestible.

indignar [indig'nar] *v* anger, annoy. **indignarse** *v* become indignant. **indignación** *sf* indignation. **indignidad** *sf* indignity. **indigno** *adj* unworthy; disgraceful.

indirecta [indi'rekta] *sf* innuendo. **indirecto** *adj* indirect.

indisciplina [indisθi'plina] *sf* indiscipline. **indisciplinado** *adj* undisciplined.

indiscreción [indiskre'θjon] *sf* indiscretion. **indiscreto** *adj* indiscreet.

indisculpable [indiskul'paβle] *adj* inexcusable.

indiscutible [indisku'tiβle] *adj* unquestionable.

indisoluble [indiso'luβle] *adj* indissoluble.

indispensable [indispen'saβle] *adj* indispensable.

*indisponer [indispo'ner] *v* upset; render unfit. **indisponerse** *v* become ill. **indisposición** *sf* indisposition. **indispuesto** *adj* indisposed, poorly.

indisputable [indispu'taβle] *adj* indisputable.

indistinto [indis'tinto] *adj* indistinct; vague.

individual [indiβi'ðwal] *adj* individual. **individualidad** *sf* individuality. **individualismo** *sm* individualism. **individualista** *s(m + f)* individualist. **individualizar** *v* individualize. **individuo, -a** *sm, sf* individual.

indivisible [indiβi'siβle] *adj* indivisible. **indiviso** *adj* undivided.

índole ['indole] *sf* nature.

indolente [indo'lente] *adj* indolent; painless. **indolencia** *sf* indolence; painlessness.

indómito [in'domito] *adj* untamed; indomitable.

indubitable [induβi'taβle] *adj* indubitable.

*inducir [indu'θir] *v* persuade; lead; infer. **inducción** *sf* induction. **inducimiento** *sm* inducement.

indudable [indu'ðaβle] *adj* unquestionable.

indulgente [indul'xente] *adj* indulgent. **indulgencia** *sf* indulgence.

indultar [indul'tar] *v* pardon; excuse. **indulto** *sm* mercy; reprieve; exemption.

indumento [indu'mento] *sm* apparel.

industria [in'dustrja] *sf* industry; business; ingenuity. **de industria** on purpose. **industrial** *adj* industrial. **industrial** *sm* industrialist. **industrialismo** *sm* industrialism. **industrializar** *v* industrialize. **industrioso** *adj* industrious.

inédito [i'neðito] *adj* unpublished.

inefable [ine'faβle] *adj* ineffable.

ineficaz [inefi'kaθ] *adj* inefficient. **eficacia** *sf* inefficiency.

ineludible [inelu'ðiβle] *adj* inevitable.

inepto [i'nepto] *adj* inept. **ineptitud** *sf* ineptitude.

inequívoco [ineˈkiβoko] *adj* unmistakable.
inercia [iˈnerθja] *sf* inertia; lifelessness.
inerme [iˈnerme] *adj* unarmed.
inerte [iˈnerte] *adj* inert.
inesperado [inespeˈraðo] *adj* unexpected, unforeseen.
inestable [inesˈtaβle] *adj* unstable. **inestabilidad** *sf* instability.
inestimable [inestiˈmaβle] *adj* invaluable.
inevitable [ineβiˈtaβle] *adj* inevitable.
inexacto [inekˈsakto] *adj* inaccurate. **inexactitud** *sf* inaccuracy.
inexcusable [inekskuˈsaβle] *adj* inexcusable; essential.
inexorable [ineksoˈraβle] *adj* inexorable.
inexperto [ineksˈperto] *adj* inexperienced.
inexplicable [inekspliˈkaβle] *adj* inexplicable.
infalible [infaˈliβle] *adj* infallible. **infalibilidad** *sf* infallibility.
infamar [infaˈmar] *v* dishonour. **infamación** *sf* defamation. **infame** *adj* infamous. **infamia** *sf* infamy.
infante [inˈfante] *sm*, *adj* infant. *sm* prince. **infancia** *sf* infancy. **infantil** *adj* infantile.
infantería [infanteˈria] *sf* infantry.
infatigable [infatiˈgaβle] *adj* indefatigable.
infausto [inˈfausto] *adj* ill-omened; ill-famed.
infectar [infekˈtar] *v* infect. **infección** *sf* infection. **infeccioso** *adj* infectious.
infeliz [infeˈliθ] *adj* unhappy. *s(m+f)* luckless person.
inferior [infeˈrjor] *adj* inferior; lower. *sm* inferior. **inferioridad** *sf* inferiority.
inferir [infeˈrir] *v* infer; inflict. **inferirse** *v* follow.
infernal [inferˈnal] *adj* infernal.
infestar [infesˈtar] *v* infest; overrun. **infestación** *sf* infestation.
infiel [inˈfjel] *adj* unfaithful. *s(m+f)* infidel.
infierno [inˈfjerno] *sm* hell.
ínfimo [ˈinfimo] *adj* lowest; vilest.
infinito [infiˈnito] *adj* infinite. **infinidad** *sf* infinity. **infinitivo** *sm* (*gram*) infinitive.
inflamar [inflaˈmar] *v* inflame. **inflamable** *adj* inflammable. **inflamación** *sf* inflammation.
inflar [inˈflar] *v* inflate. **inflación** *sf* inflation; swelling.
inflexible [inflekˈsiβle] *adj* inflexible. **inflexibilidad** *sf* inflexibility.
infligir [infliˈxir] *v* inflict.

*influir** [influˈir] *v* influence; affect. **influencia** *sf* influence; authority. **influente** *adj* *also* **influyente** influential. **influjo** *sm* influence; flood.
informal [inforˈmal] *adj* informal; unreliable. **informalidad** *sf* informality; unreliability.
informar [inforˈmar] *v* inform; notify. **informarse** *v* find out. **información** *sf* information; judicial inquiry. **informador, -a** *sm, sf* informant. **informe** *sm* report; testimonial. **informe** *adj* shapeless.
infortunio [inforˈtunjo] *sm* misfortune. **infortunado** *adj* unfortunate.
infracción [infrakˈθjon] *sf* breach; infringement. **infractor, -a** *sm, sf* transgressor.
infranqueable [infrankeˈaβle] *adj* impassable; insurmountable.
infringir [infrinˈxir] *v* infringe; violate.
infructuoso [infrukˈtwoso] *adj* fruitless.
infundado [infunˈdaðo] *adj* unfounded.
infundir [infunˈdir] *v* instil. **infusión** *sf* inspiration.
ingeniería [inxenjeˈria] *sf* engineering. **ingeniero** *sm* engineer.
ingenio [inˈxenjo] *sm* talent; wit; ingenuity; device. **ingeniosidad** *sf* ingenuity. **ingenioso** *adj* ingenious.
ingenuo [inˈxenwo] *adj* naïve; frank; simple. **ingenuidad** *sf* frankness; credulity.
*ingerir** [inxeˈrir] *v* (*comida*) consume. **ingerirse** *v* meddle. **ingerencia** *sf* interference.
Inglaterra [inglaˈterra] *sf* England. **inglés** *adj* English; *sm* Englishman; (*idioma*) English. **inglesa** *sf* Englishwoman.
ingrato [inˈgrato] *adj* ungrateful; unpleasant. **ingratitud** *sf* ingratitude.
ingrediente [ingreˈðjente] *sm* ingredient.
ingresar [ingreˈsar] *v* enter; join; (*hospital*) be admitted; (*dinero*) deposit. **ingreso** *sm* entrance; (*com*) deposit; admission. **derecho de ingreso** *sm* entrance fee.
inhábil [iˈnaβil] *adj* incompetent; tactless. **día inhábil** non-working day. **inhabilidad** *sf* incompetence; inability. **inhabilitar** *v* disqualify; disable.
inhabitable [inaβiˈtaβle] *adj* uninhabitable. **inhabitado** *adj* uninhabited.
inhalar [inaˈlar] *v* inhale. **inhalación** *sf* inhalation.

inherente [ine'rente] *adj* inherent. **inherencia** *sf* inherence.
inhibir [ini'βir] *v* inhibit. **inhibirse** *v* refrain. **inhibición** *sf* inhibition. **inhibitorio** *adj* inhibitive.
inhospitalario [inospita'larjo] *adj* inhospitable. **inhospitalidad** *sf* inhospitableness.
inhumano [inu'mano] *adj* inhuman. **inhumanidad** *sf* inhumanity.
inhumar [inu'mar] *v* bury.
inicial [ini'θjal] *adj*, *sf* initial. **iniciación** *sf* initiation. **iniciado, -a** *sm*, *sf* initiate. **iniciador, -a** *sm*, *sf* initiator. **iniciar** *v* initiate. **iniciativa** *sf* initiative.
inicuo [i'nikwo] *adj* wicked. **iniquidad** *sf* iniquity.
injertar [inxer'tar] *v* graft. **injerto** *sm* graft, grafting.
injuriar [inxuri'ar] *v* insult; damage; injure. **injuria** *sf* offence; harm. **injuriador** *adj* offensive. **injurioso** *adj* insulting.
injusticia [inxus'tiθja] *sf* injustice. **injusto** *adj* unjust.
inmediato [inme'ðjato] *adj* immediate. **de inmediato** immediately.
inmejorable [inmexo'raβle] *adj* unsurpassable.
inmemorial [inmemo'rjal] *adj* immemorial.
inmenso [in'menso] *adj* immense.
inmerecido [inmere'θiðo] *adj* undeserved.
inmigrar [inmi'grar] *v* immigrate. **inmigración** *sf* immigration. **inmigrante** *s(m+f)*, *adj* immigrant.
inminente [inmi'nente] *adj* imminent. **inminencia** *sf* imminence.
inmoderado [inmoðe'raðo] *adj* excessive. **inmoderación** *sf* excess.
inmodestia [inmodes'tia] *sf* immodesty. **inmodesto** *adj* immodest.
inmolar [inmo'lar] *v* sacrifice. **inmolación** *sf* sacrifice.
inmoral [inmo'ral] *adj* immoral. **inmoralidad** *sf* immorality.
inmortal [inmor'tal] *adj*, *s(m+f)* immortal. **inmortalidad** *sf* immortality. **inmortalizar** *v* immortalize.
inmóvil [in'moβil] *adj* motionless. **inmovible** *adj* immovable. **inmovilidad** *sf* immobility. **inmovilizar** *v* immobilize.
inmueble [in'mweβle] *sm* property; real estate.
inmundo [in'mundo] *adj* filthy; impure. **inmundicia** *sf* filth; impurity.

inmune [in'mune] *adj* immune; exempt. **inmunidad** *sf* immunity; exemption. **inmunización** *sf* immunization. **inmunizar** *v* immunize.
inmutar [inmu'tar] *v* change. **inmutarse** *v* change one's expression. **inmutabilidad** *sf* immutability. **inmutable** *adj* immutable.
innato [in'nato] *adj* innate.
innecesario [inneθe'sarjo] *adj* unnecessary.
innegable [in'negaβle] *adj* undeniable.
innoble [in'noβle] *adj* ignoble.
innocuo [in'nokwo] *adj* also **inocuo** innocuous.
innovar [inno'βar] *v* innovate. **innovación** *sf* innovation. **innovador, -a** *sm*, *sf* innovator. **innovador** *adj* innovative. **innovamiento** *sm* innovation.
innumerable [innume'raβle] *adj* innumerable.
inobediente [inoβe'ðjente] *adj* disobedient. **inobediencia** *sf* disobedience.
inocente [ino'θente] *adj* innocent. **innocencia** *sf* innocence.
inocular [inoku'lar] *v* inoculate; contaminate. **inoculación** *sf* inoculation.
inodoro [ino'ðoro] *adj* odourless.
inofensivo [inofen'siβo] *adj* harmless.
inolvidable [inolβi'ðaβle] *adj* unforgettable.
inoperable [inope'raβle] *adj* inoperable.
inopinado [inopi'naðo] *adj* unexpected.
inoportuno [inopor'tuno] *adj* inopportune.
inoxidable [inoksi'ðaβle] *adj* rustless; stainless. **acero inoxidable** *sm* stainless steel.
inquebrantable [inkeβran'taβle] *adj* unbreakable; unyielding.
inquietar [inkje'tar] *v* disturb; disquiet. **inquietador** *adj* disquieting. **inquietante** *adj* disquieting. **inquieto** *adj* restless. **inquietud** *sf* restlessness.
inquilino [inki'lino], **-a** *sm*, *sf* tenant. **inquilinato** *sm* lease.
***inquirir** [inki'rir] *v* investigate; examine. **inquiridor, -a** *sm*, *sf* inquirer. **inquisición** *sf* inquisition; inquiry. **inquisidor** *sm* inquisitor. **inquisitivo** *adj* inquisitive.
insaciable [insa'θjaβle] *adj* insatiable.
insalubre [insa'luβre] *adj* unhealthy. **insalubridad** *sf* unhealthiness.
insanable [insa'naβle] *adj* incurable.

insano [in'sano] *adj* insane; unhealthy. **insania** *sf* insanity.

inscribir [inskri'βir] *v* inscribe; register. **inscripción** *sf* inscription; registration.

insecto [in'sekto] *sm* insect. **insecticida** *sm* insecticide. **insectólogo, -a** *sm, sf* entomologist.

inseguro [inse'guro] *adj* insecure; unsafe; uncertain. **inseguridad** *sf* insecurity; uncertainty.

insensato [insen'sato] *adj* senseless; wild. **insensatez** *sf* folly.

insensible [insen'siβle] *adj* insensible; insensitive; imperceptible. **insensibilidad** *sf* insensibility; insensitiveness.

insertar [inser'tar] *v* insert. **inserto** *sm* insertion.

inservible [inser'βiβle] *adj* useless.

insidioso [insi'ðjoso] *adj* insidious.

insigne [in'signe] *adj* illustrious, distinguished.

insignia [in'signja] *sf* badge; banner. **insignias** *sf pl* insignia.

insignificante [insignifi'kante] *adj* insignificant. **insignificancia** *sf* insignificance.

insincero [insin'θero] *adj* insincere. **insinceridad** *sf* insincerity.

insinuar [insinu'ar] *v* insinuate, suggest. **insinuarse** *v* work one's way (into); make advances. **insinuación** *sf* insinuation; suggestiveness. **insinuante** *adj* insinuating; suggestive.

insípido [in'sipiðo] *adj* insipid, tasteless. **insipidez** *sf* tastelessness.

insistir [insis'tir] *v* insist; persist. **insistencia** *sf* insistence; persistence. **insistente** *adj* insistent; persistent.

insociable [inso'θjaβle] *adj* unsociable. **insociabilidad** *sf* unsociability, unsociableness.

insolación [insola'θjon] *sf* sunstroke. **insolar** *v* expose to the sun. **insolarse** *v* get sunstroke.

insolente [inso'lente] *adj* insolent. **insolencia** *sf* insolence.

insólito [in'solito] *adj* unusual.

insolvente [insol'βente] *adj* insolvent, penniless. **insoluble** *adj* insoluble. **insolvencia** *sf* insolvency.

insomne [in'somne] *s(m + f)*, *adj* insomniac. **insomnio** *sm* insomnia.

insondable [inson'daβle] *adj* unfathomable.

insoportable [insopor'taβle] *adj* intolerable.

inspeccionar [inspekθjo'nar] *v* inspect. **inspección** *sf* inspection. **inspector, -a** *sm, sf* inspector.

inspirar [inspi'rar] *v* inhale; inspire. **inspiración** *sf* inhalation; inspiration. **inspirador** *adj* inspirational.

instable [in'staβle] *adj* unstable. **instabilidad** *sf* instability.

instalar [insta'lar] *v* install; establish. **instalación** *sf* installation; (*fábrica*) plant. **instalador** *sm* fitter.

instancia [instan'θja] *sf* petition; application form.

instante [in'stante] *sm* instant; moment. *adj* insistent. **instantánea** *sf* snapshot. **instantáneo** *adj* instantaneous. **instantemente** *adv* insistently.

instaurar [instau'rar] *v* set up; restore. **instauración** *sf* restoration. **instaurativo** *adj* restorative.

instigar [insti'gar] *v* instigate; incite. **instigación** *sf* instigation. **instigador, -a** *sm, sf* instigator.

instintivo [instin'tiβo] *adj* instinctive. **instinto** *sm* instinct.

*****instituir** [institu'ir] *v* institute. **institución** *sf* institution. **instituto** *sm* institute; state secondary school.

*****instruir** [instru'ir] *v* instruct. **instrucción** *sf* instruction; education; knowledge. **instructivo** *adj* instructive. **instructor, -a** *sm, sf* instructor. **instruido** *adj* educated.

instrumento [instru'mento] *sm* instrument. **instrumentación** *sf* orchestration. **instrumental** *adj* instrumental. **instrumentar** *v* orchestrate. **instrumentista** *s(m + f)* instrumentalist; instrument-maker.

insubordinar [insuβorði'nar] *v* incite to rebellion. **insubordinarse** *v* rebel. **insubordinación** *sf* insubordination. **insubordinado** *adj* insubordinate.

insubstancial [insuβstan'θjal] *adj* insubstantial.

insuficiente [insufi'θjente] *adj* insufficient; inadequate. **insuficiencia** *sf* insufficiency; inadequacy.

insufrible [insu'friβle] *adj* insufferable.

insular [insu'lar] *adj* insular.

insulso [in'sulso] *adj* dull; tasteless. **insulsez** *sf* tastelessness.

insultar [insul'tar] *v* insult. **insultador** *adj* also **insultante** insulting. **insulto** *sm* insult.

insuperable [insupe'raβle] adj insuperable.

insurgente [insur'xente] s(m+f) rebel. adj rebellious. **insurrección** sf rebellion.

insurreccionarse v rebel. **insurrecto, -a** s, adj insurgent.

intacto [in'takto] adj intact.

intachable [inta'tʃaβle] adj irreproachable.

intangible [intan'xiβle] adj intangible. **intangibilidad** sf intangibility.

integrar [inte'grar] v integrate; compose; complete; repay. **integración** sf integration. **integral** adj integral. **pan integral** sm wholemeal bread. **integrante** adj integral. **integridad** sf integrity. **integro** adj entire, whole.

intelecto [inte'lekto] sm intellect. **intelectual** s(m+f), adj intellectual. **intelectualidad** sf intelligentsia. **intelectualismo** sm intellectualism.

inteligente [inteli'xente] adj intelligent. **inteligencia** sf intelligence; knowledge; comprehension. **inteligibilidad** sf intelligibility. **inteligible** adj intelligible.

intemperante [intempe'rante] adj intemperate. **intemperancia** sf intemperance.

intemperie [intem'perje] sf bad weather. **estar a la intemperie** be out in the open.

intempestivo [intempes'tiβo] adj inopportune.

intención [inten'θjon] sf intention. **primera intención** frankness. **segunda intención** duplicity. **intencionadamente** adv deliberately. **intencionado** adj deliberate. **intencional** adj intentional.

intenso [in'tenso] adj intense. **intensidad** sf intensity. **intensificar** v intensify. **intensión** sf intensity. **intensivo** adj intensive.

intentar [inten'tar] v try. **intento** sm attempt.

intercalar [interka'lar] v insert.

intercambio [inter'kambjo] sm interchange. **intercambiar** v interchange, exchange. **intercambiable** adj interchangeable.

interceder [interθe'ðer] v intercede. **intercesión** sf intercession.

interceptar [interθep'tar] v intercept; block. **intercepción** sf interception.

interdecir [interðe'θir] v prohibit. **interdicción** sf also **interdicto** sm prohibition.

interesar [intere'sar] v interest. **interés** sm interest. **llevar interés** bear interest. **interesante** adj interesting.

*****interferir** [interfe'rir] v interfere. **interferencia** sf interference.

íntertin ['interin] sm interim. **interino** adj provisional; acting.

interior [inte'rjor] adj interior; internal; inner; home. sm interior; inside; inland.

interjección [interxek'θjon] sf interjection.

intermedio [inter'meðjo] sm interval; interlude. adj intermediate. **intermediar** v mediate. **intermediario, -a** s, adj intermediary.

interminable [intermi'naβle] adj interminable.

intermisión [intermi'sjon] sf intermission.

intermitente [intermi'tente] adj intermittent.

internacional [internaθjo'nal] adj international. **internacionalismo** sm internationalism. **internacionalista** s(m+f) internationalist.

internar [inter'nar] v intern; confine. **internarse** v penetrate; intrude. **internamiento** sm internment. **interno** adj internal; domestic. **escuela interna** sf boarding school.

interpelar [interpe'lar] v appeal to, implore. **interpelación** sf appeal.

*****interponer** [interpo'ner] v interpose. **interponerse** v intervene. **interposición** sf intervention; (jur) lodging of an appeal.

interpretar [interpre'tar] v interpret. **interpretación** sf interpretation. **intérprete** s(m+f) interpreter.

interrogar [interro'gar] v question. **interrogación** sf question; question mark. **interrogativo** adj interrogative. **interrogatorio** sm interrogation.

interrumpir [interrum'pir] v interrupt. **interrupción** sf interruption. **interruptor** sm electrical switch.

intervalo [inter'βalo] sm interval; gap.

*****intervenir** [interβe'nir] v intervene; interfere; participate; happen; control; (med) operate on; (com) audit. **intervención** sf intervention; control; operation; audit. **interventor** sm auditor; inspector; supervisor.

intestado [intes'taðo] adj intestate.

intestino [intes'tino] adj internal. sm intestine. **intestinal** adj intestinal.

intimar [inti'mar] v intimate; become close friends. **intimación** sf declaration.

intimidad *sf* intimacy. **en la intimidad** privately. **íntimo** *adj* intimate.

intimidar [intimi'ðar] *v* intimidate. **intimidación** *sf* intimidation.

intolerable [intole'raβle] *adj* intolerable. **intolerancia** *sf* intolerance. **intolerante** *adj* intolerant.

intoxicar [intoksi'kar] *v* poison. **intoxicación** *sf* poisoning.

intraducible [intraðu'θiβle] *adj* untranslatable.

intranquilo [intran'kilo] *adj* restless. **intranquilidad** *sf* restlessness.

intransigente [intransi'xente] *adj* intransigent. **intransigencia** *sf* intransigence.

intransitable [intransi'taβle] *adj* impassable.

intransitivo [intransi'tiβo] *adj* (*gram*) intransitive.

intratable [intra'taβle] *adj* intractable; unsociable.

intrépido [in'trepiðo] *adj* brave. **intrepidez** *sf* valour.

intrigar [intri'gar] *v* intrigue. **intriga** *sf* intrigue. **intrigante** *adj* intriguing.

intrincado [intrin'kaðo] *adj* intricate; entangled.

intrínseco [in'trinseko] *adj* intrinsic.

***introducir** [introðu'θir] *v* introduce. **introducción** *sf* introduction. **introductor** *adj* introductory.

intruso [in'truso], **-a** *sm*, *sf* intruder. *adj* intrusive. **intrusarse** *v* intrude. **intrusión** *sf* intrusion.

intuición [intwi'θjon] *sf* intuition. **intuir** *v* feel; sense. **intuitivo** *adj* intuitive.

inundar [inun'dar] *v* flood. **inundación** *sf* flood. **inundante** *adj* flooding.

inusitado [inusi'taðo] *adj* unusual.

inútil [i'nutil] *adj* useless. **inutilidad** *sf* uselessness. **inutilizar** *v* render useless.

invadir [inβa'ðir] *v* invade. **invasión** *sf* invasion. **invasor**, **-a** *sm*, *sf* invader.

invalidar [inβali'ðar] *v* invalidate. **invalidación** *sf* invalidity. **inválido**, **-a** *sm*, *sf* invalid. *adj* invalid, void.

invariable [inva'rjaβle] *adj* invariable.

invencible [inβen'θiβle] *adj* invincible. **invencibilidad** *sf* invincibility.

inventar [inβen'tar] *v* invent. **invención** *sf* invention. **inventivo** *adj* inventive. **invento** *sm* invention. **inventor**, **-a** *sm*, *sf* inventor.

inventario [inβen'tarjo] *sm* inventory.

invernáculo [inβer'nakulo] *sm* also **invernadero** greenhouse. hothouse.

***invernar** [inβer'nar] *v* winter; hibernate. **invernada** *sf* winter; hibernation. **invernal** *adj* wintry.

inverosímil [inβero'simil] *adj* improbable. **inverosimilitud** *sf* improbability.

invertebrado [inβerte'βraðo] *sm*, *adj* invertebrate.

***invertir** [inβer'tir] *v* invert; (*com*) invest. **inversión** *sf* inversion; investment. **inverso** *adj* inverse, inverted. **por la inversa** the other way round.

investigar [inβesti'gar] *v* investigate. **investigación** *sf* investigation. **investigador**, **-a** *sm*, *sf* investigator; researcher.

***investir** [inβes'tir] *v* invest; confer upon. **investidura** *sf* investiture.

inveterado [inβete'raðo] *adj* inveterate, confirmed.

invicto [in'βikto] *adj* undefeated.

invierno [in'βjerno] *sm* winter.

inviolable [inβjo'laβle] *adj* inviolable. **inviolado** *adj* inviolate.

invisible [inβi'siβle] *adj* invisible. **invisibilidad** *sf* invisibility.

invitar [inβi'tar] *v* invite; call on. **invitar a una copa** stand a drink. **invitación** *sf* invitation. **invitado**, **-a** *sm*, *sf* guest.

invocar [inβo'kar] *v* invoke. **invocación** *sf* invocation.

involuntario [inβolun'tarjo] *adj* involuntary.

invulnerable [inβulne'raβle] *adj* invulnerable. **invulnerabilidad** *sf* invulnerability.

inyectar [injek'tar] *v* inject. **inyección** *sf* injection. **inyectado** *adj* congested.

***ir** [ir] *v* go; walk; come; suit. **irse** *v* go away. **ir a medias** go halves. **ir tirando** get by.

ira ['ira] *sf* anger. **iracundia** *sf* wrath. **iracundo** *adj* wrathful.

iris ['iris] *sm* (*anat*) iris. **arco iris** *sm* rainbow.

Irlanda [ir'landa] *sf* Ireland. **irlandés** *adj* Irish. *sm* Irishman; (*idioma*) Irish. **irlandesa** *sf* Irishwoman.

ironía [iro'nia] *sf* irony. **irónico** *adj* ironic(al).

irracional [irraθjo'nal] *adj* irrational. **irracionalidad** *sf* irrationality.

irradiar [irra'ðjar] *v* irradiate, radiate. **irradiación** *sf* irradiation.

irrazonable [irraθo'naβle] *adj* unreasonable.

irreal [irre'al] *adj* unreal. **irrealidad** *sf* unreality.

irreconciliable [irrekonθi'ljaβle] *adj* irreconcilable.

irrecuperable [irrekupe'raβle] *adj* irretrievable.

irreemplazable [irreempla'θaβle] *adj* irreplaceable.

irreflexión [irreflek'sjon] *sf* hastiness; thoughtlessness. **irreflexivo** hasty; thoughtless.

irrefrenable [irrefre'naβle] *adj* uncontrollable.

irrefutable [irrefu'taβle] *adj* irrefutable.

irregular [irregu'lar] *adj* irregular. **irregularidad** *sf* irregularity.

irreligioso [irreli'xjoso] *adj* irreligious.

irremediable [irreme'ðjaβle] *adj* incurable.

irreprimible [irrepri'miβle] *adj* irrepressible.

irresistible [irresis'tiβle] *adj* irresistible.

irresoluto [irreso'luto] *adj* irresolute. **irresoluble** *adj* unsolvable. **irresolución** *sf* irresolution, indecision.

irrespetuoso [irrespe'twoso] *adj* disrespectful.

irresponsable [irrespon'saβle] *adj* irresponsible. **irresponsabilidad** *sf* irresponsibility.

irrigar [irri'gar] *v* irrigate. **irrigación** *sf* irrigation. **irrigador** *sm* sprinkler.

irritable [irri'taβle] *adj* irritable. **irritabilidad** *sf* irritability. **irritación** *sf* irritation. **irritante** *sm, adj* irritant. **irritar** *v* irritate.

isla ['isla] *sf* island. **en isla** isolated. **isleño. -a** *sm, sf* islander.

Islandia [is'landja] *sf* Iceland. **islandés, -esa** *sm, sf* Icelander; *sm* (*idioma*) Icelandic. **islandés** *adj* Icelandic.

istmo ['istmo] *sm* isthmus.

Italia [i'talja] *sf* Italy. **italiano, -a** *s, adj* Italian.

itinerario [itine'rarjo] *sm* itinerary.

izar [i'θar] *v* hoist.

izquierda [iθ'kjerða] *sf* left; left hand; left wing. **mantenerse a la izquierda** keep left. **izquierdo** *adj* left; left-handed.

J

jabalí [xaβa'li] *sm* wild boar.

jabalina [xaβa'lina] *sf* javelin; (*zool*) wild sow.

jabón [xa'βon] *sm* soap. **jabón de tocador** toilet soap. **jabonar** *v* soap. **jabonera** *sf* soap-dish. **jabonoso** *adj* soapy.

jaca ['xaka] *sf* pony.

jacinto [xa'θinto] *sm* hyacinth.

jactarse [xak'tarse] *v* boast. **jactancia** *sf* boasting. **jactancioso** *adj* boastful.

jadear [xaðe'ar] *v* pant. **jadeante** *adj* panting. **jadeo** *sm* pant; panting.

jalear [xale'ar] *v* urge on. **jaleo** *sm* row, din. **armar un jaleo** start a row.

jamás [xa'mas] *adv* never. **nunca jamás** never ever.

jamón [xa'mon] *sm* ham. **jamón serrano** cured ham.

Japón [xa'pon] *sm* Japan. **japonés** *s(m+f)*, *adj* Japanese.

jaque ['xake] *sm* (*ajedrez*) check.

jaqueca [xa'keka] *sf* migraine. **dar jaqueca a** (*fam*) pester.

jarabe [xa'raβe] *sm* syrup.

jarana [xa'rana] *sf* spree; rumpus; trick. **dar jarabe a uno** (*fam*) butter someone up.

jardín [xar'ðin] *sm* garden. **jardinería** *sf* gardening. **jardinero, -a** *sm, sf* gardener.

jarra ['xarra] *sf* jug, pitcher. **jarro** *sm* jug; jar. **jarrón** *sm* vase.

jaula ['xaula] *sf* cage; crate; playpen.

jazmín [xaθ'min] *sm* jasmine.

jefe ['xefe] *sm* chief; head; leader. **jefa** *sf* head; manageress. **jefatura** *sf* leadership; managership; chieftaincy. **jefatura de policía** police headquarters.

jengibre [xen'xiβre] *sm* ginger.

jeque ['xeke] *sm* sheikh.

jerarquía [xerar'kia] *sf* hierarchy. **jerárquico** *adj* hierarchical.

jerez [xe'reθ] *sm* sherry.

jerga ['xerga] *sf* also **jerigonza** jargon.

jeringa [xe'ringa] *sf* syringe. **jeringar** *v* syringe; (*fam*) annoy.

jeroglífico [xero'glifiko] *s, adj* hieroglyphic.

jersey [xer'sei] *sm* jersey.

jesuita [xesu'ita] *sm, adj* Jesuit. **jesuítico** *adj* jesuitical.

jeta ['xeta] *sf* snout; thick lips; (*fam*) face, mug. **poner jeta** pull a face.

jilguero [xil'gero] *sm* goldfinch.

jinete [xi'nete] *sm* horseman; saddle horse; thoroughbred horse. **jinetear** *v* ride on horseback.

jirafa [xi'rafa] *sf* giraffe.

jocoso [xo'koso] *adj* amusing. **jocosidad** *sf* humour.

jofaina [xo'faina] *sf* washbowl.

jornada [xor'nada] *sf* journey; working day; session; expedition; (*teatro*) act. **al fin de la jornada** at the end of the day. **jornal** *sm* day's wage. **jornalero** *sm* day labourer.

joroba [xo'roβa] *sf* hump; (*fam*) pest. **jorobado, -a** *s, adj* hunchback.

jota ['xota] *sf* letter *j*; jot; Spanish dance.

joven ['xoβen] *adj* young. **jovenes** *s(m+f) pl* youth.

joya ['xoja] *sf* jewel. **joyería** *sf* jewellery. **joyero** *sm* jeweller.

jubilar [xuβi'lar] *v* retire; pension off. **jubilarse** *v* retire; rejoice. **jubilación** *sf* pension; retirement; jubilation.

jubileo [xuβi'leo] *sm* jubilee; comings and goings *pl*.

júbilo ['xuβilo] *sm* jubilation, rejoicing. **jubiloso** *adj* jubilant.

judía [xu'δia] *sf* bean. **judía blanca** haricot bean. **judía escarlata** runner bean. **judía verde** French bean.

judicial [xuδi'θjal] *adj* judicial. **judicatura** *sf* judicature.

judío [xu'δio], **-a** *sm, sf* Jew. *adj* Jewish. **judaico** *adj* Jewish. **judaismo** *sm* Judaism.

juego ['xwego] *sm* game; sport; gambling; play; (*platos, tazas, etc.*) set; service.

juerga ['xwerga] *sf* (*fam*) spree, binge. **juergista** *s(m+f)* reveller.

jueves ['xweβes] *sm* Thursday.

juez [xweθ] *sm* judge, justice. **juez de hecho** juror.

***jugar** [xu'gar] *v* play; bet; gamble. **jugarse** *v* bet; risk. **jugada** move; throw; stroke; shot; play. **mala jugada** dirty trick. **jugador, -a** *sm, sf* player; gambler.

juglar [xu'glar], **-a** *sm, sf* minstrel.

jugo ['xugo] *sm* juice; sap. **jugoso** *adj* juicy.

juguete [xu'gete] *sm* toy; plaything. **juguetear** *v* frolic. **jugueteo** *sm* frolicking. **juguetería** *sf* toyshop.

juicio ['xwiθjo] *sm* (*jur*) trial; judgment;

opinion; sense. **a juicio de** in the opinion of. **perder el juicio** lose one's mind. **juicioso** *adj* judicious.

julio ['xuljo] *sm* July.

jumento [xu'mento] *sm* ass.

junco[1] ['xunko] *sm* (*bot*) reed.

junco[2] *sm* (*mar*) junk.

jungla ['xungla] *sf* jungle.

junio ['xunjo] *sm* June.

junquera [xun'kera] *sf* (*bot*) rush.

junquillo [xun'kiʎo] *sm* (*bot*) jonquil.

juntar [xun'tar] *v* join; assemble; unite; collect. **juntarse** *v* meet; join; gather; live together. **junta** *sf* meeting; session; board; council; junta. **junto** *adj* joined, united, together. *adv* **junto a** near. **muy junto** very close.

juramentar [xuramen'tar] *v* swear in. **juramentarse** *v* take an oath. **jura** *sf* oath; swearing. **jurado** *adj* sworn; *sm* jury. **jurado de cuentas** chartered accountant. **juramento** *sm* oath; curse. **juramento falso** perjury. **jurar** *v* swear. **jurar al cargo** take the oath of office.

jurídico [xu'riδiko] *adj* juridical, legal.

jurisconsulto [xuriskon'sulto] *sm* legal expert. **jurisdicción** *sf* jurisdiction. **jurisprudencia** *sf* jurisprudence. **jurista** *sm* jurist, lawyer.

justa ['xusta] *sf* joust; contest.

justificar [xustifi'kar] *v* justify. **justificarse** *v* clear oneself. **justamente** *adv* justly; exactly. **¡justamente!** precisely! **justicia** *sf* justice; execution. **justiciable** *adj* actionable. **justiciero** *adj* just. **justificable** *adj* justifiable. **justificación** *sf* justification. **justificado** *adj* justified.

justo ['xusto] *adj* just; lawful; precise. *adv* exactly; tightly.

juvenil [xuβe'nil] *adj* youthful. *s(m+f)* junior. **juventud** *sf* youth.

juzgar [xuθ'gar] *v* judge; consider. **juzgar mal** misjudge. **juzgado** *sm* court.

K

kaki ['kaki] *sm, adj* khaki.

kilo ['kilo] *sm* kilo.

kilogramo [kilo'gramo] *sm* kilogramme.

kilolitro [kilo'litro] *sm* kilolitre.

kilómetro [ki'lometro] *sm* kilometre.
kilométrico *adj* kilometric.
kilovatio [kilo'βatjo] *sm* kilowatt.
kiosco ['kjosko] *sm* kiosk.

L

la [la] *art f* the. *pron* her, it.
laberinto [laβe'rinto] *sm* labyrinth; maze.
labio ['laβjo] *sm* lip. **labial** *adj* labial.
labor [la'βor] *sf* work; labour. **laborador** *sm* worker; farmer. **laborar** *v* work; till.
laborear *v* work; till; mine. **laboreo** *sm* working; tilling; mining. **laborioso** *adj* industrious; laborious. **laborismo** *sm* (*pol*) Labour party. **laborista** *s(m+f)* Labour-party member.
laboratorio [laβora'torjo] *sm* laboratory.
labrar [la'βrar] *v* fashion; carve; work; cultivate; build; bring about. **labrador** *adj* workable; arable. **labrador, -a** *sm, sf* peasant. **labranza** *sf* farming; farmland. **labriego** *sm* peasant; farmhand.
laburno [la'βurno] *sm* laburnum.
laca ['laka] *sf* lacquer, varnish.
lacayo [la'kajo] *sm* lackey.
lacerar [laθe'rar] *v* lacerate; harm; (*fruta*) damage. **laceración** *sf* laceration; damage.
lacio ['laθjo] *adj* limp; lank; withered.
lacónico [la'koniko] *adj* laconic.
lacrar¹ [la'krar] *v* infect; damage. **lacra** *sf* blemish.
lacrar² *v* seal. **lacre** *sm* sealing wax.
lacrimoso [lakri'moso] *adj* tearful.
lácteo ['lakteo] *adj* milky. **vía láctea** *sf* Milky Way. **productos lácteos** *sm pl* dairy products. **lactante** *adj* suckling; nursling. **lactar** *v* suckle.
ladear [laðe'ar] *v* tip, tilt, overturn; deviate; skirt. **ladeo** *sm* tipping, tilting.
ladera [la'ðera] *sf* slope; hillside.
ladino [la'ðino] *adj* multilingual; crafty.
lado ['laðo] *sm* side; way; space; direction; protection. **al lado** close. **al lado de** beside. **por el lado de** in the direction of.
ladrar [la'ðrar] *v* bark. **ladrido** *sm* bark; barking.
ladrillo [la'ðriʎo] *sm* brick, tile.
ladrón [la'ðron] **-a** *sm, sf* thief, robber. *sm* sluice gate; multiple socket.

lagarto [la'garto] *sm* lizard.
lago ['lago] *sm* lake.
lágrima ['lagrima] *sf* tear; drop. **verter lágrimas** shed tears. **lagrimoso** *adj* tearful.
laguna [la'guna] *sf* lagoon; pond; gap.
laico ['laiko] *adj* lay, secular.
lamentar [lamen'tar] *v* lament; regret; grieve. **lamentarse** *v* complain. **lamentable** *adj* deplorable. **lamentación** *sf* lamentation, lament. **lamento** *sm* lament; mourning. **lamentoso** *adj* lamentable, mournful.
lamer [la'mer] *v* lick.
lámina ['lamina] *sf* metal sheet; picture; engraving. **laminar** *v* laminate.
lámpara ['lampara] *sf* lamp; light; valve.
lana ['lana] *sf* wool; fleece. **lana de vidrio** fibreglass. **lanudo** *adj* woolly; shaggy.
lance ['lanθe] *sm* throw; event; move; stroke. **lance de fortuna** chance. **de lance** second-hand.
lanceta [lan'θeta] *sf* lancet.
lancha ['lantʃa] *sf* launch; flagstone. **lancha salvavidas** lifeboat. **lanchero** *sm* boatman.
langosta [lan'gosta] *sf* lobster; locust.
*languidecer [langiðe'θer] *v* languish. **languidez** *sf* languor. **lánguido** *adj* languid.
lanza ['lanθa] *sf* spear; lance; pike; nozzle.
lanzar [lan'θar] *v* throw; fling; evict. **lanzarse** *v* spring. **lanzamiento** *sm* launching.
lápida ['lapiða] *sf* stone slab; tablet.
lápiz ['lapiθ] *sm* pencil. **lapicero** *sm* pencil-holder.
lapso ['lapso] *sm* lapse.
lar [lar] *sm* hearth; home.
largar [lar'gar] *v* loosen; free. **largarse** *v* go away.
largo ['largo] *adj* long; (*fam*) generous. *sm* length. **a lo largo de** the length of. **dar largas** a delay. **largueza** *sf* length; generosity.
laringe [la'rinxe] *sf* larynx.
larva ['larβa] *sf* larva.
lascivo [las'θiβo] *adj* lascivious. **lascivia** *sf* lasciviousness.
laso ['laso] *adj* weary. **lasitud** *sf* lassitude.
lástima ['lastima] *sf* pity; complaint. **¡qué lástima!** what a pity! **lastimar** *v* hurt. **lastimarse** *v* pity; complain. **lastimoso** *adj* pitiable, pitiful.

lastre ['lastre] *sm* ballast.
lata ['lata] *sf* tin. can; (*fam*) nuisance. **dar la lata** (*fam*) pester.
latente [la'tente] *adj* latent.
lateral [late'ral] *adj* lateral, side.
látigo ['latigo] *sm* whip. **latigazo** *sm* whiplash.
latín [la'tin] *sm* Latin. **latinoamericano. -a** *s. adj* Latin American.
latir [la'tir] *v* beat; throb. **latido** *sm* heartbeat; throb.
latitud [lati'tuð] *sf* latitude; breadth. **lato** *adj* broad.
latón [la'ton] *sm* brass.
latoso [la'toso] *adj* (*fam*) annoying; boring.
latrocinio [latro'θinjo] *sm* theft.
laúd [la'uð] *sm* lute.
laudable [lau'ðaβle] *adj* praiseworthy.
laurel [lau'rel] *sm* laurel; laurel wreath. **laureado** *adj* laureate. **laurear** *v* honour; reward. **lauro** *sm* (*fig*) glory.
lava ['laβa] *sf* lava.
lavar [la'βar] *v* wash. **lavable** *adj* washable. **lavabo** *sm* wash-basin. **lavación** *sf* lotion; wash. **lavadero** *sm* washing-place. **lavado** *sm* wash; washing. **lavadora** *sf* washing machine. **lavandería** *sf* laundry.
laxante [lak'sante] *sm* laxative. **laxidad** *sf* laxity.
lazo ['laθo] *sm* lasso; loop; bow; knot; snare; link.
leal [le'al] *adj* loyal. **lealdad** *sf* loyalty.
lebrel [le'βrel] *sm* greyhound.
lección [lek'θjon] *sf* lesson. **lector, -a** *sm, sf* reader; lecturer. **lectura** *sf* reading matter.
leche ['letʃe] *sf* milk. **lechería** *sf* dairy. **lechero** *sm* milkman.
lecho ['letʃo] *sm* bed; layer.
lechuga [le'tʃuga] *sf* lettuce.
lechuza [le'tʃuβa] *sf* owl.
***leer** [le'er] *v* read.
legación [lega'θjon] *sf* legation. **legado** *sm* legacy; ambassador.
legal [le'gal] *adj* legal; lawful. **legalidad** *sf* legality. **legalización** *sf* legalization. **legalizar** *v* legalize.
legar [le'gar] *v* bequeath; depute.
legendario [lexen'darjo] *adj* legendary.
legible [le'xiβle] *adj* legible.
legión [le'xjon] *sf* legion.
legislar [lexis'lar] *v* legislate. **legislación** *sf* legislation. **legislador, -a** *sm, sf* legislator.

legislativo *adj* legislative. **legislatura** *sf* legislature.
legitimar [lexiti'mar] *v* prove; justify. **legitimidad** *sf* legitimacy. **legítimo** *adj* legitimate.
lego ['lego] *adj* lay. *sm* layman.
legua ['legwa] *sf* league.
legumbre [le'gumbre] *sf* vegetable.
lejía [le'xia] *sf* bleach.
lejos ['lexos] *adv* far away. **a lo lejos** in the distance. *sm* perspective; background. **lejanía** *sf* distance. **lejano** *adj* far-away.
lema ['lema] *sf* motto.
lencería [lenθe'ria] *sf* linen goods; lingerie.
lengua ['lengwa] *sf* tongue; language. **trabarse la lengua** become tongue-tied. **lenguaje** *sm* language; speech; style.
lenguado [len'gwaðo] *sm* (*zool*) sole.
lengüeta [len'gweta] *sf* (*de zapato*) tongue.
lenidad [leni'ðað] *sf* lenience; mildness.
lente ['lente] *s(m+f)* lens. **lente de aumento** magnifying glass. **lentes** *pl* glasses, spectacles. **lentes de contacto** contact lenses.
lenteja [len'texa] *sf* lentil.
lento ['lento] *adj* slow. **lentitud** *sf* slowness.
leña ['leɲa] *sf* firewood.
león [le'on] *sm* lion. **leona** *sf* lioness. **leonino** *adj* leonine.
lepra ['lepra] *sf* leprosy. **leproso** *adj* leprous.
lesión [le'sjon] *sf* injury. **lesionar** *v* injure. **lesivo** *adj* injurious.
letanía [leta'nia] *sf* litany; long list.
letargo [le'targo] *sm* lethargy. **letárgico** *adj* lethargic.
letra ['letra] *sf* letter; handwriting; lyric; (*com*) draft. **Letras** *sf pl* literature; Arts. **letra mayúscula** capital letter. **letra minúscula** lower-case letter. **letrado** *sm* lawyer. **letrero** *sm* label; sign.
leva ['leβa] *sf* (*tecn*) cam; lever. **árbol de levas** camshaft.
levadizo [leβa'ðiθo] *adj* that can be lifted. **puente levadizo** *sm* drawbridge.
levadura [leβa'ðura] *sf* leaven, yeast.
levantar [leβan'tar] *v* lift; raise; erect. **levantarse** *v* rise, get up. **levantamiento** *sm* raising; insurrection. **levantado** *adj* raised; lofty.
leve ['leβe] *adj* slight; trifling. **levedad** *sf* lightness; slightness.

léxico ['leksiko] *adj* lexical. *sm* dictionary; vocabulary.

ley [lej] *sf* law; loyalty; standard. **a toda ley** according to rule. **tener ley a** be very fond of.

leyenda [le'jenda] *sf* legend.

liar ['ljar] *v* bind; tie up; (*fam*) involve. **liarlas** *v* (*fam*) clear off. **liarse** *v* (*fam*) join; start an affair; get involved.

libélula [li'βelula] *sf* dragonfly.

liberal [liβe'ral] *adj* generous. **liberalidad** *sf* generosity.

libertar [liβer'tar] *v also* **liberar** liberate, free. **libertad** *sf* freedom; independence. **libertador, -a** *sm, sf* liberator.

libertinaje [liβerti'naxe] *sm* licentiousness. **libertino, -a** *s, adj* libertine.

libra ['liβra] *sf* (*peso*) pound. **libra esterlina** pound sterling.

librar [li'βrar] *v* free; exempt; deliver; despatch; expedite; (*com*) draw; pass sentence. **librador, -a** *sm, sf* liberator. **libramiento** *sm* delivery; rescue; (*com*) draft. **libranza** *sf* (*com*) draft. **libre** *adj* free; vacant; isolated; loose.

librería [liβre'ria] *sf* bookshop; bookselling; bookcase. **librero, -a** *sm, sf* bookseller.

libreta [li'βreta] *sf* notebook; cashbook; one-pound loaf.

libro ['liβro] *sm* book. **libro diario** journal. **libro mayor** ledger.

licenciar [liθen'θjar] *v* license. **licenciarse** *v* graduate. **licencia** *sf* licence; degree; (*mil*) leave. **licenciado, -a** *sm, sf* graduate; *sm* lawyer; discharged soldier. **licenciatura** *sf* Bachelor's degree.

licencioso [liθen'θjoso] *adj* licentious.

liceo [li'θeo] *sm* lyceum; secondary school.

licitar [liθi'tar] *v* (*subasta*) bid. **licitación** *sf* bid. **licitador, -a** *sm, sf* bidder.

lícito ['liθito] *adj* authorized.

licor [li'kor] *sm* liquor; liqueur.

líder ['liðer] *sm* leader.

lidiar [li'ðjar] *v* (*toros*) fight. **lidia** *sf* bullfight. **lidiador** *sm* bullfighter.

liebre ['ljeβre] *sf* hare. **coger una liebre** (*fam*) come a cropper.

lienzo ['ljenθo] *sm* canvas; linen.

liga ['liga] *sf* garter; league; alloy. **ligadura** *sf* ligature; bond. **ligamento** *sm* ligament; bond. **ligar** *v* bind; tie; unite; alloy. **ligarse** *v* join; band together.

ligero [li'xero] *adj* light; swift; frivolous.

ligereza *sf* lightness; swiftness; frivolousness.

lija ['lixa] *sf* sandpaper; (*zool*) dogfish. **lijar** *v* sandpaper.

lila ['lila] *sf* (*bot*) lilac. *sm* (*color*) lilac. *adj* (*fam*) foolish.

lima¹ ['lima] *sf* file; polish. **limar** *v* file; polish; undermine. **limadura** *sf* filing.

lima² *sf* lime; lime tree.

limaza [li'maθa] *sf* slug.

limitar [limi'tar] *v* limit. **limitación** *sf* limitation. **límite** *sm* limit; boundary.

limón [li'mon] *sm* lemon; lemon tree. **limonada** *sf* lemonade. **limonero** *sm* lemon tree.

limosna [li'mosna] *sf* alms *pl*.

limpiabotas [limpja'βotas] *sm invar* bootblack.

limpiadera [limpja'ðera] *sf* clothes brush.

limpiadientes [limpja'ðjentes] *sm invar* toothpick.

limpiar [lim'pjar] *v* clean; clear; wipe; prune; weed. **limpiador, -a** *sm, sf* cleaner. **limpiadura** *sf* cleaning. **limpieza** *sf* cleanness. **limpio** *adj* clean; clear; pure. **jugar limpio** play fair. **poner en limpio** copy out.

linaje [li'naxe] *sm* lineage. **linaje humano** mankind.

linaza [li'naθa] *sf* linseed.

lince ['linθe] *sm* lynx.

linchar [lin'tʃar] *v* lynch. **linchamiento** *sm* lynching.

lindar [lin'dar] *v* **lindar con** border; adjoin. **linde** *sf* boundary. **lindero** *sm* limit.

lindo ['lindo] *adj* pretty; handsome; nice. **de lo lindo** a great deal. **lindeza** *sf* beauty; niceness. **lindura** *sf* prettiness.

línea ['linea] *sf* line; boundary; class. **línea aérea** airline. **lineal** *adj* linear.

lingüista [lin'gwista] *s(m+f)* linguist. **lingüística** *sf* linguistics. **lingüístico** *adj* linguistic.

linimento [lini'mento] *sm* liniment.

lino ['lino] *sm* linen.

linóleo [li'noleo] *sm* linoleum.

linterna [lin'terna] *sf* lantern; lamp; torch; lighthouse.

lío ['lio] *sm* parcel; trouble; mess. **armar un lío** raise a rumpus.

liquidar [liki'ðar] *v* liquefy; liquidate. settle up. **liquidez** *sf* fluidity. **líquido** *sm, adj* liquid; (*com*) net. **líquido imponible** net taxable amount.

lira ['lira] *sf* lyre; inspiration.
lírica ['lirika] *sf* lyric poetry. **lírico** *adj* lyric.
lirio ['lirjo] *sm* lily.
lirón [li'ron] *sm* dormouse. **dormir como un lirón** sleep like a log.
lisiar [li'sjar] *v* cripple. **lisiado** *adj* crippled.
liso ['liso] *adj* smooth.
lisonjear [lisonxe'ar] *v* flatter. **lisonja** *sf* flattery. **lisonjero** *adj* flattering.
lista ['lista] *sf* list; stripe; band. **a listas** striped. **lista de correos** poste restante. **lista de platos** menu.
listo ['listo] *adj* ready; finished; clever.
litera [li'tera] *sf* berth; bunk; (*cama*) litter.
literato [lite'rato], **-a** *sm, sf* literary person. *adj* literary. **literatura** *sf* literature.
litigar [liti'gar] *v* go to law, litigate. **litigación** *sf* litigation. **litigio** *sm* lawsuit. **litigioso** *adj* contentious.
litografía [lito'grafja] *sf* lithograph; lithography. **litográfico** *adj* lithographic.
litoral [lito'ral] *adj* coastal. *sm* shore.
litro ['litro] *sm* litre.
liturgia [litur'xia] *sf* liturgy. **litúrgico** *adj* liturgical.
liviano [li'βjano] *adj* light; trivial; lewd. **liviandad** *sf* lightness; triviality; lewdness.
lívido ['liβiðo] *adj* livid.
lo [lo] *art m* him, it; that, what.
loable [lo'aβle] *adj* praiseworthy. **loa** *sf* praise. **loador** *adj* praising. **loar** *v* praise.
lobo ['loβo] *sm* wolf. **lobo marino** seal. **lobero** *adj* wolfish.
lóbrego [lo'βrego] *adj* gloomy, murky. **lobreguecer** *v* darken; grow dark. **lobreguez** *sf* gloom; murk.
lóbulo [lo'βulo] *sm* lobe.
local [lo'kal] *adj* local. *sm* place. **localidad** *sf* locality; (*teatro*) seat. **sacar localidades** get tickets. **localizar** *v* localize.
loción [lo'θjon] *sf* lotion.
loco ['loko], **-a** *adj* mad; excessive. *sm, sf* mad person. **volverse loco** go mad. **locura** *sf* madness; folly. **hacer locuras** act madly.
locomoción [lokomo'θjon] *sf* locomotion. **locomotora** *sf* locomotive.
locuaz [lo'kwaθ] *adj* talkative. **locuacidad** *sf* talkativeness.
locutor [loku'tor], **-a** *sm, sf* radio announcer; commentator.

lodo ['loðo] *sm* mud. **lodoso** *adj* muddy.
lógica ['loxika] *sf* logic. **lógico** *adj* logical. **lógicamente** *adv* logically; naturally. **logística** *sf* logistics.
lograr [lo'grar] *v* get; achieve. **lograrse** *v* succeed. **logrería** *sf* profiteering. **logro** *sm* success; profit; usury.
loma ['loma] *sf* hill; slope.
lombriz [lom'briθ] *sf* worm; earthworm. **lombriz solitaria** tapeworm.
lomo ['lomo] *sm* (*carne*) loin; (*animal*) back; (*libro*) spine.
lona ['lona] *sf* canvas.
Londres ['londres] *sm* London.
longaniza [longa'niθa] *sf* pork sausage.
longevidad [lonxeβi'ðað] *sf* longevity.
longitud [lonxi'tuð] *sf* longitude. **longitudinal** *adj* longitudinal.
lonja ['lonxa] *sf* (*de carne*) slice; grocer's shop; strap; church porch.
loro ['loro] *sm* parrot.
losa ['losa] *sf* stone slab; tile.
lote ['lote] *sm* (*com*) lot; share; prize.
loza ['loθa] *sf* crockery; pottery.
lozano [lo'θano] *adj* luxuriant; lush; robust; sprightly. **lozanía** *sf* luxuriance.
lubrificar [luβrifi'kar] *v* also **lubricar** lubricate. **lubricación** *sf* also **lubrificación** lubrication. **lubricante** *sm, adj* also **lubrificante** lubricant.
lúcido ['luθiðo] *adj* lucid; shining. **lucidez** *sf* lucidity; brilliance.
luciérnaga [lu'θjernaga] *sf* glow-worm.
***lucir** [lu'θir] *v* shine; gleam; excel; show off. **lucirse** *v* be successful; dress up.
lucro ['lukro] *sm* profit, gain. **lucros y daños** profit and loss.
luchar [lu'tʃar] *v* fight, struggle. **lucha** *sf* fight, struggle. **lucha libre** all-in wrestling. **luchador, -a** *sm, sf* fighter.
luego ['lwego] *adv* then; next; later; presently. *conj* as; therefore. **luego que** as soon as. **desde luego** of course. **hasta luego** so long.
lugar [lu'gar] *sm* place; occasion; chance; opportunity. **en lugar de** instead of. **tener lugar** take place.
lugarteniente [lugarte'njente] *sm* lieutenant.
lúgubre ['luguβre] *adj* lugubrious.
lujo ['luxo] *sm* luxury. **de lujo** de luxe. **lujoso** *adj* luxurious.
lujuria [lu'xurja] *sf* lust; lechery. **lujuriar** *v* lust. **lujurioso** *adj* lustful; lecherous.

lumbago [lum'bago] *sm* lumbago.
lumbre ['lumbre] *sf* fire; brightness; light;
skylight. **echar lumbres** spark. **lumbrera**
sf luminary; skylight; air vent; (*fig*) leading light.
luminoso [lumi'noso] *adj* bright; luminous.
luna ['luna] *sf* moon. **luna de miel** honeymoon. **lunar** *adj* lunar. **lunático, -a** *s, adj*
lunatic.
lunar [lu'nar] *sm* mole; beauty spot;
blemish.
lunes ['lunes] *sm* Monday.
lupa ['lupa] *sf* magnifying glass.
lupanar [lupa'nar] *sm* brothel.
lustrar [lus'trar] *v* polish; purify. **lustre**
sm lustre; gloss; splendour.
luto ['luto] *sm* mourning; bereavement. **ir
de luto** be in mourning.
Luxemburgo [luksem'burgo] *sm* Luxembourg.
luz [luθ] *sf* light; daylight; window. **a
todas luces** clearly. **dar la luz** put the
light on.

LL

llaga ['ʎaga] *sf* ulcer; sore; wound. **llagar**
v ulcerate; wound.
llama¹ ['ʎama] *sf* (*fuego*) flame. **estar en
llamas** burst into flames. **llamear** *v* blaze.
llama² *sf* (*pantano*) swamp.
llama³ *sf* (*zool*) llama.
llamar [ʎa'mar] *v* call; appeal to; name;
attract. **llamarse** *v* be called. **¿cómo se
llama?** what is your name? **llamado** *adj*
so-called. **llamada** *sf* call; summons.
llamador, -a *sm, sf* caller; messenger.
llana ['ʎana] *sf* trowel.
llano ['ʎano] *adj* flat; plain; straightforward. **número llano** Roman numeral. *sm*
plain; flatness. **llanura** *sf* evenness; flat
land.
llanta ['ʎanta] *sf* iron hoop; rim.
llanto ['ʎanto] *sm* lament; crying.
llave ['ʎaβe] *sf* key; spanner. **llave maestra** skeleton key. **llave inglesa** adjustable
spanner.
llegar [ʎe'gar] *v* arrive; reach; suffice;

happen. **llegarse** *v* come *or* go round. **llegar a** end up at. **llegar a ser** become.
llegada *sf* arrival. **a la llegada** on arrival.
llenar [ʎe'nar] *v* fill; be satisfied. **lleno** *adj*
full; covered; complete. **de lleno** completely. **llenura** *sf* abundance.
llevar [ʎe'βar] *v* take; carry; wear; deal
with; sever; charge; manage; (*tiempo*)
spend. **llevar a cabo** carry out. **llevarse** *v*
take away. **llevarse bien con** get on well
with.
llorar [ʎo'rar] *v* weep; cry; mourn. **llorón,
-ona** *adj* weepy. **lloroso** *adj* tearful.
llover [ʎo'βer] *v* rain. **llover a cántaros**
pour down. **lloverse** *v* (*tejado*) leak.
lloviznar *v* drizzle. **llovizna** *sf* drizzle.
lluvia *sf* rain. **lluvioso** *adj* rainy.

M

macabro [ma'kaβro] *adj* macabre.
macarrón [makar'ron] *sm* macaroon.
macarrones *sm pl* macaroni *sing*.
macanudo [maka'nuðo] *adj* (*fam*) terrific.
maceta [ma'θeta] *sf* flowerpot.
macilento [maθi'lento] *adj* lean; wan.
macizo [ma'θiθo] *adj* solid. *sm* mass;
flowerbed. **macizar** *v* fill up.
mácula ['makula] *sf* spot, stain. **macular** *v*
spot, stain.
machacar [matʃa'kar] *v* pound; crush;
bombard; (*fig*) harp on. **machacón, -ona**
sm, sf bore; swot. **machaconería** *sf* tire-
someness. **machaqueo** *sm* pounding;
crushing; harping.
machete [ma'tʃete] *sm* machete; hunting-
knife.
macho ['matʃo] *adj* male; masculine;
virile. *sm* (*fam*) he-man; sledgehammer;
he-mule. **machismo** *sm* virility.
machucar [matʃu'kar] *v* beat; pound;
bruise.
madeja [ma'ðexa] *sf* skein; mop of hair.
madera [ma'ðera] *sf* wood, timber; horn.
tener madera de have the makings of.
maderería *sf* timber yard. **madero** *sm*
beam; log.
madrastra [ma'ðrastra] *sf* stepmother.
madre ['maðre] *sf* mother. **madre política**
mother-in-law.

madreselva [maðre'selβa] *sf* honeysuckle.
madriguera [maðri'gera] *sf* den; warren.
madrina [ma'ðrina] *sf* godmother; patroness. **madrina de boda** bridesmaid.
madrugar [maðru'gar] *v* rise early. **madrugada** *sf* early morning. **madrugador, -a** *sm, sf* early riser.
madurar [maðu'rar] *v* mature, ripen. **madurez** *sf* maturity; wisdom. **maduro** *adj* ripe; middle-aged.
maestría [maes'tria] *sf* mastery. **maestrar** *v* direct; conduct; domineer. **maestra** *sf* mistress; schoolmistress. **maestro** *sm* master; teacher; *adj* master, main, chief. **magistral** *adj* masterly.
magia ['maxja] *sf* magic. **mágico** *adj* magic(al). **magico** *sm* magician.
magistrado [maxi'straðo] *sm* magistrate. **magistratura** *sf* judicature.
magnánimo [mag'nanimo] *adj* magnanimous. **magnanimidad** *sf* magnanimity.
magnético [mag'netiko] *adj* magnetic. **magnetismo** *sm* magnetism. **magnetizar** *v* magnetize.
magnetofón [magneto'fon] *sm* also **magnetófono** tape recorder. **cinta magnetofónica** recording tape.
magnífico [mag'nifiko] *adj* magnificent. **magnificencia** *sf* magnificence.
magnitud [magni'tuð] *sf* size. magnitude.
mago ['mago] *sm* magician, wizard.
magro ['magro] *adj* thin, lean. *sm* lean meat.
magullar [magu'ʎar] *v* bruise. **magulladura** *sf* bruise.
maíz [ma'iθ] *sm* maize. **harina de maíz** *sf* cornflour.
majadero [maxa'ðero] *adj* silly; boring. *sm* pestle. **majadería** *sf* nonsense. **majadura** *sf* crushing, pounding. **majar** *v* crush, pound.
majestad [maxes'tað] *sf* majesty; royalty; grandeur. **majestuoso** *adj* majestic; stately; solemn.
majo ['maxo], **-a** *sm, sf* dandy. *adj* sporty; swaggering; genial.
mal [mal] *adj* *v* **malo**. *adv* badly; poorly; wrongly. *sm* wrong; evil; illness; harm. **de mal en peor** from bad to worse. **echar a mal** despise; waste. **llevar a mal** take offence at. **mal que bien** somehow or other.
malaconsejado [malakonse'xaðo] *adj* ill-advised.

malacostumbrado [malakostum'braðo] *adj* spoiled.
malaventura [malaβen'tura] *sf* misfortune. **malaventurado** *adj* unlucky.
malbaratar [malβara'tar] *v* squander; undersell.
malcontento [malkon'tento], **-a** *sm, sf* malcontent. *adj* discontented.
malcriado [malkri'aðo] *adj* ill-bred. **malcriar** *v* spoil.
maldad [mal'ðað] *sf* wickedness.
***maldecir** [malðe'θir] *v* curse. **maldecir de** speak ill of. **maldición** *sf* curse. **maldito** *adj* accursed.
maleable [male'aβle] *adj* malleable. **maleabilidad** *sf* malleability.
malear [male'ar] *v* damage; spoil. **malearse** *v* go wrong.
maleficio [male'fiθjo] *sm* injury; witchcraft. **maleficiar** *v* hurt; bewitch.
malestar [males'tar] *sm* uneasiness.
maleta [ma'leta] *sf* suitcase; (*auto*) trunk. **hacer la maleta** pack up.
malévolo [ma'leβolo] *adj* malevolent. **malevolencia** *sf* malevolence.
maleza [ma'leθa] *sf* thicket; weeds *pl*.
malgastar [malgas'tar] *v* squander, waste. **malgastador, -a** *s, adj* spendthrift.
malhablado [mala'βlaðo] *adj* foulmouthed.
malhechor [male't∫or], **-a** *sm, sf* wrongdoer. **malhecho** *sm* misdeed.
malhumorado [malumo'raðo] *adj* ill-tempered.
malicia [ma'liθja] *sf* malice; slyness; mischievousness. **maliciable** *adj* suspicious. **maliciarse** *v* go bad. **malicioso** *adj* malicious; shrewd; sly.
maligno [ma'ligno] *adj* malignant; malicious. **maliguidad** *sf* malignity; malice.
malintencionado [malinten∫jo'naðo] *adj* ill-disposed.
malo ['malo] *adj* *also* **mal** bad; evil; wrong; poor; difficult; sick. **estar malo** be ill. **mala fama** ill fame. **venir de malas** have bad intentions.
malograr [malo'grar] *v* waste; miss. **malograrse** *v* fail; fall through. **malogrado** *adj* abortive. **malogro** *sm* failure.
***malquerer** [malke'rer] *v* hate. **malquerencia** *sf* ill-will; hatred.
malsano [mal'sano] *adj* unhealthy; sick; insanitary.

malta ['malta] sf malt.

Malta ['malta] sf Malta. **maltés, -esa** s. adj Maltese; sm (idioma) Maltese.

maltratar [maltra'tar] v ill-treat. **maltraer** v hurt; abuse. **maltrato** sm ill-treatment.

malva ['malβa] sf mallow. **malva real** hollyhock.

malvado [mal'βaðo], **-a** sm, sf evildoer. adj wicked.

malla ['maʎa] sf mesh; network; (de metal) mail. **mallas** sf pl tights.

mallo ['maʎo] sm mallet.

mamá [ma'ma] sf also **mama** mum(my), mother.

mamar [ma'mar] v suck; acquire. **mamarse** v get drunk; fiddle, wangle. **mamoso** adj sucking.

mamífero [ma'mifero] sm mammal.

mampostería [mamposte'ria] sf masonry. **mampuesto** sm rubble.

manada [ma'naða] sf herd, flock; crowd. **manadero** sm herdsman; shepherd.

manantial [manan'tjal] sm spring; source, origin. **manar** v flow; issue.

mancebo [man'θeβo] sm youth; shop assistant; bachelor.

manco ['manko] adj one-handed; one-armed; crippled; faulty. **mancar** v cripple.

mancomunar [mankomu'nar] v join, unite. **mancomún** adv jointly. **mancomunarse** v merge. **mancomunidad** sf association, confederation.

manchar [man'tʃar] v stain; mark. **mancha** sf stain; mark; dishonour.

mandar [man'dar] v order; command; send; bequeath. **mandarse** v manage by oneself. **mandadero, -a** sm, sf messenger. **mandado** sm order; errand. **mandamiento** sm commandment, order.

mandatario [manda'tarjo] sm attorney; agent; mandatary. **mandato** sm commandment; mandate. **mandato judicial** writ.

mandíbula [man'diβula] sf jawbone.

mando ['mando] sm command; power; authority.

manejar [mane'xar] v operate; handle; manage. **manejable** adj manageable. **manejo** sm operation; handling; control; stratagem.

manera [ma'nera] sf manner; mode; way; fashion. **a manera de** by way of. **de ninguna manera** by no means. **de todas maneras** by all means. **manera de ver** outlook.

manga ['manga] sf sleeve; hosepipe; waterspout. **manga de agua** shower. **manga de viento** whirlwind. **manguera** sf garden hose.

mango[1] ['mango] sm (bot) mango.

mango[2] sm handle; stock.

manía [ma'nia] sf mania, craze. **maníaco** adj, sm maniac.

maniatar [manja'tar] v manacle.

manicomio [mani'komjo] sm lunatic asylum.

***manifestar** [manifes'tar] v show; declare; manifest. **manifestación** sf manifestation. **manifestante** s(m+f) demonstrator. **manifiesto** adj clear, evident. **manifiesto** sm manifesto.

maniobrar [manjo'βrar] v manoeuvre; operate; manipulate; plot. **maniobra** sf manoeuvre; stratagem; handling.

manipular [manipu'lar] v manipulate. **manipulación** sf manipulation. **manipulador, -a** sm, sf manipulator.

maniquí [mani'ki] sm tailor's dummy; puppet. sf mannequin; model.

manivela [mani'βela] sf (auto) crank.

mano ['mano] sf hand; paw; (pintura) coat; (juego) hand, round, turn. **a mano** by hand. **a mano salva** without risk. **de segunda mano** secondhand. **darse las manos** shake hands. **mano a mano** in a friendly way. **manojo** sm handful.

manosear [manose'ar] v handle; paw; fondle. **manoseado** adj hackneyed.

mansión [man'sjon] sf mansion.

manso ['manso] adj tame; gentle; meek. **mansedumbre** sf tameness; meekness.

manta ['manta] sf blanket; rug; (fam) thrashing.

manteca [man'teka] sf grease; lard; butter; cream. **mantecada** sf slice of bread and butter.

mantecado [mante'kaðo] sm ice-cream; bun.

mantel ['mantel] sm tablecloth.

***mantener** [mante'ner] v maintain; hold; defend; feed; sustain. **mantenimiento** sm maintenance.

mantequilla [mante'kiʎa] sf butter. **mantequera** sf churn; butter-dish. **mantequería** sf dairy.

mantilla [man'tiʎa] sf mantilla, shawl.

manto ['manto] sm cloak. **mantón** sm shawl.

manual [ma'nwal] *sm* handbook. *adj* manual.

manubrio [manu'βrio] *sm* handle; crank.

manufactura [manufak'tura] *sf* manufacture; factory. **manufacturado** *adj* manufactured. **manufacturar** *v* manufacture.

manuscrito [manu'skrito] *sm* manuscript.

manzana [man'θana] *sf* apple; block of flats. **manzano** *sm* apple tree.

maña ['mana] *sf* skill; bad habit; cunning. **mañoso** *adj* clever; crafty.

mañana [ma'nana] *sf* morning. *sm, adv* tomorrow. **de mañana** early. **hasta mañana** see you tomorrow. **pasado mañana** the day after tomorrow.

mapa ['mapa] *sm* map; chart.

máquina ['makina] *sf* machine; locomotive; engine; car; bicycle. **a toda máquina** at full speed. **máquina de coser** sewing machine. **máquina de escribir** typewriter. **máquina registradora** cash register.

maquinación [makina'θjon] *sf* machination; plotting. **maquinal** *adj* automatic; mechanical. **maquinar** *v* plot.

mar [mar] *s(m + f)* sea. **alta mar** high seas. **baja mar** low tide.

maraña [ma'rana] *sf* thicket; tangle; perplexity. **marañar** *v* tangle. **marañoso** *adj* entangling.

maravillar [maraβi'ʎar] *v* wonder; amaze. **maravilla** *sf* marvel; wonder. **maravilloso** *adj* wonderful.

marcar [mar'kar] *v* mark; brand; show; dial; score. **marca** *sf* mark; make; gauge; label. **marca registrada** registered trademark.

marcial [mar'θjal] *adj* martial; warlike.

marco ['marko] *sm* frame; setting; (*moneda*) mark.

marchar [mar'tʃar] *v* march; go; run; work; depart. **marcharse** *v* go away. **marcha** *sf* march; course; movement; departure. **poner en marcha** set in motion.

marchitar [martʃi'tar] *v* fade; wither; shrivel. **marchitable** *adj* perishable. **marchito** *adj* faded.

marea [ma'rea] *sf* tide; light breeze; dew. **marea creciente/menguante** flood/ebb tide.

marearse [mare'arse] *v* feel (sea) sick. **mareado** *adj* (sea) sick; dizzy. **mareo** *sm* sickness; (*fam*) nuisance.

marfil [mar'fil] *sm* ivory.

margarina [marga'rina] *sf* margarine.

margarita [marga'rita] *sf* daisy; pearl.

margen [mar'xen] *sm* border; margin; verge; shoulder; fringe. **al margen de** in addition to. *sf* river bank; seashore.

marica [ma'rika] *sf* magpie. *sm* (*fam*) sissy. **maricón** *sm* homosexual.

marido [ma'riðo] *sm* husband.

mariguana [mari'gwana] *sf* *also* **marihuana** marijuana.

marina [ma'rina] *sf* navy; shore; seamanship. **marinero** *sm* sailor. **marinero** *adj* seafaring; seaworthy. **marino** *sm* sailor. **marino** *adj* marine.

mariposa [mari'posa] *sf* butterfly.

mariquita [mari'kita] *sf* ladybird.

mariscal [maris'kal] *sm* marshal. **mariscal de campo** field marshal.

marisco [ma'risko] *sm* seafood; shellfish.

marítimo [ma'ritimo] *adj* maritime.

marmita [mar'mita] *sf* stewpot.

mármol ['marmol] *sm* marble. **marmóreo** *adj* marble.

marqués [mar'kes] *sm* marquis. **marquesa** *sf* marchioness.

marrano [mar'rano] *sm* pig. *adj* filthy.

marrón [mar'ron] *adj* brown; maroon. *sm* (*color*) chestnut.

marsopa [mar'sopa] *sf* porpoise.

martes ['martes] *sm invar* Tuesday.

martillar [marti'ʎar] *v* hammer. **martillo** *sm* hammer.

martín pescador [mar'tin peska'ðor] *sm* kingfisher.

mártir ['martir] *s(m + f)* martyr. **martirio** *sm* martyrdom.

marxista [mark'sista] *s(m + f)* Marxist. **marxismo** *sm* Marxism.

marzo ['marθo] *sm* March.

mas [mas] *conj* but; yet. **mas que** although.

más [mas] *adv* more; most. **nada más** nothing else. **es más** moreover. **más bien** rather. **por más que** however much. *sm* plus.

masa ['masa] *sf* mass; volume; dough; mortar.

masaje [ma'saxe] *sm* massage. **masajista** *s(m + f)* masseur, masseuse.

mascar [mas'kar] *v* chew; (*fam*) mumble. **mascadura** *sf* chewing.

máscara ['maskara] *sf* mask. **mascarada** *sf* masquerade.

masculino [masku'lino] *adj* masculine, male. *sm* (*gram*) masculine. **masculinidad** *sf* masculinity.

masón [ma'son] *sm* freemason. **masonería**
sf freemasonry.

masoquismo [maso'kismo] *sm* masochism. **masoquista** *s(m+f)* masochist.
masoquista *adj* masochistic.

masticar [masti'kar] *v* chew. **masticación**
sf mastication.

mástil ['mastil] *sm (mar)* mast; pole; post.

mastín [mas'tin] *sm* mastiff. **mastín danés**
Great Dane.

masturbación [mastur βa'θjon] *sf* masturbation. **masturbarse** *v* masturbate.

mata ['mata] *sf* bush; shrub; grove; mop
of hair.

matafuego [mata'fwego] *sm* fire extinguisher.

matar [ma'tar] *v* kill, slaughter; tire out;
put out. **matadero** *sm* slaughterhouse.
matador *sm* bullfighter. **matanza** *sf*
slaughter.

matamoscas [mata'moskas] *sm invar* fly-
swatter.

matarratas [matar'ratas] *sm invar* rat
poison.

mate¹ ['mate] *sm* (check)mate.

mate² *adj* mat, dull.

matemáticas [mate'matikas] *sf* mathematics. **matemático, -a** *sm, sf* mathematician.
matemático *adj* mathematical.

materia [ma'terja] *sf* matter; stuff; subject. **materia prima** raw material. **en
materia de** as regards. **material** *adj* material. **material** *sm* stuff, material. **materiales de derribo** rubble *sing.* **materialismo**
sm materialism. **materialista** *s(m+f)*
materialist. **materialista** *adj* materialistic.
materializar *v* materialize.

maternal [mater'nal] *adj* maternal.
maternidad *sf* maternity. **casa de
maternidad** maternity hospital. **materno**
adj maternal.

matinal [mati'nal] *adj* morning.

matiz ['matiθ] *sm* tint; hue; shade; shade
of meaning. **matizado** *adj* variegated.
matizar *v* blend; shade.

matorral [mator'ral] *sm* bush; thicket;
scrubland.

matricular [matriku'lar] *v* enrol; register;
matriculate. **matricularse** *v* register; *(contienda)* enter. **matrícula** *sf* register; enrolment; matriculation; *(auto)* licence plate.

matrimonio [matri'monjo] *sm* matrimony,
marriage; *(fam)* married couple.

matriz [ma'triθ] *sf* matrix; womb. *adj*
mother; chief. **casa matriz** headquarters.

matrona [ma'trona] *sf* matron; midwife.

matute [ma'tute] *sm* smuggling; contraband. **matutear** *v* smuggle. **matutero, -a**
sm, sf smuggler.

matutino [matu'tino] *adj also* **matutinal**
morning.

maullar [mau'ʎar] *v* mew. **maullido** *sm*
mewing.

mausoleo [mauso'leo] *sm* mausoleum.

máxima ['maksima] *sf* maxim.

máxime ['maksime] *adv* especially; prin-
cipally. **máximo** *adj, sm* maximum.

maya ['maja] *sf* daisy.

mayo ['majo] *sm* May; maypole.

mayonesa [majo'nesa] *sf* mayonnaise.

mayor [ma'jor] *sm* head, chief. *adj* older,
elder; major, main; larger; adult. **calle
mayor** high street. **al por mayor** wholesale. **mayoral** *sm* foreman; farm manager.

mayorazgo [majo'raθgo] *sm* primogeni-
ture; first born son; entailed estate.

mayordomo [major'ðomo] *sm* butler;
steward.

mayoría [majo'ria] *sf* majority; coming of
age.

mayorista [majo'rista] *sm* wholesaler. *adj*
wholesale.

mayúscula [ma'juskula] *sf* capital letter.

maza ['maθa] *sf* mace; club; butt. **mazada**
sf blow with a club.

mazapán [maθa'pan] *sm* marzipan.

mazmorra [maθ'morra] *sf* dungeon.

me [me] *pron* me, myself.

mear [me'ar] *v (vulgar)* piss. **mearse** *v* wet
oneself. **meadero** *sm* urinal.

mecánica [me'kanika] *sf* mechanics;
machinery. **mecánico** *sm* mechanic; driver. **mecanismo** *sm* mechanism. **mecanizar**
v mechanize.

mecanógrafo [meka'nografo], **-a** *sm, sf*
typist. **mecanografía** *sf* typewriting.
mecanografiar *v* type.

mecer [me'θer] *v* rock; swing; shake; stir.
mecedor *sm* swing. **mecedora** *sf* rocking-
chair.

mecha ['metʃa] *sf* wick; fuse; match.

mechera [me'tʃera] *sf (fam)* shoplifter.

mechero [me'tʃero] *sm* cigarette lighter;
gas burner.

medalla [me'ðaʎa] *sf* medal.

media ['meðja] *sf* stocking.

mediado [me'ðjaðo] *adj* half-full; half-
way through; half-finished. **a mediados
de** in *or* about the middle of.

mediano [me'ðjano] *adj* medium; average; mediocre. **medianero** *adj* intermediate; interceding.

medianoche [meðja'notʃe] *sf* midnight.

mediante [me'ðjante] *adj* intervening. *prep* by means of. **mediar** *v* intervene; mediate; elapse.

medicina [meði'θina] *sf* medicine. **medicación** *sf* medication. **medicamento** *sm* medicament. **medicar** *v* medicate. **medicinal** *adj* medicinal. **médico** *sm* doctor. **médico** *adj* medical.

medio ['meðjo] *sm* middle; half; medium; way. **de medio a medio** completely. **medios** *sm pl* means, resources. *adv* half; partly. **medidas a medias** half-measures. *adj* half; middle; average; medium. **de medio cuerpo** half-length.

mediocre [me'ðjokre] *adj* mediocre. **mediocridad** *sf* mediocrity.

mediodía [meðjo'ðia] *sm* midday; noon; south.

medioeval [meðjoe'βal] *adj* medieval.

*medir [me'ðir] *v* measure; scan. **medirse** *v* act prudently. **medida** *sf* measure(ment); step; moderation. **a medida que** according as.

meditar [meði'tar] *v* meditate (on). **meditabundo** *adj* pensive. **meditación** *sf* meditation.

mediterráneo [meðiter'raneo] *adj* Mediterranean.

medrar [me'ðrar] *v* prosper, thrive; grow. **medra** *sf* prosperity; growth. **medro** *sm* progress; improvement.

medroso [me'ðroso] *adj* fearful; timid; frightening.

médula ['meðula] *sf also* **medula** marrow; (*fig*) essence.

medusa [me'ðusa] *sf* jellyfish.

megáfono [me'gafono] *sm* megaphone.

megalómano [mega'lomano], **-a** *sm, sf* megalomaniac. **megalomanía** *sf* megalomania.

mejilla [me'xiʎa] *sf* cheek.

mejor [me'xor] *adj* better; best. *adv* better; best; rather. **a lo mejor** probably. **mejor que mejor** better still. **tanto mejor** so much the better. **mejora** *sf* improvement. **mejorar** *v* improve; surpass. **mejorarse** *v* get better.

melancólico [melan'koliko] *adj* melancholy. **melancolía** *sf* melancholy.

melandro [me'landro] *sm* badger.

melaza [me'laθa] *sf* molasses; treacle.

melena [me'lena] *sf* mane; long hair.

melindroso [melin'droso] *adj* finicky; squeamish.

melocotón [meloko'ton] *sm* peach; peach tree.

melodía [melo'ðia] *sf* melody; tune. **melodioso** *adj* melodious.

melodrama [melo'ðrama] *sm* melodrama. **melodramático** *adj* melodramatic.

melón [me'lon] *sm* melon.

meloso [me'loso] *adj* honeyed; mild; sickly.

mella ['meʎa] *sf* notch; dent; impression. **hacer mella a** make a deep impression on.

mellizo [me'ʎiθo], **-a** *s, adj* twin.

membrana [mem'brana] *sf* membrane.

membrillo [mem'briʎo] *sm* quince; quince tree.

memorable [memo'raβle] *adj* memorable. **memorar** *v* remember. **memoria** *sf* memory; record. **de memoria** by heart. **memorial** *sm* memorial; petition.

mencionar [menθjo'nar] *v* mention, name. **mención** *sf* mention.

mendigar [mendi'gar] *v* beg. **mendicación** *sf* begging. **mendicante** *adj* begging. **mendigante** *sm* beggar. **mendigo, -a** *sm, sf* beggar.

menear [mene'ar] *v* stir; shake; sway; manage; run. **meneo** *sm* wag; shake; rearranging.

menester [menes'ter] *sm* need; want; occupation. **ser menester** be necessary. **menesteroso** *adj* needy.

menguar [men'gwar] *v* lessen; decline. **mengua** *sf* lessening; decline. **menguado** *adj* impaired; diminished; wretched.

menopausia [meno'pausja] *sf* menopause.

menor [me'nor] *adj* minor; lesser; least; younger; youngest; smaller; smallest. **al por menor** retail.

menos ['menos] *adj* less, fewer. *adv* less; minus; except. **al, a lo** *or* **por lo menos** at least. **echar de menos** miss.

menoscabar [menoska'βar] *v* lessen; impair; discredit. **menoscabo** *sm* reduction; impairment.

menospreciar [menospre'θjar] *v* underrate; despise. **menospreciable** contemptible. **menosprecio** *sm* contempt; scorn; disrespect; undervaluation.

mensaje [men'saxe] *sm* message. **mensajero, -a** *sm, sf* messenger.

menstruar [menstru'ar] *v* menstruate. **menstruación** *sf* menstruation. **menstrual** *adj* menstrual.

mensual [men'swal] *adj* monthly. **mensualidad** *sf* monthly salary.

mensurar [mensu'rar] *v* measure. **mensura** *sf* measure. **mensural** *adj* measuring.

menta ['menta] *sf* mint; peppermint.

mental [men'tal] *adj* mental; intellectual. **mentalidad** *sf* mentality. **mente** *sf* mind. **irse de la mente** slip one's mind.

mentecato [mente'kato], **-a** *sm, sf* simpleton. *adj* foolish; half-witted.

*mentir [men'tir] *v* lie. **mentir con** disagree. **mentira** *sf* lie; error. **parece mentira** it's hard to believe.

menudear [menuðe'ar] *v* repeat frequently; happen often. **menudencia** *sf* detail; minuteness; pettiness. **menudencias** *sf pl or* **menudas** *sm pl* offal *sing.* **menudo** *adj* small, tiny; petty. **a menudo** often.

meñique [me'ɲike] *sm* little finger. *adj* tiny.

meollo [me'oʎo] *sm* (*anat*) marrow; brains *pl*; (*fig*) essence.

meple ['meple] *sm* maple.

mercado [mer'kaðo] *sm* market. **Mercado Común** Common Market. **mercadear** *v* trade. **mercader** *sm* merchant. **mercadería** *sf* merchandise. **mercancía** *sf* goods *pl*. **mercante** *adj* merchant. **mercantil** *adj* mercantile.

merced [mer'θeð] *sf* mercy; favour. **merced a** thanks to.

mercenario [merθe'narjo], **-s**, *adj* mercenary.

mercero [mer'θero], **-a** *sm, sf* haberdasher. **mercería** *sf* haberdashery.

mercurio [mer'kurjo] *sm* mercury. **mercurial** *adj* mercurial.

*merecer [mere'θer] *v* deserve; be worthy of. **merecer la pena** be worthwhile. **merecimiento** *sm* merit.

*merendar [meren'dar] *v* take afternoon tea; have an afternoon snack. **merendarse a** get the better of. **merendero** *sm* open-air café. **merienda** *sf* afternoon snack.

merengue [me'renge] *sm* meringue.

meridiano [meri'ðjano] *sm, adj* meridian. **meridiana** *sf* couch. **meridional** *adj* southern.

mérito ['merito] *sm* merit; value. **hacer mérito de** mention. **meritorio** *adj* meritorious.

merla ['merla] *sf* blackbird.

merluza [mer'luθa] *sf* hake.

mermar [mer'mar] *v* decrease, reduce. **merma** *sf* reduction; wastage; loss.

mermelada [merme'laða] *sf* marmalade; jam.

mero ['mero] *adj* mere, pure.

merodear [meroðe'ar] *v* maraud. **merodeador, -a** *sm, sf* marauder.

mes [mes] *sm* month. **al mes** per month.

mesa ['mesa] *sf* table; desk. **mesa de cambios** bank. **alzar la mesa** clear the table.

meseta [me'seta] *sf* plateau; staircase landing.

mesón [me'son] *sm* inn, hostelry. **mesonero, -a** *sm, sf* innkeeper.

mestizo [mes'tiθo], **-a** *s, adj* half-caste.

mesura [me'sura] *sf* dignity; politeness; moderation.

meta ['meta] *sf* goal; aim; destination. **guardameta** *sm* goalkeeper.

metabolismo [metabo'lismo] *sm* metabolism.

metafísica [meta'fiska] *sf* metaphysics. **metafísico** *adj* metaphysical.

metáfora [me'tafora] *sf* metaphor. **metafórico** *adj* metaphorical.

metal [me'tal] *sm* metal; (*música*) brass; (*voz*) timbre. **metálico** *adj* metallic. **metalurgia** *sf* metallurgy.

meteoro [mete'oro] *sm* meteor. **meteórico** *adj* meteoric. **meteorito** *sm* meteorite. **meteorología** *sf* meteorology.

meter [me'ter] *v* insert, put in; smuggle; produce; reduce. **meterse** *v* interfere; intervene. **meterse a** turn to. **meterse con** quarrel with. **metido** *adj* compressed.

meticuloso [metiku'loso] *adj* meticulous.

metodista [meto'ðista] *s(m+f), adj* Methodist. **metodismo** *sm* Methodism.

método ['metoðo] *sm* method, manner. **metódico** *adj* methodical.

métrico ['metriko] *adj* metric(al). **metro** *sm* metre; underground railway.

metrónomo [me'tronomo] *sm* metronome.

metrópoli [me'tropoli] *sf* metropolis. **metropolitano** *adj* metropolitan.

mezclar [meθ'klar] *v* mix; blend. **mezclarse** *v* mingle; intermarry. **mezcla** *sf* mixture, medley. **mezcladora** *sf* mixer, blender. **mezcolanza** *sf* hotchpotch.

mezquino [meθ'kino] *adj* mean. **mezquindad** *sf* meanness.
mezquita [meθ'kita] *sf* mosque.
mi [mi] *adj* my. **mí** *pron* me.
miaja ['mjaxa] *sf* crumb; bit.
mico ['miko] *sm* monkey.
microbio [mi'kroβjo] *sm* microbe. **microbiología** *sf* microbiology.
micrófono [mi'krofono] *sm* microphone.
microscopio [mikro'skopjo] *sm* microscope. **microscópico** *adj* microscopic.
miedo [mi'eðo] *sm* fear. **dar miedo a** frighten. **tener miedo** be afraid. **miedoso** *adj* frightened.
miel [mi'el] *sf* honey. **miel de caña** molasses.
miembro ['mjembro] *sm* member; limb.
miente ['mjente] *sf* mind; thought. **caer en mientes** come to mind. **¡ni por mientes!** not on your life! **parar mientes en** consider.
mientras ['mjentras] *adv, conj* while; meanwhile; so long as. **mientras tanto** meanwhile.
miércoles [mi'erkoles] *sm* Wednesday. **miércoles de ceniza** Ash Wednesday.
mierda ['mjerða] *sf* (*fam*) shit; muck. **¡váyase a la mierda!** go to hell!
mies [mjes] *sf* corn. **mieses** *sf pl* cornfield.
miga ['miga] *sf* crumb; substance. **hacer buenas migas con** get on well with.
migración [migra'θjon] *sf* migration. **migratorio** *adj* migratory.
migraña [mi'graɲa] *sf* migraine.
mil [mil] *sm, adj* thousand. **milésimo** *adj* thousandth. **miles de** masses of.
milagro [mi'lagro] *sm* miracle; wonder. **milagroso** *adj* miraculous.
milano [mi'lano] *sm* (*ave*) kite.
mildeu [mil'deu] *sm* mildew.
milicia [mi'liθja] *sf* militia; military service. **militar** *adj* military. *sm* soldier.
miligramo [mili'gramo] *sm* milligramme.
milla ['miʎa] *sf* mile.
millar [mi'ʎar] *sm* thousand. **a millares en** thousands.
millón [mi'ʎon] *sm* million. **millonésimo** *adj* millionth. **millonario, -a** *sm, sf* millionaire.
mimar [mi'mar] *v* spoil; pamper.
mimbre ['mimbre] *s(m+f)* wicker.
minar [mi'nar] *y* mine. **mina** *sf* ɪnine; store; pencil lead. **minador** *sm* miner; (*mar*) minelayer. **minero** *sm* miner; mine-owner.

minarete [mina'rete] *sm* minaret.
mineral [mine'ral] *sm, adj* mineral. **mineralogía** *sf* mineralogy.
miniatura [minja'tura] *sf* miniature.
mínimo ['minimo] *sm, adj* minimum.
ministerio [mini'sterjo] *sm* ministry; office. **ministerial** *adj* ministerial. **ministrador** *sm* administrator. **ministrar** *v* minister; administer. **ministro** *sm* minister; judge. **primer ministro** prime minister.
minoría [mino'ria] *sf* minority. **minorar** *v* diminish.
minucioso [minu'θjoso] *adj* meticulous; minute.
minué [minu'e] *sm* minuet.
minúscula [mi'nuskula] *sf* small letter.
minuta [mi'nuta] *sf* memo; menu; list. **minutar** *v* make notes on.
minutía [minu'tia] *sf* carnation.
minuto [mi'nuto] *sm* minute.
mío ['mio] *adj, pron pers* mine.
miope [mi'ope] *adj* shortsighted. **miopía** *sf* myopia.
miosotis [mjo'sotis] *sm* forget-me-not.
mirar [mi'rar] *v* look; consider. **mira** *sf* sight. **estar a la mira** be on the lookout. **con miras a** with a view to. **mirada** *sf* look; glance. **miradero** *sm* centre of attention; vantage point. **mirado** *adj* circumspect. **mirador** *sm* bay window. **miramiento** *sm* look; consideration; respect.
mirasol [mira'sol] *sm* sunflower.
mirlo ['mirlo] *sm* blackbird.
mirra ['mirra] *sf* myrrh.
mirto ['mirto] *sf* mass. **misal** *sm* missal.
miserable [mise'raβle] *adj* wretched, miserable. **miseria** *sf* misery; poverty. **misericordia** *sf* mercy; compassion. **misericordioso** *adj* merciful; compassionate. **mísero** *adj* wretched.
misión [misi'on] *sf* mission.
mismo ['mismo] *adj* same; own; very; just; right. **aquí mismo** right here. **lo mismo con** the same goes for. **yo mismo** I myself.
misterio [mis'terjo] *sm* mystery. **misterioso** *adj* mysterious. **misticismo** *sm* mysticism. **místico, -a s,** *adj* mystic. **mistificación** *sf* falsification; trick. **mistificar** *v* falsify; deceive.
mitad [mi'tað] *sf* half; middle.
mítico ['mitiko] *adj* mythical. **mito** *m* myth. **mitología** *sf* mythology. **mitológico** *adj* mythological.

mitigar [miti'gar] v mitigate; relieve. **mitigación** sf mitigation. **mitigante** adj mitigating.

mitin ['mitin] sm political rally.

mitón [mi'ton] sm mitten.

mitra ['mitra] sf mitre.

mixto ['miksto] adj mixed. sm compound. **mixtura** sf mixture. **mixturar** v mix.

mobiliario [moβili'arjo] sm furniture.

mocasín [moka'sin] sm moccasin.

mocero [mo'θero] adj sensual. **mocear** v act like a youngster. **mocedad** sf youth; youthful prank.

moción [mo'θjon] sf motion.

moco ['moko] sm mucus. **mocoso** adj mucous.

mochila [mo'tʃila] sf rucksack.

mocho ['motʃo] adj shorn; lopped; (sin cuernos) hornless.

moda ['moða] sf fashion. **de moda** in fashion. **pasado de moda** old-fashioned.

modales [mo'ðales] sm pl manners.

modelo [mo'ðelo] sm, adj model. **modela** sf fashion model. **modelar** v model.

moderar [moðe'rar] v moderate; restrain. **moderación** sf moderation. **moderado** adj moderate. **moderador, -a** sm, sf moderator. **moderativo** adj moderating.

moderno [mo'ðerno] adj modern. **modernidad** sf modernity. **modernizar** v modernize. **modernizarse** v get up-to-date.

modesto [mo'ðesto] adj modest. **modestia** sf modesty.

módico ['moðiko] adj moderate. **modicidad** sf moderateness.

modificar [moðifi'kar] v modify. **modificación** sf modification.

modismo [mo'ðismo] sm idiom.

modista [mo'ðista] sf dressmaker.

modo ['moðo] sm mode; manner; method. **de modo que** so that. **de todos modos** in any case.

modorra [mo'ðorra] sf drowsiness. **modorro** adj drowsy.

modular [moðu'lar] v modulate. **modulación** sf modulation.

mofar [mo'far] v scoff; mock. **mofarse de** jeer at. **mofa** sf mockery. **mofador** adj mocking.

mohín [mo'in] sm grimace. **mohino** adj sulky.

moho ['moo] sm mould; rust. **mohoso** adj mouldy; rusty. **ponerse mohoso** go mouldy; rust.

mojar [mo'xar] v wet; moisten; soak. **mojado** adj wet; damp.

mojigato [moxi'gato], **-a** sm, sf hypocrite; prude. adj hypocritical; prudish.

mojón [mo'xon] sm landmark.

moldar [mol'ðar] v also **moldear** mould. **molde** sm mould. **moldura** sf moulding.

molécula [mo'lekula] sf molecule. **molecular** adj molecular.

*****moler** [mo'ler] v grind; crush; (fig) bore, weary. **moledura** sf grinding; milling; exhaustion.

molestar [moles'tar] v annoy; bother; disturb. **molestarse** v worry. **no se moleste** don't bother. **molestia** sf trouble. **molesto** adj tiresome; embarrassing.

molinero [moli'nero] sm miller. **molino** sm mill.

molusco [mo'lusko] sm mollusc.

mollera [mo'ʎera] sf crown of the head; (fig) brains. **cerrado de mollera** dense; obstinate.

momentáneo [momen'taneo] adj momentary. **momento** sm moment; momentum. **al momento** immediately.

momia ['momja] sf (cadáver) mummy. **momificación** sf mummification. **momificar** v mummify.

monada [mo'naða] sf kindness; flattery; dirty trick. **¡qué monada!** how lovely!

monarca [mo'narka] sm monarch. **monarquía** sf monarchy. **monárquico** adj monarchic(al).

monasterio [monas'terjo] sm monastery. **monástico** adj monastic.

mondar [mon'dar] v clean; prune; strip; trim; peel. **monda** sf pruning; trimming; cleaning. **mondadientes** m invar toothpick. **mondador, -a** sm, sf pruner; peeler; cleaner. **mondo** adj pure; bare; clean.

moneda [mo'neða] sf money; coin. **monedero** sm purse. **monedero falso** counterfeiter.

monitor ['monitor], **-a** sm, sf monitor.

monja ['monxa] sf nun. **monje** sm monk.

mono[1] ['mono] sm monkey; ape.

mono[2] adj lovely; cute.

monólogo [mo'nologo] sm monologue.

monopolizar [monopoli'θar] v monopolize. **monopolio** sm monopoly.

monosílabo [mono'silaβo] sm monosyllable.

monótono [mo'notono] adj monotonous. **monotonía** sf monotony.

monstruo ['monstruo] *sm* monster. **mon-struosidad** *sf* monstrosity. **monstruoso** *adj* monstrous.

monta ['monta] *sf* mounting; amount. **montacargas** *sm invar* service lift. **montaje** *sm* mounting.

montaña [mon'taɲa] *sf* mountain. **montañés** *adj* of mountains. **montañismo** *sm* mountaineering. **montañoso** *adj* mountainous. **monte** *sm* mountain; mount.

montar [mon'tar] *v* mount; ride; assemble; establish. **montura** *sf* mount; saddle; frame; mounting.

montera [mon'tera] *sf* cloth cap; bullfighter's hat; skylight. **montero** *sm* hunter.

montón [mon'ton] *sm* heap. pile. **a montones** lots of.

monumento [monu'mento] *sm* monument; memorial. **monumental** *adj* monumental.

moño ['moɲo] *sm* bun. topknot. **ponerse moños** put on airs.

mora¹ ['mora] *sf* blackberry; mulberry.
mora² *sf* delay.

morada [mo'raða] *sf* abode; sojourn. **morar** *v* dwell.

morado [mo'raðo] *adj* purple; violet. **ponerse morado** stuff oneself.

moral [mo'ral] *adj* moral. **morales** *sf pl* morals. **moraleja** *sf* (*de un cuento*) moral. **moralidad** *sf* morality. **moralista** *s(m+f)* moralist. **moralizar** *v* moralize.

mórbido ['morβiðo] *adj* morbid; delicate. **morbidez** *sf* tenderness. **morbilidad** *sf* morbidity. **morboso** *adj* morbid; diseased.

morcilla [mor'θiʎa] *sf* black pudding.
mordaz [mor'ðaθ] *adj* mordant; pungent.
mordaza [mor'ðaθa] *sf* (*en la boca*) gag.
*morder [mor'ðer] *v* bite. **mordedura** *sf* bite. **mordiente** *adj* biting. **mordiscar** *v* nibble. **mordiscón** *sm* nibble; mouthful.

moreno [mo'reno] *adj* brown; tanned; dark.

morera [mo'rera] *sf* mulberry tree.

morfina [mor'fina] *sf* morphine.

moribundo [mori'βundo] *adj* moribund.

*morir [mo'rir] *v* die; end; fade. **morirse por** crave.

mormón [mor'mon], **-a** *sm*, *sf* Mormon. **mormonismo** *sm* Mormonism.

moro ['moro], **-a** *sm*, *sf* Moor. *adj* Moorish.

moroso [mo'roso] *adj* slow; sluggish; late. **morosidad** *sf* slowness; inactivity.

morralla [mor'raʎa] *sf* rubbish; (*fig*) rabble.

morriña [mor'riɲa] *sf* nostalgia; homesickness.

mortaja [mor'taxa] *sf* shroud.

mortal [mor'tal] *adj* mortal; lethal; awful. *s(m+f)* mortal. **mortalidad** *sf* mortality.

mortero [mor'tero] *sm* mortar.

mortífero [mor'tifero] *adj* deadly, fatal.

mortificar [mortifi'kar] *v* mortify. **mortificación** *sf* mortification.

mosca ['moska] *sf* fly. **papar moscas** gape. **moscarda** *sf* bluebottle. **moscardón** *sm* blowfly; hornet.

mosquete [mos'kete] *sm* musket. **mosquetero** *sm* musketeer.

mosquito [mos'kito] *sm* mosquito; gnat. **mosquitero** *sm* mosquito net.

mostaza [mos'taða] *sf* mustard.

*mostrar [mos'trar] *v* show; exhibit; point out. **mostrable** *adj* demonstrable. **mostrador** *sm* (*reloj*) dial; (*tienda*) counter.

mote ['mote] *sm* nickname. **motejar** *v* label; name.

motín [mo'tin] *sm* uprising; mutiny.

motivar [moti'βar] *v* cause, give rise to; justify; explain. **motivación** *sf* motivation. **motivo** *sm* motive; grounds *pl*. **con motivo de** owing to.

motocicleta [motoθi'kleta] *sf* motor cycle. **motociclista** *s(m+f)* motor-cyclist.

motor ['motor] *sm* motor; engine. **motorista** *s(m+f)* motor-cyclist. **motorizar** *v* motorize.

motriz [mo'triθ] *adj* motive.

mover [mo'βer] *v* move; shake; stir; incite. **moverse** *v* get a move on. **movedizo** *adj* movable; inconstant. **movible** *adj* mobile. **móvil** *adj* mobile; fickle. **movilidad** *sf* mobility. **movilizar** *v* mobilize. **movilización** *sf* mobilization. **movimiento** *sm* movement; motion; activity.

mozo ['moθo] *sm* youth, lad; waiter. **moza** *sf* girl; servant.

mucoso [mu'koso] *adj* mucous. **mucosidad** *sf* mucus.

muchacho [mu'tʃatʃo] *sm* boy; chap. **muchacha** *sf* girl; servant.

muchedumbre [mutʃe'ðumbre] *sf* crowd; (*fig*) a lot.

mucho [ˈmutʃo] *adj* a lot of; much; great; many. *pron* many; a lot. *adv* much; a lot; a long time. **con mucho** by far. **por mucho que** however much.

mudar [muˈðar] *v* change; remove; shed. **mudarse** *v* move house; change one's clothes. **muda** *sf* change; moulting. **mudable** *adj* changeable; variable. **mudanza** *sf* change; removal. **camión de mudanzas** *sm* removal van.

mudo [ˈmuðo] *adj* dumb, mute. **mudez** *sf* dumbness.

mueble [ˈmweβle] *sm* piece of furniture. **muebles** *sm pl* furniture *sing*.

mueca [ˈmweka] *sf* grimace.

muela [ˈmwela] *sf* molar. **muela del juicio** wisdom tooth.

muelle [ˈmweʎe] *adj* soft; luxurious. *sm* wharf; embankment; spring.

muérdago [muˈerðago] *sm* mistletoe.

muerte [ˈmwerte] *sf* death; murder. **de mala muerte** (*fam*) rotten, lousy.

muerto [ˈmwerto] *V* **morir**. *adj* dead. *sm* corpse.

muestra [ˈmwestra] *sf* sample, example; specimen; sign.

mugir [muˈxir] *v* roar; bellow; low. **mugido** *sm* roar; bellow; lowing.

mujer [muˈxer] *sf* woman; wife.

muleta [muˈleta] *sf* crutch; bullfighter's cape.

mulo [ˈmulo] *sm* mule.

multar [mulˈtar] *v* fine. **multa** *sf* fine.

múltiple [ˈmultiple] *adj* multiple; many. **multiplicación** *sf* multiplication. **multiplicar** *v* multiply, increase.

multitud [multiˈtuð] *sf* multitude, crowd.

*mullir [muˈʎir] *v* beat; break up; loosen. **mullido** *adj* soft; fluffy.

mundo [ˈmundo] *sm* world; (*fam*) crowd. **todo el mundo** everybody. **mundanal** *adj* worldly. **mundanería** *sf* worldliness. **mundial** *adj* world; worldwide. **mundovisión** *sm* broadcasting by satellite.

municipal [muniθiˈpal] *adj* municipal. *sm* policeman. **municipalidad** *sf* municipality. **municipio** *sm* town council.

munífico [muˈnifiko] *adj* munificent; liberal. **munificencia** *sf* munificence; liberality.

muñeca [muˈɲeka] *sf* doll; dressmaker's dummy; wrist.

muralla [muˈraʎa] *sf* wall; rampart. **mural** *adj, sm* mural. **murar** *v* wall. **muro** *sm* wall.

murciélago [murˈθielago] *sm* (*zool*) bat.

murmullo [murˈmuʎo] *sm* murmur; whisper; rustle.

murmurar [murmuˈrar] *v* murmur; whisper; mutter; gossip. **murmuración** *sf* gossiping. **murmurio** *sm* murmuring.

músculo [ˈmuskulo] *sm* muscle. **muscular** *adj* muscular.

muselina [museˈlina] *sf* muslin.

museo [muˈseo] *sm* museum; art gallery.

musgo [ˈmusgo] *sm* moss.

música [ˈmusika] *sf* music. **musical** *adj* musical. **músico, -a** *sm, sf* musician. **musicología** *sf* musicology.

muslo [ˈmuslo] *sm* thigh.

mustio [ˈmustjo] *adj* withered; sad. **mustiarse** *v* wither.

mutación [mutaˈθjon] *sf* mutation; change. **mutabilidad** *sf* mutability. **mutante** *sm, adj* mutant.

mutilar [mutiˈlar] *v* mutilate; cripple. **mutilación** *sf* mutilation. **mutilado, -a** *sm, sf* cripple.

mutual [ˈmutwal] *adj* mutual. **mutuo** *adj* mutual; joint.

muy [mwi] *adv* very; quite; too; much. **muy señor mío** (*carta*) Dear Sir.

N

nabo [ˈnaβo] *sm* turnip.

nácar [ˈnakar] *sm* mother-of-pearl.

*nacer [naˈθer] *v* be born; originate. **nacido** *adj* born. **naciente** *adj* growing. **nacimiento** *sm* birth; origin.

nación [naˈθjon] *sf* nation. **nacional** *adj* national. *s(m+f)* national; native. **nacionalidad** *sf* nationality. **nacionalismo** *sm* nationalism. **nacionalizar** *v* nationalize.

nada [ˈnaða] *sf* nothing. *adv* by no means. **de nada** don't mention it. **nada más** only.

nadar [naˈðar] *v* swim. **nadador, -a** *sm, sf* swimmer.

nadie [ˈnaðje] *pron* nobody, no one.

naipe [ˈnaipe] *sm* playing-card.

nalga [ˈnalga] *sf* buttock.

naranja [naˈranxa] *sf* orange. **naranjada** *sf* orangeade. **naranjo** *sm* orange tree.

narciso [nar'θiso] *sm* narcissus. **narcisis-
mo** *sm* narcissism.

narcótico [nar'kotiko] *sm, adj* narcotic.

nariz [na'riθ] *sf, pl* **narices** nose.

narrar [nar'rar] *v* narrate. **narración** *sf*
narration. **narrador, -a** *sm, sf* narrator.
narrativa *sf* narrative.

nasal [na'sal] *adj* nasal.

nata ['nata] *sf* cream; curd; (*fig*) the best.
natillas *sf pl* custard *sing*.

natación [nata'θjon] *sf* swimming.

natal [na'tal] *adj* natal; native. *sm* birth;
birthday. **natalidad** *sf* birthrate.

nativo [na'tiβo], **-a** *s, adj* native. **natividad**
sf nativity. **nato** *adj* born.

natural [natu'ral] *s(m+f)* native; citizen.
sm nature. *adj* natural. **naturaleza** *sf*
nature; nationality. **naturalidad** *sf* naturalness; citizenship.

naufragar [naufra'gar] *v* sink; be shipwrecked. **naufragio** *sm* shipwreck.
náufrago *adj* shipwrecked.

náusea ['nausea] *sf* nausea. **nauseabundo**
adj nauseous; nauseating.

náutico ['nautiko] *adj* nautical. **náutica** *sf*
navigation.

navaja [na'βaxa] *sf* penknife; razor.
navajada *sf* stab; gash.

naval [na'βal] *adj* naval. **nave** *sf or* **navío**
sm ship. **navegable** *adj* navigable. **navegación** *sf* navigation; sailing. **navegante**
sm navigator.

neblina [ne'βlina] *sf* mist. fog.
nebulosidad *sf* nebulosity; haziness.
nebuloso *adj* nebulous.

necedad [neθe'ðað] *sf* foolishness; nonsense. **necio** *adj* foolish.

necesario [neθe'sarjo] *adj* necessary.
necesidad *sf* necessity; poverty.
necesitado *adj* needy. **necesitar** *v* need.

néctar ['nektar] *sm* nectar.

nefario [ne'farjo] *adj* nefarious.

nefasto [ne'fasto] *adj* ill-omened;
unlucky.

***negar** [ne'gar] *v* deny; refuse. **negarse** *v*
decline. **negación** *sf* negation. **negativa**
sf (*foto*) negative; refusal.

negligencia [negli'xenθja] *sf* negligence.
negligente *adj* negligent.

negociar [nego'θjar] *v* trade; negotiate.
negociable *adj* negotiable. **negociación** *sf*
transaction; negotiation. **negociado** *sm*
bureau; divison. **negociador, -a** *sm, sf*

negotiator; agent. **negociante** *sm* businessman; merchant. **negocio** *sm* business; trade; negotiation.

negro ['negro], **-a** *s, adj* black. **negrura** *sf*
blackness.

nene ['nene], **-a** *sm, sf* baby.

nenúfar [ne'nufar] *sm* waterlily.

neón [ne'on] *sm* neon.

nepotismo [nepo'tismo] *sm* nepotism.

nervio ['nerβjo] *sm* nerve; (*de una hoja*)
rib; sinew. **crisparle los nervios a uno** get
on someone's nerves. **tener los nervios en
punta** be on edge. **nerviosidad** *sf* nervous-
ness. **nervioso** *adj* nervous. **crisis nerviosa**
sf nervous breakdown.

neto ['neto] *adj* pure; clear; (*com*) net.

neumático [neu'matiko] *sm* tyre. *adj*
pneumatic.

neumonía [neumo'nia] *sf* pneumonia.

neuralgia [neu'ralxja] *sf* neuralgia.
neurálgico *adj* neuralgic.

neurótico [neu'rotiko] *adj* neurotic. **neurosis** *sf* neurosis.

neutro ['neutro] *adj* neutral; (*gram*) neuter. **neutral** *s(m+f)*, *adj* neutral. **neutralidad** *sf* neutrality. **neutralizar** *v* neutralize.

***nevar** [ne'βar] *v* snow. **nevada** *sf* snow
storm. **nevasca** *sf* snowfall. **nevera** *sf*
refrigerator. **nevisca** *sf* light snowfall.
neviscar *v* snow lightly. **nevoso** *adj*
snowy.

nexo ['nekso] *sm* link, tie.

ni [ni] *conj* neither; nor; or; not even. **ni
uno ni otro** neither one nor the other.
pron nobody.

nicotina [niko'tina] *sf* nicotine.

nicho ['nitʃo] *sm* niche.

nido ['niðo] *sm* nest. **cunas de nido** pull-
out beds. **nidada** *sf* brood; clutch. **nidal**
sm nest; nest egg.

niebla [ni'eβla] *sf* fog; mist; mildew.

nieto [ni'eto] *sm* grandson. **nieta** *sf* grand-
daughter.

nieve [ni'eβe] *sf* snow.

nilón [ni'lon] *sm* nylon.

ninfa ['ninfa] *sf* nymph.

ninguno [nin'guno] *adj also* **ningún** no;
not one. **de ninguna manera** in no way.
pron nobody.

niña ['niɲa] *sf* little girl; (*del ojo*) pupil.
niñada *sf* childishness. **niñera** *sf* nanny.
niñez *sf* childhood. **niño** *sm* little boy;
child. **desde niño** from childhood.

níquel ['nikel] *sm* nickel. **niquelar** *v* nick-
el-plate.

níspero ['nispero] *sm* medlar tree. **níspola** *sf* medlar.

nítido ['nitiðo] *adj* clear; bright. **nitidez** *sf* brightness; neatness.

nitrógeno [ni'troxeno] *sm* nitrogen. **nitrato** *sm* nitrate. **nítrico** *adj* nitric. **nitro** *sm* nitre; saltpetre. **nitroso** *adj* nitrous.

nivelar [niβe'lar] *v* level; balance. **nivelarse** *v* become level. **nivelarse con** get even with. **nivel** *sm* level; standard. **nivel de aire** spirit-level. **nivel de vida** standard of living. **paso a nivel** level-crossing. **nivelación** *sf* levelling.

no [no] *adv* no; not. **no bien** no sooner. **no más** only. **no obtante** in spite of. **que no** if only.

noble ['noβle] *adj* noble. *sm* nobleman. **nobleza** *sf* nobility.

noción [no'θjon] *sf* notion; idea. **nociones** *sf pl* smattering *sing*; rudiments.

nocivo [no'θiβo] *adj* noxious; harmful.

nocturno [nok'turno] *adj* nocturnal; night. **noctámbulo, -a** *sm, sf* sleepwalker.

noche ['notʃe] *sf* night; evening. **por la noche** at night. **Nochebuena** *sf* Christmas Eve.

nódulo ['noðulo] *sm* nodule.

nogal [no'gal] *sm also* **noguera** *sf* walnut tree.

nómada ['nomaða] *s(m+f)* nomad. *adj* nomadic.

nombrar [nom'brar] *v* name; nominate; mention. **nombradía** *sf* reputation. **nombramiento** *sm* naming; nomination. **nombre** *sm* name; title. **nombre de pila** Christian name. **nomenclatura** *sf* nomenclature; terminology; catalogue. **nómina** *sf* list; payroll. **nominación** *sf* nomination. **nominal** *adj* nominal. **nominativo** *sm* (*gram*) nominative.

non [non] *adj* (*mat*) odd. *sm* odd number.

nonagésimo [nona'xesimo] *adj* ninetieth. **nonagenario, -a** *s, adj* nonagenarian.

norabuena [nora'βwena] *sf* congratulations *pl. adv* by good fortune. **noramala** *adv* unfortunately.

nordeste [nor'ðeste] *sm* north-east; (*viento*) northeaster. *adj* north-east.

noria [no'ria] *sf* waterwheel.

norma ['norma] *sf* norm; rule. **normal** *adj* normal. **normalidad** *sf* normality. **normalizar** *v* normalize.

noroeste [noro'este] *sm* north-west; (*viento*) northwesterly. *adj* north-west.

norte ['norte] *sm, adj* north. **perder el norte** lose one's bearings. **norteño** *adj* northern.

Noruega [nor'wega] *sf* Norway. **noruego, -a** *sm, sf* (*persona*) Norwegian; *sm* (*idioma*) Norwegian.

nos [nos] *pron* us, ourselves.

nosotros [no'sotros] *pron* we; us, ourselves.

nostalgia [nos'talxja] *sf* nostalgia. **nostálgico** *adj* nostalgic; homesick.

notar [no'tar] *v* note; notice; note down. **nota** *sf* (*música, etc.*) note; mark; report; repute. **notabilidad** *sf* notability. **notable** *adj* notable. **notación** *sf* notation.

notario [no'tarjo] *sm* notary. **notaría** *sf* notary's office.

noticiar [noti'θjar] *v* notify. **noticia(s)** *sf* (*pl*) news *sing*. **noticiario** *sm* news bulletin. **noticiero, -a** *sm, sf* reporter. **notición** *sm* (*fam*) big news. **noticioso** *adj* well-informed. **notificación** *sf* notification.

notorio [no'torjo] *adj* notorious. **notoriedad** *sf* notoriety.

novato [no'βato], **-a** *s, adj* novice.

novecientos [noβe'θjentos] *adj, s* nine hundred.

novedad [nove'ðað] *sf* novelty; change. **novedades** *sf pl* latest models.

novela [no'βela] *sf* novel. **novelista** *s(m+f)* novelist.

noveno [no'βeno] *adj* ninth. **noventa** *adj* ninety.

novia ['noβja] *sf* girlfriend; fiancée; bride. **traje de novia** wedding dress. **novio** *sm* boyfriend; fiancé; bridegroom.

novicio [no'βiθjo] *sm* beginner; apprentice. **noviciado** *sm* novitiate; apprenticeship.

noviembre [no'βjembre] *sm* November.

novilla [no'βiʎa] *sf* heifer. **novillada** *sf* bullfight with young bulls. **novillero** *sm* novice bullfighter. **novillo** *sm* young bull. **hacer novillos** play truant.

nube ['nuβe] *sf* cloud. **estar por las nubes** (*precios*) be sky-high. **poner por las nubes** praise to the skies. **nublado** *adj* overcast. **nublar** *v* cloud over. **nubloso** *adj* cloudy; ill-fated.

núcleo ['nukleo] *sm* nucleus; core; (*bot*) stone. **nuclear** *adj* nuclear.

nudillo [nu'ðiʎo] *sm* knuckle.

nudo[1] ['nuðo] *sm* knot; bond; tumour.

nudo[2] *adj* nude.

nuera ['nwera] *sf* daughter-in-law.
nuestro ['nwestro] *adj* our. *pron* ours.
nueva ['nweβa] *sf* news. **nuevo** *adj* new.
de nuevo again. **nuevo flamante** brand
new.
nueve ['nweβe] *adj, sm* nine.
nuez [nweθ] *sf* nut; walnut. **nuez de la
garganta** Adam's apple.
nulo ['nulo] *adj* null; void; (*fig*) hopeless.
numerar [nume'rar] *v* number. **numeral**
sm, adj numeral. **numérico** *adj* numerical. **número** *sm* number; size; quantity.
numeroso *adj* numerous.
nunca ['nunka] *adv* never; ever. **casi nunca** hardly ever.
nuncio ['nunθjo] *sm* nuncio; (*fig*) omen.
nupcial [nup'θjal] *adj* nuptial. **nupcias** *sf
pl* nuptials.
nutria [nu'tria] *sf also* **nutra** *sf* otter.
nutrir [nu'trir] *v* nourish. **nutrición** *sf*
nutrition. **nutrimento** *sm* nutriment.

Ñ

ñaque ['ɲake] *sm* odds and ends.
ñoño ['ɲoɲo] *adj* insipid; prudish; fussy.
ñoñeria *sf also* **ñoñez** *sf* insipidity; prudery; fussiness.
ñu [ɲu] *sm* gnu.

O

o [o] *conj* or. **o ... o** either ... or. **o sea**
in other words.
obcecar [oβθe'kar] *v* blind; deceive. **obcecarse** *v* become blind; be dazzled. **obcecado** *adj* blind; obdurate.
obduración [oβðura'θjon] *sf* obduracy;
obstinacy.
***obedecer** [oβeðe'θer] *v* obey. **obediencia**
sf obedience. **obediente** *adj* obedient.
obertura [oβer'tura] *sf* (*música*) overture.
obesidad [oβesi'ðað] *sf* obesity. **obeso** *adj*
obese.
obispo [o'βispo] *sm* bishop. **obispado** *sm*
bishopric.
obituario [oβi'twarjo] *sm* obituary.

objetar [oβxe'tar] *v* object (to). **objeción**
sf objection. **objetivo** *sm* objective. **objeto**
sm object.
oblicuo [o'βlikwo] *adj* oblique. **oblicuar** *v*
slant.
obligar [oβli'gar] *v* oblige; force. **verse
obligado a** be forced to. **obligación** *sf*
obligation. **obligado** *adj* essential. **obligatorio** *adj* compulsory.
obliterar [oβlite'rar] *v* obliterate;
obstruct.
oblongo [o'βlongo] *adj* oblong.
obrar [o'βrar] *v* work; operate; make;
build; behave. **obra** *sf* work. **obra maestra** masterpiece. **obrero, -a** *sm, sf* worker.
obsceno [oβs'θeno] *adj* obscene.
obscenidad *sf* obscenity.
***obscurecer** [oβskure'θer] *v also*
oscurecer obscure, darken. **obscuridad** *sf*
obscurity. **obscuro** *adj* obscure.
obsequiar [oβseki'ar] *v* entertain; treat;
present. **obsequio** *sm* courtesy; gift. **obsequioso** *adj* obsequious; attentive.
observar [oβser'var] *v* observe. **observación** *sf* observation. **observador, -a** *sm, sf*
observer. **observancia** *sf* observance.
observante *adj* observant. **observatorio**
sm observatory.
obsesión [oβse'sjon] *sf* obsession. **obsesionante** *adj* obsessive. **obseso** *adj*
obsessed.
obsoleto [oβso'leto] *adj* obsolete.
obstáculo [oβs'takulo] *sm* obstacle.
obstante [oβs'tante] *prep* in spite of. *adv*
no obstante notwithstanding; nevertheless. **obstar** *v* hinder; oppose.
obstetricia [oβste'triθja] *sf* obstetrics.
obstétrico *adj* obstetric.
obstinarse [oβsti'narse] *v* be obstinate;
persist. **obstinación** *sf* obstinacy.
obstinado *adj* obstinate.
***obstruir** [oβstru'ir] *v* obstruct. **obstrucción** *sf* obstruction. **obstructivo** *adj*
obstructive.
***obtener** [oβte'ner] *v* obtain. **obtención** *sf*
attainment.
obturar [obtu'rar] *v* stop up, plug. **obturación** *sf* plugging; sealing. **velocidad de
obturación** (*foto*) shutter speed.
obturador *sm* plug; (*foto*) shutter.
obtuso [oβ'tuso] *adj* obtuse.
obús [o'βus] *sm* howitzer.
obvio ['oββjo] *adj* obvious. **obviar** *v* obviate.

oca ['oka] sf goose.

ocasión [oka'sjon] sf occasion; opportunity; reason. ocasional adj occasional; chance. ocasionalmente adv occasionally; accidentally. ocasionar v cause.

ocaso [o'kaso] sm sunset; decline; west.

occidental [okθiðen'tal] adj western, occidental. occidente sm west.

océano [o'θeano] sm ocean.

ocio ['oθjo] sm leisure; idleness. ociosidad sf idleness. ocioso adj idle.

ocre ['okre] sm ochre.

octágono [ok'tagono] adj octagonal. sm octagon.

octava [ok'taβa] sf octave. octavo adj eighth. octogenario, -a sm, sf octogenarian. octogésimo adj eightieth.

octubre [ok'tuβre] sm October.

ocular [oku'lar] adj ocular. testigo ocular eyewitness. sm eyepiece. oculista s(m+f) oculist.

ocultar [okul'tar] v hide. ocultación sf concealment; dissimulation. oculto adj secret; hidden; occult.

ocupar [oku'par] v occupy; employ; take over. ocuparse (de) look after; do; employ. ocupación sf occupation. ocupado adj occupied; taken; engaged. ocupante s(m+f) occupant.

occurrir [okur'rir] v occur. ocurrencia sf occurrence; (fig) witticism; idea. ocurrente adj witty.

ochenta [o'tʃenta] sm, adj eighty. ocho sm, adj eight.

oda ['oða] sf ode.

odiar [o'ðjar] v hate. odio sm hate, hatred. tener odio a uno hate someone. odiosidad sf hatefulness; odiousness. odioso adj odious; hateful.

odorífero [oðo'rifero] adj odoriferous, fragrant.

oeste [o'este] sm west.

ofender [ofen'der] v offend; insult. ofenderse v resent. ofensa sf offence; insult. ofensiva sf attack. ofensivo adj offensive; insulting. ofensor, -a sm, sf offender.

oferta [o'ferta] sf offer; bid; tender; gift. ley de la oferta y la demanda law of supply and demand.

oficial [ofi'θjal] adj, sm official. oficialía sf clerkship. oficina sf office; agency; laboratory. oficio sm job; appointment; calling. oficioso adj diligent; meddlesome.

*ofrecer [ofre'θer] v offer. ofrecerse v volunteer. ¿qué se le ofrece a usted? may I help you? ofrecimiento sm offer. ofrendar v contribute. ofrenda sf offer.

ofuscar [ofus'kar] v bewilder; dazzle.

ogro ['ogro] sm ogre.

oigo [o'igo] V oír.

*oír [o'ir] v hear; listen to. oírse v be heard. oír decir que hear that. oída sf hearing. oíble adj audible. oído sm hearing; ear. dolor de oídos earache.

ojal [o'xal] sm buttonhole.

ojalá [oxa'la] interj let's hope so! would to God! conj if only.

ojear¹ [oxe'ar] v look at. ojeada sf glance. ojear² v (en la caza) start game; (espantar) scare off.

ojo ['oxo] sm eye; opening; hole; keyhole; (puente) span. ¡ojo! look out!

ola ['ola] sf wave. ola de calor heatwave.

olé [o'le] interj bravo!

oleandro [ole'andro] sm oleander.

óleo ['oleo] sm oil. pintura al óleo sf oil painting. oleoducto sm pipeline. oleosidad sf oiliness. oleoso adj oily.

*oler [o'ler] v smell. oler bien/mal smell good/bad. olfatear v smell; sniff; sniff out. olfato sm sense of smell. olfatorio adj olfactory. oliente adj smelling. olor sm smell. oloroso adj fragrant.

oligarquía [oligar'kia] sf oligarchy.

olímpico [o'limpiko] adj Olympic. juegos olímpicos Olympic games.

oliva [o'liβa] sf olive; olive tree. olivar sm olive grove. olivo sm olive tree.

olmo ['olmo] sm elm tree. olmeda sf elm grove.

olvidar [olβi'ðar] v forget. olvidadizo adj forgetful. olvido sm forgetfulness.

olla ['oʎa] sf pot; kettle; stew; (remolino) eddy. olla exprés pressure cooker. olla podrida hotpot.

ombligo [om'bligo] sm navel; (fig) core.

ominoso [omi'noso] adj ominous.

omitir [omi'tir] v omit; neglect. omisión sf omission. omiso adj careless. hacer caso omiso de ignore; overlook.

ómnibus ['omniβus] sm omnibus.

omnipotencia [omnipo'tenθja] sf omnipotence. omnipotente adj omnipotent.

omnisciencia [omni'sθjenθja] sf omniscience. omniscio adj omniscient.

omnívoro [om'niβoro] adj omnivorous.

once ['onθe] sm, adj eleven.

onda ['onda] *sf* wave; ripple. onda corta/larga/media short/long/medium wave. onda luminosa light wave. onda sonora sound wave. ondear *v* wave. ondearse *v* swing. ondulación *sf* undulation. ondulado *adj* wavy. ondulante *adj* undulating. ondular *v* undulate; wriggle.
oneroso [one'roso] *adj* onerous.
ónice ['oniθe] *sm also* ónique, ónix onyx.
onza ['onθa] *sf* (*peso y animal*) ounce.
opaco [o'pako] *adj* opaque; dull. opacidad *sf* opacity.
opción [op'θjon] *sf* option. opcional *adj* optional.
ópera ['opera] *sf* opera.
operar [ope'rar] *v* operate. operación *sf* operation. operador, -a *sm, sf* operator; surgeon; projectionist. operante *adj* operative. operario, -a *sm, sf* operative, worker. operativo *adj* operative.
opinar [opi'nar] *v* think; judge. opinión *sf* opinion.
opio ['opjo] *sm* opium.
*oponer [opo'ner] *v* oppose; hinder; contradict. oponerse a compete for. oposición *sf* opposition. opositor, -a *sm, sf* opponent; competitor.
oportunidad [oportuni'ðað] *sf* opportunity. oportunista *adj* opportunist. oportuno *adj* opportune.
oprimir [opri'mir] *v* oppress; depress. opresión *sf* oppression. opresivo *adj* oppressive. opresor, -a *sm, sf* oppressor.
oprobio [o'proβjo] *sm* opprobrium, disgrace. oprobioso *adj* disgraceful.
optar [op'tar] *v* opt, choose.
óptico ['optiko] *adj* optic, optical. *sm* optician.
optimismo [opti'mismo] *sm* optimism. optimista *s(m+f)* optimist.
óptimo ['optimo] *adj* optimum, best.
opuesto [o'pwesto] *adj* opposed; against.
opulento [opu'lento] *adj* opulent. opulencia *sf* opulence.
oquedad [oke'ðað] *sf* hole; hollow.
ora ['ora] *conj* now.
oráculo [o'rakulo] *sm* oracle.
orangután [orangu'tan] *sm* orangutan.
orar [o'rar] *v* pray; plead; make a speech. oración *sf* oration; prayer. partes de la oración parts of speech. orador, -a *sm, sf* orator. orador sagrado preacher. oral *adj* oral.
orbe ['orβe] *sm* orb, globe.

órbita ['orβita] *sf* orbit. orbitar *v* orbit.
ordenar [orðe'nar] *v* order, command; tidy; direct; ordain. ordenarse *v* become ordained. orden *sm* order, sequence. por su orden successively. ordenación *sf* arrangement; ordination. ordenanza *sf* arrangement; ordinance.
ordeñar [orðe'nar] *v* milk.
ordinal [orði'nal] *adj* ordinal.
ordinario [orði'narjo] *adj* ordinary; common. de ordinario usually.
orear [ore'ar] *v* air, ventilate. orearse *v* get a breath of fresh air.
oreja [o'rexa] *sf* ear. bajar las orejas knuckle under.
orfebre [or'feβre] *sm* goldsmith; silversmith. orfebrería *sf* goldwork; silverwork.
orfeón [orfe'on] *sm* choral society.
orgánico [or'ganiko] *adj* organic. organismo *sm* organism. organista *s(m+f)* organist. organización *sf* organization. organizador, -a *sm, sf* organizer. organo *sm* organ.
orgasmo [or'gasmo] *sm* orgasm.
orgía [or'xia] *sf* orgy.
orgulloso [orgu'loso] *adj* proud. *sm* pride.
orientarse [orjen'tarse] *v* find one's bearings. orientación *sf* orientation. oriental *adj* oriental, eastern. oriente *sm* orient, east. Extremo Oriente Far East. Oriente Medio Middle East.
orificio [ori'fiθjo] *sm* orifice, hole.
origen [o'rixen] *sm* origin; native country. original *adj* original. originalidad *sf* originality. originar *v* originate. originarse *v* arise.
orilla [o'riʎa] *sf* edge; bank; shore. a orillas de on the banks of.
orín [o'rin] *sm* rust.
orina [o'rina] *sf* urine. orinal *sm* chamber pot. orinar *v* urinate.
oriundo [o'rjundo] *adj* native of.
orlar [or'lar] *v* border, edge. orla *sf* border, trimming.
ornamentar [ornamen'tar] *v* adorn, decorate. ornamentación *sf* ornamentation. ornamental *adj* ornamental. ornamento *sm* ornament. ornar *v* adorn. ornato *sm* adornment.
ornitología [ornitolo'xia] *sf* ornithology. ornitólogo *sm* ornithologist.
oro ['oro] *sm* gold. oro batido gold leaf. oro en bruto bullion. oropel *sm* tinsel.

orquesta [or'kesta] *sf* orchestra. **orquestación** *sf* orchestration. **orquestar** *v* orchestrate.

orquídea [or'kiðea] *sf* orchid.

ortega [or'tega] *sf* grouse.

ortodoxo [orto'ðokso] *adj* orthodox. **ortodoxia** *sf* orthodoxy.

ortografía [ortogra'fia] *sf* orthography, spelling.

ortopédico [orto'peðiko]. **-a** *sm*, *sf* orthopedist. *adj* orthopedic.

oruga [o'ruga] *sf* caterpillar.

os [os] *pron pl* you.

osa ['osa] *sf* she-bear. **oso** bear. **oso blanco** polar bear.

osar [o'sar] *v* dare. **osadía** *sf* daring. **osado** *adj* daring.

oscilar [osθi'lar] *v* oscillate, swing. **oscilación** *sf* oscillation.

oscuro [os'kuro] *adj* dark, obscure. **oscurecer** *v* darken; confuse. **oscuridad** *sf* obscurity.

ostensible [osten'siβle] *adj* ostensible; apparent. **ostentación** *sf* ostentation. **ostentar** *v* show off. **ostentativo** *adj* also **ostentoso** ostentatious.

ostra ['ostra] *sf* oyster.

otear [ote'ar] *v* make out; watch; scan.

otoño [o'toɲo] *sm* autumn. **otoñada** *sf* autumn season. **otoñal** *adj* autumnal. **otoñarse** *v* be seasoned.

otorgar [otor'gar] *v* grant; award; confer. **otorgamiento** *sm* granting; authorization.

otro ['otro] *adj* other; another. **otra vez** again. **otro tanto** the same (again). *pron* another. **algún otro** some other.

ovación [oβa'θjon] *sf* ovation. **ovacionar** *v* give an ovation to.

óvalo ['oβalo] *sm* oval; ellipse. **oval** *adj* oval.

ovario [o'βarjo] *sm* ovary.

oveja [o'βexa] *sf* ewe; sheep.

ovillo [o'βiʎo] *sm* (*de lana*) ball; heap.

oxidar [oksi'ðar] *v* oxidize. **óxido** *sm* oxide. **oxígeno** *sm* oxygen.

oye ['oje] *V* **oír**.

oyente [o'jente] *adj* hearing. *s(m+f)* listener.

ozono [o'θono] *sm* ozone.

P

pabellón [paβe'ʎon] *sm* pavilion; bell tent; summerhouse; hospital block; flag.

*pacer [pa'θer] *v* graze, pasture.

paciencia [pa'θjenθja] *sf* patience. **paciente** *s(m+f)*. *adj* patient. **pacienzudo** *adj* long-suffering.

pacificar [paθifi'kar] *v* pacify. **pacificación** *sf* pacification. **pacificador** *adj* pacifying. **pacífico** *adj* pacific, peaceful. **Oceano Pacífico** Pacific Ocean. **pacifismo** *sm* pacifism. **pacifista** *s(m+f)* pacifist.

pacotilla [pako'tiʎa] *sf* inferior goods *pl*. **de pacotilla** shoddy.

pactar [pak'tar] *v* make a pact, agree. **pacto** *sm* pact, agreement.

pachorra [pa'tʃorra] *sf* sluggishness; indolence.

*padecer [paðe'θer] *v* suffer; endure. **padecer de** suffer from. **padecimiento** *sm* suffering; ailment.

padre ['paðre] *sm* father. **padres** *sm pl* parents. **padrastro** *sm* stepfather. **Padre Nuestro** Lord's Prayer. **padrino** *sm* godfather; second; sponsor. **padrino de boda** best man.

padrón [pa'ðron] *sm* census; pattern; memorial; (*fam*) indulgent father.

pagano [pa'gano]. **-a** *sm*, *sf*, *adj* pagan.

pagar [pa'gar] *v* pay. **pagarse de** take a liking to. **paga** *sf* payment; salary. **pagadero** *adj* payable. **pagador**, **-a** *sm*, *sf* payer. **pagaduría** *sf* pay office. **pagaré** *sm* IOU. **pago** *sm* payment; reward.

página ['paxina] *sf* page.

país [pa'is] *sm* country. **paisaje** *sm* landscape; countryside. **paisanaje** *sm* peasantry. **paisano**, **-na** *sm*, *sf* compatriot; peasant.

Paises Bajos [pa'ises'βaxos] *sm pl* The Netherlands.

paja ['paxa] *sf* straw. **echar pajas** draw lots. **pajita** *sf* drinking straw.

pájaro ['paxaro] *sm* bird. **pajarera** *sf* birdcage.

paje ['paxe] *sm* (*niño*) page.

pala ['pala] *sf* shovel; spade; scoop; dustpan; bat. **palazo** *sm* blow with a stick.

palabra [pa'laβra] *sf* word. **de palabra** by word of mouth. **faltar a la palabra** break one's word. **palabreo** *sm* verbiage.

palabrista s(m+f) chatterbox. **palabrota** sf swear word.

palacio [pa'laθjo] sm palace; mansion. **en palacio** at court.

paladar [pala'ðar] sm palate. **paladear** v taste, relish.

palanca [pa'lanka] sf crowbar; lever; (fam) influence.

palangana [palan'gana] sf washbasin.

palco ['palko] sm (teatro) box.

paleta [pa'leta] sf shovel; trowel; (de pintor) palette; (de hélice) blade; (anat) shoulder blade.

paliar [pali'ar] v alleviate. **paliativo** adj palliative.

***palidecer** [paliðe'θer] v become pale. **palidez** paleness. **pálido** adj pale.

palillo [pa'liʎo] sm toothpick; small stick.

paliza [pa'liθa] sf beating, hiding.

palma ['palma] sf palm tree; (anat) palm. **palmada** sf slap; applause. **palmar** adj clear, obvious. **palmatoria** sf candlestick; cane. **palmear** v clap hands. **palmera** sf palm tree.

palmo ['palmo] sm (medida) span, hand-breadth. **palmotear** v applaud. **palmoteo** sm applause.

palo ['palo] sm stick; pole; handle; blow with a stick; mast. **dar de palos** thrash.

paloma [pa'loma] sf dove; pigeon. **palomar** sm dovecote. **palomino** sm young pigeon.

palpable [pal'paβle] adj palpable.

palpar [pal'par] v feel, touch. **palparse** v grope.

palpitar [palpi'tar] v palpitate, throb. **palpitación** sf palpitation. **palpitante** adj palpitating, throbbing.

paludismo [palu'ðismo] sm malaria.

palurdo [pa'lurðo] sm, adj rustic.

palustre[1] [pa'lustre] adj marshy.

palustre[2] sm trowel.

pan [pan] sm bread; loaf; dough. **pan ácimo** unleavened bread. **panadería** sf bread shop. **panadero, -a** sm, sf baker.

pana ['pana] sf corduroy. **pana lisa** velvet.

panal [pa'nal] sm honeycomb.

panamá [pana'ma] sm Panama hat.

panamericano [panameri'kano] adj pan-American.

pancarta [pan'karta] sf placard.

pandereta [pande'reta] sf tambourine.

pandilla [pan'diʎa] sf gang; clique.

panfleto [pan'fleto] sm pamphlet. **panfletista** s(m+f) pamphleteer.

pánico ['paniko] sm, adj panic.

pantalón [panta'lon] sm also **pantalones** trousers.

pantalla [pan'taʎa] sf lampshade; screen.

pantano [pan'tano] sm marsh; bog. **pantanal** sm marshland. **pantanoso** adj swampy.

panteísta [pante'ista] s(m+f) pantheist. **panteísmo** sm pantheism.

pantera [pan'tera] sf panther.

pantomima [panto'mima] sf pantomime.

pantorrilla [pantor'riʎa] sf (anat) calf.

pantufla [pan'tufla] sf or **pantuflo** sm slipper.

panza ['panθa] sf belly. **panzada** sf bellyful.

pañal [pa'nal] sm nappy.

pañería [pane'ria] sf drapery. **pañero** sm draper. **pañete** sm light cloth. **paño** sm cloth. **paños menores** underclothes. **pañuelo** sm handkerchief.

papa[1] ['papa] sm pope. **papado** sm papacy. **papal** adj papal.

papa[2] sf potato.

papá [pa'pa] sm daddy.

papada [pa'paða] sf double chin.

papagayo [papa'gajo] sm parrot.

papar [pa'par] v eat; gulp. **papamoscas** m invar flycatcher; (fig) simpleton. **papar moscas** gape.

papel [pa'pel] sm paper. **papel de forrar** brown paper. **papel de fumar** cigarette paper. **papeleo** sm paper work; (fam) red tape. **papelera** sf wastepaper basket. **papelería** sf stationer's.

papera [pa'pera] sf goitre. **paperas** sf pl mumps sing.

papiro [pa'piro] sm papyrus.

paquete [pa'kete] sm packet.

par [par] sm pair. adj equal. **sin par** matchless.

para ['para] prep for; towards. **para mañana** by tomorrow. **¿para qué?** why?

parábola [pa'raβola] sf parable; parabola.

parabrisas [para'βrisas] sm invar windshield.

paracaídas [paraka'iðas] sm invar parachute. **paracaidista** s(m+f) parachutist.

parochoques [para'ʃtokes] sm invar (auto) bumper.

parada [pa'raða] sf stop; stopping; (taxi) rank; pause; parade; dam. **paradero** sm whereabouts; destination; home. **parado** adj motionless; unemployed.

paradoja [para'ðoxa] *sf* paradox.
paradójico *adj* paradoxical.
parador [para'ðor] *sm* tourist hotel.
parafina [para'fina] *sf* paraffin.
paráfrasis [pa'rafrasis] *sf* *invar* paraphrase. **parafrasear** *v* paraphrase.
paraguas [pa'ragwas] *sm* *invar* umbrella.
paraíso [para'iso] *sm* paradise; (*teatro*) gallery.
paralela [para'lela] *sf* parallel. **paralelas** *sf pl* parallel bars. **paralelo** *sm, adj* parallel.
parálisis [pa'ralisis] *sf* paralysis. **paralítico** *sm, adj* paralytic. **paralizar** *v* paralyse.
páramo ['paramo] *sm* wilderness; bleak plateau. **paramera** *sf* desert.
parangón [paran'gon] *sm* comparison. **parangonar** *v* compare.
parapeto [para'peto] *sm* parapet; railing.
parar [pa'rar] *v* stop; check. **pararse** *v* stay; end up. **parar en mal** come to a bad end.
pararrayos [parar'rajos] *sm* *invar* lightning conductor.
parásito [pa'rasito] *sm* parasite. *adj* parasitic.
parasol [para'sol] *sm* parasol.
parcela [par'θela] *sf* (*de tierra*) plot. **parcelar** *v* parcel out.
parcial [par'θjal] *adj* partial. **parcialidad** *sf* partiality.
parco ['parko] *adj* frugal; mean; sparing.
parche ['partʃe] *sm* plaster; patch; drumhead.
pardo ['parðo] *adj* dark; brown.
parear [pare'ar] *v* match, pair.
***parecer** [pare'θer] *v* seem; appear. **parecerse** *v* resemble. **parecido** *adj* similar. **bien parecido** good-looking.
pared [pa'reð] *sf* wall. **paredón** *sm* large wall.
pareja [pa'rexa] *sf* pair; couple. **parejo** *adj* even; equal.
parentela [paren'tela] *sf* kindred. **parentesco** *sm* kinship.
paréntesis [pa'rentesis] *sm* parenthesis; bracket.
paridad [pari'ðað] *sf* comparison; parity.
pariente [pa'rjente] *sm* relation.
parir [pa'rir] *v* give birth to.
París [pa'ris] *s* Paris.
parla ['parla] *sf* gossip; chatter. **parlador, -a** *sm, sf* talker. **parlanchín** *adj* talkative. **parlante** *adj* chattering. **parlar** *v* chatter. **parleta** *sf* small talk.

parlamento [parla'mento] *sm* parliament. **parlamentario** *adj* parliamentary.
paro ['paro] *sm* stoppage; unemployment.
parodiar [paro'ðjar] *v* parody. **parodia** *sf* parody.
paroxismo [parok'sismo] *sm* paroxysm.
parpadear [parpaðe'ar] *v* blink; wink. **parpadeo** *sm* blinking; winking. **párpado** *sm* eyelid.
parque ['parke] *sm* park.
parra ['parra] *sf* vine. **hoja de parra** figleaf. **parra virgen** Virginia creeper.
párrafo ['parrafo] *sm* paragraph.
parricida [parri'θiða] *s(m+f)* (*criminal*) parricide. **parricidio** *sm* (*crimen*) parricide.
parrilla [par'riʎa] *sf* grill; gridiron; grate; grillroom.
párroco ['parroko] *sm* parish priest. **parroquia** *sf* parish; parish church. **parroquial** *adj* parochial. **parroquiano, -a** *sm, sf* parishioner; regular customer.
parsimonia [parsi'monja] *sf* parsimony; frugality; calmness.
parte ['parte] *sf* part; share; point; side; way; party; role; actor. **en otra parte** elsewhere. **por todas partes** everywhere. **por una parte y por otra** on the one hand and on the other.
partera [par'tera] *sf* midwife.
partición [parti'θjon] *sf* partition; division. **partible** *adj* divisible.
participar [partiθi'par] *v* participate; partake; invest; inform; announce. **participación** *sf* participation; share; announcement. **participante** *s(m+f)* participant; informant; competitor. **partícipe** *s(m+f)* participant.
participio [parti'θipjo] *sm* (*gram*) participle.
partícula [par'tikula] *sf* particle.
particular [partiku'lar] *adj* particular; peculiar; individual; personal. **casa particular** private house. *sm* matter; individual; civilian. **particularidad** *sf* peculiarity. **particularizar** *v* specify; distinguish; prefer. **particularizarse** *v* stand out. **particularamente** *adv* in particular.
partida [par'tiða] *sf* departure; certificate; (*com*) entry; item; party; game. **partida de campo** picnic. **partida doble** double entry. **partidario, -a** *sm, sf* follower; partisan.
partido [par'tiðo] *sm* (*deporte*) match;

(*pol*) party. *adj* divided. **darse a partido**
give in. **sacar partido** benefit from.
partir [par'tir] *v* leave, depart; divide;
share. **a partir de hoy** from today on.
partirse *v* differ in opinion; depart. **par-
tidor** *sm* distributor.
partitura [parti'tura] *sf* (*música*) score.
parto ['parto] *sm* childbirth; delivery;
(*fig*) brainchild.
parvo ['parβo] *adj* little. **párvulo** *adj* very
small.
pasa ['pasa] *sf* raisin. **pasa de Corinto** currant.
pasada [pa'saða] *sf* passage; (*aves*) flight.
de pasada in passing. **mala pasada** dirty
trick. **pasadero** *adj* tolerable.
pasado [pa'saðo] *sm*, *adj* past. **lo pasado,
pasado** let bygones be bygones. **pasado
mañana** the day after tomorrow.
pasador [pasa'ðor], **-a** *sm*, *sf* smuggler. *sm*
filter; colander; bolt; pin; fastener.
pasadores *sm pl* cufflinks *pl*.
pasaje [pa'saxe] *sm* passage; fare; ticket;
voyage; passengers *pl*. **pasajero, -a** *sm*, *sf*
passenger.
pasamano [pasa'mano] *sm* bannister;
handrail.
pasapasa [pasa'pasa] *sm* sleight-of-hand.
pasaporte [pasa'porte] *sm* passport.
pasar [pa'sar] *v* pass; give; spend; take;
send; run; cross; penetrate. **pasar de
moda** be out of fashion. **pasarlo bien/mal**
have a good/bad time. **pasar por** be considered. **pasar por alto** overlook. **¿qué
pasa?** what's up? **pasarse** pass off; be
over; miss. **pasarse de** be too. **pasarse
por** call in at.
pasarela [pasa'rela] *sf* footbridge; gangway.
pasatiempo [pasa'tjempo] *sm* pastime,
amusement.
pascua ['paskwa] *sf* (*rel*) feast; Christmas;
Easter; Epiphany; Passover. **¡felices pascuas y próspero año nuevo!** merry
Christmas and a happy New Year!
pase ['pase] *sm* invitation; permission;
(*autorización*) pass.
pasear [pase'ar] *v* go for a walk; take for
a walk; go for a ride. **paseo** *sm* walk;
drive; ride.
pasillo [pa'siʎo] *sm* corridor, passage.
pasión [pasi'on] *sf* passion. **pasional** *adj*
passionate.
pasivo [pa'siβo] *adj* passive. *sm* (*com*) lia-
bilities *pl*. **pasividad** *sf* passivity.

pasmar [pas'mar] *v* chill; stun; amaze.
pasmo *sm* amazement; convulsion. **pas-
moso** *adj* wonderful.
paso ['paso] *sm* step; pace; walk; passage; situation. **paso a nivel** level-crossing. **paso a paso** step by step. **salir del
paso** get out of a difficulty.
pasta ['pasta] *sf* pasta; dough; paste. **pastas** *sf pl* noodles.
pastar [pas'tar] *v* graze, pasture.
pastel [pas'tel] *sm* cake, pastry; (*color*)
pastel. **pastel de carne** meat pie. **pas-
telería** *sf* cake shop; cakes *pl*; confectionery. **pastelero, -a** *sm*, *sf* pastrycook.
pastilla [pas'tiʎa] *sf* bar; piece; tablet.
pastinaca [pasti'naka] *sf* (*bot*) turnip;
(*zool*) stingray.
pasto ['pasto] *sm* grass; pasture. **a pasto**
galore. **pastor** *sm* shepherd; pastor. **pastoral** *adj* pastoral. **pastorear** *v* pasture.
pastura [pas'tura] *sf* pasture; fodder.
pata ['pata] *sf* (*de animal*) foot; leg; paw.
meter la pata (*fam*) put one's foot in it.
tener mala pata (*fam*) be unlucky. **patada**
sf kick; stamp. **patalear** *v* stamp; kick
about. **pataleo** *sm* kicking.
patán [pa'tan] *sm* lout. *adj* churlish.
patanería *sf* boorishness.
patata [pa'tata] *sf* potato. **patatas fritas**
french fries.
patear [pate'ar] *v* kick; stamp.
patente [pa'tente] *sm* (*com*) patent. *adj*
obvious.
paternal [pater'nal] *adj* paternal.
paternidad *sf* paternity. **paterno** *adj*
paternal.
patético [pa'tetiko] *adj* pathetic.
patíbulo [pa'tiβulo] *sm* gallows *pl*.
patillas [pa'tiʎas] *sf pl* whiskers *pl*, side-
boards *pl*.
patín [pa'tin] *sm* skate. **patín de ruedas**
roller skate. **patinadero** *sm* skating rink.
patinador, -a *sm*, *sf* skater. **patinaje** *sm*
skating. **patinar** *v* skate; skid. **patinazo**
sm skid; (*fam*) blunder. **patinete** *sm*
child's scooter.
patio ['patjo] *sm* patio; yard.
pato ['pato] *sm* duck. **pagar el pato** (*fam*)
carry the can.
patochada [pato'tʃaða] *sf* blunder.
patología [patolo'xia] *sf* pathology. **patológico** *adj* pathological. **patólogo** *sm*
pathologist.

patraña [pa'traɲa] *sf* cock-and-bull story; fib.

patria ['patrja] *sf* native land. **patriota** *s(m+f)* patriot. **patriótico** *adj* patriotic. **patriotismo** *sm* patriotism.

patriarca [pa'trjarka] *sm* patriarch. **patriarcal** *adj* patriarchal.

patricio [pa'triθjo], **-a** *sm, sf, adj* patrician.

patrimonio [patri'monjo] *sm* patrimony, birthright. **patrimonial** *adj* patrimonial.

patrocinar [patroθi'nar] *v* patronize; sponsor. **patrocinador, -a** *sm, sf* patron; sponsor. **patrocinio** *sm* patronage; sponsorship.

patrón [pa'tron] *sm* patron; owner; landlord; pattern. **patronato** *sm* patronage; board of trustees; society.

patrono [pa'trono] *sm* boss; patron saint; owner.

patrulla [pa'truʎa] *sf* patrol. **patrullar** *v* patrol.

paulatino [paula'tino] *adj* slow, gradual. **paulatinamente** *adj* gradually; little by little.

pausa ['pausa] *sf* pause; (*música*) rest. **pausado** *adj* slow; deliberate. **pausar** *v* pause; interrupt.

pauta ['pauta] *sf* rule; model; lines *pl*. **pautar** *v* rule; give instructions. **papel pautado** ruled paper.

pávido ['paβiðo] *adj* timid.

pavimentar [paβimen'tar] *v* pave; surface. **pavimento** *sm* pavement.

pavo ['paβo] *sm* turkey. **pavo real** peacock. **pavonear** *v* show off.

pavor [pa'βor] *sm* terror; dread. **pavorido** *adj* terror-stricken. **pavoroso** *adj* dreadful; awful. **pavura** *sf* fear; dread.

payaso [pa'jaso] *sm* clown. **payasada** *sf* clowning.

paz [paθ] *sf* peace. **hacer las paces** make it up. **¡paz!** hush!

peaje [pe'axe] *sm* toll. **peajero** *sm* tollcollector.

peatón [pea'ton] *sm* pedestrian.

peca ['peka] *sf* spot; freckle. **pecoso** *adj* freckled.

pecar [pe'kar] *v* sin. **pecado** *sm* sin. **pecador, -a** *sm, sf* sinner. **pecaminoso** *adj* sinful.

pécora ['pekora] *sf* sheep; (*fam*) slut.

peculiar [peku'ljar] *adj* peculiar; special. **peculiaridad** *sf* peculiarity. **peculiarmente** peculiarly.

pechera [pe'tʃera] *sf* bib; shirt-front.

pecho ['petʃo] *sm* chest; bosom; breast; courage; tax. **dar el pecho** suckle. **enfermo del pecho** consumptive. **pechuga** *sf* (*de ave*) breast.

pedagogía [peðaɣo'xia] *sf* pedagogy. **pedagógico** *adj* teaching. **pedagogo** *sm* teacher.

pedal [pe'ðal] *sm* pedal. **pedalear** *v* pedal. **pedante** [pe'ðante] *s(m+f)* pedant. *adj* pedantic. **pedantería** *sf* pedantry.

pedazo [pe'ðaβo] *sm* piece. **hacerse pedazos** be smashed to bits.

pedernal [peðer'nal] *sm* flint.

pedestal [peðe'stal] *sm* pedestal.

pedestre [pe'ðestre] *adj* pedestrian.

pediatría [peðja'tria] *sf* paediatrics. **pediatra** *or* **pediatra** *sm* paediatrician.

pedicuro [peði'kuro], **-a** *sm, sf* chiropodist. *sf* chiropody.

*pedir [pe'ðir] *v* ask; ask for; order. **pedir limosna** beg. **pedir prestado** borrow. **pedido** *sm* demand; (*com*) order. **pedimento** *sm* petition.

pedo ['peðo] *sm* (*vulgar*) fart.

pedregal [peðre'gal] *sm* stony ground. **pedrea** *sf* stoning; hailstorm. **pedregoso** *adj* stony. **pedrería** *sf* jewels *pl*. **pedrero** *sm* stone-cutter. **pedrisco** *sm* hailstorm.

pegar [pe'gar] *v* hit; glue; (*med*) infect; take effect; give; let out; fire; sew on. **pegar fuego a** set fire to. **pegar un tiro** fire a shot. **pega** *sf* difficulty; hoax; snag. **poner pegas a** find fault with. **pegajoso** *adj* sticky; infectious.

peinar [pei'nar] *v* comb. **peinado** *sm* coiffure. **peinador, -a** *sm, sf* hairdresser; *sm* bathrobe. **peine** *sm* comb.

pelar [pe'lar] *v* cut; peel; shear; skin; shell. **pelar la pava** woo. **pelado** *adj* shorn; peeled; bare. **pelaje** *sm* fur. **pelambre** *sm* (*de animales*) hair. **pelambrera** *sf* fleece.

peldaño [pel'ðaɲo] *sm* stair; step.

pelear [pele'ar] *v* fight. **pelearse con alguien** fight somebody. **pelea** *sf* fight. **peleador** *sm* fight.

pelele [pe'lele] *sm* puppet; dummy.

peliagudo [pelja'guðo] *adj* (*fig*) difficult, tough.

pelícano [pe'likano] *sm* pelican.

película [pe'likula] *sf* film.

peligro [pe'ligro] *sm* danger. **peligrarse** *v* be in danger. **peligroso** *adj* dangerous.

pelmazo [pel'maθo] *sm also* **pelma** *sf* bore; crushed mass.

pelo ['pelo] *sm* hair; (*en madera*) grain; nap. **de medio pelo** low-class. **soltarse el pelo** show one's true colours. **pelón** *adj* bald.

pelota [pe'lota] *sf* ball. **echarse la pelota** pass the buck. **en pelota** naked.

pelotón [pelo'ton] *sm* platoon; squad.

peltre ['peltre] *sm* pewter.

peluca [pe'luka] *sf* wig.

peludo [pe'luðo] *adj* hairy.

peluquero [pelu'kero], **-a** *sm, sf* hairdresser. **peluquería** *sf* hairdresser's.

pelusa [pe'lusa] *sf* down; fuzz; (*fam*) jealousy.

pelleja [pe'ʎexa] *sf also* **pellejo** *sm* hide, skin. **jugarse el pellejo** risk one's neck.

pellizcar [peʎiθ'kar] *v* nip, pinch. **pellizco** *sm* nip, pinch.

pello ['peʎo] *sm* fur jacket.

pena ['pena] *sf* pain; grief; hardship; penalty; effort. **pena capital** capital punishment. **¡qué pena!** what a shame! **penable** *adj* punishable. **penado** *adj* painful. **penal** *adj* penal. **penalidad** *sf* penalty. **penar** *v* punish; suffer. **penarse** *v* grieve.

pender [pen'der] *v* hang; (*jur*) be pending. **pendiente** *adj* hanging; pending. **estar pendiente de** depend on.

péndulo ['pendulo] *sm* pendulum.

pene ['pene] *sm* penis.

penetrar [pene'trar] *v* penetrate; comprehend. **penetrarse** *v* become aware of; imbibe. **penetrable** *adj* penetrable. **penetración** *sf* penetration. **penetrante** *adj* penetrating.

penicilina [peniθi'lina] *sf* penicillin.

península [pe'ninsula] *sf* peninsula. **peninsular** *adj* peninsular.

penique [pe'nike] *sm* penny.

penitencia [peni'tenθja] *sf* penitence. **hacer penitencia** (*fam*) take pot-luck. **penitencial** *adj* penitential. **penitenciaria** *sf* penitentiary. **penitente** *adj* penitent.

penoso [pe'noso] *adj* painful; difficult.

*pensar [pen'sar] *v* think; think over; intend. **pensar en** think about. **pensado** *adj* deliberate. **de pensado** on purpose. **pensador, -a** *sm, sf* thinker. **pensamiento** *sm* thought. **pensativo** *adj* thoughtful.

pensión [pen'sjon] *sf* pension; boarding house; hardship. **pensionado, -a** *sm, sf* pensioner. **pensionar** *v* pension. **pensionista** *s(m+f)* pensioner; boarder.

pentágono [pen'tagono] *sm* pentagon.

penúltimo [pe'nultimo] *adj* penultimate.

penumbra [pe'numβra] *sf* half-light.

penuria [pe'nurja] *sf* penury; shortage.

peña ['pena] *sf* crag; rock; cliff; group of friends. **peñasco** *sm* large rock. **peñascoso** *adj* rocky. **peñón** *sm* rocky mountain. **el Peñón de Gibraltar** the Rock of Gibraltar.

peón [pe'on] *sm* unskilled labourer; pedestrian; foot-soldier; (*ajedrez*) pawn.

peonía [peo'nia] *sf* peony.

peor [pe'or] *adj, adv* worse; worst. **peoría** *sf* worsening.

pepino [pe'pino] *sm* cucumber. **no valer un pepino** not be worth a damn. **pepinillo** *sm* gherkin.

pepita [pe'pita] *sf* seed, pip; (*oro*) nugget.

pequeño [pe'keno] *adj* small; humble. **pequeñez** *sf* smallness; pettiness.

pera ['pera] *sf* pear; light-switch; (*barba*) goatee; sinecure. **peral** *sm* pear tree.

perca ['perka] *sf* (*zool*) perch.

percance [per'kanθe] *sm* mishap; profit.

percatarse [perka'tarse] *v* notice.

percibir [perθi'βir] *v* perceive; collect. **percepción** *sf* perception; collection. **perceptible** *adj* perceptible. **perceptivo** *adj* perceptive. **perceptor, -a** *sm, sf* perceiver. **percibo** *sm* collecting.

percusión [perku'sjon] *sf* percussion.

percha ['pertʃa] *sf* perch; pole; hat-stand; coat-rack.

*perder [per'ðer] *v* lose; spoil; waste. **perderse por** be inordinately fond of. **perdición** *sf* loss; perdition. **pérdida** *sf* damage; waste. **perdido** *adj* lost; dissolute.

perdiz [per'ðiθ] *sf* partridge.

perdonar [perðo'nar] *v* pardon; excuse. **pardón** *sm* pardon; mercy. **con perdón** by your leave. **perdonable** *adj* pardonable. **perdonavidas** *m invar* (*fam*) bully.

perdurar [perðu'rar] *v* endure. **perdurable** *adj* everlasting.

*perecer [pere'θer] *v* perish. **perecerse por** crave. **perecedero** *adj* perishable.

peregrinar [peregri'nar] *v* travel; go on a pilgrimage. **peregrinación** *sf* pilgrimage. **peregrino, -a** *sm, sf* pilgrim.

perejil [pere'xil] *sm* parsley.

perenne [pe'renne] *adj* perennial.

perentorio [peren'torjo] *adj* peremptory; urgent.

perezoso [pere θoso] *adj* lazy. **pereza** *sf* laziness.

perfecto [per'fekto] *adj* perfect. **perfección** *sf* perfection. **perfeccionamiento** *sm* improvement; perfection. **perfeccionar** *v* perfect; improve.

pérfido ['perfiðo] *adj* perfidious. **perfidia** *sf* perfidy.

perfilar [perfi'lar] *v* outline. **perfil** *sm* profile; outline.

perforar [perfo'rar] *v* perforate; drill; puncture. **perforación** *sf* perforation. **perforadora** *sf* drill.

perfumar [perfu'mar] *v* perfume. **perfume** *sm* perfume. **perfumería** *sf* perfume shop.

perfunctorio [perfunk'torjo] *adj* perfunctory.

pericial [peri'θjal] *adj* expert. **pericia** *sf* skill.

perico [pe'riko] *sm* parakeet; toupee.

periferia [peri'ferja] *sf* periphery.

perímetro [pe'rimetro] *sm* perimeter.

periódico [peri'oðiko] *sm* periodical; newspaper. *adj* periodic. **periodicidad** *sf* recurrence. **periodismo** *sm* journalism. **periodista** *s(m + f)* journalist. **periodístico** *adj* journalistic. **período** *or* **periodo** *sm* period. **periodo de prácticas** probationary period.

peripecia [peri'peθja] *sf* vicissitude; incident; adventure.

periscopio [peris'kopjo] *sm* periscope.

perjudicar [perxuði'kar] *v* prejudice; harm. **perjudicial** *adj* harmful. **perjuicio** *sm* prejudice; damage.

perjurar [perxu'rar] *v* perjure oneself. **perjurio** *sm* perjury. **perjuro, -a** *sm, sf* perjurer.

perla ['perla] *sf* pearl. **de perlas** perfectly.

***permanecer** [permane'θer] *v* stay; remain. **permanencia** *sf* stay; permanence. **permanente** *adj* permanent.

permitir [permi'tir] *v* permit. **¿me permite?** may I? **permisible** *adj* permissible. **permisivo** *adj* permissive. **permiso** *sm* permission; permit; leave; licence. **con permiso** if I may.

permutar [permu'tar] *v* permute; exchange. **permuta** *sf* exchange; permutation. **permutación** *sf* permutation.

perniabierto [pernia'βjerto] *adj* bandy-legged.

pernicioso [perni'θjoso] *adj* pernicious.

pernoctar [pernok'tar] *v* spend the night.

pero¹ ['pero] *conj* but; yet. **¡pero bueno! why!**

pero² *sm* pear tree.

perogrullada [perogru'ʎaða] *sf* platitude.

perorar [pero'rar] *v* make a speech. **peroración** *sf* peroration.

peróxido [per'oksiðo] *sm* peroxide.

perpendicular [perpendiku'lar] *sf, adj* perpendicular.

perpetrar [perpe'trar] *v* perpetrate. **perpetración** *sf* perpetration.

perpetuar [perpe'twar] *v* perpetuate. **perpetuación** *sf* perpetuation. **perpetuidad** *sf* perpetuity. **perpetuo** *adj* perpetual.

perplejo [per'plexo] *adj* perplexed; perplexing. **perplejidad** *sf* perplexity.

perro ['perro] *sm* dog; *(fam)* penny. **perra** *sf* bitch. **perrera** *sf* kennel; dog pound; dogcatcher's wagon. **perrero** *sm* dogcatcher.

***perseguir** [perse'gir] *v* pursue; persecute. **persecución** *sf* pursuit; persecution. **perseguidor, -a** *sm, sf* pursuer; persecutor.

perseverar [perseβe'rar] *v* persevere. **perseverancia** *sf* perseverance. **perseverante** *adj* persevering.

persiana [per'sjana] *sf* slatted shutter. **persiana veneciana** venetian blind.

persistir [persis'tir] *v* persist. **persistencia** *sf* persistence. **persistente** *adj* persistent.

persona [per'sona] *sf* person. **persona a persona** man to man. **personaje** *sm* personage; *(teatro)* character. **personal** *adj* personal. **personalidad** *sf* personality. **personalismo** *sm* partiality. **personalizar** *v* personalize. **personarse** *v* appear in person. **personificar** *v* personify.

perspectiva [perspek'tiβa] *sf* perspective; outlook.

perspicaz [perspi'kaθ] *adj* perspicacious. **perspicacia** *sf* perspicacity.

persuadir [perswa'ðir] *v* persuade. **persuasión** *sf* persuasion. **persuasivo** *adj* persuasive.

***pertenecer** [pertene'θer] *v* belong. **perteneciente** *adj* belonging. **pertenencia** *sf* ownership; property; membership.

pértiga ['pertiga] *sf* pole. **salto de pértiga** pole vault.

pertiguero [perti'gero] *sm* verger.

pertinaz [perti'naθ] *adj* pertinacious. **pertinacia** *sf* pertinacity.

pertinente [perti'nente] *adj* pertinent. **pertinencia** *sf* pertinence.

pertrechar [pertre'tʃar] *v* supply; equip. **pertrechos** *sm pl* equipment *sing*; munitions *pl*.

perturbar [pertur'βar] *v* perturb. **perturbación** *sf* perturbation. **perturbador** *adj* perturbing.

***pervertir** [perβer'tir] *v* pervert. **perversidad** *sf* perversity. **perversión** *sf* perversion. **perverso** *adj* perverse.

pesa ['pesa] *sf* weight. **pesas y medidas** weights and measures. **pesadez** *sf* heaviness; drowsiness; hardship.

pesadilla [pesa'ðiʎa] *sf* nightmare.

pesado [pe'saðo] *adj* heavy; sluggish. *sm* bore. **pesadumbre** *sf* grief.

pésame ['pesame] *sm* condolence.

pesar [pe'sar] *v* weigh. **a pesar de** in spite of. **me pesa mucho** I'm very sorry.

pescar [pes'kar] *v* fish. **pesca** *sf* fishing. **pescada** *sf* hake. **pescadería** *sf* fish shop; fish market. **pescadero** *sm* fishmonger. **pescado** *sm* fish. **pescador** *sm* fisherman. **pescador de caña** angler.

pescuezo [pes'kweθo] *sm* neck.

pesebre [pe'seβre] *sm* crib; manger.

pesimista [pesi'mista] *s(m+f)* pessimist. *adj* pessimistic. **pesimismo** *sm* pessimism.

pésimo ['pesimo] *adj* worthless.

peso ['peso] *sm* weight; balance; scales *pl*; peso. **en peso** bodily. **peso específico** specific gravity.

pesquisa [pes'kisa] *sf* inquiry.

pestañear [pestaɲe'ar] *v* blink. **pestaña** *sf* eyelash; fringe; hem. **pestañeo** *sm* blink.

peste ['peste] *sf* plague; corruption; poison. **echar pestes** curse. **pesticida** *sf* pesticide. **pestilencia** *sf* pestilence. **pestilente** *adj* pestilent; stinking.

pestillo [pes'tiʎo] *sm* bolt; latch.

petaca [pe'taka] *sf* tobacco pouch; cigarette case.

pétalo ['petalo] *sm* petal.

petardo [pe'tarðo] *sm* firework; (*fam*) swindle.

petición [peti'θjon] *sf* petition; plea. **peticionario, -a** *sm, sf* petitioner.

petirrojo [petir'roxo] *sm* robin.

peto ['peto] *sm* bib; breastplate.

petrificar [petrifi'kar] *v* petrify. **pétreo** *adj* stony.

petróleo [pe'troleo] *sm* petroleum. **petrolero** *sm* oil-tanker.

petulante [petu'lante] *adj* petulant; insolent. **petulancia** *sf* petulance; insolence.

peyorativo [pejora'tiβo] *adj* pejorative.

pez [peθ] *sm* fish. *sf* pitch, tar.

pezón [pe'θon] *sm* (*bot*) stalk; (*anat*) nipple.

pezuña [pe'θuɲa] *sf* hoof.

piadoso [pja'ðoso] *adj* pious; merciful.

piano ['pjano] *sm* piano. **pianista** *s(m+f)* pianist.

piar [pjar] *v* chirp.

piara ['pjara] *sf* herd.

pica ['pika] *sf* lance, pike; goad; pick; magpie.

picadillo [peka'ðiʎo] *sm* minced meat.

picante [pi'kante] *adj* hot; spicy; pungent; biting.

picaporte [pika'porte] *sm* door handle; latch; knocker; latch-key.

picar [pi'kar] *v* prick, pierce; sting; burn; punch; bite, eat; chop up. **picado** *adj* bitten; stung; minced; sour; bad. **picadura** *sf* bite; sting; peck.

picardear [pikar'ðjar] *v* corrupt; get up to mischief. **picardía** *sf* dirty trick; craftiness; mischief. **picaresco** *adj* roguish. **pícaro, -a** *sm, sf* rogue.

pico ['piko] *sm* beak; peak; pickaxe. **darse el pico** kiss. **pico carpintero** woodpecker. **son las cuatro y pico** it is just after four.

picotear [pikote'ar] *v* peck; chatter. **picotearse** *v* wrangle. **picotada** *sf also* **picotazo** *sm* peck. **picotero, -a** *sm, sf* chatterbox.

pichón [pi'tʃon] *sm* pigeon. **pichona** *sf* (*fam*) darling.

pie [pje] *sm* foot; base; stem. **a cuatro pies** on all fours. **dar pie a** give cause for. **de pies a cabeza** from head to foot.

piedad [pje'ðað] *sf* piety; pity.

piedra ['pjeðra] *sf* stone.

piel [pjel] *sf* skin.

pienso ['pjenso] *sm* fodder. **ni por pienso** not likely.

pierna ['pjerna] *sf* leg.

pieza ['pjeθa] *sf* piece; part; room. **dejar de una pieza** leave speechless.

pífano ['pifano] *sm* fife.

pigmento [pig'mento] *sm* pigment.

pigmeo [pig'meo], **-a** *s, adj* pygmy.

pijama [pi'xama] *sm* pyjamas *pl*.

pila¹ ['pila] *sf* heap; battery.

pila² ['pila] *sf* basin; trough; font. **nombre de pila** Christian name.

pilar [pi'lar] *sm* pillar; pier; milestone; basin.

píldora ['pilðora] *sf* pill.
pilón [pi'lon] *sm* basin; trough; mortar; pylon.
piloto [pi'loto] *sm* pilot; *(auto)* rear light, parking light.
piltrafa [pil'trafa] *sf* gristly meat. **piltrafas** *sf pl* scraps *pl*.
pillar [pi'ʎar] *v* pillage; get; run over; *(fam)* catch. **pillaje** *sm* pillage.
pillo ['piʎo], **-a** *sm, sf* scoundrel. *adj* villainous. **pillastre** *sm or* **pillastrón** *sm* rogue. **pillería** *sf* gang of villains; knavery.
pimienta [pi'mjenta] *sf* pepper. **pimiento** *sm (planta)* pepper. **pimentón** *sm* paprika.
pimpollo [pim'poʎo] *sm* sprout; sapling; *(fam)* handsome boy, pretty girl.
pináculo [pi'nakulo] *sm* pinnacle.
pinar [pi'nar] *sm* pine forest.
pincel [pin'θel] *sm* paintbrush. **pincelada** *sf* brush-stroke. **pincelar** *v* paint.
pinchar [pin'tʃar] *v* puncture. **pincharse** *v* have a puncture. **pinchazo** *sm* puncture. **pincho** *sm* point; prickle; spine.
pingo ['pingo] *sm* rag; devil. **pingos** *sm pl (fam)* togs.
pingüe ['pingwe] *adj* fatty; abundant.
pingüino [pin'gwino] *sm* penguin.
pino ['pino] *sm* pine tree. **pinocha** *sf* pine needle.
pintar [pin'tar] *v* paint. **pintarse** *v* make oneself up. **pinta** *sf* spot. **tener buena/mala pinta** look good/bad. **pintor, -a** *sm, sf* painter. **pintoresco** *adj* picturesque. **pintorrear** *v (fam)* daub. **pintura** *sf* painting; picture.
pinzas ['pinθas] *sf pl* tweezers; pincers; forceps; tongs; clothes pegs.
pinzón [pin'θon] *sm* finch.
piña ['piɲa] *sf* pineapple; pine cone.
piñón [pi'ɲon] *sm* pinion.
pío[1] ['pio] *sm* chirp.
pío[2] *adj* pious; merciful.
piojo ['pjoxo] *sm* louse. **piojoso** *adj* lousy.
pipa ['pipa] *sf* pipe; pip.
pique ['pike] *sm* pique; resentment. **echar a pique** sink; ruin.
piqueta [pi'keta] *sf* pickaxe.
piquete [pi'kete] *sm* picket; squad; sting; hole.
piragua [pi'ragwa] *sf* canoe.
pirámide [pi'ramiðe] *sf* pyramid. **piramidal** *adj* pyramidal.

pirata [pi'rata] *sm, adj* pirate.
Pirineos [piri'neos] *sm pl* Pyrenees *pl*.
piropear [pirope'ar] *v (fam)* compliment. **piropo** *sm* compliment.
pirotecnia [piro'teknja] *sf* fireworks *pl*.
pirueta [pi'rweta] *sf* pirouette. **piruetear** *v* pirouette.
pisar [pi'sar] *v* tread; trample. **pisada** *sf* footprint; step. **pisapapeles** *sm invar* paperweight.
piscina [pis'θina] *sf* swimming pool.
piscolabis [pisko'laβis] *sm invar (fam)* snack.
piso ['piso] *sm* floor; storey; flat. **piso bajo** ground floor.
pisotear [pisote'ar] *v* trample. **pisoteo** *sm* trampling.
pista ['pista] *sf* track; trail; runway; court; ring; rink. **pista de baile** dance floor.
pistola [pis'tola] *sf* pistol. **pistolera** *sf* holster. **pistolero** *sm* gunman.
pistón [pis'ton] *sm* piston.
pitar [pi'tar] *v* whistle at; blow a whistle; boo, hiss. **pitada** *sf* whistle.
pitón [pi'ton] *sm* python.
pizarra [pi'θarra] *sf* blackboard; slate.
pizca ['piθka] *sf (fam)* crumb; drop; pinch.
placa ['plaka] *sf* plate; badge; plaque. **placa de matrícula** *(auto)* number plate.
*placer [pla'θer] *v* please. *sm* pleasure. **a placer** at one's leisure.
plácido ['plaθiðo] *adj* placid; pleasant.
plagar [pla'gar] *v* plague. **plaga** *sf* plague.
plagiar [pla'xjar] *v* plagiarize. **plagio** *sm* plagiarism.
plan [plan] *sm* plan; project.
plana ['plana] *sf (imprenta)* page; *(llanura)* plain.
planchar [plan'tʃar] *v* iron, press. **mesa de planchar** *sf* ironing board. **plancha** *sf* iron. **planchado** *sm* ironing.
planear [plane'ar] *v* plan; glide. **planeo** *sm* gliding.
planeta [pla'neta] *sf* planet. **planetario** *sm* planetarium.
planincie [pla'niθje] *sf* plain; plateau.
planificar [planifi'kar] *v* plan. **planificación** *sf* planning.
plano ['plano] *adj* flat; level; smooth. *sm* map; plan; plane. **de plano** directly. **plano acotado** contour map. **primer plano** close-up.

podrir

plantar [plan'tar] v plant; erect. **plantarse** v stop; settle; stand firm. **planta** sf plant; (pie) sole; plan; floor. **plantación** sf plantation. **plante** sm strike; mutiny. **plantío** sm field; vegetable plot. **plantón** sm seedling.

plantear [plante'ar] v expound; create; institute; introduce. **planteamiento** sm exposition; introduction; layout.

plantel [plan'tel] sm (bot) nursery.

plantilla [plan'tiʎa] sf model; pattern; sole (of shoe); (com) payroll.

plasma ['plasma] sm plasma.

plasmar [plas'mar] v mould. **plasmarse** v materialize.

plástico ['plastiko] sm, adj plastic. **plasticidad** sf plasticity.

plata ['plata] sf silver; (fig) money. **hablar en plata** speak frankly.

plataforma [plata'forma] sf platform; flatcar; oilrig. **plataforma de lanzamiento** launching pad.

plátano ['platano] sm banana; banana tree; plane tree.

platea [pla'tea] sf (teatro) stalls pl.

platear [plate'ar] v silverplate. **platero** sm silversmith.

plática ['platika] sf chat; sermon.

platija [pla'tixa] sf plaice.

platillo [pla'tiʎo] sm saucer. **platillo volante** flying saucer.

platino [pla'tino] sm platinum.

plato ['plato] sm plate; course; dish. **hacer plato** serve a meal.

platónico [pla'toniko] adj platonic.

plausible [plau'siβle] adj plausible; praiseworthy. **plausibilidad** sf plausibility; praiseworthiness.

playa ['plaja] sf beach; seaside.

plaza [pla'θa] sf town square; market; town; position. ¡**plaza**! make way!

plazo ['plaθo] sm time limit; instalment. **comprar a plazos** buy on hire-purchase.

pleamar [plea'mar] sf high tide.

plebe ['pleβe] sf common people pl. **plebeyo** adj plebeian.

plebiscito [pleβis'θito] sm plebiscite.

*****plegar** [ple'gar] v fold; bend; pleat. **plegable** adj folding; collapsible; pliable. **plegadera** sf paper-knife. **pliegue** sm crease; tuck; pleat.

pleitear [pleite'ar] v litigate; plead. **pleito** sm lawsuit.

pleno ['pleno] adj complete; full. **plenamente** adv fully. **plenitud** sf fullness; abundance.

pliego ['pljego] sm sheet of paper; sealed letter. **pliego de condiciones** specifications pl.

plomo ['plomo] sm lead; fuse. **a plomo** straight down. **plomada** sf lead pencil; plumb line. **plomería** sf plumbing. **plomero** sm plumber.

pluma ['pluma] sf feather; pen. **pluma estilográfica** fountain pen. **plumaje** sm plumage.

plural [plu'ral] sm, adj plural. **pluralidad** sf majority.

plus [plus] sm bonus. **plus de carestía de vida** cost-of-living bonus.

pluscuamperfecto [pluskwamper'fekto] sm pluperfect.

plusmarca [plus'marka] (deporte) sm record. **plusmarquista** s(m+f) record-holder.

*****poblar** [po'βlar] v populate; inhabit; stock; colonize; plant. **poblarse** v bud; leaf. **población** sf population; town. **poblado** sm town; village. **poblador, -a** sm, sf settler.

pobre ['poβre] adj poor. sm pauper. ¡**pobre de tí!** you poor thing! **pobrete** adj wretched. **pobretón** adj very poor. **pobreza** sf poverty.

pocilga [po'θilga] sf pigsty.

poción [po'θjon] sf potion.

poco ['poko] adj (cantidad) little; small. adv little; not very; not long. **un poco** a little. **pocos** adj pl few. **poco antes** shortly before. **poco a poco** little by little. **por poco** nearly.

podar [po'ðar] v prune. **poda** sf pruning. **podadera** sf pruning shears.

podenco [po'ðenko] sm hound.

*****poder**[1] [po'ðer] v can, be able to; be possible. **hasta más no poder** as much as one can. **no poder más** be exhausted. **puede ser** perhaps.

poder[2] sm power; capacity; possession. **casarse por poderes** marry by proxy. **hacer un poder** make an effort. **poder disuasivo** deterrent. **poderío** sm authority; wealth. **poderoso** adj powerful.

poema [po'ema] sm poem. **poesía** sf poetry. **poeta** sm poet. **poético** adj poetic. **poetisa** sf poetess.

*****podrir** V **pudrir**.

polaco [poˈlako] *adj* Polish. *sm* Pole; (*idioma*) Polish.

polar [poˈlar] *adj* polar. **polaridad** *sf* polarity. **polarizar** *v* polarize.

polea [poˈlea] *sf* pulley.

polémica [poˈlemika] *sf* polemic; polemics *pl.* **polémico** *adj* polemical.

polen [ˈpolen] *sm* pollen.

policia [poliˈθja] *sf* police force. *sm* policeman. **policiaco** *adj* police. **novela policiaca** detective novel.

poligamia [poliˈgamja] *sf* polygamy. **polígamo** *adj* polygamous.

polígono [poˈligno] *sm* polygon. **polígono industrial** industrial estate. **poligonal** *adj* polygonal.

polilla [poˈliʎa] *sf* moth.

pólipo [ˈpolipo] *sm* polyp.

política [poˈlitika] *sf* politics; policy. **político** *sm* politician. **padre político** father-in-law.

póliza [ˈpoliθa] *sf* policy; contract; stamp. **poliza de seguros** insurance policy.

polizón [poliˈθon] *sm* stowaway.

polo [ˈpolo] *sm* (*geog*) pole; (*tecn*) terminal; (*deporte*) polo; ice lolly. **polo acuático** water polo. **Polo Norte/Sur** North/South Pole.

Polonia [poˈlonja] *sf* Poland. **polonesa** *sf* polonaise.

poltrona [polˈtrona] *sf* easy chair. **poltrón** *adj* lazy.

polvo [ˈpolβo] *sm* powder; dust. **café en polvo** instant coffee. **polvos** *sm pl* powder *sing.* **polvos de talco** talcum powder. **polvareda** *sf* dust cloud; (*fig*) to-do. **polvera** *sf* powder compact. **pólvora** *sf* gunpowder.

polla [ˈpoʎa] *sf* pullet. **pollo** *sm* chicken. **polluelo** *sm* chick.

pómez [ˈpomeθ] *sf* pumice.

pomo [ˈpomo] *sm* pommel; doorknob.

pompa [ˈpompa] *sf* pomp; bubble; display. **pomposidad** *sf* pomposity. **pomposo** *adj* pompous.

pómpulo [ˈpompulo] *sm* cheekbone.

ponche [ˈpontʃe] *sm* (*bebida*) punch.

poncho [ˈpontʃo] *sm* poncho. *adj* listless.

ponderar [pondeˈrar] *v* weigh up; praise highly. **ponderable** *adj* praiseworthy. **ponderación** *sf* weighing up; exaggerated praise. **ponderado** *adj* measured; prudent. **ponderativo** *adj* excessive; deliberative.

ponente [poˈnente] *sm* reporter. **ponencia** *sf* report.

***poner** [poˈner] *v* put; set. **poner al día** bring up to date. **poner casa** move (house). **poner de comer** feed. **ponerse** *v* turn oneself; dress; get down to; arrive. **ponerse bueno** recover. **ponerse guapo** smarten oneself up.

poniente [poˈnjente] *sm* west.

pontificado [pontifiˈkaðo] *sm* papacy. **pontifical** *adj* pontifical. **pontífice** *sm* pope.

pontón [ponˈton] *sm* (*puente*) pontoon.

ponzoña [ponˈθoɲa] *sf* poison. **ponzoñoso** *adj* poisonous.

popa [ˈpopa] *sf* stern. **a popa** astern.

popelina [popeˈlina] *sf* poplin.

populacho [popuˈlatʃo] *sm* rabble.

popular [popuˈlar] *adj* popular. **popularidad** *sf* popularity. **popularizar** *v* popularize.

por [por] *prep* for; by; through; during; in exchange for. **por ciento** per cent. **por más que** however. **por si acaso** in case. **por supuesto** of course.

porcelana [porθeˈlana] *sf* porcelain.

porcentaje [porθenˈtaxe] *sm* percentage.

porción [porˈθjon] *sf* portion.

porche [ˈportʃe] *sm* porch.

pordiosero [porðjoˈsero], **-a** *sm, sf* beggar.

porfiar [porˈfjar] *v* insist; persist; argue. **porfía** *sf* insistence. **porfiado** *adj* stubborn.

pormenor [pormeˈnor] *sm* detail. **al pormenor** retail.

pornografía [pornograˈfia] *sf* pornography.

poro [ˈporo] *sm* pore. **poroso** *adj* porous.

porque [ˈporke] *conj* because.

porqué [porˈke] *sm* reason.

porquería [porkeˈria] *sf* disgusting mess; muck.

porra [ˈporra] *sf* club; truncheon. **porrazo** *sm* blow.

porro [ˈporro] *sm* leek.

porrón [poˈrron] *adj* dull, stupid. **a porrones** (*fam*) galore.

portador [portaˈðor] *sm* (*com*) bearer. **portar** *v* bear, carry. **portarse** *v* behave oneself. **portátil** *adj* portable.

portal [porˈtal] *sm* entrance hall, portal.

portamonedas [portamoˈneðas] *sm invar* wallet.

portavoz [portaˈβoθ] *sm* megaphone; spokesman.

portazgo [por'taθgo] *sm* toll.

portazo [por'taθo] *sm* slam. **dar un portazo** slam the door.

porte ['porte] *sm* transport; carriage; conduct.

portento [por'tento] *sm* marvel. **portentoso** *adj* marvellous.

portería [porte'ria] *sf* porter's lodge. **portero, -a** *sm, sf* porter.

portezuela [porte'θwela] *sf (auto)* door.

pórtico ['portiko] *sm* portico.

portilla [por'tiʎa] *sf* porthole.

Portugal [portu'gal] *sm* Portugal. **portugués, -esa** *s, adj* Portuguese; *sm (idioma)* Portuguese.

porvenir [porβe'nir] *sm* future. **sin porvenir** without prospects.

pos [pos] *adj* **en pos de** behind.

posada [po'saða] *sf* inn; lodging. **posadero, -a** *sm, sf* innkeeper.

posar [po'sar] *v* alight; pose; lodge; lay down. **posarse** *v* settle; land.

*****poseer** [pose'er] *v* possess; hold; master. **posesión** *sf* possession. **posesiones** *sf pl* property *sing*.

posible [po'siβle] *adj* possible. **posibilidad** *sf* possibility. **posibilitar** *v* facilitate.

posición [posi'θjon] *sf* position.

positivo [posi'tiβo] *adj, sm* positive.

*****posponer** [pospo'ner] *v* postpone; value less.

postal [pos'tal] *adj* postal. *sf* postcard. **giro postal** *sm* money order; postal order.

postdata [post'ðata] *sf* postscript.

poste ['poste] *sm* pole; pillar; post. **poste indicador** signpost.

postergar [poster'gar] *v* pass over; postpone; adjourn. **postergación** *sf* postponement; adjournment.

posteridad [posteri'ðað] *sf* posterity. **posterior** *adj* posterior; subsequent; later.

postizo [pos'tiθo] *adj* false; artificial; assumed. *sm* hairpiece. **pierna postiza** *sf* artificial leg.

postrar [pos'trar] *v* prostrate. **postrarse** *v* kneel down; weaken. **postración** *sf* prostration. **postrado** *adj* prostrate.

postre ['postre] *sm* dessert.

postremo [pos'tremo] *adj* last. **postrimería** *sf* end, death.

postular [postu'lar] *v* postulate; request; apply for; collect. **postulación** *sf* collection. **postulado** *sm* postulate. **postulante, -a** *sm, sf* collector; applicant.

póstumo ['postumo] *adj* posthumous.

postura [pos'tura] *sf* posture; attitude.

potable [po'taβle] *adj* drinkable.

potaje [po'taxe] *sm* stew; soup.

potasio [po'tasjo] *sm* potassium.

pote ['pote] *sm* jar; jug.

potencia [po'tenθja] *sf* power; ability; potential. **potencial** *adj* potential. **potentado** *sm* potentate. **potente** *adj* powerful.

potestad [potes'tað] *sf* authority; power.

potro ['potro] *sm* colt; instrument of torture.

pozo ['poθo] *sm* hole; well; shaft; bilge.

práctica ['praktika] *sf* practice; method. **practicabilidad** *sf* practicability. **practicable** *adj* practicable. **practicante** *s(m + f)* nurse; practitioner. **practicar** *v* practise; play; perform; subsequent; experienced. **práctico** *adj* practical;

pradera [pra'ðera] *sf* meadow; prairie. **prado** *sm* field, meadow.

pragmático [prag'matiko] *adj* pragmatic. **pragmatismo** *sm* pragmatism.

preámbulo [pre'ambulo] *sm* preamble.

precario [pre'karjo] *adj* precarious. **precariedad** *sf* precariousness.

precaución [prekau'θjon] *sf* precaution. **con precaución** cautiously. **precaver** *v* forestall. **precaverse** *v* be on one's guard (against).

preceder [preθe'ðer] *v* precede. **precedencia** *sf* precedence; preference. **precedente** *adj* precedent.

precepto [pre'θepto] *sm* precept; regulation. **preceptivo** *adj* compulsory.

preciar [pre'θjar] *v* value. **preciarse** *v* boast. **preciado** *adj* prized; boastful. **precio** *sm* price; esteem. **preciosidad** *sf* excellence. **precioso** *adj* precious; witty.

precipicio [preθi'piθjo] *sm* precipice.

precipitar [preθipi'tar] *v* precipitate. **precipitarse** *v* rush. **precipitación** *sf* precipitation; haste. **precipitado** *adj also* **precipitoso** hasty, rash.

precisar [preθi'sar] *v* need; be necessary; define; fix. **precisamente** *adv* precisely; necessarily. **precisión** *sf* precision; necessity. **preciso** *adj* precise; necessary.

*****preconcebir** [prekonθe'βir] *v* preconceive. **preconcebido** *adj* preconceived.

preconizar [prekoni'θar] *v* praise; recommend; suggest. **preconización** *sf* recommendation; praise.

precoz [pre'koθ] *adj* precocious. **precocidad** *sf* precocity.

precursor [prekur'sor] *sm* forerunner.

predecesor [preðeθe'sor], **-a** *sm, sf* predecessor.

*predecir [preðe'θir] *v* predict. **predicción** *sf* prediction.

predestinar [preðesti'nar] *v* predestine. **predestinación** *sf* predestination.

prédica ['preðika] *sf* sermon; preaching. **predicación** *sf* preaching. **predicaderas** *sf pl* (*fam*) eloquence *sing*. **predicador, -a** *sm, sf* preacher. **predicar** *v* preach.

predicado [preði'kaðo] *sm* (*gram*) predicate.

predicamento [preðika'mento] *sm* predicament; prestige.

predilección [preðilek'θjon] *sf* predilection.

*predisponer [preðispo'ner] *v* predispose. **predisponer contra** prejudice against. **predisposición** *sf* predisposition.

predominar [preðomi'nar] *v* predominate. **predominancia** *sf* predominance. **predominante** *adj* predominant.

preeminente [preemi'nente] *adj* pre-eminent. **preeminencia** *sf* pre-eminence.

prefabricar [prefaβri'kar] *v* prefabricate. **prefabricación** *sf* prefabrication.

prefacio [pre'faθjo] *sm* preface.

prefecto [pre'fekto] *sm* prefect. **prefectura** *sf* prefecture.

*preferir [prefe'rir] *v* prefer. **preferencia** *sf* preference. **preferente** *adj* preferential; preferable. **preferible** *adj* preferable. **preferido** *adj* favourite.

prefigurar [prefigu'rar] *v* prefigure, foreshadow. **prefiguración** *sf* prefiguration.

prefijo [pre'fixo] *adj* prefixed. *sm* prefix. **prefijar** *v* prefix; prearrange.

pregonar [prego'nar] *v* proclaim, announce. **pregón** *sm* proclamation. **pregonero** *sm* town crier.

preguntar [pregun'tar] *v* ask; query; inquire. **preguntarse** *v* wonder. **pregunta** *sf* question. **preguntador, -a** *sm, sf* questioner.

prehistórico [preis'toriko] *adj* prehistoric.

prejuicio [pre'xwiθjo] *sm* prejudice. **prejuzgar** *v* prejudge.

prelado [pre'laðo] *sm* prelate.

preliminar [prelimi'nar] *adj, sm* preliminary. **preliminarios** *sm pl* preliminaries *pl*.

preludio [pre'luðjo] *sm* prelude.

prematuro [prema'turo] *adj* premature.

premeditar [premeði'tar] *v* premeditate. **premeditación** *sf* premeditation.

premiar [pre'mjar] *v* reward. **premio** *sm* reward; prize; (*com*) premium. **premio gordo** first prize.

premisa [pre'misa] *sf* premise, assumption.

premonición [premoni'θjon] *sf* premonition.

premura [pre'mura] *sf* urgency; tightness.

prenda ['prenda] *sf* pledge; (*com*) security; garment; darling. **en prenda** as a token of. **prendar** *v* pledge; pawn; please. **prendarse de** fall in love with. **prendería** *sf* second-hand shop. **prendero, -a** *sm, sf* second-hand dealer; pawnbroker.

prensa ['prensa] *sf* press; printing press. **dar a la prensa** publish. **prensar** *v* press.

prensil [pren'sil] *adj* prehensile.

preñado [pre'ɲaðo] *adj* pregnant; bulging; full. **preñar** *v* become pregnant; impregnate. **preñez** *sf* pregnancy.

preocupar [preoku'par] *v* preoccupy; worry; get worried. **¡no se preocupe!** don't worry! **preocupación** *sf* preoccupation; prejudice; worry. **preocupado** *adj* preoccupied; worried.

preparar [prepa'rar] *v* prepare. **preparación** *sf* preparation. **preparativo** *adj* also **preparatorio** preparatory.

preponderar [preponde'rar] *v* preponderate, prevail. **preponderancia** *sf* preponderance. **preponderante** *adj* preponderant.

preposición [preposi'θjon] *sf* (*gram*) preposition.

prerrogativa [prerroga'tiβa] *sf* prerogative.

presa¹ ['presa] *sf* capture; prey; victim; quarry; seizure. **presas** *sf pl* fangs *pl*; talons *pl*. **ave de presa** bird of prey.

presa² *sf* dam; weir. **presa de contención** reservóir.

presagiar [presa'xjar] *v* presage. **presagio** *sm* omen.

présbita ['presβita] *adj* also **présbite** long-sighted. **presbicia** *sf* longsightedness.

presbítero [pres'βitero] *sm* priest. **presbiterado** *sm* priesthood.

prescindir [presθin'dir] *v* do without. **prescindible** *adj* dispensable.

prescribir [preskri'βir] *v* prescribe; determine. **prescripción** *sf* prescription. **prescrito** *adj* prescribed.

presenciar [presen'θjar] v attend; witness.
presencia sf presence; appearance.
presencia de ánimo presence of mind.
presentar [presen'tar] v present; introduce; submit; propose; tender. **le presento a** may I introduce you to. **presentarse** v present oneself; arise; turn up; report; apply. **presentable** adj presentable. **presentación** sf presentation; introduction. **presente** adj present. **mejorando lo presente** present company excepted.
*presentir [presen'tir] v have forebodings of. **presentimiento** sm presentiment.
preservar [preser'βar] v preserve; protect. **preservación** sf preservation; protection. **preservador** adj preservative. **preservativo** sm condom.
presidencia [presi'ðenθja] sf presidency. **presidente** sm president.
presidiario [presi'ðjarjo] sm convict. **presidio** sm prison; penal servitude.
presidir [presi'ðir] v preside over; dominate.
presilla [pre'siʎa] sf loop; fastener.
presión [pre'sjon] sf pressure.
preso ['preso] sm prisoner. adj captured.
prestar [pres'tar] v lend. **prestación** sf lending. **prestado** adj loaned. **dar/pedir prestado** lend/borrow. **prestador, -a** sm, sf lender. **prestamista** s(m+f) moneylender. **préstamo** sm loan. **prestario, -a** sm, sf borrower.
presteza [pres'teθa] sf promptness.
prestidigitador [prestiðixita'ðor] sm conjurer; magician. **prestidigitación** sf conjuring; magic.
prestigio [pres'tixjo] sm prestige; trick. **prestigiado** adj also **prestigioso** prestigious.
presto ['presto] adj prompt; ready. adv promptly.
presumir [presu'mir] v presume, assume. **según cabe presumir** presumably. **presumirse** v swank; be presumptuous. **presumible** adj presumable. **presunción** sf assumption; presumptuousness. **presunto** adj presumed. **presuntuosidad** sf conceit. **presuntuoso** adj conceited.
*presuponer [presupo'ner] v presuppose; budget. **presupuesto** sm budget; reason; supposition.
presura [pre'sura] sf promptness; persistence. **presuroso** adj prompt; hasty.

pretender [preten'der] v claim; aspire to; seek; want; apply for; allege; pretend. **pretendiente** sm pretender; claimant; suitor. **pretensión** sf pretension; claim.
pretérito [pre'terito] sm (gram) past.
pretexto [pre'teksto] sm pretext.
*prevalecer [preβale'θer] v prevail. **prevaleciente** adj prevailing.
prevaricar [preβari'kar] v prevaricate. **prevaricación** sf prevarication; breach of trust. **prevaricador, -a** sm, sf prevaricator.
*prevenir [preβe'nir] v prevent; warn; prepare; foresee. **prevención** sf prevention; warning; preparation; prejudice; police station. **prevenido** adj prepared; forewarned. **bien prevenido** full. **preventivo** adj preventive.
*prever [pre'βer] v foresee; anticipate. **previsión** sf foresight; forecast. **caja de previsión** sf social security.
previo ['preβjo] adj previous. **previo pago** after payment.
prieto ['prjeto] adj dark; mean.
prima ['prima] sf premium; bonus.
primado [pri'maðo] sm (rel) primate.
primario [pri'marjo] adj primary.
primavera [prima'βera] sf spring.
primer [pri'mer] adj first. **primeramente** adv first; mainly. **primero** adj first; best; principal. **de primera** first-class.
primitivo [primi'tiβo] adj primitive; original.
primo ['primo] adj prime. sm cousin.
primogénito [primo'xenito] adj first-born.
primor [pri'mor] sm beauty; delicacy; skill. **primoroso** adj exquisite; skilful.
princesa [prin'θesa] sf princess.
principal [prinθi'pal] adj, sm principal.
príncipe ['prinθipe] sm prince.
principiar [prinθi'pjar] v start. **principiante** s(m+f) novice. **principio** sm beginning.
pringar [prin'gar] v stain with grease; wound; involve; slander. **pringarse** v embezzle. **pringón** adj greasy. **pringoso** adj fatty; greasy. **pringue** s(m+f) grease stain; dripping.
prior [pri'or] sm (rel) prior. adj prior. **priora** sf prioress. **priorato** sm priory. **prioridad** sf priority.
prisa ['prisa] sf hurry. **darse prisa** hurry. **tener prisa** be in a hurry.
prisión [pri'sjon] sf prison; imprisonment. **prisionero, -a** sm, sf prisoner.

prisma [prisma] *sm* prism. **prismático** *adj* prismatic.

privar[1] [pri'βar] *v* deprive; prohibit. **privación** *sf* deprivation. **privado** *adj* private.

privar[2] *v* be in favour; be popular.

privilegiar [priβile'xjar] *v* grant a favour to. **privilegio** *sm* privilege.

pro [pro] *sm* benefit, profit. **en pro de** on behalf of. **hombre de pro** *sm* honest man.

proa [proa] *sf* (*mar*) prow, bow, bows *pl*. **mascarón de proa** *sm* figurehead.

probable [pro'βaβle] *adj* probable. **probabilidad** *sf* probability.

***probar** [pro'βar] *v* test; try; taste; prove. **probarse** *v* try on. **probador** *sm* fitting-room. **probanza** *sf* proof. **probeta** *sf* test tube.

probidad [proβi'ðað] *sf* probity, integrity.

problema [pro'βlema] *sm* problem.

proceder [proθe'ðer] *v* proceed; behave; originate. **procedencia** *sf* origin; port of departure. **procedente** *adj* originating; reasonable; proper. **procedimiento** *sm* process.

procesar [proθe'sar] *v* prosecute. **procesado, -a** *sm, sf* accused. **procesal** *adj* procedural. **procesamiento** *sm* prosecution.

procesión [proθe'sjon] *sf* procession.

proclamar [prokla'mar] *v* proclaim. **proclama** *sf also* **proclamación** proclamation.

procrear [prokre'ar] *v* procreate. **procreación** *sf* procreation. **procreador, -a** *sm, sf* procreator.

procurar [proku'rar] *v* cause; attempt; obtain; succeed; give. **procura** *sf* power of attorney. **procurador, -a** *sm, sf* lawyer.

prodigar [proði'gar] *v* squander; lavish. **prodigalidad** *sf* prodigality.

prodigio [pro'ðixjo] *sm* prodigy. **prodigioso** *adj* prodigious.

pródigo ['proðigo] *adj* prodigal; wasteful.

***producir** [proðu'θir] *v* produce. **producirse** *v* happen. **producción** *sf* production. **productivo** *adj* productive. **producto** *sm* product. **productor, -a** *sm, sf* producer.

proeza [pro'eθa] *sf* deed; feat.

profanar [profa'nar] *v* profane. **profanación** *sf* profanation. **profano** *adj* profane.

profecía [profe'θia] *sf* prophecy. **profeta** *sm* prophet. **profético** *adj* prophetic. **profetisa** *sf* prophetess. **profetizar** *v* prophesy.

***proferir** [profe'rir] *v* utter.

profesar [profe'sar] *v* profess; manifest; practise a profession. **profesión** *sf* profession. **profesional** *adj* professional. **profesor, -a** *sm, sf* professor, teacher. **profesorado** *sm* professorship; teaching staff.

prófugo ['profugo], **-a** *s, adj* fugitive.

profundizar [profundi'θar] *v* deepen. **profundidad** *sf* depth. **profundo** *adj* deep.

profusión [profu'sjon] *sf* profusion. **profuso** *adj* profuse.

progenie [pro'xenje] *sf* progeny. **progenitor** *sm* progenitor. **progenitores** *sm pl* ancestors *pl*; parents *pl*. **progenitura** *sf* offspring.

programa [pro'grama] *sm* programme.

progresar [progre'sar] *v* progress. **progresión** *sf* progression. **progresivo** *adj* progressive. **progreso** *sm* progress.

prohibir [proi'βir] *v* prohibit. **se prohibe fumar** no smoking. **prohibición** *sf* prohibition. **prohibitivo** *adj* prohibitive.

prohijar [proi'xar] *v* adopt. **prohijamiento** *sm* adoption.

prójimo ['proximo] *sm* fellow man; neighbour; (*fam*) bloke.

prole ['prole] *sf* offspring.

prolapso [pro'lapso] *sm* prolapse.

proletario [prole'tarjo], **-a** *s, adj* proletarian.

prolífico [pro'lifiko] *adj* prolific.

prolijo [pro'lixo] *adj* tedious; long-winded. **prolijidad** *sf* long-windedness.

prólogo ['prologo] *sm* prologue.

prolongar [prolon'gar] *v* prolong. **prolongación** *sf* prolongation. **prolongado** *adj* prolonged.

promediar [prome'ðjar] *v* bisect; average out; mediate. **promedio** *sm* middle; average.

promesa [pro'mesa] *sf* promise. **prometer** *v* promise. **prometerse** *v* expect; become engaged. **prometérselas felices** have high hopes. **prometida** *sf* fiancée. **prometido** *sm* fiancé.

prominencia [promi'nenθja] *sf* prominence; projection; bulge. **prominente** *adj* prominent.

promiscuo [pro'miskwo] *adj* promiscuous; ambiguous.

promontorio [promon'torjo] *sm* promontory.

***promover** [promo'βer] *v* promote. **promoción** *sf* promotion. **promotor, -a** *sm, sf* promoter.

promulgar [promul'gar] *v* promulgate. **promulgación** *sf* promulgation.
pronombre [pro'nombre] *sm* pronoun.
pronosticar [pronosti'kar] *v* prognosticate. **pronosticación** *sf* prognostication, forecast. **pronóstico** *sm* prediction.
prontitud [pronti'tuð] *sf* promptness. **pronto** *adv* quickly, at once. **¡hasta pronto!** see you soon!
pronunciar [pronun'θjar] *v* pronounce. **pronunciarse** *v* rebel. **pronunciación** *sf* pronunciation. **pronunciamiento** *sm* rising; (*jur*) pronouncement.
propagar [propa'gar] *v* propagate. **propagación** *sf* propagation. **propaganda** *sf* propaganda.
propalar [propa'lar] *v* publish; divulge.
propenso [pro'penso] *adj* prone. **propender** *v* incline. **propensión** *sf* inclination.
propicio [pro'piθjo] *adj* propitious. **propiciación** *sf* propitiation. **propiciar** *v* propitiate.
propiedad [propje'ðað] *sf* property; ownership; propriety; resemblance. **propietario, -a** *sm, sf* landlord/lady.
propina [pro'pina] *sf* (*dinero*) tip.
propio ['propjo] *adj* proper; own; particular. **nombre propio** *sm* proper noun. **ser propio de** be typical of. **sus propias palabras** his very words. **propiamente** *adv* properly.
*proponer [propo'ner] *v* propose. **proponente** *s(m+f)* proposer. **proposición** *sf* proposition; proposal.
proporción [propor'θjon] *sf* proportion. **proporcionado** *adj* proportionate. **bien proporcionado** well proportioned. **proporcional** *adj* proportional. **proporcionar** *v* supply; cause; adapt.
propósito [pro'posito] *sm* purpose; intention. **a propósito** by the way. **a propósito de** with regard to. **de propósito** on purpose.
propuesta [pro'pwesta] *sf* proposal.
propulsar [propul'sar] *v* propel. **propulsión** *sf* propulsion. **propulsor** *sm* propeller.
prorrata [pro'rrata] *sf* quota. **a prorrata** pro rata.
prórroga ['prorroga] *sf* prorogation, extension. **prorrogar** *v* prorogue, adjourn.
prorrumpir [prorrum'pir] *v* break out.
prosa ['prosa] *sf* prose. **prosaico** *adj* prosaic.

proscribir [proskri'βir] *v* proscribe, ban. **proscripción** *sf* proscription, prohibition. **proscrito** *adj* outlawed, banished.
prosecución [proseku'θjon] *sf* pursuit; continuation. **proseguir** *v* pursue; continue.
prosélito [pro'selito] *sm* proselyte.
prospecto [pros'pekto] *sm* prospectus.
prosperar [prospe'rar] *v* prosper. **prosperidad** *sf* prosperity. **próspero** *adj* prosperous.
prosternarse [proster'narse] *v* prostrate oneself.
*prostituir [prostitu'ir] *v* prostitute. **prostíbulo** *sm* brothel. **prostitución** *sf* prostitution. **prostituta** *sf* prostitute.
protagonista [protago'nista] *s(m+f)* protagonist.
proteger [prote'xer] *v* protect. **protección** *sf* protection. **protector** *adj* protective. **protegido** *sm* protégé.
proteína [prote'ina] *sf* protein.
protestar [protes'tar] *v* protest. **protesta** *sf* protest. **protestación** *sf* protestation. **protestante** *s(m+f)*, *adj* Protestant. **protestantismo** *sm* Protestantism.
protocolo [proto'kolo] *sm* protocol.
prototipo [proto'tipo] *sm* prototype.
protuberancia [protuβe'ranθja] *sf* protuberance. **protuberante** *adj* protuberant.
provecho [pro'βetʃo] *sm* advantage; profit. **de provecho** useful. **sacar provecho de** benefit from. **provechoso** *adj* profitable.
proveer [proβe'er] *v* provide; deal with; decide; fill. **proveedor, -a** *sm, sf* supplier.
*provenir [proβe'nir] *v* originate. **proveniente** *adj* originating.
proverbio [pro'βerβjo] *sm* proverb. **proverbial** *adj* proverbial.
providencia [proβi'ðenθja] *sf* providence; foresight. **providencial** *adj* providential. **providente** *adj* provident.
provincia [pro'βinθja] *sf* province. **provincial** *adj* provincial. **provincialismo** *sm* provincialism.
provisión [proβisi'on] *sf* provision. **provisional** *adj* provisional. **provisionalmente** *adv* provisionally. **provisor** *sm* purveyer. **provisto** *adj* supplied.
provocar [proβo'kar] *v* provoke; cause. **provocación** *sf* provocation. **provocador** *adj* provocative. **provocante** *adj* provoking.

próximo ['proksimo] *adj* next; neighbouring. **la semana próxima** next week. **proximamente** *adv* closely; soon. **proximidad** *sf* proximity.

proyectar [projek'tar] *v* project; plan; throw. **proyección** *sf* projection. **proyectil** *sm* projectile. **proyecto** *sm* project. **proyector** *sm* projector; searchlight; spotlight.

prudencia [pru'ðenθja] *sf* prudence. **prudencial** *adj* (*fam*) moderate. **prudente** *adj* prudent.

prueba ['prweβa] *sf* test; proof; tasting; (*deporte*) event. **a prueba** on trial. **a prueba de** proof against.

prurito [pru'rito] *sm* itch; urge.

psicoanálisis [psikoa'nalisis] *sm invar* psychoanalysis. **psicoanalista** *s(m + f)* psychoanalyst. **psicoanalizar** *v* psychoanalyse.

psicología [psikolo'xia] *sf* psychology. **psicológico** *adj* psychological. **psicólogo, -a** *sm, sf* psychologist.

psiquiatría [psikja'tria] *sf* psychiatry. **psiquiatra** *s(m + f)* psychiatrist. **psiquiátrico** *adj* psychiatric.

púa ['pua] *sf* prong; barb; thorn; sharp point.

pubertad [puβer'tað] *sf* puberty.

publicar [puβli'kar] *v* publish. **publicación** *sf* publication. **publicidad** *sf* publicity; advertising. **público** *sm, adj* public. **dar al público** publish.

puchero [pu'tʃero] *sm* stew; cooking-pot. **ganarse el puchero** earn one's daily bread.

pucho ['putʃo] *sm* cigarette *or* cigar end; fag-end.

púdico ['puðiko] *adj* chaste; modest. **pudicia** *sf* chastity; modesty.

pudiente [pu'ðjente] *adj* rich.

pudín [pu'ðin] *sm* pudding.

pudor [pu'ðor] *sm* modesty; shame. **pudoroso** *adj* modest.

*pudrir [pu'ðrir] *v* rot, decay. **pudrición** *sf* putrefaction. **pudrimiento** *sm* rotting.

pueblo ['pweβlo] *sm* people; town; village. **de pueblos** from the country.

puente ['pwente] *sm* bridge. **puente colgante** suspension bridge.

puerco ['pwerko] *sm* pig. *adj* filthy. **puerca** *sf* sow. **puerco espín** porcupine.

pueril [pue'ril] *adj* childish. **puerilidad** *sf* childishness.

puerro ['pwerro] *sm* leek.

puerta ['pwerta] *sf* door; entrance. **puerta principal** front door. **puerta trasera** back door.

puerto ['pwerto] *sm* port; harbour; mountain pass.

pues [pwes] *adv, conj* then; since; because; well; so; yes. **pues bien** OK. **¡pues claro!** of course! **¿pues qué?** so what?

puesta ['pwesta] *sf* (*del sol*) setting; bet; putting. **puesta en escena** staging.

puesto ['pwesto] *sm* small shop; place; stall; job. **puesto de periódicos** newspaper stand.

pugnar [pug'nar] *v* fight; struggle. **pugna** *sf* fight. **pugnaz** *adj* pugnacious.

pujar [pu'xar] *v* strain; strive; outbid. **pujante** *adj* strong. **pujanza** *sf* strength.

pulcritud [pulkri'tuð] *sf* neatness; care. **pulcro** *adj* neat, tidy.

pulga ['pulga] *sf* flea. **pulgoso** *adj* flea-ridden.

pulgada [pul'gaða] *sf* inch. **pulgar** *sm* thumb.

pulir [pu'lir] *v* polish; adorn. **pulidez** *sf* polish; neatness. **pulido** *adj* polished; smooth; neat. **pulidor** *sm* polisher. **pulimentar** *v* polish. **pulimento** *sm* polish, shine.

pulmón [pul'mon] *sm* lung. **pulmonía** *sf* pneumonia.

pulpa ['pulpa] *sf* pulp.

púlpito ['pulpito] *sm* pulpit.

pulpo ['pulpo] *sm* octopus.

pulsar [pul'sar] *v* pulsate. **pulso** *sm* pulse; wrist; steady hand.

pulsera [pul'sera] *sf* bracelet; watch strap. **reloj de pulsera** *sm* wristwatch.

pulverizar [pulβeri'θar] *v* pulverize; spray. **pulverización** *sf* pulverization. **pulverizador** *sm* spray; atomizer.

pulla ['puʎa] *sf* taunt; obscenity.

punción [pun'θjon] *sf* (*med*) puncture.

punición [puni'θjon] *sf* punishment. **punible** *adj* punishable. **punitivo** *adj* punitive.

punta ['punta] *sf* point; tip; head; end; nail. **horas punta** *sf pl* rush hours *pl*. **sacar punta a** sharpen. **velocidad punta** *sf* top speed.

puntada [pun'taða] *sf* stitch.

puntapié [punta'pje] *sm* kick. **echar a puntapiés** kick out.

puntear [punte'ar] *v* stitch; tick off; perforate. **punteado** *sm* (*música*) plucking.

puntería [punte'ria] *sf* aim; marksmanship. **puntero** *adj* outstanding.

puntilla [pun'tiʎa] *sf* tack; nib; fine lace. **de puntillas** on tiptoe.

punto ['punto] *sm* point; full stop; stitch; mark; honour; matter; item. **al punto** at once. **dos puntos** colon. **en punto** on the dot. **¡punto en boca!** mum's the word!

puntual [puntu'al] *adj* punctual; reliable. **puntualidad** *sf* punctuality; reliability.

puntualizar [puntwali'θar] *v* arrange; determine; perfect; settle.

puntuar [pun'twar] *v* punctuate. **puntuación** *sf* punctuation. **signos de puntuación** *sm pl* punctuation marks *pl*.

punzar [pun'θar] *v* pierce. **punzada** *sf* prick; twinge. **punzante** *adj* sharp. **punzón** *sm* awl. punch.

puñado [pu'naðo] *sm* handful. **puñada** *sf* also **puñetazo** *sm* blow, clout. **puño** *sm* fist; cuff. **de propio puño** in one's own handwriting.

puñal [pu'nal] *sm* dagger. **puñalada** *sf* stab.

pupila [pu'pila] *sf* (*anat*) pupil.

pupilaje [pupi'laxe] *sm* boarding-house; tutelage.

pupitre [pu'pitre] *sm* desk.

puré [pu're] *sm* purée. **puré de patatas** mashed potatoes *pl*.

pureza [pu'reθa] *sf* purity. **purificación** *sf* purification. **purificar** *v* purify. **purista** *s*(*m* + *f*) purist. **puro** *adj* pure; simple.

purgar [pur'gar] *v* purge; purify. **purgante** *sm* purgative. **purgativo** *adj* purgative. **purgatorio** *sm* purgatory.

puritano [puri'tano], -**a** *s, adj* puritan. **puritanismo** *sm* puritanism.

púrpura ['purpura] *sf* purple.

pus [pus] *sm* pus, matter.

pusilánime [pusi'lanime] *adj* cowardly. **pusilanimidad** *sf* cowardliness.

pústula ['pustula] *sf* (*med*) pustule, pimple.

puta ['puta] *sf* (*fam*) whore, prostitute. **puto** *sm* (*fam*) bugger.

putrefacción [putrefak'θjon] *sf* putrefaction. **putrefacto** *adj* rotten. **pútrido** *adj* putrid.

puya ['puja] *sf* goad; (*fig*) gibe.

Q

que [ke] *pron* who; whom; that; which. *conj* that; because; than. **que sí** of course. **más que** more than.

qué [ke] *pron, adj* what. **¿qué pasa?** what's going on? **¡qué miedo!** what a fright! **¡qué raro!** how extraordinary!

*****quebrar** [ke'βrar] *v* break; go bankrupt. **quebrado** *adj* broken; bankrupt. **quebradura** *sf* crack; gap. **quebrantar** *v* shatter. **quebranto** *sm* exhaustion.

queda ['keða] *sf* curfew.

quedar [ke'ðar] *v* stay; remain; sojourn. **quedarse** *v* stay behind. **quedar en nada** come to nothing.

quedo ['keðo] *adj* quiet; still. *adv* quietly.

quehaceres [kea'θeres] *sm pl* chores; duties.

quejarse [ke'xarse] *v* complain; moan. **queja** *sf* complaint. **quejido** *sm* groan. **quejoso** *adj* plaintive; complaining.

quemar [ke'mar] *v* burn; scorch. **quema** *sf* burning; fire. **quemadura** *sf* burn; scald. **quemante** *adj* burning. **quemazón** *sf* burning; burn.

querella [ke'reʎa] *sf* quarrel; (*jur*) complaint. **querellarse** *v* lodge a complaint.

*****querer** [ke'rer] *v* love; want; try; determine. *sm* affection. **querido** *adj* dear.

queso ['keso] *sm* cheese. **queso rallado** grated cheese.

quiá [ki'a] *interj* never! surely not!

quicio ['kiθjo] *sm* hinge. **fuera de quicio** out of order.

quiebra [ki'eβra] *sf* bankruptcy; slump; fissure.

quien [ki'en] *pron* who; whom; whoever. **quién** *pron interrog* who. **¿quién sabe?** who knows? **quienquiera** *pron* whoever, whosoever.

quieto [ki'eto] *adj* still, quiet. **quietud** *sf* stillness.

quijote [ki'xote] *sm* quixotic person; idealist.

quilate [ki'late] *sm* carat.

quilla ['kiʎa] *sf* keel.

quimera [ki'mera] *sf* hallucination; quarrel. **quimérico** *adj* fantastic.

química ['kimika] *sf* chemistry.

quincalla [kin'kaʎa] *sf* hardware; ironmongery. **quincallero, -a** *sm, sf* ironmonger.

quince ['kinθe] *sm, adj* fifteen. **quincena** *sf* fortnight. **quincuagésima** *adj* fiftieth. **quinientos** *adj invar* five hundred.
quinta ['kinta] *sf* country house; conscription; (*música*) fifth.
quintal [kin'tal] *sm* hundredweight.
quinto ['kinto] *adj* fifth.
quiosco [ki'osko] *sm* kiosk.
quirúrgico [ki'rurxiko] *adj* surgical.
quisquilla [kis'kiʎa] *sf* quibble; trifle; (*zool*) shrimp.
quiste ['kiste] *sm* (*med*) cyst.
quitamanchas [kita'mantʃas] *sm invar* stain-remover.
quitar [ki'tar] *v* remove; take off; take away. **quitarse** *v* get rid of; withdraw; abstain. **de quita y pon** easily detachable.
quitasol [kita'sol] *sm* parasol, sunshade.
quizá(s) [ki'θa(s)] *adv* perhaps, maybe.

R

rábano ['raβano] *sm* radish.
rabiar [ra'βjar] *v* rave, rage. **rabiar por** long for. **rabia** *sf* rage, fury; (*med*) rabies. **rabioso** *adj* rabid.
rabino [ra'βino] *sm* rabbi.
rabo ['raβo] *sm* tail; stalk. **hacer rabona** play truant.
racial [ra'θjal] *adj* racial.
racimo [ra'θimo] *sm* bunch; cluster.
raciocinar [raθoθi'nar] *v also* **racionar** ration. **ración** *sf* portion, ration.
racional [raθjo'nal] *adj* rational. **racionalidad** *sf* rationality. **racionalista** *adj* rationalist.
racista [ra'θista] *s(m+f)* racist.
racha ['ratʃa] *sf* gust of wind; streak of luck; split.
radiactivo [raðjak'tiβo] *adj* radioactive. **radioactividad** *sf* radioactivity.
radiar [ra'ðjar] *v* radiate; broadcast. **radiación** *sf* radiation; broadcasting. **radiador** *sm* radiator. **radiante** *adj* radiant.
radicar [raði'kar] *v* take root; settle. **radicación** *sf* taking root.
radical [raði'kal] *adj* radical, fundamental. **radicalismo** *sm* radicalism.
radio¹ ['raðjo] *sm* radius.

radio² *sm* radium.
radio³ *sf* radio. **radiodifusión** *sf* broadcasting. **radiomisora** *sf* radio station. **radioyente** *s(m+f)* listener.
*raer [ra'er] *v* scrape; erase.
raíz [ra'iθ] *sf* root. **bienes raíces** real estate *sing*.
rajar [ra'xar] *v* slit; crack; slice. **raja** *sf* crack; slice.
ralea [ra'lea] *sf* sort; breed.
rallar [ra'ʎar] *v* grate. **rallador** *sm* grater. **rallo** *sm* rasp.
rama ['rama] *sf* (*bot*) branch, bough.
rambla ['rambla] *sf* avenue; gully.
ramificarse [ramifi'karse] *v* branch out. **ramificación** *sf* ramification.
ramillete [rami'ʎete] *sm* bunch of flowers, posy; cluster.
ramo ['ramo] *sm* (*bot*) branch; cluster; bouquet.
rampa ['rampa] *sf* ramp.
ramplón [ram'plon] *adj* coarse, vulgar.
rana ['rana] *sf* frog.
rancio ['ranθjo] *adj* rancid, rank, stale.
rancho ['rantʃo] *sm* (*comida*) mess; farm; ranch. **ranchero** *sm* rancher.
rango ['rango] *sm* class, rank.
ranura [ra'nura] *sf* groove.
rapaz [ra'paθ] *adj* rapacious. **rapacidad** *sf* rapacity.
rapé [ra'pe] *sm* snuff.
rápido [ra'piðo] *adj* rapid. **rapidez** *sf* speed.
rapiña [ra'piɲa] *sf* robbery with violence.
rapsodia [rap'soðja] *sf* rhapsody.
raptar [rap'tar] *v* carry off, abduct; kidnap. **rapto** *sm* abduction. **raptor, -a** *sm, sf* kidnapper.
raquero [ra'kero] *sm* beachcomber.
raqueta [ra'keta] *sf* racket.
raro ['raro] *adj* rare. **rareza** *sf* rarity.
ras [ras] *sm* level. **a ras de tierra** at ground level.
rascacielos [raska'θjelos] *sm invar* skyscraper.
rascar [ras'kar] *v* scratch; scrape. **rascadura** *sf* scratching.
rasgar [ras'gar] *v* tear; rip; slash.
rasgo ['rasgo] *sm* feature; feat; (*de pluma*) stroke.
raso ['raso] *adj* flat; level; smooth.
raspar [ras'par] *v* rasp. **raspa** *sf* rasp. **raspadura** *sf* rasping.
rastra ['rastra] *sf* trail; trace; sledge.

rastrear [rastre'ar] *v* trace; track; rake.
rastrillar [rastri'ʎar] *v* rake. **rastrillo** *sm* rake.
rastro ['rastro] *sm* track; trail.
rastrojo [ras'troxo] *sm* stubble.
rasurar [rasu'rar] *v* shave. **rasura** *sf* shaving.
rata ['rata] *sf* rat.
ratería [rate'ria] *sf* larceny, petty thieving. **ratero, -a** *sm, sf* petty thief.
ratificar [ratifi'kar] *v* ratify. **ratificación** *sf* ratification.
rato ['rato] *sm* a little while, short period of time. **al poco rato** shortly after.
ratón [ra'ton] *sm* mouse. **ratonera** *sf* mousetrap.
rayar [ra'jar] *v* rule; draw lines on; underline. **raya** *sf* line; stripe; limit. **a raya** within bounds. **rayado** *adj* lined; striped.
rayo ['rajo] *sm* beam, ray of light; flash of lightning.
raza ['raθa] *sf* race; lineage; breed.
razón [ra'θon] *sf* reason; rationale. **tener razón** be right. **razonable** *adj* reasonable. **razonar** *v* reason; justify.
reacción [reak'θjon] *sf* reaction. **reaccionar** *v* react. **reaccionario** *s(m + f)* reactionary. **reactor** *sm* reactor.
reacio [re'aθjo] *adj* obstinate.
real[1] [re'al] *adj* real.
real[2] *adj* royal.
realce [re'alθe] *sm* (*arte*) relief; highlight; importance.
realizar [reali'θar] *v* realize; make; perform.
realzar [real'θar] *v* raise; emboss; dignify.
reanimar [reani'mar] *v* revive; encourage.
reanudar [reanu'ðar] *v* renew. **reanudarse** *v* start again.
*reaparecer [reapare'θer] *v* reappear. **reaparición** *sf* reappearance.
rebajar [reβa'xar] *v* lessen, reduce; lower; allow discount; (*bebida*) weaken. **rebaja** *sf* reduction.
rebanada [reβa'naða] *sf* slice. **rebanar** *v* slice.
rebaño [re'βaɲo] *sm* flock; herd.
rebasar [reβa'sar] *v* go beyond, exceed; overtake; surpass.
rebatir [reβa'tir] *v* rebut, refute; repel. **reboto** *sm* (*mil*) alarm, call to arms; surprise attack.
rebeca [re'βeka] *sf* cardigan.

rebelarse [reβe'larse] *v* rebel. **rebelde** *adj* rebellious. **rebeldía** *sf* rebelliousness. **rebelión** *sf* rebellion.
rebosar [reβo'sar] *v* overflow. **rebosadura** *sf* overflowing.
rebotar [reβo'tar] *v* bend back; rebound; bounce. **rebotación** *sf* bouncing. **rebote** *sm* bounce.
rebozar [reβo'θar] *v* muffle. **rebozo** *sm* muffler. **sin rebozo** *openly*.
rebuscar [reβus'kar] *v* search for. **rebusca** *sf* search. **rebuscado** *adj* elaborate.
rebuznar [reβuθ'nar] *v* bray. **rebuzno** *sm* bray.
recado [re'kaðo] *sm* errand; message. **recadista** *s(m + f)* messenger.
*recaer [reka'er] *v* relapse. **recaída** *sf* relapse.
recalcar [rekal'kar] *v* cram; pack; stress. **recalcadura** *sf* pressing; packing.
recalcitrante [rekalθi'trante] *adj* recalcitrant.
*recalentar [rekalen'tar] *v* reheat; rekindle. **recalentarse** *v* overheat.
recambio [re'kambjo] *sm* re-exchange. **piezas de recambio** *sf pl* spare parts.
recargar [rekar'gar] *v* reload; overload; increase; recharge. **recarga** *sf* refill. **recargable** *adj* refillable. **recargo** *sm* additional load; surcharge.
recatarse [reka'tarse] *v* be cautious. **recatar** *v* cover up. **recatado** *adj* prudent. **recato** *sm* prudence.
recaudar [rekau'ðar] *v* collect. **recaudación** *sf* collection. **recaudador** *sm* tax collector. **a buen recaudo** in safe keeping.
recelar [reθe'lar] *v* suspect; fear. **recelo** *sm* mistrust. **receloso** *adj* suspicious.
recepción [reθep'θjon] *sf* reception; receipt; admission.
receptáculo [reθep'takulo] *sm* receptacle.
receptor [reθep'tor] *sm* recipient, receiver.
recesión [reθe'sjon] *sf* recession.
receta [re'θeta] *sf* formula; recipe; prescription.
recibir [reθi'βir] *v* receive. **recibidor, -a** *sm, sf* receiver. **recibo** *sm* reception; (*com*) receipt. **acusar recibo** (*com*) acknowledge receipt.
recién [re'θjen] *adv* recently, lately, just. **recién llegado** *sm* newcomer. **reciente** *adj* recent, new.
recinto [re'θinto] *sm* enclosure; precinct, district.

recio [ˈreθjo] *adj* tough. strong. *adv* loudly.

recipiente [reθiˈpjente] *sm* receptacle; recipient.

reciprocar [reθiproˈkar] *v* reciprocate. **recíproco** *adj* reciprocal.

recitar [reθiˈtar] *v* recite. *sm* recital. **recitación** *sf* recitation.

reclamar [reklaˈmar] *v* claim; demand; appeal. **reclamación** *sf* claim; protest. **reclamo** *sm* call; advertisement.

reclinar [rekliˈnar] *v* lean. recline. **reclinación** *sf* leaning.

reclusión [rekluˈsjon] *sf* seclusion; imprisonment. **recluso. -a** *sm. sf* recluse; convict.

recluta [reˈkluta] *sm* recruit; conscript. **reclutamiento** *sm* recruitment. **reclutar** *v* recruit; conscript.

recobrar [rekoˈβrar] *v* recover; recuperate; regain. **recobro** *sm* recovery.

recoger [rekoˈxer] *v* pick up; gather; collect; confiscate; take in; shrink. **recogerse** *v* withdraw within oneself. **recogida** *sf* collection; harvest; withdrawal. **recogido** *adj* short; small; secluded. **recogimiento** *sm* withdrawal.

recolección [rekolekˈθjon] *sf* gathering; harvest; recollection; compilation. **recolectar** *v* harvest.

***recomendar** [rekomenˈdar] *v* recommend; commend. **recomendación** *sf* recommendation. **recomendado. -a** *sm. sf* protégé/protégée.

recompensar [rekompenˈsar] *v* recompense. reward. **recompenso** *sf* compensation; recompense.

reconciliarse [rekonθiˈljarse] *v* reconcile oneself. **reconciliación** *sf* reconciliation.

recóndito [reˈkondito] *adj* secret; obscure.

***reconocer** [rekonoˈθer] *v* recognize; acknowledge; examine closely. **reconocible** *adj* recognizable. **reconocimiento** *sm* recognition; acknowledgement; examination.

reconquista [rekonˈkista] *sf* reconquest. **reconquistar** *v* reconquer.

reconsiderar [rekonsiðeˈrar] *v* reconsider.

***reconstituir** [rekonstituˈir] *v* reconstitute. **reconstitución** *sf* reconstitution.

***reconstruir** [rekonstruˈir] *v* reconstruct.

***reconvenir** [rekonβeˈnir] *v* reproach; rebuke. **reconvención** *sf* reproach.

recopilar [rekopiˈlar] *v* compile; summarize. **recopilación** *sf* compilation; summary. **recopilador** *sm* compiler.

***recordar** [rekorˈðar] *v* remember; commemorate; remind. **recordarse** *v* wake up. **para recordar** in memory. **recordable** *adj* memorable. **recordativo** *adj* reminiscent.

recorrer [rekorˈrer] *v* go over; traverse; examine; survey; repair. **recorrido** *sm* journey; run; revision.

recortar [rekorˈtar] *v* cut out; cut down; clip; trim; stand out. **recorte** *sm* cutting; outline.

recoveco [rekoˈβeko] *sm* bend; nook; recess.

recrearse [rekreˈarse] *v* amuse oneself. **recreación** *sf* recreation. **recreo** *sm* recreation; amusement.

recriminar [rekrimiˈnar] *v* recriminate. **recriminación** *sf* recrimination.

***recrudecer** [rekruðeˈθer] *v* recur; break out again.

rectángulo [rekˈtangulo] *sm* rectangle. **rectangular** *adj* rectangular.

rectificar [rektifiˈkar] *v* rectify; correct. **rectificación** *sf* rectification.

rectitud [rektiˈtuð] *sf* rectitude; rightness. **recto** *adj* right; just; straight.

rector [rekˈtor] *sm* rector; principal; governor. **rectoría** *sf* rectory.

recua [ˈrekwa] *sf* drove. herd; (*fig*) gang.

recuento [reˈkwento] *sm* recount; calculation; inventory.

recuerdo [reˈkwerðo] *sm* recollection; memory. **recuerdos** *sm pl* regards *pl*.

recular [rekuˈlar] *v* recoil. **reculada** *sf* recoil.

recuperar [rekupeˈrar] *v* recuperate. **recuperación** *sf* recovery.

recurrir [rekurˈrir] *v* revert; resort (to). **recurrir a** have recourse to. **recurso** *sm* recourse; appeal.

recusar [rekuˈsar] *v* refuse; reject. **recusación** *sf* refusal; rejection.

rechazar [retʃaˈθar] *v* repel; deny. **rechazamiento** *sm* repulsion. **rechazo** *sm* rebound; rejection.

rechinar [retʃiˈnar] *v* creak; squeak; (*los dientes*) gnash. **rechinamiento** *sm* creaking; squeaking.

rechoncho [reˈtʃontʃo] *adj* squat; chubby.

red [reð] *sf* net; grid; grille; grating; snare. **caer en la red** fall into the trap. **red ferroviaria** railway system.

redactar [reðak'tar] *v* edit. **redacción** *sf* editing; journalism. **redactor. -a** *sm*, *sf* editor; writer.

redención [reðen'θjon] *sf* redemption; help; salvation. **redentor. -a** *sm*, *sf* redeemer.

redimir [reði'mir] *v* redeem; ransom. **redimible** *adj* redeemable.

rédito ['reðito] *sm* income. **rédito imponible** taxable income.

redoblar [reðo'βlar] *v* double; redouble; repeat. **redobladura** *sf* redoubling.

redondear [reðonde'ar] *v* round; round off. **redondo** *adj* round; spherical. **negocio redondo** *sm* square deal.

***reducir** [reðu'θir] *v* reduce; lessen; compress; scale down **reducción** *sf* reduction. **reducido** *adj* reduced; abridged.

redundar [reðun'dar] *v* redound; overflow.

reembolsar [reembol'sar] *v* reimburse, repay. **reembolso** *sm* reimbursement; refund. **contra reembolso** cash on delivery.

reemplazar [reempla'θar] *v* replace. **reemplazable** *adj* replaceable. **reemplazo** *sm* replacement.

referencia [refe'renθja] *sf* reference; account; allusion. **referente** *adj* referring. **referido** *adj* aforementioned; in question. **referéndum** [refe'rendum] *sm* referendum.

***referir** [refe'rir] *v* refer; narrate; describe.

refinar [refi'nar] *v* refine; polish; perfect. **refinación** *sf* refinement. **refinado** *adj* refined; slick. **refinadura** *sf* refinement. **refinería** *sf* refinery.

reflectar [reflek'tar] *v* reflect. **reflector** *sm* reflector; searchlight.

reflejar [refle'xar] *v* reflect; show. **refleja** *sf* reflection. **reflejo** *sm* reflection; reflex; glare.

reflexión [reflek'sjon] *sf* reflection. **reflexionar** *v* reflect. **reflexivo** *adj* (*gram*) reflexive.

reflujo [re'fluxo] *sm* ebb.

reformar [refor'mar] *v* reform; amend; remake; improve; repair. **reforma** *sf* reform, reformation. **reformación** *sf* reformation. **reformador. -a** *sm*, *sf* reformer. **reformativo** *adj* reformative **reformatorio** *sm* reformatory

***reforzar** [refor'θar] *v* reinforce; strengthen; encourage; boost. **reforzado** *adj* reinforced.

refractario [refrak'tarjo] *adj* refractory. **refracción** *sf* refraction. **refractar** *v* refract.

refrán [re'fran] *sm* proverb, saying.

***refregar** [refre'gar] *v* rub; scour; scold. **refregadura** *sf* rubbing, friction.

refrenar [refre'nar] *v* curb, control. **refrenamiento** *sm* restraint.

refrescar [refres'kar] *v* refresh; cool; repeat; revise. **refrescadura** *sf* refreshing. **refrescante** *adj* refreshing; cooling. **refresco** *sm* refreshment; cold drink.

refuerzo [re'fwerθo] *sm* reinforcement; backing; help.

refugiarse [refu'xjarse] *v* shelter. **refugio** *sm* refuge. **refugio de peatones** traffic island. **refugiado. -a** *sm*, *sf* refugee.

refulgir [reful'xir] *v* shine, gleam. **refulgencia** *sf* brilliance. **refulgente** *adj* brilliant.

refundir [refun'dir] *v* recast; adapt; refurbish. **refundición** *sf* recasting; adaptation.

refunfuñar [refunfu'ɲar] *v* grumble; grouse. **refunfuñadura** *sf* *also* **refunfuño** *sm* grumbling.

refutar [refu'tar] *v* refute. **refutable** *adj* refutable. **refutación** *sf* refutation.

regadera [rega'ðera] *sf* watering-can; channel; irrigation ditch. **regadero** *sm* irrigation ditch. **regadío** *sm* irrigated land. **regadizo** *adj* irrigable. **regadura** *sf* irrigation. **regar** *v* water; irrigate; sprinkle.

regalar [rega'lar] *v* give; treat; regale; entertain. **regalador. -a** *sm*, *sf* entertainer. **regalo** *sm* gift; pleasure; treat; entertainment.

regaliz [rega'liθ] *sm* liquorice.

regañar [rega'ɲar] *v* scold; quarrel; growl; grumble. **regaño** *sm* scolding; quarrel; growl; grumble.

regata [re'gata] *sf* regatta.

regatear [regate'ar] *v* haggle; bargain; retail; begrudge; dodge. **regate** *sm* dodge. **regateo** *sm* haggling. **regatería** *sf* retail. **regatero. -a** *sm*, *sf* retailer.

regazo [re'gaθo] *sm* lap.

regencia [re'xenθja] *sf* regency.

regenerar [rexene'rar] *v* regenerate. **regeneración** *sf* regeneration. **regenerativo** *adj* regenerative.

regentar [rexen'tar] *v* manage; govern; boss. **regente** *sm* regent; director; professor. **regentear** *v* domineer.

régimen ['reximen] *sm* regime; system; rate; diet; performance.

regimiento [rexi'mjento] *sm* regiment; administration; government; town council. **regimentación** *sf* regimentation. **regimental** *adj* regimental. **regimentar** *v* regiment.

región [re'xjon] *sf* region; territory; area; space. **regional** *adj* regional.

***regir** [re'xir] *v* govern; manage; control; obtain; prevail; steer.

registrar [rexis'trar] *v* register; inspect; record; search; show. **registración** *sf* registration. **registrado** *adj* registered; examined. **registrador** *sm* registrar; inspector. **registradora** *sf* cash register. **registro** *sm* register; registry; inspection.

reglar [re'glar] *v* rule; regulate; control. **reglarse** *v* conform; reform. **regla** *sf* rule; method; discipline; menstruation. **a regla** by rule. **regla de cálculo** slide rule. **regladamente** *adv* regularly. **reglado** *adj* regular; regulated; temperate. **reglamentación** *sf* regulation. **reglamentar** *v* regulate. **reglamentario** *adj* statutory. **reglamento** *sm* statute; rules and regulations *pl*.

regocijar [regoθi'xar] *v* rejoice; gladden. **regocijarse** *v* rejoice; exult. **regocijador** *adj* cheering. **regocijo** *sm* joy, gladness.

regresar [regre'sar] *v* return.

regular [regu'lar] *adj* regular; average; ordinary. **por lo regular** as a rule. *v* regulate; control; adjust. **regulación** *adj* regulation; control. **regulación a distancia** remote control. **regulado** *adj* regulated; regular. **regulador** *sm* regulator; throttle. **regulador de volumen** volume control. **regularidad** *sf* regularity; ordinariness. **regularización** *sf* regularization. **regularizar** *v* regularize.

rehabilitar [reaβili'tar] *v* rehabilitate. **rehabilitación** *sf* rehabilitation.

***rehacer** [rea'θer] *v* remake; recover; renovate; repair. **rehacerse** *v* recuperate. **rehecho** *adj* remade; squat.

rehén [re'en] *sm* hostage.

***rehuir** [re'wir] *v* flee; shrink from; avoid; shirk. **rehuida** *sf* flight.

rehusar [reu'sar] *v* refuse; reject.

reimprimir [reimpri'mir] *v* reprint. **reimpresión** *sf* reprint. **reimpreso** *adj* reprinted.

reinar [rei'nar] *v* reign; prevail. **reina** *sf* queen. **reinante** *adj* reigning. **reinado** *sm* reign. **reino** *sm* kingdom, reign. **reino animal** animal kingdom.

reincidir [reinθi'ðir] *v* backslide; relapse into; reiterate. **reincidencia** *sf* backsliding; reiteration. **reincidente** *adj* backsliding; relapsing; reiterating.

reintegrar [reinte'grar] *v* reintegrate; reimburse; recover. **reintegrarse** *v* recoup oneself. **reintegrable** *adj* reimbursable. **reintegración** *sf* reintegration; restoration. **reintegro** *sm* recovery; reimbursement.

***reír** [re'ir] *v* laugh. **reírse de** make fun of.

reiterar [reite'rar] *v* reiterate. **reiteración** *sf* reiteration.

reivindicar [reiβindi'kar] *v* reclaim; claim; rehabilitate. **reivindicación** *sf* claim; recovery.

reja ['rexa] *sf* grating; grille; ploughshare; lattice. **rejado** *sm* grating; railing. **rejería** *sf* ornamental ironwork. **rejilla** *sf* small grating; (*tren*) luggage rack.

***rejuvenecer** [rexuβene'θer] *v* rejuvenate. **rejuvenecimiento** *sm* rejuvenation.

relación [rela'θjon] *sf* relation; connection; report; narrative; intercourse; relationship. **relaciones** *sf pl* courtship *sing*; engagement *sing*. **relacionado** *adj* related. **relacionar** *v* relate; report; connect. **relacionarse** *v* be related; be connected.

relajar [rela'xar] *v* relax; remit; loosen; debauch. **relajación** *sf* relaxation; loosening; laxity; rupture. **relajadamente** *adv* loosely, dissolutely. **relajado** *adj* lax; ruptured. **relajador** *adj* relaxing.

relámpago [re'lampago] *sm* lightning. **relámpago difuso** sheet lightning.

relatar [rela'tar] *v* report; relate; tell. **relatador, -a** *sm*, *sf* narrator.

relatividad [relatiβi'ðað] *sf* relativity.

relevar [rele'βar] *v* relieve; absolve; replace; free; emboss. **relevación** *sf* relief; liberation; remission. **relevante** *adj* outstanding. **relevo** *sm* relay race. **relieve** *sm* relief; prominence. **en relieve** embossed.

relicario [reli'karjo] *sm* reliquary, shrine; locket.

religión [reli'xjon] *sf* religion; faith; creed.

religioso [reli'xjoso] *sm* friar, monk; religious person. *adj* religious.

reliquia [re'likja] *sf* relic; memento; ailment. **reliquia de familia** heirloom.

reloj [re'lox] *sm* clock; watch. **reloj de caja** grandfather clock. **reloj de cuclillo** cuckoo clock. **reloj despertador** alarm clock. **reloj pulsera** wristwatch. **relojería** *sf* watchmaker's shop. **relojero** *sm* watchmaker.

***relucir** [relu'θir] *v* shine; excel. **sacar a relucir** show off. **reluciente** *adj* gleaming.

reluctante [reluk'tante] *adj* reluctant.

relumbrar [relum'brar] *v* dazzle; glare. **relumbrante** *adj* dazzling. **relumbre** *sm* sparkle; flash. **relumbro** *sm* glare; tinsel. **relumbroso** *adj* dazzling.

rellenar [reʎe'nar] *v* refill; fill; stuff; cram. **rellenable** *adj* refillable. **relleno** *sm* filling; stuffing; packing.

remachar [rema'tʃar] *v* rivet; stress. **remachado** *adj* riveted; (*fam*) quiet. **remache** *sm* rivet.

remanente [rema'nente] *sm* remains *pl*.

remanso [re'manso] *sm* backwater; sluggishness.

remar [re'mar] *v* row; toil.

rematar [rema'tar] *v* finish; kill; knock down at auction. **rematado** *adj* completely ruined. **rematante** *sm* highest bidder. **remate** *sm* end; finishing touch; highest bid.

remediar [reme'ðjar] *v* remedy; help; prevent. **remediable** *adj* remediable. **remedio** *sm* remedy. **no hay remedio** it can't be helped.

***remendar** [remen'dar] *v* repair; patch; darn. **remendado** *adj* spotty; patched. **remendón, -ona** *sm, sf* mender; repairer. **remiendo** *sm* repair; patch. **echar un remiendo a** put a patch on.

remero [re'mero] *sm* oarsman.

remesa [re'mesa] *sf* remittance; consignment; shipment. **remesar** *v* remit; ship.

remilgado [remil'gaðo] *adj* mincing; prim; squeamish. **remilgarse** *v* simper. **remilgo** *sm* smirk; primness.

reminiscencia [remini'sθenθja] *sf* reminiscence.

remirado [remi'raðo] *adj* considerate; cautious; discreet. **remirar** *v* review. **remirarse** *v* take great pains; enjoy looking over.

remisión [remi'sjon] *sf* remission; pardon; reference. **remisible** *adj* pardonable. **remiso** *adj* remiss.

remitir [remi'tir] *v* send; pardon; adjourn; abate. **remitirse a** quote from. **remitido** *sm* dispatch.

remo ['remo] *sm* oar; paddle; rowing. **remos** *sm pl* limbs *pl*.

remojar [remo'xar] *v* soak; steep. **remojo** *sm* soaking; steeping.

remolcha [remo'latʃa] *sf* beetroot.

remolcar [remol'kar] *v* tow; haul. **remolcador** *sm* tug.

remolino [remo'lino] *sm* whirlwind; whirlpool; (*fig*) throng. **remolinar** *v* eddy.

remontar [remon'tar] *v* remount; mend; go back in time; raise; frighten. **remonte** *sm* repair; remounting; rising.

remordimiento [remorði'mjento] *sm* remorse.

remoto [re'moto] *adj* remote; improbable.

***remover** [remo'βer] *v* remove; move; stir; discharge. **removimiento** *sm* removal.

remunerar [remune'rar] *v* remunerate. **remuneración** *sf* remuneration. **remunerativo** *adj* remunerative.

***renacer** [rena'θer] *v* be reborn; recover. **renacimiento** *sm* rebirth; renaissance.

renacuajo [rena'kwaxo] *sm* tadpole.

rencilla [ren'θiʎa] *sf* squabble; feud. **rencilloso** *adj* quarrelsome.

rencor [ren'kor] *sm* rancour. **rencoroso** *adj* rancorous.

***rendir** [ren'dir] *v* conquer; yield; surrender. **rendirse** *v* wear oneself out. **rendición** *sf* surrender; (*com*) profit. **rendido** *adj* submissive. **rendimiento** *sm* humility; weariness; output.

***renegar** [rene'gar] *v* disown; detest; curse. **renegado, -a** *sm, sf* renegade. **renegador, -a** *sm, sf* blasphemer.

renglón [ren'glon] *sm* written or printed line. **leer entre renglones** read between the lines.

reno ['reno] *sm* reindeer.

renombre [re'nombre] *sm* renown; surname. **renombrado** *adj* renowned.

***renovar** [reno'βar] *v* renovate; renew. **renovable** *adj* renewable. **renovación** *sf* renovation; renewal. **renuevo** *sm* renewal; sprout.

rentar [ren'tar] *v* yield an income or profit. **renta** *sf* income; profit. **rentero, -a** *sm,* *sf* tenant farmer. **rentista** *s(m + f)* stockholder. **rentístico** *adj* financial.

renunciar [renun'θjar] *v* renounce; resign. **renuncia** *sf* renunciation; resignation.

***reñir** [re'ɲir] *v* scold; quarrel. **reñido** *adj* on bad terms. **reñidor** *adj* quarrelsome.

reo ['reo]. **-a** *sm, sf* defendant. *adj* guilty.

reojo [re'oxo] *sm* **mirar de reojo** look askance.

reorganizar [reorgani'θar] *v* reorganize. **reorganización** *sf* reorganization.

reparar [repa'rar] *v* repair; restore; correct; make amends for; observe; parry. **reparable** *adj* noteworthy. **reparador. -a** *sm, sf* repairer; faultfinder. **reparo** *sm* repair; remedy; observation; protection.

repartir [repar'tir] *v* share; distribute. **repartición** *sf* distribution. **repartidor. -a** *sm, sf* distributor. **reparto** *sm* distribution; (*teatro*) cast.

repasar [repa'sar] *v* revise; review; retrace. **repaso** *sm* review; (*fam*) reprimand.

repatriar [repa'trjar] *v* repatriate. **repatriación** *sf* repatriation. **repatriado. -a** *sm, sf* repatriate.

repeler [repe'ler] *v* repel. **repelente** *adj* repellent.

repente [re'pente] *sm* sudden impulse. **de repente** suddenly.

repercutir [reperku'tir] *v* re-echo; rebound. **repercusión** *sf* repercussion; reverberation.

repertorio [reper'torjo] *sm* repertory; repertoire.

***repetir** [repe'tir] *v* repeat; recite. **repetición** *sf* repetition; recital.

repisa [re'pisa] *sf* shelf; ledge; bracket. **repisa de chimenea** mantelpiece. **repisa de ventana** window sill.

***replegar** [reple'gar] *v* refold; (*mil*) retreat. **replegable** *adj* folding. **repliegue** *sm* fold, crease; retreat.

repleto [re'pleto] *adj* replete; plump.

réplica ['replika] *sf* answer; replica. **replicar** *v* argue; answer back. **replicato** *sm* argument; answer.

repoblación [repoβla'θjon] *sf* repopulation; restocking; reforestation. **repoblar** *v* repopulate; restock; reforest.

repollo [re'poʎo] *sm* cabbage.

***reponer** [repo'ner] *v* replace; restore. **reponerse** *v* recover.

reportar [repor'tar] *v* restrain; obtain; bring. **reportarse** *v* contain oneself. **reportamiento** *sm* restraint.

reposar [repo'sar] *v* rest; lie down; settle; lie buried. **reposo** *sm* repose.

repostería [reposte'ria] *sf* pastry shop; pantry. **repostero. -a** *sm, sf* pastrycook; confectioner.

reprender [repren'der] *v* reprimand. **reprensible** *adj* reprehensible. **reprensor** *adj* reproachful.

represalia [repre'salja] *sf* reprisal.

representar [represen'tar] *v* represent; signify; describe; express; perform; appear to have. **representarse** *v* imagine. **representable** *adj* representable; performable. **representación** *sf* representation; performance. **representante** *s(m + f)* representative; actor, actress. **representativo** *adj* representative.

represión [repre'sjon] *sm* repression; control. **represivo** *adj* repressive.

reprimenda [repri'menda] *sf* reprimand.

reprimir [repri'mir] *v* repress; suppress. **reprimible** *adj* repressible.

***reprobar** [repro'βar] *v* reprove; condemn; (*examen*) fail. **reprobable** *adj* reprehensible. **reprobación** *sf* reproof; failure. **reprobado. -a** *sm, sf* also **réprobo. -a** *sm, sf* reprobate.

reprochar [repro'tʃar] *v* reproach; challenge. **reprochable** *adj* reproachable; reproachful. **reprochador. -a** *sm, sf* reproacher.

***reproducir** [reproðu'θir] *v* reproduce. **reproducible** *adj* reproducible. **reproducción** *sf* reproduction. **reproductor. -a** *sm, sf* breeder.

reptil [rep'til] *sm* reptile.

república [re'puβlika] *sf* republic. **republicanismo** *sm* republicanism. **republicano. -a** *sm, sf* republican.

repudiar [repu'ðjar] *v* repudiate. **repudiación** *sf* repudiation.

repuesto [re'pwesto] *sm* supply; store; sideboard. **de repuesto** spare, extra. *adj* replaced; secluded; recovered.

repugnar [repug'nar] *v* contradict; object to; be repugnant. **repugnarse** *v* conflict. **repugnacia** *sf* repugnance; opposition. **repugnante** *adj* repugnant.

repulsivo [repul'siβo] *adj* repulsive. **repulsa** *sf* refusal; rebuke. **repulsar** *v* reject; refuse. **repulsión** *sf* rejection; refusal.

reputar [repu'tar] *v* repute; consider; esteem. **reputación** *sf* reputation. **reputado** *adj* reputed.

*****requebrar** [reke'βrar] *v* woo; flatter; flirt with. **requebrador, -a** *sm, sf* flirt.

requemar [reke'mar] *v* scorch; inflame; overcook. **requemarse** *v* smoulder; become tanned. **requemado** *adj* burnt; tanned. **requemamiento** *sm* bite; sting. **requemante** *adj* burning; stinging.

*****requerir** [reke'rir] *v* request; require; urge; notify; summon; examine. **requeriente** *adj* requiring. **requerimiento** *sm* requisition; summons; notification; request.

requesón [reke'son] *sm* curd; cottage cheese.

requisar [reki'sar] *v* requisition. **requisa** *sf* tour of inspection; requisition. **requisición** *sf* requisition. **requisito** *adj* requisite.

res [res] *sf* head of cattle; animal.

resabio [re'saβjo] *sm* bad habit; unpleasant aftertaste. **resabiado** *adj* crafty; wicked; spoiled. **resabiar** *v* pervert; become vicious. **resabiarse** *v* become annoyed.

resaca [re'saka] *sf* undertow; surf; surge.

resaltar [resal'tar] *v* rebound, stand out. **resalte** *sm* projection. **resalto** *sm* rebound.

resarcir [resar'θir] *v* compensate. **resarcirse de** make up for. **resarcimiento** *sm* compensation.

resbalar [resβa'lar] *v* slide; skid; slip. **resbaladero** *also* **resbaladizo**, **resbalante** *adj* slippery. **resbalador** *adj* sliding. **resbaldura** *sf* skid mark. **resbalón** *sm* slide; slip; skid.

rescatar [reska'tar] *v* rescue; recover; save; ransom; make up for. **rescate** *sm* redemption; rescue; ransom.

rescindir [resθin'dir] *v* rescind. **rescisión** *sf* annulment.

rescoldo [res'kolδo] *sm* misgiving; embers *pl.*

resecar [rese'kar] *v* dry thoroughly. **reseco** *adj* desiccated.

*****resentirse** [resen'tirse] *v* feel the effects; be weakened.

reseñar [rese'ɲar] *v* review; outline. **reseña** *sf* review; outline.

reservar [reser'βar] *v* reserve; preserve; conceal. **reserva** *sf* reserve; reservation. **a reserva de** with the intention of. **reserva de asiento** reservation. **sin reserva** frankly. **reservado** *adj* reserved; discreet.

resfriar [resfri'ar] *v* cool; turn cold. **resfriarse** *v* catch cold. **resfriado** *m* (*med*) cold.

resguardar [resgwar'δar] *v* defend; preserve. **resguardarse** *v* protect oneself. **resguardo** *sm* defence; protection; guarantee. **reguardo de correos** postal receipt.

residencia [resi'δenθja] *sf* residence; boarding house. **residencial** *adj* residential. **residente** *s(m+f)* resident. **residir** *v* reside.

residuo [re'siδwo] *sm* residue. **residuos** *sm pl* refuse *sing.* **residual** *adj* residual.

resignar [resig'nar] *v* resign; renounce. **resignarse** *v* resign oneself. **resigna** *sf* renunciation. **resignación** *sf* resignation.

resina [re'sina] *sf* resin.

resistir [resis'tir] *v* resist; refuse. **resistencia** *sf* resistance; stamina. **resistente** *adj* resistant.

resolución [resolu'θjon] *sf* resolution; decision. **resoluto** *adj* resolute; skilled.

*****resolver** [resol'βer] *v* resolve; decide; analyse. **resolverse** *v* make up one's mind.

*****resollar** [reso'ʎar] *v* pant; puff; snort.

*****resonar** [reso'nar] *v* resound. **resonancia** *sf* resonance. **resonante** *adj* resonant.

resoplar [reso'plar] *v* snort; puff. **resoplido** *sm* snort; puff.

resorte [re'sorte] *sm* resort; means; motive; (*mec*) spring; elasticity.

respaldar [respal'δar] *v* back; support; endorse. **respaldarse** *v* lean. **respaldo** *sm* chair back; support.

respecto [res'pekto] *sm* respect. **con respecto a** with regard to.

respetar [respe'tar] *v* respect. **respetabilidad** *sf* respectability. **respetable** *adj* respectable. **respetador** *adj* respectful. **respeto** *sm* respect. **respetuoso** *adj* respectful.

respirar [respi'rar] *v* breathe. **respiración** *sf* respiration; breath. **respiro** *sm* breathing. **respiradero** *sm* ventilator.

*****resplandecer** [resplanδe'θer] *v* glitter. **resplandeciente** *adj* glittering. **resplandor** *sm* glitter.

responder [respon'der] *v* respond. **responder por** vouch for. **respondón** *adj* saucy. **responsivo** *adj* responsive. **respuesta** *sf* reply; refutation.

responsable [respon'saβle] *adj* responsible. **responsabilidad** *sf* responsibility.

*resquebrajar [reskeβra'xar] *v also* **resquebrar** split; crack. **resquebra(ja)dura** *sf* crack.

resquemar [reske'mar] *v* sting the tongue. *vm* sting in the mouth; remorse; resentment.

resquicio [res'kiθjo] *sm* crack; chink; (*fig*) slight chance.

*restablecer [restaβle'θer] *v* re-establish. **restablecerse** *v* recover from illness. **restablecimiento** *sm* re-establishment; recovery.

restallar [resta'ʎar] *v* crack; crackle.

restante [res'tante] *adj* remaining. *sm* remainder.

restar [res'tar] *v* subtract; remain.

restaurante [restau'rante] *sm* restaurant. **restauración** *sf* restoration. **restaurar** *v* restore; recover; repair.

*restituir [restitu'ir] *v* restore; pay back. **restituirse** *v* return. **restituición** *sf* restitution.

resto [resto] *sm* rest, remainder.

*restregar [restre'gar] *v* rub; scrub; wipe. **restregón** *sm* rubbing; scrubbing; wiping.

restricción [restrik'θjon] *sf* restriction. **restrictivo** *adj* restrictive.

restringir [restrin'xir] *v* restrict.

resucitar [resuθi'tar] *v* resuscitate. **resucitación** *sf* resuscitation.

resuello [re'sweʎo] *sm* breathing.

resuelto [re'swelto] *adj* resolute; resolved; firm.

resultar [resul'tar] *v* result; happen; turn out; go. **resulta** *sf* result, effect. **resultado** *vm* result. **resultante** *adj* resultant.

resumir [resu'mir] *v* summarize; abbreviate. **resumen** *sm* summary. **en resumen** in brief. **resumido** *adj* summarized.

retablo [re'taβlo] *sm* altarpiece.

retaguardia [reta'gwarðja] *sf* rearguard.

retal [re'tal] *sm* remnant.

retama [re'tama] *sf* (*bot*) broom.

retardar [retar'ðar] *v* retard, delay; (*reloj*) put back. **retardación** *sf* delay. **retardo** *vm* delay.

retén [re'ten] *sm* spare, reserve.

*retener [rete'ner] *v* retain; deduct; detain; arrest. **retención** *sf* retention; deduction; detention. **retentiva** *sf* memory. **retentivo** *adj* retentive.

retina [re'tina] *sf* retina.

retintín [retin'tin] *sm* jingle.

retirar [reti'rar] *v* withdraw. **retirarse** *v* go into seclusion. **retirada** *sf* retreat. **retirado** *adj* retired; remote. **retiro** *sm* retirement; retreat.

reto ['reto] *sm* challenge.

retocar [reto'kar] *v* retouch. **retoque** *sm* retouching.

*retorcer [retor'θer] *v* twist; distort. **retorcerse** *v* writhe. **retorcimiento** *sm* contortion.

retórica [re'torika] *sf* rhetoric. **retórico** *adj* rhetorical.

retornar [retor'nar] *v* return. **retorno** *sm* return; remuneration.

retractar [retrak'tar] *v* retract. **retracción** *sf* retraction. **retractable** *adj also* **retráctil** retractable.

*retraer [retra'er] *v* dissuade; bring again. **retraerse** *v* shelter; retreat. **retraído** *adj* retiring; unsociable. **retraimiento** *sm* retirement; retreat.

retrasar [retra'sar] *v* delay; put back; (*reloj*) be slow. **retrasarse** *v* be late. **retraso** *sm* delay; lateness.

retratar [retra'tar] *v* portray. **retratista** *s*(*m*+*f*) portrait painter. **retrato** *sm* portrait.

retrete [re'trete] *sm* lavatory.

*retribuir [retriβu'ir] *v* recompense; repay. **retribución** *sf* retribution; recompense.

retroceder [retroθe'ðer] *v* recede; fall back. **retroceso** *sm* retreat; (*com*) slump. **retrogresión** *sf* retrogression.

retruécano [retru'ekano] *sm* pun.

retumbar [retum'bar] *v* resound. **retumbante** *adj* resounding. **retumbo** *sm* rumble.

reuma ['reuma] *sm* rheumatism. **reumático** *adj* rheumatic. **reumatismo** *sm* rheumatism.

reunir [reu'nir] *v* reunite; unite; gather; reconcile. **reunión** *sf* meeting.

revalidar [reβali'ðar] *v* ratify; confirm. **revalidación** *sf* ratification.

revancha [re'βantʃa] *sf* revenge.

revelar [reβe'lar] *v* reveal; (*foto*) develop. **revelación** *sf* revelation. **revelador** *adj* revealing.

revendedor [reβende'ðor], **-a** *sm*, *sf* retailer. **revender** *v* retail.

*reventar [reβen'tar] *v* burst. **reventarse** *v* blow up. **reventón** *sm* burst; blowout.

reverberar [reβerβe'rar] *v* reverberate. **reverberación** *sf* reverberation. **reverbero** *sm* reverberation; reflector.

*reverdecer [reβerðe'θer] v grow green again; revive.

reverenciar [reβeren'θjar] v reverence, venerate. **reverencia** sf reverence. **reverendo** adj reverend. **reverente** adj reverent.

reversión [reβer'sjon] sf reversion. **reversible** adj revertible. **reverso** adj reverse.

revés [re'βes] sm reverse; back; setback. **al revés** upside down; inside out; back to front. **revesado** adj complicated; unruly.

revisar [reβi'sar] v revise; review. **revisión** sf revision; review; (com) audit. **revista** sf review; journal.

revivir [reβi'βir] v revive. **revivicar** v revive.

revocar [reβo'kar] v revoke; dissuade.

*revolcar [reβol'kar] v knock down; defeat; (fam) fail an exam. **revolcarse** v wallow.

revoltillo [reβol'tiʎo] sm also **revoltijo** jumble; mess.

revoltoso [reβol'toso] adj mischievous; unruly.

revolución [reβolu'θjon] sf revolution. **revolucionario, -a** sm, adj revolutionary.

*revolver [reβol'βer] v revolve; stir; disturb. **revolverse** v turn round.

revólver [re'βolβer] sm revolver.

revoque [re'βoke] sm plaster; stucco; whitewash.

revuelta [re'βwelta] sf revolt; turn; bend; change. **revuelto** adj difficult; unruly; upside down; disturbed.

rey [rej] sm king.

reyerta [re'jerta] sf quarrel; brawl.

rezagar [reθa'gar] v defer; postpone; leave behind. **rezagarse** v straggle. **rezagado** sm (mil) straggler. **rezago** sm remainder.

rezar [re'θar] v pray, pray for. **rezo** sm prayer; prayers pl.

rezumarse [reθu'marse] v ooze, drip; leak out.

riachuelo [rja'tʃwelo] sm brook. **ría** sf estuary.

ribera [ri'βera] sf river bank; shore.

ribete [ri'βete] sm (de ropa) border, edging; trimmings pl. **ribetear** v border; edge.

ricino [ri'θino] sm castor-oil plant. **aceite de ricino** sm castor oil.

rico ['riko], **-a** sm, sf rich person. adj rich; handsome; tasty.

ridiculizar [riðikuli'θar] v ridicule. **ridículo** adj ridiculous.

riego ['rjego] sm irrigation.

riel [rjel] sm ingot; (ferro) rail.

rienda ['rjenda] sf rein. **a rienda suelta** at full speed. **llevar las riendas** be in control.

riesgo ['rjesgo] sm risk.

rifar [ri'far] v raffle. **rifa** sf raffle.

rifle ['rifle] sm rifle.

rígido ['rixiðo] adj rigid. **rigidez** sf rigidity.

rigor [ri'gor] sm severity; rigour. **rigorismo** sm austerity. **riguroso** adj rigorous.

rimar [ri'mar] v rhyme. **rima** sf rhyme.

rimbombante [rimbom'bante] adj grandiloquent; bombastic. **rimbombancia** sf grandiloquence.

rincón [rin'kon] sm corner. **rinconada** sf corner table.

rinoceronte [rinoθe'ronte] sm rhinoceros.

riña ['riɲa] sf brawl; fight; quarrel.

riñón [ri'ɲon] sm kidney.

río ['rio] sm river. **río arriba** upstream.

ripio ['ripjo] sm rubble; refuse; residue. **no perder ripio** not to miss a trick.

riqueza [ri'keθa] sf wealth.

risa ['risa] sf laughter; laugh. **riseño** adj smiling; happy.

ristre ['ristre] sm **en ristre** at the ready.

ritmo ['ritmo] sm rhythm. **rítmico** adj rhythmic.

rito ['rito] sm rite. **ritual** sm ritual. **ritualismo** sm ritualism. **ritualista** adj ritualistic.

rival [ri'βal] s(m + f), adj rival. **rivalidad** sf rivalry. **rivalizar** v vie. **rivalizar con** rival.

rizar [ri'θar] v (pelo) curl. **rizado** sm curling. **rizador** sm curling-iron. **rizo** adj curly.

robar [ro'βar] v rob, steal; kidnap. **robo** sm robbery.

roble ['roβle] sm oak.

*robustecer [roβuste'θer] v strengthen. **robustecerse** v gain strength. **robustecimiento** sm strengthening. **robustez** sf robustness. **robusto** adj robust.

roca ['roka] sf rock.

roce ['roθe] sm friction; rubbing; chafing.

rociar [ro'θjar] v sprinkle; spray; strew; moisten. **rociada** sf sprinkling; spraying; dew. **rociadera** sf watering can. **rociador** sm sprinkler.

rocín [ro'θin] sm nag; hack.

rodapié [roða'pje] sm skirting-board.

*__**rodar**__ [ro'ðar] v roll; revolve; rotate. **rodado** adj (auto) run-in. **tránsito rodado** sm road traffic. **rodaja** sf small wheel. **rodaje** sm wheels pl.

rodear [roðe'ar] v encircle; enclose; go round. **rodearse** v surround oneself. **rodeo** sm detour; evasion; rodeo.

rodezno [ro'ðeθno] sm waterwheel; cogwheel.

rodilla [ro'ðiʎa] sf knee. **de rodillas** kneeling.

rodillo [ro'ðiʎo] sm rolling pin; roller; mangle.

*__**roer**__ [ro'er] v gnaw; nibble. **roerse** v bite. **roedor** adj gnawing.

*__**rogar**__ [ro'gar] v beg; pray. **rogación** sf petition. **rogativa** sf supplication.

rojo ['roxo] adj red. sm red; rouge. **rojear** v redden. **rojizo** adj reddish.

rollizo [ro'ʎiθo] adj chubby; plump.

rollo ['roʎo] sm roll; cylinder; (foto) film.

romance [ro'manθe] sm, adj romance. sm ballad. **romancero** sm ballad collection; ballad singer. **romántico** adj romantic.

romería [rome'ria] sf pilgrimage. **romero, -a** sm, sf pilgrim; sm rosemary.

romo ['romo] adj snub-nosed; blunt; dull.

rompecabezas [rompeka'βeθas] sm invar puzzle; jigsaw; riddle.

rompeolas [rompe'olas] sm invar breakwater.

romper [rom'per] v break; fracture; break out. **rompimiento** sm break; breach.

ron [ron] sm rum.

roncar [ron'kar] v snore; roar; boast. **ronca** sf bellow. **ronquido** sm snore.

ronco ['ronko] adj hoarse. **ronquedad** sf hoarseness.

rondar [ron'dar] v patrol; go round; pursue; haunt; serenade. **rondador** sm patrolman. **ronda** sf patrol; round of drinks.

ronronear [ronrone'ar] v purr.

ronzal [ron'θal] sm halter.

roña ['roɲa] sf filth; mange; rust; (fam) meanness. adj stingy. **roñoso** adj mangy; filthy; stingy.

ropa ['ropa] sf clothes pl, clothing. **ropa de cama** bed linen. **ropa interior** underclothes. **ropero** sm wardrobe.

roque ['roke] sm (ajedrez) rook.

rosa ['rosa] sf rose. **novela rosa** sf romantic novel. **rosado** adj rose-coloured. **rosal** sm rosebush.

rosario [ro'sarjo] sm rosary.

rosca ['roska] sf thread of a screw; doughnut; bread roll.

rostro ['rostro] sm countenance, face. **hacer rostro a** face.

rotación [rota'θjon] sf rotation. **rotativo** adj rotary.

roto ['roto] adj broken; torn. sm hole.

rotular [rotu'lar] v label. **rótula** sf label; placard.

rotundo [ro'tundo] adj round; (fig) emphatic. **rotundidad** sf roundness.

roturar [rotu'rar] v (tierra) break up. **rotura** sf breaking.

rozar [ro'θar] v graze; scrape. **rozarse** v be tongue-tied; trip over one's feet. **rozamiento** sm rubbing, friction.

rubí [ru'βi] sm, pl **rubíes** ruby.

rubio ['ruβjo] sm, adj blond. **rubia** sf blonde.

rubor [ru'βor] sm blush. **ruborizarse** v blush. **ruboroso** adj blushing.

rúbrica ['ruβrika] sf rubric; heading; flourish after a signature. **rubricar** v sign with a flourish.

rudeza [ru'ðeθa] sf roughness, rudeness. **rudo** adj rough; coarse; crude.

rudimento [ruði'mento] sm rudiment.

rueca [ru'eka] sf distaff.

rueda [ru'eða] sf wheel. **rueda de recambio** spare wheel.

ruedo [ru'eðo] sm edge; hem; round mat.

ruego [ru'ego] sm request; supplication.

rugir [ru'xir] v roar; bellow; howl. **rugido** sm roar; bellow; howl.

rugoso [ru'goso] adj wrinkled.

ruibarbo [rui'βarβo] sm rhubarb.

ruido [ru'iðo] sm noise; rumour. **meter ruido** make a noise. **ruidoso** adj noisy.

ruin [ru'in] adj mean; foul; puny. **ruindad** sf meanness; villainy.

ruina [ru'ina] sf ruin; ruins pl. **ruinoso** adj ruinous.

ruiseñor [ruise'ɲor] sm nightingale.

rumbo ['rumbo] sm course; direction; (fam) pomp. **hacer rumbo** set a course. **rumboso** adj splendid; lavish.

rumiar [ru'mjar] v ruminate; chew; grumble. **rumiante** sm ruminant.

rumor [ru'mor] sm rumour; noise; murmur. **rumorear** v rumour. **rumoroso** adj murmuring.

ruptura [rup'tura] *sf* rupture; break.
rural [ru'ral] *adj* rural.
Rusia ['rusja] *sf* Russia. **ruso, -a** *sm, sf* Russian.
rústico ['rustiko] *adj* rustic.
ruta ['ruta] *sf* route; road.
rutina [ru'tina] *sf* routine. **rutinario** *adj* routine; unimaginative.

S

sábado ['saβaðo] *sm* Saturday.
sabana [sa'βana] *sf* savannah.
sábana ['saβana] *sf* sheet.
sabanilla [saβa'niʎa] *sf* small cloth, napkin.
sabañón [saβa'ɲon] *sm* chilblain.
*saber [sa'βer] *v* know; know how to; be aware of. **a saber** namely. **sabedor** *adj* well-informed. **sabidillo, -a** *sm, sf (fam)* know-all. **sabido** *adj* known; learned. **sabiduría** *sf* knowledge; wisdom. **sabio** *adj* wise.
sabor [sa'βor] *sm* taste; flavour. **saborear** *v* taste; savour. **saborearse** *v* smack one's lips. **saboroso** *adj* tasty; savoury.
sabotear [saβote'ar] *v* sabotage. **saboteador, -a** *sm, sf* saboteur. **sabotaje** *sm* sabotage.
sabroso [sa'βroso] *adj* delicious; tasty; pleasant; racy.
sabueso [sa'βweso] *sm* bloodhound.
sacabocados [sakaβo'kaðos] *sm invar (tecn)* punch.
sacacorchos [saka'kortʃos] *sm invar* corkscrew.
sacamanchas [saka'mantʃas] *sm invar* stain-remover.
sacar [sa'kar] *v* get out; put out; draw; publish; take out; buy tickets; *(tenis)* serve. **saca** *sf* extraction; exportation.
sacarina [saka'rina] *sf* saccharine.
sacerdote [saker'ðote] *sm* priest. **sacerdocio** *sm* priesthood. **sacerdotal** *adj* priestly. **sacerdotisa** *sf* priestess.
saciar [sa'θjar] *v* satiate. **saciedad** *sf* satiety.
saco ['sako] *sm* sack; bag; plunder. **entrar a saco** plunder.
sacramento [sakra'mento] *sm* sacrament. **sacramental** *adj* sacramental.

sacrificar [sakrifi'kar] *v* sacrifice. **sacrificadero** *sm* slaughterhouse. **sacrificio** *sm* sacrifice; slaughter.
sacrilegio [sakri'lexjo] *sm* sacrilege. **sacrílego** *adj* sacrilegious.
sacro ['sakro] *adj* sacred. **sacrosanto** *adj* sacrosanct.
sacudir [saku'ðir] *v* shake, jolt. **sacudirse** *v* shake off; repel. **sacudida** *sf* shake, jolt.
sádico ['saðiko] *adj* sadistic. **sadismo** *sm* sadism. **sadista** *s(m+f)* sadist.
saeta [sa'eta] *sf* arrow; watch *or* clock hand. **saetada** *sf* arrow wound. **saetera** *sf* loophole. **saetero** *sm* bowman.
sagacidad [sagaθi'ðað] *sf* shrewdness. **sagaz** *adj* shrewd, wise.
sagrado [sa'graðo] *adj* sacred, holy. *sm* sanctuary.
sajón [sa'xon], **-ona** *s, adj* Saxon.
sal [sal] *sf* salt; wit; charm. **salero** *sm* salt cellar; wit; charm. **saleroso** *adj (fam)* witty; charming.
sala ['sala] *sf* hall; drawing-room; *(med)* ward; *(teatro)* house. **sala de conferencias** lecture hall. **sala de espera** waiting-room.
salacidad [salaθi'ðað] *sf* lechery.
salar [sa'lar] *v* salt. **salado** *adj* salty; witty.
salario [sa'larjo] *sm* salary, pay.
salchicha [sal'tʃitʃa] *sf* sausage. **salchichón** *sm* salami.
saldar [sal'ðar] *v* settle; liquidate; pay off. **saldo** *sm* payment; balance; bargain sale.
salida [sa'liða] *sf* departure; exit; start; outskirts *pl*; pretext; *(del sol)* rising; outcome; projection; witticism. **calle sin salida** *sf* cul-de-sac. **dar salida a** sell. **tener buenas salidas** be full of witty remarks. **saliente** *adj* projecting.
salina [sa'lina] *sm* salt mine. **salino** *adj* saline.
*salir [sa'lir] *v* leave; emerge; *(astron)* rise; happen. **salir para** leave for. **salir por alguien** vouch for someone. **salirse** *v* leak; overflow; escape.
saliva [sa'liβa] *sf* saliva. **salivar** *v* salivate.
salmo ['salmo] *sm* psalm. **salmista** *s(m+f)* psalmist. **salmodia** *sf* psalmody.
salmón [sal'mon] *sm* salmon.
salmuera [sal'mwera] *sf* brine.
salón [sa'lon] *sm* large hall; drawing-room.
salpicar [salpi'kar] *v* splash; sprinkle. **salpicadura** *sf* splash; spatter.
salpimentar [salpimen'tar] *v* season with salt and pepper.

salpullido [salpuˈʎiðo] *sm (med)* rash.

salsa [ˈsalsa] *sf* sauce. gravy.

saltamontes [saltaˈmontes] *sm invar* grasshopper.

saltar [salˈtar] *v* jump; skip; break; explode. **salto** *sm* jump; hop; chasm. **salto de agua** waterfall. **salto de altura** high jump. **salto con garrocha** pole vault. **salto mortal** somersault.

saltear [salteˈar] *v* rob; assault. **salteador** *sm* highwayman. **salteamiento** *sm* highway robbery.

salubre [saˈluβre] *adj* salubrious, healthy. **salubridad** *sf* wholesomeness. **salud** *sf* health. **¡salud!** cheers! **saludable** *adj* salutary. **saludador** *sm* quack doctor.

salvaguardar [salβagwarˈðar] *v* safeguard. **salvaguardia** *sf* safeguard.

saludar [saluˈðar] *v* salute; greet. **le saluda atentamente** yours faithfully. **saludo** *sm* greeting; salute. **saludos** *sm pl* regards *pl*, best wishes *pl*. **salutación** *sf* greeting.

salvaje [salˈβaxe] *adj* wild; uncultivated; savage. **salvajada** *sf* barbarity. **salvajería** *sf* savagery.

salvamanteles [salβamanˈteles] *sm invar* table mat.

salvar [salˈβar] *v* save. rescue; except; cross; overcome. **salvarse** *v* escape. **salvamento** *sm* salvation; salvage. **salvador** *adj* healing; saving.

salvavidas [salβaˈβiðas] *sm invar* lifebelt; life buoy; lifeboat.

salvedad [salβeˈðað] *sf* proviso; reservation; distinction.

salvia [ˈsalβja] *sf* sage.

salvo [ˈsalβo] *adv* except, saving. *adj* safe. **a salvo** safe. **poner a salvo** rescue. **salvo que** unless.

salvoconducto [salβokonˈdukto] *sm* safeconduct.

san [san] *adj* saint; holy. *V* **santo**.

sanar [saˈnar] *v* heal; cure; get better. **sanable** *adj* curable. **sanatorio** *sm* sanatorium.

sanción [sanˈθjon] *sf* sanction. **sancionar** *v* sanction.

sandalia [sanˈdalja] *sf* sandal.

sandía [sanˈdia] *sf* watermelon.

sanear [saneˈar] *v* guarantee; drain; repair. **saneado** *adj* unencumbered; nett. **saneamiento** *sm* surety; drainage.

sangrar [sanˈgrar] *v* bleed; drain off. **sangradera** *sf* lancet. **sangre** *sf* blood. **a sangre fría** in cold blood. **sangriento** *adj* bloody. **sanguinario** *adj* bloodthirsty. **sanguinolento** *adj* bloody.

sangría [sanˈgria] *sf* bleeding; drink made of fruit and red wine.

sanguijuela [sangiˈxwela] *sf* leech.

sanidad [saniˈðað] *sf* health; sanitation. **sanitario** *adj* sanitary. **sano** *adj* healthy; wholesome; sound; good.

santiamén [santjaˈmen] *sm* instant. **en un santiamén** in a jiffy.

santificar [santifiˈkar] *v* sanctify, consecrate. **santificación** *sf* sanctification.

santiguar [santiˈgwar] *v* bless. **santiguarse** *v* cross oneself.

santo [ˈsanto], **-a** *sm, sf* saint. *adj* sacred; saintly; holy. **santo y bueno** all well and good.

santuario [sanˈtwarjo] *sm* sanctuary, shrine.

saña [ˈsaɲa] *sf* rage; cruelty. **sañoso** *adj* furious; cruel.

sapo [ˈsapo] *sm* toad.

saquear [sakeˈar] *v* plunder. **saqueo** *sm* plunder. **saqueador, -a** *sm, sf* looter.

sarampión [saramˈpjon] *sm* measles.

sarcasmo [sarˈkasmo] *sm* sarcasm. **sarcástico** *adj* sarcastic.

sarcófago [sarˈkofago] *sm* sarcophagus.

sardina [sarˈðina] *sf* sardine.

sardónico [sarˈðoniko] *adj* sardonic.

sargento [sarˈxento] *sm* sergeant.

sarna [ˈsarna] *sf* scabies; itch. **sarnoso** *adj* mangy.

sartén [sarˈten] *sf* frying pan.

sastre [ˈsastre] *sm* tailor. **sastrería** *sf* tailoring; tailor's shop.

satélite [saˈtelite] *sm* satellite.

sátira [ˈsatira] *sf* satire. **satírico** *adj* satirical. **satirizar** *v* satirize.

*satisfacer [satisfaˈθer] *v* satisfy; please. **satisfacerse** *v* satisfy oneself; take revenge. **satisfacción** *sf* satisfaction. **satisfactorio** *adj* satisfactory. **satisfecho** *adj* satisfied.

saturar [satuˈrar] *v* saturate. **saturación** *sf* saturation.

sauce [ˈsauθe] *sm* willow.

saúco [saˈuko] *sm (bot)* elder.

savia [ˈsaβja] *sf* sap.

saxófono [sakˈsofono] *sm* saxophone.

saya [ˈsaja] *sf* skirt, petticoat. **sayo** *sm* smock.

sazonar [saθoˈnar] *v (culin)* season; ripen.

sazón *sf* season; (*culin*) flavour; mellowness. **a la sazón** at the time. **sazonado** *adj* tasty; well seasoned.

se [se] *pron* himself; herself; yourself; oneself; itself; themselves; yourselves; one another; each other. **se dice** they say. **se habla inglés** English is spoken.

sebo ['seβo] *sm* grease. **seboso** *adj* greasy.

secar [se'kar] *v* dry. **secarse** *v* dry oneself; dry up. **seca** *sf* drought; sandbank. **secador** *sm* hair-dryer. **secadora** *sf* clothes-dryer. **secano** *sm* dry land. **secante** *sm* blotting paper. **seco** *adj* dry; lean; hoarse. **en seco** high and dry.

sección [sek'θjon] *sf* section.

secretario [sekre'tarjo], **-a** *sm, sf* secretary. **secretaría** *sf* secretariat.

secreto [se'kreto] *adj* secret; private; hidden. *sm* secrecy, secret knowledge. **secreto a voces** open secret. **secreteo** *sm* private conversation.

secta ['sekta] *sf* sect. **sectario, -a** *sm, sf* sectarian.

secuaz [se'kwaθ] *sm* follower, supporter.

secuestrar [sekwes'trar] *v* kidnap; hijack. **secuestrador, -a** *sm, sf* kidnapper; hijacker. **secuestro** *sm* kidnap; hijack.

secular [seku'lar] *adj* secular. **secularizar** *v* secularize.

secundar [sekun'dar] *v* second, support.

sed [seð] *sf* thirst. **tener sed** be thirsty. **sediento** *adj* thirsty.

seda ['seða] *sf* silk. **sedoso** *adj* silky.

sedante [se'ðante] *sm* sedative. *adj* calming.

sede ['seðe] *sf* (*rel*) see; (*de gobierno*) seat. **Santa Sede** Holy See.

sedentario [seðen'tarjo] *adj* sedentary.

sedería [seðe'ria] *sf* silk trade; drapery.

sedición [seði'θjon] *sf* sedition. **sedicioso** *adj* seditious.

sedimento [seði'mento] *sm* sediment. **sedimentar** *v* deposit.

*seducir [seðu'θir] *v* seduce; attract. **seducción** *sf* seduction. **seductivo** *adj* seductive. **seductor, -a** *sm, sf* seducer.

*segar [se'gar] *v* reap; mow. **segadora** *sf* mower; reaper.

seglar [se'glar] *sm* layman. *adj* secular.

segmento [seg'mento] *sm* segment.

segregar [segre'gar] *v* segregate. **segregación** *sf* segregation.

*seguir [se'gir] *v* follow; pursue; continue. **seguida** *sf* continuation. **en seguida** at once. **seguido** *adj* successive; straight.

cuatro días seguidos four days running. **seguimiento** *sm* pursuit; following.

según [se'gun] *prep* according to. *adv* it all depends. *conj* as.

segundo [se'gundo] *adj, sm* second.

segundón [segun'don] *sm* second son.

seguro [se'guro] *adj* sure; safe. *sm* safety catch; insurance. **seguridad** *sf* safety; certainty.

seis ['seis] *sm, adj* six.

selección [selek'θjon] *sf* selection. **seleccionar** *v* select. **selectivo** *adj* selective. **selecto** *adj* select.

selva ['selβa] *sf* forest; jungle. **selvoso** *adj* wooded, forested.

sello ['seʎo] *sm* stamp; seal. **selladura** *sf* sealing. **sellar** *v* stamp; seal.

semáforo [se'maforo] *sm* semaphore; traffic lights *pl*.

semana [se'mana] *sf* week. **semanal** *adj* weekly. **semanario** *sm* weekly publication.

semblante [sem'blante] *sm* face; appearance.

*sembrar [sem'brar] *v* sow; scatter. **sembradera** *sf* seed-drill. **sembrador, -a** *sm, sf* sower.

semejar [seme'xar] *v* resemble. **semejante** *adj* similar. **semejanza** *sf* similarity.

semen ['semen] *sm* semen. **semental** *sm* sire. **sementera** *sf* sowing; seed-time.

semestre [se'mestre] *sm* semester. **semestral** *adj* half-yearly.

semicírculo [semi'θirkulo] *sm* semicircle. **semicircular** *adj* semicircular.

semilla [se'miʎa] *sf* seed. **semillero** *sm* seedbed.

seminario [semi'narjo] *sm* seminary; seminar; seedbed.

senado [se'naðo] *sm* senate. **senador** *sm* senator.

sencillo [sen'θiʎo] *adj* simple; easy. **sencillez** *sf* simplicity.

senda ['senda] *sf* path. **sendero** *sm* path.

sendos ['sendos] *adj pl* each.

senectud [senek'tuð] *sf* old age.

senil [se'nil] *adj* senile. **senilidad** *sf* senility.

seno ['seno] *sm* bosom, breast; haven, refuge.

sensación [sensa'θjon] *sf* sensation. **sensacional** *adj* sensational.

sensatez [sensa'teθ] *sf* good sense. **sensato** *adj* sensible.

sensibilidad [sensiβili'ðað] *sf* sensibility; sensitivity. **sensible** *adj* sensitive; sensible; considerable.

sensiblería [sensiβle'ria] *sf* sentimentality. **sensiblero** *adj* sentimental.

sensitivo [sensi'tiβo] *adj* relating to the senses; sensitive.

sensual [sen'swal] *adj* sensual. **sensualidad** *sf* sensuality.

*****sentar** [sen'tar] *v* seat; place; locate; establish; press; suit; fit. **sentarse** *v* sit down; settle. **sentada** *sf* sit-in. **sentado** *adj* seated; established.

sentencia [sen'tenθja] *sf* (*jur*) sentence. **sentenciar** *v* (*jur*) sentence. **sentencioso** *adj* sententious.

sentido [sen'tiðo] *sm* sense; meaning; direction; feeling. **sin sentido** meaningless. **tener sentido** make sense. *adj* heartfelt; moving; sincere.

sentimiento [senti'mjento] *sm* feeling; emotion; sentiment; grief. **sentimental** *adj* sentimental.

*****sentir** [sen'tir] *v* feel; hear; regret. **lo siento mucho** I am very sorry. **sentirse** *v* feel; suffer from. **sentirse enfermo** feel ill. **sentirse obligado a** feel obliged to.

seña ['sena] *sf* mark; sign; signal; password. **señas** *sf pl* address *sing*.

señal [se'nal] *sf* signal; sign; mark. **en señal de** in proof of. **señaladamente** *adv* signally. **señalado** *adj* famous. **señalar** *v* mark; signal; point out; denote. **señalarse** *v* distinguish oneself.

señor [se'nor] *sm* mister; gentleman; lord; master. **El Señor** the Lord. **señora** *sf* lady; wife; mistress; madam. **la señora de García** Mrs García. **señorear** *v* domineer. **señorearse** *v* take possession. **señoría** *sf* lordship. **señorío** *sm* dominion; stateliness. **señorita** *sf* miss; young lady.

separar [sepa'rar] *v* separate; divide; discharge. **separable** *adj* separable. **separación** *sf* separation; dismissal. **separado** *adj* separate. **por separado** separately.

septentrional [septentrjo'nal] *adj* northern.

séptico ['septiko] *adj* septic.

septiembre [sep'tjembre] *sm* September.

séptimo ['septimo] *adj* seventh.

septuagésimo [septwa'xesimo] *adj* seventieth.

sepulcro [se'pulkro] *sm* tomb; grave.

sepultar [sepul'tar] *v* bury. **sepultura** *sf* grave; burial. **sepulturero** *sm* gravedigger.

sequedad [seke'ðað] *sf* dryness; curtness. **sequía** *sf* drought.

séquito ['sekito] *sm* entourage; followers *pl*.

*****ser** [ser] *v* be; exist; occur. **a no ser por** but for. **sea lo que sea** come what may. **si no es que** unless.

seráfico [se'rafiko] *adj* seraphic. **serafín** *sm* seraph.

serenar [sere'nar] *v* calm; settle. **sereno** *adj* serene; calm. **serenidad** *sf* serenity; calmness.

serenata [sere'nata] *sf* serenade.

serie ['serje] *sf* series. **fabricación en serie** *sf* mass production.

serio ['serjo] *adj* serious. **tomar en serio** take seriously. **seriedad** *sf* seriousness; sincerity.

sermón [ser'mon] *sm* sermon.

serpiente [ser'pjente] *sf* serpent. **serpiente de cascabel** rattlesnake. **serpentear** *v* wriggle. **serpentino** *adj* serpentine.

serrano [se'rrano] *adj* of the mountains. *sm* highlander. **serranía** *sf* mountainous country.

*****serrar** [se'rrar] *v* saw. **serrado** *adj* serrated. **serrín** *sm* sawdust.

servicio [ser'βiθjo] *sm* service; attendance. **estar de servicio** be on duty. **servicios** *sm pl* toilet *sing*. **servible** *adj* serviceable. **servidor, -a** *sm, sf* servant. **su seguro servidor** yours faithfully. **servidumbre** *sf* household staff; servitude. **servil** *adj* servile. **servilismo** *sm* servility.

servilleta [serβi'ʎeta] *sf* napkin.

*****servir** [ser'βir] *v* serve. **para servir a usted** at your service. **servir de** act as. **servirse** *v* help oneself. **servirse de** make use of.

sesenta [se'senta] *sm, adj* sixty.

sesgar [ses'gar] *v* slant; twist. **sesgo** *sm* slant; twist.

sesión [se'sjon] *sf* session; conference.

seso ['seso] *sm* brain; sense; understanding; wisdom. **perder el seso** go mad.

seta ['seta] *sf* mushroom.

setenta [se'tenta] *sm, adj* seventy.

setiembre *V* **septiembre**.

seto ['seto] *sm* fence.

seudónimo [seu'ðonimo] *sm* pseudonym. **seudo** *adj* (*fam*) pseudo.

severo [se'βero] *adj* severe; harsh. **severidad** *sf* severity.

sexagésimo [seksa'xesimo] *adj* sixtieth. **sexagenario, -a** *sm, sf* sexagenarian.

sexo ['sekso] *sm* sex. **sexual** *adj* sexual. **sexualidad** *sf* sexuality.

sexto ['seksto] *adj* sixth. **sexteto** *sm* sextet.

si [si] *conj* if; whether. **si bien** although.

sí¹ [si] *adv* yes; indeed. **eso sí que es yes,** that's it. *sm* consent. **dar el sí** agree.

sí² *pron* himself; herself; itself; yourself; oneself; themselves; yourselves. **de por sí** in itself. **entre sí** among themselves. **metido en sí** pensive.

sibilante [siβi'lante] *adj* sibilant.

siderurgia [siðe'rurxja] *sf* iron and steel industry.

sidra ['siðra] *sf* cider.

siega ['sjega] *sf* reaping, harvesting.

siembra ['sjembra] *sf* sowing.

siempre ['sjempre] *adv* always. **siempre jamás** for ever and ever. **siempre que** whenever; provided that.

sien [sjen] *sf* (*anat*) temple.

sierra ['sjerra] *sf* saw; mountain range.

siervo ['sjerβo] *sm* slave; servant.

siesta ['sjesta] *sf* siesta.

siete ['sjete] *adj, sm* seven.

sífilis ['sifilis] *sm* syphilis. **sifilítico, -a** *s, adj* syphilitic.

sifón [si'fon] *sm* soda water; syphon.

sigilar [sixi'lar] *v* conceal. **sigilo** *sm* secrecy. **sigiloso** *adj* secretive.

siglo ['siglo] *sm* century. **siglo de oro** golden age.

signar [sig'nar] *v* sign, seal. **signarse** *v* cross oneself. **signatura** *sf* signature.

significar [signifi'kar] *v* signify; notify. **significado** *sm* meaning; significance. **significativo** *adj* significant.

signo ['signo] *sm* sign; symbol.

siguiente [si'gjente] *adj* following, next.

sílaba ['silaβa] *sf* syllable.

silbar [sil'βar] *v* whistle; hiss. **silbido** *sm* whistle, hiss.

silencio [si'lenθjo] *sm* silence. **silenciador** *sm* (*de arma*) silencer. **silenciar** *v* silence. **silencioso** *adj* silent.

silueta [si'lweta] *sf* silhouette, outline.

silvestre [sil'βestre] *adj* wild. **silvicultura** *sf* forestry.

silla ['siʎa] *sf* chair; seat; saddle. **silla de tijera** deck chair. **sillón** *sm* armchair.

sima ['sima] *sf* abyss.

símbolo ['simbolo] *sm* symbol. **simbólico** *adj* symbolic. **simbolismo** *sm* symbolism. **simbolizar** *v* symbolize.

simetría [sime'tria] *sf* symmetry. **simétrico** *adj* symmetrical.

simiente [si'mjente] *sf* seed.

símil ['simil] *adj* similar. *sm* comparison; simile. **similar** *adj* similar. **similitud** *sf* similarity.

simpatía [simpa'tia] *sf* affection; sympathy; friendliness; charm. **simpático** *adj* charming; friendly; nice. **simpatizar** *v* sympathize; get on.

simple ['simple] *adj* simple; pure; naïve. **simplemente** *adv* merely. **simpleza** *sf* simplicity; simpleness; silly thing. **simplicidad** *sf* simplicity. **simplificar** *v* simplify. **simplón, -ona** *sm, sf* simpleton.

simulacro [simu'lakro] *sm* image; semblance.

simular [simu'lar] *v* simulate. **simulación** *sf* pretence. **simulado** *adj* sham.

simultáneo [simul'taneo] *adj* simultaneous. **simultaneidad** *sf* simultaneousness.

sin [sin] *prep* without; but for; apart from. **sin embargo** nevertheless. **sin falta** without fail. **sin que** without.

sinagoga [sina'goga] *sf* synagogue.

sincero [sin'θero] *adj* sincere. **sinceridad** *sf* sincerity.

síncopa ['sinkopa] *sf* syncopation. **sincopar** *v* syncopate.

sindicato [sindi'kato] *sm* trade union; syndicate. **sindical** *adj* trade-union. **sindicalismo** *sm* trade-unionism. **síndico** *sm* trustee.

sinfín [sin'fin] *sm* endless number.

sinfonía [sinfo'nia] *sf* symphony. **sinfónico** *adj* symphonic.

singular [singu'lar] *adj* singular; exceptional; unique; excellent. **singularidad** *sf* singularity; excellence. **singularizar** *v* single out. **singularizarse** *v* distinguish oneself.

siniestro [si'njestro] *adj* (*dirección*) left; sinister. *sm* catastrophe. **siniestrado, -a** *sm, sf* victim of an accident.

sinnúmero [sin'numero] *sm* endless number.

sino¹ ['sino] *conj* but, except. **no sólo ... sino ...** not only ... but also ... .

sino² *sm* fate.

sinónimo [si'nonimo] *sm* synonym. *adj* synonymous.

sinopsis [si'nopsis] *sf* synopsis (*pl* -ses).

sinrazón [sinra'θon] *sf* injustice.

sinsabor [sinsa'βor] *sm* trouble.

sintaxis [sin'taksis] *sf* syntax. **sintáctico** *adj* syntactic.

síntesis ['sintesis] *sf* synthesis (*pl* -ses). **sintético** *adj* synthetic.

síntoma ['sintoma] *sm* symptom. **sintomático** *adj* symptomatic.

sintonizar [sintoni'θar] *v* (*radio*) tune in. **sintonía** *sf* signature tune.

sinvergüenza [sinβer'gwenθa] *adj* shameless. *s*(*m*+*f*) cad.

siquiera [si'kjera] *adv* at least; even; just. **ni siquiera** not at all. *conj* even if; even though. **siquiera ... siquiera ...** whether ... or whether ...

sirena [si'rena] *sf* (*ninfa*) siren, mermaid; (*tecn*) siren, fog-horn.

sirviente [sir'βjente] *sm* servant.

sisar [si'sar] *v* pilfer; cheat. **sisa** *sf* theft, pilfering.

sísmico ['sismiko] *adj* seismic. **sismógrafo** *sm* seismograph.

sistema [sis'tema] *sm* system, method. **sistemático** *adj* systematic.

sitiar [si'tjar] *sm* besiege; surround.

sitio ['sitjo] *sm* place; room, space; siege. **no hay sitio** there is no room.

situar [si'twar] *v* situate; put. **situación** *sf* situation.

so [so] *prep* under. **so pena de** under penalty of.

sobaco [so'βako] *sm* armpit.

sobado [so'βaðo] *adj* kneaded; (*fam*) shabby, well-worn. **sobar** *v* knead; thrash; crumple; fondle.

soberanía [soβera'nia] *sf* sovereignty. **soberano, -a** *s, adj* sovereign.

soberbia [so'βerβja] *sf* pride; magnificence, pomp. **soberbio** *adj* proud; superb.

sobornar [soβor'nar] *v* bribe. **soborno** *sm* bribe; bribery.

sobrar [so'βrar] *sf* surplus. **de sobra** in excess. **sobras** *sf pl* remains *pl*. **sobradamente** *adv* excessively. **sobrado** *adj* abundant; superfluous. **sobrancero** *adj* unemployed. **sobrante** *adj* spare.

sobre¹ ['soβre] *prep* on; upon; over; above; about. **sobre las diez** about ten o'clock. **sobre todo** above all.

sobre² *sm* envelope.

sobrecama [soβre'kama] *sm* bedspread.

sobrecargar [soβrekar'gar] *v* overload. **sobrecarga** *sf* extra burden. **sobrecargo** *sm* purser.

sobrecejo [soβre'θexo] *sm* frown.

sobrecoger [soβreko'xer] *v* surprise, take aback. **sobrecogerse** *v* be startled.

sobredicho [soβre'ðitʃo] *adj* aforesaid.

sobrehumano [soβreu'mano] *adj* superhuman.

sobremanera [soβrema'nera] *adv* exceedingly.

sobremesa [soβre'mesa] *sf* dessert; table cover; after-dinner chat.

sobrenatural [soβrenatu'ral] *adj* supernatural.

sobrepasar [soβrepa'sar] *v* surpass.

*****sobreponer** [soβrepo'ner] *v* superimpose. **sobreponerse a** overcome. **sobrepuesto** *adj* superimposed.

sobreprecio [soβre'preθjo] *sm* surcharge.

*****sobresalir** [soβresa'lir] *v* excel. **sobresaliente** *adj* outstanding.

sobresaltar [soβresal'tar] *v* attack; frighten. **sobresalto** *sm* sudden attack; shock. **de sobresalto** suddenly.

sobrescrito [soβre'skrito] *sm* (*en un sobre*) address.

sobretodo [soβre'toðo] *sm* overcoat.

*****sobrevenir** [soβreβe'nir] *v* happen suddenly.

sobrevivir [soβreβi'βir] *v* survive. **sobreviviente** *s*(*m*+*f*) survivor.

sobriedad [soβrie'ðað] *sf* sobriety. **sobrio** *adj* sober, moderate.

sobrino [so'βrino] *sm* nephew. **sobrina** *sf* niece.

socarrón [sokar'ron] *adj* sarcastic; sly. **socarronería** *sf* sarcasm; slyness.

socavar [soka'βar] *v* undermine. **socavón** *sm* excavation.

sociable [so'θjaβle] *adj* sociable. **sociabilidad** *sf* sociability.

social [so'θjal] *adj* social. **socializar** *v* socialize. **socialismo** *sm* socialism. **socialista** *s*(*m*+*f*) socialist.

sociedad [soθje'ðað] *sf* society. **socio, -a** *sm, sf* associate.

sociología [soθjolo'xia] *sf* sociology. **sociólogo, -a** *sm, sf* sociologist.

socorrer [sokor'rer] *v* help. **socorrido** *adj* helpful; handy. **socorro** *sm* succour; relief. **¡socorro!** help!

soda ['soða] *sf* soda-water.

soez [so'eθ] *adj* obscene; vulgar.

sofá [so'fa] *sf* sofa, settee.

sofocar [sofo'kar] *v* suffocate. **sofocación** *sf* suffocation. **sofocado** *adj* breathless. **sofoco** *sm* suffocation.

soga ['soga] *sf* rope, cord. **hacer soga** lag behind.

soja ['soxa] *sf* soya.

sojuzgar [soxuθ'gar] *v* subdue.

sol [sol] *sm* sun; sunlight. **hace sol** it's sunny. **tomar el sol** sunbathe.

solamente [sola'mente] *adv* only. **no solamente** not only.

solapa [so'lapa] *sf* flap; lapel; (*fig*) pretext. **solapado** *adj* sly. **solapar** *v* overlap; (*fig*) cover up, hide.

*****solar** [so'lar] *adj* solar. *sm* lot; plot; building site.

solaz [so'laθ] *sm* recreation; solace. **a solaz** with pleasure. **solazar** *v* distract; amuse; solace.

soldado [sol'ðaðo] *sm* soldier.

*****soldar** [sol'ðar] *v* solder; weld; (*huesos*) knit. **soldador** *sm* soldering iron. **soldadura** *sf* welding.

soledad [sole'ðað] *sf* loneliness, solitude.

solemne [so'lemne] *adj* solemn. **solemnidad** *sf* solemnity. **solemnizar** *v* solemnize.

*****soler** [so'ler] *v* be in the habit of; usually be *or* do. **suele comer mucho** he usually eats a lot.

solera [so'lera] *sf* prop; stone pavement; tradition; strong old wine.

solicitar [soliθi'tar] *v* request; pursue; canvass. **solicitación** *sf* solicitation; application. **solicitador, -a** *sm, sf or* **solicitante** *sm* petitioner; applicant. **solícito** *adj* solicitous. **solicitud** *sf* solicitude.

solidaridad [soliðari'ðað] *sf* solidarity. **solidar** *v* consolidate. **solidario** *adj* mutual. **solidez** *sf* solidity. **solidificar** *v* solidify. **sólido** *adj* solid.

solitario [soli'tarjo], **-a** *sm, sf* hermit, recluse. *adj* lonely; solitary; alone; single.

solo ['solo] *adj* alone; single; unique; only; (*música*) solo. *sm* (*música*) solo.

sólo ['solo] *adv* only, merely.

*****soltar** [sol'tar] *v* release; free; loosen; break; shed. **soltarse** *v* break loose; become unscrewed; lose one's inhibitions.

soltero [sol'tero] *sm* bachelor. *adj* single. **soltera** *sf* spinster. **soltería** *sf* celibacy. **solterona** *sf* old maid.

soltura [sol'tura] *sf* looseness; agility; fluency. **con soltura** fluently.

soluble [so'luβle] *adj* soluble. **solubilidad** *sf* solubility. **solución** *sf* solution. **solucionar** *v* solve.

solvencia [sol'βenθja] *sf* solvency; settlement. **solvente** *adj* solvent.

sollo ['soʎo] *sm* sturgeon.

sollozar [soʎo'θar] *v* sob. **sollozo** *sm* sob.

sombra ['sombra] *sf* shadow; shade. **dar sombra a** shade.

sombrero [som'brero] *sm* hat.

sombrilla [som'briʎa] *sf* parasol.

sombrío [som'brio] *sm* shady spot. *adj* shady; gloomy. **sombroso** *adj* shady.

somero [so'mero] *adj* superficial.

someter [some'ter] *v* submit; subdue. **sometimiento** *sm* submission.

somnífero [som'nifero] *sm* sleeping pill.

somnolencia [somno'lenθja] *sf* sleepiness. **somnámbulo, -a** *sm, sf* sleepwalker. **somnolente** *adj* sleepy.

son [son] *sm* sound; rumour; manner. **por este son** by this means.

*****sonar** [so'nar] *v* sound; ring; chime. **sonarse** *v* blow one's nose. **sonante** *adj* sounding; ringing.

sondear [sonde'ar] *v* fathom; sound out.

soneto [so'neto] *sm* sonnet.

sonido [so'niðo] *sm* sound.

sonoro [so'noro] *adj* sonorous; resonant. **sonoridad** *sf* sonority.

*****sonreír** [sonre'ir] *v* smile. **sonriente** *adj* smiling. **sonrisa** *sf* smile.

sonrojar [sonro'xar] *v* blush; flush. **sonrojo** *sm* blush.

*****soñar** [so'nar] *v* dream. **soñador, -a** *sm, sf* dreamer. **soñera** *sf* drowsiness. **soñoliento** *adj* drowsy.

sopa ['sopa] *sf* soup. **como una sopa** soaked to the skin. **sopero** *sm* soup plate.

sopapo [so'papo] *sm* (*fam*) blow, punch. **sopapear** *v* chuck under the chin; punch.

soplar [so'plar] *v* blow; blow out; blow away; prompt. **sopladura** *sf* blowing. **soplillo** *sm* fan; blower. **soplo** *sm* blowing; puff of wind. **soplón, -ona** *sm, sf* informer.

sopor [so'por] *sm* drowsiness.

soportar [sopor'tar] *v* support; tolerate; endure. **soporte** *sm* support; stand.

sor [sor] *sf* (*rel*) sister.

sorber [sor'βer] *v* sip; suck; soak up. **sorbete** *sm* sherbet; water ice. **sorbetón**

sm large draught. **sorbo** *sm* sip; swallow; gulp.

sordera [sor'ðera] *sf* deafness. **sordo** *adj* deaf; muffled.

sórdido ['sorðiðo] *adj* squalid. **sordidez** *sf* squalor.

sordomudo [sorðo'muðo]. **-a** *sm, sf* deaf-mute. *adj* deaf and dumb.

sorprender [sorpren'der] *v* surprise. **sorprendente** *adj* surprising. **sorpresa** *sf* surprise.

sortear [sorte'ar] *v* cast lots for; avoid, get round. **sorteable** *adj* avoidable. **sorteo** *sm* raffle; casting of lots; dodging.

sortija [sor'tixa] *sf* ring; (*de pelo*) curl.

sortilegio [sorti'lexjo] *sm* sorcery; charm. **sortilega** *sf* sorceress. **sortilego** *sm* sorcerer.

*****sosegar** [sose'gar] *v* calm, quieten. **sosiego** *sm* calm, quiet.

soslayar [sosla'jar] *v* place obliquely; dodge; avoid. **soslayo** *adj* oblique.

soso ['soso] *adj* tasteless; dull.

sospechar [sospe'tʃar] *v* suspect. **sospecha** *sf* suspicion. **sospechoso** *adj* suspicious, suspect.

*****sostener** [soste'ner] *v* support; sustain. **sostén** *sm* support; brassière. **sostenedor, -a** *sm, sf* supporter. **sostenido** *adj* sustained; constant.

sota ['sota] *sf* (*deporte*) jack; (*fam*) hussy.

sotana [so'tana] *sf* cassock.

sótano ['sotano] *sm* basement, cellar.

soto ['soto] *sm* thicket, copse.

soviet [so'βjet] *sm* Soviet. **soviético** *adj* Soviet.

spaghettis [spa'getis] *sm pl* spaghetti *sing*.

su [su] *adj* his; her; its; your; their; one's.

suave ['swaβe] *adj* smooth; soft; mild. **suavidad** *sf* smoothness; softness. **suavizar** *v* soften; smooth; strop.

*****subarrendar** [suβarren'dar] *v* sublet, sublease. **subarriendo** *sm* subletting.

subasta [su'βasta] *sf* auction. **subastar** *v* auction.

subcampeón [subkam'pjon]. **-ona** *sm, sf* runner-up.

subconsciencia [subkons'θjenθja] *sf* subconscious. **subconsciente** *adj* subconscious.

subdesarrollado [suβðesarro'ʎaðo] *adj* underdeveloped. **subdesarrollo** *sm* underdevelopment.

súbdito ['suβðito] *sm* subject, citizen.

subdividir [suβðiβi'ðir] *v* subdivide. **subdivisión** *sf* subdivision.

subir [su'βir] *v* climb; go up; rise; lift; promote. **subir al coche** get into the car. **subirse** *v* rise; become conceited. **subida** *sf* ascent. **subido** *adj* (*color*) bright.

súbito ['suβito] *adj* sudden. *adv* suddenly.

subjuntivo [subxun'tiβo] *sm* (*gram*) subjunctive.

sublevar [suβle'βar] *v* incite to rebellion. **sublevarse** *v* rebel. **sublevación** *sf* rebellion.

sublime [su'βlime] *adj* sublime, lofty. **sublimación** *sf* sublimation. **sublimidad** *sf* sublimity.

submarino [suβma'rino] *adj* underwater. *sm* submarine.

subordinado [suβorði'naðo] *adj* subordinate. **subordinar** *v* subordinate.

subproducto [suβpro'ðukto] *sm* by-product.

subrayar [suβra'jar] *v* underline, underscore; emphasize. **subrayado** *sm* underlining; emphasis.

subsanar [suβsa'nar] *v* excuse; redeem.

subscribir [suβskri'βir] *v* subscribe; sign. **subscripción** *sf* subscription.

*****subseguir** [suβse'gir] *v* follow. **subsiguiente** *adj* subsequent.

subsidiario [suβsi'ðjarjo] *adj* subsidiary.

subsidio [suβ'siðjo] *sm* subsidy, grant, allowance.

subsistir [suβsis'tir] *v* subsist; exist. **subsistencia** *sf* permanence; subsistence. **subsistente** *adj* subsisting.

substancia [suβ'staθja] *sf* substance. **en substancia** briefly. **substancial** *adj* substantial. **substanciar** *v* summarize; substantiate. **substancioso** *adj* substantial.

*****substituir** [suβstitu'ir] *v* substitute. **substitución** *sf* substitution. **substitutivo** *adj* substitute.

*****substraer** [suβstra'er] *v* subtract; remove; steal. **substraerse** *v* evade; withdraw. **substracción** *sf* subtraction; stealing.

subterfugio [suβter'fuxjo] *sm* subterfuge.

subterráneo [suβter'raneo] *adj* subterranean.

subtítulo [suβ'titulo] *sm* subtitle.

suburbio [suβ'urβjo] *sm* outskirts *pl*; slum. **suburbano** *adj* suburban.

subvención [suββen'θjon] *sf* subsidy. **subvencionar** *v* subsidize.

subvertir [suββer'tir] v subvert. **subversión** sf subversion. **subversivo** adj subversive.

subyugar [suβju'gar] v subjugate. **subyugación** sf subjugation.

suceder [suθe'ðer] v succeed; follow; happen. **sucedido** sm event. **sucediente** adj following. **sucesión** sf succession; offspring. **sucesivamente** adv successively. **sucesivo** adj successive. **en lo sucesivo** hereafter. **suceso** sm event; outcome.

suciedad [suθje'ðað] sf dirt, dirtiness. **sucio** adj dirty; vile, mean.

sucinto [su'θinto] adj succinct, brief.

sucumbir [sukum'bir] v succumb.

sucursal [sukur'sal] sm branch.

sud [suð] adj, sm south.

sudamericano [suðameri'kano], **-a** s, adj South American.

sudar [su'ðar] v sweat. **sudar tinta** (fam) sweat blood. **sudor** sm sweat. **sudoroso** adj sweaty.

sudeste [su'ðeste] adj, sm south-east.

sudoeste [suðo'este] sm, adj south-west.

Suecia ['sweθja] sf Sweden.

sueco ['sweko], **-a** sm, sf Swede. sm (idioma) Swedish. adj Swedish.

suegro ['swegro] sm father-in-law.

suela ['swela] sf (de zapato) sole. **suelas** sf pl sandals pl.

sueldo ['swelðo] sm salary; wage; pay. **a sueldo** paid.

suelo ['swelo] sm ground; soil; floor. **echar al suelo** demolish.

suelto ['swelto] adj free; loose; separate; agile.

sueño ['sweɲo] sm dream; sleep. **tener sueño** be sleepy.

suero ['swero] sm serum; whey.

suerte ['swerte] sf luck; fate; chance; kind; manner; quality. **¡buena suerte!** good luck! **de otra suerte** otherwise. **de tal suerte que** in such a way that.

suéter ['sweter] sm sweater.

suficiencia [sufi'θjenθja] sf sufficiency; ability; self-importance. **suficiente** adj sufficient; capable.

sufragar [sufra'gar] v help; finance. **sufragar por** vote for. **sufragio** sm suffrage.

sufrir [suf'rir] v suffer; endure. **sufrido** adj long-suffering. **sufrimiento** sm suffering; patience.

*sugerir [suxe'rir] v suggest, hint. **sugerencia** sf suggestion. **sugerente** adj suggestive. **sugestión** sf suggestion. **sugestionable** adj suggestible. **sugestionar** v influence. **sugestivo** adj suggestive; stimulating.

suicidarse [swiθi'ðarse] v commit suicide. **suicida** s(m + f) (persona) suicide. **suicidio** sm suicide.

Suiza ['swiθa] sf Switzerland. **swizo, -a** s, adj Swiss.

sujetar [suxe'tar] v secure; hold; fasten; seize; tie; restrain; subordinate. **sujetarse** v hang on; hold up; subject oneself to; abide by. **sujerción** sf subjection; control. **sujetapapeles** sm invar paperclip. **sujeto** sm subject; individual.

sumar [su'mar] v add, add up. **sumarse** v join in. **suma** sf sum; summary; essence. **en suma** in short. **sumadora** sf adding machine. **sumamente** adv extremely. **sumaria** sf (jur) indictment. **sumario** sm summary.

sumergir [sumer'xir] v submerge, plunge. **sumersión** sf submersion.

suministrar [suminis'trar] v supply, provide. **suministro** sm supply. **suministros** sm pl supplies pl, provisions pl.

sumir [su'mir] v submerge; sink.

sumisión [sumi'sjon] sf submission. **sumiso** adj submissive.

sumo ['sumo] adj greatest; supreme. **tribunal supremo** sm supreme court.

suntuoso [sun'twoso] adj sumptuous. **suntuosidad** sf sumptuousness.

supeditar [supeði'tar] v subdue; subordinate. **supeditación** sf subjection.

superar [supe'rar] v surpass; overcome. **superable** adj surmountable. **superación** sf overcoming.

superávit [supe'raβit] sm surplus.

superchería [supertʃe'ria] sf fraud; swindle.

superficial [superfi'θjal] adj superficial. **superficie** sf surface; area.

superfluo [super'fluo] adj superfluous. **superfluidad** sf superfluity.

superior [supe'rjor] adj better; superior. sm superior.

superlativo [superla'tiβo] adj superlative.

supermercado [supermer'kaðo] sm supermarket.

supersecreto [superse'kreto] adj top secret.

superstición [supersti'θjon] *sf* superstition. **supersticioso** *adj* superstitious.
supervivencia [superβi'βenθja] *sf* survival. **superviviente** *s(m+f)* survivor.
supino [su'pino] *adj* supine.
suplantar [suplan'tar] *v* supplant; forge.
suplemento [suple'mento] *sm* supplement. **suplementario** *adj* supplementary; extra. **horas suplementarias** *sf pl* overtime *sing*.
suplente [su'plente] *s, adj* substitute.
súplica ['suplika] *sf* supplication; petition. **suplicación** *sf* supplication; wafer biscuit. **suplicante** *s(m+f)* supplicant. **suplicar** *v* implore; beseech.
suplicio [su'pliθjo] *sm* torture.
suplir [su'plir] *v* make up for; substitute.
***suponer** [supo'ner] *v* suppose; believe; mean; guess. **suposición** *sf* supposition; slander.
supremo [su'premo] *adj* supreme. **supremacía** *sf* supremacy.
suprimir [supri'mir] *v* suppress; delete; omit; eliminate. **supresión** *sf* suppression; deletion.
supuesto [su'pwesto] *adj* supposed; so-called; hypothetical; feigned. **¡por supuesto!** of course! **supuesto que** since; if. *sm* hypothesis (*pl* -ses).
sur [sur] *adj* southern. *sm* south.
surcar [sur'kar] *v* plough; cleave.
surgir [sur'xir] *v* rise; spring forth; appear; anchor. **surgidero** *sm* anchorage.
surrealista [surreal'ista] *s(m+f)* surrealist. **surrealismo** *sm* surrealism.
surtido [sur'tiðo] *adj* assorted. **bien surtido** well stocked. *sm* stock; range; assortment. **surtidor** *sm* jet; fountain; petrol pump. **surtir** *v* supply. **surtir un pedido** fill an order.
susceptibilidad [susθeptiβili'ðað] *sf* susceptibility. **susceptible** *adj* susceptible.
suscitar [susθi'tar] *v* agitate; stir up. **suscitar interés** arouse interest.
suscribir *V* subscribir.
susodicho [suso'ðitʃo] *adj* aforementioned.
suspender [suspen'der] *v* suspend; adjourn; hang; fail; interrupt. **suspensión** *sf* suspension. **suspenso** *sm* (*examen*) failure.
suspicacia [suspi'kaθja] *sf* suspicion; misgiving. **suspicaz** *adj* suspicious.
suspirar [suspi'rar] *v* sigh. **suspirado** *adj* longed for; wished for. **suspiro** *sm* sigh.

sustancia *V* **substancia.**
sustentar [susten'tar] *v* sustain; maintain. **sustentamiento** *sm* sustenance; maintenance. **sustento** *sm* sustenance.
***sustituir** *V* **substituir.**
susto ['susto] *sm* fright. **dar susto a** frighten.
susurrar [susur'rar] *v* whisper; murmur. **susurrarse** *v* be rumoured. **susurrante** *adj* whispering. **susurro** *sm* whisper; murmur.
sutil [su'til] *adj* subtle; sharp; slender; delicate. **sutileza** *sf* subtlety; thinness; sharpness. **sutilizar** *v* thin down; polish; sharpen.
sutura [su'tura] *sf* suture.
suyo ['sujo] *adj* of his; of hers; of yours; of theirs. *pron* his; hers; yours; its; theirs. **lo suyo** one's share. **muy suyo** typical of one.

T

tabaco [ta'βako] *sm* tobacco. **tabacalero, -a** *sm, sf* tobacconist.
tábano ['taβano] *sm* horsefly.
taberna [ta'βerna] *sf* tavern; public house.
tabique [ta'βike] *sm* partition; dividing wall. **tabicar** *v* wall up.
tabla ['taβla] *sf* board, plank; tablet; slab; index; vegetable plot. **tablas** *sf pl* (*teatro*) stage *sing*. **pisar las tablas** go on the stage. **tablado** *sm* wooden platform; bedstead; gallows. **tablaje** *sm* boards *pl*. **tablajería** *sf* gambling. **tablear** *vb* saw into planks. **tablero** *sm* planking; blackboard; gambling den. **tableta** *sf* tablet. **tablilla** *sf* notice-board. **tablón** *sm* beam.
tabú [ta'βu] *sm* taboo.
tabular [tabu'lar] *adj* tabular. *v* tabulate.
taburete [taβu'rete] *sm* stool.
tacaño [ta'kaɲo] *adj* mean, stingy. **tacañería** *sf* meanness.
tácito ['taθito] *adj* tacit. **taciturnidad** *sf* taciturnity. **taciturno** *adj* taciturn.
taco ['tako] *sm* wad; plug; billiard cue; draught; oath. **soltar un taco** utter an oath.

tacón [ta'kon] *sm* heel. **taconazo** *sm* blow *or* tap with the heel.

tacto ['takto] *sm* touch; sense of touch; tact.

tachar [ta'tʃar] *v* accuse; erase. **tacha** *sf* fault; tack, small nail. **poner tacha** find fault. **tachón** *sm* (*carpintería*) stud. **tachonado** *adj* studded. **tachonar** *v* stud. **tachoso** *adj* defective. **tachuela** *sf* small tack.

tahona [ta'ona] *sf* bakery.

taimado [tai'maðo] *adj* sly, crafty; sullen.

tajar [ta'xar] *v* cut; hew; cleave. **taja** *sf* incision. **tajada** *sf* slice. **sacar tajada** profit. **tajadero** *sm* chopping-block. **tajador** *sm* chopper.

tal [tal] *adj* such; such a. **el tal** that fellow. **tal como** such as. **tal vez** perhaps. *pron* someone; such a person *or* thing. **como tal** as such. *adv* so; as though.

taladrar [tala'ðrar] *v* bore, drill. **taladro** *sm* bore, drill.

talante [ta'lante] *sm* mood; look; grace. **de buen/mal talante** in a good/bad mood.

talar[1] [ta'lar] *v* cut down, fell.

talar[2] *adj* full-length.

talco ['talko] *sm* tinsel; talcum powder.

talega [ta'lega] *sf* money bag; nappy.

talento [ta'lento] *sm* talent. **talentoso** *adj* talented. **talentudo** *adj* over-talented.

talón [ta'lon] *sm* heel; counterfoil; voucher; coupon.

talud [ta'luð] *sm* slope.

tallar [ta'ʎar] *v* carve; appraise; deal cards.

tallarín [taʎa'rin] *sm* noodle.

talle ['taʎe] *sm* figure; waist.

taller [ta'ʎer] *sm* workshop; studio.

tallo ['taʎo] *sm* stem, stalk.

tamaño [ta'maɲo] *sm* size. **de tamaño natural** life-size.

tambalearse [tambale'arse] *v* stagger; wobble; sway.

también [tam'bjen] *adv* also, too.

tambor [tam'bor] *sm* drum. **tambor-mayor** drum major.

Támesis ['tamesis] *sm* Thames.

tamiz [ta'miθ] *sm* sieve. **pasar por tamiz** sift.

tampoco [tam'poko] *adv* neither.

tan [tan] *adv* so. **tan siquiera** even if only.

tanda ['tanda] *sf* turn; shift; relay; gang.

tangente [tan'xente] *sm*, *adj* tangent.

tangerina [tanxe'rina] *sf* tangerine.

tangible [tan'xiβle] *adj* tangible.

tanque ['tanke] *sm* tank.

tantear [tante'ar] *v* try; test; sound; keep score. **tantearse** *v* think carefully. **tanteo** *sm* calculation; score.

tanto ['tanto] *adj* as much; so much; as great; so great. *adv* so much; as much; so; thus. **tanto como** as much as. **por lo tanto** therefore. *sm* amount; sum. **otro tanto** as much again.

***tañer** [ta'ɲer] *v* (*música*) play. **tañido** *sm* tune; twanging.

tapacubo [tapa'kuβo] *sm* hub-cap.

tapar [ta'par] *v* cover up; plug; cap; cork. **tapa** *sf* lid; cover. **tapadero** *sm* stopper. **taparrabo** *sm* loincloth. **tapón** *sm* cork; stopper.

tapia ['tapja] *sf* garden wall. **tapiar** *v* wall up.

tapicería [tapiθe'ria] *sf* tapestry; upholstery. **tapicero, -a** *sm*, *sf* upholsterer. **tapiz** *sm* tapestry. **tapizar** *v* hang with tapestry; upholster.

taquigrafía [takigra'fia] *sf* shorthand. **taquígrafo, -a** *sm*, *sf* stenographer.

taquilla [ta'kiʎa] *sf* box office; till.

tararear [tarare'ar] *v* hum.

tardar [tar'ðar] *v* delay; take a long time. **tardanza** *sf* slowness.

tarde ['tarðe] *sf* afternoon; evening. *adv* late. **se hace tarde** it's getting late. **tardecer** *v* grow late.

tarea [ta'rea] *sf* task; homework.

tarifa [ta'rifa] *sf* tariff; price list; rate.

tarima [ta'rima] *sf* stand; platform.

tarjeta [tar'xeta] *sf* card. **tarjeta postal** postcard.

tarro ['tarro] *sm* jar.

tarta ['tarta] *sf* cake, tart.

tartamudear [tartamuðe'ar] *v* stammer, stutter. **tartamudeo** *sm* stammer, stutter. **tartamudo, -a** *sm*, *sf* stutterer.

tasar [ta'sar] *v* appraise; value. **tasa** *sf* rate; valuation. **sin tasa** without limit. **tasación** *sf* valuation.

tatarabuelo [tatara'βwelo] *sm* great-great-grandfather. **tatarabuela** *sf* great-great-grandmother.

tatuaje [ta'twaxe] *sm* tattoo. **tatuar** *v* tattoo.

tauromaquia [tauro'makja] *sf* bullfighting.

taxidermia [taksi'ðermja] *sf* taxidermy. **taxidermista** *s(m + f)* taxidermist.

taxi ['taksi] *sm* taxi. **taxímetro** *sm* taximeter. **taxista** *s(m+f)* taxi-driver.

taza ['taθa] *sf* cup.

te [te] *pron* you; to you; yourself; to yourself.

té [te] *sm* tea.

teatro [te'atro] *sm* theatre. **teátrico** *adj* theatrical. **teatrero, -a** *sm, sf* theatregoer.

tecla ['tekla] *sf* key. **teclado** *sm* keyboard. **teclear** *v* strum; try.

técnica ['teknika] *sf* technique. **técnico, -a** *sm, sf* technician. **tecnología** *sf* technology. **tecnólogo, -a** *sm, sf* technologist.

techado [te'tʃaðo] *sm* roof; ceiling. **bajo techado** under cover. **techar** *v* put a roof on. **techo** *sm* roof; ceiling.

tedio ['teðjo] *sm* tedium. **tedioso** *adj* tedious.

teja ['texa] *sf* tile. **tejado** *sm* tiled roof. **tejar** *v* tile. **tejaroz** *sm* eaves *pl*.

tejer [te'xer] *v* knit; weave. **tejedor, -a** *sm, sf* weaver. **tejedura** *sf* texture; weaving.

tejón [te'xon] *sm* (*zool*) badger.

tela ['tela] *sf* cloth; material. **tela de araña** spider's web. **telar** *sm* loom.

telaraña [tela'raɲa] *sf* cobweb.

telefonear [telefone'ar] *v* telephone. **teléfono** *sm* telephone.

telegrafiar [telegra'fjar] *v* telegraph. **telegrafía** *sf* telegraphy. **telégrafo** *sm* telegraph.

telegrama [tele'grama] *sm* telegram.

telemando [tele'mando] *sm* remote control.

telepatía [telepa'tia] *sf* telepathy. **telepático** *adj* telepathic.

telescopio [tele'skopjo] *sm* telescope. **telescópico** *adj* telescopic.

telestudio [tele'stuðjo] *sm* television studio.

televisión [teleβi'sjon] *sf* television. **televisar** *v* televise. **televisor** *sm* television set.

telina [te'lina] *sf* clam.

telón [te'lon] *sm* curtain. **telón de acero** Iron Curtain.

tema ['tema] *sm* theme. **temático** *adj* thematic.

*****temblar** [tem'blar] *v* tremble; shiver; shake. **temblor** *sm* shudder. **temblor de tierra** earthquake. **tembloroso** *adj* trembling; shuddering.

temer [te'mer] *v* fear; be afraid. **temeridad**

sf temerity. **temeroso** *adj* fearful. **temor** *sm* fear.

temperamento [tempera'mento] *sm* temperament; nature. **temperancia** *sf* temperance. **temperar** *v* temper.

temperatura [tempera'tura] *sf* temperature.

tempestad [tempes'taθ] *sf* storm. **tempestuoso** *adj* stormy.

templar [tem'plar] *v* temper; moderate. **templado** *adj* temperate.

temple ['temple] *sm* temperature; mood; distemper. **pintura al temple** *sf* painting in distemper.

templo ['templo] *sm* temple.

temporada [tempo'raða] *sf* space of time; season; period.

temporal [tempo'ral] *adj also* **temporáneo** temporary; temporal; worldly; secular. *sm* bad weather.

temprano [tem'prano] *adj, adv* early.

tenaz [te'naθ] *adj* tenacious. **tenacidad** *sf* tenacity. **tenazas** *sf pl* pincers pl.

tendedero [tende'ðero] *sm* clothes line; place for drying clothes.

tendencia [ten'denθja] *sf* tendency.

*****tender** [ten'der] *v* spread out; extend; hang up; lay; set.

tendero, -a *sm, sf* shopkeeper.

tendón [ten'don] *sm* (*anat*) tendon.

tenebroso [tene'βroso] *adj* dark, gloomy. **tenebrosidad** *sf* gloom.

tenedor [tene'ðor] *sm* fork; holder. **tenedor de libros** bookkeeper. **teneduría** *sf* bookkeeping.

tenencia [te'nenθja] *sf* tenancy. occupancy; tenure.

*****tener** [te'ner] *v* have; possess; hold; spend. **tener en mucho** esteem. **tener para sí** think. **tener puesto** wear.

tenería [tene'ria] *sf* tannery.

tenia ['tenja] *sf* tapeworm.

teniente [te'njente] *sm* lieutenant. **teniente coronel** *sm* lieutenant-colonel.

tenis ['tenis] *sm* tennis.

tenor¹ ['tenor] *sm* tenor.

tenor² *sm* meaning; purport.

tenso ['tenso] *adj* tense; taut. **tensión** *sf* tension. **tensión arterial** blood pressure.

*****tentar** [ten'tar] *v* tempt; feel; attempt; examine. **tentación** *sf* temptation. **tentador** *sm* tempter. **tentadora** *sf* temptress. **tentativa** *sf* attempt. **tentativo** *adj* tentative.

tentáculo [ten'takulo] *sm* tentacle.

tentempié [tentempi'e] *sm* (*fam*) snack.

tenue ['tenwe] *adj* tenuous; faint; subdued. **tenuidad** *sf* slightness.

***teñir** [te'ɲir] *v* dye, stain, colour. **teñidura** *sf* dyeing.

teología [teolo'xia] *sf* theology. **teólogo** *sm* theologian.

teorema [teo'rema] *sf* theorem.

teoría [teo'ria] *sf* theory. **teórico** *adj* theoretical. **teorizar** *v* theorize.

teosofía [teoso'fia] *sf* theosophy.

tercero [ter'θero] *adj, sm* third.

terapéutico [tera'peutiko] *adj* therapeutic. **teurapéutica** *sf* therapeutics.

terciar [ter'θjar] *v* tilt sideways; divide into three; mediate. **tercio** *adj* third.

terciopelo [terθjo'pelo] *sm* velvet. **terciopelado** *adj* velvety.

terco ['terko] *adj* stubborn.

tergiversar [terxiβer'sar] *v* misrepresent; distort. **tergiversación** *sf* distortion.

terminar [termi'nar] *v* finish, end; complete. **terminación** *sf* end. **terminal** *adj* terminal. **terminante** *adj* decisive. **terminología** *sf* terminology.

término ['termino] *sm* end. **dar termino a** bring to an end. **termino medio** average.

termita [ter'mita] *sf* also **termite** *sm* termite.

termo ['termo] *sm* vacuum flask.

termodinámica [termoði'namika] *sf* thermodynamics.

termómetro [ter'mometro] *sm* thermometer.

termonuclear [termonukle'ar] *adj* thermonuclear.

termostato [termo'stato] *sm* thermostat.

ternero [ter'nero] *sm* calf; veal.

terneza [ter'neθa] *sf* tenderness; endearment.

ternilla [ter'niʎa] *sf* gristle.

terquedad [terke'ðað] *sf* stubbornness, obstinacy.

terraplén [terra'plen] *sm* terrace; embankment.

terraza [ter'raθa] *sf* terrace.

terremoto [terre'moto] *sm* earthquake.

terreno [ter'reno] *sm* terrain; land. **ceder terreno** give ground.

terrestre [ter'restre] *adj* terrestrial.

terrible [ter'riβle] *adj* terrible. **terrífico** *adj* terrifying.

territorial [territo'rjal] *adj* territorial. **territorio** *sm* territory.

terrón [ter'ron] *sm* lump of sugar; clod of earth.

terror [ter'ror] *sm* terror. **terrorismo** *sm* terrorism. **terrorista** *s(m+f)* terrorist.

terso ['terso] *adj* smooth; glossy; polished. **tersar** *v* smooth. **tersura** *sf* smoothness.

tertulia [ter'tulja] *sf* social gathering; company.

tesis ['tesis] *sf invar* thesis.

tesón [te'son] *sm* tenacity; persistence; inflexibility. **tesonería** *sf* doggedness.

tesoro [te'soro] *sm* treasure. **tesorería** *sf* treasury. **tesorero, -a** *sm, sf* treasurer.

testa ['testa] *sf* head.

testar [tes'tar] *v* make a will. **testamento** *sm* will, testament.

testarudo [testa'ruðo] *adj* stubborn, obstinate. **testarudez** *sf* obstinacy.

testificar [testifi'kar] *v* testify; witness. **testigo** *sm* witness. **testimonial** *adj* bearing witness. **testimoniar** *v* bear witness to. **testimonio** *sm* witness; testimony.

testículo [tes'tikulo] *sm* testicle.

teta ['teta] *sf* teat, nipple; mammary gland; udder.

tetera [te'tera] *sf* teapot.

tétrico ['tetriko] *adj* gloomy; grave; sullen.

textil [teks'til] *sm, adj* textile.

texto ['teksto] *sm* text; textbook.

textura [teks'tura] *sf* texture.

tez [teθ] *sf* complexion, skin.

ti [ti] *pron* (*fam*) you. **de ti para mi** between you and me.

tía ['tia] *sf* aunt; old mother; (*fam*) tart. **no hay tu tía** nothing doing.

tibio ['tiβjo] *adj* lukewarm. **tibieza** *sf* tepidity.

tiburón [tiβu'ron] *sm* shark.

tiempo ['tjempo] *sm* time; weather; (*gram*) tense. **al poco tiempo** soon after. **tiempo atrás** some time ago. **tiempo de perros** filthy weather.

tienda ['tjenda] *sf* shop, store; tent. **tienda de modas** boutique.

tienta ['tjenta] *sf* probe. **andar a tientas** feel one's way.

tiento ['tjento] *sm* feel, tough; tact. **a tiento** by touch.

tierno ['tjerno] *adj* tender; fresh. **pan tierno** fresh bread.

tierra ['tjerra] *sf* earth; land; country; ground. **echar por tierra** wreck. **tierra vegetal** topsoil.

tieso ['tjeso] *adj* stiff; firm. **adv** strongly. **tiesura** *sf* stiffness.

tiesto ['tjesto] *sm* flower pot.

tifo ['tifo] *sm* typhus.

tifoideo [tifoi'ðeo] *adj* typhoid. **fiebre tifoidea** *sf* typhoid fever.

tifón [ti'fon] *sm* typhoon.

tigre ['tigre] *sm* tiger.

tijeras [ti'xeras] *sf pl* scissors; shears.

tilín [ti'lin] *sm* ting-a-ling. **en un tilín** in a flash.

tilo ['tilo] *sm* lime, linden tree.

timar [ti'mar] *v* cheat. **timador** *sm* swindler.

timbrar [tim'brar] *v* stamp; seal. **timbre** *sm* bell; postage stamp.

tímido ['timiðo] *adj* timid. **timidez** *sf* timidity.

timo ['timo] *sm* cheat; swindle.

timón [ti'mon] *sm* helm; rudder. **timonear** *v* (*mar*) steer. **timonero** *sm* helmsman.

tímpano ['timpano] *sm* (*anat*) eardrum; (*música*) kettledrum.

tina ['tina] *sf* tub. **tinaja** *sf* large earthen jar.

tinglado [tin'glaðo] *sm* shed; platform.

tinieblas [ti'njeβlas] *sf pl* darkness *sing*; (*fig*) confusion *sing*.

tino ['tino] *sm* tact; moderation; skill. **sin tino** stupidly.

tinta ['tinta] *sf* ink; hue, colour. **tinte** *sm* dye; stain; shade. **tintero** *sm* inkstand, inkwell. **tintorería** *sf* dyeing; dry-cleaning. **tintorero, -a** *sm, sf* dyer; dry-cleaner. **tintura** dye; rouge.

tintín [tin'tin] *sm* tinkle. **tintinear** *v* tinkle.

tinto ['tinto] *adj* dyed. **vino tinto** *sm* red wine.

tiña ['tiɲa] *sf* ringworm.

tío ['tio] *sm* uncle.

tiovivo [tjo'βiβo] *sm* merry-go-round.

típico ['tipiko] *adj* typical; characteristic.

tiple ['tiple] *sm* (*música*) treble. *sf* soprano.

tipo ['tipo] *sm* type, pattern; model; standard; (*fam*) fellow. **tipo de cambio** rate of exchange.

tipografía [tipogra'fia] *sf* printing. **tipógrafo** *sm* printer.

tira ['tira] *sf* long strip, band.

tirada [ti'raða] *sf* throw; stretch; circulation. **tirador** *sm* marksman; handle.

tirado [ti'raðo] *adj* streamlined; (*fam*) dead easy; (*fam*) dirt cheap.

tiranía [tira'nia] *sf* tyranny. **tirano, -a** *sm, sf* tyrant. **tiranizar** *v* tyrannize.

tirante [ti'rante] *adj* taut. **tirantez** *sf* tautness.

tirar [ti'rar] *v* throw, fling; pull. **tirar por una calle** turn down a street.

tiritar [tiri'tar] *v* shiver. **tiritón** *sm* shiver.

tiro ['tiro] *sm* throw; shot; discharge; report; blow; practical joke. **tiro al blanco** target practice.

tiroides [ti'rojðes] *sm* thyroid.

tirón [ti'ron] *sm* haul, jerk; cramp; tyro, beginner. **de un tirón** straight off.

tiroteo [tiro'teo] *sm* firing, crossfire. **tirotear** *v* snipe at.

tisis ['tisis] *sf* tuberculosis.

títere ['titere] *sm* puppet; marionette.

titubear [tituβe'ar] *v* vacillate; totter, stagger; stammer. **titubeo** *sm* staggering; hesitation.

título ['titulo] *sm* title; license, diploma; degree. **titular** *adj* titular.

tiza ['tiθa] *sf* chalk.

tiznar [tiθ'nar] *v* stain, tarnish. **tiznado** *adj* stained, grimy. **tiznajo** *sm* smudge.

toalla [to'aʎa] *sf* towel. **toalla de baño** bathtowel. **toallero** *sm* towel-rail.

tobillo [to'βiʎo] *sm* ankle.

tobogán [toβa'gan] *sm* slide; chute.

tocadiscos [toka'ðiskos] *sm invar* record-player.

tocado [to'kaðo] *sm* coiffure.

tocador [toka'ðor] *sm* dressing-table.

tocar [to'kar] *v* touch; feel; (*música*) play; belong; concern; border on; be one's turn. **tocarse** *v* put on one's hat.

tocino [to'θino] *sm* bacon; salt pork.

todavía [toða'βia] *adv* yet, still; nevertheless. **todavía más** even more.

todo ['toðo] *adj* all; entire; every; each. **todo el mundo** everybody. **todo o nada** all or nothing.

toldo ['tolðo] *sm* awning.

tolerar [tole'rar] *v* tolerate; bear. **tolerable** *adj* tolerable. **tolerancia** *sf* tolerance. **tolerante** *adj* tolerant.

tomar [to'mar] *v* take; hold; get; gather. **tomarse** *v* get rusty. **tomada** *sf* capture. **tomadura** *sf* taking.

tomate [to'mate] *sm* tomato. **tomatera** *sf* tomato plant.

tomillo [to'miʎo] *sm* thyme.

tomo ['tomo] *sm* tome, volume; bulk.

ton [ton] *sm* motive; occasion. **sin ton ni son** without rhyme or reason.

tonada [to'naða] *sf* song. **tonalidad** *sf* tonality.

tonel [to'nel] *sm* cask. barrel.

tonelada [tone'laða] *sf* ton. **tonelaje** *sm* tonnage.

tónico ['toniko] *sm, adj* (*música*) tonic. **tonificar** *v* (*med*) tone up.

tono ['tono] *sm* (*música*) pitch; tone; manner. **darse tono** put on airs.

tontería [tonte'ria] *sf* foolishness, nonsense. **tonto** *adj* foolish, silly; stupid; ignorant.

topacio [to'paθjo] *sm* topaz.

topar [to'par] *v* collide with; strike against; encounter; meet by chance. **tope** ['tope] *sm* top, summit; end. **al tope** end to end.

tópico ['topiko] *sm* topic. *adj* topical.

topo ['topo] *sm* mole. **topera** *sf* molehill.

topografía [topogra'fia] *sf* topography. **topográfico** *adj* topographical.

toque ['toke] *sm* touch; peal of bells; test, trial.

tórax ['toraks] *sm* thorax.

torbellino [torβe'ʎino] *sm* whirlwind; whirlpool.

***torcer** [tor'θer] *v* twist; turn; wrench; bend. **torcedura** *sf* twisting; sprain. **torcido** *adj* twisted; bent. **torcimiento** *sm* distortion.

tordo ['torðo] *sm* thrush.

torear [tore'ar] *v* fight the bull. **torero** *sm* bullfighter.

tormenta [tor'menta] *sf* storm. **tormentoso** *adj* stormy.

tormentar [tormen'tar] *v* torment. **tormento** *sm* torment; affliction; pain.

tornar [tor'nar] *v* turn; return; do again. **torna** *sf* return. **tornarse** *v* become.

tornasol [torna'sol] *sm* (*bot*) sunflower; litmus.

torneo [tor'neo] *sm* tournament.

tornillo [tor'niʎo] *sm* screw.

torniquete [torni'kete] *sm* tourniquet; turnstile.

toro ['toro] *sm* bull. **toros** *sm pl* bullfight.

toronja [to'ronxa] *sf* grapefruit.

torpe ['torpe] *adj* clumsy; indecent. **torpeza** *sf* clumsiness; indecency.

torpedo [tor'peðo] *sm* torpedo. **torpedero** *sm* torpedo-boat.

tórpido ['torpiðo] *adj* torpid, torpor. **torpor** *sm* torpor.

torre ['torre] *sf* tower.

torrente [tor'rente] *sm* torrent. **torrencial** *adj* torrential.

tórrido ['torriðo] *adj* torrid.

torta ['torta] *sf* cake; pie. **tortada** *sf* meat pie. **tortera** *sf* pie dish.

tortilla [tor'tiʎa] *sf* omelette.

tortuga [tor'tuga] *sf* tortoise; turtle.

tortura [tor'tura] *sf* torture. **tortuoso** *adj* tortuous.

tos [tos] *sf* cough. **tos ferina** whooping-cough. **toser** *v* cough.

tosco ['tosko] *adj* coarse; crude; clumsy. **tosquedad** *sf* roughness; crudeness.

***tostar** [tos'tar] *v* toast; roast; tan. **tostada** *sf* piece of toast.

total [to'tal] *sm* total. **totalidad** *sf* totality. **totalitario** *adj* totalitarian. **totalizar** *v* total.

tóxico ['toksiko] *sm* poison. *adj* poisonous. **toxicar** *v* poison.

toxicómano [toksi'komano], **-a** *sm, sf* drug-addict. **toxicomanía** *sf* drug-addiction.

tozudo [to'θuðo] *adj* stubborn.

traba ['traβa] *sf* link; fetter; hindrance. **poner trabas** hinder. **trabadura** *sf* bond. **trabamiento** *sm* joining. **trabar** *v* join; fetter; strike up. **trabar amistad** become friends. **trabón** *sm* fetter.

trabajar [traβa'xar] *v* work; work on; elaborate; trouble; deal in. **trabajado** *adj* elaborate. **trabajador, -a** *sm, sf* worker. **trabajo** *sm* work; toil; exertion; hardship. **trabajoso** *adj* laborious.

trabalenguas [traβa'lengwas] *sm invar* tongue-twister.

tracción [trak'θjon] *sf* traction. **tractor** *sm* tractor.

tradición [traði'θjon] *sf* tradition. **tradicional** *adj* traditional.

***traducir** [traðu'θir] *v* translate; interpret. **traducción** *sf* translation. **traductor, -a** *sm, sf* translator.

***traer** [tra'er] *v* bring; carry; fetch; result in; wear. **traer a mal traer** treat roughly. **traer a cuento** mention. **traerse** *v* be dressed; behave.

traficar [trafi'kar] *v* trade; travel. **traficante** *s*(*m* + *f*) dealer. **tráfico** *sm* trade; traffic.

tragaluz [traga'luθ] *sf* skylight.

tragar [tra'gar] *v* swallow. **no puedo tragarle** I can't stand him. **tragadero** *sm* gullet. **trago** *sm* swallow; gulp.

tragedia [tra'xeðia] *sf* tragedy. **tragico** *adj* tragic.

traicionar [traiθjo'nar] *v* betray. **traición** *sf* treason; treachery. **traicionero** *adj* treacherous. **traidor, -a** *sm, sf* traitor.

traje ['traxe] *sm* dress; suit; costume. **traje de etiqueta** evening dress. **baile de trajes** *sm* fancy-dress ball.

trajín [tra'xin] *sm* haulage; coming and going. **trajinante** *sm* (*com*) carrier.

tramar [tra'mar] *v* weave; plan, plot. **trama** *sf* weft; plot.

tramitar [trami'tar] *v* negotiate, arrange. **tramitación** *sf* arrangements *pl.* **trámite** *sm* procedure; formality.

tramo ['tramo] *sm* (*puente*) span; (*escaleras*) flight; (*terreno*) strip.

trampa ['trampa] *sf* trap; trapdoor; fraud. **tramposo** *adj* deceitful.

trampear [trampe'ar] *v* defraud; scrape by. **trampeador, -a** *sm, sf* swindler.

trampolin [trampo'lin] *sm* ski jump; springboard.

trancar [tran'kar] *v* (*puerta*) bar; stride. **tranca** *sf* stick; club; (*fam*) drunkenness. **tranco** *sm* stride.

trance ['tranθe] *sm* trance; critical situation. **a todo trance** at all costs.

tranquilizar [trankili'θar] *v* tranquillize. **tranquilidad** *sf* tranquillity. **tranquilo** *adj* tranquil.

transacción [transak'θjon] *sf* transaction.

transatlántico [transat'lantiko] *adj* transatlantic. *sm* (*mar*) liner.

transbordar [transβor'ðar] *v* transfer. **transbordo** *sm* transfer.

transcribir [transkri'βir] *v* transcribe. **transcripción** *sf* transcription.

transcurrir [transkur'rir] *v* elapse, pass. **transcurso** *sm* course *or* lapse of time.

transeúnte [transe'unte] *adj* transitory, transient. *s(m + f)* transient, passer-by.

*transferir [transfe'rir] *v* transfer. **transferible** *adj* transferable.

transfigurar [transfigu'rar] *v* transfigure. **transfiguración** *sf* transfiguration.

transformar [transfor'mar] *v* transform. **transformación** *sf* transformation.

tránsfuga ['transfuga] *sm* deserter.

*transgredir [transgre'ðir] *v* transgress, violate. **transgresión** *sf* transgression. **transgresor, -a** *sm, sf* transgressor.

transición [transi'θjon] *sf* transition.

transido [tran'siðo] *adj* overwhelmed; stricken.

transigir [transi'xir] *v* compromise. **transigencia** *sf* tolerance. **transigente** *adj* tolerant.

transistor [transis'tor] *sm* transistor.

transitar [transi'tar] *v* travel; pass. **transitivo** *adj* (*gram*) transitive. **tránsito** *sm* transit; passage; transition. **transitorio** *adj* transitory.

transmitir [transmi'tir] *v* transmit. **transmisión** *sf* transmission. **transmisor** *sm* transmitter.

transparencia [transpa'renθja] *sf* transparency. **transparente** *adj* transparent.

transpirar [transpi'rar] *v* perspire; transpire. **transpiración** *sf* perspiration.

*transponer [transpo'ner] *v* transpose; transplant. **transponerse** *v* get down; get sleepy.

transportar [transpor'tar] *v* transport; (*música*) transpose. **transportarse** get carried away. **transporte** *sm* transport. **transposición** *sf* transposition.

tranvía [tran'βia] *sm* tramway; tram.

trapaza [tra'paθa] *sf* swindle, fraud; trick. **trapacear** *v* defraud. **trapacista** *s(m + f)*, swindler.

trapecio [tra'peθjo] *sm* trapeze.

trapo ['trapo] *sm* rag. *pl* old clothes.

traquetear [trakete'ar] *v* shake up; rattle. **traqueteo** *sm* rattling; jolting.

tras [tras] *prep* after; behind; beyond. **tras de** in addition to.

*trascender [trasθen'der] *v* transcend; leak out; spread. **trascendencia** *sf* transcendence. **trascendental** *adj* momentous. **trascendente** *adj* transcendent.

*trasegar [trase'gar] *v* decant; upset.

trasero [tra'sero] *adj* rear. *sm* behind. **trasera** *sf* back; rear.

trasladar [trasla'ðar] *v* transfer; translate; postpone. **trasladarse** *v* go; move. **traslación** *sf* transfer; translation. **traslado** *sm* copy; transfer.

*traslucirse [traslu'θirse] *v* shine; show through. **traslúcido** *adj* translucent.

traslumbrar [traslum'brar] *v* dazzle.

trasmutar [trasmu'tar] *v* transmute. **trasmutación** *sf* transmutation.

trasnochar [trasno'tʃar] *v* be up all *or* most of the night.

traspasar [traspa'sar] *v* transfer; transfix; transgress. **traspasador, -a** *sm, sf* transgressor. **traspaso** *sm* transfer; transgression.

traspié [tras'pje] *sm* stumble.

trasplantar [trasplan'tar] *v* transplant. **trasplantarse** *v* migrate. **trasplante** *sm* transplant.

trasquilar [traski'lar] *v* shear, snip, clip. **trasquilado** *adj* sheared; cropped.

traste ['traste] *sm* (*música*) fret. **ir al traste** fall through, fail.

trasto ['trasto] *sm* tool; weapon; equipment; piece of furniture.

trastornar [trastor'nar] *v* upset; turn upside down. **trastornado** *adj* unbalanced. **trastorno** *sm* upheaval; inconvenience.

trasunto [tra'sunto] *sm* copy, reproduction; likeness. **trasuntar** *v* copy.

tratar [tra'tar] *v* treat; deal with; handle. **tratable** *adj* manageable. **tratamiento** *sm* treatment. **trato** *sm* treatment; behaviour; bargain. **mal trato** ill-treatment.

través [tra'βes] *sm* slant; bias; reverse. **a través de** across.

travesero [traβe'sero] *adj* transverse. **travesía** *sf* crossroad.

travesura [traβe'sura] *sf* trick, prank.

traviesa [tra'βjesa] *sf* (*ferrocarril*) sleeper; (*arq*) rafter; bet.

travieso [tra'βjeso] *adj* transverse, cross; lively; mischievous. **a campo traviesa** cross-country.

trayecto [tra'jekto] *sm* route; fare stage; distance; way; itinerary. **trayectoria** *sf* trajectory.

trazar [tra'θar] *v* draw; plot; trace; design. **traza** *sf* sketch. **bien/mal trazado** good/bad looking. **trazador, -a** *sm, sf* designer.

trébol ['treβol] *sm* clover.

trece ['treθe] *adj, sm* thirteen.

trecho ['tretʃo] *sm* space; distance; lapse; stretch.

tregua ['tregwa] *sf* truce; respite.

treinta ['treinta] *adj, sm* thirty.

tremendo [tre'mendo] *adj* tremendous.

trémulo ['tremulo] *adj* tremulous.

tren [tren] *sm* train. **tren botijo** excursion train.

trenzar [tren'θar] *v* braid. **trenza** *sf* plait, braid.

trementina [tremen'tina] *sf* turpentine.

trepar [tre'par] *v* climb. **trepa** *sf* climbing. **trepadoras** *sf pl* climbing plants.

trepidar [trepi'ðar] *v* shake, tremble. **trepidación** *sf* tremor.

tres [tres] *adj, sm* three.

triángulo [tri'angulo] *sm* triangle. **triangular** *adj* triangular.

tribu [tri'βu] *sf* tribe.

tribuna [tri'βuna] *sf* tribune; gallery; grandstand. **tribunal** *sm* tribunal.

tributar [triβu'tar] *v* pay. **tributable** *adj* tributary. **tributación** *sf* tax. **tributante** *s(m+f)* taxpayer. **tributo** *sm* tribute; tax.

triciclo [tri'θiklo] *sm* tricycle.

tricotar [triko'tar] *v* knit.

trigo ['trigo] *sm* wheat. **trigal** *sm* wheatfield.

trigésimo [tri'xesimo] *adj* thirtieth.

trigonometría [trigonome'tria] *sf* trigonometry.

trillar [tri'ʎar] *v* thresh; beat. **trilla** *sf* threshing. **trillador, -a** *sm, sf* threshing machine.

trimestre [tri'mestre] *sm* three-month term. **trimestral** *adj* quarterly.

trinar [tri'nar] *v* trill. **trinado** *sm* trill.

trincar [trin'kar] *v* break; bind; hold down.

trinchar [trin'tʃar] *v* carve. **trinchante** *sm* carving-knife. **trinchero** *adj* carving.

trinchera [trin'tʃera] *sf* trench.

trineo [tri'neo] *sm* sledge, sled, sleigh.

trinidad [trini'ðað] *sf* trinity.

trinitaria [trini'tarja] *sf* pansy.

tripa ['tripa] *sf* intestine. **tener malas tripas** be cruel.

triple ['triple] *adj* triple.

trípode ['tripoðe] *sm* tripod.

tripulación [tripula'θjon] *sf* crew. **tripulante** *sm* member of the crew.

triscar [tris'kar] *v* mingle; stamp; frisk. **trisca** *sf* crunch.

triste ['triste] *adj* sad, mournful, gloomy. **tristeza** *sf* sadness.

triturar [tritu'rar] *v* grind, crush. **trituración** *sf* grinding.

triunfar [triun'far] *v* triumph. **triunfador, -a** *sm, sf* victor. **triunfal** *adj* triumphal. **triunfante** *adj* triumphant. **triunfo** *sm* triumph.

trivial [tri'βjal] *adj* trivial. **trivialidad** *sf* triviality.

triza ['triθa] *sf* shred; particle, fragment.

trocar [tro'kar] *v* exchange. **trocarse** *v* change into. **trocamiento** *sm* exchange.

trochemoche [trotʃe'motʃe] *adv* higgledypiggledy.

trofeo [tro'feo] *sm* trophy.

trole ['trole] *sm* trolley.

tromba ['tromba] *sf* waterspout.

trombón [trom'bon] *sm* trombone.

trompa ['trompa] *sf* hunting horn; (*elefante*) trunk; proboscis.

trompada [trom'paða] *sf* bump; thump.

trompeta [trom'peta] *sf* trumpet. **trompetero** *sm* trumpeter.

*tronar [tro'nar] *v* thunder. **tronada** *sf* thunderstorm. **tronante** *adj* thunderous. **tronido** *sm* thunderclap.

tronco ['tronko] *sm* tree trunk; stalk; stern.

tronchar [tron'tʃar] *v* bring down; break up.

trono ['trono] *sm* throne.

tropa ['tropa] *sf* troop.

tropel [tro'pel] *sm* crowd. **en tropel** in a rush. **tropelía** *sf* rush, hurry.

*tropezar [trope'θar] *v* stumble; run into. **tropiezo** *sm* stumble.

trópico ['tropiko] *sm* tropic. **tropical** *adj* tropical.

trotar [tro'tar] *v* trot. **trote** *sm* trot.

trozo ['troθo] *sm* piece, fragment, bit.

truco ['truko] *sm* trick.

trucha ['trutʃa] *sf* trout; (*mec*) crane.

trueno [tru'eno] *sm* thunder.

trueque [tru'eke] *sm* exchange, barter.

trufa ['trufa] *sf* truffle.

truncar [trun'kar] *v* truncate, abridge. **truncado** *adj* truncated.

tu [tu] *adj* (*fam*) your.

tú [tu] *pron* (*fam*) you.

tubérculo [tu'βerkulo] *sm* tubercle; tuber. **tuberculosis** *sf* tuberculosis. **tuberculoso** *adj* tubercular.

tubo ['tuβo] *sm* tube, pipe. **tubería** *sf* tubing. **tubular** *adj* tubular.

tuerca ['twerka] *sf* (*mec*) nut. **tuerca a mariposa** wing nut.

tuerto ['twerto], **-a** *sm, sf* one-eyed person. *adj* one-eyed.

tuétano [tu'etano] *sm* (*anat*) marrow.

tufo ['tufo] *sm* vapour; fume; stench. **tufarada** *sf* whiff.

tul [tul] *sm* tulle.

tulipán [tuli'pan] *sm* tulip.

tullido [tu'ʎiðo] *adj* cripple. **tullirse** *v* be crippled.

tumba[1] ['tumba] *sf* tomb.

tumba[2] *sf* tumble. **tumbar** *v* knock down; tumble.

tumor [tu'mor] *sm* tumour.

tumulto [tu'multo] *sm* tumult. **tumultuoso** *adj* tumultuous.

tunante [tu'nante] *s(m+f)* rascal, crook. *adj* rascally. **tunantería** *sf* crookedness.

túnel ['tunel] *sm* tunnel.

túnica ['tunika] *sf* tunic.

tuno ['tuno] *sm* rogue.

tupé [tu'pe] *sm* toupee.

tupido [tu'piðo] *adj* thick; dense.

turba ['turβa] *sf* crowd; heap; peat. **turbal** *sm* peat bog.

turbante [tur'βante] *sm* turban.

turbar [tur'βar] *v* disturb. **turbarse** *v* be embarrassed.

turbina [tur'βina] *sf* turbine.

turbulento [turβu'lento] *adj* turbulent, disorderly. **turbulencia** *sf* turbulence.

turismo [tu'rismo] *sm* tourism. **turista** *s(m+f)* tourist.

turnar [tur'nar] *v* alternate, take turns. **turno** *sm* turn, shift. **por turno** in turn.

turón [tu'ron] *sm* polecat.

turquesa [tur'kesa] *sf* turquoise.

turrón [tur'ron] *sm* nougat.

tutear [tute'ar] *v* address as *tú*.

tutela [tu'tela] *sf* protection; tutelage. **tutelar** *adj* guardian.

tutor [tu'tor] *sm* tutor; guardian. **tutoría** *sf* guardianship.

tuyo ['tujo] *pron* (*fam*) yours; of yours.

U

u [u] *conj* or (before words beginning with *o* or *ho*).

ubicar [uβi'kar] *v* be situated; (*auto*) park. **ubicarse** *v* place oneself. **ubicuidad** *sf* ubiquity. **ubicuo** *adj* ubiquitous.

ubre ['uβre] *sf* udder.

ufanarse [ufa'narse] *v* boast. **ufano** *adj* proud, conceited. **ufanía** *sf* pride, arrogance.

ujier [u'xjer] *sm* usher.

úlcera ['ulθera] *sf* ulcer. **ulcerado** *adj* ulcerated.

ulterior [ulte'rjor] *adj* further, farther; ulterior. **ulteriormente** *adj* later.

ultimar [ulti'mar] *v* conclude, finish. **ultimación** *sf* conclusion. **últimamente**

adv finally; recently. **ultimátum** *sm* ultimatum. **último** *adj* last; latest. **por último** finally.

ultrajar [ultra'xar] *v* outrage; insult. **ultraje** *sm* outrage. **ultrajoso** *adj* outrageous.

ultramarino [ultrama'rino] *adj* overseas. **ultramar** *sm* overseas countries *pl*. **ir a ultramar** go abroad.

ultranza [ul'tranθa] *adv* **a ultranza** to the death; at all costs.

umbral [um'bral] *sm* threshold. **pisar los umbrales** cross the threshold.

umbrío [um'brio] *adj also* **umbroso** shady.

un [un] *art also* **una** a; one. *adj* one.

unánime [u'nanime] *adj* unanimous. **unanimidad** *sf* unanimity.

unción [un'θjon] *sf* anointing, unction. **extremaunción** *sf* (*rel*) extreme unction.

uncir [un'θir] *v* yoke.

undécimo [un'deθimo], **-a** *s*, *adj* eleventh.

undoso [un'doso] *adj* wavy. **undulación** *sf* undulation. **undulante** *adj* undulating. **undular** *v* undulate.

ungir [un'xir] *v* anoint. **ungimiento** *sm* unction. **ungüento** *sm* ointment.

único ['uniko] *adj* only, sole, single; unique. **únicamente** *adv* only, solely.

unicornio [uni'kornjo] *sm* unicorn.

unidad [uni'ðað] *sf* unity; union; unit. **unido** *adj* united. **unificación** *sf* unification. **unificar** *v* unify.

uniformar [unifor'mar] *v* make uniform; standardize. **uniforme** *adj*, *sm* uniform. **uniformidad** *sf* uniformity.

unión [u'njon] *sf* union; unity; marriage. **unir** *v* join; mix. **unirse** *v* join; mingle.

Unión Soviética [u'njon so'βjetika] *sf* Soviet Union.

unísono [u'nisono] *adj* harmonious. **al unísono** in unison; unanimously.

universidad [uniβersi'ðað] *sf* university. **universitario** *adj* of a university.

universo [uni'βerso] *sm* universe. **universal** *adj* universal. **universalidad** *sf* universality.

uno ['uno] *adj* one; only. *pron* one; someone. **unos** *pron pl* some; a few. **unos y otros** all.

untar [un'tar] *v* grease; smear; stain; spread. **unto** *sm* grease; ointment.

uña ['uɲa] *sf* (*anat*) nail; talon, claw; hoof. **esconder las uñas** hide one's feelings. **uñero** *sm* ingrowing toenail.

uranio [u'ranjo] *sm* uranium.

urbano [ur'βano] *adj* urban; urbane. **urbanidad** *sf* urbanity. **urbanístico** *adj* urban. **urbanización** *sf* town planning. **urbe** *sf* large city.

urdir [ur'ðir] *v* warp; (*fig*) plot, scheme.

urgencia [ur'xenθja] *sf* urgency; emergency. **urgente** *adj* urgent. **urgir** *v* be urgent; urge. **me urge el tiempo** I am pressed for time.

urinario [uri'narjo] *sm* urinal.

urna ['urna] *sf* urn; ballot box.

urogallo [uro'gaʎo] *sm* (*zool*) grouse.

urraca [ur'raka] *sf* magpie.

usar [u'sar] *v* use; employ; be accustomed. **usado** *adj* used; worn. **usanza** *sf* custom; usage. **uso** *sm* use; wear; custom; enjoyment; fashion. **al uso de** in the style of.

usted [u'steð] *pron also* **Vd** you. **¡a usted!** thank you!

usual [u'swal] *adj* usual.

usufructo [u'sufrukto] *sm* use; enjoyment.

usura [u'sura] *sf* usury. **usurero, -a** *sm*, *sf* usurer.

usurpar [usur'par] *v* usurp. **usurpación** *sf* usurpation. **usurpador, -a** *sm*, *sf* usurper.

utensilio [uten'siljo] *sm* utensil; implement, tool.

útero ['utero] *sm* uterus. **uterino** *adj* uterine.

útil ['util] *sm* tool. *adj* useful; fit. **utilidad** *sf* utility, usefulness. **utilitario** *adj* utilitarian. **utilizar** *v* utilize, use.

uva ['uβa] *sf* grape. **uva pasa** raisin.

V

vaca ['βaka] *sf* cow; beef.

vacaciones [βaka'θjones] *sf pl* vacation *sing*; holidays *pl*. **irse de vacaciones** go on holiday.

vacante [βa'kante] *adj* vacant. *sf* vacancy. **vacar** *v* fall vacant.

vacilar [βaθi'lar] *v* hesitate. **vacilante** *adj* unstable, unsteady. **vacilación** *sf* vacillation.

vacío [βa'θio] *adj* empty. *sm* void; vacuum. **vaciar** *v* empty; pour out. **vacuo** *adj* empty; vacuous.

vacunar [βaku'nar] v vaccinate. **vacunación** sf vaccination.

vadear [βaðe'ar] v wade; surmount, overcome. **vadeable** adj fordable.

vagar [βa'gar] v wander, move about. sm leisure; ease. **vagabundo, -a** sm, sf vagabond. **vagante** adj vagrant.

vago ['βago] adj vague; indolent. sm tramp; loafer. **vaguedad** sf vagueness.

vagón [βa'gon] sm railway carriage; wagon. **vagón restaurante** dining-car. **vagoneta** sf small truck.

vahear [βae'ar] v steam. **vaho** sm vapour.

vahido [βa'iðo] sm vertigo, dizziness.

vaina ['βaina] sf sheath; scabbard; pod.

vainilla [βai'niʎa] sf vanilla.

vaivén [βai'βen] sm fluctuation; sway; swinging movement.

vajilla [βa'xiʎa] sf tableware, dishes pl.

vale ['βale] sm voucher; receipt; IOU.

valedero [βale'ðero] adj valid.

valentía [βalen'tia] sf valour, courage; brave or courageous act; bragging. **valentón, -ona** sm, sf braggart.

valer [βa'ler] v be worth; cost; be equal to. **vale la pena** be worthwhile. **válgame la frase** if you don't mind my saying so. **valerse** v make use of. **valía** sf value, worth.

valeroso [βale'roso] adj brave; valuable.

validar [βali'ðar] v validate; make binding. **validación** sf validation; ratification. **válido** adj valid. **validez** sf validity.

valiente [βa'ljente] adj valiant, courageous; strong; first-rate.

valija [βa'lixa] sf valise; case; mail bag.

valimiento [βali'mjento] sm value; good will; protection; favour.

valor [βa'lor] sm value, worth; price; valour, courage. adj valuable. **valoración** sf valuation. **valorar** v value, appraise.

valsar [βal'sar] v waltz. **vals** sm waltz.

valuar [βalu'ar] v value, appraise, assess. **valuación** sf valuation.

válvula ['βalβula] sf valve.

vallar [βa'ʎar] v fence in, enclose. **valla** sf fence. **vallado** sm enclosure.

valle ['βaʎe] sm valley.

vampiro [βam'piro] sm vampire.

vanagloriarse [βanaglo'rjarse] v boast. **vanagloria** sf boasting, vainglory.

vándalo ['βandalo] sm, adj vandal. **vandalismo** sm vandalism.

vanguardia [βan'gwarðja] sf vanguard; avant-garde.

vano ['βano] adj vain; idle. **en vano** in vain. **vanidad** sf vanity. **vanidoso** adj vain.

vapor [βa'por] sm vapour; steam; (mar) steamer. **vaporización** sf evaporation. **vaporizar** v evaporate.

vaquero [βa'kero] sm cowboy. **vaquería** sf herd of cows.

vaqueta [βa'keta] sf cowhide.

vara ['βara] sf rod, pole, staff; (medida) yard. **tener vara alta** have the upper hand.

varar [βa'rar] v launch; run aground.

variar [βa'rjar] v vary, change. **variable** adj variable. **variación** sf variation. **variado** adj varied. **variante** sf variant; version.

varice [βa'riθe], sf also **várice** varicose vein.

varilla [βa'riʎa] sf small stick; jawbone; curtain rail.

vario ['βarjo] adj varied, diverse. **varios** adj several.

varón [βa'ron] sm, adj male. **varonil** adj manly, virile.

vaselina ® [βase'lina] sf Vaseline ®.

vasija [βa'sixa] sf vessel; bowl; dish. **vaso** sm glass, tumbler.

vástago ['βastago] sm stem, shoot, sprout; scion, offspring.

vasto ['βasto] adj vast. **vastedad** sf vastness.

vaticinar [βatiθi'nar] v predict, foretell. **vaticinador, -a** sm, sf prophet, seer. **vaticinio** sm divination, prophecy.

vatio ['βatjo] sm (elec) watt.

vecino [βe'θino], **-a** sm, sf neighbour. **vecinal** adj local. **vecindad** sf neighbourhood.

vedar [βe'ðar] v veto; prohibit; hinder. **veda** sf prohibition. **vedado** sm game preserve.

vega ['βega] sf plain; tract of fertile ground.

vegetación [βexeta'θjon] sf vegetation. **vegetal** adj vegetable. **vegetar** v grow; (fig) vegetate. **vegetariano, -a** sm, sf vegetarian.

vehemencia [βee'menθja] sf vehemence. **vehemente** adj vehement.

vehículo [βe'ikulo] sm vehicle.

veinte ['βeinte] sm, adj twenty.

vejar [βe'xar] v vex, harass, annoy. **vejación** sf vexation. **vejatorio** adj vexatious.

vejez [βe'xeθ] *sf* old age.
vejiga [βe'xiga] *sf* blister; bladder.
vela ['βela] *sf* vigil, watch; candle; sail.
velar *v* keep watch; stay awake.
veleidad [βelei'ðað] *sf* whim; fickleness.
veleidoso *adj* fickle.
velero [βe'lero] *sm* sailing ship; glider.
velo ['βelo] *sm* veil.
velocidad [βeloθi'ðað] *sf* velocity.
velocímetro *sm* speedometer. **veloz** *adj* fast, quick.
vello ['βeʎo] *sm* soft hair, down; fluff.
velloso *adj* dowry.
vena ['βena] *sf* vein; scan. **trabajar por venas** work in fits and starts.
venablo [βe'naβlo] *sm* javelin.
venado [βe'naðo] *sm* deer; (*culin*) venison.
venal [βe'nal] *adj* venal.
vencer [βen'θer] *v* defeat; win; (*com*) fall due. **vencerse** *v* control oneself. **vencible** *adj* beatable. **los vencidos** the losers. **vencimiento** *sm* victory; (*com*) expiration, falling due.
vendar [βen'dar] *v* bandage. **venda** *sf also* **vendaje** *sm* bandage.
vendaval [βenda'βal] *sm* gale.
vender [βen'der] *v* sell. **vendedor** *sm* seller, vendor; salesperson. **vendible** *adj* saleable.
vendimia [βen'ðimja] *sf* grape harvest; vintage.
veneno [βe'neno] *sm* venom, poison. **venenoso** *adj* poisonous.
venerar [βene'rar] *v* venerate. **venerable** *adj* venerable. **veneración** *sf* veneration.
venéreo [βe'nereo] *adj* venereal.
venero [βe'nero] *sm* spring of water; source, origin, root.
vengar [βen'gar] *v* avenge. **vengador, -a** *sm, sf* avenger. **venganza** *sf* vengeance. **vengativo** *adj* vindictive.
venia ['βenja] *sf* forgiveness, pardon; permission, leave.
***venir** [βe'nir] *v* come. **venir bien** be suitable *or* convenient. **venirse** *v* come *or* go back. **venida** *sf* arrival, coming; return. **venidero** *adj* coming, future.
venta ['βenta] *sf* sale, market; inn. **venta a plazos** hire purchase. **ventero, -a** *sm, sf* innkeeper.
ventaja [βen'taxa] *sf* advantage. **ventajoso** *adj* advantageous.
ventana [βen'tana] *sf* window.
ventilar [βenti'lar] *v* ventilate. **ventilación**

sf ventilation. **ventilador** *sm* ventilator; fan.
ventosa [βen'tosa] *sf* vent.
ventoso [βen'toso] *sf* vent.
ventoso [βen'toso] *adj* windy. **ventosidad** *sf* flatulence.
ventrílocuo [βen'trilokwo] *sm* ventriloquist. **ventriloquia** *sf* ventriloquism.
ventura [βen'tura] *sf* joy, happiness; good luck. **mala ventura** ill luck. **venturado, venturero** *or* **venturoso** *adj* lucky; happy.
***ver** [βer] *v* see. *sm* view; aspect; opinion; looks *pl*, appearance. **echar de ver** notice. **estar viendo** have a feeling. **vamos a ver** let's see.
vera ['βera] *sf* border, edge.
verano [βe'rano] *sm* summer. **veranear** *v* spend the summer. **veraneo** *sm* summer holiday.
veras ['βeras] *sf pl* truth *sing*. **de veras** indeed, really. **veracidad** *sf* veracity. **veraz** *adj* truthful.
verbo ['βerβo] *sm* verb. **verbosidad** *sf* verbosity. **verboso** *adj* verbose.
verdad [βer'ðað] *sf* truth. **verdadero** *adj* true; real, authentic; sincere; truthful.
verde ['βerðe] *adj* green; immature; fresh; young; immodest, obscene. **darse un verde** amuse oneself.
verdugo [βer'ðugo] *sm* executioner; hangman; scourge. **verdugón** *sm* weal (from whiplash).
verdulero [βerðu'lero] *sm* greengrocer. **verdulería** *sf* greengrocer's. **verdura** *sf* greenness. **verduras** *sf pl* vegetables.
veredicto [βere'ðikto] *sm* verdict.
vergüenza [βer'gwenθa] *sf* shame; affront; disgrace; shyness, timidity. **sin vergüenza** shameless. **vergonzoso** *adj* shy; shameful.
verídico [βe'riðiko] *adj* truthful.
verificar [βerifi'kar] *v* verify; examine, inspect; check. **verificarse** *v* prove true; be verified. **verificación** *sf* verification. **verificativo** *adj* corroborative.
verosímil [βero'simil] *adj* likely, probable. **verosimilitud** *sf* probability.
verruga [βer'ruga] *sf* wart.
versado [βer'saðo] *adj* versed, experienced; skilful.
versar [βer'sar] *v* go round; spin. **versar sobre** to treat of, deal with.
versátil [βer'satil] *adj* versatile; variable; inconstant. **versatilidad** *sf* versatility; changeableness.

versículo [βerˈsikulo] sm verse. **versificar** v versify. **verso** sm verse. **verso suelto** blank verse.

versión [βerˈsjon] sf version.

vértebra [ˈβerteβra] sf vertebra. **vertebrado** sm, adj vertebrate.

*verter [βerˈter] v spill, empty; pour; interpret, translate. **vertedero** sm drain. **vertedor** sm sewer.

vertical [βertiˈkal] adj vertical.

vértice [ˈβertiθe] sm apex.

vértigo [ˈβertiɣo] sm vertigo. **vertiginoso** adj giddy.

vesícula [βeˈsikula] sf (anat) vesicle; blister.

vestíbulo [βesˈtiβulo] sm vestibule, entrance hall; lobby.

vestigio [βesˈtixjo] sm vestige; footstep; trace.

*vestir [βesˈtir] v dress; clothe. **vestirse** get dressed. **vestido** sm dress.

veta [ˈβeta] sf vein of ore, etc.; grain in wood; streak.

veterano [βeteˈrano] sm, adj veteran.

veterinaria [βeteriˈnarja] sf veterinary science. **veterinario** sm vet.

veto [ˈβeto] sm veto.

vez [βeθ] sf turn; time; occasion. **a la vez** at once. **a veces** sometimes. **otra vez** once more. **tal vez** perhaps.

vía [ˈβia] sf road; way; track. **vía aérea** air mail. **en vías de** in the process of. **Vía Láctea** Milky Way.

viable [ˈβjaβle] adj viable.

viaducto [βjaˈðukto] sm viaduct.

viajar [βjaˈxar] v travel. **viajante** s(m+f) traveller. **viaje** sm trip, journey. **viajero, -a** sm, sf traveller; passenger.

víbora [ˈβiβora] sf viper.

vibrar [βiˈβrar] v vibrate, shake. **vibración** sf vibration. **vibrador** sm vibrator. **vibrante** adj vibrating; vibrant.

vicario [βiˈkarjo] sm vicar.

viciar [βiˈθjar] v vitiate; corrupt. **vicio** sm vice; defect. **de vicio** for no reason at all. **vicioso** adj vicious.

vicisitud [βiθisiˈtuð] sf vicissitude, mishap.

víctima [ˈβiktima] sf victim; sacrifice.

victoria [βikˈtorja] sf victory. **victorioso** adj victorious.

vid [βið] sf vine.

vida [ˈβiða] sf life. **en mi vida** never in my life. **nivel de vida** sm standard of living.

vidriar [βiˈðrjar] v glaze. **vidriera** sf stained glass. **vidrio** sm glass. **vidrioso** adj glassy.

viejo [ˈβjexo] adj old. sm old man. **vieja** sf old woman.

viento [ˈβjento] sm wind.

vientre [ˈβjentre] sm abdomen, belly; womb; bowels pl.

viernes [ˈβjernes] sm Friday. **Viernes Santo** Good Friday.

viga [ˈβiɣa] sf beam; timber.

vigente [βiˈxente] adj (jur) in force, valid. **vigencia** sf validity. **en vigencia** in effect; in force.

vigésimo [βiˈxesimo] adj twentieth.

vigilar [βixiˈlar] v watch over. **vigilancia** sf vigilance. **vigilante** adj vigilant. **vigilia** sf watchfulness; vigil.

vigor [βiˈɣor] sm vigour. **vigoroso** adj vigorous.

vil [βil] adj vile. **vileza** sf vileness.

vilo [ˈβilo] adv **en vilo** aloft; suspended; (fig) on tenterhooks.

villa [ˈβiʎa] sf villa; town.

villancico [βiʎanˈθiko] sm Christmas carol.

villanía [βiʎaˈnia] sf villainy; coarse expression.

vinagre [βiˈnagre] sm vinegar. **vinagroso** adj vinegary.

vínculo [ˈβinkulo] sm link; chain; tie.

vindicar [βindiˈkar] v vindicate. **vindicación** sf vindication.

vino[1] [ˈβino] sm wine. **vino tinto** red wine. **vino de solera** vintage wine. **vinícola** adj relating to wine or wine production. **viña** sf vineyard.

viñeta [βiˈɲeta] sf vignette.

violar [βjoˈlar] v violate; rape. **violación** sf violation; rape. **violador** sm rapist.

violencia [βjoˈlenθja] sf violence. **violentar** v force, open by force; violate; do violence to.

violeta [βjoˈleta] adj, sf violet.

violín [βjoˈlin] sm violin. **violinista** s(m+f) violinist. **violón** sm double-bass.

virar [βiˈrar] v veer; change direction; (mar) tack.

virgen [ˈβirxen] adj, sf virgin. **virginidad** sf virginity.

viril [βiˈril] adj virile. **virilidad** sf virility.

virtual [βirˈtwal] adj virtual; potential.

virtud [βirˈtuð] sf virtue. **virtuoso** adj virtuous. **virtuosidad** sf virtuosity.

viruela [βi'rwela] *sf* smallpox.

virulencia [βiru'lenθja] *sf* virulence. **virulento** *adj* virulent.

visado [βi'saðo] *sm* visa.

visaje [βi'saxe] *sm* smirk, grimace. **visajero** *adj* grimacing.

vísceras ['βisθeras] *sf pl* viscera *pl*.

viscoso [βis'koso] *adj* viscous. **viscosidad** *sf* viscosity.

visera [βi'sera] *sf* visor.

visible [βi'siβle] *adj* visible. **visibilidad** *sf* visibility.

visión [βi'sjon] *sf* vision, eyesight; dream, fantasy; view. **visionario, -a** *sm, sf* visionary.

visitar [βisi'tar] *v* visit; inspect. **visita** *sf* visit; visitor. **hacer una visita** pay a visit.

vislumbrar [βislum'brar] *v* catch a glimpse of. **vislumbre** *sf* glimpse; glimmer.

viso ['βiso] *sm* aspect, appearance; gleam.

víspera ['βispera] *sf* eve; (*fig*) approach. **en vísperas de** on the eve of.

vista ['βista] *sf* view; eyesight; appearance, look; gaze. **a primera vista** at first sight. **con vistas de** with a view to. **¡hasta la vista!** good-bye!

visto ['βisto] *adj* seen; obvious. **bien visto** approved of. **visto bueno** authorized. **visto que** seeing that.

vistoso [βis'toso] *adj* showy; (*fam*) loud.

visual [βi'swal] *adj* visual.

vital [βi'tal] *adj* vital. **vitalidad** *sf* vitality.

vitamina [βita'mina] *sf* vitamin.

vitela [βi'tela] *sf* vellum.

vitorear [βitore'ar] *v* shout, cheer, acclaim. **¡vítor!** bravo!

vitreo [βi'treo] *adj* vitreous. **vitrina** *sf* showcase.

vitriólico [βi'trjoliko] *adv* vitriolic. **vitriolo** *sm* vitriol.

vituperar [βitupe'rar] *v* vituperate; abuse; insult. **vituperación** *sf* blame.

viuda ['βjuða] *sf* widow. **viudo** *sm* widower. **viudez** *sf* widowhood.

vivaz [βi'βaθ] *adj* vivacious. **vivacidad** *sf* vivacity.

víveres ['βiβeres] *sm pl* provisions *pl*.

vivero [βi'βero] *sm* fishpond.

viveza [βi'βeθa] *sf* gaiety, liveliness.

vivienda [βi'βjenda] *sf* housing; dwelling; lodgings *pl*. **vividero** *adj* habitable.

vivificar [βiβifi'kar] *v* animate, bring to life.

vivir [βi'βir] *v* live. **¿quién vive?** who goes there? *sm* way of life.

vivisección [βiβisek'θjon] *sf* vivisection.

vivo ['βiβo] *adj* living, alive; vivid. **al vivo** to the life.

vizconde [βiθ'konde] *sm* viscount. **vizcondesa** *sf* viscountess.

vocablo [βo'kaβlo] *sm* word. **vocabulario** *sm* vocabulary.

vocación [βoka'θjon] *sf* vocation.

vocal [βo'kal] *adj* vocal. *sm* voter. *sf* vowel.

vocear [βoθe'ar] *v* bawl. **vocerío** *sm* bawling. **vocero** *sm* spokesman.

vociferar [βoθife'rar] *v* bawl; shout.

vocinglero [βoθin'glero] *adj* vociferous; loud-mouthed; talkative. **vocinglería** *sf* clamour, uproar.

volante [βo'lante] *adj* flying. *sm* steering-wheel; shuttlecock.

*volar [βo'lar] *v* fly; blow up, explode. **volarse** *v* become furious.

volátil [βo'latil] *adj* volatile.

volcán [βol'kan] *sm* volcano. **volcánico** *adj* volcanic.

*volcar [βol'kar] *v* upset; capsize. **volcarse** *v* fall over; bend over backwards.

volear [βole'ar] *v* volley. **voleo** *sm* volley.

volición [βoli'θjon] *sf* volition.

voltaje [βol'taxe] *sm* voltage. **voltio** *sm* volt.

voltear [βolte'ar] *v* overturn; revolve; tumble. **volteador, -a** *sm, sf* tumbler. **volteo** *sm* somersault.

voluble [βo'luβle] *adj* changeable. **volubilidad** *sf* changeable.

volumen [βolu'men] *sm* volume. **voluminoso** *adj* voluminous.

voluntad [βolun'tað] *sf* volition; affection. **a voluntad** at will. **buena voluntad** goodwill.

voluntario [βolun'tarjo] *adj* voluntary. **voluntariedad** *sf* free will.

voluptuoso [βolup'twoso] *adj* voluptuous. **voluptuosidad** *sf* voluptuousness.

*volver [βol'βer] *v* return; turn; turn over. **volver sobre sí** pull oneself together. **volverse** *v* become; go back. **volverse loco** go mad.

vomitar [βomi'tar] *v* vomit. **vómito** *sm* vomit.

voraz [βo'raθ] *adj* voracious. **voracidad** *sf* voracity.

vórtice ['βortiθe] *sm* vortex.

vosotros [βo'sotros] *pron pl* (*fam*) you.

votar [βo'tar] *v* vote. **votante** *s*(*m*+*f*) voter. **voto** *sm* vote; vow.

voz [βoθ] *sf* voice; shout; report. **a media voz** in a whisper. **dar voces** call out.

vuelco ['βwelko] *sm* upset; overturning.

vuelo ['βwelo] *sm* flight; flying; wing. **al vuelo** in flight. **en un vuelo** in a jiffy.

vuelta ['βwelta] *sf* turn; return; bend; reverse; recompense. **dar una vuelta** take a stroll. **estar de vuelta** be back.

vuestro ['βwestro] *pron* yours. *adj* your.

vulcanizar [βulkani'θar] *v* vulcanize.

vulgar [βul'gar] *adj* common; ordinary; vulgar. **el hombre vulgar** the common man.

vulnerar [βulne'rar] *v* wound. **vulnerabilidad** *sf* vulnerability. **vulnerable** *adj* vulnerable.

X

xilófono [ksi'lofono] *sm* xylophone.

Y

y [i] *conj* and.

ya [ja] *adv* already; now; yet; later. **ya que** since. **ya voy** I'm just coming.

yacimiento [jaθi'mjento] *sm* (*minerales*) bed. **yacente** *adj* recumbent.

yanqui [jan'ki] *adj*, *sm* (*fam*) Yankee.

yarda ['jarδa] *sf* yard.

yate ['jate] *sm* yacht.

yedra ['jeδra] *sf* ivy.

yegua ['jegwa] *sf* mare.

yelmo ['jelmo] *sm* helmet.

yema ['jema] *sf* yolk; bud; button. **yema del dedo** tip of the finger.

yerba ['jerβa] *sf* grass; herb.

yermo ['jermo] *sm* waste land. *adj* barren; desert.

yerno ['jerno] *sm* son-in-law.

yerro ['jerro] *sm* error; mistake.

yeso ['jeso] *sm* gypsum; plaster; plaster cast.

yo [jo] *pron* I; myself; me; ego.

yodo ['joδo] *sm* iodine.

yogur [jo'gur] *sm* yoghurt.

yugo ['jugo] *sm* yoke.

yugular [jugu'lar] *adj* jugular.

yunque ['junke] *sm* anvil.

yunta ['junta] *sf* couple, pair; (*de bueys*) yoke.

yute ['jute] *sm* jute.

*yuxtaponer [jukstapo'ner] *v* juxtapose. **yuxtaposición** *sf* juxtaposition. **yuxtapuesto** *adj* juxtaposed.

Z

zafar [θa'far] *v* loosen; free; clear; lighten. **zafarse** *v* run away.

zafio ['θafjo] *adj* uncouth.

zafiro [θa'firo] *sm* sapphire.

zaga ['θaga] *sf* rear; back.

zaguán [θa'gwan] *sm* entrance hall.

*zaherir [θae'rir] *v* censure; mock; reproach.

zahurda [θa'urδa] *sf* pigsty.

zalamería [θalame'ria] *sf* flattery. **zalamero, -a** *sm, sf* flatterer.

zamarra [θa'marra] *sf* sheepskin jacket.

zambo ['θambo] *adj* knock-kneed. *sm* half-breed; monkey.

*zambullir [θambu'ʎir] *v* dive. **zambullida** *sf* dive.

zampar [θam'par] *v* polish off; shove in; devour. **zamparse** *v* rush.

zanahoria [θana'orja] *sf* carrot.

zancada [θan'kaδa] *sf* long stride. **en dos zancadas** in a trice. **zancadilla** *sf* trip; trap. **echar la zancadilla** trip up.

zanco ['θanko] *sm* stilt.

zancudo [θan'kuδo] *adj* long-legged.

zángano ['θangano] *sm* (*insecto*) drone; (*fig*) loafer; fool.

zangolotear [θangolote'ar] *v* shake; fidget; rattle. **zangoloteo** *sm* shaking; rattling.

zanja ['θanxa] *sf* ditch; trench. **abrir las zanjas** lay the foundations.

zapa ['θapa] *sf* spade; trench. **zapapico** *sm* pickaxe. **zapar** *v* undermine.

zapatear [θapate'ar] *v* kick; ill-treat; tap-dance. **zapateado** *sm* Andalusian dance. **zapatería** *sf* shoe shop; shoe factory.

407

zapatero, -a *sm. sf* shoemaker. **zapatilla** *sf* slipper. **zapato** *sm* shoe.

zar [θar] *sm* tsar.

zarandear [θarande'ar] *v* sift; winnow; shake. **zaranda** *sf* sieve.

zaraza [θa'raθa] *sf* chintz.

zarcillo [θar'θiʎo] *sm* hoe; barrel hoop; vine tendril; ear-ring.

zarco ['θarko] *adj (ojos)* light blue.

zarpa ['θarpa] *v* claw; paw. **echar la zarpa** grab hold. **zarpar** *v* weigh anchor. **zarpazo** *sm* whack.

zarza ['θarθa] *sf* bramble, blackberry bush. **zarzamora** *sf (fruto)* blackberry.

zarzo ['θarθo] *sm* hurdle.

zarzuela [θar'θwela] *sf* light *or* comic opera.

zeta ['θeta] *sf* letter *z*.

zigzaguear [θigθage'ar] *v* zigzag. **zigzag** *sm* zigzag.

zinc [θink] *sm* zinc.

zócalo ['θokalo] *sm* plinth; skirting board.

zodiaco [θo'ðjako] *sm* zodiac.

zona ['θona] *sf* zone; area. **zona edificada** built-up area. **zonas verdes** green belt *sing.*

zoología [θoolo'xia] *sf* zoology. **zoológico**

adj zoological. **parque z** logical gardens *pl.* zoo. z zoologist.

zoquete [θo'kete] *sm* chu piece of stale bread; *(fam)*

zorro ['θorro] *sm* fox. **zorra** *s* vixen. **zorrera** *sf* foxhole.

zozobrar [θoθo'βrar] *v* wreck; capsize; founder; *(fig)* worry. **zozobra** *sf* foundering; worry.

zueco ['θweko] *sm* clog; galosh.

zumbar [θum'bar] *v* buzz; hum; strike; whack. **zumbarse de** make fun of. **zumbido** *sm* humming; buzzing.

zumbón [θum'bon], **-a** *sm. sf* jester; tease. *adj* waggish.

zumo ['θumo] *sm* juice. **zumoso** *adj* juicy.

zurcir [θur'θir] *v* darn. **zurcido** *sm* darn; stitch. **zurcidura** *sf* darning.

zurdo ['θurðo], **-a** *sm. sf* left-handed person. *adj* left-handed.

zurrar [θur'rar] *v* thrash; *(cuero)* dress; curry. **zurra** *sf* tanning; thrashing. **zurrador** *sm* tanner.

zurrón [θur'ron] *sm* leather bag; husk.

zutano [θu'tano], **-a** *sm. sf* so-and-so. **fulano, zutano y mengano** Tom, Dick, and Harry.